Lecture Notes in Artificial Intelligence   11775

Subseries of Lecture Notes in Computer Science

More information about this series at http://www.springer.com/series/1244

Christos Douligeris · Dimitris Karagiannis ·
Dimitris Apostolou (Eds.)

Knowledge Science, Engineering and Management

12th International Conference, KSEM 2019
Athens, Greece, August 28–30, 2019
Proceedings, Part I

 Springer

Editors
Christos Douligeris 🆔
University of Piraeus
Piraeus, Greece

Dimitris Karagiannis 🆔
University of Vienna
Vienna, Austria

Dimitris Apostolou
University of Piraeus
Piraeus, Greece

ISSN 0302-9743   ISSN 1611-3349   (electronic)
Lecture Notes in Artificial Intelligence
ISBN 978-3-030-29550-9   ISBN 978-3-030-29551-6   (eBook)
https://doi.org/10.1007/978-3-030-29551-6

LNCS Sublibrary: SL7 – Artificial Intelligence

This Springer imprint is published by the registered company Springer Nature Switzerland AG
The registered company address is: Gewerbestrasse 11, 6330 Cham, Switzerland

Christos Douligeris · Dimitris Karagiannis ·
Dimitris Apostolou (Eds.)

Knowledge Science, Engineering and Management

12th International Conference, KSEM 2019
Athens, Greece, August 28–30, 2019
Proceedings, Part I

Editors
Christos Douligeris 🆔
University of Piraeus
Piraeus, Greece

Dimitris Karagiannis 🆔
University of Vienna
Vienna, Austria

Dimitris Apostolou
University of Piraeus
Piraeus, Greece

ISSN 0302-9743   ISSN 1611-3349 (electronic)
Lecture Notes in Artificial Intelligence
ISBN 978-3-030-29550-9   ISBN 978-3-030-29551-6 (eBook)
https://doi.org/10.1007/978-3-030-29551-6

LNCS Sublibrary: SL7 – Artificial Intelligence

This Springer imprint is published by the registered company Springer Nature Switzerland AG
The registered company address is: Gewerbestrasse 11, 6330 Cham, Switzerland

Organisation

KSEM Steering Committee

Ruqian Lu (Honorary Chair)	Chinese Academy of Sciences, China
Chengqi Zhang (Past Chair)	University of Technology, Australia
Hui Xiong (Chair)	Rutgers University, USA
Dimitris Karagiannis (Deputy Chair)	University of Vienna, Austria
David Bell	Queen's University, UK
Yaxin Bi	Ulster University, UK
Cungen Cao	Chinese Academy of Sciences, China
Zhi Jin	Peking University, China
Kwok Kee Wei	National University of Singapore, Singapore
Claudiu Kifor	Sibiu University, Romania
Jerome Lang	Paul Sabatier University, France
Gang Li	Deakin University, Australia
Yoshiteru Nakamori	JAIST, Japan
Jorg Siekmann	German Research Centre of Artificial Intelligence, Germany
Eric Tsui	Hong Kong Polytechnic University, SAR China
Zongtuo Wang	Dalian Science and Technology University, China
Martin Wirsing	Ludwig-Maximilians-Universität München, Germany
Bo Yang	Jilin University, China
Mingsheng Ying	Tsinghua University, China
Zili Zhang	Southwest University, China

KSEM 2019 Organising Committee

General Co-chairs

Gang Li	Deakin University, Australia
Dimitrios Plexousakis	University of Crete and FORTH, Greece

Program Committee Co-chairs

Christos Douligeris	University of Piraeus, Greece
Dimitris Karagiannis	University of Vienna, Austria
Dimitris Apostolou	University of Piraeus, Greece

Publication Committee Co-chairs

Dimitrios Kallergis	University of West Attica, Greece
Themistoklis Panayiotopoulos	University of Piraeus, Greece

Publicity Committee Co-chairs

Shaowu Liu   University of Technology, Australia
Yannis Theodoridis   University of Piraeus, Greece
Ergina Kavallieratou   University of the Aegean, Greece
Yonggang Zhang   Jilin University, China

Keynote, Special Sessions and Workshop Co-chairs

Yannis Manolopoulos   Open University of Cyprus, Cyprus
                            and Aristotle University of Thessaloniki, Greece
Vassilis Plagianakos   University of Thessaly, Greece

Program Committee

Salem Benferhat   Université d'Artois, France
Paolo Bouquet   University of Trento, Italy
Remus Brad   Lucian Blaga University of Sibiu, Romania
Robert Andrei Buchmann   Babeş-Bolyai University, Romania
Hechang Chen   Jilin University, China
Paolo Ciancarini   University of Bologna, Italy
Ireneusz Czarnowski   Gdynia Maritime University, Poland
Richard Dapoigny   LISTIC/Polytech'Savoie, France
Yong Deng   Southwest University, China
Josep Domingo-Ferrer   Universitat Rovira i Virgili, Spain
Dieter Fensel   University of Innsbruck, Austria
Hans-Georg Fill   University of Fribourg, Switzerland
Yanjie Fu   Missouri University of Science and Technology, USA
Chiara Ghidini   FBK Trento, Italy
Fausto Giunchiglia   University of Trento, Italy
Knut Hinkelmann   FHNW University of Applied Sciences and Arts,
                            Switzerland
Zhisheng Huang   Vrije Universiteit Amsterdam, The Netherlands
Van Nam Huynh   JAIST, Japan
Tan Jianlong   Institute of Information Engineering, Chinese Academy
                            of Sciences, China
Zhi Jin   Peking University, China
Fang Jin   Texas Tech University, USA
Mouna Kamel   IRIT, Université Paul Sabatier, France
Krzysztof Kluza   AGH UST, Poland
Konstantinos Kotis   University of Piraeus, Greece
Yong Lai   Jilin University, China
Ximing Li   Jilin University, China
Ge Li   Peking University, China
Gang Li   Deakin University, Australia
Li Li   Southwest University, China
Huayu Li   The University of North Carolina at Charlotte, USA

Preface

The International Conference on Knowledge Science, Engineering and Management (KSEM) provides a forum for researchers in the broad areas of knowledge science, knowledge engineering, and knowledge management to exchange ideas and to report state-of-the-art research results. KSEM 2019 was the 12th in this series, building on the success of the 11 previous events in Guilin, China (KSEM 2006); Melbourne, Australia (KSEM 2007); Vienna, Austria (KSEM 2009); Belfast, UK (KSEM 2010); Irvine, USA (KSEM 2011); Dalian, China (KSEM 2013); Sibiu, Romania (KSEM 2014); Chongqing, China (KSEM2015); Passau, Germany (KSEM 2016); Melbourne, Australia (KSEM 2017); and Changchun, China (KSEM 2018).

The selection process this year was, as always, very competitive. We received 240 submissions, and each submitted paper was reviewed by at least three members of the Program Committee (PC) (including thorough evaluations by the TPC co-chairs). A total of 77 papers were selected as full papers (32%), and 23 as short papers (10%). 10 posters were also presented at the conference to allow for a more personal and extended dialogue.

Moreover, we were honored to have four prestigious scholars giving keynote speeches at the conference: Prof. Stefanos Kollias (University of Lincoln, UK), Prof. Andrea Passerini (University of Trento, Italy), Prof. Xin Geng (Southeast University, China), and Dr. Dimitrios Tzovaras (Information Technologies Institute and CERTH, Greece).

We would like to thank everyone who participated in the development of the KSEM 2019 program. In particular, we want to give special thanks to the PC, for their diligence and concern for the quality of the program, and, also, for their detailed feedback to the authors.

Moreover, we would like to express our gratitude to the KSEM Steering Committee honorary chair Prof. Ruqian Lu (Chinese Academy of Sciences, China), who provided insight and support during all the stages of this effort. The members of the Steering Committee, who followed the progress of the conference very closely, with sharp comments and helpful suggestions. The KSEM 2019 general co-chairs, Prof. Gang Li (Deakin University, Australia) and Prof. Dimitrios Plexousakis (University of Crete and FORTH, Greece), who were extremely supportive in our efforts and in the general success of the conference.

We would like to thank the members of all the other committees and, in particular, those of the local Organizing Committee, who worked diligently for more than a year to provide a wonderful experience to the KSEM participants. We are also grateful to the team at Springer led by Alfred Hofmann for the publication of this volume, who worked very efficiently and effectively with Lecturer Dimitrios Kallergis, our publication co-chair. Finally, and most importantly, we thank all the authors, who are the primary reason that KSEM 2019 was so exciting and why it remains the premier forum for presentation and discussion of innovative ideas, research results, and experience from around the world.

June 2019

Christos Douligeris
Dimitris Karagiannis
Dimitris Apostolou

Qian Li	Institute of Information Engineering, Chinese Academy of Sciences, China
Junming Liu	Rutgers University, USA
Shaowu Liu	University of Technology Sydney, Australia
Li Liu	Chongqing University, China
Bin Liu	IBM TJ Watson Research Center, USA
Weiru Liu	University of Bristol, UK
Xudong Luo	Guangxi Normal University, China
Bo Ma	Xinjiang Technical Institute of Physics and Chemistry, Chinese Academy of Sciences, China
Stewart Massie	Robert Gordon University, UK
Maheswari N	VIT University, India
Oleg Okun	Cognizant Technology Solutions GmbH, Germany
Dantong Ouyang	Jilin University, China
Guilin Qi	Southeast University, China
Sven-Volker Rehm	WHU - Otto Beisheim School of Management, Germany
Ulrich Reimer	FHS St. Gallen, University of Applied Sciences, Switzerland
Luciano Serafini	FBK Trento, Italy
Leslie Sikos	University of South Australia, Australia
Leilei Sun	Tsinghua University, China
Yanni Velegrakis	University of Trento, Italy
Lucian Vintan	Lucian Blaga University of Sibiu, Romania
Daniel Volovici	Lucian Blaga University of Sibiu, Romania
Huy Quan Vu	Victoria University, Australia
Hongtao Wang	North China Electric Power University, China
Kewen Wang	Griffith University, Australia
Zhichao Wang	Tsinghua University, China
Martin Wirsing	Ludwig Maximilian University of Munich, Germany
Robert Woitsch	BOC Asset Management GmbH, Austria
Le Wu	University of Science and Technology of China, China
Zhiang Wu	Nanjing University of Finance and Economics, China
Tong Xu	University of Science and Technology of China, China
Ziqi Yan	Beijing Jiaotong University, China
Bo Yang	Jilin University, China
Jingyuan Yang	Rutgers University, USA
Feng Yi	University of Chinese Academy of Sciences, China
Qingtian Zeng	Shandong University of Science and Technology, China
Songmao Zhang	Chinese Academy of Sciences, China
Chunxia Zhang	Beijing Institute of Technology, China
Le Zhang	Sichuan University, China
Zili Zhang	Southwest University, China
Hongke Zhao	University of Science and Technology of China, China
Jiali Zuo	Jiangxi Normal University, China

Finance and Registration Chair

Theodoros Karvounidis   University of Piraeus, Greece

Local Organising Committee

Roza Mavropodi (Chair)   University of Pireaus, Greece
Maria Eftychia Angelaki   University of Pireaus, Greece
Panagiotis Drakoulogkonas   University of Pireaus, Greece
Zacharenia Garofalaki   University of West Attica, Greece
Panos Gotsiopoulos   University of Pireaus, Greece
Apostolos Karalis   University of Pireaus, Greece
Dimitris Kotsifakos   University of Pireaus, Greece
Eleni Seralidou   University of Pireaus, Greece
Dimitra Tzoumpa   University of Pireaus, Greece
Vasilis Vasilakopoulos   University of Pireaus, Greece

Contents – Part I

Social Knowledge Analysis and Management

Contents – Part I

Social Knowledge Analysis and Management

Data Processing and Data Mining

Image and Video Data Analysis

Deep Learning

Knowledge Graph and Knowledge Management

Machine Learning

Knowledge Engineering Applications

Contents – Part II

Knowledge Theories and Models

Network Knowledge Representation and Learning

Formal Reasoning and Ontologies

Centralized Reasoning Translation and Its Computing Complexity for Heterogeneous Semantic Mappings

Xiaofei Zhao[1,2(✉)] and Zhiyong Feng[1]

[1] School of Computer Science and Technology,
Tianjin University, Tianjin, China
zhaoxiaofei1978@hotmail.com
[2] School of Computer Science and Technology,
Tianjin Polytechnic University, Tianjin, China

Abstract. Bridge rules provide an important mechanism for describing semantic mapping and propagating knowledge for distributed dynamic description logics (D3L). The current research focuses on the homogeneous bridge rules that only contain atomic elements. In this paper, the research is extended to the D3L reasoning problem with heterogeneous bridge rules that contain composite elements in subset ends. The regularity of the distributed knowledge base is defined. Through the alteration of the bridge rules and transforming different forms into existing language mechanisms, we present an algorithm that can convert the D3L knowledge base with dynamic description logic $\mathcal{DSROIQ}$ as the local ontology language into a single $\mathcal{DSROIQ}$ knowledge base. Next, we study the properties of the algorithm. We prove that the algorithm will terminate in polynomial time and that the satisfiability of the target knowledge base is equivalent to the satisfiability of the original knowledge base. Thus, we prove that the worst-case time complexity of the centralized reasoning on the regular D3L knowledge base with such bridge rules is the same as that on a single $\mathcal{DSROIQ}$ knowledge base. The method proposed in this paper makes centralized reasoning for D3L obtain the same worst-case time complexity as the existing distributed reasoning method and solves the problem that the latter cannot handle heterogeneous composite bridge rules.

1 Introduction

In a large number of distributed applications such as information integration, service integration, and semantic Web, people often want ontology to be modular or distributed rather than a single ontology; the modularization of large-scale ontology has stronger specificity and higher inference efficiency, the above two reasons make distributed and modular ontology [11, 12] one of the research hotspots in recent years. A variety of logics' foundations have been proposed, such as ε-connection framework [3–5], distributed ontology framework with conservative extension [1, 2], distributed first-order logic [10], and package-based description logic. As one of the important branches, distributed dynamic description logics (D3L) introduce the description mechanism for semantic mapping, knowledge propagation mechanisms between ontologies and reasoning

C. Douligeris et al. (Eds.): KSEM 2019, LNAI 11775, pp. 3–14, 2019.
https://doi.org/10.1007/978-3-030-29551-6_1

mechanisms for distributed environments. D3L adequately satisfy the requirements that each local information system maintain a certain degree of autonomy and that its user interface while importing and reusing knowledge from other local information systems, thereby providing a complete theoretical basis for above applications.

The mapping and reasoning of elements between ontologies is the core problem to be solved in modular ontology. Due to the diversity of semantic mappings in the real world, mappings between heterogeneous elements must be able to be modeled and reasoned. Unfortunately, none of the existing researches has provided sufficient support for this. Taking $\mathcal{E}$-connection framework as an example, although the framework provides a distributed inference algorithm based on solution, the mapping constructed by $\mathcal{E}$-connection is limited to the concepts of different ontologies, so the mapping and reasoning between heterogeneous elements cannot be realized. The reasoning provided by the distributed ontology framework with conservative extension is only applicable to the case where there is signature dependency between ontologies, and mappings that do not conform to this constraint cannot be described and reasoned. In addition, this framework only theoretically proves that the signature dependency problem is decidable and does not provide an inference algorithm.

The bridge rule mechanism of D3L provides the possibility to solve the description and reasoning problems of heterogeneous semantic mapping. According to the diversity of the mappings, D3L provide not only the homogeneous bridge rules for modeling semantic relations between homogeneous elements (such as mapping between concepts, mapping between roles, and mapping between actions) but also the heterogeneous bridge rules for describing semantic relations between heterogeneous elements (such as the mapping from a concept to an action, or vice versa). In previous work [7, 8], we have made a preliminary study on the reasoning in D3L. However, this reasoning was only employed for the case of atomic concepts/atomic actions/atomic roles, such as 1: BuyCar $\xrightarrow{\sqsubseteq}$ 2: BuyVehicle. Heterogeneous bridge rules containing composite elements, such as 1: $\exists$WorkAt.University $\xrightarrow{\sqsubseteq}$ 2:Staff; 1:PlayBall $\xrightarrow{\sqsupseteq}$ 2: PlayBasketball $\sqcup$ PlayFootball; 1: Carnivore $\sqcap$ Canidae $\xrightarrow{\sqsupseteq}$ 2: HouseDog; 1: Professor $\xrightarrow{\sqsubseteq}$ 2: $\exists$WorkAt.University, as shown in Fig. 1, are not involved. Considering the diversity of semantic mapping in the real world, the research of this problem has important theoretical and practical value.

In this paper, the research is extended to the D3L reasoning problem in the case of the heterogeneous bridge rules that contain composite elements in subset ends. To obtain the decidability of distributed Tbox DTB, we define the regularity of DTB. Aiming at D3L knowledge base with dynamic description logic $\mathcal{DSROIQ}$ as the local ontology language, through the alteration of the bridge rules and transforming different forms into existing language mechanisms, we present the algorithm, which can convert the distributed knowledge base into a single $\mathcal{DSROIQ}$ knowledge base. Next, we study the properties of the algorithm. We prove that the algorithm will terminate in polynomial time and the satisfiability of the target knowledge base is equivalent to the satisfiability of the original knowledge base. Thus, we prove that the worst-case time complexity of the centralized reasoning on regular D3L knowledge base with such bridge rules is the same as that on a single $\mathcal{DSROIQ}$ knowledge base. Our approach

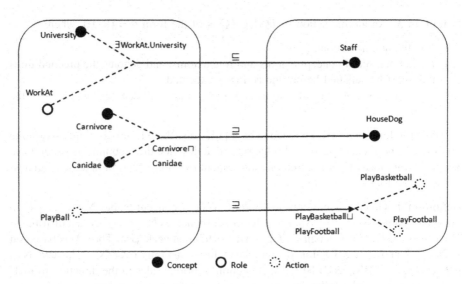

Fig. 1. Sample for heterogeneous composite bridge rules

can handle the reasoning with heterogeneous composite bridge rules effectively and can be used in the centralized reasoning on D3L knowledge bases, which will obtain the same worst-case time complexity as the existing distributed reasoning method.

2   Distributed Dynamic Description Logics

Due to the space limitations, we briefly introduce the related part of D3L used in this paper. More detailed information can be obtained in the literature [6].

Definition 1. The concepts in $\mathcal{DSROIQ}$ are expressions of one of the following forms:

$$\bot \mid \top \mid A \mid \neg C \mid C \sqcup D \mid C \sqcap D \mid \{a\} \mid \forall R.C \mid \exists R.C \mid \exists S.self \mid \;\leq nS.C \mid \;\geq nS.C$$

where A denotes an atomic concept, C and D denote general concepts, a denotes an individual, R and S denote roles, and n ranges over the nonnegative integers.

A role inclusion axiom (RIA) in $\mathcal{DSROIQ}$ is an expression of the form $S_1 \circ \ldots \circ S_n \sqsubseteq R$. The set of RIAs will constitute the role hierarchy. Given local Tbox TB, individuals t and u, a path from t to u is a non-empty sequence of roles: $R_1(x_1, x_2), \ldots, R_n(x_n, x_{n+1}) \in TB$, where $x_1 = t$, $x_{n+1} = u$ and $x_i \neq x_{i+1}$, $1 \leq i \leq n$. If there is no the path starting from individual t, t is called terminal. If there is no the path to individual t, t is called beginning.

Definition 2. If there is a partial order $\prec$ meeting the following two conditions in a role hierarchy:

(1) $S \prec R$ iff $S^- \prec R$;
(2) every RIA is of one of the forms: $R \circ R \sqsubseteq R$, $R^- \sqsubseteq R$, $S_1 \circ \ldots \circ S_n \sqsubseteq R$, $R \circ S_1 \circ \ldots \circ S_n \sqsubseteq R$, $S_1 \circ \ldots \circ S_n \circ R \sqsubseteq R$, such that $S_i \prec R$, $i = 1, \ldots, n$, then the role hierarchy is regular.

Definition 3. An atomic action in $\mathcal{DSROIQ}$ is of the form $\alpha = (P, E)$, where

(1) α is the atomic action
(2) P is a finite set of concept axioms and role axioms, and denotes the preconditions that must be satisfied before the action is executed
(3) E is a finite set of concept axioms and role axioms, and denotes the effects of the action.

The basic form of a D3L knowledge base [14] –distributed Tbox is composed of the set of local Tboxes and the set of bridge rules that describe the mappings between local Tboxes. Every local Tbox is based on independent dynamic description logic language. We have the following definition:

Definition 4. Given a non-empty index set I, a set of concept names $N_C = \cup_{i \in I} N_{ci}$, a set of role names $N_R = \cup_{i \in I} N_{Ri}$ and a set of action names $N_A = \cup_{i \in I} N_{Ai}$, a distributed Tbox over $\mathcal{DSROIQ}$ is a pair $<\{T_i\}_{i \in I}, BR>$ such that each local Tbox T_i is based on $\mathcal{DSROIQ}$ and is a collection of general inclusion axioms over N_{Ci}, N_{Ri} and N_{Ai}; $BR = \cup_{i, j \in I, i \neq j} BR_{ij}$, each BR_{ij} is a collection of bridge rules in the direction from T_i to T_j, which are of the following forms:

i: $C \xrightarrow{\sqsubseteq}$ j: D (into-concept (action) bridge rule);

i: $C \xrightarrow{\sqsupseteq}$ j: D (onto-concept (action) bridge rule);

i: $R \xrightarrow{\sqsubseteq}$ j: S (into-role bridge rule);

i: $R \xrightarrow{\sqsupseteq}$ j: S (onto-role bridge rule).

An interpretation of distributed Tbox DTB $\mathcal{I} = <\{\mathcal{I}_i\}_{i \in I}, \{r_{ij}\}_{i, j \in I, i \neq j}>$, where $\{\mathcal{I}_i\}_{i \in I}$ denotes the set of local interpretations, $\{r_{ij}\}_{i, j \in I, i \neq j}$ denotes the set of domain relations. For each $i \in I$, $\mathcal{I}_i = (\Delta^{\mathcal{I}_i}, \bullet^{\mathcal{I}_i})$. Every domain relation r_{ij} is a subset of $\Delta^{\mathcal{I}_i} \times \Delta^{\mathcal{I}_i}$, and we have $r_{ij}(d) = \{d' | <d, d'> \in r_{ij}\}$.

Definition 5. For every $i, j \in I$, an interpretation $\mathcal{I}$ satisfies the elements and axioms in a distributed Tbox DTB (denoted by $\mathcal{I} \models \bullet$), iff $\mathcal{I}$ satisfies the following clauses:

(1) $\mathcal{I} \models$ i: $C \xrightarrow{\sqsubseteq}$ j: D, if $r_{ij}(C^{\mathcal{I}_i}) \subseteq D^{\mathcal{I}_j}$;

(2) $\mathcal{I} \models$ i: $C \xrightarrow{\sqsupseteq}$ j: D, if $r_{ij}(C^{\mathcal{I}_i}) \supseteq D^{\mathcal{I}_j}$;

(3) $\mathcal{I} \models$ i: $R \xrightarrow{\sqsubseteq}$ j: S, if $r_{ij}(R^{\mathcal{I}_i}) \subseteq S^{\mathcal{I}_j}$;

(4) $\mathcal{I} \models$ i: $R \xrightarrow{\sqsupseteq}$ j: S, if $r_{ij}(R^{\mathcal{I}_i}) \supseteq S^{\mathcal{I}_j}$;

(5) $\mathcal{I} \models$ i: $C \sqsubseteq D$, if $\mathcal{I}_i \models C \sqsubseteq D$;

(6) $\mathcal{I} \models$ i: $R \sqsubseteq S$, if $\mathcal{I}_i \models R \sqsubseteq S$;

(7) $\mathcal{I} \models T_i$, if $\mathcal{I}_i \models T_i$;

(8) $\mathcal{I} \models BR$, if for every br $\in$ BR, $\mathcal{I} \models$ br;

(9) $\mathcal{I} \models DTB$, if $\mathcal{I} \models T_i$ and $\mathcal{I} \models BR$ for every $i \in I$;

(10) $DTB \models$ i: $C \sqsubseteq D$, if $\mathcal{I} \models$ DTB implies $\mathcal{I} \models$ i: $C \sqsubseteq D$ for every $\mathcal{I}$;

(11) $DTB \models$ i: $R \sqsubseteq S$, if $\mathcal{I} \models$ DTB implies $\mathcal{I} \models$ i: $R \sqsubseteq S$ for every $\mathcal{I}$.

If $\mathcal{I} \models$ DTB, then $\mathcal{I}$ is called a model of DTB.

3 Transformation Method for Heterogeneous Composite Bridge Rules

3.1 Regularity of DTB

Horrocks et al. [9] make a systematic study on $\mathcal{SROIQ}$. These researchers prove that the basic reasoning tasks in regular $\mathcal{SROIQ}$ Tbox, i.e., $\mathcal{SROIQ}$ Tbox with the regular role hierarchy, are decidable. Chang et al. [13] show that after action theory is introduced, the decidability of reasoning tasks does not change. For the purpose of obtaining the decidability of the DTB with $\mathcal{DSROIQ}$ as a local ontology language, we extend Definition 2, thus getting the definition of regularity of distributed Tbox.

Definition 6. If there is a partial order $\prec$ meeting the following three conditions in the role hierarchy of a distributed Tbox DTB:

(1) $S \prec R$ iff $S^- \prec R$;
(2) every RIA is of one of the forms: $R{\circ}R \sqsubseteq R$, $R^- \sqsubseteq R$, $S_1{\circ}...{\circ}S_n \sqsubseteq R$, $R{\circ}S_1{\circ}...{\circ}S_n \sqsubseteq R$, $S_1{\circ}...{\circ}S_n{\circ}R \sqsubseteq R$, such that $S_i \prec R$, $i = 1, ..., n$;
(3) for an arbitrary bridge rule $\mathcal{B} \xrightarrow{\sqsubseteq} R(x, y)$ or $R(x, y) \xrightarrow{\sqsupseteq} \mathcal{B}$, where $\mathcal{B}$ denotes a composite element, every $S(z, v)$ in $\mathcal{B}$ is of one of the following three cases:

> (a) there is no path from v to y;
>
> (b) $S{\prec}R$;
>
> (c) S=R (i.e., there is $R(z, v) \in \mathcal{B}$), but there is no $R(z', v') \in \mathcal{B}$ with a path from v' to y; if x=z, then there is no $C(x) \in \mathcal{B}$; if y=v, then there is no $C(y) \in \mathcal{B}$,

then the distributed Tbox DTB is regular.

3.2 Preliminary Theorem

Theorem 1. Any D3L bridge rule $\mathcal{B} \xrightarrow{\sqsubseteq} \mathcal{H}$ with $\mathcal{DSROIQ}$ as local ontology language can be transformed into a semantically equivalent bridge rule $\mathcal{B}' \xrightarrow{\sqsubseteq} \mathcal{H}$, such that all the paths in $\mathcal{B}'$ are contained in a single maximal path. If $\mathcal{H} = R(x, y)$, y is the terminal of that maximal path; if $\mathcal{H} = C(x)$, there is no path in $\mathcal{B}$.

Proof. To prove Theorem 1, we need to prove that the semantically equivalent bridge rule $\mathcal{B}' \xrightarrow{\sqsubseteq} \mathcal{H}$ can be constructed after finite steps. We can transform $\mathcal{B}$ into $\mathcal{B}'$ through the following iterative reduction steps:

> Step 1: for each variable x in $\mathcal{B}'$, iteratively compute $\mathcal{B}' = (\mathcal{B}'\backslash\mathcal{S}) \cup (C_1 \sqcap...\sqcap C_n)(x)\}$, where $\mathcal{S} = \{C_1(x), ..., C_n(x)\}$ is the set of all concept axioms that refer to x in $\mathcal{B}'$,
> Step 2: for each role axiom R(x, y) in $\mathcal{B}'$, if y is the terminal of the path in $\mathcal{B}$ and $\mathcal{H}$ is not the role axiom that has y as the second variable, then iteratively compute $\mathcal{B}' = \{\mathcal{B}'\backslash\{R(x, y), D(y)\}\} \cup \{\exists R.D(x)\}$, where D denotes all the concepts that refer to y in $\mathcal{B}$; if there is no such concept, then let D = $\top$.

The above steps reduce the number of the role axioms in $\mathcal{B}'$ during each iteration; obviously, each iteration will terminate in finite steps. After termination, $\mathcal{B}'$ cannot contain terminal individuals that are part of some path unless the individuals are the second parameter of the role axioms in $\mathcal{H}$, so all paths (if any) terminate in this terminal. If $\mathcal{H} = \mathrm{C}(x)$, according to above steps, all paths have been reduced.

Step 1, which merges concepts, is semantically equivalent transformation. During the iteration in step 2, the terminal variable y that will be deleted occurs in at most one concept axiom but not in $\mathcal{H}$ (because y is neither the second variable of the role in $\mathcal{H}$ nor the beginning in $\mathcal{B}$), so the output of each iteration is semantically equivalent to the previous bridge rule. As a result, $\mathcal{B}' \xrightarrow{\sqsubseteq} \mathcal{H}$ is semantically equivalent to $\mathcal{B} \xrightarrow{\sqsubseteq} \mathcal{H}$. $\square$

Take bridge rule worksAt(x, y) $\sqcap$ University(y) $\sqcap$ supervises(x, z) $\sqcap$ PhDStudent (z) $\xrightarrow{\sqsubseteq}$ profOf(x, z) as an example. After the above steps, $\mathcal{B}$ (worksAt(x, y) $\sqcap$ University(y) $\sqcap$ supervises(x, z) $\sqcap$ PhDStudent(z)) is transformed into $\mathcal{B}'$ $\exists$worksAt. University(x) $\sqcap$ supervises(x, z) $\sqcap$ PhDStudent(z), where z is the terminal of the single maximal path.

Bridge rules essentially describe subsumption relationships across ontologies; therefore, although Theorem 1 is for into-bridge rules, it also has similar results for onto-bridge rules. We can take the same transformation for the subset ends. The proof is similar to that of Theorem 1, and we will not cover it again.

3.3 Transformation Algorithm for D3L Knowledge Bases with Heterogeneous Composite Bridge Rules

According to Theorem 1, we can see that the role paths of every composite bridge rule can be converted into a single linear path equivalently, and each individual variable is a part of that maximal path. In the following, we assume that all bridge rules we will process are of the form described in Theorem 1.

On the basis of Theorem 1, overall, we consider the different forms of heterogeneous composite bridge rules and research their transformation semantics. In the following, we present the transformation algorithm for distributed knowledge bases. The proposed algorithm can convert the D3L knowledge base with $\mathcal{DSROIQ}$ as local ontology language into a single $\mathcal{DSROIQ}$ knowledge base.

Algorithm 1. Transformation algorithm for D3L knowledge bases

Input: DTB $<\{T_i\}_{i\in I}$, BR$>$ with $\mathcal{DSROIQ}$ as local ontology language;

Output: a single $\mathcal{DSROIQ}$ knowledge base TB$_{BR}$.

(1) Initialize TB$_{BR}=\varnothing$, initialize the set of remaining bridge rules BR'=BR,

(2) If BR'=$\varnothing$, then let TB$_{BR}$=TB$_{BR}\cup\{T_i\}_{i\in I}$, output TB$_{BR}$, algorithm terminates,

(3) Take a bridge rule $\mathcal{B}\overset{\sqsubseteq}{\longrightarrow}\mathcal{H}$ (or $\mathcal{H}\overset{\sqsupseteq}{\longrightarrow}\mathcal{B}$) from BR',

(4) We distinguish five cases:

(a) If there are two concept axioms referring to same variable z D(z) and D'(z) in $\mathcal{B}$, then remove both concept axioms from $\mathcal{B}$ and insert $(D\sqcap D')(z)$ into $\mathcal{B}$;

(b) If $\mathcal{H}$=C(x) and $\mathcal{B}$=D(x), then remove the bridge rule from BR' and insert $D\sqsubseteq C$ into TB$_{BR}$;

(c) If $\mathcal{H}$=R(x, y) and $\mathcal{B}$ is of the form: $\{R_1(x, x_2), ..., R_n(x_n, y)\}$, then remove the bridge rule from BR' and insert $R_1\circ...\circ R_n\sqsubseteq R$ into TB$_{BR}$;

(d) If $\mathcal{H}$=R(x, y) and there is D(z) in $\mathcal{B}$ such that z occurs in some role axiom of $\mathcal{B}$ or $\mathcal{H}$ (in the first or the second variable position), then the following three steps are executed:

(i) Introduce a new role S, insert D=$\exists$S.Self into TB$_{BR}$,
(ii) Introduce a new variable z', insert role axiom S(z, z') into $\mathcal{B}$, each role axiom T(x', z)$\in\mathcal{B}$ is replaced with T(x', z'), each role axiom T(z, y')$\in\mathcal{B}$ is replaced with T(z', y'),
(iii) remove D(z) from $\mathcal{B}$, if z=y, then replace $\mathcal{H}$ with R(x, z'),

(e) If $\mathcal{H}$=C(x) or $\mathcal{H}$=R(x, y) and there is D(z)$\in\mathcal{B}$ such that z occurs neither in $\mathcal{H}$ nor in any role axiom of $\mathcal{B}$, then the following two steps are executed:

(i) Introduce a new variable u; if there is R(x, t)$\in\mathcal{B}$, then let u=y; else let u=x,
(ii) Replace D(z) in $\mathcal{B}$ with $\exists$U.D(u), where U is universal role,

(5) Goto (2).

One by one, Algorithm 1 takes bridge rules from BR' and addresses them. It will not terminate until BR' is empty. During the processing of each bridge rule, five cases are distinguished. Bridge rules are transformed and reduced by (a), (d) and (e) until the precondition of (b) or (c) is satisfied. Next, they are removed from BR' by (b) or (c). After that step, we analyze whether these five cases are exhaustive. We need to show that the bridge rules that do not satisfy the preconditions of (a), (b), (c) and (d) must satisfy the precondition of (e). Assuming that the preconditions of (a), (b), (c) and (d) are all not satisfied, because the superset end of the bridge rule is a non-composite element, $\mathcal{H}$ is in two cases at most: $\mathcal{H}$ = C(x) or $\mathcal{H}$ = R(x, y). If $\mathcal{H}$ = C(x), according to Theorem 1, there are no role axioms in $\mathcal{B}$; therefore, there are only concept axioms in $\mathcal{B}$. Because the condition of (b) is not satisfied, i.e., $\mathcal{B}$ is not of the form D(x), there must be some concept axiom D(z) $\in \mathcal{B}$, where z occurs neither in $\mathcal{H}$ nor in any role axiom of $\mathcal{B}$. If $\mathcal{H} = R(x, y)$, according to Theorem 1, all paths in B are contained in a single maximal path and y is the terminal of that maximal path. Because the condition of (c) is not satisfied, i.e., $\mathcal{B}$ is not of the form $R_1(x, x_2), ..., R_n(x_n, y)$, there must be some concept axiom $D(z) \in B$. Non-applicability of (d) ensures that z does not occur in the role axioms of B and H, thus (e) is applicable again. In a word, the five cases distinguished by Algorithm 1 are exhaustive.

Take the bridge rule in Sect. 3.2 as an example. After the conversion of Algorithm 1, we can obtain the following three $\mathcal{DSROIQ}$ axioms (where S_1 and S_2 are newly introduced roles):

$$\exists worksAt.University \equiv \exists S_1.Self$$

$$PhDStudent \equiv \exists S_2.Self$$

$$S_1 \circ supervises \circ S_2 \sqsubseteq profOf$$

4 Properties of Transformation Algorithm and Complexity of D3L Centralized Reasoning

In this section, we discuss the properties of Algorithm 1 and the computational complexity of D3L centralized reasoning with complex bridge rules. The worst-case time complexity of Algorithm 1 is analyzed in Lemma 1. Lemma 2 describes that the satisfiability of target knowledge base TB_{BR} is equivalent to that of the original knowledge base DTB. Lemma 3 describes the relation between the regularity of DTB and the regularity of TB_{BR}. Thus, we obtain Theorem 2, which states that the worst-case time complexity of the centralized reasoning on DTB with composite bridge rules is the same as that on a single $\mathcal{DSROIQ}$ knowledge base.

Lemma 1. Algorithm 1 will terminate in polynomial time.
Proof. Obviously, the single step of Algorithm 1 can be done in linear time; therefore, the overall time complexity of the algorithm is affected by the number of times each step is executed. (1), (2) and (3) can be done in a polynomial number of times. We analyze step (4). (a) and (d) reduce the number of concept axioms for a bridge rule. Because no new concept axioms are introduced during the reduction, (a) and (d) can only be executed once for every concept axiom. Similarly, (b) and (c), which reduce the number of bridge rules, can be done in a polynomial number of times. (e) reduces the number of concept axioms that do not contain variables that occur in superset end. (e) can be done in a polynomial number of times because no such axioms are introduced during its execution.

In summary, Algorithm 1 will terminate in polynomial time.   □

Lemma 2. After termination of Algorithm 1, TB_{BR} and DTB are equisatisfiable.
Proof. Lemma 2 can be proved if every step of Algorithm 1 does not change satisfiability. Let TB_0/BR_0 and TB_1/BR_1 be the sets TB_{BR}/BR' before and after the execution of a transformation step. We need to prove that the satisfiability of $TB \cup TB_1 \cup BR_1$ is equivalent to the satisfiability of $TB \cup TB_0 \cup BR_0$.

Cases (a), (b) and (c) are equivalent substitutions that will not change the satisfiability of the knowledge base before and after conversions.

For case (d), $TB \cup TB_0 \cup BR_0$ and $TB \cup TB_1 \cup BR_0$ are equisatisfiable because $TB_1 = TB_0 \cup \{D \equiv \exists S.Self\}$ and S is a new role. Now let's discuss whether $TB \cup TB_1 \cup BR_0$ and $TB \cup TB_1 \cup BR_1$ have the same satisfiability. Let $\mathcal{B}_0 \xrightarrow{\sqsubseteq} \mathcal{H}_0$ and $\mathcal{B}_1 \xrightarrow{\sqsubseteq} \mathcal{H}_1$ denote a bridge rule before and after the transformation step respectively. For one direction, if $TB \cup TB_1 \cup BR_0$ is satisfiable, i.e., there is some interpretation $\mathcal{I}$ such that $\mathcal{I} \models TB \cup TB_1 \cup BR_0$, for all variable assignments π, we have $(\mathcal{B}_0 \xrightarrow{\sqsubseteq} \mathcal{H}_0)^{\mathcal{I}, \pi} = $ true. If $\pi(z) \notin D^{\mathcal{I}}$ or $\pi(z) \neq \pi(z')$, i.e., $\mathcal{B}_1^{\mathcal{I}, \pi} = $ false, obviously $(\mathcal{B}_1 \xrightarrow{\sqsubseteq} \mathcal{H}_1)^{\mathcal{I}, \pi} = $ true, so we only need to consider the cases that $\mathcal{B}_1^{\mathcal{I}, \pi} = $ true. By the construction of $\mathcal{B}_1$, we have $\mathcal{B}_0^{\mathcal{I}, \pi} = $ true. By the assumption $(\mathcal{B}_0 \xrightarrow{\sqsubseteq} \mathcal{H}_0)^{\mathcal{I}, \pi} = $ true, we get $\mathcal{H}_0^{\mathcal{I}, \pi} = $ true, thus $\mathcal{H}_1^{\mathcal{I}, \pi} = $ true, and hence $(\mathcal{B}_1 \xrightarrow{\sqsubseteq} \mathcal{H}_1)^{\mathcal{I}, \pi} = $ true. Since all other axioms in $TB \cup TB_1 \cup BR_0$ and $TB \cup TB_1 \cup BR_1$ agree, we get $\mathcal{I} \models TB \cup TB_1 \cup BR_1$, i.e., $TB \cup TB_1 \cup BR_1$ is satisfiable.

For the other direction, if $TB \cup TB_1 \cup BR_1$ is satisfiable, i.e., there is some interpretation $\mathcal{I}$ such that $\mathcal{I} \models TB \cup TB_1 \cup BR_1$, for all variable assignments π, we have $(\mathcal{B}_1 \xrightarrow{\sqsubseteq} \mathcal{H}_1)^{\mathcal{I}, \pi} = $ true. As before, we only need to consider the case that $\mathcal{B}_0^{\mathcal{I}, \pi} = $ true. Let π' be the variable assignment such that $\pi'(z') = \pi(z); \pi'(x) = \pi(x)$ (for $x \neq z'$). It is easy to see that $\mathcal{B}_1^{\mathcal{I}, \pi'} = $ true. By the assumption $(\mathcal{B}_1 \xrightarrow{\sqsubseteq} \mathcal{H}_1)^{\mathcal{I}, \pi'} = $ true, we get $\mathcal{H}_1^{\mathcal{I}, \pi'} = $ true, thus $\mathcal{H}_0^{\mathcal{I}, \pi'} = $ true. Because the assignments π' and π of all variables in $\mathcal{H}_0$ agree, we have $\mathcal{H}_0^{\mathcal{I}, \pi} = $ true, and hence $\mathcal{I} \models \mathcal{B}_0 \xrightarrow{\sqsubseteq} \mathcal{H}_0$. This shows that $\mathcal{I} \models TB \cup TB_1 \cup BR_0$, i.e., $TB \cup TB_1 \cup BR_0$ is satisfiable.

For case (e), let $\mathcal{B}_0 \xrightarrow{\sqsubseteq} \mathcal{H}$ and $\mathcal{B}_1 \xrightarrow{\sqsubseteq} \mathcal{H}$ denote a bridge rule before and after the transformation step respectively. For one direction, if $\mathcal{B}_0 \xrightarrow{\sqsubseteq} \mathcal{H}$ is satisfiable, there must be an interpretation I such that $\mathcal{I} \models \mathcal{B}_0 \xrightarrow{\sqsubseteq} \mathcal{H}$. For all variable assignments π, if $\mathcal{B}_1^{\mathcal{I}, \pi} = $ false, then $(\mathcal{B}_1 \xrightarrow{\sqsubseteq} \mathcal{H})^{\mathcal{I}, \pi} = $ true, so we only need to consider the cases that $\mathcal{B}_1^{\mathcal{I}, \pi} = $ true. $\mathcal{B}_1^{\mathcal{I}, \pi} = $ true implies $\exists U.D(u)^{\mathcal{I}, \pi} = $ true, so there must be $\delta \in \Delta^{\mathcal{I}}$ such that $\delta \in D^{\mathcal{I}}$. Let π' be the variable assignment such that $\pi'(z) = \delta$, $\pi'(x) = \pi(x)$ (for $x \neq z$). Next, we have $D(z)^{\mathcal{I}, \pi'} = $ true. Because z does not occur in any other axioms (by the applicability of (e) and the non-applicability of (a)), we get $\mathcal{B}_0^{\mathcal{I}, \pi'} = $ true. By the assumption $\mathcal{I} \models \mathcal{B}_0 \xrightarrow{\sqsubseteq} \mathcal{H}$, we find $\mathcal{H}^{\mathcal{I}, \pi'} = \mathcal{H}^{\mathcal{I}, \pi} = $ true, which implies $\mathcal{I} \models \mathcal{B}_1 \xrightarrow{\sqsubseteq} \mathcal{H}$.

For the other direction, if $\mathcal{B}_1 \xrightarrow{\sqsubseteq} \mathcal{H}$ is satisfiable, there must be an interpretation $\mathcal{I}$ such that $\mathcal{I} \models \mathcal{B}_1 \xrightarrow{\sqsubseteq} \mathcal{H}$. For all variable assignments π, if $\mathcal{B}_0^{\mathcal{I}, \pi} = $ false, then $(\mathcal{B}_0 \xrightarrow{\sqsubseteq} \mathcal{H})^{\mathcal{I}, \pi} = $ true obviously, so we only need to consider the cases that $\mathcal{B}_0^{\mathcal{I}, \pi} = $ true that imply $D(z)^{\mathcal{I}, \pi} = $ true and $\pi(z) \in D^{\mathcal{I}}$. In such cases, for any variable u we have $\exists U.D(u)^{\mathcal{I}, \pi} = $ true. Thus $\mathcal{B}_1^{\mathcal{I}, \pi} = $ true. By assumption we get $\mathcal{H}^{\mathcal{I}, \pi} = $ true, and hence

$\mathcal{I} \models \mathcal{B}_0 \xrightarrow{\sqsubseteq} \mathcal{H}$. Again we conclude that TB $\cup$ TB_0 $\cup$ BR_0 and TB $\cup$ TB_1 $\cup$ BR_1 are equisatisfiable.

Through the above analysis, we can see that every step of Algorithm 1 does not change the satisfiability of the knowledge base, so TB_{BR} and DTB are equisatisfiable. $\square$

Lemma 3. If DTB is regular, then TB_{BR} is regular.

Proof. As before, we will show every step of Algorithm 1 does not change regularity.

Cases (a) and (b) clearly do not affect regularity since they only involve concept axioms (not role axioms). By Definition 6, as long as the transformed bridge rule ($\mathcal{B} \xrightarrow{\sqsubseteq} \mathcal{H}$ or $\mathcal{H} \xrightarrow{\sqsupseteq} \mathcal{B}$) satisfies all conditions of regularity, case (c) does not affect regularity because the order of roles in the RIA $R_1 \circ ... \circ R_n \sqsubseteq R$, which is added into TB_{BR}, is the same as the original order $R_1(x, x_2)$, ..., $R_n(x_n, y)$ in $\mathcal{B}$.

For case (d), the regularity can be affected only when the new role S is $\prec$-smaller than role R(x, y) in $\mathcal{H}$ and S introduces a new terminal or beginning element to the single maximal path in $\mathcal{B}$, where role R(s, t) had been in terminal or beginning position before. However, according to the precondition of (d), in this case, the reduced concept axiom D(z) can only be D(x) or D(y). In both cases, regularity will not be changed by introducing S.

For case (e), the regularity can be affected by inserting $\exists U.D(u)$ only when the first variable of R forms the beginning of the single maximal path in $\mathcal{B}$ or the second variable of R forms the terminal of the single maximal path in $\mathcal{B}$. If the former, we set u = y (see also step (i) of (e)) and regularity is preserved because u does not replace the beginning of the previous maximum path; if the latter, we set u = x, and regularity is preserved again because u does not replace the terminal of the previous maximum path. $\square$

As mentioned earlier, it is decidable to check satisfiability of the regular $\mathcal{DSROIQ}$ knowledge base, i.e., it is decidable to check satisfiability of regular TB_{BR}. By Lemma 3 and Lemma 2, we conclude that it is decidable to check satisfiability of regular DTB. Considering that the set of bridge rules can be converted into $\mathcal{DSROIQ}$ axioms in polynomial time (Lemma 1), we conclude that the worst-case time complexity for this problem is the same as for checking satisfiability of TB_{BR}. Finally, we obtain Theorem 2.

Theorem 2. Given distributed Tbox DTB with $\mathcal{DSROIQ}$ as local ontology language, there must be a single $\mathcal{DSROIQ}$ Tbox TB_{BR} that can be computed in polynomial time in the size of BR such that TB_{BR} and DTB are equisatisfiable. If DTB is regular, then it is decidable to check satisfiability of DTB and its worst-case time complexity is the same as to check satisfiability of TB_{BR}.

5   Related Work

Grau et al. [3] and Mossakowski et al. [4] propose the distributed ontology framework that composes local ontologies by $\mathcal{E}$-connection. Claudia et al. [5] present a modalised version and develop a resolution-based reasoning algorithm by introducing a set of resolution-based inference rules. The preconditions of the $\mathcal{E}$-connection framework require that the local fields must be disjoint; hence, it is not suitable to be the logic's basis for the semantic Web, which is locally heterogeneous and partially overlapping. In addition, the expression ability of this framework is restricted in order to satisfy its preconditions. For example, an element in some ontology cannot be declared as the sub-element or the super-element of an element in other ontology, so the subset relation cannot be propagated from one ontology to another under the $\mathcal{E}$-connection framework.

Lutz et al. [1] present a distributed ontology framework in which the relations of ontologies are described by conservative extension. Ontology $T_1 \cup T_2$ is a conservative extension of ontology T_1 w.r.t. a signature Σ if and only if every consequence of $T_1 \cup T_2$ w.r.t. Σ is also a consequence of T_1. Focusing on several DLs such as ALC, ALCQI, ALCQIO and EL, they study the decidability and the complexity of deciding whether an extension of an ontology is conservative and whether two ontologies are signature inseparable. Konev et al. [2] introduce and study model-theoretic notions and related reasoning problems for Lutz's works. Conservative extension can be used in not only ontology integration but also ontology decomposition. However, the applicability of this framework is limited to the case that there are signature dependencies among distributed ontologies and the reasoning procedure considers less communications between ontologies. We think that overly strict restrictions imposed on semantic mapping reduce the ability to describe and reason about distributed features.

In addition, based on the extension of semantic mapping mechanisms, Chiara et al. [10] proposed an expressive revised version of distributed first-order logic (DFOL) that is equipped with a sound and complete theorem proving method. However, only theorem proving by natural deductive reasoning is provided, which restricts the efficient application of DFOL in practice.

6 Conclusions

In this paper, we focus on the D3L reasoning with heterogeneous bridge rules containing composite elements in subset ends. By extending the semantics of the regularity of role hierarchy, we define the regularity of DTB and provide an algorithm that can translate a D3L knowledge base with $\mathcal{DSROIQ}$ as local ontology language into a single $\mathcal{DSROIQ}$ knowledge base. Next, the properties of transformation and the complexity of D3L centralized reasoning based on our algorithm are discussed. Our work can address heterogeneous composite bridge rules effectively and shows that centralized reasoning for D3L with such bridge rules can obtain the same worst-case time complexity as the existing distributed reasoning method.

References

1. Lutz, C., Wolter, F.: Deciding inseparability and conservative extensions in the description logic EL. J. Symb. Comput. **45**(2), 194–228 (2010)
2. Konev, B., Lutz, C., Walther, D., Wolter, F.: Model-theoretic inseparability and modularity of description logic ontologies. Artif. Intell. **203**, 66–103 (2013)

3. Cuenca Grau, B., Parsia, B., Sirin, E.: Ontology integration using ε-connections. In: Stuckenschmidt, H., Parent, C., Spaccapietra, S. (eds.) Modular Ontologies. LNCS, vol. 5445, pp. 293–320. Springer, Heidelberg (2009). https://doi.org/10.1007/978-3-642-01907-4_14

4. Mossakowski, T., Kutz, O., Codescu, M.: The distributed ontology, modeling and specification language. In: 7th International Workshop on Modular Ontologies, pp. 1–21. IOS Press, Amsterdam (2013)

5. Nalon, C., Kutz, O.: Towards resolution-based reasoning for connected logics. Electron. Notes Theor. Comput. Sci. **305**, 85–102 (2014)

6. Wang, Z.: Distributed Information Retrieval Oriented Automatic Reasoning. Institute of Computing Technology, Chinese Academy of Sciences, Beijing (2010)

7. Zhao, X., Tian, D., Chen, L., Shi, Z.: Reasoning theory for D3L with compositional bridge rules. In: Shi, Z., Leake, D., Vadera, S. (eds.) IIP 2012. IAICT, vol. 385, pp. 106–115. Springer, Heidelberg (2012). https://doi.org/10.1007/978-3-642-32891-6_15

8. Zhao, X., Tian, D., Zhang, W., Shi, Z.: Properties and distributed tableaux reasoning algorithm for D3L(ccy). J. Comput. Res. Dev. **51**(3), 570–579 (2014)

9. Horrocks, I., Kutz, O., Sattler, U.: The even more irresistible $\mathcal{SROIQ}$. In: 10th International Conference on Principles of Knowledge Representation and Reasoning, pp. 57–67. AAAI, CA (2006)

10. Ghidini, C., Serafini, L.: Distributed first order logic. Artif. Intell. **253**, 1–39 (2017)

11. Stuckenschmidt, H., Parent, C., Spaccapietra, S.: Modular Ontologies-Concepts. Theories and Techniques for Knowledge Modularization. Springer, Heidelberg (2009). https://doi.org/10.1007/978-3-642-01907-4

12. Abbes, S.B., Scheuermann, A., Meilender T.: Characterizing modular ontologies. In: 6th International Workshop on Modular Ontologies, pp. 13–25. IOS Press, Amsterdam (2012)

13. Chang, L., Shi, Z., Gu, T., Zhao, L.: A family of dynamic description logics for representing and reasoning about actions. J. Autom. Reasoning **49**(1), 1–52 (2012)

14. Staab, S., Studer, R.: Handbook on Ontologies, 2nd edn. Springer, Heidelberg (2009). https://doi.org/10.1007/978-3-540-92673-3

Inconsistency Handling for Partially Preordered Ontologies: Going Beyond Elect

Sihem Belabbes[✉][iD] and Salem Benferhat[iD]

CRIL et CNRS, Université d'Artois, Lens, France
{belabbes,benferhat}@cril.fr

Abstract. We continue investigations into computing repairs for an inconsistent Description Logic (DL) knowledge base (KB). In recent work, a tractable method, called Elect, has been introduced to restore consistency of the ABox w.r.t. the TBox. Elect deals with the case of KBs expressed in DL-Lite and when a partial preorder is applied to the ABox. It has been shown that Elect generalizes the well-known IAR semantics when no priority relation over the ABox is used, and the so-called non-defeated semantics when the relation is a total preorder. In the present paper, we propose two extensions of Elect. First, we redefine Elect by using a preference-based semantics from the literature but with the drawback of losing tractability. Second, we show under which conditions Elect can be generalized to DLs that are more expressive than DL-Lite.

Keywords: Inconsistency · Description Logics · Ontologies · Partially preordered knowledge bases

1 Introduction

Description Logics (DLs) offer a variety of logic-based formalisms for representing and reasoning with knowledge that is usually specified in an ontology, also called a knowledge base (KB) [1]. Inconsistencies may arise in a KB, typically when the ABox component, issued from different sources, is inconsistent with respect to the TBox component, making the whole KB inconsistent.

Several inconsistency-tolerant semantics have been defined to allow for reasoning with inconsistent DL KBs [2,7,9,12,13]. For instance, the ABox Repair (AR) and the Intersection ABox Repair (IAR) semantics [11] are based on the notion of a repair, which is a maximal subset (in terms of set inclusion) of the ABox that is consistent w.r.t. the TBox. Using AR semantics, queries are evaluated separately on each of the repairs before intersecting the sets of answers. Using IAR semantics, queries are evaluated over the intersection of all the repairs. It is known that AR is more productive but computationally expensive, whereas IAR is tractable but more cautious.

© Springer Nature Switzerland AG 2019
C. Douligeris et al. (Eds.): KSEM 2019, LNAI 11775, pp. 15–23, 2019.
https://doi.org/10.1007/978-3-030-29551-6_2

Another line of research considers the case where a priority relation is applied to the assertions of the ABox. The so-called non-defeated repair semantics [4] has been proposed for ABoxes prioritized by way of a total preorder. The idea is to iteratively apply IAR semantics to a cumulative sequence of partitions of the ABox in order to produce a single repair. This can be done in polynomial time. Preferred repair semantics [6] also relies on total preorders to identify the most preferred repairs. Basically, it introduces variants of AR and IAR semantics by defining different preferred repairs based on: set cardinality, partitioning the ABox according to priority levels and assigning weights to the assertions.

Recently, a method called Elect [3] has been introduced for computing repairs when a partial preorder is applied to the assertions of the ABox. In the context of DL-Lite, Elect collapses with the IAR semantics for flat ABoxes (with no priority relation) and non-defeated semantics for totally preordered ABoxes. Intuitively, Elect returns the set of elected assertions, namely those that are strictly preferred to all their opponents, and does so in polynomial time. It has been shown in [3] that Elect can be defined equivalently as the result of applying the non-defeated semantics over all total extensions of the partially preordered ABox.

We propose two extensions of Elect when a partial preorder is applied to the ABox. First, instead of using the non-defeated semantics as the backbone of Elect, we consider a preferred-repair semantics based on prioritized set inclusion proposed in [6] (in the spirit of early work on prioritized propositional logic [5,8]). We call this method $Partial_{PR}$ (PR stands for Preferred Repair) and show that although it produces a repair that is larger than an Elect-repair, its computational properties are not satisfactory, even in DL-Lite. Second, we go beyond DL-Lite and consider more expressive DLs. The main difference is that conflicts between assertions are not necessarily binary as it is the case in DL-Lite [9]. We adapt the definitions and discuss the repercussions on time complexity.

After some preliminaries on DL-Lite in Sect. 2, we recall the underpinnings of Elect in Sect. 3. In Sect. 4, we introduce the method $Partial_{PR}$. In Sect. 5 we adapt Elect to DLs in general. Section 6 concludes the paper.

2   Preliminaries and Example

We briefly recall the basics of the DL-Lite$_R$ variant of DL-Lite languages [10]. We assume a finite set of *concept names* C, a finite set of *role names* R and a finite set of *individual names* I, such that C, R and I are pairwise disjoint. The language is defined as follows: $R \to P \mid P^-$; $E \to R \mid \neg R$; $B \to A \mid \exists R$; $C \to B \mid \neg B$, where $A \in$ C, $P \in$ R, and P^- is the *converse* of P. R and E are *roles*, while B and C are *concepts*. An *inclusion axiom* on concepts (resp. on roles) is a statement of the form $B \sqsubseteq C$ (resp. $R \sqsubseteq E$). Inclusions with $\neg$ in the right-hand side are called *negative inclusions*, otherwise they are called *positive inclusions*. A *TBox* $\mathcal{T}$ is a finite set of both positive and negative inclusion axioms. An *assertion* is a statement of the form $A(a)$ or $P(a,b)$, with $a, b \in$ I. An *ABox* $\mathcal{A}$ is a finite set of assertions. For a given $\mathcal{T}$ and $\mathcal{A}$, we denote a KB with $\mathcal{K} = \langle \mathcal{T}, \mathcal{A} \rangle$. A KB is *consistent* if it admits at least one model, it is *inconsistent* otherwise. A TBox $\mathcal{T}$

is *incoherent* if there is $A \in C$ such that A is empty in every model of $\mathcal{T}$, it is *coherent* otherwise. Henceforth, we shall refer to DL-Lite$_R$ simply as DL-Lite. (Refer to [10] for more details on the DL-Lite fragments.)

In this paper, we use the following running example (first proposed in [3]).

Example 1. Assume that we have the following TBox:

$$\mathcal{T} = \begin{cases} 1.\ Mdance \sqsubseteq Dance, & 2.\ Tdance \sqsubseteq Dance, \\ 3.\ Mdance \sqsubseteq DanceWoP, & 4.\ Tdance \sqsubseteq DanceWP, \\ 5.\ DanceWoP \sqsubseteq \neg DanceWP, & 6.\ DanceWoP \sqsubseteq \neg \exists HasProp, \\ 7.\ \exists HasProp^- \sqsubseteq Prop, & 8.\ \exists HasProp \sqsubseteq DanceWP \end{cases}$$

Axioms 1 and 3 (resp. 2 and 4) state that modern (resp. traditional) dances are dances without (resp. with) props. Axiom 5 means that the set of modern dances (without props) and the set of traditional dances (with props) are disjoint. Axiom 6 states that a modern dance does not have props. Axiom 7 expresses the fact that elements used by dances should belong to the set of props. Axiom 8 specifies that anything having props must be a dance with props.

The ABox is given by the following assertions:

$$\mathcal{A} = \begin{cases} Mdance(d_1), Mdance(d_2), Tdance(d_2), Tdance(d_3), \\ Tdance(d_4), DanceWP(d_3), DanceWP(d_5), DanceWoP(d_5), \\ HasProp(d_2, fl), HasProp(d_3, hat), HasProp(d_4, hk) \end{cases}$$

where each $d_i, i = 1, \ldots, 5$, represents a dance, and fl (for flowers), hat and hk (for handkerchiefs) represent props used in dances.

3 Elect Repair for Partially Preordered Assertional Bases

In Sects. 3 and 4 and unless stated otherwise, we consider a DL-Lite KB $\mathcal{K} = \langle \mathcal{T}, \mathcal{A} \rangle$ that may be inconsistent. We assume that the TBox $\mathcal{T}$ is coherent and reliable, so its elements are not questionable in the presence of conflicts. However the ABox $\mathcal{A}$ may be inconsistent w.r.t. the TBox $\mathcal{T}$.

Definition 1. *A sub-base $\mathcal{R} \subseteq \mathcal{A}$ is a maximal repair if $\langle \mathcal{T}, \mathcal{R} \rangle$ is consistent, and $\forall \mathcal{R}' \subseteq \mathcal{A}$ s.t. $\mathcal{R} \subsetneq \mathcal{R}', \langle \mathcal{T}, \mathcal{R}' \rangle$ is inconsistent. Furthermore if $\langle \mathcal{T}, \mathcal{A} \rangle$ is consistent, then there is only one repair $\mathcal{R} = \mathcal{A}$.*

Under the AR semantics, query answers are those holding in every repair. Under the IAR semantics, answers are returned from a single repair obtained by intersecting all the repairs: $IAR(\mathcal{A}) = \bigcap \{ \mathcal{R} \mid \mathcal{R} \text{ is a maximal repair of } \mathcal{A} \}$.

Definition 2. *A sub-base $\mathcal{C} \subseteq \mathcal{A}$ is an assertional conflict of $\mathcal{K}$ iff $\langle \mathcal{T}, \mathcal{C} \rangle$ is inconsistent and $\forall f \in \mathcal{C}, \langle \mathcal{T}, \mathcal{C} \setminus \{f\} \rangle$ is consistent.*

We denote by $\mathcal{C}(\mathcal{A})$ the set of conflicts in $\mathcal{A}$ w.r.t. $\mathcal{T}$. A nice feature of DL-Lite is that computing the set of conflicts is done in polynomial time and a conflict $\mathcal{C}$ involves exactly two assertions [9]. We denote a binary conflict as a pair $\mathcal{C} = \{f, g\}$ and say that f and g are conflicting assertions.

Example 2. In our running example, the set of conflicts in $\langle \mathcal{T}, \mathcal{A} \rangle$ is:

$$\mathcal{C}(\mathcal{A}) = \{\{Mdance(d_2), Tdance(d_2)\}, \{Mdance(d_2), HasProp(d_2, fl)\},$$
$$\{DanceWP(d_5), DanceWoP(d_5)\}\}.$$

One can check that the IAR-repair of $\mathcal{A}$ is:

$$IAR(\mathcal{A}) = \{Mdance(d_1), Tdance(d_3), Tdance(d_4), DanceWP(d_3),$$
$$HasProp(d_3, hat), HasProp(d_4, hk)\}.$$

□

In recent work [3], a method has been proposed for dealing with inconsistent KBs when a partial preorder (denoted $\unrhd$) is applied to the assertions of the ABox denoted $(\mathcal{A}, \unrhd)$. The method is called Elect and the repair it returns is denoted $Elect(\mathcal{A}, \unrhd)$. It relies on the notion of an elected assertion [3] like so:

Definition 3. *Let $(\mathcal{A}, \unrhd)$ be a partially preordered ABox. An assertion $f \in \mathcal{A}$ is elected iff $\forall \{f, g\} \in \mathcal{C}(\mathcal{A})$, $f \rhd g^1$.*

Henceforth, we denote by $Elect(\mathcal{A}, \unrhd) = \{f \in \mathcal{A} \text{ s.t. } f \text{ is elected}\}$ the set of elected assertions. We refer to *Elect-repair* as the result of replacing $\mathcal{A}$ by $Elect(\mathcal{A}, \unrhd)$. It has been shown that the computation of $Elect(\mathcal{A}, \unrhd)$ can be achieved in polynomial time w.r.t. the size of $\mathcal{A}$ [3].

Example 3. Let us assume a partial preorder $\unrhd$ over assertions of the ABox that are split up into the following four subsets:

- $A = \{Mdance(d_1) \overset{\unrhd}{\equiv} Tdance(d_2) \overset{\unrhd}{\equiv} Tdance(d_3) \overset{\unrhd}{\equiv} HasProp(d_3, hat)\}$
- $B = \{HasProp(d_2, fl) \overset{\unrhd}{\equiv} DanceWP(d_3) \overset{\unrhd}{\equiv} DanceWoP(d_5) \overset{\unrhd}{\equiv} DanceWP(d_5)\}$
- $C = \{Mdance(d_2)\}$
- $D = \{Tdance(d_4) \overset{\unrhd}{\equiv} HasProp(d_4, hk)\}$

where $f \overset{\unrhd}{\equiv} g$ means that the two assertions have the same priority level. Moreover, A (resp. D) contains assertions with the highest (resp. lowest) priority. Assertions of B and C are not comparable.

Using the notion of elected assertions of Definition 3, one can check that:
– Assertion $Mdance(d_2)$ is not elected since $\{Mdance(d_2), Tdance(d_2)\}$ is a conflict and $Mdance(d_2) \rhd Tdance(d_2)$ does not hold.
– Neither $DanceWoP(d_5)$ nor $DanceWP(d_5)$ is elected since the two assertions are conflicting and have the same priority level.
– Assertion $HasProp(d_2, fl)$ is not elected since $\{Mdance(d_2), HasProp(d_2, fl)\}$ is a conflict and $HasProp(d_2, fl) \rhd Mdance(d_2)$ does not hold.
All other assertions are elected: $Elect(\mathcal{A}, \unrhd) = A \cup \{DanceWP(d_3)\} \cup D$.   □

---

[1] We denote by $\rhd$ the strict preference relation associated with $\unrhd$.

It has been shown in [3] that $Elect(\mathcal{A}, \unrhd)$ can be computed equivalently by viewing the partial preorder $\unrhd$ as a family of total preorders, then computing the associated non-defeated repairs [4], and finally intersecting them.

Definition 4. *Let $(\mathcal{A}, \unrhd)$ be a partially preordered ABox.*
– A total preorder $\geq$ over $\mathcal{A}$ is a total extension of $\unrhd$ over $\mathcal{A}$ iff $\forall f, g \in \mathcal{A}$, if $f \unrhd g$ then $f \geq g$.
– Let $\mathcal{A} = (\mathcal{S}_1, \ldots, \mathcal{S}_n)^2$ be the well-ordered partition associated with a total preorder $\geq$. The non-defeated repair of $(\mathcal{A}, \geq)$ is: $nd(\mathcal{A}, \geq) = \mathcal{S}'_1 \cup \ldots \cup \mathcal{S}'_n$, where $\forall i = 1, \ldots, n$; $\mathcal{S}'_i = IAR(\mathcal{S}_1 \cup \ldots \cup \mathcal{S}_i)$.

Then $Elect(\mathcal{A}, \unrhd) = \bigcap_{\geq} \{nd(\mathcal{A}, \geq)$ s.t. $\geq$ is a total extension of $\unrhd\}$.

4   A Preference-Based Semantics for Elect

The non-defeated semantics [4] underlies the definition of Elect when a partial preorder is applied to the ABox. We propose to redefine Elect in terms of a preference-based semantics introduced in [6], which is more productive than the non-defeated repair semantics. Let us first recall the concept of preferred repairs defined for totally preordered ABoxes.

Definition 5. *Let $\mathcal{A} = (\mathcal{S}_1, \ldots, \mathcal{S}_n)$ be a prioritized ABox. Let $\mathcal{R}_1$ and $\mathcal{R}_2$ be two consistent sub-bases of $\mathcal{S}_1 \cup \cdots \cup \mathcal{S}_n$.*
– $\mathcal{R}_1$ is equally preferred to $\mathcal{R}_2$ iff $\mathcal{R}_1 \cap \mathcal{S}_i = \mathcal{R}_2 \cap \mathcal{S}_i$ for every $1 \leq i \leq n$.
– $\mathcal{R}_1$ is strictly preferred to $\mathcal{R}_2$ iff there is some $1 \leq i \leq n$ s.t. $\mathcal{R}_2 \cap \mathcal{S}_i \subsetneq \mathcal{R}_1 \cap \mathcal{S}_i$ and for all $1 \leq j < i$, $\mathcal{R}_1 \cap \mathcal{S}_j = \mathcal{R}_2 \cap \mathcal{S}_j$.
Then $\mathcal{R} \subseteq \mathcal{A}$ is a preferred repair if $\nexists \mathcal{R}' \subseteq \mathcal{A}$ s.t. $\mathcal{R}'$ is strictly preferred to $\mathcal{R}$.

Example 4. The relation $\unrhd$ of Example 3 has three total extensions as follows: in $\geq_1$ B is strictly preferred to C, in $\geq_2$ B and C are equally preferred, and in $\geq_3$ C is strictly preferred to B. Let $(\mathcal{A}, \geq_1)$, $(\mathcal{A}, \geq_2)$ and $(\mathcal{A}, \geq_3)$ be the associated ABoxes. One can check that the corresponding non-defeated repairs are:

– $nd(\mathcal{A}, \geq_1) = \mathcal{A} \cup \{HasProps(d_2, fl), DancesWP(d_3)\} \cup D$.
– $nd(\mathcal{A}, \geq_2) = \mathcal{A} \cup \{DancesWP(d_3)\} \cup D$.
– $nd(\mathcal{A}, \geq_3) = \mathcal{A} \cup \{DancesWP(d_3)\} \cup D$.

One can also check that the preferred repairs for each one of these ABoxes are:

– $\mathcal{R}_1 = \mathcal{A} \cup \{HasProp(d_2, fl), DanceWP(d_3), DanceWP(d_5)\} \cup D$
– $\mathcal{R}_2 = \mathcal{A} \cup \{HasProp(d_2, fl), DanceWP(d_3), DanceWoP(d_5)\} \cup D$.   □

---

[2] Namely, $\mathcal{S}_1 = \{f : \nexists g \in \mathcal{A}, g > f\}$ and $\forall i = 2 \ldots n, \mathcal{S}_i = \{f : \nexists g \in \mathcal{A} \backslash (\mathcal{S}_1 \cup \cdots \cup \mathcal{S}_{i-1})$ s.t. $g > f\}$, where $>$ denotes the strict relation associated with $\geq$.

The notion of preferred repairs, initially defined for total preorders, can then be used as a basis for defining a repair associated with a partial preorder $\trianglerighteq$. We call the new setting $Partial_{PR}(\mathcal{A}, \trianglerighteq)$ (where PR stands for preferred repairs). Like $Elect(\mathcal{A}, \trianglerighteq)$, $Partial_{PR}(\mathcal{A}, \trianglerighteq)$ considers all total extensions $\geq$ of $\trianglerighteq$. However instead of intersecting non-defeated repairs like in Elect, we consider the intersection of preferred repairs, denoted IPR$(\mathcal{A}, \geq)$, like so:

Definition 6. *Let $(\mathcal{A}, \trianglerighteq)$ be a partially preordered ABox. Let $\geq$ be a total extension of $\trianglerighteq$ and $(\mathcal{A}, \geq)$ a totally preordered ABox.*
– The intersection of preferred repairs associated with one total extension $(\mathcal{A}, \geq)$ is: $IPR(\mathcal{A}, \geq) = \bigcap \{\mathcal{R} \mid \mathcal{R}$ is a preferred repair of $\geq\}$.
– The preferred repair associated with $(\mathcal{A}, \trianglerighteq)$ is:
$Partial_{PR}(\mathcal{A}, \trianglerighteq) = \bigcap_{\geq} \{IPR(\mathcal{A}, \geq)$ s.t. $\geq$ is a total extension of $\trianglerighteq\}$.

Example 5. Let us continue Example 4. For $1 \leq i \leq 3$, we have:
$IPR(\mathcal{A}, \geq_i) = A \cup \{HasProp(d_2, fl), DanceWP(d_3)\} \cup D$.
Therefore $Partial_{PR}(\mathcal{A}, \trianglerighteq) = A \cup \{HasProp(d_2, fl), DanceWP(d_3)\} \cup D$.
Notice that $Partial_{PR}(\mathcal{A}, \trianglerighteq) = Elect(\mathcal{A}, \trianglerighteq) \cup \{HasProp(d_2, fl)\}$.
Hence $Elect(\mathcal{A}, \trianglerighteq) \subsetneq Partial_{PR}(\mathcal{A}, \trianglerighteq)$. $\square$

Obviously, $Partial_{PR}(\mathcal{A}, \trianglerighteq)$ is consistent, since it is the intersection of some maximal repairs which, by definition, are consistent. We now show that a repair computed by $Partial_{PR}(\mathcal{A}, \trianglerighteq)$ is larger than a base computed by $Elect(\mathcal{A}, \trianglerighteq)$.

Proposition 1. $Elect(\mathcal{A}, \trianglerighteq) \subseteq Partial_{PR}(\mathcal{A}, \trianglerighteq)$. *The converse is false.*

Proof. Consider an assertion $f \in Elect(\mathcal{A}, \trianglerighteq)$ but $f \notin Partial_{PR}(\mathcal{A}, \trianglerighteq)$. This means that there is an extension $\geq$ of $\trianglerighteq$ and a preferred repair $\mathcal{R}$ of $\geq$ s.t. $f \notin \mathcal{R}$. Let $(\mathcal{S}_1, \ldots, \mathcal{S}_n)$ be the well-ordered partition associated with $\geq$. Assume that $f \in \mathcal{S}_i$ for some $1 \leq i \leq n$. Since f is elected, then $[(\mathcal{R} \cap \mathcal{S}_1) \cup \cdots \cup (\mathcal{R} \cap \mathcal{S}_i)] \cup \{f\}$ is consistent. Hence one can construct a maximal repair $\mathcal{R}' \subseteq \mathcal{A}$ that contains $[(\mathcal{R} \cap \mathcal{S}_1) \cup \cdots \cup (\mathcal{R} \cap \mathcal{S}_i)] \cup \{f\}$. This, by definition, means that $\mathcal{R}'$ is strictly preferred to $\mathcal{R}$, which contradicts the fact that $\mathcal{R}$ is a preferred repair. Example 5 serves as counterexample to show that the converse is false. $\square$

The method $Partial_{PR}$ does not compete with Elect. Indeed, $Partial_{PR}(\mathcal{A}, \trianglerighteq)$ is intractable since when $\trianglerighteq$ is a total preorder, $Partial_{PR}(\mathcal{A}, \trianglerighteq) = IPR(\mathcal{A}, \trianglerighteq)$, and it has been shown that the complexity of $IPR(\mathcal{A}, \trianglerighteq)$ is coNP [6].

5   Elect Repair Beyond DL-Lite

We generalize Elect to partially preordered ABoxes specified in languages that are more expressive than DL-Lite. In particular, we focus on DLs where assertional conflicts $\mathcal{C} \in \mathcal{C}(\mathcal{A})$ need not be binary (i.e. involve two assertions like in DL-Lite). The obtained results also collapse with IAR (for flat ABoxes) and non-defeated repair (for totally preordered ABoxes) since they are both defined independently of the size of conflicts. However, we need to adapt the definition of an elected assertion for non-binary conflicts.

Definition 7. *Let $\mathcal{K}$ be a DL KB with a partially preordered ABox $(\mathcal{A}, \unrhd)$. An assertion $f \in \mathcal{A}$ is elected iff $\forall \mathcal{C} \in \mathcal{C}(\mathcal{A})$ where $f \in \mathcal{C}, \exists g \in \mathcal{C}, g \neq f$ s.t. $f \rhd g$.*

Note that when $\mathcal{C}$ is a binary conflict, Definition 7 amounts to Definition 3.

We now formally define the repair based on elected assertions in languages that are more expressive than DL-Lite. We refer to it as *dl-Elect repair*.

Definition 8. *Let $\mathcal{K}$ be a DL KB with a partially preordered ABox $(\mathcal{A}, \unrhd)$.
$dl\text{-}Elect(\mathcal{A}, \unrhd) = \bigcap_{\geq} \{nd(\mathcal{A}, \geq)$ s.t. $\geq$ is a total extension of $\unrhd\}$.*

Let us provide a characterization for the repair dl-Elect$(\mathcal{A}, \unrhd)$.

Proposition 2.

1. An assertion $f \in \mathcal{A}$ is elected in $(\mathcal{A}, \unrhd)$ iff $f \in dl\text{-}Elect(\mathcal{A}, \unrhd)$.
2. $dl\text{-}Elect(\mathcal{A}, \unrhd)$ is consistent w.r.t. $\mathcal{T}$.

Proof. Let $(\mathcal{A}, \unrhd)$ be a partially preordered assertional base.
(1.i) Let $f \in \mathcal{A}$ be elected. Let us show that for each total extension $\geq$ of $\unrhd$, $f \in nd(\mathcal{A}, \geq)$. Let $(\mathcal{S}_1, \ldots, \mathcal{S}_n)$ be the well-ordered partition associated with $\geq$. Assume that $f \in \mathcal{S}_i$ for some $i \in \{1, \ldots, n\}$. From Definition 7, $\forall \mathcal{C} \in \mathcal{C}(\mathcal{A})$ where $f \in \mathcal{C}, \exists g \in \mathcal{C}, g \neq f$, s.t. $f \rhd g$ and also $f > g$. So $\forall \mathcal{C} \in \mathcal{C}(\mathcal{A})$ s.t. $f \in \mathcal{C}, \exists g \in \mathcal{C}$, $g \neq f, g \in \mathcal{S}_j$ with $j > i$. Hence, $\nexists \mathcal{C} \in \mathcal{S}_1 \cup \cdots \cup \mathcal{S}_i$ where $f \in \mathcal{C}$. Removing any element from $\mathcal{C}$ leads to a consistent set of assertions w.r.t. $\mathcal{T}$. This means that $f \in IAR(\mathcal{S}_1 \cup \ldots \cup \mathcal{S}_i)$. So $f \in nd(\mathcal{A}, \geq)$, hence $f \in$ dl-Elect$(\mathcal{A}, \unrhd)$.
(1.ii) To show the converse, assume $f \in \mathcal{A}$ is not elected and let us build a total extension $\geq$ of $\unrhd$ s.t. $f \notin nd(\mathcal{A}, \geq)$. So $\exists \mathcal{C} \in \mathcal{C}(\mathcal{A})$ s.t. $f \in \mathcal{C}$ and $\forall g \in \mathcal{C}$, $g \neq f, f \rhd g$ does not hold. So there is a total extension $\geq$ of $\unrhd$ where $\forall g \in \mathcal{C}$, $g \neq f, g \geq f$. Let $(\mathcal{S}_1, \ldots, \mathcal{S}_n)$ be associated with $\geq$, and let $f \in \mathcal{S}_i$ for some $i \in \{1, \ldots, n\}$. Since $\forall g \in \mathcal{C}, g \neq f, g \geq f$, then $\forall g \in \mathcal{C}$, if $f \in \mathcal{S}_i, g \in \mathcal{S}_j$ for some $j \leq i$. Hence, $\forall k \in \{1, \ldots, n\}, f \notin IAR(\mathcal{S}_1 \cup \ldots \cup \mathcal{S}_k)$, hence $f \notin nd(\mathcal{A}, \geq)$.
(2) Assume dl-Elect$(\mathcal{A}, \unrhd)$ is inconsistent w.r.t. $\mathcal{T}$, so $\exists \mathcal{C} \subseteq$ dl-Elect$(\mathcal{A}, \unrhd)$. This means $\forall f \in \mathcal{C}, \exists g \in \mathcal{C}, g \neq f$, s.t. $f \rhd g$, which is impossible.   □

We consider the following modified version of our example.

Example 6. Let $\mathcal{T}' = \mathcal{T} \cup \{Mdance \sqsubseteq Reg_1, Tdance \sqsubseteq Reg_2, Reg_1 \sqcap Reg_2 \sqcap Reg_3 \sqsubseteq \bot\}$, that is, modern (resp. traditional) dances originate from region 1 (resp. region 2), and a dance may originate from two regions but not from three. The last axiom represents a ternary conflict. Let $\mathcal{A}' = \mathcal{A} \cup \{Reg_1(d_6), Reg_2(d_6), Reg_3(d_6), Mdance(d_6), Tdance(d_6)\}$, where d_6 represents a dance. Assume that $\unrhd$ on $\mathcal{A}'$ introduces the strict preferences: $Reg_1(d_6) \rhd Reg_2(d_6) \rhd Reg_3(d_6)$ and $Mdance(d_6) \rhd Tdance(d_6)$. $\mathcal{C}(\mathcal{A}') = \mathcal{C}(\mathcal{A}) \cup \{\{Reg_1(d_6), Reg_2(d_6), Reg_3(d_6)\}, \{Mdance(d_6), Tdance(d_6)\}\}$. One can easily check that:
dl-Elect$(\mathcal{A}', \unrhd) = Elect(\mathcal{A}, \unrhd) \cup \{Reg_1(d_6), Reg_2(d_6), Mdance(d_6)\}$.   □

From a computational point of view, maintaining tractability requires that conflicts are handled efficiently. Indeed, the complexity of dl-Elect$(\mathcal{A}, \unrhd)$ depends on the complexity of computing conflicts. If it is polynomial, then the whole process is polynomial. Notice that checking if some assertion $f \in \mathcal{A}$ is elected simply comes down to: (a) parsing all assertional conflicts, (b) checking for each conflict $\mathcal{C} \in \mathcal{C}(\mathcal{A})$ if there is some assertion $g \in \mathcal{C}$ that is strictly less preferred than f. This is done in polynomial time w.r.t. the size and number of conflicts.

6 Conclusion

This paper follows on a recent proposal of an inconsistency-tolerant semantics, named Elect [3], for partially preordered lightweight ontologies. Similarly to the well-known IAR semantics, Elect produces a single repair in polynomial time. We have extended Elect in two ways. The first extension concerns increasing the size of the repair by using a preference-based semantics as the backbone of Elect. However this impacts negatively on complexity even in DL-Lite. The second extension redefines Elect in the general context of more expressive DLs.

Another extension of Elect in the context of DL-Lite consists in applying deductive closure to produce a larger repair. This method, called CElect, is defined over the intersection of the closure of non-defeated repairs w.r.t. the positive inclusion axioms of the TBox. Interestingly, CElect is consistent and is equivalent to the closure of IAR for a flat ABox, which is different from the *Intersection Closed ABox Repair* (ICAR) [11]. And for a totally preordered ABox, CElect is equivalent to the closure of the non-defeated repair. Moreover, the Elect-repair is included in the CElect-repair. Space considerations prevent us from providing the details here and we shall do so in future work.

An ongoing work to investigate further is query answering from ontologies representing Southeast Asian dances, within the AniAge project. Experts annotate dance videos w.r.t. the TBox to capture the cultural knowledge behind postures and movements. Confidence levels are attached to annotations. However different experts may not share the same meaning of confidence scales. The whole annotation process is translated into a partially preordered ABox. Conflicts emerge when the same video is annotated differently by several experts. Inconsistencies need to be handled efficiently in order to compute query answers.

Acknowledgements. This work was supported by the European project H2020-MSCA-RISE: AniAge (High Dimensional Heterogeneous Data based Animation Techniques for Southeast Asian Intangible Cultural Heritage).

References

1. Baader, F., Calvanese, D., Mcguinness, D., Nardi, D., Patel-Schneider, P.: The Description Logic Handbook: Theory, Implementation, and Applications (2007)
2. Baget, J., et al.: A general modifier-based framework for inconsistency-tolerant query answering. In: KR, Cape Town, South Africa, pp. 513–516 (2016)
3. Belabbes, S., Benferhat, S., Chomicki, J.: Elect: An inconsistency handling approach for partially preordered lightweight ontologies. In: LPNMR, Philadelphia, USA, pp. 210–223 (2019)

4. Benferhat, S., Bouraoui, Z., Tabia, K.: How to select one preferred assertional-based repair from inconsistent and prioritized DL-Lite knowledge bases? In: IJCAI, Buenos Aires, Argentina, pp. 1450–1456 (2015)
5. Benferhat, S., Dubois, D., Prade, H.: Some Syntactic Approaches to the Handling of Inconsistent Knowledge Bases: A Comparative Study. Part 2 : The Prioritized Case, vol. 24, pp. 473–511. Physica-Verlag, Heidelberg (1998)
6. Bienvenu, M., Bourgaux, C., Goasdoué, F.: Querying inconsistent description logic knowledge bases under preferred repair semantics. In: AAAI, pp. 996–1002 (2014)
7. Bienvenu, M., Bourgaux, C.: Inconsistency-tolerant querying of description logic knowledge bases. In: Pan, J.Z., et al. (eds.) Reasoning Web 2016. LNCS, vol. 9885, pp. 156–202. Springer, Cham (2017). https://doi.org/10.1007/978-3-319-49493-7_5
8. Brewka, G.: Preferred subtheories: an extended logical framework for default reasoning. In: IJCAI, Detroit, USA, pp. 1043–1048 (1989)
9. Calvanese, D., Kharlamov, E., Nutt, W., Zheleznyakov, D.: Evolution of *DL – Lite* knowledge bases. In: Patel-Schneider, P.F., et al. (eds.) ISWC 2010. LNCS, vol. 6496, pp. 112–128. Springer, Heidelberg (2010). https://doi.org/10.1007/978-3-642-17746-0_8
10. Calvanese, D., De Giacomo, G., Lembo, D., Lenzerini, M., Rosati, R.: Tractable reasoning and efficient query answering in description logics: the DL-Lite family. J. Autom. Reason. **39**(3), 385–429 (2007)
11. Lembo, D., Lenzerini, M., Rosati, R., Ruzzi, M., Savo, D.F.: Inconsistency-tolerant semantics for description logics. In: Hitzler, P., Lukasiewicz, T. (eds.) RR 2010. LNCS, vol. 6333, pp. 103–117. Springer, Heidelberg (2010). https://doi.org/10.1007/978-3-642-15918-3_9
12. Lukasiewicz, T., Martinez, M.V., Simari, G.I.: Inconsistency handling in datalog+/- ontologies. In: ECAI, Montpellier, France, pp. 558–563 (2012)
13. Tsalapati, E., Stoilos, G., Stamou, G., Koletsos, G.: Efficient query answering over expressive inconsistent description logics. In: IJCAI, New York, USA, pp. 1279–1285 (2016)

Semantic Modeling of Textual Relationships in Cross-modal Retrieval

Jing Yu[1], Chenghao Yang[2], Zengchang Qin[2(✉)], Zhuoqian Yang[2], Yue Hu[1], and Zhiguo Shi[3]

[1] Institute of Information Engineering, Chinese Academy of Sciences, Beijing, China
{yujing02,huyue}@iie.ac.cn
[2] Intelligent Computing and Machine Learning Lab,
Beihang University, Beijing, China
{alanyang,zcqin,yzhq97}@buaa.edu.cn
[3] School of Computer and Communication Engineering,
University of Science and Technology Beijing, Beijing, China
szg@ustb.edu.cn

Abstract. Feature modeling of different modalities is a basic problem in current research of cross-modal information retrieval. Existing models typically project texts and images into one embedding space, in which semantically similar information will have a shorter distance. Semantic modeling of textural relationships is notoriously difficult. In this paper, we propose an approach to model texts using a featured graph by integrating multi-view textual relationships including semantic relationships, statistical co-occurrence, and prior relationships in knowledge base. A dual-path neural network is adopted to learn multi-modal representations of information and cross-modal similarity measure jointly. We use a Graph Convolutional Network (GCN) for generating relation-aware text representations, and use a Convolutional Neural Network (CNN) with non-linearities for image representations. The cross-modal similarity measure is learned by distance metric learning. Experimental results show that, by leveraging the rich relational semantics in texts, our model can outperform the state-of-the-art models by 3.4% on 6.3% in accuracy on two benchmark datasets.

Keywords: Textual relationships · Relationship integration ·
Cross-modal retrieval · Knowledge graph ·
Graph Convolutional Network

1 Introduction

Cross-modal information retrieval (CMIR), which enables queries from one modality to retrieve information in another, plays an increasingly important role in intelligent searching and recommendation systems. A typical solution of CMIR is to project features from different modalities into one common semantic space in order to measure cross-modal similarity directly. Therefore, feature

© Springer Nature Switzerland AG 2019
C. Douligeris et al. (Eds.): KSEM 2019, LNAI 11775, pp. 24–32, 2019.
https://doi.org/10.1007/978-3-030-29551-6_3

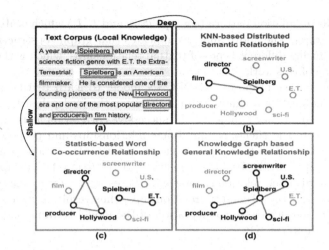

Fig. 1. (a) The original text; (b) distributed semantic relationship; (c) word co-occurrence relationship; and (d) general knowledge relationship.

representation is fundamental for CMIR research and has great influence on the retrieval performance. Recently, Deep Neural Networks (DNN) achieve superior advances in cross-modal retrieval [7,17]. For text-image retrieval, much effort has been devoted to vector-space models, such as the CNN-LSTM network [7], to represent multimodal data as "flat" features for both irregular-structured text data and grid-structured image data. For image data, CNN can effectively extract hierarchies of visual feature vectors. However, for text data, the "flat" features are seriously limited by their inability to capture complex structures hidden in texts [9] – there are many implicit and explicit textual relationships that characterize syntactic rules in text modeling. Nevertheless, the possibility of infusing prior facts or relationships (e.g., from a knowledge graph) into deep textual models is excluded by the great difficulty it imposes.

Early works attempt to learn shallow statistical relationships, such as co-occurrence [11] or location [8]. Later on, semantic relationship based on syntactic analysis [4] or semantic rules between conceptual terms are explored. Besides, semantic relationship derived from knowledge graphs (e.g., Wikidata [14]) has attracted increasing attention. A most recent work [17] models text as featured graphs with semantic relationships. However, the performance of this practice heavily relies on the generalization ability of the word embeddings. It also fails to incorporate general human knowledge and other textual relationships. To illustrate the above point, a text modeled by different types of relationships is shown in Fig. 1. It can be observed in the KNN graph (Fig. 1-b) that *Spielberg* is located relatively far away from *Hollywood* as compared to the way *director* is to *film*, whereas in the common sense knowledge graph given in (Fig. 1-d), these two words are closely related to each other as they should be. Figure 1-c shows the less-frequent subject-predicate relation pattern (e.g. *Spielberg* and *E.T.*) which is absent in the KNN-based graph. The above analysis indicates that graph construction can be improved by fusing different types of textual relationships, which is the underlying motivation of this work.

In this paper, we propose a GCN-CNN model to learn textual and visual features for similarity matching. The novelty is on the in-depth study of textual relationship modeling for enhancing the successive correlation learning. The key idea is to explore the effects of multi-view relationships and propose a graph-based integration model to combine complementary information from different relationships. Specifically, besides semantic and statistic relationships, we also exploit fusion with the relational knowledge bases for acquiring common sense about entities and their semantic relationships, thus resulting in a knowledge-driven model. TensorFlow implementation of the model is available at https://github.com/yzhq97/SCKR.

2   Methodology

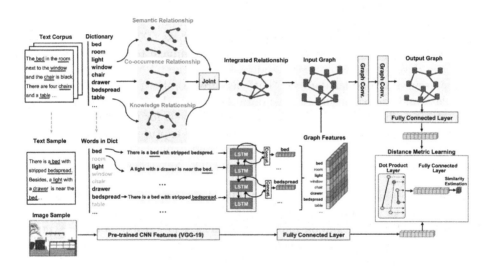

Fig. 2. The schematic illustration of our proposed framework for cross-modal retrieval.

In this paper, a dual-path neural network (as shown Fig. 2) is proposed to learn multimodal features and cross-modal similarity in an end-to-end mode. It mainly consists of three parts: (1) *Text Modeling* (top in Fig. 2): each text is represented by a featured graph by combining multi-view relationships, that is also the key idea and will be elaborated later. Graph construction is performed off-line and the graph structure is identical for all the texts in the dataset. Then we adopt Graph Convolutional Network (GCN) [2], containing two layers of convolution modules, to progressively enhance the textual representations over the constructed graph. The last FC layer projects the text features to the common semantic space; (2) *Image Modeling* (bottom in Fig. 2): we use pre-trained Convolutional Neural Network (CNN), i.e., VGGNet [13], for visual feature learning. Similar to text modeling, the last FC layer is fine-tuned to project visual features to the same semantic space as the text; (3) *Distance Metric Learning* (right in Fig. 2): the similarity between textual and visual features are measured via distance metric learning. An inner product layer is used to combine these two kinds of features, followed by a FC layer with a sigmoid activation to output the similarity scores. We use ranking-based pairwise loss function formalized in [6] for training, which can maximize the similarity of positive text-image pairs and minimizes the similarity of negative ones.

2.1   Fine-Grained Textual Relationship

In this section, we introduce the construction of graph structure to represent each text. As is mentioned above, all the texts share the same graph. Given the training texts, we extract all the nouns to form a dictionary and each noun corresponds to a vertex in the graph. The vertex set is denoted as V. Edges are the integration of the following relationships from different views.

Distributed Semantic Relationship (SR). Following the distributional hypothesis [3], words appear in similar context may share semantic relationship, which is critical for relation modeling. To model such semantic relationship, we build a semantic graph denoted as $G_{SR} = (V, E_{SR})$. Each edge $e_{ij(SR)} \in E_{SR}$ is defined as follows:

$$e_{ij(\text{SR})} = \begin{cases} 1 & \text{if } w_i \in N_k(w_j) \text{ or } w_j \in N_k(w_i) \\ 0 & \text{otherwise} \end{cases} \quad (1)$$

where $N_k(\cdot)$ is the set of k-nearest neighbors computed by the cosine similarity between words using *word2vec* embedding and k is the neighbor numbers, which is set to 8 in our experimental studies.

Word Co-occurrence Relationship (CR). Co-occurrence statistics have been widely used in many tasks such as keyword extraction and web search. Although the appearance of word embeddings seems to eclipse this method, we argue that it can serve as effective backup information to capture infrequent but syntax-relevant relationships. Each edge $e_{ij(CR)} \in E_{CR}$ in the graph $G_{CR} = (V, E_{CR})$ indicates that the words w_i and w_j co-occur at least ϵ times. The CR model can be formulated as below:

$$e_{ij(\text{CR})} = \begin{cases} 1 & \text{if } Freq(w_i, w_j) \geq \epsilon \\ 0 & \text{otherwise} \end{cases} \quad (2)$$

where $Freq(w_i, w_j)$ denotes the frequency that w_i and w_j appear in the same sentence in the dataset, we define ϵ as the threshold to rule out noise, which aims to achieve better generalization ability and improve computation efficiency. We empirically set ϵ to be 5.

General Knowledge Relationship (KR). General knowledge can effectively support decision-making and inference by providing high-level expert knowledge as complementary information to training corpus. However, it is not fully covered by task-specific text. In this paper, we utilize the triples in Knowledge Graphs (KG), i.e. (Subject, Relation, Predicate), which well represent various relationships in human commonsense knowledge. To incorporate such real-world relationships, we construct the graph $G_{KR} = (V, E_{KR})$ and each edge $e_{ij(KR)} \in E_{KR}$ is defined as below:

$$e_{ij(\text{KR})} = \begin{cases} 1 & \text{if } (w_i, relation(w_i, w_j), w_j) \in D \\ 0 & \text{otherwise} \end{cases} \tag{3}$$

where D refers to a given knowledge graph. In this paper, we adopt wikidata [14] in our experiments. For simplification, we ignore the types of relationships in KG and leave it for the future work.

Graph Integration. Different textual relationships capture information from different perspectives. It is conceivable that the relationship integration will fuse semantic information. We simply utilize the union operation to obtain multi-view relationships. $G = (V, E)$, where the edge set E satisfying:

$$E = E_{SR} \cup E_{CR} \cup E_{KR} \tag{4}$$

2.2 Graph Feature Extraction

Previous work [17] adopts Bag-of-Words (BoW), i.e., the word frequency, as the feature of each word in the text. However, this kind of feature is not informative enough to capture the rich semantic information. In this paper, we propose a kind of context-aware features for word-level representations. We first pretrain a Bi-LSTM in the text parts of the training set to predict the corresponding category labels, then sum up the concatenated outputs of Bi-LSTM of each word over every mention in the text to obtain the word representation. Such representation is context-relevant and can better incorporate the content-specific semantics in the text. From our experiment observation, our proposed context-aware graph features can achieve +2% overall retrieval performance lift compared with traditional BoW features. Due to the space limitation, we omit the BoW experimental results and focus on our proposed Bi-LSTM features.

3   Experimental Studies

Datasets. In this section, we test our models on two benchmark datasets: Cross-Modal Places [1] (CMPlaces) and English Wikipedia [10] (Eng-Wiki). CMPlaces is one of the largest cross-modal datasets providing weakly aligned data in five modalities divided into 205 categories. We follow the way in [17] for sample generation, resulting in 204,800 positive pairs and 204,800 negative pairs for training, 1,435 pairs for validation and 1,435 pairs for test. Eng-Wiki is the most widely used dataset in literature. There are 2,866 image-text pairs divided into 10 categories. We generate 40,000 positive samples and 40,000 negative samples respectively from the given 2,173 pairs for training. The remaining 693 pairs are for test. We use MAP@100 to evaluate the performance. The density for all models over two datasets is much less than 1%, indicating that our models are not trivial dense matrix.

Implementation Details. We set the dropout ratio 0.2 at the input of the last fully connected layer, learning rate 0.001 with an Adam optimization, and regularization weight 0.005. The parameters setting for loss function follows [17]. In the final semantic mapping layers of both text path and image path, the reduced dimensions are set to 1,024 for both datasets. The Bi-LSTM model is pretrained on classification task on Eng-wiki and CMPlaces, respectively.

Table 1. MAP score comparison on two benchmark datasets.

Method	Q_T	Q_I	Avg.	Dataset
CCA [10]	18.7	21.6	20.2	Eng-Wiki
SCM [10]	23.4	27.6	25.5	
LCFS [16]	20.4	27.1	23.8	
LGCFL [5]	31.6	37.8	34.7	
GMLDA [12]	28.9	31.6	30.2	
GMMFA [12]	29.6	31.6	30.6	
AUSL [18]	33.2	39.7	36.4	
JFSSL [15]	41.0	**46.7**	43.9	
GIN [17]	76.7	45.3	61.0	
SR [ours]	83.5	41.4	62.4	
SCR [ours]	84.3	42.6	63.4	
SKR [ours]	83.9	42.0	62.9	
SCKR [ours]	**84.9**	44.0	**64.4**	
BL-ShFinal [1]	3.3	12.7	8.0	CMPlaces
Tune(Free) [1]	5.2	18.1	11.7	
TuneStatReg [1]	15.1	22.1	18.6	
GIN [17]	19.3	16.1	17.7	
SR [ours]	18.6	15.8	17.2	
SCR [ours]	25.4	20.3	22.8	
SKR [ours]	24.8	20.5	22.6	
SCKR [ours]	**28.5**	**21.3**	**24.9**	

Comparison with State-of-the-Art Methods. In the Eng-Wiki dataset, we compare our model to some state-of-the-art (SOTA) retrieval models, which are listed in Table 1. We observe that SCKR achieves the best performance on the average MAP scores and slightly inferior to JFSSL on the image query (Q_I), which confirms that our relation-aware model can bring an overall improvement over existing CMIR models. Especially, text query (Q_T) gains remarkable 8.2% increase over the SOTA model GIN, which proves that our model leads to better representation and generalization ability for the text query. In the large CMPlaces dataset, compared with the previous SOTA models, SCKR also achieves 6.3% improvement compared to TuneStatReg [1].

Ablation Study. In this section, we conduct ablation experiments to evaluate the influence of the components in our proposed SCKR model. We compare SCKR model to three ablated versions, i.e., SR, SCR and SKR. The retrieval performance is also listed in Table 1. Compared to SR, both SCR and SKR achieve a significant improvement on both datasets (i.e., +5% on CMPlaces and +2% on Eng-Wiki). It indicates that either co-occurrence or the common-sense knowledge could provide complementary information to the distributed semantic relationship modeling. By integrating all kinds of textual relationships (SCKR), we obtain further promotion on MAP scores, especially on the relation-rich CMPlaces dataset. It is because that SR, CR or KR alone focuses on different views of relationships and their integration could bring more informative connections to the relational graph, thus facilitating information reasoning.

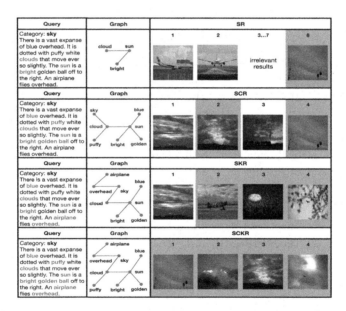

Fig. 3. Some samples of text query results using four of our models on the CMPlaces dataset. The corresponding relation graphs are shown in the second column. The retrieval results are given in the third column.

Qualitative Analysis. Fig. 3 gives an example for the text-query task on SCKR and three baseline models. We show the corresponding relation graphs and the retrieved results. We observe that SR captures the least relationships and the results are far from satisfaction, which necessitates the exploration of the richer textual relationship. SCR can effectively emphasize the descriptive textual relationship (e.g. *"sun-ball"* and *"sun-bright"*), which is infrequent but informative for better understanding the content. Notice that, only SKR incorporates the relationship between *"overhead"* and *"airplane"* through *"sky-overhead-airplane"* inference path, which indicates that general knowledge is beneficial in relation inference and information propagation. The SCKR model leverages the advantages of different models and achieves the best performance.

4   Conclusions

In this paper, we proposed a graph-based approach to integrate multi-view textual relationships, including the semantic relationship, statistical co-occurrence, and pre-defined knowledge graph, for text modeling in the CMIR tasks. A GCN-CNN framework is proposed for feature learning and cross-modal correlation modeling. Experimental results on both two benchmark datasets show that our model can significantly outperforms the state-of-the-art models, especially for text queries. In the future work, we can extend this model to other cross-modal areas such as automatic image captioning and video captioning.

Acknowledgement. This work is supported by the National Key Research and Development Program (Grant No. 2017YFB0803301).

References

1. Castrejon, L., Aytar, Y., Vondrick, C., Pirsiavash, H., Torralba, A.: Learning aligned cross-modal representations from weakly aligned data. In: CVPR (2016)
2. Defferrard, M., Bresson, X., Vandergheynst, P.: Convolutional neural networks on graphs with fast localized spectral filtering. In: NIPS, pp. 3837–3845 (2016)
3. Harris, Z.S.: Distributional structure. Word **10**(2–3), 146–162 (1954)
4. Jiang, C., Coenen, F., Sanderson, R., Zito, M.: Text classifcation using graph mining-based feature extraction. Knowl. Based Syst. **23**(4), 302–308 (2010)
5. Kang, C., Xiang, S., Liao, S., Xu, C., Pan, C.: Learning consistent feature representation for cross-modal multimedia retrieval. TMM **17**(3), 370–381 (2015)
6. Kumar, V.B.G., Carneiro, G., Reid, I.: Learning local image descriptors with deep siamese and triplet convolutional networks by minimizing global loss functions. In: CVPR, pp. 5385–5394 (2016)
7. Li, S., Xiao, T., Li, H., Yang, W., Wang, X.: Identity-aware textual-visual matching with latent co-attention. In: ECCV, pp. 1908–1917 (2017)
8. Mihalcea, R., Tarau, P.: Textrank: bringing order into text. In: EMNLP, pp. 404–411 (2004)
9. Qin, Z., Yu, J., Cong, Y., Wan, T.: Topic correlation model for cross-modal multimedia information retrieval. Pattern Anal. Appl. **19**(4), 1007–1022 (2016)
10. Rasiwasia, N., et al.: A new approach to cross-modal multimedia retrieval. In: ACMMM, pp. 251–260. ACM (2010)
11. Rousseau, F., Vazirgiannis, M.: Graph-of-word and TWIDF: new approach to ad hoc IR. In: CIKM, pp. 59–68 (2013)

12. Sharma, A., Kumar, A., Daume, H., Jacobs, D.W.: Generalized multiview analysis: a discriminative latent space. In: CVPR, pp. 2160–2167 (2012)
13. Simonyan, K., Zisserman, A.: Very deep convolutional networks for large-scale image recognition. In: ICLR (2015)
14. Vrandečić, D., Krötzsch, M.: Wikidata: a free collaborative knowledgebase. Commun. ACM **57**(10), 78–85 (2014)
15. Wang, K., He, R., Wang, L., Wang, W., Tan, T.: Joint feature selection and subspace learning for cross-modal retrieval. PAMI **38**(10), 2010–2023 (2016)
16. Wang, K., He, R., Wang, W., Wang, L.: Learning coupled feature spaces for crossmodal matching. In: ICCV, pp. 2088–2095 (2013)
17. Yu, J., et al.: Modeling text with graph convolutional network for cross-modal information retrieval. In: Hong, R., Cheng, W.-H., Yamasaki, T., Wang, M., Ngo, C.-W. (eds.) PCM 2018. LNCS, vol. 11164, pp. 223–234. Springer, Cham (2018). https://doi.org/10.1007/978-3-030-00776-8_21
18. Zhang, L., Ma, B., He, J., Li, G., Huang, Q., Tian, Q.: Adaptively unified semi-supervised learning for cross-modal retrieval. In: IJCAI, pp. 3406–3412 (2017)

A Smart Search-Based Ontology Visualization Tool Using SPARQL Patterns

Mariem Neji[1(✉)], Fatma Ghorbel[1,2], and Bilel Gargouri[1,2]

[1] MIR@CL Laboratory, University of Sfax, Sfax, Tunisia
`maryam.fsegs@gmail.com`
[2] CEDRIC Laboratory, Conservatoire National des Arts et Mtiers, Paris, France

Abstract. We are proposing a semantic approach that aims to identify valid linguistic web services composition scenarios. It targets both linguistic and software engineering experts. It is based on an OWL2 multilingual ontology, named LingOnto which models and reasons about linguistic knowledge. However, users especially non-ontology experts have difficulty to make sense of LingOnto as they do not understand its syntax. Hence, we decide to visualize LingOnto to attempt this issue. Nevertheless, the heterogeneity and the amount number of linguistic knowledge make the visualisation hard to comprehend due to visual clutter and information overload. In this paper, we propose a user-friendly ontology visualisation tool, named Ling-Graph. It targets both ontology and non-ontology experts and addresses the readability and understandability requirements. Ling-Graph is based on a "smart" search interaction technique, to extract and visualize, from LingOnto, a dynamic ontological view that contains only components corresponding to the user's need. It is relied on a SPARQL patterns-based approach which takes the user's need materialized by a set of search criteria as input and generates the ontological view that matches these criteria. The obtained tool is also applied to visualize the PersonLink ontology for non-ontology experts and a large-scale ontology DBpedia for ontology experts. Finally, we discuss the promising results derived from the evaluation of Ling-Graph.

Keywords: Ontology visualization · "Smart" search interaction · SPARQL patterns · Linguistic ontology

1 Introduction

The **Lingu**istic **W**eb **S**ervices *(LingWS)* are a kind of web services related to the linguistic information system [1]. Such services are used to compose other LingWS(s) corresponding to well-known **N**atural **L**anguage **P**rocessing *(NLP)* applications such as Text Summarization and Machine Translation.

In our previous work [2], we proposed a semantic approach that aims to identify valid LingWS(s) composition scenarios. It targets both linguistic and

© Springer Nature Switzerland AG 2019
C. Douligeris et al. (Eds.): KSEM 2019, LNAI 11775, pp. 33–44, 2019.
https://doi.org/10.1007/978-3-030-29551-6_4

software engineering experts. It is based on an OWL2 multilingual ontology, called LingOnto, which models and reasons about linguistic knowledge (i.e., linguistic data and linguistic processing). This approach consists of three steps. The first step consists in generating, from LingOnto, a dynamic ontological view that aims to highlight only components that correspond to the user's need. In the second step, this ontological view is used to identify an initial composition scenario by selecting a sequence of linguistic processing. The final step helps discover LingWS(s) corresponding to each selected linguistic processing while proposing alternative scenarios once one or more LingWS(s) are not found.

LingOnto is the angular stone of identifying valid LingWS composition scenarios. However, users especially non-ontology experts have difficulty in navigating it as they do not understand its syntax. We decide to visualize this ontology as ontology visualizations facilitate its sense-making [3]. Nevertheless, the heterogeneity and the amount number of linguistic knowledge make the visualisation hard to comprehend due to the visual clutter and information overload. Hence, there is a need for a user-friendly ontology visualization tool which has the particularity to be understandable and readable not only for ontology experts but also non-ontology experts.

In this context, several ontology visualization tools have been developed in the last two decades such as NavigOWL [4], BioOntoVis [5] OWLeasyViz [6] and Protégé VOWL [7] and Memo Graph [8]. Nevertheless, the majority of the available tools (i) target only ontology experts. (ii) They do not take into account the readability requirement. For instance, most of them require the loading of the entire visualization in the limited space provided by the computer screen. (iii) They overlook the importance of the understandability issue. For instance, VOM[1] and OWLGrEd [9] offer a UML-based ontology visualization which require knowledge about UML.

In the present paper, we propose Ling-Graph, a user-friendly ontology visualisation tool that addresses the readability and understandably requirements. It targets both ontology and non-ontology experts. It is based on a "smart" search interaction technique, to extract and visualize, in a dynamic way, only components corresponding to the user's need to offer a readable and understandable ontological view of LingOnto. It is relied on a SPARQL patterns-based approach which takes the user's need materialized by a set of search criteria as input and generates the ontological view that matches these criteria.

The remainder of the paper is organized as follows. Section 2 details our previous work. Section 3 presents some related works on the field of ontology visualization. Section 4 describes Ling-Graph. Then, Sect. 5 includes an evaluation of Ling-Graph. Finally, in Sect. 6, we summarized our work and outline some research possibilities.

---

[1] (Visual Ontology Modeler) http://thematix.com/tools/vom.

2   Background

We proposed an ontology-based approach that aims to assist both linguistic and software engineering experts to identify valid LingWS(s) composition scenarios.

2.1   Our LingOnto Ontology

We proposed a multilingual (i.e., English, French and Arabic) OWL 2 ontology, called LingOnto that allows modeling and reasoning about linguistic knowledge. To create LingOnto, first, we identified some linguistic concepts as well as the appropriate relations between them. The latter ones are extracted from [10] (LMF-ISO 24613 and DCR-ISO 12620) standard and some proposals from the literature such as [11] and [12]. We proceeded by classifying these linguistic concepts into linguistic data concepts and linguistic processing concepts. For each linguistic data concept, we presented the linguistic concepts that are related to it as well as the name of the associated relations. For example, the linguistic data concept 'verb' is in relation with the linguistic data concept 'PartOfSpeech' through the relation 'is-a'. In order to express the semantics of the NLP domain, we identified a set of semantic relations between the linguistic processing which present a strong exchange of knowledge between them. For instance, we cannot identify the part of speech of a word in a particular text without segmenting the latter into words. Hence, the linguistic processing concept 'segmentation' is in relation 'allows-to' with the linguistic processing concept 'PartOfSpeech-tagging'. Moreover, each linguistic processing manipulates various linguistics data as inputs and others as outputs. For instance, the linguistic processing concept 'segmentation' is in relation with the linguistic data concept 'text' through the relation 'hasInput' and in relation with the linguistic data concept 'word' through the relation 'hasOutput'. The current version of LingOnto includes 80 classes, 136 object properties and 326 SWRL rules. It is extensible, which means that we can add other linguistic knowledge.

2.2   Our Approach of Constructing Valid LingWS(s) Scenarios

Our approach is composed mainly of three steps. The first one consists in generating a dynamic ontological view from LingOnto in order to limit the number of visible components and preserve only the ones that correspond to the user's need. The selection of this view is based on a set of search criteria such as the "language" (i.e., English, French and Arabic) and "dichotomy level" (i.e., Linguistic data and linguistic processing). The second step helps identify an initial composition scenario by selecting a sequence of linguistic processing from the generated ontological view. This sequence is validated by a set of defined SWRL rules. We should mention that the composition scenario identified in this step represents a high level service process model. Finally, the third step helps discover LingWS(s) corresponding to each selected linguistic processing while proposing alternative scenarios once one or more LingWS(s) are not found. This step explores the LingWS registry [1] by taking into account the functional and non-functional properties of each LingWS.

3   State of the Art: Ontology Visualization Tools

Quite a number of ontology visualization tools have been proposed in the last couple of decades. We classify them, according to the target users, into **"Ontology visualisation targeting ontology expert users"** and **"Ontology visualisation targeting non-ontology expert users"**.

3.1   Ontology Visualisation Targeting Ontology Expert Users

Many proposed ontology visualization tools are designed to be used only by ontology expert users. However, most of them overlook the importance of the readability and understandability requirements. These issues becomes worse for non-ontology experts. According to [7], the generated visualizations "are hard to read for casual users". For instance, most graph-based tools, as SOVA[2] IsaViz[3] and RDF Gravity[4], require the loading of the whole graph in the limited space provided by the computer screen which generates an important number of nodes and a large number of crossing edges. Without applying any filter, the generated graph appears very dense and crowded, which have a negative impact on its readability and understandability. According to [7], all RDF visualizations are hard to read due to their large size (the RDF visualizations quickly become large in size, with a lot of nodes and edges). OWLGrEd, ezOWL [13] and VOM reuse and adapt popular diagram type to visualize the ontology, such as UML class diagrams. A major drawback of these tools is that they require knowledge about UML. Thus, they are not understandable for non-ontology expert users.

GrOWL and SOVA are intended to offer an understandable visualization by defining notations using different symbols, colors, and node shapes for each ontology key-element. However, the proposed notations contain many abbreviations and symbols from the Description Logic. As a consequence, the generated visualizations are not suitable for casual users.

OWLViz[5], OntoTrack [14], KC-Viz [15] and OntoViz [16] show only specific element(s) of the ontology. For instance, the OWLViz and KC-Viz visualize only the class hierarchy of ontology while OntoViz shows only inheritance relationships between the graph nodes. This is different with TGViz Tab [17] and NavigOWL which provide visualizations representing all the key elements of the ontology. However, these tools do not make a clear visual distinction between the different ontology key-elements. For instance, they use a plain node-link diagram where all the links and nodes look the same except for their color. This issue has a bad impact on the understandability of the generated visualization.

3.2   Ontology Visualisation Targeting Non-ontology Expert Users

Only very few visualisation tools are designed to be used by non-ontology experts: OWLeasyViz, ProtégéVOWL, WebVOWL [7] and Memo Graph. How-

---

[2] http://protegewiki.stanford.edu/wiki/SOVA.
[3] https://www.w3.org/2001/11/IsaViz/overview.html.
[4] http://semweb.salzburgresearch.at/apps/rdf-gravity/.
[5] http://protegewiki.stanford.edu/wiki/OWLViz.

ever, OWLeasyViz is not available for downloading. On the other hand, Web-VOWL and ProtégéVOWL visualize only the schema of the ontology. Besides, they use some Semantic Web words. Moreover, ProtégéVOWL is implemented as Protégé plug-in. Thus, it cannot be integrated in the prototype of our approach of constructing valid LingWS(s) scenarios. Finally, Memo Graph is designed to be used only by Alzheimer's disease patients.

Most of these tools offer a basic keyword-based search interaction technique. It is based on a simple matching between ontology's elements and the keyword that the user is looking for. However, they do not offer advanced search by extracting a combination of elements by taking into account more than one criterion that correspond to the user's need.

4   Ling-Graph Ontology Visualisation Tool

Our Ling-Graph is a user-friendly ontology visualisation tool that aims to offer a readable and understandable visualisation to both ontology and non-ontology experts. It visualizes ontology as graphs. This visualization is displayed using a force-directed method. It uses a facile-to-understand wording. Indeed, it does not use a semantic web vocabulary. It aims also to addresses the readability requirement. The aim is to alleviate the generated graphs. It is based on our "smart" search interaction technique which extract and visualise a dynamic view containing only components corresponding to the user's need. this latter is relied on a SPARQL patterns-based approach that takes the user's need materialized by a set of search criteria as input and generates the ontological view that match these criteria. This visualisation tool offers a simple layout in which its interfaces is divided into three parts: the "Ling-Graph Viewer" displaying the visualization, the "Ling-Graph details" listing details about a selected graph node, and the " Ling-Graph search criteria" providing a set of search criteria. In order to make these three parts distinguishable, we use different color for each frame. Moreover, this tool provides the seven interaction techniques detailed by Shneiderman [18] as well as other more advanced techniques.

4.1   Our "Smart" Search Interaction Technique

Our "smart" search interaction technique is relied on a SPARQL patterns-based approach. It aims to extract and visualize an ontological view, from LingOnto, that contains only components corresponding to the user's need. This need is materialized by a set of search criteria $C = (C_1, C_2, C_3, ..., C_n)$. For each search criterion C_i ($i \in [1, n]$), a set of preferences $CP = (CP_{i/1}, CP_{i/2}, CP_{i/3}, ..., CP_{i/m})$ is associated. For example, the preferences associated with the criterion "language" are : "English", "French" and "Arabic".

We proposed a set of SPARQL patterns $P = (P_1, P_2, P_3, ..., P_k)$ that defines a combination of these criteria. The proposed patterns are modular since each of them P_j ($j \in [1, k]$) is composed of a set of "sub-patterns" $SP = (SP_{j/1}, SP_{j/2}, SP_{j/3}, ..., SP_{j/n})$. Each sub-pattern $SP_{j/i}$ defines a single criterion C_i and can be optional or repeatable in the generated SPARQL query.

SPARQL Pattern Definition. A pattern P_j is a 3-tuple (G,SP,S) where:

- G = (G_n, G_e) is an oriented graph that describes the general structure of the pattern and represents a family of SPARQL queries. It contains a subset of nodes G_n, where each node refers to a search criterion C_i, and a subset of edges G_e where each edge refers to a relation between two search criteria.
- SP = $(SP_{j/1}, SP_{j/2}, SP_{j/3},...,SP_{j/n})$ is a set of n sub-patterns of P where $\forall$ $SP_{j/i} = (SG, cardmin, cardmax) \in P_j$,then, we have SG as a subgraph of G and cardmin, cardmax are respectively the minimal and maximal cardinalities of $SP_{j/i}$ where $0 \le cardmin \le cardmax$. The minimal cardinality is 0 and means that the user does not choose any preference of the criterion C_i defined by the "sub pattern" SP_i. The maximal cardinality of 1 means that the users selects just one preference of G_i and the maximal cardinality greater than 1 means that the user selects a set of preferences of C_i.
- S = $((SW_1, SW_2, SW_3, ..., SW_n), (W_1, W_2, W_3,...,W_l))$ is a template of a descriptive sentence in which n substrings SW_i corresponds to the n sub-patterns of the pattern, l distinct substrings W_k $(k \in [1, (n-1)])$ corresponds to the pattern elements *(i.e. nodes and edges)*.

Fig. 1 shows a SPARQL pattern composed of four "sub-patterns" that define four search criteria : C_1 = "treatments level", C_2 = "language", C_3 = "granularity level" and C_4 = "dichotomy level". All the sub-patterns are optional and repeatable. In the descriptive sentence template, sub-patterns sentences are represented between square brackets and the sub-pattern identifier as an index. The pattern elements are underlined, with an index referring to the graph element.

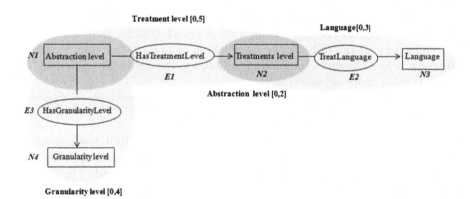

S = [Granularity level *C4*]Granularity level [of Abstraction level *C1* [has a Treatment level *C2*]Treatments level [treat the language *C3*]Language] Abstraction level

Fig. 1. Example of a SPARQL query pattern.

SPARQL Pattern Instantiation. The SPARQL query pattern is instantiated into a SPARQL query graph. For instance, the user expresses his need to develop an automatic summarization application which transforms the most significant sentences in an Arabic text. Consequently, the user selects the following preferences, $CP_{1/1}$ = morphological level, $CP_{2/1}$ = "Arabic", $CP_{3/1}$ = "SubclassOf concepts" and $CP_{4/1}$ = "Linguistic processing". Subsequently, Ling-Graph applies the instantiation of the pattern presented as shown in Fig. 2. Figure 3 presents the generated SPARQL query graph and its associated ontological view.

S = SubClassOf   Linguistic processing has a Morphological level   treat the language Arabic

The generated template of the descriptive sentence allows the final SPARQL query to be built:

SELECT DISTINCT (?x)
WHERE {?x rdfs:subClassOf* :MorphologicalLevelProcessing.
FILTER {:TreatLanguageArabic rdfs:domain ?x }}

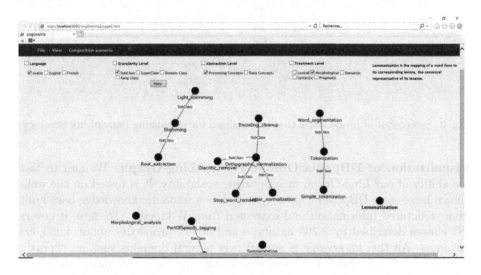

Fig. 2. Screenshot of the generated ontological view.

4.2   Other Applications of Ling-Graph

Ling-Graph is mainly proposed to be integrated in the prototype of our approach of constructing valid LingWS(s) composition scenarios. As consequential effects, it can be used by ontology and non-ontology expert users to offer readable and understandable visualizations not only of small-scale inputs, but also for the large-scale ones thanks to our "smart" search interaction technique.

Integration of Ling-Graph in CAPTAIN MEMO. We integrated Ling-Graph into CAPTIN MEMO [8] to visualize the PersonLink [19] ontology for non-ontology experts, precisely Alzheimer's disease patients. This ontology is used for modeling and reasoning about "family relationships" which are completely dependent on the culture and the language. We set three search criteria : C_1 = "language", C_2 = "culture" and C_3 = "photo". Then, we successively selected the preference(s) associated with each criterion : $CP_{1/1}$ = "French", $CP_{2/1}$ = "France" and $CP_{3/1}$ = "yes", as shown in Fig. 4.

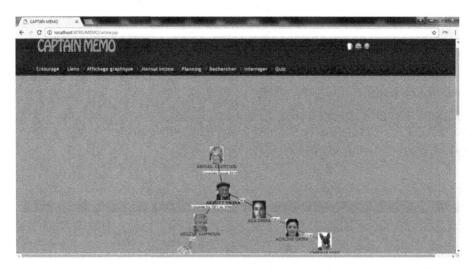

Fig. 3. Screenshot of Ling-Graph that it is utilized for visualizing PersonLink ontology.

Visualization of DBpedia Ontology with Ling-Graph. We aim to test the ability of our Ling-Graph in supporting scalability. It is tested on the well-known large-scale DBpedia [6] ontology which is a semantic knowledge base built from structured information and extracted from Wikipedia. To date, it covers 685 classes described by 2,795 datatype and object properties about 4,233,000 instances. All this knowledge is spread over several domains such as "Sport", "Tourism", "City", etc. We set two search criteria : C_1 = "domain" and C_2 = "number of instance". Then, we successively selected the preference(s) associated with each criterion : $CP_{1/1}$ = "sport", $CP_{2/1}$ = "30", as shown in Fig. 5.

5   Evaluation of Ling-Graph

First, we evaluated its usability using the standard System Usability Scale (SUS) questionnaire [20]. Then, we evaluated the efficiency of the "smart" search interaction technique offered by Ling-Graph using the precision evaluation metric.

---

[6] http://dbpedia.org/.

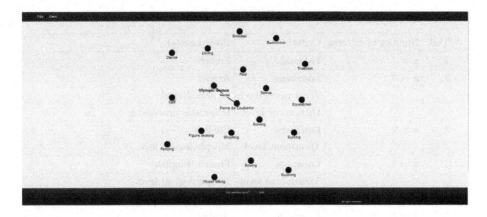

Fig. 4. Screenshot of Ling-Graph that it is utilized for visualizing DBpedia ontology.

This study included 35 participants. Most of them were computer science students of the National School of Engineers of Sfax, and linguistic experts of the Faculty of Arts and Humanities of Sfax. None of the participants had a prior experience with Ling-Graph.

This evaluation is done in the context of our approach of constructing valid LingWS(s) composition scenarios.

5.1   Usability Evaluation

Participants filled out a questionnaire to describe their opinion about the usability of Ling-Graph. In fact, we used the SUS questionnaire which is a well-known and widely used method for the measurement of the user's perception of usability evaluation of systems [20]. A 10-item attitude Likert scale is used to measure the usability of any system. Scores range on a scale from 1 to 5.

According to the SUS formula, the mean usability score of Ling-Graph is **70, 9 (28, 36 * 2, 5)** indicating a high level of usability.

5.2   "Smart" Search Interaction Technique Evaluation

The evaluation of the usability of our "smart" search interaction technique was carried out by comparing the ontological views produced by Ling-Graph against the ones generated by a linguistic expert. Let us consider $(T_1, ..., T_{10})$ where T_i is a task presented in Table 1.

To carry out the evaluation, two scenarios are proposed:

- "Golden standard scenario" : The linguistic expert is requested to identify the ontological view associated with each task T_i.
- "Smart search scenario" : For each task T_i, our Ling-Graph determines the associated ontological view to each task T_i automatically.

Table 1.

Task	Number of criteria	Criteria	Preference(s)
1	n = 1	Language	French
2	n = 3	Language	Arabic
		Treatments level	Semantic level
		Dichotomy level	Linguistic processing
3	n = 2	Language	English
		Treatment level	Morphological level
4	n = 3	Language	French, English
		Treatments level	Morphological level
		Granularity level	Subclass Of
5	n = 2	Language	Arabic
		Treatments level	Syntactic level
6	n = 3	Language	English
		Treatments level	Semantic level
		Granularity level	Subclass Of, Ranges concepts
7	n = 1	Treatments level	Lexical level
8	n = 3	Language	Arabic
		Dichotomy level	Linguistic processing, Linguistic data
		Granularity level	Subclass Of
9	n = 4	Language	Arabic, French
		Treatments level	Subclass Of
		Granularity level	Domain concepts
		Dichotomy level	Linguistic processing
10	n = 2	Language	English, French
		Treatments level	Lexical level

We compared the generated ontological views with Ling-Graph against the golden standard ones. We used the evaluation metric precision PR_i (PR_i represents the precision related to T_i). It is defined in terms of a set of components recorded as important for the user's need according to the two scenarios and the important components recorded according to Ling-Graph. The results are presented in Table 2.

The mean of the precision measures is 76,6%. Overall, it indicates that our "smart" interaction technique is efficient in determining the ontological view corresponding to the user's need.

Table 2. Evaluation's results.

PR_1	PR_2	PR_3	PR_4	PR_5	PR_6	PR_7	PR_8	PR_9	PR_{10}	Mean
60%	75%	90%	75%	85%	85%	78%	62%	76%	81%	76,6%

6 Conclusion

This paper introduced a user-friendly ontology visualisation tool, Ling-Graph, which aims to offer a readable and understandable visualisation to both ontology and non-ontology experts. It is based on a "smart" search interaction technique that aims to extract and visualize, from LingOnto, an ontological view that contains only components corresponding to the user's need. This interaction technique is relied on a SPARQL patterns-based approach which takes the user's need materialized by a set of search criteria as input and generates the associated ontological view.

Ling-Graph is mainly proposed to be integrated in the prototype of our approach of constructing valid LingWS(s) composition scenarios to visualize LingOnto. However, it can be also used by ontology and non-ontology experts to offer readable and understandable visualizations not only of small-scale inputs, but also for the large-scale ones thanks to our "smart" search interaction technique.

Future research will be devoted to ameliorate the actual version of the Ling-Graph. More specifically, we intend to extend the proposed approach to automatically generate the specific search criteria associated to each given ontology.

References

1. Baklouti, N., Gargouri, B., Jmaiel, M.: Semantic-based approach to improve the description and the discovery of linguistic web services. Eng. Appl. AI **46**, 154–165 (2015)
2. Neji, M., Gargouri, B., Jmaiel, M.: A semantic approach for constructing valid composition scenarios of linguistic web services. In: Knowledge-Based and Intelligent Information & Engineering Systems: Proceedings of the 22nd International Conference KES-2018, Belgrade, Serbia, 3–5 September 2018, pp. 685–694 (2018)
3. Lanzenberger, M., Sampson, J., Rester, M.: Visualization in ontology tools. In: 2009 International Conference on Complex, Intelligent and Software Intensive Systems, pp. 705–711 (2009)
4. Hussain, A., Latif, K., Rextin, A.T., Hayat, A., Alam, M.: Scalable visualization of semantic nets using power-law graphs. Appl. Math. Inf. Sci. **8**(1), 355 (2014)
5. Achich, N., Algergawy, A., Bouaziz, B., König-Ries, B.: BioOntoVis: an ontology visualization tool
6. Catenazzi, N., Sommaruga, L., Mazza, R.: User-friendly ontology editing and visualization tools: the owleasyviz approach. In: 2009 13th International Conference Information Visualisation, pp. 283–288 (2009)
7. Lohmann, S., Negru, S., Haag, F., Ertl, T.: Visualizing ontologies with vowl. Semantic Web **7**(4), 399–419 (2016)
8. Ghorbel, F., Ellouze, N., Métais, E., Hamdi, F., Gargouri, F., Herradi, N.: Memo graph: an ontology visualization tool for everyone. Procedia Comput. Sci. **96**, 265–274 (2016)
9. Bārzdiņš, J., Bārzdiņš, G., Čerāns, K., Liepiņš, R., Sproģis, A.: OWLGrEd: a UML style graphical notation and editor for OWL 2. In: Proceedings 7th International Workshop OWL: Experience and Directions (OWLED-2010). http://www.webont.org/owled/2010/papers/owled2010_submission_5.pdf

10. Crasborn, O., Windhouwer, M.: ISOcat data categories for signed language resources. In: International Gesture Workshop, pp. 118–128 (2011)
11. Habash, N.Y.: Introduction to arabic natural language processing. Synthesis Lectures on Human Language Technologies **3**(1), 1–187 (2010)
12. Pasha, A., Al-Badrashiny, M., Diab, M.T., El Kholy, A., Eskander, R., Habash, N., Pooleery, M., Rambow, O., Roth, R.: Madamira: a fast, comprehensive tool for morphological analysis and disambiguation of arabic. LREC **14**, 1094–1101 (2014)
13. Chung, M., Oh, S., Kim, K.-I., Cho, H., Cho, H.-K.: Visualizing and authoring owl OWL in ezOWL. In: The 7th International Conference on Advanced Communication Technology, ICACT 2005, vol. 1, pp. 528–531 (2005)
14. Liebig, T., Noppens, O.: Ontotrack: a semantic approach for ontology authoring. Web Seman. Sci. Serv. Agents World Wide Web **3**(2–3), 116–131 (2005)
15. Peroni, S., Motta, E., d'Aquin, M.: Identifying key concepts in an ontology, through the integration of cognitive principles with statistical and topological measures. In: Asian Semantic Web Conference, pp. 242–256 (2008)
16. Singh, G., Prabhakar, T., Chatterjee, J., Patil, V., Ninomiya, S., et al.: OntoViz: visualizing ontologies and thesauri using layout algorithms. In: The Fifth International Conference of the Asian Federation for Information Technology in Agriculture (AFITA 2006) (2006)
17. Alani, H.: TGVizTab: an ontology visualisation extension for protégé (2003)
18. Shneiderman, B., Plaisant, C., Cohen, M., Jacobs, S., Elmqvist, N., Diakopoulos, N.: Designing the user interface: strategies for effective human-computer interaction (2016)
19. Herradi, N., Hamdi, F., Métais, E., Ghorbel, F., Soukane, A.: Personlink: an ontology representing family relationships for the captain memo memory prosthesis. In: International Conference on Conceptual Modeling, pp. 3–13 (2015)
20. Brooke, J.: Sus: a retrospective. J. Usability Stud. **8**(2), 29–40 (2013)

Recommendation Algorithms and Systems

PRTIRG: A Knowledge Graph for People-Readable Threat Intelligence Recommendation

Ming Du[1,2], Jun Jiang[1], Zhengwei Jiang[1,2(✉)], Zhigang Lu[1,2],
and Xiangyu Du[1,2]

[1] Institute of Information Engineering, Chinese Academy of Sciences,
Beijing 100093, China
{duming,jiangjun860,jiangzhengwei}@iie.ac.cn
[2] School of Cyber Security, University of Chinese Academy of Sciences,
Beijing 100029, China

Abstract. People-Readable Threat Intelligence (PRTI) recommender Systems aim to address the problem of information explosion of PRTIs and make personalized recommendation for users. In general, PRTI is highly condensed, and consists of security items, network entities and emerging hacker organizations, attacks, etc. PRTI may also contain many Machine-Readable Threat Intelligence (MRTI). However, existing methods are unaware of such external knowledge and cannot fully discover latent knowledge-level connections among PRTIs. Under this scenario, the existing generic knowledge graphs will introduce too much noise and can not consider the entity relationship in terms of the attack chain. To solve the problems above, in this paper, we propose a knowledge graph for People-Readable Threat Intelligence recommendation (PRTIRG) and incorporates knowledge graph representation into PRTI recommender system for click-through prediction. The key components of PRTIRG are the denoising entity extraction module and the knowledge-aware long short-term memory neural network (KLSTM). Through extensive experiments on real-world datasets, we demonstrate that the PRTIRG is more effective and accurate than baselines.

Keywords: People-Readable Threat Intelligence recommendation ·
Knowledge graph ·
Knowledge-aware long short-term memory neural network ·
Denoising entity extraction

1 Introduction

The definition of threat intelligence given by Gartner is given in Definition 1. Threat intelligence can be divided into MRTI and PRTI according to the different reading objects. PRTI needs to provide more context, background information, and analysis results. For example, an analysis report for an active APT (Advanced Persistent Threat) organization is a typical PRTI.

© Springer Nature Switzerland AG 2019
C. Douligeris et al. (Eds.): KSEM 2019, LNAI 11775, pp. 47–59, 2019.
https://doi.org/10.1007/978-3-030-29551-6_5

Definition 1. *Threat intelligence is evidence-based knowledge, including context, mechanisms, indicators, implications and actionable advice, about an existing or emerging menace or hazard to assets that can be used to inform decisions regarding the subject's response to that menace or hazard.*

With the development of technologies such as big data, the term threat intelligence came into being, which has a milestone significance for the development of network security protection systems. Faced with the grim security situation, security experts need to change the traditional security defense ideas, identify and defend new threats to network security by tracking and analyzing the characteristics, methods and modes of network security threats timely and effectively. But the explosive growth of online content and services has created an overwhelming choice for users. Recommender systems intend to solve the problem of information explosion by filtering out a small amount of content from a huge amount of data to meet their personalized interests. The traditional Collaborative Filtering predict the interests of long-tail users by collaboratively learning from interests of related users [11] and have achieved significant success in various fields. In practical applications, the user-item matrix which encodes the user's individual preferences for items is usually very sparse, causing CF-based methods to degrade significantly in recommendation performance [7]. To address these problems, researchers have proposed incorporating side information into CF, such as social networks, user/item attributes, images and contexts [18].

Generally, PRTI recommendation is quite difficult as it poses three major challenges. First, PRTI is highly time-sensitive and will expire in a short period of time. In particular, it notes that security events described during the same period are more likely to be relevant, which requires traditional methods to effectively scale on time dynamics issues. Second, the PRTI language is highly condensed and consists of security terms, network entities, new types of hacking organizations, attack methods, attack tools, and so on. The correlation between intelligence is not only based on co-occurrence or clustering structure, but also on attack chain association. For example, as shown in Fig. 1, a user clicks a piece of PRTI in the lower right corner. In fact, the user may also be interested in another piece of PRTI on the left side of the clicked PRTI. By observing the entities marked as red, it can be seen that they are more similar and share the same C&C server. For the top piece of PRTI, it looks less similar to historical concerns by comparing the entities marked as green, but the C&C server 82.137.255.56 mentioned in this piece of PRTI belongs to the APT-C-27 organization as the other C&C server 31.9.48.183. At this point, the user is also likely to be interested in the top PRTI. Third, existing general-purpose knowledge Graphs are not suitable for PRTI recommender systems, such as Google Knowledge Graph and Microsoft Satori. These knowledge graphs are successfully applied in scenarios of machine reading, text classification, and word embedding [19]. However, there are a large amount of noise in them that is not related to the security field. What is more, they do not consider the association of entities at the attack chain level. If we take Fig. 1 as an example, they don't consider that the two servers belong to the same attack organization.

Fig. 1. Illustration of three pieces of Chinese-English mixed PRTIs connected through knowledge graph entities.

To extract deeper logical connections among PRTI, it is necessary to introduce additional knowledge graph information into PRTI recommendation. Knowledge graphs are often constructed from semi-structured knowledge, such as Wikipedia, or harvested from the web with a combination of statistical and linguistic methods [15].

Considering the above challenges in PRTI recommendation and inspired by the wide success of leveraging knowledge graphs, in this paper, we construct a knowledge graph for the PRTI recommendation, in which a denoising entity extraction module is proposed, specifically for every piece of PRTI. We first extract the principal components of PRTIs through the LDA topic model, and then conduct entity extraction such as network entities and hacker organizations entities, which will remove noise, retain the principal components, and reduce the scope of entity extraction. Then, we propose a novel framework that takes advantage of external knowledge for PRTI recommendation, namely the knowledge-aware long short-term memory neural network (KLSTM). KLSTM is a content-based model for click-through prediction. It takes one piece of candidate PRTI and user's click history as input, and outputs whether the user clicks on the candidate PRTI. KLSTM differs from LSTM in that it uses information from the knowledge graph as an auxiliary input. Specifically, for each input PRTI, there are several entities in the knowledge graph corresponding to it, we use these entities to characterize it.

Empirically, we applied PRTIRG to the PRTI recommendation, and the experimental results show that PRTIRG achieves 11.8% and 18.3% ACC gain compared to no external knowledge introduced.

In summary, our contributions in this paper are as follows:

- To the best of our knowledge, this is the first work to build a knowledge graph for PRTI recommendation which combined LDA model with KG-aware LSTM.
- We propose a denoising entity extraction module, and the main contribution of our work focuses on the processing of mixed PRTIs in Chinese and English. Firstly, the principal components of PRTI are extracted through the

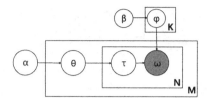

Fig. 2. Graphical model representation of LDA.

LDA topic model. Then, we extract entities like network entities and hacker organizations entities, which removes the noise and reduces the entity extraction range to some extent.

- We proposed KLSTM, a click prediction model that uses KG as an auxiliary information and discusses the impact of user preference shifts on recommendations. Then we conducted experiments on real data. The results demonstrate that our method, which combined PRTIRG with KLSTM in PRTI recommendation, is totally effective.

2   Preliminaries

In this section, we present several concepts and models related to this work, including LDA topic model, knowledge graph embedding and long short-term memory neural network.

2.1   LDA Topic Model

LDA (Latent Dirichlet Allocation) is a topic model proposed by Blei et al. in 2003 [2]. LDA is a three-level hierarchical Bayesian model, it is represented as a probabilistic graphical model in Fig. 2. In the Fig. 2, θ represents the topic distribution, and α is the Dirichlet distribution parameter of the topic distribution θ. β is the Dirichlet distribution parameter of the word probability φ. M represents the total number of documents, N represents the repeated choice of topics and words within a document, K represents the total number of topics.

The LDA model represents document as a mixed distribution of a series of topics, denoted as $p(\tau)$ and each topic is a probability distribution over the word, denoted as $p(\omega|\tau)$. Therefore, the probability distribution of each word in the document is as shown in Eq. (1):

$$p(\omega_i) = \sum_{j=1}^{K} p(\omega_i|\tau_i = j)p(\tau_i = j) \tag{1}$$

Therefor, given the parameters α and β, the joint distribution of a set of N topics τ, and a set of N words ω is given by:

$$p(\omega, \tau|\alpha, \beta) = p(\omega|\tau, \beta)p(\tau|\alpha) = \int p(\tau|\theta)p(\theta|\alpha)d\theta \int p(\omega|\tau, \varphi)p(\varphi|\beta)d\varphi \tag{2}$$

2.2 Knowledge Graph Embedding

A typical knowledge graph consists of triples of the form (h, r, t), in which h, r and t represent the head, the relation, and the tail. Knowledge graph embedding represents each entity and each relation as a low-dimensional representation vector that preserves the original structural information of the knowledge graph. In fact, in addition to representation learning, there is an easier way to represent data, it is one-hot representation. However, one-hot cannot effectively use the semantic similarity information between objects, and there is a problem that the vector dimension is too high, representation learning has advantages over the one-hot method. For knowledge representation learning, researchers have proposed a variety of models, such as structured embedding (SE), neural tensor network (NTN), translation-based knowledge graph embedding. Due to the significant advantages of the translation-based model in terms of performance, we briefly review several translation-based methods in Table 1.

Table 1. Summary of several translation-based methods.

Method	Scoring function $f_r(h,t)$	Motivation & solved problem
TransE [3]	$||h + r - t||_2^2$	Baseline
TransH [20]	$||(h - w_r^T h w_r) + r - (t - w_r^T t w_r)||_2^2$	N-1 and 1-N relationships
TransR [10]	$||M_r h + r - M_r t||_2^2$	Nodes and relationships not be in a vector space
TransD [9]	$||(w_r w_h^T + I)h + r - (w_r w_t^T + I)t||_2^2$	The relationship r represents different meanings

3   Problem Formulation

The typical recommender system generates an interaction matrix $Y = \{y_{uv} | u \in U, v \in V\}$ based on users interaction with items, where

$$y_{uv} = \begin{cases} 1, & \text{if interaction (u, v) is observed;} \\ 0, & \text{otherwise.} \end{cases} \tag{3}$$

A value of 1 for y_{uv} means that the user has implicit feedback on the item, such as clicking behavior and browsing behavior. In addition, we also add the knowledge graph as an auxiliary information to the recommender system. Under the PRTI recommendation scenarios, we extract each piece of PRTI and the output of denoising entity extraction module into entities, which are h and t in the triples (h, r, t). The relationships between PRTI and the output of denoising entity extraction module, and the relationships between different outputs of denoising entity extraction module are r in triples. The subgraph about APT-C-27 mentioned in Fig. 1 is shown in Fig. 3. The center yellow circles represent the PRTI entities, and the circles around them are the principal component entities and special entities which will be introduced in Sect. 4.2. We define a variety of

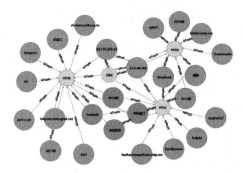

Fig. 3. Subgraph about APT-C-27 PRTI in PRTIRG.

entity relationships, such as the triple (Delphi, isTopic, PRTI1) states the fact that Delphi is one of the topics of PRTI1 and the triple (31.9.48.183, isBind, C&C) states the fact that 31.9.48.183 used to be the C&C server address of APT-C-27.

Given the above interaction matrix Y and knowledge graph, our purpose is to predict whether user u has interest in item v that has not been interacted with before.

4   Knowledge Graph for PRTI Recommendation

In this section, we describe the proposed PRTIRG in detail. We first introduce the overall framework of PRTIRG, and then discuss and introduce our related work from raw data crawling and knowledge graph construction, denoising entity extraction and knowledge-aware LSTM design. We will describe the process of raw data preparation and denoising entity extraction module in Sect. 4.2 and knowledge graph construction in Sect. 4.3.

4.1   PRTIRG Framework

The framework of PRTIRG is illustrated in Fig. 4. The input of PRTIRG are PRTIs that as many as possible, including PRTIs of historical interest to users and candidate PRTIs. For each piece of PRTI, we use a specially designed denoising entity extraction module to extract entities that can better represent PRTI, based on that, we use our entity relationship library to build a knowledge graph for PRTI recommendation. By projecting the entities or relationships of the PRTI knowledge graph into the low-dimensional vector space, we can represent the semantic information of the entities and relationships, and input them as auxiliary information to the recommendation system. It will avoid the cold start and sparse interaction matrix to some extent. The candidate PRTI embedding and the user embedding are concatenated and fed into a long short-term memory neural network (LSTM) to predict whether the user will click on the candidate PRTI. The details will be introduced in Sect. 4.3.

4.2   Raw Data Preparation and Denoising Entity Extraction

Our raw data was obtained by collecting Internet data, including PRTIs posted on Weibo, Twitter and Security Forum over the past five years and users who have forwarded, commented or liked the PRTIs. The collected data includes both pure English PRTIs and Chinese-English mixed PRTIs. Obviously, it is more difficult to deal with the PRTIs described mixed Chinese and English. In this paper, we focus on the PRTIs that mixed description of Chinese and English.

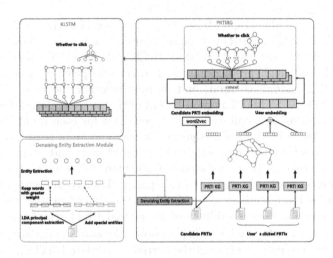

Fig. 4. PRTIRG's overall framework description.

Compared with English named entity recognition, Chinese-English hybrid named entity recognition has more challenges, more unresolved problems, and the general system of recognizing multiple types of named entity is also poor. Another problem is that existing methods extract all the entities in the text, which may bring noise in to the recommended task and increase the overhead of knowledge graph update and maintenance. In view of this, we propose a denoising entity extraction module, as show in Fig. 5. Firstly, the denoising entity extraction module we propose uses the LDA topic model to eliminate the secondary content in the text, retaining the main components that can better characterize the PRTI. And because the word segmentation method we use is for Chinese, English truncation may occur, so we delete all words that do not contain Chinese, and the English words are added back in the third step. Secondly, for the extracted list of subject words, we discard the words with lower weights. Thirdly, all IP addresses, domains, English phrases, etc. in the original PRTIs are matched, we call them special entities. In particular, the English phrases take the longest match. Finally, the principal components extracted in the second step are combined with the special entities as the output of the module.

4.3   Knowledge Graph Construction and Knowledge-Aware LSTM

Except for extracting the output of the denoising entity extraction module mentioned in Sect. 4.2 into entities, we extract each piece of PRTI into an entity to better map to a particular PRTI. PRTI knowledge graph defines a variety of entity relationships, the most representative relationships are isEqual, isTopic, isin, isBind, etc. For example, the relationship 'isEqual' connects two coreferential entities. The maintenance of the network security entity relationship library also plays a positive role in the construction of the knowledge graph. Our update of the knowledge graph is long-term and timely.

Given the knowledge graph above, we propose KLSTM that takes advantage of external knowledge for PRTI recommendation, namely the knowledge-aware long short-term memory neural network (KLSTM). KLSTM is a content-based model for click-through prediction, which takes one piece of candidate PRTI and user's click history as input, and outputs whether the user clicks on the candidate PRTI. KLSTM differs from LSTM in that it uses information from the knowledge graph as an auxiliary input. Specifically, for each input PRTI, there are several entities in the knowledge graph corresponding to it, we use these entities to characterize it. This will avoid the cold start and sparse interaction matrix to some extent. Many knowledge graph embedding methods can be used for entity representation learning. In this paper, TransH [20] which can better solve 1-n and n-1 probelms is selected. Given the clicked history $\{I_1^i, I_2^i, \ldots, I_{N_i}^i\}$ of the user u_i, the embeddings of his clicked PRTIs can be expressed as $e(I_1^i), e(I_2^i), \ldots, e(I_{N_i}^i)$ where $e(I_1^i)$ denotes the *entity embedding* learned by TransH. To represent the user u_i of the current candidate PRTI I_j, one method is to normalize the vector sum of his historical clicked PRTIs:

$$e(u_i) = Normalization(\sum_{k=1}^{N_i} e(I_k^i)) \tag{4}$$

Fig. 5. Illustration of the denoising entity extraction process.

For the I_j mentioned above, we can simply denote it as $e(I_j) = w_{1:n}^j = [w_1^j\ w_2^j \ldots w_n^j]$, where w_n^j is the word embedding. But when all the PRTIs in knowledge graph contain many words, the vector dimension will be too high. We simply average all the word embeddings of $w_{1:n}^j = [w_1^j\ w_2^j \ldots w_n^j]$:

$$e(I_j) = \frac{1}{n} \sum_{k=1}^{n} w_k^j \tag{5}$$

Finally, the input of KLSTM contains user u_i's embedding $e(u_i)$ and candidate PRTI I_j's embedding $e(I_j)$. The output of KLSTM is whether u_i will click on PRTI I_j.

5   Experiments

In this section, we introduce our experiments and results in order to verify the validity of our PRTIRG.

5.1   Dataset Description

Since there is no publicly available PRTI datasets in both the recommended and cybersecurity areas, we have built an objective and realistic PRTI dataset. Our datasets are obtained by collecting public data, including PRTIs posted on Weibo, Twitter, Security Forums and users who have forwarded, commented or liked the PRTIS, and the longest time span of the data is five years. A value of 1 for y_{uv} in interaction matrix Y means the user has forwarded, commented or liked the PRTI. But we can't simply set all PRTIs that have not interacted to 0. Because these PRTIs are likely to be published before the user follows the publisher, a more rigorous approach is to set all PRTIs between the user's earliest attention and the latest attention to 0. For user data, in order to better describe the user, we reserve users who have paid attention to at least 10 PRTIs. The above work will alleviate some user data imbalance problems. For further improvement, we also combined a certain proportion of positive sampling.

We collected a total of 25,000 PRTIs and more than 4,800 users. Use the labeling method described above to mark up and get more than 65,000 pieces of structured data.

5.2   Experiment Setup

We choose TransH [20] to learn the embedding of knowledge entities. In KLSTM, the entity embedding dimension is 100 and the word vector dimension is 200. In order to compare KLSTM with baselines, the evaluation metrics we used are ACC and F1.

To compare the effect of introducing the knowledge graph as an auxiliary information on the experimental results, we set the baselines Collaborative-LSTM and Collaborative-DNN, whose input data only retain the word vector with a dimension of 200. We set up KDNN to compare the performance of LSTM and DNN in this scenario to see if the PRTIs in a certain period of time are more relevant. We also designed several baseline experiments to compare the user's experimental results when retaining different proportions of the tested user's data and all data of other non-tested users as a training set. We will show the experimental results in Sect. 5.3.

5.3 The Prediction Accuracy and F1 Comparison

The comparison results of different baselines are shown in Table 2. The results are the average of the five experimental cases which the data of the tested users is divided into training sets and test sets according to the ratio: 9:1, 8:2, 7:3, 6:4, 5:5. Of course, the training sets here should also add all the data of other non-tested users in order to mine the interests of similar users and supplement the recommendation results.

Compared with the method of PRTI word vector information alone, the KLSTM on the accuracy and F1 are increased by 11.8% and 17.1%, and KDNN's accuracy and F1 increased by 18.3% and 3.3%, respectively. This result illustrates that the introduction of our PRTIRG helps to improve the recommended effect. Then we compare KLSTM with KDNN, KLSTM performs better, with 1.8% and 16.2% growth in accuracy and F1. We think this is because PRTIs are more similar in the same time interval, and KLSTM can retain information within a certain step.

5.4 User Preferences Shift

Table 2. Comparison with baseline experiment.

Modules	ACC	F1
KLSTM	**62.1%**	**69.6%**
Collaborative-LSTM	50.3%	52.5%
KDNN	**60.3%**	**53.4%**
Collaborative-DNN	42%	50.1%

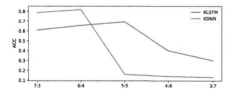

Fig. 6. Model accuracy when training sets and test sets have different size ratios.

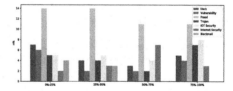

Fig. 7. User preference distribution.

Another factor that affects the effectiveness of the recommender system is the historical interaction between the user and the item. We compare the performance of KSLTM and KDNN when we use different proportions of training sets and test sets of tested user in Fig. 6. It can be seen that when the training set and test set size is 5:5, the accuracy of KDNN drops rapidly, while KLSTM reaches its highest level at this time, and then slowly declines. Interestingly, keep the current training set and the test set is top 10% of the original test set, the accuracy of KDNN is still around 81.6%. We suspect that in addition to the reduction in the size of the training set, it is possible that user preferences have shifted, and KLSTM delays the rate of decline in accuracy because it retains some historical information. In Fig. 7, user data is arranged in chronological order and divided into four parts, facing different parts of data we found that the theme of PRTIs gradually changed from hack and blackmail to Internet security and IOT security, and in the last 50% of the data, the concern for blackmail is 0. This proves the conjecture of the above user preference have shifted.

6 Related Work

Knowledge graph is a structured semantic knowledge base that has been widely used in the industrial field, such as Google Knowledge Graph and Microsoft Satori, as well as other knowledge graphs such as NELL, DBPedia, YAGO, NELL, Probase. In academia, researchers have also proposed various research points. For knowledge representation learning, [8] propose Rule-Guided Embedding (RUGE), a novel paradigm of knowledge graph embedding with iterative guidance from soft rules. For the construction of the knowledge graph, Google's knowledge graph has caused a lot of research, but because of the limited technical details of the disclosure, it is difficult to understand the connotation and value of this technology. [16] introduces the bottom-up knowledge graph construction technology architecture, abstracting the entire build process into three levels, including information extraction layer, knowledge integration layer and knowledge processing layer. For the application of knowledge graph, KG are used in a variety of areas, such as recommendation [14], question answering [1,6], and assisted judgment [17], text classification [12]. As far as we know, this paper is the first work in the PRTI recommendation.

The rise of deep learning has completely changed the recommender systems. Deep learning can effectively capture non-linear and non-trivial user-item relationships and catch the intricate relationships within the data itself. Recently, many companies have integrated deep learning into their recommendation system to improve their recommendation quality [4,5,13]. Yahoo News proposes a news recommendation system based on RNN [5], and YouTube uses a video recommendation algorithm based on deep neural network [13]. We can see a significant revolution in deep learning in industrial recommended applications.

7 Conclusions and Future Work

In this paper, we propose PRTIRG, a knowledge graph that can be used for PRTI recommendation, and naturally incorporate knowledge graph as auxiliary information into recommender systems. By using the LDA topic model, PRTIRG eliminates noise and secondary entities, retains the main components that can better characterize PRTI. Then combined it with the extracted special entities which complement the important features missed by co-occurrence or clustering structure. We conducted extensive experiments on real data and the results proved the significant superiority of PRTIRG.

For future work, we plan to (1) research and enrich PRTIRG to explore its potential in cyber security threat warnings; (2) investigate the combination of KLSTM and attention mechanism to more effectively explore user's interests and improve performance.

Acknowledgment. This work is supported by the Key Research Program of Beijing Municipal Science & Technology Commission (Grant No. D18110100060000, D181100000618003), the Strategic Priority Research Program of Chinese Academy of Sciences (Grant No. XDC02040100, XDC02030200, XDC02020200), the National Key Research and Development Program of China (Grant No. 2017YFC08218042, 2018YFB0803602, 2016QY06X1204). This research was also partially supported by Key Laboratory of Network Assessment Technology, Chinese Academy of Sciences and Beijing Key Laboratory of Network Security and Protection Technology.

References

1. Aditya, S., Yang, Y., Baral, C.: Explicit reasoning over end-to-end neural architectures for visual question answering. In: Thirty-Second AAAI Conference on Artificial Intelligence (2018)
2. Blei, D.M., Ng, A.Y., Jordan, M.I.: Latent dirichlet allocation. J. Mach. Learn. Res. **3**, 993–1022 (2003)
3. Bordes, A., Usunier, N., Garcia-Duran, A., Weston, J., Yakhnenko, O.: Translating embeddings for modeling multi-relational data. In: Advances in Neural Information Processing Systems, pp. 2787–2795 (2013)
4. Cheng, H.T., Koc, L., Harmsen, J., Shaked, T., Shah, H.: Wide & deep learning for recommender systems (2016
5. Covington, P., Adams, J., Sargin, E.: Deep neural networks for youtube recommendations. In: Proceedings of the 10th ACM Conference on Recommender Systems, pp. 191–198. ACM (2016)
6. Dong, L., Wei, F., Zhou, M., Xu, K.: Question answering over freebase with multi-column convolutional neural networks. In: Proceedings of the 53rd Annual Meeting of the Association for Computational Linguistics and the 7th International Joint Conference on Natural Language Processing (Volume 1: Long Papers), vol. 1, pp. 260–269 (2015)
7. Dong, X., Yu, L., Wu, Z., Sun, Y., Yuan, L., Zhang, F.: A hybrid collaborative filtering model with deep structure for recommender systems. In: Thirty-First AAAI Conference on Artificial Intelligence (2017)
8. Guo, S., Wang, Q., Wang, L., Wang, B., Guo, L.: Knowledge graph embedding with iterative guidance from soft rules. In: Thirty-Second AAAI Conference on Artificial Intelligence (2018)
9. Ji, G., He, S., Xu, L., Liu, K., Zhao, J.: Knowledge graph embedding via dynamic mapping matrix. In: Proceedings of the 53rd Annual Meeting of the Association for Computational Linguistics and the 7th International Joint Conference on Natural Language Processing (Volume 1: Long Papers), vol. 1, pp. 687–696 (2015)
10. Lin, Y., Liu, Z., Sun, M., Liu, Y., Zhu, X.: Learning entity and relation embeddings for knowledge graph completion. In: Twenty-Ninth AAAI Conference on Artificial Intelligence (2015)
11. Lu, Z., Dou, Z., Lian, J., Xie, X., Yang, Q.: Content-based collaborative filtering for news topic recommendation. In: Twenty-Ninth AAAI Conference on Artificial Intelligence (2015)

12. Ma, Y., Peng, H., Cambria, E.: Targeted aspect-based sentiment analysis via embedding commonsense knowledge into an attentive LSTM. In: Thirty-Second AAAI Conference on Artificial Intelligence (2018)
13. Okura, S., Tagami, Y., Ono, S., Tajima, A.: Embedding-based news recommendation for millions of users. In: Proceedings of the 23rd ACM SIGKDD International Conference on Knowledge Discovery and Data Mining, pp. 1933–1942. ACM (2017)
14. Palumbo, E., Rizzo, G., Troncy, R.: Entity2rec: learning user-item relatedness from knowledge graphs for top-n item recommendation. In: Proceedings of the Eleventh ACM Conference on Recommender Systems, pp. 32–36. ACM (2017)
15. Paulheim, H.: Knowledge graph refinement: a survey of approaches and evaluation methods. Semant. Web 8(3), 489–508 (2017)
16. Qiao, L., Yang, L., Hong, D., Yao, L., Zhiguang, Q.: Knowledge graph construction techniques. J. Comput. Res. Dev. 53(3), 582–600 (2016)
17. Szekely, P., et al.: Building and using a knowledge graph to combat human trafficking. In: Arenas, M., et al. (eds.) ISWC 2015. LNCS, vol. 9367, pp. 205–221. Springer, Cham (2015). https://doi.org/10.1007/978-3-319-25010-6_12
18. Wang, H., et al.: RippleNet: propagating user preferences on the knowledge graph for recommender systems. In: Proceedings of the 27th ACM International Conference on Information and Knowledge Management, pp. 417–426. ACM (2018)
19. Wang, H., Zhang, F., Xie, X., Guo, M.: DKN: deep knowledge-aware network for news recommendation. In: Proceedings of the 2018 World Wide Web Conference on World Wide Web, pp. 1835–1844. International World Wide Web Conferences Steering Committee (2018)
20. Wang, Z., Zhang, J., Feng, J., Chen, Z.: Knowledge graph embedding by translating on hyperplanes. In: Twenty-Eighth AAAI Conference on Artificial Intelligence (2014)

Social-Aware and Sequential Embedding for Cold-Start Recommendation

Kexin Huang[1], Yukun Cao[1], Ye Du[1], Li Li[1(✉)], Li Liu[2], and Jun Liao[2]

[1] School of Computer and Information Science,
Southwest University, Chongqing, China
{huangkexin,cykkyc,duye99}@email.swu.edu.cn, lily@swu.edu.cn
[2] School of Big Data and Software Engineering, Chongqing University,
Chongqing 400044, People's Republic of China
{dcsliuli,liaojun}@cqu.edu.cn

Abstract. Cold-start problem and sparse, long-tailed datasets are inevitable issues in recommendation systems. The solution to these problems is not to predict them in isolation, but to exploit the additional information from relevant activities. Hence recent sequential actions and social relationships of the user can be used to improve the effectiveness of the model. In this paper, we develop a novel approach called Socially-aware and sequential embedding (SASE) to fill the gap by leveraging convolutional filters to capture the sequential pattern and learning the individual social features from the social networks simultaneously. The core idea is to determine which item is relevant to the user's historical actions and seek who is the user's intimate friend, then make predictions based on these signals. Experimental results on several real-world datasets verify the superiority of our approach compared with various state-of-the-art baselines when handling the cold-start issues.

Keywords: Recommendation systems · Sequence pattern ·
Social network · Cold-start

1 Introduction

Recommendation system is a significant technology in different fields, e.g. e-commerce and music player software utilizes recommendation technology for providing personalized services to users. In this paper, the question we solved is which item user will react at the next time after giving the previous items and user's social relationships. It is a challenging work to capture sequence pattern and social dynamics effectively, for the input space dimension shows exponential growth when the quantity of users' activities and their social relations is on the sharp increase. In addition, the cold-start problem is an inevitable problem in recommendation system. The most common solution is to take advantage of social information and assume that user's preference is influenced by their friends as they may have similar preference (Fig. 1).

© Springer Nature Switzerland AG 2019
C. Douligeris et al. (Eds.): KSEM 2019, LNAI 11775, pp. 60–71, 2019.
https://doi.org/10.1007/978-3-030-29551-6_6

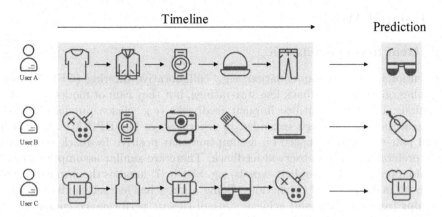

Fig. 1. The core idea of the model. SASE predicts the user's preference by modeling the user's (user A) sequential actions and their friends (user B, user C).

In order to improve model's effectiveness, most of the exiting methods are based on Markov chain and regularize the related sequential behaviors, which assumes that user's next action depends on the previous actions. One of the representative model is *Factorized Personalized Markov Chains* (FPMC) [1] proposed by Rendle et al. FPMC models the user's sequence with personalized MC, but the model doesn't perform well when the number of users and items is very few. Another intelligent way is *Socially-Aware Personalized Markov Chains* (SPMC) [2] also based on MC, which tackling the cold-start problem by combining social and sequential signals simultaneously.

At present, the state-of-the-art model is to embed the user actions and utilize the length of deep learning algorithm (Caser [3], SASRec [4]) to predict the user's next action. These models outperform the sequential recommendation baselines, yet they fail to improve predications when the observations of items and users are too few, in addition, previous approaches do not consider extra context information or model these signals separately.

In this paper, we propose a new model to address the problems mentioned above. The main difference between our work and the socially-aware recommendation models is that our approach is sequentially-aware, which not only enables the model to be expert in predicting in a sequential pattern but also performs well in cold-start issues. In addition, we model the impact of social relationships between user and their friends. Ultimately, we make an empirical comparison of several advanced socially-aware recommendation models and prove the effectiveness of the proposed model. In the rest of the paper, we review related work in Sect. 2 and describe the specific implementation details of the model in Sect. 3. Then we discuss the experimental performance in Sect. 4. Finally, we conclude the paper in Sect. 5.

2   Related Work

2.1   Item Recommendation

Conventional item recommendation, e.g., collaborative filtering (CF) [5], usually relies on explicit feedback like star-ratings, but they cannot model the order of actions. In order to utilize implicit feedbacks (e.g. clicks, purchases), conventional models had been extended in several ways like BPR-MF [6], which model pair-wise actions based on assumption that positive feedback should be more preferable than unobserved feedback. There are similar assumptions have been adapted to utilize implicit signals, e.g. SBPR [7] handles the implicit social signals to make the final predictions. Some approaches learned similarity relationships from the data and achieve state-of-the-art performance compared to relevant baselines. In order to deal with sparsity, Kabbur et al. [8] explored the similarity matrix as the product of two low-dimensional latent factor matrices. SLIM [9] is proposed by Ning et al. learned a sparse matrix of aggregation coefficients that is analogous to item-item similarity matrix for top-N recommendation system.

2.2   Sequential Recommendation

The Markov Chains is a general approach to model sequential pattern in recommendation system. Rendle et al. proposed Factorized Personalized Markov Chains (FPMC [1]) that combine the strength of Factorization Machine and the power of Markov Chains to extract the user's personalized preference and sequential pattern. TransRec [10] is proposed by He et al. also devote to the sequential recommendation system and it models user's actions as translation vectors through a shared item embedding space. The above methods are all improved on the traditional sequential model, and the advanced models leverage the neural network to model the sequence and extract the sequence features. Ruslan et al. proposed Restricted Boltzmann Machine [11] that applied 2-layers neural network successfully for the first time. A lot of advanced works model user's short time preference by Attention Mechanisms of the neural network [4,12]. Moreover, Tang's work [3] showed state-of-the-art results by utilizing CNN on sequential pattern instead of capturing user's preference from reviews and the images of items [3,13], but it ignored the social relationships of users.

2.3   Social Recommendation

There are a large number of work that leverage the social networks to alleviate the cold-start issues and long-tailed problems in recommendation system [14–16]. For instance, Cai et al. [2] proposed Socially-Aware Personalized Markov Chains (SPMC), which not only works well in cold-start settings, but also outperforms in sequential pattern. Simultaneously, joint factorization [17,18] attempt to find the social network matrix factorization so that the representation of social relationships is beneficial for interpreting users' preference. Regularization methods assume that users' preference is identical to their social circles, it enabled user's preference factors to be approach to their friends' by regularizing.

Our work differs from existing methods but mainly focus on social, sequential, dynamics information. And the crucial contributions are summarized as follows:

- We propose a Sequential and Socially-aware embedding recommendation model, as a solution to cold-start issues. The core idea is to exploit the signals from user's more recent activities and social relationships as well as adjusting the latent factors of cold-start users.
- Our approach combines CNN and Node2vec to embed sequential patterns and social factors simultaneously.
- We implement extensive experiments on different real-world datasets, showing that our model outperforms the state-of-the-art recommendation techniques.

3   Proposed Methodology

In this paper, we focus on implicit feedback, e.g. clicks, purchases, thumbs-up. We also assume that the user's action is affected by the actions of user's social relationship and the timestamp of each action is available.

3.1   Embedding Layer

We assume that the user's action in the next step is only influenced by the previous n actions, hence we convert the input sequence $(S_1^u, S_2^u, ..., S_{|S^u|-1}^u)$ into a fixed length sequence $s = (s_1, s_2, ..., s_n)$, where n represents the most appropriate processing length of the model. Therefore, if the sequence length is greater or less than n, we truncates actions or pads zero vector until the length is n. For the CNN training, we extract each item $M_i \in R^d$ in L consecutive items from the item sequence of user u at time step t as input in each training and retrieve the subsequence $\hat{E}^{(u,t)} \in R^{L \times d}$ of the input sequence embedding matrix $E^{(u,t)} \in R^{n \times d}$, where d is the dimension of the latent factor and L can be understood as the size of the "sliding window":

$$\hat{E}^{(u,t)} = \begin{bmatrix} M_{i-L} \\ \vdots \\ M_{i-2} \\ M_{i-1} \end{bmatrix} \tag{1}$$

3.2   Sequential Recommendation

Inspired by sentence embedding of textCNN in Natural Language Processing [19], we leverage CNN to capture the local features in sequential recommendation issues. After completing the construction of "image" of item sequence, our model explores the sequential patterns by sliding convolution filters of various heights. In this paper, the convolutional operation involve m filters $W^k \in R^{h \times d}$, which is applied to a window of $h \in [1, L]$ items to pick up the significant signals regardless of location and the stride is fixed to 1. The transform of each layer is defined by:

$$c_i = f(E_{i:i+h-1} \cdot W + b) \tag{2}$$

where $f(\cdot)$ denotes the activation function and $b \in R$ is the bias term. Meanwhile, E_{i+h-1} refer to the sequence of items $E_i, E_{i+1}, ..., E_{i+h-1}$. The filter is used by every possible "window" of items in the purchase sequence to produce a convolution result:

$$\mathbf{c} = [c_1, c_2, ..., c_{m-h+1}] \tag{3}$$

Then we apply a max-over-time pooling layer over the $\mathbf{c}$ to capture the most essential feature, and the final result of one filter is:

$$\mathbf{e} = max\{\mathbf{c}\} \tag{4}$$

Our approach leverage multiple filters with different "window" to obtain multiple features. By applying various filters, we can pick up the crucial sequential patterns regardless nonessential signals. Consequently, the value of final convolutional sequence embedding after the k filters is (Fig. 2):

$$\hat{\mathbf{e}} = \left\{ \mathbf{e}^{(1)}, \mathbf{e}^{(2)}, ..., \mathbf{e}^{(k)} \right\} \tag{5}$$

3.3 Social Network

Intuitively, mining users' social network information is helpful to recommend items because users' herd mentality and social interests will affect users' next action. Therefore, we construct a graph of users and represent similarity of demand among users' social relationships.

In this paper, we use the Node2vec [20] to generating embedding so that we can encode user node into a low dimensional vector. Node2Vec is similar to DeepWalk [21], and the main innovation is to improve the strategy of random walk. Node2vec defines two new hyperparameters p and q, which make the results of random walk reach a balance in BFS and DFS, but also take into account the local and macro signal, which makes the model have a strong adaptability.

Hence we define the social graph of users as $G = (V, E)$ to represent the social relationships among users, and the set of users U are the nodes $V = U$, $E \in V \times V$ is the edge set that denotes user u and v have a friend relation. For each node u_i, we can learn the d'-dimensional feature F_u by Node2vec, and F_u represent the extent of which the preferences of the user is influenced by the his or her friends in graph G. Finally, we feed the pre-trained embedding into the global network to make predictions.

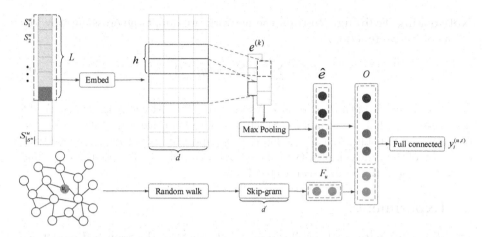

Fig. 2. The network architecture of SASE. The dashed lines with purple are sliding window and the previous actions and target action in item sequence are represented by the yellow squares and gray square, respectively. The red circles and green circles represent different convolution results with various filters ($h = 2, 3$) and the rectangular box with circles stands for concat embedding.

3.4 Prediction Component

Prediction Layer. In order to capture the sequential pattern and social relationship simultaneously, we concatenate the output of convolutional layer $\hat{e}$ and user's social network embedding F_u, and $\oplus$ denotes concatenate operation:

$$O = \hat{\mathbf{e}} \oplus F_u \tag{6}$$

The goal of our work is to predict the next item s_{t+1} when given the most recent item sequence (i.e. $s_1, s_2, \cdots, s_t,$), so we feed O into the fully connected layer to get the final prediction value:

$$y_i^{(u,t)} = \sigma(W'O_u + b') \tag{7}$$

where W' and b' are learnable parameters, $\sigma(x)$ is the sigmoid function define as $\sigma(x) = 1/(1 + e^{-x})$ and $y_i^{(u,t)}$ denotes the correlation of the next item is i by giving previous t items of user u. The higher value of $y_i^{(u,t)}$ indicates that the user is more likely to prefer item i.

In order to capture the specific preference of the user, we consider to insert the user embedding before the output layer, but we found introducing user embedding doesn't improve the final performance by doing experiments (Probably because the model has taken into account all of the user's activities).

Networking Training. To train the network, we adopt the cross-entropy loss as the objective function:

$$L = \sum_{i,j \in S^u} y_j^{(u,t)} log(y_i^{(u,t)}) \tag{8}$$

And the model is optimized by the Adam (Adaptive Moment Estimation) [22] optimizer, which is a variant of Stochastic Gradient Descent (SGD) for fast convergence and the batch size is 256 in this paper. In order to avoid over-fitting and control the time complexity of the model, we apply the Dropout [23] method with 0.5 drop ratio on fully-connected layers.

4   Experiments

In order to evaluate the feasibility and effectiveness of the proposed model, we conduct extensive experiments on three real-word datasets and compared them with the state-of-the-art socially-aware and sequential recommendation models. All datasets and code are available online[1,2].

4.1   Datasets

We experiment on a series of datasets contain substantial user feedback, timestamps and social relations.

Epinions. Epinions.com is a general consumer review site. The Epinions dataset is collected by [7] that comprising user review, timestamps, trust values, and spans from January 2001 to November 2013.

Ciao. Ciao is a European-based online-shopping portal with websites. This dataset also include user ratings, social data and time signals [24].

Flixster. Flixster is a social movie site for discovering and learning about movies. This dataset is also consistent with the main demand of our experiment that include user ratings, social information and timestamps.

In this paper, we are not concerned about the impact of ratings hence we convert all observed interactions to positive instances and the final result of the experiment is the ranking of recommendation lists. The dataset statistics are showed in Table 1.

Table 1. Dataset statistics.

Dataset	Users ($|U|$)	Items ($|I|$)	Actions	Trusts
Epinion	5,261	25,996	46,732	23,915
Ciao	1,708	16,485	34,494	35,753
Flixster	60,692	48,549	7956,727	840,141

---

[1]   https://www.cse.msu.edu/~tangjili/trust.html.
[2]   http://www.cs.ubc.ca/~jamalim/datasets/.

4.2 Baselines

To evaluate the effectiveness of SASE, we compare against four state-of-the-art recommendation models.

Factorized Personalized Markov Chains (FPMC): FPMC [1] is introduced by Rendle et al. that combine the matrix factorization and factorized Markov Chains as its recommender, which captures users' long-term preference as well as sequential continuity.

Socially-Aware Personalized Markov Chains (SPMC): SPMC [2] is a recent method that make full use of the information from social relationships and the sequence of recent activities. This model also assumes that user's next action is affected by their own feedback sequence as well as their friends' preference.

Bayesian Personalized Ranking (BPR-MF): BPR-MF [6] is a classic model described by Rendle et al. and it models user's preference for personalized ranking from implicit pairwise feedback. In contrast experiment, we use the biased matrix factorization as the underlying recommender.

Social Bayesian Personalized Ranking (SBPR): SBPR [7] is a state-of-the-art method suppose that users are inclined to interact with items that their friends enjoy. It leverages social connection to assign ranks of items to the user and recommend these items to users.

4.3 Evaluation Metrics

AUC (*Area Under the ROC curve*) metric is one of the important indicators to evaluate the effectiveness of the model, and it is also widely used in recommendation predictions. We create test set T_u and validation set V_u with the most recent actions of each user on three datasets: the most recent actions for testing and the previous actions for validation. Besides, the rest of the data is assigned to training set. We report the performance of SASE via AUC on the test set:

$$AUC = \frac{1}{|U|} \sum_{u \in |U|} \frac{1}{|I \setminus S^u|} \sum_{j \in I \setminus S^u} \mathbf{I}(y_{j,l}^{(u,t)} > y_{i,l}^{(u,t)}), \qquad (9)$$

where $\mathbf{I}(\cdot)$ denote the indicator function that returns 1 if the ground truth item j are ranked before the unobserved item i, 0 otherwise. l is the item ahead of the test items of the user $u's$ historical feedback in time t.

4.4 Performance Analysis

Our work is to alleviate the cold-start problem of the user in several datasets. The method that we obtain the cold-start datasets is similar to previous work [2], and we set a threshold N, which is the maximum number of recent feedback instances that each user can retain in their feedback history. First of all, the reason why we give up the instances where the number of feedback is less than

4 for a user is that 4 feedback instances can form a sequence in the training set at least for a user. Then if the observations outnumber the threshold N, we only preserve the recent N feedbacks and we ignore the users with feedback between 4 and N.

For the sake of fairness, the dimensions of latent factors in all models are same and we set dimension $D = 64$, since these datasets are sparse and larger dimensions does not result in significant improvements to the comparative methods. In order to choose the value that makes the model perform best we experiment with different learning rates $\alpha = \left\{1, 10^{-1}, 10^{-2}, 10^{-3}, 10^{-4}\right\}$ and regularization hyperparameters is from $\left\{1, 10^{-1}, 10^{-2}, 10^{-3}, 10^{-4}\right\}$, latent dimensions d' is from $\{10, 25, 50, 75, 100\}$, the number of filters is chosen from $\{3, 4, 5\}$ and the batch size is 256. The rest of all hyperparameters and initialization method we adopt are those suggested by the original papers.

Table 2. Performance comparison on three "cold-start" datasets

Dataset	N	FPMC	BPR-MF	SBPR	SPMC	SASE	Improvement
Epinions	5	0.503011	0.514541	0.525640	<u>0.595317</u>	**0.640591**	7.6%
	10	0.519503	0.532994	0.526204	<u>0.589500</u>	**0.649204**	10.1%
	15	0.527076	0.545447	0.538011	<u>0.580287</u>	**0.640234**	10.3%
Ciao	5	0.491940	0.504614	0.509185	<u>0.593383</u>	**0.687785**	15.9%
	10	0.551231	0.576186	0.548679	<u>0.588934</u>	**0.688069**	16.8%
	15	0.569248	<u>0.610123</u>	0.562466	0.591179	**0.683316**	11.9%
Flixster	5	0.887483	0.898370	0.894095	<u>0.900146</u>	**0.945161**	5.0%
	10	0.927250	0.929493	<u>0.939176</u>	0.939046	**0.944662**	0.5%

The average AUC of our model and baselines on cold-start datasets with diverse threshold N are showed in Table 2. We also summarize the improvement of the proposed model relative to the best baseline highlighted with a sliding line on each row. By comparing and analyzing the experimental results of the baselines and SASE, we can conclude that our model outperforms other methods in cold-start settings. In addition, SASE also outperforms state-of-the-art sequential model FPMC and socially-aware sequential model SPMC, which implies the extra information such as sequential and social signals play an important role in cold-start scenes and it's necessary to model these signals. We also come to an additional conclusion that our model not only can be superior to other baselines on Ciao and Flixster because these datasets have more social and sequential signals but also outperform on the cold-start dataset implies our the proposed SASE is good at handling cold-start issue.

In the following experiments, we discuss the influence of latent dimensionality d' and sliding window L focus on AUC metric.

The Influence of Dimension d'. In our experiment, we ignore the dimensions of the sequential latent factor because it has been discussed in previous work [3].

Hence we only discuss the influence of the social factor dimensions d' varying from 10 to 100 by showing AUC of all models. We vary d' and other optimal hyperparameters hold on. As shown in Fig. 3, when d' is around 75, it seems to get the best performance on all datasets and we see that our models usually perform better with larger latent dimensions. On the other hand, we conclude that too large dimension ($d' > 75$) has little effect on the performance of SASE, because if d' is far from than 75, it does not fully represent the social latent factor of users.

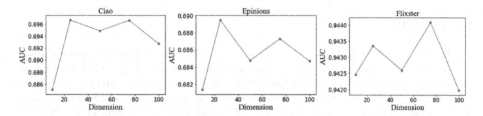

Fig. 3. AUC on the three datasets obtained by SASE when dimension $= d'$.

The Influence of "Sliding Window" L Size. Next we explore how much information SASE can obtain from high-order information when the other hyper-parameters in the model remain unchanged. Figure 4 shows the results. Due to the high sparsity of our datasets, our model does not work well in larger L. This is reasonable because the high sparse dataset is likely to introduce additional useless information and noises. It can be seen from Fig. 4 that the model achieve the best performance when L is around 4, which means that the adjacent items have greater influence on the current item.

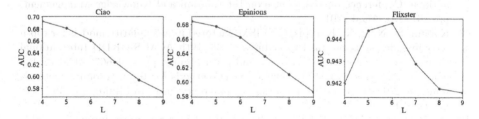

Fig. 4. The AUCs on the three datasets when we vary the hyperparameter L.

5   Conclusion

In this paper, we exploited sequential information social connections to improve the recommendation effectiveness for next item recommendation and cold-start issues. We learned the sequence pattern and social embedding in latent space by convolutional filters and network representation. Substantial experimental results on sparse and long-tailed datasets show that our approach outperforms state-of-the-art baselines and solves the cold-start problem effectively. For future work, we devote to extending our model by aggregating more context information such as locations, action types and so on. We also plan to investigate an approach to incorporate the rating information to capture user personalized preference.

Acknowledgement. This work was supported by NSFC (grant No. 61877051), CSTC (grant No. cstc2018jscx-msyb1042, cstc2017zdcy-zdyf0366 and cstc2017rgzn-zdyf0064). Li Li is the corresponding author for the paper.

References

1. Rendle, S., Freudenthaler, C., Schmidt-Thieme, L.: Factorizing personalized markov chains for next-basket recommendation. In: Proceedings of the 19th International Conference on World Wide Web, pp. 811–820. ACM (2010)
2. Cai, C., He, R., McAuley, J.: SPMC: socially-aware personalized markov chains for sparse sequential recommendation. arXiv preprint arXiv:1708.04497 (2017)
3. Tang, J., Wang, K.: Personalized top-n sequential recommendation via convolutional sequence embedding. In: Proceedings of the Eleventh ACM International Conference on Web Search and Data Mining, pp. 565–573. ACM (2018)
4. Kang, W.-C., McAuley, J.: Self-attentive sequential recommendation. In: 2018 IEEE International Conference on Data Mining (ICDM), pp. 197–206. IEEE (2018)
5. Ekstrand, M.D., Riedl, J.T., Konstan, J.A., et al.: Collaborative filtering recommender systems. Found. Trends® Hum.-Comput. Interact. **4**(2), 81–173 (2011)
6. Rendle, S., Freudenthaler, C., Gantner, Z., Schmidt-Thieme, L.: BPR: Bayesian personalized ranking from implicit feedback. In: Proceedings of the Twenty-fifth Conference on Uncertainty in Artificial Intelligence, pp. 452–461. AUAI Press (2009)
7. Zhao, T., McAuley, J., King, I.: Leveraging social connections to improve personalized ranking for collaborative filtering. In: Proceedings of the 23rd ACM International Conference on Conference on Information and Knowledge Management, pp. 261–270. ACM (2014)
8. Kabbur, S., Ning, X., Karypis, G.: FISM: factored item similarity models for top-n recommender systems. In: Proceedings of the 19th ACM SIGKDD International Conference on Knowledge Discovery and Data Mining, pp. 659–667. ACM (2013)
9. Ning, X., Karypis, G.: SLIM: sparse linear methods for top-n recommender systems. In: 2011 IEEE 11th International Conference on Data Mining, pp. 497–506. IEEE (2011)
10. He, R., Kang, W.-C., McAuley, J.: Translation-based recommendation: a scalable method for modeling sequential behavior. In: IJCAI, pp. 5264–5268 (2018)
11. Salakhutdinov, R., Mnih, A., Hinton, G.: Restricted boltzmann machines for collaborative filtering. In Proceedings of the 24th international conference on Machine learning, pp. 791–798. ACM (2007)
12. Zhou, C., et al.: ATRank: an attention-based user behavior modeling framework for recommendation. In: Thirty-Second AAAI Conference on Artificial Intelligence (2018)
13. Geng, X., Zhang, H., Bian, J., Chua, T.-S.: Learning image and user features for recommendation in social networks. In: Proceedings of the IEEE International Conference on Computer Vision, pp. 4274–4282 (2015)

14. Chaney, A.J.B., Blei, D.M., Eliassi-Rad, T.: A probabilistic model for using social networks in personalized item recommendation. In: Proceedings of the 9th ACM Conference on Recommender Systems, pp. 43–50. ACM (2015)
15. Jamali, M., Ester, M.: A matrix factorization technique with trust propagation for recommendation in social networks. In: Proceedings of the Fourth ACM Conference on Recommender Systems, pp. 135–142. ACM (2010)
16. Ma, H., King, I., Lyu, M.R.: Learning to recommend with social trust ensemble. In: Proceedings of the 32nd International ACM SIGIR Conference on Research and Development in Information Retrieval, pp. 203–210. ACM (2009)
17. Tang, J., Gao, H., Hu, X., Liu, H.: Exploiting homophily effect for trust prediction. In: Proceedings of the Sixth ACM International Conference on Web Search and Data Mining, pp. 53–62. ACM (2013)
18. Ma, H., Yang, H., Lyu, M.R., King, I.: SoRec: social recommendation using probabilistic matrix factorization. In: Proceedings of the 17th ACM Conference on Information and Knowledge Management, pp. 931–940. ACM (2008)
19. Kim, Y.: Convolutional neural networks for sentence classification. arXiv preprint arXiv:1408.5882 (2014)
20. Grover, A., Leskovec, J.: Node2vec: scalable feature learning for networks. In: Proceedings of the 22nd ACM SIGKDD International Conference on Knowledge Discovery and Data Mining, pp. 855–864. ACM (2016)
21. Perozzi, B., Al-Rfou, R., Skiena, S.: DeepWalk: online learning of social representations. In: Proceedings of the 20th ACM SIGKDD International Conference on Knowledge Discovery and Data Mining, pp. 701–710. ACM (2014)
22. Kingma, D.P., Ba, J.: Adam: a method for stochastic optimization. arXiv preprint arXiv:1412.6980 (2014)
23. Srivastava, N., Hinton, G., Krizhevsky, A., Sutskever, I., Salakhutdinov, R.: Dropout: a simple way to prevent neural networks from overfitting. J. Mach. Learn. Res. 15(1), 1929–1958 (2014)
24. Tang, J., Gao, H., Liu, H.: mTrust: discerning multi-faceted trust in a connected world. In: Proceedings of the Fifth ACM International Conference on Web Search and Data Mining, pp. 93–102. ACM (2012)

Sequential Recommendation Based on Long-Term and Short-Term User Behavior with Self-attention

Xing Wei[1,2], Xianglin Zuo[1,2], and Bo Yang[1,2(✉)]

[1] College of Computer Science and Technology,
Jilin University, Changchun 130012, China
247334537@qq.com , ybo@jlu.edu.cn
[2] Key Laboratory of Symbolic Computation and Knowledge
Engineering Attached to the Ministry of Education,
Jilin University, Changchun 130012, China

Abstract. Product recommenders based on users' interests are becoming increasingly essential in e-commerce. With the continuous development of the recommendation system, the available information is further enriched. In the case, user's click or purchase behavior could be a visual representation of his or her interest. Due to the rapid update of products, users' interests are not static, but change over time. In order to cope with the users' interest changes, we propose a desirable work on the basis of representative recommendation algorithm. The sequence of user interaction behavior is thoroughly utilized, and the items that users interact at different times have different significance for the reflect of users' interests. By considering the user's sequential behaviors, this paper focuses on the recent ones to obtains the real interest of user. In this process, user behavior is divided into long-term and short-term, modeled by LSTM and Attention-based model respectively for user's next click recommendation. We refer this model as LANCR and analyze the model in experiment. The experiment demonstrates that the proposed model has superior improvement compared with standard approaches. We deploy our model on two real datasets to verify the superior performance made in predicting user preferences.

Keywords: Recommender system · Long short-term memory ·
Sequential recommendation

1 Introduction

Recommendation system plays an essential role in current shopping websites and e-commerce. Network platform hopes to recommend products that may be of interest to users. Nowadays, users have exploded numbers of social network, and the information generated by users has also proliferated. To effectively solve this problem, various personalized recommenders have been made to provide

© Springer Nature Switzerland AG 2019
C. Douligeris et al. (Eds.): KSEM 2019, LNAI 11775, pp. 72–83, 2019.
https://doi.org/10.1007/978-3-030-29551-6_7

users with high quality items. Among the traditional personalized recommendation algorithms, the collaborative filtering algorithm [5] is undoubtedly successful. The collaborative filtering recommendation algorithm is based on similarity preference between users, but it cannot effectively recommend when facing with user's dynamically changing interest characteristics. Traditional recommendation system can be mainly divided into two methods: analyzing user's social relationship or calculating the similarity of goods. There are also algorithms that take both into account. These classical algorithms do open up the scope of recommendation and relief the problem of cold start to a certain extent. However, with the increase of user amount and the renewal of commodities, both user's social relationship and his preference to goods will change with time, which should be taken into consideration.

Recommender algorithm based on user behavior is of great importance in personalized recommendation system. Before utilizing user behavior data to design the algorithm, researchers first need to analyze the user behavior data to understand the general rules contained in the data, so that they could have the design of recommender model. Recommendation system obtains the user's interest through their behavior. Network information categories and new topics increase day by day. How to grasp the change of user is the key to improve the accuracy of recommendation results.

In the personalized recommendation system, acquiring users' interests is fundamental. In large data-intensive networks, user's preferences can be described by his or her historical behavior [4]. Initial research often extracts features from user's actions manually and aggregates them to get his attributes. However, manual extraction may not fully represent the feature itself. After extracting features by algorithmic techniques, most of current technologies deal with each user's historical behavior separately, but they do not reflect the information that users share among different behaviors [6]. In real life, the historical behavior of users is often related with others. It is proposed that the customer's purchase behavior may change with time [1], and the user's click doings in the previous and current period can be extracted separately. In other words, the predicted results to users will be influenced by both long-term and short-term interests of users. In recent studies, when dealing with top-N recommendation problems [3], it is found that the user interaction order plays an imperative role in describing his interest. The concept of perceiving user sequence intention is also proposed, and is commendably applied in next item recommendation [9].

Some of classical algorithms have been applied when facing with the problem that users' interests change along with time. Markov chain method can predict the next action of user by describing the user's latest behaviors. With the development of deep learning, RNN and LSTM algorithms [13] have been used to receive sequential input [2]. In addition to NLP applications, they can also be used for sequence recommendation. The attention mechanism was proposed in the process of neuro-machine translation (NMT) while using the encoder-decoder structure [17]. At present, attention machine is common in deep learning, which is not limited to encoder-decoder hierarchy. The algorithm of learning natural language from images is introduced [16], and the experimental results are improved by adding attention mechanism. The most advanced sentence representation model has been significantly improved by applying the same mechanism to a single sentence [15]. Attention mechanism connects two different modules by learning the weight between data.

In this paper, a new temporal recommendation model is proposed for user's sequential click actions. Our main contributions are as follows:

- The user's interest is divided into long-term and short-term, which enhances the interpretability of products recommended to users.
- A sequence recommendation is proposed, which masters the potential links between projects, and grasps the overall preferences of users, so that it focuses on both the user's global interests, and his recent actions.
- We completed our experiments on CiaoDVD and Amazon-Books datasets. The experimental results demonstrate the performance of the model.

Section 2 introduces the related algorithms and work. Section 3 describes the details of our model and gives the loss function. In Sect. 4, we have a comparative experiment to analyze the experimental results on real data sets. Finally, Sect. 5 summarizes the full text.

2   Related Works

2.1   Next Item Recommendation

In traditional recommendation system, collaborative filtering based on matrix factorization outputs the similarity matrix of users or commodities by studying the relationship matrix obtained from the user's behavior log. The recommendation algorithm based on naive bayesian classification is relatively simple to implement and has high accuracy, but it is suitable for classification problems with small amount of data and fewer categories.

The goal of sequential recommendation system could be broadly expressed as a linear combination of the users' long-term and short-term preferences [7]. Compared with a large number of previous models, which focus on users' long-term interests, session-based recommendation system is combined with GNN [8], emphasizing the importance of modeling short-term user preferences. RNNs for session-based recommendations [21] evaluated several improvements on basic RNN, and multiaspect experiments demonstrates that accounting for user's temporal shift behavior is possible to improve the performance of session-based recommendation system. In mobile application recommendation, user's historical data can also provide conspicuous assistance [23]. Combined with user's sequence of applications operated recently, the historical application can provide high accuracy in prediction scheme. User-based RNN is a new framework extended on RNN, which models user behavior, captures the dependencies between user events to full advantage, and shows the development of the original architecture in the field of recommendation [24].

Sequential recommendation predicts consecutive items according to user's historical behavior and the key work is to capture interactions within users and commodities. Markov chain predicts the next-time action by observing users' recent behaviors. The probability distribution of the next state is only determined by the current state, but the actions before this in the time series is irrelevant. MC [20] algorithm belongs to the property of no memory. In the process of improving recommender algorithm. There was a classical algorithm, which combines MC with matrix factorization for next item recommendation. In sequential recommendation field, recurrent neural network and its two most widely used variants, LSTM and GRU, are more commonly applied at present.

In online stores, recommending proper product is the core issue of recommendation system, accurately recommending the next product to users means attracting more customers and promoting the sales of products efficiently. According the market requirement, [10] proposes a long-term demand perception model, which considers that repeat purchase action represents the long-term needs of users, while complementary purchase means short-term needs. Through the analysis of customers' behaviors, the existing methods mainly use short-term feedback, but do not fully consider users' long-term stable preferences [11], or simply analyze users' long-term habits, but do not pay attention to the changes of users' favorite things over time.

The key point of our work is dividing the user's behaviors into long-term and short-term when considering their temporality, and we take different deep learning methods to model items. After joint training, the system eventually recommends the next item.

2.2 Long-Term and Short-Term Interests

Long short term memory network (LSTM) is a particular type of recurrent neural network, which learns long-term dependence information for a specific work. When facing with sequential problems, LSTM has obtained correct success and has been proverbially spreaded. It avoids completely long-term dependency problems through deliberate design. In practice, keeping the long-term information in memory is the core behavior of LSTM, rather than consuming a large amount of manpower. In standard RNN, this replication module has only one simple structure, such as a *tanh* layer. LSTM has the same mode, but the repetitive modules have a different frame. They have four layers of nervous system, coordinating and assisting each others to determine the output results. The specific principles will be introduced later.

The analysis and calculation of users' short-term interests is pretty to be accomplished by attention mechanism. Attention-based model is actually a measure of similarity. The more similar to the target state, the greater the weight of the current input is, indicating that the output depends more on the current input. Attention model has been originally applied in the field of image [14]. Subsequently, it was introduced into the field of NLP and applied to machine translation, and its main function is to learn the relationship between words. On this basis, the concept of soft attention model was introduced, which means each item is required, then a probability distribution of attention is calculated and weighted. Attention mechanism can be used not only to process the encoder or the hidden layer in front of it, but also to obtain the distribution of other features without additional information.

Self-attention mechanism is a special case, which focuses on itself and extract relevant information from its own project. Self-attention is also often referred as intra attention and has been widely used in machine learning. It refines the representation by matching a single sequence with itself. Attention-based also takes an advantage in learning context embedding. According to the items observed in the current transaction, they are weighted by different correlations to output a suitable next item [26]. In the case of limited background knowledge, self-attention can preserve the context sequence information and capture the relationship between elements. It has been proved that the model combining self-attention with sequential series can be superior to the state-of-the-art technologies in both sparse and dense datasets [25].

In our work, LSTM aims at users' long-term interests, whereas self-attention mechanism corresponding the dependency relationship of the users' short-term sequential behavior.

3   The Proposed Model

We now propose a sequential recommender system that combines LSTM and self-attention for user next click recommendation, named LANCR. The structure of this section is as follows: first, code and classify each commodity, the method selected in which is one-hot code. Next, introduce the technology proposed in detail and give the model diagram. Finally, we present the recommender results and the metrics arised in the process of building the model.

3.1   Embedding Layer

For each project, its own attributes such as movie categories, directors, actors, as well as abstracts, authors, and fields of the paper, can be together invested in describing the product itself. In machine learning application tasks, non-contiguous data is often encoded by numbers. The above attributes do not have a mathematically continuous relationship between each other, but in another aspect, they are considered as a mathematical order relationship. One-hot coding, also known as one-bit effective coding, using an N-bit status register to encode N states, each state being independent of its register bits, and at any time, only one of them is valid. One-hot encodes a value corresponding to the discrete feature to a point in Euclidean space. For example, there is a discrete form representing a movie, and the input entry is [category = action, director = Joe Russell, actor = Robert Downey&Chris Evans], which will be mapped to European space and the result of coding is as follows:

$$[0,0,1,0,...,0][0,1,0,0,...,0][0,1,0,1,...,0] \tag{1}$$

Such three binary parts correspond to the three features of the original data as a vector form, which can be linked to the neural network. Given a sequence of user's click behaviors $V = \{V_1, V_2, \ldots, V_n\}$, where V_i represents the ith item that the user clicked and n is the total number of user click sequences. After one-hot coding mentioned above, the result of item embedding layer is as follows:

$$\mathbf{e} = [e_1, e_2, \ldots, e_n] \tag{2}$$

e_i is the embedding result of V_i, which is later incorporated into the model as input of new time.

3.2   Sequence Recommendation with Self-attention

The input of model is user's click behavior sequence, and after encoding, we get the sequential embedding $\mathbf{e}$. LSTM system receives the embedding of input ordered by time, and then calculates the output of hidden layer through forget gate, input gate and output gate. In this process, the cell state is updated and the calculation results are transmitted to the next cycle. The LSTM part of our proposed model is shown in Fig. 1, where shows a structure of one time step. The new cell state and output gate determine the output of the new hidden layer.

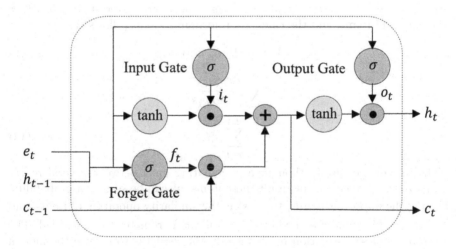

Fig. 1. The LSTM part of model [13].

The first step of LSTM is to select the information to be discarded in the sequence, which is determined by the forget gate. The gate receives the hidden layer content of the previous moment h_{t-1} and the new input vector e_t, getting a value between 0 and 1. If the value is 1, it means complete reservation while 0 means abandonment. After discarding elements, input gate determines which new information should be stored and updated. Then, a *tanh* layer creates a new candidate value vector, which is added to the state. The old cell state will be updated. The previous steps have decided what will be done, and now actually going to complete. The model then discards the information that needs to be abandoned. In the end, the LSTM system computes the output value. This result is based on cell state. The model is conveyed as follows [13]:

$$i_t = \sigma(W_{ei}e_t + W_{hi}h_{t-1} + b_i) \tag{3}$$

$$f_t = \sigma(W_{ef}e_t + W_{hf}h_{t-1} + b_f) \tag{4}$$

$$c_t = f_t \cdot c_{t-1} + i_t \cdot tanh(W_{ec}e_t + W_{hc}h_{t-1} + b_c) \tag{5}$$

$$o_t = \sigma(W_{eo}e_o + W_{ho}h_{t-1} + b_o) \tag{6}$$

$$h_t = o_t \cdot tanh(c_t) \tag{7}$$

where σ is the sigmoid function, e_t is the input item at time t, f_t expresses the forgetting vector, i_t is the input gate vector, which means the retention of new information, c_t is the updated cell state, o_t represents the output gate vector, h_t is the hidden layer state at new time, and it is provided to next part.

Next, we will calculate the latest hidden layer outputs. Through the self-attention mechanism, the hidden output is obtained as $h = \{h_1, h_2, \ldots, h_n\}$. For several recent outputs of the LSTM, $\{h_n - step + 1, h_n - step + 2, \ldots, h_n\}$ is used as the memory and input to calculate the attention output r_i, where $step$ is the step size we choose to model the user's short-term interest (e.g. 5, 10), n is the length of items, and the calculation formulas are as follows [14]:

$$s_j^i = V' relu(W_j h_j + W_i h_i) \tag{8}$$

$$a_j^i = \frac{exp(s_j^i)}{\sum_{j=1}^{n} exp(s_j^i)} \tag{9}$$

$$r_i = \sum_{j=1}^{step} a_j^i h_j \tag{10}$$

The formulas could be thought as calculating links between several recent commodities, r_i is the output result these items, a_j^i can be seen as a probability, reflecting the importance of h_j to r_i, s_j^i is the similarity operation of items, and V' is the combination of embedding $\mathbf{e}$, W_i is the parameter to be learned. The work process of self-attention mechanism in the model is to receive the hidden layer set of the previous part, each row represents a vector representation of an item, and the similarity calculation is performed between the rows and rows to obtain the weights. The weights and corresponding items are summed to get the results after analyzing the attention. We recommend the next item according to the sequence clicked by users. The model diagram is as Fig. 2.

After learning the long-term interest of the user, the latter projects are separately captured, so that the recent projects include not only the order relationship of the time, but also the interaction between each others. This part calculates the next item affected by the short-term actions. Its prediction result becomes Eq. (11):

$$\hat{y}_i = \frac{r_i}{step} \tag{11}$$

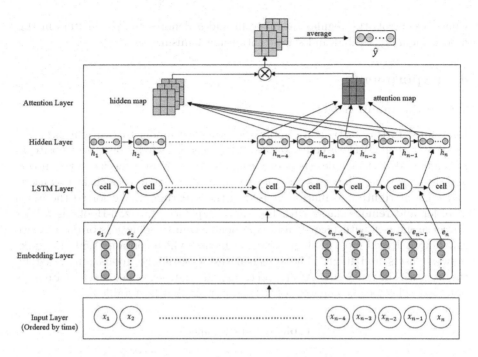

Fig. 2. The sequential recommender framework. This example takes the short-term step value of the user as 5.

$\hat{y}_i$ is the result predicted for user i. Let y_i be the next actual interactive item of the user i, and we predict the probability distribution of the next item by using the derived $\hat{y}_i$ as a softmax regression. It is the average value obtained by finding relations between recent projects. As shown in Fig. 2, when *step* is 5, all items embedding obtains the hidden layer through LSTM part, then calculates the weight of the $\{h_{n-4}, h_{n-3}, \ldots, h_n\}$, adds up the average, and takes the mean value as prediction result, instead of only removing the last output as the result. The definition of loss function is given as:

$$\mathscr{L} = -\frac{1}{N} \sum_{i=1}^{N} y_i^T log\sigma(w\hat{y}_i + b) \tag{12}$$

where y_i denotes the tag of the ith item, which is set to 1 if user clicks the result, while 0 means not, where w and b are the parameters of softmax regression and $\sigma = 1/(1 + exp(-x))$, to calculate the probability distribution. N is the total number of user's click items. We sum up losses to optimize our model. For each user, there is a loss function in the same format, setting the total number of users to M. The training process is to minimize the objective function as follow:

$$\mathscr{F} = \sum_{j=1}^{M} \mathscr{L}_j + \lambda \|\theta\| \tag{13}$$

where λ controls the regularization term and θ denotes the parameters in this model, including LSTM and self-attention mechanism.

4   Experiments

4.1   Experiment Setup

Datasets. In this section, we apply the proposed model to two real datasets. CiaoDVD is a DVD category dataset that was crawled from the website in December 2013. It includes the movie category, 72,655 users' clicks on the movie, and the click time. The cases for training and testing are movies clicked by users, and some attribute information is used in the experiment. We sorted the items in order and remove datas with too short sequence. Amazon-Books is a user purchase dataset with records and comments. Due to some loss of dataset, we randomly selected most of them for experiments, which contains 1,507,155 links between users and items. The screened test case is the goods purchased by the user within ten years. After processing the dataset, a sequence of items is obtained. The specific capacity of the datasets is shown in Table 1.

Table 1. Dataset capacity

Dataset	#Users	#Items	#User-Item actions
CiaoDVD	17,615	16,108	72,655
Amazon-Books	57,015	98,570	1,507,155

Evaluation Metrics. Two evaluation metrics are used in the experiments: Logloss (cross entropy) and AUC (Area Under ROC). A common application of AUC is an offline assessment of CTR. The evaluation of CTR plays an important role in the company's technical processes. The sigmoid function is used to relate the feature input to the probability. The probability of this output is the estimated value of the click rate.

Model Comparison. We compare this model with multiple recommendation algorithms. First, FM [18] is a classic algorithm for click rate prediction. And then BPR [19] is a personalized sorting algorithm for project prediction. At the same time, the matrix factorization recommendation algorithm based on Markov Chain [2] is compared. Finally, it is compared with the basic LSTM model. Besides paralleling with other models, we choose different *step* to find the best length of users' short-term action to the result.

4.2   Results and Analysis

The experimental results of LANCR and the comparative experiments are shown in Table 2, and we have selected several different *step* (the step size of user short-term length) and tested our models separately. The results of the test are in Table 3.

Accuracy of Proposed Model. Table 2 shows the comparison results of two baselines and the proposed method on two real datasets. From Table 2, it can be seen that LANCR is better than the basic regression model FM and bayesian probability model BPR. Among the next recommender problems, it also surpasses representative models. And the model with self-attention mechanism is more effective than the single LSTM.

Table 2. Comparative results

Dataset	Metric	FM	BPR	FPMC	LSTM	LANCR
CiaoDVD	AUC	0.7541	0.7634	0.7726	0.7943	**0.7951**
	LogLoss	0.3524	0.3351	0.327	0.3081	**0.2979**
Amazon-Books	AUC	0.8051	0.8262	0.8313	0.8526	**0.8623**
	LogLoss	0.298	0.2751	0.2538	0.2341	**0.2243**

Impact of Step Length. Table 3 shows the impact of the short-term *step*. We find that the appropriate step size can achieve higher accuracy, which means that the definition of user's short-term interest is not arbitrary. The experimental results show that the proper *step* is dependent on the datasets. For dataset Ciao, when the user's short-term step size is defined as 5, we get better results. In other words, focusing on the analysis of users' latest 5 clicks is more helpful for the next recommendation result. However, we can see that there are different results on Amazon-book dataset. When $step = 10$, the best result is achieved. Compared with Ciao, Amazon-Book dataset has a larger capacity and a relatively large number of clicked items. It cannot be deemed absolutely that the selection of *step* is affected by sample size, but we will then validate this conclusion with more datasets than before.

Table 3. Result of different steps

Dataset	Model	Metric	Step=3	Step=5	Step=8	Step=10
CiaoDVD	LANCR	AUC	0.7182	**0.7951**	0.7763	0.7523
Amazon-Books	LANCR	AUC	0.8367	0.8521	0.8514	**0.8623**

The proposed model integrates extracted features in the training process with large datasets in the experimental process. Facing a long item sequence, we choose the information that should be selected, and discard the information which has lost reference value for a long time, and deploy attention mechanism to capture the potential links between recent items, instead of compressing all of them into a hidden layer, and the model can obtain more abundant information. In terms of the association within our model, self-attention receives the global association of the items. Since the user's long-ago interest may change over time, short-term item selection is more representative of his real interest. Through the joint modeling of user's interaction, more accurate recommendation results will be provided.

5   Conclusion and Future Work

In this paper, we propose LANCR, a sequential recommendation algorithm based on long-term and short-term interest of users. The model applies LSTM to filter users' long-term interests, and uses the self-attention mechanism to calculate the user's short-term intentions and finally predicts his next click. By conducting experiments on real datasets and comparing experimental results, we believe that taking user's sequential click items into consideration has a great impact on the recommendation results. There may be some links within short-term items, not just the time order. In addition, as time progresses, user's recent click behavior is more valuable on expressing user's true intentions. So it is necessary to focus on the relationship between recent click items. In the future work, in order to observe experimental results more accurately, we will build a multi-dimensional item embedding, considering more attributes of the projects, and in the case of datasets, it's optative to add the user's own attributes to get more accurate prediction, as well as its interpretability.

Acknowledgements. This work was supported in part by National Natural Science Foundation of China under grants 61876069 and 61572226, and Jilin Province Key Scientific and Technological Research and Development project under grants 20180201067GX and 20180201044GX.

References

1. Liu, D.R., Lai, C.H., Lee, W.J.: A hybrid of sequential rules and collaborative filtering for product recommendation. Inf. Sci. **179**(20), 3505–3519 (2009)
2. Rendle, S., Freudenthaler, C., Schmidt-Thieme, L.: Factorizing personalized markov chains for next-basket recommendation. In: Proceedings of the 19th International Conference on World Wide Web, pp. 811–820. ACM (2010)
3. Tang, J., Wang, K.: Personalized top-n sequential recommendation via convolutional sequence embedding. In: Proceedings of the Eleventh ACM International Conference on Web Search and Data Mining, pp. 565–573. ACM (2018)
4. Zhou, C., et al.: ATRank: an attention-based user behavior modeling framework for recommendation. In: Proceeding of the 32nd AAAI Conference on Artificial Intelligence (2018)
5. Breese, J.S., Heckerman, D., Kadie, C.: Empirical analysis of predictive algorithms for collaborative filtering. In: Proceedings of the 14th Conference on Uncertainty in Artificial Intelligence, pp. 43–52 (1998)
6. Ni, Y., et al.: Perceive your users in depth: learning universal user representations from multiple e-commerce tasks. In: Proceedings of the 24th ACM SIGKDD International Conference on Knowledge Discovery & Data Mining, pp. 596–605. ACM (2018)
7. Villatel, K., Smirnova, E., Mary, J., et al.: Recurrent neural networks for long and short-term sequential recommendation. arXiv preprint arXiv:1807.09142 (2018)
8. Wu, S., Tang, Y., Zhu, Y., Wang, L., Xie, X., Tan, T.: Session-based recommendation with graph neural networks. arXiv preprint arXiv:1811.00855 (2018)
9. Zhang, S., Tay, Y., Yao, L., Sun, A.: Next item recommendation with self-attention. arXiv preprint arXiv:1808.06414 (2018)

10. Bai, T., Du, P., Zhao, W.X., Wen, J.R., Nie, J.Y.: A long-short demands-aware model for next-item recommendation. arXiv preprint arXiv:1903.00066 (2019)
11. Li, Z., Zhao, H., Liu, Q., Huang, Z., Mei, T., Chen, E.: Learning from history and present: next-item recommendation via discriminatively exploiting user behaviors. In: Proceedings of the 24th ACM SIGKDD International Conference on Knowledge Discovery & Data Mining, pp. 1734–1743. ACM (2018)
12. Chung, J., Ahn, S., Bengio, Y.: Hierarchical multiscale recurrent neural networks. arXiv preprint arXiv:1609.01704 (2016)
13. Hochreiter, S., Schmidhuber, J.: Long short-term memory. Neural Comput. **9**(8), 1735–1780 (1997)
14. Vaswani, A., et al.: Attention is all you need. In: Advances in Neural Information Processing Systems, pp. 5998–6008 (2017)
15. Wang, S., Zhang, J., Zong, C.: Learning sentence representation with guidance of human attention. arXiv preprint arXiv:1609.09189 (2016)
16. Yang, Z., He, X., Gao, J., Deng, L., Smola, A.: Stacked attention networks for image question answering. In: Proceedings of the IEEE Conference on Computer Vision and Pattern Recognition, pp. 21–29 (2016)
17. Bahdanau, D., Cho, K., Bengio, Y.: Neural machine translation by jointly learning to align and translate. arXiv preprint arXiv:1409.0473 (2014)
18. Rendle, S.: Factorization machines. In: 2010 IEEE International Conference on Data Mining, pp. 995–1000. IEEE (2010)
19. Rendle, S., Freudenthaler, C., Gantner, Z., Schmidt-Thieme, L.: BPR: Bayesian personalized ranking from implicit feedback. In: Proceedings of the Twenty-Fifth Conference on Uncertainty in Artificial Intelligence, pp. 452–461. AUAI Press (2009)
20. Gilks, W.R., Richardson, S., Spiegelhalter, D.: Markov Chain Monte Carlo in Practice. Chapman and Hall/CRC, Boca Raton (1995)
21. Tan, Y.K., Xu, X., Liu, Y.: Improved recurrent neural networks for session-based recommendations. In: Proceedings of the 1st Workshop on Deep Learning for Recommender Systems, pp. 17–22. ACM (2016)
22. Hidasi, B., Karatzoglou, A.: Recurrent neural networks with top-k gains for session-based recommendations. In: Proceedings of the 27th ACM International Conference on Information and Knowledge Management, pp. 843–852. ACM (2018)
23. Pu, C., Wu, Z., Chen, H., Xu, K., Cao, J.: A sequential recommendation for mobile apps: what will user click next app?. In: 2018 IEEE International Conference on Web Services (ICWS), pp. 243–248. IEEE (2018)
24. Donkers, T., Loepp, B., Ziegler, J.: Sequential user-based recurrent neural network recommendations. In: Proceedings of the Eleventh ACM Conference on Recommender Systems, pp. 152–160. ACM (2017)
25. Kang, W.C., McAuley, J.: Self-attentive sequential recommendation. In: 2018 IEEE International Conference on Data Mining (ICDM), pp. 197–206. IEEE (2018)
26. Wang, S., Hu, L., Cao, L., Huang, X., Lian, D., Liu, W.: Attention-based transactional context embedding for next-item recommendation. In: Thirty-Second AAAI Conference on Artificial Intelligence (2018)

Multi-attention Item Recommendation Model Based on Social Relations

Yuan Li[(✉)] [ID] and Kedian Mu[(✉)]

School of Mathematics Sciences, Peking University, Beijing, China
ly1993@pku.edu.cn, mukedian@math.pku.edu.cn

Abstract. Incorporating social relations in recommendation provides a promising way to alleviate problems of sparsity and cold start in collaborative filtering methods. However, most existing methods do not yet take into account social relations in a relative complete way. Besides the differences between preferences of friends, connection strength and expertise differences of users on a given item also have impacts on the spread of preference between friends. In this paper, we propose a social-aware recommendation model named *Multi-Attention Item Recommendation model based on Social relations* (MAIRS) which allows us to select more informative friends from the perspectives of their preferences, connection strengths, and expertise on items by their own respective attention models. And then, the three attention models are fused together by utilizing an aggregation function. We compare our method with state-of-the-art models on three real-world datasets: Delicious, Ciao and Epinions. The experimental results show that our method consistently outperforms state-of-the-art models in terms of several ranking metrics.

Keywords: Recommendation · Attention mechanism · Social relations

1 Introduction

As the overload of product and service information, it makes users exhausted to find products suitable for their unique taste and needs. To alleviate this information overload, recommender systems (RS) can provide an effective way to help users discover items of interest from a large resource collection. Collaborative filtering (CF), one of the most popular techniques in RS [18], recommend items for users by inferring users' preference according to their historical behaviors, such as clicks, purchases, ratings or likes.

The boom of social media fosters the research of the social-aware recommendation, which aims to improve the recommendation quality by incorporating social relations from social media in RS. The social media provides platforms for users to spread their preference or taste to their social connections, i.e., friends. Meantime, it is convenient for users to seek suggestions from their friends when shopping. Accordingly, the preference of users can be inferred not only from users' historical behaviors but also from friends' in social networks. Much effort has been devoted in social-aware recommendation, including [3,4,12].

© Springer Nature Switzerland AG 2019
C. Douligeris et al. (Eds.): KSEM 2019, LNAI 11775, pp. 84–95, 2019.
https://doi.org/10.1007/978-3-030-29551-6_8

However, most existing methods consider social influence strength for social connections equally or under the forms of constant weights or a predefined heuristic weighting function [17]. These models focus only on the similarity of friends but ignore their differences. They cannot capture the intuition that user's social influence-aware preferences on items may vary with their social connections. Therefore, a more suitable way to model social influence is that pay different attentions to different friends' influences on user's preferences for specific items. Specifically, we need to distinguish social influence among friends from the perspectives of preference, connection strength and expertise.

Generally, the basic paradigm of social-aware recommender systems is that users would be interested in the items favored by their friends. This phenomenon is known as homophily in social networks [14], which illustrates that friends are more likely to have similar preferences with each other than strangers. However, the preferences of user and his friends are not always completely alike [2]. Due to the diversity of interests and backgrounds of users and their friends [4], it's inevitable that user's and friends' preferences diverge [5]. Therefore, it's practical to consider that different friends have different degrees of similarity with users in preference. Intuitively, users are more likely to accept the suggestions from friends who have more similar preference. Hence, to better characterize social influence on users, we need to pay different attentions on different friends based on differences of their preference.

Granovetter has argued that the different connection strengths have different impacts on information spread over social networks [7]. Then, as a kind of information flowing through social networks, the spread of preference is also influenced by the different connection strengths in social networks. This implies that we should take connection strengths into account when inferring user preference from his friends.

Given an item, users tend to follow the opinions of the selected friends (leaders/experts) rather than opinions from all friends based on their own respective expertise levels on the given item. Based on this intuition, a desirable model should pay different attentions to user's friends by considering their different expertises on a specific item.

In this paper, we propose a new social-aware recommendation method, named Multi-Attentive Item Recommendation model based on Social relations (MAIRS), which provides a multi-attention framework to dynamically model social influence based on differences of preference, connection strength and expertise among users and their friends. Specifically, given a user-item pair, the framework considers the following factors to model social influence on the user's preference on the item by their own respective attention models. First, we adopt preference attention model to adaptively identify the more informative friends for the user based on their preference difference. Second, we leverage *node2vec* [8] to learn user connection strength in network. And then, we employ connection attention model to select friends based on connection strength. Third, the expertise attention is used to model social influence strength based on diverse expertise levels of friends on specific items. It makes the influence strength dynamic and sensitive to specific contexts. Last, an aggregation function is applied to combine all the three attention models to make the final choice on the user's friends for modeling the user's preference on the item. We compare MAIRS with state-of-the-art models on three public datasets: Delicious, Ciao and Epinions. The experimental results show that our method consistently outperforms state-of-the-art models in terms of several ranking metrics. Moreover, a set of quantitative experiments also confirms the importance of each type of differences in social influence strength modeling. In summary, the contributions of our work are as follow:

- We design a multi-attention framework to model the social influence strength from multiple aspects together.
- We consider the different influence from friends on user preference modeling from three perspectives: preference, connection strength and expertise differences in the social-aware recommendation.
- We conduct extensive experiments on three real-world datasets. Results indicate the effectiveness of the proposed MAIRS. Moreover, a set of quantitative experiments also demonstrate that the three types of difference play important roles in social influence strength modeling.

The rest of this paper is organized as follows. Section 2 introduces the related work in brief. Our method is presented in Sect. 3. Section 4 presents the experiment setup and analyzes results. Section 5 concludes this paper.

2   Related Work

In this section, we give brief introductions to recent progress in the social-aware recommendation and deep learning based recommendation models, respectively.

Incorporating social relations into recommendations has been extensively discussed and justified in many works [3,4]. Zhao et al. extend the BPR [16] framework based on the assumption that users tend to click the items which his friends prefer [23]. Jamali et al. proposed SocialMF model which incorporates trust propagation in the matrix factorization approach [12]. An attentional memory network was introduced by Chen et al. [4] considers the influence of friends on the user based on friend-level and aspect-level difference. However, most existing methods focus only on the similarity among friends but ignore their differences. Moreover, they cannot capture the intuition that the social influence on an individual user may vary with his friends preferences and expertises. To the best of our knowledge, we are the first to dynamically model social influence strength from preference, connection strength and expertise differences together.

Deep learning techniques have been extensively applied to RS thanks to their high quality recommendations [6,9–11]. Deep learning can help us capture non-linear and non-trivial relationships between users and items, which provides insights into user preference and item property, as well as the interactions between them [20]. A number of approaches to integrating deep learning into RS have been proposed so far. For example, NCF [11] is proposed by He et al. replaces the inner product in matrix factorization with a neural architecture. NAIS model [10] employed attention mechanism in item-based model for recommendation. A comprehensive summary can be found in [13, 22].

3 MAIRS Model

3.1 Preliminaries

In this section, we introduce Multi-Attentive Item Recommendation Model based on Social relations (MAIRS). Let's start with some necessary notations. We consider the most common social-aware recommendation scenario with implicit feedbacks. Generally, we have a set of users $\mathcal{U} = \{u_1, u_2, \ldots, u_N\}$, a set of items $\mathcal{V} = \{v_1, v_2, \ldots, v_M\}$, and a social network $\mathcal{G}$. The network $\mathcal{G} = (\mathcal{U}, \mathcal{E})$ is generated by users and their relations, where $\{u_i, u_j\} \in \mathcal{E}$ indicates that user u_i has social connection with user u_j, or user u_j has social connection with user u_i, or both. Let $\Omega = \{(u_i, v_j) | u_i \in \mathcal{U}, v_j \in \mathcal{V}\}$ represent the set of user-item pairs which have implicit feedbacks in the past. We use $r_{(i,j)}$ to indicate the preference score which user u_i shows on item v_j. For implicit feedbacks, there only positive observations are avaliable, such as user's video viewing, clicks, likes, or purchase history. Therefore, if a user-item pair (u_i, v_j) is in Ω, $r_{(i,j)}$ is assigned as 1; otherwise, $r_{(i,j)}$ is 0. For a user $u_i \in U$, let $\mathcal{V}_i^+ = \{v_1^i, v_2^i, \cdots, v_{m_i}^i\}$ denote the set of m_i items interacted by user u_i, and $\mathcal{V}_i^- = \mathcal{V} - \mathcal{V}_i^+$ denote the remaining items.

The task of social-aware recommendation is formulated as follows: given user set $\mathcal{U}$, item set $\mathcal{V}$, and network $\mathcal{G}$, for each user $u_i \in \mathcal{U}$, we aim to recommend a ranked list of items from $\mathcal{V}_i^-$ that are of interests to the user.

Next, we present a layer-by-layer description of MAIRS. The overall model architecture is illustrated in Fig. 1(a).

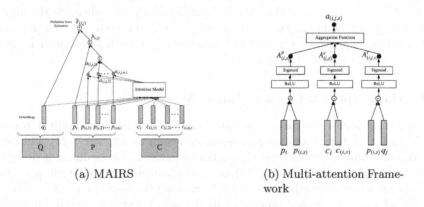

(a) MAIRS

(b) Multi-attention Framework

Fig. 1. The architecture of MAIRS.

3.2   User and Item Embedding Layer

Users and items are mapped as low-dimension vector representations after the embedding layer. Inputs of users and items are represented as one-hot encoded vectors where encoding corresponding to a unique index key of each user and item. At the embedding layer, this one-hot encoded vector is converted into a d-dimensional dense vector representation, where d is the dimension of the user and item embeddings. Let $P \in \mathbb{R}^{d \times N}$ and $Q \in \mathbb{R}^{d \times M}$ represent the user and item embeddings, respectively. Given user u_i and item v_j, $p_i \in P$ and $q_j \in Q$ denote user preference embedding and item property embedding, respectively.

3.3   Social Embedding Layer

In social networks, users often spread their preference to their friends in social networks. However, according to the research in social sciences [7], the spread of preferences between friends is affected by the strength of the connection between two friends in social networks. Therefore, how to measure the connection strength becomes the fundamental task. According to the idea in [15], there are two observations about connection strength. First, connection strength is determined partly by the local network structure. Second, the stronger the connection between two users, the more their friends overlap. These observations corresponds the *first-order proximity* and the *second-order proximity* in network embedding models [19]. Inspired by these observations, we apply *node2vec* [8] to characterize the features of nodes in this paper. Since *node2vec* provides an effective way to encode network structure into low-dimensional vector representation by preserving both first and second order proximities [8]. Therefore, the vector representations of users obtained by *node2vec* can encode the structure information related to connection strength for users. Noted that other high proximity preserving network embedding models can also be employed.

Let $C \in \mathbb{R}^{l \times N}$ represent the social embeddings for users, where l is the dimension of social embedding. For each user u_i, $c_i \in C$ represents the learned user social embedding, which encodes the connection strength (structure) between user u_i and other users in graph $\mathcal{G}$.

3.4   Multi-aspect Differences Based Attention

Attention mechanism attracts increasing concerns and has been applied in many fields, such as natural language processing and computer vision [1,21]. The original idea of attention is that different parts of a model can have different contributions for the objective function [1]. In our model, attention mechanism is utilized to learn an adaptive weighting function to capture the importance of each friend in user's friend set for user preference modeling. Particularly, given a user-item pair (u_i, v_j), user u_i is associated with a friend set $\mathcal{F}_i = \{u_{(i,1)}, u_{(i,2)}, \cdots, u_{(i,n_i)}\}$, we can obtain the item property embedding q_j, the preference embeddings of the user and his friends as $\{p_i, p_{(i,1)}, p_{(i,2)}, \cdots, p_{(i,n_s)}\}$, and the social embeddings of the user and his friends as $\{c_i, c_{(i,1)}, c_{(i,2)}, \cdots, c_{(i,n_i)}\}$ respectively, where n_i

denotes user u_i has n_i friends in social network. Next, we adopt a multi-attention framework (Fig. 1(b)) to learn $a_{(i,j,s)}, 1 \le s \le n_i$, which measures how much important friend $u_{(i,s)}$ is in friend set $\mathcal{F}_i$ when infering user u_i preference on item v_j. The importance of a friend is measured from three aspects by preference, connection and expertise attention models.

Preference Attention Model. Given user-friend pair $(u_i, u_{(i,s)})$, the embedding vectors p_i and $p_{(i,s)}$ obtained after embedding layer encode the preferences of user u_i and his friend user $u_{(i,s)}$, respectively. Therefore, we parameterize the difference between p_i and $p_{(i,s)}$ as a function with p_i and $p_{(i,s)}$ as the inputs:

$$\alpha_{(i,s)} = f(p_i, p_{(i,s)}), \tag{1}$$

the function is defined as:

$$f(x,y) = \frac{x \odot y}{\|x\|\|y\|}, \tag{2}$$

where $\odot$ is the element-wise product of vectors and $\|\cdot\|$ is the ℓ_2 norm of vector. The denominator is used to normalize and make the generated vectors have the same scale. Noted that the measurements that can distinguish the difference between two vectors, such as distance metrics, can also be used here. Next, inspired by the recent success of using neural networks to model the attention weight in [10], we employ a 2-layer network to learn the preference attention score $A^p_{(i,s)}$. Therefore, the preference attention network can be defined as following:

$$A^p_{(i,s)} = \sigma((h^p)^T \text{ReLU}(W^p \alpha_{(i,s)} + b^p_1) + b^p_2), \tag{3}$$

where $h^p, b^p_1 \in \mathbb{R}^k$, $W^p \in \mathbb{R}^{k \times d}$ and $b^p_2 \in \mathbb{R}$ are model parameters. k is the dimension of attention network. $(h^p)^T$ denotes the transpose of vector h^p. And, $\sigma(x) = (1 + \exp(-x))^{-1}$ and $\text{ReLU}(x) = \max(0, x)$ are both activation functions in deep learning.

Connection Attention Model. For user-friend pair $(u_i, u_{(i,s)})$, we can obtain the social embeddings c_i and $c_{(i,s)}$ encoding their local structures in $\mathcal{G}$ after social embedding layer. Next, a social joint embedding encoding their connection strength difference is parameterized as follows:

$$\beta_{(i,s)} = f(c_i, c_{(i,s)}). \tag{4}$$

After generating social joint embedding, we can also calculate the connection attention score $A^c_{(i,s)}$ for user-friend pair $(u_i, u_{(i,s)})$ by a 2-layer network as follows:

$$A^c_{(i,s)} = \sigma((h^c)^T \text{ReLU}(W^c \beta_{(i,s)} + b^c_1) + b^c_2), \tag{5}$$

where $h^c, b^c_1 \in \mathbb{R}^k$, $W^c \in \mathbb{R}^{k \times l}$ and $b^c_2 \in \mathbb{R}$ are connection attention model parameters.

Expertise Attention Model. For a user-friend pair $(u_i, u_{(i,s)})$ and item v_j, the embedding vector $p_{(i,s)}$ encodes the preference of user $u_{(i,s)}$, and the embedding vector q_j characterizes the property of item v_j. Then, we characterize the expertise $\gamma_{(s,j)}$ of friend $u_{(i,s)}$ shown on item v_j by the following function:

$$\gamma_{(i,j,s)} = f(p_{(i,s)}, q_j). \tag{6}$$

As such, we can get the expertise vector for every user-item pair without concerning whether they have interactions or not. Similarly, the expertise attention network can be defined as the following:

$$A^t_{(i,j,s)} = \sigma((h^t)^T \text{ReLU}(W^t \gamma_{(i,j,s)} + b^t_1) + b^t_2), \tag{7}$$

where $h_t, b^t_1 \in \mathbb{R}^k$, $W^t \in \mathbb{R}^{k \times d}$ and $b^t_2 \in \mathbb{R}$ are model parameters, and $A^t_{(i,j,s)}$ is expertise attention score for friend $u_{(i,s)}$ on item v_j.

After obtaining the three attention scores, namely preference, connection and expertise attention scores, the final attention score for friend $u_{(i,s)}$ among friend set $\mathcal{F}_i$ is calculated by an aggregation function:

$$a_{(i,j,s)} = \frac{\exp(A^p_{(i,s)} + A^c_{(i,s)} + A^t_{(i,j,s)})}{\sum_{s=1}^{n_i} \exp(A^p_{(i,s)} + A^c_{(i,s)} + A^t_{(i,j,s)})}. \tag{8}$$

Then, the final user representation for user u_i to item v_j is through a weighted manner:

$$\hat{p}_{(i,j)} = p_i + \sum_{s=1}^{n_i} a_{(i,j,s)} p_{(i,s)}. \tag{9}$$

The final user representation is a mixture of the target user's interest and his friends' suggestions. It is worth mentioning that MAIRS can model more factors which influence the social influence strength by adding more attention models directly. Furthermore, the dimensions of preference, connection and expertise attention model can be set as different values to further improve the flexibility of MAIRS.

3.5   Learning

Prediction. After modeling the user final preference representation, our task is to predict the item set which the user will interact in the future. The task can be reduced to a ranking problem among user's unobserved items based on preference score estimation $\hat{r}_{(i,j)}, v_j \in V^-_i$. In MAIRS, the prediction function is built by injecting social influence into matrix factorization framework as following:

$$\hat{r}_{(i,j)} = \hat{p}^T_{(i,j)} q_j + b_j, \tag{10}$$

where b_j represents the bias of item v_j. And, the biases of all items are stored in $B \in \mathbb{R}^M$. The item set is produced by ranking $\hat{r}_{(i,j)}$ in descending order and choosing the Top-K items.

Optimization. We employ BPR pairwise learning objective as our objective function [16]. For each user-item pair $(u_i, v_j) \in \Omega$, we sample one negative item v_{j-} from $\mathcal{V}^-_i$. Then, the preference score of user u_i on item v_j should be higher than his preference score on item v_{j-}. For all users and their rated items, the objective function can be formulated as follows:

$$\mathcal{L} = \sum_{(u_i, v_j) \in \Omega} -\ln \sigma(\hat{r}_{(i,j)} - \hat{r}_{(i,j-)}) + \frac{1}{2} \mathcal{R}, \tag{11}$$

where the regularization term $\mathcal{R}$ is used to avoid overfitting, which can be formulated as following:

$$\mathcal{R} = \lambda_p \|P\|^2 + \lambda_q \|Q\|^2 + \lambda_b \|B\|^2 + \lambda_{net} (\sum_{o \in \{p,c,t\}} \|W^o\|^2 + \|h^o\|^2 + \|b^o_1\|^2 + \|b^o_2\|^2), \tag{12}$$

where $\lambda_p, \lambda_q, \lambda_b, \lambda_{net}$ are the parameters of regularization term.

4 Experiments

4.1 Experimental Settings

Datasets. We use three public recommendation datasets containing social relations: Delicious[1], Ciao[2] and Epinions[3] [4]. Since we focus on implicit feedback in this paper, we convert explicit feedback to implicit feedback as 1 if the user has rated the item once and 0 otherwise. Closely following the setup from Chen et al. [4], all the datasets were preprocessed to make sure that all items have at least five interactions. The statistics of these datasets after preprocessing are summarized in Table 1.

Table 1. Statistics of datasets.

Dataset	#User	#Item	#Interaction	#Social relationship
Delicious	1,521	1,202	8,397	10,401
Ciao	7,267	11,211	157,995	111,781
Epinions	38,089	23,585	488,917	433,416

Evaluation Metrics. We evaluate the quality of recommendation list by two popular top-K metrics, namely Recall@K [4] and the Normalized Discount Cumulative Gain@K (NDCG@K) [4], where K is the number of items in the recommendation list. These measures vary from 0.0 to 1.0 (higher is better).

Implementation Details. We implemented our model using TensorFlow. We split each dataset into three parts: test set (10%), validation set (20%), and train set (70%). The validation set was used for parameter selection. For the embedding size d, we tested the value of $\{32, 64, 128\}$. The batch size and learning rate was searched in $\{64, 128, 256\}$ and $\{0.005, 0.01, 0.02, 0.05\}$, respectively. To avoid overfitting, we turned the margins $\lambda_p, \lambda_q, \lambda_b$ and λ_{net} in $\{0.001, 0.005, 0.01, 0.02\}$. The parameters for the baseline algorithms were initialized as in the corresponding papers and were then fine tuned to achieve optimal performance.

Comparison Methods. To evaluate the effectiveness of the proposed MAIRS model on top-K item recommendation, we compare it with classic models as well as recent state-of-the-art methods, including BPR [16], SBPR [23], SocialMF [12], NCF [11], SNCF [4], NFM [9] and SAMN [4].

4.2 Experimental Results

Recommendation Performance. To evaluate the practical significance of our proposed model, we compare MAIRS with other baseline methods on the Top-K item recommendation task. We vary K in $\{10, 20, 50\}$ to evaluate the quality of recommendation exhaustively. Table 2 reports the average performances of the various competing models in terms of different metrics, over all datasets. In particular, the results

---

[1] https://grouplens.org/datasets/hetrec-2011/.
[2] http://www.jiliang.xyz/trust.html.
[3] https://alchemy.cs.washington.edu/data/epinions/.

reveal three key observations. First, MAIRS always achieves the best performance on all datasets in terms of NDCG and Recall. Specifically, MAIRS outperforms the best baseline by performance gains about 2.13% on Delicious, 2.06% on Ciao and 3.42% on Epinions on the NDCG@10 metric, respectively. This ascertains the effectiveness of MAIRS. Second, social-aware models always perform better than models without social relations. For instance, BPR v.s. SBPR, and NCF v.s. SNCF. Last, compared with state-of-the-art social-aware model SAMN, our model considers three types of differences when modeling social influence strength of different friends. Moreover, there is no complex module such as memory module built in our model. Therefore, we can attribute the performance increase to our designed three differences based attention model. The differences from preference, connection strength, and expertise provide more fine-grained social influence strength modeling, which is beneficial to distinguish friends' different contributions in user preference inference.

Table 2. Overall results of all models on three datasets. Best performance is in boldface and the second best is underlined. The results of baselines are consistent with [4].

Datasets	Methods	Recall@			NDCG@		
		10	20	50	10	20	50
Delicious	BPR	0.1301	0.1601	0.2151	0.0930	0.1013	0.1136
	SBPR	0.1358	0.1715	0.2534	0.0888	0.1024	0.1216
	SocialMF	0.1337	0.1688	0.2433	0.0952	0.1044	0.1204
	NCF	0.1280	0.1632	0.2401	0.0887	0.1002	0.1165
	SNCF	0.1473	0.1846	0.2705	0.0971	0.1086	0.1274
	NFM	0.1422	0.1789	0.2612	0.0955	0.1075	0.1147
	SAMN	<u>0.1624</u>	<u>0.2033</u>	<u>0.2837</u>	<u>0.1034</u>	<u>0.1151</u>	<u>0.1325</u>
	MAIRS	**0.1711**	**0.2275**	**0.2996**	**0.1056**	**0.1209**	**0.1365**
Ciao	BPR	0.0644	0.0994	0.1625	0.0452	0.0547	0.0711
	SBPR	0.0651	0.1011	0.1645	0.0462	0.0572	0.0721
	SocialMF	0.0657	0.1004	0.1638	0.0469	0.0568	0.0717
	NCF	0.0677	0.1013	0.1634	0.0477	0.0581	0.0729
	SNCF	0.0722	0.1051	0.1725	0.0511	0.0619	0.0792
	NFM	0.0717	0.1034	0.1697	0.0509	0.0611	0.0778
	SAMN	<u>0.0747</u>	<u>0.1083</u>	<u>0.1753</u>	<u>0.0533</u>	<u>0.0634</u>	<u>0.0806</u>
	MAIRS	**0.0775**	**0.1123**	**0.1770**	**0.0544**	**0.0658**	**0.0826**
Epinions	BPR	0.0546	0.0836	0.1399	0.0361	0.0451	0.0596
	SBPR	0.0557	0.0846	0.1411	0.0365	0.0456	0.0598
	SocialMF	0.0542	0.0822	0.1387	0.0354	0.0447	0.0585
	NCF	0.0553	0.0840	0.1404	0.0363	0.0454	0.0597
	SNCF	0.0561	0.0852	0.1415	0.0366	0.0457	0.0603
	NFM	0.0564	0.0848	0.1417	0.0371	0.0459	0.0601
	SAMN	<u>0.0575</u>	<u>0.0869</u>	<u>0.1440</u>	<u>0.0380</u>	<u>0.0469</u>	<u>0.0617</u>
	MAIRS	**0.0608**	**0.0929**	**0.1520**	**0.0393**	**0.0493**	**0.0641**

Analysis on Different Embedding Size. To investigate the influence of embedding size d to MAIRS, we conduct experiments on the validation set under different d values. Specifically, we vary d value among $\{32, 64, 128\}$. Due to space limitation, Fig. 2 only shows the results of MAIRS and other baseline models in terms of NDCG@10 and Recall@10 on Delicious. Similar results can also be found on Epinions and Ciao. Overall, our model outperforms all baseline models with different d values in terms of different metrics. Moreover, we can also find that as the embedding size increases, the performances of all models increase. The potential reason is that a larger dimension could capture more hidden features of users and items, which is beneficial to Top-K recommendation due to the increased modeling capability.

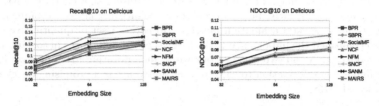

Fig. 2. Performance of our model w.r.t. different embedding size.

Analysis on Multiple Differences. According to different types of differences, there are three variants: MAIRS-ct, MAIRS-pc, and MAIRS-pt, where MAIRS-* denotes variant, p represents preference difference, c denotes connection strength difference, and t is expertise difference. Therefore, MAIRS-ct is a variant only considering connection strength and expertise differences, so do MAIRS-pt and MAIRS-pc. We conduct experiments on the three variants and MAIRS to gain a better insight into the three types of differences in MAIRS. Due to space limitation, we only present the results of the variants on the test set of delicious and ciao datasets in Fig. 3 in terms of NDCG@10 and Recall@10, respectively. Similar results can also be found on Epinions. We compare MAIRS with MAIRS-ct, MAIRS-pc, and MAIRS-pt, respectively. First, compared with MAIRS, MAIRS-ct performs inferior. It can indicate the importance of preference difference in social influence strength modeling. Since MAIRS-ct models social influence strength without considering preference difference. Similarly, the importance of connection strength (resp. expertise) can be confirmed when comparing MAIRS-pc (resp. MAIRS-pt) with MAIRS. Overall, MAIRS achieves the best performance against all the variants, which manifests that the three types of differences don't conflict with each other and can be used to model social influence collaboratively.

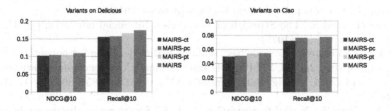

Fig. 3. Performance of variants.

5 Conclusion

In this paper, we proposed a new social-aware recommendation model MAIRS, which provides a multi-attention framework to dynamically model social influence strength with respect to preference, connection strength, and expertise differences. In MAIRS, we designed three attention models to learn attention scores of preference, connection and expertise for each user's friend when the user-item pair was given. Afterwards, an aggregation function was employed to fuse the three attention scores together to get the final attention score for each user's friend. Last, social influence can be generated by social influence strength and applied to model dynamically user preference on items. Our comparative experiments on three real-world datasets showed that MAIRS can consistently and significantly outperform state-of-the-art and classic recommendation models in terms of several evaluation metrics. Moreover, a set of quantitative experiments also confirmed the importance of the three types of differences in social influence strength modeling. As an extension of our work, incorporating attributes of users or other available side information to capture user preference is a promising development direction for MAIRS.

Acknowledgements. This work was partly supported by the National Natural Science Foundation of China under Grant No. 61572002, No. 61170300, No. 61690201, and No. 61732001.

References

1. Bahdanau, D., Cho, K., Bengio, Y.: Neural machine translation by jointly learning to align and translate. CoRR abs/1409.0473 (2014)
2. Beigi, G., Liu, H.: Similar but different: exploiting users' congruity for recommendation systems. In: Thomson, R., Dancy, C., Hyder, A., Bisgin, H. (eds.) SBP-BRiMS 2018. LNCS, vol. 10899, pp. 129–140. Springer, Cham (2018). https://doi.org/10.1007/978-3-319-93372-6_15
3. Berkani, L.: SSCF: a semantic and social-based collaborative filtering approach. In: AICCSA, pp. 1–4. IEEE (2015)
4. Chen, C., Zhang, M., Liu, Y., Ma, S.: Social attentional memory network: modeling aspect- and friend-level differences in recommendation. In: Proceedings of the Twelfth ACM International Conference on Web Search and Data Mining, WSDM 2019, Melbourne, VIC, Australia, pp. 177–185, 11–15 February 2019
5. Cocking, D., Kennett, J.: Friendship and the self. Ethics **108**(3), 502–527 (1998)
6. Covington, P., Adams, J., Sargin, E.: Deep neural networks for youtube recommendations. In: Proceedings of the 10th ACM Conference on Recommender Systems, Boston, MA, USA, pp. 191–198, 15–19 September 2016
7. Granovetter, M.S.: The Strength of Weak Ties. In: Social networks, pp. 347–367. Elsevier, Cambridge (1977)
8. Grover, A., Leskovec, J.: node2vec: scalable feature learning for networks. In: Proceedings of the 22nd ACM SIGKDD International Conference on Knowledge Discovery and Data Mining, San Francisco, CA, USA, pp. 855–864, 13–17 August 2016
9. He, X., Chua, T.: Neural factorization machines for sparse predictive analytics. In: Proceedings of the 40th International ACM SIGIR Conference on Research and Development in Information Retrieval, Shinjuku, Tokyo, Japan, pp. 355–364, 7–11 August 2017

10. He, X., He, Z., Song, J., Liu, Z., Jiang, Y., Chua, T.: NAIS: neural attentive item similarity model for recommendation. IEEE Trans. Knowl. Data Eng. 30(12), 2354–2366 (2018)
11. He, X., Liao, L., Zhang, H., Nie, L., Hu, X., Chua, T.: Neural collaborative filtering. In: Proceedings of the 26th International Conference on World Wide Web WWW 2017, Perth, Australia, pp. 173–182, 3–7 April 2017
12. Jamali, M., Ester, M.: A matrix factorization technique with trust propagation for recommendation in social networks. In: Proceedings of the 2010 ACM Conference on Recommender Systems, RecSys 2010, Barcelona, Spain, pp. 135–142, 26–30 September 2010
13. Karatzoglou, A., Hidasi, B.: Deep learning for recommender systems. In: Proceedings of the Eleventh ACM Conference on Recommender Systems, RecSys 2017, Como, Italy, pp. 396–397, 27–31 August 2017
14. McPherson, M., Smith-Lovin, L., Cook, J.M.: Birds of a feather: homophily in social networks. Ann. Rev. Sociol. 27(1), 415–444 (2001)
15. Onnela, J.P., et al.: Structure and tie strengths in mobile communication networks. Proc. Nat. Acad. Sci. 104(18), 7332–7336 (2007)
16. Rendle, S., Freudenthaler, C., Gantner, Z., Schmidt-Thieme, L.: BPR: bayesian personalized ranking from implicit feedback. In: UAI 2009, Proceedings of the Twenty-Fifth Conference on Uncertainty in Artificial Intelligence, Montreal, QC, Canada, pp. 452–461, 18–21 June 2009
17. Ricci, F., Rokach, L., Shapira, B., Kantor, P.B. (eds.): Recommender Systems Handbook. Springer, Boston (2011). https://doi.org/10.1007/978-0-387-85820-3
18. Su, X., Khoshgoftaar, T.M.: A survey of collaborative filtering techniques. Adv. Artif. Intell. 2009, 19 (2009)
19. Tang, J., Qu, M., Wang, M., Zhang, M., Yan, J., Mei, Q.: Line: large-scale information network embedding. In: Proceedings of the 24th International Conference on World Wide Web, pp. 1067–1077. International World Wide Web Conferences Steering Committee (2015)
20. Vinh, T.D.Q., Pham, T.N., Cong, G., Li, X.: Attention-based group recommendation. CoRR abs/1804.04327 (2018)
21. Vinyals, O., Toshev, A., Bengio, S., Erhan, D.: Show and tell: a neural image caption generator. In: IEEE Conference on Computer Vision and Pattern Recognition, CVPR 2015, Boston, MA, USA, pp. 3156–3164, 7–12 June 2015
22. Zhang, S., Yao, L., Sun, A., Tay, Y.: Deep learning based recommender system: a survey and new perspectives. ACM Comput. Surv. 52(1), 5:1–5:38 (2019)
23. Zhao, T., McAuley, J.J., King, I.: Leveraging social connections to improve personalized ranking for collaborative filtering. In: Proceedings of the 23rd ACM International Conference on Conference on Information and Knowledge Management, CIKM 2014, Shanghai, China, pp. 261–270, 3–7 November 2014

A Network Embedding and Clustering Algorithm for Expert Recommendation Service

Xiaolong Xu$^{(\boxtimes)}$ (iD) and Weijie Yuan

Nanjing University of Posts and Telecommunications, Nanjing 210023, China
xuxl@njupt.edu.cn

Abstract. Network embedding algorithm is dedicated to learning the low-dimensional representation of network nodes. The feature representations can be used as features of various tasks based on graphs, including classification, clustering, link prediction and visualization. Currently, network embedding algorithms have evolved from considering structures only to considering structures and contents both. However, how to effectively integrate the high-order proximity and node content of the network structure is still a problem to be solved. We propose a new network embedding and clustering algorithm in this paper. We obtain the high-order proximity representation of the information network structure, and the fusion node content completes the low-dimensional representation of the node features, so as to complete the network node clustering for the input of the spectral clustering. In order to further verify the value of the algorithm, we apply the clustering results to the field of expert recommendation, and make influence and activity assessments for domain experts to achieve more valuable expert recommendations. The experimental results show that the proposed algorithm will obtain higher clustering accuracy and excellent expert recommendation results.

Keywords: Network embedding · Clustering · Experts recommendation

1 Introduction

Information networks are ubiquitous in our daily lives, such as social networks, citation networks, and knowledge networks. A variety of useful information can be extracted by mining information networks intelligently. Typically, a network is represented in the form of a graph [1]. Different types of raw representations like adjacency matrix or adjacency list have been used as a direct input to many machine learning algorithms. Unfortunately, it is very difficult for machine learning algorithms to mine useful information from these representations as they belong to a very high dimensional space and also are highly sparse in nature. Network embedding maps the high dimensional networks to a low dimensional vector space such that the information loss is minimum in some sense.

This work was jointly supported by the Scientific and Technological Support Project of Jiangsu Province under Grant BE2016776, the "333" project of Jiangsu Province under Grant BRA2017228 and the Talent Project in Six Fields of Jiangsu Province under Grant 2015-JNHB-012.

© Springer Nature Switzerland AG 2019
C. Douligeris et al. (Eds.): KSEM 2019, LNAI 11775, pp. 96–108, 2019.
https://doi.org/10.1007/978-3-030-29551-6_9

Network embedding techniques are mostly unsupervised [1] or semi-supervised [2] in nature as it is common to encounter networks with a small number of labelled nodes or without any labelled node. Hence not much supervision is required to learn the embeddings. There are different types of network embedding methods that exist in the literature including Deepwalk [1], Line [3], node2vec [4], TADW [5], AROPE [6], and FSCNMF [7]. The study [8] of high-order proximity of network structure shows that the high-order proximities between nodes are of tremendous importance in capturing the underlying structure of the network [9–11] and thus can provide valuable information for learning the embedding vectors. It is possible to retain various network properties such as homophily [13], community structure [12] in the resultant node embeddings.

How to determine the feature matrix of the high-order proximity of the network structure, and further, how to efficiently integrate the network node content into the high-order proximity of the structure is not effectively solved.

In order to solve the above problems, the main contributions of this paper include:

- A network embedding algorithm is proposed to obtain the feature matrix, which is used as the input of spectral clustering to complete node clustering.
- In each category, the total influence and activity value of the expert are calculated separately. We use weights to combine the two values, calculate the recommended value, sort in descending order, and get the expert recommendation list.
- We provide the prototype system, complete evaluation and recommendation for the experts, and verify the value of the algorithm.

2   Related Work

In recent years, scientific research results on network embedding or network representation learning have been being born. The central idea of network embedding is to find a mapping function that converts each node in the network into a low-dimensional potential representation [14–16].

Literature [1, 3, 4, 17] provides a variety of network embedding methods. They have a common feature that they use different sampling strategies or different hyperparameters to obtain the best network embedding for a specific task. Therefore, it is difficult to find the best strategy for coherence across different types of networks. The network embedding algorithm provided by [6, 9, 18, 19] solves the problem of multi-network application to some extent.

The above unsupervised network embedding method only utilizes network structure information to obtain low-dimensional features of the network. But nodes and edges in real-world networks are often associated with additional features, called attributes. For example, in a social networking site such as Twitter, text content published by users (nodes) is available. It is therefore expected that the network embedding method also mines important features from the rich content in the node attributes and edge attributes. From the literature research, it is found that at present, there are many achievements [2, 7, 20–23] that can integrate the structure with the content expressed in the network.

In reality, many complex systems with rich internal relationships can be abstracted into complex networks and have extremely important community structures [24]. Community discovery is a process of dividing a network into multiple clusters based on a certain connection between nodes. The purpose is to discover the community structure in the network. At present, the research methods of community discovery are endless and ever-changing. The algorithms can be divided into spectrum bisection algorithm [25], hierarchical clustering algorithm [26] and heuristic algorithm [27].

Among the many classic community discovery algorithms, the most famous algorithm is the spectral clustering algorithm based on network topology [28]. The basic idea is to decompose the similarity matrix features of the network and use the main feature vector to retrieve the community.

The expert recommendation system is a recommendation system that meets the needs for experts of users in specific scenarios and helps them find relevant experts in time to solve problems. Academic social networking sites have grown rapidly in recent years. A large number of users want to make friends with other users in order to conduct potential academic exchanges and cooperation, and the Q&A community becomes the main platform for academic exchanges. The literature [29–32] shows how to find experts from the Q&A community. However, the expert recommendation system based on the Q&A community must rely on the expert's own active social behavior.

3 Network Embedding and Clustering Algorithm

3.1 Problem Modeling

This section models the problem in the context of a citation network. We assume that the set of the nodes in the citation network is $V = \{v_1, v_2, \cdots, v_n\}$. The set of the edges between nodes is $E \subset \{(v_i, v_j) | v_i, v_j \in V\}$. Let the network structure adjacency matrix be A, then A is a $n \times n$ matrix. $A = (a_{ij})$, and the value of a_{ij} is as shown in formula (1). The content matrix of the document node is C, which is a $n \times d$ matrix. The title, keyword and abstract in the document node are extracted to construct the word bag model, and C is calculated based on the word bag model. In the word bag model, the stop word is usually deleted and the stem extraction is performed as a pre-processing step. Each row of the matrix is a tf-idf vector corresponding to the text content on the node.

$$a_{ij} = \begin{cases} 0 & (v_i, v_j) \notin E \\ 1 & (v_i, v_j) \in E \end{cases} \tag{1}$$

Implement a non-negative matrix decomposition on A and C respectively, then

$$A \approx B_1 B_2 \tag{2}$$

$$C \approx UV \tag{3}$$

where, B_1 is a $n \times k$ matrix, B_2 is a $k \times n$ matrix, U is a $n \times k$ matrix, V is a $k \times d$ matrix. Usually, applied to network embedding, there is $k \ll n$.

Hence in an ideal scenario, the representations found solely based on A would match well with the representations found solely based on C. However, in reality, they may differ due to noise and topological inconsistency in the network.

3.2 Network Embedded Representation: FSCEN

Literature [6] focuses on the high-order proximity calculation of structures in information networks. Given the adjacency matrix A of an undirected network, the concept of high-order proximity is given:

$$S = F(A) = w_1 A + w_2 A^2 + \ldots + w_q A^q \tag{4}$$

where the matrix S refers to the weighted sum of various proximitys of the graph, q is the order and $w_1, \ldots w_q$ are the weights. For $\forall 1 \leq i \leq q$, $w_i \geq 0$.

Decompose for S:

$$B_1^*, B_2^* = \arg \min \left\| S - B_1^* B_2^{*T} \right\|_F^2 \tag{5}$$

where $B_1^*, B_2^* \in R^{r \times d}$ are the closest embedding vectors of content/context and d is the dimensionality of the space. Without loss of generality, we use B_1^* as the content embedding vectors.

The decomposition of the high rank matrix can generally be taken from the height of the singular value decomposition (SVD). Do SVD decomposition for S, namely:

$$S = U_s \Sigma V_s \tag{6}$$

Only the part with the highest singular value in the SVD result is intercepted, then $B_1^* = U_s \sqrt{\Sigma}$, $B_2^* = V_s \sqrt{\Sigma}$, where B_1^*, B_2^* is the result of matrix decomposition. The result of SVD can be obtained by the result of eigenvalue decomposition:

$$\begin{cases} U_s(:,i) = X(:,i) \\ \Sigma(:,i) = abs(\Lambda(i,i)) \\ V_s(:,i) = X(:,i)sign(\Lambda(i,i)) \end{cases} \tag{7}$$

where X and Λ are feature vectors and eigenvalues, respectively, and $abs(x)$ refers to the absolute value of x, namely $abs(x) = |x|$. Moreover:

$$sign(x) = \begin{cases} 1 & x > 0 \\ 0 & x = 0 \\ -1 & x < 0 \end{cases} \tag{8}$$

Therefore, as long as the eigenvalues and eigenvectors of the matrix S are calculated, the matrix decomposition result of S can be obtained, and the node embedding matrix containing the high-order neighbor information is further obtained.

If λ and x are a set of eigenvalues and eigenvectors of matrix A, then $F(\lambda)$ and x are a set of eigenvalues and eigenvectors of S. Therefore, as long as d of the top-l eigenvalues of A are greater than 0, then after calculating $F(\lambda)$, there will still be d eigenvalues in the front. The literature [6] has proved its correctness and rationality, and its further experimental results show that the weights for any order proximity can be equal. Then the formula (7) can be simplified to:

$$M = \frac{A + A^2 + \cdots + A^m}{m} \tag{9}$$

Therefore, the eigenvalues and eigenvectors of A are obtained, and the function M is applied to the eigenvalues. Replace A with M, and obtain the embedding matrix B_1^* to complete the embedding feature of the high-order proximity of the network structure.

One intuitive way to generate a single embedding of the network by using both structure and content is to use joint non-negative matrix factorization by replacing U with B_1. But that may not work in practice as large information networks are noisy and often there is significant inconsistency between structure and content. The solution is to use the content as a regularizer over structure, and vice-versa.

So given an embedding matrix U based on the content, we would like to obtain the embedding matrix B_1 based on the link structure by minimizing the following cost function:

$$D_1(B_1, B_2) = \|A - B_1 B_2\|_F^2 + \alpha_1 \|B_1 - U\|_F^2 + \alpha_2 \|B_1\|_F^2 + \alpha_3 \|B_2\|_F^2 \tag{10}$$

As we want to exploit the consistency between structure and content, the term $\|B_1 - U\|_F^2$ would try to pull B_1 close to U. The weight parameter $\alpha_1 \geq 0$ controls the importance of content while optimizing the embedding from structure. Hence the updated matrices B_1 and B_2 can be obtained as follows.

$$B_1, B_2 = \underset{B_1, B_2 \geq 0}{\arg \min} D_1(B_1, B_2) \tag{11}$$

Similarly, given an embedding matrix B_1 based on structure, embedding matrix U based on content can be found by minimizing the cost function below:

$$D_2(U, V) = \|C - UV\|_F^2 + \beta_1 \|U - B_1\|_F^2 + \beta_2 \|U\|_F^2 + \beta_3 \|V\|_F^2 \tag{12}$$

Again the term $\|U - B_1\|_F^2$ would not allow the content embedding matrix U to deviate significantly from the given structure embedding matrix B_1. The weight parameter $\beta_1 \geq 0$ controls the importance of structure while optimizing the embedding from the content. Then the updated values of U and V are calculated as:

$$U, V = \underset{U,V \geq 0}{\arg \min} D_2(U, V) \tag{13}$$

We use the above two optimizations in Eqs. (11) and (13) multiple times in an iterative way to get the final embeddings of the network. In the framework proposed above, one can easily incorporate the prior knowledge of the network quality and semantics. For example, if the content of the network is known to be more informative than the link structure, then one should give more importance to the initial representation in U than that in B_1. This can be accomplished by setting a higher value for α_1 than that of β_1. On the other hand, a higher value of β_1 gives more importance to the structure of the network than the content, and push the overall representation to be more consistent with the structure.

Set the initial B_1 to B_1^*. Note that the update of the B_1 value is independent of B_1^*. Next, we derive the necessary update rules to solve the optimization problems in Eqs. (10) and (12). It is worth noting that if B_1 is an independent variable and B_2 is a constant, the function is a concave function. In order to find the minimum value, the partial derivative is 0, and the equation is obtained:

$$B_1 = \left(A B_2^T + \alpha_1 U \right) \left(B_2 B_2^T + \alpha_1 I + \alpha_2 I \right)^{-1} \tag{14}$$

where I is an identity matrix, $B_2 B_2^T$ is a semi-definite matrix, and the inverse matrix of $B_2 B_2^T$ must exist. The proof is given as follows: the product of the matrix and its transposition is a semi-positive definite matrix, the sum of the two semi-positive matrices is semi-positive, and the multiplication of non-negative real numbers and semi-positive definite matrices is semi-positive. The determinant of a semi-definite matrix is non-negative. If 0 is set to a minimum value that tends to 0, it is invertible because it is a non-negative matrix.

To ensure the non-negativity of B_1, we further impose the following. To ensure the element wise non-negativity of B_1, we set all the negative elements to 0 to get the final update rule for B_1 as:

$$B_1 = \left[\left(A B_2^T + \alpha_1 U \right) \left(B_2 B_2^T + \alpha_1 I + \alpha_2 I \right)^{-1} \right]_+ \tag{15}$$

where $[X]_+$ represents that each element X_{ij} of the matrix X completes the following formula:

$$X_{ij} = \begin{cases} X_{ij} & X_{ij} \geq 0 \\ 0 & X_{ij} < 0 \end{cases} \tag{16}$$

Then, take B_2 as the independent variable, find the minimum value, and find the partial derivative to be 0, and get the equation:

$$B_2 = \left[\left(B_1^T B_1 + \alpha_3 I \right)^{-1} B_1^T A \right]_+ \tag{17}$$

Similarly we get the following update rules for U and V as shown below.

$$U = \left[\left(CV^T + \beta_1 B_1 \right) \left(VV^T + \beta_1 I + \beta_2 I \right)^{-1} \right]_+ \qquad (18)$$

$$V = \left[\left(U^T U + \beta_3 I \right)^{-1} U^T C \right]_+ \qquad (19)$$

At the end of the optimization, we get two different embeddings B_1 and U of the network. An convex combination of the two matrices in the form $(\gamma \times B_1 + (1 - \gamma) \times U), 0 \le \gamma \le 1$ would be a good choice for the final representation of the network.

3.3   Network Node Clustering

The final network embedding matrix is used as the input matrix of spectral clustering to complete the clustering of network nodes. The specific parameters are as follows:

(1) *n_clusters*: It is not only the target dimension of dimension reduction when performing a cut graph in spectral clustering, but also the clustering dimension of the clustering algorithm which is the last step of the spectral clustering. The numerical selection is related to a specific data set.
(2) *affinity*: The way in which similar matrices are established. The full connection method is used, using the built-in Gaussian kernel function "rbf".
(3) Kernel function parameter (*gamma*): By cross-validation, choose the appropriate value to be 0.1.
(4) *assign_labels*: The choice of the final clustering method. Use "K-Means" to complete the clustering.

4   Application Scenario: Recommending Domain Experts

4.1   Recommendation Strategy

In the same category, we separately calculate the amount of documents issued by the experts each year, and calculate the influence value of the results of the experts in the current year, based on which the recommendation index is calculated.

(1) Influence of the author

In general, a single document is completed by multiple authors. The first author's contribution is the biggest, the second author is second, and so on. By using the author contribution rate ranking formula [33], the authors of different signature sequences are calculated to contribute to the paper D_j:

$$D_j = \frac{1}{j \sum_{j=1}^{j=m} \frac{1}{j}} \qquad (20)$$

In the above formula, j represents the author's signature order, and m represents the total number of authors of the paper.

Combining the author's signature order and the influence of the paper c, the author's influence on the paper is I.

$$I = D_j \times c \tag{21}$$

The influence of the authors who published multiple papers is the sum of the influence of all papers - the Iw index, namely:

$$Iw = I_1 + I_2 + I_3 + \cdots I_s = \sum_{\alpha=1}^{\alpha=s} I_\alpha \tag{22}$$

where s is the total number of papers published by the author ($\alpha = 1, 2, 3, 4 \cdots \cdots s$).

(2) Expert recommendation index

In each year, the author completes the publication statistics and influence calculations, which are normalized separately. The normalization formula is as follows:

$$y = y_{\min} + \frac{y_{\max} - y_{\min}}{x_{\max} - x_{\min}} \times (x - x_{\min}) \tag{23}$$

where $y_{\max}$ is the maximum value of the target interval to be mapped; $y_{\min}$ is the minimum value of the target interval to be mapped; $x_{\max}$ is the maximum value of the current data; $x_{\min}$ is the minimum value of the current data; and x is assumed to be any value in the current data; y is the value after normalization mapping. Set $y_{\min}$ to 0 and $y_{\max}$ to 1, respectively, to complete the normalization of the amount of publication and influence, and the value of each author's issue and influence are set to y_1, y_2. The calculation of the expert recommendation index is derived from the formula $(t \times y_1 + (1 - t) \times y_2)$. The user determines the weight by setting the t value. If only the influence is used as the expert recommendation index, set t to 0.

By summing up the recommended index for all categories of experts of the same category, the total recommendation index of experts under the single category can be calculated. It is worth noting that different categories do not sum. Finally, the experts in all categories and their recommendation index are synthesized, and the list of expert recommendations is available in descending order.

4.2 Prototype System

Based on DBLPV, we search for experts related to "big data". We can not only get the corresponding list of expert recommendations, but also realize the statistics of the number of documents published by the target experts over the years, and use the influence of the documents signed by the experts to calculate the influence value of the experts themselves. The system of the expert recommended function is shown in Fig. 1.

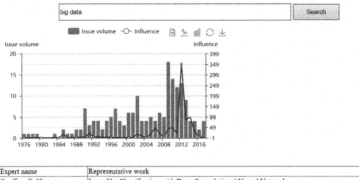

Fig. 1. Expert details function display

5   Experiments and Performance Analysis

5.1   Experimental Platform and Datasets

(1) dataset

Citeseer: 3,312 articles, 4,732 citations;
Wikipedia: 40,101 articles, 1806,377 citations;
DBLP-Citation-network V10: 3,079,007 documents, 25,166,994 citations.

(2) Software Environment

Spark1.6.2 distributed computing cluster, mysql database, python2.7.

5.2   Data Preprocessing

During the experiment, the adjacency matrix based on the network structure is a set of stable information, and no pre-processing work is required. However, the feature matrix based on the content of the network nodes will cause large interference due to some words with no specific meaning. In our experimental data, the dataset Citeseer and Wikipedia have done some denoising processing. Citeseer's content matrix consists of 3,703 words, which perform operations such as deleting stop words and extracting stems, and then deleting words with a document frequency less than 10. Based on this, we designed the preprocessing work of DBLP-Citation-network V10:

(1) Combine the title and abstract of each document.
(2) Use the English word segmentation tool (Lucene standard word breaker) to initially remove stop words.
(3) Using tfidf to calculate the word vector for each document, the matrix C calculation is complete.

5.3 Performance Comparison and Analysis

The feature matrix obtained by various network embedding algorithms is used as the input of spectral clustering, and the optimal clustering accuracy in the tuning process is extracted. The comparison is shown in Fig. 2.

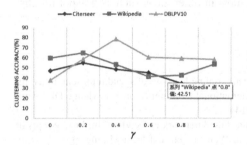

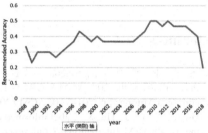

Fig. 2. Accuracy of clustering under different network embedding algorithms

Fig. 3. The effect of different (α_1, β_1) on clustering accuracy

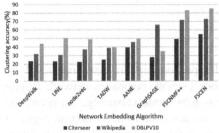

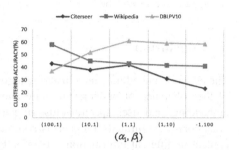

Fig. 4. The effect of different γ on clustering accuracy

Fig. 5. Recommended accuracy verification for different years

We experimented with the new FSCEN algorithm and other network embedding algorithms in different information network datasets. From the above figure, we found that the FSCEN algorithm has different degrees of improvement in clustering effect.

From Fig. 3, we find that in the Citeseer and WikiPedia datasets, when the node content matrix dominates, the clustering effect is better, which explains the reason why the clustering effect of the Citeseer and WikiPedia datasets is poor. In the DBLPV10, when the structure matrix dominates, the clustering effect is better.

From Fig. 4, we find that in the three dataset experiments, when the value of γ is small, that is, less than 0.5, better clustering effect is obtained. This means that the node content matrix still occupies a more important position than the structure matrix.

Based on the analysis of three performance graphs, the construction of the node content matrix is the most important and directly affects the clustering accuracy.

After completing the spectral clustering, we use the author to recommend the relevant formula to calculate the influence value of each expert scholar. According to different years, the size of the expert list is 30, and the accuracy change is shown in Fig. 5. After analyzing and analyzing the number of data sets, we found that the larger the amount of literature data, the more accurate the recommendation. Combined with the experimental analysis done, the larger the expert recommendation list, the higher the accuracy rate will be.

6 Conclusion

The network embedding and clustering algorithm proposed in this paper makes full use of the coherence of network structure and node content, completes network feature embedding, and uses spectral clustering to complete node clustering. However, the node content is limited to text. It is common for each node to have multiple types of content in different information networks. For example, a page in Wikipedia describes the complete content by text and multiple images. In subsequent work, we will update the formula to extend the network embedding algorithm to all types of node content. In addition to expert recommendation, we will use network embedding and clustering algorithms to make further application attempts in other areas such as hotspot mining.

References

1. Perozzi, B., Al-Rfou, R., Skiena, S.: Deepwalk: online learning of social representations. In: Proceedings of the 20th ACM SIGKDD International Conference on Knowledge Discovery and Data Mining, pp. 701–710. ACM (2014)
2. Huang, X., Li, J., Hu, X.: Label informed attributed network embedding. In: Proceedings of the Tenth ACM International Conference on Web Search and Data Mining, pp. 731–739. ACM (2017)
3. Tang, J., Qu, M., Wang, M., Zhang, M., Yan, J., Mei, Q.: Line: large-scale information network embedding. In: Proceedings of the 24th International Conference on World Wide Web, pp. 1067–1077. International World Wide Web Conferences Steering Committee (2015)
4. Grover, A., Leskovec, J.: node2vec: scalable feature learning for networks. In: Proceedings of the 22nd ACM SIGKDD International Conference on Knowledge Discovery and Data Mining, pp. 855–864. ACM (2016)
5. Yang, C., Sun, M., Liu, Z., Tu, C.: Fast network embedding enhancement via high order proximity approximation. In: Proceedings of the 2017 International Joint Conference on Artificial Intelligence, pp. 3894–3900. AAAI (2017)
6. Zhu, D., Cui, P., Zhang, Z., Pei, J., Zhu, W.: High-order proximity preserved embedding for dynamic networks. IEEE Trans. Knowl. Data Eng. **30**(11), 2134–2144 (2018)
7. Bandyopadhyay, S., Kara, H., Kannan, A., Murty, M.N.: FSCNMF: fusing structure and content via non-negative matrix factorization for embedding information networks. arXiv preprint arXiv:1804.05313 (2018)
8. Zhang, Z., Cui, P., Wang, X., Pei, J., Yao, X., Zhu, W.: Arbitrary-order proximity preserved network embedding. In: Proceedings of the 24th ACM SIGKDD International Conference on Knowledge Discovery & Data Mining, pp. 2778–2786. ACM (2018)

9. Cao, S., Lu, W., Xu, Q.: GraRep: learning graph representations with global structural information. In: Proceedings of the 24th ACM International Conference on Information and Knowledge Management, pp. 891–900. ACM (2015)
10. Cui, P., Wang, X., Pei, J., Zhu, W.: A survey on network embedding. IEEE Trans. Knowl. Data Eng. **31**(5), 833–852 (2019)
11. Ou, M., Cui, P., Pei, J., Zhang, Z., Zhu, W.: Asymmetric transitivity preserving graph embedding. In: Proceedings of the 22nd ACM SIGKDD International Conference on Knowledge Discovery and Data Mining, pp. 1105–1114. ACM (2016)
12. Wang, X., Cui, P., Wang, J., Pei, J., Zhu, W., Yang, S.: Community preserving network embedding. In: Proceedings of the 31st Conference on Artificial Intelligence, pp. 203–209. AAAI (2017)
13. McPherson, M., Smith-Lovin, L., Cook, J.M.: Birds of a feather: homophily in social networks. Ann. Rev. Sociol. **27**(1), 415–444 (2001)
14. Goyal, P., Ferrara, E.: Graph embedding techniques, applications, and performance: a survey. Knowl.-Based Syst. **151**, 78–94 (2018)
15. Hamilton, W.L., Ying, R., Leskovec, J.: Representation learning on graphs: Methods and applications. arXiv preprint arXiv:1709.05584 (2017)
16. Cai, H., Zheng, V.W., Chang, K.C.C.: A comprehensive survey of graph embedding: problems, techniques, and applications. IEEE Trans. Knowl. Data Eng. **30**(9), 1616–1637 (2018)
17. Mikolov, T., Chen, K., Corrado, G., Dean, J.: Efficient estimation of word representations in vector space. arXiv preprint arXiv:1301.3781 (2013)
18. Perozzi, B., Kulkarni, V., Chen, H., Skiena, S.: Don't walk, skip!: online learning of multi-scale network embeddings. In: Proceedings of the 2017 IEEE/ACM International Conference on Advances in Social Networks Analysis and Mining, pp. 258–265. ACM (2017)
19. Abu-El-Haija, S., Perozzi, B., Al-Rfou, R., Alemi, A.: Watch your step: Learning graph embeddings through attention. arXiv preprint arXiv:1710.09599 (2017)
20. Yang, C., Liu, Z., Zhao, D., Sun, M., Chang, E.: Network representation learning with rich text information. In: Proceedings of the 24th International Joint Conference on Artificial Intelligence, pp. 2111–2117. AAAI (2015)
21. Zhang, D., Yin, J., Zhu, X., Zhang, C.: Collective classification via discriminative matrix factorization on sparsely labeled networks. In: Proceedings of the 25th ACM International on Conference on Information and Knowledge Management, pp. 1563–1572. ACM (2016)
22. Saha, A., Sindhwani, V.: Learning evolving and emerging topics in social media: a dynamic NMF approach with temporal regularization. In: Proceedings of the 5th ACM International Conference on Web Search and Data Mining, pp. 693–702. ACM (2012)
23. Zhang, D., Yin, J., Zhu, X., Zhang, C.: User profile preserving social network embedding. In: Proceedings of the 2017 International Joint Conference on Artificial Intelligence, pp. 3378–3384 (2017)
24. Girvan, M., Newman, M.E.: Community structure in social and biological networks. Proc. Nat. Acad. Sci. **99**(12), 7821–7826 (2002)
25. Tantipathananandh, C., Berger-Wolf, T.Y.: Finding communities in dynamic social networks. In: Proceedings of the 2011 IEEE 11th International Conference on Data Mining, pp. 1236–1241. IEEE (2011)
26. Cheng, J., et al.: Voting simulation based agglomerative hierarchical method for network community detection. Sci. Rep. **8**(1), 8064 (2018)
27. de Guzzi Bagnato, G., Ronqui, J.R.F., Travieso, G.: Community detection in networks using self-avoiding random walks. Physica A **505**, 1046–1055 (2018)

28. Ng, A.Y., Jordan, M.I., Weiss, Y.: On spectral clustering: analysis and an algorithm. In: Proceedings of the International Conference on Neural Information Processing Systems, pp. 849–856. MIT Press (2001)

29. Huang, C., Yao, L., Wang, X., Benatallah, B., Sheng, Q.Z.: Expert as a service: software expert recommendation via knowledge domain embeddings in stack overflow. In: Proceedings of the 2017 IEEE International Conference on Web Services, pp. 317–324. IEEE (2017)

30. Ma, D., Schuler, D., Zimmermann, T., Sillito, J.: Expert recommendation with usage expertise. In: Proceedings of the 2009 IEEE International Conference on Software Maintenance, pp. 535–538. IEEE (2009)

31. Wang, J., Sun, J., Lin, H., Dong, H., Zhang, S.: Convolutional neural networks for expert recommendation in community question answering. Sci. China: Inf. Sci. **60**(11), 19–27 (2017)

32. Yang, B., Manandhar, S.: Tag-based expert recommendation in community question answering. In: 2014 IEEE/ACM International Conference on Advances in Social Networks Analysis and Mining (ASONAM 2014), pp. 960–963. IEEE (2014)

33. Hagen, N.T.: Harmonic allocation of authorship credit: Source-level correction of bibliometric bias assures accurate publication and citation analysis. PLoS ONE **3**(12), e4021 (2008)

Mixing-RNN: A Recommendation Algorithm Based on Recurrent Neural Network

Enhan Liu[1,2], Yan Chu[1(✉)], Lan Luan[1(✉)], Guang Li[1], and Zhengkui Wang[3]

[1] Harbin Engineering University, Harbin, China
chuyan@hrbeu.edu.cn, kellyluan@126.com
[2] Harbin University of Science and Technology, Harbin, China
[3] InfoComm Technology, Singapore Institute of Technology, Singapore, Singapore

Abstract. Collaborative filtering algorithms have been used by recommender systems for item (e.g., movie) recommendation. However, traditional collaborative filtering algorithms face challenges to provide accurate recommendation when users' interest and context suddenly changed. In this paper, we present a new Recurrent Neural Network-based model, namely Mixing-RNN that is able to capture time and context changes for item recommendation. In particular, Mixing-RNN integrates the insight from Rating-RNN and Category-RNN which are developed to predict users' interest based on rating and category respectively. Different from the traditional RNN, we integrate the forget gate and input gate in the model, where the forget gate decides what information to remain or discard and the input gate inputs rating information to the model. Our experiment evaluation on MovieLens indicates that Mixing-RNN outperforms the state-of-art methods.

Keywords: Recommender system · Collaborative filtering ·
Deep learning · Recurrent Neural Network

1 Introduction

Recommender systems have been widely used in different applications to recommend items to users [1,2]. Collaborative filtering (CF) makes automatic predictions about the interest of a user by collecting preferences from different agents, viewpoints and data sources etc. For user-based CF, intuitively, if the two users share similar interest in the past, they shall share the same interest for now as well. Many algorithms are built based on this observation such as K-Nearest Neighbor (KNN). Alternatively, item-based CF predicts user item interest based his historical item interest and what all users item interest. However, traditional

The paper is supported by National Natural Science Foundation of China under Grant No. 61771155 and Fundamental Research Funds for the Central Universities under Grant No. 3072019CF0601.

C. Douligeris et al. (Eds.): KSEM 2019, LNAI 11775, pp. 109–117, 2019.
https://doi.org/10.1007/978-3-030-29551-6_10

CF algorithms do not perform well while users interest or context suddenly changed, as they do not capture changes along time.

Take the movie recommender system as one example. Assume one user watched fifteen action movies before and then watched another five horror movies recently after his interest changed. Traditional CF algorithm will use the rating for these twenty movies and other users rating to recommend the user with new movies. When the sequence information is not considered, it is likely that the action movie will be recommended to the user instead of the horror movie, as the majority movies watched by the user are action movies. In other words, the algorithm will not differentiate the user watched the action movies first or horror movies first. However, this prediction result becomes unreasonable given that the user has changed his preference recently.

In this paper, using deep learning techniques, we present one new Recurrent Neural Network (RNN) based algorithm, Mixing-RNN which captures both the sequence information and the context information. Compared with traditional recommendation algorithms, deep learning can extract features automatically and process a large amount of data with distributed capabilities. In our model, we model the user historical data as the sequence data, which can be easily handled by RNN. The benefit of doing so is to allow the algorithm to discover the changing trends of the users' interest and preference over time. Mixing-RNN is developed based on two other proposed RNN models namely, Rating-RNN and Category-RNN. Rating-RNN is designed to take all the movie IDs watched at each time point and rating information as input to predict the movie that a user will watch next, while Category-RNN takes the movie categories that were watched at each time point as input to predict the category that the user will watch next. Additionally, we improve the traditionally RNN by adding a forget gate and an input gate. We observe that during the model training, it is important to distinguish the data importance for the input data at each time point such that the high rating movie will have more impact on the predictive decision. The aim of the forget gate is to decide what information shall be discarded or remained from previous neural network. And the aim of the input gate is to allow the model to take not only the movie ID information but also their rating information. In the end, Mixing-RNN output layer of Mixing-RNN is redesigned by the multiplication of the output probability of the movies in the output layer of Rating-RNN and the output probability of the movie categories from the Category-RNN. To improve the performance, the Rating-RNN and Category-RNN are conducted in parallel within Mixing-RNN. Our experiment evaluation indicates that Mixing-RNN is efficient and effective in personalized recommendation.

The rest of the paper is organized as follows. Section 2 summarizes the related works. Section 3 presents the details of the recommendation algorithm based on recurrent neural network. Section 4 provides the experiment evaluation. In Sect. 5, we conclude the paper.

2   Related Works

Much research has been devoted to use deep learning in various recommender systems. Hinton proposed deep learning application on structured data classification and prediction in 2006 [4–6], using Boltzmann machines and neural networks. In 2014, Netflix proposed the distributed neural network using the combination of GPU and AWS, using distributed neural networks in Netflix's recommender system [7]. The famous music platform, Spotify, uses deep learning to analyze the music style and recommend according to the style of the song, which has achieved good results [8]. The users' historical behavior can be regarded as a sequence of data, and a variety of Recurrent Neural Network [9] is undoubtedly the preferred model for the sequence data model. Google built a Youtube video recommender system based on deep neural networks [10]. In addition, Google has applied deep learning to the mobile App Store recommender system [12], which uses a large number of cross-product feature extraction based on linear regression, and then uses deep neural networks to convert a large number of category features into dense embedding vectors. MicroSoft and LinkedIn have applied deep learning to the recommendations of news and items in the world professional social networking site [13]. Compared with the traditional recommendation algorithms, the various recommendation algorithms based on deep learning have indeed been improved in terms of recommended performance.

3   The Mixing-RNN

3.1   Problem Description

The problem we study in this paper is develop solutions to predict the right movie to users based on their movie viewing history. The input of the recommendation algorithm is the user's historical viewing history and the user's rating information for the movie being viewed, and the output is the ID of the movie that the movie platform will recommend to the user.

The data set used is MovieLens, which includes user ID, movie ID, score, rating time, category information of the movie, and user gender, age, career information, and so on. First, the data in the MovieLens data set is sorted according to the rating time. For the user u_j, the movie viewing data can be abstracted into a sequence of data: (movie ID, rating, movie category), ..., (movie) ID, rating, movie category).

Therefore, the user's sequence data can be used as the input data of the input layer of the RNN, and the output layer outputs a probability vector indicating the probability that each movie will be viewed by the user in the near future. Therefore, the problem to be solved in this paper is simplified as the problem of predicting the output by the algorithm given the serialized data as an input, and the prediction accuracy is as high as possible.

3.2   Rating-RNN

In the traditional RNN, the historical information is considered in the same way as the current input information in the network. Such designs become unreasonable in the recommender system. For example, in the video platform's rating list for movies, the movies with higher ratings are those liked by the user more than those with lower ratings. If we use traditional RNN to process user sequence data, high-rated movies and low-rated movies have the same impact on the network, as the rating is not used. To tackle this challenge of RNN, we introduce an improved RNN model, Rating-RNN that captures the rating information in the model.

Figure 1 shows Rating-RNN model framework. Rating-RNN model includes various components including the raw data, preprocessing, locality sensitive hashing, input layer, RNN Layer, Dropout Layer, the softmax layer and output layer. Now, we introduce the important components of Rating-RNN in detail.

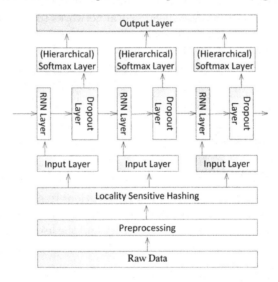

Fig. 1. Rating-RNN model

RNN Layer. Different to traditional RNN, in our RNN layer, we introduced one forget gate for the model to determine which memory needs to be discarded from the previous memory or what proportion of memories need to be discarded in the training network. For example, when one user used to watch an actor or a certain type of movie before, this information needs to be retained in the network and have a positive impact on the training of the next network. The forget Gate is developed through sigmoid function and the output of the function is between 0 and 1. The output of 1 means that all previous memories are completely preserved, when the rating of the movie is very high. The output of 0 means all memories before are discarded when the rating is very low, and a part of memory is discarded when it is between 0 and 1.

The function value formula of Forget Gate is as follows

$$f(i)^{(t)} = \sigma(b_i^f + \sum_j U_{i,j}^f x_i^{(t)} + \sum_j W_{i,j}^f h_j^{(t-1)}) \tag{1}$$

Which x_t is the current input vector, h^t contains all the memory output. b, U, W refer to the offset, the input weight and the weight of the forget gate respectively.

The next step is to decide which memory in the network can be retained. The sigmoid function layer called the input gate layer determines which information to be updated. This layer determines how much information in the current movie can be added to the new memory. If a user gives the movie a higher rating, then more information can be added, otherwise a small amount of information is added.

$$i = p * sigmoid(W_i * h_{t-1} + U_i * x_t + b_i) \tag{2}$$

The value of p is positively related to the users' score in the movie. It can be computed using a variety of functions, such as $sigmoid$, $tanh$, exp, etc. The value of p has different influences on the experimental results. The specific choice of which function can be based on experiment results. Next, the $tanh$ layer integrates the previous memory with the current input. The calculation process is as follows.

$$\hat{c}_t = tanh(W_c * h_{t-1} + U_c * x_t + b_c) \tag{3}$$

After completing the previous two steps of the design, the undesired information should be discarded through the integration of the old memory and Forget Gate. Then, the movie information currently viewed by the user should be integrated with the input gate layer, and the latest movie information viewed by the user should be added to the network.

$$c_t = f * c_{t-1} + i * \hat{c}_t \tag{4}$$

Finally, it is to determine how to output and update the memory based on previous memory. A sigmoid layer and $tanh$ layer are required to determine which part of the memory will be the output and determine which memory is suitable for backward propagation. The computation formula is as follows.

$$o = sigmoid(W_o * h_{t-1} + U_o * x_t + b_o) \tag{5}$$

$$h_t = o * tanh(c_t) \tag{6}$$

Parallel Design. To improve the neural network training process efficiency, we adopt a parallel design in the RNN model. According to the requirements, we improve the traditional RNN and add Forget Gate, Input Gate, and so on. Its calculation formula is as follows.

$$f_t = sigmoid(W_f * h_{t-1} + U_f * x_t + b_f) \tag{7}$$

$$i = p * sigmoid(W_i * h_{t-1} + U_i * x_t + b_i) \tag{8}$$

$$\hat{c}_t = tanh(W_c * h_{t-1} + U_c * x_t + b_c) \tag{9}$$

$$o = sigmoid(W_o * h_{t-1} + U_o * x_t + b_o) \tag{10}$$

From these formula, we can easily find out that apart from the slight difference of activation formula, they have the same linear operation formula, so the coefficient matrix can be combined for parallel operation.

By merging the coefficient matrices, it is possible to simply perform a single matrix that is required to be completed with four-step operation, which makes the training efficiency improved.

3.3   Category-RNN Design

As each movie has a category (e.g. Action, Horror, Adventure), Category-RNN is designed to predict the movie category. In Category-RNN, we encode the movie category into $0-1$ vector for any time t that watched by the user. The input layer of the Category-RNN is encoded vectors, and the output layer is the movie category that a user will likely watch at time $t+1$.

In the Rating-RNN, the input and output layers are the movie IDs, so both the input and output layer vectors have only one element with the value of 1 and the rest are 0. However, many movies belong to more than one categories. For example, the categories of the movie "Toy Story" are "Animation", "Children's" and "Comedy". Hence, for the "Toy Story" movie, there will be three 1 elements in the input vector. We adopt the Softmax as the output layer, where there is only one category in the output. Consider the movie may belong to multiple category. We use a new error calculation in the output layer. Assume at time t, RNN predicts the user will watch movie in category x at time $t+1$. And the real movie category the user watched is category set Y. Based on this, when the error is calculated, we use the below standard. If $x \in Y$, then the forecast is accurate, and if $x \notin Y$, then the forecast error, and the error should be calculated. Due to space constraints, we will omit the detail introduction of category-RNN.

3.4   Mixing-RNN Design

Now, we are ready to introduce Mixing-RNN which integrates the results from both the Rating-RNN and Category-RNN.

The output layer is the probability of watching each movie at the next moment in the rating-RNN, while the output layer is the probability of which category the movie belongs to at the next moment in Category-RNN. The two Softmax output layers are merged into one output to produce a unified result. The probability of the user watching the movie i is:

$$p_i = \frac{\sum\limits_{y \in Y} o_y * o_i}{\sum\limits_{i \in I} \sum\limits_{y \in Y} o_y * o_i} \tag{11}$$

where Y represents the set of categories which movie i belongs to, O_y represents the output probability of category Y in the Category-RNN output layer and O_i is the output probability of movie i in Rating-RNN.

There is no pre-defined combination of the weights of the Rating-RNN and Category-RNN outputs to merge the final results. The two RNN models can perform the training independently and merge the results in the end. This enables the parallel training which improves the training performance. Due to space constraints, we will omit the details here.

4 Experiment Results and Analysis

The dataset used in our experiment is MovieLens which includes a large amount movie user ratings. In particular, MovieLens 1M (100K) includes 10 millions (100,000) user movie ratings for 10,000 (1,700) movies from 72,000 (1000) users. Our program is developed using TensorFlow.

4.1 Evaluation on Category-RNN

Experiments are to analyze the performance of Category-RNN. In MovieLens 100 K and MovieLens 1M datasets, the movie's category information is the same. There are 18 categories, so unlike the Rating-RNN, the parameters of the Category-RNN network structure are the same on two datasets. The parameters are as follows in Table 1.

Table 1. Category-RNN parameters

Parameter	Value
Number of hidden nodes	50
Network length	3
Dropout layer	None
Output layer	Softmax
LSH layer	None

The Category-RNN is tested according based on the parameter settings in Table 1. Due to the small number of movie categories, the number of items recommended in the Rating-RNN experiment does not set to 1, 5, and 10. In this experiment, the accuracy indicators of the prediction classification are SPS@1, SPS@2 and SPS@3, respectively. As we can see from Table 2, the Category-RNN achieves 79.4% and 80.8% accuracy in predicting movie category that the user will watch at SPS@3.

Table 2. Category-RNN results

Index	MovieLens 100K	MovieLens 1M
SPS@1	46.9%	41.3%
SPS@2	71.3%	70.9%
SPS@3	79.4%	80.8%

4.2   Evaluation on Mixing-RNN

According to the design idea of mixing-RNN, the Mixing-RNN experiment is carried out according to the setting of parameters in Rating-RNN and Category-RNN.

By comparing data between the traditional recommendation algorithm and the RNN-based recommendation algorithm, it can be seen that the evaluation value of SPS and recall rate based on RNN recommendation algorithm is improved, especially in the prediction accuracy rate. Compared with the basic RNN, the Rating-RNN and Mixing-RNN proposed in this paper have achieved a better recommendation result, which shows that it is effective and feasible to adding the impact of rating data and the category characteristics of film to the RNN when analyzing the user sequence data.

5   Conclusion

Collaborative filtering has been widely used in personalized recommender system. Traditional approach of adopting collaborative filtering faces challenges when users' interest suddenly changes. We introduced the Mixing-RNN that captures both the sequence information and context information. It integrates the information from two individual RNN-based models including the Rating-RNN (a prediction model for the item recommendation based on rating) and Category-RNN (a prediction model for category recommendation). Additionally, instead of using the traditional RNN, we improved it by introducing the forget gate and input gate to determine what information to be discarded and remained in the neural network and integrate the rating information respectively. Our experiment results have indicated the Mixing-RNN outperforms baseline algorithms.

References

1. Yu, X., Chu, Y., Jiang, F., Guo, Y., Gong, D.: SVMs classification based two-side cross domain collaborative filtering by inferring intrinsic user and item features. Knowl.-Based Syst. **141**, 80–91 (2018)
2. Yu, X., Lin, J., Jiang, F., Chu, Y., Han, J.: A cross domain collaborative filtering algorithm based on latent factor alignment and two-stage matrix adjustment. In: Sun, G., Liu, S. (eds.) ADHIP 2017. LNICST, vol. 219, pp. 473–480. Springer, Cham (2018). https://doi.org/10.1007/978-3-319-73317-3_54

3. Goldberg, Y., Levy, O.: word2vec explained: deriving mikolov negative-sampling word-embedding method. CoRR, vol. abs/1402.3722 (2014)
4. Hinton, G.E., Osindero, S., Teh, Y.W.: A fast learning algorithm for deep belief nets. Neural Comput. **18**(7), 1527 (2006)
5. Hinton, G.E., Salakhutdinov, R.R.: Reducing the dimensionality of data with neural networks. Science **313**(5786), 504–507 (2006)
6. Hinton, G.E.: Learning multiple layers of representation. Trends Cogn. Sci. **11**(11), 428–434 (2007)
7. Hamel, P., Lemieux, S., Bengio, Y., et al.: Temporal pooling and multiscale learning for automatic annotation and ranking of music audio. In: ISMIR, pp. 729–734 (2011)
8. Oord, A., Dieleman, S.: Deep content-based music recommendation. In: Neural Information Processing Systems Conference, Harra 2013, pp. 2643–2651. MIT Press, Massachusetts (2013)
9. Mikolov, T., Karafit, M., Burget, L., et al.: Recurrent neural network based language model. In: INTERSPEECH 2010, Conference of the International Speech Communication Association, Makuhari, Chiba, Japan, pp. 1045–1048. DBLP, September 2010
10. Covington, P., Adams, J.: Deep neural networks for YouTube recommendations. In: ACM Conference on Recommender Systems, pp. 191–198. ACM, Boston (2016)
11. Cheng, H.T., Koc, L., Harmsen, J., et al.: Wide deep learning for recommender systems. In: The Workshop on Deep Learning for Recommender Systems, pp. 7–10. ACM (2016)
12. Elkahky, A.M., Song, Y., He, X.: A multi-view deep learning approach for cross domain user modeling in recommendation systems. In: International World Wide Web Conferences Steering Committee, pp. 278–288 (2015)
13. Zhang, X.X., Zhou, Y., Ma, Y., et al.: GLMix: generalized linear mixed models for large-scale response prediction. In: The ACM SIGKDD International Conference, pp. 363–372. ACM (2016)

SCCF Parameter and Similarity Measure Optimization and Evaluation

Wissam Al Jurdi[1]([✉])(iD), Chady Abou Jaoude[2], Miriam El Khoury Badran[1],
Jacques Bou Abdo[1], Jacques Demerjian[3], and Abdallah Makhoul[4]

[1] Department of Computer Science, Notre Dame University, Zouk Mosbeh, Lebanon
{wsjurdi,mbadran,jbouabdo}@ndu.edu.lb
[2] Faculty of Engineering, Ticket Laboratory, Antonine University, Baabda, Lebanon
chady.aboujaoude@ua.edu.lb
[3] Faculty of Sciences, LaRRIS, Lebanese University, Fanar, Lebanon
jacques.demerjian@ul.edu.lb
[4] FEMTO-ST Institute, UMR 6174 CNRS, Universite' de Bourgogne
Franche-Comte', Belfort, France
abdallah.makhoul@univ-fcomte.fr

Abstract. Neighborhood-based Collaborative Filtering (CF) is one of
the most successful and widely used recommendation approaches; however, it suffers from major flaws especially under sparse environments.
Traditional similarity measures used by neighborhood-based CF to find
similar users or items are not suitable in sparse datasets. Sparse Subspace
Clustering and common liking rate in CF (SCCF), a recently published
research, proposed a tunable similarity measure oriented towards sparse
datasets; however, its performance can be maximized and requires further
analysis and investigation. In this paper, we propose and evaluate the
performance of a new tuning mechanism, using the Mean Absolute Error
(MAE) and F1-Measure metrics, in order to show that the SCCF similarity can be radically enhanced and thus increasing its overall efficiency.
Moreover, the SCCF similarity measure was tested against several other
measures, targeted especially at sparse datasets, and the results show
how the effectiveness of a measure significantly varies with the dataset
structure and properties, and that one measure cannot be considered as
better than the other when compared with a small selection of other
measures.

Keywords: Recommender systems · Neighborhood-based CF ·
Similarity measures · Sparse datasets

1 Introduction

Throughout the years, it has been proven that neighborhood based Collaborative Filtering (CF) algorithms suffer from two major flaws [1]. The first flaw
is the limited coverage problem. Since rating correlation measures the similarity between two users by comparing their ratings for the same items, users can

© Springer Nature Switzerland AG 2019
C. Douligeris et al. (Eds.): KSEM 2019, LNAI 11775, pp. 118–127, 2019.
https://doi.org/10.1007/978-3-030-29551-6_11

be neighbors only if they have rated common items; obviously, this assumption is very limiting as some users might have a few or no common items yet still have similar preferences. Moreover, since only items rated by neighbors can be recommended, the coverage of such methods can also be limited. The second problem is the sensitivity to sparse data. The accuracy of neighborhood-based recommendation methods suffers from the lack of available ratings. Sparsity is a problem common to most recommender systems due to the fact that users typically rate only a small proportion of the available items. This is aggravated by the fact that users or items newly added to the system may have no ratings at all; a problem known as Cold-Start [2]. When the rating data is sparse, two users or items are unlikely to have common ratings, and consequently, neighborhood-based approaches will predict ratings using a very limited number of neighbors. Moreover, similarity weights may be computed using only a small number of ratings, resulting in biased recommendations.

Similarity measures are the core building block of the famous CF recommender; however, traditional and widely used measures such as the Pearson Correlation Coefficient (PCC), Cosine (COS), Spearman Rank Correlation (SRC) and their variants tend to be poor performers and claimed to be never suitable in sparse datasets [3,4].

In the paper entitled Collaborative Filtering Recommendation Based on User Trust and Common Liking Rate, Guo et al. [5] used a clustering algorithm called sparse subspace clustering [6] combined with a significantly improved, COS-based, similarity measure in order to obtain useful data with more accurate results under sparse conditions. After the clustering was done, the users retaining minimal difference in rates were selected and the similarity between them calculated according to the common liking rate set. The similarity measure was configured, balanced and executed using three parameters: alpha, beta and gamma whose values are critical for its performance, and it was compared to CJacMMD [7], COS and SRC similarities using MAE on the ML-100k dataset. The parameter optimization mechanism developed by the authors was simply to measure the effect of varying one of the parameters at a time and select the value that results in the lowest Mean Absolute Error (MAE). This developed method doesn't tune the parameters well enough to make the most out of the proposed similarity measure, and considers MAE value as the only measure of effectiveness of the recommender under sparse dataset conditions and uses merely a small subset of a larger training set to evaluate the performance.

This work is aimed at evaluating the parameter optimization mechanism developed by the authors of [5] and showing that their proposed similarity, although achieving great results on a sparse dataset - a subset of ML-100k - can still achieve even better results on a larger training set of the ML-100k by fine-tuning its parameters. The similarity is further tested on two other more sparse datasets, ML-Latest-Small and CIAO and compared with several other similarity measures where the results show that the performance of a measure depends on the size of the dataset as well as its characteristics. Moreover, this work proves that when selecting a similarity measure for a certain recommender, one cannot generalize as which similarity measure surpasses the other by merely considering the results against one or two datasets and using only one metric for evaluation. The rest of the work is organized as follows: Sect. 2 describes the SCCF algorithm, shedding light on the parts re-constructed and enhanced in our method, Sect. 3 contains the experiment details and the simulation results, and Sect. 4 concludes the work.

2   SCCF Algorithm

The SCCF algorithm was introduced in order to tackle the major flaws of the traditional CF algorithms that do not consider the common difference between users and the liking rate in their similarity measure computations. The implementation process of SCCF can be summarized as follows:

a. Apply the sparse subspace clustering method to cluster users.
b. Add the user's common liking rate.
c. Integrate the improved similarity measure and vary the balancing parameters.
d. Apply the KNN method.

The authors apply a clustering method [6] on the ML-100k dataset before initiating the similarity, rating prediction and KNN processes. The reason behind adopting the clustering algorithm is to achieve a better representation model that is able to reveal the real subspace structure of the data and eventually, achieve more accurate results. In our analysis, we did not include the clustering mechanism as we are aiming at analyzing and better-utilizing the parameters of the improved similarity measure of the algorithm isolated from SCCF. The raw similarity measure could be better utilized by varying its parameters based on the dataset structure and common rating distribution as opposed to generalizing a certain scale. With the aforementioned statement accounted for, the optimal parameter values can be considerably enhanced, and the author's simulation clearly shows what appears to be only the local minimum for the MAE results for solely a subset of the training set of the ML-100k.

2.1   Similarity Measure

The improved similarity measure approach [5] proposed by the authors is formalized as follows:

$$sim(u,v)^{SCCF} = \beta \times sim'(u,v) + (1-\beta) \times sim(u,v)^{Adj.COS} \qquad (1)$$

where
$$sim'(u,v) = LS \times sim(u,v)^{Adj.COS} \qquad (2)$$

$$LS = \alpha \times \frac{min(I_{uv},\gamma)}{\gamma} + (1-\alpha) \times \frac{min(L_{uv},I_{uv})}{I_{uv}} \qquad (3)$$

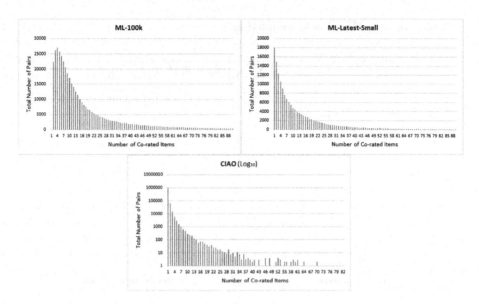

Fig. 1. Characteristics of the used datasets

$$L_{ij} = \sum_{n=1}^{m} l_n \quad and \quad l_n = \begin{cases} 1, \ if |r_{ui} - r_{vi}| <= k, \\ 0, \ otherwise \end{cases} \tag{4}$$

$$sim(u,v)^{Adj.COS} = \frac{\sum_{i \in I_{uv}} (r_{u,i} - \overline{r_u})(r_{v,i} - \overline{r_v})}{\sqrt{\sum_{i \in I_u} (r_{u,i} - \overline{r_u})^2} \sqrt{\sum_{i \in I_v} (r_{v,i} - \overline{r_v})^2}} \tag{5}$$

L_{ij} is defined by the authors as the "common liking set" and includes the sum of the data which has a minimal difference in a certain dataset. For instance, in ML-100k, the threshold for the common liking is set to 2. LS considers both the "common rate data" and the "common liking set" with a parameter α that controls the coefficient. I_{uv} represents the number of items that are commonly rated by users u and v while γ adjusts the user similarity. Finally, the original user similarity (Eq. 5) is combined with user similarity achieved after injecting the common liking data and balanced with yet another parameter β to obtain the final Eq. 1. The SCCF similarity measure was compared to three other measures only and the reason behind this choice was not stated [6]. Two of the chosen measures were traditional measures, COS and SRC, while the third was CJacMMD a new relatively similarity approach based on Mean Measure of Divergence that takes rating habits of a user into account. This concept is common with SCCF similarity measure and probably the reason why it was chosen to be compared with it. The formula of CJacMMD is defined as follows:

$$sim(u,v)^{CJacMMD} = sim(u,v)^{COS} + sim(u,v)^{Jac} + sim(u,v)^{MMD} \tag{6}$$

Where $sim(u, v)^{MMD}$ is formulated as:

$$sim(u, v)^{MMD} = \frac{1}{1 + (\frac{1}{r} \sum_{i=1}^{r} \{(\theta_u - \theta_v)^2 - \frac{1}{|I_u|} - \frac{1}{|I_v|}\})} \qquad (7)$$

Where θ is the vector that represents the sum of the total ratings of each rating value in the rating scale for users u and v.

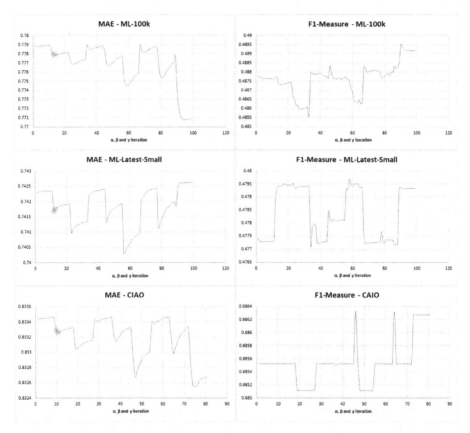

Fig. 2. MAE and F1-Measure results for each used dataset. The highlighted area on ML-100k is the minimal MAE in the SCCF study while the others show the expected results considering the same method

2.2   Evaluation Metrics

Accuracy metrics in recommender systems are divided into three categories: Predictive, Classification and Rank accuracies. The choice of certain metrics to evaluate a system is not straightforward and is quite often overlooked [8]. The efficiency and success of a certain recommender is especially dependent on its specific purpose and the characteristics of the domain it is applied to. It is very unlikely that there is a single best solution for any domain and context.

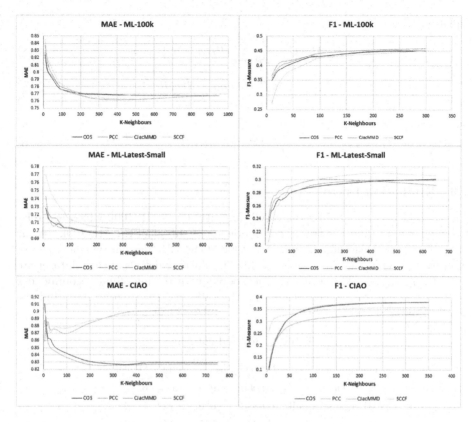

Fig. 3. Similarity measures performance comparison against the ML and CAIO datasets

The metric used to evaluate SCCF was MAE only, and the reason behind this choice was also not stated. Furthermore, MAE was interpreted as the only measure of accuracy when SCCF was compared to the other chosen similarity measures. The metrics decision is of immense importance and is made easier by defining a detailed goal and analyzing the different aspects of the system that influence such a decision [8]. In this work, we will use two evaluation metrics. The first metric is MAE in order to have our results comparable and compatible with [5]. The second metric is F1-Measure and that is to benefit from both Predictive and Classification accuracy metrics. The F1 score is interpreted as a weighted average of the precision and recall values, where it reaches its best value at 1 and worst value at 0. In light of what was mentioned, the main purpose of our work is to measure the performance of the similarity measure in order to locate the optimal parameter combination leading to the best output, and to use this output to compare SCCF with several other measures on different datasets and with two evaluation metrics. The chosen metrics are defined by the following equations:

$$MAE = \frac{1}{|S|} \sum_{i=1}^{S} |Pred_i - r_i| \tag{8}$$

$$F1 = \frac{2 \times Precision \times Recall}{Precision + Recall} \tag{9}$$

where

$$Precision = \frac{|L_r \cap L_{rev}|}{|L_r|} \ and \ Recall = \frac{|L_r \cap L_{rev}|}{|L_{rev}|} \tag{10}$$

2.3   Evaluation Data

The dataset used in running the SCCF algorithm was ML-100k which is a relatively sparse set, and the training was done on a subset of the ML-100k. In our analysis, we used the same famous ML-100k along with another two more sparse datasets, CIAO [9] and ML-Latest-Small [10]. Further details of each dataset are provided in Table 1. The train/test methodology for testing offline recommender systems was used in our algorithm and the ratio was set to 80%/20%, and the whole training set was used.

Table 1. Selected datasets

Dataset	Ratings	Users	Items	Density
ML-100k	100,000	943	1,682	6.3%
ML-Latest-Small	100,836	610	9,724	1.7%
Caio	72,345	17,615	16,121	0.03%

3   Experiment Results

The choice of the SCCF similarity parameters (mainly γ) should ultimately be a function of the total co-rated items (Eq. 3) between users and not any random range. Figure 1 shows how the distribution of pairs of users with co-rated items differs from one dataset to another. The variation in the co-rated items range and its distribution can affect the overall metric results for each of the similarity measures since the common liking factor varies dramatically especially in the case of the ML-Latest-Small dataset.

Our experiment took the above concept into consideration where the range of γ was selected according to the total number of co-rated items while varying the balancing parameters α and β (Eqs. 1 and 3). Furthermore, we iterated over all possible parameter values, a rather costly computational process, and not just incremented each alone while fixing the others as was done in the case of the SCCF results. The outputs of the MAE and F1-Measure are shown in Fig. 2. The best MAE result for ML-100k and CIAO, which show a similar co-rated dispersion (a maximum of 140 for ML-100k and 120 for CIAO), was achieved towards the highest values for all parameters ($\alpha = 1$, $\beta = 1$, $\gamma = 95$ and $\alpha = 1$, $\beta = 1$, $\gamma = 35$ respectively). As highlighted in Fig. 2, the minimum MAE value in [5] was achieved through simulating with each separate parameter and choosing a random range for gamma which resulted in the local minimum. The worst combination of parameters for ML-100k yielded 0.779 MAE and 0.485 F1 while the best one yielded 0.771 MAE and 0.49 F1. Considering only the local minimum value (0.778 - MAE of ML-100k), the similarity reaches only 12.5% of its maximum potential; therefore, based on our observations, even randomly selecting the parameters in the correct range can achieve around 80% chance of outperforming the proposed selection mechanism in [5]. Using ML-Latest-Small yielded a different performance since the distribution of the co-rated items is unique and has a greater range compared to ML-100k and CIAO (Fig. 1). It has the majority of users having a small number of co-rated items while the items with the minority having a large difference; however, the performance using our proposed parameter combination was valid and consistent on the tested datasets.

In order to measure the effectiveness of the SCCF similarity under the sparse conditions set-up in our algorithm and using the train/test mechanism, we ran the simulation against COS, PCC and CJacMMD as done in [5] using the optimal parameter configuration achieved in our previous results. The findings are presented in Fig. 3. As the case in the original work of SCCF, the similarity scored the best MAE results on the ML-100k dataset with a minimal value of 0.762 that is very close to PCC and with k = 700 neighbours. For smaller values of k (10–200), COS showed a better result until SCCF and PCC surpassed it starting at k = 250. SCCF resulted in the worst MAE score for ML-Latest-Small where PCC and CjacMMD had the best results of around 0.695 and 0.697 under k = 400. On the other hand, PCC and SCCF both had a higher MAE value for larger k on CIAO while CjacMMD scored the lowest value of 0.825 compared to the highest for PCC valued at 0.912. On the other hand, the SCCF similarity which resulted in the worst MAE on ML-Latest Small (0.701 for k = 400) and the best on ML-100k (0.69 for k = 400), achieved the highest F1 score (0.31 for k = 400) and the worst (0.44 for k = 350) on ML-Latest-Small and ML-100k respectively. CjacMMD and COS that resulted in the lowest MAE on CAIO, also scored the highest F1 score on CAIO (0.381 for k = 300). Table 2 summarizes the percentage variation of each similarity results on the lowest and highest values of k-neighbours.

Table 2. Results analysis of the similarity measures on all the used metrics for lowest and highest values of k-neighbours

ML-100k		
Measure	MAE % Decrease	F1 score % Increase
COS	6.87	30.97
PCC	8.33	20.85
CJacMMD	7.26	27.9
SCCF	9.26	65.7
ML-Latest-Small		
Measure	MAE % Decrease	F1 score % Increase
COS	4.25	36.03
PCC	6.08	24
CJacMMD	4.13	34.14
SCCF	9.06	51
CIAO		
Measure	MAE % Decrease	F1 score % Increase
COS	6.81	157.17
PCC	−2.17	105
CJacMMD	5.56	136.4
SCCF	−0.2	23

4   Conclusion

Traditional similarity measures that are sometimes used for neighborhood-based CF are not reliable in sparse environments. In our study, the SCCF similarity measure in [5] was tuned through a new proposed parameter selection mechanism. The results proved that the output can be radically enhanced and the similarity's overall efficiency increased in sparse datasets. However, the train/test methodology results for our application outlined that the performance of the similarity measure depends heavily on the quality of data contained in a dataset and their unique distribution. This makes it harder to state which measure is better than the other when comparing them in sparse environments, however, SCCF is definitely more costly to implement as its optimization requires a heavy computational process on each target dataset prior to using it to train the data. In the future, we hope to present a unified method for analyzing the quality of a dataset compared to the output of the most used metrics of evaluation in offline recommenders.

References

1. Ricci, F., Rokach, L., Shapira, B.: Recommender Systems Handbook, pp. 131–132. Springer, Boston (2011). https://doi.org/10.1007/978-0-387-85820-3

2. Schein, A., Popescul, A., Ungar, L., Pennock, D.: Methods and Metrics for Cold-Start Recommendations. SIGIR Forum (ACM Special Interest Group on Information Retrieval), pp. 253–260 (2002). https://doi.org/10.1145/564376.564421

3. Yildirim, H., Krishnamoorthy, M.: A random walk method for alleviating the sparsity problem in collaborative filtering. In: Proceedings of the 2008 ACM Conference on Recommender System RecSys08, pp. 131–138 (2008). https://doi.org/10.1145/1454008.1454031

4. Schwarz, M., Lobur, M., Stekh, Y.: Analysis of the effectiveness of similarity measures for recommender systems, pp. 275–277 (2017). https://doi.org/10.1109/CADSM.2017.7916133

5. Yubo, H., Ya, T., Sijie, W.: A collaborative filtering recommendation based on user trust and common liking rate. 186–190 (2018). https://doi.org/10.1145/3193025.3193038

6. Elhamifar, E., Vidal, R.: Sparse subspace clustering: algorithm, theory, and applications. IEEE Trans. Pattern Anal. Mach. Intell. **35** (2013). https://doi.org/10.1109/TPAMI.2013.57

7. Suryakant, Mahara, T., Kant, S.: A new similarity measure based on mean measure of divergence for collaborative filtering in sparse environment. Procedia Comput. Sci. **89**, 450–456 (2016). https://doi.org/10.1016/j.procs.2016.06.099

8. Schröder, G., Thiele, M., Lehner, W.: Setting Goals and Choosing Metrics for Recommender System Evaluations, p. 811 (2011)

9. Guo, G., Zhang, J., Thalmann, D., Yorke-Smith, N.: ETAF: An extended trust antecedents framework for trust prediction, pp. 540–547 (2014). https://doi.org/10.1109/ASONAM.2014.6921639

10. Harper, F.M., Konstan, J.: The movielens datasets: history and context. ACM Trans. Interact. Intell. Syst. (TiiS) (2015). https://doi.org/10.1145/2827872

NRSA: Neural Recommendation with Summary-Aware Attention

Qiyao Peng[1], Peiyi Wang[1], Wenjun Wang[1], Hongtao Liu[1], Yueheng Sun[1], and Pengfei Jiao[2]([✉])

[1] College of Intelligence and Computing, Tianjin University, Tianjin, China
{qypeng,wangpeiyi9979,wjwang,htliu,yhs}@tju.edu.cn
[2] Center for Biosafety Research and Strategy, Tianjin University, Tianjin, China
pjiao@tju.edu.cn

Abstract. Reviews are widely used in recommendation systems to handle the sparsity problem of rating matrix. However, learning the representations of users and items only from reviews would be challenging since there are less meaningful words and reviews while modeling users or items. In fact, in addition to reviews there are rich off-the-shelf summaries written by users along with reviews, but existing recommendation methods ignore this useful information. The summary of a review is to describe the review with shorter sentences, and can be seen as a high-level abstraction of the review. Thus the summary can play a guidance role to indicate the important parts in a review and the informativeness of the review. Hence, we propose a neural recommendation method to learn summary-aware representations of users and items from reviews. We firstly apply a summary encoder to learn representations of text summary, which will be used as the guidance indicator. We design a summary-aware review encoder to learn representations of reviews from raw words, and another summary-aware user/item encoder to learn representations of users or items from reviews. To be specific, we propose a hierarchical attention model with summary representations as attention vectors under word- and review-level to select important words and reviews for users/items respectively. We conduct extensive experiments on real-world benchmark datasets and the results demonstrate that our approach can effectively improve the performance of neural recommendation.

Keywords: Recommendation · Summary Attention · Text Mining

1 Introduction

Recently recommendation systems have been more and more important in many e-commerce platforms such as Amazon, Yelp and Alibaba [21]. The goal of the recommendation system is to predict whether the user prefers the item based on the rating matrix and the user's previous behaviors such as the reviews or summaries towards to items written by the user.

© Springer Nature Switzerland AG 2019
C. Douligeris et al. (Eds.): KSEM 2019, LNAI 11775, pp. 128–140, 2019.
https://doi.org/10.1007/978-3-030-29551-6_12

Collaborative Filtering (CF) technology has become the most commonly used method in recommendation systems. Many of the CF approaches [6,9,14] are based on Matrix Factorization (MF), which is used to find the latent features of users and items. However, these methods only utilize numeric ratings to model users and items and are affected by natural sparsity [4,21]. Therefore, to alleviate this problem, many recommendation systems utilize text information (e.g., reviews in e-commerce platforms) in conjunction with ratings to model users and items together since the text contains rich information to model user preference and item features [1,2,4,10,12,20]. For example, Zheng et al. [21] proposed DeepCoNN, which concatenated all the reviews of users or items and then adopt Convolutional Neural Networks (CNN) to extract semantic information as representations of user preference and item features. Chen et al. [1] introduced neural attention mechanism to build the recommendation model and selected the highly-useful reviews in review-level.

Fig. 1. An example of the review and summary in Amazon Website.

Despite the significant improvement of the text-based models in recommendation systems, the existing works only use reviews to learn representations of users or items, which would suffer from the useless words or reviews. Besides these existing works neglect the off-the-shell summaries along with the reviews as shown in Fig. 1, which are shorter than reviews, and can be seen as the high-level abstraction of reviews. To be specific, the reviews can provide a detailed information and the summaries can provide a more concise description about the opinions of users towards to items, which can be seen as a high-level abstraction of reviews. Thus, the summary information with less noise can help pay attention to the key parts in reviews. For example, as shown in Fig. 1, according to the summary, we can conclude that the user cares more about the price and storage of the wallet, and we should pay more attention to the parts about price and wallet in the review. Meanwhile, different reviews have different informative for users or items, and the summaries can be used to infer the usefulness of the reviews. Hence we should make full use of the summary information as the high-level guidance information of reviews for a better representations of users and items.

To this end, we integrate the summary information and propose a Neural Recommendation with Summary-aware Attention (NRSA) model to learn representations for users and items from reviews. Specifically, we firstly design a summary encoder to learn semantic representations of summaries via Convolutional Neural Networks (CNN), which will be used as the attention vectors in the following word- and review-level attention modules. Afterwards, we utilize CNN layer to extract semantic features of text reviews, and then use a word-level attention based on the summary embedding to select more informative words in a review for users and items. After learning the representations of reviews, we utilize another attention model under summary guidance to aggregate all the reviews of a user or an item to learn the summary-aware representations for the user or the item. At last, we combine the representations of a user and a target item and adopt Latent Feature Model (LFM) [7] as the prediction layer to predict the rating that the user would score the item.

The main contributions of this paper are as follows:

(1) To the best of our knowledge, we are the first to integrate the summary information of reviews as a high-level representation to enhance the representations of users and items in review-based recommendation systems.
(2) We propose a hierarchical summary-aware attention model in word-level and review-level to pay attention to those more important words and reviews, which helps to learn more precise representations of users and items.
(3) We conduct extensive experiments on three benchmark datasets and the results validate the effectiveness of our methods.

2   Related Work

In recent years, the collaborative filtering approach is popular in recommendation systems, and the most famous method in it is the matrix factorization (MF) [6,7,14,15,17]. The original MF is designed to take advantage of the user's explicit feedback data by populating users and items into latent feature space, since users and items potential features can capture the user-item relationships. Based on this, many research works have been done to enhance MF, such as Koren et al. [6] integrates it with a neighbor-based model and extends it to the factorization machine for general feature modeling.

However, the above methods only use the numerical ratings to model users and items, however the data sparsity is too high to represent users or items. Using review text is one approach to alleviate the above issues. Recently, many researchers focus on text-based recommendation systems [1,2,12,18,21]. Deep-CoNN [21] uses convolutional neural networks to process reviews and jointly model users and items through two pararrel sections of the last layer of FM coupling for rating prediction. The summary text reflects the user sentiment information towards the item. Hyun et al. [3] presents a scalable review-aware recommendation method, called SentiRec, that is guided to incorporate the sentiments of reviews when modeling the users and the items.

Attention mechanism has been shown effective in various deep learning tasks such as computer vision, nature language processing and machine learning. The principle of the attention mechanism is to learn a corresponding weight for each feature: higher weight means that this corresponding features are informative, otherwise it means that corresponding features are less informative. Seo et al. [18] proposes Dual Local and Global Attention mechanism to select informative key words and capture the global semantic meaning for modeling user preference and item features. Chen et al. [1] presents NARRE and introduces Attention-based Review Pooling to model the quality of users, which helps identify users who always write less-useful review. However, the existing methods only use reviews to model users and items, and ignore the useful summary information along with the reviews. Ma et al. [11] jointly learns text summarization and sentiment classification tasks to indicate that the summary information can be useful for learning embedding of reviews in sentiment classification. Hence in this paper, we utilize the summary information as the high-level abstraction to guide the process of modeling reviews via hierarchical attention mechanism to learn the representations of users and items.

3 Method

In this section, we introduce our NRSA approach in detail. The overview of our NRSA approach is shown in Fig. 2. Our approach contains four major components, i.e., a Summary Encoder to learn the feature representations as the guidance indicator from summaries, a User-Net to learn user representation, an Item-Net to learn item representation, and a rating prediction module to predict the rating scores based on user and item representations. Both User-Net and Item-Net contain two modules, i.e., a summary-aware Review Encoder to learn representations of reviews from words and a summary-aware User/Item Encoder to learn representations of users and items from reviews. In the following, since the User-Net and the Item-Net are similar in structure, we focus on illustrating the process for User-Net in details. The same process is applied for Item-Net with similar layers.

3.1 Problem Definition

The purpose of recommendation system in this paper is to predict the ratings of a user towards to an item according to the reviews and summaries information of users and items. Suppose there are user set U, item set I and the rating matrix $\mathbf{R} \in \mathcal{R}^{|U| \times |I|}$. For a user u, the reviews written by u can be noted as $r_u = \{r_{u,1}, \cdots, r_{u,N}\}$, since each review is along with a summary, thus the summaries of user u can be noted as $s_u = \{s_{u,1}, \cdots, s_{u,N}\}$. For an item i, the reviews towards to the item can be represented as $r_i = \{r_{i,1}, \cdots, r_{i,M}\}$, the summary for item i can be noted as $s_i = \{s_{i,1}, \cdots, s_{i,M}\}$. The rating matrix R_{ui} indicates the rating of user $u \in U$ towards to item $i \in I$.

3.2 Summary Encoder

In this section, we learn the semantic feature representations of summaries about the user towards to the item via a Summary Encoder, and the representations will be regarded as the high-level information of reviews used in the following attention modules.

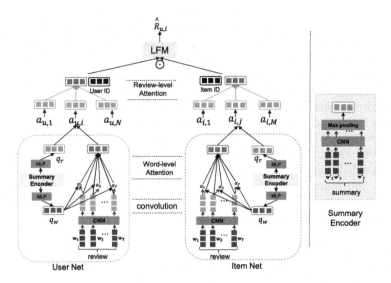

Fig. 2. The framework of our *NRSA* model. The summary encoder is to extract the semantic representation of summaries, used as the attention guidance vectors over word- and review-level. The User-Net and Item-Net learn representations from reviews for users and items.

Word Embedding. As shown in User-Net of Fig. 2, given the m-th summary, it can be denoted as a sequence with s words, noted as $S = \{W_1', W_2', \cdots, W_s'\}$ of the user towards to the item. Then we utilize word embedding to map each word W_i into a low-dimensional real-valued vector $\mathbf{W_i} \in \mathcal{R}^{d_w}$ with d_w as dimension. Thus m-th summary is transformed into an embedding matrix $\mathbf{S} \in \mathcal{R}^{s \times d_w}$.

Convolution. Following the embedding layer we utilize Convolutional Neural Networks (CNN) to extract the feature representations from the summaries named Summary-CNN. The Summary-CNN consists of K different convolution filters, denoted as $\mathbf{F} = \{\mathbf{f_1}, \mathbf{f_2}, \cdots, \mathbf{f_K}\}$, each filter is a parameter matrix $\mathbf{f_i} \in \mathcal{R}^{l \times d_w}$ which produces features by applying convolution operator on each window of word vectors $\mathbf{S}$. The convolutional result of j-th filter is computed as:

$$c_j = \text{ReLU}(\mathbf{S_{1:s}} * \mathbf{F_j} + b_j) , \tag{1}$$

where $*$ is the convolution operating, b_j is the bias and ReLU is a nonlinear activation function. Then we can obtain the features $\mathbf{C} = \{\mathbf{c_1}, \mathbf{c_2}, \cdots, \mathbf{c_K}\}$ produced by the K filters. The dimension of c_j that produced by j-th filter on the sliding window t over the embedded text is $\mathbf{c_j} \in \mathcal{R}^{s-t+1}$. Considering that summaries usually are short, we simply use the max-pooling to get the output of the j-th filter which is defined as:

$$o_j = \max(\mathbf{c_j^1}, \mathbf{c_j^2}, \cdots, \mathbf{c_j^{(s-t+1)}}) . \tag{2}$$

Then the final output is the concatenation of the output from all K filters, denoted by:

$$\mathbf{O_s} = [o_1, o_2, \cdots, o_K] . \tag{3}$$

Hence, we obtain the feature vector $\mathbf{O_s}$ of the summary which could help our model focus on more important reviews and useful review words.

3.3 Summary-Aware Review Encoder

We also adopt convolutional operation introduced above to get the semantic feature of each word in a review, and denoted as $\mathbf{C} = \{\mathbf{c_1}, \mathbf{c_2}, \cdots, \mathbf{c_T}\}$, where $\mathbf{c_i} \in \mathbf{C}$ is the semantic feature of i-th word in a review after convolution operation, and T is the length of the review sequence. Instead of max-pooling in the summary encoder, we propose the summary-aware attention model since reviews always contain quite a lot information about the user preference and item features and max-pooling operation would loss too much information.

Summary-Aware Attention over Word Level. We obtain the representations of all words in a review, and as mentioned above, not all words in a review are equally important. Therefore, we introduce the summary-aware attention to pay attention to those more informative words under the guidance of summary, which is a high-level abstraction of the review.

The attention weight α_i of the i-th word in the review text is dentoed as follows:

$$\alpha_i = \frac{\exp(g_i)}{\sum_{j=1}^{T} \exp(g_j)}, \ \alpha_i \in (0, 1) , \tag{4}$$

$$\mathbf{q_w} = \text{MLP}(\mathbf{O_s}) , \tag{5}$$

$$g_i = \mathbf{q_w} \odot \mathbf{c_i} , \tag{6}$$

where $\odot$ is the inner product operation, $\mathbf{c_i}$ is the i-th word representation in the review text. Note that we adopt a Multi Perceptron Layer (MLP) on the summary representation $\mathbf{O_s}$ as the attention query vector $\mathbf{q_w}$.

Since we have obtained all word weights of in the m-th review text above. Then, we utilize weighted summation to obtain the representation of the m-th review text:

$$\mathbf{O_{rm}} = \sum_{j=1}^{T} \alpha_j \mathbf{c_j} . \tag{7}$$

3.4 Summary-Aware User/Item Encoder

Since we obtain the representations of all reviews (i.e., $\mathbf{O_r} = \{\mathbf{O_{r1}}, \mathbf{O_{r2}}, \cdots, \mathbf{O_{rN}}\}$) and representations of all summaries (i.e., $\mathbf{O_s} = \{\mathbf{O_{s1}}, \mathbf{O_{s2}}, \cdots, \mathbf{O_{sN}}\}$) of a user, we will learn the representations of users or items according to their reviews and summaries. Since different reviews of a user are of different importance for the user, we propose our summary-aware attention over review-level to compute the informativeness of a review under the guidance of its summary. The informativeness a_{um} of each review in our approach is computed via :

$$a_{um}^* = \mathbf{h}^\mathsf{T}(\tanh(\mathbf{W_{Ir}O_{rm}} + \mathbf{W_{Is}q_r} + b_1) + b_2 \ , \qquad (8)$$

$$\mathbf{q_r} = \mathtt{MLP}(\mathbf{O_{sm}}) \ , \qquad (9)$$

where $\mathbf{h}$, $\mathbf{W_{Ir}}$ and $\mathbf{W_{Is}}$ are parameters, b_1 and b_2 are bias, and we use another MLP on the summary representation as the attention vector denoted as $\mathbf{q_r}$. Note that $\mathbf{q_r}$ and $\mathbf{q_w}$ in Eq. (9) (5), which are all derived from the summary representation $\mathbf{O_{sm}}$, can be regarded as two summary-aware indicators in word- and review-level respectively.

Finally, we normalize the informative scores of all reviews via the softmax function to obtain the weight of each review, so we can get the contributions of the m-th review to model the user preference:

$$a_{um} = \frac{\exp(a_{um}^*)}{\sum_{m=1}^{N} \exp(a_{um}^*)}, \ a_{um} \in (0,1) \ . \qquad (10)$$

Since we have obtained all reviews weights of the user towards items above. Then, we utilize weighted summation operation to obtain the summary-aware feature representations $\mathbf{p}_u$ of user u on each review:

$$\mathbf{p_u} = \sum_{m=1}^{N} a_{um}\mathbf{O_{rm}} \ . \qquad (11)$$

Likewise, we can obtain feature representation $\mathbf{q_i}$ of item i.

3.5 Rating Prediction

In this section we utilize LFM [7] to compute the rating that the user would score the item. First, we extend user preference and item features in LFM model to two components, then we introduce a neural form LFM for predicting ratings. We introduced the User-ID embedding $\mathbf{x_u}$ and the Item-ID embedding $\mathbf{y_i}$ to learn the latent factors of user and item such as user preference and item quality. By introducing the latent representation learned from the reviews, the interaction between user u and item i is modeled as:

$$\mathbf{h_0} = (\mathbf{p_u} + \mathbf{x_u}) \odot (\mathbf{q_i} + \mathbf{y_i}) \ , \qquad (12)$$

where $\mathbf{p_u}$ is user preference and $\mathbf{q_i}$ is item features, and $\odot$ denotes the element-wise product of vectors.

The rating $\hat{R}_{u,i}$ is computed by:

$$\hat{R}_{u,i} = \mathbf{W_1^\mathsf{T}h_0} + \mathbf{b_u} + \mathbf{b_i} + \mu \ . \qquad (13)$$

where $\mathbf{W_1^\mathsf{T}}$ denotes parameters of the LFM model, $\mathbf{b_u}$ denotes user bias, $\mathbf{b_i}$ denotes item bias and μ denotes global bias. LFM builds the latent features of users and items, which can further capture the potential attribute of the user and the item.

Since the task is a regression problem, we utilize the squared loss function for training our model:

$$L_{sqr} = \sum_{u,i \in \Omega} (\hat{R}_{u,i} - R_{u,i})^2 . \tag{14}$$

where Ω denotes the set of instances for training, and $R_{u,i}$ is the ground truth rating assigned by the user u to the item i.

4 Experiments

4.1 Datasets and Experimental Settings

In order to evaluate the effectiveness of our model, we use three widely used large-scale datasets from Amazon dataset[1] in our experiments, i.e., **Toys and Games**, **Kindle Store** and **Movies and TV**. All datasets contain reviews and summaries along with ratings (from 1 to 5) with respect to user-item pairs. The details of the three datasets are shown in Table 1.

Table 1. Statistical details of the three datasets.

Dataset	#users	#items	#ratings	#density(%)
Toys and Games	19,142	11,924	167,597	0.0734
Kindle Store	68,223	61,935	982,619	0.0232
Movies and TV	123,960	50,052	1,679,533	0.0271

In our experiments, we randomly split each dataset into training set, validation set and test set with 80%, 10% and 10% respectively. And we use the validation dataset to tune the hyperparameters in our model. The dimension of word embedding is set to 300, and we adopt the pre-trained word embedding which are trained on more than 100 billion words from Google News [13]. The number of filters in CNN is set to 100 and the window size of CNN is set to 3. Besides, we adopt Adam [5] to optimize our model and set 0.001 as the initial learning rate. Following many previous works [1,21], we use Root Mean Square Error (RMSE) as the evaluation metric.

4.2 Performance Evaluation

In this section, we report the performance of our method NRSA and compare it to several competitive baseline methods to evaluate our model. The baseline methods include:

---

[1] http://jmcauley.ucsd.edu/data/amazon/.

- **PMF** [16] models user and item latent factors by introducing a Gaussian distribution.
- **NMF** [8] introduces a recommendation system based on non-negative matrix factorization of rating scores.
- **SVD++** [6] proposes the recommendation system based on rating matrix via SVD with neighborhood models to model the item-item similarity.
- **HFT** [12] learns about potential factors from user or item review texts by leveraging topic distribution.
- **DeepCoNN** [21] learns user and item representations by convolutional neural networks from all user/item reviews.
- **Att-CNN** [19] uses CNN and attention mechanism over word level to learn representations of users and items from review texts.
- **NARRE** [1] introduces a item-based neural attention mechanism at the review-level, to focus on highly useful reviews.

Traditional recommendation methods, such as PMF, NMF, and SVD++, are based only on rating to learn the latent factor representations, and other methods such as HFT, DeepCoNN, Att-CNN, NARRE combine ratings and text information for recommendations.

Table 2. RMSE scores of different methods on different datasets.

Methods	Toys and Games	Kindle Store	Movies and TV
PMF	1.3076	0.9914	1.2920
NMF	1.0399	0.9023	1.1125
SVD++	0.8860	0.7928	1.0447
HFT	0.8925	0.7917	1.0291
DeepCoNN	0.8890	0.7876	1.0128
Att-CNN	0.8805	0.7796	0.9984
NARRE	0.8769	0.7783	0.9965
NRSA	**0.8542**	**0.7625**	**0.9769**

The RMSE evaluation results are summarized in the Table 2. We can find out the following observations. First, the methods utilizing the reviews (i.e., HFT, DeepCoNN, Att-CNN, NARRE and our model NRSA) perform better than those only with ratings (i.e., PMF, NMF, SVD++). This is because the rating-based methods suffer from the natural sparsity problem of rating matrix, and the review-based methods can provide more useful semantic information from texts to learn representations for users and items. Besides, we can find that the neural networks based methods can achieve better performance than those with topic models (i.e., HFT). Since the neural networks such as Convolutional Neural Networks can extract deep and non-linear semantic information of reviews, thus these CNN based methods (DeepCoNN, Att-CNN, NARRE and NRSA) can model user preference and item features more precisely from text.

Second, the attention based methods (Att-CNN, NARRE and NRSA) perform better than DeepCoNN, which regards all words and reviews the same. The reason is that for users or items, different words and reviews are of different importance and attention mechanism can help select more informative parts and pay less attention to those noise parts.

Third, our approach NRSA can always outperforms all baseline methods among all datasets. we conclude this into two reasons: (1) our approach NRSA integrates summary information and captures the high-level information of reviews via a summary encoder, which can guide the process of representing reviews. (2) NRSA contains two summary-aware attentions over word- and review-level, thus our approach can pay attention to the informative words in a review and the useful reviews of users/items under the high-level guidance of summary information. However Att-CNN only focuses on word-level attention and NARRE only select useful reviews in review-level, which are both suboptimal. Hence, our approach with hierarchical summary-aware attention can learn representations for users and items more precisely and comprehensively, which leads to a better performance in recommendation.

4.3   Effectiveness of Summary-Aware Attention

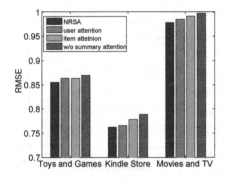
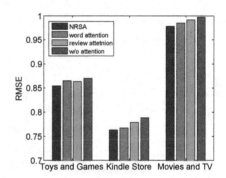

Fig. 3. Effectiveness comparison of user and item summary-aware attentions.

Fig. 4. Effectiveness comparison of word- and review-level attentions.

In this section, we analyze the effect of user/item summary-aware attention and word-/review-level attention respectively. As shown in Fig. 3, we can see that both variants incorporating only user or item summary-aware attention respectively outperform the method without any summary guidance attention (we randomly initialize the attention vector). This indicates that both user and item summary-aware attention modules can help our model to learn representations for users and items.

In addition, as shown in Fig. 4, we can see that both variants, which only include word-level attention and review-level attention, are superior to the model without any attention (we average weight of all words and reviews). This is because our word- and review-level attention can help the user to focus on the important words as well as the informative reviews towards a target item. Hence both of user and item summary-aware attention on word-/review-level are useful for our recommendation system.

Besides, our model NRSA is better than all these variants, and this indicates that the combination of user and item summary-aware attention or word- and review-level attention can further improve the performance in recommendation system.

4.4 Parameter Sensitivity Analysis

In this section, we perform parameter sensitivity analysis on the datasets to evaluate the effect of important hyperparameters in our model. We conduct experiments on the Number of latent factor and Convolution kernel size. From the result in Fig. 5, we can see that as the Number of latent factor increases, the RMSE first decreases, then reaches the best, and increases afterwards. When the Number of latent factor is too small, the model may not be able to capture the potential information about users and items. As shown in Fig. 6, with the size of Convolution kernel increases, the RMSE first decreases to best when the size is 100, it begins to increase after that. The optimal value of the Convolution kernel size is 100 and Number of latent factor is 32 regardless of different datasets.

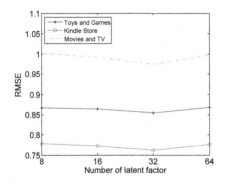
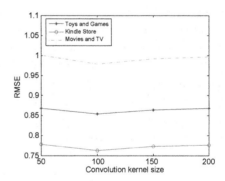

Fig. 5. Performances w.r.t. different number latent factor.

Fig. 6. Performances w.r.t. different convolution kernel size in CNN.

5   Conclusion

In this paper, we propose a Neural Recommendation with Summary-aware Attention (NRSA) to learn representations of users and items from reviews under the guidance of summaries. We adopt a CNN based summary encoder to extract the semantic representations of summaries, and we use the summary information as a high-level guidance indicator to point out the important words and reviews. In our approach, we propose a summary-aware word-level and review-level attention model under the supervision of summary to select the informative words and reviews for users and items. Extensive experiment results on three real-word datasets validate that our approach can effectively improve the performance of neural recommendation system.

Acknowledgments. This research was supported by grants from the National Key R&D Program of China (2018YFC0832101, 2018YFC0809800).

References

1. Chen, C., Zhang, M., Liu, Y., Ma, S.: Neural attentional rating regression with review-level explanations. In: WWW, pp. 1583–1592 (2018)
2. Diao, Q., Qiu, M., Wu, C.Y., Smola, A.J., Jiang, J., Wang, C.: Jointly modeling aspects, ratings and sentiments for movie recommendation (JMARS). In: KDD, pp. 193–202 (2014)
3. Hyun, D., Park, C., Yang, M.C., Song, I., Lee, J.T., Yu, H.: Review sentiment-guided scalable deep recommender system. In: SIGIRE, pp. 965–968 (2018)
4. Kim, D., Park, C., Oh, J., Lee, S., Yu, H.: Convolutional matrix factorization for document context-aware recommendation. In: RecSys, pp. 233–240. ACM (2016)
5. Kingma, D.P., Ba, J.: Adam: a method for stochastic optimization. In: International Conference on Learning Representations (2015)
6. Koren, Y.: Factorization meets the neighborhood: a multifaceted collaborative filtering model. In: SIGKDD, pp. 426–434 (2008)
7. Koren, Y., Bell, R., Volinsky, C.: Matrix factorization techniques for recommender systems. Computer **8**, 30–37 (2009)
8. Lee, D.D., Seung, H.S.: Algorithms for non-negative matrix factorization. In: NIPS, pp. 556–562. MIT Press, Cambridge (2000)
9. Linden, G., Smith, B., York, J.: Amazon. com recommendations: item-to-item collaborative filtering. IEEE Internet Comput. **1**, 76–80 (2003)
10. Lu, Y., Dong, R., Smyth, B.: Coevolutionary recommendation model: Mutual learning between ratings and reviews. In: WWW, pp. 773–782 (2018)
11. Ma, S., Sun, X., Lin, J., Ren, X.: A hierarchical end-to-end model for jointly improving text summarization and sentiment classification. CoRR (2018)
12. McAuley, J., Leskovec, J.: Hidden factors and hidden topics: understanding rating dimensions with review text. In: RecSys, pp. 165–172. ACM (2013)
13. Mikolov, T., Sutskever, I., Chen, K., Corrado, G.S., Dean, J.: Distributed representations of words and phrases and their compositionality. In: Advances in Neural Information Processing Systems, pp. 3111–3119 (2013)
14. Mnih, A., Salakhutdinov, R.R.: Probabilistic matrix factorization. In: NIPS, pp. 1257–1264 (2008)
15. Rendle, S.: Factorization machines. In: ICDM, pp. 995–1000 (2010)
16. Salakhutdinov, R., Mnih, A.: Probabilistic matrix factorization. In: NIPS, pp. 1257–1264 (2008)
17. Schafer, J.B., Frankowski, D., Herlocker, J., Sen, S.: Collaborative filtering recommender systems. In: The adaptive web, pp. 291–324 (2007)
18. Seo, S., Huang, J., Yang, H., Liu, Y.: Interpretable convolutional neural networks with dual local and global attention for review rating prediction. In: Proceedings of the Eleventh ACM Conference on Recommender Systems, pp. 297–305 (2017)

19. Seo, S., Huang, J., Yang, H., Liu, Y.: Representation learning of users and items for review rating prediction using attention-based convolutional neural network (2017)
20. Wang, C., Blei, D.M.: Collaborative topic modeling for recommending scientific articles, pp. 448–456 (2011)
21. Zheng, L., Noroozi, V., Yu, P.S.: Joint deep modeling of users and items using reviews for recommendation. In: WSDM, pp. 425–434 (2017)

Paper Recommendation with Item-Level Collaborative Memory Network

Mei Yu[1,2,3] (ID), Yue Hu[1,2,3], Xuewei Li[1,2,3], Mankun Zhao[1,2,3],
Tianyi Xu[1,2,3,4], Hongwei Liu[4], Linying Xu[1,2,3(✉)],
and Ruiguo Yu[1,2,3]

[1] College of Intelligence and Computing, Tianjin University, Tianjin, China
{yumei,huyue_ic,xuewei,zmk,tianyi.xu,
linyingxu,rgyu}@tju.edu.cn
[2] Tianjin Key Laboratory of Advanced Networking (TANKLab), Tianjin, China
[3] Tianjin Key Laboratory of Cognitive Computing and Application,
Tianjin, China
[4] Foreign Language, Literature, and Culture Studies Center,
Tianjin Foreign Studies University, Tianjin, China
liuhongwei@tjfsu.edu.cn

Abstract. The recommendation system can recommend information to users personally and efficiently, which satisfies the user's demand for information in the information age, and has become a hot topic in the current era. In the recommendation system, users and items and the interaction of their own information has a crucial impact on the efficiency and accuracy of the recommendations. However, most of the existing recommendation systems usually design the systems as user-base only, considering the user's influence on the item in the recommendation, which to some extent blurs the interaction between items and users at the item level, unknown and potential connections between items and users are not well considered. In this paper, we propose a collaborative memory network that can focus on the potential relation between items and users, and consider the impact of items' characteristics on user behavior. Experiments have shown that our improvement is better than the original method and other baseline models.

Keywords: Recommendation systems · Memory network · Collaborative filtering

1 Introduction

In the context of the era of big data, modern recommendation systems undoubtedly become an indispensable part of people's needs in their life. As an application that filters a large amount of information, the recommendation system can collect historical behavior data of users, process the data through various processing methods or using relevant recommendation technologies, in order to obtain personalized recommendation for users and recommend information or items such as movies, music, books, news, etc. to users that users may be interested in or fond of. The data of the

C. Douligeris et al. (Eds.): KSEM 2019, LNAI 11775, pp. 141–152, 2019.
https://doi.org/10.1007/978-3-030-29551-6_13

recommendation system includes explicit data and implicit data, the explicit data can more accurately reflect the user's real preference on items, such as user rating, etc., and the implicit data can reflect the user's preference after being analyzed and processed such as user clicks, watch time, etc. However, there are a large number of data and information that can be selected by users. The effective recommendation system can provide the most relevant content for users under the premise of large data volume, improve the efficiency and accuracy of the recommendation, and optimize the user experience. With the continuous development of digital libraries (DLs), many new knowledge is captured and stored in digital libraries. However, a large number of papers and related information lead to information overload, and there are a large number of papers matching the user's search query when making recommendations, but the information of many publications does not match the user's needs. Unlike other recommendations such as movie recommendations, the paper itself contains a large amount of information, and the user's history contains a lot of preference information. Such a large amount of data challenges the recommendation of the paper.

The recommendation system based on collaborative filtering can analyze the dependence between users and items, and use the similarity information between users to recommend content that users are interested in. The recommendation method also has a high degree of personalization and automation, at the same time, feedback can be used to speed up learning. Collaborative filtering technology is one of the most classic and mainstream technologies in recommendation systems. In real life, the user's rating data is very rare, that is, explicit data is much less than implicit data, so how to add implicit data to the model becomes a problem. SVD++ integrates the user's implicit behavior into the Singular Value Decomposition (SVD) model, enhancing the user's implicit feedback [1], which uses users' historical browsing data, users' historical review data, movies' historical browsing data and movies' historical score data, etc. as new parameters.

Another recommended system algorithm is the K-nearest neighbor classification algorithm (KNN). The core idea of KNN is to find the majority of the k most neighboring samples in a features space, if most of these samples belong to a certain category [2], then the sample also belongs to this category and has the characteristics of all samples in this category. When determining the classification, the KNN method only determines the category to which the sample to be classified belongs according to the categories of the nearest one or several samples. When making the category decision, it is only related to a very small number of adjacent samples, and is more suitable for a set of samples to be classified that intersect or overlap in a category.

Recently, Tay et al. [3] proposed a flexible adaptive metric learning algorithm for collaborative filtering and ranking. By learning the adaptive relationship vector between users and items interaction, find an optimal translation vector between each user-item interaction pair, while introducing a relational vector to simulate the potential relationship between users and items. Inspired by the memory network. Ebesu et al. [4] presented Collaborative Memory Network (CMN), they used the memory module as the nearest neighbor model of similar users, and used the attention mechanism based on specific users to learn the adaptive nonlinear weighting of the user neighborhood, while utilizing the adaptive neighborhood state and a non-linear interaction between users and items memory to generate recommendations.

Despite the success of CMN, it ignored some content. Each item has a connection with a group of users, and similar items do not necessarily have the same appeal to the same user. When considering the relevance between an item and a user, the CMN only considered the construction of neighborhood representation with similar users. However, in general, the problem of collaborative ranking has many-to-many nature, the item will also have a certain degree of impact on the user's choices and preferences, which may cause changes in the user's preferences. CMN ignored the potential relationships between items and users, especially those related to large data sets, it operates at the user level, with the user as the main body, and the information obtained comes from the user's clicks and the impact between similar users.

To solve this problem, we propose a network called Item-level Collaborative Memory Network (ICMN) for ranking and paper recommendation, which can fully consider the distribution of potential relationships between items and users and strengthen the relationship between the specific item and neighborhoods, it can take into account the impact of users and items on each other and their neighborhoods. Specifically, in order to be able to take into account the potential relationship between items and users, we adopt a higher-order method to obtain the weighted sum of the relationship between the specific item and the user and the neighborhoods they formed. Undoubtedly, our work has been inspired by the latest developments in NLP and recommendation systems [4]. The experimental results show that our method is better than CMN and other baseline models, it can capture the hidden semantics between implicit interactions.

Our contributions are summarized as follows:

- We propose ICMN, a new type of item-based network that is used to generate rankings for paper recommendations. For the first time, we have fully considered the distribution of potential relationships between items and users on CMN, and strengthened the relationship between specific items and neighborhoods.
- We also consider the impact of items and users on each other and their neighborhood. At the same time, neurological attention provides greater insight and interpretability for this model.
- We evaluate our proposed ICMN on a public dataset. Experiments have shown that our proposed ICMN is not only superior to CMN, but also superior to many other powerful baselines with improved performance.

2 Related Work

2.1 Collaborative Filtering

Usually, in implicit collaborative filtering, if there is an interaction between the user and the item, it is recorded as 1, otherwise 0. However, this does not indicate that the feedback between the user and the item that has generated the interaction is positive or negative. In a traditional data-based approach, all unobserved interactions are treated as negative samples and have the same weight, but unobserved interactions and data may be positive or missing data, and also have different weights. To this end, some recent efforts have focused on weighting schemes and have considered whether unobserved samples are indeed negative. For example, certain non-uniform weighting schemes on negative samples, such as user-oriented and item popularity orientation, have been proposed and proven to be more effective than uniform weighting schemes. However, one major limitation of the non-uniform weighting method is that the weighting scheme is defined based on the hypothesis proposed by the authors, which may not be correct in the actual data.

2.2   Attention Mechanism

The attention mechanism has a great improvement effect on the sequence learning task. The attention model can perform data weighted transformation on the data sequence. Xu et al. [6] proposed two attention modes, one is hard attention and the other is soft attention. Hard attention only pays attention to a certain position of the model sequence at each moment, when soft attention takes care of all the positions at a time, and the weight of each position is different. Luong et al. [6] proposed two improved attentions, namely global attention and local attention. Among them, local attention can be regarded as a mixture of hard attention and soft attention. Unlike hard attention, local attention can be differentiated almost everywhere and easy to train, it only focuses on a small part of the source position at a time, and global attention needs to scan all source hidden states each time.

2.3   Deep Learning

Deep learning stems from the research of artificial neural networks, is one of the latest trends in artificial intelligence and machine learning research, and is one of the most popular scientific research trends today. It combines low-level features to form more abstract high-level way to represent attributes categories or features to discover the distributed feature representation of the data [8]. The deep learning approach has brought historic progress to machine learning. In the study of machine learning, the motivation of deep learning lies in the establishment and simulation of a neural network for the analysis and learning of the human brain. It can mimic the mechanism of the human brain to interpret data such as images, sounds and texts, etc.

In the recommendation system, the general idea of common algorithms is to convert high-dimensional discrete features into fixed-length continuous features through the embedding layer, then pass through multiple fully connected layers, and finally convert to a 0–1 value through a sigmoid function to representing the probability of clicks. This method can fit high-order nonlinear relationships through neural networks while reducing the workload of artificial features.

2.4   Collaborative Memory Network (CMN)

CMN is a recent deep architecture that demonstrates excellent and competitive performance in several baseline tests. In this network, memory components and neural attention mechanisms are merged into neighborhood components to learn about the user's specific neighborhood. The ranking score is generated by the neighborhood and user memory [4].

CMN focuses its attention on users' information, which leads to the neglect of information about items. In the process of the user's interaction with the item, in addition to the explicit relationship, there is an implicit relationship. At the same time, in addition to the users' influence on items, the items also have a non-negligible connection with users. Similar items do not necessarily have the same appeal to the same user and items that have not interacted with the user will also affect the user's choice to some extent.

In real life, the channels through which users can accept items information are diverse, which means that different information will make the characteristics of the item have different effects on users. At the same time, it also shows that CMN cannot flexibly recommend in the case of huge data volume and dense dataset.

3   Item-Level Collaborative Memory Network

In this section, we will introduce our network model Item-level Collaborative Memory Network (ICMN) that can focus on the item's attractiveness and potential relationships to users. The overall architecture and construction process of our network model has shown in Fig. 1.

3.1   Source of Inspiration

Our inspiration comes from the CMN model which combines the memory component and the neural attention mechanism to form a neighborhood component that learns the user's specific neighborhood [4]. The model with the stacking of the two memories enables them to obtain a deeper relationship between the user and the item. In a single-layer memory, given a user u, a preference vector q_{ui} for a particular user v is formed, and then a similarity q_{uiv} of a particular user to a user in the user neighborhood is derived, which is represented by $q_{uiv} = m_u^T m_v + e_i^T m_v$. When constructing the final neighborhood representation, the CMN constructs a neighborhood representation p_{uiv} for a particular user for subsequent operations. We focus on items information and their features, embedding users and items, and using different methods to get the final neighborhood s_{iu} for a particular item. On this basis, we get the final ranking score.

3.2   User and Item Embedding

The input user and item information are embedded in the memory component of the user and the item respectively. The user's memory component is M, and the item's memory component is E, where $M \in R^{P \times d}$, $E \in R^{Q \times d}$, P and Q are the number of users and items, d is the dimension of the memory. The users' preferences are stored in the user memory component slice m_u, and the features of the item i are stored in e_i of the item memory slice to get the similarities a_{iut} for a particular item and a particular user in its given neighborhood:

$$a_{iut} = m_u^T e_t + e_i^T e_t \quad \forall t \in N(u) \tag{1}$$

Where t is a specific item in the item neighborhood with implicit feedback.

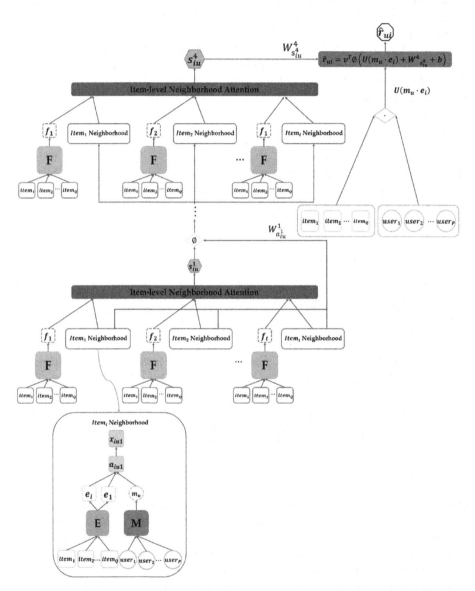

Fig. 1. Our model structure. This model can focus on item information and build with four layers of memory components.

3.3   Item Neighborhood Attention

In order to focus on the influential set of items and users in the neighborhood, the attention mechanism can learn the adaptive weighting function, which is different from the traditional neighborhood method used in Pearson correlation or cosine similarity, the function does not need to set the number of users or items. At the same time, we do not need to pre-define or set the weighting function based on past experience in the learning process of the whole attention mechanism. In this way, we can better learn the unique contribution of items:

$$x_{iut} = \frac{\exp(a_{iut})}{\sum_{g \in N(u)} \exp(a_{iut})} \quad \forall t \in N(u) \tag{2}$$

Among them, the generated neighborhood distribution can be dynamically assigned to specific item.

Then, by using the weights formed by the attention mechanism, the weights are manipulated with the neighborhood to form the neighborhood representation:

$$s_{iu} = \sum_{t \in N(u)} x_{iut} \times f_t \tag{3}$$

Where f_t is the vector of another embedded matrix of items, $\times$ is the operation at the matrix level. Focusing on the characteristics of items, the weights formed by the attention mechanism are selectively weighted to items and their neighborhoods in different ways to obtain the final weighted neighborhood.

This not only consider the impact of items on users, but also strengthens the relationship between the specific item and the neighborhood, taking into account the distribution of the potential relationship between items and user.

3.4   Memory Stack

Throughout the model building, we operate with a stack of four memories that capture deeper and broader information between items and users, improving the efficiency and performance of the entire model. Through the stacking of memories, it can dynamically assign weights to items, and capture the appeal of the item to users more comprehensively and in detail. Using the s_{iu}^y generated by the upper memory, a non-linear mapping z_{iu}^y between the memories can be formed for next memory, and then a_{iut}^{y+1} can be obtained by updating with the item neighborhood, and finally, after the four layers of memory components, the final neighborhood representation is obtained:

$$z_{iu}^y = \sigma\left(W_{a_{iu}^y}^y + s_{iu}^y + b\right) \tag{4}$$

$$a_{iut}^{y+1} = \left(z_{iu}^y\right)^T e_t \quad \forall t \in N(u) \tag{5}$$

Where $\sigma(x) = 1/(1+exp(-x))$ is the nonlinear activation sigmoid function, y is the number of memory layers, and W is a weight matrix that maps the features of items to the potential space, combined with the information of the previous layer.

3.5 Output

By capturing the local structure of items and users' neighborhood and the global interaction information between items and users, items and users have established a deeper and wider relationship, and then through a non-linear approach, the potential relationship between items and users can be more fully reflected to generate a ranking score that focuses on the items' influence:

$$\hat{r}_{iu} = v^T \emptyset \left(U(m_u \cdot e_i) + W^4_{s^4_{iu}} + b \right) \tag{6}$$

Where $\cdot$ is the operation of the element level. After obtaining the product of items and users, we learn the neighborhood representation and parameters by linear projection. We use the nonlinear activation function $\emptyset(x) = max(0,x)$, which can improve the expressive ability of the model [9], the overall structure of the model shown in Fig. 1.

3.6 Parameter Estimation

We use the Bayesian Personalized Ranking (BPR) optimization standard [12] as our loss function:

$$L = \sum_{(u,i^+,i^-)} \log \sigma(\hat{r}_{i^+u} - \hat{r}_{i^-u}) \tag{7}$$

Where $\sigma(x) = 1/(1+exp(-x))$ is the logical sigmoid function.

4 Performance Evaluation

In this section, we will introduce the dataset and baseline settings used in the experiment.

4.1 Dataset

The dataset we use is the citeulike-a dataset [9], an online service collected from CiteULike, which allows users to create their own collection of articles. Each article has a summary, title and label, and the user provides a digital catalog to save and share academic papers. And the dataset has 204,987 ratings, 5,551 users and 16,980 items.

4.2   Baselines

In this section, we will introduce the excellent baselines used in our experiments.

SVD ++: SVD ++ [1] is a hybrid model that combines neighborhood-based similarity and latent factor model.

GMF: The Generalized Matrix Factorization (GMF) [10] model is a nonlinearly extended potential factor model.

KNN: KNN [2] is a neighborhood-based method for calculating cosine item-item similarity.

BPR: Bayesian Personalized Sorting (BPR) [12] is a matrix factorization model of implicit feedback.

NeuMF: Neural Matrix Factorization (NeuMF) [10] is a matrix factorization model for item ordering through a multilayer perceptron model.

CDAE: Collaborative Denoising Automatic Encoder (CDAE) [13] is an item-based deep learning model.

FISM: Factored Item Similarity Model (FISM) [14] is a neighborhood-based model that can decompose the similarity matrix of item-item pairs and optimize the loss function.

CMN: Collaborative Memory Networking [4] is a model that fuses memory components and attention mechanisms and is the source of our ideas.

In addition, after several comparison experiments, we found that the setting of the number of negative samples has an impact on the recommended performance. The recommended performance improves with the increase of negative sample size, but will tend to stabilize at a certain negative sample size, as shown in Fig. 2. Based on the results of the comparative experiment, we set the number of negative samples as 4 and

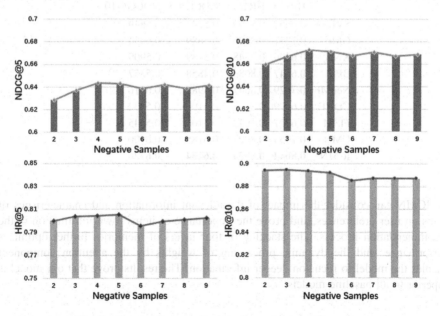

Fig. 2. Comparative experiment of negative sample number.

initialize in pre-training. In pre-training, l2's weight decay is set to 0.001. During training, l2's weight decay is set to 0.1, the embedded size d of the memory is set to 50.

We use two common ranking evaluation metrics Hit Ratio (HR) and Normalized Discounted Cumulative Gain (NDCG) [12] as the basis for the evaluation of experimental results:

$$HR@K = \frac{Number\ of\ Hits@K}{|GT|} \tag{8}$$

$$NDCG@K = \frac{DCG@K}{Ideal\ DCG@K} \tag{9}$$

Where HR can measure the presence of the positive item within the top N, $|GT|$ is all test sets and the numerator is the sum of the number of test sets belonging to each user's top-K recommendation list. NDCG can measure the items position in the ranked list and penalize the score for ranking the item lower in the list, DCG is the average Discounted Cumulative Gain, $Ideal\ DCG@K$ is the largest DCG value under ideal conditions.

4.3 Baseline Comparison

The data in Table 1 shows the experimental results of our model and each baseline model. At the same time, we also show the results of our model and other baseline models on four indicators in a more intuitive way in Fig. 3. It can be seen that our results have good results and performance on these four indicators.

Table 1. Citeulike-a dataset experiment results.

	HR@5	HR@10	NDCG@5	NDCG@10
SVD++	0.6952	0.8199	0.5244	0.5649
GMF	0.7271	0.8326	0.5689	0.6034
KNN	0.6990	0.7348	0.5789	0.5909
BPR	0.6547	0.8083	0.4858	0.5357
NeuMF	0.7629	0.8647	0.5985	0.6316
CDAE	0.6799	0.8103	0.5106	0.5532
FISM	0.6727	0.8072	0.5106	0.5545
CMN	0.7959	0.8921	0.6185	0.6500
ICMN	**0.8044**	**0.8934**	**0.6434**	**0.6726**

ICMN can consider the impact of the relevant information and characteristics of items on user preferences, and prove the importance of items' own information in the recommendation process. The stacking of four layers of memories further optimizes performance, and the dynamic processing of weights by the attention component enables the model to focus on deeper information. The results prove that our model is superior to all baseline models.

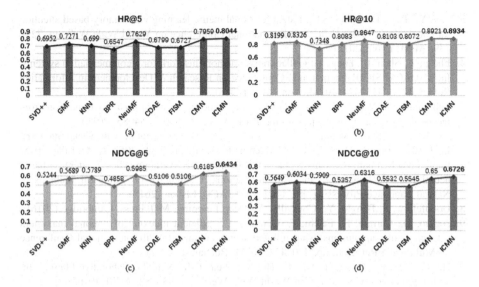

Fig. 3. Visualization of experimental results. (a) (b) (c) (d) are the results of our and other baseline models in the Citeulike-a dataset with HR@5, HR@10, NDCG@5 and NDCG@10 as the evaluation indicators.

5 Conclusion

In this paper, we propose an item-level collaborative memory network (ICMN) that can focus on the impact of the item level, which not only takes into account the attractiveness of items to users, but also fully considers the distribution of the potential relationship between items and users to strengthen the relationship between the specific item and neighborhoods and enables our network to perform well on larger data sets. Attention mechanisms can also handle items' features more rationally and dynamically to obtain more comprehensive user preference information. In future work, we want to add time information or other information that can more fully reflects the relationships between users and items to our network.

Acknowledgment. This work is supported in part by the National Natural Science Foundation of China (No. 61877043) and the National Natural Science Foundation of China (No. 61877044).

References

1. Koren, Y.: Factorization meets the neighborhood: a multifaceted collaborative filtering model. In: 14th ACM SIGKDD International Conference on Knowledge Discovery and Data mining, pp. 426–434. ACM, Las Vegas (2008)
2. Ricci, F., Rokach, L., Shapira, B.: Introduction to recommender systems handbook. In: Ricci, F., Rokach, L., Shapira, B., Kantor, P.B. (eds.) Recommender Systems Handbook, pp. 1–35. Springer, Boston, MA (2011). https://doi.org/10.1007/978-0-387-85820-3_1

3. Tay, Y., Tuan, L.A., Hui, S.C.: Latent relational metric learning via memory-based attention for collaborative ranking. In: 27th International Conference on World Wide Web, pp. 729–739. ACM, Lyon (2018)
4. Ebesu, T., Shen, B., Fang, Y.: Collaborative memory network for recommendation systems. In: 41st ACM SIGIR International Conference on Research & Development in Information Retrieval, pp. 515–524. ACM, Ann Arbor (2018)
5. Subramani, S., Wang, H., Vu, H.Q., Li, G.: Domestic violence crisis identification from facebook posts based on deep learning. IEEE Access **6**, 54075–54085 (2018)
6. Xu, K., et al.: Show, attend and tell: neural image caption generation with visual attention. In: 32nd International Conference on Machine Learning, pp. 2048–2057. ACM, Lille (2015)
7. Luong, M.-T., Pham, H., Christopher, D.: Manning effective approaches to attention-based neural machine translation. In: 12th International Conference on Empirical Methods in Natural Language Processing, pp. 1412–1421. ACL, Lisbon (2015)
8. Goodfellow, I., Bengio, Y., Courville, A.: Deep Learning. MIT Press, Cambridge (2016)
9. Amato, G., Carrara, F., Falchi, F., Gennaro, C.: Efficient indexing of regional maximum activations of convolutions using full-text search engines. In: 7th International Conference on Multimedia Retrieval, pp. 420–423. ACM, Bucharest (2017)
10. He, X., Liao, L., Zhang, H., Nie, L., Hu, X., Chua, T.-S.: Neural collaborative filtering. In: 26th International Conference on World Wide Web, pp. 173–182. ACM, Perth (2017)
11. Wang, C., Blei, D.M.: Collaborative topic modeling for recommending scientific articles. In: 17th ACM SIGKDD International Conference on Knowledge Discovery and Data mining, pp. 448–456. ACM, San Diego (2011)
12. Rendle, S., Freudenthaler, C., Gantner, Z., Schmidt-Thieme, L.: BPR: Bayesian personalized ranking from implicit feedback. In: 25th International Conference on Uncertainty in Artificial Intelligence, pp. 452–461. AUAI, Montreal (2009)
13. Wu, Y., DuBois, C., Zheng, A.X., Ester, M.: Collaborative denoising auto-encoders for top-N recommender systems. In: 9th ACM International Conference on Web Search and Data Mining, pp. 153–162. ACM, San Francisco (2016)
14. Kabbur, S., Ning, X., Karypis, G.: FISM: factored item similarity models for top-n recommender systems. In: 19th ACM SIGKDD International Conference on Knowledge discovery and Data Mining, pp. 659–667. ACM, Chicago (2013)

Social Knowledge Analysis and Management

UAFA: Unsupervised Attribute-Friendship Attention Framework for User Representation

Yuchen Zhou[1,2], Yanmin Shang[2(✉)], Yaman Cao[2], Yanbing Liu[2], and Jianlong Tan[2]

[1] School of Cyber Security, University of Chinese Academy of Sciences, Beijing, China
[2] Institute of Information Engineering, Chinese Academy of Sciences, Beijing, China
{zhouyuchen,shangyanmin,caoyanan,liuyanbing,tanjianlong}@iie.ac.cn

Abstract. The problem of user representation has received considerable attention in recent years. A variety of social networks include not only network structures (friendships) but also information about users' attributes. Previous studies have explored the integration of the two information to encode users. However, these methods focus on how to fuse the target user's friendships as a whole with its attribute information to get its representation vector, without considering the inside information of friendships, that is the influence of intimacy difference between the target user and its each friend on its representation vector. In addition, most of the above methods are supervised, which can only be applied to limited social networks analysis tasks. In this paper, we investigate a novel unsupervised method for learning the user representation by considering the influence of intimacy difference. The proposed methods take both the users' attributes and their friendships into consideration with attribute-friendship attention network. Experimental results demonstrate that the user vectors generated by the proposed methods significantly outperform state-of-the-art user representation methods on two different scale real-world networks.

Keywords: Social network analysis · User representation · Attention mechanism · User embedding

1 Introduction

Nowadays, various applications of social networks have penetrated into all aspects of life and work, and the research based on social networks is also in full swing. How to learn user representation is a key issue in social network research. Inspired by the idea of network embedding, user embedding is one of the most effective ways to learn user representation in recent years. User embedding not only can obtain distributed user representation vectors, but also solve the dimension disaster problem of user representation.

© Springer Nature Switzerland AG 2019
C. Douligeris et al. (Eds.): KSEM 2019, LNAI 11775, pp. 155–167, 2019.
https://doi.org/10.1007/978-3-030-29551-6_14

At present, the methods of learning user representation vectors by user embedding can be roughly divided into two categories. The first category uses user's single data to obtain user's representation vector, such as user attributes, user friendship, user published information, etc. Although this kind of approaches can acquire user's distribution representation vector, it only considers the user's single information and ignores the improvement of the accuracy of the user's multiple information to its representation vectors. The second category uses user's mixed data, that is, the above two or more types of data are used simultaneously to achieve user's representation vector. This article focuses on the mix of user attributes and friendship. At present, many studies have used this kind of mixed information to obtain user's representation vectors. Compared with the first kind of methods, the performance advantages of these methods have also been proved in practice. However, there are still some shortcomings in these methods: (1) the idea of these methods is to fuse multiple friend relationships of target user as a whole with its attribute information, ignoring the influence of the differences between friend relationships on the target user's representation vectors. (2) Influenced by whether the data is labeled or not, most these approaches are supervised, which greatly limits the application of these methods in different social network analysis tasks.

In order to solve above problems, this paper proposes an unsupervised user representation method (UAFA) which integrates user's attributes and user's friendships, and this method use attention mechanism to model the influence of user relationship differences on target user representation vector. Specifically, each user has two representation vectors, which are derived from user attributes and user relationship information respectively. We assume that each user's two representation vectors are similar. Based on above assumption, firstly, we design an encoder to encode each user into vector by using its own attributes, which is called ego-representation vector. Secondly, we adopt attention mechanism to transform user's friendship into vector which is called friendship-representation vector. Finally, we align the friendship-representation vector and ego-representation vector for each user to make the two vectors as similar as possible. In our method, we explored three concrete models which respectively adopt Convolutional Neural Network, Recurrent Neural Network and Deep Neural Network as encoders.

To summarize, we make the following contributions:

- As far as we know, this paper first focuses on the influence of user's friendship differences on its presentation vectors, and proposes an attribute-friendship attention framework to model the above influence. In addition, the framework is unsupervised which can eliminate the impact of data labels on model adaptability.

- Based on UAFA, we proposed three concrete models and empirically evaluate them for three tasks (gender prediction, occupation prediction and friend recommendation) on several real-world datasets.

2   Related Work

User Embedding is a special case of network embedding. Existing methods for user embedding representation learning include single data approaches and mix data approaches.

2.1   Single Data Approaches

UE model [3] and MUVR model [5] are typical single data approaches, they regard users' relations as the context of user and adopt CBOW or Skip-Gram model to learn users' representation. NMCF model [4] uses RNN to encode the content that users' post and adopts mean pool to reduce dimensions to learn users' representation. Although those approaches can acquire user representation, they only use single type of data by ignoring richer information.

2.2   Mix Data Approaches

SWE model [11], User2Vec model [10] and SBFTE model [7] integrate users' relations and content they post to acquire users' representation. While SocialEM model [9] and JUERL model [8] use users' attributes and post to acquire users' representation. All the above models are supervised. LME model [2] adopts Generalized Canonical Correlation Analysis to combine users' relations with post to generate users' representation. Although LME model is an unsupervised way, it ignores the internal differences in users' relationships. In this paper, we will propose an unsupervised user representation method by considering mix data at the same time.

3   UAFA

As we all know, on the one hand, users' attribute information on social networks reflects their essential representation. On the other hand, according to the homophily theory, users' representation are influenced by their friends' representations. In this paper, we consider users' representations from the above both perspectives, and propose an unsupervised attribute-friendship attention framework (UAFA). This framework includes two components, ego-representation and friendship-representation.

3.1   Ego-Representation

As we know, different attributes have different data formats, for example, "sex" is usually filled by one word (male or female) while "university" is always filled by two or more words. For each attribute, in order to obtain attribute vector with the same dimension, we adopt pre-trained word vectors. Specific, for attributes that have only a single word, we directly use its word vector as the attribute vector. For those attributes with more than one word, we use the weighted

158   Y. Zhou et al.

average vector of these words as the attribute vector. In this way, each attribute can be transformed into a d-dimensional vector with Look-up table.

Suppose user u_k has m attributes, according to above process, we can get m attribute vectors of u_k, denoted as $a_{k,1}, a_{k,2}, \cdots, a_{k,m}$. Here, $a_{k,t}$ represents the vector of the t-th($1 \leq t \leq m$) attribute and its dimension is d. For convenience, we use $A_k \in R^{m \times d}$ to represent u_k attributes vector matrix, and $a_{k,t}$ is a row element of A_k. We input each row element of the matrix A_k into LSTM one by one, and after encoding, we use hidden layer encoding as user u_k ego-representation ur_k (the dimension is D). It can be expressed as follows:

$$f_{k,t} = sigmoid(W_f \cdot [h_{k,t-1}, a_{k,t}] + b_f), t \in [1, m] \tag{1}$$

$$i_{k,t} = sigmoid(W_i \cdot [h_{k,t-1}, a_{k,t}] + b_i), t \in [1, m] \tag{2}$$

$$\tilde{f}_{k,t} = tanh(W_C \cdot [h_{k,t-1}, a_{k,t}] + b_C), t \in [1, m] \tag{3}$$

$$C_{k,t} = f_{k,t} * C_{k,t-1} + i_{k,t} * \tilde{f}_{k,t}, t \in [1, m] \tag{4}$$

$$o_{k,t} = sigmoid(W_o \cdot [h_{k,t-1}, a_{k,t}] + b_o), t \in [1, m] \tag{5}$$

$$h_{k,t} = o_{k,t} * tanh(C_{k,t}), t \in [1, m] \tag{6}$$

$$ur_k = h_{k,m} \tag{7}$$

The structure of ego-representation component is shown in Fig. 1.

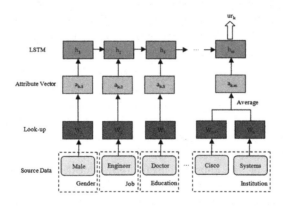

Fig. 1. Structure of Ego-representation component

3.2 Friendship-Representation

In this part, we consider the influence of user's friend representation on its representation, so as to obtain another user representation vector, namely friendship-representation. Suppose u_k has N friends denoted as $\{u_{k,1}, u_{k,2} \cdots, u_{k,N}\}$, according to the calculation process in the preceding section, we can obtain each friend's ego-representation vector $ur_{k,1}, ur_{k,2}, \cdots, ur_{k,N}$. For convenience, we use $UF_k \in R^{N \times D}$ to represent u_k's friend representations vector matrix, and $ur_{k,j(1 \leq j \leq N)}$ is a row element of UF_k. UF_k is the input of friendship-representation component.

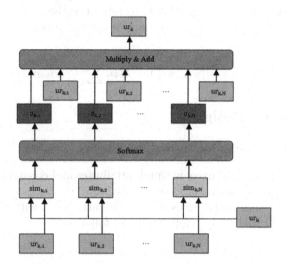

Fig. 2. Structure of friend-representation component

According to the homophily theory, the user's representation is influenced by his friends' representations. How to accurately model this influence is the problem we focus on. The most intuitive approach is to consider that each friend has the same impact on the user, that is, to use the average vector of all friend representations as the user's representation. However, this approach ignores the intimacy difference between user and different friends. In this paper, we model the influence by using attention mechanism [1]. We denote the friendship-representation of user u_k as ur'_k, it can be obtained as follows:

$$ur'_k = Attention(u_k; u_{k,1}, \cdots, u_{k,N}) = \sum_{j=1}^{N} \alpha_{k,j} * ur_{k,j} \qquad (8)$$

Where $\alpha_{k,j}$ is weight coefficient, and $\alpha_{k,j}$ represents the impact of $u_{k,j}$ on u_k, it can be expressed as (9).

$$\alpha_{k,j} = Softmax(Sim_{k,j}) = \frac{e^{Sim_{k,j}}}{\sum_{i=1}^{N} e^{Sim_{k,i}}} \qquad (9)$$

We adopt multiplicative attention and the similarity function $Sim_{k,j}$ can be expressed as (10).

$$Sim_{k,j} = Similarity(u_k, u_{k,j}) = ur_k^T W_a ur_{k,j} \qquad (10)$$

Where $W_a \in R^{D \times D}$ is the parameter of attention model. The structure of friendship-representation component is shown in Fig. 2.

3.3   Objective Function

Based on the assumption that each user's ego-representation and friendship-representation should be as similar as possible, we use cosine distance to measure similarity and define the similarity between ur_k and ur'_k as the loss function J. More formally, the objective of UAFA is to minimize the loss function J. More formally, the objective of UAFA is to minimize the loss function J, U is the total number of users.

$$MinJ = Min \sum\nolimits_{k=1}^{U} sim(ur_k, ur'_k) = Min \sum\nolimits_{k=1}^{U} cosine(ur_k, ur'_k) \qquad (11)$$

4   Experiments Design

We evaluate our method on two real-world datasets (Table 1):

- Google+: We select 1256 users with full attributes and construct a new closed social circle, and this social circle contains 54857 relations.
- Sina Weibo: We sample 16772 users with full attributes with their attributes and collect their friendships (following and followed).

Table 1. Description of two data sources

Data source	User	Relations	Average friends of each user
Google+	1256	54857	127
Sina Weibo	16772	1324988	79

To transform users' attributes into vectors, we use a set of trained English word vectors generated by using Word2Vec model on 12.7 GB Wikipedia data, and a set of trained Chinese word vectors generated by using Word2Vec model on 4.1 GB Baidu Encyclopedia.

4.1   Baselines

Word2Vec. This is the current mainstream approach to learn word embedding, it contains CBOW model and SkipGram model. In recent years, Word2Vec is also introduced in social network for user representation.

Support Vector Machine. As a classic classifier, in experiment, we use it to predict the gender and occupation attribute.

Random Forest. As a classic decision tree classifier, in the experiment, we use it to predict the gender and occupation attribute.

UE Model. This is a user embedding method proposed by Chen in 2016 [3], and the parameters of UE used in our paper are the same as [3].

DeepWalk. It is the first paper which introduces word embedding into network embedding [6], and generates node sequence by random walk. In experiments, we set the random walk length is 80 and the window size is 10.

Node2Vec. Different from DeepWalk, Node2Vec makes the node sequence contain local and macro information simultaneously by introducing two parameters p and q to achieve a balance in BFS and DFS. In experiments, we set the p is 0.5 and q is 2.

DNN-ATT (DNN). This is the first kind of concrete model of the UAFA, DNN-ATT. This model uses DNN as encoder to generate user ego-representation and uses attention mechanism to model the difference in the impact of friends on users. Moreover, we design a comparative model to verify the effectiveness of attention mechanism, DNN-AVE, which uses average strategy to obtain the friendship-representation. To highlight the use of attention mechanisms in model, we record DNN-AVE as DNN. In the above two models, the DNN network layout is 4, the middle two layers size is 512, and the last layer size is 256.

CNN-ATT (CNN). This is the second kind of concrete model of the UAFA, CNN-ATT. This model uses CNN as encoder to generate user ego-representation and uses attention mechanism to model the difference in the impact of friends on users. Similarly, we design a comparative model with CNN and average strategy, abbreviated as CNN. In the above two models, we define two convolution layers, use ReLU as activation function, adopt the max pool to reduce dimension, and use a linear function to normalize output vectors into 256 dimensions.

LSTM-ATT (LSTM). This is the third kind of concrete model of the UAFA, LSTM-ATT. This model uses LSTM as encoder to generate user ego-representation and adopts attention mechanism to model the difference in the impact of friends on users. Similarly, we design a comparative model with LSTM and average strategy, abbreviated as LSTM. In the above two models, the hidden layer size is 256.

4.2 Tasks Setup

In this paper, we select three tasks to demonstrate the effectiveness of UAFA: user gender prediction, user occupation prediction and friend recommendation.

Gender Prediction. The user's gender prediction task is to infer the missing gender attribute of a user. We partition the dataset into 10 folds, 1 fold for testing and other 9 folds for training. For each user in test set, we select the closest user in the training set and take its gender as the gender of the user in the test set. In this task, we adopt precision, recall and F1 score as the evaluation criteria.

Occupation Prediction. The user's occupation prediction task is to infer the missing occupation attribute of a user. Similar to gender prediction task, we also partition the dataset into 10 folds, 1 fold for testing and other 9 folds for training. According to these datasets, we divide occupations into 8 categories in advance. For each user in test set, we select the closest user in the training set and take its occupation as the occupation of the user in the test set. In this task, we adopt precision, recall and F1 score as the evaluation criteria.

Friend Recommendation. Friend recommendation aims to find other users that one user tend to make friends with. We partition the dataset into 10 folds, 1 fold for testing and other 9 folds for training. For each user in test set, we select the top K users closest to it as candidate friend.

5   Performance Comparison

For the above three tasks, we design the comparison methods from the perspective of using single data and mixed data. In specific, CBOW, Skip-Gram, DeepWalk, Node2Vec and UE model only use users' friendship, Random Forest and SVM only use users' attributes. In general, all of the above methods use a single type of data to represent users. In contrast, LSTM-ATT (LSTM), CNN-ATT (CNN), DNN-ATT (DNN) are the approaches which use mix type of data, and combine users' attributes and friendships to represent users.

5.1   Gender Predictions

Superiority of Mixed Data. As can be seen from Table 2, SVM is the best method to use single data and LSTM is the best method to use mixed data. For single data, the methods using attribute information (SVM and RF) are more suitable for gender prediction than methods with friendship information (CBOW, Skip-Gram, DeepWalk, Node2Vec and UE model), then, whether the combination of attribute information and friendship information will improve the performance of gender prediction? The performance of LSTM is obviously a good answer to this question. The performance of LSTM in gender prediction task is significantly higher than that of the former. This reveals that more comprehensive and accurate user representations can be achieved by using both user attributes and friend relationships. However, Table 2 also shows that the prediction precision of CNN and DNN is not higher than that of single data methods. The reason is that these two methods do not capture the long-term dependencies of attributes and relationships as LSTM does. Nevertheless, the performance of CNN and DNN is not much lower than the methods which only use single data.

Table 2. Performance comparison between single and mixed data models

Model	Google+			Sina Weibo		
	Precision	Recall	F1	Precision	Recall	F1
CBOW	0.642	0.613	0.627	0.808	0.783	0.795
DeepWalk	0.683	0.664	0.673	0.821	0.801	0.811
Node2Vec	0.701	0.682	0.691	0.857	0.834	0.845
Skip-Gram	0.734	0.709	0.721	0.843	0.826	0.834
UE Model	0.744	0.711	0.727	0.865	0.841	0.853
Random Forest	0.755	0.732	0.743	0.892	0.873	0.882
SVM	**0.764**	**0.748**	**0.756**	**0.906**	**0.886**	**0.896**
CNN	0.604	0.587	0.595	0.714	0.693	0.703
DNN	0.714	0.693	0.703	0.865	0.841	0.853
LSTM	**0.853**	**0.837**	**0.845**	**0.956**	**0.927**	**0.941**

Table 3. Performance comparison among methods with attention mechanism

Model	Google+			Sina Weibo		
	Precision	Recall	F1	Precision	Recall	F1
CNN	0.604	0.587	0.595	0.714	0.693	0.703
CNN-ATT	**0.623**	**0.605**	**0.614**	**0.756**	**0.733**	**0.744**
DNN	0.714	0.693	0.703	0.865	0.841	0.853
DNN-ATT	**0.726**	**0.707**	**0.716**	**0.879**	**0.852**	**0.865**
LSTM	0.853	0.837	0.845	0.956	0.927	0.941
LSTM-ATT	**0.875**	**0.858**	**0.866**	**0.977**	**0.953**	**0.965**

Effect of Attention Mechanisms. Table 3 shows the performance of models with hybrid data using attention mechanism. Compared with the methods without attention mechanism (CNN, DNN, and LSTM), the precision of CNN-ATT, DNN-ATT and LSTM-ATT has been improved by at least 15% and 10% on Google+ dataset and Sina Weibo dataset. This result shows that attention mechanism can better model the impact of intimacy difference between users and different friends on user representation. That is to say, CNN-ATT, DNN-ATT and LSTM-ATT assign different weights to different friends' ego-representation vector rather than the average strategy.

5.2 Occupation Predictions

Superiority of Mixed Data. Table 4 shows the performance of different models on user's occupation prediction task. Similar to gender prediction task, SVM is also the best method to use single data and LSTM is the best method to use mixed data. The performance of LSTM significantly outperforms SVM. It is reasonable to infer that LSTM captures more information to encode users' representation which is useful for enhancing the performance of occupation prediction. Similarly, the performance of CNN and DNN is not better than single data methods and the reason also relies in the problem of the long-term dependencies.

Table 4. Performance comparison between single and mixed data models

Model	Google+			Sina Weibo		
	Precision	Recall	F1	Precision	Recall	F1
CBOW	0.620	0.633	0.626	0.789	0.773	0.781
DeepWalk	0.643	0.658	0.650	0.807	0.812	0.809
Node2Vec	0.672	0.664	0.668	0.823	0.816	0.819
Skip-Gram	0.704	0.711	0.707	0.818	0.812	0.815
UE Model	0.719	0.709	0.714	0.842	0.853	0.847
Random Forest	0.730	0.724	0.727	0.863	0.859	0.861
SVM	**0.735**	**0.741**	**0.738**	**0.884**	**0.879**	**0.881**
CNN	0.601	0.614	0.607	0.751	0.735	0.743
DNN	0.688	0.668	0.678	0.816	0.804	0.810
LSTM	**0.831**	**0.837**	**0.834**	**0.918**	**0.897**	**0.907**

Effect of Attention Mechanisms. Table 5 shows the performance of models with hybrid data using attention mechanism. The F1 score of models which use attention mechanism is generally higher than that of models without attention mechanism. It has been improved by at least 10% and 8% respectively on Google+ and Sina Weibo. This result shows that different friend's representation has different contribute to the occupation prediction task and the attention mechanism can better model the impact of intimacy difference by assigning different weights to different friend's representation than the average strategy.

Table 5. Performance comparison among methods with attention mechanism

Model	Google+			Sina Weibo		
	Precision	Recall	F1	Precision	Recall	F1
CNN	0.601	0.614	0.607	0.751	0.735	0.743
CNN-ATT	**0.612**	**0.622**	**0.617**	**0.775**	**0.783**	**0.779**
DNN	0.688	0.668	0.678	0.816	0.804	0.810
DNN-ATT	**0.707**	**0.697**	**0.702**	**0.843**	**0.837**	**0.840**
LSTM	0.831	0.837	0.834	0.918	0.897	0.907
LSTM-ATT	**0.859**	**0.853**	**0.856**	**0.930**	**0.922**	**0.926**

5.3 Friend Recommendation

In this section, we compare the performance of single data (friendship) and mixed data (friendship and attributes) user representation methods on friend recommendation task. Generally speaking, the precision of these methods in friend recommendation task is lower than that in attribute prediction task. The cause lay in the fact that we delete some links when construct the social circle and the incompleteness of social links leads to the decrease of precision. But this does not prevent us from comparing the performance of these methods.

Table 6. Average accuracy comparisons of methods ($K = 10$)

Model	Google+	Sina Weibo
UE Model	0.706	0.725
Skip-Gram	0.711	0.732
Deep Walk	0.718	0.742
Node2Vec	0.724	0.754
CBOW	**0.737**	**0.763**
DNN	0.537	0.584
CNN	0.674	0.695
LSTM	**0.702**	**0.720**

Superiority of Mixed Data. From Table 6, CBOW is the best method to use single data and LSTM is the best method to use mixed data. In this task, the performance of the hybrid data methods is no better than that of the methods using only friendship data. The reason is that in the friend recommendation task, the similarity of user attributes is not the first basis for most users to consider when compared with existing friends. That is to say, most users expand their network of friends based on existing relationships. However, there are always some users who try to build new friends based on the similarity of their attributes. For these users, methods like CBOW that only use friendship information can not recommend friends very well. In this case, the mix data based methods (like LSTM, CNN and DNN) are obviously more suitable. In addition, as can be seen from Table 6, the performance of LSTM is closer to that of the methods using only friendship information, compared with CNN and DNN. The reason for this is that LSTM can capture richer temporal information.

Table 7. Average accuracy comparisons of methods with attention mechanism ($K = 10$)

Model	Google+	Sina Weibo
DNN	0.537	0.584
DNN-ATT	**0.556**	**0.608**
CNN	0.674	0.695
CNN-ATT	**0.687**	**0.704**
LSTM	0.702	0.720
LSTM-ATT	**0.718**	**0.738**

Effect of Attention Mechanism. From Table 7, we can see the effect of attention mechanism on friend recommendation task. The precision of CNN-ATT, DNN-ATT and LSTM-ATT has indeed improved. Especially LSTM-ATT, after using the attention mechanism, can more accurately adjust the weights of attribute information and friendship information, and then improve the precision of friend recommendation. It can be seen that the performance of LSTM-ATT is basically the same as that of the methods using only friendship information. At the same time, LSTM-ATT has the ability to recommend new friends to users according to their attribute similarity, which is impossible to use only friendship information.

6   Conclusion

In this paper, we proposed an unsupervised attribute-friendship attention framework for user representation, and design three concrete methods DNN-ATT, CNN-ATT and LSTM-ATT and validate the performance on three task: gender prediction, occupation prediction and friend recommendation. The experimental results show that the hybrid data model based on attention mechanism is effective and can model user representation more accurately and comprehensively.

In the future, we try to conduct more experiments on different data sets and introduce user posts in order to make user representations more informative and suitable for more tasks.

References

1. Bahdanau, D., Cho, K., Bengio, Y.: Neural machine translation by jointly learning to align and translate. arXiv preprint arXiv:1409.0473 (2014)
2. Benton, A., Arora, R., Dredze, M.: Learning multiview embeddings of Twitter users. In: Proceedings of the 54th Annual Meeting of the Association for Computational Linguistics (Volume 2: Short Papers), vol. 2, pp. 14–19 (2016)
3. Chen, L., Qian, T., Zhu, P., You, Z.: Learning user embedding representation for gender prediction. In: 2016 IEEE 28th International Conference on Tools with Artificial Intelligence (ICTAI), pp. 263–269. IEEE (2016)
4. Lefebvre-Brossard, A., Spaeth, A., Desmarais, M.C.: Encoding user as more than the sum of their parts: recurrent neural networks and word embedding for people-to-people recommendation. In: Proceedings of the 25th Conference on User Modeling, Adaptation and Personalization, pp. 298–302. ACM (2017)
5. Liu, H., Wu, L., Zhang, D., Jian, M., Zhang, X.: Multi-perspective User2Vec: exploiting re-pin activity for user representation learning in content curation social network. Signal Process. **142**, 450–456 (2018)
6. Perozzi, B., Al-Rfou, R., Skiena, S.: DeepWalk: online learning of social representations. In: Proceedings of the 20th ACM SIGKDD International Conference on Knowledge Discovery and Data Mining, pp. 701–710. ACM (2014)
7. Song, Y., Lee, C.J.: Learning user embeddings from emails. In: Proceedings of the 15th Conference of the European Chapter of the Association for Computational Linguistics: Volume 2, Short Papers. vol. 2, pp. 733–738 (2017)
8. Tang, L., Liu, E.Y.: Joint user-entity representation learning for event recommendation in social network. In: 2017 IEEE 33rd International Conference on Data Engineering (ICDE), pp. 271–280. IEEE (2017)
9. Yu, J., Gao, M., Song, Y., Fang, Q., Rong, W., Xiong, Q.: Integrating user embedding and collaborative filtering for social recommendations. In: Romdhani, I., Shu, L., Takahiro, H., Zhou, Z., Gordon, T., Zeng, D. (eds.) CollaborateCom 2017. LNICST, vol. 252, pp. 470–479. Springer, Cham (2018). https://doi.org/10.1007/978-3-030-00916-8_44
10. Yu, Y., Wan, X., Zhou, X.: User embedding for scholarly microblog recommendation. In: Proceedings of the 54th Annual Meeting of the Association for Computational Linguistics (Volume 2: Short Papers), vol. 2, pp. 449–453 (2016)
11. Zeng, Z., Yin, Y., Song, Y., Zhang, M.: Socialized word embeddings. In: IJCAI, pp. 3915–3921 (2017)

A Simple and Effective Community Detection Method Combining Network Topology with Node Attributes

Dongxiao He, Yue Song, and Di Jin[✉]

College of Intelligence and Computing, Tianjin University, Tianjin 300350, China
{hedongxiao,sy717389667,jindi}@tju.edu.cn

Abstract. Community detection is a fundamental problem in the study of complex networks. So far, extensive approaches, which use network topology alone or use both network topology and attribute information, have been designed to detect the community partitions of networks. However, existing approaches cannot work effectively for networks whose community structure does not match well with the ground-truth, or networks whose topological information contains serious noise, and networks where the difference of attribute similarity between nodes is tiny. Inspired by a force-directed network layout and community intuitive characteristics, we propose a simple while effective approach which utilizes attribute information to partition nodes into communities by maximizing network modularity. By using attributes as nodes to the network and the interaction between nodes, our novel method cannot only effectively improve community detection of networks, but also obtain the number of communities closer to the real one. Through extensive experiments on some real-world datasets, we demonstrate the superior performance of the new approach over some state-of-the-art approaches.

Keywords: Community detection · Modularity · Community structure

1 Introduction

Many complex systems can be abstracted as networks which consist of nodes and edges between nodes in modern network science. Complex networks are usually organized in communities, which have their own role and/or function such as groups of related individuals in social networks, functional modules of protein-protein interaction networks, etc. [6]. Discovering communities is useful for understanding what role they play in the network structure and dynamics, and has many real applications [7].

The primary objective of community detection is to partition the network into communities which correspond to functional modules composed of nodes. Generally, two types of information can be exploited for community detection. They are the network topology and attribute information on nodes. Therefore,

© Springer Nature Switzerland AG 2019
C. Douligeris et al. (Eds.): KSEM 2019, LNAI 11775, pp. 168–175, 2019.
https://doi.org/10.1007/978-3-030-29551-6_15

a wide variety of community detection methods based on different theories and technologies had been proposed recently [6–8,12]. Topology-oriented community detection methods can be mainly categorized into two types: measure-based methods [1,2,16,17] and probabilistic model based methods [10,13]. However, some of the real-world networks do not conform to the community structure property, and there is a lot of noise between nodes. Therefore, the above methods using network topology alone cannot work effectively in many cases. In order to improve the quality of community partitions detected, many existing methods take node attributes into account to supplement network topology information [3–5,15]. However, these methods usually need to manually adjust the effect between topology and attributes on community detection, which is typically difficult to achieve, and the similarity between nodes (calculated in these methods) in some networks are not significant. So these methods can not effectively play a role. Although some models [9,20] have been proposed, which do not need to adjust the parameters between two types of information, they cannot effectively partition nodes into communities for the network with serious noise.

Force-directed layout is a widely used technology in network layout. Its very essence is to turn structural proximities into visual proximities. Noack [18] has shown that the proximities express communities and proposes that layouts with optimal energy are consistent with clusterings with optimal modularity. The layout and clusterings of the whole network can be affected by adding or deleting nodes and edges because the structural proximity has been changed in the network. Since adding or deleting nodes and edges to the network can affect structural proximity, it may be ideal to change the community structure for community detection. But how to effectively add nodes and edges to the network for community detection is still a challenge.

To address these problems, inspired by a force-directed network layout and community intuitive characteristics, in this paper we propose a novel method with an augmented graph for community detection. Different from existing topology and attributes based approaches that using node attributes to calculate similarity, our new approach uses them as nodes to help detect communities of networks. In this way, our method not only avoids the problem that the quality of community partitions cannot be effectively improved due to the tiny difference between node attribute similarity, but also improves community structure of the network to obtain more accurate partitioning results through the interaction between nodes. We can then obtain community partition of the original network from the augmented graph using a fast and effective algorithm based on modularity optimization, e.g. Louvain. We present extensive experimental results on some real-world attributed networks to show that the new method is effective and outperforms some state-of-the-art approaches for community detection.

2   The Method

Assuming that an undirected and attributed network G is defined as a 3-tuple (V, E, X), where $V = \{v_1, v_2, \ldots, v_N\}$ is a set of N nodes, $E = \{(u, v) : u, v \in V, u \neq v\}$ is a set of e edges, which can be represented by an $N \times N$ adjacent matrix A with elements $A_{uv} = 1$ if u and v are connected, or 0 otherwise, and $X = \{x_1, x_2, \ldots, x_M\}$ is a set of M attributes, which is also binary matrix and its value is 1 if the node has the attribute, or 0 otherwise, then community detection is to partition the node set V of network G into K disjoint communities $P = \{C_1, C_2, \ldots, C_K\}$.

2.1 Motivations

Most of community detection methods mainly focus on detecting communities using network topology, and the premise is that the functional communities are consistent with community structure of networks. However, some of the real-world networks do not meet this property, and there is also typically serious noise in network topology. As shown in Table 1, we use a widely used metric modularity [17] to assess the community structure of seven widely used attributed networks [14]. We use Louvain method [1] to divide seven networks into communities to get the modularity values, and then compare it with the modularity values of the ground-truth communities. We can see that some of the real-world networks do not correspond well to what we usually say. In Table 1, it is obvious that the connections between communities are more denser for the first four networks, and the network structures contain serious noise for the latter three networks. It is not uncommon for two disconnected nodes to belong to the same community, and it is difficult to correctly divide a node connected to multiple communities for various reasons to the correct community by only relying on the topological structure. Therefore, the traditional methods based on network topology, such as modularity-based methods, cannot work effectively in this case.

Table 1. Datasets descriptions and comparison between modularity values obtained by Louvain method and ground-truth communities. Q is the Modularity value, which is between -1 and 1. The larger the value, the denser the connections within the community. N is the number of nodes, E the number of edges, M the number of attributes, K the real number of communities.

Metric	Methods	Datasets						
		Cornell	Texas	Washington	Wsicsonsin	Cora	Citeseer	UAI2010
Q	Louvain	0.647	0.552	0.561	0.639	0.809	0.883	0.455
	Ground-truth	-0.154	-0.215	-0.136	-0.118	0.640	0.543	0.258
	N	195	183	217	262	2,708	3,327	3,067
	E	283	276	366	459	5,278	4,676	28,308
	M	1,588	1,498	1,578	1,623	1,433	3,703	4,973
	K	5	5	5	5	7	6	19

As shown, the network topology reflects only one aspect of networks and usually contains noise. Fortunately, node attributes can be used to improve the results of community detection. However, this is also technically challenging to

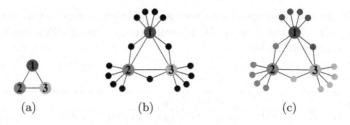

Fig. 1. Work flow of the proposed method. (a) is the original network, (b) the augmented network, and (c) the community partitions obtained by Louvain. We use large nodes to denote the original nodes in the original network and small nodes the new attribute nodes. Numbers are the ordinal numbers of nodes in the original network. Colors represent different communities. It is drawn using ForceAtlas2 [11].

effectively combine these two kinds of available information. Existing methods typically deal with network topology and node attributes separately. As a result, they need to adjust the impact of two types of information on community detection, which is difficult to achieve in real life. And most of the methods only deal with attribute information by calculating attribute similarity between nodes. However, there is no significant difference between the attribute similarity of a pair of nodes within community and that across communities in some networks in many cases. As shown in Fig. 1, Fig. 1(a) is a network with three nodes. We use the topology-based approach, such as modularity-based approach, to partition three nodes into the same community. When we improve the community partitioning result by calculating the node's attribute similarity (e.g., using cosine similarity), it does not play an effective role because the pairs of nodes have similar similarities. (The black nodes are attributes, and edges indicate that nodes have these attributes in Fig. 1(b).) Therefore, it still is not enough for community detection methods to help partition communities by calculating attribute similarity as existing methods done.

2.2 Augmented Graph Based Method

Here we develop a simple and effective community detection method that combines network topology and node attribute information by an augmented graph. The initial topological structure of the original network is augmented by new nodes called attribute nodes and new edges called attribute edges. Our method is mainly based on the following intuitive properties:

- Nodes that connected to each other are more likely to belong to the same community.
- Nodes sharing common attributes are more likely to be in the same community.
- Even if two nodes are not interconnected, they may belong to the same community through the interaction between original nodes and the interaction between original nodes and attribute nodes.

- Even if both the topological structure and attribute information contain a lot of noise, communities can be found well through the implicit interaction of these two kinds of nodes.

Algorithm 1. Augmented graph based approach.

Input: $G(V, E, X)$: undirected and attribute network. $clust$: Louvain method.
Output: A partition $P = \{C_1, C_2, \ldots, C_K\}$ of V.
1: $V_M = \{v_1, v_2, \ldots, v_M\}$ with $M = |X|$
2: $E_M \leftarrow \emptyset$
3: **for** $n = 1$ to $|V|$ **do**
4:      **for** $m = 1$ to $|X|$ **do**
5:          **if** $X_{nm} = 1$ **then**
6:              $E_M \leftarrow E_M \cup (v_n, v_m)$
7:          **end if**
8:      **end for**
9: **end for**
10: $V' \leftarrow V \cup V_M$ and $E' = E \cup E_M$ with $E_M \subseteq V \times V_M$
11: $G' = (V', E')$
12: $P' \leftarrow clust(G')$
13: $P \subset P'$ \\ P is the partition of the set V
14: **return** P

The process of the proposed new method is shown in Algorithm 1. We formally describe the work process of our method as follows. A set of attribute nodes is $V_M = \{v_1, v_2, \ldots, v_M\}$ and an attribute edge is added between node u and attribute node v_m if node u has the m-th attribute (As shown in Fig. 1(b)). There are totally M attribute nodes and $\sum_{u \in V, m \in V_M} X_{um}$ attribute edges added to the original network. In the augmented graph, two nodes are close if they are connected through many other original nodes, or if they share many common attribute nodes as neighbors. Once the augmented graph is created, we can apply some existing community detection methods, e.g., Louvain algorithm [1] based on modularity, to detect communities in the network (As shown in Fig. 1(c)).

3   Experiments

We now analyze why the new method (AUG for short) works. And then we compare it with several state-of-the-art community detection methods for evaluation. The datasets used are shown in Table 1.

3.1   Why Our Works

To validate the new method, we illustrate the original network and the augmented network of Cornell and their community partitions in Fig. 2. For the original network of the Cornell dataset in Fig. 2(a), the community structure derived is not consistent with ground-truth (i.e., the nodes within communities are sparsely connected, while ones between communities are densely connected), which results in a large number of nodes being misclassified (Fig. 2(b)). In comparison, AUG correctly assign most nodes to correct communities (Fig. 2(d)). This is because AUG uses attributes as nodes and edges which indeed improves community results (Fig. 2(c)). This validates that adding attributes as nodes and edges to the network can effectively complement the community characteristics into the network topology so as to find better communities.

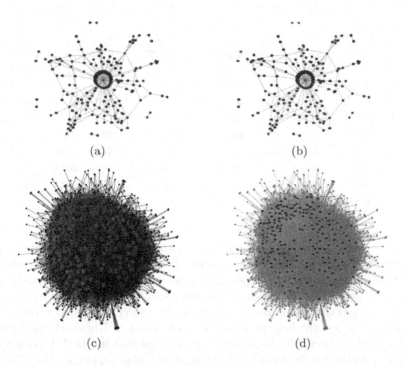

(a)   (b)

(c)   (d)

Fig. 2. An example on Cornell. (a) is the original network and (c) the augmented network. In (a) and (b), the left (right) is the real partition (predicted partition). It is drawn the same as Fig. 1.

3.2   Comparison with Existing Methods

We compared the new method with two types of the state-of-the-art community detection methods. The first, including DCSBM [13] and NetMRF [10], uses network topology alone. The second includes PCLDC [20], SCI [19] and NEMBP [9], which use both topological and attribute information. All the methods compared require the number of communities to be specified, while our method does not. Here, we set their number of communities to the ground-truth, and ran these methods with their default parameters. We used Accuracy (AC) and Normalized Mutual Information (NMI) [7] as metrics for performance evaluation.

Table 2. Comparison of the results of different community detection methods in terms of AC and NMI. ORG is the method that original networks are partitioned by using Louvain. K' is the number of communities detected. Bold font denotes the best results.

Metrics	Methods	Datasets						
		Cornell	Texas	Washington	Wsicsonsin	Cora	Citeseer	UAI2010
AC (%)	ORG	24.1	28.42	23.5	23.66	41.51	20.29	32.21
	DCSBM	37.9	48.1	31.8	32.8	38.5	26.6	2.6
	NetMRF	31.8	30.6	35	28.6	58.1	22.2	31.1
	PCLDC	30.3	38.8	30	30.2	34.1	24.9	28.8
	SCI	36.9	49.7	46.1	46.4	41.7	34.4	29.5
	NEMBP	47.2	53.6	42.9	63.4	57.6	49.5	**46.3**
	AUG	**54.87**	**57.92**	**62.21**	**71.37**	**61.26**	**58.25**	38.93
NMI (%)	ORG	14.35	8.19	10.22	8.83	42.58	32.41	28.18
	DCSBM	9.7	16.6	9.9	3.1	17.1	4.1	31.2
	NetMRF	7.3	5.5	5.8	3.2	37.2	1.2	25.8
	PCLDC	7.2	10.4	5.7	5	17.5	3	26.9
	SCI	6.8	12.5	6.8	13.3	17.8	9.2	23.4
	NEMBP	18.7	**35.1**	21.2	38	**44.1**	24.3	**47.2**
	AUG	**26.32**	30.34	**36.88**	**41.61**	42.83	**32.45**	35.32
K'	ORG	19	12	15	14	97	461	19
	AUG	6	6	7	5	10	9	6

As shown in Table 2, AUG is far superior to ORG, confirming that the new method can effectively improve the quality of community structure detected by adding attributes as nodes to the original network. Moreover, compared with ORG, AUG can find the number of communities (Table 2) which is much closer to that of ground truth communities (Table 1). Moreover, compared with existing methods, AUG has the best performance on 6 and 4 of 7 networks in terms of AC and NMI, respectively. Generally, the methods that use both topology and attribute information perform better than those using topology alone. We like to highlight that among the methods using both two types of information, our AUG is on average 26.8%, 17.2%, and 6.3% more accurate than PCLDC, SCI and NMEBP in AC; and 24.3%, 22.3% and 2.5% more accurate than PCLDC, SCI and NMEBP in NMI. These results further validates the superiority of our new approach over others in finding communities.

4   Conclusion

In this paper, we proposed an efficient and simple method for community detection by adding attributes as nodes to the original network. It is able to make fully use of network topology and attribute information especially when the topology contains serious noise. The extensive experimental results demonstrated that our method outperformed the state-of-the-art approaches for community detection and validated the superior performance of our method on 7 real-world networks.

Acknowledgments. This work was supported by Natural Science Foundation of China (61876128, 61772361).

References

1. Blondel, V.D., Guillaume, J.L., Lambiotte, R., Lefebvre, E.: Fast unfolding of communities in large networks. J. Stat. Mech-Theory E **P10008**, 1–12 (2008)
2. Chakraborty, T., Dalmia, A., Mukherjee, A., Ganguly, N.: Metrics for community analysis: a survey. ACM Comput. Surv. **50**(4), 54:1–54:37 (2017)
3. Combe, D., Largeron, C., Géry, M., Egyed-Zsigmond, E.: I-Louvain: an attributed graph clustering method. In: Fromont, E., De Bie, T., van Leeuwen, M. (eds.) IDA 2015. LNCS, vol. 9385, pp. 181–192. Springer, Cham (2015). https://doi.org/10.1007/978-3-319-24465-5_16
4. Falih, I., Grozavu, N., Kanawati, R., Bennani, Y.: Anca : Attributed network clustering algorithm. In: Complex Networks, pp. 241–252 (2018)
5. Falih, I., Grozavu, N., Kanawati, R., Bennani, Y.: Community detection in attributed network. In: Proceedings of the WWW, pp. 1299–1306 (2018)
6. Fortunato, S.: Community detection in graphs. Phys. Rep. **486**, 75–174 (2010)
7. Fortunato, S., Hric, D.: Community detection in networks: a user guide. Phys. Rep. **659**, 1–44 (2016)
8. Girvan, M., Newman, M.E.J.: Community structure in social and biological networks. Proc. Natl. Acad. Sci. **99**(12), 7821–7826 (2002)
9. He, D., Feng, Z., Jin, D., Wang, X., Zhang, W.: Joint identification of network communities and semantics via integrative modeling of network topologies and node contents. In: Proceedings of the AAAI, pp. 116–124 (2017)
10. He, D., You, X., Feng, Z., Jin, D., Yang, X., Zhang, W.: A network-specific Markov random field approach to community detection. In: Proceedings of the AAAI, pp. 306–313 (2018)
11. Jacomy, M., Venturini, T., Heymann, S., Bastian, M.: Forceatlas2, a continuous graph layout algorithm for handy network visualization designed for the gephi software. PLoS One **9**(6), e98679 (2014)
12. Jin, D., Wang, H., Dang, J., He, D., Zhang, W.: Detect overlapping communities via ranking node popularities. In: Proceedings of the AAAI, pp. 172–178 (2016)
13. Karrer, B., Newman, M.E.J.: Stochastic blockmodels and community structure in networks. Phys. Rev. E **83**, 016107 (2011)
14. Leskovec, J.: Stanford network analysis project (2016). http://snap.standford.edu
15. Muslim, N.: A combination approach to community detection in social networks by utilizing structural and attribute data. Soc. Networking **05**, 11–15 (2016)
16. Newman, M.E.J.: Modularity and community structure in networks. Proc. Natl. Acad. Sci. **103**, 8577–8582 (2006)
17. Newman, M.E.J., Girvan, M.: Finding and evaluating community structure in networks. Phys. Rev. E **69**, 026113 (2004)
18. Noack, A.: Modularity clustering is force-directed layout. Phys. Rev. E **79**, 026102 (2009)
19. Wang, X., Jin, D., Cao, X., Yang, L., Zhang, W.: Semantic community identification in large attribute networks. In: Proceedings of the AAAI, pp. 265–271 (2016)
20. Yang, T., Jin, R., Chi, Y., Zhu, S.: Combining link and content for community detection: a discriminative approach. In: Proceedings of the ACM SIGKDD, pp. 927–936 (2009)

Location-Interest-Aware Community Detection for Mobile Social Networks Based on Auto Encoder

Ming Chen(iD), Wenzhong Li$^{(\boxtimes)}$(iD), Sanglu Lu$^{(\boxtimes)}$, and Daoxu Chen

State Key Laboratory for Novel Software Technology,
Nanjing University, Nanjing, China
mchenflood@gmail.com, {lwz,sanglu}@nju.edu.cn

Abstract. Community detection partitions users in social networks into sub-groups according to structural or behavioral similarities, which had been widely adopted by a lot of applications such as friend recommendation, precision marketing, etc. In this paper, we propose a location-interest-aware community detection approach for mobile social networks. Specifically, we develop a spatial-temporal topic model to describe users' location interest, and introduce an auto encoder mechanism to represent users' location features and social network features as low-dimensional vectors, based on which a community detection algorithm is applied to divide users into sub-graphs. We conduct extensive experiments based on a real-world mobile social network dataset, which demonstrate that the proposed community detection approach outperforms the baseline algorithms in a variety of performance metrics.

Keywords: Location based service · Mobile social network ·
Interest community detection

1 Introduction

Community detection is an important topic in mobile social network, which could help us to understand mobile social network structures and provide good location based services. Community detection in mobile social network has a broad range of applications such as Ad pushing, crowd-sourcing, marketing etc. There are two types of community detection algorithms in mobile social network. The first type is graph-based community detection algorithms such as Newman algorithm [11], Louvain algorithm [2] and Label Propagation Algorithm (LPA) [14]. These state-of-the-art graph-based community detection algorithms could find cohesive subgroups in a network based on graph theory, while ignore the characteristics of node in the network. The second type is semantic-based community detection method [1] can explore overlapping semantic communities from the perspective of characteristics analysis. In mobile social network, users' location interest is very important for location-based services which indicate users' location preference.

© Springer Nature Switzerland AG 2019
C. Douligeris et al. (Eds.): KSEM 2019, LNAI 11775, pp. 176–184, 2019.
https://doi.org/10.1007/978-3-030-29551-6_16

Many existing community detection approaches [6,8,9] did not take mobile users' location interest into account, that cannot support personalized location-based services.

We take mobile users' location interest into account which could support personalized location-based services. In this paper, we propose an location-interest-aware community detection approach for mobile social networks. Specially, we develop a spatial-temporal topic model to describe users' location interest, and introduce an auto encoder mechanism to represent users' location features and social network features as low-dimensional vectors, based on which a community detection algorithm is applied to divide users into sub-graphs. We conduct extensive experiments based on a real-world mobile social network dataset, which demonstrate that the proposed community detection approach outperforms the baseline algorithms in a variety of performance metrics.

Our main contributions are summarized as follows.

- A novel idea of community detection approach based on location interest mining.
- A spatial-temporal topic model to extract users' interests.
- Comprehensive feature representations.
- An auto encoder based location-interest-aware community detection approach.
- Experiments based on real-world dataset.

2   Related Work

In this section, we review related work of community detection models. The input of the community detection algorithm is a graph (a set of nodes representing individuals, they are connected by edges), and the output is a list of node groups representing the communities. Usually everyone belongs to a community. The community detection algorithm in social networks can be divided into graph-based methods and semantic-based methods. Graph-based community detection methods, such as Newman algorithm [11], Louvain algorithm [2] and Label Propagation Algorithm (LPA) [14], these graph-based community detection algorithms [11,12], which only use graph theory, have obvious limitations. For example, they ignore the characteristics of user interest which can lead to the lack of interest cohesiveness in the community detection results. Semantic-based community detection methods [1,14] can explore overlapping semantic communities from the perspective of characteristics analysis. Community detection can also transform users into vectors, use unsupervised clustering algorithms for community segmentation, and classify similar users into the same cluster. Clustering algorithms could be K-means [7], DBSCAN [5], spectral clustering [13], etc. The more similar or closer the users in the same cluster, the better the result is. Many community detection approaches did not take mobile users' location interest into account, that cannot support personalized location-based services.

3 Our Work

The solution framework shows in Fig. 1, including the following subsection: data cleaning, extract location interest feature by LDA, extract location distribution features, extract user relation features, user representation by auto encoder, interest community clustering and visualization.

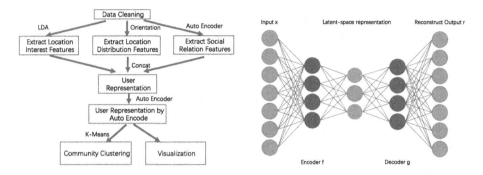

Fig. 1. The solution framework   **Fig. 2.** Auto encoder architecture

3.1 Data Cleaning

We use the mobile social network dataset from Gowalla [3], a location-based social networking service through which users share their locations by checking-in. The Gowalla dataset contains a total of 6,442,890 check-ins of 196,591 users over the period of Feb. 2009 - Oct. 2010.

In our work, we extract users from San Francisco. Since some of the users rarely check-in, we filter out users with fewer than 10 check-in locations. Because some locations have few associated check-ins, we filter out locations with fewer than 10 check-ins. After filtering out the unqualified users and locations, the dataset has 1,995 users, 3,251 locations, and 106,098 check-ins.

3.2 Extract Location Interest Features by LDA

As we found in [10], check-ins at a location at different time represent different degrees or different types of location interest. In order to extract users' interests, we consider both time and location factors. We propose a temporal-spacial LDA (Latent Dirichlet Allocation) model to extract interests. Specifically, we treat the combination time and location of a check-in event as a word, and view the historical trajectory of a user as a document.

We apply LDA to all users' document, and convert their check-in trajectories into interest distribution represented by K topics. The user distribution on each location are shown in the user-location matrix, which is obtained by counting the trajectories. The users' interest distribution is shown in user-interest matrix,

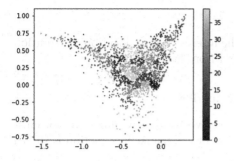

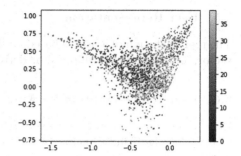

Fig. 3. Community visualization, $Q = 0.379313$

Fig. 4. Community visualization at low dimension, $Q = 0.720976$

where the number in the i-th row and j-th column represents the interest degree of the i-th user in the j-th topic. The interest distribution at each location is shown in the interest-location matrix. These latter two matrices come from the LDA process which use Gibbs sampling [4] as inference technique. To determine the best number of K for LDA, we use cross validation to determine the likelihood. It is observed that the maximum likelihood achieved for $K = 40$. Therefore 40 topics are selected in our experiments. In our experiment after 30,000 iterations the LDA model converges.

3.3 Extract Location Distribution Features

Here we use the way of dividing the map into $N * M$ grids, extracting the user's position distribution to form a position vector. The dimension of each user location vector is $N * M$. Here we set it to $N * M = 6 * 6$.

3.4 Extract User Relation Features

The representation of the user relationship can be represented by the adjacency matrix. In this case, if the number of users is N_u, the user relationship can be represented by an adjacency matrix of $N_u * N_u$. Each user's friend relationship vector dimension is N_u. Since the dimension of the user relationship is very high here, the dimensionality reduction is performed by auto encoder (Fig. 4).

The algorithm principle of user friend relationship vector dimension reduction is shown in Fig. 2. Auto encoder is neural network that intended to replicate the output of the inputs. It works by compressing the input into a latent-space representation, and then reconstructing the output of this representation.

We set the user's friend relationship vector by the auto encoder. We set the size of input layer to 1995, and set the size of hidden layer to 40, with the structure of $1995 - 128 - 64 - 40$. The network convert user vector from 1995 dimensions to 40 dimensions.

3.5 User Representation

The representation of a user is based on the interest vector, location distribution vector, and user relationship vector derived from last three steps.

3.6 User Representation by Auto Encoder

Here we use auto encoder to convert the user vector to low dimension for clustering. The algorithm principle of the user vector dimension reduction is shown in the Fig. 2.

3.7 Community Clustering and Visualization

After the user vector is encoded by auto encoder, we then cluster the users according to the K-Means algorithm. After clustering, We plot the user vector of 2 dimensions, and we can see the visual location community. Different colors represent different clustering groups, which intuitively visualizes the distance relationship between users, as shown in Fig. 3.

4 Experiment

4.1 Experimental Setting

Dataset. We use the mobile social network dataset from Gowalla [3]. Gowalla is a location-based social networking service where users share their locations by checking-in. The Gowalla dataset contains a total of 6,442,890 check-ins of 196,591 users over the period of Feb. 2009 - Oct. 2010.

Default Parameters. Each user and location have at least 10 check-ins. The number of LDA topics is 40. The vector dimension of the user's geographic location distribution is $6 * 6 = 36$ dimension. The user friend relationship vector is converted to 40 dimensions by auto encoder. The user vector is convert to 116-dimensional via auto encoder. The K-Means parameter K is 120.

4.2 Baseline Algorithms

We compare the proposed method with the following algorithm.

- Graph model based algorithm-FastNewman [11], LPA [14].
- Spectral clustering based on interest. The user's interest vector is extracted using the topic model algorithm LDA, and then the user interest vector is classified by spectral clustering [13].
- Geographic location based algorithm. Each user's most frequent geographic location is used as the classification basis.

4.3   Metric

We use an improved community module metric for performance evaluation. It includes original community modularity, community location similarity, and community interest similarity scores.

The original metric of community modularity [12], which measures the quality of community clustering, is defined as follows:

$$Q_q = \frac{1}{2m} \sum_{vw} \left[A_{vw} - \frac{k_v k_w}{2m} \right] \delta(c_v, c_w) \tag{1}$$

A is the adjacency matrix of the network, k_v is the degree of node v, and m is the number of edges in network A. c_v represents the community to which the node v belongs. If $i = j, \delta(i, j) = 1$, otherwise $\delta(i, j) = 0$. In our approach, we adopt improved community modularity performance metrics taking user's interests, locations, and social relations into account.

$$Q = Q_q + Q_\alpha + Q_\beta \tag{2}$$

$$Q_\alpha = \frac{1}{2m_e} \sum_{vw} \alpha(v, w) \delta(c_v, c_w), \tag{3}$$

$$Q_\beta = \frac{1}{2m_e} \sum_{vw} \beta(v, w) \delta(c_v, c_w) \tag{4}$$

$\alpha(v, w)$ means that if different users v, w interest are similar, then $\alpha(v, w) = 1$, otherwise $\alpha(v, w) = 0$. Since the user self comparison is not meaningful, set $\alpha(v, v) = 0$ so that when the number of communities equals the number of users, the Q_α value must be zero. $\beta(v, w)$ means that if different users v, w are similar in orientation, $\beta(v, w) = 1$, otherwise $\beta(v, w) = 0$. Similarly, $\beta(v, v) = 0$ is set so that when the number of communities is equal to the number of users, the Q_β value must be zero. Whether the different users' v, w interests are similar or not, is determined by whether the user v, w is most interested in the same topic. Whether the user's v, w orientation is similar or not, is determined by whether the user's v, w is most often in the same orientation. m_e represents the number of vw pairs that make $\delta(c_v, c_w)$ not equal zero. This makes the value of $2m_e$ increase dramatically when the number of clustering is too small, which can penalize the modularity. Intuitively, two users with similar interests and similar locations will lead to higher probability of being assigned to same community. If two users are assigned to same community, the more similar they are, the higher the module metric. Therefore, considering the social similarity degree of the user's location, the higher modularity indicates that the community clustering performance is better. Q_q value range $[-1/2, 1]$, Q_α value range $[0, 1/2)$, Q_β value range $[0, 1/2)$, so Q generally takes the range of $[-1/2, 2)$.

4.4   Experimental Result

We compare the performance of our algorithm with the benchmark algorithms. According to Table 1, the performance of the proposed algorithm is better than

Table 1. Algorithm performance comparison

Algorithms	Q	Q_q	Q_α	Q_β
FastNewman	0.662	**0.466**	0.018	0.176
LPA	0.619	0.433	0.018	0.168
Interest spectral clustering	0.659	0.094	**0.330**	0.234
Geographic location	0.575	0.052	0.023	**0.499**
Our algorithm	**0.720**	0.058	0.289	0.373

the benchmark algorithms. The Fast Newman algorithm achieved the highest Q_q value of 0.466334, but it is far behind our proposed algorithm in terms of community interest score and community geographic location score. The LPA graph model algorithm also achieved high Q_q values, but it is far behind our proposed algorithm in terms of Q_α and Q_β. Based on the geographic location algorithm, each user's most frequently visited geographic location is used as a classification basis, it get the highest Q_β score of 0.499253. However, the algorithm does not take into account the network modularity and interest similarity, so it does not perform well on other scores. The interest spectral clustering method uses the topic model algorithm LDA to extract the user's interest vector, and then clusters the users with spectral clustering. So get the highest Q_α score of 0.330194. However, the algorithm does not take into account the location module, so it does not perform well on other scores. The algorithm we proposed takes into account the interest, location, and friend relationship. Due to dimension reduction to reduce complexity, not only the computational efficiency is high, but also the overall performance is best in terms of Q. Overall, our approach is better than traditional benchmark algorithms by combining location interests, location, and friendships.

4.5 Parameter Sensitivity Analysis

Next, we perform parameter sensitivity analysis by comparing system performance under different parameters, including K-means clustering parameter K, fused data type.

K-means Clustering Parameter K. K-means clustering parameter K is an important system parameter of the model. The K-means clustering algorithm depends on the clustering group number K. In the experiment, we increased K from 60 to 480. The result is shown in Table 2. The K-means parameter K has an impact on performance. The performance is best when the K-means parameter $K = 120$. This means that bigger or smaller community number cannot improve clustering performance. Small community number means that users with different interests are assigned to the same community, making the interests of the communities different. Big community number shows that the network module degree Q_q value not perform well.

Table 2. The influence of K

K	Q	Q_q	Q_α	Q_β
60	0.613	0.067	0.196	0.349
120	**0.720**	0.058	0.289	0.373
240	0.716	0.041	0.308	0.367
480	0.684	0.028	0.302	0.353

Table 3. Fused types of data

Data	Q	Q_q	Q_α	Q_β
Loc.	0.500	0.012	0.041	**0.446**
Int.	0.703	0.050	**0.422**	0.229
Int. & Loc.	0.704	0.058	0.275	0.370
ALL	**0.720**	**0.058**	0.289	0.373

Fused Types of Data. Our model incorporates user interests, location, and social information. The types of data fused in the model is an important system parameter of the model. In the experiment, we increased this parameter from only the location information to all kinds of data participated in the operation. The result is shown in Table 3. The more types of data is fused, the better our approach performs: based on the interest and location, the method is slightly better than only the interest-based method. After adding the social vector, the overall Q performance is the best. Overall, our approach is better than traditional benchmark algorithms by combining location interests, location, and friendships. The types of data has an impact on performance. When the number of data types is too small, it means that the amount of information considered in clustering is few, so that the clustering performance is not high under comprehensive consideration. The model performs best when all types of data is included. This means more data can bring more information and improve performance.

5 Conclusion

In this paper, we propose a location-interest-aware community detection approach for mobile social networks. We develop a spatial-temporal topic model to describe users' location interest, and introduce an auto encoder mechanism to represent users' location features and social network features as low-dimensional vectors, based on which a community detection algorithm is applied to divide users into sub-graphs. We conduct extensive experiments based on a real-world mobile social network dataset, which demonstrate that the proposed community detection approach outperforms the baseline algorithms in a variety of performance metrics.

Acknowledgment. This work was partially supported by the National Key R&D Program of China (Grant No. 2018YFB1004704), the National Natural Science Foundation of China (Grant Nos. 61672278, 61832008, 61832005), the Key R&D Program of Jiangsu Province, China (Grant No. BE2018116), the science and technology project from State Grid Corporation of China (Contract No. SGSNXT00YJJS1800031), the Collaborative Innovation Center of Novel Software Technology and Industrialization, and the Sino-German Institutes of Social Computing.

References

1. Ahn, Y.Y., Bagrow, J.P., Lehmann, S.: Link communities reveal multiscale complexity in networks. Nature **466**(7307), 761 (2010)
2. Blondel, V.D., Guillaume, J.L., Lambiotte, R., Lefebvre, E.: Fast unfolding of communities in large networks. J. Stat. Mech. Theory Exp. **2008**(10), P10008 (2008)
3. Cho, E., Myers, S.A., Leskovec, J.: Friendship and mobility: user movement in location-based social networks. In: Proceedings of the 17th ACM SIGKDD International Conference on Knowledge Discovery and Data Mining, pp. 1082–1090. ACM (2011)
4. Darling, W.M.: A theoretical and practical implementation tutorial on topic modeling and GIBBs sampling. In: Proceedings of the 49th Annual Meeting of the Association for Computational Linguistics: Human Language Technologies, pp. 642–647 (2011)
5. Duan, L., Xu, L., Guo, F., Lee, J., Yan, B.: A local-density based spatial clustering algorithm with noise. Inf. Syst. **32**(7), 978–986 (2007)
6. He, D., Yang, X., Feng, Z., Chen, S., Fogelman-Soulié, F.: A network embedding-enhanced approach for generalized community detection. In: Liu, W., Giunchiglia, F., Yang, B. (eds.) KSEM 2018. LNCS (LNAI), vol. 11062, pp. 383–395. Springer, Cham (2018). https://doi.org/10.1007/978-3-319-99247-1_34
7. Jain, A.K.: Data clustering: 50 years beyond k-means. Pattern Recogn. Lett. **31**(8), 651–666 (2010)
8. Jin, D., Liu, Z., He, D., Gabrys, B., Musial, K.: Robust detection of communities with multi-semantics in large attributed networks. In: Liu, W., Giunchiglia, F., Yang, B. (eds.) KSEM 2018. LNCS (LNAI), vol. 11061, pp. 362–376. Springer, Cham (2018). https://doi.org/10.1007/978-3-319-99365-2_32
9. Ma, H., Xie, M., Wei, J., He, T.: An overlapping microblog community detection method using new partition criterion. In: Liu, W., Giunchiglia, F., Yang, B. (eds.) KSEM 2018. LNCS (LNAI), vol. 11062, pp. 313–323. Springer, Cham (2018). https://doi.org/10.1007/978-3-319-99247-1_28
10. Chen, M., Li, W., Qian, L., Lu, S., Chen, D.: Interest-aware next POI recommendation for mobile social networks. In: Chellappan, S., Cheng, W., Li, W. (eds.) WASA 2018. LNCS, vol. 10874, pp. 27–39. Springer, Cham (2018). https://doi.org/10.1007/978-3-319-94268-1_3
11. Newman, M.E.: Fast algorithm for detecting community structure in networks. Phys. Rev. E **69**(6), 066133 (2004)
12. Newman, M.E.: Modularity and community structure in networks. Proc. Natl. Acad. Sci. **103**(23), 8577–8582 (2006)
13. Ng, A.Y., Jordan, M.I., Weiss, Y.: On spectral clustering: analysis and an algorithm. In: Advances in Neural Information Processing Systems, pp. 849–856 (2002)
14. Raghavan, U.N., Albert, R., Kumara, S.: Near linear time algorithm to detect community structures in large-scale networks. Phys. Rev. E **76**(3), 036106 (2007)

Retweet Prediction Using Context-Aware Coupled Matrix-Tensor Factorization

Bo Jiang[1], Feng Yi[2(✉)], Jianjun Wu[3], and Zhigang Lu[1,4]

[1] Institute of Information Engineering, Chinese Academy of Sciences, Beijing, China
{jiangbo,luzhigang}@iie.ac.cn
[2] School of Computer Science, University of Electronic Science and Technology
of China, Zhongshan Institute, Zhongshan, China
bjstarbow@gmail.com
[3] Beijing College of Politics and Law, Beijing, China
wjjyun@gmail.com
[4] School of Cyber Security, University of Chinese Academy of Sciences,
Beijing, China

Abstract. Retweet behavior plays an important role in the process of information diffusion on social networks. Although many researches have been studied the problem of retweet prediction, these studies ignore the important characteristic of multiple contextual dimensions for user's decision in the modeling process. To this end, we propose a novel multiple dimensions retweet prediction model based on context-aware coupled matrix-tensor factorization (RCMTF). This model first introduces a reference tensor based on the historical retweet behavior patterns to alleviate the problem of data sparsity, and then constructs three contextual factor matrices from user and message and influence dimensions on basis of network structure, message content and historical interactions to further improve the prediction accuracy. Finally, we collaboratively factorizes these contextual factors under matrix and tensor factorization models framework for predicting user's retweet behaviors. Extensive experiments are conducted to demonstrate the effectiveness of the proposed method on two real-world datasets. The results show that our proposed model outperforms the state-of-the-art methods.

Keywords: Retweet prediction · Social network ·
Tensor factorization · Matrix factorization · Contextual information

1 Introduction

With the widespread adoption application of social network, a growing number of people share interesting messages, and participate in online activities, and discuss hot events in these platforms. Social networks have become powerful platforms for information diffusion, where the retweet behavior has been proved to be play an important part in the process of information spreading [26]. Thus, it is a significant but challenging task to understanding and modeling users'

© Springer Nature Switzerland AG 2019
C. Douligeris et al. (Eds.): KSEM 2019, LNAI 11775, pp. 185–196, 2019.
https://doi.org/10.1007/978-3-030-29551-6_17

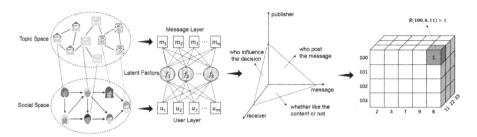

Fig. 1. An example of user's retweet behaviors with rich contextual information in social network. The publisher represents the user who posts message, and the receiver represents the user who receives message.

retweet behaviors, which in turn contributes more knowledge to support many practical applications, including behavior analysis [27], topic identification [7] and online marketing [20].

Many studies have been explored to identify the affecting factors of retweet behavior on social networks by user survey [11] and statistical analysis [19,25]. We sum up these research results, which suggest that the intention of users to retweet is positively affected by the content of message, user's topic interests, social influence between users and social relationships. We call these information as context, as shown in Fig. 1. On the other hand, researchers are more interested in predicting retweet behavior in social networks. For instance, representative research work is that the retweet prediction is considered as a classification problem [6,27]. However, one obvious drawback of these methods is that the process of extracting feature set by heuristic strategy is usually too expensive and may be bring irrelevant noise information. Another strategy is to learn recommend system, such that retweet prediction is converted to the problem of matrix completion based on the observed non-zero entities [22]. However, these models either don't take into account influence from user interactions or fail to discover individual correlations between users and messages. Moreover, matrix factorization cannot fully take context information into consideration. Besides, other models and their variants have also been studied extensively for the task, including pairwise influence-based method [27], graph-based method [26], conditional random fields [13], hierarchical Dirichlet process [28] and deep learning method [29]. However, none of these approaches to date fully holds the contextual information in the prediction process. Context-aware modeling such as tensor factorization model is characterized by seamlessly integrating contextual information that may influence the user's retweet behaviors in social networks.

In this paper, we propose a novel multiple dimensions retweet prediction model based on context-aware matrix-tensor factorization by incorporating network structure, message content, and pairwise influence. The model introduces a reference tensor based on the historical retweet behavior patterns to alleviate the data sparseness. Besides, three contextual factor matrices are designed to further improve the prediction performance, where the user similarity is learned from network structure and user's topic interests, and the message similarity is inferred by leveraging distributed vectors representation for short texts, and the pairwise influence is measured based on network structure and historical interactions. Finally, we integrate all these factors into a unified prediction model.

As a result, the main contributions of this paper are summarized as follows:

- We propose a new retweet prediction model based on context-aware coupled matrix-tensor factorization by using reference tensor and three contextual factor matrices from user-based and content-based dimensions to improve the prediction results. To the best of our knowledge, this is the first model to consider this problem with coupled matrix-tensor factorization.
- We introduce a reference tensor representing the average of retweet behaviors between publishers and receivers in a given time window based on the historical retweet behaviors to alleviate the problem of retweet data sparsity.
- We conduct experimental evaluations on two real-world social network datasets to verify the effectiveness of our proposed model. Experimental results demonstrate the proposed model outperforms the state-of-the-art methods.

The rest of this paper is organized as follows. We presents related work in Sect. 2. Then, Sect. 3 describes our proposed model and give the inference details. Section 4 introduces the experimental methodology and shows the results obtained. Finally, Sect. 5 lists our conclusions.

2 Related Work

2.1 Tensor Factorization Methods

Tensor factorization models have been proved successful in solving various application tasks, such as relational learning [12], topic modeling [9] and community detection [1]. Meanwile, tensor factorization methods have also shown excellent prediction capabilities in several important applications. For example, Karatzoglou et al. [4] propose a multiverse recommendation model based on tensor factorization using the higher-order Tucker decomposition [21]. Rendle et al. [14–16] introduce the notion of factorization machine for a general predictor task with any real valued feature vector and present pairwise interaction tensor factorization for tag recommendation. Lei et al. [8] apply matrix and tensor factorization to sparsity reduction in syntactic dependency parsing. Schein et al. [18] present a Bayesian tensor factorization model for inferring latent group structures from dynamic pairwise interaction patterns. Hidasi et al. [3] use a general factorization framework by incorporating any recommendation context with explicit and implicit feedback data. Xiong et al. [24] propose a Bayesian probabilistic tensor factorization algorithm for modeling evolving relational data. Sahebi et al. [17] propose a feedback-driven tensor factorization approach for modeling students' learning process and predicting student performance. In summary, tensor factorization can be viewed as generalizations of large classes of latent factor models, and they have found increasing popularity for context-sensitive applications and achieved great success in the these domain.

2.2 Retweet Prediction Methods

Predictive studies are to predict how message will be retweeted in a given network by learning from past diffusion patterns. For example, Yang et al. [26] propose a factor graph model to predict retweet behavior by analyzing the influence of user, information, and time, respectively. Luo et al. [10] use rank-based learning framework to discover the potential forwarded users. Can et al. [2] predict the expected retweet count of a message by using visual cues of an image linked in that message in addition to content and structure-based features. Zhang et al. [27] predict retweet behavior based on social influence locality via a logistic regression classifier. Zhang et al. [28] propose a nonparametric Bayesian model adapted from the hierarchical Dirichlet process to combine textual, structural, and temporal information for the task. Subsequently, Zhang et al. [29] also propose a attention-based deep neural network to incorporate the user, author, user interests, and similarity information between the tweet and user interests. Besides, other studies use matrix factorization to solve the problem. For instance, Wang et al. [23] utilize nonnegative matrix factorization to predict retweet behavior from user and content dimensions by employing strength of social relationship. Wang et al. [22] incorporate message embedding into co-factor matrix factorization for retweeting prediction. However, social relationship with weak tie hinders the contribution of social regularization. We notice that retweet behavior models may have to deal with more than two types of entities such as user, message, time in social networks. It is naturally that tensor factorization method is applied by considering contextual information for improving the prediction performance.

3 The Proposed Model

In this section, we present our proposed RCMTF model using the framework shown in Fig. 2. We first briefly introduce tensor factorization for retweet prediction. Then we learn reference tensor and context-aware matrices for user, message and influence. Finally, RCMTF collaboratively factorizes retweet and reference tensors, and context-aware matrices to model user's retweet behavior.

3.1 Model Description

Tensor Modeling. Given a three-order retweet tensor $R_o = [r_{ijk}] \in \mathbb{R}^{M \times N \times K}$, where M, N, K are the number of receivers, messages and publishers, respectively. The (i, j, k)-th entry in R_o is represented as $r_{ijk} \in \{0, 1\}$, where the value 1 denotes true retweet, and 0 otherwise. Let $C \in \mathbb{R}^{d_U \times d_V \times d_S}$, $U \in \mathbb{R}^{M \times d_U}$, $V \in \mathbb{R}^{N \times d_V}$ and $S \in \mathbb{R}^{K \times d_S}$ be the core tensor, latent receiver-factor matrix,

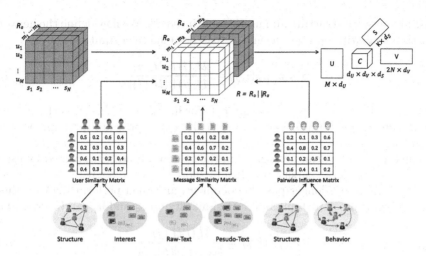

Fig. 2. The framework of context-aware coupled matrix-tensor factorization for retweet prediction.

latent message-factor matrix and latent publisher-factor matrix respectively, where $d_U = d_V = d_S = d$ is the rank of latent factors. Tensor factorization based retweet prediction solve the following problem:

$$\mathcal{L} = \frac{1}{2} \|R_o - C \times_U U \times_V V \times_S S\|_F^2 + \frac{\lambda}{2}(\|C\|_F^2 + \|U\|_F^2 + \|V\|_F^2 + \|S\|_F^2) \tag{1}$$

where $\lambda(\|C\|_F^2 + \|U\|_F^2 + \|V\|_F^2 + \|S\|_F^2)$ is introduced to avoid overfitting, controlled by the parameter λ. Retweet prediction can be modeled as a tensor completion task $\hat{R} = C \times_U U \times_V V \times_S S$.

Reference Tensor. Intrinsically, the retweet tensor R_o is very sparse. To alleviate the problem of data sparsity, we introduce a reference tensor $R_a \in \mathbb{R}^{M \times N \times K}$ based on the historical retweet behavior patterns among users. Each entry $r'_{ijk} \in R_a$ indicates the average frequency of retweet behaviors between users in given time window L (e.g. 1 week, 1 month), which can be defined as

$$r'_{ijk} = \frac{|\mathcal{S}(u, s) \cap \mathcal{T}(u)|}{|\mathcal{S}(u, s)|} \tag{2}$$

where $\mathcal{S}(u, s)$ is the set of messages sent from s to u, and $\mathcal{T}(u)$ is the set of messages retweeted by u, $|\cdot|$ denotes the number of messages.

R_a has the same structure as R_o, which can collaboratively factorize. According to statistical analysis in our dataset, R_a is much denser than R_o. Hence, the decomposing R_o and R_a together can alleviate the data sparsity and reduce the error of prediction.

User Similarity Matrix. The user-user similarities are used for improving the prediction performance by focusing the similar preferences. The similarities consist of network structure and user's topic interests. We now define the network structure similarity on users u_i and u_j based on Jaccard similarity as

$$S_{structure}(i,j) = \frac{|\mathcal{U}_s(i) \bigcap \mathcal{U}_s(j)|}{|\mathcal{U}_s(i) \bigcup \mathcal{U}_s(j)|} \tag{3}$$

where $\mathcal{U}_s(i)$ is the set of friends who u_i following. $|\mathcal{U}_s(i) \bigcap \mathcal{U}_s(j)|$ is the number of common friends both u_i and u_j. $|\mathcal{U}_s(i) \bigcup \mathcal{U}_s(j)|$ represents the number of all friends on u_i and u_j.

The topic interest can be profiled in the content of messages posted by users. To alleviate the data sparsity problem in short texts, we aggregate a collection of short texts into a longer pesudo-document, and then perform LDA on these pesudo-documents. The topic interests similarity on u_i and u_j can be defined as

$$S_{topic}(i,j) = \frac{\mathcal{U}_t(i)\mathcal{U}_t(j)}{\|\mathcal{U}_t(i)\| \, \|\mathcal{U}_t(j)\|} \tag{4}$$

where $\mathcal{U}_t(i) = \frac{1}{|D(i)|} \sum_{a \in D(i)} T_a$, $D(i)$ is the set of messages posted by user u_i, T_a is the learned vector representations.

We construct the user-user similarity matrix $X \in \mathbb{R}^{M \times M}$, in which the (i,j)-th entry is measured by a linear combination as

$$X_{ij} = \delta S_{structure}(i,j) + (1 - \delta)S_{topic}(i,j) \tag{5}$$

where δ is the parameter controlling the contribution of each factor.

Message Similarity Matrix. Similarly, the message-message similarities can shorten the semantic distance. Here, we choose N retweeted messages from the collection of document, and consist of a new set of original and retweeted messages documents with size $2N$. To solve the data sparsity problem, our strategy is to employ Doc2Vec [5] to obtain vector representation of messages.

After obtaining the sentence-level vector representation of message, we can build the message-message similarity matrix $W \in \mathbb{R}^{2N \times 2N}$, and the (i,j)-th entry in W can be calculated as

$$W_{ij} = T_{ik} \times T_{jk} \tag{6}$$

where T_{ik} denotes the vector of message m_i with k dimension.

Pairwise Influence Matrix. The pairwise influence indicates the strength of social influence both users, which consist of social relationship and interaction behavior. Specifically, we use PageRank method to measure the structure influence of node v_i as

$$PR(v_i) = \frac{1 - \sigma}{\mathcal{N}} + \sigma \sum_{v_j \in \mathcal{L}^{in}(v_i)} \frac{PR(v_j)}{\mathcal{L}^{out}(v_j)} \tag{7}$$

where $\mathcal{L}^{in}(v_i)$ represents the set of users who following v_i, $\mathcal{L}^{out}(v_j)$ represents the set of users who v_j is followed, and $\mathcal{N}$ represents the number of all users, and

$\sigma = 0.85$ represents the damping factor. Until convergence, we can obtain the steady state probability transfer matrix $F_{structure} \in \mathbb{R}^{M \times K}$. Besides, to quantify the influence of interaction behavior, we calculate the percentage of interacted messages from publisher s to user u:

$$F_{behavior}(i, j) = \frac{|\mathcal{S}(u, s) \cap \mathcal{A}(u)|}{|\mathcal{S}(u, s)|} \tag{8}$$

where $\mathcal{S}(u, s)$ is the set of messages sent from s to u, and $\mathcal{A}(u)$ is the set of messages interacted by u.

Similar, we construct pairwise influence matrix $F \in \mathbb{R}^{M \times K}$, in which the (i, j)-th entry can be calculated as

$$F_{ij} = \theta F_{structure}(i, j) + (1 - \theta)F_{behavior}(i, j) \tag{9}$$

where θ is the parameter controlling the contribution of each factor. Note that F is a nonsymmetric matrix.

3.2 Model Optimization

Finally, we factorize $R = R_o || R_a$ with context-aware matrices W, X and F collaboratively. Finally, the objective function is defined as

$$\mathcal{L} = \frac{1}{2} \left\| R - C \times_U U \times_V V \times_S S \right\|_F^2$$
$$+ \frac{\alpha}{2} \left\| X - UU^T \right\|_F^2 + \frac{\beta}{2} \left\| W - VV^T \right\|_F^2 + \frac{\gamma}{2} \left\| F - US^T \right\|_F^2 \tag{10}$$
$$+ \frac{\lambda}{2} (\|C\|_F^2 + \|U\|_F^2 + \|V\|_F^2 + \|S\|_F^2)$$

where $R \in \mathbb{R}^{M \times 2N \times K}$, and $V \in \mathbb{R}^{2N \times K}$ is low rank latent factor matrix for message feature; α, β, γ and λ are parameters controlling the contributions of the regularization.

We use stochastic gradient descent method to solve the optimum values of parameters in U, V, and S. Finally, the update of the individual components of the model as

$$\frac{\partial \mathcal{L}}{\partial U} = (Z - R)C \times_V V \times_S S + \lambda U + 2\alpha(UU^T - X)U + \gamma(US^T - F)S \tag{11}$$

$$\frac{\partial \mathcal{L}}{\partial V} = (Z - R)C \times_U U \times_S S + \lambda V + 2\beta(VV^T - W)V \tag{12}$$

$$\frac{\partial \mathcal{L}}{\partial S} = (Z - R)C \times_U U \times_V V + \lambda S + \gamma(US^T - F)U \tag{13}$$

$$\frac{\partial \mathcal{L}}{\partial C} = (Z - R)U \otimes V \otimes S + \lambda C \tag{14}$$

where $Z = C \times_U U \times_V V \times_S S$. The symbol $\times$ denotes matrix multiplication. The symbol $\times_V$ denotes tensor-matrix multiplication, where the subscript V stands for the direction. The symbol $\otimes$ denotes the tensor outer product. Using these terms to normalize the regularization terms results in better convergence.

Table 1. Statistics of experimental dataset.

Dataset	#Users	#Messages	#Relations	#Retweetings	Sparseness
Weibo	1,825	1,743,902	15,691,594	598,836	0.02%
Twitter	981	1,068,442	827,553	570,314	0.05%

4 Experiment

4.1 Experimental Setup

Datasets. We use two social network datasets to evaluate the effectiveness of our method: (1) Weibo is a social network in China like Twitter, and we use publicly available Weibo dataset from [27]. (2) We collect a large number of tweets from Twitter based on crawler by randomly choosing 100 seed users, and crawl their tweets and social relationships. Due to space limit, we directly present the basic statistical information about the two datasets in Table 1.

Baselines. Our proposed method is tested against the following state-of-the-art retweeting prediction models:

- **SVM.** The model considers message content, retweet history, followers status, followers active time and followers interests based on learning-to-rank for the task [10].
- **LRC-BQ.** The method uses a logistic regression classifier to predict user's retweet behavior based on pairwise influence and structural diversity [27].
- **MNMFRP.** This method utilizes nonnegative matrix factorization to predict retweet behavior from user and content dimensions, respectively, by using strength of social relationship to constrain objective function [23].
- **SUA-ACNN.** The model proposes attention-based deep neural network to incorporate user's attention interests and social information by embedding to represent user, user's attention interests, author and message [29].

Besides, we also compare different regularization strategies to demonstrate the effectiveness of our proposed method as

- **RCMTF-A.** This method removes the reference tensor. That is, we use R_o instead of R in Eq. (10).
- **RCMTF-U.** This method doesn't take into account user similarity factor by setting $\alpha = 0$ in Eq. (10).
- **RCMTF-M.** This method doesn't take into account message similarity factor by setting $\beta = 0$ in Eq. (10).
- **RCMTF-F.** This method doesn't take into account social influence factor by setting $\gamma = 0$ in Eq. (10).

Evaluation Metrics. In this scenario, we use precision (Pre.), recall (Rec.), F1-measure (F_1) and Accuracy (Acc.) to evaluate the performance of retweet classification prediction. We randomly split each dataset into two disjoint sets, 80% for training and 20% for testing, and perform 5-fold cross validation.

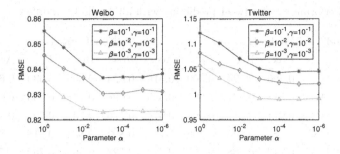

Fig. 3. RMSE vs. parameter α on Weibo and Twitter datasets.

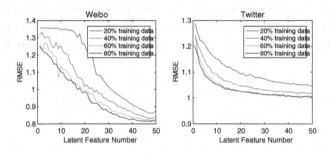

Fig. 4. RMSE vs. latent feature number on Weibo and Twitter datasets.

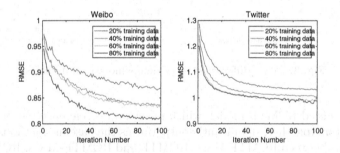

Fig. 5. RMSE vs. iteration number on Weibo and Twitter datasets.

4.2 Experiments and Analysis

Parameters. In our model, the change of parameters has a great influence on the experiment. Hence, we try to find the best parameters to balance our proposed model performance and computation cost. Due to limited space, we directly show the experimental results as shown Figs. 3, 4 and 5. From the figures, we set $\alpha = \beta = \gamma = 10^{-3}$ and $\lambda = 10^{-2}$ and set the number of latent features to 30 and set the number of iterations to 100 on two datasets (Fig. 5).

Performance Comparison for Retweet Prediction. We compare our RCMTF model with other baseline methods. Here, we list the average results of each method with 5 runs in Table 2. From these results, we can observe that:

Table 2. Performance of retweet prediction with all methods on different datasets.

Method	Weibo Dataset				Twitter Dataset			
	Prec.	Rec.	F_1	Acc.	Prec.	Rec.	F_1	Acc.
SVM	0.496	0.524	0.509	0.516	0.624	0.656	0.639	0.658
LRC-BQ	0.518	0.677	0.587	0.535	0.698	0.770	0.733	0.698
MNMFRP	0.674	0.715	0.694	0.674	0.796	0.791	0.793	0.792
SUA-ACNN	0.787	0.805	0.796	0.782	0.802	0.834	0.818	0.813
RCMTF-A	0.712	0.768	0.739	0.723	0.722	0.803	0.760	0.734
RCMTF-U	0.785	0.815	0.799	0.785	0.799	0.829	0.814	0.729
RCMTF-M	0.783	0.804	0.809	0.788	0.790	0.804	0.797	0.794
RCMTF-F	0.787	0.802	0.805	0.781	0.792	0.807	0.799	0.795
RCMTF	**0.801**	**0.827**	**0.814**	**0.832**	**0.806**	**0.853**	**0.829**	**0.851**

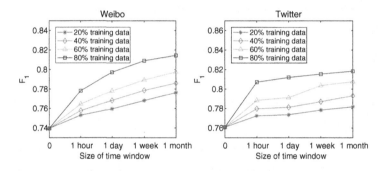

Fig. 6. F_1 vs. different sizes of time windows on datasets.

(1) The proposed RCMTF model, which incorporates reference tensor and contextual factors together, significantly outperforms the baseline methods. (2) The comparisons between RCMTF-U v.s. RCMTF and RCMTF-M v.s. RCMTF and RCMTF-F v.s. RCMTF, reveal that combining user, message and influence factors are more effective compared with the single social factor. (3) RCMTF can outperform RCMTF-A, indicating that current coarse-grained behavior can be indicated from its historical behavior patterns. (4) Among the different prediction models, SUA-ACNN performs better than most of methods, which indicate that the attention-based deep neural network can benefit the performance. We conclude that RCMTF can alleviate the data sparsity and improving the prediction performance by incorporating contextual information.

Impact of Time Windows. We try different time windows L (1 h, 1 day, 1 week, 1 month) in reference tensor R_a to test and verify the influence of retweet behavior patterns for the performance. Figure 3 illustrates the experimental results. From the results, we can see that (1) F_1 values on two datasets increase gradually as time interval enlarges, which suggest that current decision can be inferred from its historical patterns. (2) The values are relatively stable over time. This phenomenon might explain that users often purposefully retweet a message for specific users due to their limited time and attention.

5   Conclusion

In this paper, we propose a novel multiple dimensions retweet prediction model based on context-aware coupled matrix-tensor factorization by incorporating rich contextual information. We introduce a density reference tensor based on historical retweet behaviors to alleviate the data sparsity. We also design three contextual factor matrices for user similarity and message similarity and pairwise influence. Finally, we collaboratively factorise reference tensor and these factor matrices for the task. Experimental results on two real-world datasets demonstrate that the proposed method can achieve better performance than the state-of-the-art methods.

Acknowledgement. This work is supported by Natural Science Foundation of China (No. 61702508, No. 61802404). This work is also partially supported by Key Laboratory of Network Assessment Technology, Chinese Academy of Sciences.

References

1. Anandkumar, A., Ge, R., Hsu, D., Kakade, S.: A tensor spectral approach to learning mixed membership community models. In: COLT, pp. 867–881 (2013)
2. Can, E.F., Oktay, H., Manmatha, R.: Predicting retweet count using visual cues. In: CIKM, pp. 1481–1484 (2013)
3. Hidasi, B., Tikk, D.: General factorization framework for context-aware recommendations. Data Min. Knowl. Disc. **30**(2), 342–371 (2016)
4. Karatzoglou, A., Amatriain, X., Baltrunas, L., Oliver, N.: Multiverse recommendation: n-dimensional tensor factorization for context-aware collaborative filtering. In: RecSys, pp. 79–86. ACM (2010)
5. Le, Q., Mikolov, T.: Distributed representations of sentences and documents. In: ICML, pp. 1188–1196 (2014)
6. Lee, K., Mahmud, J., Chen, J., Zhou, M., Nichols, J.: Who will retweet this? detecting strangers from Twitter to retweet information. ACM Trans. Intell. Syst. Technol. (TIST) **6**(3), 31 (2015)
7. Lee, R.K.-W., Hoang, T.-A., Lim, E.-P.: On analyzing user topic-specific platform preferences across multiple social media sites. In: WWW, pp. 1351–1359. International World Wide Web Conferences Steering Committee (2017)
8. Lei, T., Xin, Y., Zhang, Y., Barzilay, R., Jaakkola, T.: Low-rank tensors for scoring dependency structures. ACL **1**, 1381–1391 (2014)
9. Liu, Y.-K., Anandkumar, A., Foster, D.P., Hsu, D., Kakade, S.M.: Two SVDs suffice: spectral decompositions for probabilistic topic modeling and latent Dirichlet allocation. In: NIPS (2012)
10. Luo, Z., Osborne, M., Tang, J., Wang, T.: Who will retweet me? finding retweeters in Twitter. In: SIGIR, pp. 869–872 (2013)

11. Metaxas, P.T., Mustafaraj, E., Wong, K., Zeng, L., O'Keefe, M., Finn, S.: What do retweets indicate? results from user survey and meta-review of research. In: ICWSM, pp. 658–661 (2015)
12. Nickel, M., Tresp, V., Kriegel, H.-P.: A three-way model for collective learning on multi-relational data. In: ICML, pp. 809–816 (2011)
13. Peng, H.-K., Zhu, J., Piao, D., Yan, R., Zhang, Y.: Retweet modeling using conditional random fields. In: ICDM, pp. 336–343. IEEE (2011)
14. Rendle, S.: Factorization machines. In: ICDM, pp. 995–1000. IEEE (2010)
15. Rendle, S., Marinho, L.B., Nanopoulos, A., Schmidt-Thieme, L.: Learning optimal ranking with tensor factorization for tag recommendation. In: KDD, pp. 727–736. ACM (2009)
16. Rendle, S., Schmidt-Thieme, L.: Pairwise interaction tensor factorization for personalized tag recommendation. In: WSDM, pp. 81–90. ACM (2010)
17. Sahebi, S., Lin, Y.-R., Brusilovsky, P.: Tensor factorization for student modeling and performance prediction in unstructured domain. In: EDM, pp. 502–506. IEDMS (2016)
18. Schein, A., Paisley, J., Blei, D.M., Wallach, H.: Bayesian poisson tensor factorization for inferring multilateral relations from sparse dyadic event counts. In: KDD, pp. 1045–1054. ACM (2015)
19. Shi, J., Chen, G., Lai, K.K.: Factors dominating individuals' retweeting decisions. In: CyberC, pp. 161–168. IEEE (2016)
20. Stephen, A.T.: The role of digital and social media marketing in consumer behavior. Curr. Opin. Psychol. **10**, 17–21 (2016)
21. Tucker, L.R.: Some mathematical notes on three-mode factor analysis. Psychometrika **31**(3), 279–311 (1966)
22. Wang, C., Li, Q., Wang, L., Zeng, D.D.: Incorporating message embedding into co-factor matrix factorization for retweeting prediction. In: IJCNN, pp. 1265–1272. IEEE (2017)
23. Wang, M., Zuo, W., Wang, Y.: A multidimensional nonnegative matrix factorization model for retweeting behavior prediction. Math. Prob. Eng. **2015**, 10 (2015)
24. Xiong, L., Chen, X., Huang, T.-K., Schneider, J., Carbonell, J.G.: Temporal collaborative filtering with Bayesian probabilistic tensor factorization. In: ICDM, pp. 211–222. SIAM (2010)
25. Yang, C., Liu, L., Jiao, Y., Chen, L., Niu, B.: Research on the factors affecting users' reposts in microblog. In: ICSSSM, pp. 1–6. IEEE (2017)
26. Yang, Z., et al.: Understanding retweeting behaviors in social networks. In: CIKM, pp. 1633–1636 (2010)
27. Zhang, J., Tang, J., Li, J., Liu, Y., Xing, C.: Who influenced you? predicting retweet via social influence locality. ACM Trans. Knowl. Disc. Data (TKDD) **9**(3), 25 (2015)
28. Zhang, Q., Gong, Y., Guo, Y., Huang, X.: Retweet behavior prediction using hierarchical Dirichlet process. In: AAAI, pp. 403–409 (2015)
29. Zhang, Q., Gong, Y., Wu, J., Huang, H., Huang, X.: Retweet prediction with attention-based deep neural network. In: CIKM, pp. 75–84. ACM (2016)

A New Multi-objective Evolution Model for Community Detection in Multi-layer Networks

Xuejiao Chen[1], Xianghua Li[1], Yue Deng[1], Siqi Chen[2], and Chao Gao[1(✉)]

[1] School of Computer and Information Science,
Southwest University, Chongqing 400715, China
cgao@swu.edu.cn
[2] College of Intelligence and Computing, Tianjin University, Tianjin 300072, China

Abstract. In reality, many complex network systems can be abstracted to community detection in multi-layer networks, such as social relationships networks across multiple platforms. The composite community structure in multi-layer networks should be able to comprehensively reflect and describe the community structure of all layers. At present, most community detection algorithms mainly focus on the single layer networks, while those in multi-layer networks are still at the initial stage. In order to detect community structures in multi-layer networks, a new multi-objective evolution model is proposed in this paper. This model introduces the concept of modularity in different decision domains and the method of local search to iteratively optimize each layer of a network. Taking NSGA-II as the benchmark algorithm, the proposed multi-objective evolution model is applied to optimize the genetic operation and optimal solution selection strategies. The new algorithm is denoted as MulNSGA-II. The MulNSGA-II algorithm adopts the locus-based representation strategy, and integrates the genetic operation and local search. In addition, different optimal solution selection strategies are used to determine the optimal composite community structure. Experiments are carried out in real and synthetic networks, and results demonstrate the performance and effectiveness of the proposed model in multi-layer networks.

Keywords: Community detection · Multi-layer networks · Multi-objective optimization · Evolutionary algorithm

1 Introduction

Complex networks are a simple and effective formalism in representing the fundamental structure among interacting units of real-world systems (e.g., social networks [1], biological networks [2], traffic networks [3]). Nodes and edges of a network represent objects in systems and relationships between objects,

C. Douligeris et al. (Eds.): KSEM 2019, LNAI 11775, pp. 197–208, 2019.
https://doi.org/10.1007/978-3-030-29551-6_18

respectively. Community structure is an important feature of networks, which reflects some important properties, such as the network topology [4], the law of network existence [5].

At present, lots of algorithms have been proposed for community detection in single layer networks [6]. However, the same entity in a real complex system often presents multi-dimensional characteristics. For example, in social networks, people often communicate through different social platforms, e.g., microblog, QQ, and email. Multi-layer networks can more accurately describe the relationship between different systems and reflect the different properties of the same entity, which have gradually become one of the newest research trend in the field of complex networks [7–10].

A multi-layer network consists of a collection of different layers in which connections between nodes are mutually independent. Each layer of a network represents a relationship between entities and reflects an attribute of entities. Different interpretations of multi-layer networks have been proposed, such as multidimensional networks [11], multi-relational networks [12] and multiplex networks [13]. Community detection in multi-layer networks has not yet been defined uniformly, which faces more challenges compared with single-layer networks. Each layer of multi-layer networks has its own community structure, but it cannot reflect the overall structures accurately.

In order to explore the integrated communities in multi-layer networks, according to the concept of community detection (i.e., nodes within the community are closely connected and connections between communities are sparse [14]), community detection is naturally defined as a multi-objective optimization problem [15]. In this paper, in order to solve multi-objective optimization problems in multi-layer networks, a multi-objective evolutionary computing model for community detection in multi-layer networks is introduced. This model finds the community structure of each layer by iteratively optimizing the modularity of each layer of the network, which adopts the locus-based representation strategy, to integrate genetic operation and multilevel local search. Meanwhile, different optimal solution selection strategies are used to solve the compound community structure in multi-layer networks.

The rest of this paper is organized as follows. The problem definition is given in Sect. 2. Section 3 presents a multi-objective evolution model for community detection in multi-layer networks, and then proposes the MulNSGA-II algorithm based on the multi-objective model. Comprehensive experiments are performed to show the effectiveness of MulNSGA-II algorithm in various networks in Sect. 4. Finally, basic concluding remarks are discussed in Sect. 5.

2   Problem Definition

A multi-layer network can be modeled as a graph $N = (\{G_1, ...G_m\}, R)$, where $G_m = (V_l, E_l)$ represents the networks at m layer with V_l node and E_l intra-layer links. And $R = \{E_{ij} \subset V_i \times V_j, i, j \in 1, ...m, i \neq j\}$ denotes the connections between the nodes of layer G_i and layer G_j. The elements of R are called the interlayer or crossed layers links. That is, a multi-layer network contains m subnetworks and there are connections among these m networks. Multi-layer networks have different network types according to the node sets of each layer and inter-layer relationships [16], as shown in Fig. 1. This paper mainly studies multi-layer networks with the same set of nodes in each layer, as shown in Fig. 1(a). Therefore, multi-layer networks can be formalized as follows.

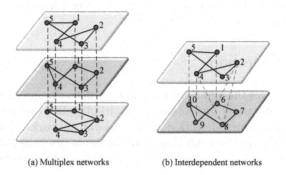

(a) Multiplex networks   (b) Interdependent networks

Fig. 1. An example of multi-layer networks with different types of nodes. (a) The multiplex networks which have the same nodes at all layers, and (b) the interdependent networks which have different sets of nodes at different network layers.

$$N = G_\delta, \quad \delta \in \{1, ..., m\}$$
$$G_\delta = (V_l, E_l) \quad l \in \{1, ..., m\} \tag{1}$$

Suppose $\Omega = \{S_1, ..., S_k\}$ is a set of feasible partitions in a multiplex network G and $F = \{F_1, F_2, ..., F_d\}$ is a set of objective functions. A many-objective community detection problem in a multi-layer network can be defined as follows:

$$\begin{cases} min \quad F\{S_i'\} = min(F_1(S_i'), ...F_m(S_i')); \\ s.t., \quad S_i' \in \Omega; \end{cases} \tag{2}$$

Each F_δ: $\Omega \to R$ evaluates the objective function only in the layer G_δ. Since F is a set of competing for objective functions that must be simultaneously optimized, it shows that the obtained non-dominated solutions of the Pareto front may be the best modularity of each layer.

Simplified composite modularity function is adopted here as the optimization function, so $F_\delta(P) = -Q_\delta(P)$. Given a multi-layer network and community index, the community index can be maximized under non-overlapping conditions (i.e, each node can only be assigned to one community). Simplified composite modularity Q_e' is calculated in Eq. (3).

$$Q_e' = \frac{1}{2M} \sum_{i,j}^{n} (A_{ij}' - \frac{d_i \times d_j}{2M}) \delta(X_i, X_j) \tag{3}$$

M is the total number of communication connection. n represents the number of communication layers or dimensions of a network. The average difference between the true fraction and the expected fraction of edges belonged to the composite community structure is calculated by a simplified multilevel modularity in a multi-layer network. The larger the value of Q'_e is, the higher the quality of the composite community structure is. A simplified composite modularity Q'_e instead of the multiplex modularity is used to evaluate the quality of integrated community structure in a multi-layer network, which ignores coupling factors (i.e., the second term $\delta(X_i, X_j)$ in Eq. (3)).

3 Proposed Method

This paper transforms the multi-layer community detection problem into a multi-objective optimization and presents a new multi-objective evolutionary computing model for community detection in multi-layer networks. This section will describe the multi-objective evolution model in detail from the aspects of encoding mode, genetic operation, local search, and optimal solution selection strategy.

3.1 Encoding Scheme

The encoding scheme of the solution is a key step to the success of an algorithm. The label-based and locus-based representation schemes are the two main encoding methods for community partition. However, the label-based representation is redundant, because if there are p labels in the diagram, then $p!$ different chromosomes may correspond to the same partition [17]. For example, the vector [1, 1, 3, 3, 3, 3, 2, 2, 2] and [3, 3, 1, 1, 1, 1, 2, 2, 2] represent the same community division. Therefore, this paper adopts the locus-based adjacency representation which makes full use of the information in the diagram to express the division of communities. It is assumed that the chromosome or solution in the population is set as $S = \{s_1, s_2, ...s_N\}$. The gene length is N, and each gene i can be any integer from 1 to N, i.e., $1 < i < N$. The value of the ith gene can be j, provided that i and j connected on at least one layer of the network.

3.2 Genetic Operators

Crossover is an important step in the genetic operation, and the uniform crossover is adopted in this paper. Uniform crossover actually belongs to the category of multi-point crossover, which has been proved to be an effective operator in evolutionary algorithms (EAs). The uniform crossover operation is as follows. First, a binary mask of the same length as the chromosome is randomly generated. The offspring is generated by selecting genes from the parent chromosome according to the mask. If the mask is equal to 0, the gene is selected from the first parent chromosome; otherwise, the gene is selected from the second parent chromosome. Figure 2(a) shows a simple example of a uniform crossover operator.

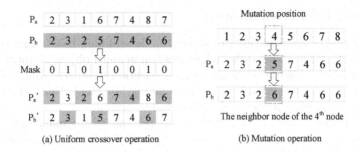

Fig. 2. An example of uniform crossover and mutation operation with 8 nodes. (a) Based on the mask, the parent chromosomes (i.e., P_a and P_b) produce two offspring chromosomes (i.e., P_a' and P_b') by uniform crossover operation. (b) According to a certain probability, the mutation location is randomly selected on the P_a chromosome, of which the node becomes its neighbor randomly to produce P_a' chromosome.

Mutation combines the knowledge of the layer nodes neighborhood, which mutates with a random probability. The ith gene on a chromosome is randomly selected with predefined probability and mutates into the jth neighbor node of the ith gene. A simple example of the proposed mutation operator is given in Fig. 2(b).

3.3 Local Search Operation

The hill climbing method (HC) is incorporated into the proposed multi-objective evolution model. First, the neighbors of a chromosome are defined as follows: Given a chromosome $S_k = \{S_k^1, S_k^2, ..., S_k^n\}$, node S_k^i is randomly selected from chromosome S_k. Then the gene S_k^i is replaced with other neighbor nodes S_k^j of the location i, where $S_k^j \neq S_k^i$. The new generated partition is defined as the neighbor of chromosome S_k. In the local search process, a chromosome is randomly selected for refinement and all possible neighbor chromosomes are identified. Compared with the original chromosome, the newly generated one is selected to replace this chromosome if it can achieve better solutions. The details of HC procedure are given in Algorithm 1.

Algorithm 1 Hill climbing procedure

1: **Input:** chromosome C_k, the local search probability p_i
2: $flag \leftarrow FALSE$
3: **for** $l = 1 : p_i * len(C_k)$ **do**
4:    Randomly select a node and location: $C_k^i \in C_k$ and j, where $j \neq i$
5:    Replace: $C_k' = C_k \leftarrow C_k^i$
6: **if** $Eval(C_k') > Eval(C_k)$ **then**
7:    Assign: $C_k = C_k \leftarrow C_k'$
8: **else**
9:    Assign: $flag \leftarrow TRUE$

3.4 Optimal Selection Strategy

In multi-objective optimization problems [18], determining how to find the optimal solution from the Pareto set is a key problem in multi-objective optimization. This paper adopts different optimal solution selection strategies. Multi-objective optimization and multi-criterion decision-making are divided into three types, namely, *a posteriori*, *a priori*, and *an interactive* [19].

In the strategy based on *a priori*, this paper selects the maximum value of the objective function, i.e., the maximum modularity, in the Pareto set as the optimal solution. In this case, the method is called *prik*.

Suppose $S_i = (s_1, s_2, ..., s_m)$ is the fitness value of the ith solution on the Pareto front. Based on *an interactive* method, the average value $mvt = ((\sum_i s_x)/d)$ is calculated for each S_i in the optimization process, and the solution with the highest value max_s is selected as the optimal solution at the end. This optimization algorithm is called *postk*.

The *posteriori* decision-making method mainly introduces the approach of k-means clustering, which can group a set of data obtained through different models to improve the quality of the results. First, MulNSGA-II algorithm is used to discover community detection at all layers, so as to form the Pareto front. Then, this strategy can find a consistent community clustering from detected communities, namely, to determine the optimal solution from the Pareto front. ot change or the maximum number of iterations is reached.

4 Experiment

4.1 Network Datasets

The synthetic network is generated by the benchmark function proposed by Bródka and Grecki [20], which is an extension of the LFR benchmark [21]. By changing parameters, networks with different structures and layers are generated respectively. Parameter settings are shown in Table 1. The mixed parameter u represents the connection part between a node and all nodes of a community. Generally speaking, the quality of the community divided will decrease with the increase of u. The degree change chance Dc will control how different the node degrees at different network layers are. The higher the Dc parameter value is, the more different nodes in different layers may be. In general, the mixing parameter u and the degree change chance Dc jointly control the network structure of each layer in a multi-layer network.

There are two real-world networks, which can be downloaded from the website[1]. The first real multi-layer network is the KAPFERER TAILOR SHOP network, which records the interaction of people in a tailor shop. The network consists of 39 nodes, 1108 links, and four layers, that is, two instrumental attribute networks (i.e., work and assistance) and two social attribute networks (i.e., friendship and social emotion). The second real multi-layer network is the

---

[1] http://vlado.fmf.uni-lj.si/pub/networks/data/UciNet/UciData.htm#kaptail.

Table 1. The m-LFR128 Parameter Settings.

Parameter	Value	Parameter	Value
Number of nodes	128	Overlapping nodes	0
Node average degree	8	Overlapping memberships	0
Number of layers	[2, 3, 4]	Maximal community size	32
Mixing parameter	[0.1, 0.2, 0.3, 0.4, 0.5]	Minimal community size	8
Exponent for power law creating degree sequence	2	Node maximal degree	16
Exponent for power law creating community sizes	2	Exponent for power law of nodes through layers	2
Degree change chance	[0.2, 0.4, 0.6, 0.8]	Membership swap chance	0

CS-AARHUS social network, which consists of 61 nodes, 620 connections, and five layers networks, namely, online Facebook relationship and offline relationship (i.e., leisure, work, co-authorship and lunch).

4.2 Evaluation Metrics

Redundancy index [22] used as an evaluation metrics calculates the proportion of redundant links in multi-layer networks. The intuitive implication of this metric is that composite communities should have more connections in multiple layer networks. Redundancy (denoted by Rc) is expressed in Eq. (4).

$$Rc = \frac{1}{d \times \|p\|} \sum_{G_\delta \in G} \sum_{\{u,v\} \in S'_i} \beta(u, v, E_l) \tag{4}$$

$\|p\|$ is the total number of communities in a multi-layer network. S'_i is the set $\{u, v\}$ that connects at least one layer in G community. If $\{u, v\} \in E_l$, $\beta(u, v, E_l) = 1$, 0 otherwise. The higher the value of R_c is, the better the quality of the partition is.

The Normalized Mutual Information (NMI) used as the other evaluation metrics can evaluate the similarity between the current clusters and the previous ones [23]. Assuming that c_1 and c_2 are two network partitions, then $NMI(A, B)$ can be calculated as Eq. (5).

$$NMI(c_1, c_2) = \frac{-2 \sum_{i=1}^{l_{c_1}} \sum_{j=1}^{l_{c_2}} F'_{ij} log(F'_{ij} N / F'_{i.} F'_{.j})}{\sum_{i=1}^{l_{c_1}} F'_{i.} log(F'_{i.}/N) + \sum_{j=1}^{l_{c_2}} F'_{.j} log(F'_{.j}/N)} \tag{5}$$

F' is a confusion matrix. $F'_i (F'_j)$ is the number of elements in the ith row (or the jth column) of F'. $l_{c_1}(l_{c_2})$ represents the total number of clustering in a partition $c_1(c_2)$. The value of NMI ranges from 0 to 1. The larger the value of NMI is, the more similar the original and optimized networks are.

4.3 Experiments Result

The proposed method is to obtain the final results by averaging the values in 10 runs. Population size, iteration number, crossover and mutation probability are set as 200, 100, 0.8 and 0.2, respectively. These parameter values are obtained by the trial-and-error method on the benchmark function to get the best result.

Figure 3 shows the results of NMI in 12 different network structures based on different parameters in the mLFR dataset. The first experiment is mainly used to compare the three strategies of MulNSGA-II algorithm (i.e., MulNSGA-*prik*, MulNSGA-*clu*, MulNSGA-*postk*) and MLMaOP-*proj*, MLMaOP-*cspa*, MLMaOP-*mf* [24], under the different network structures formed by the interaction of the layers of multi-layer networks, the mixing parameters u and the degree change chance Dc.

Table 2. The comparison results of MulNSGA-*prik*, MulNSGA-*clu*, MulNSGA-*postk* algorithm, and MOEA-MultiNet, BGLL algorithm on KAPFERER TAILOR SHOP NETWORK. The evaluation indexes are Q_m and R_c.

Strategies	Algorithms	Q_m	R_c
One-layer	BGLL/L_1	0.2179	0.3964
	BGLL/L_2	0.2006	0.4717
	BGLL/L_3	0.1380	0.2657
	BGLL/L_4	0.0932	0.4094
Multi-layer	MOEA-MultiNet	0.2094	0.4735
	MulNSGA-*prik*	0.4343	0.3705
	MulNSGA-*clu*	0.4698	0.3511
	MulNSGA-*postk*	0.4810	0.3134

It is obvious that the increase of network layers hardly affects the performances of MulNSGA-*prik*, MulNSGA-*clu*, MulNSGA-*postk* in Fig. 3. Dc controls the network structure, and the algorithm can find the best community division under different network structures. The performance of MulNSGA-II algorithm (i.e., MulNSGA-*prik*, MulNSGA-*clu*, MulNSGA-*postk*) is much better than that of MLMaOP-*proj*, MLMaOP-*cspa*, MLMaOP-*mf* algorithm [24] in different network structures and layers.

Tables 2 and 3 show that the comparison results between the proposed MulNSGA-II algorithm (i.e., MulNSGA-*prik*, MulNSGA-*clu*, MulNSGA-*postk*) and the MOEA-MultiNet [25], BGLL algorithms [26] in one of real multi-layer networks.

It can be seen from the data in Tables 2 and 3 that the compound community structure obtained by the proposed MulNSGA-II algorithm (i.e., MulNSGA-*prik*, MulNSGA-*clu*, MulNSGA-*postk*) is overall superior to the MOEA-MultiNet [25] and the BGLL algorithms [26] based on a single layer.

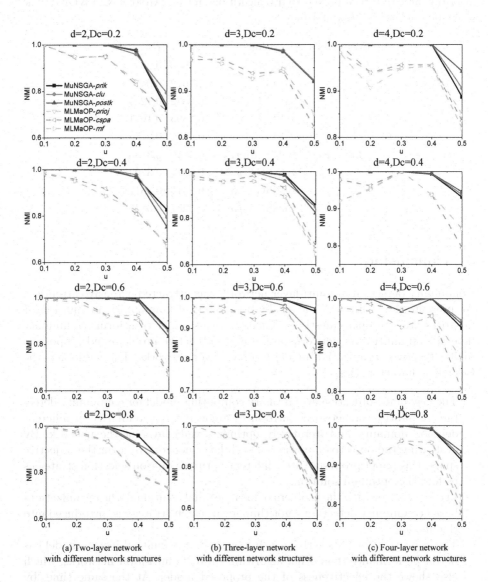

Fig. 3. The NMI results for mLFR-128 networks with the increase of network layers (i.e., d = 2, 3, 4) and the change of network structure (mixing parameter u and degree change chance Dc jointly control the network structure). Obviously, the results show that the improved MulNSGA-*prik*, MulNSGA-*clu*, MulNSGA-*postk* algorithm are much better than that of MLMaOP-proj, MLMaOP-cspa, MLMaOP-mf algorithm in different network structure and layers.

Table 3. The comparison results of MulNSGA-*prik*, MulNSGA-*clu*, MulNSGA-*postk* algorithm and MOEA-MultiNet, BGLL algorithm on CS-AARHUS NETWORK. The evaluation indexes are Q_m and R_c.

Strategies	Algorithms	Q_m	R_c
One-layer	BGLL/L_1	0.4685	0.2852
	BGLL/L_2	0.1672	0.0472
	BGLL/L_3	0.0832	0.1205
	BGLL/L_4	0.2893	0.1611
	BGLL/L_5	0.4115	0.2715
Multi-layer	MOEA-MultiNet	0.4010	0.3186
	MulNSGA-*prik*	0.2316	0.3703
	MulNSGA-*clu*	0.2315	0.3617
	MulNSGA-*postk*	0.2287	0.3847

5   Conclusion

Community detection in multi-layer networks has attracted extensive attention. At present, the definition and evaluation index of community in multi-layer networks are still open questions. Therefore, this paper transforms community detection in multi-layer networks into a multi-objective problem and proposes a multi-objective optimization model in multi-layer networks. The model has the following characteristics.

- The new multi-objective evolutionary computing model for community detection in multi-layer networks introduces a concept of modularity in different decision domains, and iteratively optimizes each layer of the network. By evaluating the objective function of each layer network to form the objective space, this paper proposes three different optimal solution selection strategies to find the optimum solution.
- In order to overcome the problem of local optimal solution in the optimization-based community detection algorithm, local search strategy is introduced into this model.
- The improved MulNSGA-II algorithm based on the multi-objective model has better performance than other algorithms in real multi-layer networks, which also shows the effectiveness of the proposed model. At the same time, by changing the network structure and layers in synthetic networks, the model is still able to find high-quality communities. When applied to layer 3 and 4 networks, the performance of the algorithm is almost unchanged. Experiments show that the improved MulNSGA-II algorithm may be applied to higher dimensional multilayer networks.

Acknowledgment. This work is supported by National Natural Science Foundation of China (Nos. 61602391, 61402379), Natural Science Foundation of Chongqing (No.

cstc2018jcyjAX0274), and in part of Southwest University Training Programs of Innovation and Entrepreneurship for Undergraduates (No. X201910635045).

References

1. Gao, C., Liu, J.M.: Network-based modeling for characterizing human collective behaviors during extreme events. IEEE Trans. Sys. Man Cybern. Syst. **46**(1), 171–183 (2017)
2. Chiti, F., Dobson, C.M.: Protein misfolding, amyloid formation, and human disease: A summary of progress over the last decade. Annu. Rev. Biochem. **86**, 27–68 (2017)
3. Strano, E., Viana, M.P., Sorichetta, A.: Mapping road network communities for guiding disease surveillance and control strategies. Sci. Rep-UK **8**(1), 4744 (2018)
4. Li, Z.T., Liu, J., Wu, K.: A multiobjective evolutionary algorithm based on structural and attribute similarities for community detection in attributed networks. IEEE Trans. Cybern. **48**(7), 1963–1976 (2017)
5. Liu, C.L., Liu, J., Jiang, Z.Z.: A multiobjective evolutionary algorithm based on similarity for community detection from signed social networks. IEEE Trans. Cybern. **44**(12), 2274–2287 (2014)
6. Gao, C., Liang, M.X., Li, X.H.: Network community detection based on the Physarum-inspired computational framework. IEEE/ACM Trans. Comput. Bi. **15**(6), 1916–1928 (2018)
7. Bravobenitez, B., Alexandrovakabadjova, B., Martinezjaramillo, S.: Centrality measurement of the mexican large Value payments system from the perspective of multiplex networks. Comput. Econ. **47**(1), 19–47 (2016)
8. Yao, Y., Zhang, R., Fan, Y.: Link prediction via layer relevance of multiplex networks. Int. J. Mod. Phys. C **28**(08), 1750101 (2017)
9. Ma, L.J., Gong, M.G., Yan, J.N., Liu, W.F., Wang, S.F.: Detecting composite communities in multiplex networks: a multilevel memetic algorithm. Swarm Evol. Comput. **39**, 177–191 (2018)
10. Taylor, D., Shai, S., Stanley, N., Mucha, P.J.: Enhanced detectability of community structure in multilayer networks through layer aggregation. Phys. Rev. Lett. **116**(22), 228301 (2016)
11. Xuan, Q., Ma, X.D., Fu, C.B., Dong, H., Zhang, G.J.: Heterogeneous multidimensional scaling for complex networks. Int. J. Mod. Phy. C. **26**(02), 1550023 (2015)
12. Dai, C.Y., Chen, L., Li, B., Li, Y.: Link prediction in multi-relational networks based on relational similarity. Inform. Sci. **394**, 198–216 (2017)
13. Pitsik, E., et al.: Inter-layer competition in adaptive multiplex network. New J. Phy. **20**(7), 075004 (2018)
14. Boutemine, O., Bouguessa, M.: Mining community structures in multidimensional networks. ACM Trans. Knowl. Discov. Data **11**(4), 51 (2017)
15. Li, Z.T., Liu, J., Wu, K.: A multiobjective evolutionary algorithm based on structural and attribute similarities for community detection in attributed networks. IEEE Trans. Cybern. **48**(7), 1963–1976 (2017)
16. Wang, Z., Wang, L., Szolnoki, A., Perc, M.: Evolutionary games on multilayer networks: A colloquium. Eur. Phys. J. B **88**(5), 124 (2015)
17. Pizzuti, C.: Evolutionary computation for community detection in networks: A review. IEEE Trans. Evol. Comput. **22**(3), 464–483 (2018)

18. Chen, X.J., Liu, Y.X., Li, X.H., Wang, Z., Wang, S.X., Gao, C.: A new evolutionary multiobjective model for traveling salesman problem. IEEE Access. **7**, 66964–66979 (2019). https://doi.org/10.1109/ACCESS.2019.2917838. https://ieeexplore.ieee.org/abstract/document/8718296

19. Purshouse, R.C., Deb, K., Mansor, M.M., Mostaghim, S., Wang, R.: A review of hybrid evolutionary multiple criteria decision making methods. In: 2014 IEEE Congress on Evolutionary Computation (CEC), pp. 1147–1154 (2014)

20. Bródka, P.: A method for group extraction and analysis in multi-layered social networks. Ph.D. disertation, Wroclaw, Poland, arXiv.org:1302.1369 (2012). https://www.ii.pwr.edu.pl/~brodka/index-en.html

21. Lancichinetti, A., Fortunato, S., Radicchi, F.: Benchmark graphs for testing community detection algorithms. Phys. Rev. E **78**(4), 046110 (2008)

22. Newman, M.E.J., Girvan, M.: Finding and evaluating community structure in networks. Phys. Rev. **69**(2), 026113 (2004)

23. Amelio, A., Pizzuti, C.: Community detection in multidimensional networks. In: 2014 IEEE Proceedings of the 26th International Conference on Tools with Artificial Intelligence, pp. 352–359 (2014)

24. Pizzuti, C., Socievole, A.: Many-objective optimization for community detection in multi-layer networks. In: 2017 IEEE Congress on Evolutionary Computation (CEC), pp. 411–418 (2017)

25. Liu, W.F., Wang, S.F., Gong, M.: An improved multiobjective evolutionary approach for community detection in multilayer networks. In: 2017 IEEE Congress on Evolutionary Computation (CEC), pp. 443–449 (2017)

26. Lancichinetti, A., Fortunato, S.: Consensus clustering in complex networks. Sci. Rep. **2**, 336 (2012). https://www.nature.com/articles/srep00336

Jointly Modeling Community and Topic in Social Network

Yunlei Zhang, Nianwen Ning, Jinna Lv, Chenguang Song, and Bin Wu$^{(\boxtimes)}$

Beijing Key Laboratory of Intelligence Telecommunications Software and Multimedia,
School of Computer Science, Beijing University of Posts and Telecommunications,
Beijing 100876, China
{yunlei0518,nianwenning,lvjinna,scg,wubin}@bupt.edu.cn

Abstract. Social networks contain not only link information, but also text information. It is an important task to discover communities in social network analysis. Moreover, it is helpful to understand the community by finding its topics of interest. In fact, social networks are always dynamic. However, there are still few method to detect communities and their topics by combining link and text information in dynamic network. In this paper, we formulate the problem of detecting communities and their topics and propose a dynamic topical community detection (DTCD) method to solve the problem. DTCD integrates link, text and time in a unified way by using generative model. The community and the topic are modeled as latent variables which are learned by collapsed Gibbs sampling. DTCD can not only find communities and their topics, but also capture the temporal variations of communities and topics. Experimental results on two real-world datasets demonstrate the effectiveness of DTCD.

Keywords: Social network · Dynamic community detection ·
User generated content · Generative model · Collapsed Gibbs sampling

1 Introduction

Recently, social network has become a necessary tool for users to communicate with each other and obtain information, such as twitter, weibo and wechat. These social networks contain not only link information, but also text information. Some users in social network may have dense links and have the same interests which are extracted from text information. As in pioneer works [4], we call these users as a community. Community structure is an important property of social networks. Obviously, communities in social network are dynamic. Discovering dynamic community structure is an important task in social network analysis. Many methods have been proposed to detect dynamic community, e.g., [3,7,10,14,16]. However, these methods only detect dynamic community based on link information with ignoring text information. Although these methods may perform well in finding communities in which there are dense links, they may fail to find communities in which there are not that dense links, but users share

C. Douligeris et al. (Eds.): KSEM 2019, LNAI 11775, pp. 209–221, 2019.
https://doi.org/10.1007/978-3-030-29551-6_19

the same interests. To solve the problem, we propose a dynamic topical community method which integrates network structure and node content in dynamic
networks.

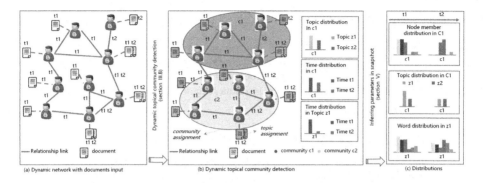

Fig. 1. Overview of dynamic topical community detection.

Figure 1 shows an overview of dynamic topical community detection process.
The input is dynamic network with node content. And it aims to reveal the latent
communities, topics and their temporal variations. Dynamic topical community
detection is challenging. Both communities and topics are hidden and changing
over times. Moreover, there are correlation between community and topic.

To detect communities and extract topics simultaneously, a generative model
is proposed, called DTCD (Dynamic Topical Community Detection), and it integrates link, node content and time stamp information in a unified way. The
community and topic are modeled as latent variables, and a generative process
is proposed to observe link, text, and time stamp to find the communities, to
extract topics and to characterize their temporal variations.

The basic idea of our model consists of two assumptions: (1) The users affiliate
to different communities with different degree; (2) A community is associated
with multiple topics. To summarize, we make the following contributions: (1) We
define the problem of dynamic topical community detection, and paves the road
to explore the relationship between community evolving and topic changing; (2)
We proposed a generative model to integrate the link, text and time stamp in a
unified way to discover community and topic and their temporal variation; (3) We
conduct experiments on two real-world networks, and our method outperforms
other baseline methods.

2   Related Work

For detailed reviews of community detection, please refer to [4,12]. We briefly
review the related works in two categories. The first category is dynamic community detection. They include random walk based method [14], local view based

method [7], evolutionary nonnegativematrix factorization methods [9,10], multiobjective based method [16]. Most of these above methods detect dynamic community by only using network structures. Only Wang et al. [14] proposed a method considering network structures and node content, but it ignores the topics in the communities. The second category is community detection with node content. They include matrix factorization based methods [11,15], probabilistic model based methods [2,6,8]. All the above methods considering node content detect community in static network, but it is not easy to extend these methods to dynamic networks.

3   Dynamic Topical Community Detection Method

3.1   Problem Formulation

In this section, we will give some definitions.

Definition 1. *A **social network** is $G = (U, E, D, T)$, where U is a set of users, E is a set of edges representing the relationship between users such as friendship, cooperation, D is a set of documents which are associated with users in U and T is a set of time stamps representing the generation time of E and D. When $|T| = 1$, we call it **snapshot network**.*

Definition 2. *A **topic** z is a $|W|$-dimensional multinomial distribution over words, denoted as ϕ_z, where each entry $\phi_{z,w}$ denotes the probability of a word $w \in W$ generated by topic z.*

A topic has different popularity at different time which is characterized by a temporal distribution defined as follows:

Definition 3. *A **topic z's temporal variation** is a $|T|$-dimensional multinomial distribution over the time stamps, denoted as Ψ_z, where each entry $\Psi_{z,t}$ is the probability of a topic z occurring at time stamp t.*

In this paper, community is characterized by link, topic and time stamp. First, a community consists of a set of users with dense links. Second, community is correlated with a mixture of topics extracted from node content, instead of one topic. Finally, community is characterized by a time stamp distribution. We give the definitions from these three aspects as follows:

Definition 4. *A **community** c is a $|U|$-dimensional multinomial distribution over users, denoted as η_c, where each entry $\eta_{c,u}$ represents the significance of the user u in the community c.*

Definition 5. *A **community c's topic profile** is a $|Z|$-dimensional multinomial distribution over topics, denoted as ψ_c, where each entry $\psi_{c,z}$ represents the extent of community c's interest in topic z;*

Definition 6. *A **community** c's **temporal variation** is a $|T|$-dimensional multinomial distribution over time stamps, denoted as Ω_c, where each entry $\Omega_{c,t}$ denotes the popularity of community c at time t.*

In social networks, users usually are affiliated to different communities with different degree. Users are modeled in *mixed-membership* manner.

Definition 7. *A **user** u's **community membership** is a $|C|$-dimensional multinomial distribution over communities, denoted as π_u, where each entry $\pi_{u,c}$ indicates user u's affiliation degree to c.*

Problem 1. Given a social network $G = (U, E, D, T)$, the task of dynamic topical community detection is to infer: (1) each topic z's distribution over words ϕ_z; (2) each topic z's temporal variation Ψ_z; (3) each community c's distribution over users η_c; (4) each community c's temporal variation Ω_c; (5) each user u's community membership π_u; (6) each community c's topic profile ψ_c.

3.2   Model Structure

DTCD models two types of user behaviors over time, i.e., one behavior is when a user publishes a document on what topic; another one is when a user interact with whom. We assume that the user behaviors are controlled by the latent community and topic. Specifically, the topic of the document published by a user is governed by the topics of the community to which the user belong, a user interacts with whom is governed by the relationship between community and user. Figure 2 shows the graphical structure of DTCD consisting of three blocks: the *text-time block* reveals the topics underlying node content, and characterizes their temporal variations; the *network-time block* reveals communities underlying link, and characterizes their temporal variations; the *user membership block* reveals the relationship between the users and the communities, which provides community labels to the neighbors and documents of the corresponding user.

3.3   Generative Process

(1) for each community $c \in C$:
   (a) draw its $|U|$-dimensional user distribution from a Dirichlet prior parameterized by β: $\eta_c|\beta \sim Dir_{|U|}(\beta)$
   (b) draw its $|Z|$-dimensional topic distribution from a Dirichlet prior parameterized by γ: $\psi_c|\gamma \sim Dir_{|Z|}(\gamma)$
   (c) draw its $|T|$-dimensional time stamp distribution from a Dirichlet prior parameterized by τ: $\Omega_c|\tau \sim Dir_{|T|}(\tau)$
(2) for each topic $z \in Z$:
   (a) draw its $|W|$-dimensional word distribution from Dirichlet prior parameterized by δ: $\phi_z|\delta \sim Dir_{|W|}(\delta)$
   (b) draw its $|T|$-dimensional time stamp distribution from Dirichlet prior parameterized by μ: $\psi_z|\mu \sim Dir_{|T|}(\mu)$
(3) for each user $u \in U$:

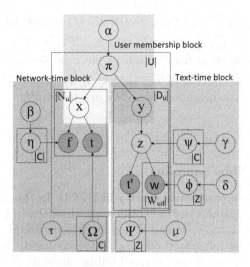

Fig. 2. Graphical model of DTCD.

(a) draw its $|C|$-dimensional community distribution from a Dirichlet prior parameterized by α: $\pi_u|\alpha \sim Dir_{|C|}(\alpha)$

(b) for each neighbor $i \in N_u$ of user u:

  (i) draw a community assignment $x_{ui}|\pi_u \sim Multi(\pi_u)$, by user u's multinomial community distribution π_u

  (ii) draw the neighbor $f_{ui}|\eta_{x_{ui}} \sim Multi(\eta_{x_{ui}})$, by community x_{ui}'s multinomial user distribution $\eta_{x_{ui}}$

  (iii) draw time stamp of the neighbor i, $t_{ui}|\Omega_{x_{ui}} \sim Multi(\Omega_{x_{ui}})$, by community x_{ui}'s multinomial time stamp distribution $\Omega_{x_{ui}}$

(c) for each document $d \in D_u$ associated with user u:

  (a) draw a community assignment $y_{ud}|\pi_u \sim Multi(\pi_u)$, by user u's multinomial community distribution π_u

  (b) draw a topic assignment $z_{ud}|\psi_{y_{ud}} \sim Multi(\psi_{y_{ud}})$, by community y_{ud}'s multinomial topic distribution $\psi_{y_{ud}}$

  (c) draw each word $w_{udj}|\phi_{z_{ud}} \sim Multi(\phi_{z_{ud}})$, $\forall j = 1, \ldots, |W_{ud}|$, by z_{ud}'s multinomial word distribution $\phi_{z_{ud}}$

  (d) draw time stamp of the document d associated with user u, $t'_{ud}|\Psi_{z_{ud}} \sim Multi(\Psi_{z_{ud}})$, by topic z_{ud}'s multinomial time stamp distribution $\Psi_{z_{ud}}$.

3.4   Inferring Communities in Snapshot Network

We use the parameters π and η to calculate the probability of generating neighbors of users in snapshot network via each community. We can obtain the community membership of the users in the snapshot network. We assume that the community membership proportions of a user equal to the expectation of the community membership proportions of neighbors linked to the user,

$P(c|i, t_i = t) = \sum_f (P(c|f)P(f|i, t_i = t))$, $P(c|f)$ is calculated by Bayes' formula $P(c|f) = \frac{P(c)P(f|c)}{\sum_c P(c)P(f|c)}$, where $P(c) = \pi_{i,c}$, $P(f|c) = \eta_{c,f}$. $P(f|i, t_i = t)$ is estimated via the empirical distribution of the neighbor nodes of the users in current snapshot network. $P(f|i, t_i = t) = \frac{n_{i,t}(f)}{\sum_f n_{i,t}(f)}$, where $n_{i,t}(f)$ denotes the number of user f in the neighbors of node i in t-th snapshot network.

4   Model Inference

4.1   Collapsed Gibbs Sampling

It is hard to inference parameters exactly in DTCD. In this paper, Gibbs sampling is used to infer parameters in DTCD approximately. In DTCD, nine latent variables π, η, x, y, z, ψ, ϕ, Ω and Ψ are need to be sampled. However, π, η, ψ, ϕ, Ω and Ψ can be integrated out due to the conjugate priors α, β, γ, δ, τ and μ by using the technique of collapsed Gibbs sampling [5]. Consequently, we only have to sample the community assignment x, y for each user and each document respectively, topic assignment z for each document from their conditional distribution given the remaining variables.

First, we need to calculating the joint posterior distribution of DTCD:

$$
\begin{aligned}
&p(w, f, t, t', x, y, z | \alpha, \beta, \gamma, \delta, \tau, \mu) \\
&= p(x, y | \alpha) p(w | z, \delta) p(z | y, \gamma) p(f | x, \beta) p(t' | z, \mu) p(t | x, \tau),
\end{aligned}
\tag{1}
$$

where $p(w|z)$ is the probability of the word w generated by the topic z; $p(z|y, \gamma)$ is the probability of the topic z generated by the community y; $p(f|x, \beta)$ is the probability of the user f generated by the community x; $p(t'|z, \mu)$ is the probability of the time stamp t' generated by the topic z;

We monitor the convergence of the inference progress by periodically computing the likelihood of training data [5]. At each iteration of our Gibbs sampler, DTCD samples both the corresponding community indicator y_{ud} and the topic indicator z_{ud} for each document D_{ud} generated by user u. DTCD samples the corresponding community indicators x_{ui} for each neighbor i. The sampling formulas are given as follows.

Sampling community indicator x_{ui} for the i-th neighbor of user u according to,

$$
\begin{aligned}
&p(x_{ui} = c* | x_{\neg ui}, f, t, \alpha, \beta, \tau) \\
&\propto \frac{n_{u(f), \neg ui}^{(c*)} + n_{u(d)}^{(c*)} + \alpha}{n_{u(f), \neg ui}^{(\cdot)} + n_{u(d)}^{(\cdot)} + |C|\alpha} \cdot \frac{n_{c*(f), \neg ui}^{(u)} + \beta}{n_{c*(f), \neg ui}^{(\cdot)} + |U|\beta} \cdot \frac{n_{c*(f), \neg ui}^{(t)} + \tau}{n_{c*(f), \neg ui}^{(\cdot)} + |T|\tau}
\end{aligned}
\tag{2}
$$

where $n_{u(f), \neg ui}^{(c*)}$ and $n_{u(d)}^{(c*)}$ denotes the number of neighbors and documents of user u assigned to community $c*$ respectively, $n_{c*(f), \neg ui}^{(u)}$ denotes the number of user u generated by community $c*$, $n_{c*(f), \neg ui}^{(t)}$ denotes the number of times that time stamp t is generated by community $c*$. Marginal counts are represented with dots; e.g., $n^{(\cdot)}_{u(f),\neg ui}$ denotes the number of neighbors of user u. $\neg ui$ represents the node ui excluded.

Sampling community indicator y_{ud} for the d-th document associated with user u according to,

$$p(y_{ud} = c * | y_{\neg ud}, x, z, \alpha, \gamma) \propto \frac{n^{(c*)}_{u(f)} + n^{(c*)}_{u(d),\neg ud} + \alpha}{n^{(\cdot)}_{u(f)} + n^{(\cdot)}_{u(d),\neg ud} + |C|\alpha} \cdot \frac{n^{(z)}_{c*(d),\neg ud} + \gamma}{n^{(\cdot)}_{c*(d),\neg ud} + |Z|\gamma} \quad (3)$$

where $n^{(z)}_{c*(d),\neg ud}, n^{(\cdot)}_{c*(d),\neg ud}$ denotes the number of documents assigned to community $c*$ and generated by topic z and any topic with document ud excluded, respectively.

Sampling topic indicator z_{ud} for the d-th document associated with user u according to,

$$p(z_{ud} = z * | y_{ud} = c*, t, z_{\neg ud}, \gamma, \delta, \mu)$$

$$\propto \frac{n^{(z*)}_{c*,\neg ud} + \gamma}{n^{(\cdot)}_{c*,\neg ud} + |Z|\gamma} \cdot \frac{n^{(t)}_{z*,\neg ud} + \mu}{n^{(\cdot)}_{z*,\neg ud} + |T|\mu} \cdot \frac{\prod_{w=1}^{|W|} \prod_{i=0}^{n^{(w)}_{ud}-1} (n^{(w)}_{z,\neg ud} + \delta + i)}{\prod_{i=0}^{n_{ud}-1} (n^{(\cdot)}_{z,\neg ud} + |W|\delta + i)} \quad (4)$$

where $n^{(t)}_{z*,\neg ud}, n^{(\cdot)}_{z*,\neg ud}$ denote the number of times that time stamp t and any time stamp of documents is generated by topic $z*$ with document ud excluded respectively, $n^{(w)}_{z,\neg ud}, n^{(\cdot)}_{z,\neg ud}$ denote the number of word w and any word is generated by topic $z*$ with document ud excluded respectively, $n^{(w)}_{ud}$ denotes the number of word w in document ud.

4.2 Time Complexity

We compute the community assignments and topic assignments of each document of each user, it takes $O(|D| \times |C| + |Z| \times |W|)$. We sample the community assignments of each neighbor node of each user, it takes $O(|C| \times |E|)$. Let I denote the number of iterations. The time complexity of the whole inference algorithm is $O((|D| \times |C| + |Z| \times |W| + |C| \times |E|) \times I)$.

5 Experiments

Experiments are conducted on two real-world datasets to evaluate the performance of the proposed approach. All experiments are conducted on a PC with Windows 10, a dual core 3.6 GHz CPU and 8G memory.

5.1   Set Up

Datasets. We use two real-world dynamic social networks, Reddit[1] and DBLP[2]: (1) The Reddit dataset consists of a part of three discussion blocks from August 25, 2012 to August 31, 2012, namely *Science, Politics, Movies*. The users are taken as nodes. Posts published by users are taken as node contents. The reply to posts are taken as edges. We obtain a word dictionary of size 5922 words after removing stop words and stemming. We partition the network into 7 time stamps where each day is taken as a time stamp. In all, 3080 users who participate in the discussions generate 5236 edges between them. The ground truth communities of users are extracted from the three discussion blocks. We set the number of community to be 3. (2) The DBLP dataset contains academic papers published on 11 conferences[3] from 2001 to 2011, it includes the fields of *DM&DB, AI&ML* and *CV&PR*. The researchers are taken as nodes. We take titles of papers as node contents. Co-author relationship between researchers is taken as edges. We only select the researchers with no less than 5 papers published in all the conferences. We obtain a word dictionary of size 7317 after removing words and stemming. Finally, we obtain 2554 nodes (researchers) and 9963 edges in the entire network. We partition the dataset into 11 time stamps where each year is taken as a time stamp. We consider the field of the conference as the ground truth. We set the number of community to be 3.

Baselines. We compare DTCD method with several baseline methods.

Latent Dirichlet Allocation (LDA) [1]. It defines a generative process for text. We set $\alpha = 50/|Z|$ and $\beta = 0.1$ [5]. We adopt LDA for topic modeling.

FacetNet [9]. It detects dynamic communities with temporal smoothness. We set parameter $\alpha = 0.9$ to balance the cost of snapshot and temporal. We adopt FacetNet for dynamic community detection.

NEIWalk [14]. NEIWalk detects dynamic communities based on heterogeneous random walk. We adopt the default value of parameters in [14] i.e., trade-off parameters $\alpha = 1/3$, $\beta = 1/3$, $\gamma = 1/3$, and random walk parameters $l = 100$, $h = 100$. We adopt NEIWalk for dynamic community detection.

Community Profiling and Detection (CPD) [2]. CPD detects communities and their topics. We adopt the default value of parameters in [2] provided by the authors, where $\alpha = 50/|Z|$, $\rho = 50/|C|$ and $\beta = 0.1$. We adopt CPD for both dynamic community detection and topic modeling.

Dynamic Topical Community Detection (DTCD). It is our method. Like in [5], we set $\alpha = 50/|C|$, $\gamma = 50/|Z|$, $\beta = 0.1$, $\delta = 0.1$, $\tau = 0.1$ and $\mu = 0.1$.

---

[1] https://www.reddit.com.
[2] https://dblp.uni-trier.de/.
[3] The 11 conferences include CVPR, ICCV, ECCV, NIPS, AAAI, IJCAI, ICML, KDD, ICDE, ICDM, VLDB and SIGMOD.

5.2   Community Detection

Metric. We use normalized mutual information (NMI) [13] to evaluate the performance of the methods.

$$NMI(X;Y) = \frac{2I(X;Y)}{H(X) + H(Y)}, \tag{5}$$

where X and Y denote the partition of communities, $I(X;Y)$ is the mutual information of random variable X and Y, and $H(X)$ denotes the entropy of X. The larger NMI is, the better the result is.

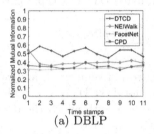
(a) DBLP

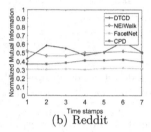
(b) Reddit

Fig. 3. The NMI values of methods on realworld networks.

Results. We display the comparison of NMI values in each snapshot network on two datasets in Fig. 3, Firstly, it is seen that the methods based on network structure and node content (DTCD, NEIWalk and CPD) achieved better result than the method only base on network structure (Facetnet) does; secondly, our method DTCD achieves the highest NMI on all snapshot network from DBLP and on most of the snapshot network from Reddit. The reason is that topic information contained in the node content helps DTCD to uncover the communities underlying network structures. DTCD does not consider temporal smoothness between consecutive snapshot networks, which leads to that the result achieved by DTCD is more fluctuant.

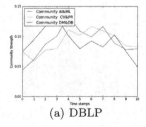
(a) DBLP

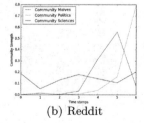
(b) Reddit

Fig. 4. Community temporal variation

DTCD finds both communities in each snapshot network and characterize the community temporal variation. We can see the different communities with different strength at each time stamp in Fig. 4. In Fig. 4(a), lines represent dome-like shape which describes the real situation. Actually we can obtain that there is more researcher in the middle stage (2004–2009) than preliminary stage (2001–2003) and late stage (2010–2011) from the data. In Fig. 4(b), we can conclude that community *movies* changes slightly over that 7 days. While community *politics* and community *sciences* rise drastically.

5.3   Topic Extraction

Metric. Like in [1], we use *perplexity* to evaluate DTCD's topic extraction performance.

$$perplexity(D_{test}) = \exp\{-\frac{\sum_{d=1}^{M} \log p(w_d)}{\sum_{d=1}^{M} N_d}\}, \tag{6}$$

where N_d denotes the number of words in the test document d, and $p(w_d)$ is the probability of the words in the document; for DTCD, it is calculated as $p(w_d) = \sum_c \pi_{uc} \sum_z \psi_{cz} \prod_l \phi_{zw_{dl}}$, where u is the user with which the document d is associated. The lower perplexity is, the better the model is.

We adopt 5-fold cross validation strategy to calculate the average value of perplexity. We use 80% of all the documents and all of the edges in network as the train set, and use the remaining 20% of all of documents as the test set.

Results. In Fig. 5(a), it shows the perplexity values with fixed number of community and varying number of topics. We can see that DTCD ($|C| = 3$, $|Z| = 20$) achieves the lowest perplexity value which shows that DTCD finds the closest distributions to the real distribution than other methods do. In Fig. 5(b), DTCD ($|C| = 3$, $|Z| = 20$) achieves the lowest perplexity value. DTCD assigns one topic to a short document, and gather similar documents via the community, so it can find better topics than LDA. In addition, DTCD takes a series of snapshot network as a whole network with time stamp, while CPD treats the snapshot network as separated one which leads to more perplexity scores than DTCD.

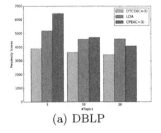
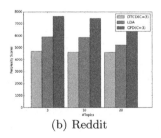

(a) DBLP   (b) Reddit

Fig. 5. Perplexity scores on realworld networks. (The less, the better)

DTCD both find topics and their temporal variations. We can see the different topics with different strength at each time stamp in Fig. 6. It is noticed that each line represents the changing trend of a topic in a relative topic strength on each time stamp, while there are no relationship between any two topics (lines). In Fig. 6(a), lines represent rising trend which describes the real situation. Actually, there are more and more publications on these three topics from 2001 to 2011. In Fig. 6(b), we have conclusions as follows: topic *movies* changes slightly over that 7 days; topic *politics* and topic *sciences* rise drastically.

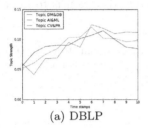
(a) DBLP

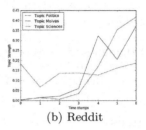
(b) Reddit

Fig. 6. Topic temporal variation

5.4   Community Distribution over Topics

DTCD assumes a community associated with a mixture of topics, instead of a topic. DTCD obtains community distribution over topics via parameter ψ, whose entry $\psi_{c,z}$ denotes the probability of user u belong to community c discussing topic z. In Fig. 7, we give the relationship between communities and topics on DBLP and Reddit datasets. We can observe that, the researchers in community *CV&PR* only focuses on topic *CV&PR*; the researchers in community *AI&ML* mainly focus on topic *AI&ML* and few researchers focus on topic *DM&DB*; the researchers in community *DM&DB* mainly focus on topic *DM&DB* and few researcher focus on topic *AI&ML*.

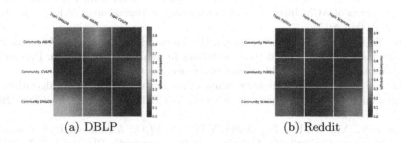
(a) DBLP   (b) Reddit

Fig. 7. Community distribution on topic

6   Conclusion

We formulated the problem of dynamic topical community detection and presented a generative model to discover community and topic and their temporal variation. And the experimental results show the effectiveness of our model. The dynamic topical community detection is a new perspective for dynamic community detection, and there are still several promising future directions. For example, it is necessary to study relationship between community evolving and topic changing; It is interesting to find topical influential users in the community which could be applied to viral marketing; another direction is to improve the efficiency of inference process in DTCD.

Acknowledgments. The work was supported by National Key R&D Program of China (2018YFC0831500), the National Natural Science Foundation of China (61772082), and Big Data Research Foundation of PICC.

References

1. Blei, D.M., Ng, A.Y., Jordan, M.I.: Latent Dirichlet allocation. J. Mach. Learn. Res. **3**, 993–1022 (2003)
2. Cai, H., Zheng, V.W., Zhu, F., Chang, K.C., Huang, Z.: From community detection to community profiling. Proc. VLDB Endow. **10**(7), 817–828 (2017)
3. Cheng, J., Wu, X., Zhou, M., Gao, S., Huang, Z., Liu, C.: A novel method for detecting new overlapping community in complex evolving networks. IEEE Trans. Syst. Man Cybern. Syst. **99**, 1–13 (2018)
4. Fortunato, S.: Community detection in graphs. Phys. Rep. **486**(3–5), 75–174 (2010)
5. Griffiths, T.L., Steyvers, M.: Finding scientific topics. Proc. Natl. Acad. Sci. **101**(Suppl. 1), 5228–5235 (2004)
6. He, D., Feng, Z., Jin, D., Wang, X., Zhang, W.: Joint identification of network communities and semantics via integrative modeling of network topologies and node contents. In: Proceedings of AAAI Conference on Artificial Intelligence, pp. 116–124 (2017)
7. Hu, Y., Yang, B., Lv, C.: A local dynamic method for tracking communities and their evolution in dynamic networks. Knowl.-Based Syst. **110**, 176–190 (2016)
8. Hu, Z., Yao, J., Cui, B., Xing, E.P.: Community level diffusion extraction. In: Proceedings of ACM International Conference on Management of Data, pp. 1555–1569. ACM (2015)
9. Lin, Y., Chi, Y., Zhu, S., Sundaram, H., Tseng, B.L.: Facetnet: a framework for analyzing communities and their evolutions in dynamic networks. In: Proceedings of International World Wide Web Conference, pp. 685–694 (2008)
10. Ma, X., Dong, D.: Evolutionary nonnegative matrix factorization algorithms for community detection in dynamic networks. IEEE Trans. Knowl. Data Eng. **29**(5), 1045–1058 (2017)
11. Nan, D.Y., Yu, W., Liu, X., Zhang, Y.P., Dai, W.D.: A framework of community detection based on individual labels in attribute networks. Physica A **512**, 523–536 (2018)
12. Rossetti, G., Cazabet, R.: Community discovery in dynamic networks: a survey. ACM Comput. Surv. **51**(2), 35 (2018)

13. Strehl, A., Ghosh, J.: Cluster ensembles - a knowledge reuse framework for combining multiple partitions. J. Mach. Learn. Res. **3**, 583–617 (2002)
14. Wang, C., Lai, J., Yu, P.S.: Neiwalk: community discovery in dynamic content-based networks. IEEE Trans. Knowl. Data Eng. **26**(7), 1734–1748 (2014)
15. Wang, X., Jin, D., Cao, X., Yang, L., Zhang, W.: Semantic community identification in large attribute networks. In: Proceedings of AAAI Conference on Artificial Intelligence, pp. 265–271 (2016)
16. Zhou, X., Liu, Y., Li, B., Li, H.: A multiobjective discrete cuckoo search algorithm for community detection in dynamic networks. Soft. Comput. **21**(22), 6641–6652 (2017)

A Social Relationships Enhanced Credit Risk Assessment Approach

Caihong Sun⬚, Chengcheng Deng, Wei Xu, and Jun Su$^{(\boxtimes)}$

School of Information, Renmin University of China, Beijing 100872, China
{chsun, weixu, sujun}@ruc.edu.cn,
dengchengchengruc@163.com

Abstract. With the rapid growth of personal loan applications, credit risk assessment has become very crucial both in academic and industrial domain. Research literatures show that besides "hard" information, such as individual socio-demographic information and loan application information, "soft" information such as social relationships of the borrowers is a key factor to the credit risk assessment as social capital. In social networks, a user's position and its influence are affected not only by the direct relationships (its friends) but also the indirect relationships (friends' friends). A user's importance and influence in his communities are attractive and valuable for credit assessment. But due to data deficiency in real life, social relationships are rarely considered in lending markets. By leveraging data from various sources, we proposed a social relationship enhanced credit risk assessment system, by building a social network from users' geolocation data, extracting social relationship features at three different levels: ego, community and global level to capture a user's position and influence from direct relationships, community and whole network perspectives. A real-life loan granting dataset is utilized for verifying the performance of the system. The experiment results show that, by combining the conventional financial indicators along with the proposed social network features, our system outperforms benchmark methods. Novel social network features we proposed make a good contribution to the loan default prediction. The research highlights the power of social relationships in detecting the default loans.

Keywords: Credit risk assessment · Feature engineering · Social network · Community detection

1 Introduction

Credit risk assessment is a crucial process for financial institutions for their operations and sustainable growth. Both the increasing volume of individual unsecured loans and fast-growing default risk highlight the importance of credit risk assessment. For instance, in China, the number of bad loans is 1.83% by the end of 2018 based on the China Banking Insurance Regulatory Commission's (CBIRC) report, higher than 1.74% in 2017. How to assess the credit risk more accurately has been a crucial and hot topic both in academic and industrial domain.

At the beginning, the assessment of credit risk mainly depended on subjective judgments such as the 5Cs rules which referring as character, capacity, capital,

C. Douligeris et al. (Eds.): KSEM 2019, LNAI 11775, pp. 222–233, 2019.
https://doi.org/10.1007/978-3-030-29551-6_20

condition and collateral, and LAPP which referring as liquidity, activity, profitability and potentialities. However, the booming of the credit industry made it impossible to assess thousands of applicants completely manually but to automate the process. Hence various machine learning credit scoring models have emerged to help financial institutions enforcing efficient credit approval [1, 2]. The main concern of credit risk assessment is how to classify the applicants into two types of groups: default and non-default. Then, the evaluator may decide to reject the loan application or approve it. For these binary classification problems, besides classification models, the feature selection is a key factor for the accuracy of models. In a traditional credit risk assessment system, individual socio-demographic information and loan application information are designed as input for feature engineering; however, in online lending market, such "hard" information is often deficient and not easy to be acquired and "soft" features are needed to enhance the performance. As Seth and Ginger [3] argued that "soft" information such as social relationships among borrowers, could make up for the devoid of some "hard" information. The importance of social relationships, i.e., social network, in credit assessment, has been proved by many researchers in online P2P lending market [2, 3, 11–13]. Due to deficiency of social network data in real life, social network features are not commonly used in credit risk assessment model yet. In this paper, we proposed a method to build social network from users' geolocation log, and then proposed novel social network features from the community, i.e. social group perspectives to enhance prediction ability.

We propose an assessment method that incorporates both conventional data, such as individual socio-demographic information and loan application information, and data of applicants' social relationships. Our method acquires social relationships by establishing social network from applicants' geolocations information. By proposing a social relationship enhanced credit risk assessment system, the main contribution of this research is in two areas: first, this work demonstrates how social relationships could be obtained from geolocation information, and different types of data (structured data and network data) could be fused to train machine learning algorithms. Second, we propose several novel network features at community level, to capture users' social group features. Five frequently used classification models are employed in our experiments and the experiment results show that social network features matter in credit risk assessment systems.

This paper proceeds as follows. Section 2 outlines previous studies related to this work. Section 3 introduces our system framework and the extraction method for social relationships. Section 4 analyzes the empirical results with using this method and Sect. 5 provides conclusions, discusses the limitations and identifies future work.

2   Related Work

Our work focuses on introducing social relationship to enhance the effectiveness of credit assessment risk. We mainly talk about literatures in two areas: features of credit risk assessment and measurements of social networks.

2.1 Features of Credit Risk Assessment

The accuracy of a predictive model depends heavily on the feature extraction and engineering. When it comes to credit risk assessment, three types of features have been explored in academic domain: personal, behavioral and social network features.

Personal features are about the personal characteristics of applicants (borrowers). In traditional credit market, banks utilized a set of credit scoring mechanism to evaluate the credit level of applicants, such as 5Cs rule and LAPP. Many researchers have used personal features in their predictive models, including age, income, telephone, marital condition, career, gender, family size, credit history, assets, saving account, residence, the number of credit cards etc. [4–9].

Behavioral features are about what the applicants have done, which include data about financial and transaction history. Avery et al. [4] used both personal information and transaction history (customers' usage history for a six months period and its aggregation), the local economic situation and personal circumstances (like medical emergency) into a linear probability regression to assess credit risk. Sustersic et al. [8] considered transaction history such as cash inflows, outflows and their aggregation into a NN algorithm to predict the credit risk. Financial histories and transaction data are considered as important features for their credit risk assessment [5–7, 9].

Besides above "hard" information, social network features, capturing the social relationships of the applicants, are mainly introduced in online P2P lending market. Social network is a kind of soft information which can be produced and used without financial intermediaries [13]. Granovette [10] argued that when solving financial problems, it should consider not only individual himself, but also the social embeddedness of the individuals, i.e., the individuals' social capital. Lin [11] found that in internet lending markets, social relationships did affect the borrower's behavior after lending. Lin et al. used the data from Proper.com, which is an American internet financial credit market platform, and found that social network information is highly related to the borrowers' credit [12]. Further studies showed that the more trustworthy their friends are, the more trustable the applicants are. In online P2P credit market, information of social networks (or social capital) could help predict the default risk [11, 13].

To sum up, besides "hard" information, social network features are useful for credit risk assessment [11–13]. But since social relationships are hard to acquire in offline financial market, few previous studies incorporate social network features into credit risk predictive models. We use information technology to harden the soft information. By using users' geolocation information reported by their mobile phones, we build applicants' social relationships and incorporate novel social network features into the credit risk predictive models.

2.2 Social Network Measurements

Social network measurements could be classified at different levels: ego network, community network, and whole network. Measurements of whole network tell the position and roles of a node in global level. While "Ego" is an individual "focal" node, if we want to understand variation in the behavior of individuals, we need to take a closer look at their local circumstances, neighborhood [14]. "Neighborhood" is the collection of ego and all nodes to whom ego has a connection at some path length (in our case we set path length to 1). Communities are associated with more highly interconnected parts in a social network. Identifying communities is crucial to the understanding of the structural properties of networks [18].

Network measures for ego networks consist of size, density, clustering coefficient etc., while network measures for whole networks mainly include betweenness, degree, average path length and degree distribution [13]. Community network measurements consist of size, density, the link ratio in and out community to measure the tightness of his community membership.

3   Social Relationships Enhanced Credit Risk Assessment Framework

Figure 1 illustrates the framework of our proposed system. There are four phases in the framework: data acquisition, data cleaning and processing, feature engineering and prediction models.

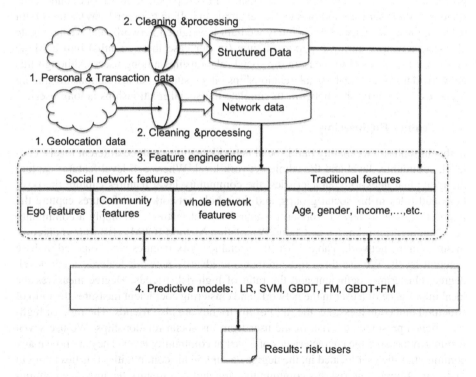

Fig. 1. Proposed credit risk assessment framework

3.1 Data Acquisition

The first phase is data acquisition. We picked a real-world credit data set, which contains two types of data: users' basic features and users' geolocation log data. The former consists of age, gender, years of working, the numbers of credit cards, marital status, which are the conventional features for credit risk prediction. The latter, users' geolocation data are gained by an app software. Via this app, users report the information about their geolocations and time which contain wifi name they connected, wifi address, check-in time and check-in location.

3.2 Data Cleaning and Processing

In the second phase, we clean and process the acquired data. Since basic features in our case are kinds of structured data, we just extract them into the structured database. We use the users' geolocation data to build social relationships among users. Inspire by [15–17], friendship network structure could be inferred by using mobile phone data and physical location. Hence, we use this spatial-temporal location information reported by users to presume users' social connections in real life. As friends tend to visit same places, we consider the number of co-occurrences and the number of locations that two people cooccurred as indicators of friendship. In this paper, if two users connect the same wifi at the same period of time (for example in half an hour, or 1 day), a tie is built between these two users. For each day we built a weighted network, and we aggregate all these networks during a period of time (in our case three months) into a whole network which is used to measure the social relationships among users. Although this network data is not real social relationships, it presumes some relationship among users. Here, we used this network to simulate the social relationships among users.

3.3 Feature Engineering

In the third phase, we mainly build social network features at three different levels: ego-level, community-level and the whole network level. Where ego-level features capture the individual network characteristics, the community level features capture the positions and roles in his social groups, and the whole network level features capture the importance in a society. To obtain community level features, we apply a community detection algorithm known as Clique Percolation Method (CPM) [18] to find all communities in the network. Table 1 lists the social network features we composed in three different levels. We use three measurements to identify network features at ego level: degree, clustering coefficient and the ratio of high-risk friends. Degree measures the local importance of a user in the network, and clustering coefficient measures the ratio of structural embeddedness, i.e. the ratio of his friends are also friends. The ratio of high-risk friends presumes the risk of the user from his social relationships. We use seven features to measure the characteristics of a user at community level. They are how many communities the user located in, the degree he sunk in his communities (his ties in or out of communities), how risk his communities are, and community features like community size, community density and degree dispersion. Finally, we use betweenness centrality to measure the user whole network characteristics. Betweenness centrality is to measure how importance a user is in controlling network communication aspect.

Table 1. Social network features.

Dimensions		Network features
Ego level (individual level)		Degree
		Clustering coefficient
		Ratio of high-risk friends
Community level	Individual	Number of communities he is in
		Number of neighbors in his communities
		Number of neighbors not in his communities
	Community	Ratio of high-risk users in communities
		Community size
		Community density
		Degree dispersion in community
Whole network level		Betweenness Centrality

Table 2. Basic features

Features	Descriptions
Age	User's age
Gender	Female: 0, Male: 1
Income	Annual income
Marital Status	Married: 1, Other: 0
The years he/she worked	Total years the user worked
Number of credit cards	How many credit cards the user has

Moreover, the basic features we extracted are listed in Table 2. They consist of users' age, gender, income, marital status, the years he/she worked, and the number of credit cards.

3.4   Predictive Models

In the fourth phase, we apply both social network and basic features into the predictive models and evaluate their performance. In our framework, five state-of-the-art models are used to test the effectiveness of our proposed social network features, i.e., LR, SVM, GBDT, FM and GBDT+FM.

We choose six measurements to evaluate the effectiveness of the predictive models: Accuracy, Recall, Precision, F-score, AUC and Logloss. The former four are measurements of model accuracy. AUC plots the true positive rate against the false positive rate. An AUC of 1 means a perfect classification whereas 0.5 refers to a random guess. Being more robust against prior distributions, AUC is considered by many researchers to be one of the best indicators of a classifier's performance. Logloss is a measure defined as the negative log-likelihood of the true labels given a probabilistic classifier's predictions, the smaller the value is, the better the prediction.

4 Experiment Analysis

In this section, we conduct several experiments to validate the effects of social network features based on LR, SVM, GBDT, FM and GBDT+FM models. We do the experiments by adding social network features or not to demonstrate the effectiveness of our proposed method.

4.1 Data Description and Basic Statistics

Two data sources provided by a company are used. One is the personal information of applicants for credit, which contains user ID, six basic features listed in Table 2 and one class label (1 as risk user and 0 as normal user). The other data is a user log data recording users' spatial-temporal location information reported by a mobile phone app software from February 1st to April 30th in an area of Guangzhou, China. Totally the users' geolocation data have 6361 users, and 2890096 log records containing information about user ID, wifi name, wifi address and connecting time, check-in time and check-in location. Among 6361 users, there are 993 high risk users are identified. As mentioned in Sect. 3.2, these geolocation data are used to build a social network among users. By deleting isolated users, we obtained a network with 2666 nodes (each node is an individual user), and 34683 links. There are 672 high-risk users. The average degree is around 26.

By applying CPM algorithm [18] to social network data (we set k = 6), we obtain 126 overlapped communities. There are 1212 users not belong to any community. The largest community contains 1272 users. One user locates in 90 communities. 442 of 672 high-risk users are located in at least one community. Three communities have no high-risk users and one community has 85.7% high-risk users which could be labelled as high-risk community.

Furthermore, we compute social network features mentioned in Table 1 and get basic features listed in Table 2 (Sect. 3.3). All the social network features and basic features are as our input features, and class label is 1 or 0 (1: high-risk users and 0: normal users). Now our credit risk assessment could be taken as a binary classification problem. We randomly choose 80% data as training set and the other 20% as testing data.

4.2 Evaluation Criteria

Any item in the prediction can be described with 4 types: True Positive (TP), False Positive (FP), False Negative (FN), and True Negative (TN). In credit risk assessment, a high FP is a serious problem for the prediction model, because it would lead to a high risk of capital loss for banks when lending money to a person who would actually default on the loan. In this paper, six commonly employed measures are applied to evaluate the model: Accuracy, Precision, Recall, F-score, AUC and Logloss. These evaluation criteria are introduced as follows:

$$Accuracy = \frac{(TP + TN)}{(TP + TN + FP + FN)} \tag{1}$$

$$Precision = \frac{TP}{(TP + FP)} \tag{2}$$

$$Recall = \frac{TP}{(TP + FN)} \tag{3}$$

$$F - score = \frac{2}{\frac{1}{Precision} + \frac{1}{Recall}} = \frac{2 * TP}{2 * TP + FP + FN} \tag{4}$$

The Area Under the Receiver Operating Characteristic (ROC) Curve (AUC) is a primary indicator when measuring the classifier without the influence of class distribution. The ROC curve is plotted to reveal the relation between the sensitivity and specificity, with sensitivity on the x-axis and specificity on the y-axis. AUC is the area under the ROC curve, ranging from 0 (no discrimination ability) to 1 (perfect discrimination ability).

Logloss is defined as $-\frac{1}{N} \sum_{i=1}^{N} (y_i \log p_i + (1 - y_i) \log(1 - p_i))$, where y_i is real class of data x_i, and p_i is the probability that sample x_i belongs to positive class. The smaller the value is, the better the prediction.

4.3 Experimental Design and Analysis

4.3.1 Experimental Design

We classified the model input as three parts: basic features, social network features (ego level + whole network level) and community level network features. To test the effectiveness of social network features, we set basic features input as baseline model, and then introduce social network features (ego level + whole network level) and community level network features respectively to explore the impacts of these network features impact on credit risk assessment. Table 3 summarizes our designed experiments. Baseline model only contains basic features, Model 1 inputs basic features with ego and whole network features, Model 2 inputs basic features and community network features, and Model 3 contains all the features. For each experiment in Table 3, we apply them into 5 state-of-the-art prediction models.

4.3.2 Experimental Results

Accuracy

Table 4 gives out the accuracy results of our experiments. We can see that except SVM, the accuracy of other 4 algorithms are improved by adding social network features. The accuracy performance of these 5 predictive models demonstrates SVM>GBDT+FM>GBDT>FM>LR. For further investigation, we found that SVM classify all the test data into normal users (class labeled 0), with both Recall and Precision equal to 0. The AUC of SVM is 0.5. So, the high accuracy of SVM is meaningless. we remove SVM algorithm from our further evaluation and discussion.

Table 3. Experimental design

Experiments	Input Features
Baseline	Basic features
Model 1	Basic features + Social network features (ego+whole)
Model 2	Basic features + Social network features (Community)
Model 3	Basic features + All Social network Features

Table 4. Accuracy metric

	LR	SVM	GBDT	FM	GBDT+FM
Baseline	0.533	0.7598	0.665	0.568	0.731
Model 1	0.578	0.7598	0.683	0.638	0.740
Model 2	0.598	0.7598	0.728	0.623	0.754
Model 3	0.602	0.7598	0.704	0.630	0.746

Recall, Precision and F-score

Figure 2 shows the Recall, Precision and F-score performance of LR, GBDT, FM and GBDT+FM in different 4 experiment settings. In LR, by adding social network features, Recall has almost no change, but Precision and F-Score performance improve a little. In GBDT and GBDT+FM, by comparison of baseline model, Recall, Precision and F-score improve by adding social network features. But in FM, there is no improvement in Recall, Precision and F-score which are need to be investigated further. LR has the highest Recall and F-score value, and GBDT+FM has the highest Precision and Accuracy value.

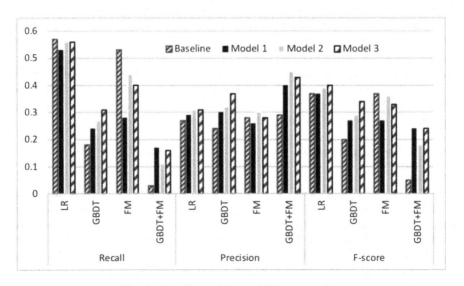

Fig. 2. Recall, precision and F-score metrics

AUC and Logloss

AUC and Logloss are two indicators for the model quality. Figure 3 shows that in the same algorithm, social network features could improve AUC and Logloss values. Among the four algorithms, GBDT+FM demonstrates the higher value of AUC. Logloss has no change in LR algorithm by adding social network features, but in GBDT, FM and GBDT+FM, logloss improve a little. Among the four algorithms, LR has the lowest logloss and accuracy.

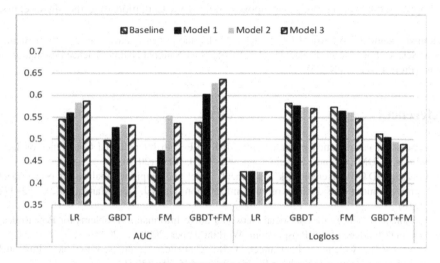

Fig. 3. AUC and logloss metrics

In sum, our experiment results demonstrate that by introducing social network features, except SVM, which cannot identify the high-risk users, all other four predictive models outperform the baseline model (without social network features) by examining six evaluation metrics. Social network features have impact on credit risk prediction.

5   Conclusions, Limitations and Future Work

In this study, we proposed a social relationship enhanced credit risk prediction framework by collecting data from different sources. By building a social network from users' geolocation data, we extract social network features in dimensions at ego, community and the whole network level. Credit risk prediction improves by introducing the novel social network features. Our study demonstrates that social network features are valuable to credit risk prediction and gives out a practical way to acquire social network data and employ feature engineering. Our work gives an insight on obtaining soft information for credit risk assessment performance improvement, such as how to build social relationships from users' mobile phone check in data, and how to construct network features at different levels, especially in community level.

But from the experiment results, the improvement by adding social network features is not large. The method we used to build social network is naïve, further we can apply the algorithms mentioned in [15–17] to rebuild the social network.

Future work can be developed in the following directions. Firstly, although this work has verified the significance of social network features on credit risk assessment, further study needs to done in extracting network features automatically. For instance, we plan to test our data on graph-based deep learning methods, such as Graph Neural Network (GNN), and Deep FM for their powers of feature engineering. Moreover, we will apply more datasets on our proposed framework to demonstrate its effectiveness.

Acknowledgement. We would like to acknowledge the partial financial support from Beijing Social Science Foundation (Project No. 17GLC056) and National Natural Science Foundation of China (Project No. 91546125).

References

1. Rendle, S.: Factorization machines. In: 2010 IEEE 10th International Conference on Data Mining (ICDM), Sydney, Australia, pp. 995–1000. IEEE (2010)
2. Li, Z.: GBDT-SVM credit risk assessment model and empirical analysis of peer-to-peer borrowers under consideration of audit information. Open J. Bus. Manag. **06**(2), 362–372 (2018)
3. Freedman, S., Jin, G.Z.: Do Social Networks Solve Information Problems for Peer-to-Peer Lending? Evidence from Prosper.com. Working Paper, 2008.11 (2008)
4. Avery, R.B., Calem, P.S., Canner, G.B.: Consumer credit scoring: do situational circumstances matter. J. Banking Finance **28**(4), 835–856 (2004)
5. Harris, T.: Quantitative credit risk assessment using support vector machines: broad versus narrow default definitions. Expert Syst. Appl. **40**(11), 4404–4413 (2013)
6. Liberati, C., Camillo, F.: Personal values and credit scoring: new insights in the financial prediction. J. Oper. Res. Soc. **69**(12), 1994–2005 (2018)
7. Sinnha, A.P., Zhao, H.: Incorporating domain knowledge into data mining classifiers: an application in indirect lending. Decis. Support Syst. **46**(1), 287–299 (2008)
8. Susterstic, M., Mramor, D., Zupan, J.: Consumer credit scoring models with limited data. Expert Syst. Appl. **36**(3), 4736–4744 (2008)
9. Zhang, T., Zhang, W., Xu, W., Hao, H.: Multiple instance learning for credit risk assessment with transaction data. Knowl.-Based Syst. **161**, 65–77 (2018)
10. Granovette, M.: Economic action and social structure: the problem of embeddedness. Am. J. Sociol. **91**(3), 481–510 (1985)
11. Lin, M.F.: Peer-to-peer lending: an empirical study. In: The 15th Americas Conference on Information Systems, AIS eLibrary, P8, San Francisco, USA (2009)
12. Greiner, M.E., Wang, H.: The role of social capital in people-to-people lending marketplaces. In: International Conference on Information Systems, DBLP (2009)
13. Lin, M.F., Prabhala, N., Viswanathan, S.: Judging borrowers by the company they keep: friendship networks and information asymmetry in online peer-to-peer lending. Soc. Sci. Electron. Publishing **59**(1), 17–35 (2013)
14. Hanneman, R., Riddle, M.: Introduction to Social Network Methods. University of California, Publisher (2005)

15. Eagle, N., Pentland, A.S., Lazer, D.: Inferring friendship network structure by using mobile phone data. Proc. Nat. Acad. Sci. **106**(36), 15274–15278 (2009)
16. Cranshaw, J., Toch, E., Hong, J., Kittur, A., Sadeh, N.: Bridging the gap between physical location and online social networks. In: Proceedings of the 12th ACM International Conference on Ubiquitous Computing, pp. 119–128. ACM (2010)
17. Crandall, D.J., Backstrom, L., Cosley, D., Suri, S., Huttenlocher, D., Kleinberg, J.: Inferring Social Ties from Geographic Coincidences. Proc. Nat. Acad. Sci. **107**(52), 22436–22441 (2010)
18. Palla, G., Derényi, I., Farkas, I., Vicsek, T.: Uncovering the overlapping community structure of complex networks in nature and society. Nature **435**(7043), 814–818 (2005)

Context Aware Community Formation for MAS-Oriented Collective Adaptive System

Wei Liu[1,2(✉)], Jingzhi Guo[2], Longlong Xu[2], and Deng Chen[2]

[1] Hubei Province Key Laboratory of Intelligent Robot,
Wuhan Institute of Technology, Wuhan, China
liuwei@wit.edu.cn
[2] School of Computer Science and Engineering,
Wuhan Institute of Technology, Wuhan, China

Abstract. Forming an effective collaboration community is the key to any successful collaborative process. However, community formation approaches for the closed multi-agent systems may be not fit the need of collective adaptive system comprising multi-agent in open environment. We propose a context aware community formation approach (CFAgentColla) for agent collaboration in open MAS. We employ ontology-based matching and calculation techniques to search for an optimized alternative capability of an agent or to generate a commitment according to the capabilities of two collaborative agents. Then, we define an adaptive goal model and propose an executable tree strategy to generate an optimal collaboration protocol according to the goals, capabilities and commitments. Additionally, we illustrate CFAgentColla approach with a real-world medical waste automated guided vehicle transportation scenario and evaluate the feasibility of our approach by validating the mainly executive parameters and by comparing with the planning approach.

Keywords: Agent collaboration · Semantic calculation ·
AGV-based simulation

1 Introduction

Collective adaptive system (CAS) is inherently scalable, and its boundaries are fluid in the sense that components may enter or leave the collective at any time; thus, CAS must dynamically adapt to environmental conditions and contextual data [1]. In terms of multi-agent systems (MAS), "they are especially suited to develop software systems that are decentralized, can deal flexibly with dynamic conditions and are open to system components that come and go" [2]. These properties make agent-based techniques valuable for the development of CAS. An autonomous agent has the ability to perceive its environment, which helps to monitor the parameters of the context that may vary [3]. As the components of CAS, autonomous agents must be capable of adapting their individual behaviors or coordinating their social behaviors over time to achieve a set of goals in an ever-changing environment.

Agent-oriented adaptation approaches have gone through the process from goal/action selection for individual goal to goal/commitment selection for a shared goal.

© Springer Nature Switzerland AG 2019
C. Douligeris et al. (Eds.): KSEM 2019, LNAI 11775, pp. 234–246, 2019.
https://doi.org/10.1007/978-3-030-29551-6_21

The goal/action selection mechanisms, such as the BDI (Belief-Desire-Intention) approach [4] and GAAM-based approach [5], help an agent select a suitable task from a task list to pursue an individual goal and it holds the key for the behavior autonomy of an agent. The goal/commitment selection approaches originate from the insight that agents' interactions, including creating and processing commitments according to what is called the commitment lifecycle. The commitment protocol to be created among participants is to combine the collaborative patterns [6]. Dalpiaz et al. [7] consider subsets of the goal model and consequently select a subset of the known commitments predefined in design time. Akin et al. [8] provide an algorithm to generate possible commitment protocols by selecting the one of generated protocol that best suits the agent. However, most previous works assume that the possible participants are researched from single neighborhood systems [9]. Although these solutions do not limit agents to communicate with only a subset of operating agents in the system, they are not efficient when the number of agents in the system increases.

In CAS, agents need to form effective collaboration communities consisting of agents which are willing to collaborate for the globe goal and do not have any conflicting goals. Most community formation approaches for the closed multi-agent systems do not readily apply to CAS applications for two major reasons. (i) Shared goals are necessary for CAS. Shared goals enable all participating agents to synchronize to achieve more complex goals that require collaborative execution. Most of the previous approaches make no reference to shared goals and only focus on the goals of individual agents [8, 10, 11]. Global goals, including individual goals and shared goals, must be modeled for agent collaboration in CAS. (ii) New neighborhoods for uncertain collaboration community. Agents in uncertain collaboration community have the option to change their behaviors from one community to another when they cannot achieve their goals (individual/shared) in the initial collaboration community. The single neighborhood and disjoint neighborhoods [12] approaches defined static structures, which are impractical in open system, because agents join and leave the community unpredictably.

To address these challenges, we proposed a goal-capability-commitment (GCC) mediation approach called GCCM [13]. There are three kernel elements in GCC model: goal, capability and commitment. The goal defined in GCCM is global goal, which is divided into two categories, individual goal and shared goal. An individual goal could be achieved by a capability; besides, the collaboration between agents provides a possibility for achieving the shared goal by a commitment which is a larger-grained element than the capability. However, global goals in the previous approaches denote the goals that are shared among all participating agents in the system. Ignorance of agent neighborhood structure was impractical in an open system for the too large search scope for the capabilities or the commitments in the whole system, which results in too long execution time and hinders the availability of the system. Furthermore, the executed annotation represented with flow expressions should be appended to the tree structure of the goal model, which enables goals to be viewed as runtime artifacts for representing and reasoning about CAS requirements. In this context, we proposed a context aware community formation for MAS-oriented adaptive collaboration systems called CFAgentColla. The main contributions of this article includes: (1) a strategy for organizing the agents as overlap neighborhood in CFAgentColla and consider either collaborative dependency when forming collaboration community; (2) a framework for introducing runtime goal modeling into collective decision making to capture the real-time requirements and generating a executive decision flow at runtime.

2   Goal-Capability-Commitment Model

Goal, capability and commitment are three kernel elements in GCC model. The goals defined in the GCC model are global goals. Individual goal (IG) describes the states that an agent wants to achieve or the states that it wants to maintain, which is achieved by the execution of capabilities from a single agent. For example, AGV charging is a typical IG. Shared goal (SG) describes the states that a system wants to achieve or the states that it wants to maintain, which is achieved by the execution of the commitments from the agents in the same collaboration community. For example, obstacle avoidance with machine vision is a typical SG. Figure 1 describes the relationships between the three kernel elements and the environment. A shared goal is decomposed into shared goals or individual goals. After an IG is achieved, it will only affect the states of the agent itself. After a SG is achieved, it will affect the states of the system or the environment.

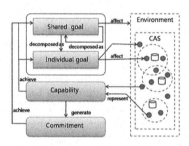

Fig. 1. The function of GCC elements for CAS

Definition 1 (Goals). Let Π_A be the set of agents participating in the system, Π_C be a finite set of context snapshots, G be the set of goal names, and Π_G be the set of globe goals defined as follows:

$$\Pi_G = \{g(S_a, C_T, S_F) | g \in G \;\&\; S_a \sqsubseteq \Pi_A \;\&\; C_T, S_F \sqsubseteq \Pi_C\}$$

$g(S_a, C_T, S_F)$ means that a context snapshot in the final states S_F will be held by the agents S_a when the context snapshots in the trigger conditions C_T are held. If S_a has only one agent, then g is a individual goal; if S_a includes more than two agents, then g is a shared goal.

Definition 2 (Capability). Let Π_A be the set of agents participating in the system, Π_{CS} be a finite set of context snapshots, L_a be the set of lists of activities C be the set of capability names, and Π_C be the set of capabilities defined as follows:

$$\Pi_C = \{c(Act, C_I, C_U, P) | c \in C \& Act \sqsubseteq \Pi_A \& C_I, C_U \sqsubseteq \Pi_{CS} \& P \in L_a\}$$

$c(Act, C_I, C_U, P)$ means that a capability c held by an agent Act provides knowledge about that agent's ability to perform an activity. In-constraints C_I denote the preconditions for the capability to execute. Out-constraints C_U include the goal states achieved by and the effects of executing c. P is an ordered sequence of n activities (p $\{a_1, \ldots a_n\}, a_1, \ldots a_n \in A$), where A is the set of activities. The various plans of an agent for achieving the same goal under different environments can be represented abstractly by different capabilities.

In order to overcome the limitations of invariant number of primitive capabilities of agents, composite capabilities will be generated in some future world when the agents act rationally. Commitment means that an agent as a debtor is committed to another agent as a creditor for the consequence if the antecedent holds. In GCC model, commitment represents a collaborative relationship between two agents according to their capabilities.

Definition 3 (Commitment). Let Π_A be the set of agents participating in the system, Π_{Ca} be the set of agent capabilities, Co be the set of capability names, and Π_{Co} be the set of commitments defined as follows:

$$\Pi_{Co} = \{co(D, C, O, Q) | co \in Co \ \&Ant, Con \sqsubseteq \Pi_C \ \& \ D, C \in \Pi_A\}$$

D is the debtor of the commitment, C is the creditor of the commitment, O is the antecedent of the commitment, and Q is the consequence of the commitment. Compared with previous representations of agent commitment [8], the antecedent and consequent of commitment in GCC model are not propositional variables but context snapshots. The commitment generation at runtime depends on the semantic matchmaking between the constraints of agent capabilities for achieving the shared goal.

In our previous work [13], the semantic implication among the sets of context snapshots is analyzed through the similarity degree of two concepts in context snapshots. Similarity degree of two concepts is calculated by a tree based concept similarity measurement approach (RNCVM) [14]. There are two sets of context snapshots S_i and S_j. S_j semantically implies S_i (denoted as $S_j \Rightarrow S_i$) means that if all the context snapshots in S_j are all held, then all the context snapshots in S_i must also be held. Analyzing the semantic implication relation among the sets of context snapshots can play a key role in determining what state constraints of GCC elements (goal, capability and commitment) can be met in the current environment.

3 Community Formation Framework for Agent Collaboration

The steps of community formation for CFAgentColla approach are summarized in Fig. 2. At the beginning (step 1), the states of all the goals are checked according to the rules of invalidation diagnosis with the assistant of goal model and context snapshot model. Then, the executed goal flow expression (*gfe*) is generated by using the recursion algorithm of depth-first traversal. Step 1 and step 2 are the mainly subprocesses of *goal model update*. If all the goals in the *gfe* could be achieved under current agent community, the next process will go to the step 5 to generate a protocol. If some goals in *gfe* could not be achieved by all the capabilities of agents in the same community, the next step will translate into generation of the commitment according to the capabilities of agents in the same community and choice of optimum achievers for all executed goals with the assistant of capability and commitment (C&C) model (step 3). If some goals are still could not be achieved in one community, then the next step will try to negotiate with other agents outside the community and enrich the community ontology to achieve the goal (step 4). Finally, an adaptive protocol is generated by representing as a C&C execution flow expression in step 5. Step 3 to step 5 are the mainly sub-processes of *participant nomination*.

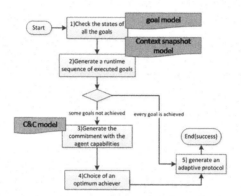

Fig. 2. Steps of CFAgentColla approach

3.1   Goal Model Update

In the multi-tree of goals, the goals represented as branch nodes, are achieved by the sub-goals, and the sub-goals without sub-goals, represented as leaf nodes, are achieved by capabilities or commitments. The executed annotation represented with flow expressions is added to each goal as an attachment, which enables goals to be viewed as runtime artifacts for representing and reasoning about CAS requirements. In flow expressions, the operators; (sequential), | (alternative), opt() (optional), * (zero or more), + (one or more), and # (shuffle) allow us to specify sequences of global goals that constitute a valid execution at runtime [15].

Definition 4 (Goal tree). Let Π_G be the set of goals and L_{fe} be the language of flow expression

$$G_T = \{n(g_A, fe) \mid g_A \in \Pi_G \& fe \in L_{fe}\}$$

$n(g_A, fe)$ means that a tree node representing a goal g_A and the decomposed information of its sub-goals are described in fe. The flow expressions fe represent the control construct among goals. If the fe of a goal represents the control construct among its sub-goals, then the C_T and S_F of the goal are empty, which means the goal will be achieved by the sub-goals. If the fe of a goal is null, the goal should be achieved by the capability of an individual agent or by a commitment of collaboration among agents.

For example in Fig. 3, the C_T and S_F of transport_medical_waste (g_0, "$g_1;g_2;g_3;$opt(g_4) $g_5;g_6$") are empty, and a shared goal transport_cart_with_elevator (g_9, "") has null fe.

Achieving the executed goal is the mainly reason for collaboration community formation. The goal model update process includes 2 sub-processes: invalids diagnoser and executed goal flow generation.

In first sub-process, we use invalidation diagnoser to check the states of all the goals. The following rules are utilized in the invalidation diagnosis in the following situations. (1) If a change in the environment context causes the trigger condition of a goal to be not true, then the goal need not be achieved. (2) If a change in the environment context or agent context causes the constraints of a capability (or a commitment) to be not true, then the capability (or the commitment) cannot achieve any goal. (3) If the debtor capability or the creditor capability of the commitment is in $Inactive(I)$, then the executing commitment has no ability to achieve the goal under the current state. In the result of invalidation diagnoser, the goals in $Terminated(T)$ will be check in the future states of environment and the goals in $Suspend(U)$ will be denoted as be valid.

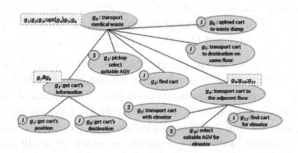

Fig. 3. A goal model with the flow expressions for AGV-MST

In second sub-process, according to the valid goals, we use flow generation component to generate a runtime sequence of executed goals. (1) After using the depth-first traversal of a multi-tree, a multi-tree of goal G_T is built in which the sequence of valid goals with the same super goal at the same level follow the flow expressions of their super goal. For example, the sequence of g_1–g_5 is set up following the flow expressions of super goal g_0. (2) We use a recursion algorithm of depth-first traversal and generate a flow expression containing the executed goals. For example, when hasStatus(currentPath, smooth) = true, the flow expression "$g_7\#g_8;g_2;g_3;g_5;g_6$" is generated; when hasStatus(currentPath, block) = true, the goal flow expression (gfe) "$g_7\#g_8;g_2;g_3;g_9;g_{10};g_{11};g_5;g_6$" is generated. The flow expression of a goal represents the execution order of sub-goals.

3.2 Participant Nomination

The collaboration community is formed based on the request of the first agent, called the initiator, which decides to collaborate with other agents. The initiators invoke the related agents, by knowing about the agents' capabilities, choose the collaborator and establish some commitments to form the community.

Nominated agents include initiators and collaborators. Initiator nomination and collaborator nomination are implemented by commitment compensation. In an open environment, the share goal is not constant, depending on whether the capabilities provided by the agent in the community can meet the goal individually. The process of commitment compensation comprises the following steps.

The first step is generation of the commitment according to the capabilities. Different collective forms may generate different types of commitments. Two types of commitments exist according to the generating methods: cooperated commitment and assisted commitment.

Definition 5 (Commitment generation). Given a goal g (S_a, C_T, S_F, fe) and a capability $c_i(Act_i, C_{Ii}, C_{Ui}, P_i)$,

(1) if there is the other capability $c_j(Act_j, C_{Ij}, C_{Uj}, P_j)$, $C_T \Rightarrow C_{Ii} \cup C_{Ij}$ and $C_{Ui} \cup C_{Uj} \Rightarrow S_F$, then a **cooperated commitment** co_c (D, C, O, Q) is generated, $C_C = a_i$, $D = a_j$, $O = C_{Ii} \cup C_{Ij}$ and $Q = C_{Ui} \cup C_{Uj}$;
(2) if there is another capability $c_j(Act_j, C_{Ij}, C_{Uj}, P_j)$, $C_T \Rightarrow C_{Ii}$, $C_T \cup C_{Ui} \Rightarrow C_{Ij}$ and $C_{Ui} \cup C_{Uj} \Rightarrow S_F$, then an **assisted commitment** co_a (D, C, O, Q) is generated, $C = a_i$, $D = a_j$, $O = C_{Ii}$ and $Q = C_{Ui} \cup C_{Uj}$.

The two types of commitment are generated in different situations. On the one hand, a cooperated commitment is generated in the situation, in which each of the two capabilities of the collaborative agents supports part of the goal and they can execute simultaneously. Either of the agent Act_i and the agent Act_j can have the capabilities can be nominated as initiator, and the other as a collaborator. On the other hand, an assisted commitment is generated in the other situation, in which the result of one capability will invoke the other capability. Since only the capability of the agent Act_i to execute will trigger conditions of the agent Act_i's capability. We will nominate Act_i as initiator and nominate Act_j as collaborator.

The semantic matching between a goal and a commitment is analyzed by determining the semantic implication between the contextual constraints of the goal and the commitment.

Definition 6 (Commitment matching). Consider a goal $g(S_a, C_T, S_F, fe)$ and a commitment co (D, C, O, Q). Commitment co semantically matches Goal g:

$Match_{plug-in}$ $(co, g) \bigwedge As = C_C.actor \cup D_C.actor$ iff$] = (C_T \Rightarrow O) \bigwedge (Q \Rightarrow S_F)$

$Match_{plug-in}$ (co, g) means the trigger conditions of $g(C_T)$ semantically imply the antecedent of $co(O)$, and the consequent of $co(Q)$ semantically implies the final states of $g(U)$. The debtor and creditor of co are different agents with different capabilities. When two capabilities belonging to an agent can work together to achieve a goal, not a new commitment but rather a new capability with greater granularity consisting of the two capabilities will be generated.

The second step is choice of the optimum commitment. When a goal cannot be achieved by any single agent, an agent must try to form a community with other agents. The achiever of a goal may be a capability from a single agent or a commitment from a community. If there are more than one capability (or commitment) could achieve a goal. We need to choose an optimum achiever to achieve the goal. An optimum achiever with the highest semantic matching degree (*SMD*) implies that it is best suited to achieving the goal under the current state.

We use RNCVM as the foundation to calculate the *SD* between two context snapshots and calculate the *SMD*. We calculate the *SMD* through the following two steps: (1) calculate the semantic distance (*SD*) between two context snapshots and (2) calculate the *SMD* between a goal and a capability (or a commitment).

First, the prerequisite for calculating the *SD* between two context snapshots cs_i and cs_j is that they have a semantic contains relation, which is denoted as $SD(cs_i, cs_j)$. Two forms of context snapshots exist: $C(x)$ and $P(x, y)$. Second, the calculation of the *SMD* between a goal and a matched capability is based on the *SD* between the context snapshots belonging to the constraints of the goal and capability. The *SMD* between a goal $g(S_a, C_T, S_F, fe)$ and a capability $c(Act, C_I, C_U, P)$ is calculated by Eq. 1:

$$SMD(g,c) = \frac{\sum_1^m SD(cs_i, cs_t) + \sum_1^n SD(cs_f, cs_u)}{m+n} \tag{1}$$

Where m is the number of context snapshots in C_I, while $cs_f \in C_I$ and $cs_t \in C_T$, and n is the number of context snapshots in S_F, while $cs_f \in S_F$ and $cs_u \in C_U$. All the *SMDs* between the goal and matched capabilities are calculated, and the capability with the highest *SMD*, which implies that the capability is most suitable to achieve the goal under the current state, is chosen.

The *SMD* between a goal $g(S_a, C_T, S_F, fe)$ and a commitment $co\ (D_C, C_C, O, Q)$ is calculated by Eq. 2:

$$SMD(g,co) = \frac{\sum_1^p SD(cso, csi) + \sum_1^q SD(csu, csf)}{p+q} \tag{2}$$

Where p is the number of context snapshots in O, while $cs_o \in O$ and $cs_i \in CT$; and q is the number of context snapshots in S_F, while $cs_u \in Q$ and $cs_f \in S_F$.

Agents that provide two capabilities for generating the commitment with the highest *SMD* form the community. Under ever-changing environment, when the goals in *Terminated(T)* or the commitment is in *Pending(P)*, the community will be disband. In addition, when an agent supports a capability in another commitment, the agent also belongs to another community. In the ideal case, every goal in *gfe* can be achieved by at least a capability or a commitment, and, likewise, the corresponding capability and commitment are active under the current context states. The adaptive protocol is represented by the operators in the flow expressions and the elements in $\Pi_C \times V_{SMD}$ or $\Pi_{Co} \times V_{SMD}$. V_{SMD} is the set of *SMD* values.

4   Evaluation

In this section we describe the prototype implementation. We introduce the evaluation of experiments carried out to evaluate CFAgentColla approach in the medical waste automated guided vehicle (AGV) transportation domain. We performed these experiments on an Intel Core (TM) i5-6200 2.4 GHz processor with 8 GB memory running Windows 10 professional edition.

4.1   Experiment 1

In the first experiment, we observed the effect of goals quantity and capability quantity on the execution performance of the goal and capability modeling without commitment (GoCo) and the on the execution performance of CFAgentColla. The matching rate of all goals (*MRG*) and the execution time were the main focus of the evaluation.

We investigated the *SMD* and *MRG* of GoCo and CFAgentColla. Because the 2D scatter plot has a large number of overlapping results, we use a 3D scatter plot to clearly visualize each goal's *SMD*. Including more capabilities in the C&C model can result in higher *MRG*; thus, in this experiment, we set $\alpha = 30$. The *MRG* in CFAgentColla (shown in Fig. 4(b)) is higher than the *MRG* in GoCo (shown in Fig. 4(a)) for the same number of executed goals. For example, when $\alpha = 30$ and $\beta = 9$, the *MRG* of GoCo is 0.88 and the *MRG* of CFAgentColla is close to 1. When $\alpha = 30$ and $\beta = 18$, the *MRG* of GoCo is 0.44 and the *MRG* of CFAgentColla is 0.67. When $\alpha = 30$ and $\beta = 36$, the *MRG* in GoCo is 0.22 and the MRG in CFAgentColla is 0.36. The most plausible reason for this phenomenon is related to the limited capabilities and unlimited commitments. When the goals of CASs are constructed as a dynamic goal model containing a large number of goals, then the *MRG* in CFAgentColla has additional remarkable advantages.

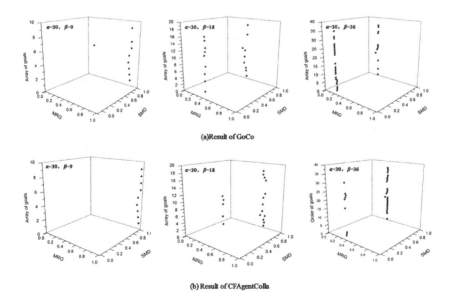

(a)Result of GoCo

(b) Result of CFAgentColla

Fig. 4. Comparison of the MRG/SMD in TR and CFAgentColla based on the number of goals (β) and number of capabilities (α)

Figure 4 shows that the *MRG* gradually decreases with multifold growth in the number of assistant goals, which is the limitation of our experiment cases, in which the assistant goals are modeled by randomly changing the constraints of the executed goals and the assistant capabilities are modeled by randomly changing the constraints of the kernel capabilities. As more assistant goals are introduced into the goal model, it becomes difficult to increase *MRG* significantly by increasing the number of assistant capabilities alone. However, the evidence suggests that the degree of closeness between capabilities and goals has a direct influence on the execution effect of CFAgentColla.

4.2   Experiment 2

In the second experiment, we compared our previous protocol generation approach (CCP) [16] and the CFAgentColla approach. Under an open environment, the CFAgentColla approach tends to have a faster response speed and less impact on other modules than does CCP approach.

In our previous work, a graph-plan-based capability compensation planning (CCP) approach was proposed to generate collaborative protocols for the self-adaptation of multi-agent cooperative systems. The CCP approach defined the meta-model of capability and commitment model for self-adaptation (CC-SA) and proposed a CCP algorithm to generate an adaptive protocol under a dynamic environment. The CCP approach improved the traditional graph planning method, which first expanded and then optimized. CCP can select an appropriate optimization execution scheme for the current environment and enrich the executability of CAS by means of capability cooperation among agents.

We implemented the MWT-AGV scenario in both the CCP approach and the CFAgentColla approach. The experiment is based on the assumption that the path to the destination waste dump is clear in case I and blocked in case II. We build two context snapshot ontologies and denote them as csmodel1.owl and csmodel2.owl. We suppose that the environment changes from "currentPath is smooth" to "currentPath is block". When hasStatus (currentPath, block) = true, cs_{10}: sameFloor (AGV_floor, destination _floor) is not in *csmodel2.owl*, so a capability or a commitment is acquired to translate the current context snapshots into cs_{10}. No existing capability can achieve this task; thus, a commitment *co* need to be is generated.

Figure 5 shows the analysis processes of CCP and CFAgentColla for the adaptive protocol generation. A new planning graph is generated when the *csmodel1.owl* file is replaced by the *csmodel2.owl* file. A new execution flow expression *efe* adding a commitment is generated, which is reflected in the change of planning graph. In Fig. 5 (a), the goal model is presented as an executable tree in CFAgentColla approach. First, the *goalmodel.owl* file and the csmodel1.owl file are input into *Protocol generation* component; then, the *csmodel1.owl* file is replaced by the *csmodel2.owl* file. In this case, g_4 is awakened. A new gfe "$g_7 \# g_8; g_2; g_3; g_9; g_{10}; g_{11}; g_5; g_6$" is generated to achieve the goals in case II. Then a new execution flow expression *efe* is generated when the context snapshot model changes, which is the same as the *efe* in the CCP approach. Two *efe* both include a commitment and some capabilities.

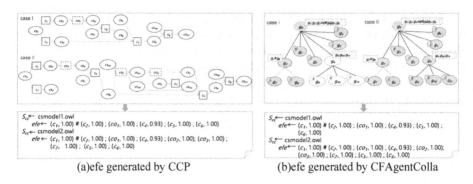

(a)efe generated by CCP   (b)efe generated by CFAgentColla

Fig. 5. CCP and CFAgentColla under changing environment

We conducted another experiment in which we used the same scenario and fixed the number of capabilities in CCmodel.owl to compare the response times of the CCP approach and the CFAgentColla approach. Response time (T_R) refers to the time cost of the generation of an adaptive protocol when the context snapshot model changes. We assume that the environment changes from case I to case II. Under this assumption, the T_R required for the two approaches is compared. The results in Fig. 6 show that the T_R of each approach does not change substantially with the change in the number of capabilities. However, given the same number of capabilities, the T_R of the E-Tree approach is less than one-half that in the CCP approach. We believe that in the case of a change in environment, CFAgentColla needs only to rematch new capabilities or generate new commitments for failed goals, whereas CCP needs to re-execute all the subsequent planning steps, which increases T_R.

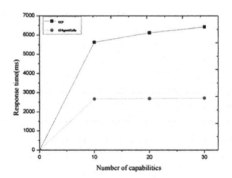

Fig. 6. Comparison of T_R with CCP and CFAgentColla based on the number of capabilities

5   Conclusion

In this paper, we have introduced a context aware community formation approach for agent collaboration in collective adaptive system. On the one hand, GCC modeling provides a foundation for employing ontology-based matching and calculation techniques to generate commitments or search for an optimized alternative capability (or commitment) to achieve the global goals under ever-changing environments. It overcomes the shortage of the previous approaches which make no reference to shared goals and focus on the goals of individual agents. On the other hand, community formation framework for agent collaboration put forwards a strategy for organizing the agents as overlap neighborhood in CFAgentColla according to their collaborative relationship based on generated commitments at runtime. It better than the single neighborhood and disjoint neighborhoods approaches defined static structures.

Acknowledgment. This work was supported by the National Natural Science Foundation of China under Grant (No. 61502355), Science and Technology Research Project of Hubei Provincial Department of Education (No. Q20181508).

References

1. Abd Alrahman, Y., Nicola, R.D., Loreti, M.: A behavioural theory for interactions in collective-adaptive systems (2017)
2. Weyns, D., Haesevoets, R., Helleboogh, A., et al.: The MACODO middleware for context-driven dynamic agent organizations. ACM Trans. Auton. Adapt. Syst. **5**(1), 3 (2010)
3. Liu, J.: Autonomous agents and multi-agent systems: explorations in learning. Self-organization and Adaptive Computation. Phys. Med. Biol. **32**(3), 327–334 (2001)
4. Singh, D., et al.: Learning context conditions for BDI plan selection. In: International Conference on Autonomous Agents and Multi-agent Systems DBLP, pp. 325–332 (2010)
5. Salehie, M., Tahvildari, L.: Towards a goal-driven approach to action selection in self-adaptive software. Softw. Pract. Exp. **42**(2), 211–233 (2012)
6. Fornara, N., Viganò, F., Colombetti, M.: Agent communication and artificial institutions. Auton. Agent. Multi-Agent Syst. **14**(2), 121–142 (2007)
7. Dalpiaz, F., Chopra, A.K., Giorgini, P., Mylopoulos, J.: Adaptation in open systems: giving interaction its rightful place. In: Parsons, J., Saeki, M., Shoval, P., Woo, C., Wand, Y. (eds.) ER 2010. LNCS, vol. 6412, pp. 31–45. Springer, Heidelberg (2010). https://doi.org/10.1007/978-3-642-16373-9_3
8. Akin, G., Michael, W., Yolum, P.: Dynamically generated commitment protocols in open systems. Auton. Agent. Multi-Agent Syst. **29**(2), 192–229 (2015)
9. Ye, D., Zhang, M., Sutanto, D.: Self-adaptation-based dynamic coalition formation in a distributed agent network: a mechanism and a brief survey. IEEE Trans. Parallel Distrib. Syst. **24**(5), 1042–1051 (2013)
10. Bucchiarone, A., Mezzina, C.A., Raik, H.: A goal model for collective adaptive systems. In: IEEE Eighth International Conference on Self-Adaptive and Self-Organizing Systems Workshops, pp. 20–25. IEEE (2014)
11. Loreti, M., Hillston, J.: Modelling and analysis of collective adaptive systems with CARMA and its tools. In: Bernardo, M., De Nicola, R., Hillston, J. (eds.) SFM 2016. LNCS, vol. 9700, pp. 83–119. Springer, Cham (2016). https://doi.org/10.1007/978-3-319-34096-8_4
12. Gaston, M.E., des Jardins, M.: Agent-organized networks for dynamic team formation. In: Proceedings of the Fourth International Joint Conference on Autonomous Agents and Multiagent Systems, pp. 230–237. ACM (2005)
13. Liu, W., Chen, D., Guo, J.Z.: Goal-capability-commitment based mediation for multi-agent collaboration. In: Proceedings of 2018 IEEE 22nd International Conference on Computer Supported Cooperative Work in Design, pp. 749–854 (2018)

14. Liu, H.Z., Hong, B., De, X.: Concept vector for similarity measurement based on hierarchical domain structure. Comput. Inform. **30**(5), 881–900 (2012)
15. Dalpiaz, F., Borgida, A., Horkoff, J., Mylopoulos, J.: Runtime goal models. In: Proceedings of the IEEE 7th International Conference on Research Challenges in Information Science, pp. 1–11. IEEE (2013)
16. Liu, W., Wang, J. and Li, S.: Concept vector's semantic similarity based capability planning for multi-agent cooperative systems. In: Proceedings of International Conference on Semantics, Knowledge and Grids (SKG). 2017 13th, IEEE (2017)

Data Processing and Data Mining

ProteinA: An Approach for Analyzing and Visualizing Protein Conformational Transitions Using Fuzzy and Hard Clustering Techniques

Silvana Albert[(✉)] [iD] and Gabriela Czibula [iD]

Department of Computer Science,
Babeş-Bolyai University, 1, M. Kogalniceanu Street, 400084 Cluj-Napoca, Romania
{albert.silvana,gabis}@cs.ubbcluj.ro

Abstract. It is not easy finding arguments against the common belief that *Proteomics* and *Genomics* are the most challenging and important research fields, posing interesting problems for our current era. Gaining insight into the protein folding process has been the goal of many in the past few decades. Understanding completely how proteins come alive and behave will revolutionize modern medicine. With the main goal of understanding the importance of the protein folding problem and uncovering hidden patterns in protein data, we are analyzing protein conformational transitions with unsupervised learning tools, by applying different types of hard and fuzzy clustering algorithms and comparing the results. As an additional goal, the paper describes a software that can perform on demand analysis on protein data and display the results in a web interface. It is a proof of concept for potential useful features that make software algorithms available for researchers of all domains.

Keywords: Proteomics · Unsupervised learning · Clustering · Fuzzy C-means · Birch · Protein software

1 Introduction

Personalized genetic sequencing has never been more accessible or affordable than today. Multiple private companies make huge profits by analyzing samples of saliva from regular people all around the world. They are telling us more and more about ourselves, our ancestors and our predisposition to various conditions. With this in mind, a future where every single dose of administered medication is custom tailored to serve the patient, is not that hard to imagine. However, the road to that future is still paved with unanswered questions about how exactly the *genotype* relates to the *phenotype*. The genes are "recipes" but the actual meal are the resulting proteins. The creation of an amino acid sequence from the DNA is just the beginning of the story. The protein undergoes lots of changes

© Springer Nature Switzerland AG 2019
C. Douligeris et al. (Eds.): KSEM 2019, LNAI 11775, pp. 249–261, 2019.
https://doi.org/10.1007/978-3-030-29551-6_22

until reaching its final stable form. We will refer to those changes as *conformations* and they serve as input data for our approach. Uncovering patterns in protein conformations helps to better understand how proteins change and evolve. It is already common knowledge that shape dictates the biological function, so any anomaly during the folding process can lead to a malformed, defective protein that, in time, can cause illness or even death for the organism. That is why we need to investigate computational methods and develop solutions that can help the researchers to gain a better understanding into the mysterious world of protein folding. We have previously investigated in [26] the use of two clustering methods (*k-means* and *hierarchical agglomerative clustering* (HAC)) and the relevance of the residues' *relative solvent accessibility* (RSA) values to analyze protein internal transitions. We obtained an empirical evidence that RSA values are slowly modifying as a protein undergoes conformational changes [26]. The contribution of this paper is twofold. First, with the main goal of providing an understanding of the importance of the protein folding problem and uncovering hidden patterns in protein conformational transitions, we are further extending our previous approach from [26] by considering new proteins as case studies and two new clustering algorithms: *fuzzy c-means* and *Birch*. Through the proposed clustering algorithms we aim: (1) to analyze if a *fuzzy* approach would be helpful in increasing the performance of the unsupervised learning process; and (2) to compare the effectiveness of the proposed clustering algorithms with the existing related work, particularly with the approach from [26]. An additional goal of the paper is to describe a straightforward approach *ProteinA* for performing on the spot analysis on protein data, as an exemplification for the idea of shared, easy to understand software for analyzing biological data. As far as we are aware of, the previously stated research questions have not been answered, so far, in the literature. The rest of the paper is structured as follows. Section 2 presents the fundamental background concepts related to proteins, as well as the applicability of clustering in protein analysis. Our approach, along with implementation details is available in Sect. 3. The experimental results, as well as advantages of our proposal are highlighted by the description of the current state of art (Sect. 4.1). The final Sect. 5 presents the key points of this paper along with some ideas for future development.

2   Background

This section introduces some core concepts required to understand the approach we are proposing. First, a brief background on proteins and their conformational transitions is provided in Sect. 2.1. Then, the fundamental concepts related to the *clustering* methods used in this paper for protein data analysis are summarized in Sect. 2.2.

2.1   Proteins and Conformational Transitions

Also known as the building blocks of life, proteins have crucial roles in all living organisms. They begin their life cycle from a linear sequence of *amino acids*, which can have various lengths; from as little as 20 pieces to 35000. In a matter of seconds after the sequence of aminio acids is built, the protein folds. It goes through a large number of changes until it reaches it's final stable 3D form. Those changes are called: *protein conformational transitions* and computing them through molecular simulations is very time and cost consuming. That is why so many people focus on trying to predict the final form of a protein, starting from the initial amino acid sequence. In order to acquire the final protein shape, proteins undergo significant structural changes, caused by inter molecular forces along with external factors such as temperature, humidity, etc. A conformation is considered to be the shape of the protein at one moment in time. There are 20 possible amino acids involved in protein genesis [7] that make the *primary structure of a protein*. They can be represented by an alphabet of 20 letters, $\mathcal{A} = \{g, p, a, v, l, i, m, c, f, y, w, h, k, r, q, n, e, d, s, t\}$ [3]. The number of possible permutations for these amino acids is huge thus predicting the final shape of the protein from it is a very tricky task. Machine Learning algorithms come to the rescue by attempting to uncover hidden patterns in the consecutive conformations. According to [20], some conformations for small fragments occur regularly and they were called *states*. They were encoded in Structural Alphabets (SA) and they transform the three dimensional representation of the protein into a manageable one dimensional array that can be used for further analysis. Each four amino acids result in one letter when converted in the structural alphabet representation. The outcome is a sequence of structural letters, transcribed using another alphabet of 25 letters $A, B, C, D, E, F, G, H, I, J, K, L, M, N, O, P, Q, R, S, T, U, V, W, X, Y$. This is not the same as the amino acids one. For avoiding confusion, the amino acids one is lowercase and the conformations are upper case. The protein Pr has a primary sequence composed of n amino acids: $Pr = p_1 p_2 \cdots p_n$ and a coon formation is a sequence of letters of length $n - 3$, each such leather representing 4 amino acids from the initial amino acid sequence $Pr = s_1 s_2 \cdots s_{n-3}$ [26].

2.2 Clustering

The process of grouping similar objects in a way that they have more in common inside their group (cluster) than they have with objects from the other groups is called *clustering*. In the machine learning literature, *clustering* methods [15] are commonly used as *unsupervised classification* techniques and descriptive models, for discovering in an unsupervised manner a structure in data. Clustering can be viewed as an exploratory technique [17] and it is represented by multiple algorithms that differ in methodology. The two main classes of clustering methods are *partitional* and *hierarchical*. The goal of *partitional* methods is mainly to maximize the similarity within the clusters (i.e. minimizing the so called *intra-cluster* distance), while the *hierarchical* methods are minimizing the similarity between the clusters (i.e. maximizing the so called *inter-cluster* distance).

2.3 Fuzzy C-Means

Fuzzy c-means clustering [1,16] (FCM) is a partitional clustering technique which employs fuzzy partitioning such that a data instance can belong to all clusters with certain membership degrees between 0 and 1. FCM differs from the classical *k-means* algorithm in which the clusters are disjoint, since it is relate to *overlapping* clustering. It uses fuzzy sets to cluster data, such that each instance may belong to more clusters with different degrees of membership. In this case, an instance will be assigned to the cluster with the maximum membership value. As in the classical clustering approach, the *fuzzy* approach uses a *distance* function for discriminating between the instances. If n represents the number of data instances and k denotes the number of clusters that we want to discover in the data set, FCM uses a membership matrix denoted by $U = (u_{ij})_{\substack{i=\overline{1,k} \\ j=\overline{1,n}}}$, such that

$$\sum_{i=1}^{k} u_{ij} = 1, \forall j \in \{1, 2, ..., n\}.\ u_{ij}\ (i \in \{1, 2, \dots k\}, j \in \{1, 2, \dots, n\})$$ represents the membership degree of instance i to cluster j. The FCM algorithm iteratively updates the clusters' centroids (centers) and the membership degrees for each instance [1]. In computing the centroids at each step, FCM uses a hyper- parameter $m \geq 1$ (called the *fuzzifier*) that controls how fuzzy the cluster will be (a large m lead to fuzzier clusters). The higher it is, the fuzzier the cluster will be in the end. As the hard $k - means$ clustering algorithm, FCM does not ensure the convergence towards an optimal solution, because the initial centroids (the initial values for matrix U) are randomly initialized. The final values for the matrix U will be used for determining the final partition reported by FCM. The number of clusters reported by FCM is less or equal to k (the user provided initial number of clusters), since there is a possibility to obtain empty clusters.

2.4 Birch Clustering

Birch clustering is a clustering approach that stands out by reducing the run time and necessary memory for analyzing large sets of data [33].

BIRCH (Balanced Iterative Reducing and Clustering using Hierarchies) [32] is a clustering algorithm which does not require the entire data set to be initially available and is shown to be suitable for very large data sets. BIRCH is a hierarchical clustering method, known as one of the fastest clustering algorithms [19]. It uses the concept of *Clustering Feature* (CF) tree which is originally built on the initial data set and afterwards is incrementally enlarged with new multi-dimensional instances which are added to the data set. An entry from the CF tree represents a cluster of instances. BIRCH incrementally and dynamically includes newly added instances into appropriate clusters, performing a single scan of the data set. The clusters' quality is then improved through additional scans of the data set [32].

As the partitional clustering methods, BIRCH requires the number of clusters in advance.

3   Our Approach

We are conducting several experiments on two protein data sets with the goal to empirically show, using *fuzzy c-means* and Birch clustering methods, that RSA values slowly change when a protein goes through conformational changes. The end goal is proving that consecutive conformations are closer and the protein evolves linearly.

3.1   Protein Data Sets

The two proteins used in our experiments are: *6EQE* - a "High resolution crystal structure of a polyethylene terephthalate degrading hydrolase from Ideonella sakaiensis" [10] and *4CG1* - a "Thermostable polyethylene terephthalate degrading hydrolase from Thermobifida fusca" [30].

Both proteins are being investigated for their roles in PET degradation and the fact that they have a lot in common leads us to expect similar results when applying unsupervised algorithms. Studies were made to prove that by altering PETase to look more like the Cutinase's would lead to better PET Degradation [10]. Their 3D shapes are illustrated in Fig. 1a and b and by computing the structural similarity as provided by the FATCAT algorithm (Flexible structure AlignmenT by Chaining Aligned fragment pairs allowing Twists) [31], the result is: Similarity = 63.57% and Identity = 49.44%.

(a) 3D view of protein 6EQE. Image from the RCSB PDB [13] of PDB ID 6EQE [10].

(b) 3D view of protein 4CG1. Image from the RCSB PDB [13] of PDB ID 4CG1 [31].

Fig. 1. Proteins 6EQE and 4CG1.

Each of the two proteins has a data set of 10000 conformational transitions encoded in Structural Alphabet Letters along with the corresponding *relative solvent accessibility* (RSA) values. RSA quantifies the amplitude of "burial or exposure" [27] for each residue and has proven to be useful for us in previous experiments [2].

3.2   Experimental Methodology

On each protein data set described in Sect. 3.1 and consisting of 10000 conformational transitions, FCM and Birch clustering methods will be applied. Before applying the clustering techniques, each protein data has been normalized using the standard deviation based normalization.

The number k of clusters is used as a parameter in the clustering process. Since successive conformations of a protein have a high degree of similarity from a biological viewpoint, we expect that its near conformations will cluster together. For instance, if $k = 2$, we would expect to obtain two classes (clusters) of conformations: one cluster containing conformations from 1 to 5000 and the second cluster containing conformations from 5001 to 10000. In the general case, for a given k (number of clusters), we consider that in the perfect partition the j-th class is formed by the conformations from $\left[\frac{10000 \cdot (j-1)}{k}\right] + 1$ to $\left[\frac{10000 \cdot j}{k}\right]$.

In both clustering algorithms, the *Euclidian distance* will be used for expressing the dissimilarity between two conformational transitions. Regarding the FCM algorithm, the final partition $C_1, C_2, \ldots, C_k$ is computed by assigning a conformation to the cluster to which it has the maximum membership degree, i.e. $C_i = \{j \mid j \in \{1, 2, \ldots, n\}$ and $u_{ij} > u_{lj}, \forall l \in \{1, 2, \ldots, n\}, l \neq j\} \; \forall 1 \leq i \leq k$.

For evaluating the clustering results, we will consider a two dimensional visualization of the clustered protein data sets, using a *Principal component analysis* (PCA) [21]. The two dimensional PCA reduces the dimensionality of the protein data sets, considering the 2 principal components that are containing the highest variance from the original data [13]. Two additional evaluation measures are used, *V-measure* and *Silhouette coefficient*. *V-measure* is an external evaluation measure used for assessing the completeness and homogeneity of the resulting clusters, compared to the expected (ideal) partition [23]. *Silhouette coefficient* is an internal evaluation measure which expresses, for each instance, its similarity to the designated cluster by comparing it to the remaining clusters [24].

3.3   *ProteinA* Software Solution

For capturing protein conformational transitions by clustering, we are proposing the software solution *ProteinA*. It is a web application that allows users to start custom cluster analyses and download the results. A clustering analysis takes about 5 min, however the idea behind the software is to allow more complex processing and delivering the results when ready. The clustering methods currently available in *ProteinA* are: k-means, *hierarchical agglomerative clustering* (HAC), FCM and Birch.

The solution is publicly running at [6]:[1]. The code is available on Github at [5][2]. Another option for easily running it on a local machine is by accessing the

---

[1] Protein clustering online http://proteinclusters.online/proteins.

[2] Protein clustering web application https://github.com/albusilvana/proteinclustering webapp.

public docker image at [4][3]. The application is written in Python and is benefiting from the advantages of the *Scikit-learn* module [21]. It employs the available clustering algorithms and each new analysis started in the web interface, triggers the creation of a new thread. The output of these threads are images like those in Figs. 2 and 3 making them available for inspecting and downloading in the web application. Building a web application that performs heavy machine learning algorithms behind the scenes was the general idea behind this software. After auditioning other alternatives, we chose Flask, a "micro-framework" for building Python web applications [14]. In order to facilitate the replication of our solution, we created a *Docker image* and published it on *Docker Hub*. Docker is a platform agnostic abstraction layer providing extremely lightweight virtual machines, thus enabling the quick deployment of a newer version of the tool in any cloud or local medium [9].

According to some initial feedback from scientists with chemical and biological background, such a software would be useful to them by allowing machine learning based analysis of protein data.

4   Results and Discussion

This section presents the results of our experiments described in Sect. 3, as well as a discussion regarding the obtained results and a comparison to related work.

We are comparatively displaying in Figs. 2 and 3 the 2D PCA visualization of the clustering results on proteins 4CG1 (Fig. 2) and 6EQE (Fig. 3) using both FCM (left side images) and Birch (right side images) and two different number k of clusters (100 and 250). For each cluster, the conformations that belong to it from the original data set are searched and displayed sequentially. The image is built sequentially by layering all the points that match a cluster, then moving to the next cluster, by using the corresponding color in the given gradient. The most visible ones are the final clusters and some of the first ones might be underneath. The range of conformations that belong to each color is available on the right hand side of each image. We would expect that the colors which are visible on the plots (i.e. the colors for the proteins' configurations which are closer to the last one - 10000) to be from the upper side of the gradient of colors, i.e. shapes of yellow.

Table 1. Clustering proteins 4CG1 and 6EQE with Birch and FCM clustering algorithms, using 100 and 250 clusters.

Protein	k	Clustering method	*V-measure*	Protein	K	Clustering method	*V-measure*
4CG1	100	FCM	0.436	6EQE	100	FCM	0.439
		Birch	**0.844**			Birch	**0.851**
	250	FCM	0.438		250	FCM	0.448
		Birch	**0.873**			Birch	**0.874**

---

[3] Protein clustering docker image on Docker hub https://hub.docker.com/r/salbert/proteinclustering.

As shown in Sect. 3.2, a cluster in the ideal partition with 100 clusters would be composed by 100 conformations, while in the partition with 250 clusters about 40 conformations are expected in a class. Analyzing the clustering results depicted in Figs. 2 and 3 we observe that the clusters provided by Birch (right side images) have better shapes and are more compact than those obtained using FCM (left side images) and this stands independent of the analyzed protein (4CG1 or 6EQE) and of the number of clusters (100 or 250). Clearly, the clusters provided by FCM are more spread out than those obtained using Birch, which are more dense. In addition, we observe that the Birch clusters from the partition with 250 clusters (Fig. 2(d) for protein 4CG1 and Fig. 3(d) for protein 6EQE) are more homogeneous and sharper than those from the partition with 100 clusters (Fig. 2(b) for protein 4CG1 and Fig. 3(b) for protein 6EQE). This is foreseeable, since as the number of clusters increases (and the conformations anticipated in a cluster decreases, as presented in Sect. 3.2), it is more likely that the clusters will be more homogeneous (i.e composed by near conformations

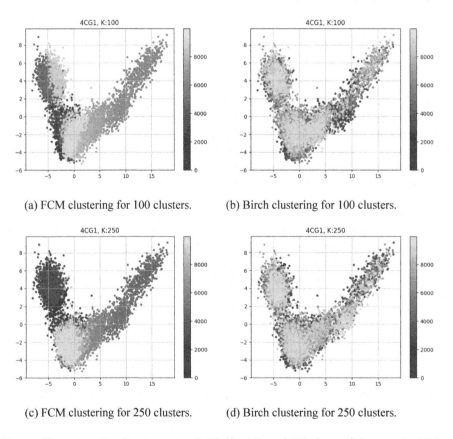

(a) FCM clustering for 100 clusters.   (b) Birch clustering for 100 clusters.

(c) FCM clustering for 250 clusters.   (d) Birch clustering for 250 clusters.

Fig. 2. Clustering visualization using PCA (for 100 and 250 clusters) for protein 4CG1: FCM (left side) and Birch (right side) (Color figure online)

which have high similarities). The previous remarks are confirmed in Table 1 where we are presenting the values for *V-measure* and *Silhouette coefficient* for proteins 4CG1 and 6EQE, using Birch and FCM clustering algorithms, for 100 and 250 clusters. From Table 1 we observe that the *V-measure* values for both cluster numbers are higher for Birch clustering than for FCM. *V-measure* is also higher for 250 clusters than for 100 clusters (for both proteins). Thus, better clusters are obtained using Birch and 250 clusters.

We note that the fuzzy operation does not improve as expected. This is possibly due to the fact that the input data is not necessary suitable for data fuzzification, considering the chosen representation. Future work will be carried out in this direction, for identifying other enhanced representations more for the fuzzy perspective. Analyzing the plots form Figs. 2 and 3 we can notice that both the shapes and the results of the two proteins are very similar. We assume this is due to the fact that the biological structure of the two proteins is also significantly similar. Besides, the *fuzzy* perspective does not improve the effectiveness of the clustering process. More experiments will be further carried out in this direction.

4.1 Comparison to Related Work

The related work from the literature which is the most similar to our approach is [26], where *k-means* and HAC clustering methods are applied for analyzing protein conformational transitions. For an accurate comparison of the results, we applied *k-means* and HAC for the proteins 4CG1 and 6EQE used in this paper. In addition, Birch was applied using the same setting as in [26] using *Silhouette coefficient* as an additional evaluation measure for computing the clustering quality. *Silhouette coefficient* is an internal evaluation measure which expresses, for each instance, its similarity to the designated cluster by comparing it to the remaining clusters [24]. Table 2 presents the comparative results between Birch and *k-means*. The best results are highlighted.

From Table 2 we observe that higher values for *V-measure* (the most relevant evaluation measure) are generally obtained using Birch, excepting several partitions for which the values provided by the two algorithms are slightly equal. The values obtained with HAC [26] were not displayed in Table 2, as they are exactly the same as using Birch (i.e. the partitions provided by HAC and Birch are identical). That makes sense because they are both hierarchical clustering techniques and the only difference between them is how they make use of the available memory. Our current available data set is small enough to be all loaded from the start in memory, thus not profiting of Birch's performance advantage. However, the efficiency of Birch with respect to other hierarchical clustering techniques (as discussed in [19,22,29]) will be visible on larger data sets. Future experiments will be carried out to empirically validate this hypothesis.

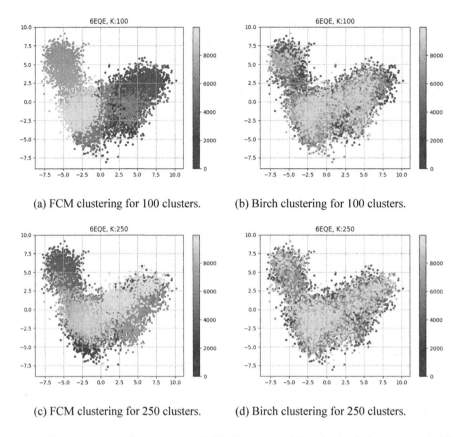

(a) FCM clustering for 100 clusters.   (b) Birch clustering for 100 clusters.

(c) FCM clustering for 250 clusters.   (d) Birch clustering for 250 clusters.

Fig. 3. Clustering visualization using PCA (for 100 and 250 clusters) for protein 6EQE: FCM (left side) and Birch (right side) (Color figure online)

To the best of our knowledge, a software solution like *ProteinA* (see Sect. 3.3) that analyzes protein conformational transitions is not available.

There are however software solutions for inspecting and modeling proteins such as Prodock [28]. Multiple solutions useful for drug design are presented in [8]. A fast prototyping molecular modeling software is *Rosetta* [18] and it performs also biological structure prediction for molecules.

The software proposed in [25] is designed to predict probabilities for Xaa-Pro peptide bonds "cis or trans" conformations. *Preditor* [11] is a web server that predicts torsion angles from input data containing either chemical shift assignments or protein data in FASTA format.

Table 2. Comparative results using Birch and *k-means*.

Protein	k	Clustering method	V measure	Silhouette coefficient	Protein	k	Clustering method	V measure	Silhouette coefficient
4CG1	4	*k-means* [26]	0.698	0.046	6EQE	4	*k-means*[26]	0.587	0.041
		Birch	**0.735**	0.043			Birch	**0.625**	0.040
	10	*k-means* [26]	**0.732**	0.033		10	*k-means* [26]	0.660	0.033
		Birch	0.690	0.037			Birch	**0.684**	0.029
	20	*k-means* [26]	0.740	0.037		20	*k-means* [26]	**0.741**	0.038
		Birch	**0.771**	0.033			Birch	0.713	0.036
	100	*k-means* [26]	**0.850**	0.047		100	*k-means* [26]	0.846	0.045
		Birch	0.844	0.048			Birch	**0.851**	0.046
	200	*k-means* [26]	**0.871**	0.047		200	*k-means*[26]	0.861	0.043
		Birch	0.869	0.048			Birch	**0.872**	0.049

5   Conclusions and Future Work

In this paper we have investigated two clustering methods (FCM and Birch) for protein data analysis and showcased our results for two proteins: PETase (6EQE) and Cutinase (4CG1). In addition, we have proposed a clustering based software solution *ProteinA* that analyses protein conformational transitions based on the user's filters and compared it to other similar solutions. We described the biological background and motivated the need for this kind of software.

In the future, more machine learning algorithms should be available and more proteins in the data set. Autoencoders and Self Organizing Maps could be employed instead of clustering and the results automatically compared. The user should be able to also pick to use only the Structural Alphabet representation, or only RSA values, or both. Also the number of conformations should be configurable, the user could say that he wants to analyze only even or odd confirmations, or only the first 1000. A feature for sending the results (when the analysis is ready), by email to the submitter, would also be useful and allowing scientists to upload their own structural alphabet.

The current format of the software solution *ProteinA* showcases a simple technology stack: Python, Scikit-learn, Flask and Docker and this format can be considered a proof of concept for fast prototyping multidisciplinary software.

Acknowledgments. The authors thank lecturer Alessandro Pandini from Brunel University, London for providing the protein data sets used in the experiments.

References

1. Albayrak, S., Amasyali, F.: Fuzzy c-means clustering on medical diagnostic systems. In: Turkish Symposium on Artificial Intelligence and Neural Networks - TAINN (2003)
2. Albert, S., Czibula, G., Teletin, M.: Analyzing the impact of protein representation on mining structural patterns from protein data. In: IEEE 12th International Symposium on Applied Computational Intelligence and Informatics (SACI 2018), pp. 533–538 (2018)

3. Albert, S., Teletin, M., Czibula, G.: Analysing protein data using unsupervised learning techniques. Int. J. Innovative Comput. Inf. Control **14**(3), 861–880 (2018)
4. Albert, S.: Protein clustering docker image (2018). https://hub.docker.com/r/salbert/proteinclustering
5. Albert, S.: Protein clustering git repository (2018). https://github.com/albusilvana/proteinclusteringwebapp
6. Albert, S.: Protein clustering analysis (2019). http://proteinclusters.online/proteins
7. Ambrogelly, A., Palioura, S., Söll, D.: Natural expansion of the genetic code. Nat. Chem. Biol. **3**(1), 29–35 (2007)
8. Anderson, A.C.: The process of structure-based drug design. Chem. Biol. **10**(9), 787–797 (2003)
9. Anderson, C.: Docker [software engineering]. IEEE Softw. **32**(3), 102–c3 (2015)
10. Austin, H.P., et al.: Characterization and engineering of a plastic-degrading aromatic polyesterase. Proc. Nat. Acad. Sci. **115**(19), E4350–E4357 (2018)
11. Berjanskii, M.V., Neal, S., Wishart, D.S.: PREDITOR: a web server for predicting protein torsion angle restraints. Nucleic Acids Res. **34**(Web Server), W63–W69 (2006)
12. Berman, H., et al.: The protein data bank. Nucleic Acids Res. **28**, 235–242 (2000)
13. Goodfellow, I., Bengio, Y., Courville, A.: Deep Learning. MIT Press, Cambridge (2016). http://www.deeplearningbook.org
14. Grinberg, M.: Flask Web Development: Developing Web Applications with Python. O'Reilly Media Inc., Sebastopol (2014)
15. Han, J.: Data Mining: Concepts and Techniques. Morgan Kaufmann Publishers Inc., San Francisco (2005)
16. Jain, A., Dubes, R.: Algorithms for Clustering Data. Prentice Hall, Englewood Cliffs (1998)
17. Kaufman, L., Rousseeuw, P.J.: Finding Groups in Data. Wiley, Hoboken (1990)
18. Leaver-Fay, A., et al.: ROSETTA3. In: Computer Methods, Part C, pp. 545–574. Elsevier (2011)
19. Lorbeer, B., Kosareva, A., Deva, B., Softić, D., Ruppel, P., Küpper, A.: Variations on the clustering algorithm BIRCH. Big Data Res. **11**, 44–53 (2018)
20. Pandini, A., Fornili, A., Kleinjung, J.: Structural alphabets derived from attractors in conformational space. BMC Bioinformatics **11**(97), 1–18 (2010)
21. Pedregosa, F., et al.: Édouard Duchesnay: Scikit-learn: machine learning in Python. J. Mach. Learn. Res. **12**, 2825–2830 (2011)
22. Pitolli, G., Aniello, L., Laurenza, G., Querzoni, L., Baldoni, R.: Malware family identification with BIRCH clustering. In: 2017 International Carnahan Conference on Security Technology (ICCST), October 2017, pp. 1–6 (2017)
23. Rosenberg, A., Hirschberg, J.: V-measure: a conditional entropy-based external cluster evaluation measure. In: Proceedings of the 2007 Joint Conference on Empirical Methods in Natural Language Processing and Computational Natural Language Learning (EMNLP-CoNLL), pp. 410–420 (2007)
24. Rousseeuw, P.J.: Silhouettes: a graphical aid to the interpretation and validation of cluster analysis. J. Comput. Appl. Math. **20**, 53–65 (1987)
25. Schubert, M., Labudde, D., Oschkinat, H., Schmieder, P.: A software tool for the prediction of Xaa-Pro peptide bond conformations in proteins based on ^{13}C chemical shift statistics. J. Biomol. NMR **24**(2), 149–154 (2002)

26. Teletin, M., Czibula, G., Albert, S., Bocicor, I.: Using unsupervised learning methods for enhancing protein structure insight. In: International Conference on Knowledge Based and Intelligent Information and Engineering Systems (KES), pp. 19–28 (2018)
27. Tien, M.Z., Meyer, A.G., Sydykova, D.K., Spielman, S.J., Wilke, C.O.: Maximum allowed solvent accessibilites of residues in proteins. PLoS One **8**(11), e80635 (2013)
28. Trosset, J.Y., Scheraga, H.A.: PRODOCK: software package for protein modeling and docking. J. Comput. Chem. **20**(4), 412–427 (1999)
29. Venkatkumar, I.A., Shardaben, S.J.K.: Comparative study of data mining clustering algorithms. In: 2016 International Conference on Data Science and Engineering (ICDSE), August 2016, pp. 1–7 (2016)
30. Wei, R., Oeser, T., Then, J., Föllner, C.G., Zimmermann, W., Sträter, N.: Structural and functional studies on a thermostable polyethylene terephthalate degrading hydrolase from thermobifida fusca. Appl. Microbiol. Biotechnol. **98**, 7815–7823 (2014)
31. Ye, Y., Godzik, A.: FATCAT: a web server for flexible structure comparison and structure similarity searching. Nucleic Acids Res. **32**, 582–585 (2004)
32. Zhang, T., Ramakrishnan, R., Livny, M.: BIRCH: an efficient data clustering method for very large databases. In: Proceedings of the 1996 ACM SIGMOD International Conference on Management of Data, SIGMOD 1996, pp. 103–114. ACM, New York (1996)
33. Zhang, T., Ramakrishnan, R., Livny, M.: Data Min. Knowl. Disc. **1**(2), 141–182 (1997)

Software Defect Prediction Using a Hybrid Model Based on Semantic Features Learned from the Source Code

Diana-Lucia Miholca$^{(\boxtimes)}$ ⓘ and Gabriela Czibula ⓘ

Department of Computer Science,
Babeş-Bolyai University, 1, M. Kogalniceanu Street, 400084 Cluj-Napoca, Romania
{diana,gabis}@cs.ubbcluj.ro

Abstract. Software defect prediction has extensive applicability thus being a very active research area in Search-Based Software Engineering. A high proportion of the software defects are caused by violated couplings. In this paper, we investigate the relevance of semantic coupling in assessing the software proneness to defects. We propose a hybrid classification model combining Gradual Relational Association Rules with Artificial Neural Networks, which detects the defective software entities based on semantic features automatically learned from the source code. The experiments we have performed led to results that confirm the interplay between conceptual coupling and software defects proneness.

Keywords: Software defect prediction · Machine learning · Conceptual coupling

1 Introduction

Software defect prediction consists in identifying defective software components. It is essential to software quality assurance [26] and has been actively researched [13] in two main directions: designing new features encoding relevant characteristics of programs [25] and proposing novel and improved machine learning algorithms [20,22]. Identifying software modules which are likely to be defective guides the code review and testing processes [6] to those locations in the software system's source code which require particular attention and, therefore, contributes to efficient resources allocation.

A high percentage of software defects are caused by violated dependencies. The two dimensions of these dependencies are technical and organizational [5]. Technical dependencies between software entities are expressed by coupling measures. Most of the existing coupling measures are *structural*, but there are also several alternative coupling measures that fall under the categories of *dynamic*, *semantic* (or *conceptual*) and *change* (*logical* or *evolutionary*) coupling. Bavota et al. [1] have empirically proved that dependencies captured by change and dynamic coupling are mostly captured by structural or conceptual coupling, while these two are complementary.

© Springer Nature Switzerland AG 2019
C. Douligeris et al. (Eds.): KSEM 2019, LNAI 11775, pp. 262–274, 2019.
https://doi.org/10.1007/978-3-030-29551-6_23

Along the technical dimension of the software defect prediction, the literature has extensively exploited software metrics including measures of structural coupling (e.g. the Chidamber and Kemerer object-oriented metric *Coupling Between Objects* (CBO), the McCabe metrics [19]), whereas only limited work has focused on the relationship between *change* coupling, as expression of alternative dependencies, and failure proneness [5,15]. *Change* coupling has been empirically confirmed to have superior impact on software defect proneness compared to structural coupling [2]. However, the software defect prediction approaches based on co-change metrics are subject to the following main limitation: they depend on historical data as well as on the attributes of the involved software tools (e.g. version control systems) [5].

Under these circumstances, the contribution of this paper is twofold. First, it investigates the relevance of *semantic* (or *conceptual*) dependencies on a system's predilection for failure. For the automatic and unsupervised extraction of the semantic features from the minimally pre-processed source code *Paragraph Vector* (or Doc2Vec) [17] and *Latent Semantic Indexing* (LSI) [23] are comparatively evaluated. The relevance of the semantic features on defect proneness is analyzed using *t-Distributed Stochastic Neighbor Embedding* (t-SNE) visualization technique. Second, the paper proposes a novel hybrid supervised software defect prediction model, *DePSem*, which combines *Gradual Relational Association Rules* (GRARs) and *Artificial Neural Networks* (ANNs) in a solution to software defect prediction which is based on the unsupervisedly learned semantic features and, thus, independent on other software artifacts.

The remainder of the paper is organized as follows. Section 2 gives background on GRARs, accompanied by an example of GRARs mining. Section 3 elaborates on the methodology *DePSem* is based on. The experimental results are pointed out in Sect. 4. Our *DePSem* approach is discussed and compared to related work in Sect. 5. Finally, we draw conclusions and indicate directions for further work in Sect. 6.

2   Background on *Gradual Relational Association Rules*

This section presents the *Gradual Relational Association Rules* (GRARs) mining approach, which has been introduced in [8] and is combined, in the current paper, with ANNs so as to obtain a software defect prediction model.

Let $\mathcal{E} = \{e_1, e_2, \ldots, e_n\}$ be a set of n *entities* (or *instances*), each entity being characterized by p *attributes* (or *features*), $\mathcal{A} = (a_1, \ldots, a_p)$ and let $\Phi(e_j, a_i)$ denote the value of the attribute a_i in e_j. A *Gradual Relational Association Rule*, $\mathcal{G}Rule$, is a sequence $(a_{i_1} \; \mathcal{G}_1 \; a_{i_2} \; \mathcal{G}_2 \; a_{i_3} \ldots \mathcal{G}_{\ell-1} \; a_{i_\ell})$, where $\{a_{i_1}, a_{i_2}, a_{i_3}, \ldots, a_{i_\ell}\} \subseteq \mathcal{A} = \{a_1, \ldots, a_p\}$, $a_{i_j} \neq a_{i_k}$, $j, k = 1..\ell$, $j \neq k$ and $\mathcal{G}_j \in \mathcal{F}$ is a binary fuzzy relation over $D_{i_j} \times D_{i_{j+1}}$, D_{i_j} being the domain of the attribute a_{i_j}. By $\mathcal{F}$ we denote a set of binary fuzzy relations that can be defined between any two attribute domains.

The *membership* of a GRAR, $\mathcal{G}Rule$, *for an instance* $e \in \mathcal{E}$ is defined as $\mu_{\mathcal{G}Rule}(e) = \min\{\mu_{\mathcal{G}_j}(\Phi(e, a_{i_j}), \Phi(e, a_{i_{j+1}})), j = 1, 2, \ldots, \ell - 1\}$ and expresses the magnitude to which the rule is satisfied.

If $a_{i_1}, a_{i_2}, a_{i_3}, \ldots, a_{i_\ell}$ are non-missing in k instances from $\mathcal{E}$ then we call $s = \frac{k}{n}$ the *support* of the GRAR $\mathcal{G}Rule$. If $\mathcal{E}' \subseteq \mathcal{E}$ is the set of all instances in $\mathcal{E}$ for which $a_{i_1}, a_{i_2}, a_{i_3}, \ldots, a_{i_\ell}$ are non-missing and $\mu_{\mathcal{G}Rule}(e) > 0$ for each instance e from $\mathcal{E}'$, then we call $c = \frac{|\mathcal{E}'|}{n}$ the *confidence* of the rule. We call

$$m = \frac{\sum\limits_{e \in \mathcal{E}'} \mu_{\mathcal{G}Rule}(e)}{n}$$ the rule's *membership at the level of the data set* $\mathcal{E}$.

A GRAR is called *interesting* [21] if its *support*, *confidence* and *membership* are greater than the given thresholds s_{min}, c_{min} and m_{min}.

For effectively mining all the interesting GRARs within a data set, an Apriori algorithm, called *Gradual Relational Association Rules Miner* (GRANUM), has been introduced in [8].

2.1 Example

We exemplify the GRARs mining approach in the following. The data sample is extracted from the publicly available Ant defect prediction data set [24] and consists of 10 non-defective instances characterized by three software metrics [7]:*Weighted Methods per Class* (WMC), *Coupling between objects*(CBO) and *Response for a Class* (RFC).

No.	WMC	CBO	RFC
1.	5	4	13
2.	1	1	3
3.	8	13	20
4.	1	1	1
5.	4	5	19
6.	2	3	4
7.	4	7	15
8.	5	5	16
9.	4	3	18
10.	3	4	19

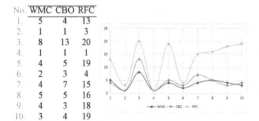

GRAR	Confidence	Membership
WMC $\lesssim$ CBO	0.8	0.8
WMC $\approx$ CBO	1	0.7096
WMC $\lesssim$ RFC	1	1
CBO $\lesssim$ RFC	1	1
WMC $\lesssim$ CBO $\lesssim$ RFC	0.8	0.8
WMC $\approx$ CBO $\lesssim$ RFC	1	0.7096
WMC $\lesssim$ RFC $\gtrsim$ CBO	0.9	0.9

Fig. 1. Example of GRARs mining: data sample, graphical representation of data and interesting GRARs mined by GRANUM for $c_{min} = 1$, $c_{min} = 0.8$ and $m_{min} = 0.7$.

Semantically interpreting, for instance, the first two binary GRARs, we deduce that CBO tends to be only slightly greater than WMC.

3 Methodology

In this section we introduce our *DepSem* approach for classifying software entities as either defective or non-defective, based on conceptual features automatically extracted from the source code. As illustrated in Fig. 2, the approach involves two main steps: (a) an unsupervised *data collection* step and (b) a supervised *classification* step.

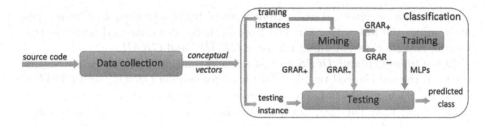

Fig. 2. Overview of *DepSem* approach.

3.1   Data Collection

During *data collection*, the source code afferent to the software entities is transformed into numeric vectors of *semantic* (or *conceptual*) *features* as described below.

Let a software system $Syst$ be as a set of *software entities* (classes, modules, methods), $Syst = \{e_1, e_2, \ldots, e_n\}$. The software entities are represented as *conceptual vectors*. The conceptual vectors consist of numeric values corresponding to a set of semantic features $S = \{s_1, s_2, \ldots, s_l\}$ unsupervisedly learned from the source code.

For extracting the conceptual vectors corresponding to the software entities, unsupervised learning models (such as *Paragraph Vector* or *Latent Semantic Indexing*) may be used. Both *Paragraph Vector* (or Doc2Vec) [17] and *Latent Sematic Indexing* (LSI) [9] - also known as *Latent Semantic Analysis* (LSA) - are models aimed to represent texts of variable lengths as fixed-length numeric vectors capturing semantic characteristics, but Doc2Vec is a prediction based model trained using backpropagation together with the stochastic gradient descent, while LSI is a statistical, count based model.

The set S represents the automatically learned feature set used for characterizing the software entities from $Syst$. Accordingly, an entity e_i is represented as an l-dimensional vector $e_i = (e_{i1}, \cdots, e_{il})$, where e_{ij} ($\forall 1 \leq j \leq l$) denotes the value of the semantic feature s_j computed for the entity e_i.

3.2   Classification

There are two possible target classes for the software defect classifier: the *positive* ("+") class corresponding to the *defective* entities and the *negative* ("−") class corresponding to the *non-defective* entities.

The *classification* step of *DePSem* is divided into three successive phases:

(1) *mining* sets of interesting GRARs that discriminate between defective and non-defective software entities;
(2) *training Multilayer Perceptrons* (MLPs) to detect defective entities based on the GRARs mined at (1);
(3) *testing* if a software instance is defective or non-defective using the classification model built at (2).

In the *mining* phase, starting from a set of fuzzy relations, $DePSem$ separately mines the interesting GRARs from both the defective and non-defective training subsets thus obtaining two sets: $GRAR_+$ and $GRAR_-$.

In the *training* phase, $DePSem$ first extracts multiple perfectly balanced subsets from the unbalanced training data used for mining $GRAR_+$ and $GRAR_-$. Then, for each perfectly balanced subset s, it builds a new data set s' in the following way. For each training instance $e = (e_1 \dots e_l) \in s$, an instance $e' = (e'_1 \dots e'_g, class) \in s'$ is constructed, where g is the cardinality of the set $\mathcal{R} = \{R_1, \dots, R_g\} = (GRAR_+ \cup GRAR_-) \backslash (GRAR_+ \cap GRAR_-)$, $e'_i = \mu_{R_i}(e)$ (i.e. the membership degree of GRAR R_i for the instance e), for $i = 1, 2, \dots, g$, and *class* is the corresponding class label. Each data set s' is next used to train one MLP. In the subsequent *testing* phase, each MLP will predict two values, p^+ and p^- expressing the likelihood of a testing instance to belong to the *defective* and *non-defective* classes, respectively.

The classification of a testing instance e_{est} (as being *positive* or *negative*) is based on the membership degrees of each rule in $\mathcal{R}$ for the test instance. Assuming that k MLPs have been trained, $DePSem$ classifies e_{test} as *defective* if $\sum_{i=1}^{k} p_i^+ > \sum_{i=1}^{k} p_i^-$ and as *non-defective* on the contrary.

Testing. In order to evaluate the performance of $DepSem$, experiments are performed on several case studies (software systems), using three vectorial models for representing as *conceptual vectors* the software entities:

M1 In the first model, each software entity is modeled as the numerical vector given by its Doc2Vec representation.

M2 In the second model, each software entity is modeled as the numerical vector given by its LSI representation.

M3 The third model we propose combines M1 and M2. Thus, a software entity is modeled as the vector obtained by concatenating its Doc2Vec and LSI representations.

Through the performed experiments, we aim to test if the Doc2Vec and LSI representations express different semantic characteristics useful for defect prediction. If this stands, then we would expect that model **M3** would lead to better classification results.

On each case study, *leave-one-out* (LOO) cross-validation is applied. On each testing set, the confusion matrix for the two possible classes (*fault* and *non-fault*) is computed, considering that the *fault* class is the *positive* one and the *non-fault* class is the *negative* one. Let us denote in the following by TF the number of *true faults* (*true positives*), FF the number of *false faults* (*false positives*), TN the number of *true non-faults* (*true negatives*) and FN the number of *false non-faults* (*false negatives*).

Based on the values from the confusion matrix, the following evaluation measures for the binary defect prediction task will be used [11]: *Precision* for the positive class, $Prec = \frac{TF}{TF+FF}$); *Sensitivity* (or *recall*, $Sens = \frac{TF}{TF+FN}$); *Negative predictive rate* $NPR = \frac{TN}{TN+FN}$ (the precision for the *negative* class); *Specificity* (or *true negative rate, Spec* $= \frac{TN}{TN+FF}$); *F-score* as the average between *F-score*$^+ = \frac{1}{\frac{1}{Prec} + \frac{1}{Sens}}$ (*F-score* for the positive class) and *F-score*$^- = \frac{1}{\frac{1}{NPR} + \frac{1}{Spec}}$ (*F-score* for the negative class); and *Area under the ROC curve* (*AUC*) defined as the area under the *Receiver Operating Characteristics* curve computed as $\frac{(Spec+Sens)}{2}$.

All the previously described evaluation measures range from 0 to 1 and larger values indicate better classifiers. *AUC* is indicated in the defect prediction literature [10,16] as the best evaluation measure for comparing the predictive performance of different software defect predictors [12].

4   Experimental Results

This section presents the experimental results obtained by applying *DePSem* classifier introduced in Sect. 3.

4.1   Case Studies

The case studies considered in our experimental evaluation use publicly available software defect prediction data sets. The data sets correspond to the following open-source Java software systems: JEdit, Ant and Tomcat. For each of the three systems, we have considered all the version available at [24], namely versions 3.2, 4.0, 4.1, 4.2 and 4.3 for JEdit, version 1.7 for Ant and version 6.0 for Tomcat.

The available software defect prediction data sets for JEdit, Ant and Tomcat software systems contain the application classes from each system, characterized by 20 object-oriented software metrics and the corresponding number of bugs. For our experiments, we have transformed the number of bugs into a binary feature denoting if the entity is defective or not ant we replaced the software metrics with the semantic features learned during *data collection*, after a minimal pre-processing of the source code (i.e. by removing multiple white spaces).

Table 1 describes the data sets used in our experiments and indicates, for each system, the number of *faulty* and *non-faulty* software entities for which the source code was available, the percentage of software *faults*, as well as the system's difficulty. As the literature suggests [3], the *difficulty* of software defect data set may be considered to be the proportion of faulty software entities for which the nearest neighbor is non-defective. The *difficulty* of a software defect data set is a measure of how difficult is to discriminate between its *defects* and *non-defects* using a certain vectorial representation for the software entities. Certainly, the value for the *difficulty* measure depends on the representation of the software entities. We computed the difficulty of each data considering three representations for the software entities: (1) the software metrics available at [24] (the fifth column from Table 1); (2) the vectorial representation obtained using Doc2Vec (the sixth column from Table 1); and (3) the vectorial representation obtained using LSI (the last column from Table 1).

Table 1. Description of the used data sets.

Data set	#Defects	#Non-defects	%Defects	Difficulty		
				(software metrics)	(Doc2Vec)	(LSI)
JEdit 3.2	90	170	34.6%	0.4667	0.0888	0.3222
JEdit 4.0	75	218	25.6%	0.6800	0.4667	0.6133
JEdit 4.1	80	221	26.6%	0.5696	0.4430	0.4810
JEdit 4.2	48	307	13.5%	0.6875	0.2291	0.6667
JEdit 4.3	11	476	2.3%	1.0000	0.2727	0.5455
Ant 1.7	166	575	22.4%	0.6024	0.5783	0.6084
Tomcat 6.0	77	726	9.6%	0.8182	0.6234	0.6234

Table 1 clearly emphasizes that the structural relationships from the source code expressed through software metrics differ from the conceptual (semantic) relations. For instance, JEdit 4.3 is the most difficult data set represented using software metrics, but is the second most simple if represented using the Doc2Vec conceptual vectors. Much more, Doc2Vec and LSI seem to capture slightly different characteristics of conceptual information. As an example, JEdit 4.2 has about the same high enough difficulty using software metrics and LSI based representation (0.6875 and 0.6667, respectively), but it has a much smaller difficulty using Doc2Vec representation (0.2291). Still, excepting JEdit 3.2, all case studies have high difficulties (above 0.48) using the LSI-based conceptual representation. As shown in Table 1, the most difficult systems are Ant 1.7 and Tomcat 6.0, as all three difficulty measures (structural and conceptual) are above 0.57.

Figs. 3, 4, 5 and 6 give the t-SNE [18] visualizations of the data corresponding to Ant and Tomcat systems as well as to JEdit versions 3.2 and 4.3, when represented using the first vectorial model (M1). *t-Distributed Stochastic Neighbor Embedding* (t-SNE) is a non-linear data visualization technique focused on retaining the local structure, while also preserving the global structure. The visualizations have been obtained for a perplexity (i.e. a parameter balancing attention between local and global structure) of 30, after 1000 iterations. Note that a large proportion of the defective instances (coloured in yellow) are located in the same sparser region, while in very crowded portions there are no or very few defective instances. This could indicate, on one hand, that the conceptual vectors capture aspects relevant in the context of software defect prediction and, on the other hand, that the software entities that are highly conceptually coupled with other software entities that are also highly coupled among themselves are less likely to be defective. The second result has been also observed in [5] and explained as follows. The consistently interdependent files form units whose quality is influenced by the technical dependencies, indicating a good modular design. An alternative explanation is that as consistently inter-coupled software components emerge, developers become more aware of such dependencies and so they know how changes propagate and where to look in order to reduce the probability of introducing defects elsewhere.

Fig. 3. t-SNE representation for *Ant 1.7* - model M1 (Color figure online)

Fig. 4. t-SNE representation for *Tomcat 6.0* - model M1 (Color figure online)

4.2 Results

For evaluating the predictive performance of the defect predictor introduced in Sect. 3, the experiments described in Sect. 4 have been conducted on the data sets presented in Sect. 4.1.

The Doc2Vec and LSI models used for *data collection* have been parameterized so as to produce vector representations of length 10. For training the Doc2Vec models, 20 epochs with a learning rate of 0.025 were used. The *mining* algorithm has been fed with the set of fuzzy binary relations $\mathcal{F} = \{\lesssim$ *(fuzzy less)* $\gtrsim$ *(fuzzy greater)*, $\approx$ *(fuzzy equal)*$\}$ and parameterized with the following minimum threshold values: $s_{min} = 1$, $c_{min} = 0.9$ and $m_{min} = 0.6$. In the *training* phase, MLPs with $g = |(GRAR_+ \cup GRAR_-)\backslash(GRAR_+ \cap GRAR_-)|$ input neurons, $\lfloor\sqrt{2 \cdot g}\,\rceil$ neurons activated by *sigmoid* functions on the hidden layer and 2 output neurons were trained using backpropagation in conjunction with stochastic gradient descent. The training process has been parameterized with a learning rate of 0.1, a momentum term of 0.1 and a decay factor of 0.1, the maximum number of training epochs being 500.

Table 2 summarizes the experimental results obtained by evaluating *DePSem* classifier. Due to the randomness produced by the stochastic nature of the optimization technique used for training the MLPs, the LOO cross-validation process has been executed multiple times and the average value of the evaluation

Fig. 5. t-SNE representation for *JEdit 3.2* - model M1 (Color figure online)

Fig. 6. t-SNE representation for *JEdit 4.3* - model M1 (Color figure online)

measures were computed, together with their 95% confidence interval (CI) [4]. The best values for the *F-score* and *AUC* evaluation measures are highlighted.

Table 2. Experimental results. The values for *F-score* and *AUC* are provided with 95% CIs

Data set	Model	*Sens*	*Spec*	*Prec*	*NPR*	*F-score*	*AUC*
JEdit 3.2	M1	0.858	0.673	0.581	0.899	0.731±0.004	0.765 ± 0.003
	M2	0.908	0.663	0.588	0.932	0.744±0.005	0.786±0.006
	M3	0.859	0.713	0.613	0.905	0.757 ±0.005	0.786 ± 0.005
JEdit 4.0	M1	0.651	0.769	0.493	0.865	0.687 ± 0.005	0.710 ± 0.005
	M2	0.919	0.463	0.371	0.943	0.575 ± 0.003	0.691 ± 0.003
	M3	0.784	0.677	0.455	0.901	0.674 ± 0.008	0.730 ± 0.009
JEdit 4.1	M1	0.846	0.742	0.540	0.931	0.742± 0.003	0.794± 0.003
	M2	0.915	0.645	0.479	0.955	0.700± 0.002	0.780± 0.003
	M3	0.890	0.705	0.519	0.947	0.732± 0.005	0.797± 0.006
JEdit 4.2	M1	0.742	0.770	0.337	0.950	0.657± 0.011	0.756± 0.008
	M2	0.904	0.457	0.207	0.968	0.479± 0.002	0.681± 0.002
	M3	0.873	0.615	0.262	0.969	0.578± 0.004	0.744± 0.002
JEdit 4.3	M1	0.695	0.656	0.045	0.989	0.436± 0.002	0.676± 0.010
	M2	0.891	0.654	0.056	0.996	0.448± 0.002	0.772± 0.014
	M3	1.000	0.766	0.090	1.000	0.516± 0.002	0.883± 0.001
Ant 1.7	M1	0.783	0.715	0.443	0.920	0.685 ±0.002	0.749 ±0.001
	M2	0.789	0.478	0.304	0.887	0.530 ±0.001	0.634 ±0.002
	M3	0.808	0.704	0.441	0.927	0.686 ±0.003	0.756 ±0.002
Tomcat 6.0	M1	0.757	0.756	0.247	0.967	0.611 ±0.003	0.756 ±0.002
	M2	0.682	0.659	0.175	0.951	0.528 ±0.001	0.670 ±0.002
	M3	0.822	0.713	0.233	0.974	0.594 ±0.003	0.768 ±0.007

From Table 2 we observe that, for most of the considered software systems, the combined representation (model M3) provided the highest *AUC* values. For only one system, *JEdit 4.2*, the best *AUC* was obtained using the Doc2Vec representation of the software entities (model M1) and was slightly better than the *AUC* obtained using M3. This sustains our assumption that Doc2Vec and LSI express slightly different features, thus a combined representation would be beneficial. In addition, we observe a good correlation between the *AUC* and the *F-score* values, for all case studies.

5   Discussion and Comparison to Related Work

The software defect prediction literature contains numerous approaches for detecting software faults using machine learning based classifiers. Most of these use software metrics for expressing structural relationships between software components. We start by comparing our approach to existing related work from the defect prediction literature which consider non-structural dependencies between software entities. Then, the experimental results from Sect. 4.2 are compared to the results of existing defect predictors based both on structural and conceptual software characteristics.

Cataldo et al. [5] have comparatively evaluated syntactic, logical and work dependencies in terms of their impact on software defect proneness. The comparative evaluation has been performed using logistic regression models. The experimental results indicate that logical dependencies are significantly more relevant than syntactic dependencies in predicting the software systems' propensity for failure.

Kirbas et al. [15] have also studied the effect of evolutionary coupling on defect proneness. The authors considered, as a case study, a large financial legacy software system. They performed both correlation and regression analyzes to quantify the association between evolutionary coupling and software defects. The correlation analysis resulted in indicating a positive correlation between evolutionary coupling and defect measures, while the regression analysis pointed out that evolutionary coupling measures can contribute to explaining software defects, but to extents which are highly dependent on their correlations. These results have been strengthened by a later study [14] which pointed out that the explanatory power of the evolutionary coupling with respect to defect propensity is also dependent on defect type and process metrics.

Our approach is related to the previously mentioned approaches [5,14,15] only in the sense that it exploits dependencies different than the ones expressed by the widely used traditional coupling measures and, presumably, the dependencies captured by the *change* coupling measures used in these studies are also partially captured by the *semantic* dependencies [1]. The main difference consists in the fact that the semantic features we use are automatically learned from the source code, whereas the change coupling measures are manually designed based on historical data.

An approach that automatically learns semantic features from token vectors extracted from the programs' Abstract Syntax Trees (ASTs) has been proposed by Wang et al. [25]. The semantic features are learned using Deep Belief Networks (DBN) and then used, on ten open source Java projects, in the context of both within-project and cross-project defect prediction. The tokens extracted from the ASTs consist of nodes of method invocations and class instance creations, method, type and enum declarations and control-flow nodes such as *if* and *while* statements, etc., while all the other nodes are ignored. As DBN requires numeric features, the authors have build a mapping between integers and tokens thus encoding tokens vectors as integer vectors which have been also completed with zeros for having consistent lengths. The semantic features have been comparatively evaluated against traditional features (software metrics in the *Promise* repository) and AST features, the results obtained confirming the superior relevance of the semantic features.

The main common characteristic of our approach and the one previously described, [25], is that the semantic features are learned automatically and unsupervisedly. The differences are the following. In our approach, the semantic representations of the software entities are learned directly from the minimally pre-processed source code, using Doc2Vec, while the semantic representations used in [25] are learned from token vectors extracted from ASTs, using DBN. This means that we are also considering the comments and identifiers which are considered in the literature to express the intent of the software entities [23] thus being relevant in expressing semantic relations. Moreover, unlike the features generation in [25], which is dependent on the programming language, the feature generation step of our approach is programming language independent. On the other hand, our approach has not yet been validated in the context of cross-project defect prediction.

Besides the previously described approaches, a lot of work has been conducted in the software defect prediction literature considering software metrics for expressing the structural relationships between software entities. The performance of several defect predictors based on software metrics and evaluated on part of the case studies considered in our paper (JEdit versions 4.0, 4.2, 4.3, Ant 1.7 and Tomcat 6.0) are summarized in the research paper [20]. Table 3 presents the performance (considering the AUC value) of $DePSem$ classifier compared to similar approaches which are providing results on the data sets evaluated in the current study. For $DePSem$, the values provided by model M3 are considered. For each classifier, the second column from Table 3 depicts the type of features (*semantic* or *software metrics*) used for prediction. The last three rows from the table present the highest, the lowest and the average AUC value taken from the research paper [20]. By "–" we indicate the approaches that do not provide results for a particular data set.

Table 3. Comparison to related work.

Approach	Type of features	JEdit 3.2	JEdit 4.0	JEdit 4.1	JEdit 4.2	JEdit 4.3	Ant 1.7	Tomcat 6.0
DePSem	semantic	**0.786**	**0.730**	**0.797**	**0.744**	**0.883**	**0.756**	**0.768**
ADTree [25]	semantic	–	0.607	0.6265	–	–	0.9445	–
ADTree [25]	software metrics	–	0.59	0.566	–	–	0.5945	–
Highest AUC taken from [20]	software metrics	–	0.858	–	0.903	0.815	0.926	0.921
Lowest AUC taken from [20]	software metrics	–	0.305	–	0.666	0.5	0.633	0.51
Average AUC taken from [20]	software metrics	–	0.660	–	0.698	0.658	0.754	0.753

Table 3 reveals that $DePSem$ outperforms the semantic features based approach from [25] on JEdit 4.0 and JEdit 4.1 systems. We mention that, unlike in [25], we have not reduced the difficulty of the data sets by eliminating instances with possibly incorrect labels. Compared to the defect predictors which are using software metrics $DePSem$ outperforms the highest available AUC [20] on JEdit 4.3 and the average AUC on all case studies. Overall, out of 21 comparisons, $DePSem$ wins (i.e. provides a better AUC value) in 15 cases.

6 Conclusions and Future Work

The paper presented a novel approach to software defect prediction based on semantic, or conceptual, features extracted automatically from the source code. The experiments performed on seven data sets have confirmed that conceptual coupling impacts the proneness to software defects.

As a first direction of further work, we aim to extend the experimental evaluation by considering additional large-scale software systems and different granularities (e.g. method-level defect prediction). As a second direction, we also intend to investigate combining the conceptual features with structural coupling metrics, since they have been shown to be complementary.

References

1. Bavota, G., Dit, B., Oliveto, R., Di Penta, M., Poshyvanyk, D., De Lucia, A.: An empirical study on the developers perception of software coupling. In: Proceedings of the 2013 International Conference on Software Engineering, ICSE 2013, pp. 692–701. IEEE Press, Piscataway (2013)
2. Bishnu, P., Bhattacherjee, V.: Software fault prediction using quad tree-based k-means clustering algorithm. IEEE Trans. Knowl. Data Eng. **24**(6), 1146–1150 (2012)
3. Boetticher, G.D.: Improving the credibility of machine learner models in software engineering. In: Zhang, D. (ed.) Advances in Machine Learning Applications in Software Engineering, pp. 52–72. IGI Global, Clear Lake (2007)
4. Brown, L., Cat, T., DasGupta, A.: Interval estimation for a proportion. Stat. Sci. **16**, 101–133 (2001)
5. Cataldo, M., Mockus, A., Roberts, J.A., Herbsleb, J.D.: Software dependencies, work dependencies, and their impact on failures. IEEE Trans. Software Eng. **35**(6), 864–878 (2009)
6. hua Chang, R., Mu, X., Zhang, L.: Software defect prediction using non-negative matrix factorization. JSW **6**(11), 2114–2120 (2011)
7. Chidamber, S.R., Kemerer, C.F.: Towards a metrics suite for object-oriented design. In: Conference Proceedings on OOP Systems, Languages, and Applications, pp. 197–211 (1991)
8. Czibula, G., Czibula, I.G., Miholca, D.L.: Enhancing relational association rules with gradualness. Int. J. Innovative Comput. Commun. Control **13**, 289–305 (2016)
9. Deerwester, S.C., Dumais, S.T., Landauer, T.K., Furnas, G.W., Harshman, R.A.: Indexing by latent semantic analysis. JASIS **41**, 391–407 (1990)
10. Fawcett, T.: An introduction to ROC analysis. Pattern Recogn. Lett. **27**(8), 861–874 (2006)
11. Gu, Q., Zhu, L., Cai, Z.: Evaluation measures of the classification performance of imbalanced data sets. In: Cai, Z., Li, Z., Kang, Z., Liu, Y. (eds.) Computational Intelligence and Intelligent Systems, pp. 461–471. Springer, Heidelberg (2009)
12. Haghighi, A.S., Dezfuli, M.A., Fakhrahmad, S.: Applying mining schemes to software fault prediction: a proposed approach aimed at test cost reduction. In: Proceedings of the World Congress on Engineering. WCE 2012, pp. 1–5, IEEE Computer Society, Washington (2012)

13. Hall, T., Beecham, S., Bowes, D., Gray, D., Counsell, S.: A systematic literature review on fault prediction performance in software engineering. IEEE Trans. Software Eng. **38**(6), 1276–1304 (2011)
14. Kirbas, S., et al.: The relationship between evolutionary coupling and defects in large industrial software. J. Softw. Evol. Process **29**(4), 1–19 (2017)
15. Kirbas, S., Sen, A., Caglayan, B., Bener, A., Mahmutogullari, R.: The effect of evolutionary coupling on software defects: an industrial case study on a legacy system. In: Proceedings of the 8th ACM/IEEE International Symposium on Empirical Software Engineering and Measurement, ESEM 2014, pp. 6:1–6:7. ACM, New York (2014)
16. Lavrač, N., Kavšek, B., Flach, P., Todorovski, L.: Subgroup discovery with CN2-SD. J. Mach. Learn. Res. **5**, 153–188 (2004)
17. Le, Q.V., Mikolov, T.: Distributed representations of sentences and documents. CoRR abs/1405.4053 (2014)
18. van der Maaten, L., Hinton, G.: Visualizing data using t-SNE. J. Mach. Learn. Res. **9**, 2579–2605 (2008)
19. McCabe, T.J.: A complexity measure. IEEE Trans. Software Eng. **2**(4), 308–320 (1976)
20. Miholca, D.L., Czibula, G., Czibula, I.G.: A novel approach for software defect prediction through hybridizing gradual relational association rules with artificial neural networks. Inf. Sci. **441**, 152–170 (2018)
21. Miholca, D.: An adaptive gradual relational association rules mining approach. Studia Universitatis Babeş-Bolyai Informatica **63**(1), 94–110 (2018)
22. Panichella, A., Oliveto, R., Lucia, A.D.: Cross-project defect prediction models: L'union fait la force. In: IEEE Conference on Software Maintenance, Reengineering and Reverse Engineering (CSMR-WCRE), February 2014, pp. 164–173 (2014)
23. Poshyvanyk, D., Marcus, A., Ferenc, R., Gyimóthy, T.: Using information retrieval based coupling measures for impact analysis. Empirical Softw. Eng. **14**(1), 5–32 (2009)
24. Tera-promise repository. http://openscience.us/repo/
25. Wang, S., Liu, T., Tan, L.: Automatically learning semantic features for defect prediction. In: Proceedings of the 38th International Conference on Software Engineering, pp. 297–308. ICSE 2016. ACM, New York (2016)
26. Zubrow, D., Clark, B.: How good is the software : a review of defect prediction techniques. In: Software Engineering Symposium, pp. 1–7. Carreige Mellon University (2001)

A Novel Method for Highly Imbalanced Classification with Weighted Support Vector Machine

Biao Qi[1,2], Jianguo Jiang[1,2], Zhixin Shi[1,2(✉)], Meimei Li[1,2], and Wei Fan[1,2]

[1] Institute of Information Engineering, Chinese Academy of Sciences, Beijing, China
{qibiao,jiangjianguo,shizhixin,limeimei,fanwei}@iie.ac.cn
[2] School of Cyber Security,
University of Chinese Academy of Sciences, Beijing, China

Abstract. In real life, the problem of imbalanced data classification is unavoidable and difficult to solve. Traditional SVMs based classification algorithms usually cannot classify highly imbalanced data accurately, and sampling strategies are widely used to help settle the matter. In this paper, we put forward a novel undersampling method i.e., granular weighted SVMs-repetitive under-sampling (GWSVM-RU) for highly imbalanced classification, which is a weighted SVMs version of the granular SVMs-repetitive undersampling (GSVM-RU) once proposed by Yuchun Tang et al. We complete the undersampling operation by extracting the negative information granules repetitively which are obtained through the naive SVMs algorithm, and then combine the negative and positive granules again to compose the new training data sets. Thus we rebalance the original imbalanced data sets and then build new models by weighted SVMs to predict the testing data set. Besides, we explore four other rebalance heuristic mechanisms including cost-sensitive learning, undersampling, oversampling and GSVM-RU, our approach holds the higher classification performance defined by new evaluation metrics including G-Mean, F-Measure and AUC-ROC. Theories and experiments reveal that our approach outperforms other methods.

Keywords: Highly imbalanced classification · Undersampling · GWSVM-RU · Information granules · Weighted SVMs

1 Introduction

In the field of data mining and machine learning, imbalanced data classification problem [9] is still troublesome and difficult to solve effectively, and still one leading challenge for knowledge discovery. The class imbalance problem arises when the class of interest is relatively rare as compared with other class(es) [1], embodied in different data quantity between classes. Without the loss of generality, we define the class of minority class samples as positive samples; meanwhile, we define the class of majority class samples as negative samples. The

C. Douligeris et al. (Eds.): KSEM 2019, LNAI 11775, pp. 275–286, 2019.
https://doi.org/10.1007/978-3-030-29551-6_24

phenomenon of imbalanced data is always common in many practical applications, such as bioinformatics, e-business, and disease diagnosis and information security. Class imbalance leads to different cost-sensitive learning between different classes, which have significant effects in machine learning. Misclassifying a positive sample will be more serious than misclassifying a negative sample. For example, in rare disease diagnosis, people with diseases can be in minority so they are positive samples and we value them much more, while persons without any diseases can be in majority, so they are negative samples and we value them less. If we classify a positive sample as the negative sample, in other word, we regard the person who should be a patient as a healthy man or woman, we will suffer much more losses than that we misclassify the healthy person as a patient.

Data imbalance affects the performance of the standard SVM classifiers [14], because they fail to take the classes imbalance into consideration. Due to the amount of the negative data is highly much more than that of the positive data, a standard SVM classifier usually generates an optimal hyperplane that is more likely close to the positive data by learning the training data. Consequently, the obtained classifier would predict the unknown positive data as the negative data easily. This is a simple and intuitive reason that standard SVM has low generalization ability for solving the imbalanced data classification. Besides, there exist more comprehensive reasons to explain this phenomenon.

Breiman et al. [6] stressed that the size of data sets, class priors, cost of errors in different classes, and placement of decision boundaries are all closely connected [5]. Many existing methods for solving the imbalanced data classification are based on above four aspects. Sampling strategies including undersampling and oversampling are widely used by many scholars, their main roles are to alter the minority and majority class sizes so that the training data set is rebalanced as much as possible. Cost-sensitive learning [8] mainly reflects that different class bears unequal cost. More specific and detailed contents about solutions will be illustrated in the later chapters.

In this paper, we mainly study binary imbalanced class classification and make use of information granules techniques [13] to slightly adjust the GSVM-RU algorithm [13] to achieve imbalanced class classification task. We propose a novel and more effective approach i.e., granular weighted SVMs repetitive undersampling (GWSVM-RU), which is an improvement based on undersampling skills. The GWSVM-RU strategy not only avoids loss of information caused by undersampling while reducing information redundancy, but also has high classification precision. It should be noted that the classification precision is no longer traditional metric of classification accuracy, but some other appraise criteria, such as G-Mean, F-Measure and AUC-ROC, and these three metrics are widely used to evaluate whether one classifier can well classify a highly imbalanced data set or not. Specifically, in a training set, on the one hand, we regard the whole positive samples as a positive information granule; on the other hand, we extract some negative information granules by standard SVMs, and combine the positive granule with negative ones to compose a new training data set. Then we employ the weighted SVMs [8] to train the best model, and finally we get some testing results with the optimal model. Lots of experiments display that our approach owns an obvious advantage on the effect of imbalanced classification and outperforms other approaches.

The rest of our paper is organized as follows. Section 2 reviews some related knowledge about standard C-support vector machine (C-SVM) [7] and why standard C-SVM fails to solve the highly imbalanced classification. Besides, we also introduce some other popular tactics or techniques used to settle the highly data imbalance problems. Section 3 mainly presents our approach i.e., GWSVM-RU, and we give the reason that why our approach can behave well on classifying imbalanced data accurately. Section 4 shows the experimental results and analysis. Finally, Sect. 5 summarizes this paper.

2   Related Knowledge

It is well-known that SVM algorithm is widely used for classification problems, the algorithm owns perfect mathematical theory and extensive application value. Compared with other machine learning algorithms, such as neural network, which is built on the basis of empirical risk minimization, SVM is based on structural risk minimization, and it can get high generalization ability while ensuring minimal empirical risk. In this paper, we only give the basic formulation of C-SVM so that we can explain why it is out of work to solve imbalanced classification.

2.1   C-Support Vector Machine(C-SVM)

Given training vectors $x_i \in R^n, i = 1, 2, \ldots, l$ and label vector $y \in R^l$ in binary classes, i.e., $y_i \in \{1, -1\}$, C-SVM needs to solve the following primal problem:

$$\min_{\omega, b, \xi} \frac{1}{2}\omega^T\omega + C\sum_{i=1}^{l} \xi_i$$
$$s.t.\ y_i(\omega^T \Theta(x_i) + b) \geq 1 - \xi_i, i = 1, 2, \ldots, l,$$
$$\xi_i \geq 0, i = 1, 2, \ldots, l. \tag{1}$$

Its dual is

$$\min_{\alpha} \frac{1}{2}\alpha^T H\alpha - e^T\alpha$$
$$s.t.\ y^T\alpha = 0, 0 \leq \alpha_i \leq C, i = 1, 2, \ldots, l. \tag{2}$$

where e is a vector of all ones, C is a weight scalar quantity, which balances the empirical risk and generalization ability, α is the Lagrange multiplier vector, H is an $l \times l$ positive semi-definite matrix, $H_{ij} \equiv y_iy_jK(x_i, x_j)$, and $K(x_i, x_j) \equiv \Theta(x_i)^T\Theta(x_j)$ is the kernel function [10]. Here training vectors will be mapped into a higher or infinite dimensional space by the function Θ. And the final decision function is formula 3:

$$f(x) = sign(\sum_{i=1}^{l} y_i\alpha_iK(x_i, x) + b) \tag{3}$$

Where the function $sign(\cdot)$ is a sign function, i.e., the formula 4.

$$sign(x) = \begin{cases} 1, & if \ x \geq 0 \\ -1, & if \ x < 0 \end{cases} \tag{4}$$

2.2   Why Standard C-SVM Fails to Solve Highly Imbalanced Classification

First of all, we need to review some facts that C-SVM handles the problem of classification based on the structural risk minimization. Theoretically, in the objective function of C-SVM, the first item denotes the generalization ability, and the second item means the empirical risk. In the highly imbalanced data classification, the number of positive samples is seriously smaller than that of the negative samples, so if we sacrifice a few of positive samples and even entire positive samples, we can gain greater generalization ability, in other words, the first item in objective function reduces much more, the second item in objective function increases less, the calculated classifier can satisfy the primitive objective function to the minimum. Consequently, the decision hyperplane ought to approach to the positive points, therefore, the classifier will be unable to correctively predict the unknown positive samples which we value more.

2.3   Some Other Strategies for Coping with Highly Imbalanced Classification

As known to us, weighted SVM (WSVM) is actually a cost-sensitive learning algorithm, which is effective for class imbalance classification in certain scenario. Sampling technology is popular to be used to confront the class imbalance. It is a class of methods. Generally, there are two directions to perform sampling, the one is oversampling such as SMOTE [4] and the other one is undersampling e.g. SVM-RANDU [11]. The former mainly adds positive examples artificially so that it rebalances the whole training data set, therefore, it increases the training data set, and it needs longer time to accomplish classification. Besides, it is apt to overfit for that it repeats the positive examples [12]. The latter chiefly decreases negative examples so that it makes two classes own the similar number of samples roughly, in this case, undersampling can shorten the training time while it may lead to some loss of information, and decrease generalization ability. Both oversampling and undersampling can get a more balanced training data set so that they will gain a better result in spite of their respective drawbacks.

Granular SVMs repetitive undersampling algorithm (GSVM-RU) was proposed by Yuchun Tang et al. [13]. The main idea of the algorithm was to extract negative information granules by standard C-SVM each round loop over and over again and combine the gained negative information granules with the positive information granule that was the whole positive samples to operate a final C-SVM training, finally formed a best model which can be used to predict the testing set. It is worth noting that the algorithm GSVM-RU is simple and easy to operate, besides, it is an undersampling method. More importantly, we know that information granule is a key concept and plays a crucial role in the algorithm, for the reason that we need to find which sample or samples is or are important, in other words, this data can express part or all characteristics of the whole data set.

Generally speaking, time complexity and space complexity will increase as the data is bigger. Naturally, our direct idea to solve a complex problem is divide-and-conquer and split a huge problem into a sequence of information granules [16] which can accurately stand for the entirety. Based on this, information granules are the best candidates here. As known that when SVM classifies a data set, we can get some more important information of the data set, in other words, this information can wholly or most partly stand for the overall data set, and we call this important information as support vectors [15]. On the one hand, it should be avoided a loss of information when we employ undersampling techniques, on the other hand, we need to find and retain as much useful information as possible. In this way, we get an excellent way that owns not only a shorter training time, but also preserves mostly useful and significant information of one data set to counter imbalanced data classification. We agree with some key points in the GSVM-RU algorithm, since positive examples are seriously less than negative examples, we also regard the whole positive examples as a positive information granule while we regard the negative support vectors extracted by each round of iteration as negative information granules.

3 Our Approach

In Sect. 2, we have introduced WSVM algorithm, which can solve general class imbalance that the proportion between classes is not too big. But when the amount proportion of different classes of data is highly great, it will emerge a phenomenon that the amount of negative information granules will be much more than the positive information granule, in other words, the number of negative support vectors will be much more than that of positive samples even if we adopt GSVM-RU, if so, it will be an inferior imbalanced data classification problem, and it will not be effective for us to use standard SVM to build any model to accurately predict the testing set. However, we confirm that we could reduce the imbalance degree in this way. Therefore our idea is to combine GSVM-RU with WSVM. We use WSVM to model new training data set which is composed of negative information granules i.e., negative support vectors that are obtained by repeatedly training a C-SVM and the positive information granule i.e., the whole positive samples, we can reach the desired effect in this way. The detailed processing procedures are shown in the Algorithm 1.

It needs to note that we extract negative valuable information granules by standard SVMs, i.e., C-SVM, at the same time we reduce information redundancy, thereby we decrease the degree of imbalance between classes. And then we employ WSVM to train the optimal model after combing the negative valuable information granules and the positive valuable information granule, one classification problem considered to be less imbalanced can be solved in this way.

Algorithm 1. GWSVM-RU

Require: A set of positive class samples P, a set of negative class samples N, $|P| <$ $|N|$, test samples set T contains the same proportion of positive and negative samples with the primitive data set,

1: $i \Leftarrow 0, N_0 \Leftarrow N$,
2: **Repeat**:
3: $i \Leftarrow i + 1$,
4: Extract negative information granules NG_i by C-SVM training $\{N_i + P\}$, the rest negative samples $N_{i+1} = N_i - NG_i$, get a series of $NG_i, i = 1, 2, \ldots$.
5: Begin to run WSVM training $\{NG + P\}$, where

$$NG = \begin{cases} NG_0 & i = 0 \\ NG_0 + NG_1 & i = 1 \\ NG_0 + NG_1 + NG_2 & i = 2 \\ \vdots & \vdots \end{cases}$$

, then get $Model_i$ and predict T, and output A_i in some evaluation metric e.g. G-Mean.
6: **Until** A_i reaches to the optimal value $A^\star$
7: **return** Classifier and $A^\star$.

---

4 Experiments

The experiments are conducted on a PC with Intel Core i5-2450M (2.50GHz) and RAM 4.00GB memory. The software is based on the LIBSVM-3.1 Matlab Toolbox [3], which is available at [1]

Table 1. Confusion matrix

	Predicted positives	Predicted negatives
Real positives	TP	FN
Real negatives	FP	TN

4.1 Evaluation Metrics

As is well known to all is that it is inadvisable that we just use error rate to evaluate whether a classifier is good or bad when facing the class imbalance. In this paper, we employ G-Mean, F-Measure, and AUC-ROC [2] as our results evaluation criteria. G-Mean and F-Measure can be defined by the Table 1.

Usually, we use Accuracy $= \frac{TP+TN}{TP+TN+FP+FN}$ as the evaluation metric, however, it will be not effective here. G-Mean $= \sqrt{Sentivity * Specifity}$ (Sensitivity $= \frac{TP}{TP+FN}$, Specificity $= \frac{TN}{TN+FP}$) and F-Measure $= \frac{2*Precision*Recall}{Precision+Recall}$ (Precision $=$

---

[1] http://www.matlabsky.com/thread-17936-1-1.html.

$\frac{TP}{TP+FP}$, Recall $= \frac{TP}{TP+FN}$) are common evaluation criteria in the class imbalance problems; G-Mean is the geometric mean of sensitivity and specificity. F-Measure integrates Precision and Recall into a single metric. Besides, the area under a receiver operating characteristic curve (AUC-ROC) can also demonstrate imbalanced classification ability between sensitivity and specificity as a function of varying a classification threshold. In this paper; we use G-Mean, F-Measure and AUC-ROC as the evaluation criteria.

4.2 Data Sets

Six data sets collected from UCI are used in our experimental analysis. As shown in Table 2, positive samples account for a small percentage of the whole samples, the all data sets in Table 2 are obvious imbalanced data sets.

Table 2. Characteristics of data sets, # *vs* # represents that positive samples versus negative samples

Dataset	# of Samples	# of Positive Samples (%)	# of Features
Abalone(18 vs 9)(ab)	731	42(5.75%)	8
Yeast(ME2 vs others)(ye)	1484	51(3.44%)	8
Balance(balance vs others)(ba)	625	49(8.5%)	4
Pima(1 vs others)(pi)	768	268(34.9%)	9
Harberman(2 vs others)(ha)	306	81(26.47%)	4
Vehicle(opel vs others)(ve)	864	212(25.0%)	18

For each data set, we use G-Mean, F-Measure and AUC-ROC to evaluate the performance of classifiers. The bigger the three metrics for one classifier, the better its effectiveness. Specific experimental process is as follows, for one whole UCI data set, we firstly normalize the data to $[0, 1]$. Secondly, we randomly partition the data set into a training set and a testing set, which are both subsets of the entire data set. Usually, the number of samples in a training set is bigger than that in a testing set, besides, the positive samples and the negative samples in the training set will occupy the same proportion as that in the whole data set. In this work, we set the training set as ninety percent of the total data set, every data set will be conducted ten times in an experiment in this way, and we take the average of the ten times results as the final result, and the standard deviation is gained at the same time. For all experiments in this paper, we select nonlinear kernel function Gaussian kernel, its form is $K(x, y) = e^{(-(\gamma(x-y)^2))}$. To build the classification model, the parameter γ and C are needed to be known. Actually, the process of selecting the parameters of γ and C is the process of establishing the model. γ and C are obtained by grid search, both are selected from $\{2^i | i = -8, -7, \ldots, 7, 8\}$. In order to avoid bias, we perform tenfold cross validation that is putting the training set into ten folds, and each fold is used to test, and the remaining nine folds are used to train a model, we run this process ten times in turn, we select the best C and the best γ based on the best testing result. On the basis of knowing the best C and the best γ, we use the whole training set to build a better model and employ the model to predict the initial testing set, then we get the final result of the classifier. What calls for special attention is that we choose the best parameters based on G-Mean, F-Measure, and AUC-ROC rather than Accuracy.

4.3   Four Other Methods

In this paper, we also investigate four other algorithms which were used to solve the problem of unbalanced classification. Furthermore, we sufficiently compare the proposed method with the four other SVM modeling algorithms.

(1) SVM-WEIGHT: SVM-WEIGHT (WSVM for short) has been introduced in the previous part. This algorithm was used only once to train a total training data set. The algorithm was sufficiently stated in [8], its main motivation was to give a bigger penalty to false negatives than false positives. Usually, we set the weight of negative points as 1, and set the weight of the positive points as a variable cost w which was also chosen by grid search. The cost for an FN is usually suggested to be the ratio of negative samples over the positive samples. The algorithm was relatively stable.

(2) SVM-RANDU: The idea of SVM-RANDU (SVM-RU for short) was to extract a number of samples from the negative examples randomly and then to build a SVM model on the undersampling data set. It has an unknown parameter Ru that if there are Np positive samples, we need to select $Np * Ru$ negative samples from the training set. The parameter Ru can be gained by the grid search. SVM-RANDU was an undersampling method and fully expounded in [11]. It is not very stable since its randomness is strong.

3) SVM-SMOTE: SMOTE (SMOTE for short) needs to generate much more artificial positive examples and then to build an SVM model on the oversampling data set, SMOTE also exists an unknown parameter Ro that if there are Np positive samples, we should add $Np * Ro$ positive samples to the original training set. Similarly, Ro is decided by the grid search. SMOTE was an oversampling method and introduced in [4].

(3) GSVM-RU: GSVM-RU is the most similar to our approach, actually, our method slightly improves GSVM-RU. GSVM-RU performs the imbalanced classification by gaining negative information granules and meanwhile improving the balance degree between negatives and positives. The difference between our approach and GSVM-RU is that we use weighted SVM to train the revised data set which is composed of negative information granules and positive samples and then predict the test data. GSVM-RU was an undersampling method and fully expounded in [13].

4.4 Time Complexity

A primal SVM needs at least $O((Np + Nn)^3)$ time for training an imbalanced data set. SVM-RU roughly takes $O((Np+Nn*Ru)^3)$ time to complete a training procedure. And SMOTE takes $O((Np*(1+Ro)+Nn)^3)$ time. WSVM has the same time complexity with the standard SVM. GSVM-RU takes $O(Gr*(Np+Nn)^3)$ [13]. So GWSVM-RU ought to be the same complexity with GSVM-RU. Note that SVM-RU ought to take the least time to train a data set in all methods, and SMOTE would have a higher complexity than SVM, WSVM actually needs more time than SVM without overweighting to learn to converge. GSVM-RU requires to build an optimal SVM model to extract information granules, so it maybe take longer time to complete the training phase, similarly, GWSVM-RU seemly has the same small weakness as the GSVM-RU which needs a longer training time. In the prediction phase, if a standard SVM gains N SVs, and there are M samples to be predicted, it will take $O((N*M)^3)$ time for prediction. Both GSVM-RU and GWSVM-RU get less SVs, so it is authentic that they need less time to predict unknown testing data set. It should be noted that GWSVM-RU will take more time to finish the whole process of training and testing in theory, but it still can be tolerated. The following experimental results can illustrate this point.

4.5 Analysis of Experiment Results

Because of the existence of randomness, we carry out ten times experiments for each dataset and make the average result as the final result. As shown in Table 3, we can summarize that our method surpasses over other methods in classification precision such as G-Mean, F-Measure and AUC-ROC remarkably. It should be noted that we execute the process of extracting each negative information granule based on the optimal criterion of evaluation, for example, we regard G-Mean as the evaluation metric, we construct the best training model based on the highest G-Mean, and then we extract a negative information granule. Because time complexity will magnify as the times of negative information granules extraction processes increase, we limit the above processes ten times, or we will terminate the information granules extraction processes when negative information granules will not exist any more. In fact, WSVM has better generalization ability than standard SVM in a certain scope of parameters, so GWSVM-RU should possess preferable generalization performance. As shown in Table 3, GWSVM indeed holds better prediction results than other classification methods.

The weakness of our approach seems that it needs a little more time to complete the whole process of classification and prediction, since the process of extracting every negative information granule, besides we need to select the optimal parameters by grid search and tenfold cross validation. As shown in Table 4, we just list the computing time of one experiment, obviously, we can see that our method is a bit time consuming than that of GSVM-RU, however, it can be still tolerated. WSVM actually is more complicated than SVM, so it

Table 3. Classification performance comparison on all data sets (%). The bold fonts represent the best experimental results

Dataset	Metric	WSVM	SVM-RU	SMOTE	GSVM-RU	GWSVM-RU
ab	G-Mean	80.24±6.45	72.98±5.78	87.87±5.70	89.26±5.82	**90.0±6.0**
ye	G-Mean	84.45±6.70	80.5±6.69	86.95±5.76	90.52±6.62	**91.0±5.0**
ba	G-Mean	91.76±5.95	89.49±6.50	75.45±5.34	92.81±4.18	**93.36±5.94**
pi	G-Mean	**82.34±5.57**	75.26±6.39	77.34±5.84	81.48±4.13	81.12±0.69
ha	G-Mean	68.0±6.25	58.06±7.89	**70.76±6.32**	68.74±5.63	68.79±6.47
ve	G-Mean	83.23±4.70	76.67±5.53	80.87±5.69	81.06±3.16	**84.89±2.5**
ab	F-Measure	64.79±6.80	65.57±6.94	69.87±5.45	**90.23±5.79**	87.86±6.23
ye	F-Measure	84.36±5.76	68.35±7.65	79.34±6.02	85.56±6.3	**88.34±6.46**
ba	F-Measure	92.86±5.79	69.93±6.76	75.08±6.47	91.82±6.65	**95.59±5.66**
pi	F-Measure	80.47±5.37	80.45±6.51	89.79±6.13	93.41±5.75	**96.12±5.69**
ha	F-Measure	69.07±4.89	69.69±5.83	**75.4±5.48**	71.93±4.53	73.79±4.09
ve	F-Measure	70.27±5.82	58.06±6.58	70.28±6.04	72.7±6.54	**75.39±5.13**
ab	AUC-ROC	92.79±1.29	85.83±2.78	73.17±1.71	93.45±1.06	**94.89±1.80**
ye	AUC-ROC	97.41±0.5	60.94±2.50	92.62±2.05	97.68±1.14	**98.45±0.43**
ba	AUC-ROC	**98.07±2.57**	88.74±3.16	96.64±2.46	98.02±5.72	98.03±2.10
pi	AUC-ROC	**98.11±1.95**	88.08±3.75	94.27±2.70	96.35±3.29	98.03±2.10
ha	AUC-ROC	66.79±0.61	**72.24±4.0**	62.07±3.45	64.34±6.0	68.0±0.00
ve	AUC-ROC	95.04±2.40	90.85±2.49	75.84±1.85	92.58±1.0	**95.12±0.52**

Table 4. Classification time comparison on all data sets. (In seconds)

Dataset	Metric	WSVM	SVM-RU	SMOTE	GSVM-RU	GWSVM-RU
ab	G-Mean	204.83	5.83	183.69	168.82	170.41
ye	G-Mean	606.24	7.75	630.67	319.38	324.52
ba	G-Mean	205.88	7.51	232.55	259.16	276.5
pi	G-Mean	191.07	8.09	232.24	230.72	272.49
ha	G-Mean	52.69	16.74	133.86	258.81	271.19
ve	G-Mean	411.98	118.12	1155.99	893.69	1118.87
ab	F-Measure	205.96	5.37	184.88	201.37	235.26
ye	F-Measure	601.36	7.86	664.04	396.49	397.37
ba	F-Measure	195.21	7.61	233.84	282.06	287.39
pi	F-Measure	195.31	7.67	231.87	297.61	302.5
ha	F-Measure	52.65	16.51	136.71	197.39	229.42
ve	F-Measure	413.29	117.77	1157.02	851.65	860
ab	AUC-ROC	249.75	83.34	255.13	307.28	336.15
ye	AUC-ROC	692.15	84.83	721.96	817.69	891.33
ba	AUC-ROC	268.93	85.06	305.53	328.18	377.28
pi	AUC-ROC	269.55	85.06	305.86	399.26	479.64
ha	AUC-ROC	126.36	93.57	209.04	340.93	352.71
ve	AUC-ROC	486.83	189.32	1227.65	1239.27	1256.47

is a little slow to complete the classification process. SVM-RU takes the least time to accomplish the whole process for it reduces the training set and thus it will produce less support vectors to accelerate prediction. SMOTE needs also a little more time to model a training set for it increases more positive samples, so it produces more support vectors, and thus requires more time to predict a testing set. We can summarize that the size of a data set and the complexity of a model decide training time, while the testing time is determined by the number of support vectors, the total time is composed of training time and testing time. From Table 4, we can get a conclusion that although GWSVM-RU needs a little more time to accomplish classification process, it's not as bad as it compared to other classification methods.

5   Conclusion

In this paper, we propose a novel strategy named GWSVM-RU based on GSVM-RU. Besides, we explore other four approaches to cope with imbalance data classification. From the experimental results, the proposed approach surpasses majority of other classification methods in the aspect of performance metrics e.g. G-Mean and F-Measure. WSVM itself has a good classification performance to solve ordinary class imbalance, so it is credible that GWSVM-RU holds more excellent generalization ability. However, WSVM fails to cope with highly class imbalance, so our direct idea is that we wipe off the most useless information of training data set and retain the most valuable information of the data set, and then control the training data set into the scope that WSVM can play a role at the imbalanced classification. So we combine the WSVM with GSVM-RU to form a powerful approach GWSVM-RU that can successfully manage highly imbalanced data classification. Traditional techniques e.g. SVM-RU only plays an effective role in certain range, however, its randomness is inevitable and insoluble. Consequently it is not advisable in reality. Besides, SMOTE also cannot get rid of the same shortcoming as that of SVM-RU. From the perspective of time complexity, SVM-RU seems to own the greatest advantage for it decreases the size of training set, SMOTE likely enlarges the training set so that it needs more time to accomplish the training process. WSVM and GWSVM-RU is a bit complicated than standard SVM and GWSVM-RU may require more time to run over the learning process. Yet empirical analyses reveal that we still can put up with it. We can conclude that our approach indeed occupies certain advantages in theory and experiments. So we hope our strategy can be helpful for future research in the class imbalance domain especially highly imbalanced data classification.

Acknowledgement. We thank our anonymous reviewers for their invaluable feedback. This work was supported by the National Natural Science Foundation of China (Grant No.61502486)

References

1. Akbani, R., Kwek, S., Japkowicz, N.: Applying support vector machines to imbalanced datasets. In: Boulicaut, J.-F., Esposito, F., Giannotti, F., Pedreschi, D. (eds.) ECML 2004. LNCS (LNAI), vol. 3201, pp. 39–50. Springer, Heidelberg (2004). https://doi.org/10.1007/978-3-540-30115-8_7
2. Bradley, A.P.: The use of the area under the ROC curve in the evaluation of machine learning algorithms. Pattern Recogn. **30**(7), 1145–1159 (1997)
3. Chang, C.C., Lin, C.J.: LIBSVM: a library for support vector machines. ACM Trans. Intell. Syst. Technol. (TIST) **2**(3), 27 (2011)
4. Chawla, N.V., Bowyer, K.W., Hall, L.O., Kegelmeyer, W.P.: SMOTE: synthetic minority over-sampling technique. J. Artif. Intell. Res. **16**, 321–357 (2002)
5. Chawla, N.V., Japkowicz, N., Kotcz, A.: Special issue on learning from imbalanced data sets. ACM Sigkdd Explor. Newsl. **6**(1), 1–6 (2004)
6. Chen, C., Liaw, A., Breiman, L., et al.: Using random forest to learn imbalanced data, vol. 110, pp. 1–12. University of California, Berkeley (2004)
7. Cortes, C., Vapnik, V.: Support-vector networks. Mach. Learn. **20**(3), 273–297 (1995)
8. Domingos, P.: MetaCost: a general method for making classifiers cost-sensitive. KDD **99**, 155–164 (1999)
9. Japkowicz, N., Stephen, S.: The class imbalance problem: a systematic study. Intell. Data Anal. **6**(5), 429–449 (2002)
10. Keerthi, S.S., Lin, C.J.: Asymptotic behaviors of support vector machines with Gaussian kernel. Neural Comput. **15**(7), 1667–1689 (2003)
11. Kubat, M., Matwin, S., et al.: Addressing the curse of imbalanced training sets: one-sided selection. In: ICML, vol. 97, pp. 179–186. Nashville, USA (1997)
12. Tang, Y., Zhang, Y.Q.: Granular SVM with repetitive undersampling for highly imbalanced protein homology prediction. In: 2006 IEEE International Conference on Granular Computing, pp. 457–460. IEEE (2006)
13. Tang, Y., Zhang, Y.Q., Chawla, N.V., Krasser, S.: SVMs modeling for highly imbalanced classification. IEEE Trans. Syst. Man Cybern. Part B Cybern. **39**(1), 281–288 (2009)
14. Vapnik, V., Vapnik, V.: Statistical Learning Theory, pp. 156–160. Wiley, New York (1998)
15. Vapnik, V.N.: An overview of statistical learning theory. IEEE Trans. Neural Networks **10**(5), 988–999 (1999)
16. Yao, Y., Zhou, B.: A logic language of granular computing. In: 6th IEEE International Conference on Cognitive Informatics, pp. 178–185. IEEE (2007)

A Study on Applying Relational Association Rule Mining Based Classification for Predicting the Academic Performance of Students

Liana Maria Crivei[ID], Gabriela Czibula[(✉)][ID], and Andrei Mihai[ID]

Department of Computer Science, Babeş-Bolyai University,
1, M. Kogalniceanu Street, 400084 Cluj-Napoca, Romania
{liana.crivei,gabis,mihai.andrei}@cs.ubbcluj.ro

Abstract. Predicting the students' academic achievements is of great interest within the Educational Data Mining (EDM) field, having the main goal of extracting patterns relevant in deciding the students' performance at a certain academic course. This paper analyses a classification model SPRAR (Students Performance prediction using Relational Association Rules) for predicting the academic results of students using relational association rules. *Relational association rules* represent an extension of classical *association rules* able to capture binary relationships between the attribute values. Three new classification scores are introduced in this paper and used in the classification stage of SPRAR. Their performance is analyzed using three real academic data sets from Babes-Bolyai University, Romania and compared to similar existing results from the literature.

Keywords: Educational Data Mining ·
Students' performance prediction · Supervised learning ·
Relational association rules

1 Introduction

Educational Data Mining (EDM) is an emerging research field focusing on developing models to identify and extract valuable information from educational related data. Research in EDM aims to reveal patterns in students' learning and enhance their academic achievements. Students' academic success and performance can be predicted through data mining techniques [8] using *supervised* or *unsupervised* learning.

There are many approaches on student performance prediction using machine learning models such as: artificial neural networks [9], [14], decision trees [9], [7], Naive Bayes [9], [14], support vector machines [14] and K-nearest neighbour [14]. Recent work on predicting the students' academic performance investigate the performance of ensemble learning methods [4] and association rule mining [5].

© Springer Nature Switzerland AG 2019
C. Douligeris et al. (Eds.): KSEM 2019, LNAI 11775, pp. 287–300, 2019.
https://doi.org/10.1007/978-3-030-29551-6_25

The students' performance prediction task is often a difficult one as it is highly dependent on various factors. One factor is the imbalanced nature of the training data set which means that the number of instances for the students who passed the examination is generally higher than the number of instances of the students that failed the examination. Other factors that affect the performance prediction could be the fact that the instructors have different evaluation mechanisms and standards or that the students' learning process may be discontinue throughout the semester.

A non-linear classification model, *SPRAR* (*Students Performance prediction using Relational Association Rules*) was introduced in [5] for predicting if a student will pass or fail at a certain academic discipline based on the students' grades received during the semester. The proposed classifier [5] used relational association rule mining for predicting the most appropriate output class (*pass* or *fail*) for a student. At the classification stage, *SPRAR* assigned to a new query instance a *score* expressing how close is that instance to the target classes. In this paper we extend the *SPRAR* classification model, by introducing three alternative scores which can be used in the classification stage of *SPRAR* for deciding if a student will *pass* or *fail* a certain course. Three real case studies are used for experimenting the performance of *SPRAR* considering the newly proposed classification scores. With the goal of empirically determining which is the the most appropriate classification score, the proposed scores are comparatively analyzed and evaluated against the original variant introduced in [5]. The study performed in this paper is new in the *educational data mining* literature.

The remainder of the paper is comprised of several sections as follows. The background concepts regarding the relational association rule (RAR) mining as well as the classification model *SPRAR* are presented in Sect. 2. In Sect. 3, which is the methodology, we introduce three methods for computing the score used in the classification stage of *SPRAR* for determining the similarity of a query instance to the classes of students which *pass* or *fail* a course. The experimental evaluation is elaborated in Sect. 4, while Sect. 5 includes the interpretation of the results obtained. Section 6 outlines the conclusions of our study and the directions for future work.

2 Background

This section starts by introducing in Sect. 2.1 the main background concepts related to *relational association rule* (RAR) mining. *SPRAR* classifier for students' performance prediction is then briefly described in Sect. 2.2.

2.1 Relational Association Rule Mining

We define the *Relational Association Rules* (RARs) concept in the following. Let us consider $D = \{s_1, s_2, \ldots, s_q\}$ a set of *records* or *instances* [3]. For every instance of the data set, we consider a sequence of m attributes $A = (a_1, \ldots, a_m)$ that describes the data set D. Each attribute a_i takes values from a non-empty and non-fuzzy domain Δ_i. *Null* (*empty*) values may also be included in the domain Δ_i. The value of attribute a_i for an instance s_j is expressed by $\Psi(s_j, a_i)$.

The set of all possible relations which are not necessarily ordinal and can be defined between two domains Δ_i and Δ_j is denoted by $\mathcal{T}$.

Definition 1. *A relational association rule [13] is an expression* $(a_{i_1}, a_{i_2}, a_{i_3},$ $\dots, a_{i_h}) \Rightarrow (a_{i_1} \tau_1 a_{i_2} \tau_2 a_{i_3} \dots \tau_{h-1} a_{i_h})$, *where* $\{a_{i_1}, a_{i_2}, a_{i_3}, \dots, a_{i_h}\} \subseteq A$, $a_{i_k} \neq a_{i_j}$, $k, j = 1, \dots, h$, $k \neq j$ *and* $\tau_k \in \mathcal{T}$ *is a relation over* $\Delta_{i_k} \times \Delta_{i_{k+1}}$, *where* Δ_{i_k} *is considered the domain of the attribute* a_{i_k}.

(a) *If* $a_{i_1}, a_{i_2}, \dots, a_{i_h}$ *are non-missing in* ω *instances from the data set then we call* $Supp = \frac{\omega}{q}$ *the* support *of the rule.*

(b) *If we denote by* $D' \subseteq D$ *the set of instances where* $a_{i_1}, a_{i_2}, a_{i_3}, \dots, a_{i_h}$ *are non-missing and all the relations* $\Psi(s_j, a_{i_1}) \tau_1 \Psi(s_j, a_{i_2})$, $\Psi(s_j, a_{i_2}) \tau_2$ $\Psi(s_j, a_{i_3})$, $\dots$, $\Psi(s_j, a_{i_{h-1}}) \tau_{h-1} \Psi(s_j, a_{i_h})$ *hold for each instance* s *from* D' *then we call* $Conf = \frac{|D'|}{q}$ *the* confidence *of the rule.*

To illustrate the notion of RARs, we use a synthetically generated data set containing four attributes denoted by a_1, a_2, a_3 and a_4 and six instances. The maximal interesting RARs identified as well as the corresponding sample data set are given in Fig. 1. $DRAR$ algorithm for RARs mining is applied using a minimum support threshold of $Supp_{min} = 1$ and a minimum confidence threshold of $Conf_{min} = 0.6$. Our attributes a_1, a_2, a_3 and a_4 have integer values therefore two possible binary relations between these attributes are used: $<$ and $\geq$. Table 1 depicts all RARs discovered in our sample data set with their respective length and confidence value. For example, the first RAR from Table 1 $a_1 \geq a_3$ having length **2** is interpreted as follows: for the analysed data set the value of the attribute a_1 is greater than or equal to the value of the attribute a_3 in 66% of instances. i.e. in 4 out of 6 instances.

No.	a_1	a_2	a_3	a_4
1.	8.50	7.00	8.00	7.80
2.	9.00	8.30	8.70	8.60
3.	7.95	5.40	8.00	7.50
4.	9.50	10.00	9.40	9.60
5.	10.00	9.20	9.60	9.80
6.	7.20	8.75	8.10	8.50

Length	Rule	Confidence
2	$a_1 \geq a_3$	0.66
2	$a_1 \geq a_4$	0.66
3	$a_1 \geq a_2 < a_3$	0.66
3	$a_1 \geq a_2 < a_4$	0.66

Fig. 1. Sample data set (left) and interesting maximal RARs mined for $Supp_{min} = 1$ and $Conf_{min} = 0.6$ (right).

2.2 *SPRAR* Classifier for Students' Performance Prediction

In this section we review the classification model $SPRAR$ introduced in [5] for deciding if a student will pass or fail at a certain academic discipline based on the students' grades received during the semester.

The classification problem is a binary classification one. The two possible classes are denoted by "+" (the class representing *positive* instances, corresponding to students that *pass* a certain course) and "−" (the class consisting of *negative* instances, corresponding to students that *fail*). The data set D used for training the $SPRAR$ classifier consists of a set of instances (students), $D = \{s_1, s_2, \ldots, s_q\}$ and each instance s_i describes the performance of a student, during the academic semester, at a given course. The attribute set characterizing D is $A = \{a_1, a_2, \ldots, a_m\}$ and represents the grades obtained by the students during the semester evaluations. Accordingly, each s_i is visualized as an m-dimensional vector $s_i = (s_{i1}, s_{i2}, \ldots, s_{im})$, s_{ij} representing the grade received by student s_i at the j-th semester evaluation. The subset of *positive* instances from D is denoted by D_+ and a subset of *negative* instances from D is denoted by D_-. These sets will be used for training the $SPRAR$ classifier.

First, as a **data pre-processing** step of $SPRAR$ the set of attributes A is enlarged with four additional attributes: $a_{m+1} = 5$, $a_{m+2} = 6$, $a_{m+3} = 7$ and $a_{m+4} = 8$). Since the algorithm for mining interesting RARs considers only binary relations between attribute values, the newly added attributes $(a_{m+1}, \ldots, a_{m+4})$ allow the uncovery of relations between attributes and specific thresholds (in our case thresholds for the grades 5, 6, 7, 8). Afterwards, the training step of $SPRAR$ consists of mining from the training data set D two sets of interesting RARs: RAR_+ represents the set of interesting RARs discovered from D_+ (i.e. the students that *pass* the course) and RAR_- represents the interesting RARs discovered from D_- (i.e. the set of students that *fail* to pass the course).

At the classification stage, when a new query instance s has to be classified, two scores are computed $score_+(s)$ and $score_-(s)$ expressing the probability that the query instance belongs to the *positive* and *negative* classes, respectively. The computation proposed in [5] for $score_+$ and $score_-$ is given in Formula (1).

$$score_+(s) = \frac{v^+(s) + nv^-(s)}{n_+ + n_-}, \quad score_-(s) = \frac{v^-(s) + nv^+(s)}{n_+ + n_-} \quad (1)$$

In Formula (1) n_+ represents the sum of confidences of the RARs from RAR_+; n_- is the sum of confidences of the RARs from RAR_-; $v^+(s)$ is the sum of confidences of the rules from RAR_+ which are verified in s and $v^-(s)$ represents the sum of confidences of the rules from RAR_- which are verified in s.

When instance s has to be classified, if $score_+ > score_-$ then instance s will be classified as a *positive* one, otherwise it will be classified as *negative*. It has to be mentioned that $score_+$ and $score_-$ represent probabilities, i.e. $score_+(s) + score_-(s) = 1$.

3   Methodology

Let us consider the problem of predicting if a student will *pass* or *fail* a certain course and the theoretical model from Sect. 2.2. If c is one class, by $\neg c$ we denote the class which is the opposite of c.

As shown in Sect. 2.2, after training the $SPRAR$ classifier two sets RAR_+ and RAR_- of interesting relational association rules are discovered in the training data D. Let us consider that $c_1^+, c_2^+, \ldots, c_p^+$ are the confidences of the RARs from the set RAR_+ and $c_1^-, c_2^-, \ldots, c_r^-$ are the confidences of the RARs from the set RAR_-.

After the training of $SPRAR$ was completed, when a new student (instance) s has to be classified (as "+" or "−"), two scores, $score_+(s)$ (indicating the similarity degree of s to the "+" class) and $score_-(s)$ (indicating the similarity degree of s to the "−" class), are computed. In the following we introduce three alternative methods to compute the *positive* and *negative scores* (denoted in the following by $score1$, $score2$ and $score3$) which can be used in the classification stage of $SPRAR$ for deciding how "close" is a student to the set D_+ of *positive* and D_- of *negative* instances from the training data set D. For deciding if a student belongs to a certain class we base our decision on the confidence of the RARs relevant for that class verified by the grades of the student. Furthermore we also consider the confidence of the RARs relevant for the opposite class which are not verified by its grades.

The first two scores we propose ($score1$ and $score2$) are defined based on the intuition that the similarity of an instance s to a particular class c is very likely to be influenced by the confidences of the rules from RAR_c that are verified in the instance s, but also by the rules from $RAR_{\neg c}$ that are not verified in the instance s. Starting from this intuition, $score_c(s)$ will measure not only how "close" the instance s is to the class c, but also how "far" it is from the opposite class.

Unlike $score1$ and $score2$, the third score ($score3$) will be defined based only on the similarity of an instance s to a particular class c, discarding the opposite class $\neg c$.

3.1 First Method Proposed ($score1$)

The first method proposed for computing $score$ is denoted by $score1$ and is an adaptation of the original score from [5] which was described in Sect. 2.2. The underlying idea behind extending the original $score$ is the following. Instead of considering only the confidence of the RARs which are entirely verified in a query instance s (as in Formula (1)), we will consider the "partial" confidence of the subrules verified in the instance s too.

Let us denote by n_+ the sum of confidences of the RARs from RAR_+ and by n_- the sum of confidences of the RARs from RAR_-. Thus, for the i-th rule r from RAR_+ ($1 \le i \le p$) we express by $v_i^+(s)$ the strength of the binary subrules of r in s. If k represents the number of binary rules from r verified in s and l the number of binary rules from r, $v_i^+(s)$ is defined as $k \cdot \frac{c_i^+}{l}$. Intuitively, if the entire rule r is verified in s (i.e. k is equal to l), then $v_i^+(s) = c_i^+$. In addition, if none of the binary subrules from r are verified in s, then $v_i^+(s)$ is 0. Similarly, for the i-th rule r from RAR_-, $v_i^-(s)$ is defined as $k \cdot \frac{c_i^-}{l}$. Analogously, by $nv_i^+(s)$ and $nv_i^-(s)$ we denote the sum of the "partial" confidences for the binary subrules from the i-th rule from RAR_+ and RAR_-, respectively, which are not verified in s. Accordingly, the computation proposed for $score1_+$ and $score1_-$ is given in Formula (2).

$$score1_+(s) = \frac{\sum_{i=1}^{p} v_i^+(s) + \sum_{i=1}^{r} nv_i^-(s)}{n_+ + n_-}, \; score1_-(s) = \frac{\sum_{i=1}^{p} nv_i^+(s) + \sum_{i=1}^{r} v_i^-(s)}{n_+ + n_-} \tag{2}$$

3.2 Second Method Proposed ($score2$)

For the query instance s and each rule r (from RAR_+ and RAR_-) we aim to compute the degree to which r together with its subrules is verified in the instance s. As for $score2$ (Sect. 3.2), we are considering not only the entire RARs verified in s, but also their binary subrules which are verified in s. When computing the similarity of instance s to a particular class (e.g. "+") we consider not only the "similarity" of s to the class, but also the "dissimilarity" of s to the opposite class ("−" in our example). Using the notations introduced in Sect. 3, the dissimilarity of s to the *positive* class ($diss_+(s)$) and the dissimilarity of s to the *negative* class ($diss_-(s)$) are computed as described in Formulae (3) and (4), respectively.

$$diss_+(s) = \sqrt{\sum_{i=1}^{p}(c_i^+ - v_i^+(s))^2 + \sum_{i=1}^{r}(v_i^-(s))^2} \tag{3}$$

$$diss_-(s) = \sqrt{\sum_{i=1}^{p} v_i^+(s))^2 + \sum_{i=1}^{r}(c_i^- - v_i^-(s))^2)} \tag{4}$$

Subsequently, based on the previously defined dissimilarity degrees, the score $score2_c(s)$ representing the probability that s belong to a class c ("+" or "−") is defined as in Formula (5). By $\neg c$ we denote the opposite class of c.

$$score2_c(s) = \frac{diss_{\neg c}(s)}{diss_c(s) + diss_{\neg c}(s)} \tag{5}$$

We mention that $score2_+$ and $score2_-$ represent probabilities, i.e. $score2_+(s) + score2_-(s) = 1$.

3.3 Third Method Proposed ($score3$)

Unlike $score1$ and $score2$, the third introduced score ($score3$) will be defined based only on the similarity of an instance s to a particular class c, discarding the dissimilarity from its opposite class $\neg c$. Thus, the computation proposed for $score3_+$ and $score3_-$ is given in Formula (6).

$$score3_+(s) = \frac{\sum_{i=1}^{p} v_i^+(s)}{p}, \; score3_-(s) = \frac{\sum_{i=1}^{r} v_i^-(s)}{r} \tag{6}$$

We observe that unlike $score1$ and $score2$, $score3_+$ and $score3_-$ do not represent probabilities, i.e. $score3_+(s) + score3_-(s) \neq 1$.

3.4 Example

For a better understanding of the classification process using $SPRAR$ with the score computation methods previously described, we are considering a simplified example. Figure 2 illustrates a sample data set containing only ten instances characterized by four attributes (5 positive and 5 negative instances extracted from data set D2). For each instance, the final examination grade and the class ("+" or "−") are provided. The middle and rightmost tables from Fig. 2 present the sets of interesting RARs mined from the positive and negative instances from the sample data for a minimum confidence threshold of 0.8 [5].

Tables 1, 2 and 3 depict the classification process of $SPRAR$ for two test instances selected from data set D2, together with their actual classes and the classes predicted by $SPRAR$ using $score1$, $score2$ and $score3$, respectively. In our example, the number of rules from RAR_+ is $p = 12$ and the number of rules from RAR_- is $r = 11$.

a_1	a_2	a_3	a_4	Final grade	Class
9.625	10	10	9.25	9	
10	10	10	10	10	
5.5	8.69	10	1	7	"+"
9.625	8.63	9.25	10	6	
2.50	6	5.70	5	5	
2.50	9.50	10	10	4	
2.50	5.71	10	5	4	
2.50	9.64	7	9	4	"−"
5.00	7.96	9.10	8.50	4	
7.3	4.8	4.6	10	4	

Rule	Confidence
$a_2 \geq a_4$	0.8
$a_2 \geq 8$	0.8
$a_3 \geq a_4$	0.8
$a_3 \geq 8$	0.8
$a_1 \geq 5$	0.8
$a_2 \geq 5$	1
$a_2 \geq 6$	1
$a_2 \geq 7$	0.8
$a_3 \geq 5$	1
$a_3 \geq 6$	0.8
$a_3 \geq 7$	0.8
$a_4 \geq 5$	0.8

Rule	Confidence
$a_1 < 8$	1
$a_1 < 6$	0.8
$a_1 < 7$	0.8
$a_1 < a_4 \geq 8$	0.8
$a_1 < a_2 \geq 5$	0.8
$a_1 < a_3 \geq 5$	0.8
$a_1 < a_3 \geq 6$	0.8
$a_1 < a_3 \geq 7$	0.8
$a_1 < a_4 \geq 5$	1.0
$a_1 < a_4 \geq 6$	0.8
$a_1 < a_4 \geq 7$	0.8

Fig. 2. Sample data (left), the sets RAR_+ (middle) and RAR_- (right) mined for a minimum confidence threshold of 0.8 [5].

Table 1. The classification of $SPRAR$ trained on the data set from Fig. 2 using $score1$ for the scores' computation.

Test instance	Actual class	v_+/nv_-	v_-/nv_+	$score1_+$	$score1_-$	Predicted class
($a_1 = 9.53$, $a_2 = 6.07$, $a_3 = 10$, $a_4 = 9.05$)	"+"	7.8/4.7	4.5/2.4	0.65	0.35	"+"
($a_1 = 5.0$, $a_2 = 1.0$, $a_3 = 10.0$, $a_4 = 7.0$)	"−"	5.8/1.2	7.9/4.4	0.36	0.64	"−"

Table 2. The classification of $SPRAR$ trained on the data set from Fig. 2 using $score2$ for the scores' computation.

Test instance	Actual class	$diss_+$	$diss_-$	$score2_+$	$score2_-$	Predicted class
($a_1 = 9.53$, $a_2 = 6.07$, $a_3 = 10$, $a_4 = 9.05$)	"+"	1.37	1.78	0.56	0.44	"+"
($a_1 = 5.0$, $a_2 = 1.0$, $a_3 = 10.0$, $a_4 = 7.0$)	"−"	1.98	0.89	0.31	0.69	"−"

Table 3. The classification of $SPRAR$ trained on the data set from Fig. 2 using $score3$ for the scores' computation.

Test instance	Actual class	$\sum_{i=1}^{p} v_i^+$	$\sum_{i=1}^{r} v_i^-$	$score3_+$	$score3_-$	Predicted class
($a_1 = 9.53$, $a_2 = 6.07$, $a_3 = 10$, $a_4 = 9.05$)	"+"	7.8	4.5	0.65	0.41	"+"
($a_1 = 5.0$, $a_2 = 1.0$, $a_3 = 10.0$, $a_4 = 7.0$)	"−"	5.8	7.9	0.48	0.73	"−"

4   Experimental Evaluation

In this section three different data sets that are used in our experiments are briefly described and the experimental setup is explained. Then the results are presented, for the three different scores introduced in Sect. 3.

4.1   Data Sets and Experimental Setup

For our experiments we used three different data sets, containing real academic data collected from Babeş-Bolyai University, Romania. The data represents grades obtained by students at three different undergraduate courses offered in the *first*, *second* and *third* semester respectively. One instance in any of the data sets represents the grades of one student. The attributes of the instance, therefore, are the different grades. While the number of grades is different from course to course (thus the number of attributes per instance is different for the three data sets), the last grade (last attribute) is always the *final examination grade*, based on which it is decided if the student passed the course. The last attribute for each instance will be used as its label during the training of $SPRAR$.

The first data set (D1) was obtained during the time frame of one academic year (2016–2017), for a course offered in the first semester. This data set contains a number of only 384 instances, significantly fewer than the other data sets, due to the shorter time frame in which the data was collected. The second data set (D2) is comprised of the grades the students obtained during a third semester course offered by the university. The data was collected in a time frame of four academic years (2014–2018). This data set contains a total of 863 instances.

The third data set (D3) contains 1154 instances collected during a time frame of six academic years (2012–2018). All data sets are available at [2]. While we modeled the prediction of students' performance as a binary classification problem, the solution is far from trivial, mainly due to the difficulty of the data sets and the imbalance of the classes (the ratio is $\sim 3 : 1$). In order to better understand the data sets and their difficulty we create a graphical visualisation of the data sets using Principal Component Analysis (PCA) [6] to transform the attribute space so that it contains only two independent attributes (principal components) which express the maximum variance in data. The results can be seen in the Figures from 3, 4, 5 and 6. The blue dots represent instances where the students passed the course (have a *final examination grade* of 5 or higher), and the red dots represent instances where the students failed the course (have a *final examination grade* lower than 5). In Fig. 3 we can see the visualization of data set D3, which has the highest number of instances. While there is a hint of class separation between the left side and the right side of the image, it is clear that the two classes are heavily intertwined, and difficult to discern one from the other. The data set D1 is visualised in Fig. 4. This visualisation seems to be quite similar to the one in Fig. 3, but it can be observed that the data set D1 has the lowest number of instances and the highest class imbalance, which may make it the most difficult data set of the three.

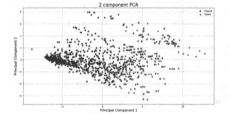

Fig. 3. PCA applied to the data set D3. (Color figure online)   **Fig. 4.** PCA applied to the data set D1. (Color figure online)

In Fig. 5 is presented the visualisation of the data set D2. It seems to be a very odd data set, given the image. This results occur because of the high number outliers in the data set. Most of the instances are actually found in the red dot in the lower left corner of the image. In Fig. 6 is presented a zoomed-in version of this part of the visualisation of the D2 data set. It is clear that Fig. 6 is a much better representation of the second data set and that most points in Fig. 5 are outliers, their respective instances could even be considered noisy data.

This noise in the data from data set D2 is not completely unexpected. We have observed that the data set contains some instances for which there is a significant level of discordance between the grades obtained during the semester evaluations and the final examination grade. This might indicate either a biased evaluation of the laboratory and practical activities either a passing criterion that might be slightly different according to the examinators' bias and might be the source of the outliers.

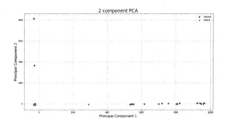
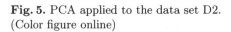
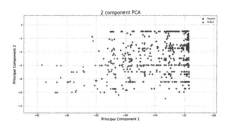

Fig. 5. PCA applied to the data set D2.   **Fig. 6.** Zoom in of left corner from Fig. 5.
(Color figure online)   (Color figure online)

4.2 Results

For training the $SPRAR$ classifier, a training subset was randomly selected from
each data set. The instances which were not selected for training, were used for
testing. The structure of the training/testing subsets from data sets D1, D2 and
D3 is described in the first columns from Table 4. For generating the sets RAR_+
and RAR_- the following parameters were used: 1 for the minimum support
threshold, 0.6 for the minimum confidence threshold and two possible binary
relations between the attributes ($<$ and $\geq$). After $SPRAR$ classifier has been
trained, it is applied on data sets D1, D2 and D3, considering all three methods
for computing the score used for deciding the classification of an instance (i.e.
$score1$, $score2$ and $score3$ introduced in Sect. 3). For evaluating the performance
of $SPRAR$, three evaluation measures specific to binary classifiers are used:
sensitivity or *recall* (Sens), *specificity* (Spec) and *Area under the ROC curve*
(AUC). The obtained experimental results are provided in the table from Fig. 7.
The AUC values are provided with a 95% confidence interval (CI) [1].

Table 4. Description of training and testing sets.

Data set	# of training instances		# of testing instances	
	negative	positive	negative	positive
D1	34	260	15	75
D2	112	571	40	140
D3	240	528	70	316

Data set	Score	TP	TN	FP	FN	Sens	Spec	AUC
D1	score1	55	10	5	20	0.73	0.67	**0.70 ± 0.09**
	score2	45	12	3	30	0.60	0.80	**0.70 ± 0.09**
	score3	55	10	5	20	0.74	0.67	**0.70 ± 0.09**
D2	score1	97	29	11	43	0.69	0.73	**0.71 ± 0.07**
	score2	80	36	4	60	0.57	0.90	**0.74 ± 0.06**
	score3	103	27	13	37	0.74	0.68	**0.71 ± 0.07**
D3	score1	240	63	7	76	0.76	0.90	**0.83 ± 0.04**
	score2	235	59	11	63	0.79	0.84	**0.82 ± 0.04**
	score3	237	64	6	79	0.75	0.91	**0.83 ± 0.04**

Score	Win	Lose	Tie
score1	1	1	4
score2	**2**	**2**	**2**
score3	1	1	4

Fig. 7. The results of $SPRAR$ using $score1$, $score2$ and $score3$ (Sect. 3) on all data sets. 95% CIs are used for AUC.

Fig. 8. Performance comparison of $SPRAR$ using different methods for score computation

5 Discussion

An advantage of the $SPRAR$ method, in contrast to other data mining models, is the interpretability of the mined knowledge. In our case, the mined RARs express relationships between the students' grades received during the semester, each rule being specific to students which either *passed* or *failed* the final examination. For instance, from the data set D3, two of the interesting discovered RARs are: $a_1 < a_3 \geq 6$ (having a confidence of 0.624 in the set of students which passed the examination) and $a_3 \geq a_4 < 5$ (having a confidence of 0.636 in the set of students which failed the examination). We could read these rules in the following way: if a student has the *seminar score* (a1) smaller than the *project status score* (a3) which is grater or equal to 6, then the student will probably pass (with confidence of 0.624), but if the student's *project status score* (a3) is grater than the *written test score* (a4) which is less than 5, then the student will probably fail (with a confidence of 0.624). Since the rules are not mutually exclusive we need a *score* to determine if the student will pass or fail depending on which rules it respects and their confidence.

The experimental results provided in the table from Fig. 7 reveal that the performance of $SPRAR$ classifier using all three scores ($score1$, $score2$ and $score3$) is about the same. For assessing the best score, we computed for each score (considering each data set) how many times it *wins* and *loses* the comparison with respect to other scores (i.e. the AUC value is greater than and less than, respectively) as well as the number of times the comparison is *tied*. The comparative results are depicted in the table from Fig. 8, which highlights that the best predictive performance of $SPRAR$ was obtained when using $score2$ for deciding the target class. That is why we will compare in the table from Fig. 9 the results provided by $SPRAR$ with $score2$ with similar approaches from the literature. For a precise comparison, we applied the methods from the related work (DTs [7], ANNs [11] and SVMs [15]) on our data sets D1, D2 and D3.

For the ANN we used the implementation from the Keras Deep learning API [10] using the Tensorflow neural networks framework, and for the DT and SVM we used the implementation from the Scikit-learn [12] framework. For the ANN we used the following parameter settings [11]: 2 hidden layers with 17 and 35 neurons, respectively, using the Sigmoid activation function; one output neuron with the linear activation function, thus the output being the predicted grade of the student; the mean squared error loss and the predefined adadelta optimizer; we trained the network for 30 epochs using a batch of 1 instance. For the SVM and DT classifiers we used the predefined settings. For all the classifiers we set weights for the classes, in order to reduce the class imbalance problem; we used a 4:1 weight ratio in favor of the negative class. Figure 10 depicts the comparison of $SPRAR$ with $score2$ and the approaches from related work considering the AUC measure. The AUC values are provided with 95% CIs.

Data	Model	Sens	Spec	AUC
D1	SPRAR (score2)	0.60	0.63	**0.70 ± 0.09**
	DT [7]	0.95	0,60	**0.77 ± 0.09**
	ANN [11]	1.00	0.27	**0.63 ± 0.10**
	SVM [15]	0.97	0.60	**0.79 ± 0.08**
	Original SPRAR [5]	0.91	0.67	**0.79 ± 0.08**
	Average on related work	0.96	0.54	**0.75 ± 0.09**
D2	SPRAR (score2)	0.57	0.90	**0.74 ± 0.06**
	DT [7]	0,79	0,43	**0,61 ± 0.07**
	ANN [11]	0,81	0,53	**0,67 ± 0.07**
	SVM [15]	0,75	0,55	**0,65 ± 0.07**
	Original SPRAR [5]	0.70	0.70	**0.70 ± 0.07**
	Average on related work	0.76	0.55	**0.66 ± 0.07**
D3	SPRAR (score2)	0.79	0.84	**0.82 ± 0.04**
	DT [7]	0.82	0.43	**0.63 ± 0.05**
	ANN [11]	0,87	0.87	**0.87 ± 0.03**
	SVM [15]	0.61	0.39	**0.50 ± 0.05**
	Original SPRAR [5]	0.74	0.88	**0.81 ± 0.05**
	Average on related work	0.76	0.64	**0.70 ±0.04**

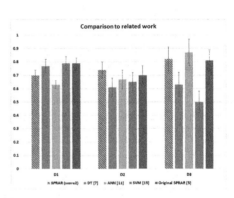

Fig. 9. $SPRAR$ with $score2$ compared to related work. 95% CIs are used for AUC.

Fig. 10. AUC comparison of $SPRAR$ with $score2$ and different algorithms from related work. The AUC values are provided with 95% CIs.

Analyzing the comparative results presented in the table from Fig. 9 and graphically illustrated in Fig. 10 we observe the following. Out of 12 comparisons, considering the AUC value, $SPRAR$ with $score2$ outperforms the related work in 8 cases (67%), while in only 4 cases our AUC is smaller than the AUC from the literature. In addition, for data sets D2 and D3, the AUC of $SPRAR$ with $score2$ is above the average AUC value from the literature. We also note that for the students' performance prediction task we aim to obtain a high *specificity*, more precisely to maximize the number of students that were correctly classified as *fail*. Considering the Spec values, our approach is better than the related work in 9 cases (75%), while in only 3 cases it provides a smaller Spec. As observed from Fig. 10, our approach obtained the best result on data set D2, which is the most difficult one from the classification viewpoint, as highlighted in Figs. 5 and 6 by the 2D PCA plots.

6 Conclusions and Future Work

This paper extended the classification model SPRAR (Students Performance prediction using Relational Association Rules) [5] for predicting students' achievement to a particular course based on *relational association rule* (RAR) mining [13]. The membership of a query instance to a pass or fail class is determined using academic data sets obtained from Babes-Bolyai University, Romania. Three new classification scores are introduced and used in the classification stage of SPRAR for deciding if a student will *pass* or *fail*. SPRAR performance is evaluated using several evaluation measures: *sensitivity, specificity* and *Area under the ROC curve*. The best prediction score is identified and compared to existing results from the current literature.

Through several experiments performed on real academic data from Babes-Bolyai University, Romania we obtained an empirical evidence that relational association rules are relevant for distinguishing between the academic performance of students. We also observed that the classification methodology (identifying the best score for discriminating between students' performance) is dependent on the data sets, therefore we could further investigate the possibility to automatically learn it using supervised methods. As future research directions we also aim to extend our experiments on other data sets, to add additional attributes and relationships in the RAR mining process for improving SPRAR's predictive performance.

References

1. Brown, L., Cat, T., DasGupta, A.: Interval estimation for a proportion. Stat. Sci. **16**, 101–133 (2001)
2. Crivei, L.: Data (2018). http://www.cs.ubbcluj.ro/~liana.crivei/AcademicData Sets/SPRAR/
3. Crivei, L.M.: Incremental relational association rule mining of educational data sets. Studia Universitatis Babes-Bolyai Series Informatica **63**(2), 102–117 (2018)
4. Crivei, L.M., Ionescu, V.S., Czibula, G.: An analysis of supervised learning methods for predicting students' performance in academic environments. ICIC Express Lett. **13**, 181–190 (2019)
5. Czibula, G., Andrei, M., Crivei, L.M.: SPRAR: a novel relational association rule mining classification model applied for academic performance prediction. In: KES2019. Procedia Computer Science (2019). to be published
6. Goodfellow, I., Bengio, Y., Courville, A.: Deep Learning. MIT Press (2016)
7. Hajizadeh, N., Ahmadzadeh, M.: Analysis of factors that affect the students academic performance - data mining approach. CoRR abs/1409.2222 (2014). http://arxiv.org/abs/1409.2222

8. Huebner, R.A.: A survey of educational data-mining research. Res. High. Educ. J. **19**, 1–13 (2013)
9. Jishan, S.T., Rashu, R.I., Haque, N., Rahman, R.M.: Improving accuracy of students' final grade prediction model using optimal equal width binning and synthetic minority over-sampling technique. Decis. Anal. **2**(1), 1–25 (2015)
10. Keras: The Python Deep Learning library. https://keras.io/
11. Pauziah Mohd Arsad, N.B., lail Ab Manan, J.: A neural network students' performance prediction model (NNSPPM). In: Proceedings of ICSIMA, pp. 1–5. IEEE Computer Society (2013)
12. Scikit-learn: Machine learning in Python. http://scikit-learn.org/stable/
13. Serban, G., Câmpan, A., Czibula, I.G.: A programming interface for finding relational association rules. IJCCC **1**(S), 439–444 (2006)
14. Shahiri, A.M., Husain, W., Rashid, N.A.: A review on predicting student's performance using data mining techniques. Procedia Comput. Sci. **72**, 414–422 (2015)
15. Tran, T.O., Dang, H.T., Dinh, V.T., Truong, T.M.N., Vuong, T.P.T., Phan, X.H.: Performance prediction for students: a multi-strategy approach. Cybern. Inf. Technol. **17**(2), 164–182 (2017)

Strict Subspace and Label-Space Structure for Domain Adaptation

Ying Li[1], Pei Zhang[1], Lin Cheng[1], Yaxin Peng[2], and Chaomin Shen[3(✉)]

[1] School of Computer Engineering and Science,
Shanghai University, Shanghai 200444, China
[2] Department of Mathematics, School of Science,
Shanghai University, Shanghai 200444, China
[3] Department of Computer Science, East China Normal University,
Shanghai 200062, China
cmshen@cs.ecnu.edu.cn

Abstract. One of the most important issues of transfer learning is domain adaptation which aims at adapting a classifier or model trained in the source domain for use in the target domain, while two domains may be different but related. Intuitively, a good feature representation across domain is crucial. In this paper, we put forward a novel feature representation approach for unsupervised domain adaptation, namely Strict Subspace and Label-space Structure for Domain Adaptation (SSLS). SSLS learns two feature representations that project the source domain and target domain into two different subspaces where marginal and conditional distribution shift can be reduced effectively. Specially, we make the distances of corresponding points in the projection subspaces as well as the label space close by Laplacian graph, which will guarantee the strictness of subspace structure and the quality of the pseudo labels. Extensive experiments verify that our method is superior to several state-of-the-art methods on three real world cross-domain visual recognition tasks Office+Caltech, USPS+MNIST, and PIE.

Keywords: Transfer learning · Unsupervised · Domain adaptation · Laplacian graph

1 Introduction

In the traditional machine learning framework, the task of learning is to learn a classification model based on sufficient training data; then use the learned model to classify and predict test documents. Machine learning algorithms have a key problem: a large amount of training data in some emerging fields is very difficult to obtain. Besides, traditional machine learning assumes that training data and test data obey the same data distribution. In many cases, however,

Supported by the National Natural Science Foundation of China (Nos. 11601315 and 11771276), and Shanghai Sailing Program (16YF1404000).

© Springer Nature Switzerland AG 2019
C. Douligeris et al. (Eds.): KSEM 2019, LNAI 11775, pp. 301–313, 2019.
https://doi.org/10.1007/978-3-030-29551-6_26

the same distribution assumption does not hold. This requires to re-label a large amount of training data to meet the needs of training, but marking new data is very expensive and requires a lot of manpower and material resources. From another point of view, it is very wasteful to completely discard previous data. How to make reasonable use of this data is the main problem solved by transfer learning through domain adaptation [1]. The goal of domain adaptation is to use the knowledge learned from a domain to help with learning tasks in the new domain.

Domain adaptation has been widely used in image classification [2], object recognition [3], feature learning [4], sentiment analysis [5], document categorization across different customer data sets [6], and 3D pose estimation [7]. It can be generally divided into semi-supervised and unsupervised domain adaptation based on the availability of target labeled data. We focus on the unsupervised domain adaptation which is considered to be more challenging. Approaches to domain adaptation can be summarized into four situations: instance transfer, feature representation transfer, parameter transfer, and relational knowledge transfer. We pay attention to the most popular approach: feature representation transfer, aiming at finding a good feature representation to minimize domain divergence and classification on model error.

In this paper, we put forward a potential feature space extraction method (SSLS) that simultaneously projects the source domain and target domain into two different subspaces. Its purpose is not only to minimize the marginal and conditional distribution shifts, but also to preserve data attributes in the original spaces. In particular, we use Laplacian graph to guarantee the structure of the corresponding points in the projection subspaces of the source and target domain by making their distance as close as possible for better domain adaptation. The objective function can be solved efficiently in a closed form. A number of experiments have proved that our method is superior to several state-of-the-art methods on three real world cross-domain visual recognition tasks: Office+Caltech, USPS+MNIST, and PIE.

The rest of the paper is organized as follows. Section 2 describes related work and highlights their difference. Our proposed approach is covered in Sect. 3 in detail. Experiment results and discussions are presented in Sect. 4 and finally we draw the conclusion in Sect. 5.

2   Related Work

In this section, we discuss relevant works on domain adaptation and highlight their difference.

Several domain adaptation approaches for learning the dimension reduction feature space are proposed. Transfer component analysis (TCA) [11] attempts to learn a set of common transfer components underlying both domains, so that the difference between data distributions in different domains can be significantly reduced when projected onto the subspace. Joint Distribution Adaptation (JDA) [12] goes one step further and proposes to minimize the mismatch between marginal probability distributions and conditional probability distributions simultaneously. Geodesic Flow Kernel (GFK) [13] proposes a geodesic flow kernel method, where the source and target data are projected into the intermediate subspace along the shortest path connected to the two original spaces. With the idea of manifold alignment [8], Manifold Alignment and Distribution Adaptation for Unsupervised Domain Adaptation (MBDA) [14] effectively combines manifold regularization with distribution adaptation, behaving much better than JDA. Besides, Subspace Alignment (SA) [15] addresses the issue of data centric methods that exploit common features of two domains by aligning the subspaces. Subspace distribution alignment (SDA) [16] improves SA by considering the variance of the orthogonal principal components. Different from SA and SDA, Joint Geometrical and Statistical Alignment (JGSA) [17] proposes a unified framework that learns two coupled projections to map the source and target data into their respective subspaces.

In particular, we not only reduce both the marginal and conditional distribution divergences between source and target domains, but also strict two subspaces and the label space by making close the distances of corresponding points in the projection subspaces as well as the pseudo labels in the label space by Laplacian graph.

3 Approach

3.1 Problem Statement

We define terminologies firstly. A domain $\mathcal{D}$ is composed of a d-dimensional feature space $\mathcal{X}$ and a marginal probability distribution $P(x)$, i.e., $\mathcal{D} = \{\mathcal{X}, P(x)\}$, where $x \in \mathcal{X}$. Given a specific domain $\mathcal{D}$, a task $\mathcal{T}$ consists of a label space $\mathcal{Y}$ and an objective predictive function $f(x)$, i.e., $\mathcal{T} = \{\mathcal{Y}, f(x)\}$. From a probabilistic viewpoint, $f(x)$ can be written as $Q(y|x)$, which can be interpreted as the class conditional probability distribution for each input sample x.

In unsupervised domain adaptation, we denote the source domain as $\mathcal{D}_{\mathcal{S}} = \{(x_i^s, y_i^s)_{i=1}^{n_s}\}$ with n_s labeled samples. Similarly, we denote the target domain by $\mathcal{D}_{\mathcal{T}} = \{(x_j^t)_{j=1}^{n_t}\}$ with n_t unlabeled samples. The problem we focus on is under the assumption that the source domain $\mathcal{D}_{\mathcal{S}}$ and the target domain $\mathcal{D}_{\mathcal{T}}$ are different, i.e., $\mathcal{X}_{\mathcal{S}} = \mathcal{X}_{\mathcal{T}}, \mathcal{Y}_{\mathcal{S}} = \mathcal{Y}_{\mathcal{T}}, P(\mathcal{X}_{\mathcal{S}}) \neq P(\mathcal{X}_{\mathcal{T}}), Q(\mathcal{Y}_{\mathcal{S}}|\mathcal{X}_{\mathcal{S}}) \neq Q(\mathcal{Y}_{\mathcal{T}}|\mathcal{X}_{\mathcal{T}})$.

The aim of the proposed method is to learn two latent feature spaces in which the distribution differences between marginal probability and conditional probability are explicitly reduced.

3.2 Main Idea

Target Variance Maximum. We apply PCA for maximizing the variances of target domain in the respective subspaces while preserving data attributes. Thus, the target variance maximization can be written as:

$$\max_{B} \mathrm{tr}(B^T S_t B), \tag{1}$$

where $B \in \mathbb{R}^{m \times k}$ is the orthogonal transformation matrix, and the target domain scatter matrix S_t is

$$S_t = X_t H_t X_t^T. \tag{2}$$

Here H_t is the centering matrix $H_t = I_t - \frac{1}{n_t} 1_t 1_t^T$, $1_t \in \mathbb{R}^{n_t}$ is the column vector with all ones, and $X_t = [\boldsymbol{x}_1, ..., \boldsymbol{x}_{n_t}] \in \mathbb{R}^{m \times n_t}$ is the input data matrix, Finally, the target data X_t is projected into the optimal k-dimensional subspace using $Z_t = B^T X_t$.

Source Linear Discriminant Information Preservation. In the proposed method, we apply LDA to the source domain by minimizing distances between samples of the same class and maximizing the distances between samples from different classes, i.e.,

$$\max_A \frac{\mathrm{tr}(A^T S_b A)}{\mathrm{tr}(A^T S_w A)}, \tag{3}$$

where

$$S_b = \sum_{c=1}^C n_s^{(c)} (m_s^{(c)} - \overline{m}_s)(m_s^{(c)} - \overline{m}_s)^T, \quad S_w = \sum_{c=1}^C X_s^{(c)} H_s^{(c)} (X_s^{(c)})^T. \tag{4}$$

Here S_b is the between class scatter matrix, S_w is the within-class scatter matrix, $m_s^{(c)} = \frac{1}{n_s^{(c)}} \sum_{i=1}^{n_s^{(c)}} \boldsymbol{x}_i$, $\overline{m}_s = \frac{1}{n_s} \sum_{i=1}^{n_s} \boldsymbol{x}_i$, $H_s^{(c)} = I_s^{(c)} - \frac{1}{n_s^{(c)}} 1_s^{(c)} (1_s^{(c)})^T$ is the centering matrix of data within class c, $X_s^{(c)} \in \mathbb{R}^{m \times n_s^{(c)}}$ is the set of source samples from class c, $n_s^{(c)}$ is the number of source samples of class c, $I_s \in \mathbb{R}^{n_s^{(c)} \times n_s^{(c)}}$ is the identity matrix, and $1_s \in \mathbb{R}^{n_s^{(c)}}$ is the number of source samples in class c. Finally, the source data is projected into the optimal k-dimensional subspace using $Z_s = A^T X_s$.

Marginal and Conditional Shift Minimization. Projecting the target and source domain into subspaces does not guarantee the reduction of their distribution mismatch. We adopt the Maximum Mean Discrepancy (MMD) on the Reproducing Kernel Hilbert Space (RKHS) as the criteria for minimizing the marginal distribution shift between domains. MMD estimates the distance between the means of two samples mapped into RKHS as:

$$\min_{A,B} \left\| \frac{1}{n_s} \sum_{i=1}^{n_s} A^T \boldsymbol{x}_i - \frac{1}{n_t} \sum_{j=n_s+1}^{n_s+n_t} B^T \boldsymbol{x}_j \right\|_F^2. \tag{5}$$

Certainly, the conditional distribution shift takes an important role in domain adaptation. We utilize the classifiers trained by the source domain with labeled data for predicting the pseudo labels of the target domain. Similarly, the sum of empirical distances over sub-domains of same class c is defined as:

$$\min_{A,B} \sum_{c=1}^{C} \left\| \frac{1}{n_s^{(c)}} \sum_{x_i \in X_s^{(c)}} A^T x_i - \frac{1}{n_t^{(c)}} \sum_{x_j \in X_t^{(c)}} B^T x_j \right\|_F^2 . \tag{6}$$

Hence, the final marginal and conditional shift term can be rewritten as:

$$\min_{A,B} \operatorname{tr} \left(\begin{bmatrix} A^T & B^T \end{bmatrix} \begin{bmatrix} M_s & M_{st} \\ M_{ts} & M_t \end{bmatrix} \begin{bmatrix} A \\ B \end{bmatrix} \right), \tag{7}$$

where

$$M_s = X_s \left(L_s + \sum_{c=1}^{C} L_s^{(c)} \right) X_s^T, \ L_s = \frac{1}{n_s^2} 1_s 1_s^T, \ \left(L_s^{(c)} \right)_{ij} = \begin{cases} \frac{1}{(n_s^{(c)})^2}, & x_i, x_j \in X_s^{(c)} \\ 0, & \text{otherwise} \end{cases} \tag{8}$$

$$M_t = X_t \left(L_t + \sum_{c=1}^{C} L_t^{(c)} \right) X_t^T, \ L_t = \frac{1}{n_t^2} 1_t 1_t^T, \ \left(L_t^{(c)} \right)_{ij} = \begin{cases} \frac{1}{(n_t^{(c)})^2}, & x_i, x_j \in X_t^{(c)} \\ 0, & \text{otherwise} \end{cases} \tag{9}$$

$$M_{st} = X_s \left(L_{st} + \sum_{c=1}^{C} L_{st}^{(c)} \right) X_t^T, \ L_{st} = -\frac{1}{n_s n_t} 1_s 1_t^T,$$

$$\left(L_{st}^{(c)} \right)_{ij} = \begin{cases} -\frac{1}{n_s^{(c)} n_t^{(c)}}, & x_i \in X_s^{(c)}, x_j \in X_t^{(c)} \\ 0, & \text{otherwise} \end{cases} \tag{10}$$

$$M_{ts} = X_t \left(L_{ts} + \sum_{c=1}^{C} L_{ts}^{(c)} \right) X_s^T, \ L_{ts} = -\frac{1}{n_s n_t} 1_t 1_s^T,$$

$$\left(L_{ts}^{(c)} \right)_{ij} = \begin{cases} -\frac{1}{n_s^{(c)} n_t^{(c)}}, & x_j \in X_s^{(c)}, x_i \in X_t^{(c)} \\ 0, & \text{otherwise} \end{cases} \tag{11}$$

Subspace Divergence Minimization. The source and target domains are represented by subspaces described by eigenvectors. Similar to SA, we want to reduce the difference between the two domains by minimizing their subspace divergence. Hence, we have

$$\min_{A,B} \|A - B\|_F^2 , \tag{12}$$

which can be rewritten as:

$$\min_{A,B} \operatorname{tr} \left(\begin{bmatrix} A^T & B^T \end{bmatrix} \begin{bmatrix} A \\ B \end{bmatrix} \right). \tag{13}$$

Strict Subspaces Structure. In the previous process, we have projected samples of the source and target domain by PCA and LDA respectively with linear transformation. Furthermore, we want to guarantee the structure of the corresponding points in the projection subspaces of the source and target domain by making their distances as close as possible for better domain adaptation.

With the idea of Laplacian graph, we construct a discrete weight graph to calculate the distances between samples. In the graph, the nodes characterize embedded samples, and the edges represent the weight which is measured by Euclidean distances. Meanwhile, we choose Gaussian similarity to measure the relationship between two samples as weighting coefficients. The cost function can be written as:

$$\sum_{i,j} W_{i,j}^{X_s} \|z_{si} - z_{sj}\|^2 + \sum_{i,j} W_{i,j}^{X_t} \|z_{ti} - z_{tj}\|^2, \tag{14}$$

where z_{si}, z_{ti} are corresponding samples of the source and target domain after projection. Hence, the optimization formula can be written as:

$$\min_{A,B} \mathrm{tr}(A^T X_s L^S X_s^T A) + \mathrm{tr}(B^T X_t L^T X_t^T B), \tag{15}$$

where

$$L^S = D_S - W_S, \ D_S^{ii} = \sum_j D_s^{ij}, \ W_S^{ij} = e^{-\frac{\|x_{si} - x_{sj}\|^2}{t}}, \tag{16}$$

$$L^T = D_T - W_T, \ D_T^{ii} = \sum_j D_t^{ij}, \ W_T^{ij} = e^{-\frac{\|x_{ti} - x_{tj}\|^2}{t}}. \tag{17}$$

Here L_S, L_T are Laplacian graph matrices which are real symmetric matrices for eigenvalue decomposition. D_S^{ii}, D_T^{ii} are the diagonal elements of D_S, D_T, which are the sum of the corresponding vertexes from the same column in the adjacency matrix. W_S, W_T are Gaussian similarity coefficients defined by heat kernel coefficient, and W_S^{ij}, W_T^{ij} are the matrix elements.

Strict Label Space Structure. A good classifier is crucial to final results of the model, let alone updating the pseudo labels for the target domain during each iteration in our model. In the proposed method, we assign each sample a label corresponding to the class when the sample belongs to it has the highest probability. Furthermore, we want to guarantee the structure of the label space. With the idea of Laplacian graph, we construct a discrete weight graph to calculate the distances between labels. Thus, the formula could be written as:

$$\sum_{i=1}^{n_s+n_t} \sum_{j=1}^{C} \left\| Y_{i,j}^{(T)} - Y_{i,j}^{(0)} \right\| + \sum_{i,j=1}^{n_s+n_t} W_{i,j}^l \|y_i - y_j\|^2, \tag{18}$$

which can be rewritten as

$$\sum_{i=1}^{n_s+n_t} \sum_{j=1}^{C} \left\| Y_{i,j}^{(T)} - Y_{i,j}^{(0)} \right\| + \mathrm{tr}(Y^T L^l Y), \tag{19}$$

where

$$L^l = D_l - W_l, \ D_l^{ii} = \sum_j D_{ll}^{ij}, \ W_l^{ij} = e^{-\frac{\|y_i - y_j\|^2}{t}}. \tag{20}$$

Algorithm 1. SSLS: Strict Subspaces and Label-space Structure for Domain Adaptation

---

Input: Source feature matrix X_s; Target feature matrix X_t; Source label vector Y_s; Iteration T; Dimension k; parameters $\mu, \alpha, \sigma, \beta, \lambda$;

Output: Transformation matrices A, B; Target domain labels Y_t^T

1: Construct S_t, S_b, S_w by (2), (4), MMD matrix M_s, M_t, M_{st}, M_{ts} by (8)(9)(10)(11) and Graph G for L^S, L^T by (16) and (17);

2: **repeat**

3:    Solve the eigenvalue decomposition in (23) and select the k corresponding eigenvectors to construct the adaptation matrix W, and obtain subspaces A, B;

4:    Map the original data to respective subspaces to get the embedding: $Z_s = A^T X_s, Z_t = B^T X_t$;

5:    Update pseudo target labels

6:    **if** $\sim$ empty(Y_s) **then**

7:       construct label matrix $Y_t^{(0)}$

8:       construct Graph G for L_l by (20)

9:       solve Y_{opt} by (24)

10:       updating $Y_t^{(T)}$

11:    **end if**

12: **until** Convergence

13: **return** Adaptation matrices A, B, Embedding Z_s, Z_t, Target labels $Y_t^{(T)}$

Here $Y_{i,j}^{(T)}$ is the probability of i-th sample belonging to j-th class after T-th iteration. $Y_{i,j}^{(0)}$ is the original probability prediction, and we assign it 1 only when the i-th sample belonging to j-th class at initial state, otherwise 0.

3.3   Learning Algorithm

Optimization of Overall Objective Function. Our proposed method summarizes the above quantities (1), (3), (7), (13), (15), and we rewrite $[A^T\ B^T]$ as W^T, then the overall object function can be written as:

$$\max_W \frac{\mathrm{tr}\left(W^T \begin{bmatrix} \beta S_b & 0 \\ 0 & \mu S_t \end{bmatrix} W\right)}{\mathrm{tr}\left(W^T \begin{bmatrix} M_s + \alpha I + \sigma X_s L^S X_s^T + \beta S_w & M_{st} - \alpha I \\ M_{ts} - \alpha I & M_t + (\alpha + \beta)I + \sigma X_t L^T X_t^T \end{bmatrix} W\right)}. \tag{21}$$

Here $\mu, \beta, \alpha, \sigma$ are trade-off parameters to balance the weight of each quantity. $I \in \mathbb{R}^{d \times d}$ is the identity matrix. We optimize this overall objective function by updating two projection matrices A and B iteratively, end up with more accurate pseudo labels for domain adaptation. Based on the generalized Rayleigh quotient, we establish the Lagrange function as:

$$\mathcal{L} = \mathrm{tr}\left(W^T \begin{bmatrix} \beta S_b & 0 \\ 0 & \mu S_t \end{bmatrix} W\right)$$
$$+ \mathrm{tr}\left(W^T \begin{bmatrix} M_s + \alpha I + \sigma X_s L^S X_s^T + \beta S_w & M_{st} - \alpha I \\ M_{ts} - \alpha I & M_t + (\alpha + \beta)I + \sigma X_t L^T X_t^T \end{bmatrix} W\right). \tag{22}$$

Table 1. Accuracy (%) on cross-domain databases: Office+Caltech, USPS+MNIST.

Datasets	NN	PCA	GFK	TCA	JDA	MBDA	JGSA	SSLS
C → A	23.70	36.95	41.02	38.20	44.78	47.29	51.46	**57.93**
C → W	25.76	32.54	40.68	38.64	41.69	41.02	45.42	**64.41**
C → D	25.48	38.22	38.85	41.40	45.22	49.04	45.86	**52.87**
A → C	26.00	34.73	40.25	37.76	39.36	40.78	41.50	**41.67**
A → W	29.83	35.59	38.98	37.63	37.97	40.00	45.76	**58.64**
A → D	25.48	27.39	36.31	33.12	39.49	43.31	47.13	**55.41**
W → C	19.86	26.36	30.72	29.30	31.17	31.37	33.21	**40.34**
W → A	22.96	31.00	29.75	30.06	32.78	40.08	39.87	**44.68**
W → D	59.24	77.07	80.89	87.26	89.17	**92.36**	90.45	90.45
D → C	26.27	29.65	30.28	31.70	31.52	33.21	29.92	**33.48**
D → A	28.50	32.05	32.05	32.15	33.09	33.51	38.00	**42.48**
D → W	63.39	75.93	75.59	86.10	89.49	**93.22**	91.86	91.86
USPS → MNIST	44.70	44.95	46.45	51.05	59.65	61.40	**68.15**	66.15
MNIST → UPSP	65.94	66.22	67.22	56.28	67.28	74.44	80.44	**84.67**
Average (Object)	31.37	39.79	42.95	43.61	46.31	48.75	50.04	**56.19**
Average (Digit)	55.32	55.59	56.84	53.67	59.91	67.92	74.30	**75.41**

By setting the derivative $\frac{\partial \mathcal{L}}{\partial W} = 0$, we obtain generalized eigenvalue decomposition:

$$\begin{bmatrix} \beta S_b & 0 \\ 0 & \mu S_t \end{bmatrix} W = \begin{bmatrix} M_s + \alpha I + \sigma X_s L^S X_s^T + \beta S_w & M_{st} - \alpha I \\ M_{ts} - \alpha I & M_t + (\alpha + \beta)I + \sigma X_t L^T X_t^T \end{bmatrix} W\Phi, \tag{23}$$

where $\Phi = \mathrm{diag}(\lambda_1, ..., \lambda_k)$ are the k leading eigenvalues. Finally, the optimal matrix W is reduced to solving (23) for the k leading eigenvectors, obtaining the subspaces transform matrix A, B. The complete procedure is summarized in Algorithm 1.

Optimization of Label Classifier. Inspired by [9,10], the optimal solution to the problem can be obtained by setting the derivative of (19) for W to 0. Thus the optimal label obtained by the classifier could be represented by :

$$Y_{opt} = (\mathcal{D}_l - \lambda W_l)^{-1} Y^{(0)}. \tag{24}$$

Table 2. Accuracy (%) on cross-domain databases: PIE.

Datasets	NN	PCA	GFK	TCA	TSL	JDA	JGSA	SSLS
PIE05 → PIE07	26.09	24.80	26.15	40.76	44.08	58.81	73.91	**76.00**
PIE05 → PIE09	26.59	25.18	27.27	41.79	47.49	54.23	**68.44**	65.07
PIE05 → PIE27	30.67	29.26	31.15	59.63	62.78	84.50	87.20	**93.15**
PIE05 → PIE29	16.67	16.30	17.59	29.35	36.15	49.75	51.84	**53.98**
PIE07 → PIE05	24.49	24.22	25.24	41.48	46.28	57.62	75.06	**82.32**
PIE07 → PIE09	46.63	45.53	47.37	51.47	57.60	62.93	74.57	**81.37**
PIE07 → PIE27	54.07	53.35	54.25	64.73	71.43	75.82	84.80	**91.53**
PIE07 → PIE29	26.53	25.43	27.08	33.70	35.66	39.89	59.68	**63.11**
PIE09 → PIE05	21.37	20.95	21.82	34.69	36.94	50.96	**71.16**	69.60
PIE09 → PIE07	41.01	40.45	43.16	47.70	47.02	57.95	**73.97**	71.64
PIE09 → PIE27	46.53	46.14	46.41	56.23	59.45	68.45	**88.59**	86.36
PIE09 → PIE29	26.23	25.31	26.78	33.15	36.34	39.95	61.40	**70.04**
PIE27 → PIE05	32.95	31.96	34.24	55.64	63.66	80.58	**91.18**	89.74
PIE27 → PIE07	62.68	60.96	62.92	67.83	72.68	82.63	**92.20**	91.22
PIE27 → PIE09	73.22	72.18	73.35	75.86	83.52	87.25	**89.89**	86.15
PIE27 → PIE29	37.19	35.11	37.38	40.26	44.79	54.66	**77.39**	75.25
PIE29 → PIE05	18.49	18.85	20.35	26.98	33.28	46.46	**72.00**	62.73
PIE29 → PIE07	24.19	23.39	24.62	29.90	34.13	42.05	70.23	**74.46**
PIE29 → PIE09	28.31	27.21	28.49	29.90	36.58	53.31	71.63	**75.43**
PIE29 → PIE27	31.24	30.34	31.33	33.64	38.75	57.01	83.15	**83.87**
Average (PIE)	34.76	33.85	35.35	44.73	49.43	60.24	75.91	**77.15**

4 Experiments

In this section, abundant experiments on 34 cross-domain image classification
data sets generated by three real world cross-domain visual recognition tasks
(Office+Caltech [13], USPS+MNIST [20,21], PIE) validate the effectiveness of
our proposed domain adaptation model.

Baseline Methods. We compare our approach with several start-of-the-art
methods for domain adaptation problem. They are: (1) 1-Nearest Neighbor
Classier (NN); (2) Principal Component Analysis (PCA) + NN; (3) Geodesic
Flow Kernel (GFK) + NN; (4) Transfer Component Analysis (TCA) + NN;
(5) Transfer Subspace Learning (TSL) + NN; (6) Joint Domain Adaptation
(JDA) + NN; (7) Manifold Alignment and Distribution Adaptation for Unsupervised Domain Adaptation (MBDA) + NN; (8) Joint Geometrical and Statistical Alignment for Visual Domain Adaptation (JGSA) + NN. Specifically, TCA
and TSL can be viewed as special case of JDA with $\mathcal{C} = 0$. With the idea of

manifold regularization, MBDA combines manifold alignment with distribution adaptation, behaving much better than JDA. JGSA learns two coupled projections simultaneously for reducing the source domain and the target domain, while JDA only considers a same projection for both domains. However, our approach enhance the source and target domain adaptation by making closer the distance between the projection subspaces, as well as considering the label space structure.

Results Analysis. The classification accuracies of our approach and several baseline methods on the Office+Caltech data sets of objects are shown in Table 1, while illustrated in Fig. 1 for the clarity of comparison. Office and Caltech-256 are two standard data sets for object recognition which contain four domains, i.e., C(Caltech-256), A(Amazon), W(Webcam), and D(DSLR). We observe that SSLS achieves an average classification accuracy of 56.19%, which is a significant error reduction of 6.15% compared to the best baseline method JGSA. This is because the NN classifier is usually based on $L1$ or $L2$ distance without considering the data structure, whereas SSLS maintains the consistency of label space structure.

Besides, our approach achieves an average classification accuracy of 75.41% on the USPS and MNIST data sets which are standard data sets of handwritten digits recognition, as shown in Table 1 and Fig. 1. It can be seen that SSLS does not perform well with little improvement of 1.11% points. This is because the USPS and MNIST data sets are just different in distribution probabilities and their data properties are similar with each other.

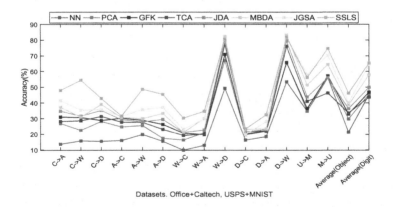

Fig. 1. Accuracy (%) on cross-domain databases: Office+Caltech, USPS+MNIST.

What's more, we conduct considerable experiments on the PIE face database with different face poses, and the results are shown in Table 2 and Fig. 2. We adopt five subsets of PIE, i.e., PIE05 (left pose), PIE07(upward pose), PIE3 (downward pose), PIE4 (frontal pose), and PIE5 (right pose). It is worth noting

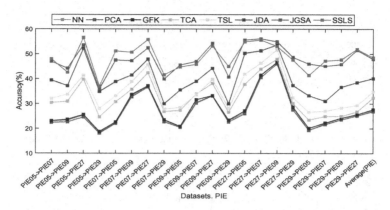

Fig. 2. Accuracy (%) on cross-domain databases: PIE.

that SSLS depicts 93.15% accuracy on PIE05 → PIE27 and achieves a classification accuracy of 77.15% on average.

In general, our approach achieves much better performance than the eight baseline methods. To begin with, our method outperforms TCA and TSL by almost 24 points in terms of average accuracy, since that both of them fail to consider conditional distribution shift. Though better considering conditional distribution shift, JDA obtains 14 points less than our average accuracy in that a unified transformation is not proper for both reducing condition shift as well as margin shift. Thirdly, our method improves JGSA significantly by roughly 3 points in that we consider the subspaces structure and the label space structure consistency.

Parameter Sensitivity. With USPS → MNIST, C → W and PIE27 → PIE05, we analysis parameter sensitivity of SSLS, while similar trends on other data sets are not shown here.

Figure 3 illustrates the relationship between parameter $T, \beta, \sigma, \lambda$ and accuracy on three data sets. For the number of iterations T, the results of SSLS can be stable after ten times, while some small fluctuations. It shows that our method could obtain a good performance within limited iterations. For the trade-off parameter β, the consequences are steady in the range of 0.001 to 1 while declining extremely when β is too large. Since that β controls the variance of within and between class from source domain, the model will be overfit easily without proper adjustment. In terms of the parameter σ which controls the weight of strict subspaces structure, it shows a steady trend in the range of 0.001 to 1. Owing to that we set this part in the denominator of the final objective function, guaranteeing the distance of corresponding points in the projection subspaces occupies an important role. λ is a weight parameter for Laplacian graph of the label space, and we can obtain from the last subgraph that when λ is bigger than 0.1, the performance is stable.

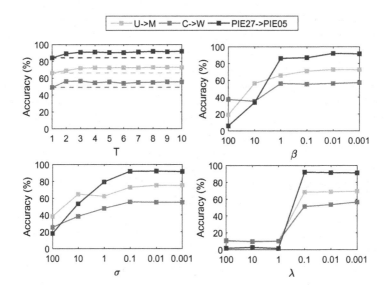

Fig. 3. Parameter sensitivity on different types of data sets.

5   Conclusion and Future Work

In this paper, we propose a new feature extraction method, namely Strict Sub-space and Label-space Structure for Domain Adaptation (SSLS), to reduce the domain shift by considering the properties of the source and target domains as well as the structure of both subspaces and label-space. Comprehensive exper-iments on three real world visual recognition tasks validate the effectiveness of SSLS with several state-of-the-art domain adaptation methods.

We have noticed that neural networks, such as Deep Adaptation Network (DAN) [15] and Joint Adaptation Network (JAN) [16], perform well in domain adaptation, while they use deep features and incorporate the latest transfer methods. Therefore, a series work such as the latest research mentioned above is essential, and combining our theory with neural networks is the direction of our future research.

References

1. Pan, S.J., Yang, Q., et al.: A survey on transfer learning. IEEE Trans. Knowl. Data Eng. **22**(10), 1345–1359 (2010)
2. Wang, H., Nie, F., Huang, H., Ding, C.H.: Dyadic transfer learning for cross-domain image classification. In: International Conference on Computer Vision, vol. 2011, pp. 551–556 (2011)
3. Gopalan, R., Li, R., Chellappa, R.: Domain adaptation for object recognition: an unsupervised approach. In: International Conference on Computer Vision, vol. 2011, pp. 999–1006 (2011)

4. Qui, Q., Patel, V.M., Turage, P.K., Chellappa, R.: Domain adaptive dictionary learning. In: European Conference on Computer Vision, vol. 2012, pp. 631–645 (2012)
5. Chen, M., Xu, Z., Sha, F.: Marginalized denoising autoencoders for domain adaptation. In: International Conference on Machine Learning, vol. 2012, pp. 1627–1634 (2012)
6. Chidlovskii, B., Clinchant, S., Csurka, G.: Domain adaptation in the absence of source domain data. Knowl. Discov. Data Min. **2016**, 451–460 (2016)
7. Yamada, M., Sigal, L., Raptis, M.: Covariate shift adaptation for discriminative 3D pose estimation. IEEE Trans. Pattern Anal. Mach. Intell. **36**(2), 235–247 (2014)
8. Ying, S., Wen, Z., Shi, J., Peng, Y., Qiao, J.: Manifold preserving: an intrinsic approach for semisupervised distance metric learning. IEEE Trans. Neural Netw. Learn. Syst. **29**(7), 2731–2742 (2018)
9. Yang, C., Zhang, L., Lu, H., Ruan, X., Yang, M.H.: Saliency detection via graph-based manifold ranking. In: Computer Vision and Pattern Recognition, vol. 2013, pp. 3166–3173 (2013)
10. Luo, L., Wang, X., Hu, S., Wang, C., Chen, L.: Close yet distinctive domain adaptation. In: Computer Vision and Pattern Recognization (2017)
11. Pan, S.J., Tsang, I.W., Kwok, J.T., Yang, Q.: Domain adaptation via transfer component analysis. IEEE Trans. Neural Networks **22**(2), 199–210 (2011)
12. Long, M., Wang, J., Ding, G., Sun, J., Yu, P.S.: Transfer feature learning with joint distribution adaptation. In: International Conference on Computer Vision, vol. 2013, pp. 2200–2207 (2013)
13. Gong, B., Shi, Y., Sha, F., Grauman, K.: Geodesic flow kernel for unsupervised domain adaptation. In: Computer Vision and Pattern Recognition, vol. 2012, pp. 2066–2073 (2012)
14. Li, Y., Cheng, L., Peng Y., Wen Z., Ying S.: Manifold alignment and distribution adaptation for domain adaptation. In: Accepted by International Conference on Multimedia and Expo (2019)
15. Fernando, B., Habrard, A., Sebban, M., Tuytelaars, T.: Unsupervised visual domain adaptation using subspace alignment. In: International Conference on Computer Vision, vol. 2013, pp. 2960–2967 (2013)
16. Sun, B., Saenko, K.: Subspace distribution alignment for unsupervised domain adaptation. In: British Machine Vision Conference (2015)
17. Zhang, J., Li, W., Ogunbona, P.: Joint geometrical and statistical alignment for visual domain adaptation. In: IEEE Conference on Computer Vision and Pattern Recognition (2017)
18. Long, M., Cao, Y., Wang, J.: Learning transferable features with deep adaptation networks. In: International Conference on Machine Learning, pp. 97–105 (2015)
19. Long, M., Zhu, H., Wang, J., Jordan, M. I.: Deep transfer learning with joint adaptation networks. In: International Conference on Machine Learning, pp. 2208–2217 (2017)
20. Lecun, Y.L., Bottou, L., Bengio, Y.: Gradient-based learning applied to document recognition. Proc. IEEE **86**(11), 2278–2324 (1998)
21. Hull, J.J.: A database for handwritten text recognition research. IEEE Trans. Pattern Anal. Mach. Intell. **16**(5), 550–554 (1994)

Multi-view Locality Preserving Embedding with View Consistent Constraint for Dimension Reduction

Yun He, Weiling Cai$^{(\boxtimes)}$, Ming Yang, and Fengyi Song

Nanjing Normal University, Nanjing 210097, People's Republic of China
caiwl@nuaa.edu.cn

Abstract. With the diversification of data sources, the multi-view data with multiple expressions have been appeared in various application scenarios. These multi-view data generally have high dimensions, large amounts and often lack of label information. Therefore, it is very important to learn multi-view data in an unsupervised way so as to analyze and excavate the potential valuable information. In this paper, we propose a multi-view locality preserving embedding algorithm with view similarity constraint for data dimension reduction. This algorithm not only preserves the local structure into low-dimensional space for each view, but also implements the similarity constraints between different views. On this basis, the algorithm looks for a joint embedding of low-dimensional subspace, so that the neighborhood among samples in original high-dimensional space can be maintained in the subspace, and the structures corresponding to different views are consistent with each other. This algorithm achieves good experimental results both in artificial data sets and multi-view data sets, which prove the correctness and feasibility of the algorithm.

Keywords: Multi-view learning · Multi-view dimensional reduction · Subspace learning

1 Introduction

Affected by the 'curse of dimensionality', the dimension of the data is getting higher and higher in practical application, which leads to many disadvantages of attribute redundancy, high computational complexity and state explosion. Therefore, the effective dimensional reduction for multi-view high-dimensional data has become a hot topic in current research [1–3]. The existing multi-view dimensional reduction algorithms usually adopt the methods of collaborative learning or searching for joint embedding in low-dimensional space to reduce the dimension of data. Recently, a multi-view discriminant analysis algorithm based on collaborative learning framework (CoKmLA) [4] was proposed, which combined the collaborative learning with the learning of discriminant subspace in order to produce a clustering strategy with the greatest consistency among views. In this algorithm, the labels of samples on one view can guide the learning of discriminant subspace on another view, and find the own discriminant subspace of each view through interactive learning of labels information between different views. In [5], a multi-view discriminant analysis algorithm based on

© Springer Nature Switzerland AG 2019
C. Douligeris et al. (Eds.): KSEM 2019, LNAI 11775, pp. 314–326, 2019.
https://doi.org/10.1007/978-3-030-29551-6_27

joint embedding in low-dimensional space (MVDA) was proposed, the algorithm attempted to project samples from different views into a joint common discriminant subspace by finding V linear projections related to views. In this discriminant subspace, the algorithm took the distribution characteristics of the data in and between views into account simultaneously, which makes the similar samples are as close as possible and the different samples are as far as possible. In [6], a canonical correspondence analysis (CCA) was proposed to project the data from two views into a low dimensional common space by maximizing the correlations between two views.

The above algorithms often ignore the similarity information of structure among multiple views. Based on the above considerations, this paper proposes a multi-view locality preserving embedding algorithm with view consistent constraints for dimension reduction (MPVD). The algorithm constructs a weighted adjacency graph on each view to reflect the local structures of the multi-view data, and on this basis, finding a joint embedding of the low dimensional subspace to preserve the neighborhood relationship of the high dimensional space. What's more, for the sake of maintaining the similarity structures among multiple views in dimension reduction process, the algorithm incorporates the similarity constraint information [7] into the local preservation information of multiple views, so that the similarity constraints of structures between different views can be maintained to a certain extent. This novel algorithm can not only form a joint low-dimensional space for preserving the neighborhood relationship of the multiple views, but also keep the structural similarity among different views. The experimental results on several artificial and real datasets prove the feasibility and superiority of the algorithm.

2   Related Work

Sometimes, we want to discuss the correlations between multiple linear spaces sometimes. For example, we will extract various features from the image, and each feature can form a linear space. For discovering the correlations between these spaces, we can use CCA to analyze. CCA is proposed to find two linear transformations corresponding to two sets of variables, so that the correlation coefficient between these two combined variables is the largest.

Suppose there is an unlabeled multi-view data set X, which has n samples and can be expressed as two views, $X = \{X^{(1)}, X^{(2)}\}$, $X^{(v)} = [x_1^{(v)}, x_2^{(v)}, \ldots, x_n^{(v)}]$, $v = 1, 2$. Where $x_i^{(v)} \in R^{d^{(v)}}$, $v = 1, 2$, represents the ith sample from the vth view in $d^{(v)}$ dimensionality. Two linear transforms w_1, w_2 are used to project these two views into a low dimensional common embedding spaces through maximizing the correlations between $w_1^T X^{(1)}$ and $w_2^T X^{(2)}$, that is:

$$\max w_1^T X_1 X_2^T w_2,$$
$$s.t. \ w_1^T X_1 X_1^T w_1 = 1, \ w_2^T X_2 X_2^T w_2 = 1. \tag{1}$$

After applying the Lagrange multiplier, the formula (1) can be solved by eigenvalue decomposition. By arranging the eigenvalues in descending order, a series of typical variables can be obtained. The larger the eigenvalue is, the stronger the correlations of typical variables are.

3 Multi-view Locality Preservation Embedding

The MPVD algorithm integrates the similarity constraints of structures among views on the basis of preserving local neighbor information of multi-view data. The processes of this algorithm are as follows: firstly, the weighted adjacency graph and the weighted matrix are constructed on each view to represent local information. On this basis, the locality preserving embedding is established for multi-view data. Secondly, the structural similarity constraints of multi-view data are achieved by minimizing the differences between the structural descriptions of any two views. Finally, the objectives of local information preserving and similarity constraints of structures between different views are combined together. By solving the objective function, the joint dimension reduction subspace is finally obtained.

3.1 Multi-view Locality Preserving Embedding

Suppose the multi-view dataset $X = \{X^{(v)} | v = 1, 2, \ldots, V\}$, $X^{(v)} = [x_1^{(v)}, \ldots, x_n^{(v)}]$. Each sample belonging to the vth view has $d^{(v)}$ attributes. By constructing a weighted adjacency graph, the local neighborhood relationships in the high-dimensional space are maintained in the subspace. Suppose the multi-view dataset in the subspace after mapping is described as $Y = \{Y^{(v)} | v = 1, 2, \ldots, V\}$, $Y^{(v)} = [y_1^{(v)}, \ldots, y_n^{(v)}]$. Firstly, an adjacency graph G is constructed on each view, where each vertex represents each sample $x_i^{(v)}(i = 1, \ldots, n)$, and each edge represents the similarity measure between the $x_i^{(v)}$ and $x_j^{(v)}$. If $x_i^{(v)}$ and $x_j^{(v)}$ are the two vertices of adjacent edges, then there is an edge between $x_i^{(v)}$ and $x_j^{(v)}$, otherwise there is no connective structure. The nearest neighbor structure is determined by k-nearest neighbor method. That means if $x_i^{(v)}$ is included in the nearest k samples of $x_j^{(v)}$ in the feature space, or $x_j^{(v)}$ is included in the nearest k samples of $x_i^{(v)}$ in the feature space, then $x_i^{(v)}$ and $x_j^{(v)}$ are neighbor structures. Secondly, constructs the weighted matrix $W^{(v)}$ on each adjacency graph. $W^{(v)}$ is a sparse matrix of $n*n$. If there is an edge between $x_i^{(v)}$ and $x_j^{(v)}$, then $W_{ij}^{(v)} = e^{-\|x_i^{(v)} - x_j^{(v)}\|^2 / t}$. Let's define that $a^{(v)}$ is a projection vector, $Y^{(v)T} = a^{(v)T} X^{(v)}$. Finally, the description of local information preserving in the subspace can be construction as follows:

$$\min \sum_{v=1}^{V} \sum_{i=1}^{n} \sum_{j=1}^{n} (y_i^v - y_j^v)^2 W_{ij}^v \tag{2}$$

Now we expand the formula (2) as:

$$\sum_{v=1}^{V}\sum_{i=1}^{n}\sum_{j=1}^{n}(y_i^v - y_j^v)^2 W_{ij}^v$$

$$= \sum_{v=1}^{V}\sum_{i=1}^{n}\sum_{j=1}^{n}((a^T)^v x_i^v - (a^T)^v x_j^v)^2 W_{ij}^v \qquad (3)$$

$$= 2\sum_{v=1}^{V}(\sum_{i=1}^{n}(a^T)^v x_i^v (x_i^T)^v a^v \sum_{j=1}^{n}W_{ij}^v - \sum_{i=1}^{n}\sum_{j=1}^{n}(a^T)^v x_i^v (x_j^T)^v a^v W_{ij}^v)$$

We convert the Σ in the last step of Eq. (3) to a matrix form in each view. For the convenient observation, $R^{(v)}$ is used to replace the content of the left half of the minus sign in the equation, and $Q^{(v)}$ represents the right:

$$R^v = (a^T)^v [x_1^v, x_2^v, \ldots, x_n^v] \begin{bmatrix} \sum_1 W_{11} & 0 & 0 & 0 \\ 0 & \sum_2 W_{22} & 0 & 0 \\ 0 & 0 & \ldots & 0 \\ 0 & 0 & 0 & \sum_n W_{nn} \end{bmatrix} \begin{bmatrix} x_1^v \\ x_2^v \\ \ldots \\ x_n^v \end{bmatrix} a^v \qquad (4)$$

$$Q^v = (a^T)^v [x_1^v, x_2^v, \ldots, x_n^v] \begin{bmatrix} W_{11} & W_{12} & \ldots & W_{1n} \\ W_{21} & \ldots & \ldots & W_{2n} \\ \ldots & \ldots & \ldots & \ldots \\ W_{n1} & W_{n2} & \ldots & W_{nn} \end{bmatrix} \begin{bmatrix} x_1^v \\ x_2^v \\ \ldots \\ x_n^v \end{bmatrix} a^v \qquad (5)$$

Bring the Eqs. (4), (5) into (3) to rewrite (3):

$$\sum_{v=1}^{V}\sum_{i=1}^{n}\sum_{j=1}^{n}(y_i^v - y_j^v)^2 W_{ij}^v = 2\sum_{v=1}^{V}(R - Q)$$

$$= 2\sum_{v=1}^{V}((a^T)^v X^v D^v (X^T)^v a^v - (a^T)^v X^v W^v (X^T)^v a^v) \qquad (6)$$

$$= 2\sum_{v=1}^{V}((a^T)^v X^v (D - W)^v (X^T)^v a^v)$$

Therefore, the Eq. (2) can be converted into the following form:

$$\sum_{v=1}^{V}(a^T)^v X^v L^v (X^T)^v a^v \qquad (7)$$

Where, L^v is the Laplace matrix, D^v is the diagonal matrix, and $a^{(v)}$ is the projection vector under each view. Finally, the objective function of the multi-view local preserving projection with view-similarity reduction is represented as follows:

$$\min \sum_{v=1}^{V} (a^T)^v X^v L^v (X^T)^v a^v \tag{8}$$

3.2 Similarity Constraints of Structures Between Different Views

Since each view of the multi-view data corresponds to the same object, there should be some correspondence between multiple views. For this reason, the MPVD algorithm incorporates the similarity constraints of structures among views on the basis of multi-view local information preserving. Assuming that there is a multi-view dataset with two views from different angles, which are represented by $X^{(1)}$ and $X^{(2)}$ respectively. Obviously, one view of the dataset can be rotated to be represented by another, that is, $X^{(1)} = RX^{(2)}$, where R is a transform matrix that can convert the one of the view into another. At the same time, the projections of the two views obtained through Eq. (8) should also have the similar correspondence, for example, $a^{(1)} = Ra^{(2)}$ ($a^{(1)}$ and $a^{(2)}$ are obtained from Eq. (8)). According to the representation theorem, the projection $a^{(v)}$ for the vth view can be equally replaced by the following forms:

$$a^{(v)} = X^{(v)} \beta_v \tag{9}$$

Where, β_v is the structural description of each projection $a^{(v)}$. Therefore, the following Eq. (10) can be accordingly obtained:

$$X^{(1)} \beta_1 = RX^{(2)} \beta_2 = X^{(1)} \beta_2 \tag{10}$$

It can be proved from above, that $\beta_1 = \beta_2$. In other words, the structure of each transform $a^{(v)}$ captured by β_v of different views is the same. Without loss of generality, suppose that $X^{(1)}, X^{(2)}, ..., X^{(V)}$ are V different views under the same object, then all of them should have the similar structures, which means the structure descriptions of projections among different views should also be similar. Let β_v as the structure description of projection for the vth view, then the structure descriptions of projection for V views can be $\beta_1, \beta_2, ...\beta_V$, and any two of them should be similar. The expression of similar constraints of structures among various views is expressed as follows:

$$\sum_{i,j=1}^{V} \|\beta_i - \beta_j\|_2^2 \tag{11}$$

Another form of β_v can be derived from Eq. (9),

$$\beta_v = ((X^{(v)})^T X^{(v)})^{-1} (X^{(v)})^T a^{(v)} = P_v a^{(v)} \tag{12}$$

Where $P_v = ((X^{(v)})^T X^{(v)})^{-1} (X^{(v)})^T$, then the Eq. (11) can be transformed into Eq. (13),

$$\sum_{i,j=1}^{V} \|\beta_i - \beta_j\|_2^2 = Tr(A^T M A) \tag{13}$$

Where, A is the joint matrix of each view, $A = [a^{(1)}, a^{(2)}, ..., a^{(V)}]$. M can be detailed as:

$$M = \begin{pmatrix} M_{11} & M_{1V} \\ \cdots \\ M_{V1} & M_{VV} \end{pmatrix}, \quad M_{ij} = \begin{cases} 2(V-1)P_i^T P_i, & i = j \\ -2P_i^T P_j, & i \neq j \end{cases} \tag{14}$$

From what has been discussed above, the final objective function of multi-view local preservation projection with view-similarity reduction can be expressed as:

$$\min Tr(A^T M A) \tag{15}$$

3.3 The Objective Function of MPVD

By minimizing the sum of the differences between the structure descriptions of projections between any two views, we incorporate the similar constraints of structures among views and multi-view local information preserving, then the following objective function can be obtained further:

$$\begin{aligned} &\arg \min Tr(A^T X L X^T A + \alpha A^T M A), \\ &s.t. \ AA^T = E \end{aligned} \tag{16}$$

In Eq. (16), the two terms represent the multi-view local information preserving and the similarity constraints of structures among different views, respectively. By combining these two parts, a subspace with local information preserving and similar constraints of structures among several views can be obtained, where X and L are diagonal matrices. Under the constraint of $AA^T = E$, the Lagrange multiplier is introduced to transform Eq. (16) into the extremum problem of Lagrange function:

$$L(A, \lambda) = A^T (XLX^T + \alpha M)A + \lambda(A^T A + c) \tag{17}$$

Take the partial derivative for A, so that the Eq. (17) can satisfy the following conditions at extreme value:

$$\partial L(A, \lambda)/\partial(A) = 0 \tag{18}$$

After Eq. (18), the Eq. (16) can be transformed into the following form:

$$(XLX^T + \alpha M)a = \lambda a \tag{19}$$

Solve the eigenvalues and eigenvectors for $(XLX^T + \alpha M)$. Ordering the eigenvalues as an ascending sort, and then selects the eigenvectors corresponding to the smaller eigenvalues to form the mapping matrix A, $A = [a^{(1)}, a^{(2)}, ..., a^{(V)}]$.

3.4   Algorithm Description

The steps of the multi-view local preservation projection with view-similarity reduction algorithm (MPVD) are as follows:

Algorithm: MPVD

Input: A multi-view data set X with n samples, $X=\{X^{(v)}|v=1, 2, ...,V\}$, $X^{(v)}=\{x_1^{(v)},..., x_n^{(v)}\}$, the clusters C, the labels *on views*.

Initialization: The number of neighbors k, the population mean t of each view .

  1: calculate the weight matrix of the adjacency graph W and diagonal matrix D;

  2: capture the local information preserving according to equation (8);

  3: capture the view-similarity constraints according to equation (15);

  4: according to equation (17), the Lagrangian multiplier is used to obtain the eigenvalues and eigenvectors.

Output: The projections of subspace A.

---

4   Experimental and Analysis

The MPVD algorithm can be well applied in many fields such as clustering, retrieval and so on. The experiments include the following three aspects. Firstly, select the multi-view datasets Wine and Texas, project them into two-dimensional subspace by MPVD algorithm respectively. By this step, we can observe the circumstance of local information preserving and verify the correctness of the algorithm. Secondly, compare the clustering performance of MPVD with some other multi-view clustering algorithms on webKB, 3source and other multi-view datasets. Finally, the retrieval results among MPVD and other algorithms are compared on Texas.

4.1   Visualization of Dimension Reduction

To verify the correctness of MPVD, we will examine whether the neighborhood of the original space is maintained in low-dimensional space on multi-view data sets Wine and Texas. During the experiment, the first two dimensions of the original data set will be visualized firstly, and then we mark a sample and its nearest neighbor randomly. After this step, we can observe the relative positions of the sample and its neighbor in two dimensional subspaces through MPVD algorithm.

In Wine and Texas, we select a sample in original space randomly and mark it by a blue rectangle. Its nearest neighbor sample is represented by a red diamond, and the remaining samples are all green. Firstly, we take the visualization of the first two dimensions of Wine and Texas on view 1 of original space, which are as shown in Figs. 1a and 2a. Secondly, we take the visualization of the experimental results after running the MPVD algorithm in two-dimensional subspace, which are as shown in Figs. 1b and 2b.

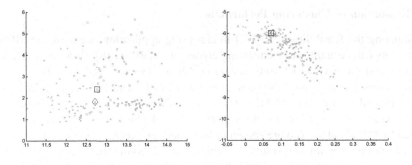

(a) Two adjacent points in the original view 1   (b) The distribution of these two points in subspace

Fig. 1. The distribution of two neighbors on Wine

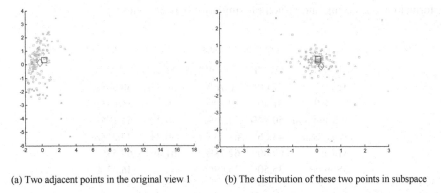

(a) Two adjacent points in the original view 1   (b) The distribution of these two points in subspace

Fig. 2. The distribution of two neighbors on Texas

As it can be seen from Fig. 1a that in the original space of the multi-view data set Wine, the blue rectangle is close to the red diamond. And in the subspace after running the MPVD algorithm, we can observe that the position of the blue rectangle is also close to the red diamond from Fig. 1b. Since the sample with blue is selected by random, it can be determined that the nearest-neighbor relationships of the samples in the original space are preserved in the subspace for the Wine data set.

As seen from Fig. 2a, in the original space of Texas, the blue rectangle and the red diamond are neighbors. Furthermore, in the subspace after the MPVD algorithm, the position of the blue rectangle is close to the red diamond from Fig. 2b. Since the sample with blue is also selected randomly, it can be determined that the neighborhood relationships of the samples in the original space are also preserved in subspace.

4.2 Evaluation of Clustering Performance

For validating the feasibility of MPVD in clustering application, we compare MPVD with the other three multi-view clustering algorithms (DEMK [8], CoKmLA, MKBD [9]) on several multi-view data sets, including Mfeat, 3Source, and webKB.

The Tables 1 and 2 show the comparison results of clustering accuracy and normalized mutual information (NMI) of several multi-view clustering algorithms on different data sets. Among them, the highest value of clustering accuracy and NMI obtained by MPVD algorithm are shown in bold, and the second is italicized. As it can be seen from the experimental results in Tables 1 and 2, compared with the other three multi-view clustering algorithms, the MPVD algorithm has achieved higher values of clustering accuracy and NMI in Texas, Cornell, Washington and 3Source data sets. Besides, the experimental results of the MPVD are close to the results of DEMK on M-feat data set. All of these experimental results have shown that the MPVD algorithm can achieve good clustering effects on most datasets due to the constraints of local information preserving and structural similarity between views.

Table 1. The accuracies of different multi-view clustering algorithms on several datasets

MPVD	DEMK	CoKmLDA	MKBD	MPVD
Texas	57.00%	56.76%	59.33%	**60.00%**
Cornell	41.40%	39.49%	40.76%	**56.69%**
Washington	50.24%	54.75%	59.42%	**66.18%**
Wiscousin	43.06%	61.33%	50.23%	**75.27%**
Mfeat	69.80%	62.78%	61.49%	*69.53%*
3Source	35.50%	36.09%	43.79%	**46.37%**

4.3 Evaluation of Retrieval Performance

Let's define that the unsupervised data set $X = \{X^{(v)} | v = 1, 2, ..., V\}$, $X^{(v)} = [x_1^{(v)}, ..., x_n^{(v)}]$, a query sample q, $q = \{q^{(1)}, q^{(2)}, ..., q^{(v)}\}$. The retrieval method tries to return the first t samples with the highest confidence belonging to the same person from X. If the dimension of X is too high, then the PCA is used on each view to reduce the dimension of data set, the projections of PCA are recorded as $P_{PCA(1)}, P_{PCA(2)}$. After pre-processing, we use MPVD to obtain the final projections which are recorded as $P_{MPVD(1)}, P_{MPVD(2)}$, here we suppose the number of views is two. In the subspace, $y_i^{(v)}$ represents the i-th sample in the v-th view, the specific expression is:

$$y_i^v = (P_{mlppvc}^{(v)})^T (P_{pca}^{(v)})^T (x_i^{(v)} - u^{(v)}) \tag{23}$$

Table 2. The NMI of different multi-view clustering algorithms on several datasets

MPVD	DEMK	CoKmLDA	MKBD	MPVD
Texas	0.1364	0.1422	0.1401	**0.1530**
Cornell	0.0745	0.1224	0.1151	**0.2433**
Washington	0.1583	0.1983	0.2476	**0.3118**
Wiscousin	0.0477	0.2716	0.1161	**0.3314**
Mfeat	0.7019	0.6368	0.5983	*0.6915*
3Source	0.2825	0.2831	0.3320	**0.3652**

Here, $u^{(v)}$ is the mean vector of $X^{(v)}$. And the expression of query sample $q^{(v)}$ in the subspace is:

$$z^{(v)} = (P_{mlppvc}^{(v)})^T (P_{pca}^{(v)})^T (p^{(v)} - u^{(v)}) \qquad (24)$$

Calculate the cosine similarity between $z^{(v)}$ and each $y_i^{(v)}$:

$$s_i^{(v)} = \frac{z^{(v)} \cdot y_i^{(v)}}{\|z^{(v)}\| \|y_i^{(v)}\|} \qquad (25)$$

In (25), $s_i^{(v)}$ denotes the similarity between $z^{(v)}$ and $y_i^{(v)}$ in the subspace, and the value range is from -1 to 1. MPVD returns the first t samples with the highest confidence. Because MPVD can obtain the similar local information structures of each view, the retrieval results on each view are matched, but not necessarily identical. In other words, the fusion model of retrieval results on all views may get a better balance or improve retrieval performance. The fusion mode is expressed as follows:

$$s_i = \alpha s_i^{(1)} + \lambda s_i^{(2)} + \ldots + \gamma s_i^{(V)} \qquad (26)$$

Where, $s_i^{(v)}$ ($v = 1, 2, \ldots, V$) represents the retrieval results on each view, s_i represents the retrieval results obtained by the fusion mode on all views, and α, λ, γ are the weighted parameter of the retrieval results of each view, with the value range from 0 to 1, and $(\alpha + \lambda + \ldots + \gamma) = 1$.

We compare MPVD with the other four dimension reduction methods (KCCA [10], CCA, LPP, PCA) in terms of retrieval performance on Texas datasets. For LPP and PCA, the multiple feature spaces of multi-view data are spliced into a large feature space for dimensionality reduction. For five dimensional reduction methods (KCCA, CCA, LPP, PCA, MPVD), each of them is tested for 50 times on Texas dataset respectively. During each test, one sample is selected randomly from 150 samples as a query sample, and the remaining 149 samples are as target dataset. The most common evaluation criteria of effect for information retrieval are accuracy rate and recall rate. Here, we use the recall rate to represent the information retrieval effect in each round, that is, the ratio of the number of samples retrieved which are consistent with the query sample category to the number of samples in the target dataset consistent with the category of query samples.

Table 3 shows that when dimension of subspace varies from 1 to 100, the best results of retrieval performance (recall rate) and the corresponding dimensions of subspace obtained by the five methods in both single view and fusion model on Texas. From Table 3, we can see that comparing the three multi-view dimensional reduction algorithms KCCA, CCA and MPVD, the retrieval performance of CCA and KCCA are approximate. The recall rates are (0.67, 0.68) and (0.68, 0.69) under the single views and (0.69, 0.68) under the fusion model which are obtained by these two methods respectively. However, the recall rates obtained by MPVD are (0.87, 0.78) under single views and 0.8 under the fusion model. The results of retrieval experiments of MPVD are much better than CCA and KCCA algorithm obviously. Second, compared with the other four dimensional reduction algorithms, the recall rates obtained by MPVD algorithm are the highest in either single view or fusion model. The reason may be concluded from that the MPVD algorithm considers not only the local information preserving, but also the structural similarity between different views, so that the dataset can maintain the neighborhood relationship in subspace and refer to the structural similarity information of multiple views. Fixing these two thoughts is very important for improving the retrieval performance of datasets. Finally, by observing the last column of Table 3, it can be found that the recall rates obtained from the fusion model are in the median of the recall rates obtained from the single view when the five dimensional reduction algorithms are used, which shows that the fusion model has played a balancing role in the retrieval results between multiple views.

Table 3. The comparison of recall rates of different algorithms on Texas

	View 1	View 2	Fusion
PCA	**0.84**(23)	0.71(46)	0.78(94)
LPP	0.68(11)	**0.72**(20)	0.69(70)
CCA	0.67(60)	0.68(20)	**0.69**(36)
KCCA	0.68(11)	**0.69**(4)	0.68(34)
MPVD	**0.87**(32)	0.78(21)	0.80(49)

Figure 3 indicates the trend of recall rates of five algorithms running on Texas both in the single view and the fusion model with the change of dimension of the subspace. Among them, the green and pink broken lines represent the MPVD and PCA algorithm, the yellow, red and blue represent the KCCA, CCA and LPP algorithm, respectively. It can be seen from Fig. 3 that, on the one hand, no matter in the single view or in the fusion model, with the difference of subspace dimensions, the recall rates of MPVD and PCA algorithm are higher than that of CCA, KCCA and LPP algorithm. What's more, with these algorithms stabilize, the recall rates of MPVD is the highest among these five dimensional reduction algorithms. On the other hand, by observing the Fig. 3a, b and c, it can be found that for these five dimensional reduction algorithms, when the dimensions of the subspace increase from 1 to 10, the recall rate increases rapidly. While after reaching 10, the recall rates show a gentle fluctuation with the increase of the dimensions. It may result from that the data set in the subspace contains only a small part of effective information when the dimension of the subspace is too low, and with the dimension increasing, the valid information contained in the subspace is gradually enriched. In addition, when the dimension of subspace gets to 50, the recall rate obtained by MPVD reaches to its highest value, 80%.

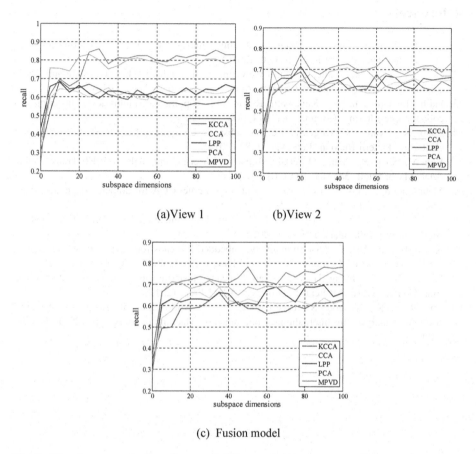

(a)View 1   (b)View 2

(c) Fusion model

Fig. 3. The change trend of recall rates of different algorithms on Texas (Color figure online)

5 Conclusion

In this paper, we propose a novel dimensional reduction algorithm, named MPVD algorithm. The algorithm firstly preserves the neighborhood relationship among samples in dimension reduction for each view, and then employs the structural similarity constraint to maintain the consistency between multiple views. Finally, combining these two thoughts, a joint embedding low-dimensional subspace is found. The results of visualization experiments on multi-view data sets Wine and Texas prove the correctness of the algorithm. And the clustering performance tests on webKB, Mfeat and other data sets, as well as the retrieval rates on Texas with four dimensional reduction algorithms, both of these experimental results confirm the feasibility of the algorithm.

Acknowledgments. This work was supported by Natural Science Foundation of Jiangsu Province under grant nos. BK20161560, BK20171479, BK20161020 and National Science Foundation of China under grant nos. 61003116, 61432008, 61603193.

References

1. Yan, F., Wang X., Zeng, Z., Hong, C.: Adaptive multi-view subspace clustering for high-dimensional data. Pattern Recogn. Lett. (2019)
2. Dong, X., Yang, M., Zhang, G.: Multi-view dimensional reduction based on semi-supervised canonical correlation analysis. Comput. Appl. Res. **12**, 3686–3712 (2016)
3. Falih, I., Grozavu, N., Kanawati, R., et al.: Topological multi-view clustering for collaborative filtering. Comput. Sci. **144**, 306–312 (2018)
4. Zhao, X., Evans, N., Dugelay, J.L.: A subspace co-training framework for multi-view clustering. Pattern Recogn. Lett. **41**, 73–82 (2014)
5. Kan, M., Shan, S., Zhang, H., et al.: Multi-view discriminant analysis. IEEE Trans. Pattern Anal. Mach. Intell. **38**, 188–194 (2015)
6. Mehrkanoon, S., Jak, S.: Regularized semipaired kernel CCA for domain adaptation. IEEE Trans. Neural Netw. Learn. Syst. **99**, 1–15 (2017)
7. Kan, M., Shan, S., Zhang, H., et al.: Multi-view discriminant analysis. IEEE Trans. Pattern Anal. Mach. Intell. **38**(1), 188–194 (2015)
8. Xu, J., Han, J., Nie, F.: Discriminatively embedded k-means for multi-view clustering. In: IEEE Conference on Computer Vision and Pattern Recognition (CVPR). IEEE (2016)
9. Cai, X., Nie, F., Huang, H.: Multi-view k-means clustering on big data. In: International Joint Conference on Artificial Intelligence. AAAI Press (2013)
10. Chaudhuri, K., Kakade, S., Livescu, K., et al.: Multi-view clustering via canonical correlation analysis. In: International Conference on Machine Learning, pp. 129–136. ACM (2009)

Research on Ship Classification Based on Trajectory Association

Tao Zhang$^{(\boxtimes)}$, Shuai Zhao, and Junliang Chen

State Key Laboratory of Networking and Switching Technology,
Beijing University of Posts and Telecommunications, Beijing 100876, China
{zhangtao89,zhaoshuaiby}@bupt.edu.cn

Abstract. Many ships have AIS devices that can provide information
such as the types of ships, which can help the maritime authorities manage the marine traffic in a better way. However, when some ships do not
have AIS devices installed or turn off these devices, it is desirable to
identify the types of ships by the trajectory features provided by radar.
In order to achieve this goal, first, the trajectories are generated based
on the obtained AIS points and radar points, and then the radar trajectories are associated with the AIS trajectories to obtain the labels of
the radar trajectories. Next, three types of features of radar trajectories
are extracted. Due to the small amount of experimental data and the
problem of class imbalance, this paper proposes a heterogeneous ensemble learning method based on EasyEnsemble and SMOTE when training
the ship classification model. The experimental results show that the
proposed method is superior to homogeneous ensemble learning and heterogeneous ensemble learning without SMOTE methods. Moreover, the
method can identify almost all the minority class samples and has certain
application value.

Keywords: Ship classification · Trajectory association ·
Trajectory features · Heterogeneous ensemble learning

1 Introduction

In order to ensure the safety of ships during navigation, most of ships are
equipped with Automatic Identification System (AIS), AIS can continuously
send data containing static and dynamic information of ships. The static information mainly includes the type, length, width of the ship, and the dynamic
information mainly includes the location, speed, direction of the ship. AIS can
also provide the identity of the ship, i.e. MMSI (Maritime Mobile Service Identify) number. Through the AIS data, the maritime authorities can obtain the
ship's attributes and navigational status. However, not all ships are equipped

This work has been supported by Beijing Natural Science Foundation (Grant
No. 4182042), National Key Research and Development Program of China (No.
2018YFB1003804).

© Springer Nature Switzerland AG 2019
C. Douligeris et al. (Eds.): KSEM 2019, LNAI 11775, pp. 327–340, 2019.
https://doi.org/10.1007/978-3-030-29551-6_28

with AIS, even some ships deliberately turn off the AIS transponders in order to escape supervision [9]. In this case, maritime authorities need to obtain information of ships from data provided by other sensors, among them, radar is often used as an alternative sensor for maritime surveillance near the ports [2]. The radar can obtain dynamic information of ships such as position, running direction, and radial velocity, these dynamic information can further form the trajectories of ships and can reflect the motion features of ships. However, the static information, such as types of ships, cannot be obtained by radar, and this information is very important for the maritime authorities. For example, when it is known that the type of ship is fishing boat, maritime authorities will focus on monitoring whether the fishing behavior of the ship is in compliance with the fishing regulations. Therefore, in the absence of AIS data, how to identify the types of ships based on the data acquired by the radar is a valuable issue.

Currently, the research on the target classification based on trajectory features become common. When inferring transportation modes, [14] first partitioned GPS trajectory into several segments and then extracted a set of valuable trajectory features, experimental results showed that the combination of these features extracted had better inference performance. [13] proposed a method of classifying user outdoor transportation modes based on GPS and accelerometer data from smart devices, and experimental evaluation showed that the method obtained a relatively high classification accuracy. Ship classification based on AIS trajectory is an important branch of the research. [11] extracted three categories of trajectory features and used logistic regression model to construct a ship classifier based on AIS data, experiment showed that the accuracy achieved by the method can meet the requirements when classifying two types of ships. After extracting the features of the AIS trajectories, [5] used the random forest algorithm to train the ship classification model. [8] introduced deep learning into the field of ship classification based on AIS data, and [6] compared the effects of several common classification methods when studying the ship classification based on AIS data. The above research showed that the categories of moving targets can be identified by trajectory features, which provided a theoretical basis for our research. However, many studies on ship classification were based on AIS data, but the AIS data itself contains the types and other static information of ships, these studies had more theoretical value than application value.

Therefore, in this paper, we focus on how to identify the ship type based on the trajectory features acquired by radar when the ship does not have AIS devices installed or turn off these devices. First, since the data collected by radar does not include types of ships, it is necessary to associate radar trajectories with AIS trajectories so that the radar trajectories can be labeled by the corresponding ship types. Second, the features of radar trajectories are extracted, and the Relief algorithm is used to measure the importance of the feature. Third, due to the large difference between the two types of ships and the small amount of experimental data, when training the classification model, this paper proposes a heterogeneous ensemble learning method based on EasyEnsemble and SMOTE. The rest of this paper is organized as follows. Section 2 describes the association between radar trajectories and AIS trajectories. Section 3 extracts the features of radar trajectories. Section 4 proposes a heterogeneous ensemble learning classification method based on EasyEnsemble and SMOTE. Section 5 conducts the ship classification experiment and compares the classification results of different ensemble learning algorithms. Section 6 summarizes the paper and provides an introduction to future work.

2   Trajectory Association

Radar and AIS can provide the motion states of ships, for example, AIS can directly provide the longitude, latitude, course over ground, heading, speed over ground of the ship, while radar provides the radial speed, horizontal angle and straight-line distance between the ship and the radar. In order to generate and associate trajectories more conveniently, the ship information provided by radar need to be converted into the longitude and latitude of the ship. The conversion formula is as follows.

$$a = (direction \times \pi)/180, b = (90 - R_{lat}) \times \pi/180, c = distance/R \quad (1)$$

$$d = \arccos(\cos b \times \cos c + \sin b \times \sin c \times \cos a), e = \arcsin(\sin c \times \sin a/\sin d) \quad (2)$$

$$ship_{lon} = R_{lon} + (e \times 180)/\pi, ship_{lat} = 90 - (d \times 180)/\pi \quad (3)$$

Among them, R_{lon} and R_{lat} are the longitude and latitude of the radar, R is the radius of the earth. Before the trajectory association, the AIS trajectories and radar trajectories should be generated based on these trajectory points provided by AIS and radar.

2.1   The Generation of AIS Trajectory

Since the AIS data contains the unique identification of the ship (MMSI number), during the generation of the AIS trajectory, when a new AIS point arrives, if the MMSI number of the AIS point is the same as the MMSI number of a formed trajectory (line 04), and the time difference between the new AIS point and the last point of the trajectory satisfies the time threshold (line 05), and then new incoming AIS point should be added to this trajectory (line 06). If all of the generated trajectories do not meet the above conditions, a new AIS trajectory is created and the AIS point should be added to the newly created AIS trajectory (line 11–15). By repeating the above process, the AIS trajectories can be generated. The left side of Fig. 1 shows some of the results of the AIS trajectory generation, and the right half is the corresponding pseudo code.

2.2   The Generation of Radar Trajectory

Since the data collected by radar does not contain the unique identification of the ship, the generation process of the radar trajectory is relatively complicated. When a new radar point arrives, the time difference between the last point in

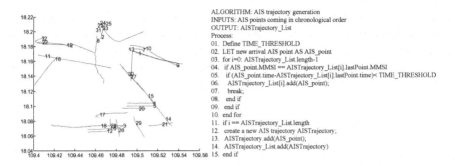

Fig. 1. Some of the results of the AIS trajectory generation and the corresponding pseudo code.

each radar trajectory and the new point is computed. If the difference satisfies the time threshold, the distance between the radar trajectory and the new radar point is computed. If this distance is less than the shortest distance recorded previously, the distance is recorded as the shortest distance and the identification number of the corresponding trajectory is recorded too (line 05–13). After this process, the shortest distance can be obtained. If the shortest distance is less than the distance threshold, then the trajectory with the shortest distance is considered as the best matched trajectory, and the point is added to the best matched trajectory. Otherwise, it means that the new radar point is the starting point of a new radar trajectory, at this time, a new radar trajectory is created and the radar point should be added to the newly created radar trajectory (line 14–20). By repeating the above process, the radar trajectories can be generated. The left side of Fig. 2 shows some of the results of the radar trajectory generation, and the right half is the corresponding pseudo code.

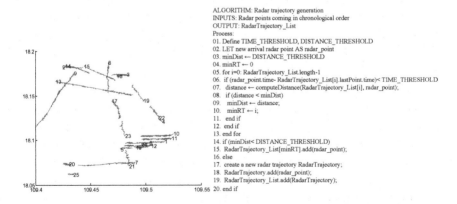

Fig. 2. Some of the results of the radar trajectory generation and the corresponding pseudo code.

2.3   Trajectory Association Algorithm

After AIS trajectories and radar trajectories are generated, the trajectory association can be conducted. First, AIS trajectories and radar trajectories are saved in radarTracksMap and aisTracksMap. The type of radarTracksMap and ais-TracksMap is HashMap (Using JAVA programming language), which both use the trajectory id as the key and the trajectory as the value. For each AIS trajectory in aisTracksMap, the distance between the AIS trajectory and each radar trajectory in radarTracksMap is computed, if the distance is less than the inter-trajectories distance threshold, an object of class named Distance is created, which contains the AIS trajectory id, the radar trajectory id, and the distance between the two trajectories, the object is stored in the distanceSet (the type of distanceSet is TreeSet), the objects in the distanceSet are arranged from small to large according to distance (line 01–11). When the distance between any pair of radar trajectory and AIS trajectory is computed, the objects in the distanceSet are taken out in order, this means that the object with the shortest distance is first taken out. If radar trajectory id and AIS trajectory id of the object taken out have not appeared in fusionMap (the type fusionMap is HashMap), these two trajectories are considered to be a pair of associated trajectories, and the association relationship is stored in fusionMap with the combination of the AIS trajectory id and the radar trajectory id as key and the distance between the trajectories as value (line 12–21). The left side of Fig. 3 shows some of the results of the trajectory association, and the right half is the corresponding pseudo code.

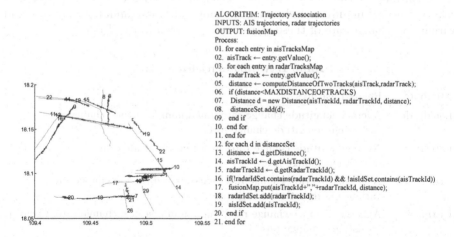

ALGORITHM: Trajectory Association
INPUTS: AIS trajectories, radar trajectories
OUTPUT: fusionMap
Process:
```
01. for each entry in aisTracksMap
02.   aisTrack ← entry.getValue();
03.   for each entry in radarTracksMap
04.     radarTrack ← entry.getValue();
05.     distance ← computeDistanceOfTwoTracks(aisTrack,radarTrack);
06.     if (distance<MAXDISTANCEOFTRACKS)
07.       Distance d = new Distance(aisTrackId, radarTrackId, distance);
08.       distanceSet.add(d);
09.     end if
10.   end for
11. end for
12. for each d in distanceSet
13.   distance ← d.getDistance();
14.   aisTrackId ← d.getAisTrackId();
15.   radarTrackId ← d.getRadarTrackId();
16.   if(!radarIdSet.contains(radarTrackId) && !aisIdSet.contains(aisTrackId))
17.     fusionMap.put(aisTrackId+","+radarTrackId, distance);
18.     radarIdSet.add(radarTrackId);
19.     aisIdSet.add(aisTrackId);
20.   end if
21. end for
```

Fig. 3. Some of the results of the trajectory association and the corresponding pseudo code. (Color figure online)

In Fig. 3, the red curves represent the AIS trajectories and the blue curves represent the radar trajectories. For example: AIS trajectory 11 is successfully associated with radar trajectory 13, AIS trajectory 19 is successfully associated with radar trajectory 15. When the trajectories are associated, the radar trajectories can be labeled by the corresponding ship types.

3   Feature Extraction

After obtaining the labeled radar trajectories, the features of the radar trajectories should be extracted. In this paper, the features are mainly divided into three categories, namely attributes related features, speed and acceleration related features, and shape related features.

3.1   Attributes Related Features

Through the ship information collected by radar and the location of the radar, we can obtain the longitude, latitude, radial velocity of the ship, and the direction and distance of the ship relative to the radar. In general, all types of ships are likely to appear anywhere in the ocean and sail in any direction. Therefore, in the radar trajectory, longitude, latitude, direction, and distance are not good enough to distinguish ship types. However, the change rate of these attributes can reflect the running speed and steering speed of ship, different types of ships often have different running and steering speeds. Therefore, the change rate of these attributes can be extracted as the trajectory features to distinguish ship types. In addition to these features, the radial speed itself can also distinguish the ship types to some extent.

According to the knowledge of mathematical statistics, these attributes related features mainly include average change rate, maximum change rate and variance of change rate of these attributes, as shown in the Table 1.

Table 1. Attributes related features

Attribute	Related features
Longitude	Average longitude change rate, maximum longitude change rate, variance of longitude change rate
Latitude	Average latitude change rate, maximum latitude change rate, variance of latitude change rate
Direction	Average direction change rate, maximum direction change rate, variance of direction change rate
Distance	Average distance change rate, maximum distance change rate, variance of distance change rate
Radial speed	Average radial speed, maximum radial speed, variance of radial speed; average radial speed change rate, maximum radial speed change rate, variance of radial speed change rate

The distributions of change rates of attributes in different types of ship trajectories tend to be different, so in trajectories generated by different types of ships, the ratios that change rates of attributes exceeding a certain threshold will be different. Therefore, referring to [3], when classifying ships, the ratios that change rates of attributes exceeding a certain threshold are also important trajectory features. These features mainly include the ratio that longitude change rate exceeding a certain threshold (R-LonCR), the ratio that latitude change rate exceeding a certain threshold (R-LatCR), the ratio that the direction change rate exceeding a certain threshold (R-DirCR), the ratio that the distance change rate exceeding a certain threshold (R-DistCR), the ratio that the radial speed change rate exceeding a certain threshold (R-RadCR).

The values of these features will vary with the thresholds, and they have different importance in ship classification. Therefore, when extracting these features, the thresholds need to be selected reasonably, in other words, the importance scores of features need to be computed according to certain criteria, so that the features under the selected thresholds can better identify ship types. Relief [4] is an important feature selection method for two-class problem, it computes the importance score of a feature by comparing the feature distance between sample and its homogeneous samples and the feature distance between the sample and its heterogeneous samples. The Relief method can independently compute the importance score of each feature and has high operational efficiency, therefore, this paper uses the Relief method to compute the importance scores of features under different thresholds. (a)–(e) in Fig. 4 show the Relief values of R-LonCR, R-LatCR, R-DirCR, R-DistCR, R-RadCR at different thresholds, respectively, the threshold with the largest Relief value is taken as the final selected threshold.

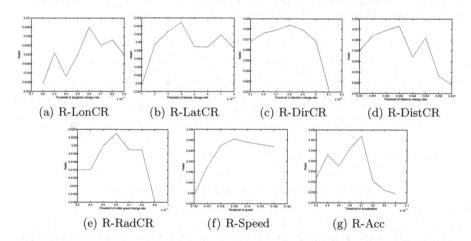

(a) R-LonCR   (b) R-LatCR   (c) R-DirCR   (d) R-DistCR

(e) R-RadCR   (f) R-Speed   (g) R-Acc

Fig. 4. Relief values of R-LonCR, R-LatCR, R-DirCR, R-DistCR, R-RadCR at different thresholds

As can be seen from Fig. 4, the thresholds of R-LonCR, R-LatCR, R-DirCR, R-DistCR and R-RadCR are $8.6*10^{-7}$, $4*10^{-8}$, 0.00058, 0.053, 0.00066, respectively. After getting these appropriate thresholds, corresponding trajectory features can be obtained.

3.2 Speed and Acceleration Related Features

The speed and acceleration of ship cannot be directly obtained by radar, but they can be computed by the distance and time difference between two adjacent points in radar trajectory. Different types of ships often have different speeds and accelerations due to their different weights and powers. Therefore, the correlation statistics of speed and acceleration can also be extracted to distinguish ship types. These features mainly include average speed, maximum speed, variance of speed, average acceleration, maximum acceleration and variance of acceleration.

The distributions of speeds and accelerations in different types of ship trajectories also tend to be different. Therefore, the ratio that speed exceeding a certain threshold (R-Speed) and the ratio that acceleration exceeding a certain threshold (R-Acc) are also important trajectory features when identifying ship types. (f)–(g) in Fig. 4 show the Relief values of R-Speed and R-Acc at different thresholds, respectively.

3.3 Shape Related Features

The shapes of trajectories generated by different types of ships also tend to be different, For example, the sailing routes of cargo ships and passenger ships tend to be close to straight lines, and fishing boats tend to reciprocate in a certain areas when they are working. Therefore, the shape related features can also be used to identify ship types, these features mainly include the range of the trajectory, the length of the trajectory, and the coefficients of the fitted curve of the trajectory. The shape related features are shown in Fig. 5.

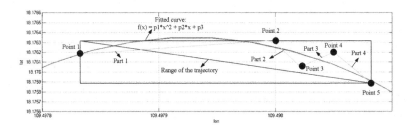

Fig. 5. Shape related features (Color figure online)

In Fig. 5, point 1–point 5 are trajectory points, the rectangle of the black border is the smallest rectangle containing these trajectory points. The diagonal of this rectangle is the range of the trajectory, as shown by the purple line in Fig. 5. The length of trajectory is defined as the sum of the distances of all the two adjacent points in the trajectory. As shown in Fig. 5, part 1–part 4 are the connecting lines between adjacent trajectory points, and the sum of the lengths of these line segments is the length of the trajectory. The formula for computing the trajectory length is: $\sum_{i=0}^{n-2} distance(P_{r_i}, P_{r_{i+1}})$, n is the number of points in the trajectory. In addition to range and distance, the trajectory also has geometric features. This paper uses the coefficients of the fitted curve of the trajectory as geometric features. The blue curve in Fig. 5 is the fitted curve of these trajectory points, the coefficients of this curve are the geometric features needed to be extracted.

As mentioned earlier, the trajectories of cargo ships and passenger ships are close to straight lines, the quadratic coefficient of the fitted curve approaches 0, and its navigating range and distance are large. When the fishing boat is working, it is often reciprocating in a certain area, and its sailing distance is relatively large, while the sailing range is relatively small. Therefore, the above features can distinguish ship types to some extent.

4   Heterogeneous Ensemble Learning Based on EasyEnsemble and SMOTE

After extracting the trajectory features, we can use these features to train the ship classification model. In the trajectory data collected in this paper, the number of ships of each type is quite different. For example, among the 242 pairs of trajectories that were successfully associated, there were 139 pairs of fishing boats (positive samples) and 18 pairs of pleasure crafts (negative samples). Due to the large difference in the number of positive and negative samples, the classification problem in the paper is a class imbalance problem, and the traditional classification method is no longer applicable, because if all samples are predicted as positive samples, since the number of positive samples is much larger than the negative samples, at this point, a higher accuracy can be obtained, but this is meaningless.

Therefore, for the class imbalance problem, we need to preprocess these class imbalance data before the model training so that the number of samples in each class is as equal as possible. At present, there are mainly two methods for processing unbalanced data, namely under-sampling and over-sampling. Over-sampling balance the number of samples by generating a portion of the minority samples, this method may lead to overfitting of the classification model due to the automatic generation of minority samples, SMOTE [1] is a common over-sampling algorithm that generates more minority samples by interpolating the minority samples, since this method doesn't resample the minority samples simply, overfitting of the classification model can be avoided to some extent. Under-sampling balances positive and negative samples by removing some of the majority samples, this method may result in the loss of important information, in order to avoid this problem, EasyEnsemble [7] divides the majority samples into sets, where the number of samples in each set is equal to the number of the minority samples, then the minority samples are added to each set, so that the number of samples in each set is balanced, and on the whole, there is no loss of information, EasyEnsemble is a classic under-sampling algorithm. In order to take advantage of the above two algorithms, this paper proposes a heterogeneous

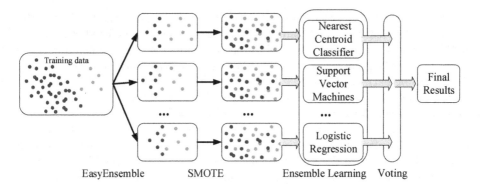

Fig. 6. Heterogeneous ensemble learning method based on EasyEnsemble and SMOTE

ensemble learning method based on EasyEnsemble and SMOTE when training the ship classification model. The process of this method is shown in Fig. 6.

In the training set, first, all the minority samples are selected; second, the same number of majority samples are selected; third, the majority and minority samples selected in the previous two steps are combined to form one training sub-set, the number of two types of samples is balanced in the sub-set; fourth, the above three steps are repeated until a certain number of training sub-sets are formed; fifth, in each training sub-set, the SMOTE algorithm is used to generate the same number of majority samples and minority samples, i.e. two types of samples are simultaneously over-sampled; sixth, the training sub-sets are trained by multiple classification algorithms, then the same number of classification models as the training sub-sets are obtained; finally, when classifying the samples in the test set, the classification models get the final classification results by voting.

In the above process, the first step to the fourth step are EasyEnsemble algorithm, which is mainly used to form a certain number of balanced training sub-sets. The fifth step is the SMOTE algorithm, which uses interpolation method to simultaneously add equal amounts of positive and negative samples in each training sub-set. In this step, the oversampling process of each training sub-set is independent, the generated noises and samples in each training sub-set are different, the noises in each sub-set can only affect the accuracy of a single classification model, while the original data participates in the training process of all classification models, therefore, the combination of EasyEnsemble and SMOTE can reduce the overfitting of the classification model caused by the noises. In ensemble learning, the greater the diversity of individual learners, the better the effect of ensemble learning algorithms. Since the samples generated in each training sub-set are different, different individual learners can be obtained by training these different sub-sets. In order to further increase the diversity of individual learners, this paper adopts heterogeneous ensemble learning method, which selects multiple classification algorithms as individual learners.

5   Case Study

5.1   Trajectory Association and Feature Extraction

This paper uses real AIS and radar data for experiments. These data were collected in the waters near Sanya, China from 2 to 7 January 2017. Among them, the number of AIS points is 418808, and the number of radar points is 151620. Based on these points and the trajectory generation algorithms in Sects. 2.1 and 2.2, 1203 AIS trajectories and 732 radar trajectories are generated. After trajectory association, 242 pairs of trajectories are successfully associated. In these successful associated trajectories, we conduct our experiment with 139 pairs of fishing boats as positive samples and 18 pairs of pleasure crafts as negative samples.

According to Sect. 3, three types of features need to be extracted from radar trajectories, and the total number of features of each radar trajectory is 36. After feature extraction, radar trajectory can be converted into feature vector.

5.2   Ship Classification Model Training

Splitting Dataset into Training and Test Sets. In order to avoid introducing additional errors, the ratio of positive and negative samples in the training set and test set should be as consistent as possible. Therefore, in this experiment, the training set contains 103 fishing boats and 14 pleasure crafts. The test set contains 36 fishing boats and 4 pleasure crafts. At the same time, in order to obtain more accurate experimental results, we repeat 50 times when splitting the data, resulting in 50 training sets and 50 test sets.

Evaluation of Classification Model. Since the classification problem in the experiment is a class imbalance problem, the traditional classification evaluation criteria cannot be used when measuring the performance of classification model. In order to obtain more accurate evaluation result, we need to increase the importance of the minority samples in the evaluation process. In the experiment, we use the balanced accuracy score [12] to compute the accuracy of classification model. In this experiment, the formula of the balanced accuracy score is: $(\frac{TF}{TotalF} + \frac{TP}{TotalP})/2$. TF is the number of correctly predicted fishing boats, $TotalF$ is the total number of fishing boats, TP is the number of correctly predicted pleasure crafts, and $TotalP$ is the total number of pleasure crafts.

Description and Training of Classification Model. Ensemble learning can achieve better performance than a single learner by combining multiple learners, it can be divided into homogeneous ensemble and heterogeneous ensemble according to whether the individual learners in them belong to the same category. As described in Sect. 4, the heterogeneous ensemble learning based on EasyEnsemble and SMOTE method selects multiple classification algorithms as individual learners. The classification algorithms used in this method mainly include nearest neighbor classifier (NNC), support vector machine (SVM), logistic regression (LR) and multi-layer perceptron classifier (MLPC). To evaluate the effectiveness of our method, the experiment performs a performance comparison between our method and other ensemble learning methods. The individual learners of our method are 10 NNCs, 10 SVMs, 10 LRs, and 10 MLPCs. The methods that need to be compared mainly include four homogeneous ensemble learning methods and one heterogeneous ensemble learning method without using SMOTE. Among them, the individual learners of the four homogeneous ensemble learning methods are 40 NCCs, 40 SVMs, 40 LRs, and 40 MLPCs, respectively. Among them, the MLPC used in the experiment has two hidden layers, the first hidden layer has 4 neurons, and the second hidden layer has 3 neurons. In the experiment, the Scikit-learn module [10] has been used. The average and maximum balanced accuracy scores of each ensemble learning algorithm in 50 experiments are shown in Table 2.

Table 2. The balanced accuracy scores of ensemble learning algorithms.

Algorithms	Number of base learners	Average score	Maximum score
Ensemble learning (NNC)	40	0.7217	0.8889
Ensemble learning (SVM)	40	0.7456	**0.9167**
Ensemble learning (LR)	40	0.7442	**0.9167**
Ensemble learning (MLPC)	40	0.7242	0.9028
Heterogeneous ensemble learning without SMOTE	40	0.7344	0.9028
Heterogeneous ensemble learning	40	**0.7689**	**0.9167**

As can be seen from Table 2, the average scores of the other five ensemble learning methods are smaller than the average score of the method proposed in the paper; the maximum scores of ensemble learning (SVM) and ensemble learning (LR) are equal to the maximum score of the method proposed in the paper, while the maximum scores of the other three ensemble learning methods are smaller than the maximum score of the proposed method. Therefore, the heterogeneous ensemble learning method based on EasyEnsemble and SMOTE proposed can better solve the class imbalance problem in the paper. The average and maximum balanced accuracy scores obtained by the method in this paper are 0.7689 and 0.9167, respectively, as shown in the last row of Table 2. The confusion matrices corresponding to the two scores are shown in Tables 3 and 4, respectively. The numbers in Tables 3 and 4 represent the number of ships. Since Table 3 is the average confusion matrix of 50 experiments, the corresponding number of ships may not be an integer.

Table 3. Confusion matrix corresponding to the average score.

Confusion matrix when the average score is 0.7689		Predicted class	
		Fishing boats	Pleasure crafts
Actual class	Fishing boats	24.94	11.06
	Pleasure crafts	0.62	3.38

Table 4. Confusion matrix corresponding to the maximum score.

Confusion matrix when the maximum score is 0.9167		Predicted class	
		Fishing boats	Pleasure crafts
Actual class	Fishing boats	30	6
	Pleasure crafts	0	4

5.3 Result Analysis

As can be seen from Table 2, the average balanced accuracy score of each classification model is not high, which is caused by the limited classification ability of the trajectory features provided by radar. But according to the above confusion matrices, almost all the minority class samples are accurately predicted. This is because when training the classification model of unbalanced dataset, the minority samples are selected more times, which improves the recognition of the classification model for the minority class samples. This is applicable in many scenarios, for example, when identifying abnormal ships (minority class), we prefer to identify as many minority class samples as possible to reduce the risk.

6 Conclusion

This paper mainly studies how to identify the type of ship by the ship's trajectory features obtained by radar when the ship does not send AIS data. First, the trajectory generation and association algorithms are used to associate the radar trajectory with the ship type, and then the heterogeneous ensemble learning method based on EasyEnsemble and SMOTE is used to complete the training of the ship classification model. By comparing the classification results in the experiment, the algorithm proposed in the paper has better results, and can solve the classification and recognition problems in specific scenarios (for example, when it is necessary to identify the minority class samples as much as possible).

Due to the limited trajectory features provided by radar, the overall accuracy of the ship classification is not very high, which limits the application scope of this method. Therefore, in the future work, we will use radar to guide the photoelectric device to obtain the photoelectric data of ships, and fuse the photoelectric data with the trajectory data to improve the accuracy of ship classification.

References

1. Chawla, N.V., Bowyer, K.W., Hall, L.O., Kegelmeyer, W.P.: Smote: synthetic minority over-sampling technique. J. Artif. Intell. Res. **16**, 321–357 (2002)
2. Habtemariam, B.K., Tharmarasa, R., Meger, E., Kirubarajan, T.: Measurement level AIS/radar fusion for maritime surveillance. In: Signal and Data Processing of Small Targets 2012, vol. 8393, p. 83930I. International Society for Optics and Photonics (2012)
3. Ji, Q., Jin, B., Cui, Y., Zhang, F.: Using mobile signaling data to classify vehicles on highways in real time. In: 2017 18th IEEE International Conference on Mobile Data Management (MDM), pp. 174–179. IEEE (2017)
4. Kira, K., Rendell, L.A.: A practical approach to feature selection. In: Machine Learning Proceedings 1992, pp. 249–256. Elsevier (1992)
5. Kraus, P., Mohrdieck, C., Schwenker, F.: Ship classification based on trajectory data with machine-learning methods. In: 2018 19th International Radar Symposium (IRS), pp. 1–10. IEEE (2018)
6. Krüger, M.: Experimental comparison of ad hoc methods for classification of maritime vessels based on real-life AIS data. In: 2018 21st International Conference on Information Fusion (FUSION), pp. 1–7. IEEE (2018)
7. Liu, T.Y.: Easyensemble and feature selection for imbalance data sets. In: 2009 International Joint Conference on Bioinformatics, Systems Biology and Intelligent Computing, pp. 517–520. IEEE (2009)
8. Ljunggren, H.: Using deep learning for classifying ship trajectories. In: 2018 21st International Conference on Information Fusion (FUSION), pp. 2158–2164. IEEE (2018)
9. McCauley, D.J., et al.: Ending hide and seek at sea. Science **351**(6278), 1148–1150 (2016)
10. Pedregosa, F., et al.: Scikit-learn: machine learning in Python. J. Mach. Learn. Res. **12**, 2825–2830 (2011)
11. Sheng, K., Liu, Z., Zhou, D., He, A., Feng, C.: Research on ship classification based on trajectory features. J. Navig. **71**(1), 100–116 (2018)
12. Urbanowicz, R.J., Moore, J.H.: ExSTraCS 2.0: description and evaluation of a scalable learning classifier system. Evol. Intel. **8**(2–3), 89–116 (2015)
13. Xia, H., Qiao, Y., Jian, J., Chang, Y.: Using smart phone sensors to detect transportation modes. Sensors **14**(11), 20843–20865 (2014)
14. Zheng, Y., Li, Q., Chen, Y., Xie, X., Ma, W.Y.: Understanding mobility based on GPS data. In: Proceedings of the 10th International Conference on Ubiquitous Computing, pp. 312–321. ACM (2008)

Learning a Subclass of Deterministic Regular Expression with Counting

Xiaofan Wang[1,2]($\boxtimes$) and Haiming Chen[1]

[1] State Key Laboratory of Computer Science, Institute of Software,
Chinese Academy of Science, Beijing 100190, China
{wangxf,chm}@ios.ac.cn
[2] University of Chinese Academy of Science, Beijing, China

Abstract. In this paper, we propose a subclass of single-occurrence regular expressions with counting (cSOREs) and give a learning algorithm of cSOREs. First, we learn a SORE. Then, we construct a *countable finite automaton* (CFA) by traversing the syntax tree of the obtained SORE. Next, the CFA runs on the given finite sample to obtain the minimum and maximum number of repetitions of the subexpressions under the iteration operators. Finally we obtain a cSORE by traversing the syntax tree and introducing the counting operators. Our algorithm not only can learn a cSORE, which is expressive enough to cover more XML data, but also has better generalization ability for smaller sample.

Keywords: Schema inference · Regular expressions · Counting

1 Introduction

The eXtensible Markup Language (XML), which has been widely used on the Web, is the lingua franca for data exchange [1]. The schema languages (such as DTD (Document Type Definitions) and XSD (XML Schema Definitions) recommended by W3C (World Wide Web Consortium) [24]) have advantages for diverse applications such as data processing, automatic data integration, and static analysis of transformations [12,21,22]. However, many XML documents on the Web are not accompanied by a schema [3,23], or valid schema [6,7], therefore, schema inference becomes an essential work.

Schema inference can be reduced to learning regular expressions from sets of positive samples. Using techniques from Gold [16], the class of regular expressions cannot be learned only from positive data. Even Bex et al. proved in [5] that the class of deterministic regular expressions cannot be learned from positive data. Therefore for practical purposes many researchers turned to focus on learning subclasses of deterministic regular expressions [4,5,8,9,13,14,25].

Work supported by National Natural Science Foundation of China under Grant No. 61472405.

© Springer Nature Switzerland AG 2019
C. Douligeris et al. (Eds.): KSEM 2019, LNAI 11775, pp. 341–348, 2019.
https://doi.org/10.1007/978-3-030-29551-6_29

Deterministic regular expressions [11] require that each symbol in the input word can unambiguously be matched to a position in the regular expression without looking ahead in the word. In practice, there are many applications of the subclass of deterministic regular expressions on the Web, including that of single-occurrence regular expressions (SOREs) [8,9]. However, SOREs, which do not support counting, are defined on standard regular expressions. Regular expressions with counting, which are used in XML Schema [10,15,17–20,25], are extended from standard regular expressions by adding counting [15]. In this paper, we propose a subclass of single-occurrence regular expressions with counting (cSOREs). Our experiments (see Table 1) showed that the proportion of cSOREs is 94.16% for 32,750 real-world XSD files grabbed from Google, Maven, and GitHub, where 378,558 regular expressions were extracted. This indicates the practicability of cSORE. Therefore, it is necessary to study a learning algorithm for cSORE.

For learning regular expressions with counting, we have proposed the class ECsores [25], and the corresponding learning algorithm *InfECsore* [25]. However, although the ECsore learnt by *InfECsore* is a precise representation of any given finite sample, the algorithm *InfECsore* has less generalization ability such that, in some cases, the learnt ECsore covers relatively less XML data[1]. Therefore, a new subclass cSORE and a new method for learning cSORE are proposed. Although the defined cSOREs have more constrains than ECsores, compared with the algorithm *InfECsore*, our algorithm not only can learn a cSORE, which is expressive enough to cover more XML data, but also has better generalization ability (higher precision and recall) for smaller sample.

The main contributions of this paper are as follows. First, we infer a SORE. Then, we present a learning algorithm for cSOREs, where the main steps are as follows: (1) Construct a countable finite automaton (CFA) [25] from the syntax tree of the learnt SORE; (2) The CFA runs on the given finite sample to obtain the minimum and maximum number of repetitions of the subexpressions under the iteration operators; and (3) Generate the cSORE by traversing the syntax tree and introducing the counting operators. Finally, we provide the evaluations in generalization ability about our algorithm.

The paper is structured as follows. Section 2 gives the basic definitions. Section 3 presents the learning algorithm of the cSORE, Sect. 4 presents experiments. Section 5 concludes the paper.

2   Preliminaries

2.1   Regular Expression with Counting

Let Σ be a finite alphabet of symbols. The class of standard regular expressions over Σ is defined in the standard way: ε, $a \in \Sigma$ are regular expressions. For any

---

[1] For instance, the original schema in XSD can be denoted by $r_0 = (a|b)^+$, given sample $S = \{ba, aa, baabaa\}$, the ECsore learnt by *InfECsore* is $r_1 = (b?a^{[1,2]})^{[1,2]}$. However, an learnt cSORE can be $r_2 = (b?a)^{[1,4]}$, $|\mathcal{L}(r_1)| = 16 < |\mathcal{L}(r_2)| = 30$. Note that $\mathcal{L}(r_0) \supseteq \mathcal{L}(r_2) \supseteq S$ and $\mathcal{L}(r_0) \supseteq \mathcal{L}(r_1) \supseteq S$.

regular expressions r_1 and r_2, the disjunction $(r_1|r_2)$, the concatenate $(r_1 \cdot r_2)$, and the Kleene-star r_1^* are also regular expressions. Usually, we omit concatenation operators in examples. The regular expressions with counting are extended from standard regular expressions by adding the counting [15]: $r^{[m,n]}$ is a regular expression for regular expression r, where $m \in \mathbb{N}$, $n \in \mathbb{N}_{/1}$, $\mathbb{N} = \{1, 2, 3, \cdots \}$, $\mathbb{N}_{/1} = \{2, 3, 4, ...\} \cup \{+\infty\}$, and $m \leq n$. $\mathcal{L}(r^{[m,n]}) = \{w_1 \cdots w_i | w_1, \cdots, w_i \in \mathcal{L}(r), m \leq i \leq n\}$. Note that r^+, $r?$, and r^* are used as abbreviations of $r^{[1,+\infty]}$, $r|\varepsilon$, and $r^{[1,+\infty]}|\varepsilon$, respectively.

2.2   SORE, ECsore and cSORE

SORE is defined as follows.

Definition 1 (SORE [8,9]). *Let Σ be a finite alphabet. A single-occurrence regular expression (SORE) is a standard regular expression over Σ in which every terminal symbol occurs at most once.*

In this paper, for a SORE r, since $\mathcal{L}(r^*) = \mathcal{L}((r^+)?)$, a SORE does not use the Kleene-star operation, and forbids the expressions of forms $(r?)?$, $(r^+)^+$, and $(r?)^+$.

Example 1. $(ab)^+$ is a SORE, while $(ab)^+a$ is not. The expressions $(a?)?$, $(a^+)^+$, and $(a?)^+$ are forbidden.

Definition 2 (ECsore [25]). *Let Σ be a finite alphabet. An ECsore is a regular expression with counting over Σ in which every terminal symbol occurs at most once. For a regular expression r, an ECsore forbids immediately nested counters, expressions of form $(r?)?$ and $(r?)^{[m,n]}$.*

ECsore does not use the Kleene-star and the iteration operations. And ECsores are deterministic by definition.

Definition 3 (cSORE). *Let Σ be a finite alphabet. A cSORE is an ECsore over Σ. For regular expressions r_1, r_2, $\cdots$, r_k ($k \geq 2$), a cSORE forbids expressions of form $(r_1 r_2^{[m_1,n_1]} r_3)^{[m_2,n_2]}$ and $(r_1(r_2^{[m_1,n_1]})?r_3)^{[m_2,n_2]}$ where $\varepsilon \in \mathcal{L}(r_1)$ and $\varepsilon \in \mathcal{L}(r_3)$, and expressions of form $(r_1?r_2? \cdots r_k?)^{[m,n]}$.*

According to the definition, cSOREs are a subclass of ECsores. ECsores are deterministic regular expressions, so are the cSOREs.

Example 2. $a?b^{[1,2]}(c|d)^{[1,+\infty]}$, $((c|d)^{[1,2]})?$, and $a?b(c|d)e$ are cSOREs, also ECsores, while $a(b|c)^+a$ is not a SORE, therefore neither a cSORE nor an ECsore. $(a^{[3,4]}|b)^{[1,2]}$ and $(a^{[3,4]}b)^{[1,2]}$ are cSOREs, also ECsores. However, the expressions $(a?b^{[1,2]}c?)^{[3,4]}$, $(a?(b^{[1,2]})?c?)^{[3,4]}$ are ECsores, not cSOREs.

Definition 4 (Countable Finite Automaton [25]). *A Countable Finite Automaton (CFA) is a tuple $(Q, Q_c, \Sigma, \mathcal{C}, q_0, q_f, \Phi, \mathsf{U}, \mathsf{L})$. The members of the tuple are described as follows:*

- *Σ is a finite and non-empty alphabet.*
- *q_0 and q_f : q_0 is the initial state, q_f is the unique final state.*
- *Q is a finite set of states. $Q = \Sigma \cup \{q_0, q_f\} \cup \{+_i\}_{i \in \mathbb{N}}$.*
- *$Q_c \subset Q$ is a finite set of counter states. Counter state is a state q ($q \in \Sigma$) that can directly transit to itself, or a state $+_i$. For each subexpression (excluding single symbol $a \in \Sigma$) under the iteration operator, we associate a unique counter state $+_i$ to count the minimum and maximum number of repetitions of the subexpression, respectively.*
- *C is finite set of counter variables that are used for counting the number of repetitions of the subexpressions under the iteration operators. $C = \{c_q | q \in Q_c\}$, for each counter state q, we also associate a counter variable c_q.*
- *$U = \{u(q) | q \in Q_c\}$, $L = \{l(q) | q \in Q_c\}$. For each subexpression under the iteration operator, we associate a unique counter state q such that $l(q)$ and $u(q)$ are the minimum and maximum number of repetitions of the subexpression, respectively.*
- *Φ maps each state $q \in Q$ to a set of tuples consisting of a state $p \in Q$ and two update instructions. $\Phi: Q \mapsto \wp(Q \times ((L \times U \mapsto (\boldsymbol{Min}(L \times C), \boldsymbol{Max}(U \times C))) \cup \{\emptyset\}) \times ((C \mapsto \{\boldsymbol{res}, \boldsymbol{inc}\}) \cup \{\emptyset\}))$. ($\emptyset$ denotes empty instruction.)*

Definition 5 (Transition Function of a CFA [25]). *The transition function δ of a CFA $(Q, Q_c, \Sigma, C, q_0, q_f, \Phi, U, L)$ is defined for any configuration (q, γ, θ) and the letter $y \in \Sigma \cup \{\dashv\}$*

(1) $y \in \Sigma$: $\delta((q, \gamma, \theta), y) = \{(z, f_\alpha(\gamma, \theta), g_\beta(\theta)) | (z, \alpha, \beta) \in \Phi(q) \wedge (z = y \vee ((y, \alpha, \beta) \notin \Phi(q) \wedge z \in \{+_i\}_{i \in \mathbb{N}}))\}$.
(2) $y = \dashv$: $\delta((q, \gamma, \theta), \dashv) = \{(z, f_\alpha(\gamma, \theta), g_\beta(\theta)) | (z, \alpha, \beta) \in \Phi(q) \wedge (z = q_f \vee z \in \{+_i\}_{i \in \mathbb{N}})\}$.

3   Inference of cSOREs

Our learning algorithm works in the following steps.

Step 1: We infer a SORE for a given finite sample, and the SORE is obtained by post-processing the result of the algorithm *Soa2Sore* [14].

The post processes for the SORE derived from algorithm *Soa2Sore* are as follows. Let r_0 denote the SORE inferred by *Soa2Sore*. Every possibly repeated subexpression of r_0 is rewritten to be under iteration ($^+$), and for regular expressions $r_1, r_2, \cdots, r_k$ ($k \geq 2$), the expressions of forms $(r_1 r_2^+ r_3)^+$ and $(r_1(r_2^+)?r_3)^+$ ($\varepsilon \in \mathcal{L}(r_1)$ and $\varepsilon \in \mathcal{L}(r_3)$) are forbidden. And the expressions of form $(r_1?r_2? \cdots r_k?)^+$ are also forbidden.

Step 2: A CFA is constructed by traversing the syntax tree of the SORE obtained from step 1.

First, the state-transition diagram G of a CFA is constructed by traversing the syntax tree of the SORE obtained from step 1. The entire process is similar to the preorder traversal of the binary tree. Then, the detailed descriptions of the CFA are presented such as like in [25]. Note that, the parameter $\Phi(q)$ in transition function of a CFA can be obtained from G.

Step 3: The CFA derived from step 2 runs on the same finite sample used in step 1 to obtain the minimum and maximum number of repetitions of the subexpressions under the iteration operators.

The CFA counts the minimum and maximum number of repetitions of the subexpressions under the iteration operators. Counting rules are given by transition functions of the CFA. We use the algorithm *Counting* proposed in [25] to run the CFA. Let $\mathcal{A}$ denote the constructed CFA and S denote the given finite sample. Let $\mathsf{C} = Counting(\mathcal{A}, S)$, where $\mathsf{C} = \{(l(q), u(q)) | q \in \mathcal{A}.Q_c\}$.

Step 4: We obtain a cSORE by traversing the syntax tree constructed in step 2 and replace the iteration operators with corresponding counting operators where the values of the lower bound and upper bound are obtained in step 3.

Note that, C is the set of pairs of the lower bound and upper bound values.

4 Experiments

In this section, first, we present the practical analysis of cSOREs. Then, we provide the evaluations in generalization ability about our algorithm. And all experiments were conducted on a ThinkCentre M8600t-D065 with an Intel core i7-6700 CPU (3.4 GHz) and 8G memory. All codes were written in C++.

4.1 Practicability

The 32,750 real-world XSD files were grabbed from Google, Maven, and GitHub. Table 1 shows that the proportion of cSOREs is 94.16% for the 378,558 regular expressions that were extracted from these XSD files. This indicates the significant practicability of cSOREs.

Table 1. Proportions of SOREs, ECsores and cSOREs.

Subclasses	% of XSDs
SOREs	93.74
ECsore	96.53
cSORE	94.16

4.2 Generalization Abilities

We evaluate the algorithms *InfECsore* and *InfcSORE* by computing the precision and recall according to the given sample. We specify that, the learnt expression with higher precision and recall has better generalization ability. The average precision and average recall, which are as functions of sample size, respectively, are averaged over 1000 expressions.

We randomly extracted the 1000 expressions from XSDs, which were grabbed from Google, Maven, and GitHub. Each one of the 1000 expressions does not contain the iteration operators ($^{+}$), but contains the counters, where the upper bounds are less than 10. To learn each extracted expression e_0, we randomly generated corresponding XML data by using ToXgene [2], the samples are extracted from the XML data, each sample size is that listed in Fig. 1. And we define precision (p) and recall (r). Let positive sample (S_+) be the set of the all strings accepted by e_0, and let negative sample (S_-) be the set of the all strings not accepted by e_0. Let e_1 be the expression derived by *InfECsore* or *InfcSORE*. A true positive sample (S_{tp}) is the set of the strings, which are in S_+ and accepted by e_1. While a false negative sample (S_{fn}) is the set of the strings, which are in S_+ and rejected by e_1. Similarly, a false positive sample (S_{fp}) is the set of the strings, which are in S_- and accepted by e_1. While a true negative sample (S_{tn}) is the set of the strings, which are in S_- and rejected by e_1. Then, let $p = \frac{|S_{tp}|}{|S_{tp}|+|S_{fp}|}$ and $r = \frac{|S_{tp}|}{|S_{tp}|+|S_{fn}|}$. Note that $\mathcal{L}(e_0)$ and $\mathcal{L}(e_1)$ are finite languages, and we can construct counter automata [15] (receptors) for e_0 and e_1, respectively. Then we can obtain $|S_{tp}|$, $|S_{fp}|$ and $|S_{fn}|$.

The plots in Fig. 1(a) show that, for a smaller sample (sample size ≤ 500), the precision for the expression derived by *InfcSORE* is higher than that for the expression learnt by *InfECsore*. But for a larger sample (sample size ≥ 600), the precision for the expression derived by *InfcSORE* is lower than that for the expression learnt by *InfECsore*. However, the plots in Fig. 1(b) illustrate that, the recall for the expression derived by *InfcSORE* is consistently higher than that for the expression learnt by *InfECsore*. The reason is that, although the cSOREs are a subclass of the ECsores, for the same sample, the learnt cSORE can have more constrains than the learnt ECsore such that some subexpressions without numerical constrains in the learnt cSORE. This will lead to that the learnt cSORE is expressive enough to cover more XML data. In general, for a smaller sample, *InfcSORE* has better generalization ability such that its result has higher precision and recall.

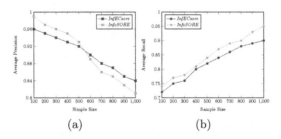

(a)   (b)

Fig. 1. (a) and (b) are average precision and average recall as functions of the sample size for each algorithm, respectively.

5   Conclusion

This paper proposed an inference algorithm for learning a subclass of deterministic regular expressions: cSOREs. The main strategies include: (1) Construct a CFA from the syntax tree of the learnt SORE; (2) The CFA runs on the given finite sample to obtain the counting operators; and (3) Generate the cSORE by traversing the syntax tree and introducing the counting operators. Compared with previous work, for any given finite language, our algorithm not only can learn a cSORE, which is expressive enough to cover more XML data, but also has better generalization ability for smaller sample. A future work is extending the SORE with counting and interleaving, studying the practical issues and the learning algorithms.

References

1. Abiteboul, S., Buneman, P., Suciu, D.: Data on the Web: From Relations to Semistructured Data and XML. Morgan Kaufmann, Burlington (2000)
2. Barbosa, D., Mendelzon, A.O., Keenleyside, J., Lyons, K.: ToXgene: an extensible template-based data generator for XML. In: WebDB (2002)
3. Barbosa, D., Mignet, L., Veltri, P.: Studying the XML web: gathering statistics from an XML sample. World Wide Web 9(2), 187–212 (2006)
4. Bex, G.J., Gelade, W., Neven, F., Vansummeren, S.: Learning deterministic regular expressions for the inference of schemas from XML data. In: Proceedings of the 17th International Conference on World Wide Web, pp. 825–834. ACM (2008)
5. Bex, G.J., Gelade, W., Neven, F., Vansummeren, S.: Learning deterministic regular expressions for the inference of schemas from XML data. ACM Trans. Web 4(4), 1–32 (2010)
6. Bex, G.J., Martens, W., Neven, F., Schwentick, T.: Expressiveness of XSDs: from practice to theory, there and back again. In: Proceedings of the 14th International Conference on World Wide Web, pp. 712–721. ACM (2005)
7. Bex, G.J., Neven, F., Van den Bussche, J.: DTDs versus XML schema: a practical study. In: Proceedings of the 7th International Workshop on the Web and Databases: Colocated with ACM SIGMOD/PODS 2004, pp. 79–84. ACM (2004)
8. Bex, G.J., Neven, F., Schwentick, T., Tuyls, K.: Inference of concise DTDs from XML data. In: International Conference on Very Large Data Bases, Seoul, Korea, pp. 115–126, September 2006
9. Bex, G.J., Neven, F., Schwentick, T., Vansummeren, S.: Inference of concise regular expressions and DTDs. ACM Trans. Database Syst. 35(2), 1–47 (2010)
10. Boneva, I., Ciucanu, R., Staworko, S.: Schemas for unordered XML on a DIME. Theor. Comput. Syst. 57(2), 337–376 (2015)
11. Brüggemann-Klein, A., Wood, D.: One-unambiguous regular languages. Inf. Comput. 142(2), 182–206 (1998)
12. Che, D., Aberer, K., Özsu, M.T.: Query optimization in XML structured-document databases. VLDB J. 15(3), 263–289 (2006)
13. Freydenberger, D.D., Kötzing, T.: Fast learning of restricted regular expressions and DTDs. In: Proceedings of the 16th International Conference on Database Theory, pp. 45–56. ACM (2013)
14. Freydenberger, D.D., Kötzing, T.: Fast learning of restricted regular expressions and DTDs. Theor. Comput. Syst. 57(4), 1114–1158 (2015)
15. Gelade, W., Gyssens, M., Martens, W.: Regular expressions with counting: weak versus strong determinism. SIAM J. Comput. 41(1), 160–190 (2012)
16. Gold, E.M.: Language identification in the limit. Inf. Control 10(5), 447–474 (1967)

17. Hovland, D.: Regular expressions with numerical constraints and automata with counters. In: Leucker, M., Morgan, C. (eds.) ICTAC 2009. LNCS, vol. 5684, pp. 231–245. Springer, Heidelberg (2009). https://doi.org/10.1007/978-3-642-03466-4_15

18. Kilpeläinen, P., Tuhkanen, R.: Towards efficient implementation of XML schema content models. In: Proceedings of the 2004 ACM Symposium on Document Engineering, pp. 239–241. ACM (2004)

19. Kilpeläinen, P., Tuhkanen, R.: One-unambiguity of regular expressions with numeric occurrence indicators. Inf. Comput. **205**(6), 890–916 (2007)

20. Latte, M., Niewerth, M.: Definability by weakly deterministic regular expressions with counters is decidable. In: Italiano, G.F., Pighizzini, G., Sannella, D.T. (eds.) MFCS 2015. LNCS, vol. 9234, pp. 369–381. Springer, Heidelberg (2015). https://doi.org/10.1007/978-3-662-48057-1_29

21. Manolescu, I., Florescu, D., Kossmann, D.: Answering XML queries on heterogeneous data sources. In: VLDB, vol. 1, pp. 241–250 (2001)

22. Martens, W., Neven, F.: Typechecking top-down uniform unranked tree transducers. In: Calvanese, D., Lenzerini, M., Motwani, R. (eds.) ICDT 2003. LNCS, vol. 2572, pp. 64–78. Springer, Heidelberg (2003). https://doi.org/10.1007/3-540-36285-1_5

23. Mignet, L., Barbosa, D., Veltri, P.: The XML web: a first study. In: Proceedings of the 12th International Conference on World Wide Web, pp. 500–510. ACM (2003)

24. Thompson, H., Beech, D., Maloney, M., Mendelsohn, N.: XML Schema Part 1: Structures, 2nd edn. W3C Recommendation (2004)

25. Wang, X., Chen, H.: Inferring deterministic regular expression with counting. In: Trujillo, J.C., et al. (eds.) ER 2018. LNCS, vol. 11157, pp. 184–199. Springer, Cham (2018). https://doi.org/10.1007/978-3-030-00847-5_15

Aggregately Regularized Multi-task Matrix Factorization for Household Energy Breakdown

Hongtao Wang, Miao Zhao, Chunlan Niu, and Hongmei Wang[✉]

School of Control and Computer Engineering,
North China Electric Power University, Baoding, China
{wanght,zhaom,Niucl,wanghm}@ncepu.edu.cn

Abstract. Household energy breakdown aims to disaggregate the monthly energy consumption into appliance level usage. It is an important but challenging issue due to the cost of hardware deployments. Existing approaches shed light on decomposing the energy in a non-intrusive way and utilizing matrix factorization. However, traditional matrix factorization methods overlook the relations among appliances and aggregations. In this paper, we propose an novel aggregately regularized Multi-task model, Non-negative Matrix Factorization (MultiNMF), to address this issue. By combining the per-appliance tasks with regularizations, Multi-NMF can simultaneously infer the appliance level energy usage for users. The model is evaluated on both synthetic and real world datasets with different settings, and the experimental results demonstrate the effectiveness of our approach.

1 Introduction

The recent big smart meter data has encouraged many new applications that help analyzing household energy usage and discover hidden knowledge. Energy breakdown has been one of the foci of both smart grid and data science research community. Household energy breakdown aims to disaggregate the monthly energy usage into appliance level, namely, decompose the energy consumption of aggregated loads of home into individual usage of appliances, such as air-conditioning(HVAC), lighting, washing machine, refrigeration, to name a few. Energy breakdown necessitates individuals to plan their energy usage rationally in order to lower their monthly bill. It is reported that such breakdown feedback can bring about a 10–15% saving in energy consumption costs [2]. On the other hands, energy breakdown could also help power supplier for both short-term and long-term load prediction, and help up to determine when conventional and renewable generation asserts must be added to the power grid [14].

Traditional techniques that perform an energy breakdown are expensive and not scalable: they require houses to install sensors on each individual appliance [9], or on each circuit in the breaker box [12]. One more practical approach

ⓒ Springer Nature Switzerland AG 2019
C. Douligeris et al. (Eds.): KSEM 2019, LNAI 11775, pp. 349–356, 2019.
https://doi.org/10.1007/978-3-030-29551-6_30

is called non-intrusive load monitoring (NILM) [8], which uses statistical methods to disaggregate the energy measured by a single smart meter. Unfortunately, NILM would also require installing a high-frequency smart meter and would thus cost up to $500 per home to deploy [4], which not practical for many areas.

Recently, there are several works on studying energy breakdown without any hardware installation [3,4], just utilizing the monthly electricity bills and a few training data from homes which already have an energy breakdown results. Batra et al. proposed Gemello [3], a clustering-based method which estimates the energy breakdown for a home by matching it with similar homes that do have a hardware-based disaggregation solution. But Gemello is limited by the weak features to define a similarity measure. As the advances in the domain of collaborative filtering technique, a matrix factorization (MF) method [4] was proposed by a matrix containing the appliance energy consumption and the aggregate energy consumption across different months. However, both Gemello and MF neglect the relationships among different appliances.

To address this issue, in this paper, we propose an aggregately regularized Multi-task Non-negative Matrix Factorization (MultiNMF) model. With the proposed model, multiple energy breakdown tasks are combined to simultaneously optimize a single objective. To build the relations among tasks, we introduce a aggregated regularization term into matrix factorization, and propose an effective algorithm for model optimization. We perform extensive experiments and evaluate our approach on both synthetic and the publicly available Dataport dataset. Results show that the performance of our MultiNMF approach outperforms several baselines.

The major contributions of this paper can be summarized as follows:

- We formalize and build a novel approach called MultiNMF, a multi-task matrix factorization based method to perform monthly energy analytics.
- We conduct an aggregate regularization term into the matrix factorization objective to address relations among tasks.
- We evaluate the proposed approach and conduct extensive experiments on both synthetic and real-world datasets.

The rest of the paper is organized as follows. In Sect. 2 we briefly review the related work. Then in Sect. 3 we formally introduce the energy breakdown problem, and propose our approach to solve it. In Sect. 4, we evaluate the proposed model and report the analysis results. Finally in Sect. 5 we conclude the paper.

2 Related Works

In the past decades various techniques for measuring home energy consumption in appliance level have been extensively studied. According to the types of sensors used for load monitoring, these efforts can fall into three classes: (1) appliance-level sensors based approach: installing appliance level sensors on all appliances in home that monitor and report appliance energy consumption; (2) home-level sensor based approach: only using a single sensor on the power signal measured at a single point (home mains), and then disaggregating the signal into appliance level consumption data; and (3) non sensor based approach: directly breaking down the appliance level consumption from the aggregated home consumption data.

For appliance-level sensors based approach, various metering hardwares and methods for energy breakdown have been proposed in the past decades. The simplest method is to install power sensors on each individual appliance directly [5], or on each circuit in the breaker box [12]. An alternative way is to use ambient sensors to instrument the power of an appliance via some side channel signals generated by power suppliers, such as sound, light, temperature, radio frequency [6], and EMI noise [7], etc.

For home-level sensor based approach, the most influential framework is proposed by Hart [8] in the 1980s named non-intrusive load monitoring (NILM). Then in the past three decades the research community has proposed a vast amount of sensors and solutions to scale up energy breakdown under NILM framework [2]. NILM solutions work under the assumption that we have to perform source separation on the power signal measured at a single point (home mains). Then they perform disaggregation that infer the power or energy of individual appliance based on aggregate load measurements. It should be noted that both previous types of work require instrumentation across each home and could not scale up.

To address this issues, several approaches are proposed recently without any extra sensors installed in home. These approaches can provide an energy breakdown just using the monthly electricity bills and a few training data that already have an energy breakdown. Batra et al. proposed Gemello, a system that estimated the energy usage of one home based on other homes that were very similar and used kNN based clustering algorithms for matching [3]. As the advances of collaborative filtering technique in the domain of recommender systems [1], a matrix factorization (MF) method [4] is proposed by a matrix containing the appliance energy consumption and the aggregate energy consumption across different months. However, both Gemello and MF did not consider relations among appliances to conduct their energy breakdown.

3   Approach

In this section, we first introduce the problems of energy breakdown in Sect. 3.1. Then we formulate the key idea of our MultiNMF model in Sect. 3.2.

3.1   Problem Statement

Given the aggregated energy consumptions of a home across several months, the goal of energy breakdown is to predict the monthly energy usage per appliance. We partition energy consumption dataset into two parts. One subset consists of energy consumption records with only aggregated values from different months, and the other consists of the detailed energy consumption values for each type of alliance as well as the aggregated values. Examples of raw data are shown in Fig. 1.

	Hvac1	Hvac2	⋯	Hvac12	⋯⋯	Agg1	⋯	Agg12	f1	f2	f3
PU	?	?	??	?	???	45	⋯	56	3	5	102
TU1	13	6	⋯	25	⋯	40	⋯	49	3	5	110
TU2	10	8	⋯	29	⋯	48	⋯	61	4	5	99
TU3	34	31	⋯	42	⋯	78	⋯	93	5	8	140
TU4	30	29	⋯	45	⋯	82	⋯	86	5	8	144
⋮	⋮	⋮	⋮	⋮	⋮	⋮	⋮	⋮	⋮	⋮	⋮

Fig. 1. Data examples

In Fig. 1, each row denotes a record from a user(or home). PU represents the predicted users and TU represents the training users. Each column demotes an attribute, ranging from energy consumption of every appliance across months, aggregated energy across months and a few extra features. For example, 'Hvac1' denotes energy consumption from heating, ventilation and air-conditioning at month 1. 'Agg1' denotes the aggregated energy consumption at month 1. While 'f1', 'f2' and 'f3' denote number of occupants, number of rooms and house square footage respectively. The question marks represent values need to be predicted. Note that there are only a few PUs and comparably more TUs in the table.

3.2 Our Approach

Non-negative matrix factorization (MF) based approach can predict per-appliance energy consumption for a test user, without requiring any measuring devices. The basic assumption of this genre of approach is that the energy consumption values are determined by some common and shared patterns across a broad range of homes [4]. These patterns can be learned and represented from two low-dimensional matrices: the user factor matrix and the appliance factor matrix. A record of a home can be reconstructed from these factor matrices using only a small amount of data, such as several monthly aggregated meter readings.

For an energy dataset we assume it contains n homes, including n_1 PUs and n_2 TUs $(n_1 < n_2)$. We classify all appliances into s categories and the number of months in this dataset is t. $A_i \in R^{n \times t}$ denotes the energy consumption for the ith appliance across t months, $i = 1, \cdots, s$. $B \in R^{n \times t}$ denotes the aggregated energy consumption across t months. Let $M_i = (A_i, B) \in R^{n \times m}$ be the concatenated original matrix that need to complete, where $m = 2t$. The aim of matrix factorization is to fill the absent values in M_i. Since energy is a non-negative quantity, we formulate our task as a non-negative matrix factorization (NMF) problem [11].

Assume there are k latent factors. We aim to learn two factor matrices $U_i \in R^{n \times k}$ and $V_i \in R^{k \times m}$, such that $M_i \approx U_i V_i$, where $U_i \geq 0$, $V_i \geq 0$ and $k \leq n, m$.

The MF problem can be formulated as the following optimization problem [4]:

$$\underset{U_i, V_i}{\mathrm{argmin}} \parallel M_i - U_i V_i \parallel_2^2 + \lambda_1 (\parallel U_i \parallel_2^2 + \parallel V_i \parallel_2^2)$$

$$s.t.\ U_i, V_i \geq 0$$

(1)

where λ_1 is the regularization parameter to alleviate over-fitting, and $\parallel \cdot \parallel_2$ denotes the l_2 norm. Once U_i and V_i are learned, we can multiply U_i and V_i to derive a completed matrix that the entries with absent values in M are filled. These new values are the predicted energy breakdown results per-appliance.

Although MF approach is effective in the energy breakdown task, the relations among appliances and aggregation values are neglected. Specifically, the appliance matrix M_i is constrained by the aggregation of all appliances. Thus, for the learned factor matrices U_i and V_i, it could also be subjected to this rule. Let S be the aggregation matrix. Suppose there are l appliances. Then the multi-task NMF can be formulated as the following optimization problem:

$$\underset{U_i, V_i, i=1 \cdots l}{\mathrm{argmin}} \sum_{i=1}^{l} (\parallel M_i - U_i V_i \parallel_2^2 + \lambda_1 (\parallel U_i \parallel_2^2 + \parallel V_i \parallel_2^2))$$

$$+ \lambda_2 \parallel \sum_{i=1}^{l} U_i V_i - S \parallel_2^2 \quad s.t.\ U_i, V_i \geq 0$$

(2)

where λ_2 is the regularization parameter controlling the contribution of relations among appliances.

Equation 2 is a non-convex optimization problem. To solve the optimization problem, we adopt Alternating Least Squares (ALS) [10] optimization method as there is no closed form solution for finding the optimal result. We perform ALS method to update each latent variable by fixing the other tasks and variables when minimizing the objective function, since it become convex in this scenario.

4   Performance Evaluation

In order to illustrate the effectiveness of the proposed approach, we present the dataset and baselines in Sect. 4.1, followed by the evaluation metric and results in Sects. 4.2 and 4.3.

4.1   Datasets and Baselines

We test the performance of the proposed energy breakdown approach on both synthetic and real world datasets described as follows.

For synthetic datasets, we generate 1000 samples from multivariate normal distributions each time. These samples are from multiple number of clusters. For real world dataset, we use the publicly available Dataport [13] in our experiment. Dataport is a large public datasets for household energy data. It includes energy consumptions from 586 homes in Austin, Texas, USA for the year 2015. We compare the performance of our approach against **MF**[4], which is the state-of-the-art technique based on non-negative matrix factorization that does not require any additional hardware installation.

4.2 Evaluation Metric

We use the same evaluation metric PEC as prior works [3,4]. PEC calculates the Percentage of Energy Correctly assigned, indicating how close the predicted energy breakdown results are to ground-truth values. The formula of PEC for home, appliance, month ($< h, a, m >$) triplet is as follows:

$$PEC(h,a,m) = \frac{|E(h,a,m) - \hat{E}(h,a,m)|}{E(h,aggregate,m)} \times 100\% \qquad (3)$$

where $E(h,a,m)$ and $\hat{E}(h,a,m)$ denote the ground-truth consumptions and the predicted consumptions by appliance a for home h in month m, respectively. $E(h,aggregate,m)$ denotes the ground truth aggregate home energy usage for home h in month m.

Instead of using the RMS errors in prediction accuracy, we calculating RMS errors in PEC metric. For an appliance a, the RMS of $PEC(h,a,m)$ is defined across different months and homes, and is given by the following:

$$RMS\ PEC(a) = \sqrt{\frac{\sum_h \sum_m PEC(h,a,m)^2}{n \times t}} \qquad (4)$$

where n is the number of homes and t indicates the number of months. Lower RMS error in PEC means better energy breakdown performance.

4.3 Results

Synthetic Data. Each synthetic dataset contains 1000 samples from normal distribution with different components. The means of components follows a uniform distribution ranging from 10 to 100, and we set the covariance matrix to $5 * I_n$ where I_n is the identity matrix. The parameters are set as follows: $\lambda_1 = 0.01$, $\lambda_2 = 0.01$. The above parameters are not sensitive to the results and we directly set to the bests. We vary the number of rank and the number of simulated appliances as variables for evaluation. The results are shown in Table 1 and Fig. 2.

Table 1 shows the RMS PEM error on different number of components, when fix missing rate as 0.1 and we chose the best results for different ranks. We can see that the RMS become larger for both MF and MultiNMF, when the number of components increases. But our MultiNMF model outperforms MF for all scenarios as the number of components increases. Then we fix number of components to 2 and missing rate to 0.1, and vary the rank k. The results are shown in Fig. 2(a). We can clearly see that the performances of both MF

Table 1. RMS results on different number of components (Appliances).

	$c=2$	$c=3$	$c=4$	$c=5$	$c=6$
MF	13.828	21.69	6.397	7.804	6.746
MultiNMF	10.342	19.013	7.201	7.236	5.917

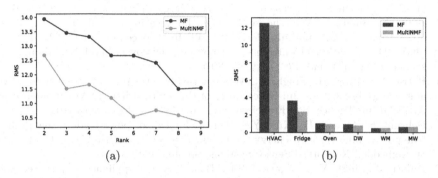

(a)   (b)

Fig. 2. Performances on synthetic and real-word datasets

and MultiNMF are declined as the ratio of missing values increases. But our MultiNMF can utilize the relations and performs better than MF.

Real-World Data. We perform our experiments on six typical appliances: heating, ventilation and air-conditioning (HVAC), fridge, washing machine (WM), microwave (MW), dish washer (DW) and oven, as done in prior work [4]. All homes have 12 month values for each appliance. Since some values are missing in this data, we randomly complete these values to compute the aggregations. The results shown in Fig. 2(b) also demonstrates that our model has improvements than previous MF method in most appliances.

5   Conclusion

In this paper, we propose a novel multi-task non-negative matrix factorization model, named MultiNMF. With this model, multiple energy breakdown tasks for single appliance are connected and learned simultaneously. To model the connections between tasks, we introduce an aggregation regularization term to induce a multi-task objective. Extensive experiments on both synthetic and real-world datasets demonstrate the effectiveness of our approach on household energy breakdown tasks.

Acknowledgments. This work was supported in part by the National Natural Science Foundation of China (Grant No.61802124), and the Fundamental Research Funds for the Central Universities (2019MS126).

References

1. Abdi, M.H., Okeyo, G.O., Mwangi, R.W.: Matrix factorization techniques for context-aware collaborative filtering recommender systems: a survey. Comput. Inf. Sci. **11**(2), 1–10 (2018)
2. Armel, K.C., Gupta, A., Shrimali, G., Albert, A.: Is disaggregation the holy grail of energy efficiency? The case of electricity. Energy Policy **52**(1), 213–234 (2013)
3. Batra, N., Singh, A., Whitehouse, K.: Gemello: creating a detailed energy breakdown from just the monthly electricity bill. In: Proceedings of the 22nd ACM SIGKDD International Conference on Knowledge Discovery and Data Mining, San Francisco, pp. 431–440, 13–17 August 2016
4. Batra, N., Wang, H., Singh, A., Whitehouse, K.: Matrix factorisation for scalable energy breakdown. In: Proceedings of the Thirty-First AAAI Conference on Artificial Intelligence, San Francisco, pp. 4467–4473, 4–9 February 2017
5. Debruin, S., Ghena, B., Kuo, Y.S., Dutta, P.: Demo: powerblade a low-profile, true-power, plug-through energy meter. In: Proceedings of the ACM Conference on Embedded Networked Sensor Systems, pp. 463–464 (2015)
6. Gulati, M., Singh, V.K., Agarwal, S.K., Bohara, V.A.: Appliance activity recognition using radio frequency interference emissions. IEEE Sens. J. **16**(16), 6197–6204 (2016)
7. Gupta, S., Reynolds, M.S., Patel, S.N.: Electrisense: single-point sensing using EMI for electrical event detection and classification in the home. In: Proceedings of the 12th International Conference on Ubiquitous Computing, UbiComp 2010, Copenhagen, Denmark, pp. 139–148, 26–29 September 2010
8. Hart, G.W.: Nonintrusive appliance load monitoring. Proc. IEEE **80**(12), 1870–1891 (1992)
9. Kim, Y., Schmid, T., Charbiwala, Z., Srivastava, M.B.: ViridiScope: design and implementation of a fine grained power monitoring system for homes. In: Proceedings of the 11th International Conference on Ubiquitous Computing, UbiComp 2009, pp. 245–254 (2009)
10. Koren, Y., Bell, R.M., Volinsky, C.: Matrix factorization techniques for recommender systems. IEEE Comput. **42**(8), 30–37 (2009)
11. Lee, D.D., Seung, H.S.: Algorithms for non-negative matrix factorization. In: Proceedings of the Neural Information Processing Systems 2000, Denver, pp. 556–562 (2000)
12. Marchiori, A., Hakkarinen, D., Han, Q., Earle, L.: Circuit-level load monitoring for household energy management. IEEE Pervasive Comput. **10**(1), 40–48 (2011)
13. Parson, O., et al.: Dataport and NILMTK: a building data set designed for non-intrusive load monitoring. In: Proceedings of the 2015 IEEE Global Conference on Signal and Information Processing, GlobalSIP 2015, Orlando, pp. 210–214, 14–16 December 2015
14. Tabatabaei, S.M., Dick, S., Xu, W.: Toward non-intrusive load monitoring via multi-label classification. IEEE Trans. Smart Grid **8**(1), 26–40 (2017)

Learning Continuous User and Item Representations for Neural Collaborative Filtering

Qinglin Jia[1,2](✉) (iD), Xiao Su[3], and Zhonghai Wu[1,2]

[1] School of Software and Microelectronics, Peking University, Beijing, China
{jiaql,wuzh}@pku.edu.cn
[2] National Research Center of Software Engineering,
Peking University, Beijing, China
[3] Academy for Advanced Interdisciplinary Studies, Peking University, Beijing, China
sugarshaw951018@pku.edu.cn

Abstract. Collaborative filtering (CF) is one of the most successful approach commonly used by many recommender systems. Recently, deep neural networks (DNNs) have performed very well in collaborative filtering for recommendation. Conventional DNNs based CF methods directly model the interaction between user and item features by transforming users and items into binarized sparse vectors with one-hot encoding, then map them into a low dimensional space with randomly initialized embedding layers and automatically learn the representations in training process. We argue that randomly initialized embedding layers can not capture the contextual relations of user interactions. We propose an approach that uses the optimized representations of user and item generated by doc2vec algorithm to initialize embedding layers. Items with similar contexts (i.e., their surrounding click) are mapped to vectors that are nearby in the embedding space. Our experiments on three industry datasets show significant improvements, especially in high-sparsity recommendation scenarios.

Keywords: Deep learning · Distributed representation ·
Recommender systems · Collaborative filtering

1 Introduction

Due to the explosive growth of internet services, recommender systems which help users quickly discover items of interest, now play a pivotal role [7]. One of the most promising technologies for recommendation is collaborative filtering [6].

Matrix factorization (MF) is a kind of popular CF model which has shown its effectiveness and efficiency in many applications [2]. MF transforms user-item rating matrix into the same latent factor space, then models user interactions on an item as the inner product of their latent vectors. In the latent factor space, MF assumes each dimension is independent of each other and simply combines

© Springer Nature Switzerland AG 2019
C. Douligeris et al. (Eds.): KSEM 2019, LNAI 11775, pp. 357–362, 2019.
https://doi.org/10.1007/978-3-030-29551-6_31

them with the same weight in linear. In this setting, MF may not be sufficient to model the complex non-linear relations of user-item rating matrix. Compared with MF, DNNs can model users' implicit feedback with a high level of non-linearities. In this work, we present the fusion of DNNs and MF to combine the benefits.

For the pure collaborative filtering setting, the input feature is usually transformed to a binarized sparse vector with one-hot encoding, which often results in an unrealistic amount of computational resource requirement. To overcome the aforementioned problem, the embedding layer is always above the one-hot encoding input layer. which can transform one-hot encoding of users and items to continuous, low dimensional vectors as representations. Embedding layers are randomly initialized and automatically learn the representations of user and item in a multi-dimensional space. But the automatically learning process only concerns the co-occurrence of items. It can not capture the contextual relations of user action sequence which is more important to model user preference. This contextual information has the potential to greatly improve the recommendation.

In the field of natural language processing (NLP), several researchers have found that words with same or similar set of surrounding words are conceptually similar. Partially motivated by this idea, we believe that the context of an item can be defined by its surrounding items. Thus, two $item_1$ and $item_2$ are similar if they have the same or similar context. Our intuition is simple, i.e., items with similar context should be nearby in the embedding space. Contextual information can facilitate finding better item representations which can help CF model judge the similarity of items.

For recommender systems, the sequence of user visited items can indicate the shifting of user interest with time. Different item sequences indicate different user interest, and we should differentiate the users who visited the same item set but different item sequences. We try to utilize the ordering of user visited items and embed time information into user representations for CF model.

We propose an approach that optimizes the representations of user and item through doc2vec algorithm in order to improve the performance of the state-of-the-art neural collaborative filtering. We first generate user and item representations with doc2vec. Then, the generated vectors are used to initialize the latent vectors of neural collaborative filtering for training. We name the neural collaborative filtering with improved representation model IR-NCF.

2   Proposed Approaches

In this section, we describe our model that allows us to efficiently model user-item interactions and their contextual relationships, called IR-NCF. First, we propose to utilize the ordering of user visited items and embed contextual information into user and item representations for recommendation tasks. Then, we extend neural collaborative filtering framework by incorporating the learned representations. The overall architecture of IR-NCF is shown in Fig. 1. We will present detailed illustration of the proposed approach in the rest of this section.

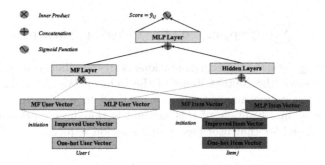

Fig. 1. Architecture of IR-NCF model

2.1 Notation and Problem Formulation

In this work, we focus on implicit feedback and take it as the training and test data. Every item is mapped to a unique vector, represented by a column in a N-by-S matrix $\mathbf{Q}$ where S is the vector size and N is the total number of items. Similarly, the entire collection of M users is represented by a M-by-S matrix $\mathbf{P}$, where row m is the vector $\mathbf{p}_m$ for user m. They share the same vector size S. We define a M-by-N binary rating matrix $\mathbf{Y} = [\mathbf{Y}_{ij}]_{M*N}$. For example, a value of 1 for y_{ij} indicates that there is an interaction between user i and item j. Given part of the ratings in $\mathbf{Y}$, the problem is to predict the other ratings in $\mathbf{Y}$. It is defined as:

$$\hat{y}_{ij} = f(\mathbf{p}_i, \mathbf{q}_j | \mathbf{P}, \mathbf{Q}, \Theta_f). \tag{1}$$

where $\hat{y}_{ij}$ denotes the predicted score. $\mathbf{P} \in \mathbb{R}^{M*S}$ and $\mathbf{Q} \in \mathbb{R}^{N*S}$ stores the latent factors for users and items respectively. Θ_f denotes model parameters, and f is the mapping function. $\mathbf{p}_i$ and $\mathbf{q}_j$ denotes the latent vector that describes user i and item j.

2.2 User and Item Representations

Inspired by the recent progress on word embedding, we adopt doc2vec algorithm to embed contextual information into user and item representations for recommendation. Doc2vec [4] introduces a unique, randomly initialized numeric vector as another input of the model to represent the document that the target word is part of. The same method can be used to learn user representations by modeling user as a dedicated element in the learning process to predict items in user action sequence.

Given a uses action sequence $s = \{e_1, ..., e_i, ..., e_{|s|}\}$. User vectors are considered as a global context to predict the action from their action sequence and updated during training. Item vectors are learned to predict the neighborhood based on co-occurrence in a fixed-length window. Following doc2vec, we can learn item representations by maximizing the log-likelihood over the set S of all user action sequences in the training data.

$$\mathcal{L} = \sum_{s \in S} (log\mathbb{P}(\mathbf{p}_u | \mathbf{q}_{e_1} : \mathbf{q}_{e_n})) + \sum_{e_i \in s} log\mathbb{P}(\mathbf{q}_{e_i} | C(e_i), \mathbf{p}_u)) \tag{2}$$

where $\mathbf{p}_u$ and $\mathbf{q}_{e_i}$ denote the representations corresponding to user u and item e_i. $C(e_i)$ represents the context items of the item e_i. We can learn the representations by leveraging any optimization method to maximize this objective function. The main advantage of this method is that user representations are specifically tailored for that user based on his action sequence.

2.3 Integrating Neural Collaborative Filtering with Improved Representations

We build our predictor based on neural collaborative filtering framework with learned low-dimensional user and item representations which can effectively achieve better recommendation performance. The neural collaborative filtering framework has two components.

The matrix factorization component computes the score of a user i on an item j as the linear combination of an element-wise product of two latent vectors. The deep component is multi-layer perceptron (MLP) network. The latent vectors are fed into the hidden layers of a neural network in the forward pass.

The MF component and deep component are concatenated and then fed to one common loss function for joint training. We use binary cross-entropy loss to learn model parameters.

$$L_s = - \sum_{(i,j) \in N_s} \log \hat{y}_{ij} - \sum_{(i,j) \in N_s^-} \log (1 - \hat{y}_{ij}) \tag{3}$$

N_s is the positive pairs set in $\mathbf{Y}$. We generate a set of N_s^- of negative pairs by sampling items from the entire item. We sample items in proportion of their popularity.

2.4 Experimental Setup

We performed experiments on two publicly accessible datasets and a private dataset. AOTM is a dataset containing listening records of users from artofthemix. Tracks in the playlist are usually arranged in a specific sequence which can indicate users' interest. TMALL is an open e-commerce dataset used in the TMall competition. In TMALL dataset, users can click, add-to-cart, add-to-favourite and purchase. The original data is very large and sparse. So we only consider the action type which is purchasing. B2C is a private dataset that comes from a B2C e-commerce website like Amazon. It contains user behaviors much like TMALL, but not as sparse as TMALL. We refer to this dataset as B2C. The evaluation is done by *leave-one-out* evaluation. We adopt *Hit Ratio (HR)@10* and *Normalized Discounted Cumulative Gain (NDCG)@10* as metrics.

We compared our IR-NCF model against several baselines, namely ItemKNN, Matrix Factorization (MF) and NCF.

- **ItemKNN** [5]. It is a standard collaborative filtering method by recommending similar items based on user histories. This method adopts doc2vec to model users and items. It has been reported to show superior performance over the traditional ItemKNN [6].
- **MF** [3]. It is the classic matrix factorization model for explicit feedback. We use the cross-entropy loss as the optimization loss for implicit feedback setting.
- **NCF** [1]. NCF combines a deep component with MF which is reported as the state-of-the-art method.

2.5 Performance Evaluation

The experimental results on all three datasets are shown in Table 1. Results show that IR-NCF gives the best performance across all datasets. This corroborates the relevance of taking into account the contextual information of the user-item interaction as a core feature. For baseline method, NCF outperforms ItemKNN and MF. This clearly demonstrates the effectiveness of DNNs. A major contribution of IR-NCF is the incorporation of DNNs, which can utilize the learned representations.

Table 1. Results of effectiveness experiments on three datasets.

Dataset	ATOM		TMALL		B2C	
M@10	HR	NDCG	HR	NDCG	HR	NDCG
ItemKNN	0.3096	0.1810	0.3038	0.1924	0.8628	0.7460
MF	0.4797	0.2960	0.4816	0.2960	0.9532	0.8323
NCF	0.4857	0.3001	0.4875	0.2973	0.9544	0.8429
IR-NCF	0.5606	0.3507	0.5843	0.3837	0.9578	0.8538

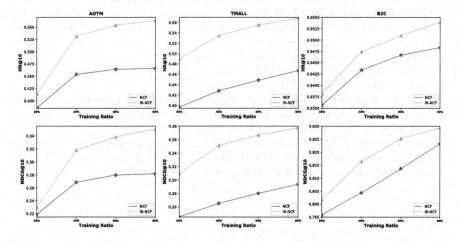

Fig. 2. Performance change of different methods when gradually decrease train set.

The performance are strong related with the quality of datasets. For sparse datasets, performance will significantly decrease We randomly partition the entire training set into five equal folds. and vary the amount of training data from one fold to five folds, corresponding to 20%, 40%, 60%, 80%, 100% data as training sets. As shown in Fig. 2, the more data there is available and the less the sparsity of the data, the better CF can recognize patterns and perform the predictive task. We can see that IR-NCF is consistently better than the baseline. The results indicate that learned continuous representations is effective to recommendation performance in sparsity recommendation scenarios.

3   Conclusion

In this paper, we focus on finding good representations for users and items. We explore to generate user and item representations by doc2vec algorithm to effectively utilize contextual information from user action sequences for recommendation. The learned representations are further integrated into a neural collaborative filtering framework. NCF with improved representations shows great potential to improve recommendations. Extensive experiments demonstrate the effectiveness of our proposed model. We also verify the superiority of our method when training data is sparse.

References

1. He, X., Liao, L., Zhang, H., Nie, L., Hu, X., Chua, T.S.: Neural collaborative filtering. In: Proceedings of the 26th International Conference on World Wide Web, pp. 173–182. International World Wide Web Conferences Steering Committee (2017)
2. Koren, Y., Bell, R.: Advances in collaborative filtering. In: Ricci, F., Rokach, L., Shapira, B. (eds.) Recommender Systems Handbook, pp. 77–118. Springer, Boston (2015). https://doi.org/10.1007/978-1-4899-7637-6_3
3. Koren, Y., Bell, R., Volinsky, C.: Matrix factorization techniques for recommender systems. Computer **8**, 30–37 (2009)
4. Mikolov, T., Sutskever, I., Chen, K., Corrado, G.S., Dean, J.: Distributed representations of words and phrases and their compositionality. In: Advances in Neural Information Processing Systems, pp. 3111–3119 (2013)
5. Phi, V.T., Chen, L., Hirate, Y.: Distributed representation based recommender systems in e-commerce. In: DEIM Forum (2016)
6. Sarwar, B., Karypis, G., Konstan, J., Riedl, J.: Item-based collaborative filtering recommendation algorithms. In: Proceedings of the 10th International Conference on World Wide Web, pp. 285–295. ACM (2001)
7. Zhang, W., Sun, H., Liu, X., Guo, X.: Temporal QOS-aware web service recommendation via non-negative tensor factorization. In: Proceedings of the 23rd International Conference on World Wide Web, pp. 585–596. ACM (2014)

Partial Alignment of Data Sets Based on Fast Intrinsic Feature Match

Yaxin Peng[1], Naiwu Wen[1], Xiaohuang Zhu[1], and Chaomin Shen[2]([✉])

[1] Department of Mathematics, School of Science,
Shanghai University, Shanghai, China
[2] Department of Computer Science, East China Normal University,
Shanghai, China
cmshen@cs.ecnu.edu.cn

Abstract. Point Feature Histograms (PFH) is a statistic and geometric invariant descriptor that has been widely used in shape analysis. Current PFH based feature extraction methods are highly affected by the time scale and become less effective for unbalanced cases, which limits their performance. In this paper, we focus on finding a framework for partial registration by an adaptive partition of point set algorithm. Firstly, we propose an adaptive partition method base on PFH coding. Secondly, we conduct a series of fast parallel implementations for efficiency. Thirdly, we plug in the PFH based partition method and trimmed strategy to our modified iterative closest point method. Experiments demonstrate that our algorithms are robust and stable.

Keywords: Partial registration · PFH coding · ICP · Trimmed method

1 Introduction

Point set registration is a technique widely used in the fields of computer vision and pattern recognition [3,9,18]. The purpose of registration between two point sets is to find their correspondence and space transformation, which can transform one point set to its counterpart.

A variety of point set registration algorithms have appeared. Iterative Closest Point (ICP) [4,6] is well known for its efficient frame to find a proper correspondence and space transformation iteratively. The ICP algorithm, however, is only applicable to rigid registration, and sensitive to noise, missing points, outliers and large transformation. Regarding these issues, many improved ICP algorithms have been proposed [11,12,15–17].

All these algorithms work only when the overlap rate between two point sets is low. For the overlap large than 60%, the Trimmed ICP (TrICP) algorithms have been proposed [7,10]. TrICP neglects outliers and then conducts ICP by minimizing the Trimmed Squared Distance (TSD). [8,14] introduce an initial transformation based on PCA and conduct an optimization framework of TrICP

ⓒ Springer Nature Switzerland AG 2019
C. Douligeris et al. (Eds.): KSEM 2019, LNAI 11775, pp. 363–367, 2019.
https://doi.org/10.1007/978-3-030-29551-6_32

to complex global transformations. However, this initial process may lead to miss-alignment when there is partial registration, since the distribution of object is not necessarily consistent with that of partial object, such as the barycenter.

To settle this problem, a subICP algorithm based on subset registration between the partitions of point set [5] is proposed. The performance of subset ICP is sensitive to the number of subsets and the partition pattern. For avoiding the unbalance of data caused by missing points and outlier, we need an adaptive partition method to divide the point cloud to subpartition. A proper criterion for cutting point set into subset, for example, the number of partitions and how to cut the point set, is very important. Curvature and normal direction are widely used geometric features in point set registration [6,13]. The distance between two normal directions is also introduced as a criterion for point set registration. Although curvature and the angle between normal direction are rigid invariant features of point set and need only simple computation, they are sensitive to noise.

In this paper, we propose a framework for partial registration by an adaptive partition of point set algorithm named as OICP. We introduce an adaptive partition method based on PFH for missing data or outlier, increasing the accuracy, and propose a series of parallel methods for K nearest neighbors search, normal direction and PFH descriptor estimation.

2   Adaptive Partition Method to Point Sets

Normal direction is a widely used feature for point sets. A PFH representation is based on the relationships between the points in the k-neighborhood and their estimated surface normals. Being a high dimensional hyperspace, PFH provides an informative signature for the feature representation. It is invariant to the 6D pose of the underlying surface, and copes very well with different sampling densities or noise levels in the neighborhood.

For carrying on our subICP methods smoothly, we need an adaptive partition method to divide the point cloud to k subpartition. Firstly, we need to capture PFH code of point sets pairs. Then, we implement the PFH feature matching between them, then pick up those point pairs with high matching accuracy, and make these picked points as the centers of subpartition. We collect all these centers and its k-neighbor points as subpartition of source point set.

3   Proposed Method Based on Adaptive Partition

The classical ICP method and its modification cannot get satisfied performance. We propose a normal direction weighted ICP method. Let $X = \{x_i, x_2, \cdots, x_m\}$ be the model point set, and $Y = \{y_i, y_2, \cdots, y_n\}$ be the target point set. We conduct PCA for original point set pair to find the initial transformation R^1 and t^1.

(1) Updating correspondence
Fixing the transformation, we update the correspondence by minimizing the direction objective function:

$$f = \frac{1}{m} \sum_{i=1}^{m} d_i^2,$$

where $d_i^2 = \|x_{c(i)} - (Ry_i + t)\|^2$ is the squared distance between $x_{c(i)}$ and Ty_i, and $c(i)$ is the correspondence point of y_i.

(2) Updating overlap ratio between data sets pair
Fix correspondence, update overlap ratio by minimizing the mean trimmed squared distance (MTSD)

$$\epsilon(r) = \frac{1}{r^{\lambda+1}m_r} \sum_{i=1}^{m_r} d_i^2, \tag{1}$$

where r is the overlap ratio, and $m_r = m \times r$. Sort d_i^2 increasingly, find r reaches the minimum of $\epsilon(r)$ by adding point pair one-by-one in P_r, then select the first $m_r = |P_r|$ point pairs.

(3) Updating Transformation
Fixing correspondence and overlap point pair set P_r, updating T^{k+1} by minimizing

$$\underset{R \in SO(n), t \in R^n}{\arg \min} \sum_{i=1}^{m_r} \|R \cdot y_i^k + t - x_i\|^2,$$

where R is the transformation, t is the transition, and $SO(n)$ is a rotation group.

Parallelize and Accelerate
The acquisition of normal direction and PFH descriptor give us a good initialization, then get higher accuracy and need less iteration number, but it is still time consuming especially for large scale data. Moreover, larger neighbor also takes much more time. So we introduce GPU accelerate algorithm.

With the help of CUDA (Compute Unified Device Architecture), we could implement our parallel PFH computation conveniently on NVIDIA GPUs. The main idea of designing the parallel PFH is that every thread in the GPU takes control of every point in a point cloud data. Nearest neighborhood search, normal computation and PFH descriptors can be conducted every point parallelled.

4   Implementation

In order to show the effectiveness of our algorithm, we compare it with ICP and TrICP. We perform several experiments on 3D point sets such as Stanford dragon, bunny and Happy Buddha [1,2]. From Fig. 1 and Table 1, our algorithm can achieve satisfactory results comparing with ICP, TrICP. Random noise is also generated for one or both copies of the original data set in the second raw of Fig. 1. It demonstrates that our algorithms are robust, especially under the random noise. In Table 1, we also compare the quantity result under random noise for different methods. Notice that ICP and TrICP fail to register no matter with noise or not. Visual inspection shows that our algorithm performs best.

We compare the computation times for ICP, modified TrICP and our method, as shown in Table 1. Our method has a good performance in terms of accuracy, stability and speed. The hardware for implementation are Intel(R) Core(TM) i7-8750H CPU @ 2.20 GHz, 8 GB RAM, GeForce GTX 1060 and 6 GB RAM.

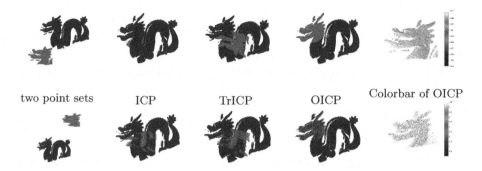

Fig. 1. Comparison of results for registration. The first column is the original data; the second column is the result for ICP; the third is for TrICP; the fourth and fifth are for our method.

Table 1. Comparison results for different methods

Point set	Noise (Y/N)	Point number	ICP		TrICP		OICP	
			Error	Time (s)	Error	Time (s)	Error	Time (s)
Dragon	N	41,841/11,449	1.84	18.6	1.39	37.0	$<10^{-6}$	2.2
	Y	41,841/11,449	1.86	42.0	1.46	52.1	0.02	2.7
Cat	N	24,321/7,468	2.76	22.2	1.42	22.6	$<10^{-6}$	1.1
	Y	24,321/7,468	2.84	59.7	1.46	29.1	0.40	1.6
Happy	N	54,353/17,212	4.22	76.5	1.22	74.8	$<10^{-6}$	2.5
	Y	54,353/17,212	4.51	75.0	1.42	88.9	0.08	3.2
Horse	N	48,485/7,510	2.17	48.9	2.02	51.2	$<10^{-6}$	2.9
	Y	48,485/7,510	2.34	55.8	2.12	49.0	0.05	2.3

5   Conclusions

In this paper, we have focused on finding a fast framework for partial registration. We propose an adaptive partition method base on intrinsic PFH coding; then, we conduct a series of fast parallel implementation for reducing time consuming; we plug in this PFH based partition method and trimmed strategy to our modified iterative closest point method and it performs well.

Acknowledgements. This work was supported by the National Natural Science Foundation of China under Grant No. 11771276.

References

1. http://graphics.stanford.edu/data/3Dscanrep/
2. https://www.cc.gatech.edu/projects/
3. Belongie, S., Malik, J., Puzicha, J.: Shape matching and object recognition using shape contexts. IEEE Trans. Pattern Anal. Mach. Intell. **24**(4), 509–522 (2002)

4. Besl, P., McKay, N.: A method for registration of 3-D shapes. IEEE Trans. Pattern Anal. Mach. Intell. **14**(2), 239–256 (1992)
5. Chen, J., Belaton, B., Pan, Z.: A robust subset-ICP method for point set registration. In: Zaman, H.B., Robinson, P., Olivier, P., Shih, T.K., Velastin, S. (eds.) IVIC 2013. LNCS, vol. 8237, pp. 59–69. Springer, Cham (2013). https://doi.org/10.1007/978-3-319-02958-0_6
6. Chen, Y., Medioni, G.: Object modelling by registration of multiple range images. Image Vis. Comput. **10**(3), 145–155 (1992)
7. Chetverikov, D., Stepanov, D., Krsek, P.: Robust Euclidean alignment of 3D point sets: the trimmed iterative closest point algorithm. Image Vis. Comput. **23**(3), 299–309 (2005)
8. Dong, J., Peng, Y., Ying, S., Hu, Z.: LieTrICP: an improvement of trimmed iterative closest point algorithm. Neurocomputing **140**, 67–76 (2014)
9. Du, S., Guo, Y., Sanroma, G., Ni, D., Wu, G., Shen, D.: Building dynamic population graph for accurate correspondence detection. Med. Image Anal. **26**(1), 256–267 (2015)
10. Du, S., Zhu, J., Zheng, N., Liu, Y., Ce, L.: Robust iterative closest point algorithm for registration of point sets with outliers. Opt. Eng. **50**(8), 087001 (2011)
11. Du, S.Y., Zheng, N.N., Meng, G.F., Yuan, Z.J., Li, C.: Affine registration of point sets using ICP and ICA. IEEE Signal Process. Lett. **15**, 689–692 (2008)
12. Du, S.Y., Zheng, N.N., Ying, S.H., Liu, J.Y.: Affine iterative closest point algorithm for point set registration. Pattern Recogn. Lett. **31**, 791–799 (2010)
13. Johnson, A.E., Hebert, M.: Surface registration by matching oriented points. In: Proceedings of the International Conference on Recent Advances in 3-D Digital Imaging and Modeling, NRC 1997, p. 121. IEEE Computer Society (1997)
14. Peng, Y., Ying, S., Qin, J., Zeng, T.: Trimmed strategy for affine registration of point sets. J. Appl. Remote Sens. **7**(1), 073468 (2013)
15. Ying, S., Peng, J., Du, S., Qiao, H.: A scale stretch method based on ICP for 3D data registration. IEEE Trans. Autom. Sci. Eng. **6**(3), 559–565 (2009)
16. Ying, S., Peng, Y., Wen, Z.: Iwasawa decomposition: a new approach to 2D affine registration problem. Pattern Anal. Appl. **24**(2), 127–137 (2011)
17. Zha, H., Ikuta, M., Hasegawa, T.: Registration of range images with different scanning resolutions. In: Proceedings of the IEEE International Conference on System, Man, Cybernetics, Nashville, Tennessee, USA, pp. 1495–1500 (2000)
18. Zhang, Z.: Iterative point matching for registration of free form surfaces. Int. J. Comput. Vision **13**(2), 119–152 (1994)

Image and Video Data Analysis

Implicit Rating Methods Based on Interest Preferences of Categories for Micro-Video Recommendation

Jie Chen[1], Junjie Peng[1,2,3]($\boxtimes$), Lizhe Qi[4], Gan Chen[1], and Wenqiang Zhang[4,5]

[1] School of Computer Engineering and Science, Shanghai University, Shanghai, China
{ces_chenjie,jjie.peng,cgclio}@shu.edu.cn
[2] Shanghai Institute for Advanced Communication and Data Science,
Shanghai University, Shanghai, China
[3] Lab of Intelligent Techonology and Systems, Shanghai Computer Society,
Shanghai, China
[4] Academy for Engineering and Technology, Fudan University, Shanghai, China
{qilizhe,wqzhang}@fudan.edu.cn
[5] School of Computer Science and Technology, Fudan University, Shanghai, China

Abstract. Collaborative filtering (CF) without explicit information is one of the most challenging research directions in the field of video recommendation, as the effectiveness of traditional CF methods strongly depend on the ratings of videos for users. However, in the actual online video platforms, explicit ratings are very rare or even completely unavailable in most cases. This makes the effects of traditional recommendation algorithms are not satisfactory. In addition, micro-videos have attracted wide attention, while they have not be considered differently by the traditional recommendation algorithms. It is meaningful to study the recommendation methods for micro-videos. Considering that micro-videos have categories, two implicit rating methods based on interest preferences of categories are proposed to improve the performance of recommendation for micro-videos under implicit feedback. Its core idea is to construct a rating matrix based on implicit information by mining users' implicit interest preference information for different categories of micro-videos, and use it as the basis of recommendation algorithms. The proposed rating methods are validated on a large online video content provider, and they are correct and can effectively mine users' preferences without explicit ratings according to the experimental results. They can bring better results than some existing algorithms, and can be better applied to the video recommendation system.

Keywords: Collaborative filtering · Implicit information ·
Micro-video · Category · Rating method

1 Introduction

The scale of online video industry has grown unprecedentedly. An research report [3] points out that the scale of online video users in China alone has

© Springer Nature Switzerland AG 2019
C. Douligeris et al. (Eds.): KSEM 2019, LNAI 11775, pp. 371–381, 2019.
https://doi.org/10.1007/978-3-030-29551-6_33

reached more than 500 million, and more than 95% of them will choose mobile phones to watch online videos. However, as huge number of videos emerge every year, it is not easy for users to find videos that they are interested in. And for the video content providers, it is also difficult to continuously attract users to watch more videos which is important to increase their revenue.

In view of the above difficulties, video recommender system [15] was proposed and applied in video industry. And the most widely used well-known methods of it are methods of collaborative filtering [6,13], such as the user-based [22], the item-based [5], and matrix factorization-based [7,9–11,14,17,19,23] collaborative filtering methods. Rating matrix is their input and basis, so the quality of it (whether it contains more abundant and accurate preference information) is an important prerequisite for them to achieve good results. However, in the actual online video platform, explicit ratings are very rare or even completely unavailable in most cases. Under this condition, the rating matrix of existing methods can only reflect whether users have interactions with videos, that is, there are only two values (0 and 1) of the item in it. And it can not reflect the degrees of interactions and the different preferences of users. This makes the effects of traditional recommendation algorithms unsatisfactory. This condition is called implicit feedback-based recommendation [21].

In addition, micro-video [16] has gradually become a new fashion of entertainment. The number of users of micro-video applications in China alone has reached more than 600 million [3], which shows that micro-video industry is booming. However, the traditional video recommendation methods mainly focus on the long videos such as movies and TV series, and do not consider micro-videos. Compared with long videos, besides the short duration, micro-videos usually lack some important information such as directors list, actors list and so on. Therefore, if the implicit recommendation methods are used for micro-videos, the effects of them will inevitably be worse than that of long videos. So it is necessary to analyze and process micro-videos separately.

Through the observations of information of micro-videos in a real large online video platform, what can be found is that micro-videos have categories. Then two implicit rating methods based on interest preferences of categories are proposed. With the rating methods the rating matrices can be generated and used as the bases of collaborative filtering algorithms to improve the performances of them for micro-video recommendation. The interest preferences of categories for users can be extracted from user logs in the platform by data analysis technologies.

2   Related Work

Recommendation system has been widely used in many fields, such as social network, service recommendation [2], academic paper recommendation [12], online shopping [8], and so on. Video has more implicit information than other products, such as visual information, text descriptions, comments, and so on. There are many kinds of recommendation methods based on these implicit information. Among them, the widely used are the methods based on user profile [18], knowledge graph [20], social network [4], deep learning [1], and matrix factorization [7,9–11,14,17,19,23]. The most frequently used method is matrix factorization.

Assume Y is the rating matrix of matrix factorization under implicit feedback ($Y \in \mathbb{R}^{N_1 \times N_2}$, N_1 and N_2 are the number of users and micro-videos respectively), in which the value of j-th column in i-th row is y_{ij} which is defined in formula (1):

$$y_{ij} = \begin{cases} 1, & \text{user } i \text{ has interactions with video } j \\ 0, & \text{user } i \text{ has no interaction with video } j \end{cases} \tag{1}$$

According to the actual situation, interactions may include watching, commenting, etc. In this paper, interaction refers to watching.

Existing matrix factorization methods assume that there are K latent factors ($K \in Z^+$) that can potentially affect the watching of users, and convert users and videos into a space with K dimensions. For any user i and video j, they are mapped to two vectors (p_i and q_j) with real numbers about latent factors separately. These methods model predicted rating $\hat{y}_{ij}$ of i to j according to these vectors, and recommend videos based on the predicted ratings. For example, $\hat{y}_{ij}$ of the classical matrix factorization algorithm [23] is modelled and shown in formula (2):

$$\hat{y}_{ij} = p_i^T q_j \tag{2}$$

In order to obtain the above latent vectors, some objective functions and optimize methods were proposed by existing methods. For example, function J and alternating least squares (ALS) are used in algorithm [23] as shown below:

$$J = \sum_{i=1}^{N_1} \sum_{j=1}^{N_2} (y_{ij} - \hat{y}_{ij})^2 + \lambda (\sum_{i=1}^{N_1} ||p_i||^2 + \sum_{j=1}^{N_2} ||q_j||^2) \tag{3}$$

3   Interest Preferences of Categories (IPoC)

In order to clearly describe our rating methods, some basic definitions are given.

Assume the time length threshold L ($L \in Z^+$) is used to partition micro-videos in all videos. N_1 is the number of all users ($N_1 \in Z^+$), the i-th user is referred to i ($i \in Z^+$). N_2 is the number of all micro-videos ($N_2 \in Z^+$), the j-th micro-video is referred to j ($j \in Z^+$), and its composition as formula (4) shows:

$$(L_j, C_j), L_j \leq L \tag{4}$$

where L_j is the time length of j, C_j is its list of categories (C_j is a set of positive integers, where each element represents the unique index of a category).

Assume N_3 is the size of the set of watching logs of user i ($N_3 \in Z^+$), the k-th log of them is shown in formula (5) ($k \in Z^+$):

$$(T_{ik}, L_{ik}, X_{ik}) \tag{5}$$

where T_{ik} is the start time, L_{ik} is the length of watching time, and X_{ik} is the index of the micro-video that user i watched ($X_{ik} \in Z^+$ and $X_{ik} \in [1, N_2]$).

Assume F_{ij} is the watching completion degree of user i ($i = 1, 2, ..., N_1$) to micro-video j ($j = 1, 2, ..., N_2$) which means the percentage of micro-video j watched by user i. It is defined in formula (6):

$$F_{ij} = \begin{cases} f, & 0 \leq f < 1 \\ 1, & f \geq 1 \end{cases}, f = \sum_{k=1}^{N_3} \frac{L_{ik}}{L_j}, X_{ik} = j \tag{6}$$

where f is the sum of all parts of watching completion degree of i to j, N_3 is the number of watching logs of i. And for k-th watching log, if the index of micro-video in this log equals j, then L_{ik}/L_j is the watching completion degree of this log (L_{ik} is the length of watching time and L_j is the time length of j).

W_{ic} is the total position weighted preference on c-th category ($c \in Z^+$ and $c \in [1, |\bigcup_{k=1}^{N_3} C_{ik}|]$) for user i. It reflects the total preference of category c for user i, in which the position weight is introduced to distinguish the order of categories in the categories list of a micro-video as formula (7) shows:

$$W_{ic} = \sum_{j=1}^{N_2} F_{ij} \times \alpha_c \tag{7}$$

where $\bigcup_{k=1}^{N_3} C_{ik}$ is the set of all categories that i watched ($|\cdot|$ is the size of a set), N_2 is the number of all micro-videos, for j-th micro-video, F_{ij} is the watching completion degree of i to j, α_c is a position weight of category c. In this paper, $\alpha_c = 1/Loc(c)$, where $Loc(c)$ is the index (it begins from 1) of c in C_j (the categories list of j), and α_c gets 0 if c is not in C_j.

I_{ic} is the Interest Preference of Category (IPoC) of c-th category ($c \in Z^+$ and $c \in [1, |\bigcup_{k=1}^{N_3} C_{ik}|]$) for user i. It quantifies interests in different categories of user i. Based on the above W_{ic}, it normalizes the preferences of users to unify them of different users to one scale so that I_{ic} can be compared directly, as in formula (8).

$$I_{ic} = \begin{cases} 0, & W_i = 0 \\ \dfrac{W_{ic}}{W_i}, & W_i > 0 \end{cases}, W_i = \sum_{c' \in \bigcup_{k=1}^{N_3} C_{ik}} W_{ic'} \tag{8}$$

where $\bigcup_{k=1}^{N_3} C_{ik}$ is the set of all categories of micro-video that i watched ($|\cdot|$ is the size of a set), W_{ic} is the total position weighted preference of c and W_i is the sum of all total position weighted preferences of all watched categories.

4   Implicit Rating Methods Based on Interest Preferences of Categories

4.1   Non-confidence Based IPoC Method

The rating matrix created by the implicit rating method based on Interest Preferences of Categories for micro-videos is Y' ($Y' \in \mathbb{R}^{N_1 \times N_2}$, N_1 and N_2 are the number of users and micro-videos respectively), in which the value of j-th column ($j \in Z^+$ and $j \in [1, N_2]$, represents a micro-video) in i-th row ($i \in Z^+$ and $i \in [1, N_1]$, represents a user) is y'_{ij} which is defined in the formula (9):

$$
y'_{ij} = \begin{cases} 1 \times I_{ij}, & j \in \bigcup_{k=1}^{N_3} X_{ik} \\ 0, & j \notin \bigcup_{k=1}^{N_3} X_{ik} \end{cases} \tag{9}
$$

where $\bigcup_{k=1}^{N_3} X_{ik}$ represents all indexes of the micro-videos that i watched. I_{ij} is the sum of all Interest Preferences of each category in C_j (the categories list of j) of user i.

4.2 Confidence Based IPoC Method

Assume Y'' is the rating matrix created by the implicit rating method based on Interest Preferences of Categories and their confidences for micro-videos ($Y'' \in \mathbb{R}^{N_1 \times N_2}$), in which the value of j-th column in i-th row is y''_{ij} which is shown in the formula (10).

$$
y''_{ij} = \begin{cases} I_{ij} \times (1 + \beta_{ij}), & j \in \bigcup_{k=1}^{N_3} X_{ik} \\ 0, & j \notin \bigcup_{k=1}^{N_3} X_{ik} \end{cases}, \beta_{ij} = \begin{cases} 1, & |C_i| = 1 \\ 0, & \sigma^2 = 0 \\ \dfrac{I_{ij} - \overline{I_i}}{|C_i| \times \sigma^2}, & \sigma^2 > 0 \end{cases} \tag{10}
$$

where $\bigcup_{k=1}^{N_3} X_{ik}$ represents all indexes of the micro-videos that i watched. I_{ij} is the sum of all Interest Preferences for each category in C_j (the categories list of j) of user i. β_{ij} is the confidence of I_{ij}. C_i is the set of all categories of micro-videos that user i watched (it's size is $|C_i|$). $\overline{I_i}$ and σ^2 are the average and variance value of the IPoC of all categories in C_i for user i respectively.

As is shown in formula (10), the confidence of user i of one category equals 1 when i has only watched this category of micro-videos ($|C_i| = 1$), and equals 0 when the user has no preference ($\sigma^2 = 0$, it indicates that interest preferences of various categories for micro-videos are the same). Obviously, $\beta_{ij} \in [0, 1]$.

The above two IPoC based implicit rating methods consider interest preferences of different categories for users to micro-videos. The rating matrices (Y' and Y'') generated by them contain a lot of user preference information, and can be used as bases of existing video recommendation algorithms to improve the performances of them.

5 Experiment and Result Analysis

5.1 Experiment Environment

A real dataset of a large online video content provider is built for micro-video recommendation. It contains more than 70,000 micro-videos, which are less than 10 min, and cover sports, entertainment, news and other categories. In order to

Table 1. Datasets.

Dataset	Number of interactions	Number of users	Number of mirco-videos	Scale of rating matrix	Sparsity of rating matrix
Dataset 1	1135322	1971	49047	96671637	0.988256
Dataset 2	2804929	8106	77284	626464104	0.995523

compare the performances of the proposed two IPoC based rating methods on datasets with different scales, the original dataset is divided into two sub-datasets (Dataset 1 and 2), as shown in Table 1.

In this experiment, L (time length threshold of micro-videos) is set to 600 s. In the two datasets, the first 80% data are as the training set and the remaining 20% are as testing set. For each comparison algorithm, the maximum number of iterations is set to be 10 (if any), the regularization parameter is set to be 0.01 (if any), the learning rate is set to be 0.01 (if any) and $TopN$ (the maximum length of recommended list) is set to be 20.

The experimental environment is listed in Table 2.

Table 2. Experimental environment.

Configuration name	Configuration details
CPU	Intel(R) Core(TM) i7-8750H CPU @ 2.20 GHz 6 cores
RAM	8 GB DDR4 2666 MHz
Disk	250 GB SSD
OS	Windows 10 Family Edition 64 bits
JDK	JDK 1.8.0_74 64 bits

The evaluating indicator of the experiment is $NDCG$ (Normalized Discounted Cumulative Gain) defined as follows [21]:

$$NDCG@TopN = Z_{TopN} \times \sum_{k=1}^{TopN} \frac{2^{r_k}-1}{log_2(k+1)} \tag{11}$$

where $TopN$ is the maximum length of recommended list, Z_{TopN} is a regular term to ensure that $NDCG$ has a value of 1 in the best case, $r_k \in \{0,1\}$ and it indicates whether the k-th recommended item appears in the testing set. $NDCG$ takes into account the sequence of videos in the recommended list. The higher the $NDCG$ is, the more satisfactory the comprehensive performance of the recommended list is, and that is, users prefer videos in front of the recommended list.

5.2   Baselines

The rating matrix Y of traditional rating method under implicit feedback (according to formula (1)) is used as input, and $NDCG@20$ is used as evaluation indicator. The following recommendation algorithms are applied separately, and their results under different implicit factor numbers (K) are used as baselines.

(1) ALS [23], classical matrix factorization algorithm.
(2) PMF [19], probabilistic matrix factorization algorithm.
(3) BiasedMF [17], the matrix factorization algorithm with bias value.
(4) SVDPP [11], SVD with implicit feedback (SVD++).
(5) RankSGD [9], mixing of different collaborative filtering algorithms.
(6) FISMauc [10], factored item similarity model.

They are widely used well-known approaches of matrix factorization recommendation algorithms about some implicit factors, and the implements used in this experiment of them is LibRec [6]. In this experiment, the number of implicit factors (K) is set to 10, 20, 30, 40 and 50, respectively. The rating matrices $Y^{'}$ and $Y^{''}$ created by the proposed rating methods are used as inputs of above algorithms separately, and the results of them are used as comparisons.

5.3   Experimental Result Analysis

The graphs show the results of ALS (Figs. 1 and 2), PMF (Figs. 3 and 4), BiasedMF (Figs. 5 and 6), SVDPP (Figs. 7 and 8), RankSGD (Figs. 9 and 10), and FISMauc (Figs. 11 and 12) with different rating methods under K factors on the two datasets about micro-videos. Among them, the logarithmic scale is used to enlarge smaller values of BiasedMF and SVDPP for easy observation.

It should be noted separately that, as shown in Figs. 9 and 10, the $NDCG@20$ obtained by RankSGD with Non-confidence Based IPoC Method are much lower than those obtained by RankSGD with traditional rating method both on Dataset 1 and 2. That is to say, using RankSGD with Non-confidence based IPoC rating method simply can not achieve better results. On the Dataset 1 and 2, the $NDCG@20$ obtained by RankSGD with Confidence Based IPoC Method are higher than that of RankSGD with traditional rating method except when k equals 10. On the whole, using RankSGD with Confidence Based IPoC Method can bring more effective results.

The following points can be summarized from the experimental results:

(1) $NDCG@20$ obtained by some widely used well-known recommendation algorithms (such as ALS, PMF, BiasedMF, SVDPP and FISMauc) with Non-confidence Based IPoC Method are higher than that with traditional rating methods both on the Dataset 1 and 2. This proves that the Non-confidence Based IPoC Method can obtain more accurate and effective recommendation results after considering interest preferences of categories for users to micro-videos and giving the rating matrix more information of preferences.

(2) The Confidence Based IPoC Method has better performances than traditional rating methods, when it is used with some effective methods (such as ALS, PMF, BiasedMF, SVDPP, BiasedMF and FISMauc) both on the Dataset 1 and 2. This is due to the influences of interest preferences of categories too.

(3) Generally speaking, the performances of the Confidence Based IPoC Method are better than that of the Non-confidence Based IPoC Method both on the Dataset 1 and 2 with some useful methods (such as ALS, BiasedMF, SVDPP, BiasedMF, and FISMauc). This shows that the confidences of interest preferences of categories can help to improve the performances.

(4) On Dataset 1 and 2, at least one of the two proposed rating methods based on IPoC can improve the performances of the above comparison algorithms. For example, the Confidence Based IPoC Method with RankSGD can bring better results while the Non-confidence Based IPoC Method with RankSGD cannot (Figs. 9 and 10).

(5) The influence of scale and sparsity of datasets on the proposed rating methods can be observed by doing experiments on two datasets with different scales and sparseness. Although the effectiveness of the proposed rating methods are lower with larger and sparser matrix than that with smaller and more intensive matrix, they are still better than traditional rating method.

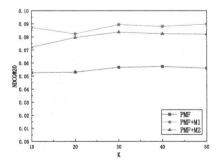

Fig. 1. ALS on Dataset 1.

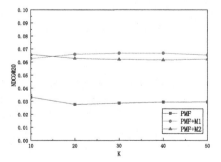

Fig. 2. ALS on Dataset 2.

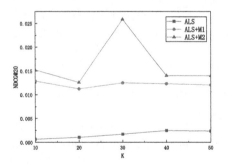

Fig. 3. PMF on Dataset 1.

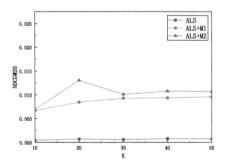

Fig. 4. PMF on Dataset 2.

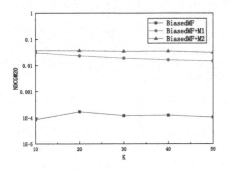

Fig. 5. BiasedMF on Dataset 1.

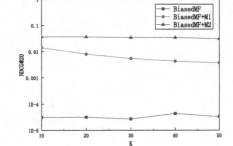

Fig. 6. BiasedMF on Dataset 2.

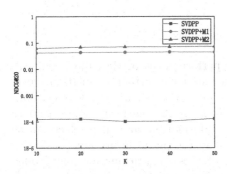

Fig. 7. SVDPP on Dataset 1.

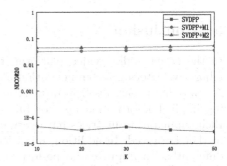

Fig. 8. SVDPP on Dataset 2.

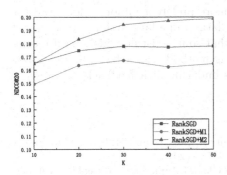

Fig. 9. RankSGD on Dataset 1.

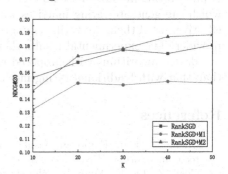

Fig. 10. RankSGD on Dataset 2.

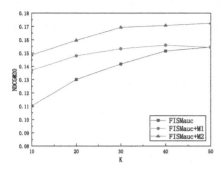

Fig. 11. FISMauc on Dataset 1.

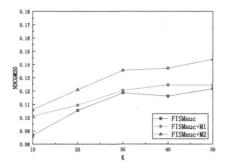

Fig. 12. FISMauc on Dataset 2.

6 Conclusion

In the actual online video platform, the performances of the traditional collaborative filtering recommendation algorithms have further room to improve. As they often lack explicit ratings, and a large number of user logs containing implicit information are not fully utilized in the platform. These lead to their input rating matrices have very little information, and their effect can be further improved. In addition, micro-videos in the platform are not considered differently. To improve the performances of these algorithms for micro-video recommendation, considering the category characteristics of micro-videos, two implicit rating methods based on interest preferences of categories are proposed, which can generate rating matrices with more preference information. And the effectiveness of them are verified on a real dataset of a large online video content provider. The experimental results show that some existing widely used recommendation algorithms with proposed rating methods can achieve better results than that with traditional rating methods under implicit feedback.

References

1. Chen, X., et al.: Exploiting visual contents in posters and still frames for movie recommendation. IEEE Access **6**, 68874–68881 (2018)
2. Chen, Z., Lu, F., Yuan, X., Zhong, F.: TCMHG: topic-based cross-modal hypergraph learning for online service recommendations. IEEE Access **6**, 24856–24865 (2018)
3. China National Security Agency: China network audio-visual development research report 2018 (2018)
4. Cui, L., Dong, L., Fu, X., Wen, Z., Lu, N., Zhang, G.: A video recommendation algorithm based on the combination of video content and social network. Concurr. Comput. Pract. Exp. **29**(14), e3900 (2017)
5. Deshpande, M., Karypis, G.: Item-based top-N recommendation algorithms. ACM Trans. Inf. Syst. **22**(1), 143–177 (2004)
6. Guo, G., Zhang, J., Sun, Z., Yorke-Smith, N.: LibRec: a Java library for recommender systems. In: UMAP Workshops. CEUR Workshop Proceedings, vol. 1388. CEUR-WS.org (2015)

7. Haque, M.E., Zobaed, S.M., Tozal, M.E., Raghavan, V.: Divergence based non-negative matrix factorization for top-N recommendations. In: HICSS, pp. 1–10. ScholarSpace/AIS Electronic Library (AISeL) (2019)
8. Huang, S., Wang, Z., Jiang, Y.: Guess your size: a hybrid model for footwear size recommendation. Adv. Eng. Inform. **36**, 64–75 (2018)
9. Jahrer, M., Töscher, A.: Collaborative filtering ensemble for ranking. In: KDD Cup. JMLR Proceedings, vol. 18, pp. 153–167. JMLR.org (2012)
10. Kabbur, S., Ning, X., Karypis, G.: FISM: factored item similarity models for top-N recommender systems. In: KDD, pp. 659–667. ACM (2013)
11. Koren, Y.: Factor in the neighbors: scalable and accurate collaborative filtering. TKDD **4**(1), 1:1–1:24 (2010)
12. Li, S., Brusilovsky, P., Su, S., Cheng, X.: Conference paper recommendation for academic conferences. IEEE Access **6**, 17153–17164 (2018)
13. Lin, C.-H., Chi, H.: A novel movie recommendation system based on collaborative filtering and neural networks. In: Barolli, L., Takizawa, M., Xhafa, F., Enokido, T. (eds.) AINA 2019. AISC, vol. 926, pp. 895–903. Springer, Cham (2020). https://doi.org/10.1007/978-3-030-15032-7_75
14. Loepp, B., Donkers, T., Kleemann, T., Ziegler, J.: Interactive recommending with Tag-Enhanced Matrix Factorization (TagMF). Int. J. Hum. Comput. Stud. **121**, 21–41 (2019)
15. Lu, W., Chung, F., Jiang, W., Ester, M., Liu, W.: A deep Bayesian tensor-based system for video recommendation. ACM Trans. Inf. Syst. **37**(1), 7:1–7:22 (2019)
16. Ma, J., Li, G., Zhong, M., Zhao, X., Zhu, L., Li, X.: LGA: latent genre aware micro-video recommendation on social media. Multimedia Tools Appl. **77**(3), 2991–3008 (2018)
17. Paterek, A.: Improving regularized singular value decomposition for collaborative filtering. In: Proceedings of KDD Cup and Workshop, vol. 2007, pp. 5–8 (2007)
18. Sahu, A.K., Dwivedi, P.: User profile as a bridge in cross-domain recommender systems for sparsity reduction. Appl. Intell. **49**, 2461–2481 (2019)
19. Salakhutdinov, R., Mnih, A.: Probabilistic matrix factorization. In: NIPS, pp. 1257–1264. Curran Associates, Inc. (2007)
20. Wang, H., et al.: RippleNet: propagating user preferences on the knowledge graph for recommender systems. In: CIKM, pp. 417–426. ACM (2018)
21. Zhang, Y., Zuo, W., Shi, Z., Yue, L., Liang, S.: Social Bayesian personal ranking for missing data in implicit feedback recommendation. In: Liu, W., Giunchiglia, F., Yang, B. (eds.) KSEM 2018. LNCS (LNAI), vol. 11061, pp. 299–310. Springer, Cham (2018). https://doi.org/10.1007/978-3-319-99365-2_27
22. Zhao, Z., Shang, M.: User-based collaborative-filtering recommendation algorithms on Hadoop. In: WKDD, pp. 478–481. IEEE Computer Society (2010)
23. Zhou, Y., Wilkinson, D., Schreiber, R., Pan, R.: Large-scale parallel collaborative filtering for the Netflix prize. In: Fleischer, R., Xu, J. (eds.) AAIM 2008. LNCS, vol. 5034, pp. 337–348. Springer, Heidelberg (2008). https://doi.org/10.1007/978-3-540-68880-8_32

An Enhanced Deep Hashing Method for Large-Scale Image Retrieval

Cong Chen[1,2]🆔, Weiqin Tong[1,2(✉)]🆔, Xuehai Ding[1]🆔, and Xiaoli Zhi[1]🆔

[1] School of Computer Engineering and Science, Shanghai University, Shanghai, China
{cchenmy,wqtong,dinghai,xlzhi}@shu.edu.cn
[2] Shanghai Institute for Advanced Communication and Data Science,
Shanghai, China

Abstract. Hashing-based image retrieval plays an important role in approximate nearest neighbor search because of its storage and retrieval efficiency. Efficient image features are of vital importance for image retrieval task. However, the features of images may not directly suitable for image retrieval due to the illumination or cluttered background in images. In this paper, we propose an enhanced deep hashing method for image retrieval to promote the retrieval accuracy, in which we adopt an enhanced feature module that selects the attractive areas in images. It jointly explores the hashing learning, enhanced feature module, and batch normalization module in a unified framework, which can guarantee the optimal compatibility of hash coding and feature learning. The proposed deep model contains three parts: (1) a convolutional subnetwork consists of several convolutional-pooling layers and the proposed enhanced feature module; (2) a batch normalization module is utilized to control the quantization errors of hash codes at a moderate level; (3) a more comprehensive loss function is introduced to enhance the discriminative of image features and minimize the prediction errors of the learned hash codes. The experimental results on three datasets show that the proposed method can achieve competitive performance compared to other hashing approaches.

Keywords: Image retrieval · Enhanced feature module ·
Hashing learning · Convolutional neural network

1 Introduction

With the explosive increasing of web images, many efforts have been devoted to content-based image retrieval, especially in image databases with millions to billions of images. In order to achieve better performance for image retrieval, it is critical to extract discriminative features to ensure that the derived features of images are focused on the attractive areas, and the images with similar contents

---

This work is supported in part by science and technology committee of shanghai municipality under grant No. 16010500400.

© Springer Nature Switzerland AG 2019
C. Douligeris et al. (Eds.): KSEM 2019, LNAI 11775, pp. 382–393, 2019.
https://doi.org/10.1007/978-3-030-29551-6_34

are close to each other and the different contents are far from each other. Another challenging problem in large-scale image retrieval task is the cost of storage and computational time.

For the above problems, hashing can identify binary codes for images efficiently. Most existing hashing methods mainly try to find more suitable hand-crafted visual features (e.g., GIST [1], SIFT [2]) to represent the contents of images. Unfortunately, the hand-crafted visual features have limited performance improvements when handling complex image changes. Recently, deep convolutional neural network(CNN) has demonstrated excellent performance in many computer vision tasks [3,4]. It is acknowledged that the semantic information of images can be described by widely used CNN features [3]. The CNN models trained on large annotated datasets can capture rich information at higher semantic levels and achieve superior performance compared to hand-crafted features. However, the dimensions of the extracted CNN features are generally high. Therefore, deep hashing methods have been explored which consider above problems simultaneously. The learned hash codes have shown the encouraging performance for large-scale image retrieval.

Toward this end, we put forward an enhanced deep hashing (EDH) method for image retrieval via a deep architecture that encodes input images to discriminative binary codes. The framework of the proposed EDH method is illustrated in Fig. 1. A deep network properly stacking several convolutional-pooling layers with the input of images and the labels. The desired image representations are obtained by the outputs of the enhanced feature module. In order to obtain higher retrieval accuracy, we introduce a batch normalization (BN) module to accelerate the convergence of the object function and control the quantization error moderately. In addition, we explore a more comprehensive loss function including softmax loss, quantization loss and center loss to enhance the discriminative ability of the learned binary codes. The results on three widely used datasets demonstrate that the proposed EDH method has superior performance gains over some other hashing methods.

The remainder of this paper is organized as follows. In Sect. 2, we briefly review the related works. We elaborate the proposed EDH method for large-scale image retrieval in Sect. 3. In Sect. 4, we report the evaluation results of the proposed EDH method and several hashing approaches on publicly image datasets. Finally, Sect. 5 concludes this paper.

2   Related Work

Hashing methods have become a leading approach for large-scale image retrieval and they can be divided into data-independent methods and data-dependent methods. Compared to data-independent approaches, data-dependent (learning-based hashing) methods are able to achieve excellent performance by exploring the data distribution. According to the available label information, learning-based hashing methods can be categorized into unsupervised, supervised and semi-supervised methods.

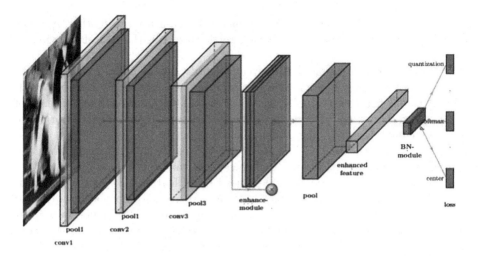

Fig. 1. The architecture of the proposed network

Unsupervised hashing methods learn hashing functions by preserving the data similarity from the unlabeled data. Representative unsupervised methods including the notable Locality Sensitive Hashing(LSH) [5], Spectral Hashing (SH) [6], Iterative Quantization (ITQ) [7].

Semi-Supervised hashing methods exploit the information from the labeled data and unlabeled data simultaneously to generate binary image features. In [8], a hash framework is proposed by introducing an information theoretic regularizer over the labeled and unlabeled data and minimizing the error over the labeled data.

Supervised hashing methods leverage supervised information (e.g., class labels, pairwise similarities) to learn better image representations and achieve higher retrieval accuracy. By utilizing the label information, the supervised discrete hashing (SDH) [9] produces compact hash codes and optimal classifier simultaneously. Recently, most existing deep hashing approaches are supervised by imposing constraints on the networks, such as point-wised constraints [10], pair-wised constraints [11–14] and ranking-wised constraints [15]. They utilize the supervised information of pairs or triplets training images to learn the binary codes. In [16], a two-stage supervised hashing method CNNH is proposed which learns binary codes by preserving the pairwise similarity over training images firstly. Based on the learned codes, the hash functions are then learned by the CNN network. Some deep hashing methods have been proposed in an end-to-end learning framework. In [12], NINH promotes the two-stage CNNH by feature learning and hash coding simultaneously, so that image representations and hash codes can be optimized in one learning process. In [11], NINH is improved by using the CNN architecture to learn binary codes and hash functions which preserve the pairwise similarity. In [13], DHN introduces a pairwise cross-entropy loss function to learn hash functions for the learned image representations. In [15], a ranking-based hashing method is proposed to learn hash functions that maintain multi-level semantic similarity between images.

3 The Proposed Method

In this section, we elaborate the details of the proposed EDH method as show in Fig. 1, which incorporates the feature learning and hash coding.

3.1 The Network Architecture

Encouraged by the performance of deep features, we construct a hashing network by stacking three convolutional-pooling layers. The first several convolutional layers can learn the mid-level representations of images, pooling layers can enhance the robustness of the image representations to local transformations, and the top layer of the sub-network can extract the higher-level and global image features.

Following the outputs of the top layer in convolutional sub-network, we add an enhanced feature select module inspired by the concept of RoI (Region of Interest) [17], which automatically obtains the most interest response in images. To be more specific, we assume that the top layer of the convolutional sub-network outputs L feature maps and each size is h × w. Then, we get the sum feature map S of L along the channel by a 1 × 1 convolutional, a softmax layer and a threshold layer follow the S and have the same size h × w. The softmax layer is able to get the feature map W which forms a probability distribution and the softmax function is defined in Eq. (1). It can be easily verified that $W_{i,j} \geq 0$ and $\sum_{i=1}^{h} \sum_{j=1}^{w} W_{i,j} = 1$, where $0 \leq i \leq h$ and $0 \leq j \leq w$. The threshold layer discretizes the elements in W to obtain the M with the elements either 1 or 0, we denote $M_{i,j} = 1$ if $M_{i,j} > \alpha$, otherwise $M_{i,j} = 0$.

$$W_{i,j} = \frac{e^{(F_{i,j})}}{\sum_{i=1}^{h} \sum_{j=1}^{w} e^{(F_{i,j})}} \tag{1}$$

where the α is a control factor for selecting the more attractive areas in images. The regions with the elements 1 indicate that the corresponding areas of images are more attractive. Then we put the M through the outputs of the last pooling layer along channel side to generate a specified dimension feature vector that focuses on the interest areas of images. We will test the effectiveness of the control factor α in experiment part.

With the expectation that the label of the image is well inferred by the learned binary codes, we incorporate the feature learning part and the BN module in a unified framework. So equipped with the extracted features from the sub-network, we employ a full-connected layer named the enhanced feature layer as show in Fig. 1. Following the enhanced feature layer, a BN module is introduced to generate more discriminative hash codes. The details of the BN module are shown in Fig. 2(a), where the BN-layer is the batch normalization layer [18] and the HASH-layer is a full-connected layer to generate q-bit code. To speed up the convergence of the objective function, many deep models, such as Inception [18], use BN layer. As for AC-layer, we use the tanh function as the activation function that restricts each of the output elements to the range $[-1, 1]$. The output vector of tanh is a real-value approximate hash code which can be converted to a q-bit hash code by quantization. More specifically, we can let the output vector $\mathbf{B(I)}$ of the AC-layer represents the input image $\mathbf{I}$, then the q-bit hash code $\mathbf{b}$ can be calculated by Eq. (2), where $\mathbf{B(I)}_i$ and $\mathbf{b}_i$ are the i-th elements of $\mathbf{B(I)}$ and $\mathbf{b}$, respectively. The $\mathbf{sgn}(\cdot)$ function: $\mathbf{sgn}(b) = 1$ if $b > 0$ and $\mathbf{sgn}(b) = -1$ otherwise.

$$\mathbf{b_i} = \mathbf{sgn}(\mathbf{B(I)}_i)(i = 1, 2, ..., q) \tag{2}$$

In addition, the quantization loss is controlled by the outputs of the BN-layer and we connect the outputs of the AC-layer to the softmax loss.

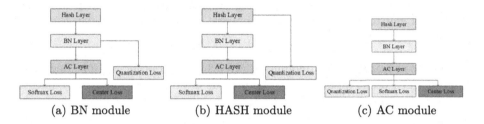

(a) BN module   (b) HASH module   (c) AC module

Fig. 2. Structure of different modules

3.2 Loss Function

Loss function determines the direction of parameter optimization in the deep model, so different objective functions yield different features with varying discriminative power in same model. We assume that the dataset has $\mathbf{n}$ training images $\{\mathbf{x_i}\}_{i=1}^n$ belonging to $\mathbf{m}$ classes, the label $\mathbf{y}_i \in \mathbf{R}^m$, the label matrix indicated by $\mathbf{Y} = [\mathbf{y}_1, ..., \mathbf{y}_n] \in \mathbf{R}^{m \times n}$, so $\mathbf{I}_{(y_i=j)} = 1$ if $\mathbf{x}_i$ belongs to the $\mathbf{j}$-th class and 0 otherwise. We use $\mathbf{X}$ represents the data matrix with $\mathbf{n}$ images, and the hashing learning is to learn hash functions $H : R \rightarrow \{-1, 1\}$, which can map the images into binary Hamming Space. Through the hash functions, we can obtain the discrete binary codes of images $\mathbf{b_i} \in \{-1, 1\}^k$, in which k is the dimension of the Hamming Space. With the requirements that $\mathbf{b_i}$ can well predicts its label for the image x_i, we utilize the outputs of BN module as the discrete binary codes $\mathbf{B}$ as show in Fig. 2(a).

$$\mathbf{B} = g(\mathbf{X}) \in \{-1, 1\}^{k \times n} \tag{3}$$

where $g(\cdot)$ is the transformation of the proposed deep model. To predict the label of the image, θ_j is used as the prediction function for the $\mathbf{j}$-th class, so we define the softmax loss function in Eq. (4), in which $b_i \in \{-1, 1\}^k$.

$$\mathbf{L_s} = \sum_{i=1}^n \sum_{j=1}^m -\mathbf{I}_{(y_i=j)} \log \frac{e^{\theta_j^T \mathbf{b}_i}}{\sum_{l=1}^m e^{\theta_j^T \mathbf{b}_i}} \tag{4}$$

Unfortunately, it is difficult to optimize the problem in Eq. (4) due to the discrete constraints. Consequently, we introduce the relaxation strategy [11] that slackens the binary code $\mathbf{B}$ to be continuous, but the strategy introduces the quantization loss between the original binary code $\mathbf{B}$ and the continuous binary code $\mathbf{B}$. We attempt to impose a regularization term on the continuous values to approach the desired discrete values $(+1/-1)$. So the Eq. (4) is rewritten as Eq. (5), where $|\cdot|$ is the element-wise absolute value operation, 1 is a vector of ones and $\|\cdot\|_1$ is the l_1-norm of one vector and γ is a weight parameter that is used to control the quantization loss.

$$\mathbf{L}_s = \sum_{i=1}^{n}\sum_{j=1}^{m} -\mathbf{I}_{(y_i=j)} \log \frac{e^{\theta_j^T \mathbf{b}_i}}{\sum_{l=1}^{m} e^{\theta_j^T \mathbf{b}_i}} + \gamma \sum_{i=1}^{n} \||\mathbf{b}_i| - 1\|_1 \tag{5}$$

If we train the model supervised by Eq. (5), we can only ensure that the derived features are separable to some extent, regardless of the intra-class compactness that is of great significance for discriminative features. So the center loss [19] is considered on the basis of softmax loss. The center loss is defined in Eq. (6), where c_{y_i} is the feature center of the y_i class. Each class has a feature center and we minimize the L_c by clustering features in the same class around the feature center as close as possible.

$$\mathrm{L}_c = \frac{1}{2}\sum_{i=1}^{n} \|\mathbf{b}_i - c_{y_i}\|_2^2 \tag{6}$$

In general, the overall loss function of all training images is obtained as show in Eq. (7), in which η is a weight parameter to control the importance of the center loss.

$$\mathbf{L} = \mathbf{L}_s + \frac{\eta}{2}\mathbf{L}_c =$$

$$\sum_{i=1}^{n}\sum_{j=1}^{m} -\mathbf{I}_{(y_i=j)} \log \frac{e^{\theta_j^T \mathbf{b}_i}}{\sum_{l=1}^{m} e^{\theta_j^T \mathbf{b}_i}} + \gamma \sum_{i=1}^{n} \||\mathbf{b}_i| - 1\|_1 + \frac{\eta}{2}\sum_{i=1}^{n} \|\mathbf{b}_i - c_{y_i}\|_2^2 \tag{7}$$

To optimize the above formulation, we adopt the back-propagation scheme with mini-batch gradient descent algorithm to train the developed deep hashing network. Once the training process of the hashing network is done, we can obtain the q-bit hash codes for any input image.

4 Experiment

To verify the effectiveness of the proposed hashing method, experiments are conducted on three publicly datasets including CIFAR-10 [20], NUS-WIDE [21] and Flickr [22]. We implemented all the experiments with the Tensorflow framework on a NVIDIA Tesla P100 with CUDA9.0 and cuDNN v7.0.

4.1   Datasets

CIFAR-10: a dataset containing 60,000 images belonging to 10 classes. Each class has 6,000 images in size 32×32.

NUS-WIDE: a dataset containing 269,648 images. Each image belongs to at least one of the 81 classes. Following [12], we use the images associated with the 21 most frequent concepts, resulting in a total of 195,834 images.

Flickr: a dataset containing 25,000 images downloaded from Flickr.com. Each image has one or multiple labels in 38 object categories (e.g. tree, clouds, lake, night).

In CIFAR-10 and NUS-WIDE, we follow the experimental protocols in [12], [23] that we randomly select 100 images per class as the test query set and 500 images per class as the training set. In Flickr, we randomly select 1000 images as the test query set, and 4000 images as the training set.

4.2   Experimental Setting

We compare the proposed EDH with several hashing methods, including two unsupervised methods (LSH, ITQ) and several supervised methods (NINH, DDQH [24], etc). All of these methods are implemented on the source code provided by the authors, respectively. The parameter in these baseline methods are set according to the suggestions in the original publications.

To train the developed deep model, some details of implementation should be confirmed in advance. For the activation function, besides the final BN layer, all the convolutional layers and full-connected layers utilize the rectification linear unit [25]. During training, the batch size is fixed to 100, the filter size is set to 5×5 with stride 1 in the first two convolutional layers and 3×3 with stride 1 in the other convolutional layers. For all the convolutional layers, the number of feature maps are set to 64, 128, 128, respectively. The initial learning rate is set to 0.001 and the parameter η, γ, α are set to 1, 1, 0.1, respectively.

4.3   Experimental Results

We use mean average precision (MAP) which is a widely-used metric in image retrieval to validate the performance of all hashing methods on three datasets. AP is the average precision score for a set of retrieved images. Table 1 shows the comparison results for all hashing methods with varying length hash codes within {12, 24, 32, 48} bits.

Firstly, we can observe that the performance of the proposed EDH is the best, EDH0 is the model without the BN module and also shows the better performance than other baseline methods because it can extract better image features, which is a good proof of the effectiveness of the improvements. Compared EDH with EDH0, the performance of EDH is about 1% higher than that of EDH0 on three datasets, which indicates that the BN module does boost the performance. Secondly, compared to the shallow hashing methods with hand-crafted features, the deep hashing methods have better performance, which shows the superiority of the deep features. Thirdly, EDH and EDH0 are both superior to CNNH, because EDH and EDH0 learn hash functions and prediction functions simultaneously, while CNNH is a two-stage method. In addition, in some cases, we can find that the performance with longer binary codes is still worse than EDH and EDH0 with shorter binary codes, which shows that EDH and EDH0 can uncover compact binary codes. It also indicates that the extra consideration of center loss does play a role to some extent. Finally, the proposed EDH method is able to learn discriminative and compact binary codes by jointly exploiting the feature extraction, BN module and hash learning in an end-to-end manner simultaneously.

Table 1. Mean Average Precision (MAP) on three image datasets

Datasets	CIFAR-10				NUS-WIDE				Flickr			
HashBits	12	24	32	48	12	24	32	48	12	24	32	48
LSH	0.121	0.126	0.120	0.120	0.403	0.421	0.426	0.441	0.499	0.513	0.521	0.548
ITQ	0.162	0.169	0.172	0.175	0.452	0.468	0.472	0.477	0.544	0.555	0.560	0.570
CNNH	0.465	0.521	0.521	0.532	0.617	0.663	0.657	0.688	0.749	0.761	0.768	0.776
NINH	0.552	0.566	0.558	0.581	0.674	0.697	0.713	0.715	0.773	0.806	0.814	0.818
DQN	0.554	0.558	0.564	0.580	0.768	0.776	0.783	0.792	0.839	0.848	0.854	0.863
DHN	0.555	0.594	0.603	0.621	0.708	0.735	0.748	0.758	0.810	0.828	0.829	0.841
DSH	0.616	0.651	0.661	0.676	0.652	0.656	0.658	0.663	0.806	0.811	0.802	0.827
DDQH	0.713	0.707	0.716	0.724	0.776	0.781	0.785	0.786	0.841	0.844	0.849	0.853
EDH0	0.732	0.748	0.746	0.741	0.798	0.806	0.810	0.815	0.852	0.857	0.860	0.863
EDH	**0.746**	**0.757**	**0.754**	**0.749**	**0.806**	**0.813**	**0.821**	**0.826**	**0.857**	**0.861**	**0.867**	**0.873**

Moreover, the performance is evaluated by using the precision curves with respect to different numbers of top returned images. Figure 3 shows the results on different datasets. We can observe that the MAP is insensitive to the number of top returned images, and the proposed method achieves higher performance which is consistent with the results in Table 1.

4.4 Comparison of Different BN Module

In order to verify the BN module can improve the retrieval accuracy, experiments are conducted with/without the BN module and investigate the effects of different BN module schemes as show in Fig. 2. The hash bits is fixed to 24 bits. For the HASH module, the quantization loss is imposed on the outputs of the hash layer as show in Fig. 2(b), and the quantization loss is imposed on the outputs of the activation layer in AC module as show in Fig. 2(c). The results of different BN modules are show in Fig. 4(a) and the results reveal that the performance of AC module and HASH module are both worse than the BN module.

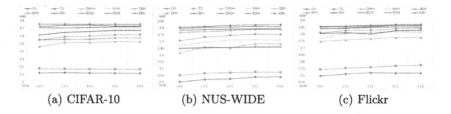

(a) CIFAR-10   (b) NUS-WIDE   (c) Flickr

Fig. 3. Results of different number of top returned images

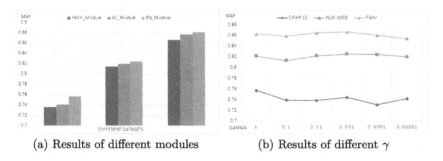

(a) Results of different modules   (b) Results of different γ

Fig. 4. Results of different parameters on three datasets

From the Fig. 4(a), we can also observe that the performance obtained varying improvements by utilizing different modules to control the quantization loss. Moreover, the best MAP of the BN module outperforms HASH module on three datasets by substantial margins of 2.1%, 1.0%, 1.6%, respectively.

4.5   Parameter Sensitivity

In the proposed deep hashing network, we use trade-off parameters including η, γ in the comprehensive loss function. In this part, experiments are conducted to investigate the effects on the model by setting different values of η and γ. We first explore the influence of parameter γ, which controls the importance of the regularization term and is equivalent to controlling the importance of quantization loss. In experiments, the values of γ are set within {1, 0.1, 0.01, 0.001, 0.0001, 0.00001}. The results of different datasets with varying γ show in Fig. 4(b). We can observe that parameter γ has little influence on results because the performance discrepancy within 1% and the best results are obtained by BN module with $\gamma = 1$. Since the parameter γ is not sensitive to the final performance, we investigate the influence of parameter η on the model while setting γ to 1. From the Fig. 5(a), the performance has some fluctuations on different datasets when the values of parameter η are limited to {0, 0.2, 0.4, 0.6, 0.8, 1}. It is noting that the performance of $\eta = 0$ is inferior than the η set to other values, which reveals that the center loss is not considered in objection function and the center loss does play a role in learning discriminative and compactness binary codes. In Fig. 5(a), we also find that the retrieval performance with η

is relatively distinct on three datasets. The best performance achieved on three datasets corresponds to the different values of η, and the η is simply set to 1 in experiments in other subsections for a more fair comparison.

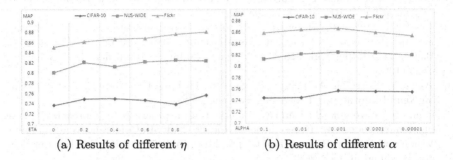

(a) Results of different η (b) Results of different α

Fig. 5. Results of different parameters on three datasets

Furthermore, the influence of the parameter α in the enhance module is explored. The comparison results show in Fig. 5(b), from which the better performance obtained by the smaller α in range (0.001, 0) can be observed since the feature maps can select more attractive areas in images. When the α is set too small, the performance becomes worse because all the areas in images are selected and the derived features are not discriminative.

5 Conclusion

In this paper, we put forward the EDH method for image retrieval which integrates feature learning, hashing learning into one unified framework. The image features are obtained from the convolutional sub-network firstly. Then in order to generate more discriminative features, we construct an enhance feature module to select the more attractive areas in images. Finally, following the enhance module, we adopt the BN module and the more comprehensive loss function to accelerate the network convergence and boost the retrieval accuracy. The evaluation results on several benchmark datasets show that the EDH method achieves encouraging performance for large-scale image retrieval.

References

1. Oliva, A., Torralba, A.: Modeling the shape of the scene: a holistic representation of the spatial envelope. Int. J. Comput. Vision **42**(3), 145–175 (2001)
2. Lowe, D.G.: Object recognition from local scale-invariant features. In: Proceedings of the International Conference on Computer Vision-Volume 2, ICCV 1999, pp. 1150. IEEE Computer Society, Washington, DC (1999)

3. Krizhevsky, A., Sutskever, I., Hinton, G.E.: ImageNet classification with deep convolutional neural networks. In: Proceedings of the 25th International Conference on Neural Information Processing Systems - Volume 1, NIPS 2012, pp. 1097–1105. Curran Associates Inc. (2012)

4. Long, J., Shelhamer, E., Darrell, T.: Fully convolutional networks for semantic segmentation. CoRR, abs/1411.4038 (2014)

5. Gionis, A., Indyk, P., Motwani, R.: Similarity search in high dimensions via hashing. In: Proceedings of the 25th International Conference on Very Large Data Bases, VLDB 1999, pp. 518–529. Morgan Kaufmann Publishers Inc., San Francisco (1999)

6. Weiss, Y., Torralba, A., Fergus, R.: Spectral hashing. In: International Conference on Neural Information Processing Systems (2008)

7. Gong, Y., Lazebnik, S.: Iterative quantization: a procrustean approach to learning binary codes. In: Proceedings of the 2011 IEEE Conference on Computer Vision and Pattern Recognition, CVPR 2011, pp. 817–824. IEEE Computer Society, Washington, DC (2011)

8. Jun, W., Sanjiv, K., Shih-Fu, C.: Semi-supervised hashing for large-scale search. IEEE Trans. Pattern Anal. Mach. Intell. **34**(12), 2393–2406 (2012)

9. Shen, F., Shen, C., Liu, W., Tao Shen, H.: Supervised discrete hashing. In: IEEE Conference on Computer Vision and Pattern Recognition, CVPR 2015, Boston, MA, USA, pp. 37–45, 7–12 June 2015

10. Lin, K., Yang, H.F., Hsiao, J.H., Chen, C.S.: Deep learning of binary hash codes for fast image retrieval. In: 2015 IEEE Conference on Computer Vision and Pattern Recognition Workshops, CVPR Workshops 2015, Boston, MA, USA, pp. 27–35, 7–12 June 2015

11. Liu, H., Wang, R., Shan, S., Chen, X.: Deep supervised hashing for fast image retrieval. In: 2016 IEEE Conference on Computer Vision and Pattern Recognition (CVPR), pp. 2064–2072. IEEE Computer Society, Los Alamitos, June 2016

12. Lai, H., Pan, Y., Liu, Y., Yan, S.: Simultaneous feature learning and hash coding with deep neural networks. In: 2015 IEEE Conference on Computer Vision and Pattern Recognition (CVPR), pp. 3270–3278. IEEE Computer Society, Los Alamitos, June 2015

13. Zhu, H., Long, M., Wang, J., Cao, Y.: Deep hashing network for efficient similarity retrieval. In: Proceedings of the Thirtieth AAAI Conference on Artificial Intelligence, AAAI 2016, pp. 2415–2421. AAAI Press (2016)

14. Li, W.J., Wang, S., Kang, W.C.: Feature learning based deep supervised hashing with pairwise labels. In: Proceedings of the Twenty-Fifth International Joint Conference on Artificial Intelligence, IJCAI 2016, New York, NY, USA, pp. 1711–1717, 9–15 July 2016

15. Zhao, F., Huang, Y., Wang, L., Tan, T.: Deep semantic ranking based hashing for multi-label image retrieval. In: IEEE Conference on Computer Vision and Pattern Recognition, CVPR 2015, Boston, MA, USA, pp. 1556–1564, 7–12 June 2015

16. Xia, R., Pan, Y., Lai, H., Liu, C., Yan, S.: Supervised hashing for image retrieval via image representation learning. In: Proceedings of the Twenty-Eighth AAAI Conference on Artificial Intelligence, Québec City, Québec, Canada, pp. 2156–2162, 27–31 July 2014

17. Ren, S., He, K., Girshick, R., Sun, J.: Faster R-CNN: towards real-time object detection with region proposal networks. In: Proceedings of the 28th International Conference on Neural Information Processing Systems - Volume 1, NIPS 2015, pp. 91–99. MIT Press, Cambridge (2015)

18. Ioffe, S., Szegedy, C.: Batch normalization: accelerating deep network training by reducing internal covariate shift. In: Proceedings of the 32nd International Conference on International Conference on Machine Learning - Volume 37, ICML 2015, pp. 448–456. JMLR.org (2015)
19. Song, K., Li, F., Long, F., Wang, J., Ling, Q.: Discriminative deep feature learning for semantic-based image retrieval. IEEE Access **6**, 44268–44280 (2018)
20. Fergus, R., Bernal, H., Weiss, Y., Torralba, A.: Semantic label sharing for learning with many categories. In: Daniilidis, K., Maragos, P., Paragios, N. (eds.) ECCV 2010. LNCS, vol. 6311, pp. 762–775. Springer, Heidelberg (2010). https://doi.org/10.1007/978-3-642-15549-9_55
21. Chua, T.S., Tang, J., Hong, R., Li, H., Luo, Z., Zheng, Y.: NUS-WIDE: a real-world web image database from National University of Singapore. In: Proceedings of the ACM International Conference on Image and Video Retrieval, CIVR 2009, pp. 48:1–48:9. ACM, New York (2009)
22. Huiskes, M.J., Lew, M.S.: The MIR Flickr retrieval evaluation. In: Proceedings of the 2008 ACM International Conference on Multimedia Information Retrieval, MIR 2008. ACM, New York (2008)
23. Cao, Y., Long, M., Wang, J., Zhu, H., Wen, Q.: Deep quantization network for efficient image retrieval. In: Proceedings of the Thirtieth AAAI Conference on Artificial Intelligence, AAAI 2016, pp. 3457–3463. AAAI Press (2016)
24. Tang, J., Lin, J., Li, Z., Yang, J.: Discriminative deep quantization hashing for face image retrieval. IEEE Trans. Neural Netw. Learn. Syst. **29**(12), 6154–6162 (2018)
25. Nair, V., Hinton, G.E.: Rectified linear units improve restricted Boltzmann machines. In: International Conference on International Conference on Machine Learning (2010)

Spatio-Temporal Correlation Graph for Association Enhancement in Multi-object Tracking

Zhijie Zhong[1,2], Hao Sheng[1,2(✉)], Yang Zhang[1,2], Yubin Wu[1,2], Jiahui Chen[1,2], and Wei Ke[3]

[1] School of Computer Science and Engineering, Beihang University, Beijing, China
[2] Beijing Advanced Innovation Center for Big Data and Brain Computing, Beihang University, Beijing, China
{zhongzhijie,shenghao,yang.zhang,yubin.wu,chenjh}@buaa.edu.cn
[3] Macao Polytechnic Institute, Macao, China
wke@ipm.edu.mo

Abstract. Due to the frequent interaction between targets in real-world scenarios, various data association problems, such as association ambiguities and association failure, are caused by potential correlation between interactive tracklets, especially during crowded and cluttered scenes. To overcome the non-intuitionistic of tracklet interaction, spatio-temporal correlation graph (STCG) is proposed to model the potential correlation between pairwise tracklets. Three primitive interactions (aggregation, abruption, stability) are defined to model the completed period of the tracklet interaction. Furthermore, STCG model is applied into network flow tracking to exploit the potential correlation between tracklets and enhance the association of the interactive tracklets, especially when overlapping or occlusion is happened. Our method is effective on MOT challenge benchmarks and achieves considerable competitive results with current state-of-the-art trackers.

Keywords: Multi-object tracking ·
Spatio-temporal correlation graph · Tracklet interaction ·
Potential correlation · Data association

1 Introduction

As tracking-by-detection paradigm becomes popular and accepted, association of detections and tracklets is a key technology which affects the accuracy and efficiency of multi-object tracking (MOT) directly. MOT is converted into association problem under this paradigm and various data association methods are proposed. Milan *et al.* propose a conditional random field (CRF) based framework [12,14] which models target exclusion both at the level of detections and at the level of trajectories for tracklet association. Multiple hypothesis tracking (MHT) based methods [4,8,18,19] keep a tree of hypotheses for each target

---

The original version of this chapter was revised: an Acknowledgement was added. The correction to this chapter is available at https://doi.org/10.1007/978-3-030-29551-6_75

© Springer Nature Switzerland AG 2019
C. Douligeris et al. (Eds.): KSEM 2019, LNAI 11775, pp. 394–405, 2019.
https://doi.org/10.1007/978-3-030-29551-6_35

(a) No overlapping tracklet association (b) With overlapping tracklet association

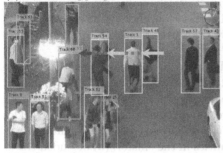 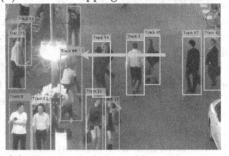

(c) No occluded tracklet association   (d) With occluded tracklet association

Fig. 1. Results of network flow tracking with/without interactive tracklet association. (a), (b): overlapping tracklet association, which penalizes the overlap between two different tracklets which are likely to be the same target. (c), (d): occluded tracklet association, which encourages the link between two different tracklets in occlusion which are belong to the same target. The solid arrow line denotes a trajectory of track 48.

to associate detections and tracklets. For the purpose of global data association, network flow based methods [2,24] are proposed. To improve the ability of data association in long-term occlusion, McLaughlin *et al.* [11] incorporate a motion model into network flow tracking. Track interaction are modeled in [3] by adding pairwise costs to network flow framework to cope with situations of occlusion and cluster. Chen *et al.* [5] propose a top-down community evolution model for network flow tracking to cope with the accumulative errors in tracklet association. Network flow based methods are popular as they have the benefit of computational efficiency and global optimality.

However, the above association methods still have some limitations in crowded and cluttered scenes. Since there exist frequent interaction between targets [9], it brings potential correlation including exclusion and inclusion between tracklets. Exclusion is a mutual exclusion correlation between close tracklets, e.g. in Fig. 1(a), there are exclusion correlation between overlapping tracklets when they are likely to be the same target. Inclusion is a long-gap association between distant tracklets, e.g. in Fig. 1(c), there are inclusion correlation between occluded tracklets when they are the fragments of one target due to long-term occlusion. Potential exclusion and inclusion correlation between interactive tracklets are often ignored or handled ineffectively in above current methods, which brings association ambiguities and association failure under overlap and occlusion conditions.

To address this problem, a spatio-temporal correlation graph (STCG) for pairwise tracklets to exploit the potential correlation between interactive tracklets is proposed. As the potential correlation is caused by interaction, we first model the tracklet interaction. The interaction is set up with three primitive interactions: aggregation I_{aggr}, abruption I_{abru}, stability I_{stab}. By constructing our STCG the interaction tendency can be effectively embodied. Then we apply our STCG model to handle the potential correlation between interactive tracklets. Tracking results using two interactive tracklet association in this paper are illustrated in Fig. 1.

In summary, this paper makes the following contributions: (1) to exploit the potential correlation between interactive tracklets, we propose a STCG including STCG initial formation and STCG refinement which explicitly models the completed tracklet interaction with primitive interaction; (2) overlapping tracklet association analyses the exclusion between overlapping tracklets which improves the ability to deal with association ambiguities in the cluster; (3) occluded tracklet association extracts the inclusion between occluded tracklets which allows the tracker to handle long-term occlusion between targets; (4) we demonstrate the effectiveness and validity of our method on MOT challenge benchmarks which achieves competitive results with current state-of-the-art trackers.

2   Related Work

Multi-object tracking has been a popular topic in computer vision for years and most recent tracking methods can be generally categorized into two groups: online approaches and offline approaches. Online approaches focus on the online processing technique, where the current tracking state is estimated using only current and past observations. Kalman filters [23] and particle filters [6] are widely applied in real tracking applications. Although online approaches is commonly applied in time-critical scenes, they have a significant weakness that online approaches cannot correct the trajectories when an early error is made.

In contrast, offline approaches take information from all frames into consideration where the entire sequence or a batch of the sequences is processed. Tracking-by-detection is one of the most popular frameworks in recent research. Detections are gained by detectors in each frame and then linked into trajectories. Therefore, the multi-object tracking can be converted into a data association problem and various methods are proposed.

Conditional random field (CRF) based methods [12,14] formulated multi-object tracking as an energy minimization problem and solved data association by energy minimization. Data association and trajectory estimation are joint in these methods. However, lacking robustness in tracking occluded targets is a common shortcoming of them.

Multiple hypothesis tracking (MHT) [8] is a classic tracking method where association decisions are delayed until they are resolved. To solve the detection failure problem, [4] modelled the correlation between detections and scenes and [19] proposed a heterogeneous association graph that fuses high-level detections and low-level image evidence for target association. However, MHT is considered impractical in current tracking task owing to the high computation complexity and consuming too much memory.

Zhang *et al.* [24] and Butt *et al.* [2] proposed a min-cost network flow based data association method for multiple object tracking by solving the optimal problem though either linear programming or Lagrangian methods. Since network flow based association methods have the benefit of finding the globally optimal solution efficiently, many methods [3,5,11] follow the network flow framework to improve association robustness in crowded scenes.

In addition, some spatio-temporal model based tracking approaches have been proposed in recent research. Ren *et al.* [15] proposed a spatio-temporal target-to-sensor data association in multiple target tracking. Zhang *et al.* [25] proposed an spatio-temporal context learning based method with self-correction under multiple views to track players in soccer videos. To deal with the problems of missed detection and improve the robustness of tracking, a combined model utilizing the information of spatial-temporal correlation is proposed in [22]. The above approaches still have some limitations in terms of interactive target association in crowded scene. In this paper, we focus on this issue and aims to cope with association ambiguities and association failure problems in crowded scene.

3   Spatio-Temporal Correlation Graph for Pairwise Tracklet Interaction

In real video surveillance, the frequent occurrence of target interaction is the main reason of tracking failure. To overcome the non-intuitionistic of tracklet interaction between targets, spatio-temporal correlation graph (STCG) is introduced for interaction modelling.

3.1   Defination of STCG

For pairwise tracklets τ_m and τ_n, when they have spatio-temporal interaction, the interaction period $P_{m,n}$ of them is defined as $P_{m,n} = \{t_s...t_i...t_e\}$ where for each time t_i the overlap of detections $O_{m,n}^{t_i} > 0$. t_s, t_e are the start and end of the interaction period. The overlap $O_{m,n}^{t_i}$ is defined as $O_{m,n}^{t_i} = (d_m^{t_i} \cap d_n^{t_i})/(\min(d_m^{t_i}, d_n^{t_i}))$ where $d_m^{t_i}, d_n^{t_i}$ are respectively the detection boxes of τ_m and τ_n at t_i. We use $\tau_{m,n}$ to denote the tracklet pair τ_m and τ_n.

According to the spatio-temporal correlation in interaction, we define three primitive interactions: aggregation I_{aggr}, abruption I_{abru}, stability I_{stab}. I_{aggr} is an interaction period where the overlap $O_{m,n}^{t_i}$ has positive correlation with time t_i. I_{abru} is an interaction period where $O_{m,n}^{t_i}$ has negative correlation with t_i. I_{aggr} and I_{abru} respectively embody an upward and an downward interaction

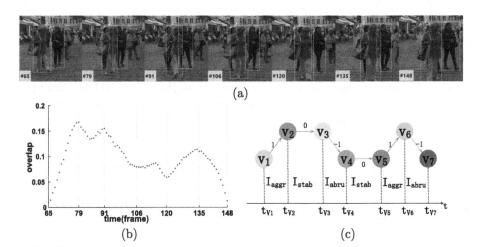

(a)

(b)   (c)

Fig. 2. (a) shows a completed period of pairwise tracklet interaction in the real scene from frame 65 to frame 148; (b) shows the trend of the overlap of pairwise tracklets in the completed interaction period in (a); (c) is the corresponding STCG for pairwise tracklet interaction in (a), (b).

tendency of tracklets $\tau_{m,n}$. I_{stab} is an interaction period where $O_{m,n}^{t_i}$ is uncorrelated with t_i. Tracklets $\tau_{m,n}$ in I_{stab} move close with the similar motion while the interaction tendency alternates between uptrend and downtrend in a stable range. An completed interaction period $P_{m,n}$ can be partitioned into multiple primitive interactions, e.g. in Fig. 2(a) and (b) an interaction period in the real scene goes through 6 primitive interactions.

A weighted directed graph called STCG $G_{\tau_{m,n}} = (V_{\tau_{m,n}}, E_{\tau_{m,n}})$ for tracklets $\tau_{m,n}$ is proposed to formulate the interaction partition, which is shown in Fig. 2(c). Each edge $e_i = <v_i, v_{i+1}>$ with two vertexes v_i, v_{i+1} linked represents an primitive interaction. v_i, v_{i+1} respectively represent the start time t_{v_i} and the end time $t_{v_{i+1}}$ of the primitive interaction. Weight w_i of edge e_i has three values: $1, -1, 0$ which respectively indicate primitive interaction $I_{aggr}, I_{abru}, I_{stab}$. Therefore, the interaction modelling problem is converted to how to construct an STCG for pairwise tracklet interaction.

3.2   STCG Construction

Polynomial Regression. STCG essentially represents an partition of interaction period which can reflect general trend of interaction, so regression analysis is proposed to get the correlation f_{corr} between overlap $O_{m,n}^{t_i}$ and time t_i during interaction $P_{m,n}$ which fits the general interaction trend. It can be formulated as $O_{m,n}^{t_i} = f_{corr}(t_i)$. As the correlation is uncertain, polynomial function $f_{\tau_{m,n}}^r(t) = \sum_{j=0}^r \omega_j t^j$ is proposed to fit the correlation f_{corr} where r and ω_j are the order and the coefficient. Given order r, we can use Least Square Method to obtain the polynomial fitting function $f_{\tau_{m,n}}^r$. We hope to get the optimal order

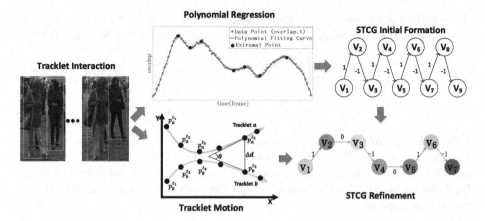

Fig. 3. Illustration of the STCG construction for tracklet interaction. An initial STCG is formed by polynomial regression. Then it is refined with the tracklet motion.

r where the corresponding polynomial fitting function $f^r_{\tau_{m,n}}$ is the best fitting, which can be formulated as an optimal problem.

$$\min \quad E_{RMS}(r) = \sqrt{\frac{\sum_{i=1}^{K}\{f^r_{\tau_{m,n}}(t_i) - O^{t_i}_{m,n}\}^2}{K}} + \lambda \sum_{j=0}^{r}{\omega_j}^2 \tag{1}$$

$$s.t. \qquad |f^r_{\tau_{m,n}}{}'(t_i)| < \Phi, \forall t_i \in P_{m,n} \tag{2}$$

$$|t_a - t_b| > \Psi, \forall t_a, t_b \in \Theta_{f^r_{\tau_{m,n}}} \tag{3}$$

$$for \quad r \in \{1, 2, ..., K\}$$

where Φ, Ψ are the constraint factors, $t_i \in P_{m,n}$, K is the size of $P_{m,n}$, $\Theta_{f^r_{\tau_{m,n}}}$ is the extremal point set of function $f^r_{\tau_{m,n}}$

$$\Theta_{f^r_{\tau_{m,n}}} = \{t|t \in [t_s, t_e], f^r_{\tau_{m,n}}{}'(t) = 0, f^r_{\tau_{m,n}}{}''(t_i) \neq 0\} \tag{4}$$

As shown in Eq. 1, Root Mean Square Error with a regularization term penalizing the overfitting is minimized to obtain a suitable fitting function $f^r_{\tau_{m,n}}$. Besides, the overlap of pairwise tracklets does not change significantly over time in the real scene so the best fitting polynomial function should take this factor into consideration like Eqs. 2 and 3 show.

STCG Initial Formation. With the polynomial function gained we can generate an initial STCG $G_{\tau_{m,n}}$. The extreme point of function $f^r_{\tau_{m,n}}$ is potential critical point of interaction period $P_{m,n}$, so $V_{\tau_{m,n}}$ represents the extreme point set $\Theta_{f^r_{\tau_{m,n}}}$ with addition of the start t_s and the end t_e of $P_{m,n}$. Setting the elements of $V_{\tau_{m,n}}$ in an ascending order, the edge set $E_{\tau_{m,n}}$ of STCG is formulated as $E_{\tau_{m,n}} = \{< v_i, v_{i+1} > |v_i, v_{i+1} \in V_{\tau_{m,n}}\}$. As $I_{aggr}, I_{abru}, I_{stab}$ are defined by the correlation between $O_{m,n}^{t_i}$ and t_i, edge $e_i = <v_i, v_{i+1}>$ can be weighted according to the monotonicity of $f_{\tau_{m,n}}^r$ by the initial weighting function $W_{\tau_{m,n}}^{init}$

$$W_{\tau_{m,n}}^{init}(e_i) = \begin{cases} 1 & \forall t \in (t_{v_i}, t_{v_{i+1}}) f_{\tau_{m,n}}^{r\ \prime}(t) > 0 \\ -1 & \forall t \in (t_{v_i}, t_{v_{i+1}}) f_{\tau_{m,n}}^{r\ \prime}(t) < 0 \\ 0 & \forall t \in (t_{v_i}, t_{v_{i+1}}) f_{\tau_{m,n}}^{r\ \prime}(t) = 0 \end{cases} \tag{5}$$

STCG Refinement. In I_{stab} interaction, tracklets $\tau_{m,n}$ move close with the similar motion while $O_{m,n}^{t_i}$ alternates between uptrend and downtrend due to the drift of detection boxing. Edges indicating I_{stab} cannot be weighted correctly in Eq. 5. So we use the tracklet motion to get the perfect weighting function $W_{\tau_{m,n}}$ which is defined as

$$W_{\tau_{m,n}}(e_i) = \begin{cases} 0 & ||p_t(\tau_m) - p_t(\tau_n)|| < \xi, cos(\tau_m, \tau_n) > 0 \\ W_{\tau_{m,n}}^{init}(e_i) & otherwise \end{cases} \tag{6}$$

where $p_t(\tau)$, ξ, $cos(\tau_m, \tau_n)$ are respectively the position of tracklet τ at time $t \in [t_{v_i}, t_{v_{i+1}}]$, the threshold of distance and the cosine of angle between τ_m and τ_n. Then adjacent vertexes and edges with the same weight are merged to get the revised STCG. Figure 3 illustrates our STCG construction.

4   Interactive Tracklet Association via STCG

Interaction of trajectories obviously involve partial overlap among trajectories and occlusion between targets, which are the primary cause of tracking failure. In this section, STCG is applied to exploit the potential correlation both of them and enhance the association with interaction modelling.

4.1   Overlapping Tracklet Association

When two tracklets of the same target have overlap interaction, the overlap often begins with a high value, keeps changing in a high range and ends with a high value as the false overlapping detections happen suddenly. With STCG $G_{\tau_{m,n}}$ a pairwise cost for overlapping tracklets $\tau_{m,n}$ is defined as

$$C_{\tau_{m,n}} = O_{m,n}^{t_s} + \sum_{e_i \in E_{\tau_{m,n}}} avg(e_i)\delta(W_{\tau_{m,n}}(e_i) = 0) \\ + O_{m,n}^{t_e} + sim(app_{\tau_m}, app_{\tau_n}) \tag{7}$$

where δ is an indicator function, app_τ is the appearance feature vector which is extracted by VGG16 [20] for tracklet τ, $sim(app_{\tau_m}, app_{\tau_n})$ is the cosine distance between app_{τ_m} and app_{τ_n}, $avg(e_i)$ which is the average overlap between $\tau_{m,n}$ in the primitive interaction period that edge e_i indicates is calculated as

$$avg(e_i) = \frac{1}{t_{v_{i+1}} - t_{v_i} + 1} \sum_{t=t_{v_i}}^{t_{v_{i+1}}} O_{m,n}^t \tag{8}$$

where $e_i = <v_i, v_{i+1}>$, t is the time frame.

The pairwise cost $C_{\tau_{m,n}}$ is used to discourage tracklets $\tau_{m,n}$ when they are likely to be the same target. The term $O_{m,n}^{t_s}$ and $O_{m,n}^{t_e}$ penalize the situation that the overlap begins and ends with a high value in the completed interaction. The term $\sum_{e_i \in E_{\tau_{m,n}}} avg(e_i)\delta(W\tau_{m,n}(e_i) = 0)$ and $sim(app_{\tau_m}, app_{\tau_n})$ indicate that the continuously highly overlapping tracklets with high similarity will be discouraged. The pairwise cost can be incorporated into network flow methods by [3] to enhance overlapping tracklet association.

4.2   Occluded Tracklet Association

Occluded tracklet association is proposed to associate occluded tracklets when they are fragments of the same trajectory. Since there are no direct interaction between them, we propose to use the occluding tracklet which causes the occlusion to recover the indirect interaction. Occluded tracklet association is based on our overlapping tracklet association above to ensure tracklets in occlusion are unambiguous.

For two tracklets in the same occlusion, the tracklet getting into occlusion is called pre-occluded tracklet while the tracklet getting out of occlusion is called post-occluded tracklet. The interaction between pre-occluded tracklet and occluding tracklet is I_{aggr} or I_{stab} with the beginning of occlusion while the interaction between post-occluded tracklet and occluding tracklet is I_{abru} or I_{stab} with the end of occlusion. Given a tracklet τ_i and each tracklet τ_j occluded by τ_i, we construct a STCG $G_{\tau_{i,j}}$ for each pair $\tau_{i,j}$ to get the pre-occluded tracklet set $pre(\tau_i)$ and the post-occluded tracklet set $post(\tau_i)$. $pre(\tau_i), post(\tau_i)$ are defined as

$$pre(\tau_i) = \{\tau_j | W_{\tau_{i,j}}(e_k) \geq 0, \forall e_k \in E_{\tau_{i,j}}\} \tag{9}$$

$$post(\tau_i) = \{\tau_j | W_{\tau_{i,j}}(e_k) \leq 0, \forall e_k \in E_{\tau_{i,j}}\} \tag{10}$$

Occluded tracklet association is to associate each pre-occluded tracklet with corresponding post-occluded tracklet when they are belong to the same trajectory. It can be formulated as a binary graph mapping problem and applied to network flow tracking method with the mapping results.

5   Experiments

Dataset. We test our approach both on the MOT16 and MOT17 benchmark [13] and achieve competitive results. They are widely used for a fair comparison in recent years and both of them contain video sequences in unconstrained environments filmed with both static and moving cameras. There are 14 sequences (7 training, 7 test) in MOT16 benchmark and 42 sequences (21 training, 21 test) in MOT17 benchmark. We first demonstrate the evaluation results on MOT16 train sequences to verify the effectiveness of our method in Sect. 5.2. Moreover, in Sect. 5.3, our method is compared with other state-of-art tracking methods.

For a fair comparison, we use the public detection set given by MOT16 and MOT17. All tracking approaches are based on the same input.

Evaluation Metrics. We use the standard CLEAR MOT metrics [1] for evaluating tracking performance. MOTA↑ (multiple object tracking accuracy) combines three kinds of errors including FP↓ (false positives), FN↓ (false negatives) and IDs↓ (identity switches). MOTP↑ (multiple object tracking precision) is the precision of the output trajectories against ground truth. IDF1 [16] is the ratio of correctly identified detections over the average number of ground truth and computed detections. MT↑ (the number of mostly tracked trajectories), ML↓ (the number of mostly lost trajectories), FM↓ (track fragmentations) are also reported. The indicator ↑ means the higher the better while ↓ means the lower the better.

5.1   Computational Time

We implemented our approach in Matlab without code optimization or parallelization and tested it on a PC with 3.0 GHz CPU and 16 GB memory. It took 1210 s for all seven MOT16 training sequences and 810 s for all seven MOT16 testing sequences. Note that the time of object detection and appearance feature extraction are not included.

5.2   Framework Verification

We first verify our method on MOT16 training sequences. One baseline method, one intermediate result and final result are shown in Table 1. The baseline method is the current published network flow tracking method [5]. To verify the ability to handle association ambiguities in clusters, we first add the overlapping tracklet association. Compared to results of baseline, FP decreases nearly by 20% while FN slightly increases, so the false and ambiguous tracklets are handled. Besides, the identity switching with overlapping tracklets accordingly decreases and MOTA increases by 0.9. Then the occluded tracklet association is added. Compared to the previous result, IDs decreases from 393 to 329, IDF1 increases by 4.1 and FM falls from 477 to 447 as a result of associating tracklet fragments caused by target occlusion. And trajectories in the occlusion are mostly tracked, so FN decreases by 3026. Although FP increases by 1291 and MOTP decreases by 0.5 as a result of detection interpolation in the gap between trajectory fragments, MOTA and IDF1 increase more obviously. The results prove that our occluded tracklet association allows the tracker to deal with long-term occlusion between tracklets. Compared to the original baseline method, most of our final evaluation indicators are better. It proves the effectiveness of our model.

5.3   Benchmark Comparison

Our proposed method is tested on both MOT16 and MOT17 benchmarks, and the quantitative evaluations of our approach, as well as the best previously published approaches, are provided in Tables 2 and 3. The comparison can also be found in the MOT Challenge website and our tracker is named STCG.

Table 1. Results on MOT16 training dataset

Method	MOTA↑	MOTP↑	IDF1↑	MT↑	ML↓	FP↓	FN↓	IDs↓	FM↓
baseline	40.2	78.2	44.5	76	232	5329	60235	408	480
+overlapping tracklet association	41.1	**78.3**	45.0	75	231	**4241**	60404	393	477
+occluded tracklet association	**42.7**	77.8	**49.1**	**82**	**224**	5532	**57378**	**329**	**447**

Table 2. Results on MOT challenge 2016 benchmark (1/5/2019)

Method	MOTA↑	IDF1↑	MT↑	ML↓	FP↓	FN↓	IDs↓	FM↓
ours (STCG)	**49.3**	52.0	16.2%	41.4%	6886	84979	515	775
HCC [10]	49.3	50.7	17.8%	39.9%	**5333**	86795	**391**	**535**
AFN [17]	49.0	48.2	**19.1%**	**35.7%**	9508	**82506**	899	1383
LMP [21]	48.8	51.25	18.2%	40.1%	6654	86245	481	595
TLMHT [18]	48.7	**55.3**	15.7%	44.5%	6632	86504	413	642
EHAF16 [19]	47.2	52.4	18.6%	42.8%	12586	83107	542	787
MHT_DAM [8]	45.8	46.1	16.2%	43.2%	6412	91758	590	781
INTERA_MOT [9]	45.4	47.7	18.1%	38.7%	13407	85547	600	930
EDMT [4]	45.3	47.9	17.0%	39.9%	11122	87890	639	946

Table 3. Results on MOT challenge 2017 benchmark (1/5/2019)

Method	MOTA↑	IDF1↑	MT↑	ML↓	FP↓	FN↓	IDs↓	FM↓
ours (STCG17)	51.1	54.5	20.4%	38.6%	32258	241916	**1702**	**2483**
AFN17 [17]	51.5	46.9	20.6%	**35.5%**	22391	248420	2593	4308
eHAF17 [19]	**51.8**	**54.7**	**23.4%**	37.9%	33212	**236772**	1834	2739
jCC [7]	51.2	54.5	20.9%	37.0%	25937	247822	1802	2984
MHT_DAM [8]	50.7	47.2	20.8%	36.9%	22875	252889	2314	2865
TEM [5]	49.1	45.4	17.0%	38.3%	**22119**	261797	3439	3881

Table 2 shows our experimental results on MOT16 benchmark. Our tracker achieves competitive results as opposed to the published state-of-the-art trackers. MOTA and IDF1 are two aggregative metrics to evaluate the performance of trackers. Our proposed STCG tracker takes the first place sorted by MOTA score (49.3) and the third place sorted by IDF1 score (52.0). Besides, on most other metrics including IDs, FM, FN our method is comparable with other current best published tracking methods.

On the more recent MOT17 benchmark, our results are shown in Table 3. Our tracker achieves the second highest IDF1 (54.5), the lowest IDs (1702) and the lowest FM (2483), which shows state-of-the-art performance of our method on tracklet association. TEM [5] is the network flow based tracking method which is our baseline method as well. Compared to [5], our tracking result has significant improvements and outperforms [5] on almost all metrics. The results prove that our method can considerably benefit the overall tracking performance.

6 Conclusion

This paper proposes a STCG-based interaction modelling method that can exploit the potential correlation between interactive tracklets for tracklet association enhancement. Interaction features are embodied by constructing STCG including STCG initial formation and STCG refinement. Furthermore, we show practical benefits of our method for two interactive tracklet association: overlapping tracklet association and occluded tracklet association. We also demonstrate our method on the MOT challenge benchmarks, and the competitive results prove that our model is effective and advanced.

Acknowledgement. This study is partially supported by the National Key R&D Program of China (No. 2017YFC0806500), the National Natural Science Foundation of China (No. 61861166002), the Science and Technology Development Fund of Macau SAR (File no. 0001/2018/AFJ) Joint Scientific Research Project, the Macao Science and Technology Development Fund (No.138/2016/A3), the Fundamental Research Funds for the Central Universities, the Open Fund of the State Key Laboratory of Software Development Environment (No. SKLSDE-2019ZX-04) and the China Scholarship Council State-Sponsored Scholarship Program (Grant No. 201806025026). Thank you for the support from HAWKEYE Group.

References

1. Bernardin, K., Stiefelhagen, R.: Evaluating multiple object tracking performance: the CLEAR MOT metrics. EURASIP J. Image Video Process. **2008**(1), 246309 (2008)
2. Butt, A.A., Collins, R.T.: Multi-target tracking by Lagrangian relaxation to min-cost network flow. In: IEEE Conference on Computer Vision and Pattern Recognition (2013)
3. Chari, V., Lacostejulien, S., Laptev, I., Sivic, J.: On pairwise costs for network flow multi-object tracking. In: IEEE Conference on Computer Vision and Pattern Recognition (2015)
4. Chen, J., Hao, S., Yang, Z., Zhang, X.: Enhancing detection model for multiple hypothesis tracking. In: Computer Vision and Pattern Recognition Workshops (2017)
5. Chen, J., Sheng, H., Zhang, Y., Ke, W., Xiong, Z.: Community evolution model for network flow based multiple object tracking. In: 2018 IEEE 30th International Conference on Tools with Artificial Intelligence (ICTAI), pp. 532–539. IEEE (2018)
6. Fu, Z., Feng, P., Angelini, F., Chambers, J., Naqvi, S.M.: Particle PHD filter based multiple human tracking using online group-structured dictionary learning. IEEE Access **6**, 14764–14778 (2018). https://doi.org/10.1109/ACCESS.2018.2816805
7. Keuper, M., Tang, S., Andres, B., Brox, T., Schiele, B.: Motion segmentation & multiple object tracking by correlation co-clustering. IEEE Trans. Pattern Anal. Mach. Intell. (2018). https://doi.org/10.1109/TPAMI.2018.2876253
8. Kim, C., Li, F., Ciptadi, A., Rehg, J.M.: Multiple hypothesis tracking revisited. In: IEEE International Conference on Computer Vision (2015)
9. Lan, L., Wang, X., Zhang, S., Tao, D., Gao, W., Huang, T.S.: Interacting tracklets for multi-object tracking. IEEE Trans. Image Process. **27**, 4585–4597 (2018)

10. Ma, L., Tang, S., Black, M.J., Van Gool, L.: Customized multi-person tracker. In: Jawahar, C.V., Li, H., Mori, G., Schindler, K. (eds.) ACCV 2018. LNCS, vol. 11362, pp. 612–628. Springer, Cham (2019). https://doi.org/10.1007/978-3-030-20890-5_39

11. McLaughlin, N., Del Rincon, J.M., Miller, P.: Enhancing linear programming with motion modeling for multi-target tracking. In: 2015 IEEE Winter Conference on Applications of Computer Vision (WACV), pp. 71–77. IEEE (2015)

12. Milan, A., Schindler, K., Roth, S.: Multi-target tracking by discrete-continuous energy minimization. IEEE Trans. Pattern Anal. Mach. Intell. **38**(10), 2054–2068 (2016)

13. Milan, A., Leal-Taixé, L., Reid, I.D., Roth, S., Schindler, K.: MOT16: a benchmark for multi-object tracking. CoRR abs/1603.00831 (2016). http://arxiv.org/abs/1603.00831

14. Milan, A., Schindler, K., Roth, S.: Detection- and trajectory-level exclusion in multiple object tracking. In: Computer Vision and Pattern Recognition (2013)

15. Ren, G., Schizas, I.D., Maroulas, V.: Distributed spatio-temporal multi-target association and tracking. In: 2015 IEEE International Conference on Acoustics, Speech and Signal Processing (ICASSP), pp. 4010–4014, April 2015. https://doi.org/10.1109/ICASSP.2015.7178724

16. Ristani, E., Solera, F., Zou, R., Cucchiara, R., Tomasi, C.: Performance measures and a data set for multi-target, multi-camera tracking. In: Hua, G., Jégou, H. (eds.) ECCV 2016. LNCS, vol. 9914, pp. 17–35. Springer, Cham (2016). https://doi.org/10.1007/978-3-319-48881-3_2

17. Shen, H., Huang, L., Huang, C., Xu, W.: Tracklet association tracker: an end-to-end learning-based association approach for multi-object tracking. CoRR abs/1808.01562 (2018)

18. Sheng, H., Chen, J., Zhang, Y., Ke, W., Xiong, Z., Yu, J.: Iterative multiple hypothesis tracking with tracklet-level association. IEEE Trans. Circuits Syst. Video Technol. **14**, 1–13 (2015)

19. Sheng, H., Zhang, Y., Chen, J., Xiong, Z., Zhang, J.: Heterogeneous association graph fusion for target association in multiple object tracking. IEEE Trans. Circuits Syst. Video Technol. **PP**(99), 1 (2018)

20. Simonyan, K., Zisserman, A.: Very deep convolutional networks for large-scale image recognition. Computer Science (2014)

21. Tang, S., Andriluka, M., Andres, B., Schiele, B.: Multiple people tracking by lifted multicut and person re-identification. In: 2017 IEEE Conference on Computer Vision and Pattern Recognition (CVPR), pp. 3701–3710, July 2017. https://doi.org/10.1109/CVPR.2017.394

22. Wei, J., Yang, M., Liu, F.: Learning spatio-temporal information for multi-object tracking. IEEE Access **5**, 3869–3877 (2017). https://doi.org/10.1109/ACCESS.2017.2686482

23. Weng, S.K., Kuo, C.M., Tu, S.K.: Video object tracking using adaptive Kalman filter. J. Vis. Commun. Image Represent. **17**, 1190–1208 (2006). https://doi.org/10.1016/j.jvcir.2006.03.004

24. Zhang, L., Li, Y., Nevatia, R.: Global data association for multi-object tracking using network flows. In: IEEE Conference on Computer Vision and Pattern Recognition (2008)

25. Zhang, P., Zheng, L., Jiang, Y., Mao, L., Li, Z., Sheng, B.: Tracking soccer players using spatio-temporal context learning under multiple views. Multimedia Tools Appl. **77**(15), 18935–18955 (2018). https://doi.org/10.1007/s11042-017-5316-3

Finger Gesture Recognition Based on 3D-Accelerometer and 3D-Gyroscope

Wenchao Ma[1], Junfeng Hu[1], Jun Liao[1], Zhencheng Fan[1], Jianjun Wu[2], and Li Liu[1]([✉])

[1] School of Big Data & Software Engineering,
Chongqing University, Chongqing 401331, China
dcsliuli@cqu.edu.cn
[2] KCT Smart Wearable Technology Chongqing Research Institute Co., Ltd.,
Chongqing 401329, China

Abstract. Gesture-based interaction, as a natural way for human-computer interaction, has a wide range of applications in the ubiquitous computing environment. The latest research findings reveal that user's arm and hand gestures are likely to be identified with ease using the motion sensors worn on the wrist, but it is not clear how much of user's finger gestures can be recognized. This paper presents a method, which is capable of recognizing the bending of fingers, based on input signals from the 3D-accelerometer and 3D-gyroscope worn on the wrist. Features from Time-domain and Frequency-domain are extracted. Gestures are recognized by five classifiers, and the recognition results were then compared with each other. In this paper, maximal information coefficient is adopted for examining the effect of features on the gesture classification. Besides, we work out a faster calculation method, which is based on the features of top 30 maximal information coefficient. Our present results can be widely applied for medical rehabilitation and consumer electronics control based on gesture interaction.

Keywords: Gesture recognition · Feature extraction · Accelerometer · Gyroscope

1 Introduction

Hand gesture as a natural, intuitive, and convenient way of human-computer interaction (HCI) will greatly ease the interaction process. In recent years, smart devices such as smartphones and smartwatches which both have motion sensors in them, have developed rapidly. Thus, gesture recognition from the motion sensor is an emerging technique for gesture-based interaction, which suits well the requirements in ubiquitous computing environments. It has been verified that smartwatch would be able to identify the user's arm and hand gestures with ease [15], however, it is not clear if we can recognize the user's finger gestures using accelerometer and gyroscope worn on the wrist. The finger gestures are

© Springer Nature Switzerland AG 2019
C. Douligeris et al. (Eds.): KSEM 2019, LNAI 11775, pp. 406–413, 2019.
https://doi.org/10.1007/978-3-030-29551-6_36

especially challenging to be detected using above motion sensors since when a gesture occurs, the movement on the wrist is delicate and it is not clear whether it can be recognized uniquely. If feasible, there can be a plethora of applications ranging from medical rehabilitation to consumer electronics control.

In this paper, we investigate the following questions: Can accelerometer and gyroscope sensors worn on the wrist be used for identifying the user's finger gestures? To solve this question, we carry out a series of experiments. A glove that has bending sensors on the five fingers and motion sensor (3D-accelerometer and 3D-gyroscope) on the wrist is developed to capture and segment the data. To compress data and to minimize the influence of variations resulted from gestures made by different users, features from Time-domain and Frequency-domain are extracted. Five classifiers were evaluated on our data set. We further extend our experiment to analyze the features' effectiveness on classifying the gestures using maximal information coefficient, and a faster calculation method was conducted utilizing features with top 30 maximal information coefficient.

2   Related Work

The related research on gesture recognition has gained a lot of interest in recent years. Existing sensing techniques for hand gesture recognition and interaction could be categorized into three main groups: vision-based, movement-based, and EMG-based techniques. Vision-based techniques can track and recognize hand gestures effectively [7]. At the same time, they are sensitive to user's circumstances such as background texture, color, and lighting, which limits their extensive application. It is expected that EMG based techniques would be able to identify user's finger and hand gestures with ease [4,16]. But for ordinary smartwatches and most wearable computing devices, there is no EMG sensor, which hinders the convenience and naturalness of it. The movement-based approach utilizes different sensors to measure movement. In the movement-based gesture recognition, accelerometer and gyroscopes are embedded in various devices are used for gesture recognition. Weiss et al. [15] identify the user's arm and hand gestures using a smartwatch, but it is not clear if we can recognize the user's finger gestures. Gummeson et al. [9] introduced a wearable ring platform which can be used to understand user's finger gestures and writing. However, this limits the gestures to a specific finger, and gestures using other fingers like little finger or thumb cannot be identified. In this work, it is shown that our gesture recognition method is more general as it allows us to recognize gestures from all fingers only with an accelerometer and a gyroscope worn on the wrist, which can be easily satisfied by a smartwatch or a smart wristband. Such device-free gesture recognition is difficult to be applied to identify low-intensity finger gestures.

3   Data Preprocessing

3.1   Data Collection

Here we have developed a glove that has bending sensors on five fingers and 6-D sensor (3-D accelerometer and 3-D gyroscope) MPU6050 on the wrist to capture and segment the motion signal of gestures. Bending sensors output the voltage values to indicate the bending of the fingers. The sensor data is collected at 100 Hz on the glove and transferred to a computer via Bluetooth. The sampling frequency of 100 Hz for our glove is not too high since the typical sampling frequency for the accelerometer on current smartwatches is 100 Hz [1]. This means that our glove closely resembles a smartwatch in terms of the motion sensors. As shown in Fig. 1, we selectively place the MPU6050 above the wrist, so the sensor on our glove is positioned on the same position as the sensor of the smartwatch. For ease of expression, the gestures in our study are named after the two-letter logograms of their English descriptions (refer to Table 1). Ten people participated in the data collection, including two female and eight male students aged between 20 and 24. Each subject performed 5 hand gestures defined above in a sequence by their left hand. Every gesture action lasted about 1 s and the action interval was about 0.5–1 s. Each gesture was repeated 10 times for training the recognition system. The data we obtained has 11 columns including three-axis acceleration, three-axis angular velocity, and the five values of the bending sensors.

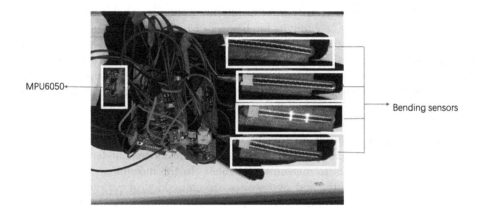

Fig. 1. The glove we used for experiment

Table 1. Brief description of gestures

Description	Brief description
Thumb bending	TB
Forefinger bending	FB
Middle finger bending	MB
Ring finger bending	RB
Little finger bending	LB

3.2 Data Segmentation

The start and the end of a gesture were labeled by the variation of the corresponding bending sensor. According to our observation, when the gesture action occurs, the value of the corresponding bending sensor will increase first and then decrease. Figure 2 shows the signal segment index of five fingers according to the variation of bending sensors. gestures. In our experiment, the length of the gesture signal was set to 70.

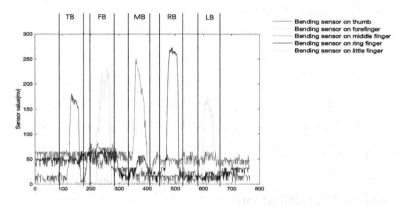

Fig. 2. Illustration for the signal segments of five finger gestures.

3.3 Feature Extraction

Feature extraction is carried out to reduce the data dimensionality while preserving the signal patterns which help to differentiate between the gesture classes. The motion energy is a frequency domain feature that can be measured for smartwatch's accelerometer and gyroscope as shown in [14], The energy is computed as:

$$Energy = \sum_{i=1}^{windowlength/2} (magnitude_i)^2 \qquad (1)$$

where magnitude values are the Fast Fourier Transform (FFT) coefficients calculated over the time window. The energy is only calculated for half the window since the remaining magnitude values are redundant which follows from the symmetry of FFT. As shown in Fig. 3, it is obvious that at the Z-axis of gyroscope, the gesture TB's minimum appears following the appearance of the maximum, but for the gesture LB is contrary, so we use the maximum index and the minimum index as two time domain features. Afterward, three frequency features are extracted from a gesture: Mean, Median Frequency and Entropy, Bao, et al. [2] have successfully applied the four frequency domain features mentioned above in activity recognition. Many previous studies have demonstrated that time domain feature such as average, standard deviation, root mean square, mean absolute deviation, maximum, minimum, range, interquartile range, skewness, kurtosis, upper quartile, lower four Quantile and correlation coefficient are also well suited to acceleration and gyroscope signal modeling. All features are calculated for both accelerometer and gyroscope, correlation coefficient calculated across all three axes while the others for all three axis individually. Finally, we make our feature set by combining all the features we have mentioned above in a sequence.

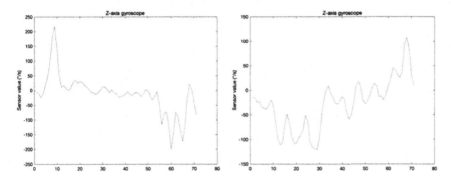

Fig. 3. Z-axis gyroscope signal of gesture TB and gesture LB

4   Gesture Classification

We chose the Feed-forward Neural Network (FNN) [10], Support Vector Machine (SVM) [3] and k-Nearest Neighbor (KNN) [6] to carry out experiments with feature extraction, and we also use two series models, Long Short-Term Memory (LSTM) [11] and Gated Recurrent Unit (GRU) [5], which recognize the gestures without feature extraction. Firstly, the data was normalized so that it conforms to the normal distribution. Then randomly confuses the data set, dividing it into the training set and test set. A four-layer FNN was developed, which consists of an input layer, two hidden layers with 50 units and an output layer. The activation functions of the hidden layer and the output layer are Relu [8] and softmax [13], respectively. The grid cross-validation was used to verify the performance of the SVM classifier under different kernel functions and penalty coefficients. Finally, We carried out our experiments with 5-fold cross-validation, and the average results of the 5-fold cross-validation of the five classifiers are given in Table 2. The 4-layer FNN get the highest accuracy of 94.3%. The methods with feature extraction get much higher accuracy than the methods without feature extraction. This demonstrates that our feature exaction stage can effectively reduce the intra-class variation of gestures to help us classify the gestures. For all classifiers, it is easier to misclassify between gesture MB and gesture RB. Since gesture MB and gesture RB have a similar influence on the wrist, and for many people, the middle finger and the ring finger cannot be bent alone, the bending of one finger inevitably drives the bending of another finger. Thus our result is acceptable. Maximal information coefficient [12] is a method of measuring the correlation between variables. We calculate the Maximal information coefficient for all features we used above and order them

Table 2. Total and respective recognition accuracy for the five methods

	TB	FB	MB	RB	LB	Total
4-layer neural network	100%	94.4%	80.7%	87.5%	100%	94.3%
SVM	100%	92.7%	73.3%	76.4%	100%	89.3%
KNN	97.6%	89.8%	52.1%	58.2%	96.8%	85.4%
LSTM	39.4%	27.4%	35.6%	33.9%	45.7%	37.1%
GRU	42.5%	34.4%	38.6%	32.4%	44.3%	38.4%

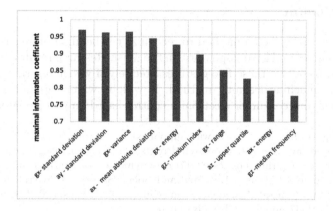

Fig. 4. Maximal information coefficient of top 10 features

in decreasing order of their Maximal information coefficient. Figure 4 shows the Maximal information coefficient of top 10 features. It is observed that features of stand deviation, energy, variance and maximum index have more maximal information coefficient on distinguishing the gestures, while features such as skewness, kurtosis are of little use in classification. And the classification of these five gestures depends more on the x-axis and z-axis of the accelerometer and gyroscope. In order to reduce the computational cost and speed up the recognition, we conducted experiments to train the FNN with the maximal information coefficient of top10, top15, top30, and top60 features, respectively. The results are shown in Table 3. Top 30 features can get the accuracy of 91.7%, and then the accuracy rate increases or decreases randomly within a small range as the number of features increases. In general, the classification accuracy of approximately 94.3% with all features and 91.7% with top30 features indicates that our method is efficient on classifying the bending of fingers.

Table 3. Respective recognition accuracy of different number of features

	TB	FB	MB	RB	LB	Total
Top10	85.3%	72.1%	60.3%	55.2%	78.4%	70.9%
Top15	89.7%	83.3%	65.6%	64.2%	91.2%	78.6%
Top30	99.5%	90.2%	79.4%	83.5%	100%	91.7%
Top40	99.3%	88.9%	81.3%	80.9%	99.5%	90.9%

5   Conclusion

This paper has proposed a method to recognize the bending of fingers, based on the accelerometer and gyroscope worn on the wrist. Research results demonstrate that we can recognize these five gestures precisely if we choose the appropriate features and machine learning method. It will be widely applied for medical rehabilitation and consumer electronics control based on gesture interaction.

Acknowledgement. This work was supported by grants from the Fundamental Research Funds for the Key Research Programm of Chongqing Science & Technology Commission (grant nos. cstc2017rgzn-zdyf0064, cstc2017rgzn-zdyfX0042), the Chongqing Provincial Human Resource and Social Security Department (grant no. cx2017092), the Central Universities in China (grant nos. 2019CDJGFDSJ001, CQU0225001104447 and 2018CDXYRJ0030).

References

1. http://developer.getpebble.com
2. Bao, L., Intille, S.S.: Activity recognition from user-annotated acceleration data. In: Ferscha, A., Mattern, F. (eds.) Pervasive 2004. LNCS, vol. 3001, pp. 1–17. Springer, Heidelberg (2004). https://doi.org/10.1007/978-3-540-24646-6_1
3. Burges, C.J.: A tutorial on support vector machines for pattern recognition. Data Min. Knowl. Disc. **2**(2), 121–167 (1998)
4. Chen, X., Zhang, X., Zhao, Z.Y., Yang, J.H., Lantz, V., Wang, K.Q.: Multiple hand gesture recognition based on surface EMG signal. In: 2007 1st International Conference on Bioinformatics and Biomedical Engineering, pp. 506–509. IEEE (2007)
5. Chung, J., Gulcehre, C., Cho, K., Bengio, Y.: Empirical evaluation of gated recurrent neural networks on sequence modeling. arXiv preprint arXiv:1412.3555 (2014)
6. Cover, T.M., Hart, P.E., et al.: Nearest neighbor pattern classification. IEEE Trans. Inf. Theory **13**(1), 21–27 (1967)
7. Institute of Electrical and Electronics Engineers: IEEE Trans. Syst. Man Cybern. Part A: Syst. Hum. (1900)
8. Glorot, X., Bordes, A., Bengio, Y.: Deep sparse rectifier neural networks. In: Proceedings of the Fourteenth International Conference on Artificial Intelligence and Statistics, pp. 315–323 (2011)
9. Gummeson, J., Priyantha, B., Liu, J.: An energy harvesting wearable ring platform for gestureinput on surfaces. In: Proceedings of the 12th Annual International Conference on Mobile Systems, Applications, and Services, pp. 162–175. ACM (2014)

10. Haykin, S.: Neural Networks: A Comprehensive Foundation. Prentice Hall PTR, Upper Saddle River (1994)
11. Hochreiter, S., Schmidhuber, J.: Long short-term memory. Neural Comput. 9(8), 1735–1780 (1997)
12. Kinney, J.B., Atwal, G.S.: Equitability, mutual information, and the maximal information coefficient. Proc. Natl. Acad. Sci. 111(9), 3354–3359 (2014)
13. Krizhevsky, A., Sutskever, I., Hinton, G.E.: ImageNet classification with deep convolutional neural networks. In: Advances in Neural Information Processing Systems, pp. 1097–1105 (2012)
14. Munguia Tapia, E.: Using machine learning for real-time activity recognition and estimation of energy expenditure. Ph.D. thesis, Massachusetts Institute of Technology (2008)
15. Weiss, G.M., Timko, J.L., Gallagher, C.M., Yoneda, K., Schreiber, A.J.: Smartwatch-based activity recognition: a machine learning approach. In: 2016 IEEE-EMBS International Conference on Biomedical and Health Informatics (BHI), pp. 426–429. IEEE (2016)
16. Zhang, X., Chen, X., Wang, W.H., Yang, J.H., Lantz, V., Wang, K.Q.: Hand gesture recognition and virtual game control based on 3D accelerometer and EMG sensors. In: Proceedings of the 14th International Conference on Intelligent User Interfaces, pp. 401–406. ACM (2009)

Deep Learning

DST: A Deep Urban Traffic Flow Prediction Framework Based on Spatial-Temporal Features

Jingyuan Wang, Yukun Cao, Ye Du, and Li Li[✉]

School of Computer and Information Science,
Southwest University, Chongqing, China
{wjykim,cykkyc,duye99}@email.swu.edu.cn, lily@swu.edu.cn

Abstract. Traffic flow prediction is an interesting and challenging problem in transportation modeling and management. The complex topological structure of urban road network makes it more complicated. The performance of traditional traffic flow prediction models like time series models is not satisfactory, for those methods cannot describe the complicated nonlinearity and uncertainty of the traffic flow precisely. With the rapid development of deep learning, many researchers try to apply deep learning methods to traffic flow prediction. However, those deep learning models neither consider both spatial relation and temporal relation, nor do they combine spatial relation and temporal relation in an effective way. In this paper, we propose a deep urban traffic flow prediction framework (DST) based on spatial-temporal features. In our framework, we use a local convolutional neural network (CNN) method which only considers spatially nearby regions to extract the spatial features and a long short-term memory (LSTM) model to extract the temporal features. In addtion to the traffic flow data, we also use external context data when predicting traffic flow. The experiments on a large-scale taxi trajectory dataset *TaxiCQ* show that our proposed model significantly outperforms other comparison models.

Keywords: Urban traffic flow prediction · Local CNN · LSTM · Spatial-temporal features

1 Introduction

Urban transportation system is the artery of social and economic activities in city. As an important part of urban computing [1,2], traffic flow prediction is one of the most fundamental technologies in intelligent transportation system. The complex topological structure of urban road network makes traffic flow prediction in urban area more complicated. The study of urban traffic flow prediction has an important significance in real-time route guidance and reliable traffic control strategies [3,4].

© Springer Nature Switzerland AG 2019
C. Douligeris et al. (Eds.): KSEM 2019, LNAI 11775, pp. 417–427, 2019.
https://doi.org/10.1007/978-3-030-29551-6_37

In this paper, we study the urban traffic flow prediction problem. The aim of traffic flow prediction is to predict the number of vehicles within a given time interval on the basis of the historical traffic information. Traffic flow prediction is a typical temporal and spatial process. On the one hand, traffic flow data is time series data [5]. On the other hand, traffic flow is significantly affected by the topological structure of road network. The traditional methods for traffic flow prediction are time series methods. With the rapid development of deep learning, many researchers try to apply deep learning methods to traffic flow prediction. However, none of them consider spatial relation and temporal sequential relation simultaneously. Unlike the existing approaches, our study takes both spatial features and temporal features into consideration when predicting urban traffic flow.

We propose a deep urban traffic flow prediction framework (DST) based on spatial-temporal features. In our framework, we use a local CNN model to extract the spatial features and a LSTM model to extract the temporal features. The prediction process of our framework is shown in Fig. 1. The process includes two phases: the offline training phase and the online predicting phase. During the offline training phase, we first transform historical trajectories into historical traffic flow by calculating flow. Then, we combine historical traffic flow and historical context data (e.g., weather and events) to train the prediction framework DST. During the online predicting phase, we first transform real-time trajectories (trajectories in the last few time intervals) into real-time traffic flow by calculating flow. Then we feed the real-time traffic flow and real-time context data to the trained model, and we can get the predicting result.

The remainder of this paper is organized as follows: Sect. 2 includes a review of related work. Our model is described in detail in Sect. 3. In Sect. 4, we introduce the experiments and analyze the results. We conclude our work in Sect. 5.

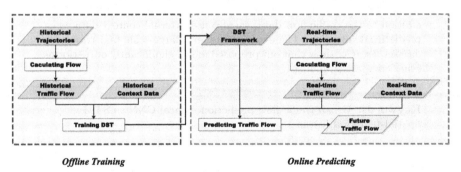

Fig. 1. The prediction process of our framework

2   Related Work

Many approaches on traffic flow prediction have been proposed. These approaches can be roughly classified into two categories: parametric and nonparametric methods. The traditional methods for traffic flow prediction are parametric approaches.

In earlier studies, linear time series models have been widely applied. Time series methods, such as the autoregressive integrated moving average (ARIMA), were employed to forecast short-term traffic flow. Moreover, some improved ARIMA models like space-time ARIMA [6] and seasonal ARIMA (SARIMA) [7] were also proposed to predict traffic flow. Due to the stochasticity and nonlinearity of the traffic flow, parametric approaches cannot describe traffic flow precisely. Thus, some researchers tried to use nonparametric methods. Jin et al. [8] employed support vector regression (SVR) to predict traffic flow. Leshem et al. [9] developed a random forest regression (RF) method.

In the past decade, deep learning has achieved great development and successful application in several domains that has not been seen before. Many researchers made the attempt to apply deep learning methods to traffic flow prediction. Huang et al. [10] incorporated multitask learning (MTL) into deep belief networks (DBN) for traffic flow prediction. Lv et al. [11] proposed a stacked auto-encoder (SAE) model. Polson et al. [12] developed a deep learning architecture which combined a linear model and a sequence of *tanh* layers. Wang et al. [13] used a bidirectional LSTM (BiLSTM) model to extract deep features of traffic flow. Zhang et al. [14] proposed to use residual CNN (ST-ResNet) on the images of traffic flow. A multi-view network was creatively proposed in [15]. Liang et al. [16] predicted the readings of a geo-sensor over several future hours by using a multi-level attention-based recurrent neural network. However, those deep learning models neither consider both spatial relation and temporal relation, nor do they combine spatial relation and temporal relation in an effective way.

3 Deep Urban Traffic Flow Prediction Framework: DST

3.1 Problem Definition

In this part, we show some notations to be used in our work and define the urban traffic flow prediction problem. They are fundamental and vital to the models in the following sections.

- **Location set:** We define the set of non-overlapping locations $L = \{l_1, l_2, ..., l_N\}$ as rectangle partitions of a city.
- **Time interval set:** We define the set of time intervals as $\mathcal{I} = \{I_1, I_2, ..., I_T\}$.
- **Trajectory data:** The raw data is trajectory data, which contains the longitude, latitude and timestamp information of vehicles. The longitude and latitude information of the raw trajectory should be mapped into the relative location. After the transformation process, we can gain the data of a vehicle as a tuple $(v.t, v.l)$, where $v.t$ is the timestamp and $v.l$ is the location.
- **Traffic flow:** We define traffic flow as the number of vehicles at one location per time interval, i.e., $y_t^i = |\{v : v.t \in I_t \wedge v.l \in l_i\}|$, where $|\cdot|$ denotes the cardinality of the set. To simplify the formulation, we use the index of time interval t representing I_t, and the index of location i representing l_i for the rest of the paper.

- **Traffic flow prediction:** The aim of traffic flow prediction problem is to predict the number of vehicles at time interval $t + 1$, given the data until time interval t. In addition to historical traffic flow data, we can also take advantage of context features such as temporal features, spatial features and weather features. The context features for a location i and a time interval t are denoted as a vector $e_t^i \in \mathbb{R}^r$, where r is the number of context features. Our task is to predict $y_{t+1}^i = F(\mathcal{Y}_{t-m...,t}^L, \varepsilon_{t-m...,t}^L)$, where $\mathcal{Y}_{t-m...,t}^L$ are historical traffic flow and $\varepsilon_{t-m...,t}^L$ are historical context features for all locations L from time interval $t-m$ to time interval t.

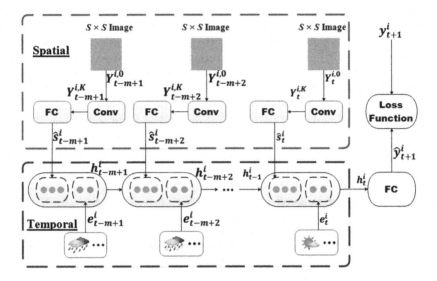

Fig. 2. The prediction framework: DST

3.2 Spatial Perspective: Local CNN

Traffic flow is significantly affected by the topological structure of road network. Thus, it is essential to extract the spatial features of traffic flow while predicting. If we treat the traffic in a city as an image and the traffic volume for time interval as pixel values, we can extract the spatial features. However, including regions with weak correlations to predict a target region may lead to decrease of performance and reliability of the prediction model. Therefore, we propose a local convolutional neural network (CNN) method which only considers spatially nearby regions. This idea is supported by *the first law of geography*: near things are more related than those distant things.

As the spatial part in Fig. 2, at each time interval t, we treat one location i with its surrounding neighborhoods as one $S \times S$ single-channel image of traffic flow values (i is as the center of the image), where S controls the size of spatial window. And zero padding is employed for locations at boundaries of the city.

Then, we have an single-channel image as a tensor $Y_t^i \in \mathbb{R}^{S \times S \times 1}$, for each location i and time interval t. The local CNN takes Y_t^i as input $Y_t^{i,0}$ and feeds it into K convolutional layers. The process at each layer k is defined as follows:

$$Y_t^{i,k} = f(Y_t^{i,k-1} * W_t^k + b_t^k) \tag{1}$$

where $*$ denotes the convolutional operation and $f(\cdot)$ is ReLU activation function. The parameters $W_t^{1,\dots,K}$ and $b_t^{1,\dots,K}$ are shared across all regions $i \in L$.

After K convolution layers, we transform the output $Y_t^{i,K} \in \mathbb{R}^{S \times S \times \lambda}$ to a feature vector $s_t^i \in \mathbb{R}^{S^2\lambda}$ (λ is the number of filters) by a flatten layer. Then, we reduce the dimension of the feature vector by a fully connected layer, which can be defined as

$$\hat{s}_t^i = f(W_t^{fc} s_t^i + b_t^{fc}) \tag{2}$$

For each time interval t, $\hat{s}_t^i \in \mathbb{R}^d$ are as the spatial features for region i.

3.3   Temporal Perspective: LSTM

Traffic flow data is time series data. Long short-term memory (LSTM) network [17] is an effective way to handle sequential data. In addition to the traffic flow data, we also use external context data when predicting traffic flow.

The memory block of LSTM consists of one or more self-connected memory cells c_t^i and three multiplicative units: the input gate i_t^i, forget gate f_t^i and output gate o_t^i. The multiplicative gates allow LSTM memory cells to keep the information for long periods of time. The following equations mathematically abstract the process.

$$i_t^i = \sigma(W_i x_t^i + U_i h_{t-1}^i + V_i c_{t-1}^i + b_i) \tag{3}$$

$$f_t^i = \sigma(W_f x_t^i + U_f h_{t-1}^i + V_f c_{t-1}^i + b_f) \tag{4}$$

$$o_t^i = \sigma(W_o x_t^i + U_o h_{t-1}^i + V_o c_t^i + b_o) \tag{5}$$

$$c_t^i = f_t^i \circ c_{t-1}^i + i_t^i \circ tanh(W_c x_t^i + U_c h_{t-1}^i + b_c) \tag{6}$$

$$h_t^i = o_t^i \circ tanh(c_t^i) \tag{7}$$

where $\sigma(\cdot)$ is sigmoid function, $\circ$ is Hadamard product and $tanh(\cdot)$ is hyperbolic tangent function. And the output of LSTM for the region i after m time intervals is h_t^i.

As the temporal part in Fig. 2, we concatenate spatial features with context features and get the input of LSTM $x_t^i \in \mathbb{R}^{r+d}$ for region i at time interval t.

$$x_t^i = \hat{s}_t^i \oplus e_t^i \tag{8}$$

where $\oplus$ is the concatenation operation.

3.4 The Prediction Framework: DST

As shown in Fig. 2, we feed the output of LSTM h_t^i to the fully connected layer and then we get the prediction value $\hat{y}_{t+1}^i$ of traffic flow.

$$\hat{y}_{t+1}^i = \sigma(W_{fc}h_t^i + b_{fc}) \tag{9}$$

where $\sigma(\cdot)$ is sigmoid function. W_{fc} and b_{fc} are learnable parameters. We use mean square loss as loss function. It is defined as

$$\mathcal{L}(\theta) = \frac{1}{N}\sum_{i=1}^{N}(y_{t+1}^i - \hat{y}_{t+1}^i)^2 \tag{10}$$

where y_{t+1}^i is the observation (real) value of traffic flow, and $\hat{y}_{t+1}^i$ is the prediction value of traffic flow. N is the number of samples.

4 Experiments and Results

4.1 Data Description

In this paper, we evaluate our model and other comparison models on a large-scale trajectory dataset *TaxiCQ*. *TaxiCQ* is the taxicab GPS data in the main urban area of Chongqing from January to June in 2017. The main urban area of Chongqing includes nine districts: Yuzhong District, Dadukou District, Jiangbei District, Nan'an District, Shapingba District, Jiulongpo District, Beibei District, Yubei District and Banan District. The total area is about 5472 km². After the transformation process, we get the traffic flow data. There are 25 × 25 regions (including zero padding for locations at boundaries of the main urban area of Chongqing) in our data. The size of each region is 3 km × 3 km. The context features used in our experiment include temporal features, spatial features and weather features (e.g., precipitation condition) [18].

We use the data of five months (from January to May) in 2017 as the training set and the later one month (June) as the testing set.

4.2 Evaluation Metric

To evaluate the effectiveness of the traffic flow prediction models, we use two performance indexes, which are the Mean Absolute Percentage Error (MAPE) and the Root Mean Square Error (RMSE). They are defined as follows.

$$MAPE(f, \hat{f}) = \frac{1}{n}\sum_{i=1}^{n}\frac{|f_i - \hat{f}_i|}{f_i} \tag{11}$$

$$RMSE(f, \hat{f}) = \left[\frac{1}{n}\sum_{i=1}^{n}(|f_i - \hat{f}_i|)^2\right]^{\frac{1}{2}} \tag{12}$$

where f is the observation (real) value of traffic flow, and $\hat{f}$ is the prediction value of traffic flow.

4.3   Methods for Comparison

The models used in comparison experiments are explained as follows.

- **Historical average (HA):** Historical average is an intuitive method. It predicts the traffic flow using average values of previous traffic flow at the location at the same time interval of the day.
- **Autoregressive integrated moving average (ARIMA):** ARIMA combines moving average and autoregressive components for modeling time series to predict traffic flow.
- **Support vector regression (SVR):** The Support Vector Regression uses the same principles as the Support Vector Machine (SVM) for classification, with only a few minor differences.
- **Bidirectional long short-term memory (BiLSTM)** [13]: Bidirectional long short-term memory is a typical deep learning method to process sequential data.
- **ST-ResNet** [14]: ST-ResNet treats the traffic in a city as an image and the traffic volume for a time interval as pixel values. Given a set of historical traffic images, the model predicts the traffic image for the next timestamp.

4.4   Parameters Setting

In the spatial part, the size of spatial window S is set to 11, which means one location i with its surrounding neighborhoods is as one 11×11 single-channel image of traffic flow values. The number of convolutional layers K is set to 2. The number of filters λ is set to 32, and the size of filter is 2×2. The dimension of the output d is set to 32.

In the temporal part, 30 min is as the length of time interval and the sequence length m is set to 6, which means that we use the previous 6 time intervals (3 h) to predict the traffic flow in the next time interval.

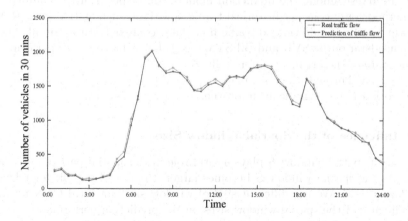

Fig. 3. The comparison between real traffic flow and prediction of traffic flow

4.5 The Prediction Accuracy Comparison

To intuitively evaluate the prediction performance of the DST model, we use DST to predict 30-min interval traffic flow of a whole day (June 1, 2017) using the data collected from No. 313 observation location (the center of the main urban area of Chongqing). As shown in Fig. 3, the red line represents the real traffic flow, and the blue line shows the prediction of traffic flow. From Fig. 3, we can notice that the performance of the DST model is quiet good during most of the day. Besides, there are mainly four fluctuating periods, which are around 7:00, 12:00, 15:00 and 18:30 respectively. Those fluctuating periods are all peak traffic periods during which the performance of the DST framework is not as stable as other periods.

Table 1. The comparison results on *TaxiCQ*

Models	MAPE (%)	RMSE
HA	16.33	138.96
ARIMA	11.21	95.95
SVR	7.94	68.48
BiLSTM	6.55	56.92
ST-ResNet	5.91	48.72
DST	**4.09**	**33.63**

Then the performance of our model and other comparison models is tested on all observation locations of the main urban area of Chongqing and the results of them are listed in Table 1. As shown in Table 1, both MAPE and RMSE of DST are lowest among the prediction models. More specifically, we notice that the methods only consider historical traffic flow data, such as HA and ARIMA, perform poorly. In addition to traffic flow data, context features are also taken into consideration by SVR and BiLSTM. And they achieve better performance. As the state-of-the-art method for traffic flow prediction, ST-ResNet gains good performance. Through the combination of local CNN and LSTM, our proposed framework achieves significant improvement over ST-ResNet.

4.6 Influence of the Spatial Window Size

The size of spatial window S plays a vital role in the spatial part of our framework. As the spatial window S becomes larger, the model may fit for relations in a larger area. We use different spatial window sizes for local CNN to study the influence of the spatial window sizes on the prediction performance.

As shown in Fig. 4, our framework achieves the best performance when the size of spatial window S is 11 (i.e., one location i with its surrounding neighborhoods is as one 11×11 single-channel image of traffic flow values). The prediction

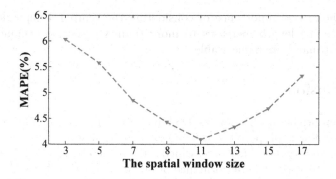

Fig. 4. Influence of the spatial window size

error increases as the spatial window size decreases, which may be caused by the fact that locally correlated neighboring locations are not fully covered. Besides, the prediction error increases significantly (more than 1.23%), as the spatial window size increases to 17 (where each area approximately covers more than 46% of the space in the main urban area of Chongqing). The result suggests that locally significant correlations may be averaged as the spatial window size increases. Thus, there exists an optimal border for the spatial window size, not the larger the better.

4.7 Influence of the Sequence Length

The sequence length m of LSTM is an important hyperparameter in the temporal part of our framework. We use different sequence lengths for LSTM to study the influence of sequence length on the prediction performance.

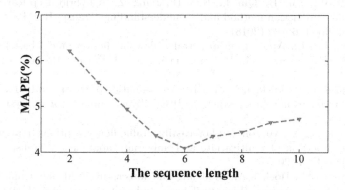

Fig. 5. Influence of the sequence length

As shown in Fig. 5, our framework achieves the best performance when the sequence length m is 6 (i.e., 3 h). The decreasing trend in MAPE as the length increases shows the importance of considering the temporal dependency. Furthermore, as the length increases to more than 3 h, the performance slightly degrades but mainly remains stable.

5   Conclusion

A novel deep prediction framework DST based on spatial-temporal features for urban traffic flow is proposed in this paper. Our framework considers both spatial features and temporal features, which are modeled by local CNN and LSTM respectively. To verify the performance of our model, we evaluate the proposed model and other five comparison models (HA, ARIMA, SVR, BiLSTM, ST-ResNet) on a large-scale taxi trajectory dataset *TaxiCQ*. The experiment results show that our proposed model significantly outperforms other comparison models.

Our method can be used to a wide range of applications, including traffic forecasting, vehicle navigation devices, vehicle routing, and congestion management.

In the follow-up work, we attempt to combine trajectory data with more additional features from commercial maps (e.g. Google Maps). And we will validate the generalization ability of our model on more large-scale datasets.

Acknowledgement. This work was supported by NSFC (grant No. 61877051) and CSTC (grant No. cstc2018jscx-msyb1042, cstc2017zdcy-zdyf0366).

References

1. Zheng, Y., Mascolo, C., Silva, C.T.: Guest editorial: urban computing. IEEE Trans. Big Data **3**(2), 124–125 (2017)
2. Zheng, Y.: Urban computing: enabling urban intelligence with big data. Frontiers Comput. Sci. **11**(1), 1–3 (2017)
3. Yuankai, W., Tan, H., Qin, L., Ran, B., Jiang, Z.: A hybrid deep learning based traffic flow prediction method and its understanding. Transp. Res. Part C Emerg. Technol. **90**, 166–180 (2018)
4. Guo, Y., Lu, L.: Application of a traffic flow prediction model based on neural network in intelligent vehicle management. Int. J. Pattern Recogn. Artif. Intell. (2018)
5. Mackenzie, J., Roddick, J.F., Zito, R.: An evaluation of HTM and LSTM for short-term arterial traffic flow prediction. IEEE Trans. Intell. Transp. Syst. **99**, 1–11 (2018)
6. Kamarianakis, Y., Vouton, V.: Forecasting traffic flow conditions in an urban network: comparison of multivariate and univariate approaches. Transp. Res. Rec. **1857**(1), 74–84 (2003)
7. Williams, B.M., Hoel, L.A.: Modeling and forecasting vehicular traffic flow as a seasonal arima process: theoretical basis and empirical results. J. Transp. Eng. **129**(6), 664–672 (2003)
8. Jin, X., Zhang, Y., Yao, D.: Simultaneously prediction of network traffic flow based on PCA-SVR. In: Liu, D., Fei, S., Hou, Z., Zhang, H., Sun, C. (eds.) ISNN 2007. LNCS, vol. 4492, pp. 1022–1031. Springer, Heidelberg (2007). https://doi.org/10.1007/978-3-540-72393-6_121

9. Leshem, G., Ritov, Y.: Traffic flow prediction using adaboost algorithm with random forests as a weak learner. In: Proceedings of World Academy of Science, Engineering and Technology, vol. 19, pp. 193–198 (2007)
10. Huang, W., Song, G., Hong, H., Xie, K.: Deep architecture for traffic flow prediction: deep belief networks with multitask learning. IEEE Trans. Intell. Transp. Syst. **15**(5), 2191–2201 (2014)
11. Lv, Y., Duan, Y., Kang, W., Li, Z., Wang, F.Y.: Traffic flow prediction with big data: a deep learning approach. IEEE Trans. Intell. Transp. Syst. **16**(2), 865–873 (2015)
12. Polson, N.G., Sokolov, V.O.: Deep learning for short-term traffic flow prediction. Transp. Res. Part C Emerg. Technol. **79**, 1–17 (2017)
13. Wang, J., Hu, F., Li, L.: Deep bi-directional long short-term memory model for short-term traffic flow prediction. In: Liu, D., Xie, S., Li, Y., Zhao, D., El-Alfy, E.-S.M. (eds.) ICONIP 2017. LNCS, vol. 10638, pp. 306–316. Springer, Cham (2017). https://doi.org/10.1007/978-3-319-70139-4_31
14. Zhang, J., Zheng, Y., Qi, D.: Deep spatio-temporal residual networks for citywide crowd flows prediction. In: AAAI, pp. 1655–1661 (2017)
15. Yao, H., et al.: Deep multi-view spatial-temporal network for taxi demand prediction. In: 2018 AAAI Conference on Artificial Intelligence (AAAI 2018) (2018)
16. Liang, Y., Ke, S., Zhang, J., Yi, X., Zheng, Y.: GeoMAN: multi-level attention networks for geo-sensory time series prediction. In: IJCAI, pp. 3428–3434 (2018)
17. Hochreiter, S., Schmidhuber, J.: Long short-term memory. Neural Comput. **9**(8), 1735–1780 (1997)
18. Koesdwiady, A., Soua, R., Karray, F.: Improving traffic flow prediction with weather information in connected cars: a deep learning approach. IEEE Trans. Veh. Technol. **65**(12), 9508–9517 (2016)

Small-Scale Data Classification Based on Deep Forest

Meiyang Zhang[1] and Zili Zhang[1,2]

[1] College of Computer and Information Science,
Southwest University, Chongqing 400715, China
zhangzl@swu.edu.cn
[2] School of Information Technology, Deakin University,
Locked Bag 20000, Geelong, VIC 3220, Australia

Abstract. Developing effective and efficient small-scale data classification methods is very challenging in the digital age. Recent researches have shown that deep forest achieves a considerable increase in classification accuracy compared with general methods, especially when the training set is small. However, the standard deep forest may experience overfitting and feature vanishing in dealing with small sample size. In this paper, we tackle this problem by proposing a skip connection deep forest (SForest), which can be viewed as a modification of the standard deep forest model. It leverages multi-class-grained scanning method to train multiple binary forest from different training sub-dataset of classes to encourage the diversity of ensemble and solve the class-imbalance problem. To expand the diversity of each layer in cascade forest, five different classifiers are employed. Meanwhile, the fitting quality of each classifiers is taken into consideration in representation learning. In addition, we propose a skip connection strategy to augment the feature vector, and use Gradient Boosting Decision Tree (GBDT) as the final classifier to improve the overall performance. Experiments demonstrated the proposed model achieved superior performance than the-state-of-the-art deep forest methods with almost the same parameter.

Keywords: Small-scale data · Deep forest · Skip connection · Diversity

1 Introduction

In recent years, the emergence of big data has attracted great attention, many fields have enormous amount of corresponding data storage. But many of the data are unlabeled so that they can not be further analyzed. To increase the available data volume, many people have jointly formed ImageNet dataset for image analysis. However, it needs expensive manual cost for each type of small-scale datasets to label a large number of data. Moreover, many tasks failed to obtain a large amount of labeled data due to personal privacy and data security.

© Springer Nature Switzerland AG 2019
C. Douligeris et al. (Eds.): KSEM 2019, LNAI 11775, pp. 428–439, 2019.
https://doi.org/10.1007/978-3-030-29551-6_38

Like some medical and military industries, they face the difficulty in carrying out effective analysis with small sample size. Therefore, it is urgent to seek a more optimized small-scale data classification method to conduct data analysis and provide policy support.

The advance of deep neural networks has achieved great success in various applications, especially in visual and speech recognition [1,2]. Inspired by deep neural networks, many methods have been proposed to classify the small-scale data using variants of deep learning approaches [3,4]. Hu et al. [5] learned facial features from a small number of images, increasing sample diversity by combining distinctive facial features. Then, these combined images and original images are used to train a convolutional neural network (CNN). Chen et al. [6] proposed a convolutional self-encoding neural network to encode original images and decode to obtain new images. The difference between the original images and the new images is minimized to train the parameters of CNN. Zhou [7] combined the neural networks ensemble with the C4.5 decision tree to improve the generalization ability and the comprehensibility of the classification model. However, a few shortcomings may limit the applications of deep neural networks in small-scale data. On one hand, deep neural networks are complicated model, and huge amounts of training data are usually required to train the model [8]. On the other hand, it is well known that deep neural networks are difficult to be theoretically analyzed, and the learning performance depends seriously on the skills of parameter tuning. These make it unruly to get prospective classification performance using deep neural networks.

To ease deficiencies of deep neural networks, recently, an alternative to deep learning structure-deep forest model, called gcForest, has been proposed [8]. In contrast to deep neural networks, gcForest not only has much fewer hyper-parameters but also is easy to be theoretically analyzed. Meanwhile, the number of cascade layers can be adaptively determined such that the model complexity can be automatically set, enabling gcForest to perform excellently even on small-scale data.

Due to the small sample size and the class-imbalance in small-scale data, two challenges may limit the application of gcForest on small-scale data. (1) If we manually define different types of classifiers to encourage the diversity of ensemble in multi-grained scanning, it may raise the risk of over-fitting. (2) In cascade forest, representation learning at each layer might result in the vanishing of important features and the burst of unimportant features. In order to take the advantages of gcForest, it is significant to modify it to work better on small-scale data. In this paper, we propose a SForest model to meet aforementioned classification problem in small-scale data. The key idea of SForest model is to encourage the diversity of ensemble and consider the augment features on each layer. Our contributions can be summarized as follows:

(1) We adopt a multi-class-grained scanning strategy to encourage the diversity of ensemble by using different class of training data to train different forest respectively. In addition, this strategy removes the risk of class-imbalance.

(2) We inject the skip connection operation into cascade forest to augment features of the next layer. Moreover, five different types of classifiers are used to improve the diversity of ensemble and boost important features in forest learning at each layer of cascade forest.

(3) We employ the GBDT [9] to find an optimal combination of the weight for the final layer.

The rest of this paper is organized as follows: Sect. 2 presents the gcForest model and some concepts. Section 3 introduces SForest and its workflow. In Sect. 4, we compare SForest with some popular machine learning models by giving experimental results and evaluations. Finally, in Sect. 5, we get conclusions for this paper.

2   Related Work

Similar to the deep neural network, gcForest [8] has multi-layer cascade structure, but each layer contains many forests instead of neurons in deep neural networks. The gcForest consists of two ensemble components: the first one is multi-grained scanning, the second one is the cascade forest.

2.1   Multi-grained Scanning

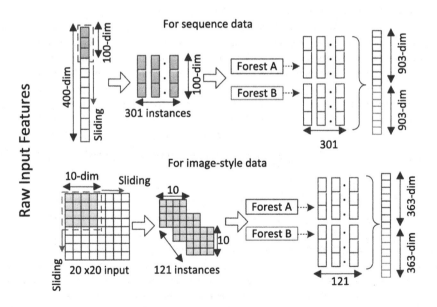

Fig. 1. Multi-grained scanning in gcForest.

Deep neural networks are powerful in handling feature relationships. Inspired by this, gcForest employs the procedure of multi-grained scanning to enhance cascade forest, which adopts sliding window to scan from high dimensionality to learn representations of input data according to different random forests (RFs). Different size of sliding windows can increase data diversity. Figure 1 only shows one size of sliding windows, including sequence data and image data.

For a given sliding window, a raw input feature will be divided into many instances with the same size and the same label, and then the instances extracted from the same window are used to train two different RFs. Hence, the output of the RFs for each sliding window is a class probability vector. For all instances from each input feature are fed through these RFs, the outputs are concatenated together to produce a new feature vector for each given input.

As Fig. 1 illustrates, suppose there are 3 classes and a 100-dimensional sliding window is used. For sequence data, 301 instances will be acquired with a 400 raw input feature, then, 301 three-dimensional class vectors are produced by each forest, leading to a 1,806-dimensional transformed feature vector corresponding to the original 400-dimensional raw input feature vector.

2.2 Cascade Forest

Unlike deep neural networks, which define numerous hidden neurons to learn representations layer-by-layer using forward and backward propagation algorithms, the cascade forest learns classification distribution (features) directly by assembling amounts of decision forests under the supervision of input features at each layer.

As illustrated in Fig. 2, each layer of cascade forest receives feature information processed by its preceding layer, and outputs its processing result concatenated with the original feature vector to the next layer. Indeed, each layer is designed to include different types of forests to encourage the diversity of the ensemble. Two types of forests, completely random forest and random forest, are employed in gcForest.

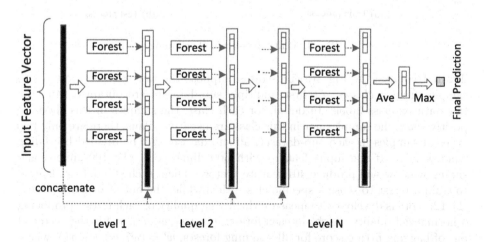

Fig. 2. Cascade forest in gcForest.

In practice, class vector produced by each forest is generated by k-cross-validation. The performance of whole cascade will be estimated on validation set when a new layer is expanded, and the expanding progress will be automatically terminated once there is no significant performance gain.

3   SForest Model

In this section we will first introduce the multi-class-grained scanning, and then the improved cascade forest is given, followed by the overall architecture.

3.1   Multi-class-grained Scanning

Although the multi-grained scanning method has been proven to be effective in feature handling, there are still some disadvantages in extracting features. (1) Considering the class-imbalance data in small-scale dataset, the decision tree will emphasize classes with a larger instance size, and ignore small-size classes. (2) The diversity of forest is determined manually, not the data itself. Model classification capabilities will be weakened because diversity is critical to the ensemble structure, especially on small-scale data. (3) All forests in the ensemble have equal contributions in multi-grained scanning, which may lead to that class distribution is sensitive to the number of forests. Therefore, we adopt the method of training forest with different training data [10].

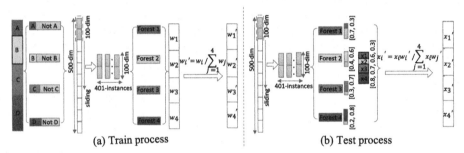

Fig. 3. Multi-class-grained scanning.

Train Process: As Fig. 3(a) illustrates, suppose the raw training data has m samples from 4 classes. At first, multiple sub-datasets are obtained from the raw data by class labels. In detail, for each class, the samples in this class are positive, and the samples not in this class are negative. Thus, there are only two types of samples in each sub-dataset, all sub-dataset will be divided by sliding window next. If the input feature with 500 dimensions, the 100-dimensional sliding window will produce 401 feature vectors. Then, each sub-dataset is used to train a forest to sense a specific class. Meanwhile, the out-of-bagging (OOB) [11,12] score is developed to measure the fitting quality of each forest, producing a normalized quality weight in each forest. $w = (w_1, w_2, w_3, w_4)$ is the vector of out-of-bagging fitting score for all scanning forests, $w' = (w'_1, w'_2, w'_3, w'_4)$, where $w'_i = w_i / \sum_{j=1}^{4} w_j$, is normalized weight vector of forests.

Test Process: As shown in Fig. 3(b), for each 100-dimensional instance after sliding window operation, each forest generates a 2-dimensional feature vector. Then a 4-dimensional feature vector is generated by selecting the possibility of positive estimation in each 2-dimensional class vector. Suppose $x = (x_1, x_2, x_3, x_4)$ is a 4-dimensional class vector, and the normalized class vector is define as $x' = (x_1', x_2', x_3', x_4')$, where $x_i' = x_i w_i' / \sum_{j=1}^{4} x_j w_j'$.

However, each instance can only produce a 4-dimensional feature vector from this forest ensemble group, which makes the feature vector dimension generated by the ensemble greatly reduce. To acquire the same dimension as gcForest, each sliding window employs two groups of forest ensemble to enhance the feature vector. Theoretically, the training time of multi-class-grained scanning with two group ensembles is the same as previous multi-class-grained scanning model.

The multi-class-grained scanning with two group ensemble forests model is shown as Fig. 4. Based on the fit forests and their quality weights, a 500-dimensional raw input feature can be transformed into two 1604-dimensional representation vectors. Thereby, we obtain a 3208-dimensional representation vector by concatenating these 1604-dimensional representation vectors. Taking training time into account, we will find that the execution time of multi-class-grained scanning with two group ensemble forests does not increase, because the two group of forests ensemble can be executed in parallel.

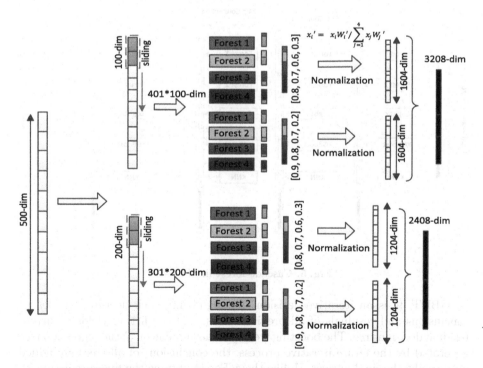

Fig. 4. Multi-class-grained scanning with two group ensemble forests.

3.2   Improved Cascade Forest

Cascade forest, which learns more discriminative representations under supervision of input representations in layer-by-layer processing, thus gives more accurate prediction by the ensemble of forests. It is well known that diversity is crucial to determine the quality of ensemble learning [13]. The ensemble classifier should be "many but different". To this end, each layer of the improved cascade structure contains five types of classifiers: random forests, completely random forests, K-nearest neighbours (KNN), logistic regression, and Xgboost [14].

In deep neural networks, the residual network (ResNet) [15] effectively solves the problem of gradient vanishing and gradient explosion in CNN, and lower training errors can be obtained even when the network becomes deeper. Since the cascade forest is similar to the CNN structure in representation learning, the feature vanishing or feature explosion also appears in the training process of cascade forest, resulting in the neglect of important features and the emphasis of unimportant features. As shown in Fig. 5, improved cascade forest infuses the skip connection as ResNet to solve feature problems. Moreover, due to the intelligibility of the decision tree, the top-k most important features information is transmitted from the trained forest to the next layer to avoid the loss of important features.

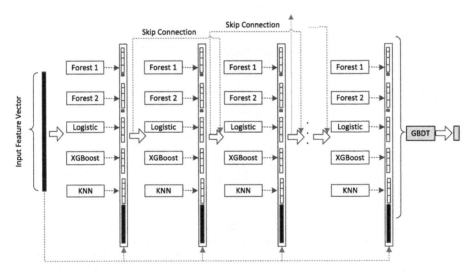

Fig. 5. Cascade forest in SForest.

GBDT [9] is an iterative decision tree algorithm, each decision tree learns conclusions and residuals of all previous trees, and the fitting yields a current residual decision tree. The boosting tree is the accumulation of the regression tree generated by the entire iterative process, the conclusions of all trees are added up to make the final answer. Unlike the gcForest obtains the final prediction by maximizing the aggregated class vector at the last level, SForest employs GBDT as final classifier to obtain the final prediction directly.

3.3   Overall Procedure

Figure 6 summarizes the overall procedure of SForest. There are 4 classes and m samples with 500-dimensional in training data, a sliding window with 100-dimensional will produce m 401×100-dimensional instances. 4 sub-datasets are generated based on the positive and negative samples of each class, and two groups of ensemble forest, each group containing 4 forests, can be trained from corresponding sub-dataset. Finally, two 1,604-dimensional feature vectors will be obtained through two groups of forest as described in Sect. 3.1, and a 3,208-dimensional feature vector is generated by concatenating two 1,604-dimensional feature vectors.

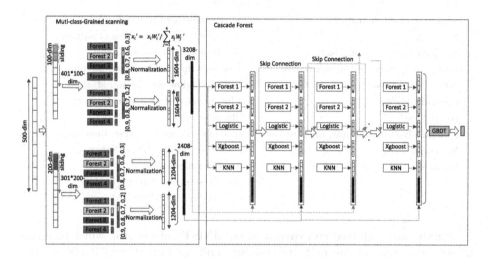

Fig. 6. Overall procedure of SForest.

Similarly, a sliding window with 200-dimensional will generate a 2,208-dimensional feature vector for each original sample. The transformed 3208-dimensional feature vectors will then be used to train the 1st-grade of cascade forest. In the following layer, the transformed feature vectors, augmented with the class vector generated by **the previous layer** and the class vector generated by **the layer before the previous layer**, will then be used to train the cascade forests. Moreover, the top-k features are selected to extract the standard deviation boosting feature in each forest. This procedure will be repeated till convergence of validation performance.

In other words, the final deep forest model is a cascade of cascade forests, where each layer in the cascade consists of multiple classifiers, each corresponding to a grain of scanning, as shown in Fig. 6. Given a test instance, it will go through the multi-class-grained scanning procedure to get its corresponding transformed feature representation, and the representation is put into the cascade forest till the last level. The final prediction will be obtained by GBDT classifier.

4   Experiments

To investigate the effectiveness of SForest, we conducted experiments on some small-scale datasets. In all experiments of this study, we used 5-fold cross-validation to evaluate the overall accuracy of different methods. gcForest and SForest configurations are shown as Table 1. Moreover, the top-5 most important features in completely random forests and random forests were considered in SForest.

Table 1. Summary of hyper-parameters and default setting. Comparison of the SForest and gcForest approaches. (d is the dimension of raw input feature)

gcForest	SForest
Multi-grained scanning:	**Multi-class-grained scanning:**
No. Forest: $\{2\}$	No. Forest: $\{2 * k \mid k$ is class of dataset$\}$
No. Tree in each forest: $\{500\}$	No. Tree in each forest: $\{1000\}$
Tree growth: until all leaves are pure	Tree growth: until all leaves are pure
Sliding window size: $[d/16], [d/8], [d/4]$	Sliding window size: $[d/16], [d/8], [d/4]$
Cascade Forest:	**The improved Cascade Forest:**
Forest type:	Classifier type:
$\{$completely-random forest, random forest$\}$	$\{$completely-random forest, random forest,
No. Forests: $\{8\}$	logistic regression, KNN, Xgboost$\}$
No. Trees in each forest: $\{500\}$	No. Classifiers: $\{5\}$
	No. Trees in each forest: $\{500\}$
	No. neighbors in KNN: $\{5\}$

Firstly, we conducted an experiment on MNIST dataset [16], which contains 60,000 images of size 28 by 28 for training (and validating), and 10,000 images for testing. Here, we chose 2000/250 and 1000/100 (train/test) for validating the availability of SForest respectively. We compared the classification performance of SForest with RF, SVM, the standard gcForest and SForest without multi-class-grained scanning (improved cascade forest) on the dataset.

Table 2. Validating SForest performance on MNIST dataset

Data size	RF	SVM (rbf kernel)	gcForest	Improved cascade forest	SForest
60000/10000	96.80%	98.6%	**99.26%**	98.54%	99.04%
2000/250	93.64%	94.8%	98.03%	97.60%	**98.62%**
1000/100	89.33%	92.4%	96.67%	97.71%	**97.83%**

As shown in Table 2, for original MINIST dataset, the gcForest achieves most high performance. However, for other MINIST sub-datasets, SForest outperforms other methods in overall accuracy prediction. What is interesting about the data in this table is that the improved cascade forest achieves almost performance to gcForest, this means that the improved cascade forest helps improve performance apparently.

4.1 Result of Binary Classification Tasks

The class of the dataset is 2 when the dataset is a binary classification task, thus the number of one group forests in multi-class-grained scanning is 2, which is the same as the number of multi-grained scanning forests in gcForest. Three datasets are selected to explore the classification effectiveness on binary classification tasks. These are two UCI datasets [16]: the Ionosphere dataset with 34 features and 351 samples, Parkinsons with 23 features and 197 samples. Colon [17] with 2000 features and 62 samples. In fairness, in each class of datasets, we use the hierarchical sampling method to extract 4/5 samples for training set, and 1/5 samples for testing data. SDF [3] set the number of trees in each forest is 1000, and set the number of pairs in training set is 1000.

Table 3. Comparison of test accuracy on binary classification datasets

Dataset	RF	gcForest	SDF [3]	Improved cascade forest	SForest
Ionosphere	78.63%	88.54%	89.51%	89.54%	**89.89%**
Parkinsons	75.00%	77.31%	79.03%	**80.47%**	80.30%
Colon	84.60%	91.62%	91.89%	92.13%	**92.76%**

Table 3 presents the classification accuracy of the proposed algorithm and other methods. Observed from Table 3, it can be seen that the improved cascade forest has a powerful classification ability to binary tasks than others on small-scale datasets. SForest has a slight improvement compared with the improved cascade structure. This phenomenon reflects that multi-class-grained scanning has a little effect on the binary classification of small-scale datasets. Compared with gcForest, the number of cascade forest layer in three dataset using SForest increased by (2, 1, 3).

4.2 Result of Multi-class Tasks

Table 4. The configuration of BCDForest.

BCDForest configuration
Multi-class-grained scanning:
No. Forest: $\{2 * k \mid k$ is class of dataset$\}$, No. Tree in each forest: $\{1000\}$
Tree growth: until all leaves are pure, Sliding window size: $[d/16], [d/8], [d/4]$
The improved Cascade Forest:
Classifier type: {completely-random forest, random forest}
No. Classifiers: {8}, No. Trees in each forest: {500}

We will discuss the multi-class tasks in the following content. Four datasets, which have three high-dimensional datasets and one low-dimensional dataset, are selected to analyze the effect of SForest in multi-class tasks. Three high-dimensional datasets come from microarray gene expression datasets [17,18]. Brain has 42 samples with 5597 features, BRCA with 3641 features and 514 samples, PANCANCER with 8026 features and 3594 samples. One low-dimensional Yeast data comes from UCI dataset [16], which contains only 8 features and 1484 samples. BCDForest [10] configuration is shown in Table 4. gcForest and SForest use the default configuration as before, except that the multi-grained scanning and multi-class-scanning are abandoned considering that the low-dimensional features do not hold spacial or sequential relationships in Yeast dataset.

Table 5. Comparison of test accuracy on multi-class datasets

Dataset	RF	gcForest	BCDForest [10]	Improved cascade	SForest
Brain	79.63%	89.25%	96.48%	93.56%	**97.26%**
BRCA	84.58%	88.14%	92.05%	90.32%	**92.93%**
PANCANCER	96.02%	96.51%	97.30%	95.36%	**98.03%**
Yeast	61.66%	63.45%	63.78%	64.63%	None

As shown in Table 5, the SForest achieves comparable or even better predictive accuracy than BCDForest. Interestingly, the SForest has a good effect on low dimensional data. It is evident that when there are small sample size or high-dimension datasets, the multi-class-grained scanning process helps improve performance apparently.

5   Conclusion

This study has shown a variant deep forest approach called SForest which has significant accuracy improvement on the small-scale dataset. We identify two deficiencies of gcForest in dealing with small-scale dataset and then come up with some solutions. On the one hand, instead of manually defining different types of RFs in multi-grained scanning, we employed multi-class-grained scanning strategy to encourage the diversity of ensemble by training multiple binary classifiers using the whole training data. Furthermore, two groups of forest ensemble are used to enhance the feature vector. Meanwhile, we considered the fitting quality of each binary classifier in the feature learning to encourage the accuracy of estimation. On the other hand, we proposed a skip connection strategy to prevent the vanishing of the important features and bursting of the unimportant features. Top-k important features are emphasized to propagate the profiles of discriminative features among cascade layers. Experiments demonstrate that our method achieves good prediction performance compared with other deep forest models. In conclusion, our method provides an option to make predictions using deep learning on small-scale datasets.

References

1. Krizhevsky, A., Sutskever, I., Hinton, G.E.: ImageNet classification with deep convolutional neural networks. In: Advances in Neural Information Processing Systems, pp. 1097–1105 (2012)
2. Hinton, G., et al.: Deep neural networks for acoustic modeling in speech recognition: the shared views of four research groups. IEEE Signal Process. Mag. **29**(6), 82–97 (2012)
3. Utkin, L.V., Ryabinin, M.A.: A siamese deep forest. Knowl. Based Syst. **139**, 13–22 (2018)
4. Dong, M., Yao, L., Wang, X., Benatallah, B., Zhang, S.: GrCAN: gradient boost convolutional autoencoder with neural decision forest. arXiv preprint arXiv:1806.08079 (2018)
5. Hu, G., Peng, X., Yang, Y., Hospedales, T.M., Verbeek, J.: Frankenstein: learning deep face representations using small data. IEEE Trans. Image Process. **27**(1), 293–303 (2018)
6. Chen, M., Shi, X., Zhang, Y., Wu, D., Guizani, M.: Deep features learning for medical image analysis with convolutional autoencoder neural network. IEEE Trans. Big Data (2017)
7. Zhou, Z.H., Jiang, Y.: NeC4.5 neural ensemble based C4.5. IEEE Trans. Knowl. Data Eng. **16**(6), 770–773 (2004)
8. Zhou, Z.H., Feng, J.: Deep forest: towards an alternative to deep neural networks. arXiv preprint arXiv:1702.08835 (2017)
9. Friedman, J.H.: Greedy function approximation: a gradient boosting machine. Ann. Stat., 1189–1232 (2001)
10. Guo, Y., Liu, S., Li, Z., Shang, X.: Towards the classification of cancer subtypes by using cascade deep forest model in gene expression data. In: 2017 IEEE International Conference on Bioinformatics and Biomedicine (BIBM), pp. 1664–1669. IEEE (2017)
11. Martínez-Muñoz, G., Suárez, A.: Out-of-bag estimation of the optimal sample size in bagging. Pattern Recogn. **43**(1), 143–152 (2010)
12. Bylander, T.: Estimating generalization error on two-class datasets using out-of-bag estimates. Mach. Learn. **48**(1–3), 287–297 (2002)
13. Mellor, A., Boukir, S.: Exploring diversity in ensemble classification: applications in large area land cover mapping. ISPRS J. Photogrammetry Remote Sens. **129**, 151–161 (2017)
14. Chen, T., Guestrin, C.: XGBoost: a scalable tree boosting system. In: Proceedings of the 22nd ACM SIGKDD International Conference on Knowledge Discovery and Data Mining, pp. 785–794. ACM (2016)
15. He, K., Zhang, X., Ren, S., Sun, J.: Deep residual learning for image recognition. In: Proceedings of the IEEE Conference on Computer Vision and Pattern Recognition, pp. 770–778 (2016)
16. LeCun, Y., Bottou, L., Bengio, Y., Haffner, P.: Gradient-based learning applied to document recognition. Proc. IEEE **86**(11), 2278–2324 (1998)
17. Maas, A.L., Daly, R.E., Pham, P.T., Huang, D., Ng, A.Y., Potts, C.: Learning word vectors for sentiment analysis. In: Proceedings of the 49th Annual Meeting of the Association for Computational Linguistics: Human Language Technologies-volume 1, pp. 142–150. Association for Computational Linguistics (2011)
18. Díaz-Uriarte, R., De Andres, S.A.: Gene selection and classification of microarray data using random forest. BMC Bioinf. **7**(1), 3 (2006)

A Text Annotation Tool with Pre-annotation Based on Deep Learning

Fei Teng[1]([✉])(iD), Minbo Ma[1], Zheng Ma[1], Lufei Huang[2], Ming Xiao[3], and Xuan Li[2]

[1] School of Information Science and Technology,
Southwest Jiaotong University, Chengdu, China
`fteng@swjtu.edu.cn`
[2] The Third People's Hospital of Chengdu, Chengdu, China
[3] School of Electrical Engineering, KTH Royal Institute of Technology,
Stockholm, Sweden

Abstract. In this paper, we introduce an open-source tool, YEDDA, supported by a pre-annotation module based deep learning. EPAD proposes a novel annotation workflow, combining pre-annotation and manual annotation, which improves the efficiency and quality of annotation. The pre-annotation module can effectively reduce the annotation time, and meanwhile improve the precision and recall of annotation. EPAD also contains some of the mechanisms to facilitate the usage of the pre-annotation module. As a collaborative design, EPAD provides administrators with annotation statistics and analysis functions. Experiments showed that EPAD shortened almost 60.0% of the total annotation time, and improved 12.7% of F-measure for annotation quality.

Keywords: Annotation tool · Deep learning · Pre-annotation

1 Introduction

Information extraction is an important part of the technology of free-text informatization in Natural Language Processing (NLP). At present, supervised learning achieves the state-of-art performance in information extraction. However, supervised learning relies on a large amount of annotated corpus, which requires enormous manual annotation to build. The manual annotation consumes a lot of labor and financial resources so that some annotation tools have been developed, aiming at shortening the annotation time. Another challenge of annotation is that the quality of annotated corpus is not guaranteed due to human error and different annotators understanding of the annotation guideline. But little research focuses on improving the precision and recall of annotation.

Supported by Sichuan Science and Technology Program (No. 2017SZYZF0002).

C. Douligeris et al. (Eds.): KSEM 2019, LNAI 11775, pp. 440–451, 2019.
https://doi.org/10.1007/978-3-030-29551-6_39

Recent works Inforex [1] and YEDDA [2] propose using string matching algorithms for annotation recommendations, however, such recommendations may introduce misconception of annotations. Taking the annotation in the medical text as an example, medical entities with the same character string may belong to different categories, such as that "anemia" can be annotated as disease or symptom, depending on the context. BRAT [3] integrates Conditional Random Field (CRF) [4] algorithm to recommend entity scope and category. However, its performance relies on a lot of manual features which are dedicatedly formulated based on domain knowledge. Therefore, it is important to provide an accurate recommendation without additional manual work, and the recommendation performance can be further improved as the annotation progresses.

In order to address the above problems, we propose the first version of EPAD, a pre-annotated, open-source[1] annotation tool. It provides a pre-annotation collaborative framework, as shown in Fig. 1, which contains administrator client and annotator client. EPAD offers pre-annotation module and analysis module for administrator client. The former performs Named Entity Recognition (NER) [5] based on learning to provides pre-annotated text. The latter statistical analysis module provides the administrator with the progress of annotation and detailed disagreement of paired annotators. For annotator client, EPAD provides a simple and multifunctional Graphical User Interface (GUI), which not only supports normal manual annotation but also prompts the annotator for pre-annotated text. EPAD mainly has two contributions as follows:

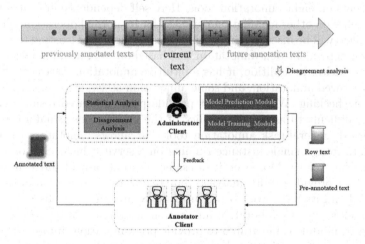

Fig. 1. Framework of EPAD.

* **Deep Learning-Based Pre-annotation:** pre-annotation can provide partially pre-annotated text before manual annotation, and dynamically recommend as long as new entity is manually annotated during the annotation process. EPAD integrates two pre-annotation modules, semantic pre-annotation

---

[1] https://github.com/cloudXia777/EPAD.

(SPA) based on deep learning and character pre-annotation (CPA) based on matching. The efficiency and quality of annotation are improved by pre-annotation, simultaneously. Experiments show that EPAD reduced at least 60% of the annotation time, compared to manual annotation with other annotation tools. Moreover, and the recall and precision of annotation were significantly improved by 18.4% and 4.8%, respectively.

* **Novel Annotation Workflow:** EPAD redefines the annotation workflow, including offline training, pre-annotation, manual annotation, and annotation fusion. The annotators no longer annotate text from scratch, and they can also learn from disagreement analysis to better understand the annotation standards and rules.

The rest of this paper is organized as follows: Sect. 2 reviews previous annotation tools supporting entity annotation. Section 3 introduces the main three features of EPAD. Section 4 describes the framework of the system and the supported modules. Section 5 shows the design and results of comparative experiments. Lastly, Section 6 gives a conclusion of this paper and future work.

2   Related Work

In the field of Natural Language Processing, there exist many text annotation tools for building an corpus. Table 1 shows a high-level overview of the five requirements on eight annotation tools. Here self dependence indicates whether the tool relies on other installation packages for its normal operation. The above requirements will be discussed in detail in the description of existing tools. BRAT [3] is a self-dependent text annotation tool based on web, installing without others dependencies. In addition, it has a intuitive annotation interface which supports structured annotation, and some annotation assistants, e.g. corpus search, constraint checking. While it cannot provide post-annotated result analysis so that it is difficult to assess the quality of the annotations. Anafora [6] is also a web-based, general-task annotation tool that allows annotators to remotely access data from a single instance running on a server which relies on a remote install of Chartreader. Moreover, it can safely annotate any plaintext file, while it also does not provide results analysis. GateTeamware [7] is a collaborative annotation tool and its framework based on Gate [8] and supports distributed annotation module and Collaborative annotation workflows. Moreover, a Machine Learning IE module is integrated to provide pre-annotation. Inforex [1] provides a web-based authorization mechanism to control the access right of annotator to data. It gives a super annotation to transform the input of multiple groups of annotator into the final annotation results. Moreover, the annotation process uses Positive Specific Agreement (PSA) [9] to calculate the disagreements between paired annotators, while EPAD not only supports analysis of inter-annotator disagreements but also statistics of detailed annotation results.

The tools mentioned above are web-based which need to be configured through complex local services, increasing the complexity of annotation. Considering this effect, there are also many non web-based annotation tools. WordFreak

Table 1. Comparison of eight different tools on five requirements

Tool	Non web-based	Self dependence	Analysis	Character PA	Semantic PA
WordFreak	√	√	×	×	×
Knowtator	√	×	√	×	×
BRAT	×	√	×	×	√
Anafora	×	×	×	×	×
GATE Teamware	×	√	×	×	√
Inforex	√	×	√	√	×
YEDDA	√	√	√	√	×
EPAD	√	√	√	√	√

PA is the abbreviation of pre-annotation.

[10] is based on plug-in architecture development which allows components to be embedded. While it cannot support the schema editing, thus unable to migrate annotation effectively. Knowator [11] is also a general-purpose annotation tool which is a plugin in the widely used knowledge representation system Protege [12] and can easily define complex annotation schema. It supports post-annotation analysis by integrating inter-annotator evaluation [13]. While the post-annotated analysis and pre-annotation are not supported. YEDDA [2] is a lightweight annotation tool what reflects in simple annotator interface and matching algorithm. It also has the capability of quality analysis because it supports multiple annotator analysis results and detailed paired annotation reports. However, it needs to merge all the annotations of the same annotator into one annotation file to support the result analysis among different annotators which is unfriendly for the administrator.

As mentioned above, some annotation tools support for shortening annotation time, which is mainly divided into two types. One applies traditional machine learning, such as Hidden Markov Model (HMM) [14] and CRF, to recognize entity from text with contextual statistics before manual annotation. The other applies matching algorithms, such as fuzzy matching and maximum forward matching, to dynamically match the set of annotated entities. EPAD has integrated two pre-annotation modules, one is Bidirectional Long Short-Term Memory-Conditional Random Field (BiLSTM-CRF) model [15] for semantical pre-annotation. The other is based on a maximum forward matching algorithm for character pre-annotation. SPA can pre-annotate before new text is manually annotated then add the predicted entities by the model to the annotated list. On the one hand, it can assists the annotator to complete part of the annotation in advance, reducing the annotation workload. On the other hand, it can recommend annotator for multi-category entities, increasing the attention of annotator to the type of entity. CPA can prompt newly annotated entities without being recommended by SPA for annotator as a supplement.

Compared with these annotation tools, EPAD provides an independent, analyzable text annotation tool with system recommendations by pre-annotation based on deep learning. In addition, it supports analyzing inter-annotator disagreement and generating a text report.

3   Features

3.1   User-Friendly Visualization

Visualization of Annotated Entity Source. The annotated entities include SPA predicted entities, CPA matching entities, and manually annotated entities. EPAD provides clear entity visualization for annotators to distinguish entities from different sources effectively. As shown in Fig. 2, the pre-annotation entities, and combined entities are shown, purple represents the SPA recommended entities, pink represents the CPA matching entities, and green represents the manually annotated entities. Through color tagging, annotators can obviously distinguish entities from plain text. The annotator can also double-click the annotated entity to make it highlighted in the text, which can quickly locate the entity. It is convenient to annotate the entity better according to its context.

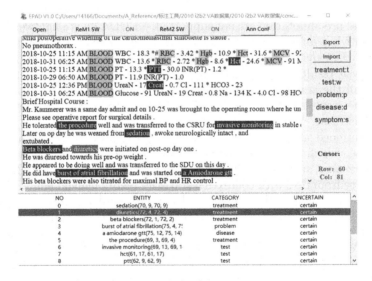

Fig. 2. Annotator interface of EPAD. The sample data is part of the 2010 I2B2 dataset and contains five concepts: treatment, test, problem, disease, symptom. (https://www.i2b2.org/NLP/DataSets/Main.php)

Convenient Configuration. The schema (entity category) of different annotation task is different, so it needs to be flexibly edited according to cognition. However, previous annotation tools are not convenient to configure by modifying the configuration file. EPAD provides a visual schema editing module to modify the schema. Instead of requiring the annotator or administrator to tediously read and write the configuration file, it writes the modified value to the configuration file through the visualization operation, directly. EPAD also offers annotators visual configuration for other modules. For example, a visual shortcut key modification for conveniently setting the shortcut key according to their habits.

3.2   Pre-annotation

Character Pre-annotation. The "blood" shown in Fig. 2, the same entity may appear multiple times, which increase the annotator unnecessary workload. CPA addresses the situation by using a dictionary and character string matching algorithm. CPA dynamically adds the annotated entities to a dictionary, then uses the established dictionary to match the subsequent texts in real time based on maximum forward matching algorithm. CPA can only get entities from the character string level, unable to resolve multi-category entity. So that EPAD merely prompts entities obtained by CPA module for annotator.

Semantic Pre-annotation. Different from CPA, SPA can recommend entities more precise, because deep learning model can learn semantic representation from training data. Therefore it can recognize entity with multi-category as long as which exist in the training data. So entities obtained by SPA are added directly to the annotated entity list before manual annotation. Even if SPA predicts incorrectly on some entities, it still can remind annotator to pay more attention to these entities. Because on the one hand, these entities have complex semantics so that the model cannot predict correctly. On the other hand, it shows that the model is not good enough on these entities and needs to be better optimized, which can assist the administrator to determine the time for retraining model. Furthermore, we evaluate the effect of pre-annotation from two aspects: annotation efficiency and annotation quality. See Sect. 5 for a detailed introduction.

3.3   Novel Annotation Workflow

EPAD proposes a novel annotation schema for pre-annotation. As shown in Fig. 3, the middle part is the pre-annotation process. An initial deep neural network model is trained when the cumulative amount of manual annotations is larger than the set threshold (Depending on different annotated texts and different deep neural network settings). In the next annotation process, manual annotation can be carried out based on the predicted text of the model. When the number of annotated texts is greater than a threshold again, the model can be trained again. The annotation workflow forms an iterative annotation process, which provides a systematic solution for pre-annotation not only limiting entity annotation.

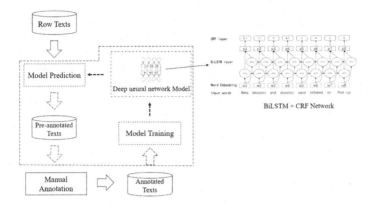

Fig. 3. Novel annotation workflow.

3.4 Pluggable and Updatable Model

EPAD has designed two mechanisms to better support pre-annotation. The SPA module is designed as a pluggable interface to facilitate the use of the state-of-art model. Incremental training is also applied to model training, which loads the model weights from the previous training directly and trains on the new annotation data, saving computer power and training time for historical training data.

4 EPAD

The front end of EPAD is based on the Tkinter module of python standard Tk GUI toolkit[2], which is characterized by the ability to run under any system with the python environment. Pre-annotation of EPAD integrates an NER module based on deep learning, which is programmed by kears library[3]. Moreover, it is a collaborative tool including annotator client and administrator client, which are introduced in detail, respectively.

4.1 Annotator Client

In this part, Fig. 2 shows the annotator interface for the entity annotation task based on clinical records. In the middle of the interface is text annotation area. The right of the text annotated area is the basic annotated control button. The list below the textual area is to display the annotated entities, which can be added, deleted, and modified by annotators.

Annotator client integrates multiple modules to improve annotation efficiency. EPAD simplifies annotation action, and using shortcut key annotation can effectively shorten the time required to select a category. The schema editing

---

[2] https://docs.python.org/3.6/library/tkinter.html.

[3] https://keras.io/.

module makes it easy for users to modify the entity category, which facilitates the migration of annotations from different domains. The followings introduce in more detail.

Shortcut Annotation. EPAD also provides both shortcut annotation and normal annotation. Shortcut annotation refers to mapping a selected textual scope to a specific category by pressing the specified key. It simplifies the process of entity annotating. Annotators only need to select the text then press the key to complete the annotation, moreover, the shortcut map can be modified by visual editing module. Annotators also can delete the annotated entity using shortcut key "Ctrl+q" and withdraw action by shortcut key "Ctrl+z".

Schema and Shortcut Editing Module. Schema and shortcut editing module supports visual modification of the schema configuration and shortcut map. Through the "Ann ConF" button, the annotator can easily make a modification to meet the needs of annotation entities in different domains.

4.2 Administrator Client

Annotation often needs multiple annotators to work together, which requires the administrator to supervise and manage the entire work process. Therefore, the administrator needs the ability to manage the pre-annotation module, evaluate the quality of annotations and the differences among annotators. EPAD provides several toolkits for administrator managing and supervising annotation process.

Model Training and Prediction. EPAD designs pre-annotation module as pluggable, which makes it easy to embed new state-of-art model. EPAD provides administrator with visual model training and model prediction, including model hyperparameters and hardware support configuration. Administrators can put the newly annotated data into the specified path for incremental training of the model. Considering the consumption of machine resources required to load the deep learning model, the prediction module does not use the way of real-time prediction to annotate text. When the model is updated, the module can be used to predict the text to be annotated, and the prediction results are distributed to each annotator.

Statistics and Disagreement Analysis. The Statistical Analysis (SA) module provides a multi-annotator statistical analysis matrix to statistics annotations among different annotators. EPAD also provides a disagreement analysis module based on inter-annotator disagreement to evaluate the difference between annotators in some situations. Situations include that both of annotation label (entity category) and position indices match completely, annotation labels do not match, but the position indices coincide, the annotation label is same but has the same end index and a different start index. As shown in Fig. 4, these analysis results are presented to the annotator in the form of text.

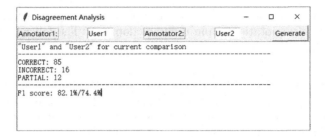

Fig. 4. Disagreement analysis.

5   Experiments

We conducted two small-scale comparative experiments to evaluate the annotation efficiency and quality of EPAD. Considering the experimental impact of language handicap, we adopt Chinese text for experimental annotation. The texts to be annotated are stratified sampling of 10 documents with overall similarity[4] from 300 Chinese documents provided by the CCKS[5] electronic medical record named entity recognition task. In addition, we select 200 documents as a training set for training deep learning model, 90 as a validation set and the F-measure achieved 85.7% on the validation set. Then we randomly extracted 7 documents to familiarize annotator with annotation tools. Three undergraduates are chosen to perform all annotations and to avoid individual differences among annotators, the inter-annotator agreements with each other was closed around at 95%.

5.1   Annotation Efficiency

In the experiment of evaluating the annotation efficiency, we measure the efficiency by annotation time. The experiment evaluates remaining three documents. We divide the experiment into two groups. One is to compare the annotation efficiency of EPAD without pre-annotation module, the other is to compare the performance of EPAD with different pre-annotation module.

Figure 5 shows the annotation time in seconds of contrast experiment between two groups in three documents. In experiment of without pre-annotation, EPAD and YEDDA achieve similar annotation time, because EPAD uses the same shortcut annotation as YEDDA. With the help of character pre-annotation, the annotation time can be reduced by 13.9% compared with without pre-annotation. With semantic pre-annotation, the annotation time can be reduced by 34.9%. One reason for this improvement is that EPAD directly adds the SPA entities to the annotated entity, which saves a long operation time. On the other

---

[4] On average, there are 24 sentences per document, 100 characters per sentence and 5 entities per sentence.

[5] https://biendata.com/competition/CCKS2018_1/.

hand, the entity distribution of the annotated documents is relatively tight then easy to be ignored. And there are some entities with misconception, which require more time to judge. This also proves that the EPAD with SPA can improve the annotation efficiency in complex entity text. In all, In the same annotation time, the annotated entities can be increased by 60% with the pre-annotation module.

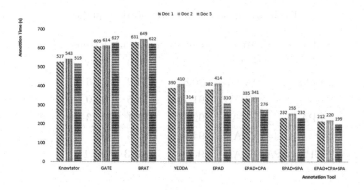

Fig. 5. Annotation time in seconds comparison.

5.2   Annotation Quality

In the experiment of evaluating the annotation quality, we use F1-measure as the evaluation criterion. F1-measure is the harmonic mean of accuracy and recall. The specific calculation formula is as follows:

$$prescision = \frac{TP}{TP + FP} \tag{1}$$

$$recall = \frac{TP}{TP + FN} \tag{2}$$

$$F1 - measure = \frac{2 \times prescision \times recall}{prescision + recall} \tag{3}$$

Among them, TP denotes the number of entities, which is annotated as an entity and matches the value of actual class exactly; FP denotes the number of entities, which is annotated as an entity but does not match the value of actual class; FN denotes the number of entities, which is not annotated as an entity but it is.

We use the revised labels for competition official data as the global standard and divide the experiment into four parts, purely manual, annotation with CPA, annotation with SPA and annotation with both CPA and SPA. Table 2 shows the evaluation results. From the table, we can observe that EPAD with full pre-annotation is the best performance which can improve F-measure by 12.7% than annotation with purely manual. Comparing character pre-annotation, semantic pre-annotation has a significant improvement in recall, an increase of 13.1%, which is attributed to the good performance of the deep neural network in entity recognition. And Compared with BRAT, EPAD with SPA has improved in both precision and recall, indicating that BiLSTM+CRF deep learning model performs better than traditional machine learning CRF. After our detailed analysis of the annotation results, we mainly focus on the improvement of recall of duplicate entities and multi-category entities, which shows that pre-annotation can improve the annotation quality in complex semantic text.

Table 2. Comparison of annotation quality

Mode	Tool	Precision	Recall	F1-measure
No PA	EPAD	90.3	70.9	79.4
CPA	YEDDA	90.8	74.2	81.6
	EPAD	91.2	74.5	82.0
SPA	BRAT	92.3	81.1	86.3
	EPAD	94.7	87.6	91
CPA+SPA	EPAD	**95.1**	**89.3**	**92.1**

6 Conclusion and Future Work

We have introduced a comprehensive entity annotation tool, EPAD, with pre-annotation based on deep neural network. In order to further improve the quality of annotation, we are going to integrate a multi-role annotation mechanism to more effectively annotate.

References

1. Marcińczuk, M., Oleksy, M., Kocoń, J.: Inforex-a collaborative system for text corpora annotation and analysis. In: Proceedings of the International Conference Recent Advances in Natural Language Processing, RANLP. INCOMA Shoumen, pp. 473–482 (2017)
2. Yang, J., Zhang, Y., Li, L., Li, X.: YEDDA: a lightweight collaborative text span annotation tool, arXiv preprint arXiv:1711.03759 (2017)
3. Stenetorp, P., Pyysalo, S., Topić, G., Ohta, T., Ananiadou, S., Tsujii, J.: BRAT: a web-based tool for NLP-assisted text annotation. In: Proceedings of the Demonstrations at the 13th Conference of the European Chapter of the Association for Computational Linguistics, pp. 102–107. Association for Computational Linguistics (2012)
4. Yu, X., Lam, W., Chan, S.-K., Wu, Y.K., Chen, B.: Chinese NER using CRFs and logic for the fourth SIGHAN bakeoff. In: Proceedings of the Sixth SIGHAN Workshop on Chinese Language Processing (2008)
5. Grishman, R., Sundheim, B.: Message understanding conference-6: a brief history. In: COLING 1996 Volume 1: The 16th International Conference on Computational Linguistics, vol. 1 (1996)
6. Chen, W.-T., Styler, W.: Anafora: a web-based general purpose annotation tool. In: Proceedings of the Conference. Association for Computational Linguistics. North American Chapter. Meeting, vol. 2013, p. 14. NIH Public Access (2013)

7. Bontcheva, K., et al.: Gate teamware: a web-based, collaborative text annotation framework. Lang. Res. Eval. **47**(4), 1007–1029 (2013)
8. Cunningham, H., Maynard, D., Bontcheva, K., Tablan, V.: GATE: an architecture for development of robust HLT applications. In: Proceedings of the 40th Annual Meeting on Association for Computational Linguistics, pp. 168–175. Association for Computational Linguistics (2002)
9. Hripcsak, G., Rothschild, A.S.: Agreement, the f-measure, and reliability in information retrieval. J. Am. Med. Inform. Assoc. **12**(3), 296–298 (2005)
10. Morton, T., LaCivita, J.: WordFreak: an open tool for linguistic annotation. In: Proceedings of the 2003 Conference of the North American Chapter of the Association for Computational Linguistics on Human Language Technology: Demonstrations-Volume 4, pp. 17–18. Association for Computational Linguistics (2003)
11. Ogren, P.V.: Knowtator: a protégé plug-in for annotated corpus construction. In: Proceedings of the 2006 Conference of the North American Chapter of the Association for Computational Linguistics on Human Language Technology: Companion Volume: Demonstrations, pp. 273–275. Association for Computational Linguistics (2006)
12. Noy, N.F., et al.: Protégé-2000: an open-source ontology-development and knowledge-acquisition environment. In: AMIA... Annual Symposium Proceedings. AMIA Symposium, vol. 2003, p. 953. American Medical Informatics Association (2003)
13. Alonso, H.M., Johannsen, A., Plank, B.: Supersense tagging with inter-annotator disagreement. In: Linguistic Annotation Workshop 2016, pp. 43–48 (2016)
14. Saito, K., Nagata, M.: Multi-language named-entity recognition system based on HMM. In: Proceedings of the ACL 2003 Workshop on Multilingual and Mixed-Language Named Entity Recognition-Volume 15, pp. 41–48. Association for Computational Linguistics (2003)
15. Huang, Z., Xu, W., Yu, K.: Bidirectional LSTM-CRF models for sequence tagging. arXiv preprint arXiv:1508.01991 (2015)

Object Detection by Combining Deep Dilated Convolutions Network and Light-Weight Network

Yu Quan, Zhixin Li[✉], and Canlong Zhang

Guangxi Key Lab of Multi-source Information Mining and Security,
Guangxi Normal University, Guilin 541004, China
lizx@gxnu.edu.cn

Abstract. In recent years, the performance of object detection algorithm has been improved continuously, and it has become an important direction in the field of computer vision. All the work in this paper will be based on a two-stage object detection algorithm. First, the dilated convolution network is added to the backbone network to form the Deep_Dilated Convolution Network (D_dNet), which improves the resolution of the feature map and the size of the receptive field. In addition, in order to obtain higher accuracy, the feature map of pretraining is compressed and a light-weight network is established. Finally, to further optimize the proposed two network models, this paper introduces the transfer learning into the pretraining. The whole experiment is evaluated based on MSCOCO dataset. Experiments show that the accuracy of the proposed model is improved by 1.3 to 2.2% points.

Keywords: Object detection · Deep dilated convolution network · Light-weight network · Transfer learning · Convolutional neural network

1 Introduction

With the research of unstructured visual data, object detection algorithm has become a classic subject in the field of image processing and computer vision. This paper is mainly based on deep learning [5]. In addition, this method gradually realizes the end-to-end object recognition and detection network from the initial R-CNN [6], Fast R-CNN [7] to the later Faster R-CNN [18], R-FCN [3], Mask R-CNN [8]. They can deal with the diversity change well, and the training and testing efficiency of the network has been greatly improved. This makes the computer vision have much room for improvement in object detection, instance segmentation and object tracking.

To further improve the accuracy and speed of object detection. Taking Mask R-CNN [8] as the research background, this paper improves the network framework from two parts: the process of generating feature maps in the backbone network part and the process of identifying candidate areas in the head network part.

© Springer Nature Switzerland AG 2019
C. Douligeris et al. (Eds.): KSEM 2019, LNAI 11775, pp. 452–463, 2019.
https://doi.org/10.1007/978-3-030-29551-6_40

Structural improvement of backbone network: This paper adds the structure of the dilated convolution network [9] while retaining the partial residual network (ResNet) [9] layer. In this way, the stability of network performance is guaranteed, and the number of network parameters is reduced by 17 times. In addition, to further obtain better semantic features, this paper adds an improved spatial feature pyramid network (FPN) [12] after convolution operation to further improve the performance of object detection and instance segmentation [24].

Head Network Structure Processing: In order to change the time-consuming and computational normality of the fully convolutional layer (FC layer), this paper compresses the classification of feature map into 10 categories (MSCOCO [2,22] datasets have 80 classifications), and changes the FC layer for classification and regression operation into single layer operation.

In this paper, a series of comparative experiments on MSCOCO datasets are carried out. The experimental results of backbone network structure improvement are improved by 1.9% and head network improvement by 1.4%. To further optimize the network model, this paper adds the transfer learning method, which improves the accuracy of the whole network model by up to 2.5%. The overall network framework of this article is shown as Fig. 1.

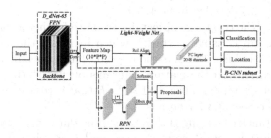

Fig. 1. D_dNet R-CNN network structure diagram

2   Related Works

In recent years, All the improvements in this paper are also two-stage object detection methods based on in-depth learning, and have achieved better results on the basis of predecessors [1,3,6–8].

Firstly, RBG [6] proposed the R-CNN network framework, which provides a new way of thinking for object detection. From then on, the deep learning method has been brought into the field of object detection. Then, Ross Girshick [7] introduced Fast R-CNN network structure, which improved the problems of long training time, large memory consumption and high complexity of R-CNN. At the end of 2017, He et al. [8] proposed Mask R-CNN network structure, and realized the instance segmentation [13] and key point detection [4,19]. In short, the implementation of Mask R-CNN algorithm is to add FCN to Faster R-CNN to generate corresponding object mask [8].

Inspired by the above related papers, this paper proposes a deep dilated convolution network and a light-weight network model. First, our basic network integrates ResNet network and dilated convolution network, which can not only avoid the problem of deep network degradation, but also reduce the number of parameters. Second, to further improve the speed of classification and regression, we compress the feature map by mapping, and reduce the number of fully connected layers and the number of operations in the process of classification and regression operation. In this paper, we obtain better results within acceptable error range.

3   Models Description

3.1   Overview

In the design of backbone network, according to the decreasing rule of feature map size, trunk network usually has five stages (p1–p5). In addition, it is known that the FPN network contains p6, while RetinaNet contains p6 and p7 (p6 and p7 have no pretraining) [11]. Even if we add the shallow to the deeper semantics, most of the semantic information will be lost. To address this issue, two additional phases (p6 participation is in pretraining) have been added to the trunk network, as detailed in Sect. 3.2.

As we all know, the two-stage object detection to further achieve higher accuracy, the head design is usually "thick", which increases the calculation of the whole network and reduces the detection speed. This paper maps and performs compression operations on the feature diagrams output in the pretraining (the MSCOCO dataset's sample is always $81 \times P \times P$ that is compressed to $10 \times P \times P$ or $5 \times P \times P$). See Sect. 3.3 for details.

In addition, transfer learning [17] can solve the data embarrassment problem well. And convolution neural network has good hierarchy. With the increase of network layer and the detection of image features, the more common the features detected by deep convolutional neural network are, the better the effect of transfer learning is. So we add the transfer learning method to the pretraining of the network. See Sect. 3.4 for details.

3.2   Deep Dilated Convolutional Neural Network

Firstly, the first four stages of Resnet-50 (1, 2, 3, 4) are still retained in the design of backbone network in this paper. The first stage passes $7 \times 7 \times 64$ convolution operation, batch normalization (BN), activation function (Rectified Linear Unit, ReLU) and maximum pooling layer (Max pooling layer). This ensures that the input image is only 1/4 of the original image after passing through stage 1, thus ensuring a sufficiently large receptive field. However, considering that the feature map obtained in the first stage is large, the corresponding time is also large. Therefore, this paper still follows the practice of the Mask R-CNN: in the first stage, we only participated in the pretraining stage. In addition, each large layer in stages 2–4 is superimposed by the same repeat convolutional layer of remaining modules 1×1, 3×3 and 1×1.

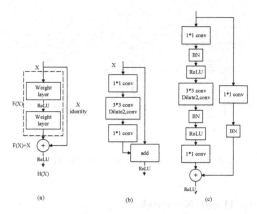

Fig. 2. Core module comparison diagram. (a) ResNet residual module, (b) DetNet core module, (c) D_dNet core module.

In stage 5–6, this paper absorbs the idea of DetNet network design [14], changes the traditional residual convolutional module operation, and increases the bottleneck network structure of dilated convolution network [21], in Fig. 2. Firstly, the size of the feature map of these two stages is consistent, which is 1/16 of the original feature map and better than the resolution and receptive field effect of the original ResNet-50 network. Second, the first layer of stage 5–6 consists of two branches: main path and bypass. On the main road, the three convolution layers of 1×1, 3×3, and 1×1 are used as basic modules. Then, a processing operation of a batch normalization and activation function is respectively added between the convolution layers. Since the input first passes through the 1×1 convolution kernel, the feature map size is not changed, then the batch normalization and activation function processing operations are performed, and then the 3×3 convolution layer is entered. Since padding $= 1$ is set here, it does not change. Enter the size of the feature map so that the size of the feature map remains the same on the main road. On the bypass, in order to ensure that the input feature map can be added to the feature map output on the main road, a $1 \times 1 \times 256$ convolution operation is set on the bypass. The second and third layers in the two stages of stage 5–6 continue to use the residual module. In addition, it is found through analysis that directly outputting a 256-dimensional layer first passes through a $1 \times 1 \times 64$ convolution layer, then passes through a $3 \times 3 \times 64$ convolution layer, and finally passes through a $1 \times 1 \times 256$ convolution layer. The output is 256 dimensions, and the parameter quantity is reduced by 1/9. Therefore, increasing the depth expansion convolution network module reduces the pressure on the amount of computation and memory requirements to a certain extent. The complete pretraining model is shown as Fig. 3.

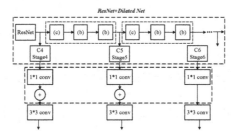

Fig. 3. D_dNet backbone network structure.

3.3   Light-Weight Head Network

This paper analyses two decisive factors affecting the complexity of head network [15]. One is that the feature map after pooling treatment is thicker and the other is that the fully connected layer is too thick. we try to compress the output feature map of pooling operation from $81 \times P \times P$ to $10 \times P \times P$ (based on MSCOCO dataset) in the framework of Mask R-CNN object detection, which is equivalent to compress more than 3900 channels to 490 channels. Then, this paper adds an 81-class fully connected layer before the classification and regression operations, and make the classification and regression operations all pass through a fully connected layer. Although the accuracy may be somewhat compromised, the design of head network structure within acceptable range is shown in Fig. 4.

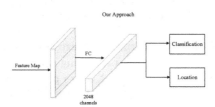

Fig. 4. Light-weight network structure diagram.

3.4   Training Model Based on Transfer Learning

This paper attempts to further optimize the first two models by adding a transfer learning method and finds that the knowledge learned by convolutional neural network is actually the weight parameters obtained through pretraining, so the essence of transfer learning in this paper is the weight transfer. In addition, studies in literature [16,23] have proved that knowledge movement among convolutional neural networks does not need to have strong semantic correlation. The definition of the source and target tasks loaded into the model training by transfer learning is as follows:

$$D_S = \{(X_S^{(n)}), y_S(n)\}_{n-1}^N \sim p_S(X, y), \tag{1}$$

$$D_T = \{X_T^{(m)}\}_{m=1}^M \sim p_T(X, y) \tag{2}$$

the two formulas are the training data of the source task and the target task respectively. In this paper, the mapping function $g(X, \theta_g)$ is firstly used to map the input X of the training samples in the two tasks to the feature space, and the parameter θ_g is optimized to minimize the difference in the input distribution of the mapped two tasks, so as to obtain the minimum loss and the optimal training results.

This paper modifies the number of output layer neurons according to the object task, and randomly initialize the weights of all connected layer neurons. At the same time, this paper initializes the parameters of other network layers using the weights that are obtained from the pre-training of MSCOCO datasets. Finally, this paper trains the whole network with the target task training set and get the final model. The whole process is shown in Fig. 5.

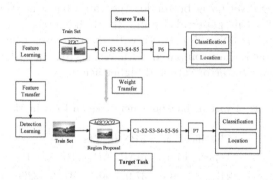

Fig. 5. Schematic diagram of the transfer learning process

4   Analysis of Experimental Results

4.1   Datasets and Evaluation Indicators

Dataset Description: This article chooses to use the extensive MSCOCO dataset, which has 80 categories in the direction of object detection. There are 80k images in the training set, 40k images in the test set and 40k images in the verification set. In addition, we combine the 80k training set with the 35k verification set and divide them into the 115k training set and the 5K small verification set. Here this paper uses the standard MSCOCO dataset indicators to evaluate the experiment. It mainly includes average precision (AP), average recall (AR) and variant criteria of different indicators.

Partial Parameter Settings: The GPU1080 configuration is selected in this paper. Due to the limitation of the processor, each GPU can only process one image at a time, and each image will set 2000 training regions of interest and 1000 test regions of interest. The learning rate is set to 0.01. The image input is still 1024×1024 size, but in a spatial pyramid operation the input size is 256×256 size feature map. The size of the pooling layer is set to 7.

Experimental evaluation criteria: This paper aims to obtain more persuasive evidence. Firstly, this paper validates and compares the proposed model and method. Then, this paper does a global comparative experiment, that is, this paper adds the transfer learning method to the two improved network models. The experimental analysis and results are as follows.

4.2 Deep Dilated Convolutional Neural Network Experiment

Experiment 1: In order to further verify the effectiveness of the proposed D_dnet-65 network in the feature space pyramid structure, the D_dNet-65 network is compared with the ResNet-50, ResNet-101, Mask R-CNN-50, Mask R-CNN-101 and DetNet networks. The specific results are shown in Table 1. The error rate of D_dNet-65 network is 23.8%, and the corresponding complexity reaches 5.2G. First of all, compared with ResNet-50 and Mask R-CNN-50, we found that the accuracy of the D_dNet-65 is better for the same basic network (up to 1.7% in mAP). Secondly, this paper also wants to further verify the effectiveness of the structure of the D_dNet-65 network with the increase of parameters. It can be seen from Table 1 that compared with resnet-101 and Mask R-CNN-101, D_dNet-65 has lower bit error rate and higher accuracy.

Table 1. Effects of various backbone networks on FPN in MSCOCO (%).

Backbone	Classification		FPN results					
	Toperr	FLops	mAP	AP_{50}	AP_{75}	AP_s	AP_m	AP_l
ResNet-50	24.1	3.8G	37.9	60.0	41.2	22.9	40.6	49.2
ResNet-101	23.0	7.6G	39.8	62.0	43.5	24.1	43.4	51.7
Mask R-CNN-50	**23.9**	**4.3G**	**37.8**	**60.2**	**41.5**	**20.1**	**41.1**	**50.4**
Mask R-CNN-101	23.6	4.6G	38.7	61.1	42.8	22.4	42.5	51.6
DetNet-59	23.5	4.8G	40.2	61.7	43.7	23.9	43.2	52.0
D_dNet-65	**23.8**	**5.2G**	**39.5**	**61.2**	**43.2**	**22.6**	**42.7**	**51.9**

Experiment 2: In this paper, in order to further verify the effectiveness of D_dNet-65 network, this paper takes Mask R-CNN network structure as the basic model, and only change its backbone network structure. Then, this paper compares their effects on border regression to prove the performance of the D_dnet-65. From Table 2, there is a slight gap between D_dNet-65 and the latest DetNet networking approach. However, the proposed the D_dNet-65 network structure can improve the performance of Mask R-CNN, even by 1.3 to 2.2% points.

Experiment 3: On backbone network, we consider the difference between the D_dNet-65 network and the Mask R-CNN network. Table 3 shows the comparison experiments of four kinds of backbone network from zero training FPN. We

Table 2. Effect of various backbone networks on border regression on MSCOCO (%).

Models	Backbone	Bounding box AP					
		mAP	AP_{50}	AP_{75}	AP_s	AP_m	AP_l
Mask R-CNN-50	ResNet-50-FPN	**39.1**	**61.7**	**42.9**	**21.3**	**42.3**	**50.7**
Mask R-CNN-101	ResNet-101-FPN	38.2	60.3	41.7	20.1	41.1	50.2
Mask R-CNN	DetNet-59-FPN	40.7	62.5	44.1	24.6	43.9	52.2
ask R-CNN	D_dNet-65-FPN	**40.4**	**62.1**	**43.5**	**22.7**	**42.8**	**52.0**

find that the D_dNet-65 network model proposed in this paper has good accuracy. Next, this paper wants to experiment further with the effectiveness of the D_dNet-65 network for different size objects.

Table 3. Results of zero-training of FPN network on MSCOCO (%).

Backbone	mAP	AP_{50}	AP_{75}	AP_s	AP_m	AP_l
ResNet-50	34.5	55.2	37.7	20.4	36.7	44.5
Mask R-CNN-50	**34.9**	**56.1**	**38.4**	**21.3**	**37.4**	**45.1**
DetNet-59	36.3	56.5	39.3	22.0	38.4	46.9
D_dNet-65	**35.6**	**56.3**	**38.9**	**21.7**	**38.1**	**46.4**

4.3 Light-Weight Head Network Experiment

Experiment 4: In order to verify the validity of the light-weight network model, we will do a series of comparative experiments on MSCOCO's small dataset. In this paper, it embeds the improved light-weight network into R-FCN, Mask R-CNN-50, D_dNet-65 and so on. In Table 4, the experimental effect of Mask R-CNN-50 was 1.8% lower than our own model. Although our results are slightly worse than those of Light-Head R-CNN, the computational speed is improved with the accuracy guaranteed. In addition, the regression loss of this paper is obviously smaller than the classified loss.

Table 4. Results of various models based on Light-weight network on MSCOCO (%).

Models	mAP	AP_s	AP_m	AP_l
R-FCN	33.1	18.8	36.9	48.1
Mask R-CNN-50	**37.9**	**21.1**	**40.5**	**51.2**
Light-Head R-CNN	41.5	25.2	45.3	53.1
D_dNet-65 R-CNN	**39.7**	**22.3**	**42.7**	**52.6**

4.4   Experiment Based on Transfer Learning Method

Experiment 5: In order to verify the effectiveness of the transfer learning method, we add the transfer learning method to the ResNet (50, 100) and the Mask R-CNN (50, 100) networks and the D_dNet-65 R-CNN networks respectively, and verify the trained model with verification set (the verification set is 5k small verification sets separated from MSCOCO dataset).

In Table 5, this paper finds that the training accuracy and object detection performance of the network with the transfer learning method are very good. The improved Mask R-CNN-50 was increased by 1% point compared with the original experimental results in [8], and our D_dNet-65 R-CNN experimental results were 1.2% higher than the Mask R-CNN-50. In addition, this paper can fine-tune the parameters of convolution layer in the training process, so as to better improve the performance of the model.

Table 5. Multiple model training results based on transfer learning (%).

Models	Training accuracy	Performance test
ResNet-50	94.9	-
ResNet-101	94.7	-
Mask R-CNN-50	**95.1**	**39.3**
Mask R-CNN-101	95.3	39.1
D_bNet-65 R-CNN	**96.3**	**39.7**

5   Analysis of Results

Here this paper will analyze the comparison experiment of the D_dNet-65 R-CNN network model in detail. Our experiment is divided into four stages. In the first stage, this paper validates the influence of network structure on FPN and border regression respectively. In order to further validate the performance of the D_dNet-65 network structure, we do experiments on the Mask R-CNN (50, 101). The results show that adding the D_dNet-65 network can effectively improve the instance segmentation performance of the Mask R-CNN (50, 101). In the second phase, in order to verify the effectiveness of light-weight network, comparative experiments were carried out on ResNet (50,100), Mask R-CNN, D_dNet-65 and so on. In the third stage, this paper adds the proposed transfer learning method into the pretraining of several models for experimental analysis. In the fourth phase, as shown in Fig. 6, we do a comparative experiment on the whole network structure. In this paper, two models and transfer learning methods are embedded in the network of the graph and validated on MSCOCO dataset. Compared with the polygonal line of the inverted triangle, the polygonal line of the positive triangle tends to approach gradually with the increase of training time. Although inverted triangles do not work as well as regular triangles, the accuracy is much improved. Generally speaking, the method proposed in this paper has achieved good results in performance and speed.

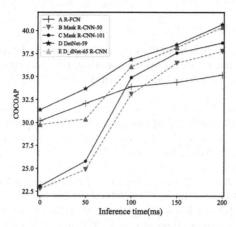

Fig. 6. Comparison of various models on MSCOCO

6   Conclusions

This paper presents a D_dNet-65 R-CNN model based on a two-stage object detection method. The model is based on MSCOCO dataset and consists of backbone network, head network and new transfer learning method. Firstly, based on the backbone network, a deep dilated convolution network is proposed. On the one hand, it can ensure the resolution of the feature map and the size of the receptive field, on the other hand, it can further reduce the number of parameters in the network. In addition, the "thickness" of the head network is reduced by compressing the feature map according to the characteristics of one-stage object detection, so that the training speed of the head network can be improved on the premise of guaranteeing the accuracy. Finally, to further optimize the model, transfer learning method is used to train the model. Through the comparative analysis of several experiments, both single training and comprehensive experiments, have achieved good results.

In addition to the proposed improved method and experimental verification, this paper also considers the next step of work. First of all, from the experimental direction, in addition to the possibility of adding multiple datasets for comparative experiments, it can also further study the effect of multi-scale images. Second, from the research direction, it can transfer the proposed object detection framework to the direction of instance segmentation and key point detection.

Acknowledgments. This work is supported by the National Natural Science Foundation of China (Nos. 61663004, 61762078, 61866004), the Guangxi Natural Science Foundation (Nos. 2016GXNSFAA380146, 2017GXNSFAA198365, 2018GXNSFDA281009), the Research Fund of Guangxi Key Lab of Multi-source Information Mining and Security (16-A-03-02, MIMS18-08), the Guangxi Special Project of Science and Technology Base and Talents (AD16380008), Innovation Project of Guangxi Graduate Education (XYCSZ2019068) and the Guangxi "Bagui Scholar" Teams for Innovation and Research Project.

References

1. Anderson, P., He, X., Buehler, C., et al.: Bottom-up and top-down attention for image captioning and visual question answering, In: Proceedings of the IEEE Conference on Computer Vision and Pattern Recognition (CVPR), pp. 6077–6086 (2018)
2. Chen, X., Fang, H., Lin, T.Y., et al.: Microsoft COCO captions: data collection and evaluation server. arXiv preprint arXiv:1504.00325 (2015)
3. Dai, J., Li, Y., He, K., et al.: R-FCN: object detection via region-based fully convolutional networks. In: Advances in Neural Information Processing Systems (NIPS), pp. 379–387 (2016)
4. Deng, Z., Li, K., Zhao, Q., et al.: Effective face landmark localization via single deep network. arXiv preprint arXiv:1702.02719 (2017)
5. Erhan, D., Szegedy, C., Toshev, A., et al.: Scalable object detection using deep neural networks. In: Proceedings of the IEEE Conference on Computer Vision and Pattern Recognition (CVPR), pp. 2147–2154 (2014)
6. Girshick, R., Donahue, J., Darrell, T., et al.: Rich feature hierarchies for accurate object detection and semantic segmentation. In: Proceedings of the IEEE Conference on Computer Vision and Pattern Recognition (CVPR), pp. 580–587 (2014)
7. Girshick, R.: Fast R-CNN. In: Proceedings of the IEEE International Conference on Computer Vision, pp. 1440–1448 (2015)
8. He, K., Gkioxari, G., Dollár, P., et al.: Mask R-CNN. In: Proceedings of IEEE International Conference on Computer Vision (ICCV), pp. 2980–2988 (2017)
9. He, K., Zhang, X., Ren, S., et al.: Deep residual learning for image recognition. In: Proceedings of the IEEE Conference on Computer Vision and Pattern Recognition (CVPR), pp. 770–778 (2016)
10. Krizhevsky, A., Sutskever, I., Hinton, G.E.: Imagenet classification with deep convolutional neural networks. In: Advances in Neural Information Processing Systems (NIPS), pp. 1097–1105 (2012)
11. Lin, T.Y., Goyal, P., Girshick, R., et al.: Focal loss for dense object detection. In: Proceedings of the IEEE International Conference on Computer Vision, pp. 2980–2988 (2017)
12. Lin, T.Y., Dollár, P., Girshick, R., et al.: Feature pyramid networks for object detection. In: Proceedings of the IEEE Conference on Computer Vision and Pattern Recognition (CVPR), pp. 2117–2125 (2017)
13. Long, J., Shelhamer, E., Darrell, T.: Fully convolutional networks for semantic segmentation. In: Proceedings of the IEEE Conference on Computer Vision and Pattern Recognition (CVPR), pp. 3431–3440 (2015)
14. Li, Z., Peng, C., Yu, G., et al.: DetNet: a backbone network for object detection. arXiv preprint arXiv:1804.06215 (2018)
15. Li, Z., Peng, C., Yu, G., et al.: Light-head R-CNN: in defense of two-stage object detector. arXiv preprint arXiv:1711.07264 (2017)
16. Oquab, M., Bottou, L., Laptev, I., et al.: Learning and transferring mid-level image representations using convolutional neural networks. In: Proceedings of the IEEE Conference on Computer Vision and Pattern Recognition, pp. 1717–1724 (2014)
17. Pan, S.J., Yang, Q.: A survey on transfer learning. IEEE Trans. Knowl. Data Eng. **22**(10), 1345–1359 (2010)
18. Ren, S., He, K., Girshick, R., et al.: Faster R-CNN: towards real-time object detection with region proposal networks. In: Proceedings of the Advances in Neural Information Processing Systems, pp. 91–99 (2015)

19. Steder, B., Rusu, R.B., Konolige, K., et al.: Point feature extraction on 3D range scans taking into account object boundaries. In: 2011 IEEE International Conference on Robotics and Automation, pp. 2601–2608. IEEE (2011)
20. Simonyan, K., Zisserman, A.: Very deep convolutional networks for large-scale image recognition. arXiv preprint arXiv:1409.1556 (2014)
21. Shrivastava, A., Sukthankar, R., Malik, J., et al.: Beyond skip connections: top-down modulation for object detection. arXiv preprint arXiv:1612.06851 (2016)
22. Vinyals, O., Toshev, A., Bengio, S., et al.: Show and tell: lessons learned from the 2015 mscoco image captioning challenge. IEEE Trans. Pattern Anal. Mach. Intell. **39**(4), 652–663 (2017)
23. Wagner, R., Thom, M., Schweiger, R., et al.: Learning convolutional neural networks from few samples. In: The 2013 International Joint Conference on Neural Networks (IJCNN), pp. 1–7. IEEE (2013)
24. Yongzhe, Z., Zhixin, L., Canlong, Z.: A hybrid architecture based on CNN for cross-modal semantic instance annotation. Multimedia Tools Appl. **77**(7), 8695–8710 (2018)

D3N: DGA Detection
with Deep-Learning Through NXDomain

Mingkai Tong[1], Xiaoqing Sun[1(✉)], Jiahai Yang[1], Hui Zhang[1], Shuang Zhu[1], Xinran Liu[2], and Heng Liu[3]

[1] Institute for Network Sciences and Cyberspace, Tsinghua University, Beijing, China
{tmk16,sxq16}@mails.tsinghua.edu.cn, {yang,hzhang,szhu}@cernet.edu.cn
[2] National Computer Network Emergency Response Center, Beijing, China
lxr@cert.org.cn
[3] China Electronics Cyberspace Great Wall Co., Ltd, Beijing, China
liuheng@cecgw.cn

Abstract. Modern malware typically uses domain generation algorithm (DGA) to avoid blacklists. However, it still leaks trace by causing excessive Non-existent domain responses when trying to contact with the command and control (C&C) servers. In this paper, we propose a novel system named D3N to detect DGA domains by analyzing NXDomains with deep learning methods. The experiments show that D3N yields 99.7% TPR and 1.9% FPR, outperforming FANCI in both accuracy and efficiency. Besides, our real-world evaluation in a large-scale network demonstrates that D3N is robust in different networks.

Keywords: DGA detection · NXDomain · Deep learning

1 Introduction

Most modern malware families make use of Domain Generation Algorithms (DGAs) rather than relying on hardcoded domains or IP addresses to invalidate preemptive defenses, such as blacklists and sinkholes. With the help of DGA, attackers can readily gain bulks of pseudo-random domain names and only need to register one or several of them to establish communication channels for malware to receive commands. However, on defenders' side, all of the domains created by DGAs are suspicious and must be monitored or even blocked, in case of the constant change of the registered ones. Facing this highly asymmetric situation, we aim to design a DGA detection system that is: (i) **Accurate**, with high accuracy and low false positive rate. (ii) **Versatile**, with no need for privileges to use sensitive information. (iii) **Automatic**, with no need for manual feature engineering. (iv) **Online**, a newly-coming domain can be classified instantly. (5) **Robust**, with high performance in different kinds of networks.

The existing proposals of DGA detection can be grouped into three categories: *DNS traffic monitoring*, *graph-based mining* and *domain name analysis*, which we will show more details in Sect. 2. However, none of them meet all the

C. Douligeris et al. (Eds.): KSEM 2019, LNAI 11775, pp. 464–471, 2019.
https://doi.org/10.1007/978-3-030-29551-6_41

above goals simultaneously. In this paper, we use deep learning methods to analyze NXDomains automatically and design a system named D3N. In summary, we make the following contributions:

(1) We compare three deep learning network models to detect DGA domains. With the CNN model, D3N can yield 99.7% TPR and 1.9% FPR, outperforming the previously proposed NXDomain analysis system named FANCI.
(2) We take NXDomains as the input of classifier, which reduces more than half DNS traffic, making real-time detection possible.
(3) We evaluate D3N prototype in CERNET2. The results show D3N can achieve high performance in real-world.

The remainder of this paper is organized as follows. In Sect. 2 we systematically outline previous work on DGA detection. Section 3 describes D3N's framework and pipeline. Section 4 shows offline experimental results while Sect. 5 presents real-world evaluation. We summarize our main jobs and discuss future work in Sect. 6.

2   Related Work

According to data sources and algorithms, the existing researches of DGA detection can be grouped into the following three categories.

DNS Traffic Monitoring. Notos [3] pioneered the use of Passive DNS and assigned reputation scores to domains by analyzing network and zone features. Pleiades [4] analyzed NXDomain traffic with a combination of clustering and classification methods. However, this type of researches need contextual information, and some even require close collaboration among DNS operators.

Graph-Based Mining. Researches in this category tend to extract graph models from DNS traffic. Khalil [5] extracted Domain Resolution Graph and tried to label by computing the weights among domain nodes. Lee et al. [6] built Domain Name Travel Graph to represent clients' communication sequences and identify domain clusters. However, graph analysis requires more computing resources and is easy to have sparse matrices or islands.

Domain Name Analysis. Researches in this group emphasize on character distribution of DGA domains. Woodbridge [14] and Lison [8] leveraged RNN models to detect DGA. However, they only used public datasets to train classifiers, making it easy for attackers to generate adversarial samples [2]. FANCI [13] is more realistic by analyzing DNS traffic of a campus network, yet it needs hand-crafted features, which is time-consuming and easy to circumvent.

3   The Overview of D3N

When trying to resolve an unregistered domain, we will receive a NXDomain response, indicating the inexistence of a corresponding IP address. For DGA-based malware, in order to get in touch with the C&C server, they need to

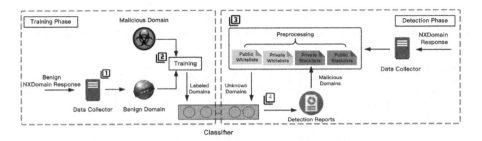

Fig. 1. The architecture of D3N

iterate through a set of DGA domains until finding the registered one, resulting in bulks of NXDomains inevitably. Thus, identifying DGA domain from NXDomain can be useful for malware detection [4]. As is shown in Fig. 1, we divide D3N's workflow into Training phase (steps 1 and 2) and Detection phase (steps 3 and 4). After data collection (step 1), we train the classifier with the labeled dataset (step 2). In Detection phase, the NXDomain responses are preprocessed (step 3) and the newly-coming domains are sent to the classifier. We analyze the detection reports (step 4) to see if an unknown domain is benign, belonging to a well-known DGA family or generated by an unrecorded one. Details of the two phases and the classifier are described in the following.

- **Training Phase.** We take domain names from DGArchive [11] as the malicious set and use the processed DNS traffic of Tsinghua Campus Network in April of 2018 as benign set for the following reasons: (1) The campus network is under close monitoring and controlling; (2) According to the network administrators' reports, no attacks occurred in April; (3) We filter these domains against DGArchive and few malicious domain is found. In step 2, we compare the performance of three deep learning models - CNN, LSTM, BiLSTM and choose the best one as the final classifier.
- **Detection Phase.** Before sending domains to the classifier, we perform a preprocess step (step 3) to improve performance and efficiency. As is shown in Fig. 1, we have public and private lists in this step. We use information from services like *malwaredomainlist.com malwaredomains.com*, etc to build our Public Blacklist and use Alexa Top 1k [1] as the Public Whitelist. As for the private whitelist, we hold the intuition that popular domains in a LAN are inclined to be benign, otherwise there will be a major attack event and will be detected. Therefore, we sort all effective second-level domain (e2TLD) [12] in the network by frequency and consider the top 5 as the private whitelist. In step 4, we analyze detection reports generated by the classifier and add malicious domains to the private blacklist. Considering an increasing number of dynamic DNS [9] or CDN [7] services are abused by attackers to perform malicious behaviors, we choose not to include them in whitelists.
- **Classifier.** Figure 2 shows the workflow of D3N's classifier in which DNN model is the core part. We test CNN, LSTM, BiLSTM and find that CNN

slightly outperforms the other two. By using DNN model in the classifier, D3N can support both binary classification and multi-classification, which means it can not only detect malicious domains but also identify the DGA family in the same time. Taking data skew and rare domain discovery into consideration, we gather DGA families with less than K (we set K as 250 in experiments) unique domains into a specific class. As shown in Fig. 2, result reports generated by the classifier contains class *Benign*, class *Rare* and several common DGA family classes. In actual operation, we will focus on domains that are assigned to *Rare* category to see if any unrecorded DGA generates them.

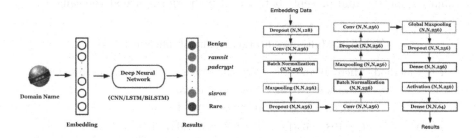

Fig. 2. Workflow of the classifier (left) and the structure of CNN model (right)

4   Experiments

D3N needs a labeled dataset in the Training Phase. In our experiments, we use domains in DGArchive as the malicious set and the processed domains in Tsinghua Campus Network (TUNET) as the benign one.

Malicious Set. DGArchive is provided by a comprehensive measurement study of Domain Generating Malware supported by Fraunhofer FKIE [11]. We got 45.7 million DGA domains in total which contains 62 different DGA families.

Benign Set. By collecting DNS traffic at the Central DNS resolver of TUNET in April 2018, we obtained 12.4 billion records and extracted 38.3 million unique domains in which 15.3 million are corresponding to NXDomains. To improve its quality, we filtered these domains through DGArchive.

4.1   DNNs Test

We test CNN, LSTM and BiLSTM based on the above dataset. In order to remit data skew, we set a ceiling C and a floor F to control data scale of each class. For a DGA family whose number of domains exceeds ceiling, we randomly sample C unique domains for its class. For families with a moderate amount of domains, that is between C and F, all of their domains are remained. As for those failing to achieve the floor, we assort domains of them together as class *Rare*. Then a random sampling is performed on the benign set. In the experiment, we set the sampling number as $5 \cdot C$. Based on the above data collecting rules, we obtain 1,471,972 domains in 64 classes by setting the ceiling $C = 30,000$ and the floor $F = 250$. In order to get more reliable metrics, we perform 5-fold cross-validation.

Table 1 provides the Micro-average metrics, Macro-average metrics and Training speed of the three DNNs while Fig. 3 shows their ROC curves and AUC. With the micro-average method, we sum up the individual true positives, false positives, and false negatives of different sets to get metrics. By contrast, the macro-average method is more straightforward by taking average of the precision and recall of each class. As can be seen, CNN slightly excels the others on evaluation metrics and presents better runtime performance at the same time.

Table 1. Multi-classification results of different DNNs

DNN method	Micro-average		Macro-average		Training speed/sample
	Precision	Recall	Precision	Recall	
CNN	0.86793	0.82789	0.85025	0.81482	89 μs
LSTM	0.85108	0.81252	0.83910	0.79631	182 μs
BiLSTM	0.85900	0.81993	0.84474	0.83466	363 μs

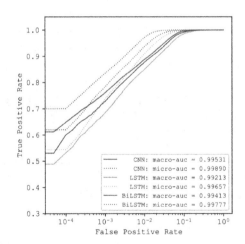

Fig. 3. ROC curves of CNN, LSTM and BiLSTM in micro-average and macro-average methods

4.2   Comparision with FANCI

In this section, we aim to compare D3N with FANCI [13], a recently proposed
NXDomain analysis system. FANCI manually extracted 21 features, such as
length, number of subdomains etc, from domain names and trained support
vector machines, random forests to detect malicious ones. Due to the limitations
of its methods, FANCI is unable to support multi-classification with no more
than one trained model. Therefore, we only compare them in the *Mixed-DGA*
scenario, namely just telling whether the domain is malicious or not.

Table 2 shows the *Accuracy, True positive rate, False positive rate* and *AUC*
of all models in D3N and FANCI. We can see that D3N is generally superior to
FANCI in all indicators. In particular, D3N with CNN model attains the best
performance in Mixed-DGA detection.

Table 2. Mixed-DGA detection results of D3N and FANCI

Methods		ACC	TPR	FPR	AUC
D3N binary-classification	CNN	0.98892	0.99788	0.01999	0.99894
	LSTM	0.98869	0.99124	0.01186	0.99890
	BiLSTM	0.98824	0.99618	0.01961	0.99882
FANCI	SVM	0.98193	0.98193	0.02621	0.99658
	RF	0.97557	0.99655	0.04548	0.98779

Apart from *how well it detects, how fast it can build a decision* is also an
important issue for detection systems. We test D3N's detection efficiency by
deploying it on a MacBook with Intel Core 2.3 GHz dual-core i5 processor, 8G
RAM and comparing it with FANCI, an applicable domain name detect system which can supervise large networks [13]. The average processing rates over
150,000 samples are shown in Table 3 indicating that D3N with CNN is the most
efficient model. With a common configured GPU involved, such as GTX 1080Ti,
a domain can be handled within 10 μs. We deem that D3N is qualified for on-line
detection.

Table 3. Detection speed of D3N and FANCI (/sample)

D3N_binary	D3N_multi	FANCI
CNN 1.21 ms	CNN 1.25 ms	SVM 1.33 ms
LSTM 1.74 ms	LSTM 2.40 ms	RF 1.46 ms
BiLSTM 2.42 ms	BiLSTM 3.79 ms	

5   Real-World Detection

Finally, we choose CERNET2, the first IPv6 national backbone network in China, to test D3N's performance in real-world. We collect 4.95 million NXdomains from DNS traffic of CERNET2 in April, 2018. After the preprocessing step, we finally get 2.80 million unknown domains. We choose the trained CNN model as the classifier to detect those uncertain domains. As shown in Table 4, 42,537 domains have been detected as DGA-related, containing 15 known DGA families and a Rare family which we treat as unknown family set.

To verify the detection results, we ask for experts' confirmation and utilize malware report services like *VirusTotal* and *Hybrid*. Besides, we queried the 360 pDNS dataset [10] to find the ever resolved IPs of the detected domains. It turns out that lots of domains have malicious IP resolution records. What's more, we pay attention to class *Rare* and find lots of domains in this class are reported by public services several months after they are detected by D3N. The real-world evaluation demonstrates that D3N is a robust detection system and can be adaptive in different networks.

Table 4. D3N detection results in CERNET2 (16 days)

Domains collected: 4954841			
Domains left after preprocessing: 2791481			
Malicious domains: (DGA families)	drye	1200	corebot	9302
	chinad	10211	gameover	10974
	rovnix	2840	murofetweekly	2436
	urlzone	440	xxhex	198
	tinynuke	48	qadars	93
	ekforward	8	pandabanker	2
	tinba	2	wd	1
	infy	1	*Rare*	4781

6   Conclusion and Future Work

In this paper, we present a detection system called D3N, which can detect DGA-generated domains by analyzing NXDomain traffic with deep learning methods. With DNN models, D3N can not only avoid the arduous feature engineering but also provide additional information about DGA family through multiclassification. We test three DNN models in D3N based on one-month benign domains extracted from TUNET and malicious domains collected by DGArchive for more than three years. The experimental results show that D3N with CNN model is superior to the others on accuracy and efficiency. Besides, in Mixed-DGA detection, D3N outperforms the recently proposed Domain detection system FANCI. In the real-world evaluation, D3N successfully handles the large scale of DNS traffic in CERNET2. The detection results demonstrate that D3N can be used as an online detection system with high accuracy and efficiency.

At present, D3N only aims to make early detection of malware by analyzing NXDomians. As further research work, we plan to strengthen its ability of registered domain detection to uncover the running malware. Besides, as labeled datasets of domains are hard to obtain, we plan to study on applying self-supervised methods in domain detection as another part of our future work.

Acknowledgment. We thank Chenxi Li, Shize Zhang, Xinmu Wang and Shuai Wang for constructive comments on experiments, valuable advice on data processing and parameters tuning. Additionally, we thank DGArchive and Information Technology Center of Tsinghua University for authorizing the use of their data in our experiments. This work is supported by the National Key Research and Development Program of China under Grant No.2017YFB0803004.

References

1. Alexa.com: Alexa Top 500 Global Sites (2019). https://www.alexa.com/topsites
2. Anderson, H.S., Woodbridge, J., Filar, B.: DeepDGA: adversarially-tuned domain generation and detection. In: Proceedings of the 2016 ACM Workshop on Artificial Intelligence and Security, pp. 13–21. ACM (2016)
3. Antonakakis, M., Perdisci, R., Dagon, D., Lee, W., Feamster, N.: Building a dynamic reputation system for DNS. In: USENIX Security Symposium, pp. 273–290 (2010)
4. Antonakakis, M., et al.: From throw-away traffic to bots: detecting the rise of DGA-based malware. In: Presented as Part of the 21st {USENIX} Security Symposium ({USENIX} Security 12), pp. 491–506 (2012)
5. Khalil, I., Yu, T., Guan, B.: Discovering malicious domains through passive DNS data graph analysis. In: Proceedings of the 11th ACM on Asia Conference on Computer and Communications Security, pp. 663–674. ACM (2016)
6. Lee, J., Lee, H.: GMAD: graph-based malware activity detection by DNS traffic analysis. Comput. Commun. **49**, 33–47 (2014)
7. Lin Jin, H.S.: CDN list [Data set] (2019). https://doi.org/10.5281/zenodo.842988
8. Lison, P., Mavroeidis, V.: Automatic detection of malware-generated domains with recurrent neural models. arXiv preprint arXiv:1709.07102 (2017)
9. Netgate.com: Services DNS Configuring Dynamic DNS pfSense Documentation (2019). https://www.netgate.com/docs/pfsense/dns/dynamic-dns.html
10. Passivedns.cn: Sign In-passiveDNS (2019). http://netlab.360.com/
11. Plohmann, D., Yakdan, K., Klatt, M., Bader, J., Gerhards-Padilla, E.: A comprehensive measurement study of domain generating malware. In: 25th {USENIX} Security Symposium ({USENIX} Security 16), pp. 263–278 (2016)
12. Publicsuffix.org: Public suffix list. https://publicsuffix.org/. Accessed 7 Jun 2019
13. Schüppen, S., Teubert, D., Herrmann, P., Meyer, U.: {FANCI}: feature-based automated NXdomain classification and intelligence. In: 27th {USENIX} Security Symposium ({USENIX} Security 18), pp. 1165–1181 (2018)
14. Woodbridge, J., Anderson, H.S., Ahuja, A., Grant, D.: Predicting domain generation algorithms with long short-term memory networks. arXiv preprint arXiv:1611.00791 (2016)

Deep Neighbor Embedding for Evaluation of Large Portfolios of Variable Annuities

Xiaojuan Cheng[1,2], Wei Luo[3(✉)], Guojun Gan[4], and Gang Li[3]

[1] Xi'an Shiyou University, Shaanxi, China
xiaojuan.cheng@tulip.org.au
[2] Xinjiang Technical Institute of Physics and Chemistry,
Chinese Academy of Sciences, Urumqi, China
[3] Deakin University, Geelong, Australia
{wei.luo,gang.li}@deakin.edu.au
[4] University of Connecticut, Storrs, CT, USA
guojun.gan@uconn.edu

Abstract. Variable annuities are very profitable financial products that pose unique challenges in risk prediction. Metamodeling techniques are popular due to the significant saving in computation time. However, the current metamodeling techniques still have a low valuation accuracy. One key difficulty is the selection of a small number of contracts that optimally represent the whole portfolio. In this paper, we propose a novel and highly effective method for selecting representative contracts. At the center of this method is a deep neighbor embedding that supports robust clustering of the contracts in a portfolio. The embedding is a low-dimensional representation that respects similarities among contracts in both contract-specific features and their historical performance, achieved through abstract representation in a deep neural network. Empirical results show that the proposed model achieves significant improvement in valuation accuracy, often 10 times or more accurate compared with the popular Kriging-based model.

Keywords: Variable annuity · Neighbor embedding ·
Deep transfer learning

1 Introduction

A variable annuity (VA) is a retirement insurance product that in the U.S. alone generated 92.9 billion sales in 2018, according to *Insured Retirement Institute* (IRI). With the product's popularity, comes the significant and complex risk due to the return guarantees embedded in variable annuities. The traditional risk estimation method based on Monte-Carlo simulation involves the prohibitive computational cost and fails to handle large policy portfolios in most insurance companies. Insurance companies are turning to machine learning for the valuation of large portfolios of variable annuity policies. In particular, metamodeling

© Springer Nature Switzerland AG 2019
C. Douligeris et al. (Eds.): KSEM 2019, LNAI 11775, pp. 472–480, 2019.
https://doi.org/10.1007/978-3-030-29551-6_42

techniques [4, 7] have been proposed to provide a portfolio-level risk estimate with a minimal amount of simulation.

With metamodeling, Monte Carlo simulation [8] is conducted only on a small number of representative policies in a large portfolio. The risk estimates on these representative policies are then used to infer the overall risk profile of the whole portfolio. Selecting the truly representative policies is crucial for successful metamodeling. Today, the most popular approach is to partition a portfolio into a number of policy clusters and then select the centroid policy from each cluster as a representative policy [4]. In the past, clustering is usually performed on a set of predefined features describing each policy and the policyholder. This choice of feature space has a number of potential issues, ranging from the presence of irrelevant features, mixed variable types, to the so-called "curse of dimensionality" when the feature set is large. In order to improve the accuracy and robustness of risk estimation, researchers have been actively searching for better ways to select representative policies [2,3,5]. Our earlier work [1] suggests that clustering on the deep-representation level greatly improves the accuracy.

Metamodeling and the Challenges. The metamodeling of a large portfolio consists of two steps. First a small number of representative policies are selected from the portfolio using clustering-based approaches or sampling-based approaches and then valued via computationally intensive MCMC. Next, a regression model extrapolate the MCMC valuation to all policies in the portfolio. Selecting the truly representative policies is the key to the success of metamodeling.

The aforementioned clustering-based approaches perform clustering on a high-dimension space, which can result imbalanced clusters (see Fig. 1b). Figure 1 illustrates clearly a low-dimensional embedding of the deep representation can generate robust clusters. We can see that the silhouette value almost surpasses the average level in a low-dimensional embedding. However in the high-dimensional representation space, it's extremely nonuniform for each cluster. In this paper, we present a novel framework integrating neighbor embedding with deep transfer learning, which achieves a significant performance improvement.

Our Contributions. In this work, we propose a novel approach to select representative policies for variable annuities, extending our work in [1]. This approach significantly improves the quality of selected representative policies, via clustering over a low-dimensional embedding of the deep representation of the portfolio. To our knowledge, it is the first time that dimension reduction has been applied to metamodeling for variable annuities. Although the idea looks deceivingly simple, we show that a naive application of dimension reduction on the original feature space does not work. It is the integration of transfer learning and local-distance preserving embedding that results in the significant performance improvement shown in this paper.

2 The Method: DR-TL

In this section, we present a *dimension-reduced transfer learning* (DR-TL) framework. Unlike TL framework in [1] performs clustering in a high-dimension space, Fig. 2 shows DR-TL framework performs clustering in a low-dimension embedding. The process consists of major steps as follows: (1) Fit a backbone deep neural network using historical Monte Carlo simulation results, then get a high-dimensional latent representation of policies from intermediate layer. (2) Apply the neighbor-based embedding to the deep representation to get a low-dimension manifold. (3) Clustering via the k-means algorithm in the low-dimension space to find representative contracts. (4) Run the Monte Carlo simulation for the valuation of representative contracts under the target market. (5) Fine-tuning

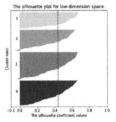 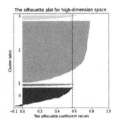

(a) Clustering in a low-dimensional space.   (b) Clustering in a high-dimensional space.

Fig. 1. The silhouette plot for four clusters respectively in low-dimensional embedding and in high-dimensional representation space. The dotted red line reflects the average silhouette score of all the values. (Color figure online)

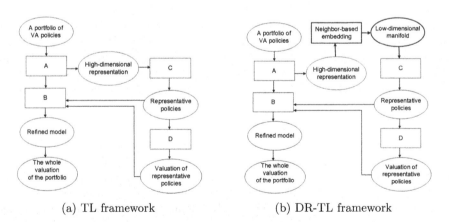

(a) TL framework   (b) DR-TL framework

Fig. 2. The TL framework in [1] and the proposed DR-TL framework, with the additional neighbor embedding step to produce a low-dimensional manifold. **A**: Fit a model with historical simulation (different market conditions). **B**: Fine-tuning the fitted model by transfer learning method (updated market conditions). **C**: Data clustering. **D**: Monte Carlo simulation.

the backbone deep neural network model using representative policies and the corresponding valuation under the target market. (6) Use the tuned model to estimate the valuation of all policies in the portfolio.

2.1 Problem Formulation

Policy and Portfolio. A VA portfolio $\mathcal{P}$ often contains a large number N of individual policies c_i sold to different customers: $\mathcal{P} = \{c_i : 1 \leq i \leq N\}$. For each policy c_i, a feature vector x_i captures the characteristics of the policy and the customer. At the same time, each policy c has an expected risk y_i. Although y_i is unknown in general, it can be very well estimated by Monte Carlo simulation, though the simulation is usually very computationally extensive and can only be performed on a small sample from $\mathcal{P}$.

Metamodeling. Metamodeling attempts to estimate the aggregated risk $\overline{Y}$ of the whole portfolio $\mathcal{P}$ using only regression models to compensate the lack of complete Monte Carlo results. It involves two subtasks: selecting a subset $\mathcal{R}$ of K representative policies of the portfolio $\mathcal{P}$, and inferring the overall risk $\overline{Y}$ from the simulated results $\{y_i : c_i \in \mathcal{R}\}$ on the representative subset.

The second subtask is relatively straightforward: instead of directly predicting $\overline{Y} = \text{mean}\left(\{y_i : 1 \leq i \leq N\}\right)$, we can pursue the unbiased estimate of each y_i. This can be achieved through fitting a regression model on $\{(x_i, y_i) : c_i \in \mathcal{R}\}$. Our prior work has shown that a deep neural network pre-trained using historical data achieved the best prediction performance so far.

The first subtask of selecting an optimal subset remains largely unsolved, hence it is the focus of this work. One natural solution is to first cluster $\mathcal{P}$ based on $\{x_i\}$ and then select only the cluster centers (similar to medoids) [4]. The prior work shows that clustering directly on the features $\{x_i\}$ can be problematic, especially when $\{x_i\}$ contains discrete features and/or high-variance features irrelevant to y_i. Instead, we have shown that transfer learning which solves the second (regression) problem also provides an opportunity to better address the first (clustering) problem, as better clustering can be obtained on the deep representation of a pre-trained model.

Although deep representation in a pre-trained model leads to better clustering results, it also brings a new challenge: the high dimensionality of the deep representation may cause sensitive clusters and cluster centers. Therefore, this paper address the following research problem: with a limited computation budget on the Monte Carlo simulation for K policies, how to find the robust K clusters and cluster centers $\{c_{ij} : 1 \leq j \leq K\}$ that allow the most accurate estimation of $\overline{Y}$ given $\{(x_{ij}, y_{ij}) : 1 \leq j \leq K\}$.

2.2 Neighbour Based Embedding

As the hidden layer representation has a high dimension, directly performing clustering algorithm may result in unstable clusters as well as sensitive cluster centers. We use neighbor based embedding to map the high-dimension representations into a lower dimensional space without losing the local structures among policies.

There are many mature neighbor based embedding methods, such as t-SNE [9], ISOMap [11] and UMAP [10]. In this paper, we use UMAP due to its superiority in embedding stability and computational efficiency. The embedding aims to preserve the local structures among observations. Many nonlinear embedding methods follow a similar two-step process: generating weighted K-neighbor graphs followed by laying out the graph in a low-dimensional space.

In UMAP, the graph weights are derived from two weighted directed graphs defined by the similarity measure $w\left(\left(x_i, x_{i_j}\right)\right) = \exp\left(\frac{-\max\left(0, d\left(x_i, x_{i_j}\right) - \rho_i\right)}{\sigma_i}\right)$, where $d\left(x_i, x_{i_j}\right)$ is the pairwise distance in the feature space, and ρ_i, σ_i are normalising constants. The layout algorithm in UMAP is the widely used force-directed graph layout algorithm. Negative sampling is used for computational efficiency. In this paper, we set the embedding space dimension as 2. At the end of the embedding step, the hidden representations are all mapped to a 2-d space on which clustering will be carried out.

3   Experiment and Analysis

In this section, we evaluate the performance of the proposed DR-TL framework using both simulated datasets and standard benchmark datasets. Then we present the numerical results to show the superiority of low-dimensional embedding of the deep representation including both simulated data and benchmark dataset.

3.1   Data Description

Simulated Dataset. The simulated dataset is generated by make_blobs function in sklearn Python library. This data is used to simulate a portfolio of $1,000$ policies with 5 features from 20 clusters. The corresponding $Y = f(x)$ is made up of a random noisy in linear and nonlinear form. In the linear form, Y_1 and Y_2 simulate respectively two different market scenarios. Forming the dependent variable coefficients are $\{2, 1, 1, 3, 5\}$ and $\{5, 2, 3, 4, 2\}$. In the nonlinear form, $\hat{Y_2}$ simulating the target market consists of a quadratic polynomial and the coefficients are $\{2, 1, 3, 1, 2\}$.

VA Benchmark Dataset. The second dataset [6] is a large synthetic benchmark dataset used extensively in metamodeling [8]. The runtime used to create these synthetic datasets would be about 3 years if only a single CPU was used. The dataset contains $1,000$ risk-neutral paths, and each path contains $38,000$ VA policies. Each policy contains a feature vector of 34 predictors, a Greeks value and a central risk metric that is the target variable for metamodeling.

3.2   Performance Metrics

To evaluate the accuracy of the proposed model, we follow the strategy in [4] and use the following two validation measures: the *percentage error* (PE) at the portfolio level and R^2. Among which, the percentage error is defined as

$$PE(\mathcal{P}) = \frac{\sum_{c_i \in \mathcal{P}}(\hat{y}_i - y_i)}{\sum_{c_i \in \mathcal{P}} y_i}, \tag{1}$$

Table 1. PE of Kriging model and DR-Kriging model on simulated data.

# clusters	$PE \downarrow$ (linear)		$PE \downarrow$ (nonlinear)	
	Kriging model	DR-Kriging model	Kriging model	DR-Kriging model
$k = 10$	−0.402	**−0.303**	**0.167**	0.178
$k = 20$	**−0.084**	−0.292	**−0.091**	0.169
$k = 30$	**0.036**	0.152	0.191	**0.069**

Table 2. R^2 of Kriging model and DR-Kriging model on simulated data.

# clusters	$R^2 \uparrow$ (linear)		$R^2 \uparrow$ (nonlinear)	
	Kriging model	DR-Kriging model	Kriging model	DR-Kriging model
$k = 10$	0.604	**0.824**	0.252	**0.289**
$k = 20$	0.832	**0.904**	0.642	**0.693**
$k = 30$	**0.954**	0.830	**0.778**	**0.778**

where y_i describes the value of policy c_i in the portfolio $\mathcal{P}$ from the high-resolution Monte Carlo simulation. and $\hat{y}_i$ is the corresponding estimate from the neural network. On the other hand, R^2 is defined as

$$R^2 = 1 - \frac{\sum_{c_i \in \mathcal{P}}(\hat{y}_i - y_i)^2}{\sum_{c_i \in \mathcal{P}}(y_i - \mu)^2}, \tag{2}$$

where $\mu = \frac{1}{n}\sum_{c_i \in \mathcal{P}} y_i$ is the average Delta value.

From the above equations we can see, PE and R^2 are complimentary measurements for the valuation performance. While R^2 indicates the fitness at the policy level, PE directly reflects the accuracy at the portfolio level. For insurance companies with a large portfolio, the hedging is commonly used to manage the portfolio level risk. Therefore minimising PE, or equivalently maximising the portfolio accuracy, is the primary objective in this work.

3.3   Results

Performance of DR-Kriging Model on Simulated Data. First, we try a *dimension-reduced Kriging* (DR-Kriging) model, which applies dimension reduction directly on the feature space, instead of the deep representation space. On the simulated data, we compared the baseline Kriging model with the DR-Kriging model. Tables 1 and 2 show PE and R^2 achieved by the Kriging model and the DR-Kriging model with different number of clusters k. These results show that dimension reduction directly applied on the feature space doesn't improve the performance.

DR-TL on Simulated Data. Unlike DR-Kriging, DR-TL applies dimension reduction on the deep represenation. Table 3 shows PE achieved by the Kriging model and the DR-TL model on the simulated data. For different numbers of clusters, DR-TL model achieves smaller absolute PE values than the baseline kriging model. the superiority of DR-TL is particularly evident on the nonlinear data. For example, with 30 clusters, DR-TL reduced the PE from 0.038 to 0.009.

Table 3. PE of Kriging model and DR-TL model on simulated data.

# clusters	$PE \downarrow$ (linear)		$PE \downarrow$ (nonlinear)	
	Kriging model	DR-TL model	Kriging model	DR-TL model
$k = 10$	0.425	**0.035**	1.268	**−0.214**
$k = 20$	0.100	**0.024**	0.529	**0.017**
$k = 30$	0.048	**0.013**	0.038	**0.009**

Table 4. R^2 of Kriging model and DR-TL model on simulated data.

# clusters	$R^2 \uparrow$ (linear)		$R^2 \uparrow$ (nonlinear)	
	Kriging model	DR-TL model	Kriging model	DR-TL model
$k = 10$	0.604	**0.987**	**0.222**	0.004
$k = 20$	0.831	**0.999**	0.725	**0.804**
$k = 30$	0.953	**0.999**	0.816	**0.926**

Table 5. PE on benchmark data

# clusters	$PE \downarrow$		
	Kriging	TL	DR-TL
50	−0.168	0.152	**0.075**
80	−0.050	0.088	**0.032**
90	0.098	0.053	**0.006**
100	−0.108	0.043	**0.003**
200	−0.032	0.024	**0.003**

Table 6. R^2 on benchmark data

$R^2 \uparrow$		
Kriging	TL	DR-TL
0.187	0.139	0.162
0.273	**0.508**	0.245
0.304	**0.504**	0.281
0.222	**0.445**	0.430
0.365	0.485	**0.507**

Table 4 shows the R^2 results on simulated data. While the PE shows the accuracy at the portfolio level, the R^2 shows the accuracy at the individual policy level, which is not a primary concern for portfolio risk valuation.

DR-TL on Benchmark Data. Tables 5 and 6 show the results on the benchmark data [4]. In addition to the Kriging model, TL model from [1] is used as another baseline. Although Table 6 shows that DR-TL does not optimise the policy-level accuracy, Table 5 shows the proposed DR-TL method significantly outperformed the two baselines on PE, the primary optimisation target of portfolio metamodeling. First, a superior PE of 0.003 is achieved with as few as 100 representative policies. This is 30 times better than what can be achieved through the mainstream Kriging method. This is a new level of accuracy that, to our knowledge, has never been achieved through metamodeling with such a small training sample. Second, the high accuracy translates to great saving in terms of simulation time. If 90 representative policies are sufficient to reach a PE less than 1%, the predicted risk can potentially be recalculated in near real-time when an insurance company needs to adjust its product portfolio.

4 Conclusions

In this work, we have proposed a novel metamodeling framework integrating neighbor embedding with deep transfer learning. Although dimension reduction seems to be an obvious option to improve clustering stability, we have shown that when directly applied to policy-level features, dimension reduction fails to improve the valuation accuracy, and sometimes even results in higher PE. Building on the transfer-learning metamodels, the new framework can locate representative policies that are not only stable, but also relevant to the risk profile.

The proposed framework enables a large portfolio to be valued in high accuracy with fewer than 50 training examples in metamodeling. This translates to 10 times or higher saving in the computational cost on simulation, and we believe that this significant improvement of the valuation accuracy can potentially bring disruptive change to how the insurance industry performs the risk evaluation.

Acknowledgement. This work was supported by the International Cooperation Project of Institute of Information Engineering, Chinese Academy of Sciences under Grant No. Y7Z0511101, and Guangxi Key Laboratory of Trusted Software (No KX201528).

References

1. Cheng, X., Luo, W., Gan, G., Li, G.: Fast valuation of large portfolios of variable annuities via transfer learning. In: Nayak, A.C., Sharma, A. (eds.) PRICAI 2019. LNCS, vol. 11672, pp. 716–728. Springer, Cham (2019)
2. Gan, G.: Application of data clustering and machine learning in variable annuity valuation. Insur. Math. Econ. **53**(3), 795–801 (2013)
3. Gan, G.: Application of metamodeling to the valuation of large variable annuity portfolios. In: Proceedings of the Winter Simulation Conference, pp. 1103–1114 (2015)
4. Gan, G., Huang, J.X.: A data mining framework for valuing large portfolios of variable annuities. In: Proceedings of the 23rd ACM SIGKDD International Conference on Knowledge Discovery and Data Mining - KDD 2017, pp. 1467–1475 (2017)

5. Gan, G., Valdez, E.: An empirical comparison of some experimental designs for the valuation of large variable annuity portfolios. Dep. Model. **4**, 382–400 (2016)
6. Gan, G., Valdez, E.: Nested stochastic valuation of large variable annuity portfolios: Monte Carlo simulation and synthetic datasets. Data **3**(3), 31 (2018)
7. Gan, G., Valdez, E.A.: Regression modeling for the valuation of large variable annuity portfolios. North Am. Actuarial J. **22**(1), 40–54 (2018)
8. Kleijnen, J.P.C.: A comment on blanning's "metamodel for sensitivity analysis: The regression metamodel in simulation". Interfaces **5**(3), 21–23 (1975)
9. van der Maaten, L., Hinton, G.: Visualizing data using t-SNE. JMLR **9**, 2579–2605 (2008)
10. McInnes, L., Healy, J., Melville, J.: UMAP: uniform manifold approximation and projection for dimension reduction. arXiv preprint arXiv:1802.03426 (2018)
11. Tenenbaum, J.B., De Silva, V., Langford, J.C.: A global geometric framework for nonlinear dimensionality reduction. Science **290**(5500), 2319–2323 (2000)

State Representation Learning for Minimax Deep Deterministic Policy Gradient

Dapeng Hu[1], Xuesong Jiang[1,2(✉)], Xiumei Wei[1], and Jian Wang[2]

[1] Qilu University of Technology,
Shandong Academy of Sciences, Jinan 250353, China
jxs@qlu.edu.cn
[2] Shandong College of Information Technology, Weifang, China

Abstract. Recently, the reinforcement learning of multi-agent has been developed rapidly, especially the Minimax Deep Deterministic Policy Gradient (M3DDPG) algorithm which improves agent robustness and solves the problem that agents trained by deep reinforcement learning (DRL) are often vulnerable and sensitive to the training environment. However, agents in the real environment may not be able to perceive certain important characteristics of the environment because of their limited perceptual capabilities. So Agents often fail to achieve the desired results. In this paper, we propose a novel algorithm State Representation Learning for Minimax Deep Deterministic Policy Gradient (SRL_M3DDPG) that combines M3DDPG with the state representation learning neural network model to extract the important characteristics of raw data. And we optimize the actor and critic network by using the neural network model of state representation learning. Then the actor and critic network learn from the state representation model instead of the raw observations. Simulation experiments show that the algorithm improves the final result.

Keywords: M3DDPG · State representation learning · SRL_M3DDPG

1 Introduction

Recently, multi-agent reinforcement learning has been developed rapidly, and many outstanding researchers have proposed multi-agent algorithms such as the counterfactual multi-agent policy gradients [1] and the Multi-Agent Deep Deterministic Policy Gradient (MADDPG) [2]. The MADDPG algorithm is not only suitable for the environment of cooperative interaction but also for the competitive or mixed interactive environment involving material and information behavior.

In addition, Minimax Deep Deterministic Policy Gradient algorithm (M3DDPG) [3] is proposed to solve the issue of Deep Reinforcement Learning (DRL) training which is often fragile and sensitive to the environment, especially in multi-agent scenarios. M3DDPG is a minimax extension of the classical MADDPG algorithm. It can force every agent to perform well during training, even if its training opponents make the worst response.

The End-to-end learning [4] reduces pre-processing and subsequent processing, providing more space for the model to automatically adjust the data and improving the

© Springer Nature Switzerland AG 2019
C. Douligeris et al. (Eds.): KSEM 2019, LNAI 11775, pp. 481–487, 2019.
https://doi.org/10.1007/978-3-030-29551-6_43

overall adaptability of the model. However, the input of end-to-end learning is not the original data, but more about the characteristics of data, especially in the case of high-dimensional data, such as image problem [5]. The high dimensionality of the data caused a dimensional disaster, thus the initial idea is to manually extract some of the key features of the image [11]. Actually, this is a process of dimensionality reduction. How to mention features is a key issue. The criticality of feature extraction is even more critical than learning algorithms. This means that features require sufficient experiences to design, which is becoming more and more difficult as data volumes increase. In order to improve the adaptability to the data, we propose the State Representation learning Minimax Deep Deterministic Policy Gradient algorithm (SRL_M3DDPG) algorithm.

Therefore, for the M3DDPG algorithm, in order to better extract the characteristics of data, we propose a new algorithm SRL_M3DDPG. We establish a deep neural network to construct a mapping of observation values and state values. The model network learns the mapping of observation-to-state through back propagation prediction errors [10]. Then the actors and critic network in M3DDPG learn from the new neural network instead of learning from the original observations. This paper introduces a method of using state representation learning of neural networks to make the network itself capture features well and adapt to the data. Linking this method to the M3DDPG algorithm produces the SRL_M3DDPG algorithm.

In the rest of the paper, we will firstly present related works in Sect. 2 and experiment and result in Sect. 3.

2 Related Work

2.1 Minimax Deep Deterministic Policy Gradient

Minimax Multi-agent Deep Deterministic Policy Gradient (M3DDPG) [3] algorithm is proposed to improve the learned policies robustness of MADDPG algorithm. For the purpose of learning robust policies, researchers propose updating policies when considering the worst situation: they optimize the accumulative reward for each agent i under the assumption that all other agents acts adversarially. This yields the minimaxlearning objective $\max_{\theta_i} J_M(\theta_i)$ where

$$J_M(\theta_i) = \mathrm{E}_{s^0 - \rho}[\min_{a^0_{j \neq i}} Q^\mu_{M,i}(s^0, a^0_1, \cdots, a^0_N)|_{a^0_i = \mu(o^0_i)}] \tag{1}$$

Update critic by minimizing the loss. The loss formula is:

$$\mathcal{L}(\theta_i) = \frac{1}{s} \Sigma_k (y^k - Q^\mu_{M,i}(X^k, a^k_1, \ldots, a^k_N))^2 \tag{2}$$

Update actor using the sampled policy gradient. The optimization formula is:

$$\nabla_{\theta_i} J \approx \frac{1}{S} \sum_k \nabla_{\theta_i} \mu_i(o^k_i) \nabla_{a_i} Q^\mu_{M,i}(x^k, a^*_1, \ldots, a_i, \ldots, a^*_N)|_{a_i = \mu_i} \tag{3}$$

Update target network parameters for each agent i:

$$\theta_i' \leftarrow \tau\theta_i + (1 - \tau)\theta_i' \tag{4}$$

2.2 State Representation Learning

The success of machine learning algorithms generally depends on data representation, learning with generic priors can help design representations, and the quest for AI is motivating the design of more powerful representation learning algorithms implementing such priors [6]. This state representation learning has advantages in feature extraction which is more convenient and will not affect the subsequent steps.

Deep reinforcement learning (deep RL) process requires a huge number of trials, especially in automating processes of complex behaviors. Researchers propose a recurrent neural network (RNN) to learn from prior data [7]. An automatic encoder is used to compress the observer into a low-dimensional state vector and has it trained to construct a mapping of the observed states [8, 9].

In this paper, state representation learning establishes mapping of observation o_t to agent real state $\tilde{s}$ through deep neural networks (DNNs). The purpose of the state prior method in this paper is to establish the mapping from state to observation. The observed state obtains observations from the environment. Given the initial state of each agent i, it can predict the next observation and reward of the agent by training. The reward helps to evaluate the action.

2.3 State Representation Learning for Minimax Deep Deterministic Policy Gradient

In this part, we systematically introduce the SRL_M3DDPG algorithm consisting of three DNNs (a model network, a critic network, and an actor network). In the first DNNs, we construct SRL model with prior and the number of input neurons is equal to that of columns in the state matrix. The number of output neurons is equal to that of columns of the observation matrix, and there are 20 neurons in the hidden layer. In the rest of DNNs (critic network and an actor network) parameters are consistent with the M3DDPG algorithm.

The SRL model are defined as a loss function $\mathcal{L}$, applied on a set of observations $(o_1, \ldots, o_n)$ that is minimized under certain conditions C, the loss is:

$$\text{loss} = \mathcal{L}_{\text{prior}}(o_1, \ldots, o_n; \theta_\varphi | C) \tag{5}$$

In this paper we take the cross entropy as a loss function and loss function trained by adadelta optimizer. The learning rate $a_{SRL} = 0.01$. The cross entropy loss function $\mathcal{L}$ is:

$$\mathcal{L}_{SRL} = -\sum_{k} y_k \log x_k \tag{6}$$

In the step t, we obtain the real state s_t and real observation o_t. The predicted value $\tilde{o}_t$ is obtained after the first DNNs [see Fig. 1]. Please note that s_t, o_t and $\tilde{o}_t$ are three different matrices. In the first DNNs, the number of input neurons is equal to that of columns in the state matrix. The number of output neurons is equal to that of columns of the observation matrix. There are 20 neurons in the hidden layer. In the rest of DNNs (the critic network, and the actor network), the actor network obtains two parameters s_t and $\tilde{o}_t$, then select an action matrix a_t according to the strategy of M3DDPG. The critic network evaluates a_t according to state information and other information such as actions of other agents, and selects an optimal action a_t^*. When the agent completes this action a_t^*, the reward value r_t and the next state s_{t+1} are obtained [see Fig. 2].

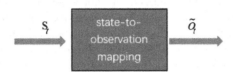

Fig. 1. The neural network model structure of state representation learning

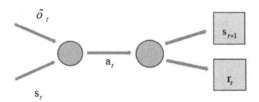

Fig. 2. The process in the rest of DNNs

In the experiment, firstly we train the SRL network model. The first DNNs is trained 10, 000 times which uses the adadelta optimizer to reduce loss and adjust weights by back propagation. When the first layer network weights are fixed, the actor and the Critic network weights are updated [see Fig. 3].

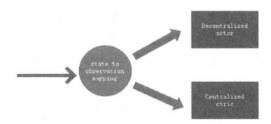

Fig. 3. The SRL_M3DDPG model

3   Experiment

MADDPG agents can learn coordinated behaviour more easily via the centralized critic. Therefore, MADDPG algorithm is more adaptable to complex and changeable environment than traditional RL algorithm. In the experiment, this algorithm outperforms traditional RL algorithms on a variety of cooperative and competitive multi-agent environments [2]. The M3DDPG algorithm improves agent robustness and solves the problem that Deep Reinforcement Learning (DRL) training is vulnerable to the training environment. Empirically, M3DDPG outperforms the MADDPG methods on mixed cooperative and competitive scenarios [3].

In order to implement our experiments, we used the grounded communication environment proposed in [2]. We are focused on the Cooperative navigation [see Fig. 4] environment. In this environment, agents must cooperate through physical actions to reach a set of L landmarks. Agents observe the relative positions of other agents and landmarks, and are collectively rewarded based on the proximity of any agent to each landmark. In other words, the agents have to 'cover' all of the landmarks. Further, the agents occupy significant physical space and are penalized when colliding with each other. Our agents learn to infer the landmark they must cover, and move there while avoiding other agents.

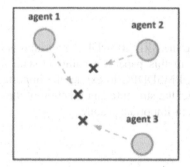

Fig. 4. Cooperative navigation

To evaluate the quality of learned policies trained by different algorithms in competitive scenarios, respectively we measure the performance of agents trained by SRL_M3DDPG algorithm and M3DDPG algorithm in cooperative navigation environment. Each of the 100 episodes outputs the corresponding mean episode reward and is denoted by a record, which is respectively saved in two files. When running up to 60,000 episodes (600 records), the operation stop. We then draw 60,000 episodes (600 records) of images of different algorithms. In the first deep neural network for SRL model the learning rate $a_{SRL} = 0.01$. The critic network and the actor network learning rate and other parameters are consistent with the M3DDPG algorithm. The final result is shown in [see Fig. 5].

We can learn from Fig. 5 that the average rewards for the two rounds are similar within the first 10,000 episodes (100 records). As the episode increases, the mean episode reward of SRL-M3DPPG algorithm is higher than M3DDPG algorithm.

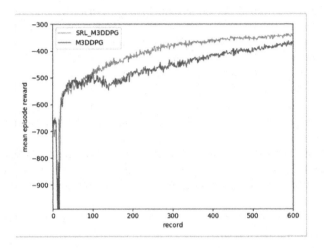

Fig. 5. Comparison of the mean episode reward of the two algorithms (making a record for every hundred episodes)

Experiments show that the SRL_M3DDPG algorithm is better than the M3DDPG algorithm in most cases. In this paper we combine state representation learning of neural networks model and M3DDPG to extract the important characteristics of data. This method does not affect the structure and function of the M3DDPG algorithm, and can help the agent to obtain important features.

4   Conclusion

In the paper we propose a new algorithm SRL_M3DDPG, which uses prior knowledge to complete the training before learning the RL task. However there are still many shortcomings in our work. In particular, how to improve the efficiency of cooperation between agents, by increasing the number of agents that are worth researching and we only use the cooperative navigation environment, by increasing the number of agents, which has no obvious effect.

In the future, we will study the situation of agents in more complex and diverse environments, especially complex and competitive environments. Other work will be further studied in the future.

Acknowledgments. This work was supported in part by National Key R&D Program of China (No. 2017YFA0700604).

References

1. Foerster, J., Farquhar, G., Afouras, T., Nardelli, N., Whiteson, S.: Counterfactual multiagent policy gradients. arXiv preprint arXiv:1705.08926 (2017)
2. Lowe, R.: Multi-agent actor-critic for mixed cooperative-competitive environments. In: Neural Information Processing Systems (NIPS) (2017)
3. Shihui, L., Yi, W., Xinyue, C., Honghua, D., Fei, F., Stuart, R.: Robust multi-agent reinforcement learning via minimax deep deterministic policy gradient. In: AAAI Conference on Artificial Intelligence (AAAI) (2019)
4. Yeung, S., Russakovsky, O., Mori, G., Fei-Fei, L.: End-to-end learning of action detection from frame glimpses in videos. In: The IEEE Conference on Computer Vision and Pattern Recognition (CVPR), pp. 2678–2687 (2016)
5. Mnih, V., Kavukcuoglu, K., Silver, D.: Playing atari with deep reinforcement learning: arXiv:1312.5602 [cs.LG]
6. Bengio, Y., Courville, A., Vincent, P.: Representation learning: a review and new perspectives. IEEE Trans. Pattern Anal. Mach. Intell. $35(8)$, 1798–1828 (2013)
7. Duan, Y., Schulman, J., Chen, X.: RL2: Fast reinforcement learning via slow reinforcement learning. arXiv:1611.02779
8. Finn, C.: Learning visual feature spaces for robotic manipulation with deep spatial autoencoders (2015)
9. Lange, S., Riedmiller, M., Voigtlander, A.: Autonomous reinforcement learning on raw visual input data in a real world application. In: International Joint Conference on Neural Networks, pp. 1–8 (2012). https://doi.org/10.1109/ijcnn.2012.6252823
10. Li, Z., Jiang, X.: State representation learning for multi-agent deep deterministic policy gradient. In: Krömer, P., Zhang, H., Liang, Y., Pan, J.-S. (eds.) ECC 2018. AISC, vol. 891, pp. 667–675. Springer, Cham (2019). https://doi.org/10.1007/978-3-030-03766-6_75
11. Akgül, C.B., Rubin, D.L., Napel, S.: Content-based image retrieval in radiology: current status and future. J. Digit. Imaging $24(2)$, 208–222 (2011)

Low-Sampling Imagery Data Recovery by Deep Learning Inference and Iterative Approach

Jiping Lin, Yu Zhou$^{(\boxtimes)}$, and Junhao Kang

Shenzhen University, Shenzhen 518060, China
lin_ji_ping@163.com, zhouyu_1022@126.com, 1800271054@email.szu.edu.cn

Abstract. Block-based compressed sensing (CS) recovery aims to reconstruct the high quality image from only a small number of observations in a block-wise manner. However, when the sampling rate is very low and the existence of additive noise, there are usually some block artifacts and detail blurs which degrades the reconstructed quality. In this paper, we propose an efficient method which takes both the advantages of deep learning (DL) framework and iterative approaches. First, a deep multi-layer perceptron (DMLP) is constructed to obtain the initial reconstructed image. Then, an efficient iterative approach is applied to keep the consistence and smoothness between the adjacent blocks. The proposed method demonstrates its efficacy on benchmark datasets.

Keywords: Compressed sensing · Deep learning · Iterative approach

1 Introduction

In block compressive sensing (BCS) [5], an image $\mathbf{X}$ is divided into a certain number of image blocks with size $B \times B$. For the ith block,

$$\mathbf{y}_i = \boldsymbol{\Phi}_B \mathbf{x}_i + \mathbf{n}_i \tag{1}$$

where $\boldsymbol{\Phi}_B \in R^{M_B \times B^2}$ represents the sensing matrix, $\mathbf{y}_i \in R^{M_B}$ is the observed vector for the ith block, $\mathbf{x}_i \in R^{B^2}$ denotes the ith vectorized block and $\mathbf{n}_i$ denotes the additive noise.

Given $\boldsymbol{\Phi}_B$, designing efficient approaches to recover $\mathbf{x}_i$ from $\mathbf{y}_i$ is very critical. It is well-known that most of existing BCS are based on the iterative approaches [2–4,6]. To further improve the quality of the reconstructed image, more comprehensive models, such as the bilevel optimization model [10], multi-objective optimization models [11] and sparsity-enhanced models [2,6] are proposed. Although proper modeling could contribute a bit in achieving very competitive results, these models are usually not easy to solve, which requires different iterative approaches, e.g. iterative thresholding shrinkage methods, gradient-based methods or some evolutionary algorithms. To obtain the satisfactory results, it is often

© Springer Nature Switzerland AG 2019
C. Douligeris et al. (Eds.): KSEM 2019, LNAI 11775, pp. 488–493, 2019.
https://doi.org/10.1007/978-3-030-29551-6_44

the case that more number of iterations are preferred, increasing the computational complexity. Moreover, the initial solution is also very important, which is currently obtained either by random initialization or by the least squares (LS) method. When the sampling rate (SR) is small (less than 20%), which makes the problem seriously ill-posed, these methods may not guide the iterative algorithm to converge to a high quality solution fast enough.

In this paper, we propose an efficient method which takes both the advantages of deep learning framework and the iterative approaches. First, a deep multi-layer perceptron (DMLP) is trained to find the mapping between BCS measurements and the original imagery blocks. Then, an efficient iterative approach is applied on the whole image to further reduce the block artifacts between the adjacent blocks. The proposed method is compared with several state-of-the-art competitors on the benchmark database and demonstrates its efficacy. The rest of our paper is organized as follows. Section 2 introduces our proposed BCS reconstruction approach, the experimental studies are presented in Sect. 3, and the conclusion is finally made in Sect. 4.

2 The Proposed Method

2.1 Deep MLP

Following the suggestions in [1], the structure of deep MLP (DMLP) is shown in Fig. 1, which consists of give layers.

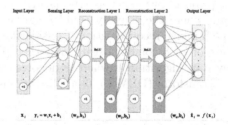

Fig. 1. Structure of the proposed DMLP

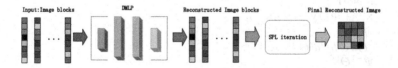

Fig. 2. Flowchart of our proposed approach

For the input layer, the number of neurons is set equal to the length of vectorized image block, B^2. The connection weights between the input layer and the sensing layer construct the sensing matrix, where the signal $\mathbf{x}_i \in R^{B^2}$ is mapped to $\mathbf{y}_i \in R^{M_B}$ ($M_B \ll B^2$). There are two reconstruction layers that perform recovery of $\mathbf{x}_i$ from $\mathbf{y}_i$ and each followed by an activation function in terms of rectified linear units (ReLU) [7]. The length of the reconstruction layer is usually determined by $B^2 \times T$, where T denotes the redundancy parameter for reconstruction. The output layer has the same size with input layer, which denotes the reconstructed signal, $\hat{\mathbf{x}}_i$. In overall, the mathematical expression of the DMLP can be written as:

$$f(\mathbf{x}) = \mathbf{W}_4 \cdot ReLU\left(\mathbf{W}_3 \cdot ReLU\left(\mathbf{W}_2\left(\mathbf{W}_1\mathbf{x} + \mathbf{b}_1\right) + \mathbf{b}_2\right) + \mathbf{b}_3\right) + \mathbf{b}_4 \quad (2)$$

where $\cdot$ denotes the product between matrix and vector and $ReLU(\mathbf{x}) = max(\mathbf{0}, \mathbf{x})$ is the activation function based on an element-wise comparison.

Table 1. Statistical results of PSNR and SSIM for BCS considering the overlap

Methods	$SR = 0.1$		$SR = 0.125$		$SR = 0.15$		$SR = 0.175$	
BCS-SPL-DDWT [6]	26.48	0.847	26.89	0.864	28.55	0.889	28.85	0.910
MS-BCS-SPL [3]	28.94	0.920	29.51	0.951	29.82	0.955	30.11	0.958
MH-BCS-BCS-SPL [2]	29.33	0.920	29.96	0.951	30.87	0.967	31.36	0.978
BCS-DNN [1]	29.47	0.943	30.38	0.955	31.16	0.969	31.58	0.981
Proposed	**30.37**	**0.955**	**30.65**	**0.963**	**31.28**	**0.971**	**31.60**	**0.983**

2.2 Smoothed Projected Landweber Algorithm

Landweber iteration algorithm is a classical approach to solve the ill-posed linear inverse problems. The projected version converts the original signal into a sparse or compressive domain where the sparsity could be enhanced, so it could be intuitively applied in CS image reconstruction. Considering removing the block artifacts, the procedure of BCS combined with smoothed projected Landweber (SPL) algorithm is given in Algorithm 1, where $\mathbf{\Psi}$ denotes the sparse basis Dual-tree Discrete Wavelet Transform (DDWT) [6] applied in our method.

Algorithm 1. BCS-SPL

1: While not terminated
2: $\hat{\mathbf{x}}^{(i)} = Wiener(\mathbf{x}^{(i)})$;
3: for each block j
4: $\hat{\mathbf{x}}_j^{(i)} = \hat{\mathbf{x}}_j^{(i)} + \mathbf{\Phi}_B^T(\mathbf{y}_j - \mathbf{\Phi}_B\hat{\mathbf{x}}_j^{(i)})$;
5: $\mathbf{\Theta}^{(i)} = \mathbf{\Psi}\hat{\mathbf{x}}^{(i)}$;
6: $\hat{\mathbf{\Theta}}^{(i)} = Threshold(\mathbf{\Theta}^{(i)}, \lambda)$;
7: $\hat{\mathbf{x}}^{(i)} = \mathbf{\Psi}^{-1}\hat{\mathbf{\Theta}}^{(i)}$;
8: for each block j
9: $\hat{\mathbf{x}}_j^{(i+1)} = \hat{\mathbf{x}}_j^{(i)} + \mathbf{\Phi}_B^T(\mathbf{y}_j - \mathbf{\Phi}_B\hat{\mathbf{x}}_j^{(i)})$;
10: $i = i + 1$;
11: End
12: **return** $\hat{\mathbf{x}}^{(i+1)}$

2.3   The Flowchart of Our Approach

As presented in Fig. 2, the proposed method is composed of two stages: at first, we establish an end-to-end deep neural network based on MLP and obtain the reconstructed image block by block based on inference. In the second stage, the reconstructed image in the first stage is used as the initial solution, $x^{(0)}$, the SPL iteration method is applied to get the ultimately recovered image.

3   Experimental Studies

3.1   Parameter Settings

In our experiment, we randomly choose 5,000,000 image blocks from 50,000 images in LabelME database [8]. The learning rate is set to 0.005, the batch size is 16 with a block size 16×16 and the redundancy parameter R is equal to 8. All the training images for DMLP are converted into grayscale images.

3.2   Numerical and Visual Results

In Table 1, the peak signal-to-noise ratio (PSNR) and structural similarity index (SSIM) [9] for 10 test images when SR is equal to 0.1, 0.125, 0.15 and 0.175 are given and each image is tested for 20 times. For simplicity, we fixed the overlap equal to 8 in all the simulations. It is demonstrated that our proposed method could achieve significantly higher PSNR and SSIM. In comparison to the DL-based method, the proposed approach could have a maximum 0.9dB gain in PSNR and the improvement is more significant when the SR is smaller. Our method utilizes the powerful regression ability of DNN in the first stage and have a very good estimated initial solution for the iterative process in the second stage especially under a very low SR.

Table 2. Average computational time for different BCS methods

Methods	Time (seconds)	Time with overlap (seconds)
BCS-SPL-DDWT	9.54	20.25
MS-BCS-SPL	103.55	231.56
MH-BCS-BCS-SPL	161.37	339.08
BCS-DNN	0.65	2.56
Proposed	0.92	4.06

3.3 Computational Time

To evaluate the efficiency of our proposed method, the computational time for different methods with and without overlap between the adjacent blocks is recorded in Table 2. BCS-DNN only needs the fast inference, which is able to be completed in around 3 s. In our method, the initial solution obtained by DNN is usually near-optimal, which largely reduces the iterative times. So, its computational time is comparative to BCS-DNN and could achieve a higher reconstruction quality.

4   Conclusion

In this paper, we proposed an efficient CS recover method. At first, a DMLP is built where the recovered image block is obtained based on the inference from the learned regression parameters and its input measurements. Then, SPL is applied on the whole image to further reduce the block artifacts and improve the pixel consistence and smoothness between the adjacent blocks. Experimental results demonstrate that our method could not only achieve competitive numerical results but also outperform the compared methods in visual quality.

Acknowledgment. This work is supported in part by the Natural Science Foundation of China under Grant 61702336, in part by Shenzhen Emerging Industries of the Strategic Basic Research Project JCYJ20170302154254147, and in part by Natural Science Foundation of SZU (grant No. 2018068).

References

1. Adler, A., Boublil, D., Elad, M., Zibulevsky, M.: A deep learning approach to block-based compressed sensing of images. arXiv preprint arXiv:1606.01519 (2016)
2. Chen, C., Tramel, E.W., Fowler, J.E.: Compressed-sensing recovery of images and video using multihypothesis predictions. In: 2011 Conference Record of the Forty Fifth Asilomar Conference on Signals, Systems and Computers (ASILOMAR), pp. 1193–1198. IEEE (2011)
3. Fowler, J.E., Mun, S., Tramel, E.W.: Multiscale block compressed sensing with smoothed projected landweber reconstruction. In: 2011 European Signal Processing Conference, pp. 564–568 (2011)
4. Fowler, J.E., Mun, S., Tramel, E.W., et al.: Block-based compressed sensing of images and video. Found. Trends Sig. Process. 4(4), 297–416 (2012)
5. Gan, L.: Block compressed sensing of natural images. In: 2007 15th International Conference on Digital Signal Processing, pp. 403–406, July 2007. https://doi.org/10.1109/ICDSP.2007.4288604
6. Mun, S., Fowler, J.E.: Block compressed sensing of images using directional transforms. In: 2010 Data Compression Conference. pp. 547–547, March 2010. https://doi.org/10.1109/DCC.2010.90
7. Nair, V., Hinton, G.E.: Rectified linear units improve restricted Boltzmann machines. In: International Conference on Machine Learning, pp. 807–814 (2010)

8. Russell, B.C., Torralba, A., Murphy, K.P., Freeman, W.T.: Labelme: a database and web-based tool for image annotation. Int. J. Comput. Vision **77**(1–3), 157–173 (2008)
9. Wang, Z., Bovik, A.C., Sheikh, H.R., Simoncelli, E.P.: Image quality assessment: from error visibility to structural similarity. IEEE Trans. Image Process. **13**(4), 600–612 (2004)
10. Zhou, Y., Kwong, S., Guo, H., Gao, W., Wang, X.: Bilevel optimization of block compressive sensing with perceptually nonlocal similarity. Inf. Sci. **360**, 1–20 (2016). https://doi.org/10.1016/j.ins.2016.03.027
11. Zhou, Y., Kwong, S., Guo, H., Zhang, X., Zhang, Q.: A two-phase evolutionary approach for compressive sensing reconstruction. IEEE Trans. Cybern. **47**(9), 2651–2663 (2017)

Knowledge Graph and Knowledge Management

Enhancing Graph-Based Keywords Extraction with Node Association

Huifang Ma[1,2,3]($\boxtimes$), Shuang Wang[1], Miao Li[1], and Ning Li[4]

[1] College of Computer Science and Engineering,
Northwest Normal University, Lanzhou 730070, Gansu, China
mahuifang@yeah.net
[2] Guangxi Key Laboratory of Trusted Software,
Guilin University of Electronic Technology, Guilin 541004, China
[3] Guangxi Key Lab of Multi-source Information Mining and Security,
Guangxi Normal University, Guilin 541004, China
[4] Institute of Information Engineering, Chinese Academy of Sciences,
Beijing 100093, China

Abstract. In this paper, we present an enhancing graph-based keywords extraction method with node association (GKENA), which strengths graph-based keywords extraction approaches by applying strong association rule mining and unifying three different node attributes into a single framework. Specifically, we regard one single document as a sequential transaction dataset, and apply an efficient algorithm to exploit closed frequent sets and the strong association rules are generated to represent the correlations among multiple terms for association graph construction. Each graph node represents combinations of two or more terms and three node attributes (i.e. graph structure, node semantics and associations) are unified to transfer extra node information into a Markov chain model to obtain the ranking. Besides, in order to avoid the semantic overlapping among top ranked candidate words, a trustworthy clustering algorithm is employed and the center word in each cluster is selected to construct the keywords sets. Our experiments on both Chinese and English datasets indicate that GKENA can boost the quality of keywords in graph-based keywords extraction techniques.

Keywords: Keywords extraction · Graph-based ranking ·
Node association mining · Graph structure

1 Introduction

Along with the popularity of Internet technology, numerous documents have been made available electronically. Extracting keywords from massive texts can help individuals obtain the worthwhile information. Keywords are highly condensed summaries that serve as meaningful and significant expressions consisting of one or more words in documents. These keywords can be highlighted within

© Springer Nature Switzerland AG 2019
C. Douligeris et al. (Eds.): KSEM 2019, LNAI 11775, pp. 497–510, 2019.
https://doi.org/10.1007/978-3-030-29551-6_45

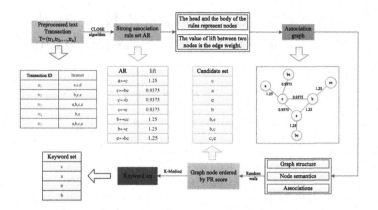

Fig. 1. The research framework for GKENA

the body of the document to facilitate users' fast browsing and reading, which have been widely used in document summarization, text categorization, full-text indexing, and cross-lingual text reuse [1].

As for supervised keyword extraction methods, they always require manually annotated training datasets, which are not easy to obtain. Furthermore, these approaches are generally domain-specific, and may require time and resource consuming retraining when the domain is changed. Unsupervised methods for keywords extraction can be categorized as statistic-based methods, latent semantic analysis methods, and graph-based methods. The statistic-based approach assess the terms' degrees of importance to the document based on internal and external characteristics in document and corpus respectively. For instance, TF-IDF(Term Frequency-Inverse Document Frequency) [2] and JSD(Jensen-Shannon Divergence) [3] are typical keywords extraction methods focusing on the internal characteristics, including word frequency, position and co-occurrence distribution between words. In terms of latent semantic analysis it [4] seeks latent semantic information among document collection under the framework of document-topic model, which construct the word-topic-document structure to capture latent semantic between word and document. For graph-based keywords extraction methods, a text is always converted into a graph whose nodes represent text units(e.g., words, phrases, and sentences) and whose edges represent the relationships between these units. Graph-based keywords extraction originates from PageRank algorithm [5], which works by counting the number and quality of links to a node to determine a rough estimate of how important the node is. They always take text structure and relations between words into consideration. A well-known graph-based method is TextRank [6], which runs PageRank on a graph specially designed for a keywords extraction or document summarization task. Recently, GraphSum [7] believes there are strong and weak association between nodes in a graph and new algorithm should discriminates between positive and negative term correlations.

Our key innovation is to take node attributes as additional to capture semantic meanings in the text. As a result, we can collect a set of good keywords candidates and further employ graph-based ranking scheme to build a document-specific keywords extraction model. Figure 1 illustrates the research framework for GKENA. More specifically, in this work, we overcome the problem of requiring document sets while still obtaining high-quality keywords. The main advantages are efficiency, domain-independence and single-document operation. GKENA leverages the benefits of graph-based keywords extraction by taking into account the structure and three different node attributes within an individual document. It boosts its effectiveness via mining the frequent closed items for graph construction and analyzing positive and negative term correlations separately, which increases the scores of words more likely to be relevant and lowers the scores of those that are negatively correlated to one another. Besides, we capture the attributes of nodes derived from internal graph structure information. Thereafter, the complex structure information such as the sum of degrees of neighbor nodes 2 steps away can be considered. The experimental results on two manually annotated datasets show that GKENA proposes high-quality keywords and outperforms several baseline and the state-of-the-art keywords extraction methods on two datasets.

The rest of this paper is organized as follows. Section 2 introduces the preliminaries for association graph construction. Then we detail the GKENA algorithm in Sect. 3. Section 4 describes the experiment evaluation and discussions. Finally, we summarize our contributions and conclude the paper in Sect. 5.

2 Preliminaries

A document can be regarded as a transaction database made up of a large number of sentences and the association graph of the document depicts the association among two or more terms. More precisely, we focus on discovering recurrent combinations of terms, in the form of frequent closed itemsets, from the transactional representation of an individual document.

2.1 Strong Association Rules Mining

We perform the basic language-dependent analysis including data denoising and stop words removal. The document can be regarded as sentence set $St = \{st_1, st_2, ..., st_n\}$, where each st_i is split by a sequence of stop marks ('$._\circ$', '?', '!', '...'). Let each sentence $st_i = \{w_{i1}, w_{i2}, ..., w_{iz}\}$ corresponds to one transaction tr_i, and w_{iq} be the q-th word in tr_i. All words in a sentence that are not stop words are the items of the sentence. Hence, the transaction database is denoted as $T = \{tr_1, tr_2, ..., tr_n\}$ for the document.

Association rule is designed for discovering interesting relations between items in a transaction database and the basic format is $A \to B$ where $A \cap B = \varnothing$, $A \neq \varnothing$ and $B \neq \varnothing$. Some formal definitions are defined follows.

Item Set Transaction, Transaction Item Set. Let $C = (D, I, R)$ denote the task of data mining, non-empty transaction subset $T \subseteq D$, non-empty item subset $X \subseteq I$, then transaction set T The set of items included is: $f(T) = \{i | \forall d \in T, i \in I, (d, i) \in R\}$. The transaction covered by item set X is represented as: $g(X) = \{d | \forall i \in X, d \in D, (d, i) \in R\}$.

Closed Item Set. Item set X is a closed item set if and only if $S(X) = f(g(X)) = X$.

k-itemset. A k-itemsets (i.e., an itemset of length k) is defined as a set of k distinct terms, which is denoted as k-itemset.

sup(A→ B). The support $sup(A \to B)$ of $A \to B$ is defined as the number of transactions containing $A \cup B$ divided by the number of the whole transactions in T.

Associated Lift. The lift of this rule is defined as:

$$lift(A \to B) = \frac{sup(A \to B)}{sup(A) \times sup(B)} \tag{1}$$

In terms of conditional probability, we can get the follow conclusions:

(1) A is dependent from B if and only if $lift(A \to B) = 1$, which indicates that there is no relationship between A and B.
(2) The posterior probability of B is higher/lower than prior probability of B if and only if $lift(A \to B) > 1 / lift(A \to B) < 1$, which shows that there exists positive/negative association between A and B.

Strong Association Rule. If $sup(A \to B) \geq minsup$ and $lift(A \to B) \subseteq [-\infty, max^{-lift}] \cup [min^{+lift}, +\infty]$, then $A \to B$ is a strong association rule where $minsup$ is the minimum support threshold, max^{-lift} is the maximum negative association threshold and min^{+lift} is minimum positive association threshold.

Frequent Closed Itemset. The itemset X is the frequent closed itemset if and only if $sup(X) \geq minsup$ and $S(X) = X$ where $S(X)$ is closure operator of X.

Given the transactional representation T of the document D and $minsup$, max^{-lift} and min^{+lift}, the frequent closed itemset mining is to extract all of the closed frequent itemsets in T. GKENA exploits an implementation to obtain frequent closed itemsets [8] and produce strong association rules. CLOSE utilizes the closure operation and breadth-first traverse to search the itemset space, and achieves fast pruning of non-frequent itemset and non-closed itemset, which lead to small scale strong association rules without information loss and can effectively deal with the problem of complex graph structure. CLOSE extract the 1-itemsets of the document and compute the closure of them at start, then remove the non-frequent itemsets and generate the next size itemsets according to the closure. In the process of generating different itemsets, the space complex of CLOSE is $O(n^2)$.

2.2 Association Graph Generation

GKENA computes the score of nodes by random walking on the association graph, so the form of association graph will directly influence on efficiency of algorithm. Let AR denote the strong association rule set of the document and all no-repeating rule heads and rule bodies in AR be AR_{head} and AR_{body} respectively, and set the whole itemset in $N = AR_{head} \cup AR_{body}$ be nodes of graph. The association graph is constructed to describe the relation between two itemsets. There is an edge between two nodes if and only if there is strong association between them. Owing to the symmetry of $lift$, the edge is bidirectional and the weight of it is defined as $lift$.

Table 1. Example of transaction database

Transaction ID	tr_1	tr_2	tr_3	tr_4	tr_5
Itemset	a, c, d	b, c, e	a, b, c, e	b, e	a, b, c, e

Table 1 shows an example of an transaction database. Let $minsup = 0.6$, $min^{+lift} = 1.2$, $max^{-lift} = 0.95$, After performing CLOSE, the frequent closed itemset $FC = \{\{a, c\}, \{b, e\}, \{c\}, \{b, c, e\}\}$, the strong association rule set $AR = \{a \leftrightarrow c, c \leftrightarrow be, c \leftrightarrow b, c \leftrightarrow e, b \leftrightarrow ce, b \leftrightarrow e, e \leftrightarrow bc\}$, and the node set $N = \{\{b, c\}, \{b, e\}, \{c, e\}, \{a\}, \{b\}, \{c\}, \{e\}\}$, the $lift$ of these rules are treated as weight of each edge. In this way, we can obtain weighted undirected association graph as shown in Fig. 2.

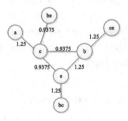

Fig. 2. Association graph of the document

3   The Proposed GKENA Algorithm

As a well-known unsupervised solution for ranking nodes based on their importance, PageRank [5] assumes that a highly ranked node is more likely to be pointed to by other highly ranked nodes. Based on the assumption, PageRank gives each node a ranking score by modeling itself using the Markov chain framework to obtain the unique converged ranking result. It outputs a probability distribution to represent the likelihood that a person randomly clicking on links will arrive at any particular page. PageRank can be calculated for collections of documents of any size. Formally, let N_i represent the i-th node in N, e indicate the number of incoming edge for N_i, $C(N_i)$ represent the outgoing degree of the node N_i and d be the damping factor which is recommended to be set to 0.85, then the PageRank score of N_i is defined as follows:

$$PR(N_i) = (1 - d)\frac{1}{|N|} + d\sum_{k=1}^{e}\frac{PR(N_k)}{N_k} \tag{2}$$

One potential drawback of PageRank is that it only propagates the near-by node scores and external information such as the attributes of nodes are not fully considered. Another limitation of PageRank is that the jumping probability of PageRank between two nodes is equal to $1/|N|$, which is not necessary the case however. There are positive associations and negative associations between nodes. GKENA improves the PageRank algorithm from the following two aspects: On one hand, more complex graph structure information such as the sum of degrees of neighbor nodes 2 steps away are considered and the semantic information of node attributes are fully revealed. On the other hand, higher scores to the nodes are assigned that are positively correlated with other term set and lower scores are set if two nodes are negatively correlated.

3.1 The Similarity Between Nodes

In terms of graph structure, if the connection form of two nodes are similar, they are more likely to be similar nodes in the form of graph structure. To quantify the graph structure attributions of one node, we define six indicators shown in Table 2, where $attr1 - attr3$ intuitively hint the ability of one node to be associated with the rest of nodes, $attr4$ reflects the similarity degree of one node with its neighbors, $attr5 - attr6$ inform the spreading ability of the node in the graph. Hence, the graph structure of node N_i can be formally represented as $Attr_i = (attr1, attr2, ..., attr6)$. To avoid large numerical scale, we take the logarithmic value of all the attributes.

Table 2. Six attribution indicators.

Attribution	Definition	Attribution	Definition
attr1	Number of nodes with distance of 1	attr4	Assortativity (attr1/average degree of neighbors)
attr2	Number of nodes with distance of 2	attr5	attr2/attr1
attr3	Number of nodes with distance of 3	attr6	attr3/attr2

From the perspective of node semantics, in our approach, the co-occurrence distribution of nodes N_i and I is $P = \{p_1, p_2, ..., p_m\}$, p_j represents the normalized value of the sentence containing N_i and w_j in the transaction set, and the co-occurrence distribution of N_j and I is $Q = \{q_1, q_2, ..., q_m\}$, The semantic distance [3] between N_i and N_j is calculated as follows:

$$
\begin{cases}
JSD(N_i, N_j) = \dfrac{1}{2}(\displaystyle\sum_{k=1}^{m} p_i \times log_2 \dfrac{p_i}{m_i} + \sum_{k=1}^{m} q_i \times log_2 \dfrac{q_i}{m_i}) \\
m_i = \dfrac{p_i + q_i}{2}
\end{cases}
\tag{3}
$$

We then optimize the distance metric of N_i and N_j considering the above two aspects as in formula (4). The L2 norm in formula (4) measures the difference of graph structure between the i-th node and j-th node. The larger the L2 norm is, the larger the difference is. The slower the s_{ij} is, the more difference of graph structure or semantic distribution between N_i and N_j is.

$$
\begin{cases}
s_{ij} = \dfrac{1}{JSD(N_i, N_j)} \times e^{-|Attr_i - Attr_j|_2^2} \\
|Attr_i - Attr_j|_2^2 = |Attr_i|^2 + |Attr_j|^2 - 2 Attr_i^T \cdot Attr_j
\end{cases}
\tag{4}
$$

A N-dimensional vector r is defined where each element r_i is defined as:

$$
\begin{cases}
r_i = \dfrac{1}{z} \sum_{j \in V} s_{ij} \\
z = \sum_{i \in V} \sum_{j \in V} s_{ij}
\end{cases}
\tag{5}
$$

We take r_i to modify the PageRank to change the jumping probability of PageRank between two nodes, i.e. the more similar two nodes are, the more likely they turn to jump. The updated formula is shown as formula (6), where $C(N_k)$ is the degree of N_k and e represents the number of neighbor of N_k.

$$
PR(N_i) = (1 - d) \times r_i + d \times \sum_{k=1}^{e} \frac{PR(N_k)}{N_k}
\tag{6}
$$

3.2 Associated Lift

Aiming to strengthening the positive association voting score and decreasing the negative association voting score at the same time, we adapt lift to formula (6) as:

$$
PR(N_i) = (1 - d) \times r_i + d \times \sum_{k=1}^{e} \frac{PR(N_k) \times lift(N_i, N_k)}{N_k}
\tag{7}
$$

where $lift(N_i, N_k)$ represents the association degree between N_i and N_k, $lift < 1$ indicates the association between N_i and N_k is negative while positive on the contrary. Hence, $lift$ could adjust the $PR(N_k)$ according to the feature of association. According to the formula (7), GKENA is performed on the association graph, and the PR score of each node is iteratively calculated until the formula is satisfied with formula (8) where δ is the random walking threshold.

$$
\sum_{i=1}^{|N|} |PR^{t+1}(N_i) - PR^t(N_i)| \leq \delta
\tag{8}
$$

3.3   Keywords Clustering

Clustering is applied to data mining tasks to explore hidden similar relationships between data. Common clustering algorithms are K-Means, K-Medoids. K-Means is sensitive to isolated points, and if it has a maximum value, it can greatly distort the distribution of data. The K-medoids algorithm is proposed to eliminate this sensitivity. The keyword candidate set of the document is formed by taking a subset of frequent itemsets of different lengths, and the k-item set contains 2^k-1 non-empty subsets, and the 1-item set must be $(k$-1$)$-item set A subset of this phenomenon can be seen as a $(k$-1$)$-item set with a semantic inclusion relationship for a 1-item set. To avoid the semantic inclusion between the extracted keywords, the sorted nodes are then clustered via K-Medoids clustering algorithm [9]. We then sort PR in descending order, and select the top P nodes. The algorithm flow is detailed in Algorithm 1.

Algorithm 1. Graph-based Keywords Extraction Method with Node Association

Require:
  the preprocessing document; $minsup$; min^{+lift}; max^{-lift}; d; K; P; δ;
Ensure:
  Keywords set
1: Extract strong association rule set AR using CLOSE;
2: Construct association graph according to AR;
3: Initialize PR score of each node to $PR(N_i) = 1/|N|$;
4: Calculate each similarity s_{ij} according to formula (4);
5: Calculate the similarity vector r according to formula (5);
6: Iteratively compute PR score of each node via formula (7) until satisfied with formula (8);
7: Sort PR in descending order, and select the top P nodes;
8: Apply K-Medoids to cluster the P nodes;
9: Return all of the cluster centers;

---

4   Experiments and Results Analysis

The experimental design consists of four parts. Firstly, we adopt authoritative Chinese and English data sets and three standard evaluation metrics. Secondly, we analyze the input parameters for the optimal association graph construction. Thirdly, we discuss the influence of scale of the keywords extraction on the optimal association graph. Finally, the proposed method will be compared with four typical keywords extraction algorithms to verify its effectiveness.

4.1   Data Sets and Evaluation Metrics

Two representative long text: the book *Origin of Species* http://vdisk.weibo.com/s/uheNHb1stTh6u (Chinese version) by Charles Darwin (Darwin'book) along with the paper —The Role of Entropy in Word Ranking [10] by Mehri and Darooneh (MD'paper) (English texts) are adopted, which have been wildly used by a large number of scholars to verify the accuracy of various keyword extraction algorithms [3,6,11]. After the preprocessing step, there are 39,599 words and 3495 sentences in Darwin'book which are distributed in 14 sections, and there are 1,185 words and 49 sentences in MD'paper. All of the corresponding transactions of sentences are then applied for strong association rules mining, association graph construction. Moreover, the glossary of Darwin'book and the title and abstract of MD'paper are analyzed, 15 important words and 9 representative terms are taken as the benchmark, respectively.

We use MAP (Mean Average Precision) [12], $Recall$ and F_β [13] score for quantitative evaluation, where MAP is defined as follows:

$$P(i) = \frac{1}{i} \sum_{j=i}^{i} g(M_{ret}(j), M_{rel})$$

$$AP(i) = \frac{\sum_{j=i}^{i} P(j) \times g(M_{ret}(j), M_{rel})}{\sum_{j=i}^{i} g(M_{ret}(j), M_{rel})} \tag{9}$$

$$MAP = \frac{1}{M_{ret}} \times \sum_{j=i}^{M_{ret}} AP(i)$$

Where M_{ret} represents the returned keyword sequence, M_{rel} denotes the keywords sequence in the glossary, $M_{ret}(j)$ denotes the j-th word in M_{ret}. $g(t, M_{rel}(j))$ is an indicator function, returns 1 if the term t appears in the original vocabulary sequence M_{rel}, otherwise returns 0. $P(i)$ and $AP(i)$ represent the accuracy and mean average accuracy.

Since the returned keywords are expected not only with high accuracy but also in the top position, we apply MAP to calculate F_β, and set $\beta = 0.5$ as follows.

$$R = \frac{|M_{ret} \cap M_{rel}|}{|M_{ret}|}$$
$$F_\beta = \frac{(1 + \beta^2) \times MAP \times R}{\beta^2 \times MAP + R} \tag{10}$$

4.2   The Model Parameters

It is worth noting that the structure of the association graph directly determines the effect of GKENA. There are many parameters for the association graph, different parameter settings lead to different association graph. For instance, a bigger $minsup$ setting may discard some relevant words, while numerous redundant words would be retained if $minsup$ is too small. Furthermore, min^{+lift} and max^{-lift} will influence the structure of the association graph, and the coefficient d will affect the result of keywords extraction. Considering the limitation of our paper, we only utilize Chinese data as an example to analyze the parameter setting.

The $minsup$ is set between [0.3%, 1.6%], and max^{-lift} starts from 0.55 and with a 0.05 step, the initial value of min^{+lift} is 2 and with a 3 step, d is set between [0.15, 0.85] according to experience. In addition, we set M_v as the keyword sequence. In order to avoid the excessive parameter change, the extraction effect analysis is complicated. The number of keywords extracted is not considered at present. When the model parameters are adjusted, The top $|M_{rel}|$ of each keyword sequence M_v is extracted as the extracted keyword sequence M_{ret}, and the input parameter of the association graph model and the change curve of the MAP are plotted.

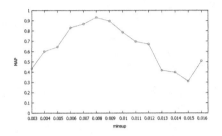

Fig. 3. Impact of $minsup$ to MAP

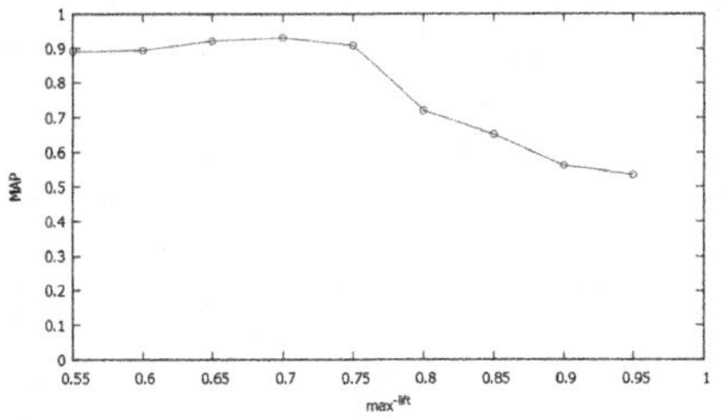

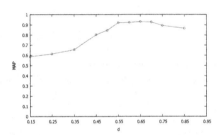

Fig. 4. Impact of max^{-lift} to MAP

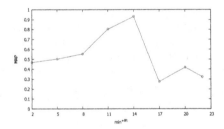

Fig. 5. Impact of min^{+lift} to MAP

Fig. 6. Impact of d to MAP

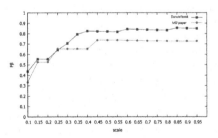

Fig. 7. Impact of scale to F_β (Color figure online)

Table 3. Keyword extracted by different algorithm on Darwin'book.

Index	Glossary	GEKNA	TextRank	GraphSum	NA	GS
1	Species	Species	Species	Species	Species	Species
2	Variation	Variation	Type	Variation	Variation	Heredity
3	Heredity	Natural selection	Animal	Living	Habitat	Habit
4	Instinct	Living environment	Change	Extinction	Heredity	Variation
5	Natural selection	Heredity	Difference	Heredity	Consanguinity	Extinction
6	Sterile hybridization	Geography distribution	Plant	Differentiation	Character	Ancestor
7	Isolation	Character	Biology	Characte	Natural selection	Natural selection
8	Extinction	Fossil	Variation	Varietas	Hybrid	Instinct
9	Character	Sterile hybridization	Living	Ancestor	Instinct	Character
10	Geography distribution	Survive struggle	Posterity	Consanguinity	Sterile hybridization	Consanguinity
11	Survive struggle	Geology	Seed	Fossil	Fossil	Population
12	Ancestor	Population	Structure	Difference	Ancestor	Biology
13	Posterity	Extinction	Gender	Posterity	Varietas	Hybridization
14	Fossil	Domestic	Natural selection	Natural selection	Extinction	Distribution
15	Population	Malaysia amphibious	Varietas	Plant	Posterity	Fossil
MAP	–	0.9334	0.7490	0.8614	0.8525	0.9003
P	–	0.7333	0.2666	0.6	0.7333	0.6666
F_β	–	0.8851	0.5501	0.7924	0.8257	0.8413

Figure 3 illustrates that the effect of GKENA when $minsup$ changes between the $[0.3, 0.8]$. It can be seen that when $minsup$ is bigger than 1%, the MAP declines rapidly. Figures 4 and 5 indicate that the MAP is gradually increasing when max^{-lift} and min^{+lift} are set in the ranges $[0.55, 0.75]$ and $[2, 14]$ respectively, and it appears to be sharply affected by slightly increasing max^{-lift} and min^{+lift}. Figure 6 shows that the keyword extraction effect of GKENA rises steadily with the increase of d, and reaches the fixed value when $d \geq 0.55$. Besides, we find that the $lift$ value may affect a dozen more than the graph structure, and the association graph model built on Chinese data can achieve the best extraction when $minsup = 0.8\%$, $min^{+lift} = 14$, $max^{-lift} = 0.7$, and $d = 0.65$.

Table 4. Keyword extracted by different algorithm on MD's paper.

Index	Glossary	GEKNA	TextRank	GraphSum	NA	GS
1	Entropy	Keyword extraction	Keyword	Word rank	Word rank	Word rank
2	Keyword extraction	Word rank	Text	Keyword extraction	Keyword extraction	Text mine
3	Complexity system	Entropy	Entropy	Entropy	Rank	Keyword extraction
4	Word rank	Entropy metric	Rank	Text entropy	Entropy	Rank
5	Text mine	Text mine	Retrieve	Information retrieve	Text	Information retrieve
6	Information theory	Statistic	System	Extraction	Information retrieve	Entropy
7	Complex systems	Information retrieve	Frequence	Metric measure	Extract	Extract
8	Systematic measure	Distance	Standard	Text keyword	Text keyword	Distance
9	Statistical mechanics	Occurrence	Extraction	Retrieve	Word retrieve	Standard
MAP	–	0.9722	0.2593	0.8703	0.9444	0.9629
P	–	0.4444	0.1111	0.4444	0.3333	0.4444
F_β	–	0.7856	0.2047	0.7301	0.6911	0.7808

4.3 The Scale of Extraction

Keyword extraction focuses on selecting the most related words to the document, so the scale of keywords appears to be critical. This paper introduces the keyword extraction parameter $scale = M_{ret}/M_v$, then $M_{ret} = scale \times M_v$ represents the scale of extracting keywords from the descending sequence M_v. Figure 7 illustrates F_β as a function of $scale$ fraction for Darwin'book (purple with squared point) and MD'paper (green with round point).

For Darwin'book, when parameters are set as optimal, 87 nodes are generated and $M_v = 23$ nodes can be retrieved, and the maximum value of $F_\beta = 0.8548$ when $scale = 85\%$. This means that, the best choice for retrieved words list of this book is a sequence which includes top $M_{ret} = 0.85 \times M_v$ of entries in the sorted list. Similar work is done on MD'paper, we have the maximum values $F_\beta = 0.7296$ at $scale = 0.8$ and $M_v = 11$ in the case of parameters setting as $minsup = 12\%$, $min^{+lift} = 5$, $max^{-lift} = 0.8$ and $d = 0.75$.

4.4 Algorithm Comparison

For a quantitative comparison between GKENA and other typical keywords extraction algorithms, we adopt TextRank, GraphSum, NA (Keywords Extraction Method by Nodes Association) and GS (Keywords Extraction Method by Graph Structure).

We choose the above four methods mainly based on the following points: (1) TextRank is the classical keywords extraction algorithm; (2) NA and GS are variants of GKENA; (3) GraphSum is the most similar to this paper. Since GraphSum is mainly used to generate the summary of document, we remove the sentence coverage steps of the original GraphSum. Besides, in order to give the comparative algorithms some advantages, all algorithms are performed on the optimal association graph obtained by GKENA.

Tables 3 and 4 show the returned keywords under three evaluation metrics on two authoritative data sets. From the experimental results, we can see that the effect of GraphSum is slightly worse compared with GKENA, which indicates that the graph structure attribute and associated $lift$ are useful to improve the performance of keywords extraction. Furthermore, due to the lack of semantic similar words clustering in GraphSum, there exits semantic similar redundant words. However, the effect of TextRank is the worst without considering graph structure and associated $lift$. It is worth noting that, although the accuracy of the NA and GS are roughly the same as the GKENA algorithm in accuracy, the MAP of GKENA is more impressive than NA and GS.

5   Conclusion

In this paper, we put forward a keywords extraction algorithm combining graph structure with nodes association. Firstly, we apply CLOSE to obtain the strong association rules for the association graph construction. Then, we design GKENA algorithm via considering the graph structure, semantic information and associated lift between nodes, which increases the jumping possibility between non-neighbor nodes. Besides, it also strengthens the positive association and decreases the negative association between neighbor nodes. Finally, we cluster the returned keywords sequence which can avoid the problem of semantic inclusion. Experiments show that our method outperforms four typical methods under MAP and F_β on two authoritative datasets. In the future, we plan to explore the new forms of association graph and optimize the efficiency of GKENA. In addition, the proper parameters setting in GKENA make a difference to the result. The advantage is that GKENA cannot adaptively generate appropriate hyperparametric values for arbitrary text, so GKENA sets the proper parameters to the empiric value. In the future, we aim to find the mapping relationship between hyper-parameters and text length to achieve the self-adaptation of GKENA.

Acknowledgments. The work is supported by the National Natural Science Foundation of China (No. 61762078, 61363058, 61802404, 61702508) Guangxi Key Laboratory of Trusted Software (No. kx201910) and Research Fund of Guangxi Key Lab of Multisource Information Mining & Security (MIMS18-08), Key Research Program of Beijing Municipal Science & Technology Commission (Grant No. D18110100060000).

References

1. Xie, F., Wu, X.D., Zhou, X.: Efficient sequential pattern mining with wildcards for keyphrase extraction. Knowl. Based Syst. **115**, 27–39 (2017)

2. Doen, Y., Murata, M., Otake, R., Tokuhisa, M.: Construction of concept network from large numbers of texts for information examination using TF-IDF and deletion of unrelated words. In: 8th International Symposium on Soft Computing and Intelligent Systems, pp. 1108–1113. IEEE Computer Society (2014)

3. Mehri, A., Jamaati, M., Mehri, H.: Word ranking in a single document by Jensen-Shannon divergence. Phys. Lett. A **379**(28–29), 1627–1632 (2015)

4. Blei, D.M., Ng, A.Y., Jordan, M.I.: Latent dirichlet allocation. J. Mach. Learn. Res. **3**(6), 993–1022 (2012)

5. Brin, S., Page, L.: Reprint of: the anatomy of a large-scale hypertextual web search engine. Comput. Netw. **56**(18), 3825–3833 (2012)

6. Li, W., Zhao, J.: TextRank algorithm by exploiting wikipedia for short text keywords extraction. In: 3rd International Conference on Information Science and Control Engineering, pp. 683–686. IEEE, Beijing (2016)

7. Baralis, E., Cagliero, L., Mahoto, N., Fiori, A.: GraphSum: discovering correlations among multiple terms for graph-based summarization. Inf. Sci. **249**(16), 96–109 (2013)

8. Pasquier, N., Bastide, Y., Taouil, R., Lakhal, L.: Efficient mining of association rules using closed itemset lattices. Inf. Syst. **24**(1), 25–46 (1999)

9. Li, P.P., Wang, H., Zhu, K.Q., Wang, Z.: A large probabilistic semantic network based approach to compute term similarity. IEEE Trans. Knowl. Data Eng. **27**(10), 2604–2617 (2015)

10. Mehri, A., Darooneh, A.H.: The role of entropy in word ranking. Physica A **390**(18–19), 3157–3163 (2011)

11. Yang, Z., Lei, J., Fan, K., Lai, Y.: Keyword extraction by entropy difference between the intrinsic and extrinsic mode. Physica A **392**(19), 4523–4531 (2013)

12. Lv, X., El-Gohary, N.M.: Semantic annotation for context-aware information retrieval for supporting the environmental review of transportation projects. J. Comput. Civil Eng. **30**(6), 332–338 (2016)

13. Liu, M., Xu, C., Luo, Y., Wen, Y.: Cost-sensitive feature selection by optimizing F-measures. IEEE Trans. Image Process. **27**(3), 1323–1335 (2018)

TransI: Translating Infinite Dimensional Embeddings Based on Trend Smooth Distance

Xiaobo Guo[1,2,3], Neng Gao[2,3], Lei Wang[3], and Xin Wang[3(✉)]

[1] School of Cyber Security,
University of Chinese Academy of Sciences, Beijing, China
[2] State Key Laboratory of Information Security,
Chinese Academy of Sciences, Beijing, China
[3] Institute of Information Engineering, Chinese Academy of Sciences, Beijing, China
{guoxiaobo,gaoneng,wanglei,wangxin}@iie.ac.cn

Abstract. Knowledge representation learning aims to transform entities and relationships in a knowledge base into computable forms, so that an efficient calculation can be realized. It is of great significance to the construction, reasoning and application of knowledge base. The traditional translation-based models mainly obtain the finite dimension vector representation of entities or relationships by projecting to finite dimensional Euclidean space. These simple and effective methods greatly improve the efficiency and accuracy of knowledge representation. However, they ignore a fact that the semantic space develops and grows forever with the passage of time. Finite dimensional Euclidean space is not enough in capacity for vectorizing infinitely growing semantic space. Time is moving forward forever, so knowledge base would expand infinitely with time. This determines that the vector representation of entities and relationships should support infinite capacity. We fill the gap by putting forward TransI (Translating Infinite Dimensional Embeddings) model, which extends knowledge representation learning from finite dimensions to infinite dimensions. It is trained by Trend Smooth Distance based on the idea of continuous infinite dimension vector representation. The Training Efficiency of TransI model is obviously better than TransE under the same setting, and its effect of Dimension Reduction Clustering is more obvious.

Keywords: Trend Smooth Distance · Training Efficiency · Dimension Reduction Clustering

1 Introduction

Knowledge Graphs such as WordNet [13], Freebase [1] and Yago [3] have become very important resources to support AI related applications, including relation extraction, question answering, semantic search and so on. Generally, a knowledge graph is a collection of relational facts that are often represented in the

© Springer Nature Switzerland AG 2019
C. Douligeris et al. (Eds.): KSEM 2019, LNAI 11775, pp. 511–523, 2019.
https://doi.org/10.1007/978-3-030-29551-6_46

form of a triplet (head entity, relation, tail entity), denoted as (h, r, t), e.g. (Bill Gates, founded, Microsoft).

As traditional knowledge base representations mainly rely on the learned logic inference rules for knowledge reasoning, numerical machine learning methods cannot be leveraged to support the computation. Research on representation learning attracts the attention. A series of translation-based embedding models, such as TransE [2], TransH [15], TransR [9], TransD [7], TranSparse [8], TranG [16], TransT [10] and other related models [4–6,14] are produced. At present, all these methods obtain the vector representation of entities or relationships by projecting to low-dimensional vector space.

Time is moving forward forever, so knowledge base would expand infinitely with time. This determines that the vector representation of entities and relationships should support infinite capacity. However, the current knowledge graph embedding models are all studying how to embed fixed-scale knowledge base, FB15k, WN18, etc. into a finité dimensional Euclidean space, where loss functions are calculated by L1 or L2 distances. This motivates us to propose a new model that can break through the constraints of finite dimensional Euclidean space.

In this paper, we propose a knowledge representation embedding model called TransI (Translating Infinite Dimensional Embeddings), which learns the vector representation of entities and relationships in an infinite dimension Euclidean space. Each entity and relationship can be fitted to obtain a continuously-differentiable function in time space with time as the independent variable, and the fluctuation trend of the function is measured by Trend Smooth Distance as a scoring function.

To summarize, we make the following contributions:

Contribution I: We propose a novel model called TransI, which extends knowledge representation learning from the finite-dimensional space to the infinite-dimensional one. As a result, the spatial embedding of knowledge base can better adapt to its nature of infinite expansion over time.

Contribution II: Trend Smooth Distance is proposed to measure the trend similarity of continuously-differentiable functions. It calculates the score function of TransI by capturing the similarity of high and low fluctuation trends expressed by infinite dimension vectors. Compared with L1 and L2 distances, the absolute size of each dimension of the vector in Trend Smooth Distance has little influence on the score function, which makes the model less sensitive to the manual-set value range.

Contribution III: We propose a local gradient descent algorithm based on Trend Smooth Distance. The experimental results show that the loss function in the training process decreases much faster than that in TransE, and the convergence efficiency of TransI is more obvious.

Compared to TransE, we focus on the global patterns, not the individual values and we emphasize the interaction between features, not their absolute sizes. This is the fundamental reason why TransI is more semantically distinguishable than TransE.

2 Related Work

Our work is related to classical translation-based methods of knowledge representation learning. Inspired by word2vec [11,12], TransE regards every entity and relation as a vector in the embedding space. It is an energy-based model and represents a relation as a translation vector indicating the semantic translation from the head entity to the tail entity. In this way, the pair of embedded entities (h, t) in a triplet (h, r, t) can be connected by r with low error. The score function is Eq. (1):

$$f_r(h, t) = |h + r - t|_{L1/L2} \tag{1}$$

Compared with previous models, TransE has fewer parameters and lower computational complexity, but it performs poorly when dealing with multiple semantic relationships. As a result, a series of improved models are proposed.

TransH [15] is proposed to enable an entity to have distinct distributed representations when involved in different relations. TransR/CTransR [9] is proposed based on the idea that entities and relations should be in two different vector spaces. KG2E [6] uses Gaussian embedding to explicitly model the certainty of entities and relations. TransD [7] uses two vectors to represent each entity/relation, the first one represents the meaning of the entity/relation, the other one is used to construct mapping matrix dynamically. TranSparse [7] considers the heterogeneity and the imbalance of knowledge graphs. TransG [16] can discover the latent semantics of a relation automatically and leverages a mixture of multiple relation-specific components for translating entity pairs to address the new issue. TransT [10] integrates the structured information and entity types to generate multiple embedding representations of each entity in different contexts and estimate the posterior probability of entity and relation prediction.

No matter putting entities and relations into different representation spaces or considering about the muti-semantics of different relationships, all the above TransE-based representation learning methods gradually improve the accuracy of finite-dimensional knowledge representation learning for fixed volume knowledge base.

The original intention of TransI is not to improve the accuracy of link prediction or triplet classification of the above TransE-based research results, but to propose a feasible scheme to extend knowledge representation learning from finite dimensions to infinite ones, hoping to inspire the extension of metric space. As TransE is a groundbreaking fundamental model of the above translation-based models, we choose it as a baseline to explore a new way to expand metric space. It is hoped that TransI will become a new fundamental model in infinite dimensional space, just like TransE in finite dimensional space.

3 TransI: Translating Infinite Dimensional Embeddings

A desirable infinite dimensional embedding model must satisfy several requirements: firstly, it must have reasonable expressions of infinite dimensional vectors;

secondly, it must have a reasonable method for calculating the distance of infinite dimensional vectors; thirdly, it must have a gradient descent method suitable for infinite dimension vector distance calculation to train vector representation.

In this section, we present a novel knowledge embedding model called TransI, which satisfies all the three requirements.

3.1   Polynomial Representation of Infinite Dimensional Vectors

This paper assumes the infinite vector representation of each entity and relationship can uniquely correspond to a unary continuously-differentiable function. The fluctuation trend of this function reflects the strong and weak action of the infinite dimensional features. As shown in Fig. 1, let f be a continuously-differentiable unary polynomial function and its independent variable is in the closed interval $[0, 1]$. The independent variable is equal to the subscript of each dimension component in a finite dimension vector. As the independent variable in f is continuous to take all the values in $[0, 1]$, that is, there are infinite subscripts between 0 and 1, so f can be used to represent an infinite dimensional vector. When the highest degree is fixed, there are infinite possibilities for the value of the coefficient of function f. That is, there are infinite possibilities for the trend of ups and downs, which can be equivalent to the infinite semantic space in terms of capacity.

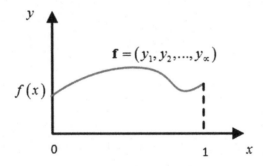

Fig. 1. Visualization of an infinite dimensional vector.

How can we get the corresponding continuously-differentiable unary polynomial functions of all entities and relationships? We can refer to the quantization method of signal in time domain or space domain. In the real world, physical objects such as waves and signals occur over time. From the point of view of time domain or space domain, they are infinite-dimensional. For example, for a spatial signal or a time signal, each dimension of the signal has a specific value, but as time or space changes, the number of values cannot be calculated. That is, it can not be directly expressed as a finite dimension vector. In this case, in a closed interval corresponding to a certain period of time, a point can be selected at a certain distance to represent its surrounding infinite points. The degree of information loss can be controlled by controlling the sampling interval.

Inspired by the above method, any infinite dimension vector representation of any entity and relationship can be expressed as a continuously-differentiable unary polynomial function f. As shown in Fig. 2, f can be obtained by separately sampling, composing point pairs and fitting functions. The independent variable of f is set to x and the sampling period is regarded as the value interval of x. The signal value collected at each time point can be regarded as the sampling point y of infinite dimension vector representing f, which is obtained by random initialization. From the above values of x and y, several pairs of sampling points (x, y) of infinite dimension vector are formed in order. As shown in Fig. 3, the polynomial function fitted by the above sampling points on the value interval of x is f.

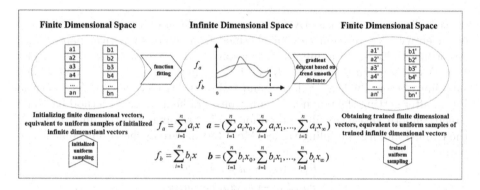

Fig. 2. TransI training model.

Given an entity or a relation, a continuously-differentiable function in a fixed closed interval can be obtained from some finite dimensional samplings through fitting operation. According to the direction from small to large of the value of the independent variable, the corresponding function value is calculated to be every dimension in the expression of infinite dimension vector. In this way, the infinite dimension vector representation of entity or relationship can be obtained. The global closed interval can be selected arbitrarily according to the convenience of calculation. The essence of this method is to capture the trend characteristics of infinite dimensional vector wave using two-dimensional mesh. Then we fit the two-dimensional lattice as a continuous differentiable function, which is smoothing the infinite vector representation in fact. This makes the vector representation not only get rid of the dependence on the absolute size of each dimension feature, but also improve the generalization ability.

The specific process is as follows: x takes values in the closed interval $[a, b]$ at intervals ρ, then the number of sampling points is $k = [b - a]/\rho$. The sampling vectors of $[b - a]/\rho$ dimensions are randomly generated, and y takes the values

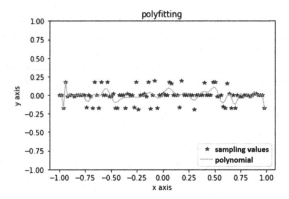

Fig. 3. Polynomial function fitting.

of each dimension in turn. By fitting process, the infinite dimension vector f of an entity or a relation can be obtained from finite numerical pairs (x, y). According to Eq. (2), the infinite dimension vector corresponding to the triplet (h, r, t) can be represented as $(f_h(x), f_r(x), f_t(x))$. $\boldsymbol{h}$, $\boldsymbol{r}$, $\boldsymbol{t}$ are k-dimensional sampling vectors for head, relation and tail of the triplet (h, r, t). As shown in Fig. 2, after getting the polynomial functions, gradient descent method based on Trend Smooth Distance will be used for model training, and the final output is the trained uniform sampling values. More Details are in shown in the next two parts.

$$
\begin{aligned}
\boldsymbol{h}_{[b-a]/\rho} &\rightarrow f_h(x), x \in [a, b] \\
\boldsymbol{r}_{[b-a]/\rho} &\rightarrow f_r(x), x \in [a, b] \\
\boldsymbol{t}_{[b-a]/\rho} &\rightarrow f_t(x), x \in [a, b]
\end{aligned}
\tag{2}
$$

What needs to be stated in particular is that the polynomial fitting process doesn't need a complex neural network training, because accurate fitting is unnecessary here. What we only need to do is to set the polynomial degree and call the polyfit function of python numpy package directly to get the approximate trend fitting curve.

3.2 Trend Smooth Distance

TransE employs a distance function $d(\boldsymbol{h} + \boldsymbol{r}, \boldsymbol{t})$ to quantify the possibility of triplets holding. The basic idea is that, if (h, r, t) holds, $\boldsymbol{t}$ should be a nearest neighbor of $\boldsymbol{h} + \boldsymbol{r}$, far away otherwise. d can be obtained with use of L1 or the L2 distance.

Previously, a series of TransE-based models used the absolute size of each dimension of the finite dimension vector to calculate the vector distance, which is not applicable to the infinite dimension vector. The fluctuation trend of vectors may reflect the essence of entities and relationships better than the absolute size of vectors. To prove that, Trend Smooth Distance is defined in Eq. (3). It means if (h, r, t) holds, the fluctuation trend of $f_h(x) + f_r(x)$ should be closest to that of $f_t(x)$. In this paper, we use the first derivative to quantify the fluctuation trend of continuously-differentiable function f and the definite integral of the square of derivative difference to quantify the distance d of infinite dimensional vectors.

$$d(\boldsymbol{h} + \boldsymbol{r}, \boldsymbol{t}) = \int_a^b [\partial(f_h(x) + f_r(x))/\partial x - \partial(f_t(x))/\partial x]^2 \, dx \qquad (3)$$

In the training process, the maximum interval method is used to optimize the objective function to enhance the distinguishing ability of knowledge representation. For each (h, r, t) and its negative sample (h', r, t'), TransI aims to minimize the hinge-loss as follows in Eq. (4):

$$\mathcal{L} = max(\gamma + d(\boldsymbol{h} + \boldsymbol{r}, \boldsymbol{t}) - d(\boldsymbol{h}' + \boldsymbol{r}, \boldsymbol{t}'), 0) \qquad (4)$$

where γ is a margin hyper-parameter and (h', r, t') is a negative sample from the negative sampling set. A negative sample can be obtained by randomly replacing the head or the tail of a correct triplet with an entity from the entity list.

3.3   Model Translation

The optimization is carried out by stochastic gradient descent (in mini-batch mode) with Trend Smooth Distance. Detailed optimization procedure is described in Algorithm 1. γ is a margin hyper-parameter of hinge-loss function, k is the number of dimensions of the sampling points, l is the highest degree of the fitting polynomials adopted, $Epoch$ is training times, and m is the size of a minibatch.

All y values of sampling points for entities and relations are first initialized following the random procedure proposed in [2]. At each main iteration of the algorithm, a small set of triplets is sampled from the training set, and will serve as the training triplets of the minibatch. For each such triplet, we then sample a single corrupted triplet. All x values of sampling points for sampling entities and relationships are obtained from the initialization process at equal intervals. Then the x values and y values make a sequential combination. According to these pairs of points, continuously-differentiable functions can be fitted. The parameters are then updated by taking a gradient step based on these functions. The algorithm can be stopped when the validation loss drops to a stable value, if the training times does not reach $Epoch$.

4   Experiments

4.1   Dataset

We use datasets commonly used in previous methods: Freebase [1]. It is a large collaborative knowledge graph of general world facts. For example, the triplet

Algorithm 1. Training TransI model

Require: Training set T, entity set E, relation set R, margin γ, dim k, polynomial times l, training times $Epoch$, the size of minibatch m

Ensure: Vector representation of all the entities and relations in a knowledge graph

$\mathbf{r}_y \leftarrow uniform(\frac{-10}{\sqrt{k}}, \frac{10}{\sqrt{k}})$ for each $r \in R$

$\mathbf{r}_y \leftarrow \mathbf{r}_y/\|\mathbf{r}_y\|$ for each $r \in R$

$\mathbf{e}_y \leftarrow uniform(\frac{-10}{\sqrt{k}}, \frac{10}{\sqrt{k}})$ for each $e \in E$

$iter = 1$

while $iter \leq Epoch$ **do**

    $\mathbf{e}_y \leftarrow \mathbf{e}_y/\|\mathbf{e}_y\|$ for each $e \in E$

    $S_{batch} \leftarrow sample(T, m)$//sample a minibatch of size b

    $T_{batch} \leftarrow \varnothing$//initialize the set of pairs of triplets

    for $(h, r, t) \in S_{batch}$ **do**

        $(h', r, t') \leftarrow$ sample $S'_{(}h, r, t)$//sample a corrupted triplet

        $T_{batch} \leftarrow T_{batch} \cup ((h, r, t), (h', r, t'))$

        $x \leftarrow (\frac{-10}{\sqrt{k}}, \frac{10}{\sqrt{k}})$// x values

        $f(x) \leftarrow plotfit(x, y, l)$ //obtain corresponding function

        $d(\mathbf{h} + \mathbf{r}, \mathbf{t}) = \int_a^b [\partial(f_h(x) + f_r(x))/\partial x - \partial(f_t(x))/\partial x]^2 dx$//obtain distance

        $\sum_{((h,r,t),(h',r,t'))\in T_{batch}} \nabla[\gamma + d(\mathbf{h} + \mathbf{r}, \mathbf{t}) - d(\mathbf{h'} + \mathbf{r}, \mathbf{t'})]_+$//obtain loss update embeddings w.r.t

    end for

    $iter + +$

end while

(Bill Gates, place of birth, Seattle) indicates that the person entity Bill Gate was born in (place of birth) the location entity Seattle. In this paper, FB15k is adopted for model performance evaluation. It contains 14951 entities and 1345 relations. The training set contains 483142 triplets, the valid set contains 50000 triplets and the test set contains 59071 triplets.

4.2 Evaluation Protocol

For evaluation, we use Training Efficiency and Dimension Reduction Clustering as evaluation indicators.

The Training Efficiency refers to the number of main iterations needed when both the partial loss of the sample data in the training set and the global loss of the verification set reach a stable state. The less the number of main iterations needed to achieve stability, the higher the convergence efficiency of the training process.

Dimension Reduction Clustering can be used to measure the overall discriminative power of a model training result. This index focuses on the multi-semantics of entities and relationships and is mainly used to reflect the semantic distinguishability of vector representation. Vectors representing different entities or relationships should be closer in the representation space than other vectors if they have the same or similar semantics. This means that after clustering in the representation space, the vectors within the same cluster tend have some common or similar semantics, and the vectors between different clusters tend to have different semantics. In this paper, t-SNE (t-distributed stochastic neighbor embedding) package is used to map the high-dimensional vectors to the two-dimensional space.

What is t-SNE? It is a machine learning method for dimensionality reduction with the main advantage of maintaining local structure. Vectors that are close to each other in a high dimensional data space are still close to each other in a low dimensional data space after using this descending dimension method. Therefore, this paper uses this method to reflect the vector distance of high-dimensional space with the clustering effect of two-dimensional space. The more obvious the clustering degree is, the higher the semantic distinguishability of vector representation is.

4.3   Training Efficiency

In this paper, both TransI and TransE select 500 triplets from the training set to form a sample set for local gradient descent operation in each main iteration process. Every 100 main iterations, sample loss and validation loss are calculated, where sample loss is the loss of the selected sample data set (including 500 triples) and validation loss is the global loss of the verification set (including 50,000 triples). To make both them appear in the diagram at the same time, sample loss is expanded by 100 times.

As shown in Fig. 4, both the sample loss and the validation loss of TransI are stable when the main iteration reaches 6000 or so. However, the validation loss of TransE is not stable until the main iteration reaches 40000 or so and its sample loss is still unstable when the main iteration reaches 80,000.

The upward jitter of validation loss is very large during the training of TransE, which indicates that TransE is sensitive to the absolute size of entity and relation vector representation. Adjusting individual vector representations by gradient descent may cause a large global shock. On the contrary, the validation loss of TransI decreases smoothly and efficiently throughout the training process, which indicates that it is insensitive to the absolute size of entities and relational vectors, and a certain amount of cumulative adjustments is needed to trigger global changes. This robustness of the objective function helps TransI to maintain better stability and generalization ability.

4.4   Dimension Reduction Clustering

The first 500 trained entity vectors and relationship vectors are taken for t-SNE dimensionality reduction analysis, and the visualization results are shown in Figs. 5 and 6.

As shown in Fig. 5, with the increase of the number of main iterations, the training results of both models show a trend of clustering gradually. The output of entity vector trained by TransI can nearly form a continuous graph with middle blank after dimension reduction. Entities divided by blanks belong to different clusters, and the distinction is very clear because of a large blank space.

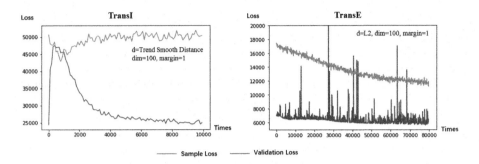

Fig. 4. Training efficiency of TransI and TransE.

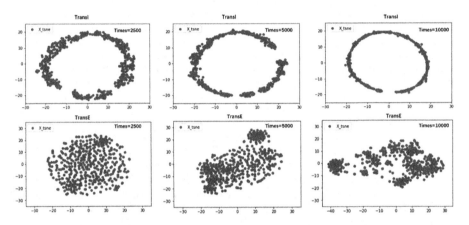

Fig. 5. Dimensionality reduction analysis of entity vectors.

The nearer entities on the same side of the blank are almost aligned, and the number of clusters can be defined according to the actual needs. This flexibility provides the possibility of adaptive multi-semantic learning. The output of entity vectors trained by TransE can also present obvious clustering phenomenon, but the resulting graph is irregular and has fewer blanks. As the points in the same cluster are connected into pieces, both its semantic discriminability and cluster definition flexibility is lower than that of TransI. As shown in Fig. 6, with the increase of the number of main iterations, the relationship vectors trained by TransI appear clustering phenomenon. However, the training results of TransE do not clusters, and the experimental results show that the clustering still does not appear even when the number of main iterations reaches 80 000. This suggests that transE has a weaker semantic discriminability in relations compared to transI.

Why is this? It is the interaction between the features of each dimension that determines the semantic nature of entity or relation, rather than the values of them. The Trend Smooth Distance adopted by TransI can well capture the strong and weak action mode of the global features. However, The L1 or L2

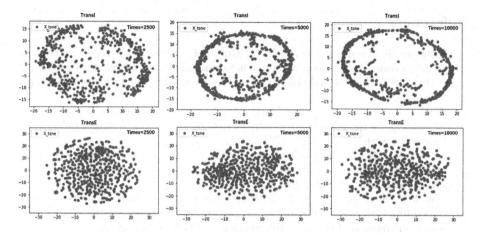

Fig. 6. Dimensionality reduction analysis of relation vectors.

distance adopted by TransE was calculated with absolute distance, making the model training too dependent on the actual value of each feature and ignoring the global consideration of feature mode. Compared to transE, we focus on the global patterns, not the individual values and we emphasize the interaction between features, not their absolute sizes. This is the fundamental reason why TransE is ineffective in training multi-semantic relations.

5   Conclusion

TransI model proposed in this paper extends knowledge representation learning from finite-dimensional space to infinite-dimensional space. Then Trend Smooth Distance is proposed to calculate the score function of TransI by capturing the similarity of high and low fluctuation trends expressed by infinite dimension vectors. Last but not the least, a local gradient descent algorithm suitable for Trend Smooth Distance is presented. The experiment results show that TransI is superior to TransE in Training Efficiency and Dimensionality Reduction Clustering. These results prove the possibility and feasibility of metric space migration in knowledge embedding research.

In the future, we will continue to study the following two aspects:

TransI model involves a lot of fitting, integral and differential operations. It takes three days to complete the above training, so the parameter adjustment is a problem. The present raw data meanrank is about 2000 under the parameter configuration shown in Fig. 4. We will try to use Tensorflow or Pytorch to optimize the algorithm and carry out a huge number of circular parameter adjustments to get a good ranking and try to make evaluation on more datasets.

Compared with TransE, TransI has a better effect on Dimensionality Reduction Clustering of relationships. This shows that TransI has potential to deal with multi-semantics of relationships. We will try to apply this model in multi-semantics relation learning.

References

1. Bollacker, K., Evans, C., Paritosh, P., Sturge, T., Taylor, J.: Freebase: a collaboratively created graph database for structuring human knowledge. In: Proceedings of the 2008 ACM SIGMOD International Conference on Management of Data, pp. 1247–1250. ACM (2008)
2. Bordes, A., Usunier, N., Garcia-Duran, A., Weston, J., Yakhnenko, O.: Translating embeddings for modeling multi-relational data. In: Advances in Neural Information Processing Systems, pp. 2787–2795 (2013)
3. Fabian, M., Gjergji, K., Gerhard, W., et al.: Yago: a core of semantic knowledge unifying wordnet and wikipedia. In: 16th International World Wide Web Conference, WWW, pp. 697–706 (2007)
4. Fan, M., Zhou, Q., Chang, E., Zheng, T.F.: Transition-based knowledge graph embedding with relational mapping properties. In: Proceedings of the 28th Pacific Asia Conference on Language, Information and Computing (2014)
5. Guo, S., Wang, Q., Wang, B., Wang, L., Guo, L.: Semantically smooth knowledge graph embedding. In: Proceedings of the 53rd Annual Meeting of the Association for Computational Linguistics and the 7th International Joint Conference on Natural Language Processing (Volume 1: Long Papers), vol. 1, pp. 84–94 (2015)
6. He, S., Liu, K., Ji, G., Zhao, J.: Learning to represent knowledge graphs with Gaussian embedding. In: Proceedings of the 24th ACM International on Conference on Information and Knowledge Management, pp. 623–632. ACM (2015)
7. Ji, G., He, S., Xu, L., Liu, K., Zhao, J.: Knowledge graph embedding via dynamic mapping matrix. In: Proceedings of the 53rd Annual Meeting of the Association for Computational Linguistics and the 7th International Joint Conference on Natural Language Processing (Volume 1: Long Papers), vol. 1, pp. 687–696 (2015)
8. Ji, G., Liu, K., He, S., Zhao, J.: Knowledge graph completion with adaptive sparse transfer matrix. In: Thirtieth AAAI Conference on Artificial Intelligence (2016)
9. Lin, Y., Liu, Z., Sun, M., Liu, Y., Zhu, X.: Learning entity and relation embeddings for knowledge graph completion. In: Twenty-Ninth AAAI Conference on Artificial Intelligence (2015)
10. Ma, S., Ding, J., Jia, W., Wang, K., Guo, M.: TransT: type-based multiple embedding representations for knowledge graph completion. In: Ceci, M., Hollmén, J., Todorovski, L., Vens, C., Džeroski, S. (eds.) ECML PKDD 2017. LNCS (LNAI), vol. 10534, pp. 717–733. Springer, Cham (2017). https://doi.org/10.1007/978-3-319-71249-9_43
11. Mikolov, T., Chen, K., Corrado, G., Dean, J.: Efficient estimation of word representations in vector space. arXiv preprint arXiv:1301.3781 (2013)
12. Mikolov, T., Sutskever, I., Chen, K., Corrado, G.S., Dean, J.: Distributed representations of words and phrases and their compositionality. In: Advances in Neural Information Processing Systems, pp. 3111–3119 (2013)
13. Miller, G.: WordNet: a lexical database for English. Commun. ACM **38**, 39–41 (1995)
14. Wang, Q., Wang, B., Guo, L.: Knowledge base completion using embeddings and rules. In: Twenty-Fourth International Joint Conference on Artificial Intelligence (2015)

15. Wang, Z., Zhang, J., Feng, J., Chen, Z.: Knowledge graph embedding by translating on hyperplanes. In: Twenty-Eighth AAAI Conference on Artificial Intelligence (2014)
16. Xiao, H., Huang, M., Zhu, X.: TransG: a generative model for knowledge graph embedding. In: Proceedings of the 54th Annual Meeting of the Association for Computational Linguistics (Volume 1: Long Papers), vol. 1, pp. 2316–2325 (2016)

A Knowledge-Based Conceptual Modelling Approach to Bridge Design Thinking and Intelligent Environments

Michael Walch[1]([envelope]), Takeshi Morita[2], Dimitris Karagiannis[1], and Takahira Yamaguchi[2]

[1] University of Vienna, Vienna, Austria
michael.walch@univie.ac.at, dk@dke.univie.ac.at
[2] Keio University, Yokohama, Japan
t_morita@keio.jp, yamaguti@ae.keio.ac.jp

Abstract. One aspect of knowledge management is concerned with the alignment between what is captured in the heads of people and what is encoded by technology. The alignment of knowledge is necessary as humans possess an efficient ability to design innovation based on business insights, while technological systems are able to operating efficiently in different environments. To support knowledge management, this study presents systematic foundations covering a knowledge-based conceptual modelling approach. On a systematic level, three procedures are presented to facilitate the alignment of knowledge between people and technology: the decomposition of concepts from design thinking in conceptual models, the abstraction of capabilities from intelligent environments in conceptual models, and the (semi-) automated, intelligent transformation of conceptual models. Furthermore, the architecture of ICT infrastructure supporting the three procedures is addressed. These systematic foundations are integrated in the OMiLAB ecosystem and instantiated in two projects. The first project revolves around PRINTEPS, which is a framework to develop practical Artificial Intelligence. The second project revolves around s*IoT, which is a unifying semantic-aware modelling environment for the Internet of Things. Additionally, two concrete cases are presented for both project. Due to employing common systematic foundations, transfer and reuse among the two projects is facilitated.

Keywords: Knowledge creation and acquisition ·
Knowledge and data integration ·
Conceptual modelling in knowledge-based systems

1 Introduction

The dedicated exploration and exploitation of knowledge has the potential to bring together people that are engaged in organizations and society with technology that acts on behalf of humans in an increasingly autonomous manner.

© Springer Nature Switzerland AG 2019
C. Douligeris et al. (Eds.): KSEM 2019, LNAI 11775, pp. 524–536, 2019.
https://doi.org/10.1007/978-3-030-29551-6_47

Combining the strengths of both is crucial for the vision of a prosperous future in which the co-creation and reciprocal influence between people and technology enables advanced benefits. In recent years, many such benefits are wished for in different application domains. Some examples are (1) distributed, collaborative and automated design & manufacturing workflows realized by Cyber-Physical System, Internet of Things, Cloud Computing and Big Data Analytics in Industry 4.0 [1], (2) urban development turned to technology, innovation, and globalization in Smart Cities [2], (3) innovative creativity and productivity support for information exploration in new media [3], and ontology evolution in the Semantic Web [4]. One general issue in these examples is that the alignment of knowledge is required between what that is captured in the heads of people and what is encoded by technology.

The conceptual framework for tackling the issue is based on two ideas. The first is to extract innovative scenarios that humans come up with from the heads of people, to capture them in design thinking artifacts, and to decompose and represent the knowledge captured by design thinking artifacts in conceptual models. The second is to enhance technical systems into constituting elements of intelligent environments, to put intelligent environments into operation, and to abstract in conceptual models the data, information, and knowledge encoded by the operation of intelligent environments. From this results the challenge that knowledge contained in conceptual models differs in form, quality, and semantic richness, which is why a conceptual model-based transformation of knowledge is required. Thereby, manual engineering tasks should be substituted by (semi-) automated, intelligent ones as human engineering effort does not scale. By searching for patterns to describe the relation between design thinking, conceptual models, and intelligent environments on a meta-level, the problem is to find and to come up with systematic foundations that enable reuse and horizontal integration across different projects addressing the topic. To explore the pattern space, the PRINTEPS [5] and s*IoT [6] project are considered as instances that realize the patterns under scrutiny. Based on these instances, the method to find and to come up with systematic foundations is an agile composition of qualitative meta-synthesis [7,8] and model-based design science research [9,10]. The validation of the identified patterns is achieved by two evaluation cases, a SWOT analysis, and the transfer of tools between PRINTEPS and s*IoT.

After the introduction, the state of the art on design thinking and intelligent environments is provided based on s*IoT and PRINTEPS in Sect. 2. Section 3 explores how PRINTEPS and s*IoT instantiate common systematic foundations from the OMiLAB ecosystem. Validation cases for the resulting patterns that employ knowledge-based conceptual modelling are presented in Sect. 4. The discussion of how common systematic foundations are useful is conducted in Sect. 5 before concluding the study.

2   Bridging Design Thinking and Intelligent Environments

The alignment of knowledge between people and technology becomes increasingly necessary and complex for building digital products like innovative

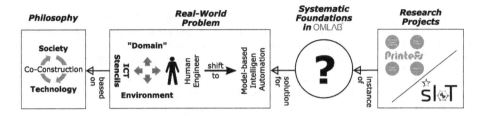

Fig. 1. Topic of the study.

product-service systems. Figure 1 illustrates the related problem of combining domain knowledge in the heads of people and environments in which this knowledge is put into operation. To tackle the problem, human engineers often use ICT systems to relate both elements. However, this approach does not scale as the speed of change increases for domain knowledge and environments. Rather, different projects like PRINTEPS and S*IoT employ knowledge-based conceptual models to bridge the gap between design thinking and intelligent environments in a (semi-) automated, intelligent manner. PRINTEPS focuses on making intelligent environments accessible to human end-users, while s*IoT focuses on extending design thinking to represent and automate the knowledge that is captured in the heads of people. By integrating PRINTEPS and s*IoT based on patterns of common systematic foundations, it is possible to realize a bridge between design thinking and intelligent environments. This requires a knowledge-based conceptual modelling approach, as described in Sect. 3. Before this explanation, details are provided on how PRINTEPS aligns knowledge between people and technology by focusing on intelligent environments, while s*IoT aligns knowledge between people and technology by focusing on design thinking.

2.1 Design Thinking in s*IoT

A topic in s*IoT [6], which is an extended conceptual modelling approach, is to support design and use of innovative scenarios in a business context. This makes it necessary to access human knowledge about, e.g., a domain, human interaction, and context; and to turn human knowledge into a core element of digital products. Therefore, s*IoT employs design thinking in collaborative workshops with the goal of finding innovative business models. This requires creativity, insight, and understanding of customer needs. However, the result of design thinking workshops rarely is a fully fledged business model. Rather, often paper-based and semantically poor design thinking specific artifacts are created. The result is a semantic gap between design thinking specific artifacts and the business models in a specific company context. To bridge the semantic gap, s*IoT employs dedicated conceptual modelling tools like, e.g., the Scene2Model tool [11]. As a consequence, it becomes possible to link design thinking artifacts with business models in the context of an enterprise. This is the input for the s*IoT and other tool which employ knowledge representation schemes, AI,

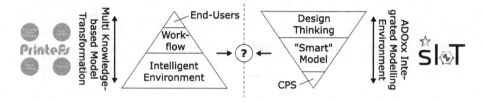

Fig. 2. Design thinking and intelligent environments in s*IoT and PRINTEPS.

and technologies from the semantic web stack to connect business models and cyber-physical systems to enable the operationalization of innovative scenarios. In summary, s*IoT employs tools for building "smart" models to put the artifacts of design thinking into operation. These "smart" models are at the centre between two layers of interpretability: one for people concerned with innovating business scenarios, the other for cyber-physical systems that operate in complex real-world settings.

2.2 Intelligent Environments in PRINTEPS

A topic in PRINTEPS [5], which is a platform to develop practical intelligent applications, is to support the setting of environments in which different AI approaches enable robots to operate. These intelligent environments are characterized by increased complexity due to a feedback loop between all the systems that interact during operation. To enable smooth operation, knowledge is encoded in intelligent environments by the function, structure, and behaviour of these systems and their connection. Business insights and end-user requirements are a part of this knowledge. However, human end-users and business experts generally do not have the skills or tools to encode their knowledge in intelligent environments. Therefore, PRINTEPS abstracts the knowledge encoded in intelligent environments by providing intricate capabilities of intelligent environments. The relation between abstract, intricate capabilities and the operation of intelligent environments again takes the form of a feedback loop. The problem is that different computational paradigms, granularity of detail, and language of presentation are used on both ends of the feedback loop. To manage this complexity, PRINTEPS employs the robot operating system, multi-knowledge based models, and the (semi-)automated, intelligent transformation between them. As a result, PRINTEPS makes it possible to encoding knowledge about intelligent environments in workflow models. Nevertheless, human end-users and business experts still wish for more intuitive means of knowledge acquisition.

2.3 Bridging the Gap

Figure 2 shows the focus of PRINTEPS and s*IoT. On the one hand, the focus of PRINTEPS is on intelligent environments that provide capabilities to human

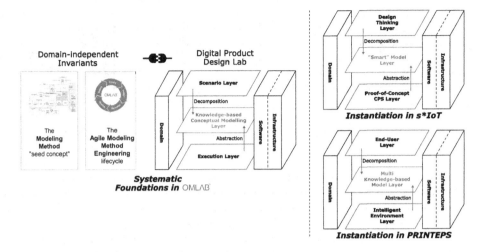

Fig. 3. Design thinking and intelligent environments in s*IoT and PRINTEPS.

end-users. As human end-users are generally not able to transform their knowledge directly into intelligent environments, conceptual models are employed as an intermediary. In particular, a multi-knowledge-based transformation is employed in PRINTEPS to align knowledge between end-users and intelligent environments. On the other hand, the focus of s*IoT is on design thinking to represent innovative scenarios. As the knowledge captured by design thinking artifacts generally cannot be directly used for operationalization in a business context, conceptual models are employed as an intermediary. In particular, an integrated conceptual modelling environment is employed in s*IoT to align knowledge between design thinking and cyber-physical systems. As PRINTEPS and s*IoT both employ knowledge-aware conceptual models to connect people and technology, a knowledge-based conceptual modelling approach is identified as an invariant between PRINTEPS and s*IoT.

3   Knowledge-Based Conceptual Modelling Approach

Additional benefits emerge by combining the strengths of PRINTEPS and s*IoT, as both focus on different aspects of aligning knowledge between people and technology when building digital products. To combine the two research projects, common systematic foundations surrounding a knowledge-based conceptual modelling approach have to be found. This section illustrates these systematic foundations and their integration with other patterns from the OMiLAB ecosystem.

3.1   Concept Synthesis in the OMiLAB Ecosystem

PRINTEPS and s*IoT are two projects that align knowledge between people and technology, as shown in Fig. 2. The combination of their different strengths can be achieved by synthesizing common systematic foundations on the meta-level [12]. These common systematic foundations can be related to PRINTEPS and s*IoT through instantiation, which facilitates cross-project reuse of results. By synthesizing common systematic foundations for PRINTEPS and s*IoT on the meta-level, a three layer pattern emerged through active design science research. Figure 3 shows the synthesized pattern, its integration with other patterns in the OMiLAB ecosystem, and its instantiation for PRINTEPS and s*IoT.

The pattern to combine PRINTEPS and s*IoT consists of three layers: scenario layer, conceptual modelling layer, and execution layer. On the scenario layer, knowledge about innovation is created by people engaged in different aspects of society. Knowledge is transformed between the scenario layer and the conceptual modelling layer by the decomposition of the former. On the conceptual modelling layer, knowledge is represented in different kinds of conceptual models. Model transformations are employed on the conceptual modelling layer to relate different conceptual models and the knowledge within them. Knowledge is also transformed between the conceptual modelling layer and the execution layer by the abstraction of the latter. On the execution layer, different systems put knowledge into operation. The name coined for this three layer pattern is *digital product design lab*, as its instantiation and consequent realization enables the creation of digital products that require an alignment of knowledge between people and technology. The pattern of the digital product design lab is integrated in the OMiLAB ecosystem. The OMiLAB ecosystem is an open platform, environment, and knowledge base to support the conceptualization and operationalization of conceptual modelling methods based on a general understanding of model values [13]. The OMiLAB ecosystem is managed by the OMiLAB NPO which is located in Berlin, Germany. Concepts of the OMiLAB ecosystem are domain-independent patterns like the modelling method seed concept [14] or the agile modelling method engineering life-cycle [15]. The pattern of the digital product design lab from the the OMiLAB ecosystem can be instantiated for PRINTEPS and s*IoT. This instantiation is beneficial as the pattern can be refined to enable the different foci from which the different strengths of the PRINTEPS and s*IoT projects emerge. Likewise, PRINTEPS refines the execution layer in a layer for intelligent environments while reducing the scope of the scenario layer layer to end-user aspects. Alternatively, s*IoT refines the scenario layer by incorporating design thinking while reducing the scope of the execution layer by merely considering proof-of-concept aspects.

3.2 Digital Product Design Lab Realization for PRINTEPS

The PRINTEPS instance of the OMiLAB ecosystem, including the pattern for a digital product design lab is realized in the OMiLAB associated partner laboratory at Keio University. Figure 4 shows the installation that realizes different patterns of the OMiLAB ecosystem instance. Next to this physical realization, a virtual component is also necessary. The essential virtual component is PRINTEPS. PRINTEPS is a user-centric platform to develop integrated intelligent applications by combining four types of modules; namely, knowledge-based

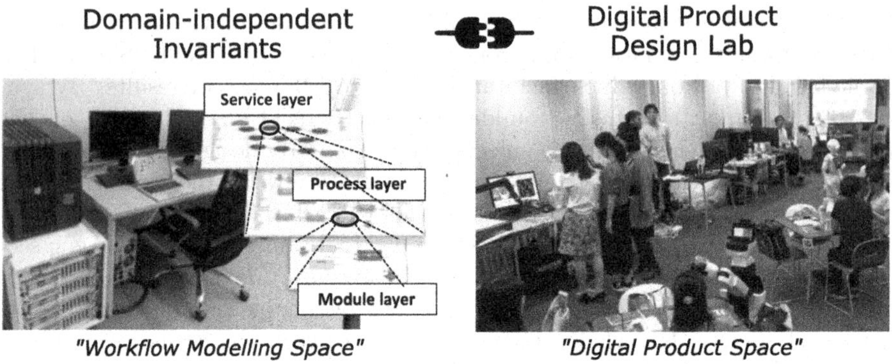

Fig. 4. Realized instance of the OMiLAB ecosystem in the OMiLAB associated partner laboratory at Keio University.

reasoning, spoken dialogue, image sensing, and motion management. PRINT-EPS provides a user-friendly workflow editor based on Robot Operating System (ROS) and Service Oriented Architecture (SOA). It supports end users in AI applications design and development.

In detail, Fig. 4 shows the realization of two patterns in the OMiLAB associated partner laboratory at Keio University. Domain-independent invariants of the OMiLAB ecosystem are realized in the *Workflow Modelling Space*, while the PRINTEPS instance of the digital product design lab is realized in the *Digital Product Space*. Since PRINTEPS workflow editor is implemented as a web application, domain experts are able to create workflows using web browsers installed on any laptop PC, at any location. The left side of Fig. 4 shows an example of *Workflow Modelling Space* in a laboratory of Keio University. The workflow editor is applied in the Digital Product Space to build digital products based on the workflows that can be converted to executable Python source codes on ROS. Some of these products have already been realized, e.g., teaching assistant robots and robot teahouse (the right side of Fig. 4) which is described in more detail in Sect. 4. Decomposing services and processes into modules in the workflows while abstracting from proof-of-concept realizations based on a myriad of existing products (Pepper humanoid robot, HSR human support robot, Jaco2 arm type robot, and several sensors), these digital products align people and technology with knowledge.

3.3   Digital Product Design Lab Realization for s*IoT

The s*IoT instance of the OMiLAB ecosystem including the pattern for a digital product design lab is realized in the OMiLAB node at the University of Vienna. Figure 5 shows the installation that realizes different patterns of the OMiLAB ecosystem instance. Next to this physical realization, virtual components are also necessary. Two essential virtual components are ADOxx and OLIVE. ADOxx is an integrated conceptual modelling environment that stretches across the meta-model hierarchy. ADOxx can be used to engineer different modelling methods for building conceptual models that represent knowledge. Furthermore, ADOxx enables the integration of knowledge-driven AI to process the knowledge that is represented in conceptual models. OLIVE is a framework that extends the capabilities of ADOxx with, e.g., dashboards, data stores on the edge, and connectivity to the IoT. Using OLIVE, it is possible to integrate conceptual models and data-driven AI. The term "smart" models has been coined for the integration of conceptual models, knowledge-driven AI, and data-driven AI. All these elements are bound together in a service-driven architecture.

Fig. 5. Realized instance of the OMiLAB ecosystem in the OMiLAB node of the University of Vienna.

In detail, Fig. 5 shows the realization of two patterns in the OMiLAB node at the University of Vienna. Domain-independent invariants of the OMiLAB ecosystem are realized in the *Modelling Method Space* and the s*IoT instance of the digital product design lab is realized in the *Digital Product Space*. The former is a manufacturing line for modelling methods inspired by the modelling method seed concept and agile modelling method engineering. The result of this manufacturing line are modelling methods and tools. These modelling methods and tools are applied in the Digital Product Space to build digital products based on "smart" models that align knowledge between people and technology. Some such digital products are already realized, e.g., a shopping assistant for disabled people, delivery on demand in Industry 4.0, and a smart city tourist guide which is described in more detail in Sect. 4. By decomposing design thinking artifacts in "smart" models while abstracting from proof-of-concept realizations based on, e.g., NAO humanoid robots, robotic arms, and flying drones, these digital products align knowledge between people and technology.

4   Case Studies

This chapter presents two demonstrative cases in which the realized PRINTEPS and s*IoT instances of the digital product design lab pattern are put to action. Thereby, a common understanding is facilitated based on the pattern for a digital product design lab from the OMiLAB ecosystem. This common understanding enables cross-project reuse, which is elaborated further in Sect. 5.

4.1   PRINTEPS Teahouse Case

A digital product space is realized in the OMiLAB associated partner laboratory at Keio University, corresponding to the PRINTEPS instances of the digital product design lab pattern. This realization is further refined according to Fig. 6 and put to action in the PRINTEPS robot teahouse case. The robot teahouse has been developed with the aim of realizing teahouses where human staff and machines work in synergy to provide services. Currently, the robot teahouse consists of six services: customer detection, greeting, guiding customers to a table, order taking, serving drinks, and cleaning up. To realize the robot teahouse, it is necessary to acquire expert knowledge from teahouse owners and express them as conceptual models using workflows, business rules, and ontologies. In the robot teahouse, the workflows are used to describe standard business procedures for robots with sensors. The business processes are used by robots to change the way they greet customers and take orders according to customers' attributes such as age, gender, and accompanying person. The ontologies are used to describe agents, objects, and environment in the robot teahouse such as robots, menus, and table positions. Although, currently, we have acquired the expert knowledge by interviewing teahouse owners, this process should be supported by tools and methods such as the design thinking approach.

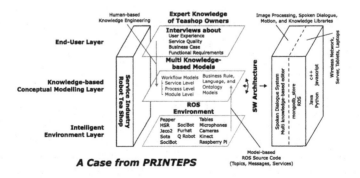

Fig. 6. Digital product design lab pattern for the PRINTEPS teahouse case.

It is also necessary to integrate multiple robots (Pepper humanoid robot, HSR human support robot, Jaco2 arm type robot, etc.) and sensors (Microphones, Kinect, omni-directional camera, etc.) with knowledge-based reasoning, image sensing, spoken dialogue, and motion management. In the robot teahouse, knowledge-based reasoning techniques are used for greeting and guiding customers to a table. Image sensing techniques are used for customer and table detection. Spoken dialogue techniques are used for order taking. Motion management techniques are used for guiding customers to a table, serving drinks, and cleaning up. Since there is a big gap between the knowledge-based conceptual modelling layer and the intelligent environment layer, we have developed PRINTEPS including multi-knowledge-based editor and spoken dialogue system to facilitate the alignment of knowledge between people and technology.

4.2   s*IoT Smart City Tour Guide Case

A digital product space is realized in the OMiLAB node at the University of Vienna, corresponding to the s*IoT instances of the digital product design lab pattern. This realization is further refined according to Fig. 7 and put to action in the s*IoT smart city tour guide case. The general idea for this case is to support tourism in a smart city by exploring the potential of new business-aware service ideas, knowledge-driven and data-driven AI, and emerging robotic systems. This case can be tackled from different angles, e.g., by conceptual model transformation and the abstraction of capabilities from drones[1] and by decomposing stakeholder requirements in smart city models to create intelligent tours using a NAO robot[2].

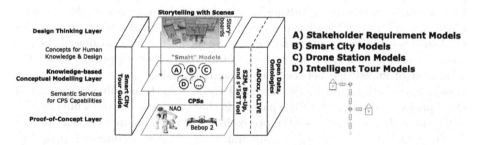

Fig. 7. Digital product design lab pattern for the s*IoT smart city tour guide case.

The integration of knowledge-driven and data-driven AI with conceptual models is crucial for the different angles that tackle the s*IoT smart city tour guide case. One concrete example is a smart tour that requires input about what human participants know or want to know, the execution of the tour supported by emerging robotic systems, and knowledge-based conceptual models that facilitate the alignment of knowledge between people and technology. Thereby, knowledge-based conceptual models support knowledge acquisition using, e.g.,

---

[1] austria.omilab.org/psm/content/XCMSmartDrone.
[2] austria.omilab.org/psm/content/XSTST.

speech and gesture recognition, the integration of open ontologies containing smart city knowledge and data, and semantic-aware services orchestration for e.g., landmark detection.

5 Discussion

Common systematic foundations between PRINTEPS and s*IoT, enable the integration of the two projects. This has been demonstrated by a concrete collaboration that made it necessary to bridge design thinking and intelligent environments. In design thinking workshops during this collaboration, the Scene2Model tool, which is a part of the s*IoT project, is used to elicit stakeholder requirements for PRINTEPS cases. This proved to be useful as knowledge acquisition is a current topic in the AI community. As a result, human knowledge about innovative scenarios could be represented in conceptual models that relate to workflow models of PRINTEPS and their decomposition in the operation of intelligent environments.

To further evaluate the knowledge-based conceptual modelling approach and its integration as a pattern in the OMiLAB ecosystem, a SWOT analysis is useful. The strength of the pattern is that it can be instantiated for different projects to enable reuse, transfer, and collaboration. Furthermore, the pattern enables the integration of knowledge-driven and data-driven AI from which the benefits of knowledge-based conceptual models emerge. The weakness of the pattern is that it might not be applicable to all kinds of projects, i.e., projects that are only interested in advancing theoretical foundations might not care about how theoretical foundations benefit from the design of innovative scenarios or about operation environments in which the theoretical foundations can be put to use. The opportunity for the pattern is that many research project tackle the alignment of knowledge between people and technology from different angles. Research, education, and application can benefit from the possible integration of these projects. The threat for the pattern is that openness and the willingness to share and collaborate are essential prerequisites. For closed projects that are not seeking relations with the bigger community only limited usefulness is provided.

6 Conclusion

This study examines the hypothesis that design and use of digital products requires scalable alignment of knowledge between what is in the heads of people and what is encoded by technology. As different projects already tackle the issue, the question is how to facilitate reuse, transfer, and combination of results. PRINTEPS and s*IoT are two such projects that employ conceptual models to focus on a subsection of knowledge alignment between people and technology. Respectively, they focus on the role that design thinking and intelligent environments play. To integrate both projects and potentially others as well, a pattern for systematic foundations on the meta-level is identified and integrated in the

OMiLAB ecosystem. At the core of this pattern lies a knowledge-based conceptual modelling approach that employs data-driven and knowledge-driven AI. From the instantiation of this pattern for PRINTEPS and s*IoT emerges the potential to bridge design thinking and intelligent environments. This potential is further illustrated by evaluation cases, a SWOT analysis, and preliminary collaboration results. The generalization of the results from this study is currently in progress as new OMiLAB nodes are spawned based on the identified pattern within an EU project. Future steps are underway to intensify the collaboration between PRINTEPS and s*IoT to realize the full vision of bridging design thinking and intelligent environments. Concrete collaboration is planned on a front-end for PRINTEPS end-users based on design thinking and an intelligent environment for s*IoT based on ROS.

Acknowledgement. A part of this study was supported by the project of "A Framework PRINTEPS to Develop Practical Artificial Intelligence," (JPMJCR14E3) the Core Research for Evolutional Science and Technology (CREST) of the Japan Science and Technology Agency (JST).

References

1. Li, G., Tan, J., Chaudhry, S.S.: Industry 4.0 and big data innovations. Enterp. Inf. Syst. **13**(2), 145–147 (2019)
2. Stephanedes, Y.J., Golias, M., Dedes, G., Douligeris, C., Mishra, S.: Challenges, risks and opportunities for connected vehicle services in smart cities and communities. In: 2nd IFAC Conference on Cyber-Physical and Human Systems CPHS 2018, vol. 51, no. 34, pp. 139–144 (2019). IFAC-PapersOnLine
3. Maiden, N., Zachos, K., Paraskevopoulos, F., Lentsek, S., Apostolou, D., Mentzas, G.: Creative information exploration in journalism. In: The 9th International Conference on Information, Intelligence, Systems and Applications, IISA2018 (2018)
4. Zablith, F., et al.: Ontology evolution: a process-centric survey. Knowl. Eng. Rev. **30**(1), 45–75 (2015)
5. Morita, T., Nakamura, K., Komatsushiro, H., Yamaguchi, T.: PRINTEPS: an integrated intelligent application development platform based on stream reasoning and ROS. Rev. Socionetwork Strat. **12**, 71–96 (2018)
6. Walch, M., Karagiannis, D.: How to connect design thinking and cyber-physical systems: the s*IoT conceptual modelling approach. In: 52nd Hawaii International Conference on System Sciences, HICSS 2019, Wailea, USA, 8–11 Jannuary 2019 (2019)
7. Nye, E., Melendez-Torres, G., Bonell, C.: Origins, methods and advances in qualitative meta-synthesis. Rev. Educ. **4**(1), 57–79 (2016)
8. Twinomurinzi, H., Johnson, R.: Meta-synthesizing qualitative research in information systems. J. Community Inf. **11**(3) (2015)
9. Hevner, A., Chatterjee, S.: Design Research in Information Systems: Theory and Practice, vol. 22. Springer Science & Business Media, Boston (2010). https://doi.org/10.1007/978-1-4419-5653-8
10. Vom Brocke, J., Buddendick, C.: Reusable conceptual models-requirements based on the design science research paradigm. In: Proceedings of the First International Conference on Design Science Research in Information Systems and Technology (DESRIST), pp. 576–604. Citeseer (2006)

11. Muck, C., Miron, E.-T., Karagiannis, D., Moonkun, L.: Supporting service design with storyboards and diagrammatic models: the Scene2Model tool. In: Joint International Conference of Service Science and Innovation (ICSSI 2018) and Serviceology (ICServ 2018), September 2018
12. Morita, T., et al.: Practice of multi-robot teahouse based on PRINTEPS and evaluation of service quality. In: 2018 IEEE 42nd Annual Computer Software and Applications Conference, COMPSAC 2018, Tokyo, Japan, 23–27 July 2018, vol. 2, pp. 147–152 (2018)
13. Bork, D., Buchmann, R., Karagiannis, D., Lee, M., Miron, E.-T.: An open platform for modeling method conceptualization: the OMiLAB digital ecosystem. Commun. Assoc. Inf. Syst. (2018)
14. Fill, H.-G., Karagiannis, D.: On the conceptualisation of modelling methods using the ADOxx meta modelling platform. Enterp. Model. Inf. Syst. Architectures Int. J. $\mathbf{8}(1)$, 4–25 (2013)
15. Karagiannis, D.: Agile modeling method engineering. In: Proceedings of the 19th Panhellenic Conference on Informatics, PCI 2015, New York, NY, USA, pp. 5–10. ACM (2015)

Named Entity Recognition in Traditional Chinese Medicine Clinical Cases Combining BiLSTM-CRF with Knowledge Graph

Zhe Jin[1], Yin Zhang[1(✉)], Haodan Kuang[2], Liang Yao[3],
Wenjin Zhang[4], and Yunhe Pan[1]

[1] College of Computer Science and Technology,
Zhejiang University, Hangzhou, China
{shrineshine,yinzh}@zju.edu.cn
[2] College of Basic Medical Science,
Zhejiang Chinese Medical University, Hangzhou, China
[3] Northwestern University, Chicago, IL, USA
[4] First Affiliated Hospital, School of Medicine,
Zhejiang University, Hangzhou, China

Abstract. Named entity recognition in Traditional Chinese Medicine (TCM) clinical cases is a fundamental and crucial task for follow-up work. In recent years, deep learning approaches have achieved remarkable results in named entity recognition and other natural language processing tasks. However, these methods cannot effectively solve the problem of low recognition rate of rare words, which is common in TCM field. In this paper, we propose TCMKG-LSTM-CRF model that utilizes knowledge graph information to strength the learning ability and recognize rare words. This model introduces knowledge attention vector model to implement attention mechanism between hidden vector of neural networks and knowledge graph candidate vectors and consider influence from previous word. The experiment results prove the effectiveness of our model.

Keywords: Named entity recognition · Knowledge graph ·
Traditional Chinese Medicine

1 Introduction

As a distinct medical system with diagnosis and treatment, Traditional Chinese Medicine (TCM) has always played a significant role in Chinese society for thousands of years [1] and has attracted more and more attention worldwide along with the development. Clinical cases constitute the main knowledge system of TCM which contain detailed and valuable information of the whole medical procedure such as how doctors diagnose and prescribe for patients.

In TCM, there are multiple types of TCM entities. For instance, a common clinical case is usually composed of patient information, diagnosis from doctor and treatment plan. Symptom entities might appear in patient information. Syndrome entities and diseases entities will exist in diagnosis. Meanwhile herb entities, prescription entities

C. Douligeris et al. (Eds.): KSEM 2019, LNAI 11775, pp. 537–548, 2019.
https://doi.org/10.1007/978-3-030-29551-6_48

and treatment method entities will be often mentioned in treatment plan part in general. Therefore, these entities cover considerable information in the clinical cases.

Named entity recognition (NER) has attracted considerable research work in recent years. Compared to the past approaches that focus on handcrafted features, the state-of-the-art approaches using deep learning architecture such as BiLSTM-CRF have archived better performance and less manual feature engineering. However, there still exist some entities that may not occur in the training set. Deep learning methods are dedicated to discovering the pattern between characters, words, phrases and their context but in TCM or other medical systems such pattern of uncommon characters and words that are simultaneously considered symptoms and diseases are difficult or unable to be learned. As a knowledge graph contains rare entities and type information of each entity, the performance of NER can be better if we incorporate the knowledge graph into neural network.

In this paper, we study the problem of named entity recognition in TCM clinical cases and we combine the information from knowledge graph with neural network. More specifically, given a set of TCM clinical cases, our goal is to identify all the six pre-defied types of entities above. We construct a Traditional Chinese Medicine knowledge graph and propose a model called TCMKG-LSTM-CRF for solving this problem.

The main contributions of this paper include:

(1) We construct a Traditional Chinese Medicine knowledge graph using TCM textbooks, dictionaries, standards and other officially released data. The knowledge graph contains 64,771 entities and 96,038 triples.
(2) We propose a novel model to incorporating knowledge graph with BiLSTM-CRF. We design a knowledge attention vector model to get information from the knowledge graph and combine it into BiLSTM-CRF. Our model outperforms the basic BiLSTM-CRF model and its improved version with pretrained embeddings, especially on the recognition of rare words.

2 Background

As a fundamental natural language processing task, NER has drawn research attention in last decades. In general, the purpose of NER is to recognize the named entities in texts such as the names of persons, organizations and locations. Traditional NER methods [2, 3] and some early clinical NER systems [4, 5] in medical field were based on hand-crafted rules which relied on a large number of experts.

From the end of the 20th century, supervised and statistical-based methods gradually became the mainstream including Hidden Markov Models [6], Decision Trees [7], Maximum Entropy [8], Support Vector Machines [9] and Conditional Random Fields (CRF) [10]. These statistical methods are very dependent on pre-defined features which need a sufficient feature engineering to adjust and find the best set of features.

In the past several years, based on Recurrent Neural Network (RNN) [11], Long Short-Term Memory neural networks (LSTM) [12] and Gated Recurrent Unit (GRU) [13] has gained a huge success on natural language processing as these models are able to handle long term dependencies. These models are widely used in language modelling [14, 15], machine translation [16–18] and other NLP tasks. BiLSTM [19] further improve LSTM by using both past and future information. Huang et al. [20] explored the combination of LSTM/BiLSTM and CRF utilizing POS and other context features. Lample et al. [21] introduced character-level word representations. Chalapathy et al. [22] applied BiLSTM-CRF to clinical concept extraction. Yang et al. [23] employs an attention mechanism with a sentinel to introduce knowledge information and achieve trade-off.

For NER in Chinese clinical texts, Wang et al. [24] started to use conditional random fields based on literal features and positional features. Wang et al. [25] further tested the performance of different features and different machine learning methods in free-text clinical records. Wang et al. [26] tried to incorporate dictionaries into BiLSTM-CRF. Wang et al. [27] used both graphical and phonetic features. There are few works concentrating on traditional Chinese clinical texts recently.

3   Methods

In this section, we present our TCMKG-LSTM-CRF model. Firstly, we provide a brief introduction of LSTMs, Bidirectional LSTMs and BiLSTM-CRF networks. We then describe how we construct TCM knowledge graph which is used in model and the details of TCMKG-LSTM-CRF model.

3.1   LSTMs, Bidirectional LSTMs and BiLSTM-CRF Networks

Recurrent Neural Networks (RNNs) are a class of neural networks that take a sequence of vectors $(x_1, x_2, \ldots, x_n)$ as input and compute another vector $(h_1, h_2, \ldots, h_n)$ at each time step based on history of inputs and the current input. Long Short-term Memory Networks (LSTMs) are a variant of RNNs and have been designed to solve the problem of long-term dependency of RNNs. LSTMs use a memory cell and three gates to control information stream, and thereby are able to capture long range dependency. The input gate controls the information added to the current memory, meanwhile the forget gate and the output gate could control what information to remove from the previous memory or to output. Usually we use the following implementation:

$$
\begin{aligned}
i_t &= \sigma(W_i \cdot [h_{t-1}, x_t] + b_i) \\
f_t &= \sigma\big(W_f \cdot [h_{t-1}, x_t] + b_f\big) \\
c_t &= f_t \odot c_{t-1} + i_t \odot \tanh(W_c \cdot [h_{t-1}, x_t] + b_c) \\
o_t &= \sigma(W_o \cdot [h_{t-1}, x_t] + b_o) \\
h_t &= o_t \odot \tanh(c_t)
\end{aligned}
\tag{1}
$$

where σ is the logistic sigmoid function, $\cdot$ is the dot product and $\odot$ is the element-wise product, i_t, f_t, c_t, o_t and h_t are input gates, forget gates, cell vector, output gates and hidden state. W_i, W_f, W_c and W_o are weight matrices. b_i, b_f, b_c are b_o are bias vectors.

Bidirectional LSTMs (BiLSTM) are an extension of LSTMs which train two LSTMs which have opposite direction. One accepts input data in forward direction calculating hidden state $\overrightarrow{h_t}$ at time step t while the other one operates in backward direction having hidden state $\overleftarrow{h_t}$. BiLSTMs concatenate them as $h_t = \left[\overrightarrow{h_t}; \overleftarrow{h_t} \right]$ which contains bidirectional information at time step t.

BiLSTM-CRF networks combine a bidirectional LSTM network and a CRF layer to improve the performance. A CRF layer has a state transition matrix A as parameters. A_{y_i, y_j} denotes the transition score between tag y_i and y_j. The probability of tag sequence could be represented as follow:

$$s(y) = \sum\nolimits_{t=1}^{n} \left(f_{t, y_t} + A_{y_{t-1}, y_t} \right) \tag{2}$$

where f_{t, y_t} is the probability of tag y_t output by BiLSTM networks at time t.

3.2   TCMKG and Entity Embeddings

In order to adding external knowledge graph information, as there is no authoritative and structured TCM knowledge graph, we construct our Traditional Chinese Medicine Knowledge Graph (TCMKG) by Neo4j. Texts from TCM textbooks, dictionaries, standards and other officially released data are extracted into triples as the basic unit of knowledge Graph. Triples are 3-tuples consisting of a subject, a predicate (or relation) and an object, usually expressed as (s, r, o). Both the subject and the object are regarded as entities and such triples contain the relationship between entities.

We pre-defined eleven types of entities based on the field of TCM: *Medicine, alias, prescription, pieces, disease, symptom, syndrome, meridian, property, flavour* and *function*. The pre-defined relations between each of them are shown as Fig. 1. *Property, flavor* and *meridian* often appear in the description text of the medicine, showing the understanding of the medicine from the perspective of Chinese medicine. *Property* refers to "four natures" containing four characteristics of cold, heat, warm and cool, which reflect body's effect of inclination of semi-interior phase change after the medicine acting on the body. *Flavor* means medicine's localization in Yin and Yang. In the five flavors, "pungent" and "sweet" belong to Yin while "sour", "bitter" and "salty" belong to Yang. *Tropism* describes the therapeutic effect of the medicine on the pathology of certain viscera and meridians. The rest entities are common and easy to define and understand.

All entities and relationships are stored in the knowledge graph as triples. We have constructed 64,771 entities and 96,038 triples in TCMKG.

We adopted TransE [25], TransH [26] and TransR [27] to learn entity embeddings for entities in TCMKG. In TransE, for each triples, relationship is represented as translation in the embedding, which means if (s, r, o) holds, $s + r$ should be close to o while $s + r$ should be far away from o otherwise. So TransE assumes the $f_r(s, o)$ is low if (s, r, o) holds

$$f_r(s, o) = \|s + r - o\|_2^2 \tag{3}$$

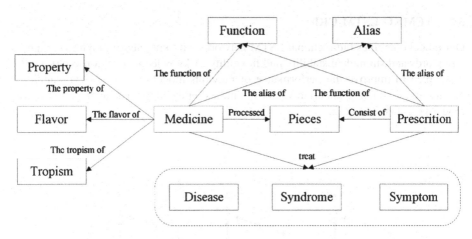

Fig. 1. Pre-defined types of entities and relations of TCMKG. Rectangles represent entities and arrows indicate relationships between two entities.

We trained embeddings by minimizing:

$$L = \sum_{(s,r,o)\in S} \sum_{(s',r,o')\in S'} [\gamma + d(s+r,o) - d(s'+r,o')]_{+} \qquad (4)$$

Where d() is the distance function, $[\,]_+$ denotes the positive part, hyperparameter $\gamma > 0$, S is training set and S' is corrupted set by randomly replacing s or o to another one.

TransH enables entities and relations to have different distributed representations. For a triple (s,r,o), the entity embeddings s and o are projected to the hyperplane of w_r and denoted as $s_\perp$ and $o_\perp$. Then $f_r(s,o)$ is defined as:

$$f_r(s,o) = \|s_\perp + r - o_\perp\|_2^2 \qquad (5)$$

Unlike TransE and TransH that assume embeddings of entities and relations within the same space R^k, TransR set up two different spaces, i.e., entity space and relation spaces, and then performs translation in relation space. Each relation r has a projection matrix $M_r \in R^{k \times d}$ where $s, o \in R^k$ and $r \in R^d$. $f_r(s,o)$ will be correspondingly defined as:

$$s_r = sM_r, \; o_r = oM_r \qquad (6)$$

$$f_r(s,o) = \|s_r + r - o_r\|_2^2 \qquad (7)$$

In recent years, there are also many methods using deep learning in graph embedding generation such as ConvE [28] and ConvKB [29]. The reason we choose TransE, TransH and TransR for entity embedding generation is that: (1) Our knowledge graph is also a large scale dataset and is updated in real time which requires embedding generation work to be completed in less time and (2) according to Dai et al. [29], TransE have the second or the third best score among several baselines in mean rank and mean reciprocal rank which means it's performance and result is acceptable.

3.3   TCMKG-LSTM-CRF

Our model combines bidirectional LSTM networks with knowledge graph to recognize rare words and strengthen stability and flexibility. A knowledge attention vector model is adopted to improve the performance of previous models which retrieve candidate entities and computing attention vector of entities' embedding. The architecture of our model is shown in Fig. 2.

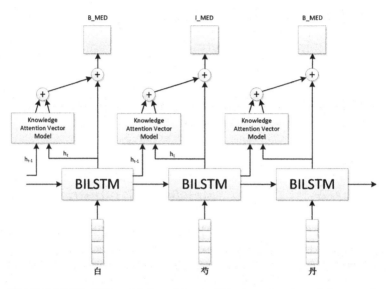

Fig. 2. TCMKG-LSTM-CRF model. h_t and h_{t-1} will be input into knowledge attention vector model to add knowledge graph information before CRF layer.

As character is the smallest unit in Chinese and words cannot be easily and precisely recognized, only character-level embedding will be used. All input Chinese characters x_t will be firstly mapped to pre-trained embedding vectors v_t. After the calculation of BiLSTM, the hidden state $h_t \in R^{d_h \times 1}$ of neural network at the time t will enter into knowledge attention vector model combined with h_{t-1} at time $t-1$. As shown in Fig. 3, in knowledge attention vector model, the candidate entities of character x_t will be retrieved in TCMKG. Each candidate entities $C_{x_t,i}$ has a embedding vector $v_{x_t,i} \in R^{d_e \times 1}$ after training of TCMKG (For character x_t which does not have any candidate entities, $v_{x_t,i}$ will be set as $\vec{0}$). With hidden state h_t, we then compute the attention score $\alpha_{h_t}(i)$ between the i-th entity vector and h_t:

$$h'_t = \tanh\left(W_f h_t + b_f\right) \tag{8}$$

$$\alpha_{h_t}(i) = \frac{\exp\left(v_{x_t,i} \cdot h'_t\right)}{\sum_{k=1}^{n} \exp\left(v_{x_t,i} \cdot h'_t\right)} \tag{9}$$

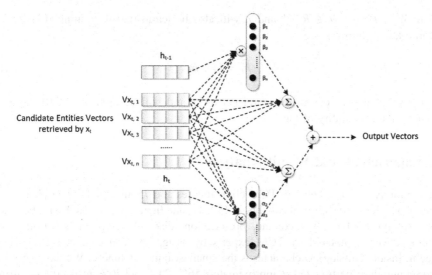

Fig. 3. Knowledge attention vector model. The representation h_t of each character will be calculated the attention between candidate words' vectors in the knowledge graph. h_{t-1} will also be calculated because the last character often participate in the composition of the word or affect the current character.

where $W_f \in R^{d_e \times d_h}$, $b_f \in R^{d_e \times 1}$ are parameters to be learned, and $v_{x_t,i} \cdot h'_t$ is the inner product of $v_{x_t,i}$ and h'_t. The entity attention vector e_{h_t} is calculated as weighted sum of attention score $\alpha_{h_t}(i)$ and embedding vector $v_{x_t,i}$:

$$e_{h_t} = \sum\nolimits_{i=1}^{n} \alpha_{h_t}(i)v_{x_t,i} \tag{10}$$

We also adopt the information of previous word because it is very common that some words will be used in combination frequently especially in ancient TCM clinical cases. So combination information will be counted in final attention vector. $e_{h_{t-1}}$ can be calculated in same way:

$$h'_{t-1} = \tanh\left(W_f h_{t-1} + b_f\right) \tag{11}$$

$$\alpha_{h_{t-1}}(i) = \frac{\exp\left(v_{x_{t-1},i} \cdot h'_{t-1}\right)}{\sum_{k=1}^{n} \exp\left(v_{x_{t-1},i} \cdot h'_{t-1}\right)} \tag{12}$$

$$e_{h_{t-1}} = \sum\nolimits_{i=1}^{n} \alpha_{h_{t-1}}(i)v_{x_{t-1},i} \tag{13}$$

We compute knowledge attention vector m_t as:

$$m'_t = \lambda e_{h_t} + (1-\lambda)e_{h_{t-1}} \tag{14}$$

$$m_t = W_r m'_t + b_r \tag{15}$$

where $W_r \in R^{d_h \times d_e}$, $b_r \in R^{d_h \times 1}$ and λ will also be learnt during training. Finally we incorporate m_t into h_t:

$$\widehat{h_t} = h_t + m_t \tag{16}$$

$\widehat{h_t}$ is regarded as output of neural networks and will be input into CRF layer to calculate the probability of tags.

4 Experiment and Result Analysis

We randomly select 75 modern TCM clinical cases and 75 ancient TCM clinical cases from two authoritative clinical case books [30, 31] and literatures in CKCEST[1]. For each case, six types of entity–medicine, prescription, disease, symptom, syndrome and treatment were annotated by TCM experts by assigning each character BIO labels (Begin, Inside, Outside) as character is the smallest unit in Chinese. We have split the data set into three parts (sized at approximately 56%, 24% and 20%, respectively), using the first part for training and the second part for validating and the third part for testing.

In TCMKG-LSTM-CRF model, the value of max epochs is set to 100 and early stopping is enabled. Dropout rate is set to 0.5. For each characters, embedding vector is trained by Word2Vec [32] and its dimension is set to 100. The hidden vector dimension is set to 100 and entity embedding vector dimension is set to 10. We have tested different settings of dimensions and the results are not sensitive to them. We use Stochastic Gradient Descent to optimize with an initial learning rate of 0.05.

In evaluation, both exact-match and inexact-match criteria are achieved to evaluate the performance of model. On exact-match criteria, all predicted tags must be as same as real tags but on inexact-match criteria, match will be counted when any part of the them overlap. For both match criteria, we use precision P, recall R and F-measure F as measures which defined as follows:

$$P = \frac{N_m}{N_p}, R = \frac{N_m}{N_r}, F = \frac{2 \times P \times R}{P + R} \tag{17}$$

where N_m is the total number of matched entities, N_p is the total number of predicted entities, N_r is the total number of real entities. We also use ACC_{tags} to measure the accuracy of tags predicted.

We compared our TCMKG-LSTM-CRF model with BiLSTM-CRF, BiLSTM-CRF with embeddings pretrained by Word2Vec (BiLSTM-CRF (Pretrained)) and we also applied three different entity embeddings generation methods to test its impact on our model. Table 1 shows the results. Among these models, original CRF model performs best in both precisions on exact-match criteria and inexact-match criteria while the recall and f-measure score are worst because CRF model identifies most of the probable characters as entities resulting in a low overall accuracy rate. BiLSTM-CRF has

---

[1] http://zcy.ckcest.cn/MedicalRecord/index.

significantly improved this phenomenon, especially in F-measure score on inexact-match criteria which means BiLSTM could effective generate representations of characters based on context. BiLSTM-CRF (Pretrained) performs much better than BiLSTM-CRF both on exact-match criteria and inexact-match criteria. BiLSTM-CRF (Pretrained) achieves 0.7238 F-measure score on exact-match criteria and 0.8350 F-measure score on inexact-match criteria, which is higher than BiLSTM-CRF by 0.0261 and 0.0273. It also achieves a better accuracy of tags predicted with accuracy of 87.03%, higher than BiLSTM-CRF by 1.04% which indicates that using pretrained vector is a very effective and simple method to improve training procedure of model.

Table 1. Named entity recognition results on test set of TCM clinical cases.

Model	Exact-match			Inexact-match			ACC_{tags}
	P	R	F	P	R	F	
CRF	**0.8350**	0.5149	0.6366	**0.8869**	0.5469	0.6761	-
BiLSTM-CRF	0.7358	0.6646	0.6977	0.8515	0.7695	0.8077	85.99
BiLSTM-CRF Pretrained	0.7418	0.7071	0.7238	0.8553	0.8163	0.8350	87.03
TCMKG-LSTM-CRF							
-TransE	0.7487	0.7155	**0.7316**	0.8557	0.8178	0.8362	**87.41**
-TransH	0.7345	0.7154	0.7243	0.8502	0.8281	0.8385	87.31
-TransR	0.7431	**0.7201**	0.7308	0.8525	**0.8556**	**0.8541**	87.90

With knowledge attention vector model, our model TCMKG-LSTM-CRF performs better than BiLSTM-CRF (Pretrained) no matter which entity embeddings generation method is applied. In both exact-match criteria and inexact-match criteria, the improvement of our model to task is mainly reflected in recall, which shows the amount of false negatives in recognition can be effectively reduced by adding the attention mechanism with knowledge graph. As a better method of generation of knowledge graph entity embeddings. TransR has also achieved better results overall combined with our model. For both F-measure score, the improvement of our model is statistically significantly by a 2-tailed paired t-test at 95% confidence.

We further explore the impact of difference size of hidden unit in BiLSTM layer and the improvement on recognizing rare words of the combination with knowledge graph. In Fig. 4 we can observe that the trends of performance are almost growing first and declining gradually. The parameters of model are increasing while the size of hidden unit adds to 100 which make the model has more learning ability. Then overfitting might happen with the growth of hidden size. Table 2 shows different performance of our model and BiLSTM-CRF model on different entity types. The most obvious improvement is reflected in the recognition of prescription entity. After analyzing the dataset, we find that among all the entity types, the proportion of rare words in the prescription entity is the highest because for common diseases, Chinese medicine doctors often give patients a list of medicines or drugs instead of specific prescriptions and such specific prescriptions usually appear only once or twice in the clinical case of a corresponding disease. So the combination of knowledge graph significantly improves the ability of the BiLSTM-CRF model to recognize rare words.

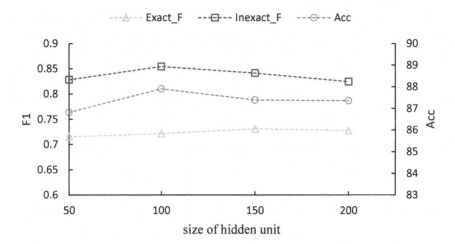

Fig. 4. The impact of difference size of hidden unit on the performance of TCMKG-LSTM-CRF with TransR in terms of Exact_F, Inexact_F and Acc.

Table 2. Comparative performance of our model and BiLSTM-CRF model on different entity types.

Entity type	Exact-match		Inexact-match	
	F(our model)	F(BiLSTM)	F(our model)	F(BiLSTM)
Symptom	0.6586	0.6368	0.7976	0.7774
Medicine	0.8383	0.8294	0.9315	0.9127
Treatment	0.5405	0.5369	0.7297	0.7179
Prescription	0.6728	0.6526	0.9230	0.8012
Disease	0.3953	0.4285	0.5348	0.5238
Syndrome	0.3333	0.3283	0.5970	0.5714

5   Conclusions

In this study, we propose a TCMKG-LSTM-CRF model for named entity recognition in TCM clinical cases, which combines bidirectional LSTM, conditional random field and TCM knowledge graph. This model adopts knowledge attention vector model to implement attention mechanism combining embeddings of candidate entities with current and previous hidden vectors of neural networks. Entity recognition results on real world TCM clinical data sets show the effectiveness and the better ability to recognize rare words of our model and the combination with knowledge base. Our model could play a better role in other natural language processing tasks on TCM texts such as entity linking and relation extraction. In future work, we plan to expand the size of the knowledge base including increasing the type of relationship and number of triples in order to further enhance the effect of the model and test the performance of more knowledge graph embedding generation approaches.

Acknowledgments. This work is supported by the China Knowledge Centre for Engineering Sciences and Technology (CKCEST) and the Natural Science Foundation of Zhejiang Province, China (No. LY17H100003).

References

1. Nestler, G.: Traditional chinese medicine. Med. Clin. North Am. **86**(1), 63–73 (2002)
2. Rau, L.F.: Extracting company names from text. In: Seventh IEEE Conference on Artificial Intelligence Applications, 1991 Proceedings, vol. 1, pp. 29–32. IEEE (1991)
3. Coates-Stephens, S.: The analysis and acquisition of proper names for the understanding of free text. Comput. Humanit. **26**(5–6), 441–456 (1992)
4. Friedman, C., Alderson, P.O., Austin, J.H.M., Cimino, J.J., Johnson, S.B.: A general natural-language text processor for clinical radiology. J. Am. Med. Inform. Assoc. **1**(2), 161–174 (1994)
5. Fukuda, K., Tamura, A., Tsunoda, T., Takagi, T.: Toward information extraction: identifying protein names from biological papers. Pac. Symp. Biocomput. 707–718 (1998)
6. Bikel, D.M., Miller, S., Schwartz, R., Weischedel, R.: Nymble: a high-performance learning name-finder. In: Proceedings of the Fifth Conference on Applied Natural Language Processing, pp. 194–201. Association for Computational Linguistics (1997)
7. Sekine, S.: Description of the Japanese NE system used for MET-2. In: Seventh Message Understanding Conference (MUC-7): Proceedings of a Conference Held in Fairfax, Virginia, April 29–May 1 1998
8. Borthwick, A., Sterling, J., Agichtein, E., Grishman, R.: Description of the MENE named entity system as used in MUC-7. In: Proceedings of the Seventh Message Understanding Conference (MUC-7), Fairfax, Virginia, April 29–May 1 1998
9. Asahara, M., Matsumoto, Y.: Japanese named entity extraction with redundant morphological analysis. In: Proceedings of the 2003 Conference of the North American Chapter of the Association for Computational Linguistics on Human Language Technology-Volume 1, pp. 8–15. Association for Computational Linguistics (2003)
10. McCallum, A., Li, W.: Early results for named entity recognition with conditional random fields, feature induction and web-enhanced lexicons. In: Proceedings of the Seventh Conference on Natural Language Learning at HLT-NAACL 2003-Volume 4, pp. 188–191. Association for Computational Linguistics (2003)
11. Goller, C., Kuchler, A.: Learning task-dependent distributed representations by backpropagation through structure. In: IEEE International Conference on Neural Networks 1996, vol. 1, pp. 347–352. IEEE (1996)
12. Hochreiter, S., Schmidhuber, J.: Long short-term memory. Neural Comput. **9**(8), 1735–1780 (1997)
13. Cho, K., et al.: Learning phrase representations using RNN encoder-decoder for statistical machine translation. arXiv preprint arXiv:1406.1078 (2014)
14. Mikolov, T., Karafiát, M., Burget, L., Černocký, J., Khudanpur, S.: Recurrent neural network based language model. In: Interspeech, vol. 2, p. 3 (2010)
15. Mikolov, T., Kombrink, S., Burget, L., Černocký, J., Khudanpur, S.: Extensions of recurrent neural network language model. In: 2011 IEEE International Conference on Acoustics, Speech and Signal Processing (ICASSP), pp. 5528–5531. IEEE (2011)
16. Sutskever, I., Vinyals, O., Le, Q.V.: Sequence to sequence learning with neural networks. In: Advances in Neural Information Processing Systems, pp. 3104–3112 (2014)

17. Liu, S., Yang, N., Li, M., Zhou, M.: A recursive recurrent neural network for statistical machine translation (2014)
18. Auli, M., Galley, M., Quirk, C., Zweig, G.: Joint language and translation modeling with recurrent neural networks. In: EMNLP, vol. 3, pp. 1044–1054 (2013)
19. Graves, A., Fernández, S., Schmidhuber, J.: Bidirectional LSTM networks for improved phoneme classification and recognition. In: Duch, W., Kacprzyk, J., Oja, E., Zadrożny, S. (eds.) ICANN 2005. LNCS, vol. 3697, pp. 799–804. Springer, Heidelberg (2005). https://doi.org/10.1007/11550907_126
20. Huang, Z., Xu, W., Yu, K.: Bidirectional LSTM-CRF models for sequence tagging. arXiv preprint arXiv:1508.01991 (2015)
21. Lample, G., Ballesteros, M., Subramanian, S., Kawakami, K., Dyer, C.: Neural architectures for named entity recognition. arXiv preprint arXiv:1603.01360 (2016)
22. Chalapathy, R., Borzeshi, E.Z., Piccardi, M.: Bidirectional LSTM-CRF for clinical concept extraction. arXiv preprint arXiv:1611.08373 (2016)
23. Yang, B., Mitchell, T.: Leveraging knowledge bases in LSTMs for improving machine reading. In: Proceedings of the 55th Annual Meeting of the Association for Computational Linguistics (Volume 1: Long Papers), vol. 1, pp. 1436–1446 (2017)
24. Wang, Y., Liu, Y., Yu, Z., Chen, L., Jiang, Y.: A preliminary work on symptom name recognition from free-text clinical records of traditional chinese medicine using conditional random fields and reasonable features. In: Proceedings of the 2012 Workshop on Biomedical Natural Language Processing, pp. 223–230. Association for Computational Linguistics (2012)
25. Wang, Y., et al.: Supervised methods for symptom name recognition in free-text clinical records of traditional chinese medicine: an empirical study. J. Biomed. Inform. **47**, 91–104 (2014)
26. Wang, Q., Xia, Y., Zhou, Y., Ruan, T., Gao, D., He, P.: Incorporating dictionaries into deep neural networks for the chinese clinical named entity recognition. arXiv preprint arXiv:1804.05017 (2018)
27. Wang, Y., Ananiadou, S., Tsujii, J.: Improve Chinese clinical named entity recognition performance by using the graphical and phonetic feature. In: 2018 IEEE International Conference on Bioinformatics and Biomedicine (BIBM), pp. 1582–1586. IEEE (2018)
28. Dettmers, T., Minervini, P., Stenetorp, P., et al.: Convolutional 2D knowledge graph embeddings. In: Thirty-Second AAAI Conference on Artificial Intelligence (2018)
29. Nguyen, D.Q., Nguyen, T.D., Nguyen, D.Q., et al.: A novel embedding model for knowledge base completion based on convolutional neural network. arXiv preprint arXiv:1712.02121 (2017)
30. Dong, J., Wang, Y.: zhongguoxiandaimingzhongyiyianjingcui (in Chinese) (2010)
31. Lu, Z., Yang, S., Wang, X., et al.: erxumingyileian (in Chinese), fumingyileian, xumingyileian
32. Mikolov, T., Sutskever, I., Chen, K., Corrado, G.S., Dean, J.: Distributed representations of words and phrases and their compositionality. In: Advances in Neural Information Processing Systems, pp. 3111–3119 (2013)

Adaptive-Skip-TransE Model: Breaking Relation Ambiguities for Knowledge Graph Embedding

Shoukang Han[1,2,3], Xiaobo Guo[1,2,3(✉)], Lei Wang[2,3], Zeyi Liu[3], and Nan Mu[1,2,3]

[1] School of Cyber Security, University of Chinese
Academy of Sciences, Beijing, China
[2] State Key Laboratory of Information Security,
Chinese Academy of Sciences, Beijing, China
[3] Institute of Information Engineering, Chinese Academy of Sciences, Beijing, China
{hanshoukang,guoxiaobo,wanglei,liuzeyi,munan}@iie.ac.cn

Abstract. Knowledge graph embedding aims to encode entities and relations into a low-dimensional vector space, obtaining its distributed vector representation for further knowledge learning and reasoning. Most existing methods assume that each relation owns one unique vector. However, in the real world, many relations are multi-semantic. We note that a reasonable adaptive learning method for the number of semantics for a given relation is lacking in knowledge graph embedding. In this paper, we propose a probabilistic model Skip-TransE, which comprehensively considers the two-way prediction ability and global loss intensity of the golden triplets. Then based on Skip-TransE, its non-parametric Bayesian extended model Adaptive-Skip-TransE is presented to automatically learn the number of semantics for each relation. Extensive experiments show that the proposed models can achieve some substantial improvements above the state-of-the-art baselines.

Keywords: Knowledge embedding · Multi-semantic relations · Adaptive learning

1 Introduction

Knowledge Graphs such as WordNet [15], Freebase [3] and Yago [6] have become very important resources to support many AI related applications, including relation extraction (RE), question answering (Q&A), etc. Generally, a knowledge graph is a collection of relational facts that are often represented in the form of a triplet (head entity, relation, tail entity) (denoted as (h, r, t), e.g. (*Obama, Born-in, Honolulu*). As traditional knowledge base representations mainly rely on the learned logic inference rules for knowledge reasoning, numerical machine learning methods cannot be leveraged to support the computation. Research on representation learning attracts the attention. These studies produced a series

© Springer Nature Switzerland AG 2019
C. Douligeris et al. (Eds.): KSEM 2019, LNAI 11775, pp. 549–560, 2019.
https://doi.org/10.1007/978-3-030-29551-6_49

of embedding models, such as TransE [4], TransH [19]. Inspired by word2vec [13,14], TransE regard every entity and relation as a translation in the embedding space. For a golden triplet (h, r, t), the head entity embedding $\mathbf{h}$ is close to the tail entity embedding $\mathbf{t}$ by adding the relation embedding $\mathbf{h}$, that is $\mathbf{h} + \mathbf{r} \approx \mathbf{t}$. TransH is proposed to enable an entity to have distinct distributed representations when involved in different relations. In fact, the above models generate only one embedded vector for each single relation, not considering the ambiguity issues caused by the multiple semantics of relations.

2   Related Work

To solve the problem of precise embedding of multiple semantic relations, TransR/CTransR [12] is proposed based on the idea that entities and relations should be in two different vector spaces. What's more, CTransR believes that the specific relation in the relational space contains more sub-relations with different meanings. The representations of the sub-relations and their numbers can be obtained by clustering the vector differences of all the head and tail entity pairs of a given relation, and the pairs in the same cluster share the same sub-relation vector. This cluster calculation may ignore a variety real-world semantics. TransD [9] considers multiple types of entities and relations simultaneously, and replaces the transfer matrix with the product of the two projection vectors of the entity-relational pair. TranSparse [10] takes into account the heterogeneity (some relations connect many entity pairs, while others do not) and imbalances (the number of head and tail entities may differ) of the complex relations, using adaptive sparse transfer matrices to embed the knowledge graph into a continuous vector space. Prior assumptions about the number of semantics is required in the above two methods at the expense of great flexibility. TransG [20], as the first generative method to address the issue of multiple relation semantics, models the different semantics of the same relation into different Gaussian distributions and assumes that all semantics of a relation contribute to the fractional function of the fact triples, but also makes the computational complexity large and blurs the boundaries between semantics.

By exploring the research process of embedding, we find that adaptive learning of the number of relational semantics is a milestone problem of embedding, which greatly affects the accuracy and flexibility of embedding. The semantic quantity of a relation should not be assumed in advance because it depends greatly on the training set. Different training set would produce different numbers of semantics of relations. The current knowledge graph embedding field lacks a reasonable adaptive learning method for semantic quantity and semantic representation. Besides, we also note that previous translation-based methods only sample a single corrupted triplet for each golden triplet. Thus they calculate local loss between each golden triplet and its single corrupted triplet in their objective function. It is insufficient for training because the local loss can just optimize the ranking error between these two triplets, while the global loss among the golden triplet and all its corrupted triplets can optimize overall ranking error for each triplet to learn better embedding vector.

In response to the above questions, we conduct a series of studies. The contributions in this paper are mainly as follows:

1. Firstly, we propose a probabilistic model Skip-TransE that considers the global ranking loss of each golden triplet, inspired by the SkipGram model of word2vec [13,14]. It can optimizes the representation vector by predicting the corresponding head-to-tail entity pair (h, t) given the relation r.
2. Secondly, we introduce Adaptive-Skip-TransE model based on Skip-TransE via stick-breaking representation, inspired by the Adaptive Skip-gram model [1]. It can automatically learns the required numbers of representations of all relations.
3. Lastly, we evaluate our models on link prediction and triple classification tasks. In experiments, Skip-TransE significantly outperforms TransE. Adaptive-Skip-TransE outperforms baselines, and comparable to or slightly better than TransG.

3 Our Models

Firstly, we define the score function for a triplet. Given a triplet (h, r, t), the score function is:

$$z(\mathbf{h}, \mathbf{r}, \mathbf{t}) = b - \tfrac{1}{2} \parallel \mathbf{h} + \mathbf{r} - \mathbf{t} \parallel^2 \tag{1}$$

where b is a bias constant, which is a model hyperparameter. If the triplet is a golden triplet, $z(\mathbf{h}, \mathbf{r}, \mathbf{t})$ is expected to be large, otherwise it is small.

3.1 Skip-TransE

Inspired by Skip-Gram model of word2vec, which uses the current word to predict the surrounding window of context words, Skip-TransE can be used to predict the head and tail entity pair (h, t) given the relation r for a triplet (h, r, t).

Firstly, we define the conditional probability of a golden triplet (h, r, t) is as follows:

$$P(h|r, t, \theta) = \frac{\exp\{z(\mathbf{h}, \mathbf{r}, \mathbf{t}|\theta)\}}{\sum_{\tilde{h} \in \Delta'} \exp\{z(\tilde{\mathbf{h}}, \mathbf{r}, \mathbf{t}|\theta)\}} \tag{2}$$

where global parameter $\theta = \{relation_i\}_{i=1}^{|\mathbf{R}|} \cup \{entity_i\}_{i=1}^{|\mathbf{E}|}$ stands for both relation and entity vector representation of the knowledge graph, Δ' represents the corresponding corrupted triplets set for the golden triplet, which is constructed by replacing the head entity with all entities in $\mathbf{R}$. Equation(2) is a softmax function essentially, and we also define $P(t|r, h, \theta)$ in the same way. Skip-TransE considers the global loss for each triplet in its objective function, that is its objective function contains more information for training to benefit knowledge graph embedding vectors.

Here, the direction of the head entity $\rightarrow$ relation $\rightarrow$ tail entity is defined as the positive direction, then the prediction of tail is forward, and that of head is reversed. For a given triple, it is intuitively known that if the forward and reverse predictions can be considered simultaneously, the representation vector can better reflect the overall establishment of the triple. The conditional probability of bidirectional prediction is defined as $P(h \Longleftrightarrow t|r,\theta) = P(t|h,r,\theta) \times P(h|t,r,\theta)$. A probability is originally a small number. The subsequent multiplication of many probabilities may cause an underflow. So the logarithm of the probability is calculated here: $\mathcal{L}_f(h \Longleftrightarrow t|r,\theta) = \log P(h \Longleftrightarrow t|r,\theta) = \log P(h|r,t,\theta) + \log P(t|r,h,\theta)$.

The probability of predicting the head and tail pairs is positively correlated with that of bidirectional prediction: $\mathcal{L}_f(h,t|r,\theta) \propto \mathcal{L}_f(h \Longleftrightarrow t|r,\theta)$. In the vector learning process, it is fluctuating trend of the scoring function that indicates the optimization direction of the vector representation. The actual value of the scoring function itself has no more practical significance. Therefore, the bidirectional probability can be used as an approximate scoring function when predicting entity pairs for a given relation, that is : $\mathcal{L}_f(h,t|r,\theta) \approx \mathcal{L}_f(h \Longleftrightarrow t|r,\theta)$.

Hence, we define the likelihood of observing a triplet given the relation r as:

$$\mathcal{L}_f(h,t|r,\theta) \approx \log P(h|r,t,\theta) + \log P(t|r,h,\theta) \tag{3}$$

The goal of the model is to maximize the conditional likelihoods of existing triplets in the knowledge graph:

$$\mathcal{L}_\mathcal{K} = \sum_{(h,r,t)\in\Delta} \mathcal{L}_f(h,t|r,\theta) \tag{4}$$

Computational Complexity. According to Eqs. (1) and (3), we can see that the score function is almost the same as the one of TransE [4], thus its computational burden mainly comes from the normalization term of Eq. (3), which can be computed efficiently with the help of negative sampling, as we will discussed in Sect. 3.3.

3.2   Adaptive-Skip-TransE

The above probabilistic model learns only one prototype per relation. But it would be problematic to assume that a single relation vector may capture all the semantics of a relation. We use the constructive definition of Dirichlet process (DP) [7] via the stick-breaking representation [16] to define a prior over the required number of prototypes of a relation automatically. The DP process assumes that each relation may have infinite number of prototypes, and the prototype probabilities are computed by dividing total probability mass into infinite number of diminishing pieces summing to 1. So the prior probability of k-th meaning of a relation r is:

$$P(z = k|r,\boldsymbol{\beta}) = \beta_{rk} \prod_{l=1}^{k-1}(1 - \beta_{rl}),$$

$$P(\beta_{rk}|\alpha) = Beta(\beta_{rk}|1,\alpha), k = 1,\ldots \tag{5}$$

z indicates which semantic the relation r takes, α controls the prior number of prototypes for a relation, specifically, larger values of α produce more prototypes of relation r. However, as the amount of training data is finite, the number of prototypes (these with non-zero prior probabilities) of relation r will be less than the number of occurrences of r in the knowledge graph, denoted as n_r.

Combining all parts together, we may write the Adaptive-Skip-TransE model as follows:

$$\mathcal{L}_{\mathcal{K}}(H, T, Z, \beta | R, \alpha, \theta)$$

$$= \sum_{r=1}^{|\mathbf{R}|} \sum_{k=1}^{\infty} \log P(\beta_{rk}|\alpha) + \sum_{i=1}^{N} \{\log P(z_i|r_i, \beta) + \log P(h_i, t_i|r_i, z_i, \theta)\} \quad (6)$$

where $R = \{r_i\}_{i=1}^{N}$, $H = \{h_i\}_{i=1}^{N}$, and $T = \{t_i\}_{i=1}^{N}$ represents N triplets and their corresponding head entity, tail entity and relation in the whole knowledge graph. $Z = \{z_i\}_{i=1}^{N}$ is a set of senses for all the relations.

Computational Complexity. Compared with TransG, which is quite complicated because it assumes that all the semantics of a relation contribute to the score function for a given triplet, our model actually only needs a specific semantic for the triplet through stick-breaking representation, and thus it has fewer parameters, and is easier to understand compared with TransG.

3.3 Training and Disambiguation

Stochastic Variational Inference. Since Z and β are latent variables, and β, θ are infinite-dimensional parameters, we cannot train the model by stochastic gradient ascent directly. Thus, we use stochastic variational inference to make the training tractable in this paper. First, we consider the evidence lower bound (ELBO) on the marginal likelihood $\mathcal{L}_{\mathcal{K}}(H, T | R, \alpha, \theta)$ of Eq. (6):

$$\mathcal{L}(q(Z), q(\beta), \theta) = \mathbb{E}_q[\log P(H, T, Z, \beta | R, \alpha, \theta) - \log q(Z, \beta)] \quad (7)$$

where $q(Z, \beta) = \prod_{i=1}^{N} q(z_i) \prod_{r=1}^{|\mathbf{R}|} \prod_{k=1}^{T} q(\beta_{rk})$ is the variational approximation to the posterior $P(Z, \beta | H, T, R, \alpha, \theta)$, each hidden variable of $q(Z, \beta)$ is independent and possible number of prototypes for each relation is truncated to T [2]. Moreover, [11] has proved that the maximization of the ELBO with respect to $q(Z, \beta)$ is equivalent to the minimization of Kullback-Leibler divergence between $q(Z, \beta)$ and the true posterior $P(Z, \beta | H, T, R, \alpha, \theta)$, that is, we can train the model through maximizing Eq. (7). Combining Eq. (7) with Eq. (6), ELBO $\mathcal{L}(q(Z), q(\beta), \theta)$ takes the following form:

$$\mathcal{L}(q(Z), q(\beta), \theta) = \mathbb{E}_q \left[\sum_{r=1}^{|\mathbf{R}|} \sum_{k=1}^{T} \log P(\beta_{rk} | \alpha - \log q(\beta_{rk})) \right.$$

$$\left. + \sum_{i=1}^{N} (\log P(z_i|r_i, \beta) - \log q(z_i) + \log P(h_i, t_i|r_i, z_i, \theta)) \right] \quad (8)$$

Take the derivatives of $\mathcal{L}(q(Z), q(\beta), \theta)$ with respect to $q(Z)$ and $q(\beta)$, we obtain their update equations:

$$\log q(z_i = k) = \mathbb{E}_{q(\beta)}\left[\log \beta_{r_i,k} + \sum_{l=1}^{k-1} \log(1 - \beta_{r_i,l})\right]$$
$$+ \log P(h_i, t_i | r_i, k, \theta) + \mathbf{const} \quad (9)$$

$$\log q(\beta) = \sum_{r=1}^{|\mathbf{R}|} \sum_{k=1}^{T} \log Beta(\beta_{rk} | a_{rk}, b_{rk}) \quad (10)$$

where natural parameters a_{rk} and b_{rk} depend on the number of occurrences of the particular sense n_{rk} [2] : $a_{rk} = 1 + n_{rk}$, $b_{rk} = \alpha + \sum_{l=k+1}^{T} n_{rl}$.

Because variational updates Eq. (9) and Eq. (10) require the full pass over training data, we employ stochastic variational inference approach [8] and online optimization algorithm [1] for the maximization of $\mathcal{L}$ to improve the training efficiency. There are two groups of parameters in our objective: $\{q(\beta_{rk})\}$ and θ are global; $\{q(z_i)\}$ are local. First, we update the local parameters with global parameters fixed according to Eq. (9) and denote the obtained distribution as $q^*(Z)$, we can obtain a function of the global parameters $\mathcal{L}^*(q(\beta), \theta) = \mathcal{L}^*(q^*(Z), q(\beta), \theta)$.

The new lower bound $\mathcal{L}^*$ contains no more local parameters, then we iteratively optimize $\mathcal{L}^*$ with respect to the global parameters using stochastic gradient estimated at a single object. Formally, stochastic gradient w.r.t. θ computed on the i-th object is computed as follows:

$$\widehat{\nabla_\theta}\mathcal{L}^* = N \sum_{k=1}^{T} q^*(z_i = k)\nabla_\theta \log P(h_i, t_i | r_i, k, \theta) \quad (11)$$

As to optimizing $\mathcal{L}^*$ w.r.t. global posterior approximation $q(\beta)$, we need to estimate the stochastic gradient with respect to natural parameters a_{rk} and b_{rk} according to Eq. (10). Based on the conclusion of [8], we assume that $q(Z)$ for all occurrences of relation r equal to $\{q(z_i)\}$. Then the stochastic gradient can be estimated by computing intermediate of natural parameters $(\widehat{a_{rk}}, \widehat{b_{rk}})$ on the i-th data point:

$$\widehat{a_{rk}} = 1 + n_r q(z_i = k), \widehat{b_{rk}} = \alpha + \sum_{l=k+1}^{T} n_r q(z_i = k) \quad (12)$$

where n_r is the total number of occurrences of relation r. The stochastic gradient then can be computed in the following simple form: $\widehat{\nabla_{a_{rk}}}\mathcal{L}^* = \widehat{a_{rk}} - a_{rk}$, $\widehat{\nabla_{b_{rk}}}\mathcal{L}^* = \widehat{b_{rk}} - b_{rk}$. It can be found that making such gradient update is equivalent to updating counts n_{rk}, i.e.,

$$\widehat{\nabla_{n_{rk}}}\mathcal{L}^* = n_r q(z_i = k) - n_{rk} \quad (13)$$

Combining all parts together, the update of $q(z_i)$ can be seen as local step, and the updates of θ and n_{rk} (essentially, it updates $q(\beta)$) are global steps. The detailed learning procedure is described in Algorithm 1.

Algorithm 1. Training Adaptive-Skip-TransE model

Require: training data $\{(h_i, r_i, t_i)\}_{i=1}^N$, hyperparameter α
Ensure: parameters θ, distributions $q(\beta)$, $q(\mathbf{z})$
   Initialize parameters θ, distributions $q(\beta)$, $q(\mathbf{z})$, learning rate λ_t
   for $i = 1$ **to** N **do**
      Select triplet (h_i, r_i, t_i)
      Local Step:
      for $k = 1$ **to** T **do**
         $\gamma_{ik} = \mathbb{E}_{q(\beta)}\big[\log \beta_{r_i,k} + \sum_{l=1}^{k-1} \log(1 - \beta_{r_i,l})\big]$
         $\gamma_{ik} \leftarrow \gamma_{ik} + \log P(h_i, t_i | r_i, k, \theta)$
      end for
      $\gamma_{ik} \leftarrow \exp(\gamma_{ik}) / \sum_l \exp(\gamma_{il})$
      Global Step:
      for $k = 1$ **to** T **do**
         Update $n_{rk} \leftarrow (1 - \lambda_t)n_{rk} + \lambda_t n_r \gamma_{ik}$
      end for
      Update
      $\theta \leftarrow \theta + \lambda_t \nabla_\theta \sum_{k=1}^T \gamma_{ik} \log P(h_i, t_i | r_i, k, \theta)$
   end for

Negative Sampling. Since their normalizers sum over all triplets in the knowledge graph which is too large, we cannot compute the normalizers in $P(h|r, t, \theta)$ and $P(t|h, r, \theta)$ efficiently. Similar to word2vec, we use negative sampling (NEG) to compute only a sample of them, denoted as negative samples.

First, we define the probability of a given triplet (h, r, t) to be true $(D = 1)$:

$$P(D = 1|h, r, t) = \sigma(z(\mathbf{h}, \mathbf{r}, \mathbf{t})) \tag{14}$$

where $\sigma(x) = \frac{1}{1+\exp\{-x\}}$ and $D \in \{0, 1\}$.

Instead of maximizing $\log P(h|r, t, \theta)$ in Eq. (3), we maximize:

$$\log P(1|h, r, t) + \sum_{i=1}^c \mathbb{E}_{\tilde{h}_i \sim P_{neg}(\tilde{h}_i)}\big[P(0|\tilde{h}_i, r, t)\big] \tag{15}$$

where c is the number of negative examples to be discriminated for each positive example, and $P_{neg}(\tilde{h}_i)$ is the noise distribution. We also replace $\log P(t|h, r, \theta)$ in Eq. (3) in the same way. NEG guarantees that maximizing Eq. (15) can approximately maximize $\log P(h|r, t, \theta)$.

Disambiguation. With use of the trained model, inferring the meaning of a relation **r** given its head entity and tail entity is achievable. The predictive probability of a meaning of relation r is computed as follows:

$$P(z = k|r, \theta, \alpha) \approx \int P(z = k|\boldsymbol{\beta}, r)q(\boldsymbol{\beta})d\boldsymbol{\beta} \tag{16}$$

where $q(\boldsymbol{\beta})$ is an approximation of $P(\boldsymbol{\beta}|\theta, \alpha)$. And $q(\boldsymbol{\beta})$ obeys an independent Beta distribution, so the integral can be taken analytically by the expectation of $q(\boldsymbol{\beta})$. Therefore, the probability of each meaning of relation r given its head and tail entity pair (h, t) can be computed as

$$\log P(z = k|r, h, t, \theta) \approx \log P(h, t|r, k, \theta) + \log P(z = k|r, \theta) \tag{17}$$

4   Experiments

Our models are evaluated on two tasks: link prediction [4] and triplet classification [17].

4.1   Data Sets

We use datasets commonly used in previous methods: WordNet [15] and Freebase [3]. In this paper, WN18 and FB15k are adopted for link prediction, WN11 and FB13 for triplet classification. The details of these datasets are listed in Table 1.

Table 1. Statistics of data sets

Datasets	Rel	Ent	Train	Valid	Test
WN18	18	40,943	141,442	5,000	5,000
FB15k	1,345	14,951	483,142	50,000	59,071
WN11	11	38,696	112,581	2,609	10,544
FB13	13	75,043	316,232	5,908	23,733

4.2   Link Prediction

Used in [4,5], link prediction aims to complete a triplet (h, r, t) with h or t missing, i.e., predict t given (h, r) or predict h given (r, t). Instead of giving one best answer, this task ranks a set of candidate entities from the knowledge graph. Similar to [4,5], WN18 and FB15k are used here for link prediction task.

Evaluation Protocol. We adopt the same protocol in TransE. For each testing triplet (h, r, t), we corrupt it by replacing the tail t with every entity e in the knowledge graph and calculate all score function value according to the Eq. (1). Then we rank the scores in ascending order, and get the rank of the original correct triplet. Similarly, we can get another rank for (h, r, t) by corrupting the head h. Aggregated over all the testing triplets, we can calculate two evaluation metrics: *the averaged rank* (denoted as *Mean Rank*), and *the proportion of correct entities ranked in top 10* (denoted as *Hits@10*). We call this raw evaluation

Table 2. Evaluation results on link prediction (%).

Datasets	WN18				FB15k			
Metric	Mean rank		Hits@10		Mean rank		Hits@10	
	Raw	Filter	Raw	Filter	Raw	Filter	Raw	Filter
TransE [4]	263	251	75.4	89.2	243	125	34.9	47.1
TransH [19]	401	388	73.0	82.3	212	87	45.7	64.4
TransR [12]	238	225	79.8	92.0	198	77	48.2	68.7
CTransR [12]	231	218	79.4	92.3	199	75	48.4	70.2
TransD [9]	224	212	79.6	92.2	194	91	53.4	77.3
TranSparse [10]	223	211	80.1	93.2	190	82	53.7	79.9
TransG [20] •	357	345	84.5	94.9	152	50	55.9	88.2
Skip-TransE (this paper)	**248**	**232**	75.2	92.3	172	**45**	50.9	78.9
Adaptive-Skip-TransE (this paper)	**228**	**211**	77.8	94.6	163	**37**	53.5	85.2

Table 3. Experimental results on FB15K by mapping properties of relations (%).

Relation category	Prediction Head (Hits@10)				Prediction Tail (Hits@10)			
	1-to-1	1-to-N	N-to-1	N-to-N	1-to-1	1-to-N	N-to-1	N-to-N
TransE [4]	43.7	65.7	18.2	47.2	43.7	19.7	66.7	50.0
TransH [19]	66.8	87.6	28.7	64.5	65.5	39.8	83.3	67.2
TransR [12]	78.8	89.2	34.1	69.2	79.2	37.4	90.4	72.1
CTransR [12]	81.5	89.0	34.7	71.2	80.8	38.6	90.1	73.8
TransD [9]	86.1	95.5	39.8	78.5	85.4	50.6	94.4	81.2
TranSparse [10]	87.1	95.8	44.4	81.2	87.5	57.0	94.5	83.7
TransG [20]	93.0	96.0	62.5	86.8	92.8	68.1	94.5	88.8
Skip-TransE (this paper)	84.5	94.3	50.6	79.8	83.9	59.4	92.7	82.3
Adaptive-Skip-TransE (this paper)	89.7	**96.5**	56.9	86.6	88.1	**66.4**	**95.5**	**88.3**

setting. In fact, a corrupted triplet may also exist in the knowledge graph, which should be also considered as correct. Hence, we should remove those corrupted triplets which exist in either training or testing set before getting the above two metrics. We call this filter evaluation setting. In both settings, a lower *Mean Rank* is better while a higher *Hits@10* is better.

Implementation. Since the data sets are the same, we directly compare our models with several baselines, including TransE, TransH, TransR, TransD, TranSparse, TransG, Unstructured model, SE, LFM and SLM. The best configuration is determined according to the mean rank. For Skip-TransE, the optimal configuration is $b = 7$, $\lambda = 0.0015$, $k = 100$, $c = 10$ on WN18 and $b = 9$, $\lambda = 0.0015$, $k = 300$, $c = 30$ on FB15k. For Adaptive-Skip-TransE, the optimal configuration is as follows: $b = 7$, $\alpha = 0.1$, $\lambda = 0.0015$, $k = 100$, $c = 10$, $p = 10$ on WN18, $b = 9$, $\alpha = 0.5$, $\lambda = 0.0015$, $k = 300$, $c = 30$, $p = 20$ on FB15k.

Results. Tables 2 and 3 show the comprehensive forecast and branch prediction separately, conclusions are as follows: (1) Skip-TransE plays better than most baseline models, and especially achieves better performance than TransE, TransH and TransR/CTransR in all types of relations (1-to-1, 1-to-N, N-to-1, N-to-N), which demonstrates that considering global loss among each golden triplet and all its corrupted triplets can significantly improve the embedding. (2) Adaptive-Skip-TransE outperforms most baseline embedding models, and achieves comparable performance relative to TransG in all types of relations, but with fewer parameters. (3) Adaptive-Skip-TransE's better performance than Skip-TransE indicates that capturing multiple relation semantics would benefit embedding.

4.3 Triplet Classification

Triplet classification aims to judge whether a given triplet (h, r, t) is correct or not. It is used in [17] to evaluate knowledge graph embeddings learned by NTN model, and WN11 and FB13 are the benchmark datasets for this task.

Evaluation Protocol. We follow the same protocol in [17]. Note that evaluation of classification needs negative labels, and WN11 and FB13 datasets already contain negative triplets, which are built by corrupting the corresponding positive observed triplets. The decision rule for triplet classification is very simple: for each triplet (h, r, t), if the value calculated by the score function Eq. 1 is above a relation-specific threshold δ_r, then the triplet will be classified as positive, otherwise it will be classified as negative. The relation-specific threshold is determined by maximizing the classification accuracy on the validation set.

Implementation. As all methods use the same datasets WN11 and FB13, we compare our model with several baselines from TransE, TransH, TransR, TransD, TranSparse, TransG, Unstructured model, SE, LFM and SLM. The best configuration is determined by the classification accuracy in validation set. We use different parameters for Skip-TransE and Adaptive-Skip-TransE. For Skip-TransE, the optimal configuration is $b = 7$, $\lambda = 0.0015$, $k = 100$, and $c = 10$ on WN18 and $b = 9, \lambda = 0.0015$, $k = 200$, and $c = 20$ on FB15k. For Adaptive-Skip-TransE, the optimal configuration is as follows: $b = 7$, $\alpha = 0.3$, and $p = 10$ on WN18, $b = 11$, $\alpha = 0.8$, and $p = 30$ on FB15k.

Results. The accuracy of triplet classification on two datasets is reported in Table 4. Conclusions are as follows: (1) Skip-TransE significantly outperforms TransE, that means global loss consideration is more suitable for knowledge graph representation learning. (2) Adaptive-Skip-TransE outperforms many baseline embedding models. Though with fewer parameters, its performance is comparable to TransG. This means it finds a better trade-off between model complexity and expressiveness on the multiple relation semantics issue.

Table 4. Triplet classification: accuracy for different embedding models (%).

Datasets	WN11	FB13
TransE	75.9	81.5
TransH	78.8	83.3
TransR	85.9	82.5
KG2E	85.4	85.3
TransD	86.4	89.1
TranSparse	86.8	87.5
TransG	87.4	87.3
Skip-TransE	85.1	86.2
Adaptive-Skip-TransE	**86.7**	**87.1**

5 Conclusion

In this paper, we introduced Skip-TransE and Adaptive-Skip-TransE used for embedding knowledge graphs into low dimensional vector space. Skip-TransE, which is a probabilistic knowledge graph embedding model, learns embeddings by predicting its corresponding head and tail entity pair given the relation. It uses all the corrupted triplets as the normalization term for each golden triplet in its probabilistic score function, and uses negative sampling to make training efficient. Adaptive-Skip-TransE is a nonparametric bayesian extension of Skip-TransE via stick-breaking representation to address the multiple relation semantics issue. It is capable to automatically learn the required number of representations for all relations and learn more distinctive meanings as larger training set comes. In experiments, we evaluate our models on link prediction and triplet classification tasks. Extensive experiments show that the proposed models achieves some substantial improvements against the state-of-the-art baselines.

According to [18], the two standard benchmarks mainly used for link prediction task suffer from inverse relation bias. In future, we will try to improve our model to have a good robustness on reverse relation deviation datasets.

References

1. Bartunov, S., Kondrashkin, D., Osokin, A., Vetrov, D.: Breaking sticks and ambiguities with adaptive skip-gram. In: Artificial Intelligence and Statistics, pp. 130–138 (2016)
2. Blei, D.M., Jordan, M.I., et al.: Variational inference for dirichlet process mixtures. Bayesian Anal. **1**(1), 121–143 (2006)
3. Bollacker, K., Evans, C., Paritosh, P., Sturge, T., Taylor, J.: Freebase: a collaboratively created graph database for structuring human knowledge. In: Proceedings of the 2008 ACM SIGMOD International Conference on Management of Data, pp. 1247–1250. ACM (2008)

4. Bordes, A., Usunier, N., Garcia-Duran, A., Weston, J., Yakhnenko, O.: Translating embeddings for modeling multi-relational data. In: Advances in Neural Information Processing Systems, pp. 2787–2795 (2013)

5. Bordes, A., Weston, J., Collobert, R., Bengio, Y.: Learning structured embeddings of knowledge bases. In: Conference on Artificial Intelligence, No. EPFL-CONF-192344 (2011)

6. Fabian, M., Gjergji, K., Gerhard, W., et al.: Yago: a core of semantic knowledge unifying wordnet and wikipedia. In: 16th International World Wide Web Conference, WWW, pp. 697–706 (2007)

7. Ferguson, T.S.: A bayesian analysis of some nonparametric problems. Ann. Stat. **1**, 209–230 (1973)

8. Hoffman, M.D., Blei, D.M., Wang, C., Paisley, J.W.: Stochastic variational inference. J. Mach. Learn. Res. **14**(1), 1303–1347 (2013)

9. Ji, G., He, S., Xu, L., Liu, K., Zhao, J.: Knowledge graph embedding via dynamic mapping matrix. In: ACL, vol. 1, pp. 687–696 (2015)

10. Ji, G., Liu, K., He, S., Zhao, J.: Knowledge graph completion with adaptive sparse transfer matrix. In: Thirtieth AAAI Conference on Artificial Intelligence (2016)

11. Jordan, M.I., Ghahramani, Z., Jaakkola, T.S., Saul, L.K.: An introduction to variational methods for graphical models. Mach. Learn. **37**(2), 183–233 (1999)

12. Lin, Y., Liu, Z., Sun, M., Liu, Y., Zhu, X.: Learning entity and relation embeddings for knowledge graph completion. In: AAAI, pp. 2181–2187 (2015)

13. Mikolov, T., Chen, K., Corrado, G., Dean, J.: Efficient estimation of word representations in vector space. arXiv preprint arXiv:1301.3781 (2013)

14. Mikolov, T., Sutskever, I., Chen, K., Corrado, G.S., Dean, J.: Distributed representations of words and phrases and their compositionality. In: Advances in Neural Information Processing Systems, pp. 3111–3119 (2013)

15. Miller, G.A.: Wordnet: a lexical database for English. Commun. ACM **38**(11), 39–41 (1995)

16. Sethuraman, J.: A constructive definition of dirichlet priors. Statistica Sinica **4**, 639–650 (1994)

17. Socher, R., Chen, D., Manning, C.D., Ng, A.: Reasoning with neural tensor networks for knowledge base completion. In: Advances in Neural Information Processing Systems, pp. 926–934 (2013)

18. Chandrahas, S.R., Talukdar, P.P.: Revisiting simple neural networks for learning representations of knowledge graphs (2017)

19. Wang, Z., Zhang, J., Feng, J., Chen, Z.: Knowledge graph embedding by translating on hyperplanes. In: AAAI, pp. 1112–1119. Citeseer (2014)

20. Xiao, H., Huang, M., Zhu, X.: Transg : A generative model for knowledge graph embedding. In: Proceedings of the 54th Annual Meeting of the Association for Computational Linguistics, Long Papers, vol. 1, pp. 2316–2325. Association for Computational Linguistics (2016). https://doi.org/10.18653/v1/P16-1219, http://aclweb.org/anthology/P16-1219

Entity Linking Based on Graph Model and Semantic Representation

Ningyu Ma[1], Xiao Liu[2], and Yulun Gao[2(✉)]

[1] Chien-shiung Wu College, Southeast University, Nanjing, China
213161006@seu.edu.cn
[2] School of Computer Science and Engineering, Southeast University, Nanjing, China
haroldliuj@gmail.com, 213162340@seu.edu.cn

Abstract. A large number of applications which bridge web data with knowledge bases have led to an increase in the entity linking research. Candidate entity disambiguation plays an important role in the typical entity linking systems. Generally, graph-based candidate disambiguation approaches applied document-level topical coherence of candidate entities. Nevertheless, they do not make full use of abundant unambiguous entities to enrich semantic information during the disambiguation. To solve this problem, we propose a graph-based model combining semantic representation learning for entity linking. Specifically, we construct a referent graph based on semantic vectors trained from RDF data, in which we introduce the dynamic PageRank algorithm with unambiguous entities to enhance the performance of entity linking. Primary experiments show that this model outperforms state-of-the-art on benchmark datasets.

Keywords: Entity linking · Candidate disambiguation · Graph based

1 Introduction

A large number of applications which bridge web data with knowledge bases have led to an increase in the entity linking research [1]. For example, news or blogs from web pages involve a large number of entities, but most of them do not have relevant descriptions. In order to help people understand the content of web pages better, many websites and authors will link the entities appearing in the web pages with the corresponding Knowledge Base (KB) terms to provide readers with the more detailed introduction. By establishing the association between the entity mention in documents and the real-world entities in the knowledge graph. Therefore, entity linking plays an important role in promoting potential applications, e.g., question answering [2,3], information extraction [4,5] and information retrieval [6,7].

N. Ma and X. Liu—Contributed equally.

© Springer Nature Switzerland AG 2019
C. Douligeris et al. (Eds.): KSEM 2019, LNAI 11775, pp. 561–571, 2019.
https://doi.org/10.1007/978-3-030-29551-6_50

Graph-based models achieve a comfortable balance between reducing the time consumption and modeling the document-level topical coherence of candidate entities. For graph-based approaches, Han et al. [8] construct a referent graph (also named mention-entity graph). It collects the initialized confidence of different entities and then propagates and enhances the confidence by the edge. Zhang et al. [9] propose an iterative graph-based algorithm to jointly model the entity detection and entity linking. It could be used in a domain-specific area by capturing the local dependency of mention-to-entity and the global interdependency of entity-to-entity. Gentile et al. [10] propose a named entity disambiguation approach based on the graph and semantic relations in KBP evaluation. Alhelbawy et al. [11] also propose a graph-based approach and the PageRank algorithm to select target entities. However, these above methods generally do not make full use of abundant unambiguous entities. With the increasing number of unambiguous entities, semantic information of referent graph is not enriched.

To solve these problems, we propose an entity linking algorithm, called ELGR, which combines graph model and semantic representation. With given documents and mentions to be linked, ELGR constructs a referent graph from RDF data. Then, the dynamic PageRank-based [12] algorithm is introduced to capture the highest-score candidate entity into the unambiguous set that contributes to the next iteration. Moreover, semantic representation learning is applied in the referent graph initialization and the update of each step. The main contributions of this paper are as follows:

1. We propose a new referent graph construction method which constitutes a basis for the entity disambiguation algorithm based on dynamic PageRank [12]. The number of vertices, the number of edges, and the weights of edges are dynamically changed according to the increasing number of unambiguous entities.
2. We introduce the notion of dynamic PageRank [12] in the referent graph for entity disambiguation that picks out the ambiguous candidate entity which gains the highest-score as the target in each round and gradually completes the selection process for candidate entity disambiguation.

2   Related Work

Candidate entity disambiguation refers to selecting the most suitable entity from the set of candidate entities of the mention. The existing entity disambiguation approaches contain graph-based approaches, probability generation model-based approaches, topic model-based approaches and deep learning-based approaches.

Graph-based models make it easier to model the document-level topical coherence of candidate entities. They consider the association consistency between candidate entities, but the strategies adopted by each one are different. AGDISTIS [13] uses a breadth-first search algorithm to obtain a set of related entities and uses these sets of associated entities to construct an association graph. The PBoH [14] is based on statistical approaches to obtain the probability that an entity pair co-occurs in the same text. The AGDISTIS only considers the literal name similarity but does not fully consider the context of the mentions and the candidate entity. The PBoH only considers the direct relationship between two entities, ignoring the indirect relationship between entities. Our method uses random walks to obtain the linkable entities of a particular entity and their relationships from the map constructed by the knowledge base. The sequences of linkable entities and relationships are used to represent the specific entity. Then the embedding approach is used to obtain the semantic representation of these entities, and the cosine similarity is used to measure the consistency of the two candidate entities. Compared with the former two, ELGR is better in capturing the semantic relationship between entities.

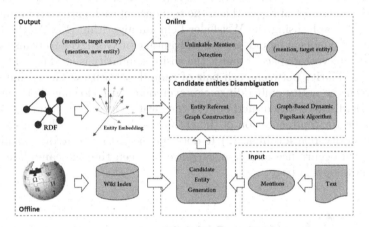

Fig. 1. Entity link algorithm framework based on graph model and semantic representation

3 Our Approach

We propose an entity linking algorithm based on graph model and semantic representation. As shown in Fig. 1, our model contains the following three main parts: (1) offline processing, (2) candidate entities generation, (3) candidate entity disambiguation, which can be divided into referent graph construction and update, graph-based disambiguation, and unlinkable mention detection.

3.1 Offline Preprocessing

In order to reduce the consumption of memory and time, we first employ the offline preprocessing to pre-store the required information. The preprocessing includes two steps: the first is to create an inverted index of all entities in the knowledge base, and the second is to represent each entity in vector space. The process is shown on the left side of Fig. 1.

Entity Index Construction. In the beginning, this module needs to build an inverted index for all entities. The index file could be divided into two parts: the document domain and the index domain. The former one is stored in the document object. The latter index domain is mainly used for searching. With the inverted index constructed, all terms could be retrieved efficiently.

Semantic Representation Learning. The method of semantic similarity calculation between candidate entities is shown in Fig. 2. We first obtain the referent entities, which are closely related to the candidate entities in the RDF graph. Then, the referent graph $G = (V, E)$ is constructed, where V is the set of vertices and E is the set of edges. Then the sequence of each entity is obtained from the referent graph, using the Weisfeiler-Lehman algorithm [15]. As the training procedure of language model, we take advantage of Word2vec to translate these sequences into vector space. Finally, the cosine similarity is used to calculate the semantic similarity between each pair of candidate entities. The cosine similarity between the entity embeddings can overcome the following shortcomings of the Google distance-based method: (1) the entity source is not limited, and the semantic vector representation of the entity can be trained as long as there are sufficient entity relationships. (2) It does not need to repeatedly calculate the frequency of occurrence and co-occurrence between the two candidate entities on the encyclopedia page.

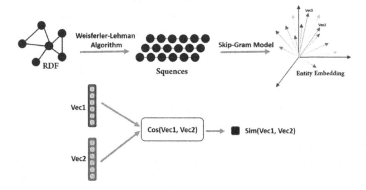

Fig. 2. Entity link algorithm framework based on graph model and semantic representation

3.2   Candidate Entity Generation

Candidate entity generation is to obtain a set of candidate entities of each ambiguous mention. Each mention in the set $M = m_1, m_2, ..., m_n$ is referred as a surface name extension. The search is performed om the index constructed by the local knowledge base, then, the index items whose names are completely matched or partially matched in the knowledge base are returned. The entities corresponding to the index items are returned as the candidate entity set $N_i = n_{i1}, n_{i2}, ..., n_{in}$, where n_{ik} represents the kth candidate entity object corresponding to the query string m_i. Finally, the set of candidate entity $N' = N_1, N_2, ..., N_n$ of the entity mention set M is obtained.

The surface name of the entity is extended and the entity refers to the mention set M after the expansion: (1) Add the original mention's surface name to the mention set. (2) From the mention in the document in which the entity is referred to, the longest new entity that returns the substring for the entity's alleged name is added to the mention set. (3) If the entity refers to the abbreviated dictionary which has been prepared, the complete mention corresponding to the abbreviation is added to the mention set. (4) If the entity is referred to as a symbolic noun, the named entity that is closest to the symbolic noun in the original document is added.

3.3   Candidate Entity Disambiguation

Entity disambiguation is the key point of entity linking. The module needs to calculate the semantic similarity between candidate entities so that the weight of each edge in the referent graph can be obtained, and then the score of each vertex is obtained by the PageRank algorithm. In each round we select the highest-score candidate entity as the best target entity for the corresponding entity. After each round, the referent graph is updated. The specific operation is to retain the best candidate entity in the graph and delete other candidate entities. At the same time, we update the new referent graph vertex and edge weight information, and then use the PageRank algorithm to compute the score of each vertex iteratively.

Entity Referent Graph Construction. The primary function of the entity referent graph construction is to construct a referent graph of all mentions and corresponding candidate entities in the text. The referent graph is served as a basis of dynamic PageRank [12] disambiguation algorithm. The underlying assumption is that there is usually a semantic correlation between entities in the same text, and the correlation is reflected in the calculation of the edge weights. Generally, referent graph construction uses Google distance as a semantic correlation measure between entities, and thus establishes the relationship between vertices. The construction of the referent graph is a core issue because the quality of the graph has a critical impact on the performance of the entity linking. The construction includes three levels of the vertex set construction as follow:

1. Vertex set construction: The referent graph used in this paper is a directed graph. The vertices are the set of related candidate entities of the mentions identified from the text, and then, the preliminary set of candidate entities N' is obtained.
2. Edge set construction: In order to involve semantic information as much as possible, a directed edge is established between each non-identical entity pair. The weight of the edge represents the conversion probability between each pair of entities, which is recorded as entity transform probability (ETP). ETP

could be measured by the semantic similarity between each pair of entities. The specific formula is as follows:

$$SM(e_a^i, e_b^j) = cos(v(e_a^i), v(e_b^j))$$

$$ETP(e_a^i, e_b^j) = \frac{SM(e_a^i, e_b^j)}{\Sigma_{k \in (V \backslash V_i)} SM(e_a^i, k)}$$

where $v(e)$ means the vector of entity e, and k means the referent graph is a K-Partite graph.

3. Additional auxiliary edge construction required by the dynamic PageRank [12] algorithm: In order to support the following dynamic PageRank [12] algorithm, we continue to add auxiliary edges, which represent the probability of randomly moving from any vertex to all other vertices except the vertex. We set the probability to δ. According to the related work in the past, the typical δ value will be set into the interval $[0.1, 0.2]$.

Algorithm 1. Dynamic PageRank Disambiguation Algorithm Based on Graph

---

Input: entity referennt graph $G = (V, E)$, number of iterations$k$.
Output: target entity set $T = \{T_1, T_2, ..., T_3\}$, each entity refers to the corresponding target entity.

1 $G = (V, E)$, $V = S \cup U$; S are ambiguous vertexes and U are unambiguous vertexes Initial checkset $P \leftarrow S$; **while** $True$ **do**
2 | **if** $|V|$ *equals* $|P|$ **then**
3 | | break;
4 | **else**
5 | | $PageRank(G(V, E), k)$;
6 | | $RankCandidatesAccordingToPRScore(V)$;
7 | | $SelecthighestPRscorePR(v) = h, v \in V and v \notin P$;
8 | | $store(T_i \leftarrow v)$;
9 | | $updateGraph(G, v)$;
10 **return** T;

Graph-Based Disambiguation. The basic idea of graph-based disambiguation is to sort the scores of the vertices after each round of PageRank algorithm. The score represents the importance of the candidate entity. We select the undiscriminating candidate entities with the highest scores per round as the best candidate entity. Progressively, it completes the disambiguation of multiple candidate entities for the unlinked mentions. Only the best candidate entities of the unlinked mentions are retained in the figure, and other candidate entity vertices that have been eliminated are deleted. With the count of unambiguous candidate entities grows, these disambiguated candidate entities contribute to the vertex score of the next round of PageRank algorithms.

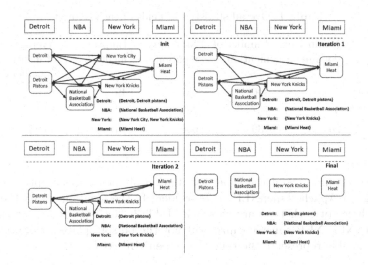

Fig. 3. Example of the overall process of entity disambiguation

Example 1. *Figure 3 shows the whole procedure of a disambiguation example. In the first step, based on the constructed entity referent graph, the first round of the PageRank algorithm is performed. Then the highest-score candidate "New York Knicks" will be picked as the disambiguated entity of this round. It means that the mention "New York" will be linked to the entity "New York Knicks". After that, as shown in "Iteration 1", the referent graph is updated and the entity node "New York City" will be removed along with relevant edges. This procedure will be executed iteratively unless all mentions are disambiguated.*

4   Experiment

We performed experiments on the ACE2004[1], AQUAINT[2] and MSNBC[3], and we compare our model with the AGDISTIS [13] and PBoH [14] algorithms. The primary experimental results show that the performance of this method is better than the existing entity linking methods, and it maintains a stable and acceptable accuracy on different datasets.

4.1   Dataset

The knowledge base used here is English Wikipedia (March 2017 version). To evaluate the performance of the proposed method, we validate our model on three benchmarks. The overall statistics of each dataset is shown in Table 1.

---

[1] https://catalog.ldc.upenn.edu/LDC2005T09.
[2] https://catalog.ldc.upenn.edu/ldc2002t31.
[3] http://kdd.ics.uci.edu/databases/msnbc/msnbc.html.

Table 1. Overall statistics of fields of each dataset

Data set	Number of documents	Number of mention	No empty mention	Empty mention	Average number of mentions per document
ACE2004	36	306	257	49	8.5
AQUAINT	50	727	727	0	14.54
MSNBC	20	739	656	83	36.95

To better understand the type distribution of each dataset entity, we take advantage of Apache OpenNLP NER to identify the mentions of each dataset. The statistics of each type are shown in Table 2. "Others" represent the type that OpenNLP NER can recognize, but not the person, place, or organization, and unavailable represents the type that OpenNLP NER cannot recognize.

Table 2. Overall statistics of types of each data set

Data set	Person	Location	Organization	Others	Unavailable
ACE2004	43	116	71	-	76
AQUAINT	61	134	96	4	432
MSNBC	213	186	144	1	195

4.2   Result and Discussion

The experimental results are analyzed from two perspectives: overall accuracy and linkable entity disambiguation performance based on standard accuracy rate, recall rate, and F1-Score.

Analysis of Overall Accuracy. This paper compares the accuracy of different methods on the whole dataset on the ACE2004, AQUAINT and MSNBC datasets. Then we use the metric to measure the experimental results of different entity linking methods, which has a certain reference value. The other evaluation criteria (precision, recall, and f1-score) are not considered here. The experimental results of each method on the data set ACE2004, AQUAINT, and MSNBC are shown in Table 3, where T is the total number of mentions, R is the total number of correct matched mentions, and A is the overall data accuracy.

As shown in Table 3, our method has achieved the highest accuracy on all three data sets, and the accuracy maintains at more than 80%. Moreover, its performance is relatively stable. Compared with the AGDISTIS and PBoH, the accuracy of our method is nearly 20.6% and 7.5% higher on the ACE2004 dataset, almost 31.9% and 1.2% higher on the AQUANT dataset, and nearly 10.3% and 1.3% higher on the MSNBC dataset. It is significantly better than AGDISTIS on the three data sets. The AGDISTIS only considers the similarity of literal

Table 3. Overall accuracy statistics for each method

	ACE2004			AQUAINT			MSNBC		
Methods	R	T	A	R	T	A	R	T	A
AGDISTIS	198	306	0.647	379	727	0.517	542	739	0.733
PBoH	238	306	0.778	598	727	0.824	608	739	0.823
Our method	**261**	**306**	**0.853**	**608**	727	**0.836**	**618**	739	**0.836**

names and does not adequately consider the context of mentions and candidate entities, which is one of the essential reasons that the experimental results are not so good.

Analysis of Linkable Entity Disambiguation. We further analyze the accuracy, recall, and F1 of linkable entities in the knowledge base. Because the core goal of the entity linking task is to disambiguate and match entities within the knowledge base, the F1 is the most important indicator for measuring the performance of the entity linking algorithm. The statistics of the experimental results are shown in Table 4.

Table 4. The results of each approach on the linkable entity

	ACE2004			AQUAINT			MSNBC		
Method	P	R	F	P	R	F	P	R	F
AGDISTIS	0.668	0.644	0.656	0.725	0.517	0.604	0.761	0.720	0.740
PBoH	0.788	**0.881**	0.832	**0.859**	0.824	0.841	0.826	**0.899**	**0.861**
Our method	**0.879**	0.856	**0.867**	0.836	**0.848**	**0.842**	**0.846**	0.832	0.839

Our method has the highest F1 on both the ACE2004 and the AQUAINT, which is 3.5% and 0.1% higher than the PBoH respectively. However, it is 2.2% lower than PBoH on the MSNBC. Combining the results of three data sets, the performance of this method is approximately the same as that of PBoH in the aspect of linkable entity disambiguation. Compared with AGDISTIS and PBoH, the F1 of the proposed method is respectively 21.1% and 3.5% higher on ACE2004, and 23.8% and 0.1% higher on AQUAINT. It is found that PBoH only considers the direct relationship between two entities, and ignores the indirect relationship between entities, while the direct relationship between entities is far less than the indirect relationship. Therefore, there is room for improvement in how to use candidate entity consistency to disambiguate, which is one of the reasons why the performance of PBoH is worse than ours in the former two datasets.

5   Conclusion and Future Work

In this paper, we proposed a graph-based model combining semantic representation learning for entity linking. Explicitly, a new referent graph construction method was proposed, in which the referent graph contains all mentions and candidate entities in the same document. In our model, the structure of the referent graph can be dynamically changed according to the increasing number of unambiguous entities. We also introduced the notion of dynamic PageRank, considering the semantic similarity between each pair of candidate entities. The algorithm picked out the ambiguous candidate entity which gained the highest-score as the target in each round, and gradually completed the selection process for candidate entity disambiguation. We performed experiments on three benchmarks, and the experimental results demonstrate that the performance of our method is better than the existing methods generally, and it maintains a stable and acceptable link accuracy on different benchmarks.

For the future work, we will construct a hybrid referent graph to incorporate multi-type resources, in which a novel network representation approach will be introduced to capture the semantic information for entity linking. Moreover, we will integrate the entity linking system to high-level applications like machine reading comprehension in natural language understanding.

References

1. Shen, W., Wang, J., Han, J.: Entity linking with a knowledge base: issues, techniques, and solutions. IEEE Trans. Knowl. Data Eng. **30**, 443–460 (2015)
2. Gattani, A.: Entity extraction, linking, classification, and tagging for social media: a wikipedia-based approach. In: Proceedings PVLDB (2013)
3. Welty, C., Murdock, J.W., Kalyanpur, A., Fan, J.: A comparison of hard filters and soft evidence for answer typing in Watson. In: Cudré-Mauroux, P., et al. (eds.) ISWC 2012. LNCS, vol. 7650, pp. 243–256. Springer, Heidelberg (2012). https://doi.org/10.1007/978-3-642-35173-0_16
4. Lin, T., Mausam, Etzioni, O.: Entity linking at web scale. In: Proceedings of NAACL, pp. 84–88 (2012)
5. Nakashole, N., Weikum, G., Suchanek, F.M.: PATTY: a taxonomy of relational patterns with semantic types. In: Proceedings of EMNLP, pp. 1135–1145 (2012)
6. Cheng, T., Yan, X., Chen-Chuan Chang, K.: EntityRank: searching entities directly and holistically. In: Proceedings of VLDB, pp. 387–398 (2007)
7. Bordino, I., Mejova, Y., Lalmas, M.: Penguins in sweaters, or serendipitous entity search on user-generated content. In: Proceedings of CIKM, pp. 109–118 (2013)
8. Han, X., Sun, L., Zhao, J.: Collective entity linking in web text: a graph-based method. In: Proceedings of SIGIR, pp. 765–774 (2011)
9. Zhang, J., Li, J.: Graph-based jointly modeling entity detection and linking in domain-specific area. In: Chen, H., Ji, H., Sun, L., Wang, H., Qian, T., Ruan, T. (eds.) CCKS 2016. CCIS, vol. 650, pp. 146–159. Springer, Singapore (2016). https://doi.org/10.1007/978-981-10-3168-7_15
10. Gentile, A.L., Zhang, Z., Xia, L., Iria, J.: Graph-based semantic relatedness for named entity disambiguation (2009)

11. Alhelbawy, A., Gaizauskas, R.J.: Graph ranking for collective named entity disambiguation. In: Proceedings of ACL, pp. 75–80 (2014)
12. Zhang, H., Lofgren, P., Goel, A.: Approximate personalized pagerank on dynamic graphs. In: Proceedings of the 22nd ACM SIGKDD International Conference on Knowledge Discovery and Data Mining, San Francisco, CA, USA, 13–17 August 2016, pp. 1315–1324 (2016)
13. Usbeck, R., et al.: AGDISTIS - graph-based disambiguation of named entities using linked data. In: Mika, P., et al. (eds.) ISWC 2014. LNCS, vol. 8796, pp. 457–471. Springer, Cham (2014). https://doi.org/10.1007/978-3-319-11964-9_29
14. Ganea, O.-E., Ganea, M., Lucchi, A., Eickhoff, C., Hofmann, T.: Probabilistic bag-of-hyperlinks model for entity linking. In: Proceedings of WWW, pp. 927–938 (2016)
15. Ristoski, P., Paulheim, H.: RDF2Vec: RDF graph embeddings for data mining. In: Groth, P., et al. (eds.) ISWC 2016. LNCS, vol. 9981, pp. 498–514. Springer, Cham (2016). https://doi.org/10.1007/978-3-319-46523-4_30

The Model-Driven Enterprise Data Fabric: A Proposal Based on Conceptual Modelling and Knowledge Graphs

Ana-Maria Ghiran[ID] and Robert Andrei Buchmann[(✉)][ID]

Business Informatics Research Center,
Babeş-Bolyai University, Cluj-Napoca, Romania
{anamaria.ghiran,robert.buchmann}@econ.ubbcluj.ro

Abstract. Enterprise data is typically located in disparate legacy systems and heterogeneous sources. Researchers and business analysts identified the importance of integrating such data sources through a semantic data fabric to support the generation of valuable insights and consolidated views. Still, this objective is hard to attain as information is dispersed in ever-growing enterprise data lakes and silos. Some solutions are very abstract, taking the form of pre-scriptive enterprise frameworks, and therefore they do not provide operational mappings between data from real systems. In other cases the integration requires technical expertise that may be format-specific and, because of this, it is hard to cover heterogeneous technologies. It would be useful if those working on the enterprise architecture level could express on a high abstraction level the involved data sources and interlinking rules. This paper proposes a solution that enables integration management in a diagrammatic view that does not require expertise with data transformations. In support of this idea, we engineer a modelling method that provides (i) a front-end interface to enable the combination of relevant data with the help of an agile modelling language and (ii) the use of RDF as a common representation that captures the output of the modelled integrations in an Enterprise Knowledge Graph.

Keywords: Data integration · Enterprise Knowledge Graphs · Conceptual modelling · Model-driven data fabric · Resource description framework

1 Introduction

The notion of "data fabric" is bridging the traditional gap between data and knowledge, by resorting to knowledge-based integration techniques (i.e., employing rules and data linking facts) in order to bring together, in an operational way, heterogeneous data that spans across a multitude of sources or formats. The knowledge expressed in a data fabric is an asset that should be managed through Knowledge Management practices – in our work we resort for this purpose to Nonaka's seminal SECI model ("Socialisation-Externalisation-Combination-Internalisation") [1].

Current digitalisation trends and enterprise architectures impose a shift in how organisations apply the SECI knowledge conversion cycle. Knowledge is not anymore

© Springer Nature Switzerland AG 2019
C. Douligeris et al. (Eds.): KSEM 2019, LNAI 11775, pp. 572–583, 2019.
https://doi.org/10.1007/978-3-030-29551-6_51

an asset to be managed or consumed only by humans – knowledge-driven systems and engineering processes need to have on-the-fly access to some machine-readable representations of knowledge [2]. Some approaches [3, 4] have (re)considered Nonaka's vision to take advantage of digitalisation and proposed novel reinterpretations of the knowledge conversion stages. In these approaches, the development of Enterprise Knowledge Graphs is enabled by specific technological support for the externalisation, combination and internalisation stages, reinterpreted as follows:

Externalisation is the articulation of knowledge such that it can be shared within organisation or further transmitted. Our approach is to replace the traditional forms of representation (i.e., natural language as the main form of expression, in poorly structured documents or mixed content reports) with customized conceptual modelling (i.e., diagrammatic models conforming a custom modelling language that governs the data fabric).

Combination is the process by which fragments of knowledge are assembled in order to enable new insights. In traditional approaches, this activity is rather an art but in our reinterpreted version it takes advantage of the opportunities provided by semantic technology, as diagrammatic models dictate how knowledge graphs are built.

Internalisation is the phase when knowledge is successfully assimilated and operationalised. Since knowledge is not anymore limited to human consumption, a reconsideration for this stage was advanced by [4] - where a representation in both diagrammatic and machine-readable form of a service enables successful knowledge transfer between stakeholders (humans) as well as between information systems.

We advocate the idea that a data fabric is fundamentally a knowledge building effort that must consider these knowledge conversion stages. In this paper we show how this can be done according to the reinterpreted SECI cycle. Specifically we propose an artefact that comprises: (i) a domain-specific modelling language for mapping data entities/sources through diagrammatically defined rules; (ii) a modelling procedure for building those mappings; (iii) mechanisms to automatically generate knowledge graph fragments from legacy data lifted according to the mapping rules.

The remainder of the paper is structured as follows: Sect. 2 introduces background concepts and formulates problem statement. Section 3 describes the approach and elaborates on its ingredients. Section 4 discusses a showcase example. Section 5 comments on related works. The paper ends with a discussion on the current limitations of the proposal and final conclusions.

2   Problem Statement

The identified problem is that enterprise IT architects that can best describe an encompassing enterprise perspective are not aware of the technical details about how to gather the required data, and for this they solicit other experts - a slow process to achieve a design solution for each identified data source. On the other hand, software engineers are aware of the means for dealing with data integration but they are missing the comprehension of the overall architecture that the data fabric must cover.

Data is generated by all constituents of an enterprise, therefore it is inherently distributed and heterogeneous in both content and format. There are two approaches to achieve enterprise data integration:

- The *top-down approach* – starting from an integrated view of the enterprise, software engineers are looking for solutions to implement an infrastructure that would enable a seamless integration of all facets of an enterprise. This is currently achieved by designing an enterprise architecture (that presents the structure and the operation of an organisation in order to determine how it can achieve its objectives [5]) using a modelling language (like Archimate [6]) to create enterprise models against which analysis can be performed. However there is no operational bridging between such models and the data sources involved at run-time;
- The *bottom-up approach* – starting from various legacy data and heterogeneous formats, engineers are looking for solutions to integrate them. This can be achieved in several ways: (i) by adopting a Service-oriented Architecture (SOA) style [7] for all applications; (ii) by lifting all data in distributed Enterprise Knowledge Graph [8]; (iii) a combination of services and graphs – i.e., data is published on the Web in RDF format [10] and is linked to legacy data sources through the use of URIs, generating a global data space [9].

Data integration is subsumed to the goal of deriving knowledge and according to Nonaka's cycle, the *Externalisation* phase should precede the *Combination* phase. In this respect a top-down approach is preferable – our proposal is to have the enterprise modelling language employed not only for understanding and analysis purposes, but for operational bottom-up integration of data sources, by generating integrative knowledge graphs based on configurations performed with conceptual modelling means. Consequently our proposition is *a model-driven approach to developing a data fabric*, one that hybridises the top-down and bottom-up approaches mentioned here.

3   Solution Overview and Technical Enablers

An overview of the proposed approach is given in Fig. 1. We employ a modelling tool to describe in diagrammatic representations the data sources that we would like to integrate, currently with some limited possibilities of fetching some of their schema (e.g., for CSV as will be discussed in a showcase example). The selected source files/descriptions need to be parsed to identify the types of the entities or attributes that are present there. In the second step the modeller will define linking rules (associations) between entities or between entities and attributes - there are several possible cases: (i) associations between concepts in the same data source; (ii) associations with newly created instances; (iii) associations between concepts across multiple data sources; (iv) associations with concepts from existing terminologies. Based on these linking rules and on transformation algorithms that are specific to each considered format, instance data is gathered into a Knowledge Graph that can be queried as per the needs of the integration case.

The following sections will elaborate on the ingredients that support us in addressing these requirements.

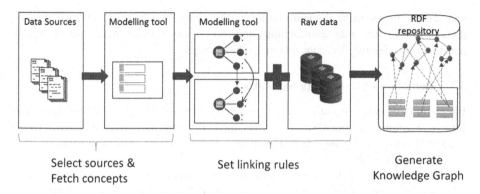

| Data Sources | Modelling tool | Modelling tool | Raw data | RDF repository |

Select sources &
Fetch concepts

Set linking rules

Generate
Knowledge Graph

Fig. 1. Overview of the approach

3.1 Conceptual Modelling of the Data Integration

We engineer a domain-specific modelling language that is tailored according to recent metamodelling practices (see a collection of such languages in [11]) with the help of Agile Modelling Method Engineering (AMME) – a methodology that enables the design and quick prototyping of agile modelling tools. The methodology was discussed in detail in [12, 13]; diagrams created with such tools are fundamentally graph-based.

A model simplifies complex reality by capturing its essence and filtering the noise [14]. Domain-specific models allow the description of a system through concepts that are relevant for an application domain. Humans may perceive diagrammatic representations easier than text, depending on the decoding effort – a well-designed modelling language should be more effective than sequences of characters [15].

Conceptual modelling in a business context has been mainly concerned with describing the activities that are supposed to be streamlined as processes (BPMN, EPC, Petri Nets etc.) [16]. Business processes are entitled to be primarily considered, but domain-specific modelling and enterprise modelling also advocate other tangible or intangible assets to be captured in diagrammatic models [17]. In our case, these are (i) data sources that are already in a structured format (such as database data, server logs, customer service logs in formats like CSV, XML and so on); (ii) the concepts extracted from those data sources schemata; (iii) concepts pertaining to the business domain either picked from an existing terminology/taxonomy or specifically created by the organisation.

3.2 Semantic Technology

Our proposal advocates an adherence to a common representation format - for this purpose we adopt RDF [10], the framework that allows us to structure both traditional data points and knowledge structures in knowledge graphs. Resources or entities take form of nodes in the graph and relations are edges. When using a reference to the same entity in multiple RDF statements, by having each of the entities uniquely identified through the URI schema, a directed graph is obtained and nodes of this graph can point to any addressable or non-addressable resource. Managing data in RDF is more flexible and can be supported by domain ontologies that bring dual benefits: (i) can represent domain knowledge in an unambiguous and formal way; (ii) can make use of logical reasoning to infer implied concepts and relationships.

3.3 Definition of Data Mapping Rules

Integration of arbitrary data sources involves either (i) a transformation from one format to another format (favoured when there is a small number of formats to be supported); or (ii) a semantic layer that allows uniform access to all data sources – this is where the data fabric approach belongs.

The second approach exposes a unified query interface to access data and is more adequate from the scalability point of view as it enables adding new data sources with little change in the architecture. Knowledge Graphs are more than a mediating layer; they make use of an ontology as a data vocabulary and they also contain instance data. Ontology-based data integration [18] is needed especially when data sources do not use the same interpretation of the information and some reconciliation is required.

Legacy data can be lifted into Knowledge Graphs by using *mapping solutions*. A simple and straightforward way to lift data from relational databases to RDF is to use Direct Mapping [19], that maps the data directly without any possibility to customize the RDF (without user interaction). Direct Mapping provides a basis for defining transformations, but it is not enough for custom-made associations - it cannot reuse the vocabulary of any existing ontology (all identifiers are generated based on the data and database schema). To create more expressive and controlled mappings, W3C recommends R2RML [20], as a mapping language that allows the user to specify relationships between relational databases and RDF triples. It creates a view over the RDF data and all applications that need to query the data will address the queries on the RDF view. R2RML can be used however only for data coming from relational databases. The RDF Mapping Language (RML) [21] was proposed to extend the R2RML applicability by supporting a broader range of inputs including CSV, XML, JSON etc.

Using mapping languages separates their definition from the implementation, according to [22]. We don't need only to access data in a uniform way (in the sense achieved by the mapping languages) but we actually want to have it replicated in a Knowledge Graph, which can make use of inferential capabilities and support knowledge creation. The next chapter will showcase our key contribution - the domain-specific modelling method that brings together these ingredients.

4   Showcase Example

The hereby proposed domain-specific modelling method considers the steps that must be performed in order to enable integration of various enterprise data in a Knowledge Graph. In order to implement the modelling method we followed the AMME methodology and we employed the ADOxx metamodeling platform [23] that also offers scripting support for model content manipulation (e.g., model transformation as required by our proposal), for implementing algorithms (e.g. the conversion of raw data based on the association rules defined by the modeller) or for external coupling (e.g., reading/writing from files, accessing data from Web services).

In the following the modelling method will be presented in a step-wise manner, according to its usage procedure.

4.1   Select Data Sources

In the first step, the modeller will choose at a high level the data sources. Figure 2 shows the selection of a single file, employees.csv (on the right side of the figure, we can also see the contents of the file) that becomes a container on the modelling canvas. ADOxx provides the possibility to read content from files in formats like CSV, TXT, XLS or even from database files through the AdoScript language. In cases when file formats are specific to certain applications we can make use of the external execution environment that can be called from ADOxx.

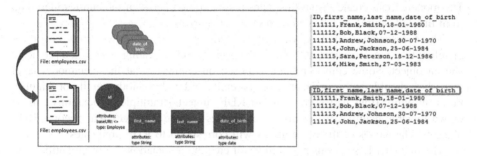

Fig. 2. Selecting a CSV data source

Information found in the CSV header can be used to generate model elements corresponding to each field. Initially these are considered generic RDF terms - represented by rectangles with rounded corners to suggest that they are placeholders for more refined concepts according to the RDF semantics (each distinguished by visual notation). The modeller must set for each one their role – i.e., if they represent an "entity" or a "feature" (a property in the entity schema) - these are high level concepts of the modelling language that can be mapped on RDF constructs. Correspondingly, the visual shapes are dynamically changing to visually reflect the nature of these: entities are depicted with circles and features with rectangles. This visualisation technique is consistent with those used for representing ontologies [24].

An entity will refer to the individuals found in a data source (e.g., the Ids that can identify a row in a table). A name for entity elements will be suggested by the modelling tool based on the identifying field name pulled from the data source (e.g., "ID"). Aligning to RDF principles [25], the modeller will specify a base URI that will be added to prefix the ID values retrieved from the data source in order to obtain individual URIs. A better approach for this is to have all instance URIs generated by a URI pattern. This will be covered in the future developments.

An "entity" has a type (the class to which the referred instances belong): this can be derived from the data source from where the entity is extracted (like Employee, as depicted in the figure) or it could be overridden by a type from a controlled vocabulary (like foaf:Person from FOAF [26]).

A "feature" corresponds to a column name and will refer to all the values taken from that column. As columns in relational databases can have a datatype, likewise features can also get a datatype which will translate to an XSD datatype (e.g. a string datatype was attached to the first_name feature). Furthermore, string datatypes can get language codes as annotations.

The modeller can choose (i) to employ only a subset of the features (ii) to combine them with others from other data sources (iii) to combine them with some newly created entities or instances created directly on the modelling canvas.

4.2   Set Linking Rules

The modeller can create visual link rules (associations) between the entities identified from the data source or between entities and features.

These associations will govern the generation of RDF triples from raw data, therefore they are consistent with the RDF specification indicating a subject, a predicate and an object. Some constraints are imposed on connectors at the metamodel level (e.g., they should always originate from an entity and end in another entity or feature). From an entity (that will correspond to RDF subjects) multiple associations can be drawn towards features or towards other entities (whose instances will become RDF objects). The names of the associations will correspond to RDF predicates.

The modeller has various possibilities of creating associations between entities and features. First, they can set relationships between concepts that were discovered from the same data source. This is the case illustrated in Fig. 3a. Three associations were created: has_first_name, has_last_name, has_date_of_birth. The semantics of these associations is as follows: for all values extracted from the Id column the property has_first_name will link the values from column first_name.

Another possibility is to create associations between concepts that were derived from different data sources, each data source being visualised as a container of its entities and features – see case b in Fig. 3: another data source called preferences.csv was selected: it contains values that represent Ids and titles of some books and the Id of the employee that borrowed that book. The new association prefers_book links all the individuals (for which we had previously modelled the construction of RDF statements) to some books for those records that show a match between the employee Id and the foreign empl_id. Connectors in ADOxx can also have attributes, and will be used when we need to specify the condition that will constrain the instance-level data joins.

We can observe that empl_id is not connected – which means that it will not contribute with data values to the generated Knowledge Graph, it is only attached to the data source because of its use in the joining condition.

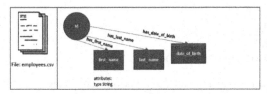

The modelled associations are:
∀Id :has_first_name ∀first_name.
∀Id :has_last_name ∀last_name.
∀Id :has_date_of_birth ∀date_of_birth.

a) associations between concepts from the same data source

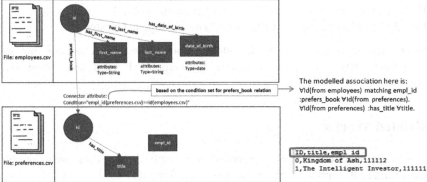

The modelled association here is:
∀Id(from employees) matching empl_id
:prefers_book ∀Id(from preferences).
∀Id(from preferences) :has_title ∀title.

b) associations between concepts from multiple data sources

Fig. 3. Setting association rules

The modeller can also link concepts from the data sources to some newly created entities, features or even instances created directly in the modelling tool. An example of a new entity can be an Organisation "entity" that is not present in any data source, but has some instance Ids typed directly in a list attribute of the modelling element representing it. Or, a specific organisation "instance" can be linked to an "entity" (i.e., in the generated data it will be linked to all its instances).

4.3 Generate the RDF Triples

Our goal is to obtain RDF statements that are readily available for uploading in the Knowledge Graph repository. As we employed ADOxx meta-modelling platform, the underlying mechanisms for understanding the modelled associations and to apply them to raw data must be defined using the AdoScript language [27], which allow us to tailor functionalities to be embedded in the custom-made modelling tool. The scripts are fairly simple as they will read diagrammatic contents, distinguish the types of elements present on the modelling canvas and will generate corresponding serialisation patterns. The script's output is the RDF serialisation that will be saved into an external file, which can be later imported in an RDF repository like RDF4J [28] or GraphDB [29].

For the first modelled associations shown in Fig. 3(a), the following triples in Turtle [30] format are generated based on the underlying graph structure of the diagrams, as exposed by the metamodelling platform on which the tool is implemented:

:E111111 rdfs:type :Employee.
:E111111 :has_first_name "Frank".
:E111111 :has_last_name "Smith".
:E111111 :has_date_of_birth "18-01-1980"^^xsd:Date.

Similarly, the association between concepts between various data sources will generate the following triples:

:E111112 :prefers_book :0. :0 :has_title "Kingdom of Ash".
:E111111 :prefers_book :1. :1 :has_title "The Intelligent Investor".

Future developments will consider adding more complex mechanisms that will allow defining RDF constructs currently not supported, such integration with ontologies.

5   Related Works

Most of the architectures that were proposed in the early days of database integration used a centralised approach which extracts, transform and loads (ETL) data from heterogeneous sources into a Data Warehouse [31].

For relational data there are two approaches that define how to access content from databases in RDF: one that stores a conversion of the database as RDF in a triple store and one that creates an RDF view over the relational data which can be accessed in the same way as any RDF data. The first approach is usually implemented in cases when the database would not be used anymore to record updated information and we need the legacy data from it.

OpenRefine [32] is a tool offered by Google as an open source project that can assist in transforming and mapping data from one format into another format. It is very useful in cleaning data, removing inconsistencies and transforming values based on some expressions written in General Refine Expression Language (GREL) or Jython [33]. The tool can be customized for a specific usage, i.e. by defining extensions, An example for this could be to export data into a specific format as it is the case with Grefine [34] which enables exporting data as RDF-XML; other serialization formats for RDF like Turtle would be very useful but currently we could not find any such implementations. OpenRefine can also be used for integration with other technologies, e.g. OntoRefine from Ontotext [30]. The tool is integrated in the GraphDB, which is an RDF triplestore, and it can be used for converting data in a similar way and afterwards importing it into a repository.

Regarding the second approach (having an RDF view), tools such as D2RQ [35], R2RML [20] provided mapping languages to allow a user to specify the relation between two data models: the ER data model and the RDF data model. These approaches iterate tables to create RDF views of them. D2RQ later evolved towards R2RML which became a W3C recommendation. Furthermore, R2RML is the basis for a new project, RML [21], which intends to broaden the recommendation and be accepted as a generic mapping language.

Each approach had its own drawbacks: the first did not support large files (as the size of the graph is proportional to the number of vertices and edges and determines the efficiency of exploring data in such a graph); and was hindered by the tendency of maintaining relational databased because of their mature stage. On the other hand, having just an RDF view would not enable taking full advantage of the potentials offered by the graph-based technologies, i.e. inferring capabilities.

Recent trends in databases [36] show a substantial increase in popularity for the graph databases, proving that industry is shifting from traditional systems to the new storing platforms. Therefore our work is oriented towards the efforts in transforming the data from legacy systems and integrating them as Knowledge Graph data fabrics with the help of a modelling tool which implements a domain-specific modelling method. Within this method we employ the existing adapters used by known mapping languages to execute the associations that are visually modelled.

6   Limitations

A modelling tool presents data in an abstract way and it has narrow capabilities of showing dynamic previews of the generated Knowledge Graph (it is more fit for graph editing than for external data visualisation).

Data value transformations, data curations in the sense achieved by OpenRefine tool are difficult to be built in a modelling tool. Also, a preview of the input data and of the results requires adding elaborated extensions of the modelling method using ADOxx script language.

There are still other rules and principles regarding the RDF constructs that have been not covered yet and need further investigation: using blank nodes, possibility of grouping generated statements in named graphs etc.

7   Conclusions

Current data integration tools are designed for specific situations and formats and most of them focus on syntactic integration, i.e. transformation from one format to another. In cases when semantic integration is considered we can find a number of mapping languages that support lifting heterogeneous data sources in RDF but surprisingly there are much less editors that support users in defining such mappings. Many data integration solutions seem rather as an afterthought and incorporating them in the information systems requires expert knowledge.

This paper proposes a visual editor that makes use of diagrammatic conceptual modelling to enable the user to select the data sources and to define linking rules between the concepts identified in those sources, with concepts from standard vocabularies or with ad-hoc created resources. These associations permit to generate RDF statements in an automated way, without requiring expertise regarding the performed transformations, by establishing a model-driven data fabric that can be further evolved with the help of the AMME methodology. The proposal can be considered as originating in the model-driven code generation paradigm, but instead of generating source code its goal is to produce Knowledge Graphs through conceptual modelling means.

In this way, we repurpose modelling methods for data integration management, an idea that crosses the traditional design-time/run-time boundary and represents a reinterpretation of Nonaka's SECI cycle through the lens of conceptual modelling.

Acknowledgements. This work was supported by a mobility grant of the Romanian Ministry of Research and Innovation, CNCS - UEFISCDI, project number **PN-III-P1-1.1-MC-2019-0465**, within PNCDI III.

References

1. Nonaka, I.: The knowledge-creating company. Harv. Bus. Rev. Press **69**, 96–104 (1991)
2. Buchmann, R.A., Cinpoeru, M., Harkai, A., Karagiannis, D.: Model-aware software engineering-a knowledge-based approach to model-driven software engineering. In: Proceedings of ENASE 2018, SciTe Press, pp. 233–240 (2018)
3. Ghiran, A.M., Osman, C.C., and Buchmann, R.A.: A semantic approach to knowledge-driven geographical information systems. In: Proceedings of ECKM 2017, ACPI, pp. 353–362 (2017)
4. Buchmann, R.A., Ghiran, A.-M.: Serviceology-as-a-service: a knowledge-centric interpretation. Serviceology for Services. LNCS, vol. 10371, pp. 190–201. Springer, Cham (2017). https://doi.org/10.1007/978-3-319-61240-9_18
5. Moser, C., Buchmann, R.A., Utz, W., Karagiannis, D.: CE-SIB: a modelling method plug-in for managing standards in enterprise architectures. In: Mayr, Heinrich C., Guizzardi, G., Ma, H., Pastor, O. (eds.) ER 2017. LNCS, vol. 10650, pp. 21–35. Springer, Cham (2017). https://doi.org/10.1007/978-3-319-69904-2_2
6. The Open Group: Archimate 3.0.1 Specification. https://publications.opengroup.org/c179. Accessed 01 Apr 2019
7. The Open Group: SOA Reference Architecture. https://publications.opengroup.org/standards/soa/c119. Accessed 01 Apr 2019
8. Pan, J.Z., Vetere, G., Gomez-Perez, J.M., Wu, H. (eds.): Exploiting Linked Data and Knowledge Graphs in large organisations. Springer, Heidelberg (2017). https://doi.org/10.1007/978-3-319-45654-6
9. Bizer, C., Heath, T., Berners-Lee, T.: Linked data - the story so far. Int. J. Semant. Web Inform. Syst. **5**(3), 1–22 (2009)
10. W3C: RDF 1.1 concepts and abstract syntax. https://www.w3.org/TR/rdf11-concepts/. Accessed 01 Apr 2019
11. Karagiannis, D., Mayr, H.C., Mylopoulos, J.: Domain-Specific Conceptual Modeling. Springer, Heidelberg (2016). https://doi.org/10.1007/978-3-319-39417-6
12. Karagiannis, D.: Agile modeling method engineering. In: Proceedings of the 19th Panhellenic Conference on Informatics, pp. 5–10. ACM (2015)
13. Karagiannis, D.: Conceptual modelling methods: the AMME agile engineering approach. In: Silaghi, G.C., Buchmann, R.A., Boja, C. (eds.) IE 2016. LNBIP, vol. 273, pp. 3–19. Springer, Cham (2018). https://doi.org/10.1007/978-3-319-73459-0_1
14. Kim, S.-K., Woolridge, R.: Enterprise knowledge modeling: challenges and research issues. J. Knowl. Manage. Pract. **13**(3) (2012). http://www.tlainc.com/articl311.htm. Accessed 01 Apr 2019

15. Moody, D.: The "physics" of notations: toward a scientific basis for constructing visual notations in software engineering. IEEE Trans. Softw. Eng. **35**(6), 756–779 (2009)
16. Dumas, M., La Rosa, M., Mendling, J., Reijers, H.A.: Fundamentals of Business Process Management, vol. 1. Springer, Heidelberg (2013)
17. Karagiannis, D., Buchmann, R.A., Walch, M.: How can diagrammatic conceptual modelling support knowledge management? In: Proceedings of ECIS 2017, pp. 1568–1583. AIS (2017)
18. Wache, H., et al.: Ontology-based integration of information-a survey of existing approaches. In: IJCAI-01 Workshop: Ontologies and Information Sharing, pp. 108–117 (2001)
19. W3C recommendation: A Direct Mapping of Relational Data to RDF. https://www.w3.org/TR/rdb-direct-mapping/. Accessed 01 Apr 2019
20. W3C recommendation: R2RML: RDB to RDF Mapping Language. http://www.w3.org/TR/r2rml/. Accessed 01 Apr 2019
21. Dimou, A., Vander Sande, M., Colpaert, P., Verborgh, R., Mannens, E., Van de Walle, R.: RML: a generic language for integrated RDF mappings of heterogeneous data. In: Proceedings of LDOW (2014)
22. Heyvaert, P., et al.: RMLEditor: a graph-based mapping editor for linked data mappings. In: Sack, H., Blomqvist, E., d'Aquin, M., Ghidini, C., Ponzetto, S.P., Lange, C. (eds.) ESWC 2016. LNCS, vol. 9678, pp. 709–723. Springer, Cham (2016). https://doi.org/10.1007/978-3-319-34129-3_43
23. BOC GmbH: The ADOxx metamodelling platform. http://www.adoxx.org/live. Accessed 01 Apr 2019
24. Lohmann, S., Negru, S., Haag, F., Ertl, T.: Visualizing ontologies with VOWL. Semant. Web **7**(4), 399–419 (2016)
25. Heath, T., Bizer, C.: Linked data: evolving the web into a global data space. Synth. Lect. Semant. Web: Theory Technol. **1**(1), 1–136 (2011)
26. FOAF Vocabulary Specification 0.99. http://xmlns.com/foaf/spec/. Accessed 01 Apr 2019
27. Adoscript Developer Reference. https://www.adoxx.org/live/adoscript-documentation. Accessed 04 Apr 2019
28. RDF4J: Java framework for processing and handling RDF data. http://rdf4j.org/. Accessed 01 Apr 2019
29. Ontotext: GraphDB. http://graphdb.ontotext.com/. Accessed 01 Apr 2019
30. W3C recommendation: RDF 1.1 Turtle Terse RDF Triple Language. https://www.w3.org/TR/turtle/. Accessed 01 Apr 2019
31. Smith, J.M., et al.: Multibase: integrating heterogeneous distributed database systems. In: Proceedings of AFIPS, national computer conference, 4-7 May 1981, pp. 487–499. ACM (1981)
32. Google News Initiative. http://openrefine.org/. Accessed 01 Apr 2019
33. OpenRefine. https://github.com/OpenRefine/OpenRefine/wiki/Documentation-For-Users. Accessed 01 Apr 2019
34. Grefine - RDF – extension. https://github.com/stkenny/grefine-rdf-extension/releases. Accessed 01 Apr 2019
35. Cyganiak, R., Bizer, C., Garbers, J., Maresch, O., Becker, C.: The D2RQ Mapping Language. http://d2rq.org/d2rq-language, Accessed 01 Apr 2019
36. DB-Engines, DBMS popularity ranking by database model – Popularity changes per category. https://db-engines.com/en/ranking_categories. Accessed 01 Apr 2019

Leveraging User Preferences for Community Search via Attribute Subspace

Haijiao Liu[1], Huifang Ma[1,2,3(✉)], Yang Chang[1], Zhixin Li[3],
and Wenjuan Wu[4]

[1] College of Computer Science and Engineering, Northwest Normal University,
Lanzhou 730070, Gansu, China
mahuifang@yeah.net
[2] Guangxi Key Laboratory of Trusted Software,
Guilin University of Electronic Technology, Guilin 541004, China
[3] Guangxi Key Lab of Multi-Source Information Mining and Security,
Guangxi Normal University, Guilin 541004, Guangxi, China
[4] School of Information, Renmin University of China, Beijing 100872, China

Abstract. In this paper, we propose a community search scheme via attribute subspace. This method utilizes not only network structure but also node attributes within a certain subspace to quantify a community from the perspective of both internal consistency and external separability, which is able to capture a user preferred community. Firstly, the attributes similarity and neighborhood information of nodes are combined, and the center node set of the target community can be obtained by extending the sample node given by the user with its neighbors. Secondly, an attribute subspace calculation method with entropy weights is established based on the center node set, and the attribute subspace of the community can thus be deduced. Finally, the community quality, which is the combination of internal connectivity and external separability is defined, based on which the target community with user's preference can be detected. Experimental results on both synthetic network and real-world network datasets demonstrated the efficiency and effectiveness of the proposed algorithm.

Keywords: Community search · User's preference · Attribute subspace · Entropy

1 Introduction

Network is a simple but powerful representation of real-world complex systems as most objects in the world are closely related. Communities serve as basic structures for understanding the organization of many real-world networks, such as social, biological, collaboration, and communication networks [1, 2]. In particular, community search focus on discovering the 'local' links within and connecting to the target community related to user's preference, which refers to a limited number of nodes in the whole network. It can be applied in scientific research, commercial promotion and other fields. For example, a marketing manager selling sports goods requires sets of communities with similar sport appetite, and then offers trial products to a few members from each

© Springer Nature Switzerland AG 2019
C. Douligeris et al. (Eds.): KSEM 2019, LNAI 11775, pp. 584–595, 2019.
https://doi.org/10.1007/978-3-030-29551-6_52

community based on their sport appetite to expect the products to be promoted in the communities. Most of recent community search methods may fail to capture the requirements of a specific application and not be able to detect the set of required communities for a specific application.

The existing conventional community detection methods can be roughly divided into two groups: global and local methods. The global methods emphasize on all the entire network topology, while the local methods focus on local positions [3, 4]. The research on community detection using graphs was started in early 1970s [5] and many algorithms based on global methods were proposed. The main limitation of these approaches is that the number of partitions in the network should be decided in advance to obtain a better result. Moreover, several measures are defined as a global objective for community detection or graph partitioning and are not applicable to individual subgraphs. Different from global methods, most existing local community detection algorithms took a seed as an initial community and they extended the community via running a greedy optimization process for a quality function. Some noticeable work includes: Baumes et al. [6] proposed an algorithm for overlapping community detection based on the iterative scan (IS) and rank removal (RaRe). Lancichinetti et al. [7] introduced Order Statistics Local Optimization Method (OSLOM) algorithm but it resulted in a significant number of singleton communities. For the community search task, the local community detection method is applicable, but it always ignores user's preference and may take a lot of time. Therefore, it is necessary to design community search algorithms for specific applications. There are several pioneer and embryonic works proposed independently and almost simultaneously. For instance, FocusCO [8] is a semi-supervised clustering method whose detection results can be steered by a domain expert. FocusCO allows user to steer the communities by providing a small set of exemplar nodes that are deemed to be similar to one another as well as similar to the type of nodes the communities of his interest should contain. TSCM [9] is a sample information extension method designed to extend the two sample nodes to a set of exemplar nodes from which the target subspace is inferred. Then the set of target communities are located and detected based on the target subspace. However, even if the existing semi-supervised community search techniques consider user's preference, only the attribute information of nodes or only some attributes of nodes are considered in the detecting process. Besides, the recent target community detection based on attribute subspace in networks [10], i.e. TC-AE, is able to detect community related to user's preference. However, TC-AE fails to consider a good neighborhood with either only a few edges at its boundary or many of the cross-edges can be "exonerated".

In this work, we propose a novel approach for community search (neighborhood, cluster) in an attributed graph, namely, Community Search via Attribute Subspace (CS-AS). We provide a formal definition of 'good community', and the way for detection 'good' community with user's preference and attribute subspace, together with a series of experiments on three large and popular real-world networks as well as synthetic network to verify the effectiveness of our method.

2   Attribute Subspace Focus Extraction

In this section, we formulate community search and present a strategy of calculating attribute subspace weights. To be specific, we consider the weight of an attribute in the target community represents the probability of contribution in forming the community. Therefore, an objective function is designed to simultaneously minimize the within community dispersion and maximize the negative weight entropy to stimulate more attributes to contribute to the identification of the community [11]. In this way, we can avoid the problem of identifying target clusters by few dimensions in sparse data.

2.1   Problem Formulation

An attributed network consists of nodes, edges and attribute vectors associated with the nodes. More formally, let $G = (V, E, F)$ denote an attributed graph, where $V = \{v_1, v_2 \ldots, v_n\}$ is the set of n nodes; $E = \{(v_i, v_j)|$ an edge between nodes v_i and $v_j\}$ is the set of edges, satisfying $|E| = m$; $A = \left[a_{ij}\right]_{n \times n}$ is the adjacency matrix of graph G, where $a_{ij} = 1$, if $(v_i, v_j) \in E$ and 0 otherwise; $F: V \rightarrow D_1 \times \cdots \times D_r$ is an attribute function which gives each node an attribute vector $f(v)$, f_{vt} denotes the value of attribute t for node v;. The attribute subspace is represented by a subspace vector $L = [l_1, l_2, \ldots, l_t, \ldots, l_r]^{\mathrm{T}}$, l_t measures the importance weight of the attribute t in the subspace. Since we only consider the relative importance between attributes, the subspace satisfies the normalized condition $\sum_{t=1}^{r} l_t = 1$, $l_t > 0$. In such a network, we wish to locate a community supervised by an exemplar node. More specifically, the user is allowed to provide an exemplar node $z \in V$ in any potential community M whose nodes are similar on some focus attributes of a specific application. $Z \subset V$ represents the seed of the community, where $Z \subseteq M \subset V$. We denote $B \subset V$ be the set of boundary nodes that are outside the target community but have at least one edge to some node in the target community, i.e. $e_{ij} \in E$, $v_i \in M$, $v_j \in B$, $M \cap B = \varnothing$.

In summary, our algorithm is given as follows:

Given: A graph $G = (V, E, F)$ with node attributes, an exemplar node $z \in V$ provided by the user;

Detection: A subspace vector $L = [l_1, l_2, \ldots, l_t, \ldots, l_r]^{\mathrm{T}}$ for exemplar node z;

Define: A measure to quantify the quality of C based on internal connectivity, boundary B, and Attribute Subspace L;

Find: Target Community with User's Preference.

2.2   Central Node Set Extraction

We first identify focused cluster, i.e. good candidate nodes that potentially belong to community. Then, attribute subspace is identified based on the focused cluster. In other words, for the target community, the internal nodes are similar to each other with its attribute subspace and are dissimilar with external nodes. To achieve this goal, we consider both attribute similarity and structural similarity between nodes, and the focused cluster is determined based on the sample nodes given by user.

Since one sample node contains limited information to accurately capture the target subspace, we design an extension method to extend the sample node to a set of connected exemplar nodes which the target subspace can be inferred. Intuitively, nodes in the focused clusters are more similar with their neighbors.

Definition 1 (Attribute similarity): The attributes similarity between nodes u and v is denoted by $s(u, v)$ as:

$$s(u, v) = \exp(-\| f(u) - f(v) \|_2) \tag{1}$$

where $\| f(u) - f(v) \|_2$ is the 2-norm between attributes vector of nodes u and v. Note that the attributes similarity is between 0 and 1.

Definition 2 (Attribute neighborhood Network): Given a node v whose attribute neighbors set is denoted as $NB(v) = \{u | (u, v) \in E \wedge s(u, v) > \beta\} \cup \{v\}$, the attribute neighborhood network of node v is defined as $NN(v) = (NB(v), NE(v))$, where the edge set $NE(v) = \{(u, w) | u \in NB(v) \wedge w \in NB(v) \wedge (u, w) \in E\}$, while β is the similarity threshold. Finally, the central node set is formed as $Z = NB(v) = \{z_1, z_2, \ldots, z_c\}$.

2.3 Attribute Subspace with Entropy Weighting

Intuitively, nodes from the same community should be similar to each other on the particular set of focus attributes [12, 13]. For the central node set Z expanded from the exemplar node, the attribute subspace that makes them similar can be deduced. Unlike the calculation of feature weights for each cluster in an iterative manner in [14], the target community attribute subspace weight objective function can be directly calculated and is defined as follows:

$$F(L) = \sum_{i=1}^{c} \sum_{j=i+1}^{c} \sum_{t=1}^{r} l_t (f_{v_i t} - f_{v_j t})^2 + \gamma \sum_{t=1}^{r} l_t \log_2 l_t \tag{2}$$

subject to $\sum_{t=1}^{r} l_t = 1$, $l_t > 0$, where c is the number of nodes in the central node set, r is the dimension of the node attributes, and l_t represents the weight of the t-th attribute. The first term in (2) is the sum within community dispersions, and the second term is the negative weight entropy. The positive parameter γ controls the strength of the incentive on dimensions.

We use the Lagrangian multiplier technique to obtain the following minimization problem:

$$\min F'(L, \delta) = \sum_{i=1}^{c} \sum_{j=i+1}^{c} \sum_{t=1}^{r} l_t (f_{v_i t} - f_{v_j t})^2 + \gamma \sum_{t=1}^{r} l_t \log_2 l_t - \delta(\sum_{t=1}^{r} l_t - 1) \tag{3}$$

where δ is the Lagrange multipliers corresponding to the constraints. By setting the gradient of $F'(L, \delta)$ with respect to l_t and δ to zero, we obtain:

$$\frac{\partial F'}{\partial \delta} = (\sum_{t=1}^{r} l_t - 1) = 0 \tag{4}$$

$$\frac{\partial F'}{\partial l_t} = \sum_{i=1}^{c} \sum_{j=i+1}^{c} (f_{v_it} - f_{v_jt})^2 + \gamma \sum_{t=1}^{r} l_t(1 + \log_2 l_t) - \delta = 0 \quad (5)$$

from (5), we obtain:

$$l_t = \exp(\frac{-D_t - \gamma + \delta}{\gamma}) = \exp(\frac{\delta - \gamma}{\gamma}) \times \exp(\frac{-D_t}{\gamma}) \quad (6)$$

where $D_t = \sum_{i=1}^{c} \sum_{j=i+1}^{c} (f_{v_it} - f_{v_jt})^2$ and $\sum_{t=1}^{r} l_t = 1$, Substituting this expression back to (5) :

$$\sum_{t=1}^{r} l_t = \sum_{t=1}^{r} \exp(\frac{\delta - \gamma}{\gamma}) \times \exp(\frac{-D_t}{\gamma}) = \exp(\frac{\delta - \gamma}{\gamma}) \times \sum_{t=1}^{r} \exp(\frac{-D_t}{\gamma}) = 1 \quad (7)$$

It follows that, $\exp(\frac{\delta-\gamma}{\gamma}) = \frac{1}{\sum_{t=1}^{r} \exp(\frac{-D_t}{\gamma})}$, substituting this expression back to (6), we obtain:

$$l_t = \frac{\exp(\frac{-D_t}{\gamma})}{\sum_{t=1}^{r} \exp(\frac{-D_t}{\gamma})} \quad (8)$$

3   Community Search with User Preference

3.1   Community Quality in Attributed Graphs

We consider a community to be of high quality from two aspects [15]: (1) internal consistency; (2) external separability. There are many internal edges between nodes within a good community and an attribute subspace makes the community members highly similar. In addition, a good community has fewer edges on its borders, or many intersecting edges that can be "removed", that is, the focus attributes that enable nodes in a community to resemble each other also make them different from or separate from border nodes.

Definition 3 (Weighted attribute similarity): The exponential kernel of attribute vectors is adopted as the attributes similarity between nodes u and v under L, denoted by s $(u,v|L)$ as:

$$s(u, v|L) = \exp(-\|f(u) - f(u)\|^L) = \exp(-\sqrt{(f(u) - f(v))^T diag(L)(f(u) - f(v))}) \quad (9)$$

where $\|f(v) - f(u)\|^L$ is the weighted Euclidean distance under the subspace L, diag(L) is the diagonal matrix whose main diagonal is L.

Definition 4 (Community quality score): Based on the above two criteria of community quality, the community quality score is quantified as:

$$Qs = \frac{1}{2(\sum_{v_i \in C, v_j \in C} A_{ij})} \times \sum_{v_i \in C, v_j \in C,} \left(A_{ij} - \frac{k_i k_j}{2m}\right) s\big(f(v_i), f(v_j)|L_C\big)$$
$$- \frac{1}{2(\sum_{v_i \in C, v_j \in B} A_{ij})} \times \sum_{\substack{i \in C, j \in B, \\ a_{ij}=1}} \left(1 - \min\left(1, \frac{k_i k_j}{2m}\right)\right) s\big(f(v_i), f(v_j)|L_C\big) = I + E \tag{10}$$

where I is the internal consistency of a target community C, if the community C with (1) many existing and (2) 'surprising' internal edges among its members where (3) (a set of) attributes make them highly similar receives a high internal consistency score. Different from internal consistency I, external separability E considers only the boundary edges and quantifies the degree that these cross-edges can be exonerated. The higher the number of cross-edges that can be exonerated, the larger the external separability (note the negative sign) and hence the quality of a community becomes.

3.2 Algorithm for Community Search

We expand the community by carefully choosing new nodes to include and continue expanding until there exist no more nodes that increase the community quality score. Algorithm 1 illustrates the initial community search process as follows:

Algorithm 1 Initial target community search

Input: An attributed graph $G = (V, E, F)$, the Central node set Z, the attribute subspace of community L, the set of boundary nodes B;

Output: A set of nodes in the initial target community M'

1. $M' = Z$;   # Initialize the initial target community set
2. $CN = B$;   # Storage candidate node
3. $\Delta Qs(M') = 0$, $\Delta Qs(M')_{best} = 0$;

#$\Delta Qs(M')$ Change value of quality score of target community, $\Delta Qs(M')_{best}$ Maximum change in quality score of target community;

4. **Repeat**
5.   bestNode=null;   # Record the best candidate node
6.   **For each** $v \in CN$ **do**
7. $\Delta Qs(M') = Qs(M', add(v)) - Qs(M')$;
8.   **If** $\Delta Qs(M') > \Delta Qs(M')_{best} > 0$
9. $\Delta Qs(M')_{best} = \Delta Qs(M')$;
Maximum change in update quality score
10.   bestNode=v;
Record the current best node
11.   **End for**
12. $M' = M' \cup \{$ bestNode$\}$;
Add the best node
13. $CN \leftarrow \{CN \cup \{v|(v,\text{bestNode}) \in E, v \notin M'\}\}/\{$ bestNode $\}$;
Update the set of candidate nodes
14. $\Delta Qs(M')_{best} = 0$;
15. **Until** bestNode=null;
16. **Return** M';

Next, a greedy strategy is adopted to adjust the target community locally. Concretely, it is possible to adjust the operation with moderate variation and select the node with the largest positive moderate in each iteration change to be included into the target community. Iterations continue until no more nodes are added leading to moderate positive changes and Community quality score are no longer increased. The addition of nodes is based on an improved optimal search strategy. Each addition of nodes is the current optimal choice. Therefore, similar to addition of nodes, a traceability strategy can be adopted to check whether there are any nodes removed, which leads to a quality score positive increase in the community.

The quality score of the community is between 0 and 1. Every time the nodes are selected to join the community or the nodes in the community are deleted, the moderate value of the target community can be increased positively, so the convergence of the algorithm is guaranteed.

4 Experiments

In this section, we thoroughly evaluate the effectiveness and efficiency of CS-AS on both synthetic network and real-world networks. Besides, we compare our method with several state-of-the-art target community detection algorithms and evaluate the performance via NMI and F1 Score.

4.1 Experiments Settings

Synthetic Network. Synthetic attributed network with ground truth communities are generated based on the LFR benchmarks [10], which have similar features to real-world networks. We generate the synthetic network with four ground-truth community structure (*NO.* 1–4). We then assign the graph clusters generated, either to one of focus attribute sets or as unfocused. It is worth noting that in real-world graphs, we expect to see more than two focuses on a variety of attribute subspaces. For each focused cluster, one of the subsets is chosen as focus attributes. We randomly use a given sample node from each community to capture the target community. The statistics of the synthetic network is shown in Table 1 [10].

Real-World Networks. Three real-world networks with ground-truth communities collected by SNAP are adopted[1]: Enron Mail, YouTube, Amazon and DBLP. Enron email communication network covers all the email communication within a dataset of around half million emails, and the ground truth corresponds to the subject of mail. YouTube indicates friendships among users and the ground truth communities are user-defined groups. Amazon is a product co-purchasing network where co-purchased products are connected by edges, and the ground truth corresponds to product

---

[1] http://snap.stanford.edu/data/.

categories. DBLP is a co-authorship network and the ground truth corresponds to authors in the same research area. A detailed description of real-world graphs used in this work is given in Table 2.

Table 1. Synthetic attributed network with ground truth communities.

No.	Number of nodes	Number of edges	Attribute subspace
1	320	35840	$\{f_1,f_2,f_3,f_{12}\}$
2	316	34950	$\{f_1,f_5,f_{10},f_{12},f_{16},f_{20}\}$
3	184	11850	$\{f_4,f_8,f_{19}\}$
4	700	156000	–
In total	1750	178829	$\{f_1,f_2,\ldots,f_{20}\}$

4.2 Evaluation Metrics

In this experiment, we use two commonly used performance metrics to evaluate the proposed algorithm: The Normalized Mutual Information (NMI) and F1 score. In order to make better evaluation, we compare our method with three works previous presented closely related to target community: FocusCO, TSCM and TC-AE. The comparison of characteristics for each algorithm are summarized in the Table 3.

Table 2. The real-world network datasets

Datasets	Number of nodes	Number of edges	Nodes	Edges	Attributes
Amazon	3250	21987	User	Co-purchasing	Product
DBLP	8030	36,658	Author	Co-authorship	Article keyword
YouTube	12412	85,239	User	Friendship	User attribute

Table 3. The comparison of different target community detection method.

Algorithm	Attribute	Structure	Attribute weight	User interest	Edge Exempt
FocusCO	√	×	√	√	×
TSCM	√	×	√	√	×
TC-AE	√	√	√	√	×
CS-AS	√	√	√	√	√

4.3 Experimental Results

Parameter Sensitivity. The proposed CS-AS contains two parameters β and γ, where β is the similarity threshold to control the size of seed community; while γ is the positive parameter that controls the strengths of the incentive for attributes in the subspace. In this paper, both of them are set to be tuning parameters and are selected through our experiments.

We first investigate the effect of parameter β by adjusting it from 0 to 1 with 0.1 as intervals. We also analyze how the parameter γ affects the performance by fixing β. The performance on NMI and F1 are calculated on both artificial networks and real-world networks with 5 different user given nodes. With the fixing β, we tested the effect of γ from 0 to 1 with 0.1 as intervals. The averaged experimental results are shown in Figs. 1 and 2 respectively.

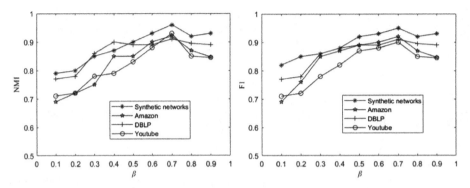

Fig. 1. NMI/F1 score of the CS-AS algorithms with different β values.

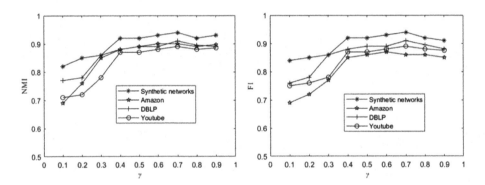

Fig. 2. NMI/F1 score of the CS-AS algorithms with different γ values.

The extension of sample highly relies on parameter β. From Fig. 1, we can see that for all the data sets, the best performance is achieved when $\beta = 0.7$, indicating that the high similarity would lead to high quality seed sets. However, if the value of β is set higher, the effect of the sample information extension technique will be attenuated during the target subspace mining process. Since the sample information extension procedure is essential for acquiring a more reasonable target subspace and target communities, thus, the best performance is achieved for $\beta = 0.7$.

According to Fig. 2, for the different data sets, we can see a high NMI/F1 is obtained in a large range of values for γ, i.e. [0.4, 0.8]. These results suggest that the increase in all judging criteria is robust across a wide range of mixing proportions and the detection results are not sensitive to the change of γ values. As a result, we set $\beta = 0.7$ and $\gamma = 0.6$, this parameter setting will be as default in the subsequent experiments.

Comparison Results. In order to further verify the effectiveness of our method, with the above parameter settings, we evaluate CS-AS, FocusCO, TSCM and TC-AE methods on both synthetic networks and real-world network datasets. The results of all the comparison algorithms are averaged over 10 runs with randomly provided exemplar nodes for each run. All other parameters of the methods are set as default described in their papers. Figure 3 displays the overall performance in terms of different metrics on different datasets.

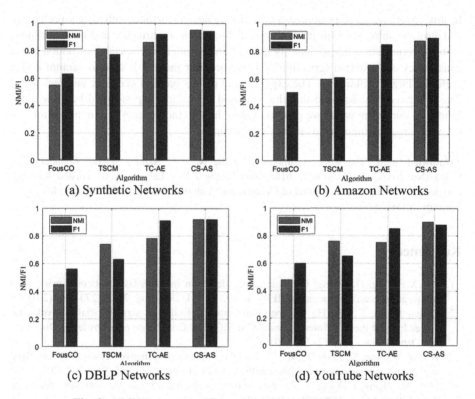

Fig. 3. NMI/F1 score on different networks with different methods.

Note that recovering a target clusters of interest in the existence of more other clusters is an increasingly challenging problem. It is observed from Fig. 3 that our approach achieves the highest performance for both evaluation criteria on all datasets. Concretely, it performs much better than TC-AE and TSCM and remarkably better than FocusCO, which suggests that our model is able to generate significantly better results by learning from exemplar nodes. TC-AE shows its relatively poor performance, the possible reason is that TC-AE equally penalize all the boundary edges irrespective of context. The subspace obtained from TSCM becomes less similar to the target, in other words, some attributes in the subspace are far from the target space. As for FocusCO, on one hand, it is difficult for user to provide more and similar sample nodes, and one the other hand, perceiving a set of exemplar nodes similar by the user is a bit subjective and may not consider the relations between the structures and attribute similarity. What is more, all algorithms performed better on YouTube network than others. This is because most egonet in YouTube network are subgraphs with low overlapping and each of them is as dense as a completed graph.

5   Conclusions and Future Work

In this paper, we have presented a community search method with user's preference and attribute subspace. Our method utilizes both network structure and node attributes within a certain subspace to quantify a community from the perspective of both internal consistency and external separability. Therefore, our method is able to capture a user preferred target community. The experimental results on both synthetic and real-world data sets have demonstrated that the proposed algorithm outperformed baseline algorithms. In our future work, we plan to explore how to incorporate community influence to exact target community with user's preference.

Acknowledgment. The work is supported by the National Natural Science Foundation of China (No. 61762078, 61363058, 61663004) Guangxi Key Laboratory of Trusted Software (No. kx201910) and Research Fund of Guangxi Key Lab of Multi-source Information Mining & Security (MIMS18-08).

References

1. Ma, X., Dong, D., Wang, Q.: Community detection in multi-layer networks using joint nonnegative matrix factorization. IEEE Trans. Knowl. Data Eng. **31**(2), 273–286 (2019)
2. Cheng, K., Li, J., Liu, H.: Unsupervised feature selection in signed social networks. In: Proceedings of the 17th International ACM SIGKDD Conference on Knowledge Discovery and Data Mining, pp. 777–786 (2017)
3. Wu, W., Kwong, S., Zhou, Y., Jia, Y., Gao, W.: Nonnegative matrix factorization with fixed hypergraph regularization for community detection. Inform. Sci. **435**, 263–281 (2018)
4. Ding, X., Zhang, J., Yang, J.: A robust two-stage algorithm for local community detection. Knowl.-Based Syst. **152**, 188–199 (2018)
5. Boorman, S., White, H.: Social structure from multiple networks. II. Role structures. Am. J. Sociol. **81**(6), 1384–1446 (1976)
6. Baumes, J., Goldberg, M., Krishnamoorthy, M., Magdon-Ismail, M., Preston, N.: Finding communities by clustering a graph into overlapping subgraph. In: Proceedings of the IADIS International Conference on Applied Computing, pp. 97–104 (2005)
7. Lancichinetti, A., Radicchi, F., Ramasco, J., Fortunato, S.: Finding statistically significant communities in networks. PLoS One **6**(4), e18961 (2011)
8. Perozzi, B., Akoglu, L., Sánchez, P., Müller, E.: Focused clustering and outlier detection in large attributed graphs. In: Proceedings of the 14th International ACM SIGKDD Conference on Knowledge Discovery and Data Mining, pp. 1346–1355 (2014)

9. Wu, P., Pan, L.: Mining target attribute subspace and set of target communities in large attributed networks (2017)
10. Liu, H., Ma, H., Chang, Y., Li, Z.: Target community detection based on attribute subspace with entropy weighting. Chin. Inform. Process. **33**(8), 114–123 (2019)
11. Li, X., Wu, Y., Ester, M., Kao, B., Wang, X., Zheng, Y.: Semi-supervised clustering in attributed heterogeneous information networks. In: Proceedings of the 26th International World Wide Web Conference on World Wide Web, pp. 1621–1629 (2017)
12. Günnemann, S., Färber, I., Raubach, S., Seidl, T.: Spectral subspace clustering for graphs with feature vectors. In: Proceedings of the 14th International on Data Mining, pp. 231–240 (2013)
13. Chen, F., Zhou, B., Alim, A., Zhao, L.: A generic framework for interesting subspace cluster detection in multi-attributed networks. In: Proceedings of the 17th IEEE International Conference on Data Mining, pp. 41–50 (2017)
14. Jing, L., Ng, M., Huang, J.: An entropy weighting k-means algorithm for subspace clustering of high-dimensional sparse data. IEEE Trans. Knowl. Data Eng. **19**(8), 1026–1041 (2007)
15. Perozzi, B., Akoglu, L.: Scalable anomaly ranking of attributed neighborhoods. In: Proceedings of the 3rd International Conference on Sustainable Design and Manufacturing, pp. 207–215 (2016)

Visualization of Customer Satisfaction Linked to Behavior Using a Process-Based Web Questionnaire

Hisashi Masuda[1]([⊠]) and Wilfrid Utz[2]

[1] Kyoto University, Yoshida-Honmachi, Sakyo-ku, Kyoto 606-8501, Japan
masuda.hisashi.4c@kyoto-u.ac.jp
[2] University of Vienna, Währinger Straße 29, 1090 Vienna, Austria
wilfrid.utz@univie.ac.at

Abstract. Advances in technology enable service providers to design diverse customer experiences. However, in the field of the hospitality and tourism industry where service providers and customers directly interact, there are issues in how to acquire, analyze and utilize individual evaluation data linked to customer experiences. Here, we propose a visualization method of customer evaluation based on customer satisfaction data linked to fragmented customer experiences, using a web-based questionnaire system that allows customers to describe the process of the customer experience by themselves. To evaluate the practical application, we constructed a prototypical environment that allows visual interaction using a business process modeling environment as an interface. In order to develop this system, we conducted a survey of customer experience regarding customer behavior by web questionnaire for service users. In this system, the linkage between the overall customer satisfaction and the partial satisfaction connected to each customer behavior are displayed visibly by applying a business process modeling tool. In the service industry, clarifying customer satisfaction in terms of customer behavior will lead to get fundamental data for the personalized/customized service.

Keywords: Customer satisfaction · Customer experience ·
Web questionnaire · Business process modeling

1 Introduction

1.1 Background

The service industry is becoming more sophisticated and complex with the advances in technology. At the same time, the function of services has expanded across sectors, breaking the barriers of the conventional industry classification. It has become possible for customer themselves get in contact with various services through smartphones. Under these circumstances, there is more room for personalization of services to customers [1–3].

In the tourism and hospitality industry, many possibilities to interact directly with customers exist. Consequently, manners to obtain customer behavior and feedback as

© Springer Nature Switzerland AG 2019
C. Douligeris et al. (Eds.): KSEM 2019, LNAI 11775, pp. 596–603, 2019.
https://doi.org/10.1007/978-3-030-29551-6_53

data are a major concern in this area. For example, in the best case that the service provider has a web service deployed, a personalized cookie is linked during interaction and the user's behavior can be grasped.

For small and medium-sized enterprises (SMEs), it is difficult to catch up with new technologies independently because of limited resources. A scheme that enables SMEs to use ICT is needed. This trend is exemplified by the evolution of simple and affordable devices, that make it possible to handle various payment scenarios. But, there are companies that cannot use a system such as digital marketing that streamlines marketing. Given such a case, a mechanism is needed that can support the diverse, experiential design of customers without expertise in ICT.

As for the evaluation of service encounters, various evaluation points have been proposed from different viewpoints [4–6]. Furthermore, in marketing, concepts for describing customer experiences such as personas [7] that abstract representative individuals into abstract figures are required. Elevating these personas into customer journey maps are a widely used practice [8, 9]. However, such research methods are labor intensive. It is difficult for organizations such as SMEs in the service industry to introduce additional resources and use these methods properly and continuously [10, 11].

Given these observations, a simple data acquisition and analysis method is required to capture the context of the customer during service evaluation. The use of a web questionnaire method has already been used in many practices and is proposed. Nevertheless, there is a need for to extend the methodology to obtain data to better understand the context in customer evaluation while utilizing such an approach.

It is necessary to provide the respondent side with the opportunity of continuous information input regarding Customer Satisfaction (CS) evaluation by reducing the input cost. On the other hand, in order to reduce the analysis cost for data analysts, it is required to perform data analysis on the acquired datasets in a smart and automated fashion and provide results immediately.

1.2   Research Purpose and Objectives

The purpose of this research project is to express the variety of evaluation for each behavior of the customer as quantitative data for the overall CS evaluation on the customer experience for a service. In customer experience, even if the same service is provided, the customer does not necessarily give a uniform rating to the service. Customers have their own evaluation criteria, some are shared by most, some are shared by several, and others are unique to each customer [12].

The first step required to solve the set research subject relates to the correction required to interpret the customer's context for the existing web questionnaire. The second step is to conceptualize the automation of data analysis and the visual confirmation method of the results utilizing the acquired data. Due to current web questionnaires mainly use static analysis methods with pre-defined question items, it is difficult to adapt to the wide range of the customers' criteria to their service provision automatically.

1.3   Approach

In order to approach the research subject, a proposal for an adaptive web questionnaire, data acquisition, analysis and visualization has been developed. The targets of data acquisition using the created web-questionnaire are retail, restaurant, and hotel industries in Japan. As data analysis and its visualization, we implemented a process modeling environment where visual click operations can be performed on the acquired data.

The proposed data acquisition approach is a two-stage web questionnaire method. Concerning the customer experience in using the service, the respondent in the first stage provides information on actions performed on the spot during the time from entering to leaving the service encounter. A form that includes special functions is used for inputting the information. Each item is described in a dedicated posting form as one line per action. In the second-stage, in addition to the face sheet and overall CS rating, as in the general web questionnaires, the CS rating associated with each action entered in the first-stage is captured. In case there are additional statements of their assessment, comments about it can be added. As a result, in any customer experience assessment, it is possible to obtain information on the point of interest from the customer point of view, the CS evaluation, and the evaluation reason to be noted as a series of structured data.

Using such a web questionnaire system, data on CS ratings were obtained by conducting a survey of customers of retail, food and drink and hotel services in Japan. The implementation period is March-April 2018. The respondents were obtained through a research agency providing marketing research monitors in Japan. Immediately after using retail, eating and drinking and accommodation services, each respondent was asked to answer the CS questionnaire. Each respondent was asked to repeat the assessment at least three times. As a result, the number of valid responses obtained was 88 for retail, 138 for food and drink, and 19 for lodging.

The acquired data were classified into two groups for each retail, restaurant, and lodging industries in the viewpoint of above or below the average value of the payment fee for each service. The CS levels linked to the behavior of each customer experience input were plotted on a numbered line from 0 to 1, representing the service encounter from entry to exit time. The evaluation of data was done visually using business process modelling. As a result, in addition to the classification of overall CS, more diverse CS rating patterns within it have become explicitly observable.

By establishing the proposed environment, it became possible to construct a method of continuous acquisition, data analysis, and confirmation. Academically, it has become possible to provide data on CS assessments that contribute to personalization and customization that is more conscious of one-to-one marketing in CS assessments. In practice, the proposed environment can be used as an interface with the customer, providing more value, based on sharing information between the customer and the service provider.

2 Methodology

2.1 Concept: Two-Tier Questionnaire System

In order to obtain feedback on customer experience evaluation, this paper demonstrates the proposed questionnaire system. The customer can input actions on their service experience as the detailed data during the service encounter. The overall concept is described in the following:

Step 1: a customer using retail, food and drink service answers the proposed web questionnaire system based on experience during the encounter,
Step 2: the data obtained from the questionnaire system are organized and managed coherently,
Step 3: the results are shown using business process models extended with different visualization options.

The core feature of the proposed data acquisition method is the web questionnaire survey divided into two tiers. In a first phase, the system listens to the behavior of the consumer when using the service. Based in the results obtained, in the second stage an adaptive web questionnaire page based on the behavior entered in the first stage is generated. Thereby, the focus point of service utilization from a customer viewpoint is extracted. At the same time, by listening to the items related to the overall opinion as in a conventional questionnaire survey, it is possible to reflect the customer's viewpoint while also considering the provider's viewpoint.

In the first stage, the respondent fills in the behavior from entry to exit during the service that he/she uses. The services supported by the questionnaire survey are currently limited to retail, food, and accommodation services. In particular, the input form of the process in one row and one action makes it possible to obtain information on the behavior as structured data during input. Respondents describe their own service usage and press submit button to move to the second stage questionnaire page. The actual questionnaire survey is conducted in Japanese.

In the second stage of the questionnaire survey, in addition to the question items of conventional CS level evaluation, the evaluation of the CS level linked to the action entered in the first stage is also performed. Here, the customer is asked for a comment on CS on a 7-level Likert scale and the reason for it, in case this is noteworthy for evaluation.

From the viewpoint of data analysis, groups are classified based on the average value of the charged amount for each of retail business, restaurant services, and the lodging. The CS pattern is linked to the behavior of the customer experience. In particular, each customer satisfaction linked to the behavior is requested customers to fill in the web questionnaire form in the range from entering to leaving the store. Here, each individual CS rating is plotted on the 0–1 number line by representing 0 when entering a store and 1 when leaving a store. In this way, by structuring the satisfaction rating linked to the customer's actions, the design can be made for comprehensive analysis and interpretation.

As a proof-of-concept, an implementation of this system using business process models as a basis to manage and analyze such data visually is available. The business process models are established using the ADOxx Metamodelling Platform [13] which is a platform to implement domain-specific metamodels for experimentation. In particular, ADOxx supports the development of hybrid modelling methods that are composed of artefacts and fragments required by a specific domain and extended to needs observed.

The openness of the platform enables the realization of the proposed visualization techniques by:

- Establishing a business process based metamodel to capture and visualize service process instance information as defined in the first stage of the questionnaire system,
- Extend the process view with statistical assessment and visualization techniques to identify overlapped or different actions.
- Support a means of interaction between customer and provider via the means of graphical models and allow for syntactic and semantic model processing (like simulation as discussed in [14] for the domain of industrial business processes) to provide insights in the historical data obtained and provide the foundation for a model-based prediction.
- Derive patterns from service process instance and understand customer segments in their service usage based on their behavior and experience.

The requirements listed above have been assessed and aligned with the development approach discussed in [15–17]. The development approach follows the conceptual design of the hybrid metamodel (composed of a questionnaire metamodel, reuse of an existing business process metamodel and integration with visualization methods). As the objective is to provide an intuitive environment, graphical tool support is required. The ADOxx platform is used as a development and deployment environment following a meta-modelling approach based on building blocks [16] utilizing conceptual structures as a formal means to identify the syntax and semantics of required constructs. Applying the Agile Modelling Method Engineering (AMME) framework [17], an iterative adaptation is supported.

2.2 Survey Design

In this paper, data was obtained by the introduced web questionnaire method through research monitors held by a marketing research company in Japan. The marketing research company owns 800,000 research monitors. The survey period was between March 29, 2018 and April 13, 2018. Participants have been asked to respond on the web questionnaire page. It has been proposed that at least three service usages are evaluated during the service period. During the period, 88 filled in questionnaires were received in the retail business (male = 34%, female = 66%), 131 in the restaurant business (male = 56%, female = 44%), and 19 in the lodging business (male = 63%, female = 37%).

3 Results

3.1 Customer Satisfaction Evaluations Linked to Customer Experience

In terms of overall CS in the retail industry, results can be distinguished as satisfied, neutral, and unsatisfactory categories of CS evaluations linked to customer experience behavior. The data obtained for service usage higher than the average price consist of a totally satisfied group (N = 12) and a neutral group (N = 7). Also data obtained for service usage below the average price consists of a comprehensively satisfied group (N = 36), a neutral group (N = 17), and a totally unsatisfactory group (N = 5).

In terms of overall CS in the restaurant industry, the data obtained for service usage higher than the average price consist of a totally satisfactory group (N = 12) and a neutral group (N = 4). Data obtained for service usage below the average price consists of a comprehensively satisfied group (N = 76), a neutral group (N = 24), and an unsatisfactory group (N = 7).

In terms of overall CS in the hotel industry, the data obtained for service usage higher than the average price consist of a totally satisfactory group (N = 11), a neutral group (N = 2) and a totally unsatisfactory group (N = 2). And also the data obtained for service usage below the average price consists of a comprehensively satisfied group (N = 3).

3.2   Extended Visualization as Business Process Models

Based on the data analysis performed above, the extended system with respect to integrated process instance visualization support are presented. An object for data visualization is generated, and then the target industry, data analysis range, data analysis method and output result are adjusted on the object (Figs. 1 and 2). This step establishes the continuous data flow from the questionnaire as semantically enriched data assets for analysis and processing.

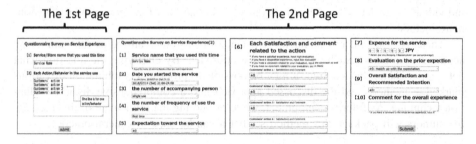

Fig. 1. Overview of the web questionnaire for service evaluation on customer behavior

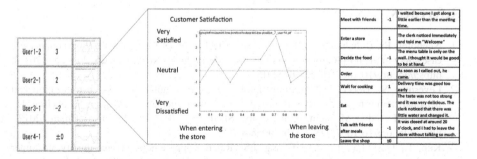

Fig. 2. Overview of the business process model as an interface of the proposed analysis

Figure 1 shows graphically the layers of visualization based on the proposed system. Using a model-based approach, the data obtained is semantically enriched through a rule-based system and provides the different visualization in an integrated fashion.

4 Conclusion

In this paper, a contribution is made to understand in more detail the trend of CS evaluation. We have designed a two-tier web questionnaire and coupled it with a graphical modelling environment using ADOxx to support diverse and interactive visualization methods. The system allows customers to describe their own service experiences and view assessment results as quantitative data. It has been observed that there are various patterns in the evaluation in each individual's experience, even for a customer who shows a comprehensive CS rating that they are satisfied, neutral, or neither. In particular, in this method, the position of the process is standardized in the range from the entry time to the exit time for each action. Therefore, data acquisition and quantitative analysis can be performed seamlessly. Since this method can be used as a web questionnaire, it can also be used in an organization with limited resources, such as a small business. The proposed method can handle more diverse features from the viewpoint of service evaluation. However, in order to generalize the tendency of the individual input data, this method requires more data than the conventional question-naire method.

There is also concern about the existence of customer attributes that cannot be acquired by methods such as the proposed approach. By clarifying the question what data can or cannot be acquired, it may be possible to propose a combination of various marketing methods and the discussed approach into a comprehensive, hybrid evalua-tion technique. As future development, while promoting the refinement of this method, the authors will package this method so that it can be used in general practice.

Acknowledgement. This work was supported by JSPS KAKENHI Grant Number 15H05396.

References

1. Neuhofer, B., Buhalis, D., Ladkin, A.: Smart technologies for personalized experiences: a case study in the hospitality domain. Electron. Mark.: Int. J. Netw. Bus. **25**, 243–254 (2015). https://doi.org/10.1007/s12525-015-0182-1
2. Levesque, N., Boeck, H.: Proximity marketing as an enabler of mass customization and personalization in a customer service experience. In: Bellemare, J., Carrier, S., Nielsen, K., Piller, F.T. (eds.) Managing Complexity. SPBE, pp. 405–420. Springer, Cham (2017). https://doi.org/10.1007/978-3-319-29058-4_32
3. Kuo, T., Tsai, G.Y., Lu, I.Y., Chang, J.S.: Relationships among service quality, customer satisfaction and customer loyalty: a case study on mobile shopping APPs. In: Proceedings of the 17th Asia Pacific Industrial Engineering and Management System Conference, pp. 7–10 (2016)

4. Shostack, G.L.: Planning the service encounter. In: Czepiel, A.J., Solomon, R.M., Surprenant, F.C. (eds.) The Service Encounter, pp. 243–254. Lexington Books, New York (1985)
5. Bitner, M.J., Booms, B.H., Tetreault, M.S.: The service encounter: diagnosing favorable and unfavorable incidents. J. Mark. **54**, 71–94 (1990)
6. Chandon, J.-L., Leo, P.-Y., Philippe, J.: Service encounter dimensions - a dyadic perspective: measuring the dimensions of service encounters as perceived by customers and personnel. Int. J. Serv. Ind. Manage. **8**(1), 65–86 (1997)
7. Pruitt, S.J., Adlin, T.: The Persona Lifecycle: Keeping People in Mind Throughout Product Design. Elsevier, Amsterdam (2006)
8. Stickdorn, M., et al.: This is Service Design Thinking: Basics, Tools, Cases, vol. 1. Wiley, Hoboken (2011)
9. Lemon, K.N., Verhoef, P.C.: Understanding customer experience throughout the customer journey. J. Mark. **80**(6), 69–96 (2016)
10. Taiminen, H.M., Karjaluoto, H.: The usage of digital marketing channels in SMEs. J. Small Bus. Enterp. Dev. **22**(4), 633–651 (2015)
11. Arendt, L.: Barriers to ICT adoption in SMEs: how to bridge the digital divide. J. Syst. Inform. Technol. **10**(2), 93–108 (2008)
12. Kluckhohn, C., Murray, H.A.: Personality in nature, society, and culture. Knopf, New York (1953)
13. ADOxx Metamodelling Platform (2019). https://www.adoxx.org
14. Utz, W., Lee, M.: Industrial business process management using adonis towards a modular business process modelling method for zero-defect-manufacturing. In: 2017 International Conference on Industrial Engineering, Management Science and Application, ICIMSA (2017). https://doi.org/10.1109/ICIMSA.2017.7985590
15. Utz, W.: Design metamodels for domain-specific modelling methods using conceptual structures, pp. 47–60 (2018). http://ceur-ws.org/Vol-2234/paper4.pdf
16. Karagiannis, D., Bork, D., Utz, W.: Metamodels as a conceptual structure: some semantical and syntactical operations. In: Bergener, K., Räckers, M., Stein, A. (eds.) The Art of Structuring, pp. 75–86. Springer, Cham (2019). https://doi.org/10.1007/978-3-030-06234-7_8
17. Karagiannis, D.: Agile modeling method engineering (2015). https://doi.org/10.1145/2801948.2802040

A Multilingual Semantic Similarity-Based Approach for Question-Answering Systems

Wafa Wali[1]([⊠]), Fatma Ghorbel[1,2], Bilel Gragouri[1], Fayçal Hamdi[2], and Elisabeth Metais[2]

[1] MIRACL Laboratory, Sfax, Tunisia
wafa.wali@fsegs.rnu.tn
[2] Cnam laboratory Cédric, Paris, France
https://www.miracl.rnu.tn, https://www.cedric.cnam.fr/

Abstract. Question-answering systems face a challenge related to the process of deciding automatically about the veracity of a given answer. This issue is particularly problematic when handling open-ended questions. In this paper, we propose a multilingual semantic similarity-based approach to estimate the similarity score between the user's answer and the right one saved in the data tier. This approach is mainly based on semantic information notably the synonymy relationships between words and syntactico-semantic information especially semantic class and thematic role. It supports three languages: English, French and Arabic. Our approach is applied to a multilingual ontology-based question-answering training for Alzheimer's disease patients. The performance of the proposed approach was confirmed through experiments on 20 patients that promising capabilities in identifying literal and some types of intelligent similarity.

Keywords: Question-answering systems · Multilingualism ·
Semantic similarity · Synonymy relationship · Semantic class ·
Thematic role

1 Introduction

In the context of the VIVA[1] project (*"Vivre à Paris avec Alzheimer en 2030 grâce aux nouvelles technologies"*), we are proposing a memory prosthesis, called Captain Memo [13], to help Alzheimer's patients to palliate mnesic problems. Data are structured semantically using an ontology, called, PersonLink [6]. It is a multilingual OWL2 ontology for storing, modeling and reasoning about interpersonal relationships (e.g., father and half-brothers) and describing people (e.g., name, age, preferences and lived events). This prosthesis supplies a set of services. Among these services, one is called Autobiographical Training [13]. It

---

[1] http://viva.cnam.fr/.

© Springer Nature Switzerland AG 2019
C. Douligeris et al. (Eds.): KSEM 2019, LNAI 11775, pp. 604–614, 2019.
https://doi.org/10.1007/978-3-030-29551-6_54

is a "question-answering" non pharmacological memory training that attempts to preserve the patient's reminding abilities.

Autobiographical Training is based on a multilingual questions database (English, French and Arabic). However, all of them are closed-ended questions and they can be answered in only one word or a simple "es" or "no" e.g., "Is Alice black-haired?" and "What is the name of your son?". We aim to extend this database by proposing open-ended questions which are ones that require more than one word answers. The answers could come in the form of a list, a few sentences or something longer such as a paragraph e.g., "Tell me about the relationship between your three children?" and "What types of decorations do you used for your birthday party?".

In this paper, we attempt the issue of allowing users to answer multilingual open-ended questions in a natural language. We estimate the semantic similarity score between the user' answer and the right one saved in the data tier by exploiting the semantic distance.

During the few previous years, several methods for sentence similarity computation have been proposed such as, [1] and [18]. However, these methods are applied only to the English language e.i., they do not support the French and Arabic languages. Moreover, many knowledge elements, e.g., the semantic class, the thematic role and the relationship between them, are not taken into account when measuring the sentence similarity. Both the semantic class and the thematic role give, for each argument, information about the relationship between words and improve the sentence meaning [3].

In this paper, we propose a multilingual semantic similarity-based approach to estimate the similarity score between the user's answers and the one saved in the data tier. Compared to related work, The proposed approach is mainly based on semantic information notably the synonymy relationships between words and syntactico-semantic information especially semantic class and thematic role. It supported three languages: English, French and Arabic. Our approach is mainly proposed to be integrated in the prototype of Autobiographical Training for Alzheimer's patients. However, it can be used in any multilingual question answering systems.

We evaluated the performance of proposed approach in terms of the Precision and Recall evaluation metrics. This evaluation is done in the context of Autobiographical Training. 20 Alzheimer's disease patients entered this study. The results are promising.

The remainder of the paper is structured as follows. Section 2 includes an outline of the available measurement approaches that describes current method for sentence similarity computation. The proposed approach is presented in Sect. 3., Sect. 4 is devoted to describe some experimentation and discuss the evaluation's results. Finally, in Sect. 5, we conclude and we give perspectives.

2   Related Work

There is extensive literature that dealt with the measurement of the similarity between sentences which can be grouped into three main categories: (*i*) syntactic based methods, (*ii*) semantic based methods and (*iii*) hybrid methods. In this paper, we just limit to present the hybrid methods to explore their advantages and their limitations. Several hybrid methods have been proposed. Li et al. [11] presented a method that takes into account the semantic and word order information implied in the sentences. The semantic similarity of two sentences is computed using information from a structured lexical database, such as WordNet [14] and corpus statistics. As for, Islam and Inkpen [7] reported on a Semantic Text Similarity (STS) measure using a corpus-based measure for semantic word similarity and a modified version of the Longest Common Subsequence (LCS) string matching algorithm. In their research, Oliva et al. [15] reported on a method called SyMSS to estimate a sentence semantic similarity. This method considers that the meaning of a sentence is made up of the meanings of its separate words and the structural way the words are combined. Furthermore, Ferreira et al. [4] proposed a measure to estimate the degree of similarity between two sentences based on three layers, such as the lexical layer, which encompasses a lexical analysis, stop word removal and stemming, the a syntactic layer, which performs syntactic analysis; and the semantic layer which describes mainly the annotations that play a semantic role. More recently, deep learning based methods became competitive. [2] estimate the similarity between sentences into takes account the synonymy relations and the word order using deep learning.

However, all of the mentioned methods are applied to the English language and they do not support the specific particularity of the French and Arabic languages. Moreover, they estimate the semantic similarity based only on the syntactic structure of sentence notably word order or the syntactic dependency and the synonymy relationship between terms. They do not take into consideration the semantic arguments notably the semantic class and thematic role in computing the semantic similarity. The proposed work falls into the latter category. It is a multilingual approach that estimates the semantic similarity between sentences based on syntactico-semantic information notably semantic class and thematic role that achieves a significant semantic similarity score.

3   The Proposed Multilingual Semantic Similarity-Based Approach

This section describes the proposed approach to estimate a semantic similarity score between the user 'answer and the right answer saved in data tier. It supports three languages: English, French and Arabic. It includes an extension of previous strategies at take account of the most important linguistic and the syntactico-semantic information. Compared to related work, it takes also into account the semantic arguments notably the semantic class and thematic role.

The proposed approach is divided into three parts: (i) "Preprocessing", (ii) "Similarity Score Attribution" and (iii) "Supervised Learning". Figure 1 summarizes this approach.

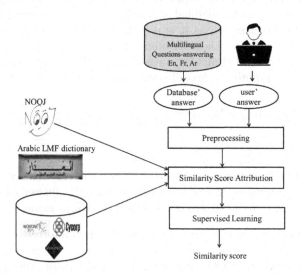

Fig. 1. The proposed multilingual approach for estimating answerings similarity.

3.1 Preprocessing

Before estimating the similarity score between the answer given by the user (A_{User}) and the right ones saved in the data tier (A_{Right}), it is essential to determine the words for comparison. Three sub-steps are proposed:

- Tokenization: the two answers A_{User} and A_{Right} are decomposed into authentication tokens (words). This step filters the answers and tags the words into their part of speech and labels them accordingly. WordNet [14] handles only relationships between noun-noun and verb-verb. The other parts of speeches are not taken onto account. Therefore, to reduce the time and space complexity of the approach, we only consider nouns and verbs to calculate the similarity.
- Removal of the punctuation signs: punctuation signs, which are being used in any text, represent unimportant information between sentences; therefore, they are eliminated for the purpose of getting more meaningful results.
- Lemmatization: morphological variables are reduced to their base form using the Stanford Morphological analyzer [12].

3.2 Similarity Score Attribution

To estimate the similarity rating between the two answers, three similarity levels are measured: lexical, semantic and syntactico-semantic. We use the content of the Arabic LMF standardized dictionary [9],WordNet [14], VerbNet [16], DBpedia [10], OpenCyc ontology[2] and the NOOJ platform [17].

The lexical similarity is computed using the lexical units that compose the answers for the purpose of extracting the words that are lexically the same. The lexical resemblance, which is defined as SL(A_{User}, A_{Right}), is computed by means of the Jaccard coefficient [8], as it is popularly used to compare the proximity of the data in the process (Data Clustering) [5] and it is sufficiently suitable to be employed in the word similarity measurement. The formula presented below explains how to compute the lexical resemblance between answers.

$$SL(A_{User}, A_{Right}) = \frac{MC}{MA_{User} + MA_{Right} - MC} \qquad (1)$$

where:

MC is the number of common words between the two answers,
MA_{User} is the number of words contained in A_{User} answer and
MA_{Right} is the number of words contained in A_{Right} answer.

The measurement of the semantic similarity is reinforced by means of the WordNet database [14] in order to extract the synonyms of each answers' words. Also, we have used the NOOJ platform [17] to determine the named entities. We have used also the OpenCyc ontology (see Footnote 2) to extract common senses facts (for instance, twins have the same birthday).

The computing process of the semantic resemblance involves primarily the creation of a set of joint words relying only on the recognizable origin of pairs of answers. A raw semantic vector is extracted for each answer using the WordNet database [14]. We calculate the semantic vector for each answer. The combined joint word from it the semantic vector is derived is called T. Moreover, since each semantic vector coincides with the stem that exists in the group of the joint words, each semantic vector entry matches the stem of the joint word series, and consequently the dimension is equal to the number of stems in the combined word set.

The entry value of the lexical semantic vector T = (T1, T2, ... Tm) is identified through the word semantic similarity that matches the word in the answer; where m is number of the vectors cells. Since is the combined joint word Wi, then, we have: if Wi found in the answer, it will be set to 1 (case1). On the other hand, if Wi does not exist in the answering, the score of the semantic similarity will be computed between Ti and all the words in the sentence by applying the synonymy link of the WordNet database (case2). Therefore, the closest word to Wi in the answering is the one that has the highest resemblance score MaxSim, then Ti is set to MaxSim.

As a consequence, for two given words, W1 and W2, it is necessary to find the semantic similarity Sim (W1 and W2). The word similarity estimation is carried out through a direct method which consists in identifying the synonymy set of

---

[2] http://www.cyc.com/opencyc/.

every word for the purpose of detecting synonyms between words. For instance, the common ones between the words "stable" and "constant" are "steady" and "firm" as the synonyms of "stable" are (steady, constant, enduring, firm, stable) whereas the synonyms of "constant" are (steady, abiding, firm, perpetual, hourly). When two synonym sets are gathered for every word, the similarity degree between them is computed applying the Jaccard coefficient [8].

$$Sim(W1, W2) = \frac{MC}{MW1 + MW2 - MC} \tag{2}$$

where:

MC is the number of common words between the two synonym sets,
MW1 is the number of words contained in the W1 synonym set and
MW2 is the number of words contained in the W2 synonym set.

On the basis of the semantic vectors previously calculated, the semantic similarity degree, which is labeled $SM(A_{User}, A_{Right})$, is computed between them by applying the Cosine similarity (Salton (1968).

$$SM(A_{User}, A_{Right}) = \frac{V1.V2}{||V1||.||V2||} \tag{3}$$

where:

V1 is the semantic vector of A_{User} answer and
V2 is the semantic vector of answer A_{Right}.

The estimation of the syntactico-semantic similarity consists of extracting the characteristics of the semantic arguments of every answer from the VerbNet database for the French and English languages [16] and LMF Arabic dictionary for the Arabic language [9]. As a consequence, a syntactic parser is used to identify, on the one hand, the syntactic behavior of the answers and, on the other hand, the semantic predicates from the databases which is very rich in semantic predicates. Moreover, the meanings of the lexical entry, such as (the verb of the answer) and the predicative representation that connects the syntactic behavior and the semantic predicate predefined in the first stage are looked up in the databases. Then, when the predicative representation is caught, the semantic arguments will be extracted. Once the pairs of semantic argument have the same thematic role and semantic class, they are considered similar. After that, the degree of the syntactico-semantic similarity between two elements of each pair of the answer is computed based on the common semantic arguments of the elements of the pair of answers, which are called $SSM(A_{User}, A_{Right})$ by using the Jaccard coefficient [8].

$$SSM(A_{User}, A_{Right}) = \frac{ASC}{ASA_{User} + ASA_{Right} - ASC} \tag{4}$$

W. Wali et al.

where :

ASC is the number of common semantic arguments between the two answers,
ASA_{User} is the number of semantic arguments contained in answer A_{User},
and
ASA_{Right} is the number of semantic arguments contained in answer A_{Right}.

3.3 Supervised Learning

We propose to use the automatic learning in order to define the appropriate coefficients for the measures described below. In this context, our aim is to apply, in a first step, a hyper plane equation (decision boundary, such as similar or not-similar) on the answers, and deduct a score similarity in the second step.

The procedure of identifying the appropriate coefficients consists of two steps: a training step, which aims at getting a hyper plane equation through the Supervised Vector Machine (SVM) learning algorithm, and a test step, (hyperplane equation) by means of the validation approach.

During the first step, the extraction vectors which describe the pairs of sentences are prepared. In most cases, any vector V is described through the collection of lexical (SL), semantic (SM) and syntactico-semantic resemblance values (SSM) defined by a score according to which any criterion matches the analysis value of the answering pair under the criterion. Every vector is complemented by a Boolean criterion, particularly D. The criterion category is set up by an expert who judges whether the pair elements are similar or different. Moreover, repeating the number of similar vectors as well as other different ones is possible. In the second phase, the SVM learning algorithm is applied to create an optimal hyper-plane which distinguishes between two classes (similar or different). At this level, the extracted vectors represent the input on which the classification equation is based that represented as follows.

$$\alpha * SL + \beta * SM + \gamma * SSM + C \tag{5}$$

where:

α is attributed weight to lexical similarity,
β is attributed weight to semantic similarity,
γ is attributed weight to syntactico-semantic similarity and C is constant.

In the utilization phase, we compute the sentence similarity measure based on the validated classification equation. Thus, we apply the generated coefficients on the computed scores, such as the lexical, semantic and syntactico-semantic similarity in order to measure the sentence similarity. After the process computing of the measure sentence similarity, we detect the similarity class as follows:

If $Sim(A_{User}, A_{Right}) \geq$ threshold, then the answers pair are similar, else if $Sim(A_{User}, A_{Right}) \ll$ threshold, then the answers pair are not similar.

4   Experimental Results

A Java-based prototype is implemented based on the proposed approach. We integrate the prototype of the proposed approach in the prototype of the Autobiographical Training memory training for Alzheimer's patients. Figure 2 shows an example of a open-ended question, the response given by the user and the decision of its correctness based on our approach.

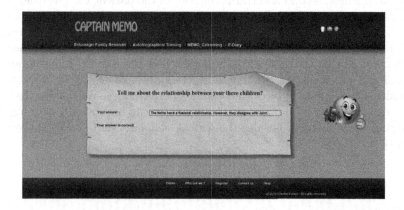

Fig. 2. A screenshot of autobiographical training.

The evaluation consisted on one test session to each patient. Its duration depends on the cognitive performance of the Alzheimer's patient. At mean, it was about one hour and 53 min. At the beginning of each session, we gave a brief introduction and a live demo of Autobiographical Training. Each patient gives the responses of 80 open-ended questions. We classify these questions according to the length of the given answers. For each patient Pi, three scenarios had been tested:

- The first scenario, called "one or two sentence(s) responses scenario" $(1/2_S)$, represents only questions which have responses formed only by one or two sentence(s). T_{S1}/i represents the total of the questions related to the patient Pi which have correct responses based on our approach. GS_{S1}/i represents the "gold standard" questions which have correct responses. there are given by the caregiver Ci.
- The second scenario, called "Three or four sentences responses scenario" $(3/4_S)$, represents only questions which have responses formed by three or four sentences. T_{S2}/i represents the total of the questions related to the patient Pi which have correct responses based on our approach. GS_{S2}/i given by the caregiver Ci represents the "gold standard" questions which have correct responses.
- The third scenario, called "More than four sentences responses scenario" $(>4_S)$, represents only questions which have responses formed by more than

four sentences. T_{S3}/i represents the total of the questions related to the patient Pi which have correct responses based on our approach. GS_{S3}/i given by the caregiver Ci represents the "gold standard" questions that have correct responses.

For each scenario, we compare the generated collection of questions against the golden standard ones. The exact Precision measures Pi@$1/2_S$ $((|T_{S1}/i \cap GS_{S1}/i| / |T_{S1}/i|))$, Pi@$3/4_S$ and Pi@$>4_S$ represent respectively, the precision values related to the first, second and third scenarios of the patient Pi. The exact Recall measures Ri@$1/2_S$ $((|T_{S1}/i \cap GS_{S1}/i| / |GS_{S1}/i|))$, Ri@$3/4_S$ and Ri@$>4_S$ represent respectively, the Recall values related to the first, second and third scenarios of the patient P_i. Figure 3 shows the results. The results obtained are encouraging. We noticed that the analysis of short sentences presents the highest measures of recall and precision. As the sentence gets longer, there will be a more complex calculation, which reduces the system's performance. We believe that these results can be improved. In fact, we think that we can improve the learning stage by adding other features besides the lexical, semantic and syntactico-semantic features.

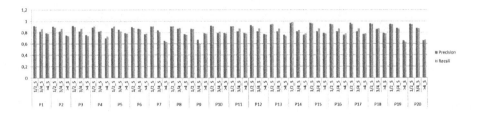

Fig. 3. The obtained rsults.

5 Conclusion and Perspectives

In this paper, we proposed a multilingual semantic similarity approach for question-answering systems. it estimates the similarity score between the user's answer and the one saved in data tier. Compared to related work, it takes into account the synonymy relations between words and the semantic arguments properties notably semantic class and thematic role. It supports three languages: English, French and Arabic. A prototype based on the approach is implemented. It is integrated in Autobiographical Training which is a multilingual ontology-based question-answering training for Alzheimer's patients. An experimental evaluation is performed. The obtained results are promising. Our approach is mainly proposed to be integrated in Autobiographical Training and it can be applied in other question-answering systems. Moreover, our approach can be incorporated in other applications, such as automatic summarization and data clustering. As for the future perspectives to our work, we will improve the approach in order to disambiguate word sense by other types of semantic relationships such as homonyms.

References

1. Agirre, E., Cer, D., Diab, M., Gonzalez-Agirre, A., Guo, W.: SEM 2013 shared task: semantic textual similarity, including a pilot on typed-similarity. In: In* SEM 2013: The Second Joint Conference on Lexical and Computational Semantics. Association for Computational Linguistics. Citeseer (2013)
2. Anjaneyulu, M., Sarma, S.S.V.N., Vijaya Pal Reddy, P., Prem Chander, K., Nagaprasad, S.: Sentence similarity using syntactic and semantic features for multi-document summarization. In: Bhattacharyya, S., Hassanien, A.E., Gupta, D., Khanna, A., Pan, I. (eds.) International Conference on Innovative Computing and Communications. LNNS, vol. 56, pp. 471–485. Springer, Singapore (2019). https://doi.org/10.1007/978-981-13-2354-6_49
3. Course, L.: Lexical semantics of verbs vi: assessing semantic determinants of argument realization, July 2009
4. Ferreira, R., Lins, R.D., Simske, S.J., Freitas, F., Riss, M.: Assessing sentence similarity through lexical, syntactic and semantic analysis. Comput. Speech Lang. **39**, 1–28 (2016)
5. Gad, W.K., Kamel, M.S.: New semantic similarity based model for text clustering using extended gloss overlaps. In: Perner, P. (ed.) MLDM 2009. LNCS (LNAI), vol. 5632, pp. 663–677. Springer, Heidelberg (2009). https://doi.org/10.1007/978-3-642-03070-3_50
6. Herradi, N., Hamdi, F., Métais, E., Ghorbel, F., Soukane, A.: PersonLink: an ontology representing family relationships for the CAPTAIN MEMO memory prosthesis. In: Jeusfeld, M.A., Karlapalem, K. (eds.) ER 2015. LNCS, vol. 9382, pp. 3–13. Springer, Cham (2015). https://doi.org/10.1007/978-3-319-25747-1_1
7. Islam, A., Inkpen, D.: Semantic text similarity using corpus-based word similarity and string similarity. ACM Trans. Knowl. Discov. Data (TKDD) **2**(2), 10 (2008)
8. Jaccard, P.: Etude comparative de la distribution florale dans une portion des Alpes et du Jura. Impr. Corbaz (1901)
9. Khemakhem, A., Gargouri, B., Hamadou, A.B., Francopoulo, G.: ISO standard modeling of a large arabic dictionary. Nat. Lang. Eng. **22**, 1–31 (2015)
10. Lehmann, J., et al.: DBpedia - a large-scale, multilingual knowledge base extracted from Wikipedia. Semant. Web J. **6**(2), 167–195 (2015). http://jens-lehmann.org/files/2015/swjdbpedia.pdf
11. Li, Y., Mclean, D., Bandar, Z., O'Shea, J., Crockett, K.: Sentence similarity based on semantic nets and corpus statistics. IEEE Trans. Knowl. Data Eng. **18**(8), 1138–1150 (2006). https://doi.org/10.1109/TKDE.2006.130
12. Manning, C.D., Surdeanu, M., Bauer, J., Finkel, J., Bethard, S.J., McClosky, D.: The stanford CoreNLP natural language processing toolkit. In: Association for Computational Linguistics (ACL) System Demonstrations, pp. 55–60 (2014). http://www.aclweb.org/anthology/P/P14/P14-5010
13. Metais, E., et al.: Memory prosthesis. Non-Pharmacol. Ther. Dement. **3**(2), 177–180 (2015). ISSN 1949-484X
14. Miller, G.A.: WordNet: a lexical database for English. Commun. ACM **38**(11), 39–41 (1995). https://doi.org/10.1145/219717.219748
15. Oliva, J., Serrano, J.I., del Castillo, M.D., Iglesias, Á.: SyMSS: a syntax-based measure for short-text semantic similarity. Data Knowl. Eng. **70**(4), 390–405 (2011)
16. Schuler, K.K.: VerbNet: a broad-coverage, comprehensive verb lexicon. Ph.D. thesis, University of Pennsylvania (2006). http://verbs.colorado.edu/~kipper/Papers/dissertation.pdf

17. Silberztein, M., Váradi, T., Tadić, M.: Open source multi-platform NooJ for NLP. In: Proceedings of COLING 2012: Demonstration Papers, pp. 401–408. The COLING 2012 Organizing Committee, Mumbai, December 2012. https://www.aclweb.org/anthology/C12-3050
18. Sultan, M.A., Bethard, S., Sumner, T.: Dls@ cu: sentence similarity from word alignment. In: Proceedings of the 8th International Workshop on Semantic Evaluation (SemEval 2014), pp. 241–246 (2014)

From Attribute Relationship Diagrams to Process (BPMN) and Decision (DMN) Models

Krzysztof Kluza[(✉)], Piotr Wiśniewski, Weronika T. Adrian, and Antoni Ligęza

AGH University of Science and Technology,
al. A. Mickiewicza 30, 30-059 Krakow, Poland
{kluza,wpiotr,wta,ligeza}@agh.edu.pl

Abstract. Business Process Model and Notation (BPMN) is a well established standard for modeling and managing process knowledge of organizations. Recently, the Decision Model and Notation (DMN) standard has been proposed as a complementary technique to enact particular type of knowledge, namely the organizational rules (decision logic). An integrated model of processes and rules may bring numerous benefits to the knowledge management systems, but the modeling process itself is not a trivial task. To this end, methods that facilitate prototyping and semi-automatic construction of the integrated model are of great importance. In this paper, we propose a method for generating business processes with decisions in BPMN+DMN standards, using a prototyping method called ARD. We present an algorithm that, starting from an ARD model, generates an executable process model along with decision specification. Such a model can be treated as a structured rule base that provides explicit inference flow determined by the process control flow.

1 Introduction

Knowledge acquisition – extracting, structuring and organizing knowledge – is a non-trivial stage of knowledge management process. When it comes to processes and rules, they are usually modeled manually by business analysts. These models are based on pieces of information acquired from structured interviews or documentation provided by the company (such as system descriptions, requirement specifications or documents describing products and services). During modeling, the analysts use their knowledge and experience, but the procedure is not a clearly defined mapping. Thus, it can be seen as it would involve the famous ATAMO[1] procedure to obtain Business Processes and Business Rules. Depending on the representation languages, resulting models must often have be significantly refined or implemented in order to be executed.

The paper is supported by the AGH UST research grant.

[1] "And then a miracle occurs" – the phrase, popularized by the Sidney Harris cartoon, is often used in BPM papers to describe procedures which take place but are hard to describe or algorithmize, e.g. [1,2].

© Springer Nature Switzerland AG 2019
C. Douligeris et al. (Eds.): KSEM 2019, LNAI 11775, pp. 615–627, 2019.
https://doi.org/10.1007/978-3-030-29551-6_55

This paper proposes a method that supports designing business processes with decisions. In particular, we propose to generate process models integrated with decision models from Attribute Relationship Diagrams (ARD) [3]. ARD is a knowledge representation method for structured specification of a system. ARD specification can be prepared manually as described in [4] or using data mining methods as proposed in [5]. ARD models preparation is out of scope for this paper, so we only give a brief overview of it using an illustrative case study. The method presented in this paper is a refinement of the one described in [6]. In particular, the original method has been adapted for the Decision Model and Notation (DMN) OMG standard.

The ARD method was proposed as a simple method for generating a knowledge base structure [4]. Based on the ARD *dependencies*, it is possible to generate schemes of decision tables. These schemes can be then filled with rules, either manually by a domain expert, or automatically – mined from some additional data (like in the case of decision models, e.g. [7,8]).

The rest of this paper is organized as follows: Sect. 2 presents an overview of the notations considered in the paper. In Sect. 3, we give an overview of the algorithm for generating a process model integrated with the decision model. Section 4 provides an illustrative example concerning the presented algorithm. The paper is summarized in Sect. 5.

2   Preliminaries

In this section, we introduce and explain all the considered notations, namely ARD, BPMN and DMN, that will be used in the generation algorithm.

2.1   Attribute Relationship Diagrams

Attribute Relationship Diagrams (ARD) is a method that aims at capturing relations between "attributes" of a considered system. These "attributes" denote the system's selected properties or variables considered in decision logic. Originally, ARD was introduced in [4] as a method for prototyping a knowledge base structure in a similar way as the relational database structure is generated from the ERD diagrams, and as a simple alternative to the classic approaches [9].

The process of creating an ARD model is iterative and hierarchical. Its aim is to define increasingly detailed models, from a general conceptualization to a very specific one, and keep the functional dependencies between the models. The fragments of the below formalization were partially presented in [10] and developed in [6].

Let us consider the set C of *conceptual attributes*, the set A of *physical attributes*, the set P of *properties*, the set D of *dependencies* and the set Q consisting of *derivations*, defined as follows.

Definition 1. *A **conceptual attribute** $c \in C$ is an attribute describing some general, abstract aspect of the specified system.*

Conceptual attribute name starts with a capital letter, e.g. `Measures`. During the design process, conceptual attributes are refined into, possibly multiple, physical attributes.

Definition 2. *A **physical attribute** $a \in A$ is an attribute describing a specific, well-defined, atomic aspect of the specified system.*

Names of physical attributes are not capitalized, e.g. `weight`. A physical attribute origins (indirectly) from one or more conceptual attributes and cannot be further refined.

Definition 3. *A **property** $p \in P$ is a non-empty set of attributes ($p \subseteq A \cup C$) describing the property and representing a piece of knowledge about a certain part of the system being designed. A **simple property** $p \in P^s$ is a property consisting of a single attribute ($|p| = 1$). A **complex property** $p \in P^c$ is a property consisting of multiple attributes ($|p| > 1$). Note that $P = P^s \cup P^c$.*

Definition 4. *A **dependency** $d \in D$ is an ordered pair of properties (f, t), where $f \in P$ is the **independent property** and $t \in P$ is the **dependent property** that depends on f. If $f = t$ the property is called **self-dependent**. For notational convention $d = (f, t), d \in D, D \subseteq P \times P$ will be presented as: $d(f, t)^2$.*

A (functional) dependency is a relation between two properties that shows that in order to determine the dependent property attribute values, values of the attributes of the independent property are needed.

Definition 5. *A **derivation** $q \in Q$ is an ordered pair of properties (f, t), where $t \in P$ is derived from $f \in P$ upon a transformation. Similarly to dependency $Q \subseteq P \times P$, however $D \cap Q = \emptyset$.*

Definition 6. *A **Design Process Diagram** G_D is a triple (P, D, Q), where:*

- *P is a set of properties,*
- *D is a set of dependencies,*
- *Q is a set of derivations.*

The DPD diagram is a directed graph with properties as nodes and both dependencies and derivations as edges.

Definition 7. *An **Attribute Relationship Diagram** G_A is a pair (P_{ARD}, D), where:*

- *there is a $G_D = (P, D, Q)$,*
- *P_{ARD} is a subset of G_D properties ($P_{ARD} \subseteq P$) such that $P_{ARD} = \{p_i \in P \colon \forall_{p_j \in P} (p_i, p_j) \notin Q\}$,*
- *and D is a set of dependencies.*

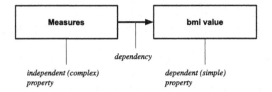

Fig. 1. An example of a simple ARD diagram

An ARD diagram can be depicted as a graph with the properties represented as nodes and dependencies represented as edges.

To illustrate the ARD concepts, a fragment of an exemplary ARD diagram with two properties and the dependency between them is presented in Fig. 1.

The diagram should be interpreted in the following way: bmi value depends on some Measures. Note that in other modeling languages, the dependency is often modeled inversely, i.e. as an arrow pointing from a dependent object to an independent one, e.g. in UML.

2.2   ARD Design Process

Specification of ARD is an iterative process that serves as a tool for diagram specification. The diagram transformations constitute the core aspects of the ARD method. They transform a property into one or more properties, specifying new derivations and dependencies into a G_D model. These transformations are also required in order to introduce new attributes. For the transformation of properties from the diagram G_A^1 into the properties in diagram G_A^2, the properties in the G_A^2 diagram are more specific than in the G_A^1.

During the design process, the ARD model becomes more and more specific. The transformations can be depicted in a hierarchical Transformation Process History (TPH) model as defined below and presented in Fig. 2.

Definition 8. *A **Transformation Process History** G_T is a pair (P, Q), where P and Q are properties and dependencies respectively from the existing $G_D = (P, D, Q)$.*

A TPH diagram forms a tree with properties as nodes and derivations as edges. It denotes what particular property or what attributes a particular property attribute is refined into. Such a diagram stores the history of the design process. ARD physical attributes may be further refined in order to specify the type of the attribute (or the domain of the attribute).

2.3   ARD Case Study Example

As a case example for presenting how the proposed method works, we will use the case based on Quetelet index or the so called Body Mass Index (BMI), which

---

[2] $d(f, t)$ denotes a dependency d from a property f to a property t.

is a value derived from the weight and height of a person. It is defined as the body mass (in kilograms) divided by the square of the body height (in metres). Using these two input values one can calculate the BMI value, which next can be interpreted based on the sex of the person. At the end, a proper health advice can be given to the specific person.

Using the ARD design process, we designed a simple "Health advisor" tool. The history of ARD transformations is presented in Fig. 2, while the final ARD model corresponding to this transformation history is shown in Fig. 3.

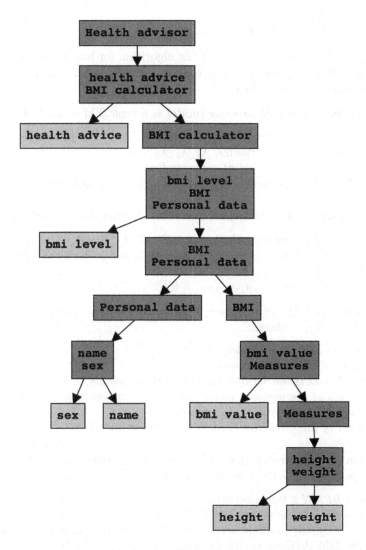

Fig. 2. Transformation process history for BMI example

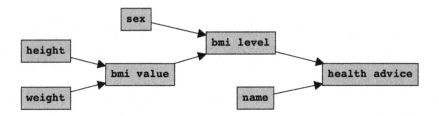

Fig. 3. Attribute relationship diagram for BMI example

2.4   BPMN and DMN Formalization

For the purpose of the description of the algorithm for integrated model generation from ARD diagrams, let us introduce a simplified business process model integrated with decision model.

Definition 9. *A **BPMN process model** is a tuple* $\mathcal{PM} = (\mathcal{O}, \mathcal{F}, \Lambda)$, *where:*

- $\mathcal{O}$ *is the set of flow objects,* $o_1, o_2, o_3, \dots \in \mathcal{O}$,
- Λ *is the set of model attributes,* $\lambda_1, \lambda_2, \lambda_3, \dots \in \Lambda$,
- $\mathcal{F} \subset \mathcal{O} \times \mathcal{O} \times 2^{\Lambda_{\mathcal{F}}}$ *is the set of sequence flows,*
  where $\Lambda_{\mathcal{F}} \subset \Lambda$ *is a subset of attributes that are used in sequence flows.*

The set $\mathcal{O}$ of flow objects is divided into three distinct sets $\mathcal{O} = \mathcal{A} \cup \mathcal{E} \cup \mathcal{G}$:

- $\mathcal{A}$ *is the set of activities such that* $\mathcal{A} = \mathcal{T} \cup \mathcal{S}$, $\mathcal{T} \cap \mathcal{S} = \emptyset$,
  where $\mathcal{T}$ is the set of tasks $(\tau_1, \tau_2, \tau_3, \dots \in \mathcal{T})$ and $\mathcal{S}$ is the set of sub-processes,
- $\mathcal{E}$ is the set of events, $e_1, e_2, e_3, \dots \in \mathcal{E}$
- $\mathcal{G}$ is the set of gateways, $g_1, g_2, g_3, \dots \in \mathcal{G}$.

Definition 10. *A **DMN decision requirement diagram** is a tuple* $\mathcal{DM} = (\mathcal{D}, \mathcal{I}, \mathcal{R}, T_{\mathcal{D}})$, *where:*

- $\mathcal{D}$ *is the set of decision nodes,*
- $\mathcal{I}$ *is the set of input data nodes,*
- $\mathcal{R} \subseteq \mathcal{D} \cup \mathcal{I} \times \mathcal{D}$ *is the set of information requirements,*
- $T_{\mathcal{D}}$ *is a set of the decision tables related to decision nodes (usually a single decision table for a specific decision node),*
- A *is a set of the attributes used in the decision model.*

Definition 11. ***Business process model integrated with the decision model*** *is a tuple:* $\mathcal{M} = (\mathcal{PM}, \mathcal{DM}, map)$, *where:*

- $\mathcal{PM}$ *is a BPMN 2.0 process model,*
- $\mathcal{DM}$ *is a decision model,*
- *map is a mapping function between the Business Rule tasks and the decisions from the* $\mathcal{DM}$ *decision model, i.e. map:* $\mathcal{T}_{BusinessRule} \to \mathcal{D}$.

This simple notation presented above will be used in the next section for description of the algorithm.

3   Algorithm for Generating Process Model Integrated With Decision Model from Attribute Relationship Diagram

The ARD method allows an expert to gradually identify the properties of a system being designed. Having the properties identified and described in terms of attributes, we adapted the algorithm presented in [6], so it can generate an executable BPMN process model with the corresponding DMN decision model.

Input for the algorithm:

- an ARD diagram G_A consisting of simple properties with physical attributes,
- additionally, the corresponding TPH diagram G_T, and the depth *level* for deriving the attributes.

Output of the algorithm:

- a business process model integrated with the decision model $\mathcal{M}$.

Goal: Automatically build a process model integrated with decision model based on the ARD diagram (optionally supported by TPH diagram).

3.1   Algorithm Draft

1. Create a new process model integrated with decision model $\mathcal{M} = (\mathcal{PM}, \mathcal{DM}, map)$.
2. Select the set A_{tmp} consisting of the *ARD* input attributes (i.e. which occur only as independent or self-dependent properties in the set of dependencies) and the set D_{tmp} consisting of dependencies with these attributes, i.e.:
   $A_{tmp} = \{a \in A\colon (a \in f_i) \wedge ((\exists_{t_j \in P}\ d(f_i, t_j) \in D \wedge \not\exists_{t_k \in P}\ d(t_k, f_i) \in D) \vee (d(f_i, f_i) \in D))\}$, $D_{tmp} = \{d(f_i, t) \in D\colon \exists_{a \in A}\ a \in f_i\}$.
3. Loop for each dependency $d \in D_{tmp}\colon d(f, t), f \neq t$:
   (a) Select all independent properties (other than f) that t depends on.
       Let $F_t = \{f_t^i \in P\colon d(f_t^i, t) \wedge f_t^i \neq f\}$.
       Remove the considered dependencies from the set: $D_{tmp} := D_{tmp} \setminus F_t$.
   (b) Select all dependent properties (other than t) that depend only on f.
       Let $T_f = \{t_f^i \in P\colon d(f, t_f^i), t_f^i \neq t, \not\exists_{f_x}\ (d(f_x, t_f^i), f_x \neq f)\}$.
       Remove the considered dependencies from the set: $D_{tmp} := D_{tmp} \setminus T_f$.
   (c) Based on F_t and T_f create Business Rule tasks and add them to the $\mathcal{T}_{BR}$ set[3]. Create also a corresponding decision ($\delta \in \mathcal{D}$) with the decision table ($t_{\mathcal{DM}} \in T_{\mathcal{DM}}$). A BR task ($\tau_{BR} \in \mathcal{T}_{BusinessRule}$) is related to the corresponding decision. For developing decision table schema, see the algorithm presented in Sect. 3.2.

---

[3] For simplicity, $\mathcal{T}_{BusinessRule}$ will be denoted as $\mathcal{T}_{BR}$, and its elements as τ_{BR}^1, τ_{BR}^2.

4. Based on the A_{tmp} set of input attributes and the TPH model, select the set C_{tmp} of high-level conceptual attributes from which these input attributes are derived, i.e. $C_{tmp} = \{c \in C \colon \exists_{a \in A_{tmp}} \ c \in derive(a, level)\}$[4].

5. For each conceptual attribute $c \in C_{tmp}$ create a new τ^c_{User} User task "Enter $name(c)$"[5], and add it to the $\mathcal{T}_{User}$ set, and connect each User task from the $\mathcal{T}_{User}$ set using control flow with the proper BR tasks that require the input attributes related to the User task (with g_+ parallel gateway if necessary[6]).

6. Create the Start event e_{Start} and connect it with all User tasks from the $\mathcal{T}_{User}$ set using control flow (with g_+ parallel gateway if necessary).

7. Select the set D_{tmp} consisting of all dependencies that have no input attributes in properties, i.e. $D_{tmp} = \{d(f_i, t_i) \in D \colon \forall_{a \in A_{tmp}} \ a \notin f_i \wedge a \notin t_i\}$, and the set A_{tmp} consisting of all the attributes occurring in these dependencies, i.e. $A_{tmp} = \{a \in A \colon \exists_{\substack{f_i \in P \\ t_i \in P \\ d(f_i,t_i) \in D}} \ a \in f_i \vee a \in t_i\}$, and go to step 3.

8. Using control flow, connect the BR tasks from the $\mathcal{T}_{BR}$ set one another (with g_+ parallel gateway if necessary) according to the following rule: two BR tasks $\tau^1_{BR}, \tau^2_{BR} \in \mathcal{T}_{BR}$ should be connected if a decision table schema in the decision corresponding to the task τ^2_{BR} contains at least one attribute a as an input attribute which is an output attribute of the decision table schema corresponding to τ^1_{BR}.

9. Select a subset $\mathcal{T}^{out}_{BR}$ of $\mathcal{T}_{BR}$, consisting of BR tasks that have no outcoming control flows[7], i.e. $\mathcal{T}^{out}_{BR} = \{\tau \in \mathcal{T}_{BR} \colon \ \nexists_{o \in \mathcal{O}} \ (\tau, o, \Lambda_{\tau, o}) \in \mathcal{F}\}$.
Select the high-level conceptual attribute c from which the output attributes of task from $\mathcal{T}^{out}_{BR}$ are derived, i.e. $c \in derive(A^{dec}_{\delta_{\mathcal{DM}}}, level)$, where $map(\tau) = \delta_{\mathcal{DM}} \wedge \tau \in \mathcal{T}^{out}_{BR}$.

10. Add a User task τ^{end}_{User} "Display $name(c)$"[8] and connect the selected tasks from $\mathcal{T}^{out}_{BR}$ with it.

11. Create the End event e_{End} and connect the User task τ^{end}_{User} with it, i.e. $(\tau^{end}_{User}, e_{End}, \Lambda_{\tau^{end}_{User}, e_{End}}) \in \mathcal{F}$.

12. Return $\mathcal{M}$.

3.2   Algorithm for Decision Table Schemes Development

A schema for a decision table $(t_{\mathcal{DM}} \in T_{\mathcal{DM}})$ corresponding to decision $\delta \in \mathcal{D}$ related to a BR task $(\tau_{BR} \in \mathcal{T}_{BusinessRule})$ can be developed as follows:

---

[4] The function $derive(a, level)$ returns a set consisting of a conceptual attribute which was finalized into the given attribute a.

[5] If a particular conceptual attribute covers a single input attribute, create a User task "Enter $name(a)$" instead.

[6] The g_+ parallel gateway is necessary if there are more than one BR tasks to be connected.

[7] This subset of output BR tasks should not be empty.

[8] If there is only one output attribute, its name should be used instead of $name(c)$.

1. if $F_t = T_f = \emptyset$, create a new τ_{BR} BR task "Determine[9] $name(t)$", where $name(t)$ is a name of the t attribute, and associate the task with the following decision $map(\tau_{BR}) = \delta_{DM}$ related to the table with the schema: $f \mid t$, i.e. $schema(t_{DM}) = (\{f\}, \{t\})$.

2. if $F_t \neq \emptyset, T_f = \emptyset$, create a new τ_{BR} BR task "Determine $name(t)$" and associate the task with the following decision $map(\tau_{BR}) = \delta_{DM}$ related to the table with the schema: $f, f_t^1, f_t^2, \ldots \mid t$, i.e. $schema(t_{DM}) = (\{f, f_t^1, f_t^2, \ldots\}, \{t\})$.

3. if $F_t = \emptyset, T_f \neq \emptyset$, create a new τ_{BR} BR task "Determine $name(T_f \cup \{t\})$", where $name(T_f)$ is a name of the lower-level conceptual attribute from which all the $T_f \cup \{t\}$ attributes are derived[10], and associate the task with the following decision: $map(\tau_{BR}) = \delta_{DM}$ related to the table with the schema: $schema(t_{DM}) = (\{f\}, \{t, t_f^1, t_f^2, \ldots\})$, and $map(\tau_{BR}) = \delta_{DM}$.

4. if $F_t \neq \emptyset, T_f \neq \emptyset$, create new two τ_{BR}^1, τ_{BR}^2 BR tasks "Determine $name(t)$" and "Determine $name(T_f)$", and associate them with the following decisions related to the decision table schemes respectively: $f, f_t^1, f_t^2, \ldots \mid t$ and $f \mid t_f^1, t_f^2, \ldots$, i.e.:
$schema(t_{DM}^1) = (\{f, f_t^1, f_t^2, \ldots\}, \{t\})$, $map(\tau_{BR}^1) = \delta_{DM}^1$,
$schema(t_{DM}^2) = (\{f\}, \{t_f^1, t_f^2, \ldots\})$, and $map(\tau_{BR}^2) = \delta_{DM}^2$.

4   Case Example

To present the described algorithm, we use a simple but illustrative BMI case study example. Figure 4 depicts the result BPMN and DMN models. The red lines depicts the main steps of the translation. In this case, we used the depth $level = 2$.

In the case of the schemes for the decision tables, these are as follows:

1. $map(\tau_{BR}^1) = \delta_{DM}^1$, $schema(\delta_{DM}^1) = (\{height, weight\}, \{bmi\ value\})$,
2. $map(\tau_{BR}^2) = \delta_{DM}^2$, $schema(\delta_{DM}^2) = (\{sex, bmi\ value\}, \{bmi\ level\})$,
3. $map(\tau_{BR}^2) = \delta_{DM}^2$, $schema(\delta_{DM}^2) = (\{bmi\ level, name\}, \{health\ advice\})$.

Figure 5 shows various results depending on different values of the depth $level$ variable. In the case of decision level, the similar concept may be considered. Adjusting the decision depth level require some changes in the algorithm for decision table schemes development as a BR task ($\tau_{BR} \in \mathcal{T}_{Business\,Rule}$) would have to correspond not to a single decision $\delta \in \mathcal{D}$, but to a subset of decisions. This will influence both process model (as shown in Fig. 6) and DMN decision model (see the groups representing various subsets of decisions depending on the considering decision depth level in Fig. 6).

---

[9] For user-friendliness of task names, if the attribute t is of the symbolic type or derived one, the word "Determine" should be used in the task name. In other cases (i.e. numeric types), one can use the word "Calculate" instead.

[10] The conceptual attribute name can be found in the corresponding TPH model, if it is available for the algorithm. In other case, in the task name the names of all the attributes from the T_f set can be used.

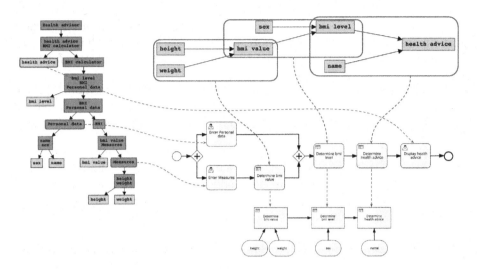

Fig. 4. BPMN and DMN models generated using the presented algorithm with the depth *level* = 2.

When it comes to the level 0, every business rule task is mapped to a single specific decision. In the case of higher decision depth levels, a single business rule task may be mapped into several tables, e.g. the model at the highest level contains exactly single Business Rule task, which is connected to a single DMN model with all decisions.

5   Summary

The paper provides an overview of the method for generation of business process model integrated with decision model. The proposed method uses an ARD diagram as a base for generating the model.

The result of the presented method is an executable process model with decision model (containing e.g. decision table with schemes for rules). Such a model can be useful for rapid prototyping or for simulation. These prototype models can be then quickly refined with information needed for complete execution (e.g. rules) and executed in any run-time environment supporting BPMN and DMN (Fig. 7).

For future work, we plan to evaluate the performance of the proposed algorithm and compare it with other existing proposals for BPMN+DMN generation [8,11,12]. Moreover, we will apply our method to a series of real-world use cases, to analyze the complexity of the generated models in realistic applications.

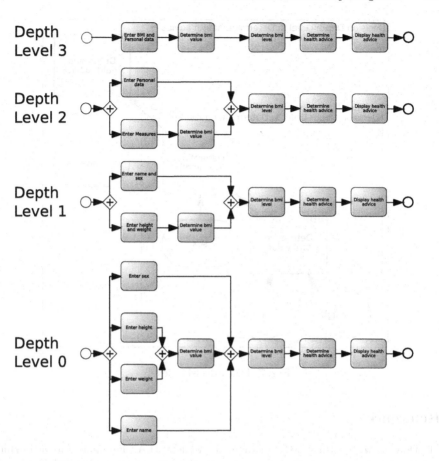

Fig. 5. BPMN model generated using the presented algorithm with various depth *level* variable.

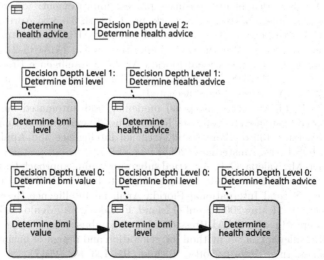

Fig. 6. BPMN decision levels

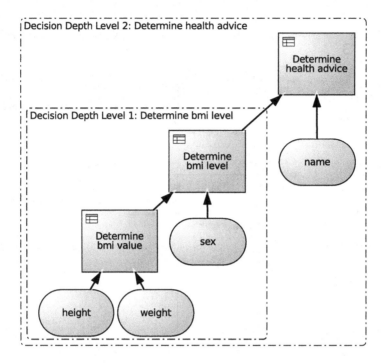

Fig. 7. DMN decision levels

References

1. Dumas, M., La Rosa, M., Mendling, J., Reijers, H.A.: Fundamentals of Business Process Management. Springer, Berlin (2013). https://doi.org/10.1007/978-3-642-33143-5
2. Forster, F.: The idea behind business process improvement: toward a business process improvement pattern framework, pp. 1–13. BPTrends, April 2006
3. Nalepa, G.J., Wojnicki, I.: Towards formalization of ARD+ conceptual design and refinement method. In Wilson, D.C., Lane, H.C. (eds.) FLAIRS-21: Proceedings of the Twenty-First International Florida Artificial Intelligence Research Society conference: 15–17 May 2008, Coconut Grove, Florida, USA, Menlo Park, California, pp. 353–358. AAAI Press (2008, accepted)
4. Nalepa, G.J., Ligęza, A.: Conceptual modelling and automated implementation of rule-based systems. In: Software Engineering: Evolution and Emerging Technologies. Volume 130 of Frontiers in Artificial Intelligence and Applications, pp. 330–340. IOS Press, Amsterdam (2005)
5. Atzmueller, M., Nalepa, G.J.: A textual subgroup mining approach for rapid ARD+ model capture. In Lane, H.C., Guesgen, H.W. (eds.) FLAIRS-22: Proceedings of the Twenty-Second International Florida Artificial Intelligence Research Society Conference: 19–21 May 2009, Sanibel Island, Florida, USA, Menlo Park, California, FLAIRS, pp. 414–415. AAAI Press (2009, to be published)
6. Kluza, K., Nalepa, G.J.: A method for generation and design of business processes with business rules. Inform. Softw. Technol. **91**, 123–141 (2017)

7. Bazhenova, E., Weske, M.: Deriving decision models from process models by enhanced decision mining. In: Reichert, M., Reijers, H.A. (eds.) BPM 2015. LNBIP, vol. 256, pp. 444–457. Springer, Cham (2016). https://doi.org/10.1007/978-3-319-42887-1_36

8. Batoulis, K., Meyer, A., Bazhenova, E., Decker, G., Weske, M.: Extracting decision logic from process models. In: Zdravkovic, J., Kirikova, M., Johannesson, P. (eds.) CAiSE 2015. LNCS, vol. 9097, pp. 349–366. Springer, Cham (2015). https://doi.org/10.1007/978-3-319-19069-3_22

9. Vanthienen, J., Wets, G.: From decision tables to expert system shells. Data Knowl. Eng. **13**(3), 265–282 (1994)

10. Kluza, K., Nalepa, G.J.: Towards rule-oriented business process model generation. In Ganzha, M., Maciaszek, L.A., Paprzycki, M. (eds.) Proceedings of the Federated Conference on Computer Science and Information Systems - FedCSIS 2013, Krakow, Poland, 8–11 September 2013, pp. 959–966. IEEE (2013)

11. Bazhenova, E., Zerbato, F., Oliboni, B., Weske, M.: From BPMN process models to dmn decision models. Inform. Syst. **83**, 69–88 (2019)

12. De Smedt, J., Hasić, F., vanden Broucke, S.K.L.M., Vanthienen, J.: Towards a holistic discovery of decisions in process-aware information systems. In: Carmona, J., Engels, G., Kumar, A. (eds.) BPM 2017. LNCS, vol. 10445, pp. 183–199. Springer, Cham (2017). https://doi.org/10.1007/978-3-319-65000-5_11

Building Chinese Legal Hybrid Knowledge Network

Sheng Bi⬤, Yanhui Huang⬤, Xiya Cheng⬤, Meng Wang$^{(\boxtimes)}$⬤,
and Guilin Qi⬤

School of Computer Science and Engineering, Southeast University, Nanjing, China
{bisheng,haungyanhui,chengxiya,meng.wang,gqi}@seu.edu.cn

Abstract. Knowledge graphs play an important role in many applications, such as data integration, natural language understanding and semantic search. Recently, there has been some work on constructing legal knowledge graphs from legal judgments. However, they suffer from some problems. First, existing work follows the Western legal system, thus cannot be applied to other legal systems, such as Asian legal systems; Second, existing work intends to build a precise legal knowledge graph, which is often not effective, especially when constructing the precise relationship between legal terms. To solve these problems, in this paper, we propose a framework for constructing a legal hybrid knowledge network from Chinese encyclopedia and legal judgments. First, we construct a network of legal terms through encyclopedia data. Then, we build a legal knowledge graph through Chinese legal judgments which captures the strict logical connections in the legal judgments. Finally, we build a Chinese legal hybrid knowledge network by combining the network of legal terms and the legal knowledge graph. We also evaluate the algorithms which are used to build the legal hybrid knowledge network on a real-world dataset. Experimental results demonstrate the effectiveness of these algorithms.

Keywords: Legal knowledge graphs · Legal judgments ·
Chinese encyclopedia · Legal hybrid knowledge network

1 Introduction

Knowledge graphs, which belong to the field of knowledge engineering, are proposed by Google in 2012. A knowledge graph is a multi-relational graph composed of entities as nodes and relations as edges with different types. Knowledge graphs are a kind of knowledge representation form, and they extract domain entities, attributes and their relationships from a large amount of text data to produce structured knowledge. The major advantage of knowledge graphs is the ability to express knowledge of complex relationships accurately and graphically, which is in line with human learning habits and can help people learn key knowledge and relationships more quickly. Therefore, knowledge graphs play an

© Springer Nature Switzerland AG 2019
C. Douligeris et al. (Eds.): KSEM 2019, LNAI 11775, pp. 628–639, 2019.
https://doi.org/10.1007/978-3-030-29551-6_56

important role in many applications, such as data integration, natural language understanding and semantic search.

Recently, there has been some work on constructing legal knowledge graphs from legal judgments. Erwin Filtz proposes a method to represent the legal data of Australia and enhances representation by semantics to build a legal knowledge graph, where unambiguous and useful interlinking of legal cases are supported [6]. European researchers start a LYNX project [13] to build a legal knowledge graph for smart compliance services in multilingual Europe. As a collection of structured data and unstructured documents, the legal knowledge graph covers different jurisdictions, comprising legislation, case law, doctrine, standards, norms, and other documents and can help companies solving questions and cases related to compliance in different sectors and jurisdictions.

However, they suffer from some problems. First, existing work follows the Western legal system, thus cannot be applied to other legal systems, such as Asian legal systems; Second, existing work intends to build a precise legal knowledge graph, which is often not effective, especially when constructing the precise relationship between legal terms. The relationship between legal terms is sometimes ambiguous and hard to be formalized.

To solve these problems, in this paper, we propose a framework for constructing a legal hybrid knowledge network from Chinese encyclopedia and legal judgments. First, we crawl many legal webs and extract original encyclopedia data, and use the high-quality encyclopedia knowledge to construct a network of legal terms. Then, we build a legal knowledge graph through Chinese legal judgments which captures the strict logical connections in the legal judgments. Finally, we combine the network of legal terms with the legal knowledge graph to produce our framework – Chinese legal hybrid knowledge network.

To sum up, in this paper, we design procedures of constructing a knowledge graph and succeed in constructing a Chinese legal hybrid knowledge network by means of data mining, text extraction, natural language processing, etc. Our contributions in this paper are listed as follows:

1. We construct a network of legal terms through encyclopedia data and build a legal knowledge graph through Chinese legal judgments which captures the strict logical connections in the legal judgments.
2. We propose a framework for constructing a legal hybrid knowledge network from Chinese encyclopedia and legal judgments.
3. We conduct extensive experiments on a real-world dataset to evaluate the algorithms which are used to build the legal hybrid knowledge network. Experimental results demonstrate the effectiveness of these algorithms.

The remainder of this paper is organized as follows. Section 2 shows a brief overview of related work. Section 3 provides the details of the approaches to building our legal hybrid knowledge network. In Sect. 4, we evaluate our algorithms and give the experimental results. In the end, Sect. 5 concludes our work.

2   Related Work

Our work is related to the work of knowledge graph construction, especially in the legal domain.

2.1   Knowledge Graph

Knowledge graph is the work on interrelated information, usually limited to a specific business domain, and managed as a graph. In the past years, there has been a large number of related work on constructing knowledge graphs. Cyc [9], one of the oldest knowledge graphs, has devoted fifteen years to build an ontology of general concepts spanning human reality in predicate logic form. Inspired by widespread used information communities like Wikipedia and The Semantic Web, the American software company Metaweb designed Freebase [4], which is a practical tuple database used to structure diverse general human knowledge with high scalability. DBPedia [1], the most famous general knowledge graph in the world, extracts structured data from Wikipedia infoboxes and makes this information accessible on the Web, supporting 125 languages and providing quantities of facts, largely focused on named entities that have Wikipedia articles. Similar to DBpedia, Yet Another Great Ontology (YAGO) [17] also extracts knowledge from Wikipedia (e.g., categories, redirects, infoboxes). Moreover, YAGO extracts information from WordNet [12] (e.g., synsets, hyponymy). Compared with DBpedia, YAGO mainly aims at an automatic fusion of knowledge extracted from diverse Wikipedia language editions, while DBpedia aims at building different knowledge graphs for each Wikipedia language edition.

Besides English knowledge graphs listed above, in recent years, many Chinese knowledge graphs have been published such as Zhishi.me, XLore and CN-DBPedia. Zhishi.me [14], the first large scale Chinese knowledge graph, extracts structural features in three largest Chinese encyclopedia sites (i.e., Baidu Baike, Hudong Baike, and Chinese Wikipedia) and proposes several data-level mapping methods for automatic link discovery. XLore [18] is a large scale multi-lingual knowledge graph by structuring and integrating Chinese Wikipedia, English Wikipedia, French Wikipedia, and Baidu Baike. Up to date, XLore contains 16284901 instances, 2466956 concepts, and 446236 properties. Since the update frequency of knowledge bases is very slow, researchers propose a never-ending Chinese Knowledge extraction system, CN-DBpedia [19]. CN-DBpedia provides the freshest knowledge with a smart active update strategy and can generate a knowledge base which is constantly updated.

2.2   Legal Knowledge Graph

With the rapid development of open knowledge graphs, researchers draw attention to knowledge graphs in specific domains, like in legal domain. Since knowledge graphs need a certain data representation so that it can be used, Erwin Filtz proposes a method to represent the legal data of Australia, mainly legal norms and court decisions in legal documents, and enhances representation by semantics to build a legal knowledge graph, where unambiguous and useful interlinking of legal cases are supported [6]. European researchers start a LYNX project [13] to build a legal knowledge graph for smart compliance services in multilingual Europe. As a collection of structured data and unstructured documents, the legal knowledge graph covers different jurisdictions, comprising legislation, case law, doctrine, standards, norms, and other documents and can help companies solve questions and cases related to compliance in different sectors and jurisdictions.

However, existing work on constructing legal knowledge graphs follows the Western legal system, thus cannot be applied to other legal systems, such as Asian legal systems. Moreover, they intend to build a precise legal knowledge graph, which is often not effective, especially when constructing the precise relationship between legal terms. The relationship between legal terms is sometimes ambiguous and hard to be formalized. In construct, in this work, we try to construct a hybrid knowledge network from Chinese encyclopedia and Chinese legal judgments, where the relationship between legal terms are not precisely defined.

3 Methods for Constructing Legal Hybrid Knowledge Network

In this section, we elaborate on our procedures of the legal hybrid knowledge network. We divide the process for building legal hybrid knowledge network into three steps. Firstly, we construct a network of legal terms through Chinese Web-based encyclopedia. Secondly, we construct a legal knowledge graph by extracting triples from legal judgments. Finally, we combine the network of legal terms and the legal knowledge graph. The overall framework is shown in Fig. 1, which indicates the general steps to develop legal hybrid knowledge network. The details of building procedures are presented in the following subsections.

3.1 Constructing Legal Terms Network

To construct a network of legal terms, we obtain a large amount of high-quality interconnected semantic data from Chinese encyclopedia, in particular, we identify important structural features in three largest Chinese encyclopedia sites (i.e., Baidu Baike[1], Hudong Baike[2], and Chinese Wikipedia[3]) for extraction and propose several data-level mapping strategies for automatic link discovery. Figure 2 shows the example of building a network of legal terms from Chinese encyclopedia. Table 1 shows the statistical results which we crawl on these websites.

From Table 1, we can see that the data sources have a wide coverage of Chinese subjects and spans many domains except legal domain. In this case, we need to select legal terms from data sources. However, it is difficult to distinguish

---

[1] https://baike.baidu.com.

[2] http://www.baike.com.

[3] https://zh.wikipedia.org.

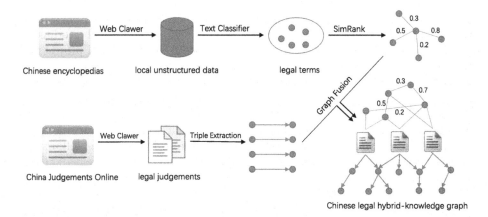

Fig. 1. The framework shows the general steps to develop the Chinese legal hybrid knowledge network. The top part is a typical process to construct a network of legal terms from Chinese encyclopedia, and the bottom part is the process to develop legal knowledge graph from legal judgments online. The lower right part indicates the final legal hybrid knowledge network.

Table 1. The statistical result of entity extracted from different Chinese encyclopedia.

Baidu Baike	Hudong Baike	Wikipedia
10434530	3728441	736540

between legal terms and common terms. What is worse, it is worthwhile to note that legal knowledge is not original data from these raw texts but should be extracted carefully from them. However, the entities extracted from Chinese encyclopedia are not clearly classified and it is to manually classify them because the size of the set of entities is too big. To solve this problem, we build a classifier to find professional legal terms from unprofessional websites.

We get legal terms in encyclopedia information by category. If the category of terms belongs to "legalese", "jurist" or "laws and articles", we consider these terms as legal related. However, these data are still not enough. To enlarge the number of legal terms, we take legal terms as seed and acquire terms that are not related to law automatically. We use these data to train a classifier.

Intuitively, the closer to legal term with the internal link, the more likely they are relevant. Assuming that the order of neighborhoods of legal terms is smaller than four, these neighborhoods are legal related and may be legal terms. In other words, the order of neighborhoods of legal entities is bigger than three, these neighborhoods have no relation with legal entities and can be regarded as negative samples. Therefore, we consider first-order, second-order and third-order neighborhoods of legal entities as possible legal entities to be classified, and other neighborhoods of legal entities as negative samples. Figure 3 indicates the structure of different order entity. For example, as for legal entities in Baidu

Baike, we consider entities whose category belongs to 'legalese', 'jurist' or 'laws and articles' as legal entities. Moreover, these legal entities have 96243 first-order neighborhoods, 1226592 second-order neighborhoods, and 8074532 third-order neighborhoods. There are 1037163 neighborhoods left which are considered to have no relation with legal entities. We select 5000 entities from 1037163 entities randomly to make a manual evaluation. The result shows that 4997 entities are irrelevant with the legal domain, which verifies the effectiveness of our hypothesis.

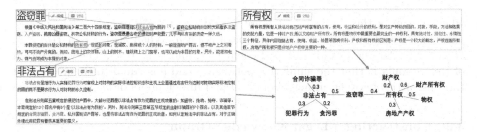

Fig. 2. The example of building network of legal terms from Chinese encyclopedia. Firstly, we obtain legal terms from three largest Chinese encyclopedia sites. Then we calculate the similarities between these legal terms. Finally, these legal terms are linked together by similarities to form a network of legal terms.

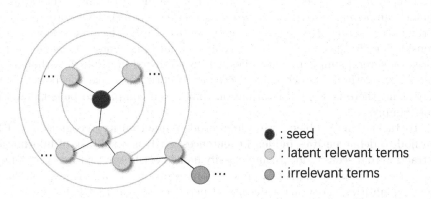

Fig. 3. We use seed as positive sample, and the neighborhoods which order bigger than three as negative sample, the rest as potential legal domain related.

We use Support Vector Machine (SVM) [16] as our classifier. We randomly select 30000 entities from 1037163 entities as negative samples, which have no relation to the legal domain. We collect 27004 professional legal terms by manual annotation as positive samples. Then we use these positive samples and negative samples to train our classifier. It is worthwhile to note that we build five classifiers and the final results are voted by these five classifiers, which improves the accuracy of classification results. Through these classifiers, we get 14925 legal entities.

After obtained enough legal entities through our classifier, we use these entities to construct our network of legal terms. In our network of legal terms, each entity is regarded as a point and entities are connected by the similarities between these entities. We use SimRank to compute similarity. The weight between entity a and entity b is computed as follows:

$$s(a,b) = \frac{C}{|I(a)||I(b)|} \sum_{i=1}^{|I(a)|} \sum_{j=1}^{|I(b)|} s(I_i(a), I_j(b)) \tag{1}$$

where $s(a,b)$ is the similarity of point a and point b. Note that when $a = b$, $s(a,b) = 1$. $I_i(a)$ is the $i - th$ in-neighbor of point a. When $I(a) = \emptyset$ or $I(b) = \emptyset$, $s(a,b) = 0$. Parameter C is damped coefficient, and $C \in (0,1)$. The description of this formula is that the similarity between a and b is equal to the average of the similarities between in-neighbors of a and in-neighbors of b.

3.2   Constructing a Legal Knowledge Graph

In this subsection, we show the details of building our legal knowledge graph. According to the definition, a knowledge graph is a special graph where nodes are entities and edges are relations. Knowledge graphs represent knowledge by using RDF-style triples (h, r, t) which describe the relation r between the first head entity h and the second tail entity t. For instance, "Beijing is the capital of China" can be represented as $(Beijing, capitalOf, China)$. Therefore, we should extract RDF-style triples from legal judgments to build a legal knowledge graph. Considering the specific standard format of legal judgments, we extract triples based on several simple manual rules, which are listed in Table 2. Although the rule-based method extracts some necessary information like the plaintiff and defendant, there is a lot of information that is too complex to be extracted by rules simply.

To tackle this problem, we adopt other named entity recognition (NER) method to define entities hidden in sentences. NER is a subtask of information extraction that seeks to locate and classify named entities in text into pre-defined categories such as the names of persons, organizations, locations, expressions of times, quantities, monetary values, and percentages. Currently, the most popular method of NER is using Conditional Random Field (CRF) [7] and Long Short-Term Memory (LSTM), which is used in this paper. Moreover, we obtain keywords and abstracts of legal judgments by the means of TextRank [10] to enrich our legal knowledge graph. TextRank is a graph-based ranking model for text processing which can be used to find the most relevant sentences in text and keywords as well. Figure 4 indicates the triple extraction and knowledge graph building process.

Fig. 4. The example of extracting triples and building knowledge graph from legal judgments. The left part is a part of legal judgment and the right part is a knowledge graph consisted of triples extracted from the legal judgment. Different relations are labelled in different colors. (Color figure online)

Table 2. Extraction rules in legal judgments.

Extraction rules	Example sentences	Triples
Plaintiff #	Plaintiff: Rose	{"subject": "xxx case", "predicate": "plaintiff", "object": "Rose"}
Defendant #	Defendant: Jack	{"subject": "xxx case", "predicate": "plaintiff", "object": "Rose"}
Judge #	Judge: Smith	{"subject": "xxx case", "predicate": "judge", "object": "Smith"}
Court clerk #	Court clerk: Nathy	{"subject": "xxx case", "predicate": "court clerk", "object": "Nathy"}

3.3 Building a Hybrid Knowledge Network

Having constructed the network of legal terms and the legal knowledge graph, we use entity links in legal judgments to combine the network and the knowledge graph to build our legal hybrid knowledge network. We use LSTM+CRF based method to recognize named entities. Then we use string matching to map these named entities to legal entities and get candidates. Note that one named entity usually corresponds to one candidate entity only. Especially, if there are more than one candidate entity corresponding to the same named entity, we should first compute the correlation between the candidate entities and the named entity respectively, then select the most relevant candidate entity. Figure 5 shows an example of the Chinese Legal Hybrid Knowledge Network.

4 Evaluation

In this section, we evaluated three algorithms used in constructing the Chinese Legal Hybrid Knowledge Network.

4.1 Evaluation of Legal Related Entity Classification

In the section of constructing a network of legal terms, we had obtained 29706 positive samples and 1037163 negative samples. For better performance, we

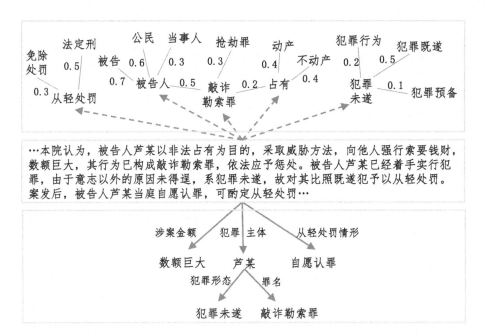

Fig. 5. The example of the Chinese legal hybrid knowledge network. We link the legal entities which are in legal judgment to network of legal terms.

built 5 classifiers totally and each classifier was trained with different features. To be specific, these features were one hot, tf-idf [15], LDA [3], doc2vec [8], word2vec [11] respectively. As mentioned above, in classification, we used SVM to perform binary classification. The training dataset included 29706 positive samples and 29706 negative samples. Note that 29706 negative samples were randomly selected from all negative samples and we updated the whole negative samples by deleting those selected samples each time. The performances of these five classifiers with different features are presented in Fig. 6.

As is shown in Fig. 6, all of our classifiers have high accuracy, recall and F1 values, which verifies the effectiveness of our methodology.

4.2   Evaluation of Named Entity Recognition

To evaluate the effect of NER, we selected 1000 legal judgments randomly as our test dataset. Three annotators who were well educated and had expertise in law were invited to find all named entities in our dataset which were used as label data. All legal judgments were annotated in IOB (short for Inside, Outside, Beginning) format. And each word was tagged with *other* or one of three entity types: *Person, Location* or *Organization*. Each line in the file represented one token with two fields: the word itself and its named entity type. In addition, we extracted chunks from source files and represented every chunk in the format of a three-element tuple: (*chunk, type, start_position*).

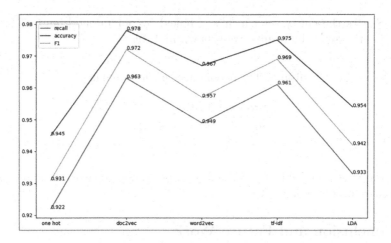

Fig. 6. The performance curves of SVM with different features.

We applied LSTM+CRF to recognize named entities. This tool first tokenized the sentences, analyzed these sentences and created their respective list of tuples. Then we compared the output list against the standard list.

We scored NER based on exact matching for entity type which measured the method's capability for accurate named entity detection. We counted TP, FP and FN, and calculated the precision and recall as follows:

$$Precision = \frac{TP}{TP + FP} \tag{2}$$

$$Recall = \frac{TP}{TP + FN} \tag{3}$$

As a result, our method took effect since the precision was 91% and the recall was 87% compared with annotated data.

4.3 Evaluation of Entity Linking

In this section, we selected 1000 legal entities randomly and there were 26000 entities labelled by law experts. The entity linking tool we used here was Fast Entity Linker Toolkit (FEL)[4]. We used recall, accuracy and F1 measure to evaluate the effect of entity linking. They were calculated as follows:

$$Precision = \frac{S_1 \bigcap T_1}{S_1} \times 100\% \tag{4}$$

$$Recall = \frac{S_1 \bigcap T_1}{T_1} \times 100\% \tag{5}$$

$$F_1 = \frac{2 * precision * recall}{precision + recall} \tag{6}$$

---

[4] https://github.com/yahoo/FEL.

where S_1 was the entity set which was linked by our method, and T_1 was the labelled entity set. The results were shown in Table 3.

Table 3. The performance of entity linking.

Precision	Recall	F1
86.21%	89.69%	87.91%

As was shown in Table 3, FEL had good performance in precision, recall and F1 measure and was of great effect.

5   Conclusion and Future Work

In this paper, we proposed a methodology for constructing a Chinese Legal Hybrid Knowledge Network. We first built a network of legal terms based on Chinese encyclopedia information and a legal knowledge graph based on the legal knowledge extracted from legal judgments online. Then we linked the network of legal terms and the legal knowledge graph by legal entities to compose our final legal hybrid knowledge network. Moreover, we evaluated the algorithms which were used to build the legal hybrid knowledge network on a real-world dataset. The results showed the effectiveness of these algorithms.

In the future, we will develop our Chinese legal hybrid knowledge network by incorporating more information. Moreover, we will try to apply our legal hybrid knowledge network to other legal applications, such as legal question answering, and similar case recommendation.

Acknowledgement. This work was supported by National Key R&D Program of China (2018YFC0830200) and National Natural Science Foundation of China Key Project (U1736204).

References

1. Auer, S., Bizer, C., Kobilarov, G., Lehmann, J., Cyganiak, R., Ives, Z.: DBpedia: a nucleus for a web of open data. In: Aberer, K., et al. (eds.) ASWC/ISWC -2007. LNCS, vol. 4825, pp. 722–735. Springer, Heidelberg (2007). https://doi.org/10.1007/978-3-540-76298-0_52
2. Benjamins, V.R., Casanovas, P., Breuker, J., Gangemi, A.: Law and the Semantic Web: Legal Ontologies, Methodologies, Legal Information Retrieval, Andapplications, vol. 3369. Springer, Heidelberg (2005). https://doi.org/10.1007/b106624
3. Blei, D.M., Ng, A.Y., Jordan, M.I.: Latent Dirichlet allocation. J. Mach. Learn. Res. **3**(Jan), 993–1022 (2003)
4. Bollacker, K., Evans, C., Paritosh, P., Sturge, T., Taylor, J.: Freebase: a collaboratively created graph database for structuring human knowledge. In: Proceedings of the 2008 ACM SIGMOD International Conference on Management of Data, pp. 1247–1250. ACM (2008)

5. Do, P.K., Nguyen, H.T., Tran, C.X., Nguyen, M.T., Nguyen, M.L.: Legal question answering using ranking SVM and deep convolutional neural network. arXiv preprint arXiv:1703.05320 (2017)
6. Filtz, E.: Building and processing a knowledge-graph for legal data. In: Blomqvist, E., Maynard, D., Gangemi, A., Hoekstra, R., Hitzler, P., Hartig, O. (eds.) ESWC 2017. LNCS, vol. 10250, pp. 184–194. Springer, Cham (2017). https://doi.org/10.1007/978-3-319-58451-5_13
7. Lafferty, J., McCallum, A., Pereira, F.C.: Conditional random fields: probabilistic models for segmenting and labeling sequence data (2001)
8. Le, Q., Mikolov, T.: Distributed representations of sentences and documents. In: International Conference on Machine Learning, pp. 1188–1196 (2014)
9. Lenat, D.B.: CYC: a large-scale investment in knowledge infrastructure. Commun. ACM **38**(11), 33–38 (1995)
10. Mihalcea, R., Tarau, P.: TextRank: bringing order into text. In: Proceedings of the 2004 Conference on Empirical Methods in Natural Language Processing (2004)
11. Mikolov, T., Chen, K., Corrado, G., Dean, J.: Efficient estimation of word representations in vector space. arXiv preprint arXiv:1301.3781 (2013)
12. Miller, G.A.: WordNet: a lexical database for English. Commun. ACM **38**(11), 39–41 (1995)
13. Montiel-Ponsoda, E., Gracia, J., Rodríguez-Doncel, V.: Building the legal knowledge graph for smart compliance services in multilingual Europe. In: CEUR workshop proceedings No. ART-2018-105821 (2018)
14. Niu, X., Sun, X., Wang, H., Rong, S., Qi, G., Yu, Y.: Zhishi.me - weaving chinese linking open data. In: Aroyo, L., et al. (eds.) ISWC 2011. LNCS, vol. 7032, pp. 205–220. Springer, Heidelberg (2011). https://doi.org/10.1007/978-3-642-25093-4_14
15. Ramos, J., et al.: Using TF-IDF to determine word relevance in document queries. In: Proceedings of the First Instructional Conference on Machine Learning, Piscataway, NJ, vol. 242, pp. 133–142 (2003)
16. Sánchez A, V.D.: Advanced support vector machines and kernel methods. Neurocomputing **55**(1–2), 5–20 (2003)
17. Suchanek, F.M., Kasneci, G., Weikum, G.: YAGO: a core of semantic knowledge. In: Proceedings of the 16th International Conference on World Wide Web, pp. 697–706. ACM (2007)
18. Wang, Z., et al.: XLore: a large-scale English-Chinese bilingual knowledge graph. In: International semantic web conference (Posters & Demos), vol. 1035, pp. 121–124 (2013)
19. Xu, B., et al.: CN-DBpedia: a never-ending Chinese knowledge extraction system. In: Benferhat, S., Tabia, K., Ali, M. (eds.) IEA/AIE 2017. LNCS (LNAI), vol. 10351, pp. 428–438. Springer, Cham (2017). https://doi.org/10.1007/978-3-319-60045-1_44

Machine Learning

Evidential Artificial Immune Recognition System

Abir Lahsoumi[(✉)] and Zied Elouedi

LARODEC, Institut Supérieur de Gestion de Tunis, Université de Tunis,
41 Avenue de la liberté, cité Bouchoucha, 2000 Le Bardo, Tunisia
Lahsoumi.abir10@gmail.com, zied.elouedi@gmx.fr

Abstract. Uncertainty is one of the main classification issues that
must be handled carefully and not rejected in order to make better
decisions. Artificial immune recognition system (AIRS) is an immune-
inspired supervised learning classifier that has shown good and competitive classification results. It works perfectly in a certain context, however
it is quite the opposite in an environment pervaded with uncertainty.
To overcome this limitation, we propose a new approach combining the
AIRS and belief function theory one of the well-know theories managing
uncertainty. Experimentations on real data sets from the U.C.I machine
learning repository show good performances of the proposed approach.

Keywords: Artificial immune recognition system (AIRS) ·
Classification · Uncertainty · Belief function theory

1 Introduction

Classification is a supervised learning technique used for predicting the label that
should be given to a new unlabeled data pattern after training and understanding
the data. AIRS was introduced in 2001 as one of the first immune systems
approaches to classification [10], it appeared to work quite well on different
classification issues and provided good results in several contexts as medical
diagnosis problems [13,19], software fault prediction problems [17], intrusion
detection problems [18], etc.

Despite the standard AIRS works very well in a certain environment, it is
not able to cope in an uncertain one, this issue has attracted a lot of attention
since handling uncertainty improves the performance and helps in better decision
making. Therefore, many research have been dealt with this kind of imperfection
in order to increase the accuracy of AIRS and to identify the significant components of AIRS that could empower it for better performance. Among these
research, we mention AIRS Fuzzy Resource Allocation [11] which is based on
the idea that resource allocation is done linearly with affinities and this linearity
requires excess resource usage in the system, which results in long classification
time and high number of memory cells. To get rid of this problem, authors in [11]
proposed to replace the linear resource allocation by fuzzy resource allocation to

© Springer Nature Switzerland AG 2019
C. Douligeris et al. (Eds.): KSEM 2019, LNAI 11775, pp. 643–654, 2019.
https://doi.org/10.1007/978-3-030-29551-6_57

improve its classification performance in two aspects namely the classification time and the reduction of the number of memory cells. This method has shown a better improvement in the majority of datasets [12]. The same authors in [13] proposed a tournament selection method into the resource competition phase by applying a fuzzy weighted preprocessing procedure based on sample means of each feature values before the application of AIRS. Two membership functions are defined known as input and output membership functions which are allowed to assign a new feature value for each feature according to its old value.

More than that, AIRS with Fuzzy KNN [14] was proposed to overcome the limitation of the original KNN used in the classification procedure to identify the diabetes diseases. The basis of the algorithm is to assign membership as a function of the vector's distance from its k-nearest neighbors and those neighbors' membership in the possible classes [14]. On the other hand, a Possibilistic AIRS was proposed in [3], which is a new classification technique based on the AIRS method within the possibility theory for handling uncertainty existing in attribute and class values of training instances via possibility distributions. This combination increased the accuracy of the classifier.

Despite the improvement of the existing works and available approaches of AIRS under uncertain environment, AIRS does not provide promising classification results due to the increase of imprecision and uncertainty in the class assignment decision procedure.

The belief function theory provides a very powerful framework to deal with epistemic uncertainty, it offers a flexible tool for modeling imperfect information and handling nicely the case of total ignorance, this theory has been successfully combined with classification techniques such as belief decision tree [15], belief neural networks [16], etc.

Therefore, in this paper, we propose a new version of AIRS combined with belief function theory to deal with uncertainty. The proposed approach is called the Evidential AIRS.

The rest of the paper is organized as follows: Sect. 2 introduces the Artificial immune recognition system. Section 3 provides some background on belief theory. Section 4 details our approach. Section 5 presents experiments and discusses the results and Sect. 6 concludes the paper.

2 The Artificial Immune Recognition System

Artificial Immune Recognition System (AIRS) is a supervised learning technique inspired by the immune system metaphors [1] including clonal selection, resource allocation, affinity maturation, etc. AIRS has shown good and competitive classification results when compared to other well-established classification techniques like decision trees, artificial neural networks, naive Bayes classifiers, etc [2].

In this work, we will use the AIRS2 which is a revisiting version of AIRS. This second version offers simplicity of implementation, more data reduction and minimizes the processing time [3].

2.1 AIRS2 Algorithm

AIRS2 is widely applied to a variety of problems in artificial intelligence, it is considered as one of the most powerful techniques of supervised learning due to its efficiency in the classification area. In this section, we succinctly describe the AIRS2 algorithm steps. Starting with the first step, namely, the learning step (the reduction phase), then the classification step which is based on the K-nearest-neighbor classifier [4].

The Learning Procedure: presents the main step in the AIRS [5]. The input of the learning step is the training set T where each instance of the training data is considered as an antigen which follows the same representation as an antibody [1]. It produces as an output a reduced data set named memory cell pool (MC). This procedure is composed of four stages: (1) initialization, (2) Memory cell identification and Artificial Recognition Balls (ARB) generation, (3) Competition for resources and development of a candidate memory cell, (4) Memory cell introduction. We will explain these stages in details:

Initialization: This stage is known as the pre-processing stage which consists of normalizing all continuous attributes in the data set such that the Euclidean distance between two data points is in the range of [0, 1]. The normalized Euclidean distance is also used as an affinity measure between two cells.

$$affinity(x,y) = Edist(x,y) = \sqrt{\sum_{i=1}^{p}(x_i - y_i)^2} \tag{1}$$

where x and y are the two attribute vectors representing two instances (cells) and p is the number of attributes.

After normalization, the affinity threshold is calculated by:

$$affinity_t hreshold(AT) = \frac{\sum_{i=1}^{n}\sum_{j=i+1}^{n} affinity(ag_i, ag_j)}{\frac{n*(n-1)}{2}} \tag{2}$$

This equation represents the mean affinity between all antigens in the training set, where n is the number of training instances (antigens), ag_i and ag_j are the ith and j^{th} antigens, and affinity(ag_i, ag_j) returns the Euclidean distance (or any other adequate distance) between the two antigens'attribute vectors. The value of AT will be used in the next stages.

The final part of this stage is the initialization of the memory cell pool (MC) by randomly choosing 0 or more antigens from the training set to be added to the set of memory cells.

Memory Cell Identification and ARB Generation: From now on, antigens (training instances) will be presented to the algorithm one by one:

– Clonal selection: each *mc* in the memory cell pool having the same class as the antigenic pattern *ag*, determines its affinity to *ag*. $(Stim(ag, mc) = 1 - affinity(ag, mc))$, *mc* with the highest stimulation is selected as the best match memory cell (*mc_match*) and it will be used in the affinity maturation process. If in the memory cell pool there is no *mc* having the same class as the antigen, this antigen will be added directly to *MC*.
– Affinity Maturation: Once the *mc_match* is selected, the number of mutated clones is computed by:

$$mc.Num\_Clones = ClonalRate * HyperClonalRate * Stim(ag, mc\_match) \quad (3)$$

Where *ClonalRate* and *HyperClonalRate* are user-defined parameters and *Stim* is the stimulation value between the *mc_match* and the antigen. According to this number, the *mc_match* will be cloned by a mutation process and the mutated clones of *mc_match* will be placed on the Artificial Recognition Balls Pool (ARB).

The mutation process is done randomly by generating a random value between [0.1] for each feature value. If this value is lower than the *MutationRate* (user-defined parameter) then mutation will take place. Only the attribute values are allowed to be mutated.

Competition for Resources and Development of a Candidate Memory Cell: At this moment, there is a set of ARBs including *mc_match* and mutations of *mc_match*.

The main of this stage is to develop a candidate memory cell (*mc_candidate*) which is the most successful in correctly classifying a given antigen.

This is achieved through the following steps:

– Stimulation level between each ARB and the actual antigen will be computed and normalized. Then the resource number of each ARB is measured by:

$$ARB.resources = ClonalRate * Stim\_normalized(ag, ARB) \quad (4)$$

– Then the ARB pool will be following a survival mechanism based on a limited number of resources (user-defined parameter). If the total number of resources of all the ARBs exceeds the allowed one, the surplus resources will be removed from the weakest ARB (ARB with the smallest stimulation level) until the number of resources becomes equal to the allowed number of resources. ARBs left with zero resources will be removed from the system and only those ARBs that are most stimulated are capable of competing for resources.
– After this competition, the stop criterion is evaluated. This latter is reached if the average stimulation of all existing ARBs with the antigen is higher than Stimulation_threshold (user-defined parameter). If the opposite is true, the ARBs will be mutated and the mutated clones will be added to the

ARBs pool, then the competition for resources processes will take place and only survived ARBs are going to pass through the clonal expansion and the mutation procedures until the stop criterion is met. Here the number of clones is computed by:

$$ARB.Num\_Clones = Stim(ag, ARB) * ClonalRate \qquad (5)$$

- Once the stop criterion is reached, the ARB with the highest stimulation level will be selected as the candidate memory cell (mc_candidate).

Memory Cell Introduction: This is the final stage of the training process, it consists in updating in the memory cell pool. If the affinity between the selected mc_candidate and the training antigen is higher than of the mc_match. Then the mc_candidate will be added to MC and will become a long-lived memory cell. In addition, if the affinity value between and mc_candidate and mc_match is also less than the product of the affinity threshold and the affinity threshold scalar (user-defined parameter) mc_candidate will replace mc_match in the set of memory cells.

The ARB pool is cleared after each new antigenic presentation.

The Classification Step: with the training completed, classification will be done by applying the K-nearest neighbor algorithm on the evolved memory cell pool. The classification of a test instance will be achieved by the majority vote between the most stimulated memory cells.

3   The Belief Function Theory

The belief function theory is considered as an efficient theory for dealing with all kinds of imperfect knowledge, especially, uncertain knowledge. This theory, known as Dempster-Shafer theory or evidence theory, was firstly proposed by Dempster in the frame of the theory of statistical inference [7]. It has been formalized then by Shafer [20] as a general framework for representing uncertainty. In this section, we briefly provide the basics of belief function theory.

3.1   The Frame of Discernment

let $\Omega = \{H_1,...,H_n\}$ be a finite non-empty set containing all the elementary events to a specific problem and which are assumed to be exhaustive and mutually exclusive. It is called the frame of discernment and also referred to as the universe of discourse or the domain of reference. All the subsets of Ω belong to the power set denoted by 2^Ω and defined as follows:

$$2^\Omega = \{A/A \subseteq \Omega\} = \{\emptyset, \{H_1\}, \{H_2\}, ..., \{H_1 \cup H_2\}, ..., \Omega\} \qquad (6)$$

where the power set 2^Ω serves as a repository definition for all variables used in the belief function theory to assess the veracity of any statement.

3.2   Basic Belief Assignment (bba)

A basic belief assignment (bba) represents the impact of a piece of evidence on the different subsets of the frame of discernment Ω. The bba, called initially basic probability assignment [7]. such that:

$$m : 2^{\Omega} \to [0, 1] \tag{7}$$

$$\sum_{A \subseteq \Omega} m(A) = 1 \tag{8}$$

$m(A)$, a quantity named basic belief mass (bbm), is a part of belief exactly allocated to the event A of Ω without being apportioned to any of its subset. Thereupon, the proposition $m(\Omega)$ measures the part of belief assigned to the whole frame Ω.

3.3   Dempster's Combination Rule

Dempster's combination rule was first introduced in [7] and then reinterpreted by Shafer [20] as a basis for belief function theory. It is a commutative and associative rule that allows combining bba's of the same frame of discernment expressed from different independent sources. The induced bba reflects a conjunctive combination of the underlying evidence [21].

Let m_1 and m_2 be the mass functions induced by distinct pieces of evidence which are defined over the same frame of discernment Ω. The mass function $m_1 \oplus m_2$, combined according to Dempster's combination rule, is defined as:

$$m_{1 \oplus} m_2(A) = \frac{1}{1 - K_{12}} \sum_{B \cap C = A} m_1(B) m_2(C), \forall A \subseteq \Omega, A \neq \emptyset \tag{9}$$

$$K_{12} = \sum_{B \cap C = \emptyset} m_1(B) m_2(C) \tag{10}$$

where K_{12} is the degree of conflict. A high degree of conflict indicates that the sources might be in disagreement [6].

4   The Evidential AIRS Approach

In this section, we introduce the Evidential AIRS concept by representing its definition and motivations. Then we define the used notations. Finally, the Evidential AIRS method will be described and its algorithm will be presented.

4.1   Definition

The Evidential AIRS approach is based on the idea of adapting the AIRS2 to an uncertain environment in order to improve its performance. This method is done by firstly pointing to uncertainty in AIRS then dealing with it in the belief function context.

4.2   Motivations

In this paper, uncertainty in AIRS2 lies in the classification step, which is based on the K-nearest neighbors algorithm (KNN). In fact, this step used the distance information only in the selection of the K-nearest neighbors and it does not play a role in the final class assignment decision [6]. KNN is based on a voting method and the majority of votes gives the assignment decision which means that the vote of each K-nearest neighbor has the same weight. Thus, the vote of a neighbor which is very near to the test sample and that of one which extremely far carries the same weight if they are among the chosen K-nearest neighbors [6]. Also, there is a possibility of a tie occurring as a result of voting. This can only be resolved by randomly assigning a class to the test sample from among the classes getting the same number of maximum votes.

In order to handle these issues, we develop an Evidential AIRS approach as a new classification technique, which is a combination of AIRS2 and the Evidential K-nearest neighbor's algorithm (EKNN) [8], which is a nonparametric supervised classification algorithm based on the belief function theory.

4.3   Notations

We define the notations that will be used in our work:

- $\Omega = \{c_1, ..., c_p\}$, is the frame of discernment considered as the set of classes and p is the number of classes.
- $MC = \{(mc^{(1)}, c^{(1)}), ..., (mc^{(n)}, c^{(n)})\}$ is the memory cell pool including the available information of n memory cells and their corresponding class labels $c^{(i)}$, i = 1,...,n taking values in Ω.
- $m(\{c_q\}|mc^{(i)})$ is basic belief mass assigned to class c_q.

4.4   The Evidential AIRS Algorithm

Our approach takes place after the learning procedure, which means that it is based on the reduced establish data set "MC pool". This latter will be taken as input for the EKNN and according to its test samples (antigens) will be classified. To ensure the assignment of the appropriate class to each unlabeled antigen and to handle the total ignorance that characterized a situation when we are totally undecided about the decision to make, a distance measure between each memory cell in the MC pool and a test sample will be considered as the weight of evidence attributed to each class. Then, K-nearest neighbors will be selected and their pieces of evidence will be combined to decide the assigned class.

Let ag be a test sample (antigen) to classify based on information in MC, a certain distance function d (usually the Euclidean distance) is used to measure the similarity between ag and the MC samples, according to the relevant metric d the K-nearest neighbors are selected and $I_K = \{i_1,...,i_K\}$ is the set of K-nearest neighbors indexes. Each pair $(mc^{(i)}, c^{(i)})$ of the K-nearest neighbors represents a distinct piece of evidence concerning the class membership of ag. Therefore, this piece of evidence can be applied to generate the K basic belief assignment (bba) $m(.|mc^{(i)})$ over Ω denoted by:

$$m(\{c_q\} \mid mc^{(i)}) = \alpha\phi_q(d^{(i)})$$
$$m(\Omega \mid mc^{(i)}) = 1 - \alpha\phi_q(d^{(i)}) \tag{11}$$
$$m(\{A\} \mid mc^{(i)}) = 0, \forall A \in 2^{\Omega} \setminus \{\Omega, \{c_q\}\}$$

Where $d^{(i)} = d(ag, mc^{(i)})$, c_q is the class of $mc^{(i)}$ ($c^{(i)} = c_q$), α is a user predefined parameter between [0,1] and ϕ_q is a decreasing function verifying $\phi_q(0) = 1$ and $\lim_{d \to \infty} \phi_q(d) = 0$ [9]. Note that $m(.|mc^{(i)})$ reduces to the vacuous bba $(m(\Omega|x^{(i)}) = 1)$ when the distance between ag and $mc^{(i)}$ tends to infinity, reflecting a state of total ignorance [9]. ϕ_q is computed by:

$$\phi_q(d) = \exp(-\gamma_q d^2)$$
$$\gamma_q = \frac{1}{d_q} \tag{12}$$

γ_q being the reciprocal of the mean distance d_q between any two training samples belong to the same class c_q.

After computing the K bba's corresponding to the K-nearest neighbors, these have to be combined using Dempster's combination rule to get the final bba. The assigned class to the test sample is the one with the maximum mass.

The Evidential AIRS approach is summarized by the following algorithm.

Algorithm 1. Evidential AIRS Algorithm

Input: MC = memory cell pool, n = number of MC samples, p = number of classes, c = class labels, ag = test sample

Output: y = class label

1 **begin**
2   **for** $i = 1$ **to** n **do**
3 | Compute distance $d(mc^{(i)}, ag)$.
4   **end**
5   Find the set I_K containing indices for the K smallest distance $d(mc^{(i)}, ag)$.
6   Compute K bba's of the K-nearest neighbors (using Eqs. 11 and 12).
7   Combine the K bba's using the Dempster rule.
8   **return** the label (y) with the maximum mass.
9 **end**

---

5   Experimental Results

5.1   The Framework

We have performed several tests on real data sets obtained from the U.C.I. repository to evaluate our approach and to confirm its performance comparing to the standard AIRS2 [1] and the Fuzzy AIRS [14]. Since this latter is a combination of AIRS2 and Fuzzy K-nearest neighbor, which is quite similar to our approach in the fact that both approaches are interested in the classification step and get the same input (MC pool). Yet, each method has it own treatment procedure that provides the final class assignment decision. Therefore, a comparison must take place to show the improvement of Evidential AIRS over the Fuzzy one an the standard AIRS2.

We have used seven data sets namely Cryotherapy (C), Iris (I), Breast Cancer (BC), Indian Liver patient (ILP), Wine (W), Breast Concer Coimba (BCC) and Connectionist Bench (CB).

Table 1 presents the characteristics of the used data sets which are #nbInstances, #nbAttributes and #nbclass respectively, the number of antigens, the number of attributes and the number of class labels of a data set.

Table 1. The characteristics of used data sets

Data set	#nbInstances	#nbAttributes	#nbClass
C	90	6	2
I	150	5	3
BC	569	9	2
ILP	584	10	2
W	178	13	3
BCC	119	9	2
CB	208	60	3

For all data sets, we choose to work with the most used parameter values for AIRS2, Fuzzy AIRS, Evidential AIRS:

Clonal rate = 10, Mutation rate = 0.2, HyperClonal Rate = 2, Number of resources = 200, Stimulation threshold = 0.8, Affinity threshold scalar = 0.5. Regarding the value of K in the K-nearest neighbor component, we have tested different values for the different data sets therefore $K = [1, 2, 3, 5, 7, 9,$ number of attribute+1].

5.2   Evaluation Criterion

The evaluation of our approach is mainly based on the classification accuracy, expressed by the percentage of correct classification (PCC).

In our simulations, in order to obtain an unbiased estimation of the PCC, we have used the cross-validation technique. This technique consists of running a certain number of tests and computing the final PCC as the average of all obtained ones.

5.3   Experimental Results

In this section, we compare the Evidential AIRS to the standard AIRS2 and to
the Fuzzy AIRS using the accuracy criterion through the results of PCC of the
different used K-values. Then, we analyze these results.

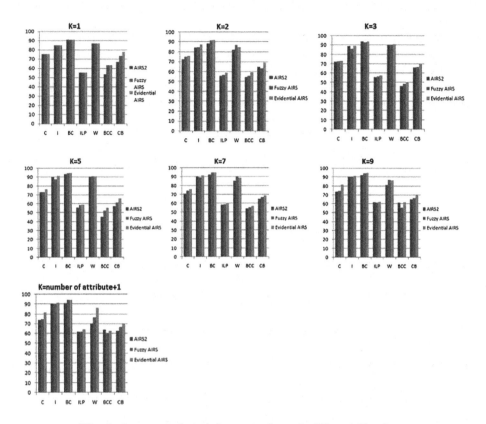

Fig. 1. Accuracy of used data sets through different K-values

From Fig. 1 we remark that the Evidential AIRS gives better accuracy in the
majority of data sets through different choosing K-values.

The following table is dedicated to representing the comparison results of
the average PCC of the different used K-values as well as the percentage of the
improvement of Evidential AIRS over AIRS2 (Improvement 1) and over Fuzzy
AIRS (Improvement 2).

Through the results shown in Table 2, we can notice that the Evidential AIRS
outperforms the standard AIRS2 in terms of classification accuracy for all used
data sets (the improvement is from 1.26% for the Iris data set (I) to 6.1% for
the Connectionist Bench data set (CB)). As well the results have outlined the
improvement of our approach over the fuzzy one in the majority of data sets.

Table 2. The average PCC (%) of Evidential AIRS VS AIRS2 and Fuzzy AIRS

Data sets	AIRS2	Fuzzy AIRS	Evidential AIRS	Improvement 1	Improvement 2
C	72.97	74.36	**76.42**	**+3.45**	**+2.03**
I	88.21	86.98	**89.50**	**+1.29**	**+2.52**
BC	91.73	93.50	**93.69**	**+1.96**	**+0.16**
ILP	57.91	59.68	**61.20**	**+3.29**	**+1.52**
W	83.68	**87.14**	86.50	**+2.82**	**−0.64**
BCC	54.52	57.09	**59.64**	**+5.12**	**+2.55**
CB	63.81	66.79	**69.90**	**+6.1**	**+3.11**

For example for the data set Cryotherapy (C) the PCC reaches 76.42%, however it reaches respectively 72.97%, 74.36% for AIRS2 and Fuzzy AIRS and for Connectionist Bench (CB) data set the Evidential AIRS gives the highest accuracy rate 69.90% while Fuzzy AIRS and AIRS2 gives respectively 66.79% and 63.81%. These results highlight the importance of handling uncertainty within the belief function framework and its impact on classification accuracy.

6   Conclusion

In this work, we have defined a new classification approach adapted to an environment characterized by uncertainty called the Evidential AIRS, which is based on the AIRS2 and the belief function theory to handle uncertainty in AIRS, especially in the classification step. More precisely this approach is a combination of AIRS2 and Evidential k-nearest neighbors. Based on the evaluation method the Evidential AIRS has shown better classification accuracy compared to AIRS2 and Fuzzy AIRS.

Finally, some future work has to be mentioned including handling uncertainty in the learning procedure, especially in the maturation process.

References

1. Watkins, A., Timmis, J., Boggess, L.: Artificial immune recognition system (AIRS): an immune-inspired supervised learning algorithm. Genet. Program. Evolvable Mach. **5**(3), 291–317 (2004)
2. Meng, L., van der Putten, P., Wang, H.: A comprehensive benchmark of the artificial immune recognition system (AIRS). In: Li, X., Wang, S., Dong, Z.Y. (eds.) ADMA 2005. LNCS (LNAI), vol. 3584, pp. 575–582. Springer, Heidelberg (2005). https://doi.org/10.1007/11527503_68
3. Hentech, R., Jenhani, I., Elouedi, Z.: Possibilistic AIRS induction from uncertain data. Soft Comput. **20**(1), 3–17 (2016)
4. Dasarathy, B.V.: Nearest Neighbour NN Norms: NN Pattern Classification Techniques. IEEE Computer Society Press, Washington (1991)
5. Jenhani, I., Elouedi, Z.: Re-visiting the artificial immune recognition system: a survey and an improved version. Artif. Intell. Rev. **42**(4), 821–833 (2012)

6. Faziludeen, S., Sankaran, P.: ECG beat classification using evidential K-nearest neighbours. Proc. Comput. Sci. **89**, 499–505 (2016)
7. Dempster, A.P.: Upper and lower probabilities induced by a multivalued mapping. Ann. Math. Stat. **38**, 325–339 (1967)
8. Denoeux, T.: A k-nearest neighbor classification rule based on Dempster-Shafer theory. IEEE Trans. Syst. Man Cybern. **25**, 804–813 (1995)
9. Zouhal, L.M., Denoeux, T.: An evidence theoretic kNN rule with parameter optimization. IEEE Trans. Syst. Man Cybern. **28**(2), 263–271 (1998)
10. Watkins, A.: A resource limited artificial immune classifier. In: The 2002 Congress on Evolutionary Computation, pp. 926–931 (2002)
11. Polat, K., Gunes, S.: Automated identification of diseases related to lymph system from lymphography data using artificial immune recognition system with fuzzy resource allocation mechanism (fuzzy-airs). Biomed. Signal Process. Control **1**(4), 253–260 (2006)
12. Golzari, S., Doraisamy, S., Sulaiman, M.D.N., Udzir, N.I.: Effect of fuzzy resource allocation method on AIRS classifier accuracy. Theor. Appl. Inform. Technol. **5**(4), 18–24 (2005)
13. Polat, K., Güneş, S.: Principles component analysis, fuzzy weighting pre-processing and artificial immune recognition system based diagnostic system for diagnosis of lung cancer. Expert Syst. Appl. **34**(1), 214–221 (2008)
14. Chikh, M., Saidi, M., Settouti, N.: Diagnosis of diabetes diseases using an artificial immune recognition system2 (AIRS2) with fuzzy k-nearest neighbor. J. Med. Syst. **36**(5), 2721–2729 (2012)
15. Elouedi, Z., Mellouli, K., Smets, P.: Belief decision trees: theoretical foundations. Int. J. Approx. Reason. **28**(2–3), 91–124 (2001)
16. Lee, H., Grosse, R., Ranganath, R., Ng, A.Y.: Convolutional deep belief networks for scalable unsupervised learning of hierarchical representations. In: The 26th Annual International Conference on Machine Learning, pp. 609–616 (2009)
17. Catal, C., Diri, B.: Software defect prediction using artificial immune recognition system. In: The 25th Conference on IASTED International MultiConference: Software Engineering, pp. 285–290 (2007)
18. Sabri, F., Norwawi, N.M., Seman, K.: Hybrid of rough set theory and artificial immune recognition system as a solution to decrease false alarm rate in intrusion detection system. In: 7th International Conference on Information Assurance and Security (IAS), pp. 134–138 (2011)
19. Polat, K., Sahan, S., Kodaz, H., Günes, S.: A new classification method for breast cancer diagnosis: feature selection artificial immune recognition system (FS-AIRS). In: Wang, L., Chen, K., Ong, Y.S. (eds.) ICNC 2005. LNCS, vol. 3611, pp. 830–838. Springer, Heidelberg (2005). https://doi.org/10.1007/11539117_117
20. Shafer, G.: A Mathematical Theory of Evidence. Princeton University Press, New Jersey (1976)
21. Reineking, T.: Belief functions: theory and algorithms. Doctoral dissertation, Staats-und Universitätsbibliothek Bremen (2014)

Gated Self-attentive Encoder for Neural Machine Translation

Xiangpeng Wei[1,2], Yue Hu[1,2(✉)], and Luxi Xing[1,2]

[1] Institute of Information Engineering, Chinese Academy of Sciences, Beijing, China
{weixiangpeng,huyue,xingluxi}@iie.ac.cn
[2] School of Cyber Security, University of Chinese Academy of Sciences, Beijing, China

Abstract. Neural Machine Translation (NMT) has become a popular technology in recent years, and the RNN-based encoder-decoder model is its actual translation framework. However, it remains a major challenge for RNNs to handle long-range dependencies. To address this limitation, we propose a gated self-attentive encoder (GSAE) for NMT that aims to directly capture the dependency relationship between any two words of source-side regardless of their distance. The proposed GSAE gains access to a wider context and ensures the better representation in the encoder. We extensively evaluate the proposed model using three language pairs. Experiments on WMT'14 English-German and WMT'14 English-French tasks show that our shallow model achieves BLEU = 26.54 and BLEU = 38.94 respectively, which are comparable with the state-of-the-art deep models. On WMT'17 English-Chinese translation task, our GSAE-NMT outperforms two strong baselines by 1.61 and 1.15 BLEU points, respectively.

Keywords: Neural Machine Translation · Gated Self-attentive Encoder · Dependency relationship

1 Introduction

Recently, attention-based neural machine translation has achieved significant improvements in translation quality of many language pairs such as English-German, English-French and Chinese-English [2, 21]. In NMT model, an encoder represents the source sentences of various lengths into sequences of intermediate hidden vectors. Then these hidden vectors are summarized by attention mechanism to synthetise context vectors that are used by the decoder to generate translations. In most cases, both encoder and decoder are implemented as recurrent neural networks (RNNs) or their variants such as gated recurrent units (GRUs) and long-short term memory networks (LSTMs).

The capacity of modeling temporal dependencies makes RNNs applicable for sequence modeling tasks with arbitrary length, however, it remains challenges for RNNs to handle inherent structure of sentences and long-range dependencies. As a result, several methods have been proposed to enrich the representations produced by NMT model with explicit dependency structures inherent in sentences. For example, [28] enrich each encoder state from both child-to-head and head-to-child with syntactic knowledge from source dependency trees. [4] propose a novel attentional NMT with source dependency

© Springer Nature Switzerland AG 2019
C. Douligeris et al. (Eds.): KSEM 2019, LNAI 11775, pp. 655–666, 2019.
https://doi.org/10.1007/978-3-030-29551-6_58

representation that captured by developing a CNN network from source dependency trees to improve translation performance. [27] introduce a sequence-to-dependency meth-od to jointly generate the target translations and their syntactic dependency trees to facilitate word generation. Despite recent success, these dependency tree based methods have limitations on training in end-to-end way. As the dependency trees are constructed firstly, and then used as additional inputs of NMT model. Thus the errors made along the dependency parsing process will quickly accumulate during translation.

In this paper, we propose a gated self-attentive encoder (GSAE) to improve translation performance. More specifically, in addition to the bidirectional RNN layer, we enhance the representation of source-side with an extra self-attention layer to capture the global dependencies of inputs. A major advantage of the self-attention is that it allows distant elements interact with each other by shorter paths ($O(1)$ vs. $O(n)$ in RNNs), which is augmented to RNNs. Then, these two representations produced by RNN layer and self-attention layer are properly blended by a gate network that can automatically tunes the weights of them. The whole model, including the self-attention layer and the gate network, can be learned in end-to-end fashion.

We extensively evaluate the proposed model using three language pairs. On WMT'-14 English-German and WMT'14 English-French tasks, our shallow model achieves 26.54 and 38.94 BLEU points respectively, which are comparable with the state-of-the-art deep models. On WMT'17 English-Chinese task, our GSAE-NMT outperforms two strong baselines by 1.61 and 1.15 BLEU points, respectively. The contributions of this paper can be summarized as follows:

- We propose to augment the standard RNN-based encoder with self-attentive connections to capture global dependency information, which can be crucial for correctly understanding the source sentences.
- We demonstrate consistent improvements over two baselines and comparable results over the state-of-the-art Transformer on three language pairs.

2 Neural Machine Translation

Neural machine translation models are typically implemented with a RNN-based encoder-decoder framework. Such a framework directly models the translation probability $P(y|x)$ of a target sentence $y = \{y_1, y_2, ..., y_{T_y}\}$ conditioned on the source sentence $x = \{x_1, x_2, ..., x_{T_x}\}$, where T_x and T_y are the lengths of sentences x and y.

The encoder of NMT bidirectionally encodes the source sentence x into a sequence of hidden vectors $H = \{h_1, h_2, ..., h_{T_x}\}$, where $h_i = [\overrightarrow{h}_i; \overleftarrow{h}_i]$, $\overrightarrow{h}_i$ and $\overleftarrow{h}_i$ are calculated by two RNNs from left-to-right and right-to-left respectively as follows,

$$\begin{aligned} \overrightarrow{h}_i &= f_{\rightarrow}(x_i, \overrightarrow{h}_{i-1}) \\ \overleftarrow{h}_i &= f_{\leftarrow}(x_i, \overleftarrow{h}_{i+1}) \end{aligned} \tag{1}$$

where $f_{\rightarrow}$ and $f_{\leftarrow}$ can be Gated Recurrent Unit (GRU) [6] or Long Short-Term Memory (LSTM) [10]. In this paper, we use GRU for all RNNs.

Afterwards, the decoder of NMT computes the conditional probability of each target word y_t conditioned on previously translated words $y_{<t}$ as well as the source sentence x:

$$p(y_t|y_{<t}, x) \propto \exp\{y_{t-1}, r_t, c_t\}$$
$$r_t = g(r_{t-1}, y_{t-1}, c_t) \tag{2}$$

where r_t is the decoder RNN hidden representation at step t, and g is a conditional GRU unit [16] with attention, which consists of two GRU blocks and an attention model in between. An attention function Attn can be described as mapping a query and a set of key-value pairs to an output, and is proposed to softly align each decoder state with the encoder states, where the attention score α_{tk} is computed to explicitly quantify how much each source word contributes to the target word y_t

$$\alpha_{tk} = \frac{\exp(e_{tk})}{\sum_{j=1}^{T_x} \exp(e_{tj})}$$
$$e_{tk} = v_a^T \tanh(W_a r_{t-1} + U_a h_k) \tag{3}$$

where v_a, W_a, U_a are the trainable parameters. The context vector c_t is the weighted sum of all encoder states

$$c_t = \sum_{k=1}^{T_x} \alpha_{tk} h_k \tag{4}$$

Denote all the parameters to be learned in the encoder-decoder framework as Θ, and denote D as the training dataset that contains source-target sentence pairs. The training process aims at seeking the optimal parameters Θ^* to correctly encode a source sentence and decode it into the target sentence. We use the maximum likelihood estimation in this paper:

$$\Theta^* = \arg\max_{\Theta} \prod_{(x,y)\in D} P(y|x;\Theta)$$
$$= \arg\max_{\Theta} \prod_{(x,y)\in D} \prod_{t=1}^{T_y} P(y_t|y_{<t}, x;\Theta) \tag{5}$$

3   Gated Self-attentive Encoder for Neural Machine Translation

Our gated self-attentive encoder (GSAE) NMT model, illustrated in Fig. 1, leverages the power of both short and long-rang dependencies to achieve the goal of correctly understanding source sentences. The backbone of the design is a RNN-based NMT (as described in Sect. 2) with the advantage of modeling temporal dependencies, and the self-attention component empowers the RNN-based model with the abilities to capture the dependency relationship between two arbitrary words of source-side. Further, we develop a gate annotation layer for properly blending the contextual representation produced by bidirectional RNN layer and the long-range self-attentive representation produced by self-attention layer.

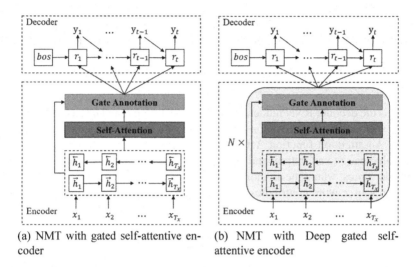

(a) NMT with gated self-attentive encoder

(b) NMT with Deep gated self-
attentive encoder

Fig. 1. Left is our novel NMT model with one-layer gated self-attentive encoder, which consists of hidden states from bidirectional RNN and long-range dependencies from self-attention. Right is our novel NMT model with deep N-layers gated self-attentive encoder. We apply conditional GRU (as described in Sect. 2) in decoder.

3.1 Source Self-attentive Representation

As long-range dependencies can be crucial for correctly understanding source sentences, hence we adopt the self-attention mechanism to compute the source dependency representation. Self-attention is a special case of the attention mechanism introduced in Sect. 2, in which all of the keys, values and queries come from the same place, in this case, the output of the bidirectional RNN layer in the encoder.

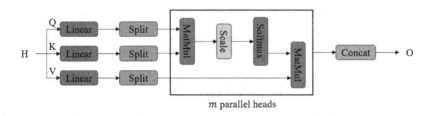

Fig. 2. The computation graph of multi-head self-attention mechanism.

Inspired by the success and methodology of Transformer, we adopt the multi-head attention formulated by [25]. Figure 2 depicts the computation graph of the multi-head attention mechanism. The core of the multi-head attention is the scaled dot-product operation. Formally, given a matrix of a set of queries $Q \in \mathbb{R}^{n \times d}$, keys $K \in \mathbb{R}^{n \times d}$ and values $V \in \mathbb{R}^{n \times d}$, the scaled dot-product operation summarizes self-attentive context vectors as

$$\text{Attention}(Q, K, V) = \text{softmax}(\frac{QK^T}{\sqrt{d}})V \tag{6}$$

That is, we compute the dot products of each query with all keys, divide each by $\sqrt{d}$, apply a softmax function to obtain the weights on the values, and weighted sum the values to obtain the self-attentive representation.

Instead of performing a single attention function with d-dimensional keys, values and queries, multi-head attention maps the matrix of input vectors $H \in \mathbb{R}^{n \times d}$ to a set of queries, keys and values with d' dimensions by using m different linear projections. Formally,

$$\begin{aligned} O &= \text{MultiHead}(Q, K, V) \\ &= \text{Concat}(o_1, o_2, ..., o_m) \\ o_i &= \text{Attention}(QW_i^Q, KW_i^K, VW_i^V) \end{aligned} \tag{7}$$

where the matrices $W_i^Q \in \mathbb{R}^{d \times d'}$, $W_i^K \in \mathbb{R}^{d \times d'}$ and $W_i^V \in \mathbb{R}^{d \times d'}$ are parameters of i-th linear projection, and $d' = d/m$.

As formulated above, it is obvious that the distance between any two positions is 1 in self-attention. Thus, the self-attention directly captures the soft dependencies between any two words of source-side regardless of their distance and gains access to a wider context, which can be crucial for correctly understanding source sentences.

3.2 Gate Annotation

To utilize multiple representations produced by RNN layer and self-attention layer, one feasible solution is summing or concatenating of them. However, the information contained in these two representations may have duplicated parts, thus, a simple addition (or concatenation) may lead to over translation [12,24]. In this paper, we develop a gate network for properly blending these two representations.

Formally, given the recurrent representation $H \in \mathbb{R}^{T_x \times d}$ and the self-attentional representation $O \in \mathbb{R}^{T_x \times d}$, in which T_x indicates the length of the source sentence and d indicates the hidden size. The computation of the gated annotation can be specified as

$$A = g_0 \odot H + g_1 \odot O \tag{8}$$

where g_0 and g_1 are gated units, formulated as

$$\begin{aligned} g_0 &= \sigma(HW_{g_0} + OU_{g_0}) \\ g_1 &= \sigma(HW_{g_1} + OU_{g_1}) \end{aligned} \tag{9}$$

where $W_{g_0} \in \mathbb{R}^{d \times d}$, $U_{g_0} \in \mathbb{R}^{d \times d}$, $W_{g_1} \in \mathbb{R}^{d \times d}$ and $U_{g_1} \in \mathbb{R}^{d \times d}$ are trainable parameters.

3.3 Depth in Space

Previous works pointed out that deep topology is essential to achieve good performance [25,26,29]. In this paper, we investigate deep gated self-attentive encoder, which are constructed by stacking blocks on the top of each other, as illustrated in Fig. 1(b). Each block consists of three sub-layers. The first is a simple bidirectional GRU, the second is the self-attention layer, and the third is the gate annotation layer. We employ a residual connection [9] around each of the first two sub-layers, followed by layer normalization [1]. Specifically, for the first two sub-layers, the output Y of each sub-layer is computed as

$$Y = \text{LayerNorm}(X + \text{SubLayer}(X)) \tag{10}$$

where X is the input of each sub-layer.

4 Experiments

We perform experiments on three WMT translation tasks, WMT'14 English-German (En-De), WMT'14 English-French (En-Fr) and WMT'17 English-Chinese (En-Zh).

4.1 Datasets

WMT'14 English-German: we use the same dataset as [11,15] which comprises 4.5M sentence pairs for training. The concatenation of *newstest2012* and *newstest2013* is used as the development set and *newstest2014* is used as the test set. Both side of the corpora are truecased and tokenized. As vocabulary we use 32K sub-word tokens based on Byte-Pair Encoding [17].

WMT'14 English-French: we use the full training set of 36M sentence pairs, and remove sentences longer than 80 words. Models are evaluated on the concatenation of *newstest2012* and *newstest2013*, and results are reported on *newstest2014*. The same as English-German, both side of the corpora are truecased and tokenized. We use a source and target vocabulary with 32K BPE (Byte-Pair-Encoding) types.

WMT'17 English-Chinese: the parallel training data consists of 24.2M sentence pairs. We remove sentences with repetition or more than 50 words, which results in 22M sentence pairs for training. We choose *newsdev2017* as development set, and the *newstest2017* as our test set. The Stanford Chinese word segmenter [23] is used to segment the Chinese training data. The English side of the corpora is truecased and tokenized. We experiment with word-based models using both source and target vocabularies of 30K most frequent words.

4.2 Model Parameters and Optimization

The dimension of word embeddings is set to 512, the number of hidden units is 1024. The number of heads m is set to 8. We use Adam optimizer with $\beta_1 = 0.9$, $\beta_2 = 0.999$ and $\epsilon = 10^{-8}$. The size of mini-batch is 80 and gradients are re-scaled if their norm exceeds 5.0. We use dropout for GRUs as suggested by [31], and dropout rate is set to 0.3. Inspired by [29], we initialize all trainable parameters uniformly between $[-0.04, 0.04]$.

We train our models on single NVIDIA 1080Ti GPU. For English-German, each training step takes about 0.6 s, the models are trained 300,000 steps or 2 days.

For English-French, each training step takes about 0.6 s, the models are trained 1,000,000 steps or 7 days. For English-Chinese translation, each training step takes about 0.4 s and the models are trained for 5 epochs or about 6 days.

During test time, we simply decode until the end-of-sentence symbol *eos* occurs, using beam search with a beam width of 10.

4.3   Models and Techniques

We compare our GSAE-NMT with two baselines. The first one is a classic baseline model implemented by ourselves with a bidirectional GRU based encoder and a conditional GRU based decoder (mentioned in Sect. 2), denoted as BaseNMT. To enhance this BaseNMT, we assemble it with some advanced techniques, such as training with dynamic learning rate [25] and initializing all word embeddings with word2vec[1]. The second one [4] creates a dependency unit to learn dependency representation for each source word from dependency trees and then incorporates long-distance dependency constraints into NMT for improving translation performance, denoted as SDRNMT. In this paper, both SDRNMT and GSAE-NMT were implemented on the BaseNMT model. We train each model 4 times repeatedly and for each repetition we obtain a well-trained model by averaging the last 10 checkpoints, which resulted in 4 well-trained models. We report BLEU scores averaged over these 4 well-trained models on test set. For comparison, we also implement models with deep topology and ensemble (ensemble of 4 models that differ in random initializations) techniques.

Table 1. BLEU scores of various models on the En-De and En-Fr experiments. GSAE-NMT is our gated self-attentive encoder based model. To further demonstrate the effectiveness of our method, we also compare GSAE-NMT with various existing models, such as *GNMT* [29], *ConvS2S* [8] and *Transformer* [25], and list their results reported in their papers. The highest score per dataset of our models is marked in bold. $|\Theta|$ indicates the number of parameters per model.

Model	$|\Theta|$ $\times 10^6$	BLEU En-De	En-Fr
GNMT [29]	–	24.60	39.92
ConvS2S [8]	–	25.16	40.46
Transformer Base [25]	65	27.30	38.10
Transformer Big [25]	213	28.40	41.00
BaseNMT	80	24.42	37.05
SDRNMT	91	25.18	37.70
GSAE-NMT	109	26.54	38.94
+ Deep GSAE	157	27.28	39.63
+ *Ensemble*(4)	–	**28.55**	**40.96**

---

[1] https://code.google.com/archive/p/word2vec/.

Table 2. BLEU scores of various models on the En-Zh experiments. We also list results from another two recently published open source models *Transformer* and *ConvS2S* for comparison. (The "IMP" column presents the improvement of test compared to the BaseNMT.)

Model	Newstest17	IMP
ConvS2S [8]	17.57	−
Transformer Base [25]	17.95	−
Transformer Big [25]	18.66	−
BaseNMT	16.28	−
SDRNMT	16.74	+0.46
GSAE-NMT	17.89	+1.61
+ Deep GSAE	18.40	+2.12
+ *Ensemble*(4)	19.38	+3.10

4.4 Overall Results

The detailed results are shown in Tables 1 and 2. Compared to the BaseNMT and SDRNMT, our GSAE-NMT achieves significant improvements. For English-German and English-French tasks, GSAE-NMT outperforms BaseNMT by about 2.12/1.89 BLEU points. As the only difference between the two models is that our GSAE-NMT additionally uses the output of self-attention layer to enhance the representation of source-side, we can conclude that such additional long-range dependency representation provides useful information to help NMT model. And our method outperforms SDRNMT by about 1.36/1.24 BLEU points. Since SDRNMT incorporates hard dependencies between words extracted from pre-obtained parser trees into NMT, our proposed gated self-attentive encoder which considers soft dependencies between arbitrary words is more powerful. The performance of our GSAE-NMT is also better than BaseNMT and SDRNMT on English-Chinese translation, which outperforms BaseNMT by about 1.61 BLEU points and outperforms SDRNMT by about 1.15 BLEU points.

We also test our gated self-attentive encoder on a deep NMT model in which the encoder is stacked 4-layer GSAEs. The results show that our deep model can get 0.74, 0.69 and 0.51 BLEU improvements upon the shallow GSAE-NMT model for English-German, English-French and English-Chinese tasks respectively. Besides, the ensemble technique also improves the shallow GSAE-NMT model by 2.01/2.02/1.49 BLEU points on these three translation tasks, respectively. These results demonstrate the effectiveness and robustness of the proposed gated self-attentive encoder.

To further prove the effectiveness of our method, we compare GSAE-NMT with various existing state-of-the-art models, such as GNMT [29], ConvS2S [8] and Transformer [25]. As shown in Tables 1 and 2, our best model achieves performance superior or comparable to the existing Deep RNN-based, Deep CNN-based and Deep Attention-based NMT models.

Table 3. Results of different combinations of the two representations produced by the bidirectional RNN layer and the self-attention layer.

Model	$\|\Theta\|$ $\times 10^6$	BLEU
GSAE-Add	92	25.91
GSAE-Concat	104	25.82
GSAE-NMT	109	26.54

Table 4. BLEU scores of BaseNMT and GSAE-NMT with different model sizes. L_{enc} indicates the depth of encoder.

MODEL	L_{enc}	width	BLEU
1 BaseNMT	1	1024	24.42
2 BaseNMT	2	1024	24.95
3 BaseNMT	4	1024	25.17
4 GSAE-NMT	1	512	26.31
5 GSAE-NMT	1	1024	26.54
6 GSAE-NMT	2	1024	26.85
7 GSAE-NMT	4	1024	27.28
8 GSAE-NMT	6	1024	27.13

4.5   Analysis on Gated Self-attentive Encoder

We further look into the proposed gated self-attentive encoder and conduct some analysis to better understand it on English-German task.

Add (Concat) vs. Gate. At first, we study the appropriate combinations of the two representations produced by the bidirectional RNN layer and the self-attention layer. For comparison, we develop two variants of our GSAE-NMT: (1) GSAE-Add: to verify the effectiveness of the gate annotation layer of GSAE, we remove the gate network and obtain the output of encoder by simply adding the two representations (i.e., replace A in Eq. 8 by $H + O$) produced by RNN layer and self-attention layer; (2) GSAE-Concat: similar to GSAE-Add, we obtain the output of encoder by simply concatenating the two representations (i.e., replace A in Eq. 8 by $[H; O]$) produced by RNN layer and self-attention layer. Table 3 shows the effect of various combinations. Although GSAE-NMT introduces more parameters, it remarkably surpasses the GSAE-Add by 0.63 BLEU points and surpasses the GSAE-Concat by 0.72 BLEU points. We can conclude that by developing a gate network to automatically tune the weights of different representations can significantly improve translation performance.

Depth vs. Width. Next, we will study the model size. In Table 4, starting from $L_{enc} = 1$ and gradually increasing the model depth, we can achieve substantial improvements in terms of BLEU. With $L_{enc} = 4$, our GSAE-NMT yields the best BLEU score. We tried to increase the model depth with the same hidden size but failed to see further improvements. Besides, GSAE-NMT introduces more parameters than BaseNMT. In order to figure out the effect of GSAE-NMT comparing models with the same parameter size, we decrease the number of hidden units in GSAE-NMT model. Row 3 shows that, after reducing the size of hidden layer by half, the BLEU score is 26.31, which still outperforms the deep 4 layers BaseNMT model that with more parameters.

5   Related Work

Machine Translation. Several works had investigated the potential of using inherent structure of sentences in Statistical Machine Translation (SMT) [14, 18]. Recently, some efforts have been done to incorporate syntactic structures into NMT to enhance translation. [7] incorporate source-side parse trees into NMT by developing a tree-to-sequence attentional architecture and achieve promising improvements. [3] propose a bidirectional tree encoder and tree-coverage based decoder for using explicit source-side syntactic trees in NMT. [27] introduce a sequence-to-dependency method to jointly generate the target translations and their syntactic dependency trees to facilitate word generation. Our method differs from them significantly. We propose to model soft long-range dependencies of source-side with self-attention mechanism, which is augmented to RNN based models.

Self-attention. Self-attention have been successfully used in many natural language processing tasks. [5] use LSTMs and self-attention to facilitate the task of machine reading. [13] propose self-attentive sentence embedding and applied them to author profiling, sentiment analysis and textual entailment. [25] propose a self-attention based neural machine translation model. More recently, [19] apply self-attention to language understanding task and achieve the state-of-the-art performance on various datasets. [22] apply self-attention mechanism in semantic role labeling to capture long-range dependencies and achieve superior performance on previous state-of-the-art models. [20] propose a bi-directional block self-attention network for RNN-CNN-free sequence modeling. [30] propose a new QA architecture, in which convolution models local interactions and self-attention models global interactions.

6   Conclusion

In this paper, we propose a gated self-attentive encoder (GSAE) to enhance the neural machine translation. To enable the encoder to capture the dependency relationship between two arbitrary words, besides the contextual information of the RNN, we develop a self-attention layer to model the long-range dependencies. And for composition, a gate annotation network is developed to learn the weights of the two representations produced by RNN layer and self-attention layer automatically. Furthermore, we also equipped the proposed GSAE with deep topology and ensemble techniques. Experiments on extensive English-Chinese translation tasks show that GSAE improves the quality of translation and our best single model beats the BaseNMT by 2.12 BLEU points. And fair comparisons on English-German and English-French translations indicate that our shallow GSAE based model achieves performance superior or comparable to various existing state-of-the-art neural machine translation systems.

References

1. Ba, J.L., Kiros, J.R., Hinton, G.E.: Layer normalization. In: CoRR (2016)
2. Bahdanau, D., Cho, K., Bengio, Y.: Neural machine translation by jointly learning to align and translate. In: Proceedings of the International Conference on Learning Representations 2015. San Diego, USA (2015)
3. Chen, H., Huang, S., Chiang, D., Chen, J.: Improved neural machine translation with a syntax-aware encoder and decoder. In: Proceedings of the 55th Annual Meeting of the Association for Computational Linguistics, Vancouver, Canada, pp. 1936–1945. Association for Computational Linguistics (2017)
4. Chen, K., et al.: Neural machine translation with source dependency representation. In: Proceedings of the 2017 Conference on Empirical Methods in Natural Language Processing, Copenhagen, Denmark, pp. 2846–2852. Association for Computational Linguistics (2017)
5. Cheng, J., Dong, L., Lapata, M.: Long short-term memory-networks for machine reading. In: Proceedings of the 2016 Conference on Empirical Methods in Natural Language Processing, Austin, Texas, pp. 551–561. Association for Computational Linguistics (2016)
6. Cho, K., Caglar Gulcehre, B.V.M., Bahdanau, D., Holger Schwenk, F.B., Bengio, Y.: Learning phrase representations using RNN encoder-decoder for statistical machine translation. In: Proceedings of the 2014 Conference on Empirical Methods in Natural Language Processing, Doha, Qatar, pp. 1724–1734. Association for Computational Linguistics (2014)
7. Eriguchi, A., Hashimoto, K., Tsuruoka, Y.: Tree-to-sequence attentional neural machine translation. In: Proceedings of the 54th Annual Meeting of the Association for Computational Linguistics, Berlin, Germany, pp. 823–833. Association for Computational Linguistics (2016)
8. Gehring, J., Auli, M., Grangier, D., Yarats, D., Dauphin, Y.N.: Convolutional sequence to sequence learning. In: Proceedings of the 34th International Conference on Machine Learning ICML 2017 (2017)
9. He, K., Zhang, X., Ren, S., Sun, J.: Deep residual learning for image recognition. In: Proceedings of the IEEE Conference on Computer Vision and Pattern Recognition, pp. 770–778 (2016)
10. Hochreiter, S., Schmidhuber, J.: Long short-term memory. In: Neural Computation, pp. 1735–1780 (1997)
11. Jean, S., Cho, K., Memisevic, R., Bengio, Y.: On using very large target vocabulary for neural machine translation. In: Proceedings of the 53rd Annual Meeting of the Association for Computational Linguistics and the 7th International Joint Conference on Natural Language Processing, Beijing, China, pp. 1–10. Association for Computational Linguistics (2015)
12. Koehn, P., Och, F.J., Marcu, D.: Statistical phrase-based translation. In: Conference of the North American Chapter of the Association for Computational Linguistics on Human Language Technology, pp. 48–54. Association for Computational Linguistics (2003)
13. Lin, Z., et al.: A structured self-attentive sentence embedding. In: Proceedings of International Conference on Learning Representations 2017 (2017)
14. Liu, Y., Liu, Q., Lin, S.: Tree-to-string alignment template for statistical machine translation. In: Proceedings of the 21st International Conference on Computational Linguistics and 44th Annual Meeting of the ACL, Sydney, Australia, pp. 609–616. Association for Computational Linguistics (2006)
15. Luong, M.T., Pham, H., Manning, C.D.: Effective approaches to attention-based neural machine translation. In: Proceedings of the 2015 Conference on Empirical Methods in Natural Language Processing, Lisbon, Portugal, pp. 1412–1421. Association for Computational Linguistics (2015)

16. Sennrich, R., et al.: Nematus: a toolkit for neural machine translation. In: Proceedings of the 15th Conference of the European Chapter of the Association for Computational Linguistics, EACL 2017 (2017)

17. Sennrich, R., Haddow, B., Birch, A.: Neural machine translation of rare words with subword units. In: Proceedings of the 54th Annual Meeting of the Association for Computational Linguistics, Berlin, Germany, pp. 1715–1725. Association for Computational Linguistics (2016)

18. Shen, L., Xu, J., Weischedel, R.M.: A new string-to-dependency machine translation algorithm with a target dependency language model. In: Proceedings of ACL-08: HLT, Columbus, Ohio, USA, pp. 577–585. Association for Computational Linguistics (2008)

19. Shen, T., Zhou, T., Long, G., Jiang, J., Pan, S., Zhang, C.: Disan: directional self-attention network for RNN/CNN-free language understanding. In: Proceedings of the Thirty-Second AAAI Conference on Artificial Intelligence. New Orleans, Lousiana, USA (2018)

20. Shen, T., Zhou, T., Long, G., Jiang, J., Zhang, C.: Bi-directional block self-attention for fast and memory-efficient sequence modeling. In: Proceedings of International Conference on Learning Representations 2018 (2018)

21. Sutskever, I., Vinyals, O., Le, Q.V.: Sequence to sequence learning with neural networks. In: Advances in Neural Information Processing Systems, vol. 27, pp. 3104–3112 (2014)

22. Tan, Z., Wang, M., Xie, J., Chen, Y., Shi, X.: Deep semantic role labeling with self-attention. In: Proceedings of the Thirty-Second AAAI Conference on Artificial Intelligence. New Orleans, Lousiana, USA (2018)

23. Tseng, H., Chang, P., Andrew, G., Jurafsky, D., Manning, C.: A conditional random field word segmenter for sighan bakeoff 2005. In: In Fourth SIGHAN Workshop on Chinese Language Processing, pp. 168–171 (2005)

24. Tu, Z., Lu, Z., Liu, Y., Liu, X., Li, H.: Modeling coverage for neural machine translation. In: Proceedings of the 54th Annual Meeting of the Association for Computational Linguistics, Berlin, Germany, pp. 78–85. Association for Computational Linguistics (2016)

25. Vaswani, A., et al.: Attention is all you need. In: Advances in Neural Information Processing Systems 30: Annual Conference on Neural Information Processing Systems 2017 (2017)

26. Wang, M., Lu, Z., Zhou, J., Liu, Q.: Deep neural machine translation with linear associative unit. In: Proceedings of the 55th Annual Meeting of the Association for Computational Linguistics, Vancouver, Canada, pp. 136–145. Association for Computational Linguistics (2017)

27. Wu, S., Zhang, D., Yang, N., Li, M., Zhou, M.: Sequence-to-dependency neural machine translation. In: Proceedings of the 55th Annual Meeting of the Association for Computational Linguistics, Vancouver, Canada, pp. 698–707. Association for Computational Linguistics (2017)

28. Wu, S., Zhou, M., Zhang, D.: Improved neural machine translation with source syntax. In: Twenty-Sixth International Joint Conference on Artificial Intelligence, pp. 4179–4185. Melbourne, Australia (2017)

29. Wu, Y., et al.: Google's neural machine translation system: bridging the gap between human and machine translation. In: CoRR (2016)

30. Yu, A.W., et al.: Qanet: combining local convolution with global self-attention for reading comprehension. In: Proceedings of International Conference on Learning Representations 2018 (2018)

31. Zaremba, W., Sutskever, I., Vinyals, O.: Recurrent neural network regularization. In: Proceedings of International Conference on Learning Representations 2015, pp. 1310–1318. San Diego, California (2015)

RGCN: Recurrent Graph Convolutional Networks for Target-Dependent Sentiment Analysis

Junjie Chen[1,2], Hongxu Hou[1($\boxtimes$)], Jing Gao[2], Yatu Ji[1], and Tiangang Bai[1]

[1] College of Computer Science, Inner Mongolia University, Hohhot, China
chenjj@imau.edu.cn, cshhx@imu.edu.cn, jiyatu0@126.com
[2] College of Computer Science and Information Engineering,
Inner Mongolia Agricultural University, Hohhot, China

Abstract. With the increasing numbers of user-generated content on the web, identifying the sentiment polarity of the given aspect provides more complete and in-depth results for businesses and customers. Existing deep learning methods ignore that the sentiment polarity of the target is related to the entire text structure, and prevalent approaches among them cannot effectively use the syntactic information. In this paper, we propose to use a novel framework named as recurrent graph convolutional network (RGCN) for target-dependent sentiment classification in which the given text is considered as a graph based on its syntactic structure and recurrent graph convolutional networks are used to encode the text and target. We conduct comprehensive experiments on publicly accessible datasets, and results demonstrate that our model outperforms the state-of-the-art baselines.

Keywords: Recurrent Graph Convolutional Networks ·
Graph structure · Target-dependent sentiment analysis

1 Introduction

Sentiment analysis [16], also known as opinion mining [10,17], is a vital task in text mining. Typically, users write both positive and negative aspects in the same review, although the general sentiment may be positive or negative. Given the review that *"the food is so good and so popular that waiting can really be a nightmare."* It expresses negative sentiment towards "waiting" while holding positive sentiment towards "food". Target-dependent sentiment analysis, also known as aspect based sentiment analysis, is a fine-grained task in the field of sentiment classification [10,19]. The goal of this subtask is to predict the sentiment polarity of targets that appear in a given text.

Supported by Inner Mongolia Natural Science Foundation of China (2018MS06005, 2015MS0628) and Inner Mongolia Autonomous Region Key Laboratory of Big Data Research and Application of Agriculture and Animal Husbandry.

C. Douligeris et al. (Eds.): KSEM 2019, LNAI 11775, pp. 667–675, 2019.
https://doi.org/10.1007/978-3-030-29551-6_59

Neural networks have the ability of learning continuous text features to generate new representations through multiple hidden layers. In recent years, more and more deep learning approaches have been explored in this task, which have more scalable way than feature based methods. Prevalent methods based on Neural Network [2,4,7,11,12,20–22,24] don't use syntactic information. However, it is important to consider the entire text structure and the importance of the specific regional structure related to target words. In this paper we propose a novel framework, called RGCN, in which we introduce a hidden state like recurrent neural network, and the node state is the representation of the hidden state and neighbor nodes information. In our work, the result of the dependency parsing is used to construct a text graph, and the target is treated as a specific region of the entire graph. Recurrent graph convolutional neural networks are used to encode the text and targets, and then the sentiment classification are obtained by these representations. Experimental results on two publicly available datasets show that our model outperforms state-of-the-art methods.

2   Graph Convolutional Networks

In recent years, there has been a surge of interest in Graph Convolutional Network (GCN) approaches, which is generally used for representation learning of graphs and node classification [5,6]. Due to the success of GCN in node and graph representation, they have been introduced into the NLP tasks, such as semantic role labeling [14,15], machine translation [1,13] and so on. In GCN, the graph structure is represented by an adjacent matrix, and the convolution operation is performed on the graph structure. Kipf and Welling [6] describe GCN as:

$$H^{(l+1)} = f(LH^{(l)}W^{(l)}) \tag{1}$$

Where L is the adjacency matrix of the graph and $H^{(l)}$ is regarded as the hidden layer vectors. The hidden representation of a single-layer GCN can only capture information about direct neighbors. Li et al. [8] proposed that the GCN model mix the graph structure and the node features in the convolution, which makes the output features of the nodes in the same cluster more similar. Although the GCN model is powerful in feature extraction, it is not entirely appropriate for the target-dependent sentiment analysis task.

3   Our Model

Our framework is shown in Fig. 1. It can be divided into two parts, one is the representation of the text graph, and the other is the representation of target words. We employ RGCN to get features of nodes, then the representation of text is obtained by mean pooling layer of all nodes, and the representation of the target is by the max pooling layer of the aspect words.

3.1 Graph Construction

Let $W = \{w_1, w_2, \ldots w_N\}(|W| = N)$ denotes words set in the corpus. W_s is words set of the given text, $W_s = \{w_{s1}, w_{s2}, \ldots w_{sM}\}$ ($|W_s| = M, W_s \subset W$) and $W_t = \{w_{t1}, w_{t2}, \ldots w_{tK}\}(W_{ti} \in W_s)$ indicates words set of the target. As shown in Fig. 1, given the sentence *"the food is so good and so popular that waiting can really be a nightmare"*, $W_t = \{food\}$ and $W_s = \{the, food, is, so, good, and, popular, that, waiting, can, really, be, a, nightmare\}$.

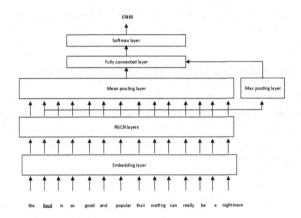

Fig. 1. The architecture of our model.

More formally, an undirected text graph is defined as $G = (V, E)$, where V and E are sets of nodes and edges, respectively. The text graph is constructed as follows: first, each vertex corresponds to a word in W_s, and then a connection is established for the syntactic dependency relation where the two words belong to the set of specific part of speeches. Finally, self-loops are added to the text graph.

3.2 RGCN

After the graph construction, the given text is converted to a graph. The word or the node w_{si} in the graph is represented by the vector x_i after the embedding layer. Usually, the length N of the set W in the corpus is larger than the length M of the set W_s in the text. Since it is not necessary to build the adjacency matrix $A \in \mathbb{R}^{N \times N}$ for each given text, we covert nodes sequence to the current text words sequence, then the adjacency matrix A becomes $\mathbb{R}^{M \times M}$.

The output of embedding layer is denoted as X_{embed}. We introduce a hidden state for the node, and the initial hidden representation of nodes is defined as $H^{(0)} = X_{embed} \in \mathbb{R}^{M \times F}$, and F is the feature size. The initial state of nodes in the graph is defined as:

$$X^{(0)} = f(U_0 H^0) \tag{2}$$

Where U_0 is a weight matrix, and $X^{(0)} \in \mathbb{R}^{M \times F}$. For RGCN layers, the propagation rule is defined as:

$$H^{(l+1)} = f(LH^l U_{l1} + X^l V_{l1})$$ (3)

$$X^{(l+1)} = f(H^{l+1} U_{l2} + X^l V_{l2})$$ (4)

Where U_{l1}, U_{l2}, V_{l1} and V_{l2} are trainable parameters. It can be seen from the equation that in RGCN, the node hidden state is updated by the node last hidden state and the neighbor node state. The node state is updated by the nodes hidden state and the last node state. It not only contains information of graph structure like GCN, but also uses the last hidden state like RNN.

3.3 The Representation of the Text and the Target

We design aggregate functions as pooling operations, which are the element operation on feature vectors. After pooling operations, the hidden feature vectors of nodes is denoted as $H^{(p)} \in \mathbb{R}^F$, which is the representation of the text graph. In our work, we apply a mean pooling layer to the given text and a max pooling layer to the target words.

4   Experiments and Results

4.1   Experimental Setting

We test our model on public datasets from SemEval 2014 [19], including user-generated reviews of laptop and restaurant domains. Following previous work [2, 11,12,21], we removed a few examples having the "conflict" label. The statistics of the datasets are shown in Table 1. In our experiments, five-layer RGCN with RELU activation function is developed. The hidden dimension is set to 200 for the model. The dropout and early stop techniques are used to ease overfitting. 300-dimensional word embeddings pre-trained by GloVe [18] are utilized, which are not tuned during training time.

Table 1. Statistics of aspects in different datasets

Datasets	Positive		Negative		Neutral	
	Train	Test	Train	Test	Train	Test
Restaurant	2164	728	805	196	633	196
Laptop	987	341	866	128	460	169

4.2   Compared Methods

We compare our model with following baseline methods:

AdaRNN [3] is used for feature learning over a target-dependent dependency tree based on recursive neural networks, where composition functions are adaptively selected according to the inputs.

TD-LSTM [20] is a model based on LSTM network, in which two LSTM models are used to model the preceding and following contexts surrounding the target string for sentiment classification.

ATAE-LSTM [22] uses attention mechanism in LSTM network in which different aspects attend different parts of a sentence.

MemNet [21] is a neural attention model over an external memory, which consists of multiple computational layers.

RAM [2] is a framework that adopts multiple-attention mechanism on recurrent neural network.

IAN [12] is an interactive attention networks model. It uses two attention networks to model the target and context interactively.

Cabasc [11] is based on the memory model, which can solve the semantic mismatch problem through two attention mechanisms, namely sentence-level content attention mechanism and context attention mechanism.

GCAE [23] is based on convolutional neural networks and gating mechanisms.

To reveal the capability of models, the same word vectors are used in all models. Models which implementation are not provided by authors, are re-implemented in Pytorch. We follow the hyperparameter settings reported in the original paper, and set the unreported parameters to be the same as ours.

Table 2. Results of our model against baselines.

Methods	Restaurant	Laptop
AdaRNN	75.20	66.52
TD-LSTM	75.17	66.94
ATAE-LSTM	76.14	67.17
MemNet[a]	76.88	68.18
IAN	76.96	67.86
RAM	76.87	67.24
Cabasc	_77.05_	_68.65_
GCAE[a]	76.12	_68.65_
RGCN	**79.46**	**71.03**

[a] denotes that the results are obtained by running the code released by authors.

4.3 Main Results

For all methods accuracy evaluation is used as metric, and results are shown in Table 2. The best scores are highlighted in bold and the underlines indicate the second best performances.

As the results show, our model RGCN consistently outperforms all comparison methods on these datasets. This may be due to the fact that the syntactic dependency graph establishes a connection between two long distance words, shortening the distance between the aspect and the related words.

In LSTM-based models, TD-LSTM, ATAE-LSTM, and IAN, IAN has better results than other models because IAN uses context and target attention mechanisms, which make better use of important parts of a sentence for aspect words.

MemNet is based on memory network, containing multiple attention layers, superior to LSTM-based models on Laptop. Compared with RAM and MemNet, Cabasc enhances the ability to capture important information about a given aspect from a global perspective by sentence-level content attention mechanism and context attention mechanism, thus has a best performance in all baselines on Laptop and Restaurant. GCAE utilizes convolutional neural network with gating mechanisms, obtaining the best result as Cabasc on Laptop.

Although AdaRNN utilizes results of dependency parsing, it performs worse than others especially on Laptop. Compared with AdaRNN, our method holds the entire text information in the RGCN, and the target focus on the specific region of aspects to avoid noise of other graph parts.

4.4 Analysis of Our Model

To illustrate the effectiveness of our approach, we designed more relevant models to compare the results. The models replacing the RGCN layer with the GCN layer and the gated graph neural network (GGNN) [9] layer are denoted as GCN and GGNN, respectively. In our model, the RGCN layer updates the node state by last node state and hidden state, which is different from RNN. The implementation of the node state is update by the hidden state is named TRGCN. RGCN(x) is a model that passes nodes state to the pooling layer instead of hidden states. The best performance of these models is shown in Table 3.

Table 3. Analysis of our model.

Methods	Restaurant	Laptop
GCN	78.30	69.43
GGNN	78.39	70.06
TRGCN	79.29	70.06
RGCN(x)	78.75	69.12
RGCN	**79.46**	**71.03**

The results show that GCN is worse than other models because it is difficult to distinguish different node features as the layer increases. The accuracy of our model is higher than all models, which indicates that it can get better nodes representation in the graph structure. The results of TRGCN are superior to other models, which shows that introducing hidden states into GCN does improve performance.

4.5 Effect of Layers

We studied the impact of the layers on performance of GCN and RGCN as shown in Fig. 2. The hidden representations of a single-layer can only capture the information for the immediate neighbors, while models with K-layers can incorporate nodes that are at most K hops information. Figure 2 shows that the when the layer is set to 2 GCN is better than RGCN. As the layer increases, the accuracy of GCN is lower than RGCN, and the GCN line is flatter than RGCN, which is consistent with the previous analysis. We also observed that the accuracy does not improve with the increase of layers.

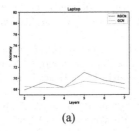
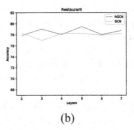

(a)   (b)

Fig. 2. Effect of layers on GCN and RGCN

5   Conclusion

In this paper, we present a novel framework for the task of target-dependent sentiment analysis. Compared with baselines on public datasets, the experimental results show that our model outperforms the state-of-the-art. Syntactic information can improve performance as demonstrated in traditional feature-based machine learning methods. We provide a way to integrate syntactic information in deep learning framework. The attention mechanism has proven to be useful in NLP tasks, and in the future we will study graph-based attention mechanisms for RGCN.

References

1. Bastings, J., Titov, I., Aziz, W., Marcheggiani, D., Simaan, K.: Graph convolutional encoders for syntax-aware neural machine translation. In: Proceedings of the 2017 Conference on Empirical Methods in Natural Language Processing, Copenhagen, Denmark, pp. 1947–1957. Association for Computational Linguistics, September 2017. https://www.aclweb.org/anthology/D17-1209

2. Chen, P., Sun, Z., Bing, L., Yang, W.: Recurrent attention network on memory for aspect sentiment analysis. In: Proceedings of the 2017 Conference on Empirical Methods in Natural Language Processing, pp. 452–461 (2017)
3. Dong, L., Wei, F., Tan, C., Tang, D., Zhou, M., Xu, K.: Adaptive recursive neural network for target-dependent twitter sentiment classification. In: Proceedings of the 52nd Annual Meeting of the Association for Computational Linguistics (Volume 2: Short Papers), vol. 2, pp. 49–54 (2014)
4. Fan, C., Gao, Q., Du, J., Gui, L., Xu, R., Wong, K.F.: Convolution-based memory network for aspect-based sentiment analysis. In: The 41st International ACM SIGIR Conference on Research & Development in Information Retrieval, pp. 1161–1164. ACM (2018)
5. Hamilton, W., Ying, Z., Leskovec, J.: Inductive representation learning on large graphs. In: Advances in Neural Information Processing Systems, pp. 1024–1034 (2017)
6. Kipf, T.N., Welling, M.: Semi-supervised classification with graph convolutional networks. arXiv preprint arXiv:1609.02907 (2016)
7. Li, L., Liu, Y., Zhou, A.: Hierarchical attention based position-aware network for aspect-level sentiment analysis. In: Proceedings of the 22nd Conference on Computational Natural Language Learning, pp. 181–189 (2018)
8. Li, Q., Han, Z., Wu, X.M.: Deeper insights into graph convolutional networks for semi-supervised learning. In: Thirty-Second AAAI Conference on Artificial Intelligence (2018)
9. Li, Y., Tarlow, D., Brockschmidt, M., Zemel, R.: Gated graph sequence neural networks. In: International Conference on Learning Representations (2016)
10. Liu, B.: Sentiment analysis and opinion mining. Synth. Lect. Hum. Lang. Technol. 5(1), 1–167 (2012)
11. Liu, Q., Zhang, H., Zeng, Y., Huang, Z., Wu, Z.: Content attention model for aspect based sentiment analysis. In: Proceedings of the 2018 World Wide Web Conference on World Wide Web, pp. 1023–1032. International World Wide Web Conferences Steering Committee (2018)
12. Ma, D., Li, S., Zhang, X., Wang, H.: Interactive attention networks for aspect-level sentiment classification. In: Proceedings of the 26th International Joint Conference on Artificial Intelligence, pp. 4068–4074. AAAI Press (2017)
13. Marcheggiani, D., Bastings, J., Titov, I.: Exploiting semantics in neural machine translation with graph convolutional networks. In: Proceedings of the the 16th Annual Conference of the North American Chapter of the Association for Computational Linguistics: Human Language Technologies (NAACL-HLT 2018), New Orleans, US. Association for Computational Linguistics, June 2018
14. Marcheggiani, D., Frolov, A., Titov, I.: A simple and accurate syntax-agnostic neural model for dependency-based semantic role labeling. In: Proceedings of the 21st Conference on Computational Natural Language Learning (CoNLL 2017), Vancouver, Canada, pp. 411–420. Association for Computational Linguistics, August 2017. http://aclweb.org/anthology/K17-1041
15. Marcheggiani, D., Titov, I.: Encoding sentences with graph convolutional networks for semantic role labeling. In: Proceedings of the 2017 Conference on Empirical Methods in Natural Language Processing, Copenhagen, Denmark, pp. 1507–1516. Association for Computational Linguistics, September 2017. https://www.aclweb.org/anthology/D17-1159
16. Nasukawa, T., Yi, J.: Sentiment analysis: capturing favorability using natural language processing. In: Proceedings of the 2nd International Conference on Knowledge Capture, pp. 70–77. ACM (2003)

17. Pang, B., Lee, L., et al.: Opinion mining and sentiment analysis. Found. Trends®
Inf. Retr. **2**(1–2), 1–135 (2008)
18. Pennington, J., Socher, R., Manning, C.: Glove: global vectors for word representation. In: Proceedings of the 2014 Conference on Empirical Methods in Natural
Language Processing (EMNLP), pp. 1532–1543 (2014)
19. Pontiki, M., Galanis, D., Pavlopoulos, J., Papageorgiou, H., Androutsopoulos, I.,
Manandhar, S.: Semeval-2014 task 4: aspect based sentiment analysis. In: Proceedings of International Workshop on Semantic Evaluation, pp. 27–35 (2014)
20. Tang, D., Qin, B., Feng, X., Liu, T.: Target-dependent sentiment classification with
long short term memory. CoRR, abs/1512.01100 (2015)
21. Tang, D., Qin, B., Liu, T.: Aspect level sentiment classification with deep memory
network. In: Proceedings of the 2016 Conference on Empirical Methods in Natural
Language Processing, pp. 214–224 (2016)
22. Wang, Y., Huang, M., Zhao, L., et al.: Attention-based LSTM for aspect-level sentiment classification. In: Proceedings of the 2016 Conference on Empirical Methods
in Natural Language Processing, pp. 606–615 (2016)
23. Xue, W., Li, T.: Aspect based sentiment analysis with gated convolutional networks. In: Proceedings of the 56th Annual Meeting of the Association for Computational Linguistics (Volume 1: Long Papers), ACL 2018, Melbourne, Australia,
pp. 2514–2523, 15–20 July 2018. https://aclanthology.info/papers/P18-1234/p18-
1234
24. Zhang, M., Zhang, Y., Vo, D.T.: Gated neural networks for targeted sentiment
analysis. In: AAAI, pp. 3087–3093 (2016)

An Evidential Semi-supervised Label Aggregation Approach

Lina Abassi[(⊠)] and Imen Boukhris

LARODEC Laboratory, Institut Supérieur de Gestion de Tunis,
University of Tunis, Tunis, Tunisia
lina.abassi@gmail.com, imen.boukhris@hotmail.com

Abstract. Crowdsourcing is a powerful concept that typically takes advantage of human intelligence to deal with problems in many fields most importantly in machine learning. Indeed, it enables to collect training labels in a fast and cheap way for supervised algorithms. The only major challenge is that the quality of the contributions is not always guaranteed because of the expertise heterogeneity of the participants. One of the basic strategies to overcome this problem is to assign each task to multiple workers and then combine their answers in order to obtain a single reliable one. This paper provides a new iterative approach that aggregates imperfect labels using the supervision of few gold labels under the evidence theory. Besides of inferring the consensus answers, the workers' accuracies and the questions difficulties are as well estimated. A comparative evaluation on synthetic and real datasets confirms the effectiveness of our semi-supervised approach over the baselines.

Keywords: Crowdsourcing · Answer aggregation · Evidence theory · Gold labels

1 Introduction

Over the past few years, crowdsourcing has provided easy and affordable access to human intelligence to solve a variety of basic tasks in different areas of computer science [1–3]. Computers and algorithms can be quite productive in performing some functions including identifying patterns in a picture or executing complex computations, but other processes are still best carried by humans such as recognizing contents of an image or ambiguous text/writing. Platforms such as Amazon Mechanical Turk or Crowdflower simplified crowdsourcing tasks such as audio transcription, image categorization, product reviews, text translation and so on. The resultant labelled data serves generally as training data for supervised learning algorithms. In these platforms, employers typically post their tasks and workers are asked to give a reliable answer in order to get small amount of money in return. Unfortunately, accuracy of the participants is often more or less divergent owing to factors such as skill, motivation, poor task design or task complexity. This leads to imperfect results since that the quality of a crowdsourced

© Springer Nature Switzerland AG 2019
C. Douligeris et al. (Eds.): KSEM 2019, LNAI 11775, pp. 676–686, 2019.
https://doi.org/10.1007/978-3-030-29551-6_60

task strongly depends on the quality of humans involved in its execution. It has been affirmed that combined answers when assigning the same task to more than one contributor (i.e redundancy) [5] is as effective as experts answers [3]. This latter is among the first techniques to be applied in crowdsourcing platforms in order to encounter inferior quality contributions. However, redundancy needs a competent combination method to deliver best results. Plus, it is important to take into account the skill levels of the involved employees.

In this work, we propose a new approach of answer aggregation under the assumption that few answers on gold standards (i.e a priori labelled tasks) are available. For this, we resort to the evidence theory. The advantage of this theory is that, it allows to model uncertainty in data and provides operations to both revise and fuse information. Our proposal has as main purposes to infer consensus labels by iteratively combining submissions while joining the workers' skills and tasks complexity rates. Therefore, the evidence theory is well suited to deal with this paper objectives.

This paper is organized as follows: In Sect. 2, we provide an overview of existing label aggregation techniques. Section 3, briefly reviews the basic concepts of the evidence theory. Section 4 introduces our proposed approach in details. The experimental study is presented in Sect. 5 and finally, conclusion is given in Sect. 6.

2 Related Work

One of the fundamental technical issues of crowdsourcing is quality control. Because labellers could have mixed abilities or dedication, obtaining accurate responses is no longer assured. Since assigning the same task to several contributors was allowed by the majority of platforms, aggregation methods became a necessity. As a consequence, many proposals were released. They are referred to as inference algorithms. A lot of them not only estimate the label of instances but also generate other parameters such as abilities of jobbers, the difficulty of instances and so on. Some are only based on the contributed labels involving no prior gold information, said unsupervised methods. Among them, a non iterative method, Majority Decision (MD) which is the most used technique and it can most of the time achieve good results. Its only limitation is that it considers the max votes locally (i.e for each task separately) [4]. The Belief Label Aggregation (BLA) [23] calculates the worker levels of expertise regarding majority votes and integrate them to infer true reponses under the evidence theory. Another method [13] based on linear algebra estimates both true answers and workers abilities. Alternatively, we find iterative methods based on the EM algorithm [19] which is widely used to infer latent variables [20,21]. For instance, the Dawid & Skene (DS) [12] method considers the expertise of labellers which is estimated in the Maximization phase (M) and then integrated in the Expectation phase (E) to generate consensus labels. Also based on the EM algorithm, a variety of approaches has proposed ways to assess the abilities of participants [11] and/or difficulty of task such as the Generative model of Labels, Abilities and Difficulties (GLAD) [22] and the Iterative Belief Label Aggregation (I-BLA) [25].

This latter, is based on the evidence theory. A different category of methods is of those which fully depend on gold information gathered from experts to estimate the true answers, called supervised methods such as the one proposed by Snow [3] and the Supervised Learning from Multiple Experts (SLME) [14]. However, this complete supervision can be expensive which comes against the whole purpose of crowdsourcing. While collecting a large amount of labels from experts is not a practical solution, it may be useful to get a small number of gold data from experts. This concept has inspired several methods mainly non iterative, referred to as semi-supervised techniques like the Expert Label Injected Crowd Estimation (ELICE) [15] which infers the reliabilities of workers and questions complexities using some gold data similarly to a set of other methods [16,28]. Recent works within the evidence theory also depend on gold information to guess the final responses namely (GS-BLA) [24], (CGS-BLA) [26], and (CAS-CAD) [28]. For instance, The (CGS-BLA) [26] uses gold input to predict the worker skill and consider it as an attribute to cluster workers then integrate their labels according to their relative cluster. Table 1 outlines the related work methods.

In this paper, we propose a new approach that takes advantage of the iterative algorithm (i.e EM) principle and the supervision of a few gold standards hence making it an iterative semi-supervised technique. Based on the evidence theory, our proposal namely the Iterative Gold Standards-based Belief Label Aggregation estimates through a series of iterations the task true label, the skill levels of contributors and the complexity of tasks. The evidence theory has a lot of assets when coping with imperfect data as it enables their representation, update and fusion. Methods like [18,27,28] have adopted the evidence framework and succeeded in gathering quality results.

Table 1. Related work methods

	Iterative	Non-iterative
Unsupervised (no gold data)	DS, GLAD, I-BLA	MD, BLA, KOS
Semi-supervised (few gold data)	IGS-BLA	ELICE, CASCAD, GS-BLA, CGS-BLA
Supervised (with gold data)	Snow et al., SLME	-

3 The Evidence Theory

3.1 Definition

The evidence theory [6,7] also known as the belief function theory is a theoretical framework for reasoning with partial and unreliable information. It models the uncertainty on given decision options and provides operations to manipulate them. We adopt the most commonly used model namely Transferable Belief Model (TBM) [17].

Let $\Theta = \{\theta_1, \theta_2, ..., \theta_k\}$ be a finite set of elementary values θ called frame of discernment.

A mass function or a basic belief assignment (*bba*) denoted by m, represents the knowledge committed to the elements of 2^Θ given a source of information. It is defined as a mapping function m from 2^Θ to $[0, 1]$ satisfying:

$$\sum_{A \subseteq \Theta} m(A) = 1 \tag{1}$$

The subset A of Θ such that $m(A) > 0$ is the focal sets of m. The belief committed to a singleton A represents a certain *bba* such that $m(A) = 1$. A state of total ignorance is defined by $m(\Theta) = 1$. A *bba* is conflictual when $m(\emptyset) > 0$. If the *bba* has at most one focal element A different from Θ, it is called a simple support function:

$$m(A) = 1 - \theta, m(\Theta) = \theta \tag{2}$$

for some A and $\theta \in]0, 1[$.

3.2   Evidential Operations

Discounting Evidence. Discounting [6] consists in incorporating the reliability of a source contributing a piece of information represented by a mass function m. The discounting factor α belongs to $[0, 1]$ and the discounted mass function m^α is defined by:

$$\begin{cases} m^\alpha(A) = (1 - \alpha)m(A), \quad \forall A \subset \Theta, \\ m^\alpha(\Theta) = (1 - \alpha)m(\Theta) + \alpha. \end{cases} \tag{3}$$

Combination of Evidence. The evidence theory provides several combination rules in order to combine distinct reliable sources $m_1, ..., m_n$ such as:

- *Conjunctive rule of combination* proposed by Smets [10] and defined by:

$$m_1 \textcircled{\cap} m_2(A) = \sum_{B \cap C = A} m_1(B)m_2(C) \tag{4}$$

- *Dempster rule of combination* proposed by Dempster [7]. It is the normalized version of conjunctive rule as it does not allows a mass on the empty set. It is defined by:

$$m_1 \oplus m_2(A) = \begin{cases} \dfrac{m_1 \textcircled{\cap} m_2(A)}{1 - m_1 \textcircled{\cap} m_2(\emptyset)} & \text{if } \emptyset \neq A \subseteq \Theta \\ 0 & \text{otherwise.} \end{cases} \tag{5}$$

- *The Combination With Adapted Conflict rule* (CWAC) [9] defined by:

$$m_{\textcircled{\ominus}}(A) = (\textcircled{\ominus} m_i)(A) = Dm_{\textcircled{\cap}}(A) + (1 - D)m_\oplus(A) \tag{6}$$

It actually performs the same way as the conjunctive rule or the Dempster rule depending on the maximum Jousselme distance [8] between two *bbas* defined as $D = \max\ [\mathrm{d}(m_i,\ m_j)]$ such that:

$$d(m_1, m_2) = \sqrt{\frac{1}{2}(m_1 - m_2)^t \mathrm{D}(m_1 - m_2)}, \tag{7}$$

with D is called the Jaccard index defined as:

$$\mathrm{D}(A, B) = \begin{cases} 0 & \text{if } A = B = \emptyset, \\ \frac{|A \cap B|}{|A \cup B|} & \forall\, A, B \in 2^\Theta. \end{cases} \tag{8}$$

Decision Making. To make a decision when dealing with mass functions, the Transferable Belief Model includes the pignistic probability ($BetP$) that consists in transforming the mass functions into a probability space. It is defined as follows:

$$BetP(\theta_i) = \sum_{A \subseteq \Theta} \frac{|A \cap \theta_i|}{|A|} \cdot \frac{m(A)}{(1 - m(\emptyset))} \quad \forall\, \theta_i \in \Theta \tag{9}$$

The hypothesis having the highest $BetP$ is chosen as the final decision.

4   IGS-BLA: Iterative Gold Standards-Based Belief Label Aggregation

Consider a set of N single choice questions performed by M labellers. Each answer a_{ij} given by a labeller l_j (with $j \in \{1,2, ..., M\}$) to a question q_i (with $i \in \{1,2, ..., N\}$) belongs to $\{1,2, ..., K\}$ (with $K \in \mathbf{N}$). A_i is the final answer to a question q_i. In addition, since our scenario involves some supervision, we consider another set of n gold standards (questions labelled by experts) is available such that $n \ll N$. In the rest of this paper, we refer to gold standards as labelled questions and the remaining as unlabelled ones.

Our suggested approach the Iterative Gold Standards based Belief Label Aggregation allows the estimation of consensus labels as well as the abilities and difficulty rates through a series of iterations summarized in Algorithm 1. As described, the procedure begins by modelling all the contributed answers under the evidence theory transforming them into mass functions (*bbas*). Furthermore, the labellers ability scores ($x_j \in [0, 1]$) are initialized to 1, considering them as fully reliable and the question difficulty rates ($y_i \in [0, 1]$) are initialized to 0, considering them as very easy. After that, two main steps iterate until no changements occur. The first step consists in label inferring incorporating the workers expertise scores and questions complexities. Label inferring is actually done by aggregating all answers on unlabelled questions. Next, in the second step, given the true labels of the few labelled questions and the aggregated labels of unlabelled questions, the abilities of workers are calculated. As for the questions difficulties, they are measured regarding a conflict rate generated in the aggregation phase. Owing to the iterations, the computation of labels and parameters is jointly reinforced which results in the betterment of the estimation process. In what follows, the steps of our approach are explained thoroughly:

Algorithm 1. IGS-BLA Algorithm

Input: A set of answers a_{ij} to N unlabelled questions and a set of n gold labels to labelled questions.

Output: The final aggregated labels A_i, the abilities x_j and the difficulty rates y_i

1: Labels transformation to mass functions (*bbas*)
2: Initialize labellers ability scores with $x_j = 1$ (assuming each one is perfect) and question complexities with $y_i = 0$ (assuming that they are all very easy)
3: **repeat**
4:    Step 1: Aggregate all answers on unlabelled questions integrating x_j and y_i
5:    Step 2: Update all x_j and all y_i given the aggregated labels and gold labels
6: **until** Convergence
7: **return** A_i, x_j and y_i for all unlabelled questions

4.1 Label Representation

This pre-step enables the transformation of the answers into mass functions under the evidence theory. Accordingly, each answer is represented as *bba* m_{ij}^{Θ} with $\Theta = \{\theta_1, \ldots, \theta_n\}$. To simplify, we assume dealing with binary labels hence $\Theta = \{1, 2\}$.

So, when $a_{ij} = 1$, it becomes $m_{ij}(\{1\}) = 1$ and when $a_{ij} = 2$, it is changed to $m_{ij}(\{2\}) = 1$. These transformed *bbas* are certain.

4.2 Step 1: Label Assessment

Throughout this step, all unlabelled questions final answers are estimated joining two parameters notably labellers ability rates and questions complexities. In order to take them into account, we resort to the discounting operation (Eq. 3). Hence, the converted mass functions are updated using the ability values x_j combined with the difficulty rates y_i such that the discounted rate α_j is computed as follows:

$$\alpha_j = \beta(1 - x_j) + (1 - \beta)y_i \tag{10}$$

Noting that $(1 - x_j)$ represents the error rate of a worker. Plus, we fixed β to 0.5 to give both parameters the same importance.

Example 1. We suppose labeller l_1 is bad having an ability score $x_1 = 0.2$ and he answered 2 on question q_1 which is considered hard as it has a difficulty $y_1 = 0.8$. Hence, the discounting rate is $\alpha_1 = 0.4 + 0.4 = 0.8$. Accordingly, the certain *bba* representing his answer will be changed to a simple support function as follows:
$m_{11}^{\alpha}(\{2\}) = (1 - 0.8) \cdot 1 = 0.2,$
$m_{11}^{\alpha}(\{1, 2\}) = 0.8 + (1 - 0.8) \cdot 0 = 0.8$

Once the discounting step completed, all answers on unlabelled questions in form of mass functions are combined using the combination with adapted conflict (CWAC) rule (Eq. 6) to obtain one final mass function such as $\ominus_{j=1}^{M} m_i = m_{i1}^{\alpha}$ $\ominus m_{i2}^{\alpha} \ominus m_{ij}^{\alpha} \ominus \ldots m_{iM}^{\alpha}$. A conflict rate $c_i \in [0, 1]$ is produced by this combination rule that basically represents the mass on the empty set of the aggregated mass functions. The (CWAC) rule allows to generate a rational conflict rate that reveals the contradiction of *bbas*. That is the reason why we adopted this rule over the conjunctive rule which has an absorbing power causing it to generate a very high conflict degree.

Finally, we have recourse to the pignistic probability (*BetP*) (Eq. 9) to make a decision regarding the final label, which is the one having the higher value.

Example 2. We consider the following mass function as the one obtained after applying the (CWAC) rule on question q_1:
$m_1(\varnothing) = 0.17$,
$m_1(\{2\}) = 0.83$
The obtained pignistic probability is:
$\text{BetP}(\{1\}) = 0$
$\text{BetP}(\{2\}) = 1 \cdot (0.83/(1 - 0.17)) = 1$,
Hence, the final label is $A_i = 2$.

4.3 Step 2: Parameters Assessment

Given the inferred labels in the previous step and the set of gold labels we acquire, the workers levels of ability x_j are computed and that by comparing his answers to them as follows:

$$x_j = \frac{Number\ of\ correct\ labels}{Number\ of\ labelled\ +\ unlabelled\ questions} \tag{11}$$

Then, concerning the difficulty rate of questions $y_i \in [0, 1]$, we consider the conflict rate generated by the (CWAC) rule as the indicator of the complexity of a question. Actually, the more a question is hard the more answers are mixed and hence reflect a high conflict. As a result, the difficulty of a question is the same level of conflict deduced when aggregating answers (i.e $y_i = c_i$).

5 Experimentation

Since the evaluation of our approach requires that the totality of questions be answered by all labellers, we conducted experiments on two synthetic datasets from the UCI repository [30] namely IRIS (100 instances) and Mushroom (8124 instances), as well as a real world balanced dataset called Bluebird [29] (108 questions answered by 39 workers).

We compare our proposal, the Iterative Gold Standards-based Belief Label Aggregation (IGS-BLA) with related work methods namely (MD), (ELICE), (BLA), (GS-BLA) and (CGS-BLA) regarding two evaluation metrics:

– accuracy; which reflects how much labels have been correctly estimated.
– bad participants resistance; which tests accuracy with different proportions of low quality labellers.

Simulated Datasets

We investigated the performance of our method with different base workers ratios. In fact, we assume that low quality participants have less than 20% accuracy, as for good ones it is above 70%. We simulated data accordingly for 20 workers and we made a random selection of the gold questions each time in the same manner as ELICE [15]. We display the results in terms of accuracy with different ratio intervals of bad participants in Table 2. Results manifestly show that with less than 40% of poor quality workers, all methods perform greatly. But accuracy begins to decrease with a ratio between 40% and 70%, notably for (MD) and (BLA) mainly because they involve the vote of majority and continuously drops above 70%, but still IGS-BLA records best results and outperforms the CGS-BLA method with 0.65 accuracy for the IRIS dataset.

Real Dataset

Besides the investigation on simulated data, we evaluated our approach on a real world dataset, Bluebird. As for gold questions, we selected 8 questions randomly and measured accuracy.

As depicted in Fig. 1, our approach (IGS-BLA) records superior accuracy as the number of workers increases (64% accuracy with 39 workers).

Table 2. Average accuracies of baseline methods on simulated datasets for three ratio intervals of bad labellers

Bad workers	Dataset # GS	Mushroom 20	IRIS 4
<40%	MD	0.98	0.95
	ELICE	0.97	0.98
	BLA	0.95	0.97
	GS-BLA	0.98	1
	CGS-BLA	1	1
	IGS-BLA	1	1
40%–70%	MD	0.4	0.35
	ELICE	0.91	0.9
	BLA	0.45	0.43
	GS-BLA	0.97	0.98
	CGS-BLA	1	1
	IGS-BLA	1	1
>70%	MD	0.01	0.02
	ELICE	0.35	0.32
	BLA	0.13	0.1
	GS-BLA	0.57	0.38
	CGS-BLA	0.56	0.43
	IGS-BLA	0.64	0.65

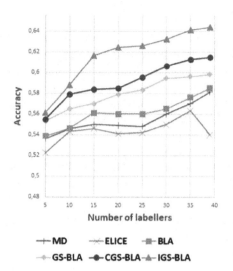

Fig. 1. Accuracies as function of the number of workers for Bluebird dataset

6   Conclusion

In this work, we proposed a novel semi-supervised label aggregation approach based the evidence theory. It allows the estimation of the true labels, while at the same time calculating the participants levels of ability and the difficulty of questions. This procedure is reinforced through iterations. Moreover, parameters are assessed with the supervision of few gold data provided by experts. As a result, accuracy has been significantly improved allowing our approach to outperform the baseline methods.

References

1. Zheng, Y., Wang, J., Li, G., Feng, J.: QASCA: a quality-aware task assignment system for crowdsourcing applications. In: International Conference on Management of Data, pp. 1031–1046 (2015)
2. Yan, T., Kumar, V., Ganesan, D.: Designing games with a purpose. Commun. ACM **51**(8), 58–67 (2008)
3. Snow, R., O'Connor, B., Jurafsky, D., Ng, A.Y.: Cheap and fast but is it good? Evaluation non-expert annotations for natural language tasks. In: The Conference on Empirical Methods in Natural Languages Processing, pp. 254–263 (2008)
4. Kuncheva, L., Whitaker, C., Shipp, C., Duin, R.: Limits on the majority vote accuracy in classifier fusion. Pattern Anal. Appl. **6**, 22–31 (2003)
5. Sheng, V.S., Provost, F., Ipeirotis, P.G.: Get another label? Improving data quality and data mining using multiple, noisy labellers. In: International Conference on Knowledge Discovery and Data Mining, pp. 614–622 (2008)
6. Shafer, G.: A Mathematical Theory of Evidence, vol. 1. Princeton University Press, Princeton (1976)

7. Dempster, A.P.: Upper and lower probabilities induced by a multivalued mapping. Ann. Math. Stat. **38**, 325–339 (1967)
8. Jousselme, A.-L., Grenier, D., Bossé, É.: A new distance between two bodies of evidence. Inf. Fusion **2**, 91–101 (2001)
9. Lefèvre, E., Elouedi, Z.: How to preserve the confict as an alarm in the combination of belief functions? Decis. Support Syst. **56**, 326–333 (2013)
10. Smets, P.: The combination of evidence in the transferable belief model. IEEE Trans. Pattern Anal. Mach. Intell. **12**(5), 447–458 (1990)
11. Raykar, V.C., Yu, S.: Eliminating spammers and ranking annotators for crowd-sourced labelling tasks. J. Mach. Learn. Res. **13**, 491–518 (2012)
12. Dawid, A.P., Skene, A.M.: Maximum likelihood estimation of observer error-rates using the EM algorithm. Appl. Stat. **28**, 20–28 (2010)
13. Karger, D.R., Oh, S., Shah, D.: Budget-optimal task allocation for reliable crowd-sourcing systems. Oper. Res. **62**, 1–24 (2014)
14. Raykar, V.C., et al.: Supervised learning from multiple experts: whom to trust when everyone lies a bit. In: Proceedings of the 26th Annual International Conference on Machine Learning, pp. 889–896 (2009)
15. Khattak, F.K., Salleb, A.: Quality control of crowd labelling through expert evaluation. In: The Neural Information Processing Systems 2nd Workshop on Computational Social Science and the Wisdom of Crowds, pp. 27–29 (2011)
16. Lee, K., Caverlee, J., Webb, S.: The social honeypot project: protecting online communities from spammers. In: International World Wide Web Conference, pp. 1139–1140 (2010)
17. Smets, P., Mamdani, A., Dubois, D., Prade, H.: Non Standard Logics for Automated Reasoning, pp. 253–286. Academic Press, London (1988)
18. Ben Rjab, A., Kharoune, M., Miklos, Z., Martin, A.: Characterization of experts in crowdsourcing platforms. In: Vejnarová, J., Kratochvíl, V. (eds.) BELIEF 2016. LNCS (LNAI), vol. 9861, pp. 97–104. Springer, Cham (2016). https://doi.org/10.1007/978-3-319-45559-4_10
19. Watanabe, M., Yamaguchi, K.: The EM Algorithm and Related Statistical Models, p. 250. CRC Press, Boca Raton (2003)
20. Li, J., Li, X., Yang, B., Sun, X.: Segmentation-based image copy-move forgery detection scheme. IEEE Trans. Inf. Forensics Secur. **10**, 507–518 (2015)
21. Liu, K., Cheung, W.K., Liu, J.: Detecting multiple stochastic network motifs in network data. Knowl. Inf. Syst. **42**, 49–74 (2015)
22. Whitehill, J., Wu, T., Bergsma, J., Movellan, J.R., Ruvolo, P.L.: Whose vote should count more: optimal integration of labels from labellers of unknown expertise. In: Neural Information Processing Systems, pp. 2035–2043 (2009)
23. Abassi, L., Boukhris, I.: Crowd label aggregation under a belief function framework. In: Lehner, F., Fteimi, N. (eds.) KSEM 2016. LNCS (LNAI), vol. 9983, pp. 185–196. Springer, Cham (2016). https://doi.org/10.1007/978-3-319-47650-6_15
24. Abassi, L., Boukhris, I.: A gold standards-based crowd label aggregation within the belief function theory. In: Benferhat, S., Tabia, K., Ali, M. (eds.) IEA/AIE 2017. LNCS (LNAI), vol. 10351, pp. 97–106. Springer, Cham (2017). https://doi.org/10.1007/978-3-319-60045-1_12
25. Abassi, L., Boukhris, I.: Iterative aggregation of crowdsourced tasks within the belief function theory. In: Antonucci, A., Cholvy, L., Papini, O. (eds.) ECSQARU 2017. LNCS (LNAI), vol. 10369, pp. 159–168. Springer, Cham (2017). https://doi.org/10.1007/978-3-319-61581-3_15
26. Abassi, L., Boukhris, I.: A worker clustering-based approach of label aggregation under the belief function theory. Appl. Intell. **49**, 53–62 (2018)

27. Abassi, L., Boukhris, I.: Imprecise label aggregation approach under the belief function theory. In: Abraham, A., Cherukuri, A.K., Melin, P., Gandhi, N. (eds.) Intelligent Systems Design and Applications, vol. 941, pp. 607–616. Springer, Cham (2018)
28. Koulougli, D., HadjAli, A., Rassoul, I.: Handling query answering in crowdsourcing systems: a belief function-based approach. In: Annual Conference of the North American Fuzzy Information Processing Society (NAFIPS), pp. 1–6 (2016)
29. Welinder, P., Branson, S., Perona, P., Belongie, S.J.: The multidimensional wisdom of crowds. In: Neural Information Processing Systems, pp. 2424–2432 (2010)
30. Frank, A.: UCI machine learning repository (1987). http://archive.ics.uci.edu/ml

Knowledge Engineering Applications

Improved Feature Selection Algorithm for Biological Sequences Classification

Naoual Guannoni[1,2]([✉]) [iD], Faouzi Mhamdi[2,3], and Mourad Elloumi[2]

[1] Faculty of Sciences of Tunis (FST), Tunis El-Manar University, Tunis, Tunisia
nawel.gannouni90@gmail.com
[2] Laboratory of Technologies of Information and Communication and Electrical
Engineering (LaTICE) ENSIT, University of Tunis, Tunis, Tunisia
faouzi.mhamdi@ensi.rnu.tn, Mourad.Elloumi@gmail.com
[3] Higher Institute of Applied Languages and Computer Science of Beja,
University of Jendouba, Jendouba, Tunisia
https://fr.overleaf.com/project/5ced19f73f8fb07b2db14280

Abstract. Biological data is undergoing exponential growth in both
the volume and complexity. Indeed, the selection of biological features
is an important step that aims to reduce the curse of dimensionality to
improve prediction performance in classification systems. In this paper,
we focus on protein sequence classification which constitutes an important problem in biological sciences. We represent in first a comparative
study between classical filter feature selection algorithms and feature
selection methods based on new correlation techniques in order to identify relevant, not redundant features. Then, we propose an improved
version of Strong Relevant Algorithm for Subset Selection (STRASS)
algorithm called "optimized STRASS algorithm" that uses new correlation metrics to reduce irrelevant and redundant features.

Experimental results show the effectiveness of this work. The proposed method can be applied to high-dimensional data. The final aim
of this study is to select the best pairwise combination of filter feature
selection method and the best classifier that enhances the accuracy of
protein classification.

Keywords: Feature selection · Filter method · Classification ·
Protein sequence

1 Introduction

Feature selection is the process of selecting a subset of relevant features and discarding the irrelevant for use in the predictive model. This process has several
advantages such as improving the performance of a classification algorithm, providing a better understanding of the process that generated the data [6,12,19].

There are three main classes of feature selection algorithms: wrapper, filter,
and embedded method [10]. This distinction is based on their dependence or
independence from the induction algorithm. In this paper, we focus on filter

© Springer Nature Switzerland AG 2019
C. Douligeris et al. (Eds.): KSEM 2019, LNAI 11775, pp. 689–700, 2019.
https://doi.org/10.1007/978-3-030-29551-6_61

feature selection methods. These techniques use such criteria to select a subset of features which are relevant and non-redundant [6,12].

Several classical filter feature selection algorithms are available in the literature such as relief, information gain, chi-square, Symmetrical uncertainty (SU) and Correlation-based feature selection (CFS). On the other hand, a lot of studies have been undertaken to propose new methods for ranking and selecting the important features from high-dimensional data using new correlation metrics [4,6,8,17].

Protein sequence classification is one of the most important problems in biological sciences. It is the assignment of sequences to known categories based on sequence similarity. That is, it helps to find the sequential relationships included in the data [1,2,9]. The term family of a class is used to denote any collection of sequences that can share common characteristics [3]. The sequences of proteins that are extracted are stored in various databases. Each database stores a specific classification of protein sequences. Protein sequence databases characterize by their high-dimensional variables and contain a higher amount of knowledge. These biomedical data are frequently containing thousands of features (genes) yet much fewer samples. Thus, they create several problems for the researchers during the analysis of large amounts of sequence data [9]. Therefore, these databases required for a highly accurate and efficient feature selection method that can accurately classify the protein sequences into existing families [9].

In this paper, we first present a comparative study between classical filter feature selection method and existing filter methods based on new correlation metrics for protein sequence classification. This aims to select the most significant features which lead to improved classification results of our families' sequences. Then, we propose a method to optimise STRASS algorithm. This work can aid biologists to make the best decision about protein classification and to predict the disease.

This paper is organized as follow: In Sect. 2 we present we present a literature review of feature section methods based on new correlation metrics. Section 3 describes our proposed method to optimize STRASS algorithm. Section 4 follows reporting the experimental study and the results. In Sect. 5, we discuss our obtained results. Finally, in Sect. 6, we conclude by summarizing our results, and presents directions for future work.

2   Literature Review of Feature Selection Methods Based on New Correlation Methods

2.1   New Dependency and Correlation Analysis for Features

Guangzhi Qu et al. [17] proposed a new feature correlation metric $\phi_y(X_i, X_j)$ and a feature subset merit measure $e(S)$ in order to determine the relevance among features with respect to a desired data mining task. This correlation method concerning the relevance of the features and the pairwise feature correlation to improve the predictive power classification. When there is a decision Y associated with two features X_i and X_j, the correlation between them is called decision dependent correlation (DDC), and the new correlation metric is based on this measure. It given by:

$$\phi_y = \frac{I(Y;X_i) + I(Y;X_j) - I(Y;X_i,X_j)}{H(Y)} \tag{1}$$

$\phi_y = 1$ means that the features X_i and X_j are completely correlated with respect to decision Y. The proposed subset evaluation measure $e(S)$ enables to evaluate the subset feature selection to making decision. So, the bigger the value of this measure, the better the feature subset in making a decision.

$$e(S) = \frac{\sum_{\forall j \in I_m} I(Y;X_j)}{H(Y)} - \sum_{\forall i, ji, j \in I_m} \phi_y(X_i, X_j) \tag{2}$$

The feature selection method used this new correlation metric consists of two functional modules [17]: removing irrelevance features using a user-defined threshold δ_1 determine which feature is relevant to the final decision and eliminating redundancy from the features to be selected.

2.2 Feature Selection via Correlation Coefficient Clustering

Hui-Huang Hsu et al. [7], proposed a new method using a correlation coefficient instead of the Euclidean distance for clustering analysis in order to remove similar/redundant features. This feature selection method consists of two steps: In the first step, the whole feature set is separated into different groups using clustering analysis and correlation coefficient instead of the Euclidian distance. Closely related features can be put together. In the second step, the most relevant and non-redundant features from each group is selected by computing the correlation coefficient between each feature in the cluster and the class. The most related feature-class is selected. Other features in the same cluster are then removed.

2.3 Strong Relevant Algorithm for Subset Selection (*STRASS*)

Brigitte Chebel et al. [4], proposed a new filter algorithm *STRASS* based on k-way correlation between features and the class to select relevant features.

In the first, it proposed two new criteria for relevance and redundancy. The first criterion computes the discriminating capacity (DC) of a set of variables in order to extract a subset of variables with the same (DC) of all variables. The second criterion evaluates the discriminating capacity Gain (DCG) of one feature relative to a set of features. Features with the largest gains are added to the selected set, and features with null gain are redundant are discarded. DC measures the weak relevance of a set of features and DCG measures the Strong Relevance of a set of features.

Consider an input data Ω consist of n samples $W_1, \ldots W_n$. Each sample in Ω is composed of r features. The whole feature is denoted $x = \{x_1, \ldots x_n\}$.

Each sample in Ω is labeled with a class $\in C$. The set of classes is denoted $C = \{c_1, \ldots c_M\}$. Let associate to a feature x_k the Boolean function ϕ_{ij}^k, $1 \leq i$, $j \leq n$, $1 \leq k \leq r$.

$$\phi_{i,j}^k : \Omega * \Omega \to \{0,1\} \qquad w_i, w_i \to 1 \text{ if } x_k(w_i) = x_k(w_j)$$

with $x_k(w_i)$ represents the value of feature x_k in w_i.

$$\phi_{ij}^C : \Omega * \Omega \to \{0,1\} \qquad w_i, w_i \to 1 \text{ if } C(w_i) = C(w_j)$$

with $C(w_i)$ is the class of sample w_i

The discriminating capacity (DC) measure of a feature set $L = \{x_1, \ldots x_m\}$ is defined as the following formula:

$$DC(L, \Omega) = \sum_{i=1}^{n} \sum_{j=1}^{n} \overline{\prod_{i=1}^{n} \phi_{ij,}^k} \cdot \overline{\phi_{ij}^C} \tag{3}$$

The Discriminating Capacity Gain (DCG) can be defined as the following formula:

$$DCG(x_k, L, \Omega) = \sum_{i=1}^{n} \sum_{i=1}^{n} SR(x_k, L, w_i, w_j) \tag{4}$$

With SR is the Strong Relevance of a feature x_k on pairs of instances. Therefore, the proposed *STRASS* algorithm breaks up into three steps: In the first step, the features are ranked in descending order based on *DCG* and a subset of strongly relevant features is selected. In the second step, the remaining features are evaluated one by one and the weakly relevant features that have the largest discriminating capacity are combined with the previously selected features. In the third step, the algorithm consists to remove redundant features. Features having a discriminating capacity *DC* lower than a predefined threshold are removed [4]. The run-time complexity of STRASS algorithm is very high for large dataset because the pairwise data representation is inherently a combinatorial problem [4].

3   Contribution: Optimization of STRASS Algorithm

The limitation of STRASS algorithm is that it only applicable for small size databases due to the high computational complexity [4]. It cannot be executed for a higher amount of features. However, it takes a lot of time to be executed especially when we use our big data set.

In this part, we propose a new methodology to reduce the execution time of STRASS algorithm. This method is called optimized STRASS algorithm.

The proposed method consists of two major steps:

In the first step, we developed a new frequency-based feature selection method. This step consists of selecting the features that are most common in the classes. Therefore, we develop a method that select features (genes) that have an occurrence number superior to a threshold defined by the user (20%, 25%, 30%, 35%, 40%). This filter technique enables to select the most occurrence features in the instances (structure of the protein). That means this method choose the features based on their appearances in the instances.

After reducing the number of irrelevant features, in the second step, we use the new two criteria of relevance and redundancy of STRASS algorithm Eqs. (3) and (4) in order to obtain again a new final subset of relevant and non redundant features that enhance the accuracy of classification. These criteria enable to detect not only strongly relevant features but also weakly relevant one.

The final aim of the proposed method is to detect relevance, non-redundant features with less computationally complexity than original STRASS algorithm. Another aim of the proposed method is to be efficient for large dataset with reduced run time. Figure 1 illustrates the proposed method.

4 Experimental Study and Results

In this section, we present the experimental methodology, the data set, and the obtained results. Our experimental study is divided into two parts. In the first part, we illustrate the dataset used for the experimentation. In the second part, we evaluate the performances of feature selection methods for the classification of the protein sequence.

4.1 Description of the Dataset

The protein sequence database consists of 87 instances and 6600 attributes. Each instance represents a primary structure and each attribute represents a motif, i.e., a substring conserved in a family of the primary structure. The last attribute

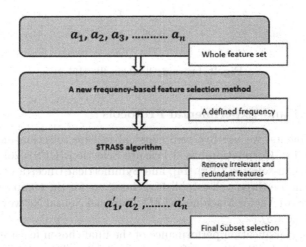

Fig. 1. The process of the new approaches of STRASS algorithm.

represents the families to which the different sequences belong (classes). We used two families of proteins that are extracted from the data bank SCOP (for example F_2 is a toll-like receptor) [15]. All proteins contained in the same family have similar structures. The protein sequence is a series of amino acids that have a specific order. There exist 20 amino acids that allow the description of a protein by a sequence of characters. Inspired by text mining we have used n-grams (a sequence of n characters) extraction technique in order to produce descriptor. However, unlike the text classification, there is no "natural" separation in the character sequences, thus n-grams technique seemed to be good in our case [14].

In our study we choose n = 3. In fact, previous works showed that n = 3 (3-grams) are a good compromise to produce a minimal motif subset with high discrimination of protein sequence capacity [14].

The Boolean data representation is used in our experiments. Each case in the data set $T[i,j]$ represents the weighting of the jth attribute in the ith instance (the importance of motif in a sequence). For example, in the case of a Boolean weighting, if $T[i,j] = 1$ then the jth attribute (motif) is present in the ith instance (sequence), otherwise it is absent. Many attributes are absent in the most instances. They can be irrelevant or redundant and can provide no information about a protein sequence. Figure 2 describe the proposed dataset.

Sequence set ↓	MLD	LDN	Motifs (3-gramms) ↓ DNT	NTR	TRL	Family ↓ Class
seq1	0	0	0	0	0	c1
seq2	0	0	1	0	0	c1
seq3	0	0	0	0	0	c2
seq4	0	0	0	0	0	c2
seq5	0	0	0	0	1	c2
seq6	0	0	0	1	1	c1
seq7	0	0	0	1	1	c1

Fig. 2. Learning boolean file [15].

4.2 Concept and Experimental Protocols

In our experiments, we use five well classical feature selection methods. They are Relief [11,13], Correlation-based Feature Selection (CFS) [20], Information Gain (IG) [5], Chi-squared (X^2) [14], and Symmetrical Uncertainty (SU) [6]. In addition, we choose three well-established classifiers for the comparison purpose. They are: Support Vector Machine *(SVM)*, Artificial Neural Network *(ANN)* and Decision Tree *(C4.5)*.

We use the classification performance of the final chosen features set. Several characteristics of classification performance have been chosen such as: Precision, Recall, and F-measure. A tenfold cross-validation model was used in order to assess the results of the experiments. All experiments are carried out using the Weka (Waikato Environment for Knowledge Analysis) tool.

In addition, Java was used to develop STRASS algorithm, Correlation coefficient clustering algorithm, Decision dependent Correlation algorithm (DDC) algorithm and the novel approach of STRASS algorithm.

Tables 1, 2 and 3, report on the performances achieved by Support Vector Machine *(SVM)*, Decision Tree *(DT)* and Artificial Neural Network *(ANN)* using classical technique of features selection as describe in Sect. 2 and feature selection methods based on new correlation technique as describe in Sect. 3. Tables 4, 5 and 6 report on the performances achieved by these classifiers using our new approach (Optimized STRASS algorithm). "F" denotes the number of attributes retained by the algorithm. "Freq" denotes frequency percentage (threshold) used in the proposed approach.

We varied the parameters of ANN algorithm. The configuration of this classifier is a clown in [18] and it gives the best results. We use the default setting value for the remaining classifier because it achieves also the best results in most cases.

5 Discussion

The tables show the performance of classification methods in terms of precision, Recall and F-measure respectively. The best results for each classifier are highlighted in red color.

For the correlation coefficient feature selection algorithm, we varied the K value between 100 and 1000 in order to detect the average subsets that can give the best results.

For the Decision dependent Correlation algorithm (DDC), we varied a threshold δ_1 between 0.04 and 0.1 [16] to determine which feature is relevant to the final decision and we set $\delta_2 = 0.99$ [16]. In this work, we used the same thresholds as described in [16] because they can achieve the best results in most cases.

From the below tables, we can notice that the classical filter methods (CFS, Relief, IG, chi-square, and SU) achieve similar performances. They give the best accuracy (0.978) when 1818 of the features were included. There is obviously a strong similarity in the feature set selected by these ranker research methods.

The classical filter methods achieved their highest values when selected 1818 features (we discard attributes whose evaluation falls below a threshold $= 0$). We chose these features subsets by involving much experimentation. This is the weakness of these ranked methods. These classical methods do not cope with redundant features.

The performance of these classical methods using SVM and ANN classifiers is superior to this method using C4.5 classifier.

Feature selection method based on correlation coefficient clustering chooses attributes that result in a higher performance for protein class when $k = 500$, $k = 600$, $k = 900$ and $k = 1000$. We can conclude that for this method, the performance of classification increase as the number of features increase.

Table 1. Results summary for the protein sequence classification using SVM.

SVM	Number of selected features	Parameters	Precision	Recall	F-measure
Correlation based feature selection	F = 62	Best first search	0.978	0.977	0.977
Relief	F = 3049	Ranker search	0.978	0.977	0.977
Information gain	F = 1818	Ranker search Threshold: 0.0	0.968	0.966	0.966
Chi-square	F = 1818	Ranker search	**0.978**	**0.978**	**0.978**
Symmetrical uncertain (SU)	F = 1818	Ranker search	**0.978**	**0.977**	**0.977**
Correlation coefficient clustering	F = 100	k = 100	0.839	0.805	0.805
	F = 200	k = 200	0.94	0.931	0.931
	F = 300	k = 300	0.94	0.931	0.931
	F = 400	k = 400	0.958	0.954	0.954
	F = 500	k = 500	**0.978**	**0.977**	**0.977**
	F = 600	k = 600	0.977	0.977	0.977
	F = 700	k = 700	0.955	0.954	0.954
	F = 800	k = 800	0.955	0.954	0.954
	F = 900	k = 900	**0.978**	**0.977**	**0.977**
	F = 1000	k = 1000	**0.978**	**0.977**	**0.977**
Decision dependent Correlation algorithm	F = 180	$\delta_1 = 0.1$	0.932	0.931	0.931
	F = 245	$\delta_1 = 0.09$	0.945	0.943	0.943
	F = 319	$\delta_1 = 0.08$	0.942	0.943	0.943
	F = 430	$\delta_1 = 0.07$	**0.977**	**0.977** (DDC)	**0.977**
	F = 514	$\delta_1 = 0.06$	**0.977**	**0.977**	**0.977**
	F = 646	$\delta_1 = 0.05$	0.966	0.966	0.966
	F = 932	$\delta_1 = 0.04$	**0.977**	**0.977**	**0.977**

In addition, It is worth noting that feature selection based on decision dependent correlation (DDC) does better when the number of features is in [430, 932] (in Tables 1, 2 and 3) and using only SVM and ANN classifiers.

Tables 4, 5 and 6 show the experimental results of our proposed approach (optimized STRASS algorithm). We choose to use a frequency interval between 20% and 40% since We did not find any occurrence of the attribute when we defined a frequency percentage over 40%.

An interesting point that our algorithm provides the best performance comparing two the other algorithms especially when we used in advance a frequency interval between 30% and 40 %.

It can be seen from Table 4 that our optimized STRASS algorithm improves the performance of SVM compared the other feature selection algorithms (precision = 0.98). Moreover, from Tables 5 and 6, the performance obtained with our proposed method is always the best when used C4.5 classifier apart from when using with ANN classifier.

Table 2. Results summary for the protein sequence classification using ANN.

ANN	Number of selected features	Parameters	Precision	Recall	F-measure
Correlation based feature selection	F = 62	Best first search	0.977	0.977	0.977
Relief	F = 3049	Ranker search	**0.978**	**0.977**	**0.977**
Information gain	F = 1818	Ranker search Threshold: 0.0	**0.978**	**0.977**	**0.977**
Chi-square	F = 1818	Ranker search	**0.978**	**0.977**	**0.977**
Symmetrical uncertain (SU)	F = 1818	Ranker search	**0.978**	**0.977**	**0.977**
Correlation coefficient clustering	F = 100	k=100	0.812	0.759	0.754
	F = 200	k = 200	0.916	0.897	0.897
	F = 300	k = 300	0.94	0.931	0.931
	F = 400	k = 400	0.949	0.943	0.943
	F = 500	k = 500	**0.978**	**0.977**	**0.977**
	F = 600	k = 600	0.968	0.966	0.966
	F = 700	k = 700	0.955	0.954	0.954
	F = 800	k = 800	0.958	0.954	0.954
	F = 900	k = 900	**0.968**	**0.966**	**0.966**
	F = 1000	k = 1000	**0.968**	**0.966**	**0.966**
Decision dependent Correlation algorithm (DDC)	F = 180	$\delta_1 = 0.1$	0.932	0.931	0.931
	F = 245	$\delta_1 = 0.09$	0.945	0.943	0.943
	F = 319	$\delta_1 = 0.08$	0.955	0.954	0.954
	F = 430	$\delta_1 = 0.07$	**0.977**	**0.977**	**0.977**
	F = 514	$\delta_1 = 0.06$	**0.977**	**0.977**	**0.977**
	F = 646	$\delta_1 = 0.05$	0.966	0.966	0.966
	F = 932	$\delta_1 = 0.04$	**0.977**	**0.977**	**0.977**

In addition, for most cases, the performance of the dataset that applied our optimized STRASS algorithm is better than the performance of the dataset that applied the other feature selection methods.

On the other hand, our proposed method is a powerful algorithm on large data set. In fact, it is computationally efficient and it has a lower execution time than the original STRASS algorithm.

Table 3. Results summary for the protein sequence classification using C4.5.

C4.5					
	Number of selected features	Parameters	Precision	Recall	F-measure
Correlation based feature selection	F = 62	Best first search	0.932	0.931	0.931
Relief	F = 3049	Ranker search	0.92	0.92	0.92
Information gain	F = 1818	Ranker search Threshold: 0.0	0.945	0.943	0.943
Chi-square	F = 1818	Ranker search	0.945	0.943	0.943
Symmetrical uncertain (SU)	F = 1818	Ranker search	0.945	0.943	0.943
Correlation	F = 900	k = 900	**0.885**	**0.874**	**0.874**
coefficient clustering	F = 1000	k = 1000	**0.871**	**0.862**	**0.862**
Decision dependent	F = 319	$\delta_1 = 0.08$	**0.896**	**0.897**	**0.897**
Correlation	F = 932	$\delta_1 = 0.04$	**0.887**	**0.828**	**0.826**

Table 4. Results summary of Optimized STRASS algorithm using SVM classifier.

SVM					
	Number of selected feature using frequency algorithm	Final number of selected features	Precision	recall	F-measure
Optimization of STRASS algorithm	Freq40% F = 5	F-final = 4	0.864	0.828	0.841
	Freq35% F = 20	F-final = 19	0.966	0.966	0.966
	Freq30% F = 45	F-final = 44	**0.98**	**0.977**	**0.98**
	Freq25% F = 117	F-final = 116	0.954	0.954	0.954
	Freq20% F = 266	F-final = 265	0.898	0.897	0.896

Table 5. Results summary of Optimized STRASS algorithm using ANN classifier.

ANN					
	Number of selected feature using frequency algorithm	Final number of selected features	Precision	Recall	F-measure
Optimization of STRASS algorithm	Freq40% F = 5	F-final = 4	0.839	0.828	0.828
	Freq35% F = 20	F-final = 19	**0.958**	**0.954**	**0.954**
	Freq30% F = 45	F-final = 44	**0.954**	**0.954**	**0.954**
	Freq25% F = 117	F-final = 116	0.943	0.943	0.943
	Freq20% F = 266	F-final = 265	0.943	0.943	0.942

Table 6. Results summary of Optimized STRASS algorithm using C4.5 classifier.

C4.5					
	Number of selected feature using frequency algorithm	Final number of selected features	Precision	Recall	F-measure
Optimization of STRASS algorithm	Freq40% F = 5	F-final = 4	0.864	0.828	0.826
	Freq35% F = 20	F-final = 19	**0.966**	**0.966**	**0.966**
	Freq30% F = 45	F-final = 44	**0.966**	**0.966**	**0.966**
	Freq25% F = 117	F-final = 116	0.954	0.954	0.954
	Freq20% F = 266	F-final = 265	0.877	0.877	0.877

6   Conclusions

In this paper, we have presented a comparative study between feature selection methods in order to ameliorate the performance of protein classification.

Then, we have proposed an optimization version of STRASS algorithm in order to reduce the computation time and/or memory space of STRASS algorithm.

Experiments results show that the classical filter methods, algorithms based on new correlation methods and our new approach of STRASS algorithm can help us to give the best classification results, especially when using SVM classifier. The worst classification performance is given when using C4.5 classifier.

On the other hand, our proposed algorithm has given a reduced run-time complexity compared to the original STRASS algorithm and it has become efficient for large data sets. Future works may consider the improvement of classification precision of protein classification by computing many classification methods, and therefore to identify most of the features related to an investigated class. Another future work may consider the development of new feature selection algorithm that is able to extract alternative and equivalent classification models.

As other feature work, we can use other kinds of features and other types of biological data, i.e. DNA and RNA sequences.

References

1. Bhavani, R., Sadasivam, G.S.: A novel feature selection based on apriori property and correlation analysis for protein sequence classification using mapreduce. Int. J. Data Min. Bioinform. **17**(3), 255–265 (2017)
2. Sadhasivam, S., Bhavani, R.: A filter based feature selection for protein sequence classification over hadoop. Int. J. Appl. Eng. Res. **14**(10), 34603–34606 (2015)
3. Blekas, K., Fotiadis, D.I., Likas, A.: Protein sequence classification using probabilistic motifs and neural networks. In: Kaynak, O., Alpaydin, E., Oja, E., Xu, L. (eds.) ICANN/ICONIP -2003. LNCS, vol. 2714, pp. 702–709. Springer, Heidelberg (2003). https://doi.org/10.1007/3-540-44989-2_84

4. Chebel-Morello, B., Malinowski, S., Senoussi, H.: Feature selection for fault detection systems: application to the tennessee eastman process. Appl. Intell. **44**(1), 111–122 (2016)
5. Grimaldi, M., Cunningham, P., Kokaram, A.: An evaluation of alternative feature selection strategies and ensemble techniques for classifying music. In: Workshop on Multimedia Discovery and Mining [MDM 2003] at ECML/PKDD-2003, p. 44 (2003)
6. Hosni, H., Mhamdi, F.: A filter correlation method for feature selection. In: 2014 25th International Workshop on Database and Expert Systems Applications (DEXA), pp. 59–63. IEEE (2014)
7. Hsu, H.-H., Hsieh, C.-W.: Feature selection via correlation coefficient clustering. JSW **5**(12), 1371–1377 (2010)
8. Hwang, Y.-S.: Wrapper-based feature selection using support vector machine. Life Sci. J. **11**(7), 632–636 (2014)
9. Iqbal, M.J., Faye, I., Samir, B.B., Md Said, A.: Efficient feature selection and classification of protein sequence data in bioinformatics. Sci. World J. **2014**, 12 (2014)
10. Jović, A., Brkić, K., Bogunović, N.: A review of feature selection methods with applications. In: 2015 38th International Convention on Information and Communication Technology, Electronics and Microelectronics (MIPRO), pp. 1200–1205. IEEE (2015)
11. Kouser, K., Lavanya, P., Rangarajan, L., et al.: Effective feature selection for classification of promoter sequences. PloS one **11**(12), e0167165 (2016)
12. Li, Y., Li, T., Liu, H.: Recent advances in feature selection and its applications. Knowl. Inf. Syst. **53**, 1–27 (2017)
13. Mhamdi, F., Mhamdi, H.: A new algorithm relief hybrid (hrelief) for biological motifs selection. In: 2013 IEEE 13th International Conference on Bioinformatics and Bioengineering (BIBE), pp. 1–5. IEEE (2013)
14. Mhamdi, H., Mhamdi, F.: Feature selection methods on biological knowledge discovery and data mining: a survey. In: 2014 25th International Workshop on Database and Expert Systems Applications (DEXA), pp. 46–50. IEEE (2014)
15. Murzin, A.G., Brenner, S.E., Hubbard, T., Chothia, C.: Scop: a structural classification of proteins database for the investigation of sequences and structures. J. Mol. Biol. **247**(4), 536–540 (1995)
16. Novaković, J.: Toward optimal feature selection using ranking methods and classification algorithms. Yugoslav J. Oper. Res. **21**(1), 119–135 (2016)
17. Qu, G., Hariri, S., Yousif, M.: A new dependency and correlation analysis for features. IEEE Trans. Knowl. Data Eng. **17**(9), 1199–1207 (2005)
18. Ramkumar, T., et al.: Analysis of multilayer perceptron machine learning approach in classifying protein secondary structures. Biomed. Res. **27**, S166–S173 (2016)
19. Sánchez-Maroño, N., Alonso-Betanzos, A., Tombilla-Sanromán, M.: Filter methods for feature selection-a comparative study. Intell. Data Eng. Autom. Learn.-IDEAL **2007**, 178–187 (2007)
20. Yildirim, P.: Filter based feature selection methods for prediction of risks in hepatitis disease. Int. J. Mach. Learn. Comput. **5**(4), 258 (2015)

DRAM: A Deep Reinforced Intra-attentive Model for Event Prediction

Shuqi Yu, Linmei Hu[⊠], and Bin Wu

Beijing University of Posts and Telecommunications, Beijing, China
shuqiatwork@gmail.com, {hulinmei,wubin}@bupt.edu.cn

Abstract. We address the problem of event prediction which aims to predict next probable event given a sequence of previous historical events. Event prediction is meaningful and important for the government, agencies and companies to take proactive actions to avoid damages. By acquiring knowledge from large-scale news series which record sequences of real-world events, we are expected to learn from the past and see into the future. Most existing works focus on predicting known events from a given candidate set, instead of devoting to more realistic *unknown event prediction*. In this paper, we propose a novel deep reinforced intra-attentive model, named DRAM, for unknown event prediction, by automatically generating the text description of the next probable unknown event. Specifically, DRAM designs a novel hierarchical intra-attention mechanism to take care not only the previous events but also those words describing the events. In addition, DRAM combines standard supervised word prediction and reinforcement learning in model training, allowing it to directly optimize the non-differentiable BLEU score tracking human evaluation and generate higher quality of events. Extensive experiments on real-world datasets demonstrate that our model significantly outperforms state-of-the-art methods.

Keywords: Event prediction · Reinforcement learning · Intra-attention

1 Introduction

An event is defined as a typical thing that happens at a specific time and place [1], which may trigger a sequence of following events. Over years, massive amount of news series containing event sequences have been accumulated and become publicly available. Reasoning these news series may show us some common or frequent patterns about how a typical event sequence developed and evolved over time. As such, we are able to learn from the past data and predict the future events given a sequence of existing events.

Event prediction is a meaningful and crucial task which can aid governments, companies and individuals to take proactive and informed actions by providing

© Springer Nature Switzerland AG 2019
C. Douligeris et al. (Eds.): KSEM 2019, LNAI 11775, pp. 701–713, 2019.
https://doi.org/10.1007/978-3-030-29551-6_62

predictive information. Take a news series "11.13 Paris Terror Attack" for example, given an event sequence, where each event is represented by a news title, i.e. "Explosion occurs outside a sports stadium in France.", "A mass shooting and hostage-taking occurred.", "President declares a state of emergency after the attacks unfold.", "ISIS claims responsibility for the attacks.". Our model generates "France", "Paris", "shooting", "sever", "emergency", "chaos", word by word, which is consistent with the real next event "Terrorist attack in France caused injuries and chaos.". Clearly, with the predicted results in place, government can thus take proactive or preventive measures to avoid casualties and damages.

Nevertheless, event prediction is non-trivial. Firstly, how can we pay attention to the critical information of previous events at both word level and event level. Secondly, how can we generate high-quality and readable events from human evaluation perspective.

Existing works on event prediction task can be described in two aspects. Some works are based on structured event construction and predict *known* events from a candidate set. For example, [5] learned coherence score between events to determine whether or not the two events appear in the same chain. [14] generated plausible future targeted event given a present news event by extracting causality relationships between two events. The other line of works adopts neural networks to directly model event sequences and predicts the next event by generating a word sequence describing it, e.g. [13] described a model for statistical script learning containing sequences of events using LSTM network. [7] proposed CH_LSTM model for event representation learning and interpreted it into next unknown event. However, the generated events are still unsatisfactory, deviating a lot from ground-truth events.

In this paper, we propose a novel **D**eep **R**einforced Intra-**A**ttentive **M**odel (**DRAM**) for event prediction by automatically generating a text description of next probable event. Particularly, DRAM designs a novel hierarchical intra-attention mechanism to capture different levels (including both event level and word level) of valuable information in previous events for next event prediction. In addition, it combines supervised word prediction and reinforcement learning (Self-critic Sequence Training [16]) in model training. This allows DRAM to directly optimize the discrete BLEU score that tracks human evaluation, and generate higher quality events that are much closer to the gold standard.

Overall, our main contributions can be summarized as follows.

- To the best of our knowledge, this is the first deep reinforced model to address the challenging unknown event prediction problem.
- We designed a new hierarchical attention mechanism to take care of both event-level and word-level information in previous event sequence for next event prediction.
- Extensive experiments on real-world datasets demonstrate that our model significantly outperforms six state-of-the-art models in unknown event prediction.

2   Problem Definition

In this section, we introduce some basic concepts and define the task of unknown event prediction. **Event**. An event is a typical thing happens at a specific time and place [1], which is usually described by a news report. In this paper, each event e_m is denoted by its description text, i.e. $e_m = (w_{m,1}, w_{m,2}, ..., w_{m,N_m})$, where $w_{m,n} \in V$ refers to the n-th word in m-th event, and V denotes the vocabulary.

Event Sequence. An event sequence s, which records how events developed and evolved, is composed of a sequence of events, represented as $s = (e_1, e_2, ..., e_m)$.

Event Prediction. Given an event sequence, $(e_1, e_2, ..., e_m)$, we aim to predict next probable unknown event e_{m+1} by automatically generating the text description of it.

3   Methodology

In this section, we present our proposed **D**eep **R**einforced Intra-**A**ttentive **M**odel (DRAM) for event prediction task in details. As illustrated in Fig. 1, our model DRAM contains an event sequence encoder for encoding the previous events, a hierarchical intra-attention mechanism for capturing the important information at different levels and a next event predictor for generating the next probable event.

To achieve satisfactory predicted events, we directly optimize the metric BLEU score that tracks human evaluation instead of minimizing the maximum-likelihood loss. As BLEU score is discrete, we use the self-critical policy gradient training algorithm [16] in our model.

3.1   Event Sequence Encoder

An event sequence always exhibits a hierarchical sequential structure: a sequence of events $S = (e_1, ..., e_M)$, and a sequence of words $e_m = (w_{m,1}, ..., w_{m,N_m})$ describing the events. To capture the different importance of information at different levels, we design a hierarchical LSTM encoder (including event encoder and sequence encoder) with a hierarchical intra-attention mechanism.

Event Encoder. The event encoder aims to map a typical event $e_m = (w_{m,1}, w_{m,2}, ..., w_{m,N_m})$ into a fixed-length vector $\mathbf{e}_m$ using LSTM [6]. It reads the words within the event sequentially and updates its hidden state iteratively as follows:

$$\mathbf{h}_{m,n}^w = \text{LSTM}_{event\_enc}^w(\mathbf{h}_{m,n-1}^w, \mathbf{w}_{m,n}), n = 1, ..., N_m, \tag{1}$$

in which $LSTM_{event\_enc}^w$ refers to the event encoder using the basic LSTM function, $\mathbf{h}_{m,n}^w$ indicates the hidden vector generated at the n-th word in the m-th event. The initial hidden state of LSTM network is set to zero $\mathbf{h}_{m,0}^w = \{0\}$, the same with the initial word state $\mathbf{w}_{m,0} = \{0\}$. $\mathbf{w}_{m,n}$ refers to the embedding of word tokens. After consuming the last word of a given event, the hidden state $\mathbf{h}^w_{m,N_m}$ is supposed to capture order-sensitive information within a typical event. We consider it as the final representation of e_m.

Sequence Encoder. Given an event sequence, $s = (e_1, e_2, ..., e_M)$, the sequence encoder takes the event representations $\mathbf{e}_m$ obtained by the event encoder as input and calculates a sequence of recurrent states $\mathbf{h}^e_m$:

$$\mathbf{h}^e_m = \text{LSTM}^e_{seq\_enc}(\mathbf{h}^e_{m-1}, \mathbf{e}_m), m = 1, ..., M, \tag{2}$$

where $LSTM^e_{seq\_enc}$ refers to the sequence encoder using the basic LSTM function, we set $\mathbf{h}^e_0 = \{0\}$, $\mathbf{e}_0 = \{0\}$ for initialization. $\mathbf{e}_m$ denotes the representation of the m-th event in an event sequence, which is obtained by the event encoder. The sequence encoder computes the current hidden state $\mathbf{h}^e_m$ after consuming the representation of the current m-th event, and thus updates its internal state iteratively. After consuming all the events in the sequence, the last hidden state is taken as the final representation of the event sequence, which is believed to condense the information at both word and event levels of all the observed events.

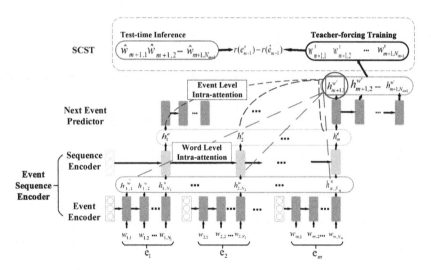

Fig. 1. Illustration of Our DRAM model. It consists of an event sequence encoder incorporating a new hierarchical attention mechanism and a next event predictor. In model training, it combines supervised word prediction and reinforcement learning which enable the optimization of the discrete BLEU score tracking human evaluation.

3.2 Hierarchical Intra-attention Mechanism

Considering the different importance of word level information in event encoder and event level information in sequence encoder, we present a hierarchical intra-attention mechanism.

By paying attention to valuable words and events in the sequence of previous events, we are supposed to get better results of next event prediction.

Word Level Intra-attention. It encourages the model to stress valuable words in previous events, instead of emphasizing the last few words, which is a severe constraint suffered by the LSTM models [6]. By linking the output of current decoding step with word tokens in previous input events, word level intra-attention mechanism highlights the words which play a key role in the next event prediction.

For a word $w_{(m,n)}$, the strength indicator $\mathbf{a}_{t,(m,n)}$ is calculated between the hidden state $\mathbf{h}^{w'}_{M+1,t}$ at the current decoding step t and the hidden state $\mathbf{h}^w_{m,n}$ for the word $w_{(m,n)}$. Formally,

$$\mathbf{a}^w_{t,(m,n)} = \mathbf{h}^{w'}_{M+1,t}{}^{\mathrm{T}}\mathbf{W}^{(att)}_w\mathbf{h}^w_{m,n}, m \in [1, M], n \in [1, N_m], \tag{3}$$

in which $\mathbf{W}^{(att)}_w$ is the model parameter.

To alleviate repetition problem, we penalize the input words $w_{(m,n)}$ that have already obtained high scores at current decoding step t according to:

$$\mathbf{a}'^w_{t,(m,n)} = \begin{cases} \exp(\mathbf{a}^w_{t,(m,n)}) & if\ t = 1 \\ \dfrac{\exp(\mathbf{a}^w_{t,(m,n)})}{\sum_{j=1}^{t-1}\exp(\mathbf{a}^w_{j,(m,n)})} & otherwise \end{cases} \tag{4}$$

Then, the normalized attention weight $\alpha^w_{t,(m,n)}$ is calculated across all the words in the input events.

$$\alpha^w_{t,(m,n)} = \frac{\mathbf{a}'^w_{t,(m,n)}}{\sum_{i=1}^M \sum_{j=1}^{N_i} \mathbf{a}'^w_{t,(i,j)}}, m \in [1, M], n \in [1, N_m]. \tag{5}$$

Finally, the word level attention vector $\mathbf{w}^{(att)}_t$ at the decoding step t can be calculated according to:

$$\mathbf{w}^{(att)}_t = \sum_{m=1}^M \sum_{n=1}^{N_m} \alpha^w_{t,(m,n)} \cdot \mathbf{h}^w_{m,n}. \tag{6}$$

The attention vector $\mathbf{w}^{(att)}_t$ captures the information of key words at current decoding step for next event prediction.

Event Level Intra-attention. This attention mechanism aims to suggest which events are more responsible for next event prediction. Specifically, at current decoding step t, the strength indicator $\mathbf{a}^e_m$ is calculated as follows:

$$\mathbf{a}^e_{t,m} = \mathbf{h}^{w'}_{M+1,t}{}^{\mathrm{T}}\mathbf{W}^{(att)}_e\mathbf{h}^e_m, m \in [1, M], \tag{7}$$

in which $\mathbf{W}^{(att)}_e$ is the model parameter.

The normalized attention weight $\alpha_{t,m}^e$ is calculated across all the events in the input sequence with softmax function.

$$\alpha_{t,m}^e = \frac{\exp(\mathbf{a}_{t,m}^e)}{\sum_{i=1}^{M} \exp(\mathbf{a}_{t,i}^e)}, m \in [1, M]. \tag{8}$$

Finally, we compute the attention vector $\mathbf{e}_t^{(att)}$ that captures the information of critical events for next event prediction, at each decoding step t:

$$\mathbf{e}_t^{(att)} = \sum_{m=1}^{M} \alpha_{t,m}^e \cdot \mathbf{h}_m^e. \tag{9}$$

3.3 Next Event Predictor

After encoding the sequence of previous events $e_{1:m}$, a decoder is designed to interpret the encoded information into word tokens describing the next probable event e_{m+1}. At each decoding step t, the hidden state of the decoder is updated with:

$$\mathbf{h}_{m+1,t}^{w'} = \text{LSTM}_{dec}(\mathbf{h}_{m+1,t-1}^{w'}, \mathbf{w}_t), \tag{10}$$

where $LSTM_{dec}$ is a LSTM decoder. The initial hidden state of the decoder, $\mathbf{h}_0^{w'} = \mathbf{h}_m^e$. The initial word state $\mathbf{w}_0 = \{0\}$.

To pay attention to the key words and critical events, we further incorporate the attentive information obtained from the hierarchical attention mechanism by concatenation. Formally, we concatenate the output of the current-step decoder $\mathbf{h_t^{w'}}$ with the hierarchical attention vectors $\mathbf{e}_t^{(att)}$ and $\mathbf{s}_t^{(att)}$ at each decoding step. Afterwards, a Softmax layer is applied to generate the final distributions of word tokens at each decoding step t based on:

$$P(w_t) = \text{Softmax}(\mathbf{W}_{out}[\mathbf{h}_{m+1,t}^{w'}||\mathbf{w}_t^{(att)}||\mathbf{e}_t^{(att)}] + \mathbf{b}_{out}), \tag{11}$$

in which $\mathbf{W}_{out}$ and $\mathbf{b}_{out}$ are the model parameters.

We adopt random sampling technique to obtain word tokens according to the probability distribution $P(w_t)$.

3.4 Reinforcement Learning

Existing methods [7,13] optimize the maximum-likelihood loss with supervised word prediction. However, the generated events are unsatisfactory, showing a discrepancy from the ground-truth. The reasons behind this phenomenon can be discussed in twofold. The first one, called exposure bias [12,15], comes from the fact that the network has knowledge of the ground truth sequence up to the next token during training but does not have such supervision when testing, hence accumulating errors as it predicts the sequence. The second reason is due to the gap between the learning objective and human evaluation. BLEU score as a metric tracking human evaluation can be applied to alleviate the problem.

Due to that BLEU score is discrete, we apply the reinforcement learning (self-critical policy gradient training [16]) algorithm to optimize it.

The core idea behind this is to utilize the output of its own test-time inference to normalize the rewards it experiences. We adopt BLEU for rewards calculation and thus the model can directly optimizes the discrete BLEU score during training process, reconciling the difference between learning objective and evaluation metrics.

In addition, by harmonizing the model with respect to its own inference procedure, this training method alleviates the "exposure bias" problem at the same time.

As Fig. 1 illustrated, we generate two sequences of words at each training iteration. One is the sampled output event, $e^s_{m+1} = (w^s_1, w^s_2, ..., w^s_{N_{m+1}})$ generated by "teacher-forcing". The other is the reference output event $\hat{e}_{m+1} = (\hat{w}_1, \hat{w}_2, ..., \hat{w}_{N_{m+1}})$, obtained by current model inference using greedy decoding. We denote $r(e^s_{m+1})$ and $r(\hat{e}_{m+1})$ as the reward scores of the output event e^s_{m+1} and the reference output $\hat{e}_{m+1}$ respectively. We minimize the reinforcement loss L_{rl} as follows:

$$L_{rl} = (r(e^s_{m+1}) - r(\hat{e}_{m+1}))L_{ml}, \tag{12}$$

in which L_{ml} refers to the supervised training loss minimizing the maximum-likelihood loss of e^s_{m+1}.

$$L_{ml} = -\sum_{s=1}^{S_{train}} \sum_{m=1}^{M} \log P(e^s_{m+1}|e^s_{1:m}). \tag{13}$$

Accordingly, the output e^s_{m+1} which obtains a higher reward than the reference output $\hat{e}_{m+1}$ will be increased in probability, while the output which gets a lower reward will be suppressed.

4 Experiments

We evaluate our proposed DRAM model by comparing it with state-of-the-art methods on benchmark data.

4.1 Dataset

We employ a large-scale real-world dataset **Chinese Sina News Series**, which is the only available benchmark dataset that has been used in [7], containing 15,254 news series and each series includes about 50 news articles in average. Following [7], we first sort the news articles in chronological order, and then use a window of size 5 to segment the news series to get non-overlapping event sequences. Finally, we obtain order-sensitive event sequences set, containing 155,358 event sequences in total. We adopt JIEBA tool[1] to perform Chinese

---

[1] https://pypi.org/project/jieba/.

708 S. Yu et al.

word segmentation, and remove the stop words and further prune the vocabulary V by dropping the words that occur in less than 100 documents. Finally, we get a vocabulary of size 8,107.

We randomly split the dataset into three parts, 80% for training set, 10% for testing set and 10% for validation set. In particular, the training set contains 124,288 event sequences, and 607,090 events; validation set contains 15,535 event sequences and 75,802 events; test set contains 15,535 event sequences and 75,957 events.

4.2 Implementation Details

Baselines. We implemented six state-of-the-art models, as well as two variants of our proposed model DRAM in order to study the individual effect of the hierarchical intra-attention mechanism and reinforcement learning:

- Backoff N-gram [17]: An N-gram $(N = 5)$ language model using backoff smoothing.
- Modified Kneser-Key [17]: An N-gram $(N = 5)$ language model using Kneser-key smoothing.
- Witten-Bell Discounting N-Gram [17]: An N-gram $(N = 5)$ language model using Witten-Bell Smothing.
- LSTM [13]: The LSTM model where we treat all the words in previous events as a whole sequence, and generates next probable event after consuming all the words in previous events.
- HLSTM [7]: A hierarchical LSTM model considering the hierarchical structure of events.
- CH_LSTM [7]: A model incorporating topic information into HLSTM model.
- DRAM w/o ATT (ours): A variant of our proposed DRAM model without attention mechanism.
- DRAM w/o RL (ours): A variant of our proposed DRAM model without reinforcement learning.

Evaluation Metrics. We choose two standard metrics, namely, the perplexity [2] and the standard BLEU score [11] to evaluate different methods. Perplexity is a standard metric which measures how well a model fits the data and thus can perform better prediction. Lower perplexity indicates a better model. BLEU counts n-gram overlap between a generated event and a ground-truth one, which has a high correlation with human judgment. We adopt standard BLEU here, which is the averaging of BLEU 1-gram, 2-gram, 3-gram and 4-gram.

Parameter Setting. The embedding dimensions of LSTM hidden states, words, and attention vectors are set to 300 for all the models discussed herein. The word embeddings are uniformly initialized with a range of $[-0.8, 0.8]$ and updated during training. We train all the supervised models by maximizing the log likelihood using ADAM [9] optimizer. The learning rate is initialized as 0.0005 and the batch size is set as 32. To avoid over-fitting, we set the dropout rate to 0.2.

For reinforcement learning of our model DRAM, we use the trained model maximizing the log likelihood as an initializer. The learning rate of the reinforcement learning is set as 0.00005.

4.3   Experimental Results

Table 1. Comparison of different models on the Chinese Sina News Series dataset in terms of Perplexity and Standard BLEU.

Model	Perplexity	BLEU
Backoff N-gram	884	9.1
Modified Kneser-Ney	870	9.3
Witten-Bell Discounting N-gram	835	9.1
LSTM	588	21.3
HLSTM	526	22.3
CH_LSTM	483	24.5
DRAM w/o ATT	418	24.7
DRAM w/o RL	286	29.1
DRAM	**282**	**30.7**

Quantitative Analysis. Table 1 shows our experiential results. We can observe that among all the methods, our proposed DRAM model yields the best performance consistently with respect to all the measures. Specifically, our model DRAM w/o RL (with only attention) improves the state-of-the-art CH_LSTM model by around 18% and 6% in terms of perplexity and BLEU score respectively, demonstrating the effectiveness of our proposed hierarchical intra-attention mechanism. The attention mechanism encourages the model to pay attention to critical information in previous events, reducing the influence of noisy information. In addition, our DRAM with both reinforcement learning and attention mechanism significantly outperforms the existing methods, improving state-of-the-art method CH_LSTM by more than 34%, 13.6% in terms of perplexity and BLEU respectively. We believe the reason is that by using reinforcement learning, we can optimize the metric matching human judgment and alleviate the "exposure bias" problem in supervised learning methods.

Qualitative Analysis. We present a qualitative analysis for the models. Figure 2 shows an example about "China win rallying race". We list the given previous events, the next event (ground-truth) and the predicted events generated by different models. Specifically, we compare our model DRAM with state-of-the-art model CH_LSTM and two variants of DRAM (i.e., w/o RL or w/o ATT). As we can observe, our model DRAM is able to predict the match result, "China win rallying race", which is consistent with ground-truth next event.

4.4 Next Event Ranking

Following [7], we also evaluate our model on next event ranking task. Given a news series, this task is to find the most probable next event within in a candidate set. Ideally, our model is expected to assign the ground-truth event with the highest probability within the candidate set.

Fig. 2. A case study about "China win rallying race".

Detailed Process. To obtain the dataset for this task, we merge the validation set and the test set, containing 31,070 news series in total. Following [7], we randomly divided the dataset (31,070 news series) into 621 non-overlapping subsets with each containing 50 news series except the last one which contains remaining 20 series (i.e., $31,070 = 621 * 50 + 20$). For each news series (consisting of a few events) in a subset, we aim to choose the best last event given its previous events. The candidate set is composed of the last events of all the series in the corresponding subset. We use the measurement $his@n$ which indicates the probability of the correct events within the top n ranked events.

Result Analysis. Table 2 illustrates the performance of our model compared with state-of-the-art neural models, in terms of hits@1, hits@5, hits@10. The results are consistent with Table 1. Our models and its variants all outperform existing neural models, which shows the effectiveness of the reinforcement learning and hierarchical attention. It is worth noticing that our model DRAM has significant improvement (more than 2%) compared to the baseline models in terms of the most important metric hits@1.

5 Related Work

5.1 Event Prediction

Event prediction has been widely investigated. Many approaches have been proposed based on structured event construction. For example, [5] extracted event chains from texts [3], and designed a coherence function to score whether or not two events appear in the same event chain. In addition, a few works try

Table 2. The performance of different models on next event ranking task with the measurements of *hits*@1, *hits*@5, *hits*@10.

Model	hits@1	hits@5	hits@10
LSTM	23.04	51.23	67.36
HLSTM	26.99	56.97	71.23
CH_LSTM	28.03	57.12	72.34
DRAM w/o ATT	28.12	57.34	72.89
DRAM w/o RL	29.05	57.78	73.5
DRAM	30.10	58.21	74.3

to exploit external knowledge (e.g., DBpedia) for event prediction. For example, [14] generated plausible future event given a present event by extracting causality relationships between the two events and generating them using ontology. [4] presented events based on Markov logic networks framework and reason the probabilities of the next event with the help of DBpedia. [10] constructed narrative event evolutionary graph to solve the script event prediction problem. All these works rely heavily on hand-crafted features. Some other works adopt neural networks to directly learn the representation of events or event sequences. [13] described a model for statistical script learning using LSTM. [7] proposed a context-aware hierarchical LSTM prediction model which directly learns event representations and generates next event with a sequence to sequence network.

Following [7,13], we propose a novel generative model DRAM for event prediction. DRAM applies a new hierarchical intra-attention mechanism to attend over information at different levels. In addition, DRAM combines standard supervised word prediction and reinforcement learning in model training, which allows the optimization of the discrete BLEU score tracking human evaluation and generates higher quality of events.

5.2 Deep Reinforcement Learning

Deep reinforcement learning, which combines reinforcement learning and deep neural networks, has been applied into a variety of tasks including image captioning [16], machine reading comprehension [8], text summarization [12,18] and so on. Specifically, [16] put forward the self-critic sequence training (SCST) algorithm for image captioning. [12] applied reinforcement learning into text summarization and generated more natural summaries. To further incorporate topic information into text summarization task, [18] proposed a topic-aware sequence to sequence model and adopted reinforcement learning for model optimization. To the best of our knowledge, our research is the first deep reinforced model for event prediction.

6   Conclusion and Future Work

In this paper, we propose a novel deep reinforced intra-attentive sequence model for unknown event prediction. To generate predictive events of high quality, we propose to optimize both the maximum likelihood and the non-differentiable BLEU score through reinforcement learning. In addition, we design a hierarchical intra-attention mechanism which enables the model to not only put emphasis on important events but also consider valuable words for predicting the next event. Extensive experiments on real-world datasets demonstrate the superiority of our model compared to state-of-the-art models.

In future work, we will improve our model to predict the exact place and time of next event.

Acknowledgements. This work is supported in part by National Key Research and Development Program of China under Grant 2018YFC0831500 and National Natural Science Foundation of China (No. 61806020), the Fundamental Research Funds for the Central Universities.

References

1. Allan, J., Papka, R., Lavrenko, V.: On-line new event detection and tracking. In: ACM SIGIR (1998)
2. Bengio, Y., Ducharme, R., Vincent, P., Janvin, C.: A neural probabilistic language model. J. Mach. Learn. Res. **3**, 1137–1155 (2003)
3. Chambers, N., Jurafsky, D.: Unsupervised learning of narrative event chains. In: ACL (2008)
4. Dami, S., Barforoush, A.A., Shirazi, H.: News events prediction using Markov logic networks. J. Inf. Sci. **44**, 91–109 (2018)
5. Granroth-Wilding, M., Clark, S.: What happens next? event prediction using a compositional neural network model. In: AAAI (2016)
6. Hochreiter, S., Schmidhuber, J.: Long short-term memory. Neural Comput. **9**, 1735–1780 (1997)
7. Hu, L., Li, J., Nie, L., Li, X., Shao, C.: What happens next? future subevent prediction using contextual hierarchical LSTM. In: AAAI (2017)
8. Hu, M., Peng, Y., Huang, Z., Qiu, X., Wei, F., Zhou, M.: Reinforced mnemonic reader for machine reading comprehension (2017)
9. Kingma, D.P., Ba, J.: Adam: a method for stochastic optimization. arXiv preprint arXiv:1412.6980 (2014)
10. Li, Z., Ding, X., Liu, T.: Constructing narrative event evolutionary graph for script event prediction. In: IJCAI (2018)
11. Papineni, K., Roukos, S., Ward, T., Zhu, W.: BLEU: a method for automatic evaluation of machine translation. In: ACL (2002)
12. Paulus, R., Xiong, C., Socher, R.: A deep reinforced model for abstractive summarization. arXiv preprint arXiv:1705.04304 (2017)
13. Pichotta, K., Mooney, R.J.: Learning statistical scripts with LSTM recurrent neural networks. In: AAAI (2016)
14. Radinsky, K., Davidovich, S., Markovitch, S.: Learning causality for news events prediction. In: WWW (2012)

15. Ranzato, M., Chopra, S., Auli, M., Zaremba, W.: Sequence level training with recurrent neural networks. arXiv preprint arXiv:1511.06732 (2015)
16. Rennie, S.J., Marcheret, E., Mroueh, Y., Ross, J., Goel, V.: Self-critical sequence training for image captioning. In: CVPR (2017)
17. Stolcke, A.: SRILM - an extensible language modeling toolkit. In: ICSLP (2002)
18. Wang, L., Yao, J., Tao, Y., Zhong, L., Liu, W., Du, Q.: A reinforced topic-aware convolutional sequence-to-sequence model for abstractive text summarization (2018)

Permission-Based Feature Scaling Method for Lightweight Android Malware Detection

Dali Zhu[1,2] and Tong Xi[1,2(✉)]

[1] Insitute of Information Engineering, Chinese Academy of Sciences,
Beijing 100086, China
{zhudali,xitong}@iie.ac.cn
[2] School of Cyber Security, University of Chinese Academy of Sciences,
Beijing 100086, China

Abstract. Android system has gained the highest market share due to its openness and portability in the mobile ecosystem. Whereas, users are suffering from serious security issues these years. Many malicious Android applications are released in popular app stores and it's hard to distinguish them. Most of the current malware detection researches are focus on collecting features as much as possible for better performance instead of mining information inside the simple features. Scaling is an effective means to improve classification results while scaling the features for a large bundle of apps remains a challenging work. In this paper, we propose a malware detection method based on Machine Learning (ML) using permission usage analysis to cope with the rapid increase in the number of Android malware, named Permission Feature Selection (PFS). PFS uses Android permission as a classification feature with high utilization. The method greatly shortens the time cost in detection without reducing the detection accuracy and makes it possible to scan large-scale samples in a short time. Besides, various experiments were designed on real-world datasets to verify the reliability of the method. The results of the evaluation show that the proposed method performed better than other feature scaling methods with 91.2% accuracy and the average time cost reduced to less than 2 s.

Keywords: Malware detection · Feature scaling · Machine Learning

1 Introduction

As of September 2018, according to StatCounter [1], Android has occupied 75.33% mobile operating system market share worldwide. It's widely used due

This work was supported in by the National Key Research and Development Program of China-the Key Technologies for High Security Mobile Terminals (Grant No.2017YFB0801903), and the Youth Star project of the Institute of Information Engineering, CAS (No. Y8YS016104).

© Springer Nature Switzerland AG 2019
C. Douligeris et al. (Eds.): KSEM 2019, LNAI 11775, pp. 714–725, 2019.
https://doi.org/10.1007/978-3-030-29551-6_63

to the principle of openness. Application developers could release feature-rich Apps to markets leading the Android ecosystem prosperity. It's true that there are two sides to everything. Third-Party markets and lax review mechanisms have led to a rapid proliferation of Android malware as well as security threats. An investigation report discovered by McAfee at the end of 2018 shows that there are more than 4,000 mobile threat families and variants in the McAfee sample database today [2]. Kaspersky Lab, a famous security research lab, detected 1,744,244 malicious installation packages which are 421,666 packages more than in the previous quarter [3].

To handle these escalating security concerns, researchers have designed many effective detection frameworks and have used most of the machine learning models to recognize malware. So far, the malware detection approaches can be classified into two categories: static analysis-based detection [4–13] and dynamic analysis-based method [14,15,17–21]. For example, Droid-Sec utilizes both static analysis and dynamic analysis to discover malware behaviors based on Deep Belief Network (DBN), which totally uses nearly two hundred features. It is a trend that researchers are more likely to extract more and more features from unzipped files and feed the features to classification models for a satisfactory result. However, we found such a strange phenomenon in reality. The detection approaches mainly used by virus vendors are the old ways based on rule matching and the fashionable machine-learning-based method plays a supporting role. The survey found that although the latter method has higher classification accuracy, it also needs to consume more testing time. As mentioned above, the number of Android apps is exploding, it's not enough to scan new applications in a short time by increasing the number of detection devices. Therefore, we believe that time cost is an urgent problem to be solved. Among the several features adopted by the previous research, Application Programming Interface (API) features can well represent program behavior. But a normal application usually contains thousands of API calls, and the dependencies between APIs are complex. It takes a lot of time to extract API calls from the sample without analysis and classification. As a result, the classification method proposed in the paper doesn't consider the API features. In addition to the API, permission is another important classification feature. A normal application usually applies no more than 20 permissions. So from the perspective of the number of features analyzed, permission is clearly superior to other features. While, legal applications often apply more permissions than they need in fact, which causes the detection system with a high false-positive rate in reality [16]. In order to solve the problem, we propose a feature scaling method, which filters the original data before feeding the feature to the classifier, It's not only further reduces the detection time of the system, but more importantly, improves the classification performance to an acceptable range. Our contributions can be summarized as follows:

– We develop Permission Feature Selection (PFS) method, a feature selection approach to detect malware using only a subset of permissions in Android. Contrast with using as much as different features, the work reduces the data redundancy by shrinking the number of permissions to get better performance in various machine learning models.

- To evaluate the result objectively and fairly, we collect a total 13,958 malware from VirusShare and Drebin datasets as well as 14000 benign samples crawled from different Android markets flited by Qihoo-360 Anti-virus engine.
- We provided various experimental results of our method to evaluate the effect in various aspects. Five experiments are conducted in total in this paper.

The rest of the paper is organized as follows: Sect. 2 introduces the design details about the proposed PFS. Section 3 shows the experimental results to show the performance of our method. Section 4 discussed related work in Android malware detection field, followed by Sect. 5 that concludes this paper.

2 The PFS Method

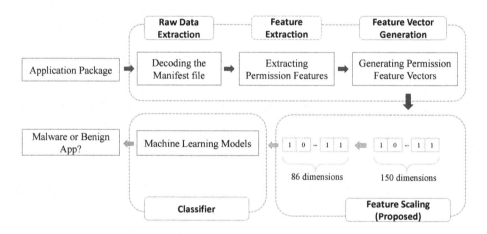

Fig. 1. The overall architecture of proposed approach

Figure 1 shows the overall architecture of our approach. The goal of the PFS system is to achieve high detection accuracy and improve the quality of the distinguishing features. Instead of using all kinds of features extracted from application packages, we focus on doing research on one of the most significant data, permission. This approach, in fact, eliminates the noise permissions we gained to minimize the number of permissions. The condition that little researchers are interested in this aspect can be ascribed to the fact that similar actions have little or no significant influence on malware detection effectiveness. However, the experimental results show that the proposed method works better than other scaling ways and has the highest detection accuracy in the test dataset. PFS is a bilayer data mining process consists of two parts: Recursive Feature Elimination (RFE) and Density Rate (DR).

2.1 Permission Feature

As a privilege-separated operating system, Android enforces the application running with a unique system identifier. A permission-based access control mechanism designed to restrict apps getting sensitive information from mobile devices. As a result, applications must apply for corresponding permissions before attaching to a system resource and the system could monitor the behaviors of programs. Due to the limit of the mechanism, common malicious behaviors such as sending short messages or invoking cameras need more private data. As a result, they usually apply more sensitive permissions than benign ones according to the statistic.

The permission feature is extracted from the Manifest file, an indispensable file for any Android application. There are two types of permission used in the file. The normal permission requested are labelled by ⟨uses-permission⟩ and ⟨/uses-permission⟩. While, the security permissions and protection levels are recorded between ⟨permission⟩ and ⟨/permission⟩ tags. In this paper, the permission feature is made up of both kinds of permissions.

2.2 Bilayer Data Mining

We propose two levels of data mining methods to filter out permissions. The first part of PFS is the RFE process to calculate the most valuable ones out of all original permissions. Though RFE is a reliable method in the feature selection field with a substantial theoretical foundation, it discards some useful information. As a result, it performs unsatisfied in malware detection. As a result of that, we put forward an innovative way to refine more significant permissions named DR after RFE to improve the accuracy of classification.

Recursive Feature Elimination (RFE). RFE is a mature feature selection method used to rank features according to some measure of their importance and remove the weakest features. The algorithm of RFE showed in Algorithm 1. in detail. Due to eliminating dependencies and collinearity with moderate computational efforts, it is widely used in various aspects. However, there are no papers using RFE in Android malware detection. One of the most dependable reasons is that this feature selector often performs badly in malware reorganization. Though so much redundancy and noises exist in all of the permissions, the removed permissions which the selector thought useless also contain a bit of information which could help to classification at the same time. The result of experiments in Sect. 3 verifies it and it even performs worse than using all features. To relief the problem, we adopt the means of cross-validated to get the best performance. After applying RFE, we find that using 91 permissions as classified feature performs nearly as well as employing 150 ones. Detailed results of the experiment showed in Sect. 3.

Algorithm 1. Recursive Feature Elimination

Input: The Original Feature (all predicts)
Output: The Subset of Original Feature (optimal predicts)
 1: Tune/train the model on the training set using all predicts
 2: Calculate model performance
 3: Calculate variable importance or rankings
 4: **for** Each subset size S_i,i=1...$|S|$ **do**
 5:    Keep the S_i most important variables
 6:    [Optional] Pre-process the data
 7:    Tune/train the model on the training set using S_i predictors
 8:    Calculate model performance
 9:    [Optional] Recalculate the rankings for each predictor
10: **end for**
11: Calculate the performance profile over the S_i
12: Determine the appropriate number of predictors
13: Use the model corresponding to the optimal S_i

Density Rate (DR). We supposed that the permission feature malware and benign programs used follow distributions distinct from one another. For example, malicious software uses more SEND_SMS permission than the good ones in frequency for sending the user's private data to the attacker's servers. Naturally, we consider utilizing this difference for detection. Two matrices, B and G, defined for this operation. B stands a table of permissions used by malware apps, while G presents a list of permissions used by benign samples. B_{ij} indicates whether the ith sample applies for the jth permission, while "1" stands yes and "0" stands no. Matrices G is created in the same way. Besides, we use (1) and (2) to calculate the density of each permission used in B and G.

$$D_B(j) = \frac{\sum_i B_{ij}}{size(B_i)} \tag{1}$$

$$D_G(j) = \frac{\sum_i G_{ij}}{size(G_i)} \tag{2}$$

where $D_B(j)$ represents the density of the jth permission used in malware dataset, and $D_G(j)$ denotes the density of the jth permission used in good software samples. The density rate discipline could be expressed as:

$$R(j) = \frac{max(D_B(j), D_G(j))}{D_B(j) + D_G(j)} \tag{3}$$

The DR algorithm is used to display the difference of permission density between malware and benign samples. The result of R(j) is a value between [0.5, 1] standing the contribution of the jth permission made. The larger the value, the more significant the corresponding permission is.

We totally select 86 permissions from original 150 permissions, about 57.3% of all. More important, the result of experiments in Sect. 3 discovers that the proposed scaling method improves nearly 2% accuracy, more effective than similar works [19] released before.

3   Evaluation

In this section, we evaluate the performance of the proposed method with different effective machine learning models. There are 25 dangerous permissions listed by Android, shown in Table. 1.

Table 1. 25 dangerous permissions provided by Android

READ_CALENDAR	WRITE_CALENDAR	READ_EXTERNAL_STORAGE
GET_ACCOUNTS	ACCESS_FINE_LOCATION	PROCESS_OUTGOING_CALLS
RECORD_AUDIO	READ_PHONE_STATE	READ_CELL_BROADCASTS
READ_SMS	WRITE_CALL_LOG	WRITE_EXTERNAL_STORAGE
READ_CALL_LOG	ADD_VOICEMALL	RECEIVE_WAP_PUSH
RECEIVE_SMS	READ_CONTACTS	ACCESS_COARSE_LOCATION
WRITE_CONTACTS	CAMERA	CALL_PHONE
USE_SIP	SEND_SMS	BODY_SENSORS
RECEIVE_MMS		

In addition, researchers further concluded 10 sensitive permissions from the total 25 dangerous permissions, shown in Table 2, used by applications to achieve user's private information. Malware samples must apply for more than one permission in Table 1 before stealing or damaging sensitive data of the devices. As a result, it's acceptable to use these sensitive permissions as a classification feature. Nonetheless, benign ones also request dangerous permissions to complete their normal behaviors such as locating users by Google Map. It's confusing to classify samples effectively depending on this merely.

3.1   Dataset

So far, there is still no standard or official dataset for Android malware detection. Researchers always use some reference resource instead such as VirusShare [22] dataset, Drebin [23] dataset and other famous malware community in this field. In this paper, we offered a malware dataset, 13,958 malware samples, combined by VirusShare and Drebin. Simultaneously, we crawled 14,000 benign ones from different Android markets including Google Plays [24], WanDouJia [25] etc. flited by VirusTotal [26] which integrates nearly 70 renowned anti-virus engines and provides APIs for scanning. Before training machine learning models, the dataset was shuffled and divided into a training set and a testing set in the ratio of 7:3.

Table 2. Top 10 sensitive permissions

Function	Permission
Get private information	ACCESS_COARSE_LOCATION
	ACCESS_FINE_LOCATION
	READ_CONTACTS
	READ_OWNER_DATA
	READ_PHONE_STATE
	READ_SMS
Send & receive short message	RECEIVE_SMS
	SEND_SMS
Call numbers	CALL_PHONE
	PROCESS_OUTGONG_CALLS

3.2 Experiments

We used an Ubuntu 16.04 machine with Intel Xeon e5-2609 CPU, GeForce GTX TITAN X GPU and 256GB RAM for experiments discussed in this paper and further research.

The requested permission vector is built by permissions extracted from Manifest files. Then, the permission information is translated into a binary vector where '1' indicates that the application applies for this permission, and '0' indicates the opposite. Details are shown in Fig. 2.

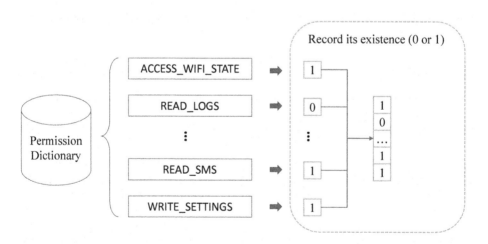

Fig. 2. The process of generating permission vector

We evaluate the performance of malware detection systems using the measures shown in Table 3. These indices are typical indicators for assessing the performance of the detection system. For the malware detection system, the FP rate is an essential evaluation reference. If the rate of FP is too high, the detection system mistook more malware to benign ones, which causes enormous damage to the ecosystem of Android. F-Score is determined by precision rate and recall rate so that it can judge the performance of the system comprehensively.

Table 3. Performance indices of Android malware detection.

Indices	Description
True Positive (TP)	# of apps correctly classified as malware
True Negative (TN)	# of apps correctly classified as benign
False Negative (FN)	# of apps mistakenly classified as malware
False Positive (FP)	# of apps mistakenly classified as benign
Accuracy	(TP + TN)/(TP + TN + FP + FN)
Precision	TP/(TP + FP)
Recall	TP/(TP + FN)
F-Score	2 × Precision × Recall/(Precision + Recall)

In order to achieve the best performance in malware detection, the paper selects some machine learning models which are commonly used in classification such as Naïve Bayes (NB), Logistic, Support Vector Machine (SVM), Random Forest (RF) and J48. As Table 4 shows, RF is more suitable in recognizing malware and reaches more than 91% detection rate in recall and accuracy.

The paper reports the effectiveness of different feature scaling methods shown in Table 5. (Note: the work of Li et al. [11], Li et al. [12] and Zhu et al. [13] will be introduced in Sect. 4 in detail). The best result of each evaluation index is typed in bold. As shown, the simple approach of simply using dangerous permissions performs badly in malware detection that recall and accuracy rates are even less than 80%. It's exhilarating that the method proposed gets the best performance in the experiment. In the methods with short detection time, the classification accuracy of the proposed method has been greatly improved. And the time consumed by the method is greatly reduced against methods with similar classification accuracy.

Table 4. Results of detection using various machine learning models

Machine learning models	Precision (%)	Recall (%)	FP (%)	TP (%)	F-Score (%)	Acc (%)	Time (s)
Naive Bayes	68.93	66.64	31.12	66.63	66.63	66.64	**0.08**
Logistic	78.37	78.45	22.93	78.41	78.32	78.37	2.14
SVM	91.16	86.15	**7.35**	86.15	88.58	90.34	1.67
Random Forest	**91.20**	**91.19**	10.5	**91.20**	**91.21**	**91.19**	2.57
J48	87.43	89.65	13.14	87.43	87.44	87.43	1.23

Table 5. Detection results using different feature scaling approaches

Approach	Num of permissions	Precision (%)	Recall (%)	FP (%)	TP (%)	F-Score (%)	Acc (%)	Time (s)
All Pers	150	90.58	83.61	6.87	83.61	86.96	88.93	4.32
Dangerous Pers	25	81.54	70.60	12.92	70.60	75.68	79.72	1.86
RFE	91	**91.75**	75.91	**5.39**	75.91	83.09	86.36	3.47
Li et al. [11]	22	80.65	82.83	13.14	71.43	73.45	78.33	**1.46**
Liet al. [12]	150	90.36	84.24	7.43	83.46	87.15	89.73	4.62
Zhu et al. [13]	150	89.12	83.82	7.39	85.33	87.23	88.34	5.49
Ours	86	91.20	**91.19**	10.5	**91.20**	**91.21**	**91.19**	1.94

Discussion: The result reflects the fact that with the improvement of applications, more benign software also applies so many sensitive permissions to complete complex functions. At the same time, the leak of private data is easier to occur through the legal channel. Besides, the improvement of precision and FPR rate after RFE proving the validity of feature selection. There is a need to make known the relevance of the number of permissions used and the result of classification. According to Fig. 2, with an increasing number of permissions, the accuracy of classification increases and stays around 91%. Meanwhile, the accuracy reaches the peak using 86 permissions and achieves 91.2% precision. The folds of cross-validation of RF also influence the result of experiments as Fig. 3 shows. With the number of permissions increases, the classification accuracy improves gradually and becomes flatter eventually. It explains the balance of positive information and noise carried by new permission (Fig. 4).

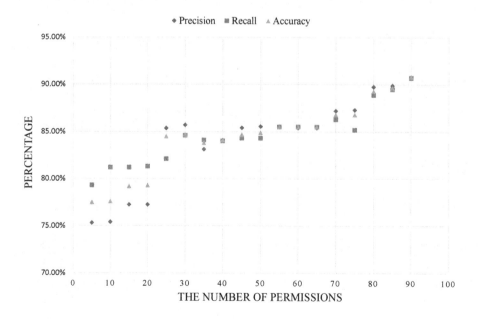

Fig. 3. Malware classification performance of PFS

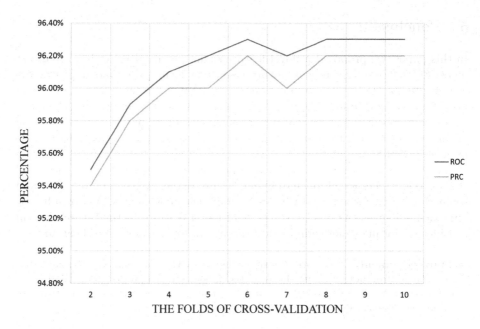

Fig. 4. RF classification performance of the PFS using cross-validation

4 Related Work

Previous papers have discussed Android permission in malware detection. Li et al. [11] supposed a Significant Permission Identification (SigPID) system using only 22 permissions selected by their feature selection method. They analysis the permission both malware and benign samples used and ranking them with a negative rate to characterize the importance of each permission. In the end, they choose the most 22 significant permissions to construct permission feature performs as well as 150 permissions using machine learning classifies. However, they abundant too many useful permissions and it is embarrassed to ameliorate the performance of classification after feature scaling.

Li et al. [12] suggested a fine-grained Android malware detection base on deep learning. Authors extract permissions from Manifest.xml file, API called and other information about the applications from classes.dex file. Then, they adopted Multi-layer Perceptron (MLP) as a classifier to recognize malware. Deep Neural Network (DNN) usually performs better than traditional machine learning methods, while, it's a pity that the authors focus on model construction instead of feature selecting.

Zhu et al. [13] explored a detection of Android malware using permissions, system events, sensitive APIs and URLs. They totally picked 9 sensitive permission using prior knowledge. After that, they employed the ensemble Rotation Forest (RF) to construct a model to detect whether an Android App is malicious or not. Finally, the proposed method achieves an accuracy of 88.26%.

5   Conclusion

In this paper, we proposed a novel feature scaling method in Android malware detection that reduces the computing resource consumption and improves the classification accuracy. The permission feature used is extracted by the analyzing file, Manifest.xml, from an APK file. Original permissions applied by the application contains lots of noises that interferences classifiers' performance. The scale of the permission feature is decreased after PFS, while machine learning models perform better than before.

In the evaluation, we carried out comparative experiments. We compared the detection accuracy of much different permission feature scaling methods and evaluated the performance of various machine learning models. As a result, our approach enhances the quality of the permission feature. In the future, we will consider exploiting other signification characters for malware classification.

Acknowledgement. This work was supported in by the National Key Research and Development Program of China-the Key Technologies for High Security Mobile Terminals (Grant No.2017YFB0801903), and the Youth Star project of the Institute of Information Engineering, CAS (No. Y8YS016104).

References

1. Statcounter.   https://gs.statcounter.com/os-market-share/mobile/worldwide. Accessed 15 Apr 2019
2. McAfee Labs Threats Report. https://www.mcafee.com/enterprise/en-us/assets/ reports/rp-quarterly-threats-dec-2018.pdf
3. IT Threat Evolution. https://securelist.com/it-threat-evolution-q2-2018-statistics /87170
4. Yuan, Z., et al.: Droid-Sec: deep learning in android malware detection. ACM SIGCOMM Comput. Commun. Rev. **44**(4), 371–372 (2014)
5. Narayanan, A., et al.: Adaptive and scalable android malware detection through online learning. In: 2016 International Joint Conference on Neural Networks (IJCNN), pp. 2484–2491. IEEE (2016)
6. Sun, J., et al.: Malware detection on Android smartphones using keywords vector and SVM. In: 16th International Conference on Computer and Information Science (ICIS), pp. 833–838. IEEE (2017)
7. Kim, T., et al.: A multimodal deep learning method for android malware detection using various features. IEEE Trans. Inf. Forensics Secur. **14**(3), 773–788 (2019)
8. Wang, C., Lan, Y.: PFESG: permission-based android malware feature extraction algorithm. In: Proceedings of the 2017 VI International Conference on Network, Communication and Computing, pp. 106–109. ACM (2017)
9. Qiao, Y., Yun, X., Zhang, Y.: How to automatically identify the homology of different malware. In: 2016 IEEE Trustcom/BigDataSE/ISPA, pp. 929–936. IEEE (2016)
10. Li, Z.-Q., et al.: A similar module extraction approach for android malware. In: DEStech Transactions on Computer Science and Engineering. MSO (2018)
11. Li, J., et al.: Significant permission identification for machine-learning-based android malware detection. IEEE Trans. Industr. Inf. **14**(7), 3216–3225 (2018)

12. Li, D., Wang, Z., Xue, Y.: Fine-grained android malware detection based on deep learning. In: 2018 IEEE Conference on Communications and Network Security (CNS), pp. 1–2. IEEE (2018)
13. Zhu, H., et al.: DroidDet: effective and robust detection of android malware using static analysis along with rotation forest model. Neurocomputing **272**, 638–646 (2018)
14. Lin, C.-H., Pao, H.-K., Liao, J.-W.: Efficient dynamic malware analysis using virtual time control mechanics. Comput. Secur. **73**, 359–373 (2018)
15. Yan, L.K., Yin, H.: DroidScope: seamlessly reconstructing the OS and Dalvik semantic views for dynamic android malware analysis. Presented as part of the 21st USENIX Security Symposium. USENIX Security, vol. 12, pp. 569–584 (2012)
16. Jordaney, R., et al.: Transcend: detecting concept drift in malware classification models. In: 26th USENIX Security Symposium. pp. 625–642 (2017)
17. Enck, W., et al.: TaintDroid: an information-flow tracking system for realtime privacy monitoring on smartphones. ACM Trans. Comput. Syst. (TOCS) **32**(2), 5 (2014)
18. De Carli, L., et al.: KALI: scalable encryption fingerprinting in dynamic malware traces. In: 2017 12th International Conference on Malicious and Unwanted Software (MALWARE), pp. 3–10. IEEE (2017)
19. Bulazel, A., Yener, B.: A survey on automated dynamic malware analysis evasion and counter-evasion: PC, mobile, and web. In: Proceedings of the 1st Reversing and Offensive-Oriented Trends Symposium, p. 2. ACM (2017)
20. Burguera, I., Zurutuza, U., Nadjm-Tehrani, S.: Crowdroid: behavior-based malware detection system for android. In: Proceedings of the 1st ACM Workshop on Security and Privacy in Smartphones and Mobile Devices, pp. 15–26. ACM (2011)
21. Petsas, T., et al.: Rage against the virtual machine: hindering dynamic analysis of android malware. In: Proceedings of the Seventh European Workshop on System Security, p. 5. ACM (2014)
22. VirusShare. https://virusshare.com/. Accessed 24 Apr 2019
23. Drebin. https://www.sec.cs.tu-bs.de/~danarp/drebin/. Accessed Feb 2014
24. Google Play. https://play.google.com/store/. Accessed Apr 2019
25. WanDouJia. https://www.wandoujia.com/. Accessed Apr 2019
26. VirusTotal. https://www.virustotal.com/ko/. Accessed Apr 2019

Agile Query Processing in Statistical Databases: A Process-In-Memory Approach

Shanshan Lu[1], Peiquan Jin[1,2(✉)], Lin Mu[1], and Shouhong Wan[1,2]

[1] University of Science and Technology of China, Hefei, China
jpq@ustc.edu.cn
[2] Key Laboratory of Electromagnetic Space Information,
Chinese Academy of Sciences, Hefei, China

Abstract. Statistical database systems are designed to answer queries on summarized data (or macro data), while queries on raw records are not allowed in such database systems. As macro data can offer aggregate information about the database, it is also an effective way to use statistical queries to provide analytical results in semantic databases. However, traditional statistical databases are proposed for security protection, i.e., hiding the raw records from user queries. Few studies are toward query optimizations on aggregate queries in statistical databases. In this paper, we propose a new process-in-memory (PIM) based processing scheme called *agile query* for accelerating queries in statistical databases. We present two new designs in the *agile query*. First, we propose an in-memory index to cache aggregate operators (e.g., sum, min, max, count, and average) in the main memory. The aggregate queries that hit in the in-memory index can be evaluated in the memory and no I/O operation will be incurred. Second, we propose to incrementally update the in-memory operator index so that we can ensure the consistency between the cached data and the original data records. We implement the *agile query* processing framework on top of MySQL and conduct experiments over various sizes of datasets to compare our design with the traditional method in MySQL. The results show that our proposal achieves up to 9 times higher throughput than MySQL under the skewed Zipf query set, and averagely gets about 2 times higher throughput under the random and uniform distributed queries.

Keywords: Query processing · Statistical database · Processing in memory

1 Introduction

A statistical data management system (DBMS) [1] is a data management system designed to explicitly handle so called "macro data," i.e., data computed by different forms of summarization, including grouping and classification, as first class objects. In a statistical data management system, there are data manipulation operators that return the macro data related results, such as sum, count, and average values [2]. As macro data can offer aggregate information about the database, it is also an effective way to use statistical queries to provide analytical results in semantic databases.

Research on statistical databases started in the 1970s and flourished in the 1980s [3]. A number of systems developed based on both relational and object-oriented data

© Springer Nature Switzerland AG 2019
C. Douligeris et al. (Eds.): KSEM 2019, LNAI 11775, pp. 726–738, 2019.
https://doi.org/10.1007/978-3-030-29551-6_64

models. Many of these systems represented statistical data by graph-based representations, where one can construct hierarchies of categories based on different attributes and calculate summarized data for each category. Traditional statistical DBMSs were mainly designed to minimize the redundancy of computation when answering a user query as well as to enhance data security so that the individual data records are not exposed to a malicious user.

However, with the increasing of the data volumes, the query performance of statistical databases is becoming a critical issue. For example, in order to calculate the average value of a given attribute, the DBMS has to traverse all the raw records. This is time-consuming especially when there are tens of millions of raw records in a table. Traditional relational DBMSs often use indices to accelerate queries, but this scheme does not work for aggregate queries, as the DBMS has to access all raw records while calculating the aggregate values.

In this paper, aiming to optimize aggregate queries in statistical databases, we propose a new approach called *agile query*. The idea of *agile query* is straightforward, i.e., we aim to utilize the main memory to let most aggregate queries be evaluated in the memory, so that costly I/O operations can be reduced and the overall performance can be enhanced. Following this general idea, we present two new designs in this paper. First, we propose an in-memory index to cache aggregate operators (e.g., sum, min, max, count, and average) in the main memory. The aggregate queries that hit in the in-memory index can be evaluated in the memory and no I/O operation will be incurred. Second, we propose to incrementally update the in-memory operator index so that we can ensure the consistency between the cached data and the original data records. In order to make our design more general, we also offer the service of registering a new aggregate operator into the query processing framework. Briefly, we make the following contributions in this paper:

(1) We propose a new approach called *agile query* that aims to optimize aggregate queries in statistical databases. An in-memory hash index is designed to cache frequently used aggregate operators, and aggregate queries hitting in the in-memory hash index can be evaluated in the memory without I/O operations. We demonstrate that this design is efficient for improving the performance of aggregate queries.

(2) We present the implemental details of the *agile query* approach, including the in-memory hash index maintenance, the query processing algorithm, and the registration of new aggregate operators. Specially, we develop an incremental updating strategy for the in-memory hash index to ensure the data consistency between the cached data and the underlying raw data. When raw data records are updated, we use triggers to automatically update the cached data to maintain the data consistency.

(3) We conduct experiments on the basis of the TPC-H benchmark and use three datasets that range from 1 GB to 30 GB and querying workloads with different distributions such as random, uniform, and Zipf. We compare the *agile query* approach with the traditional method in MySQL. The results show that our proposal can significantly increase the throughput. Particularly, the throughput of the *agile query* under the Zipf query distribution is up to 9 times higher than that of MySQL, and the throughput of the *agile query* under the random and uniform distributions is about 2 times higher than that of MySQL on average.

2 Related Work

Statistical databases, which only allow users to execute aggregate queries, were developed mainly for database security enhancement. An overview of the various concepts used in statistical databases can be found in the literature [4]. Statistical databases are firstly used for statistical analysis purposes [5, 6]. They are usually connected to scientific databases [7] and OLAP [8].

Statistical databases are typically designed to provide information about the records in the database and its subset, while preventing the disclosure of attribute values for any single record [9]. Many statistical data applications need to offer statistical information to public but also need to protect personal privacy. However, traditional SQL DBMSs are difficult to handle such needs [10]. In the literature [11], the authors proposed an efficient method to map the original data set to a new anonymous data set, which can preserve the correlation between different dimensions. The previous work [12] introduced a kind of Hippocratic security method, which managed the collection of statistical databases according to a series of management rules through the virtual community of several organizations.

While most previous work in statistical databases focused on security issues, there are few studies towards query optimization over statistical databases [13, 14]. However, in the related field, namely scientific databases [15, 16], a few methods toward scientific query optimizations have been proposed [17, 18]. As scientific databases are not focused on statistical queries, the proposed query optimizations are not suitable for statistical queries. In the literature [13], a query access plan based on the statistics of the database was proposed, but it was not specifically designed for statistical queries. In the literature [18], a query rewriting scheme was proposed to generate a transformed query that can form results without scanning the user tables, but this method assumed that the dictionary tables were in the memory, which is not practical for large databases. In the literature [14], researchers presented new query processing techniques on aggregate queries in security statistics databases. However, this work was mainly toward secure query processing.

Recently, with the advance of non-volatile memories such as flash memory [19–21] and PCM [22, 23], the processing-in-memory (PIM) architecture [24, 25] has received much attention from both academia and industry. The PIM architecture proposes to perform computation in the main memory, so as to reduce costly I/O operations and avoid the "storage wall" problem [25]. The key idea of PIM is actually to use additional memory to accelerate computation. Our work is first inspired by the PIM architecture. The proposed *agile query* approach also uses memories to reduce disk I/Os. However, the key difference of our proposal from PIM is that our work is specially designed for aggregate queries in statistical databases, while the PIM architecture is mainly for byte-based computation.

3   The *Agile Query* Approach

3.1   Design Criteria

The basic idea of the *agile query* approach is to let most aggregate computations be executed in the main memory, so that costly I/O operations can be reduced, resulting in the improvement of overall time performance.

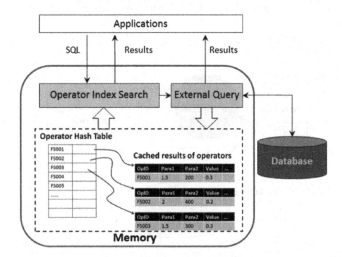

Fig. 1. Architecture of the *agile query* approach

Figure 1 shows the architecture of the *agile query* approach. We maintain an in-memory operator hash table in the memory, which stores all frequently, used aggregate operators as well as their parameters. When users issue an aggregate query, we first perform an operator index search over the in-memory operator hash table. If the query hits in the hash table, we simply retrieve the cached results corresponding to the query and return them to users. If the query is not registered in the hash table, we perform an external query, meaning that the query is delivered to the underlying DBMS for further execution. The external query processing is the same as the traditional query processing in SQL DBMSs. Note that if the external query is an insertion or update query, the in-memory hash index will be automatically updated along with the data update.

Typical aggregate operators include *sum, min, max, count*, and *average*, which are all standard operators in SQL databases. However, our approach also allows users to register new operators other than the standard five aggregate operators. When users register a new operator, the information about the new operator will be added into the in-memory hash index. In our implementation, when an operator is not found in the in-memory hash index, it will be registered into the hash index.

Figure 2 shows an example of the *agile query*. Here, we assume that the indexed operator is to retrieve the trajectory length of a given object. As the object moves with time, we have to traverse all raw records if we do not maintain the in-memory hash index in the memory. In the *agile query*, the historical trajectory information is cached in the index. Thus, when the object moves, new position records will enter into the database (more specifically, into the memory). The *agile query* processor can see that the trajectory query about the object has been maintained in the hash index. Therefore, we perform an incremental calculation in the memory over the historical trajectory and the new records to generate the up-to-date trajectory for the object, which will be returned to users. Finally, we update the cached historical trajectory using the generated real-time trajectory. Through this mechanism, we can see that trajectory length queries can be mostly answered in the in-memory hash index, leading to the increasing of the time performance.

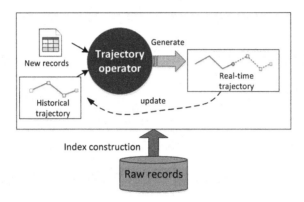

Fig. 2. An example about real-time trajectory query in the *agile query*

3.2   In-Memory Hash Index

The in-memory hash index in the *agile query* maintains the registered aggregate queries. A newly arrived query will be first evaluated in the memory-resident hash table. Basically, the in-memory hash index maintains three kinds of information about an aggregate operator, which are described as follows:

(1) **Operator information.** This kind of information includes many aspects about the registered operator, including the operator name, parameter names, and parameter values. Based on these kinds of information, we can generate the entire SQL statement for the registered aggregate operator. There are 22 types of queries in the TPC-H benchmark. Each type of query has several variables whose values are chosen by users at runtime. Once these variable values are determined, we can obtain a complete SQL statement. In real-world applications where people often make duplicated aggregate queries, the cached operator information will be much helpful to reduce query overheads.

(2) **Result information.** The second kind of information maintains the results of the indexed aggregate operator. Each indexed operator has a corresponding set of cached results. When a user query hits the in-memory hash index, the corresponding results of the query will be retrieved and returned to the user.

(3) **Timestamp.** The third kind of information is the timestamp. Each operator has an associated timestamp, which is an integer that can only be increased. When a user query hits an operator in the in-memory hash index, the timestamp of the operator will be increased to the largest value. When the in-memory hash index reaches the memory-space limitation, we select the operator that has the lowest timestamp as the victim to be replaced.

Algorithm 1 shows the process of incrementally updating the hash table. The query type can be select, insert, update, or delete. For a select query, if the query does not hit in the in-memory hash table, meaning that the query is a new query, we register the query into the hash table. If the hash table is full, we select the entry with the lowest timestamp as the victim and replace it with the new query. If the query is an insert, delete, or update, we simply update the hash table. More specifically, for a delete query, we remove the corresponding operator from the hash table. For an update query, we modify the results information and update the timestamp of the operator. For an insert query, we add a new entry in the hash table. In our implementation, we use triggers to monitor the query type. For insert, delete and update operations, as they will change the results of the raw records, the triggers can automatically update the hash table to realize the data consistency.

Algorithm 1. Incremental_Update_Hash(E, hit)

Input: E is the query type, hit is a Boolean value identifying whether the query is
       hit in the index.

Output: updated $hash$ table

1   **If** E is a select operation
2   **If** $hit = false$ //not hit
3   **If** the $hash$ table is full
4   replace the entry having the lowest timestamp in the $hash$ table;
5   register E into the $hash$ table;
6   **Else** // E is insert, delete, or update
8   update the $hash$ table;
9   **Return** the updated $hash$ table;
End   Incremental_Update_Hash

3.3 Query Processing

Algorithm 2 shows the details of the *agile query* processing. When users issue a SQL query statement, we first search the in-memory hash index to see whether there is an operator matching the query. If the query hits in the hash table, the result information about the cached operator corresponding to the query are returned to users. If the hash index does not contain the inputted query, we perform a traditional disk-based search, which is the same as usual.

If the given query does not hit in the in-memory hash index, we have to perform extra memory searches compared to the traditional query processing. However, memory search can be generally performed within a few nanoseconds, if the hash table has a limited size. To this end, the time overhead of query processing in case of no hits in the in-memory hash table can be neglected. Therefore, in our implementation, we set a memory-space threshold for the hash index, so that we can avoid the increasing time cost of the memory search over the hash table. In addition, when the size of the hash table increases, we can infer that more queries will hit in the hash index, yielding the increasing of the hit ratio and in turn the overall time performance of the system.

Algorithm 2. AgileQuery(S)

Input: S is the query statement.

Output: the query result R.

1	**For** each entry r in the *hash* table
2	**If** r matches S
3	$R \leftarrow r.results$;
4	**Return** R;
5	$R \leftarrow$ ExternalQuery(S); // perform external query
6	register S into the *hash* table;
7	**Return** R;
End	AgileQuery

---

4 Performance Evaluation

4.1 Settings

We implement the *agile query* approach on top of MySQL and use the TPC-H benchmark to evaluate performance. TPC-H is a decision support benchmark consisting of concurrent data modifications and a suite of business oriented ad-hoc queries. TPC-H evaluates the performance of various decision support systems by executing sets of queries against a standard database under controlled conditions.

The experimental system is implemented on a computer with an Intel(R) Core(TM) i5-8500 CPU @3.00 GHz with 16 GB RAM. We choose 8 query types in TPC-H, namely Q1, Q3, Q6, Q7, Q11, Q12, Q14 and Q18, which are all aggregate queries. As there are multiple variables in each query, our experiment finally includes 1194 different queries.

We conduct experiments over various sizes of datasets to compare our design with the traditional query processing method. The components of the TPC-H database are defined to consist of eight separate and individual tables. The relationships between columns of these tables are illustrated in Fig. 3.

The database size is defined with reference to the scale factor (SF). We use three SFs in the experiments, namely 1, 10, and 30. As a result, the total size of our database is 1 GB, 10 GB, and 30 GB, respectively. In addition, we manually prepare the queries in terms of different distributions, including uniform distribution, random distribution, and Zipf distribution. Consequently, we get nine data sets.

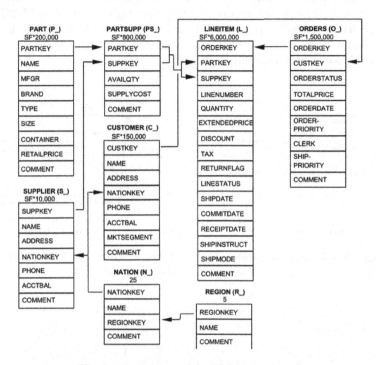

Fig. 3. The schema of the TPC-H benchmark

We evaluate the throughput, hit radio, and space cost of the *agile query* approach and compare it with the traditional query method in MySQL. The values of variables in each query are generated randomly. In each running, we first perform 300 queries as a warm-up for the system, and then collect the results of the next 1000 queries.

4.2   Throughput

In this experiment, we compare the query throughput of the *agile query* method with the traditional method on different data sets under different distributions. Since the execution efficiency of the 1 GB dataset is significantly higher than that of the 10 GB dataset and the 30 GB dataset, we show the results of the 1 GB dataset in separated figures. Figures 4 and 5 show the query throughput under the uniform distribution. Figures 6 and 7 show the performance under the random distribution. Figures 8 and 9 show the performance under the Zipf distribution. To make the figures clearer, values above 1 in Figs. 5 and 7 are displayed as 1, and values above 100 in Fig. 8 are displayed as 100.

We can see that the throughput of the *agile query* method is much better than that of the traditional method, regardless of the query distribution and the size of dataset. The throughput of the *agile query* under the random and uniform distributions is averagely about 2 times higher than that of MySQL. Specially, the throughput of the *agile query* under the Zipf distribution is up to 9 times higher than that of MySQL. This is because that the queries under the Zipf distribution are much skewed; thus most queries can hit in the in-memory hash index. to this end, the *agile query* method is more suitable for skewed querying applications.

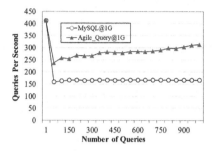

Fig. 4. QPS@1 GB uniform distributed queries

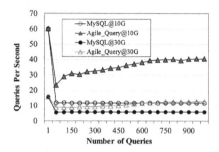

Fig. 5. QPS@10 GB/30 GB uniform distributed queries

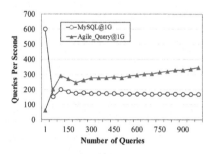

Fig. 6. QPS@1 GB random distributed queries

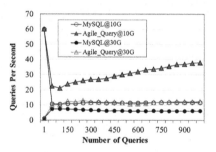

Fig. 7. QPS@10 GB/30 GB random distributed queries

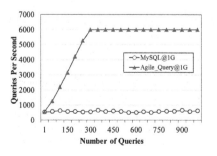

Fig. 8. QPS@1 GB Zipf distributed queries

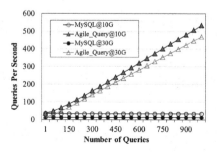

Fig. 9. QPS@10 GB/30 GB Zipf distributed queries

4.3 Hit Ratio

Next, we measure the hit ratio of queries in the in-memory hash index. The following three figures, Figs. 10, 11, and 12, show the hit ratios under three query workloads. We can find that under the uniform and the random distribution, the hit ratio after 300 times of pre-heating is around 0.5; it continues to rise slowly when executing subsequent queries. Under the Zipf distribution, the hit ratio increases rapidly after 300 times of pre-heating. Specially, after executing 500 queries, the hit ratio reaches a high value over 0.9 under all distributions.

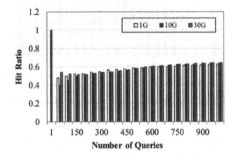

Fig. 10. Hit radio@ uniform distributed queries

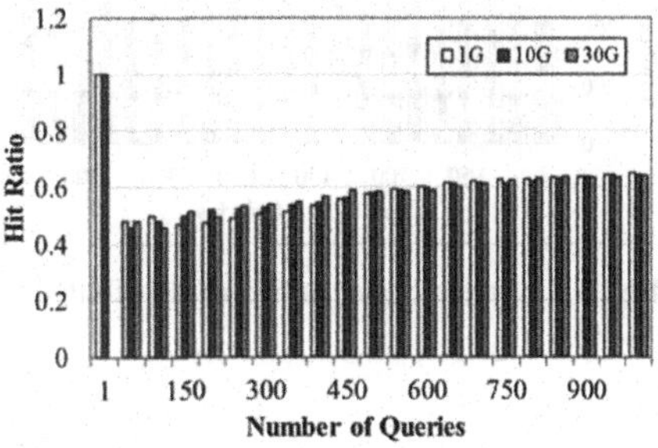

Fig. 11. Hit radio@ random distributed queries

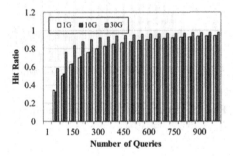

Fig. 12. Hit radio@Zipf distributed queries

4.4 Space Cost

In this experiment, we measure the memory space cost of the hash index. Figures 13, 14, and 15 show the number of entries in the hash table under different distributions. In our experiment, the maximum number of the entries in the hash table is set to 500. When the number of entries exceeds 500, we select the most recently unused entry as the victim for replacement.

Under the random and uniform query workloads, we can see in Figs. 13 and 14 that the hash index becomes full after executing about 800 queries. This is mainly because the queries in these two query workloads are not skewed; thus new queries will quickly fulfill the hash index.

Figure 15 shows the hash table size under the skewed Zipf query workload. We can see that after about 300 queries the size of the hash table becomes stable but not exceed the size limit. This result also indicates that the proposed *agile query* approach is more suitable for skewed queries.

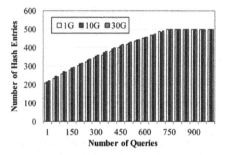

Fig. 13. Space cost@ uniform distributed queries

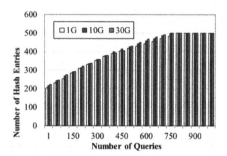

Fig. 14. Space cost@ random distributed queries

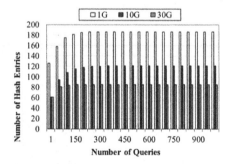

Fig. 15. Space cost@ Zipf distributed queries

5   Conclusions

In this paper, we propose a new approach called *agile query* for accelerating aggregate queries in statistical databases. A special in-memory hash index is proposed to cache aggregate operators in the memory, so that newly arrived queries can be first evaluated in the memory-resident hash table. With this mechanism, we are able to improve the performance of aggregate queries in statistical databases, especially in the applications where the distribution of queries is skewed. We conduct experiments over three data sets whose sizes range from 1 GB to 30 GB. The experimental results show that our approach is much more efficient than the traditional query processing method.

Acknowledgements. This work is partially supported by the National Key Research and Development Program of China (2018YFB0704404) and the National Science Foundation of China (61672479).

References

1. Gupta, A.: Statistical data management. In: Liu, L., Özsu, M.T. (eds.) Encyclopedia of Database Systems, 2nd edn. Springer, Boston (2018)
2. Rafanelli, M., Shoshani, A.: Storm: a statistical object representation model. In: Michalewicz, Z. (ed.) SSDBM 1990. LNCS, vol. 420, pp. 14–29. Springer, Heidelberg (1990). https://doi.org/10.1007/3-540-52342-1_18
3. Shoshani, A.: OLAP and statistical databases: similarities and differences. In: PODS, pp. 185–196 (1997)
4. Brankovic, L., Giggins, H.: Statistical database security. In: Petković, M., Jonker, W. (eds.) Security, Privacy, and Trust in Modern. Data Management Data-Centric Systems and Applications, pp. 167–181. Springer, Heidelberg (2007)
5. Shoshani, A., Olken, F., Wong, H.K.T.: Characteristics of scientific databases. In: VLDB, pp. 147–160 (1984)
6. Shoshani A. Statistical databases: characteristics, problems, and some solutions. In: VLDB, pp. 208–222 (1982)
7. Shoshani, A., Wong, H.K.T.: Statistical and scientific database issues. IEEE Trans. Software Eng. **10**, 1040–1047 (1985)
8. Lu, H., Vaidya, J., et al.: Statistical database auditing without query denial threat. INFORMS J. Comput. **27**(1), 20–34 (2015)
9. Ryan, J.: A brief survey on the contribution of Mirka Miller to the security of statistical databases. Math. Comput. Sci. **12**(3), 255–262 (2018)
10. Domingo-Ferrer, J.: Inference control in statistical databases. In: Liu, L., Özsu, M.T. (eds.) Encyclopedia of Database Systems, 2nd edn. Springer, Boston (2018)
11. Aggarwal, C.C., Yu, P.S.: A condensation approach to privacy preserving data mining. In: Bertino, E., et al. (eds.) EDBT 2004. LNCS, vol. 2992, pp. 183–199. Springer, Heidelberg (2004). https://doi.org/10.1007/978-3-540-24741-8_12
12. Skinner, G., Chang, E., et al.: Shield privacy Hippocratic security method for virtual community. In: IECON, pp. 472–479 (2004)
13. Baranczyk, S., Konik, R., et al.: Forecasting query access plan obsolescence: U.S. Patent 9, 990, 396 (2018)
14. Xike, X., Xingjun, H., Torben, P., Peiquan, J., Jinchuan, C.: OLAP over probabilistic data cubes I: Aggregating, materializing, and querying. In: ICDE, pp. 799–810 (2016)
15. Cormode, G., Korn, F., Muthukrishnan, S., Srivastava, D.: Summarizing two-dimensional data with skyline-based statistical descriptors. In: Ludäscher, B., Mamoulis, N. (eds.) SSDBM 2008. LNCS, vol. 5069, pp. 42–60. Springer, Heidelberg (2008). https://doi.org/10.1007/978-3-540-69497-7_6
16. Gemulla, R., Rösch, P., Lehner, W.: Linked bernoulli synopses: sampling along foreign keys. In: Ludäscher, B., Mamoulis, N. (eds.) SSDBM 2008. LNCS, vol. 5069, pp. 6–23. Springer, Heidelberg (2008). https://doi.org/10.1007/978-3-540-69497-7_4
17. Singh, S., Mayfield, C., Shah, R., Prabhakar, S., Hambrusch, S.: Query selectivity estimation for uncertain data. In: Ludäscher, B., Mamoulis, N. (eds.) SSDBM 2008. LNCS, vol. 5069, pp. 61–78. Springer, Heidelberg (2008). https://doi.org/10.1007/978-3-540-69497-7_7

18. Wang, F., Agrawal, G., Jin, R.: Query planning for searching inter-dependent deep-web databases. In: Ludäscher, B., Mamoulis, N. (eds.) SSDBM 2008. LNCS, vol. 5069, pp. 24–41. Springer, Heidelberg (2008). https://doi.org/10.1007/978-3-540-69497-7_5

19. Zhi, L., Peiquan, J., Xuan, S., et al.: CCF-LRU: a new buffer replacement algorithm for flash memory. IEEE Trans. Consum. Electron. **55**(3), 1351–1359 (2009)

20. Peiquan, J., Xike, X., Na, W., Lihua, Y.: Optimizing R-tree for flash memory. Expert Syst. Appl. **42**(10), 4676–4686 (2015)

21. Peiquan, J., Yi, O., Theo, H., Zhi, L.: AD-LRU: an efficient buffer replacement algorithm for flash-based databases. Data Knowl. Eng. **72**, 83–102 (2012)

22. Chen, K., Jin, P., Yue, L.: A novel page replacement algorithm for the hybrid memory architecture involving PCM and DRAM. In: Hsu, C.-H., Shi, X., Salapura, V. (eds.) NPC 2014. LNCS, vol. 8707, pp. 108–119. Springer, Heidelberg (2014). https://doi.org/10.1007/978-3-662-44917-2_10

23. Wu, Z., Jin, P., Yang, C., Yue, L.: APP-LRU: a new page replacement method for PCM/DRAM-based hybrid memory systems. In: Hsu, C.-H., Shi, X., Salapura, V. (eds.) NPC 2014. LNCS, vol. 8707, pp. 84–95. Springer, Heidelberg (2014). https://doi.org/10.1007/978-3-662-44917-2_8

24. Talati, N., Ali, A., et al.: Practical challenges in delivering the promises of real processing-in-memory machines. In: DATE, pp. 1628–1633 (2018)

25. Ahn, J., Yoo, S., Mutlu, O., et al.: PIM-enabled instructions: a low-overhead, locality-aware processing-in-memory architecture. In: ISCA, pp. 336–348 (2015)

Enhancing the Conciseness of Linked Data by Discovering Synonym Predicates

Subhi Issa$^{(\boxtimes)}$, Fayçal Hamdi, and Samira Si-said Cherfi

CEDRIC - Conservatoire National des Arts et Métiers,
292 Rue Saint Martin, Paris, France
{subhi.issa,faycal.hamdi,samira.cherfi}@cnam.fr

Abstract. In the meantime of the rapidly growing of Linked Data, the quality of these datasets is yet a challenge. A close examination of the quality of this data could be very critical, especially if important researches or professional decisions depend on it. Nowadays, several Linked Data quality metrics have been proposed which cover numerous dimensions of Linked Data quality such as completeness, consistency, conciseness and interlinking. In this paper, we propose an approach to enhance the conciseness of linked datasets by discovering synonym predicates. This approach is based, in addition to a statistical analysis, on a deep semantic analysis of data and on learning algorithms. We argue that studying the meaning of predicates can help to improve the accuracy of results. A set of experiments are conducted on real-world datasets to evaluate the approach.

Keywords: Linked Data quality · OWL2 · Conciseness ·
Ontology alignment

1 Introduction

Today, the Internet is considered as an extremely crowded place because data is clearly increasing on the web that there is much more now than ever before. The basic idea behind the Web of Data is to represent the Web content as structured data, and to provide a reasoning framework on this data. To achieve this, a set of types, properties and relationships between entities have been collected, and made by using semantic web technologies (OWL, RDF, SPARQL, etc.) available. However, the published data on the Web of Data are not as good as we could expect leading to a low add value and a low reliability of the derived results.

A high quality of data can help applications to produce more accurate results. Several approaches and tools have been proposed to evaluate varying dimensions of Linked Data quality. However, for the majority of dimensions, these approaches do not provide an in-depth study but only generic measures to evaluate data quality [22]. The conciseness of data is one of these dimensions that should be extensively examined as it prevents data redundancy. Wasteful data redundancy generally occurs when a given piece of data should not be repeated.

© Springer Nature Switzerland AG 2019
C. Douligeris et al. (Eds.): KSEM 2019, LNAI 11775, pp. 739–750, 2019.
https://doi.org/10.1007/978-3-030-29551-6_65

This is important because, on the one hand, having useless data may influence the accuracy of information negatively, and on the other hand, this requires query expansion to extract all needed information. In this work, we plan to discover repeated predicates to enhance the dataset conciseness. Our objective is to **find equivalent predicates** to remove relations which do not present new information to the dataset. The proposed approach consists of three phases. It is based, in addition to a statistical and NLP-based analysis, on a semantic analysis through studying the meaning of each predicate to detect logical conflicts.

We especially aim to analyze the meaning of the candidate predicates in order to find those that are synonyms, and exclude those having different semantic features. We take into account several semantic features such as symmetric, transitive, functional, inverse functional, disjoint domain/range and cardinality restrictions. Finally, we take into account the meaning of the predicate in a specific context using learning algorithms.

This paper is structured as the following: Sect. 2 elaborates the related work. Section 3 illustrates the motivations for our research work. In Sect. 4, we explain our proposed approach. After that, we present and discuss experiments in Sect. 5. Finally, Sect. 6 concludes this work and points out future directions.

2   Related Work

Ontology alignment is the process of identifying that several vocabularies are semantically related, which may be in one or more datasets. Different approaches [13,18] are applied to discover synonym objects. In addition to research in linking RDF at the conceptual and instance levels that have been investigated in the recent past, property alignment has not received much attention yet. There are some studies on mapping properties across RDF sources [5,8,23]. In [5], the authors identified similar relations using subject and object overlap of predicates. On the other hand, [8] also used statistical measures to identify strictly equivalent relations rather than similarity in general. In [7,23], authors provided methods to group equivalent predicates by clustering synonymous relations. PARIS [20] is another well-known approach which needs to be mentioned in this context. It combines instance and schema matching using probabilities with high accuracy. This work focuses particularly on aligning two ontologies.

Our work is motivated by the problems we have met when we have tried to reveal conceptual schemas of RDF data sources [11]. We relied on a mining approach taking into consideration the data model from a more frequent combination of predicates based on completeness measurement [12]. The idea is how to deal with predicates that have the same meaning with different names. Besides to completeness dimension, conciseness is one aspect of Linked Data quality dimensions [22] which basically aims to avoid repetition elements. The eliminating of the synonymously used predicates aims to optimize the dataset to speed up processing. Mendes et al. [16] categorized the conciseness dimension into intensional and extensional conciseness. The first type, which is the intensional conciseness, measures a number of unique dataset attributes to the total number of schema attributes, thus, this measurement is represented on the schema level. In a similar manner but on the instance level, extensional concise-ness measures the number of unique objects to the real number of objects in the dataset. In [15], the authors proposed an assessment metric by detecting the number of ambiguous instances according to those of semantic metadata sets in order to discover the duplicated instances. In the similar sense but under a different name, Füber et Hepp [6] defined the elements of representation like (classes, predicates and objects) under the domination of "uniqueness". Their definition suggested uniqueness of breadth at the schema level and uniqueness of depth at the instance level.

Indeed, the proposed metrics of conciseness assessment are based on a simple ratio, which compares the proportion of existing elements to the overall ones. Whereas, the conciseness at schema level is measured by the number of unique predicates and dataset classes to the total number of those elements in a schema [16]. On instance level, it measures the number of unique instances to the total number of instances in the dataset [6,15,16]. In [2], the authors proposed an algo-rithm to discover the synonym predicates for query expansions. This algorithm is based on mining similar predicates according to their subjects and objects. How-ever, their approach proposed a lot of predicates that are not synonyms (false positives). In this paper, we focus on extracting equivalent predicates from RDF datasets.

3   Motivating Scenario

Semantic data is usually collected from heterogeneous sources through a variety of tools for different purposes [14,17]. Unfortunately, this sort of mixing could lead to decreasing the quality of data, so that we have proposed this approach to enhance the conciseness dimension of Linked Data.

Our research on the conciseness dimension was inspired by Abedjan and Naumann's work "Synonym Analysis for Predicate Expansion" [2]. The authors proposed a data-driven synonym discovery algorithm for a predicate expansion by applying both schema analysis and range content filtering.

Range content filtering aims to represent a transaction as a distinct object with several predicates. For example, the object *Lyon*[1] city is connected with several predicates such as (*birthPlace*, *deathPlace* and *location*). The authors supposed that synonym predicates share a similar group of object values. For this reason, the proposed approach seeks the frequent patterns of predicates that share a significant number of object values.

In fact, it is not sufficient to synonymously discover the used predicates depending only on range content filtering. For example, the predicates *birthPlace* and *deathPlace* share significant co-occurrences with the same object values but they are definitely used differently. For this reason, the authors added another filter called "schema analysis" in order to overcome this problem. This filter

---

[1] Lyon is a French city.

is better in finding suitable synonym predicates. The authors supposed that the synonym predicates should not co-exist for the same instance. According to schema analysis, transactions of distinct subjects with several predicates are represented. By applying negative association rules [2], the synonym predicates appear in different transactions. For example, the subject *Michael_Schumacher* does not have two synonym predicates such as *born* and *birthPlace* in the same dataset.

Table 1. Six configurations of context and target [1]

Conf.	Context	Target
1	Subject	Predicate
2	Subject	Object
3	Predicate	Subject
4	Predicate	Object
5	Object	Subject
6	Object	Predicate

Table 2. Facts in SPO structure from DBpedia

Subject	Predicate	Object
Adam_Hadwin	*type*	*GolfPlayer*
Adam_Hadwin	*birthPlace*	*Moose_Jaw*
Adam_Hadwin	*nationality*	*Canada*
White_River	*sourceCountry*	*Canada*
White_River	*riverMouth*	*Lake_Superior*
White_River	*state*	*Ontario*

Now, we clarify the drawbacks of Abedjan and Naumann's approach through applying the following example (see Table 2). We use a sample of facts from DBpedia to discover the synonym predicates.

Based on range content filtering (Conf. 6 as illustrated in Table 1), all the predicates will be gathered into groups by each distinct object. Thus, in order to retrieve frequent candidates, results could be as in Table 3.

Table 3. Range content filtering

Object	Predicate
GolfPlayer	*type*
Moose_Jaw	*birthPlace*
Canada	*nationality, sourceCountry*
Lake_Superior	*riverMouth*
Ontario	*state*

Table 4. Schema analysis

Subject	Predicate
Adam_Hadwin	*type, birthPlace, nationality*
White_River	*sourceCountry, riverMouth, state*

As a result, we can see that *nationality* and *sourceCountry* are already in the same transaction. By applying FP-growth algorithm [9] for mining frequent itemsets (any other itemset mining algorithm could, obviously, be used), *nationality* and *sourceCountry* will be found as a frequent pattern.

The next step is performing schema analysis (Conf. 1 as illustrated in Table 1) by considering subjects as a context to get transactions of Table 4. By applying negative association rules, Abedjan and Naumann's algorithm shows that there

is no co-occurrence between *sourceCountry* and nationality predicates. Therefore, it will propose *nationality* and *sourceCountry* as a synonym predicate pair,
which is not correct because we cannot replace *nationality* predicate (that has as
domain "Person") with *sourceCountry* predicate (that has as domain "Stream"
which is a flowing body of water).

4   The Proposed Approach

In the next subsections, we explain our proposed approach that consists of three
phases. In addition to the statistical study through schema analysis and range
content filtering, we basically intend to perform a semantic analysis to understand the meaning of the candidates. Finally, we have used learning algorithms
to filter the results of the two previous phases.

4.1   Phase 1: Statistical Analysis

As we have already mentioned, our goal is to start with statistical analysis in
order to discover potential equivalent predicates. We are interested, in this part,
in studying the appearance of each predicate by finding the frequent pattern
with negative association rules. This part is basically inspired from Abedjan
and Naumann's work [2] which proposed a data-driven synonym discovery algorithm for predicate expansion. Based on mining configuration of contexts and
targets [1], the authors applied Conf. 1 and Conf. 6 as illustrated in Table 1 that
represents schema analysis and range content filtering, respectively. We use the
same method as in Sect. 3 to generate candidate pairs of synonym predicates and
semantic analysis to remove those that are actually not. In the next subsection,
we look forward to study the candidates depending on semantics features to
decrease the number of predicates by identifying strictly equivalent predicates
and eliminating inequivalent ones.

4.2   Phase 2: Semantic Analysis

Actually, some predicates are not easy to understand, share the same meaning
with different identifiers or have several meanings. For these reasons, calculating
string similarity or synonym based measurements on predicate names alone does
not suffice. Indeed, the first phase proposes candidate pairs as synonyms but
also too many false positive results, especially in the case of large cross-domain
datasets. As the previous example illustrated in Sect. 3, the predicate *nationality*
and *sourceCountry* could have the same object (Conf. 6) like *Canada*. They also
never co-occur together for the same subject (Conf. 1). However, *nationality* is
a predicate of an instance that its type is *Person* class and *sourceCountry* is a
predicate of an instance that its type is *Stream* class. Thus, they should not be
considered as synonyms.

We add an extension to Abedjan and Naumann's work by studying the meaning of each candidate. Indeed, we examine the semantic representations of the

synonym candidates that, under certain conditions, provide us with useful conclusions; for example, a predicate could not be equivalent to another predicate if they have disjoint domains or ranges. Taking the previous example of *nationality* and *sourceCountry* predicates. According to the DBpedia ontology, *Stream* class is a subclass of *Place* class, and *Place* and *Person* classes are completely disjointed. As a consequence, we cannot consider *nationality* and *sourceCountry* as equivalent predicates.

Thus, in this phase we take into account the semantic part of the predicates. This allows us to detect the incompatibility of the predicates that have opposite features such as symmetric and asymmetric. OWL 2 supports declaring two classes to be disjointed. It also supports declaring that a predicate is symmetric, reflexive, transitive, functional, or inverse functional. We take into account these features for each predicate in addition to the *max* cardinality restriction.

We prove the disjointness of predicates (thus, that these predicates could not be synonyms) using $\mathcal{SROIQ}$ description logic that models constructors which are available in OWL 2 DL [10]. We depend on studying the meaning of predicates by analyzing their features.

In the following, we give an example about the disjointness of domains between two predicates. For a given RDF triple, the *rdfs:domain* property indicates the class that appears as its subject (the predicate domain), and the *rdfs:range* property indicates the class or data value that appears as its object (the predicate range).

– **Domain of predicate**
   We use here the *rdfs:domain* property to check whether the domains of the two compared predicates are disjointed or not. If yes, we can state that these predicates cannot be synonyms.

Theorem 1. *Let p_1 & p_2 be two predicates and C_1 & C_2 be two classes. p_1 & p_2 cannot be synonyms if:*

$$\exists p_1.\top \sqsubseteq C_1 \tag{1}$$

$$\exists p_2.\top \sqsubseteq C_2 \tag{2}$$

$$C_1 \sqcap C_2 \sqsubseteq \bot \tag{3}$$

Proof. Assume $\exists x$, that:

$$p_1(x, y_1) \tag{4}$$

$$p_2(x, y_2) \tag{5}$$

We assert that:

$$(1) + (4) \Rightarrow C_1(x) \tag{6}$$

$$(2) + (5) \Rightarrow C_2(x) \tag{7}$$

$$(6) + (7) \Rightarrow C_1 \sqcap C_2 \not\sqsubseteq \bot \tag{8}$$

$$(3) + (8) \Rightarrow \bot \ absurd \tag{9}$$

As a result, we conclude that predicates that have disjointed domains are disjointed. In the same manner, we can prove the other features discussed previously (the complete list of the theorems is available here: http://cedric.cnam.fr/~hamdif/upload/KSEM19/SA_Theorems.pdf).

4.3   Phase 3: NLP-Based Analysis

The returned candidates showed that some predicates are semantically similar but non-equivalent such as *composer* and *artist*. The Domain and Range types of instances of these predicates are the same and share same features (e.g. asymmetric, non-functional). Thus, statistical and semantic analyses are not sufficient to detect that *composer* and *artist* are non-equivalent predicates. To address such issues, we have used learning algorithm to map words or phrases from the vocabulary to vectors of numbers called *word embedding*. We apply word2vec tool[2] for learning word embeddings based on a training dataset. The idea behind this tool is to assign a vector space to each unique word in the corpus where any words sharing common contexts are located close one another in the space. Therefore, if there are two words that the context in which they are used is about the same, then these words are probably quite similar in meaning (e.g. *wrong* and *incorrect*) or are at least related (e.g *France* and *Paris*).

Word2vec uses training algorithms to generate word vectors (embeddings) based on a dataset. As it would be extremely expensive to calculate the similarity of all predicate pairs of the dataset, we run Word2vec only on the resulting pairs from applying the statistical and semantic analyses in Phase 1 and Phase 2. Then, we apply cosine similarity [19] for comparing two vectors, which is defined as follows:

$$\cos(\mathbf{t}, \mathbf{e}) = \frac{\mathbf{t}\mathbf{e}}{\|\mathbf{t}\|\|\mathbf{e}\|} = \frac{\sum_{i=1}^{n} \mathbf{t}_i \mathbf{e}_i}{\sqrt{\sum_{i=1}^{n} (\mathbf{t}_i)^2}\sqrt{\sum_{i=1}^{n} (\mathbf{e}_i)^2}}$$

where similarity score will always be between 0.0 and 1.0. A high similarity value indicates that two words are closely related and the maximum similarity (1.0) that they are identical.

This phase helps to decrease the number of false positive results, through including the candidates that have a significant similarity score and excluding them otherwise.

5   Experiments

In this section, to evaluate our approach, we present two experiments performed on real-world datasets, DBpedia[3] and YAGO[4]. The metrics we use for evaluating pair accuracy are the standard precision, recall and F-measure (harmonic mean of precision and recall).

---

[2] https://code.google.com/archive/p/word2vec/.

[3] https://wiki.dbpedia.org.

[4] https://www.mpi-inf.mpg.de/departments/databases-and-information-systems/research/yago-naga/yago/.

5.1 Experimental Setup

DBpedia project is one of the largest knowledge bases on the Linked Open Data (LOD) cloud. It is composed of structured information extracted collaboratively from Wikipedia. Thus, it should represent a good challenge for our approach to find synonyms predicates, as there is a great chance that some of the data entered by different contributors is equivalent. Unfortunately, as many datasets available in LOD, DBpedia suffers from a lack of expressive OWL2 features like *functional* properties, *transitive* properties, etc. Therefore, in this case it is difficult for our approach to perform a semantic analysis. As illustrated in Table 5, only 30 functional properties, that represent 1%, have been defined. Furthermore, DBpedia neither use *max* cardinality nor *transitive* or *symmetric* properties. In addition, we have noted that, 16.3% of predicates are represented without domains and 10.2% without ranges.

To address the lack of domains and ranges, we infer, based on the approach proposed in [21], missed predicate domains (and/or ranges). By studying the instances that occur with each predicate which has no *rdfs:domain* value (and/or *rdfs:range* value), we have found that some of these instances may belong to different classes. In this case, only the class having a number of instances greater than a selected threshold will be defined as the domain (or range) of the pred-

Table 5. Features predicates of DBpedia dataset (v10-2016)

Feature	Existence
Domain	83.7%
Range	89.8%
Functional properties	1%
Transitive properties	0%
Symmetric properties	0%
Max cardinality	0%

icate. In case the number of instances is smaller than the threshold, *owl:Thing* will be selected as domain (or range) value. Besides, we applied [4,21] to enrich DBpedia with the other OWL2 properties (*functional, transitive*, etc.).

On the other hand, due to the fact that some predicates share the same features such as (artist, composer, writer, etc.), we have decided to use Word2vec, as we explained in Sect. 4.3. Our goal is to convert each predicate to a vector based on its context, and then calculate the similarity between predicate pairs. For this, we need a training dataset that contains all the predicate candidates. To create this dataset, we have chosen to concatenate data from Large Movie Review Dataset that contains 50,000 reviews from IMDB[5], and Polarity Dataset v2.0[6] that have 2,000 movie reviews. This choice is motivated by the fact that these two datasets include the majority of the candidates according to our experiments. For missed predicates or when the frequency of the predicate is very low, we have generated paragraphs from the DBpedia dataset itself and we added them to the training dataset. Indeed, Carlson et al. [3] suggest that typically 10–15 examples are sufficient to learn the meaning of the predicate from Natural Language texts. We have generated these paragraphs through the text that exists in *rdfs:comment* of both the subject and object of the triple, and *rdfs:label* of the predicate. As an example, the English phrases about *dbo:residence* predicate is generated using the following query:

---

[5] http://ai.stanford.edu/~amaas/data/sentiment/.

[6] http://www.cs.cornell.edu/people/pabo/movie-review-data/.

```
SELECT DISTINCT ?s1 ?p1 ?o1 WHERE {
   ?s dbo:residence ?o .
   ?s rdfs:comment ?s1 .
   ?o rdfs:comment ?o1 .
   dbo:residence rdfs:label ?p1 .
   FILTER (lang(?o1) = 'en')
   FILTER (lang(?s1) = 'en')
   FILTER (lang(?p1) = 'en') }
```

As a result, we have got a paragraph that contains the missed candidate to add to our training dataset. For example, the previous query generates the following paragraph (an excerpt): *"Lena Headey is an English actress...residence London is the capital of England and the United Kingdom..."*. Adding this paragraph to the dataset will help the training process to generate a vector for the predicate *residence* that has as a context the fact that *residence* connects *Person* to *Place*.

5.2 First Experiment

The objective of this first experiment is to show the improvement in detecting synonyms brought by the semantic analysis and NLP phases. As a reminder, the main goal of our approach is to enhance the statistical analyses of synonyms predicates (which is the core of Abedjan and Naumann's approach). To evaluate our results, we have used a gold standard of DBpedia synonyms predicates generated by [23]. This gold standard contains 473 true positive pairs of 10 classes in DBpedia. Compared to [23], our approach gives, for a support threshold equals 0.01%, a slightly better F-measure (0.76 for our approach and 0.75 for [23]). But as we have explained just before, the objective here is to show the interest of using semantic analysis and NLP. Thus, our approach would be rather complementary with [23] instead of being a direct concurrent.

Figures 1 and 2 illustrate the number of equivalent predicates pairs and the F-measure at each phase. To show the improvement that Phase 2 and 3 could bring better, we have chosen a low support threshold value for the statistical analyses to obtain a large number of candidates. This will increase the number of true and false positive results at Phase 1, and will show how Phase 2 and Phase 3 decrease false positive results to enhance the precision value. Besides, at Phase 3, our approach filters the candidates regarding their similarity scores that should be less than a user-specific threshold. In this experiment, we have set the value on 50%.

Figure 2 shows that, with a support threshold equals 0.01%, we obtain, after applying the statistical analysis (Phase 1), 4197 candidate pairs. Then, by performing a semantic analysis (Phase 2), this number decreases to 2006, which represents the elimination of 52.2% of false positive results. For example, the predicates *owner* and *employer* have been proposed as equivalent predicates by the statistical analysis phase; because, on the one hand, they share a significant number of object values in their range *dbo:Organisation*, and on the other hand,

748   S. Issa et al.

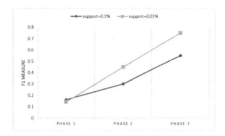
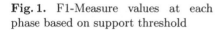
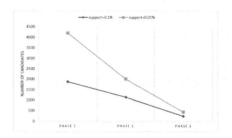

Fig. 1. F1-Measure values at each phase based on support threshold

Fig. 2. Number of candidate pair at each phase

they rarely co-occur for the same instance. By applying the semantic analysis, this pair of predicates will be excluded due to a domain disjointness. Indeed, the domain of *employer* is *dbo:Person* and the domain of *owner* is *dbo:Place*, and *dbo:Person* and *dbo:Agent* (that is a super class of *dbo:Person*) are disjoint. Thus, as explained in Sect. 4.2, *owner* and *employer* cannot be synonyms. Finally, by performing an NLP-based analysis (Phase 3), the number of candidate pairs decreases to 429, which represents the elimination of 78.6% of false positive results. This phase was able to filter the predicates that share the same semantic features but are non-equivalents such as *author* and *composer*.

Our approach works well to achieve our objective through decreasing the number of false positive results. The experiment shows that we can increase the precision value without affecting the recall.

5.3 Second Experiment

The gold standard of synonyms predicates of the first experiment is the only one that we have found in LOD. Thus, to perform more tests on our approach, we have created a new gold standard from mappings established between the predicates of different datasets. In fact, the trick consists of merging in one dataset, two or more datasets that have equivalence predicates between them. These predicates will therefore be the gold standard of the new dataset. For this experiment, we have chosen to merge DBpedia and YAGO that share a significant number of equivalent predicates. PARIS tool [20] proposes a gold standard containing 173 mappings between the predicates of these two datasets. However, this gold standard is incomplete and, thus, can only serve to see if our approach is able to find all equivalent predicates. Due to the huge number of instances that use the predicates of this gold standard, we have demanded from three experts to manually extract 35 mappings (equivalent predicates). Then, for each dataset, we have chosen a couple of categories from different natures to cover all the 35 predicates. For DBpedia, we have selected instances that have the following categories: $C = \{dbo:Person, dbo:Film, dbo:Organisation, dbo:PopulatedPlace\}$, and for YAGO the following categories that are semantically close to those of DBpedia: $C = \{yago:wordnet\_person\_105217688, yago:wordnet\_movie\_106613686, yago:wordnet\_organization\_1008008335, yago:wordnet\_urban\_area\_108675967\}$.

Figure 3 shows the obtained recall when varying the support thresholds of the Phase 1. The maximum value is obtained when the support threshold equals 0.01%. This is logical since a great number of candidates is generated. However, certainly a lot of false positives will also be generated. The reason why we do not find all the synonyms (e.g. *isbn* and *hasISBN*) relies on the fact that some predicate pairs share insufficient number

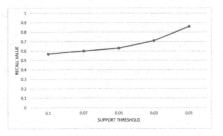

Fig. 3. Recall value based on support threshold values

of objects. The interesting result of this experiment is that our approach finds a good number of synonyms (recall at roughly 60%) even if the support threshold is relatively high (compared to 0.01%).

6   Conclusion

In this work, we have proposed a new approach to enhance the conciseness of Linked datasets by discovering synonym predicates. This approach consists of three phases: (1) performing a statistical analysis to obtain an initial set of synonyms predicates, (2) performing semantic analysis of obtained set by exploring OWL2 features (*functional, transitive, cardinality, etc.*), and (3) finally, performing similarity-based comparison between contextual vectors representing each candidate predicate. The main objective of the last two phases is to reduce the false positive candidates generated in the first phase.

The experiment results show that our approach is highly promising, as it allows eliminating around 78.6% of false positives compared to the Abedjan and Naumann's approach [2]. They also show good results in terms of F-measure. However, it failed to discover some synonym predicates that are rarely used.

For future work, we plan to add a new phase to deal with uncommon predicates or with predicates having, as an object, a data value instead of a class. We will also study how to improve the F-measure by combing our approach with others like, for example, the unsupervised data-driven method proposed by [23].

References

1. Abedjan, Z., Naumann, F.: Context and target configurations for mining RDF data. In: Proceedings of the 1st International Workshop on Search and Mining Entity-Relationship Data, pp. 23–24. ACM (2011)
2. Abedjan, Z., Naumann, F.: Synonym analysis for predicate expansion. In: Cimiano, P., Corcho, O., Presutti, V., Hollink, L., Rudolph, S. (eds.) ESWC 2013. LNCS, vol. 7882, pp. 140–154. Springer, Heidelberg (2013). https://doi.org/10.1007/978-3-642-38288-8_10
3. Carlson, A., Betteridge, J., Kisiel, B., Settles, B., Hruschka, E.R., Mitchell, T.M.: Toward an architecture for never-ending language learning. In: Twenty-Fourth AAAI Conference on Artificial Intelligence (2010)

4. Fleischhacker, D., Völker, J., Stuckenschmidt, H.: Mining RDF data for property axioms. In: Meersman, R., et al. (eds.) OTM 2012. LNCS, vol. 7566, pp. 718–735. Springer, Heidelberg (2012). https://doi.org/10.1007/978-3-642-33615-7_18

5. Fu, L., Wang, H., Jin, W., Yu, Y.: Towards better understanding and utilizing relations in DBpedia. Web Intell. Agent Syst. Int. J. **10**(3), 291–303 (2012)

6. Fürber, C., Hepp, M.: SWIQA-a semantic web information quality assessment framework. In: ECIS, vol. 15, p. 19 (2011)

7. Galárraga, L., Teflioudi, C., Hose, K., Suchanek, F.M.: Fast rule mining in ontological knowledge bases with AMIE+. VLDB J. Int. J. Very Large Data Bases **24**(6), 707–730 (2015)

8. Gunaratna, K., Thirunarayan, K., Jain, P., Sheth, A., Wijeratne, S.: A statistical and schema independent approach to identify equivalent properties on linked data. In: Proceedings of the 9th International Conference on Semantic Systems, pp. 33–40. ACM (2013)

9. Han, J., Pei, J., Yin, Y., Mao, R.: Mining frequent patterns without candidate generation: a frequent-pattern tree approach. Data Min. Knowl. Discov. **8**(1), 53–87 (2004)

10. Horrocks, I., Kutz, O., Sattler, U.: The even more irresistible SROIQ. Kr **6**, 57–67 (2006)

11. Issa, S., Paris, P., Hamdi, F., Cherfi, S.S.S.: Revealing the conceptual schemas of RDF datasets. In: 31st International Conference on Advanced Information Systems Engineering (CAiSE), Italy, pp. 1–15, June 2019

12. Issa, S., Paris, P.-H., Hamdi, F.: Assessing the completeness evolution of DBpedia: a case study. In: de Cesare, S., Frank, U. (eds.) ER 2017. LNCS, vol. 10651, pp. 238–247. Springer, Cham (2017). https://doi.org/10.1007/978-3-319-70625-2_22

13. Kalfoglou, Y., Schorlemmer, M.: Ontology mapping: the state of the art. Knowl. Eng. Rev. **18**(1), 1–31 (2003)

14. Lei, Y., Sabou, M., Lopez, V., Zhu, J., Uren, V., Motta, E.: An infrastructure for acquiring high quality semantic metadata. In: Sure, Y., Domingue, J. (eds.) ESWC 2006. LNCS, vol. 4011, pp. 230–244. Springer, Heidelberg (2006). https://doi.org/10.1007/11762256_19

15. Lei, Y., Uren, V., Motta, E.: A framework for evaluating semantic metadata. In: Proceedings of the 4th International Conference on Knowledge Capture, pp. 135–142. ACM (2007)

16. Mendes, P.N., Mühleisen, H., Bizer, C.: Sieve: linked data quality assessment and fusion. In: Proceedings of the 2012 Joint EDBT/ICDT Workshops, pp. 116–123. ACM (2012)

17. Mika, P.: Flink: semantic web technology for the extraction and analysis of social networks. Web Semant. Sci. Serv. Agents WWW **3**(2), 211–223 (2005)

18. Rahm, E., Bernstein, P.A.: A survey of approaches to automatic schema matching. VLDB J. **10**(4), 334–350 (2001)

19. Salton, G.: Automatic text processing (1988)

20. Suchanek, F.M., Abiteboul, S., Senellart, P.: PARIS: probabilistic alignment of relations, instances, and schema. Proc. VLDB Endowment **5**(3), 157–168 (2011)

21. Töpper, G., Knuth, M., Sack, H.: DBpedia ontology enrichment for inconsistency detection. In: Proceedings of the 8th International Conference on Semantic Systems, pp. 33–40. ACM (2012)

22. Zaveri, A., Rula, A., Maurino, A., Pietrobon, R., Lehmann, J., Auer, S.: Quality assessment for linked data: a survey. Semant. Web **7**(1), 63–93 (2016)

23. Zhang, Z., Gentile, A.L., Blomqvist, E., Augenstein, I., Ciravegna, F.: An unsupervised data-driven method to discover equivalent relations in large linked datasets. Semant. web **8**(2), 197–223 (2017)

A Comparative Analysis Methodology for Process Mining Software Tools

Panagiotis Drakoulogkonas$^{(\boxtimes)}$ ⓘ and Dimitrios Apostolou ⓘ

University of Piraeus, 80, M. Karaoli & A. Dimitriou Street,
18534 Piraeus, Greece
{drakoulogkonas, dapost}@unipi.gr

Abstract. Process mining is a research discipline situated at the intersection of data mining and computation intelligence on the one hand, and process modelling and analysis on the other hand. The aim of process mining is to use information stored in event logs of information systems in order to discover, monitor, and improve processes [1]. The field of process mining has gained attention over the last years and new process mining software tools, both academic and commercial, have been developed. This paper provides an extensive list of process mining software tools. Moreover, it identifies and describes many criteria that can be used in order to compare process mining software tools. Additionally, this paper introduces a new methodology that can be used for the comparative analysis of any number of process mining software tools, using any number of criteria. Furthermore, this paper describes Analytic Hierarchy Process (AHP), which can be used in order to help users decide which software tool best suits their needs.

Keywords: Process mining · Software tools ·
Comparative analysis methodology · Comparison criteria ·
Analytic Hierarchy Process (AHP)

1 Introduction

Process mining is a concretization of Business Process Intelligence (BPI) using system-generated event logs as a starting point. Process mining includes process discovery (i.e., the extraction of process models from event logs), conformance checking (i.e., the monitoring of deviations by comparing model and log), model repair, model extension, case prediction, recommendations, and social network/organizational mining [1].

Several works have surveyed process mining software tools. Turner, Tiwari, Olaiya, and Xu [2] presented a comparison of a number of business process mining tools. They provided an outline of the practice of business process mining and an analysis of business process mining techniques. Kebede [3] proposed a framework enabling the comparison of process mining software tools and made a comparative evaluation of some tools. Verstraete [4] made a comparative study of a number of software tools, namely ProM, Disco, Celonis Discovery, Perceptive Process Mining, QPR ProcessAnalyzer, ARIS Business Process Analysis, Fujitsu Process Analytics, XMAnalyzer, StereoLOGIC Discovery Analyst. Claes, and Poels [5] surveyed the

© Springer Nature Switzerland AG 2019
C. Douligeris et al. (Eds.): KSEM 2019, LNAI 11775, pp. 751–762, 2019.
https://doi.org/10.1007/978-3-030-29551-6_66

following software tools: ARIS Process Performance Manager, BPMOne, Disco, Futura Reflect, Interstage Automated Process Discovery, Nitro, ProM, ProM Import, QPR ProcessAnalyzer/Analysis, XESame.

Our work is motivated by the apparent lack of a rigorous methodology for examining, comparing and ultimately selecting among the plethora of process mining software tools. This paper provides an extensive list of existing software tools and identifies and describes criteria that can be used for the comparison of process mining software tools. Furthermore, this paper proposes a new comparative analysis methodology. This methodology can be used for the comparative analysis of any number of software tools using any number of criteria. Using the proposed methodology and AHP, the paper makes a comparative analysis of three process mining software tools, namely ProM, Disco, and Celonis Process Mining.

In Sect. 2, a list of existing software tools is provided. Section 3 describes the comparative analysis methodology and criteria, and AHP. Section 4 makes a comparative analysis of the three process mining software tools mentioned above, using the proposed comparative analysis methodology, a number of criteria, and AHP. In Sect. 5, a discussion is made. Section 6 concludes the paper.

2 Software Tools for Process Mining

Over the last years, event data have become readily available, process mining techniques have matured, and process mining algorithms have been implemented in various academic and commercial systems. Today, there is an active group of researchers working on process mining and it has become one of the "hot topics" in Business Process Management (BPM) research. Furthermore, there is a huge interest from industry in process mining and more and more software vendors are adding process mining functionality to their tools [1]. Table 1 outlines prominent software tools that can be used in order to execute operations related to process mining.

Table 1. Software tools that can be used for executing operations related to process mining.

Name	Website	University/Company
ARIS Process Mining	https://www.softwareag.com/corporate/products/process/process_mining/default.html	Software AG
Automated Process Discovery Service	https://www.fujitsu.com/global/products/software/middleware/application-infrastructure/interstage/solutions/bpmgt/bpm-services/apd/	Fujitsu
Celonis Process Mining	https://www.celonis.com/try-or-buy/	Celonis
CoBeFra	http://processmining.be/cobefra/	KU Leuven
Dbminer	http://people.ac.upc.edu/msole/homepage/dbminer.html	Universitat Politècnica de Catalunya, Barcelona, Spain

(continued)

Table 1. (*continued*)

Name	Website	University/Company
Disco	https://fluxicon.com/disco/	Fluxicon
DiscoverIQ	https://www.openconnect.com/discoveriq	OpenConnect
Enterprise Discovery Suite	http://www.stereologic.com/products/enterprise-discovery-suite/	StereoLOGIC
ILOG JViews Enterprise	https://www.ibm.com/developerworks/downloads/ws/jviews/	IBM
Interstage Business Process Manager	https://www.fujitsu.com/global/products/software/middleware/application-infrastructure/interstage/solutions/bpmgt/bpm/	Fujitsu
LANA Process Mining	https://lanalabs.com/en/	Lana Labs
Minit	https://www.minit.io/	Minit
myInvenio	https://www.my-invenio.com/	Cognitive Technology
Process Analytics Software	https://www.fujitsu.com/global/products/software/middleware/application-infrastructure/interstage/solutions/bpmgt/bpma/	Fujitsu
ProcessGold	https://processgold.com/en/	ProcessGold
ProM	http://www.promtools.org/doku.php	Eindhoven Technical University
ProM for RapidMiner	http://www.processmining.org/rapidminer/start	Eindhoven University of Technology
QPR ProcessAnalyzer	http://www.qpr.com/products/qpr-processanalyzer	QPR Software
Rialto Process	http://www.exeura.eu/en/products/rialto-process/	Exeura
WorkIQ	https://www.openconnect.com/workiq	OpenConnect
XMAnalyzer	http://xmpro.com/xmpro-releases-new-ibos-process-mining-module-xmanalyzer/	XMPRO

3 Comparative Analysis

In this section, we propose a comparative analysis methodology and identify comparative analysis criteria. Using the proposed methodology and any number of criteria, a comparative analysis of any number of process mining software tools can be made.

3.1 Comparative Analysis Methodology

The methodology is composed of two phases:

- **Phase 1: Selection of Comparative Analysis Criteria.** The aim of phase 1 is the selection of the criteria to be used for the comparative analysis of the tools.

- **Phase 2: Selection of Software Tool(s) Using AHP.** The aim of phase 2 is the selection of one or more of the software tool(s) using AHP and the criteria selected in phase 1.

The two phases of the comparative analysis methodology are described in the following sections.

3.2   Phase 1: Selection of Comparative Analysis Criteria

During phase 1, we select the criteria that we want to use in the comparative analysis of the process mining software tools. In the following lines, we provide a list of comparative analysis criteria that can be selected for the comparison of the software tools. We have classified the criteria in three main categories: General Information; Process Mining Types; Discovery Problems Addressed. The main categories and the comparative analysis criteria are illustrated in Fig. 1.

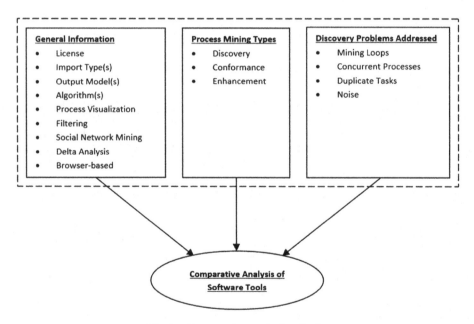

Fig. 1. Comparative analysis criteria.

A description of each of the comparative analysis criteria follows:

- **License.** The license type of the software tool [6, 7].
- **Import Type(s).** The input format types supported by the software tool (e.g. csv, xls, xes) [6, 8, 9].
- **Output Model(s).** The output model(s) notation supported by the software tool (e.g. Petri Nets, BPMN, Transition Systems, Fuzzy Model) [1, 10, 11].
- **Algorithm(s).** The supported algorithm(s) [6, 9–11].

- **Process Visualization.** Check if process visualization is supported [8, 12, 13].
- **Filtering.** Check if the software tool supports filtering of data [6, 14–16].
- **Social Network Mining.** Check if the software tool can perform social network mining, based on information, recorded in the event log, about the users executing the activities [17].
- **Delta Analysis.** Check if the software tool can provide delta analysis, which compares the derived process model with a reference model (e.g. the model used to configure the system). In this way, business process alignment can be checked [3].
- **Browser-Based.** Check if the software tool is browser-based, i.e. if it can run using a browser, without requiring installation.
- **Discovery.** Check if the software tool supports discovery. A discovery technique can take an event log and produce a model without using any other a-priori information. Typically, the discovered model is a process model (e.g. Petri net, UML, EPC, BPMN). However, this model can also describe other perspectives [1, 6, 9].
- **Conformance.** Check if conformance is supported. Conformance checking techniques use both an event log and a model as input. The output comprises diagnostic information demonstrating commonalities and differences between event log and model. Conformance checking can be useful in order to show if reality, as recorded in the event log, conforms to the model and vice versa. Specifically, conformance checking can be used in order to detect, locate and explain deviations, and to measure the severity of the detected deviations [1, 6, 9].
- **Enhancement.** Check if the software tool supports enhancement. Model enhancement techniques use both an event log and a model as input and produce an improved or extended model as output. The idea of enhancement is to use information about actual processes recorded in event logs, in order to extend or improve an existing process model. One type of enhancement is extension, i.e. cross-correlating process model with the event log in order to add new perspectives to the process model. Another type of enhancement is repair, i.e. modifying the process model in order to better reflect reality [1, 6, 9].
- **Mining Loops.** Check if the software tool is able to deal with loops, i.e. to accurately discover a model containing loops. Some process discovery algorithms have limitations on loops. For example, the α-algorithm requires a pre- and post-processing step in order to deal with short loops [6, 9].
- **Concurrent Processes.** Check if the software tool can discover and represent a model containing concurrent processes. Some models, like transition systems and flow charts may not allow for the modeling of concurrency other than enumerating the possible interleavings [6, 9].
- **Duplicate Tasks.** Check if the "Duplicate Tasks" problem can be addressed. "Duplicate tasks" refers to the situation, in which more than one task of a process have the same label. Duplicate tasks are typically registered with the same label in the log and algorithms may need an extra effort to discover which events of the log belong to which transitions and to discover the model that better fits the log [18].

- **Noise.** Check if the specific software tool can deal with noise. The discovered model should not include noisy behavior, i.e. infrequent/exceptional behavior. Users typically want to know the main behavior. It is difficult to deduce meaningful information based on extremely rare patterns or activities. Some mature algorithms address this issue by abstracting from infrequent/exceptional behavior [6, 9].

3.3   Phase 2: Selection of Software Tool(s) Using AHP

During phase 2, we select one or more software tool(s), using AHP and all the criteria selected in phase 1. AHP is a structured technique that can be used for the organization and analysis of complex decisions. It provides a comprehensive framework for structuring a decision problem, for representing its elements, for relating the elements to overall goals, and for evaluating the alternative solutions [19]. Instead of providing a "correct" decision, AHP helps stakeholders to find out the decision that best suits their goal and their perception of the problem. AHP provides a rational and comprehensive framework for structuring a decision problem, for quantifying and representing its elements, for relating the elements to the goal(s), and for evaluating the alternative solutions [20]. The decision problem is decomposed into a hierarchy of sub-problems, each of which can be comprehended more easily and analyzed independently. AHP can be implemented in the following steps [21]:

1. Developing a model for the decision: The first step of an AHP analysis is to create a hierarchy consisting of goal(s), criteria, and alternatives.
2. Deriving priorities (weights) of the criteria: In order to derive their relative priorities (weights), the criteria are pairwise compared with respect to their importance in reaching the goal. Pairwise comparisons are made using a scale ranging from 1 to 9 with 1 meaning equal importance and 9 meaning extreme importance [22]. Then, judgments are reviewed to ensure a reasonable level of consistency in terms of transitivity and proportionality.
3. Deriving local priorities (preferences) of the alternatives: In order to derive their relative local priorities, the alternatives are pairwise compared with respect to their importance for each criterion separately. Pairwise comparisons are done, using the scale described above [22]. Afterwards, if required, the consistency of judgments can be checked and adjusted.
4. Deriving overall priorities (model synthesis): The local priorities (preferences) of the alternatives derived in step 3 are combined as a weighted sum - considering the priorities of the criteria derived in step 2 - in order to calculate the overall priorities. The alternative having the highest overall priority constitutes the best choice.
5. Performing sensitivity analysis: Perform a study of how changes in the weights of the criteria affect the result, in order to comprehend the reasoning behind the derived results.
6. Making the final decision: Based on the overall priorities (step 4) and the sensitivity analysis (step 5), the final decision can be made.

After the judgments have been entered, we need to check that they are consistent. For example, if we assign 3 as the value of preference of the criterion A with respect to the criterion B, and we assign 2 as the value of preference of the criterion B with respect to the criterion C, then the value of preference of the criterion A with respect to the criterion C should be 3 × 2 = 6. If we had assigned a value such as 4 or 7, there would be a level of inconsistency in the judgments. Some inconsistencies are allowed and expected in AHP analysis, because the numeric values are derived from the subjective preferences of individuals. The question is how much inconsistency can be acceptable. For this purpose, AHP calculates a Consistency Ratio (CR), comparing the Consistency Index (CI) of our judgments with the consistency index of a Random-like Matrix (RI). A random matrix is a matrix where the judgments have been entered randomly and hence it is expected to be highly inconsistent. In AHP, the CR is calculated by the formula CR = CI/RI. Saaty has shown that if the CR is less than or equal to 0.10, then it is acceptable to continue the AHP analysis. If the CR is greater than 0.10, then we need to revise the judgments and improve the consistency [21].

4   Comparative Analysis Methodology Example

In this section, we use the comparative analysis methodology described above in order to make a comparative analysis of three process mining software tools, namely ProM, Disco, and Celonis Process Mining:

- **ProM:** It is an open source framework that supports the development of process mining plug-ins [16], which can be used for the implementation of process mining algorithms [11]. ProM aims largely the academic and research community. Some of its features are: process discovery, conformance checking, process analysis, social network analysis [3], simulation, filtering etc. We selected ProM because of its popularity, its many features and capabilities, and its availability for evaluation.
- **Disco:** It is a commercial process mining tool, developed by Fluxicon. Some of its features are: process discovery, event log filtering using various parameters, project management, animation, detailed statistics etc. [3]. We selected Disco because of its usability [15], capabilities, features, and its availability for evaluation.
- **Celonis Process Mining:** It is a commercial process mining tool, developed by Celonis. Some of its features are: Real-time surveillance of business transactions, process analysis, automated integration of source data, process reporting, filtering [3], browser-based, real-time optimization etc. We selected Celonis Process Mining because of its usability, features, capabilities, and its availability for evaluation.

4.1   Phase 1: Selection of Comparative Analysis Criteria

In our example, we selected nine of the comparative analysis criteria described in Sect. 3.2, namely License, Process Visualization, Filtering, Social Network Mining, Delta Analysis, Browser-based, Discovery, Conformance, and Enhancement. Anyone can add and/or remove any number of criteria. Table 2 shows an overview of the features of the three tools.

Table 2. Overview of software tools ($\checkmark$ = yes, $\times$ = no).

Criteria	Software Tools		
	ProM	Disco	Celonis Process Mining
License	Open source	Evaluation/Commercial	Evaluation/Commercial
Process Visualization	$\checkmark$	$\checkmark$	$\checkmark$
Filtering	$\checkmark$	$\checkmark$	$\checkmark$
Social Network Mining	$\checkmark$	$\times$	$\times$
Delta Analysis	$\checkmark$	$\checkmark$	$\checkmark$
Browser-based	$\times$	$\times$	$\checkmark$
Discovery	$\checkmark$	$\checkmark$	$\checkmark$
Conformance	$\checkmark$	$\checkmark$	$\checkmark$
Enhancement	$\checkmark$	$\checkmark$	$\checkmark$

4.2 Phase 2: Selection of Software Tool(s) Using AHP

In our example, we created an AHP hierarchy, consisting of:

- A goal: Select software tool(s).
- Nine Criteria: License; Process Visualization; Filtering; Social Network Mining; Delta Analysis; Browser-based; Discovery; Conformance; Enhancement.
- Three Alternatives (the software tools): ProM; Disco; Celonis Process Mining.

In our case, we used the AHP Online System – BPMSG [23, 24]. We created the hierarchy and we pairwise compared the nine criteria with respect to their importance for the selection of the software tool. We then pairwise compared the alternatives with respect to their importance for each of the nine criteria separately. In order to make the comparisons, we used a scale ranging from 1 to 9. For example, the pairwise comparisons with respect to license can be seen in Fig. 2 [23–25]. We then clicked the "Check Consistency" button and the system automatically calculated the CR. In a number of cases, the CR was not acceptable, and the system highlighted some judgments and informed us to adjust the highlighted judgments to improve consistency. We adjusted them and the calculated CR was finally acceptable [23–25].

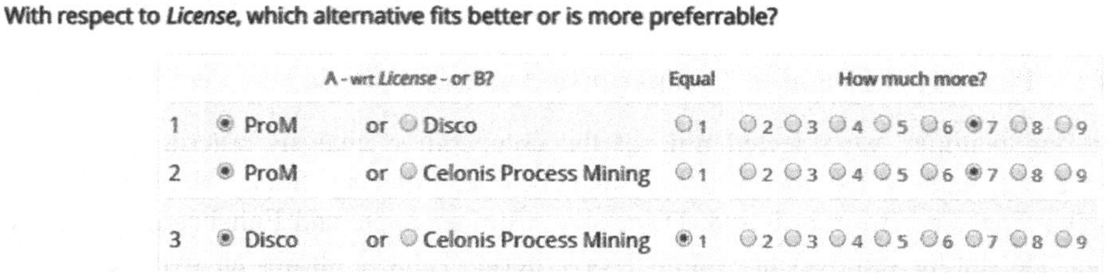

With respect to *License*, which alternative fits better or is more preferrable?

Fig. 2. Pairwise comparisons of the alternatives with respect to license [23–25]

The derived priorities of the nine criteria and the three alternatives are illustrated in Fig. 3 [23, 24, 26].

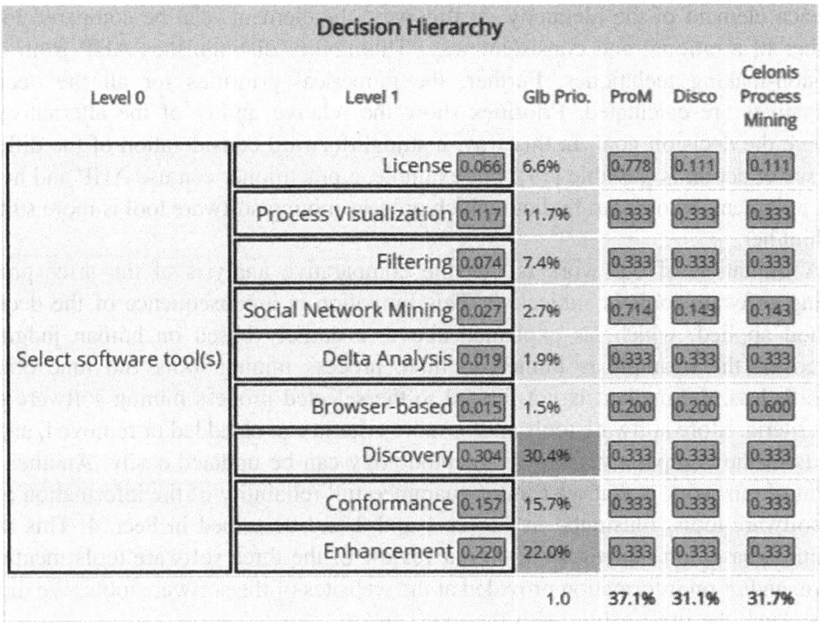

Decision Hierarchy					
Level 0	Level 1	Glb Prio.	ProM	Disco	Celonis Process Mining
Select software tool(s)	License 0.066	6.6%	0.778	0.111	0.111
	Process Visualization 0.117	11.7%	0.333	0.333	0.333
	Filtering 0.074	7.4%	0.333	0.333	0.333
	Social Network Mining 0.027	2.7%	0.714	0.143	0.143
	Delta Analysis 0.019	1.9%	0.333	0.333	0.333
	Browser-based 0.015	1.5%	0.200	0.200	0.600
	Discovery 0.304	30.4%	0.333	0.333	0.333
	Conformance 0.157	15.7%	0.333	0.333	0.333
	Enhancement 0.220	22.0%	0.333	0.333	0.333
		1.0	37.1%	31.1%	31.7%

Fig. 3. Decision hierarchy [23, 24, 26]

According to Fig. 3 [23, 24, 26], the ranking of the three process mining software tools is: 1. ProM (37,1%); 2. Celonis Process Mining (31,7%); 3. Disco (31,1%). Therefore, the process mining software tool that best suits our needs is ProM. It is important to point out that the result is based on our own judgments. If someone else had made different judgments, then the software tool that best suits his/her needs could be Disco or Celonis Process Mining or ProM.

5 Discussion

The comparative analysis methodology consists of two phases. The aim of phase 1 is the selection of the comparative analysis criteria. The aim of phase 2 is the selection of one or more software tool(s), using AHP and all the criteria selected in phase 1 and their values.

AHP can help users to decompose a decision problem into a hierarchy of easier understood sub-problems, each of which can then be analyzed independently. After the hierarchy is built, users can evaluate the elements by comparing them to each other two at a time, with respect to their impact on an element above them in the hierarchy. When making the comparisons, users can use their own judgments about the relative meaning and importance of the elements. Therefore, AHP uses the human judgments, and not only the underlying information, in order to perform the evaluations. AHP converts human judgments to numerical values and the numerical values can be processed and compared over the entire decision problem. A numerical weight or priority is created for each element of the hierarchy. In this way, the elements can be compared to one another in a rational and consistent way. This ability distinguishes AHP from other decision-making techniques. Further, the numerical priorities for all the decision alternatives are calculated. Priorities show the relative ability of the alternatives to achieve the decision goal. In this way, a straightforward consideration of the different courses of action is possible [19]. For example, a practitioner can use AHP and his/her own judgments in order to find out which process mining software tool is more suitable for him/her.

A limitation of our work is that the comparative analysis of the three process mining software tools is subjective. This limitation is a consequence of the decision method applied, which, as explained above, is largely based on human judgment. Moreover, the example is limited to three process mining tools and nine criteria. Nevertheless, the method is not limited to the selected process mining software tools and criteria. More software tools and/or more criteria can be added or removed, and the results of the comparative analysis methodology can be updated easily. Another limitation of our work is that we cannot guarantee full reliability of the information about the software tools, illustrated in Tables 1 and 2 and described in Sect. 4. This information is based on our research, on our review of the three software tools mentioned above, and/or on information provided at the websites of the software tools. We did not cross check the information with the tool vendors.

This paper is useful to practitioners because it describes prominent software tools that can be used for process mining. Moreover, the description of the criteria and the new comparative analysis methodology introduced in this paper can help practitioners to decide which process mining software tool best suits their needs. A possible extension to our work is to collect feedback from the actual use of the tools by practitioners. Feedback from field usage can shed some light with respect to: (i) possible problems of process mining software tools; (ii) the importance of the different features of the tools; (iii) new features that may be required by practitioners. The results of this analysis could be used to extend the comparative analysis methodology described herein. Furthermore, the comparative analysis methodology introduced in this paper, could be extended by researchers in the future, in order to include more comparative analysis methods.

6 Conclusions

This paper describes existing process mining software tools and proposes a new methodology enabling their comparative analysis using a number of criteria. Compared to other related works, this paper provides a more extensive list of process mining software tools. Moreover, our work identifies and describes many criteria that can be used in order to compare the software tools. The proposed methodology can help users to make comparative analyses of process mining software tools and decide which tool best suits their needs. This methodology uses AHP and provides a framework that allows users to compare any number of software tools using any number of criteria. More software tools and/or more criteria can be added or removed, and the results of the comparisons can be updated easily. To the best of our knowledge, there is no related work providing a detailed comparative analysis methodology like the one described in this paper.

Acknowledgement. This work has been partly supported by the University of Piraeus Research Center.

References

1. van der Aalst, W., et al.: Process mining manifesto. In: Daniel, F., Barkaoui, K., Dustdar, S. (eds.) BPM 2011. LNBIP, vol. 99, pp. 169–194. Springer, Heidelberg (2012). https://doi.org/10.1007/978-3-642-28108-2_19
2. Turner, C.J., Tiwari, A., Olaiya, R., Xu, Y.: Process mining: from theory to practice. Bus. Process Manag. J. **18**(3), 493–512 (2012)
3. Kebede, M.: Comparative evaluation of process mining tools. University of Tartu (2015)
4. Verstraete, D.: Process mining in practice: comparative study of process mining software, Doctoral dissertation, MS thesis, Faculty of Economics and Business Administration, Ghent University, Ghent, Belgium (2014). https://lib.ugent.be/fulltxt/RUG01/002/165/042/RUG01-002165042_2014_0001_AC.pdf)
5. Claes, J., Poels, G.: Process mining and the ProM framework: an exploratory survey. In: La Rosa, M., Soffer, P. (eds.) BPM 2012. LNBIP, vol. 132, pp. 187–198. Springer, Heidelberg (2013). https://doi.org/10.1007/978-3-642-36285-9_19
6. Van der Aalst, W.M.: Process Mining: Data Science in Action. Springer, Heidelberg (2016). https://doi.org/10.1007/978-3-662-49851-4
7. Verbeek, H.M.W., Buijs, J.C.A.M., Van Dongen, B.F., van der Aalst, W.M.: Prom 6: the process mining toolkit. In: Proceedings of BPM Demonstration Track, vol. 615, pp. 34–39 (2010)
8. Günther, C.W., Rozinat, A.: Disco: discover your processes. BPM (Demos) **940**, 40–44 (2012)
9. Van Der Aalst, W.: Process Mining: Discovery, Conformance and Enhancement of Business Processes. Springer Science+Business Media, Heidelberg (2011). https://doi.org/10.1007/978-3-642-19345-3
10. Augusto, A.: Automated discovery of process models from event logs: review and benchmark. IEEE Trans. Knowl. Data Eng. **31**, 686–705 (2019)
11. van Dongen, B.F., de Medeiros, A.K.A., Verbeek, H.M.W., Weijters, A.J.M.M., van der Aalst, W.M.P.: The ProM framework: a new era in process mining tool support. In: Ciardo, G., Darondeau, P. (eds.) ICATPN 2005. LNCS, vol. 3536, pp. 444–454. Springer, Heidelberg (2005). https://doi.org/10.1007/11494744_25
12. Aguirre, S., Parra, C., Alvarado, J.: Combination of process mining and simulation techniques for business process redesign: a methodological approach. In: Cudre-Mauroux, P., Ceravolo, P., Gašević, D. (eds.) SIMPDA 2012. LNBIP, vol. 162, pp. 24–43. Springer, Heidelberg (2013). https://doi.org/10.1007/978-3-642-40919-6_2
13. Aalst, W.M.P.: Business process simulation revisited. In: Barjis, J. (ed.) EOMAS 2010. LNBIP, vol. 63, pp. 1–14. Springer, Heidelberg (2010). https://doi.org/10.1007/978-3-642-15723-3_1

14. Leemans, S.J.J., Fahland, D., van der Aalst, W.M.P.: Exploring processes and deviations. In: Fournier, F., Mendling, J. (eds.) BPM 2014. LNBIP, vol. 202, pp. 304–316. Springer, Cham (2015). https://doi.org/10.1007/978-3-319-15895-2_26

15. Rubin, V.A., Mitsyuk, A.A., Lomazova, I.A., van der Aalst, W.M.: Process mining can be applied to software too! In: Proceedings of the 8th ACM/IEEE International Symposium on Empirical Software Engineering and Measurement, p. 57. ACM, September 2014

16. Van der Aalst, W.M., van Dongen, B.F., Günther, C.W., Rozinat, A., Verbeek, E., Weijters, T.: ProM: the process mining toolkit. BPM (Demos) **489**(31), 2 (2009)

17. van der Aalst, W.M.P., Song, M.: Mining social networks: uncovering interaction patterns in business processes. In: Desel, J., Pernici, B., Weske, M. (eds.) BPM 2004. LNCS, vol. 3080, pp. 244–260. Springer, Heidelberg (2004). https://doi.org/10.1007/978-3-540-25970-1_16

18. Vázquez-Barreiros, B., Mucientes, M., Lama, M.: Mining Duplicate Tasks from Discovered Processes (2015)

19. Saaty, T.L.: Analytic hierarchy process. Encycl. Biostatistics **1** (2005)

20. Majumder, M.: Impact of Urbanization on Water Shortage in Face of Climatic Aberrations. Springer, Singapore (2015). https://doi.org/10.1007/978-981-4560-73-3

21. Mu, E., Pereyra-Rojas, M.: Understanding the analytic hierarchy process. Practical Decision Making. SOR, pp. 7–22. Springer, Cham (2017). https://doi.org/10.1007/978-3-319-33861-3_2

22. Saaty, T.L.: Decision making with the analytic hierarchy process. Int. J. Serv. Sci. **1**(1), 83–98 (2008)

23. Goepel, K.D: Implementation of an online software tool for the analytic hierarchy process (AHP-OS). Int. J. Anal. Hierarchy Process **10**(3) (2018)

24. https://bpmsg.com/academic/ahp.php. Accessed 20 April 2019

25. https://bpmsg.com/academic/ahp_altcalc.php?n=3&t=License&c[0]=ProM&c[1]=Disco&c[2]=Celonis+Process+Mining. Accessed 19 April 2019

26. https://bpmsg.com/academic/ahp-group.php?sc=anEbap. Accessed 20 April 2019

Multimodal Learning with Triplet Ranking Loss for Visual Semantic Embedding Learning

Zhanbo Yang[1], Li Li[1(✉)], Jun He[1], Zixi Wei[1], Li Liu[2], and Jun Liao[2]

[1] School of Computer and Information Science, Southwest University,
Chongqing 400715, People's Republic of China
`perphyoung@email.swu.edu.cn`, `lily@swu.edu.cn`
[2] School of Big Data and Software Engineering, Chongqing University,
Chongqing 400044, People's Republic of China
{`dcsliuli,liaojun`}`@cqu.edu.cn`

Abstract. Semantic embedding learning for image and text has been well studied in recent years. In this paper, we present a simple while effective dual-encoder (image encoder and text encoder) framework to unify image and text into a common embedding space. Inspired by deep metric learning, we utilize triplet ranking loss to minimize the gap between the two embedding spaces. We train and test our proposed framework on Flickr8k, Flickr30k and MS-COCO datasets respectively, and evaluate the framework on the Corel1k benchmark dataset as an application. Using VGG-19 for image encoder, GRU for text encoder and triplet ranking loss, we gained obvious improvement versus baseline model on image annotation and image search tasks. Additionally, we explore the vector generated by our image encoder and the one by word embedding of plain word for some arithmetic operations. The above experiments demonstrate the effectiveness of our proposed learning framework.

Keywords: Visual semantic embedding · Triplet ranking loss · Multimodal learning · Word embedding

1 Introduction

There are multiple form of stuff surrounding us. They come in the way as sight, hearing, touch, smell, taste form and so on. For humans, we are naturally combine these multiple sense into a whole one, while these may be viewed as unrelated for visual recognition systems. In order to tackle this problem, multimodal representation learning is proposed. In the visual semantic domain, the datasets usually offer image-label (single word) or even image-text (multiple words) pairs, which make it possible for unifying the image representation [1] and word representation/embedding [2] into a common embedding space, called visual semantic embedding learning.

© Springer Nature Switzerland AG 2019
C. Douligeris et al. (Eds.): KSEM 2019, LNAI 11775, pp. 763–773, 2019.
https://doi.org/10.1007/978-3-030-29551-6_67

In order to project the two form into a common embedding space, metric learning offers some helpful loss function to minimize the gap between the two modality spaces, they are usually referred as pair-based metric learning. With the rising of deep learning [3], deep metric learning [4] is proposed. The two most typical pair-based deep metrics are contrastive loss [5] and triplet loss [6]. For the visual semantic task, their variants are usually called contrastive ranking loss and triplet ranking loss.

In this paper, we unifying the multimodal space (image and text) into a common embedding space, by taking advantage of triplet ranking loss and word embedding tools.

Concretely, our main contributions are twofold:

- We investigate triplet ranking loss for learning visual semantic embedding, which get better image annotation and image search performance.
- We take advantage of the pre-trained word embedding model to initial the text encoder, which improve the representation quality in our experiments.

The remainder of this paper is organized as follows. The related works are provided in Sect. 2. In Sect. 3, we introduce the proposed learning framework. Section 4 describes our experiments, and in Sect. 5, we evaluate our model as an interesting application. We conclude the paper in Sect. 6.

2   Related Works

2.1   Deep Metric Learning

Metric learning encourages similar samples to be closer and dissimilar ones to apart from each other. With the rising of deep learning [3], deep metric learning are getting more attentions. Deep metric learning is first explored by [7] for signature verification. Contrastive loss in [5] learns a globally coherent nonlinear function that maps the data evenly to the output manifold. Triplet loss in [6] is an improvement version of contrastive loss [5] that learns useful representations by distance comparisons, and can be used for unsupervised learning as well. In our proposed framework, we use triplet ranking loss (variant of triplet loss [6]) for exploring the visual semantic embedding learning.

2.2   Multimodal Representation Learning

The information in real world usually comes as multiple modalities. Thus multimodal learning model is capable to fill the missing modality given the observed ones. Kiros et al. [8] using log-bilinear models for representation of joint multimodal probability distribution. AutoEncoder is introduced in [9] for learning multimodal representations over audio and video. In our proposed framework, we evaluate the multimodal representation learning over image and text. And this is most related to the following visual semantic embedding part.

2.3 Visual Semantic Embedding

The visual semantic embedding is a set of models for learning common embedding space over image and sentence (or only label in previous year). DeViSE [10] is proposed as a mean to perform zero-shot image classification with image and its label word by word2vec [2]. DeFrag [11] using a R-CNN [12] detector as the image feature extractor. VSA [13] take advantage of both R-CNN [12] and BRNN [14] to encode the image and text, respectively. Our proposed framework is a direct extension of UVSE [15], which uses a VGG-19 [16] to extract image feature and a LSTM [17] to encode text, with a contrastive ranking loss [5]. Instead, the main difference is that we utilize a more powerful loss function, the triplet ranking loss [6], to minimize the gap of the common embedding space.

2.4 Word Embedding

Word embedding is one of the most breakouts in Natural Language Processing (NLP) domain. Its representation format is a kind of vector of single word. The most straightforward form of word embedding is one-hot representation, but it does not concern the relationship of the context of the specific word. In 2013, a powerful tool called word2vec [2] is proposed by Mikolov et al. to tackle this issue. The word2vec provides two training mechanism for computing vector representations of word, one for continuous bag-of-word and the other for skip-gram. More recently, GloVe [18] proposed by Stanford in 2014 and FastText [19] by Facebook in 2016 are aimed to improve the representation quality for word embedding. Our model uses the most common word2vec[1] to initial the embedding layer for the text encoder.

3 Proposed Learning Framework

We propose to learn a dual-normalized visual semantic embedding for an image-text pair with a deep neural network framework, as showed in Fig. 1.

Our proposed framework has two branches, one for image and the other for corresponding description text. For image branch, we first utilize a CNN to extract the image feature map as a vector, following by a fully-connected transformation layer and a normalization at the end. And for text branch, word embedding is firstly processing the text, then a RNN mechanism is performed to encode the processed word embedding. Afterward, we apply the encoded vector into a normalization layer. Finally, we unify the two vectors from the two branches into the common embedding space, by means of the triplet ranking loss.

For the rest of this section, we will explain some basis to understand our proposed framework.

---

[1] https://code.google.com/archive/p/word2vec/.

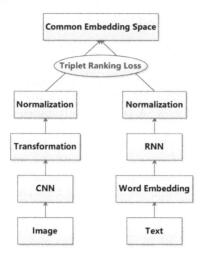

Fig. 1. Our proposed framework for visual semantic embedding learning

3.1   Convolutional Neural Network for Semantics

A typical convolutional neural network (CNN) usually consisted with 3 network layers, namely *convolution layer, max-pooling layer* and *fully-connected layer*. These layers can be formalized as following equations:

$$y_c^{(l)} = w_c^{(l)} \otimes x_c^{(l-1)} + b_c^{(l)} \tag{1}$$

where $x_c^{(l-1)}$ and $y_c^{(l)}$ denote the input and output of the convolution layer, $w_c^{(l)}$ and $b_c^{(l)}$ indicate the learning weight and bias we will learn. The signal $\otimes$ denotes the convolution operation.

$$y_{m,n}^d = \max_{i \epsilon R_{m,n}^d}(x_i) \tag{2}$$

where x_i and $y_{m,n}^d$ denote the input and output of the max-pooling layer, m and n indicate the sizes of pool kernel.

$$x_f^{(l)} = w_f^{(l)} \cdot f_{l-1}(x_f^{(l-1)} + b_f^{(l)}) \tag{3}$$

where x_f denotes the output of the fully-connected layer, $w_f^{(l)}$ and $b_f^{(l)}$ is consisted with Eq. 1.

In our proposed framework, we take the classic VGG-19 network [16], which won the second place of the ImageNet Large Scale Visual Recognition Challenge 2014 (ILSVRC-2014), for extracting 4096-dimensional image features.

3.2   Recurrent Neural Network for Semantics

For sequence-based learning task, recurrent neural network (RNN) is usually one of the best options. However, traditional RNN is unable to *memorize* the long term dependency, thus the improved-type RNN are proposed, such as Long Short-Term Memory (LSTM) [17] and its simplified version, Gated Recurrent Unit (GRU) [20]. In our proposed framework, we use the simpler GRU as the text encoder. The GRU architecture in this work can be formalized as following:

$$z_t = \sigma(W_z \cdot [h_{t-1}, x_t]) \tag{4}$$
$$r_t = \sigma(W_r \cdot [h_{t-1}, x_t]) \tag{5}$$
$$\widetilde{h_t} = tanh(W_h \cdot [r_t * h_{t-1}, x_t]) \tag{6}$$
$$h_t = (1 - z_t) * h_{t-1} + z_t * \widetilde{h_t} \tag{7}$$

where z_t, r_t, $\widetilde{h_t}$ and h_t denote the update gate, reset gate, candidate state and hidden state, respectively. x_t indicate the layer input and Ws the learning weights we should learn.

In our learning framework, we use the GRU to encode the text into a 300-dimensional vector.

3.3 Triplet Ranking Loss for Semantics

Deep metric learning [4] is well applied to various deep learning task. Its two most commonly used types are contrastive loss [5] and triplet loss [6].

In [4], a contrastive loss is defined as:

$$L_{contrast} = (1 - L_{ij})[S_{ij} - \lambda]_+ - L_{ij}S_{ij} \tag{8}$$

where L stands for loss function, $[x]_+ = max(0, x)$, S_{ij} denote the similarity matrix of sample i and j. $L_{ij} = 1$ indicates a positive pair, and 0 for negative one. Negative pairs are apart from each other over a given margin, λ.

And a triplet loss in [4] is represented as:

$$L_{triplet} = [S_{an} - S_{ap} + \lambda]_+ \tag{9}$$

where S_{an} and S_{ap} denote the similarity of a negative pair x_a, x_n, and a positive pair x_a, x_p, with an anchor sample x_a.

For the visual semantic embedding task in our proposed framework, similar to Eq. 9, we define the loss function of our model as:

$$L_{model} = [S_{i,\widehat{t}} - S_{i,t} + \lambda]_+ + [S_{\widehat{i},t} - S_{i,t} + \lambda]_+ \tag{10}$$

where i and t stand for paired image and correlative text, and $\widehat{t}$ and $\widehat{i}$ denote unpaired one, respectively.

4 Experiments

Consistent with UVSE [15], we perform the following query tasks: image annotation (image to text, i2t), and image search (text to image, t2i). The former task can be view as, given an image, retrieve its corresponding text from a database, and the latter is, given a description text, find its paired image.

4.1 Datasets

We evaluate the tasks above in three most commonly used datasets: Flickr8k [21], Flickr30k [22] and MS-COCO [23]. These datasets above contain 8,000, 31,000 and 123,000 images respectively, and each image is annotated with 5 description text using Amazon Mechanical Turk. For the former two Flickr-based datasets, we use 1,000 images for validation, the other 1,000 images for testing, and the rest for training. For the MS-COCO, 5,000 images for validation and the other 5,000 for testing. The dataset split is consistent with [13].

Additionally, we apply our trained model for a interesting application in next section, namely arithmetic operation between vectors generated by image encoder of our framework and by word embedding tool, on a benchmark dataset Corel1k [24], which contains 1,000 images of common objects for standard image testing task. See Table 1 for more detailed datasets information.

Table 1. Details of datasets

Dataset name	Size		
	Train	Validation	Test
Flickr8k	6,000	1,000	1,000
Flickr30k	29,000	1,000	1,000
MS-COCO	123,000	5,000	5,000
Corel1k	-	-	1,000

4.2 Image Encoder and Text Encoder

For image encoder in our proposed framework, we first resize the images to $224 * 224 * 3$, then use the VGG-19 model [16] pre-trained on ImageNet to extract the initial 4096-dimensional vector. And then a fully-connected transformation layer with 1024-dimension is added, following by a L2 normalization, as showed in Fig. 1.

While for text encoder, we first convert all texts to lower case and discard the non-alphanumeric characters. This operation results in 3178, 8481 and 10006 words in each vocabulary size for dataset Flickr8k, Flickr30k and MS-COCO, respectively. When getting the preprocessing text token, if the token is contained in pre-trained word embedding model (in our case, word2vec [2]), we use its embedding vector for better representation. If the token does not occur in the word embedding model, we just eliminate it, and use padding to feed the gap. Then we feed the previous vectors into the GRU model (similar but simpler than one used in UVSE [15]) to extract the 300-dimensional vector. Afterward, a L2 normalization layer is added.

When getting the vectors above, we can project these vectors into the common embedding space with 1024-dimension through triplet ranking loss.

4.3 Training Details

We evaluate our model for at most 30 epochs, with batch size 128 for all datasets. We use Adam optimizer method [25] with initial learning rate 2e-4, and decay the learning rate to its 10% for every 10 epochs. For GRU encoder, we compare the performance of only 1 layer versus 2 layer. We use cosine similarity score to measure the distance of image and text embedding, with fixed margin 0.2 in Eq. 10, to stay consistent with UVSE [15].

4.4 Experiment Results

On image annotation and image search tasks, usually the **Recall@K** (**R@K**, higher is better) and **Median rank** (**Med r**, lower is better) are taken as the metrics.

We select the models mentioned on Sect. 2.3 for comparison, namely DeViSE [10], DeFrag [11], VSA [13] and UVSE [15].

Results on Flickr8k. Table 2 describes the compare results on the Flickr8k dataset. The last 2 lines show the results of our model. The second column list the main features used in the specific model. The number after our model name represents the number of layers in our GRU encoder. DeViSE [10] is chosen as the baseline model in DeFrag [11], we following the convention. The UVSE [15] model has 2 version, the better one take advantage of the VGG-19 (denote as UVSE(VGG) in the table) for image encoder. From Table 2, our 1-layered and 2-layered model gain 5.0% and 23.3% improvement in R@1 metric (higher is better) on image annotation task compared with UVSE(VGG) [15] model, and gain 12.8% and 28.0% improvement on image search task. This proves that the triplet ranking loss used in our framework is more effective than the contrast ranking loss.

Table 2. Results on the Flickr8k dataset

Model	Features	Image annotation				Image search			
		R@1	R@5	R@10	Med r	R@1	R@5	R@10	Med r
Random ranking	-	0.1	0.6	1.1	631	0.1	0.5	1.0	500
DeViSE	word2vec	4.8	16.5	27.3	28	5.9	20.1	29.6	29
DeFrag	rcnn	12.6	32.9	44.0	14	9.7	29.6	42.5	15
VSA	rcnn+brnn	16.5	40.6	54.2	7.6	11.8	32.1	44.7	12.4
UVSE	contrast_loss	13.5	36.2	45.7	13	10.4	31	43.7	14
UVSE(VGG)	contrast_loss	18.0	40.9	55.0	8	12.5	37.0	51.5	10
Ours-1	triplet_loss	18.9	44.3	58.9	7	14.1	37.5	51.0	10
Ours-2	triplet_loss	**22.2**	**47.5**	**61.1**	**6**	**16.0**	**41.0**	**54.9**	**8**

Results on Flickr30k. Table 3 depicts the results on the Flickr30k dataset. We also gain 30.4% and 35.2% improvement in R@1 metric compared with UVSE(VGG) on image annotation task, and 32.7% and 36.9% improvement on image search task. Compare to the results on Flickr8k dataset, we get more improvement, such as 30.4% to 5.0% in R@1 on image annotation task and 32.7% to 12.8% on image search task. Moreover, we get lower Med r (lower is better) results in both query tasks. This indicates that our proposed model can benefit from the data increment for Flickr-based datasets.

Table 3. Results on the Flickr30k dataset

Model	Features	Image annotation				Image search			
		R@1	R@5	R@10	Med r	R@1	R@5	R@10	Med r
Random Ranking	-	0.1	0.6	1.1	631	0.1	0.5	1.0	500
DeViSE	word2vec	4.5	18.1	29.2	26	6.7	21.9	32.7	25
DeFrag	rcnn	14.2	37.7	51.3	10	10.2	30.8	44.2	14
DeFrag(ft)	rcnn	16.4	40.2	54.7	8	10.3	31.4	44.5	13
VSA	rcnn+brnn	22.2	48.2	61.4	4.8	15.2	37.7	50.5	9.2
UVSE	contrast_loss	14.8	39.2	50.9	10	11.8	34.0	46.3	13
UVSE(VGG)	contrast_loss	23.0	50.7	62.9	5	16.8	42.0	56.5	8
Ours-1	triplet_loss	30.0	57.3	67.4	4	22.3	47.4	58.4	6
Ours-2	triplet_loss	**31.1**	**58.6**	**70.0**	4	**23.0**	**48.7**	**60.4**	6

Results on MS-COCO. Table 4 portrays the results on the MS-COCO dataset. UVSE [15] does not show its results on MS-COCO dataset, so we take the VSA model [13] for comparison. The line of VSA model is direct taken from its publication. We gain 11.5% and 17.4% improvement on image annotation task, and 19.0% and 23.4% on image search task, on R@1 metric. We can see that, except the *Med r* metric, we overwhelm all of the others. This may indicate the tricks used specifically on VSA [13], or just a wrong record of the result.

Table 4. Results on the MS-COCO dataset

Model	Features	Image annotation				Image search			
		R@1	R@5	R@10	Med r	R@1	R@5	R@10	Med r
VSA	rcnn+brnn	38.4	69.9	80.5	**1.0**	27.4	60.2	74.8	3.0
Ours-1	contrast_loss	42.8	74.0	84.5	2	32.6	66.3	79.0	3
Ours-2	contrast_loss	**45.1**	**75.8**	**85.3**	2	**33.8**	**67.4**	**80.2**	3

5 Application

Our proposed framework can be used for image encoder and/or text encoder in common semantic task. In this section, we will evaluate the vector from our image encoder and the one from word2vec [2], by doing arithmetic operation between them. The result of this experiment is shown in Fig. 2.

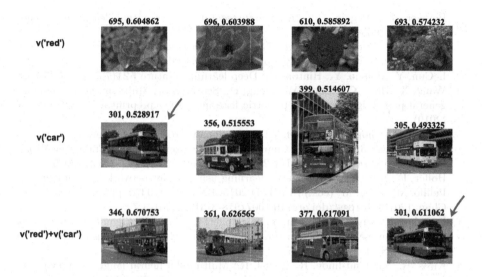

Fig. 2. Illustration of arithmetic operation between image vector and text vector (Color figure online)

In Fig. 2, the first line is the images we choosing from Corel1k dataset [24] which get the most high cosine similarity score of $v('red')$ from word2vec. The second line lists the ones from the $v('car')$. And the last line takes the element-wise average of $v('red')$ and $v('car')$. The numbers above the image represent the name of image (such as '695.jpg') and the cosine similarity score (higher is better). We should notice that, the first image in second line and the last image in third line (denote by red arrow) are the same image, but the third line one gets higher score. This demonstrates that the image encoder of our proposed framework can benefit from more semantic words for image search task.

6 Conclusion

In this paper, we propose a simple while effective framework to unify image and correlated text into the common embedding space, inspired by triplet ranking loss, using VGG-19 as image encoder and GRU as text encoder. The experiments on image annotation and image search tasks demonstrate the effectiveness of our proposed framework over the baseline models.

Acknowledgments. The authors would also like to thank the anonymous referees for their valuable comments and helpful suggestions. This work was supported by NSFC (grant No. 61877051) and CSTC (grant No. cstc2018jscx-msyb1042, cstc2017zdcy-zdyf0366 and cstc2017rgzn-zdyf0064).

References

1. Beymer, D., Poggio, T.: Image representations for visual learning. Science **272**(5270), 1905–1909 (1996)
2. Mikolov, T., Chen, K., Corrado, G., Dean, J.: Efficient estimation of word representations in vector space. arXiv preprint arXiv:1301.3781 (2013)
3. LeCun, Y., Bengio, Y., Hinton, G.: Deep learning. Nature **521**(7553), 436 (2015)
4. Wang, X., Han, X., Huang, W., Dong, D., Scott, M.R.: Multi-similarity loss with general pair weighting for deep metric learning. arXiv preprint arXiv:1904.06627 (2019)
5. Hadsell, R., Chopra, S., LeCun, Y.: Dimensionality reduction by learning an invariant mapping. In: 2006 IEEE Computer Society Conference on Computer Vision and Pattern Recognition (CVPR 2006), vol. 2, pp. 1735–1742. IEEE (2006)
6. Hoffer, E., Ailon, N.: Deep metric learning using triplet network. In: Feragen, A., Pelillo, M., Loog, M. (eds.) SIMBAD 2015. LNCS, vol. 9370, pp. 84–92. Springer, Cham (2015). https://doi.org/10.1007/978-3-319-24261-3_7
7. Bromley, J., Guyon, I., LeCun, Y., Säckinger, E., Shah, R.: Signature verification using a "siamese" time delay neural network. In: Advances in Neural Information Processing Systems, pp. 737–744 (1994)
8. Kiros, R., Salakhutdinov, R., Zemel, R.: Multimodal neural language models. In: International Conference on Machine Learning, pp. 595–603 (2014)
9. Ngiam, J., Khosla, A., Kim, M., Nam, J., Lee, H., Ng, A.Y.: Multimodal deep learning. In: Proceedings of the 28th International Conference on Machine Learning (ICML-11), pp. 689–696 (2011)
10. Frome, A., Corrado, G.S., Shlens, J., Bengio, S., Dean, J., Mikolov, T., et al.: DeViSE: a deep visual-semantic embedding model. In: Advances in Neural Information Processing Systems, pp. 2121–2129 (2013)
11. Karpathy, A., Joulin, A., Fei-Fei, L.: Deep fragment embeddings for bidirectional image sentence mapping. In: Advances in Neural Information Processing Systems, pp. 1889–1897 (2014)
12. Girshick, R., Donahue, J., Darrell, T., Malik, J.: Rich feature hierarchies for accurate object detection and semantic segmentation. In: Proceedings of the IEEE Conference on Computer Vision and Pattern Recognition, pp. 580–587 (2014)
13. Karpathy, A., Fei-Fei, L.: Deep visual-semantic alignments for generating image descriptions. In: Proceedings of the IEEE Conference on Computer Vision and Pattern Recognition, pp. 3128–3137 (2015)
14. Schuster, M., Paliwal, K.K.: Bidirectional recurrent neural networks. IEEE Trans. Signal Process. **45**(11), 2673–2681 (1997)
15. Kiros, R., Salakhutdinov, R., Zemel, R.S.: Unifying visual-semantic embeddings with multimodal neural language models. arXiv preprint arXiv:1411.2539 (2014)
16. Simonyan, K., Zisserman, A.: Very deep convolutional networks for large-scale image recognition. arXiv preprint arXiv:1409.1556 (2014)
17. Hochreiter, S., Schmidhuber, J.: Long short-term memory. Neural Comput. **9**(8), 1735–1780 (1997)

18. Pennington, J., Socher, R., Manning, C.: GloVe: global vectors for word representation. In: Proceedings of the 2014 Conference on Empirical Methods in Natural Language Processing (EMNLP), pp. 1532–1543 (2014)
19. Bojanowski, P., Grave, E., Joulin, A., Mikolov, T.: Enriching word vectors with subword information. Trans. Assoc. Comput. Linguist. **5**, 135–146 (2017)
20. Cho, K., et al.: Learning phrase representations using rnn encoder-decoder for statistical machine translation. arXiv preprint arXiv:1406.1078 (2014)
21. Hodosh, M., Young, P., Hockenmaier, J.: Framing image description as a ranking task: data, models and evaluation metrics. J. Artif. Intell. Res. **47**, 853–899 (2013)
22. Young, P., Lai, A., Hodosh, M., Hockenmaier, J.: From image descriptions to visual denotations: new similarity metrics for semantic inference over event descriptions. Trans. Assoc. Comput. Linguist. **2**, 67–78 (2014)
23. Lin, T.-Y., et al.: Microsoft COCO: common objects in context. In: Fleet, D., Pajdla, T., Schiele, B., Tuytelaars, T. (eds.) ECCV 2014. LNCS, vol. 8693, pp. 740–755. Springer, Cham (2014). https://doi.org/10.1007/978-3-319-10602-1_48
24. Wang, J.Z., Li, J., Wiederhold, G.: Simplicity: semantics-sensitive integrated matching for picture libraries. IEEE Trans. Pattern Anal. Mach. Intell. **9**, 947–963 (2001)
25. Kingma, D.P., Ba, J.: Adam: a method for stochastic optimization. arXiv preprint arXiv:1412.6980 (2014)

IDML: IDentifier-Based Markup Language for Resource-Constrained Smart Objects in WoT

Wuming Luo$^{(\boxtimes)}$

School of Software, Tsinghua University, Beijing 100086, China
lwml6@mails.tsinghua.edu.cn

Abstract. Data representation for resource-constrained Smart Objects (SOs) in Web of Things (WoT) requires compatibility, interoperability, scalability and high efficiency. However, general methods of data representation on web plane have rich extra information for data and they are not efficient; and current methods on Smart Objects are not flexible and they cannot represent complex data structures, such as relational data and hierarchical data. To represent data in resource-constrained Smart Objects flexibly and efficiently, this paper presents IDentifier-based Markup Language (IDML). When constructing the framework for IDML, three ideas are proposed, i.e., structuralization of associations between keys and their values, shortening the length of metadata identifiers, utilization nonprinting characters to control the structure of data block. In IDML, three kinds of data representation methods are designed, including sequential data, relational data, and hierarchical data. Evaluation by comparison and calculation shows that, IDML not only has the scalability and flexibility of general data representation languages on web plane, but also has high efficiency on Smart Objects. Compared with ANSI10.8.2 and JSON in a case scenario, IDML can improve efficiency up to 37.4% and 50.4% respectively.

Keywords: Web of Things · Internet of Things · Smart Object · Data representation · Resource-constrained object · IDentifier-based Markup Language

1 Introduction

In the age of Internet of Everything, Smart Objects [1] are the core components of Web of Things (WoT) [2]. They include Barcode labels, RFID tags, smart sensors or actuators, Smart Products [3], Intelligent Products [4], Cooperating Objects [5], u-Things [6] with all kinds of AEB (Attachment, Embedded, Blending) objects and all kinds of devices, products or equipment etc. Smart Objects are accessed and access heterogeneous system movably and randomly, and data in these Smart Objects should be semi-structured for flexibility and scalability.

At present, XML, JSON, EDI, and YAML, JSON's derivative JSON-LD and JSON-TD, are heavyweight data representation or data interchange language. These languages have much extra information about semantic and format, and they are highly scalable data representation. However, they have poor efficiency due to much extra

© Springer Nature Switzerland AG 2019
C. Douligeris et al. (Eds.): KSEM 2019, LNAI 11775, pp. 774–786, 2019.
https://doi.org/10.1007/978-3-030-29551-6_68

information. Many Smart Objects in IoT have limited computation, memory and communication resource, and all of the languages mentioned above are not fit for data representation of Smart Objects. Meanwhile, the lightweight data representation methods, such as EPC and TEDS, are not flexible for Smart Objects due to fixed data templates. The identifier methods, such as Application Identifier (AI) and Data Identifier (DI), can only represent sequential data model and cannot represent complex relationship among data, such as relational data model or hierarchical data model. Therefore, all the current data representation cannot meet the requirements of resource-constrained Smart Objects.

To design data representation for resource-constrained Smart Objects, however, there are two challenges. On one hand, this method must have high representation efficiency for limited capability of computation and storage in Smart Objects. On the other hand, this method should flexibly represent all kinds of data models to meet the diversities of practical requirements, i.e., relational data, hierarchical data. To some extent, these two challenges contradict each other in nature. Therefore, the data presentation for the Smart Objects is a tradeoff solution to meet both of them.

Focusing on the above challenges, this paper presents the IDentifier-based Markup Language (IDML). This language is designed for the resource-constrained Smart Objects. There are three ideas to design IDML, i.e., structuralization of associations between Keys and their Values, shortening the length of metadata identifiers and utilization nonprinting characters to control data structure. In IDML, three data representation methods of sequential data, relational data, and hierarchical data are designed. The representation system of this scalable markup language can solve the challenges of data representation for the resource-constrained Smart Objects.

There is an application conceptual graph for IDML shown in Fig. 1. On web or host-devices plane, with rich computing and storage resource, the data representation languages are XML or JSON with Semantic Web. On resource-constrained Smart Object plane, the data representation languages are IDML with Semantic Smart Object. IDML can represent three data models for Smart Objects, i.e., sequential data, relational data and hierarchical data.

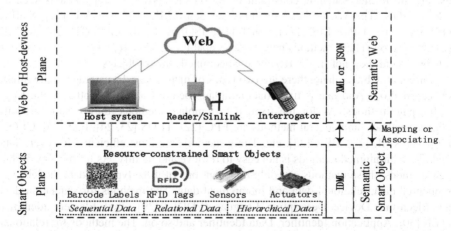

Fig. 1. Application conceptual graph of IDentifier-based Markup Language (IDML)

The remainder of this paper is organized as follows: Sect. 2 introduces related work. Section 3 presents overview and main design ideas of IDML. And Sect. 4 design method for three data models in IDML. Section 5 evaluates IDML by comparison and computation. Finally, conclusions are drawn in Sect. 6.

2   Related Work

The current methods of data representation are analyzed and classified, as shown in Fig. 2. There are two types of methods for data representation. i.e., byte-aligned methods and bit-aligned methods. And data representation methods also fall into two categories: one is for Web or host-devices plane, and another is for Smart Object plane.

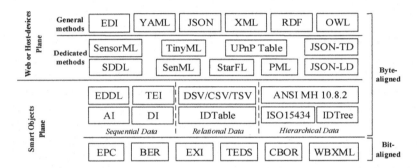

Fig. 2. The classification and relationship of different data representation methods

On Web or host-devices plane, the methods also subdivide into general methods and dedicated methods, and they all are byte-aligned methods. As for the general methods, the data representation system about XML [7], RDF [8] and OWL [9], and popular methods such as EDI [10], JSON [11] and YAML [12], are heavy-weight data semantic representation methods on Web plane. As for the dedicated methods, they usually are further semantic constraint based on the above general methods such as XML, JSON. The WoT-related methods are SensorML [13], TinyML [14], StarFL [15], PML [16], UPnP Table [17], SDDL [18], JSON-LD [19], JSON-TD [20], SenML [21], and so on. These methods have strong capability of data representation with poor efficiency and they not fit for Resource-constrained Smart Objects.

On Smart Object plane, there are two types of methods of data storage in the Smart Object in WoT. And one is fixed data template methods and the another is the Key-Value pair methods. As for the fixed data template methods, they usually are bit-aligned methods, and general methods are EPC [22], TEDS [23, 24], EXI [25], CBOR [26], WBXML [27], BER [28], etc. These methods are most efficient. However, data with these bit-aligned methods is not easy to retrieve and modify. As for the Key-Value pair methods, these methods can only represent one of three types of data models, i.e. sequential data, relational data and hierarchical data. The methods for sequential data are Electronic Device Description Language(EDDL) [29], Text Element Identifier (TEI) [30], Application Identifier, Data Identifier and so on. The methods for relational data are IDTable [31], Delimiter-Separated Values (DSV) and so on. The methods for hierarchical data are ISO15434 [32], American Standard ANSI MH 10.8.2 [33] and IDTree methods. However, there is no method to represent all of above three data models.

It is shown that there is no method to satisfy all high scalability, flexibility and efficiency for Smart Objects. Focusing on the above challenges, this paper presents an identifier-based and Smart Object-oriented markup language IDML.

3 Overview of IDML

3.1 System Framework of IDML

The system framework on IDML is shown in Fig. 3. There are Web or host-devices plane and Smart Object plane. The Web or host-devices plane is the host of Smart Objects. It is the associated specific domain knowledge of Smart Objects. On Web or host-devices plane, the domain knowledge includes domain ontologies models, metadata dictionary A and data models.

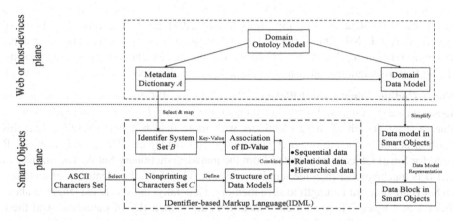

Fig. 3. System framework of IDentifier-based Markup Language (IDML)

On Smart Object plane, some metadata are selected from domain metadata dictionary A. They are used possibly in Smart Object. The identifiers of these metadata in the metadata dictionary are too long to occupy much memory. Therefore, these identifiers of metadata are recoded with shorter length which is called identifier ID of metadata. These identifier IDs constitute set B. These IDs in set B are the one-to-one mapping with the metadata selected from A. The ID can associate with its corresponding value, which may be an ID-Value pair, or mapping relationship between fields of table header and values of table record. Meanwhile, some nonprinting characters are selected from ASCII Characters Set and constitute set C. These nonprinting characters are defined to control the structure of data model or the relationship among data. By combining the association of ID-Value and nonprinting characters, three data models can be described in Smart Object, i.e., sequential data, relational data and hierarchical data. The details are formalized in Sect. 4. With IDML method, the data model simplified from data model on Web plane, can be represented as data block and stored in Smart Object.

3.2   Design Highlights

For any markup languages, there are four aspects to impact the representation of data model, i.e., self-describing information about data for scalability, the identifiers of metadata, the values of metadata, and the structure of data model. As a general markup language for IDML, the uncontrollable values of metadata is out of consideration in this paper. In DML framework, the other three aspects are the design highlights to the challenges. They are illustrated as follows.

Associations of ID-Value for Flexibility. The key is the unique identifier of metadata. These associations are the self-describing information about data. when these associations lie in the Smart Objects instead of in the Web or other storage space, they can reduce the coupling between Smart Object and their host systems. In IDML framework, the associations of ID-Value are designed and stored in Smart Objects to improve the flexibility of data representation. By this self-describing information, the host system can parse these data without any priori format information. There are two kinds of associations in IDML. One is the popular ID-Value pair as we known. The other is the mapping relationship between table fields in table header and values in table records. These two associations can construct three kinds of data models described in Sect. 4.

Short Coding Length for Efficiency. In XML and JSON, the whole identifiers of metadata are represented directly in data documents. They are consumed much memory due to string length of these identifiers with more than 6 bytes generally. And this method is not fit for the resource-constrained Smart Objects. The metadata in Set B used for Smart Objects are selected from the metadata dictionary Set A. The number of Set B is much smaller than the number of Set A. Therefore, the identifiers of metadata in Set B are reduced in length to save memory. Generally, the shortened length is about from 1 to 4 bytes. These shortened identifiers are named IDs of metadata. And these IDs and corresponding values construct the association of ID-Value pairs. In order to distinguish these IDs from other characters' strings, all IDs are underlined.

Nonprinting Characters for Efficiency. In XML, Controlling the structure among data is with beginning tag <metadata> and closing tag <\metadata>; and in JSON, Controlling the structure among data is the brace "{" and "}", colons and quotation marks. The complex separators of controlling the structure consume too much memory for both of them. In order to reduce the consumption of memory, some nonprinting characters are selected from ASCII set and are used to control the structure of data models. They are one byte in length. By defining the controlling functions of these nonprinting characters, they can represent data models for sequential data, relational data and hierarchical data. For example, control character GS is used to separate two ID-Value pairs, and controlling characters HT and VT pair is used to define the table header, and controlling characters STX and ETX pair is used to control structure relationship of hierarchical data. They not only represent the complex structure but also save memory space and improve the efficiency. In order to distinguish these non-printing characters from the other characters, all the nonprinting characters are bold and capital.

4 Design of IDML

4.1 Construction of Identifier System

The collection of all the metadata in a specific domain is the domain metadata dictionary. Assume that there is a metadata dictionary set A which consist of n metadata. The metadata $a_i (i = 1, \ldots, n)$ in set A is m-tuple, which describes the attributes of the metadata a_i. The m-tuple of metadata a_i includes a unique string $MID_i (i = 1, \ldots, n)$ to distinguish the metadata a_i from the others in the namespace of set A, and whose length is L bytes. The m-tuple also includes the variables $Vlen_i$, which is the length of the metadata a_i corresponding value, and other attributes $Attri_{ij} (i = 1, \ldots, N; j = 3, \ldots, m)$ of the metadata a_i. This is, the metadata dictionary $A = \{a_1, a_2, a_3, a_4, \ldots, a_n\}$.

The identifier set B is the collection of all the metadata used possibly in Smart Object. The identifiers Set is $B = \{b_1, b_2, \ldots, b_k\}$, and the identifier tuple is $b_i = (\underline{ID}_i, Vlen_i')(i = 1, \ldots, k)$, and the length of the unique string ID_i is $|\underline{ID}_i| = l$, and $l < L$.

These metadata are selected from the domain metadata dictionary A to shorten coding of their identifiers with a small number of metadata. The relationship between set A and set B is shown in Fig. 4.

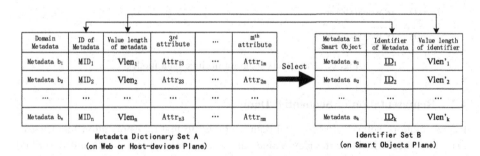

Domain Metadata	ID of Metadata	Value length of metadata	3rd attribute	...	mth attribute		Metadata in Smart Object	Identifier of Metadata	Value length of identifier
Metadata b₁	MID₁	Vlen₁	Attr₁₃	...	Attr₁ₘ	Select	Metadata a₁	ID₁	Vlen'₁
Metadata b₂	MID₂	Vlen₂	Attr₂₃	...	Attr₂ₘ		Metadata a₂	ID₂	Vlen'₂
...	...	...	...	...	...		...	...	...
Metadata bₙ	MIDₙ	Vlenₙ	Attrₙ₃	...	Attrₙₘ		Metadata aₖ	IDₖ	Vlen'ₖ

Metadata Dictionary Set A
(on Web or Host-devices Plane)

Identifier Set B
(on Smart Objects Plane)

Fig. 4. The relation between metadata dictionary A and identifier Set B

For arbitrary metadata b_i in set B, there exists a corresponding metadata a_j in set A, $\underline{ID}_i \rightarrow MID_{j'}$, and $Vlen_i' = Vlen_j$.

In order to represent and parse the structure among data, some nonprinting controlling characters set C is introduced. The characters in set C are nonprinting characters, which are selected from ASCII characters set. These nonprinting characters are used to identify beginning and closing, separating $\underline{ID}$-Value pairs and controlling structure etc. The nonprinting character set is $C = \{\mathbf{GS}(0x1D), \mathbf{RS}(0x1E), \mathbf{STX}(0x02), \mathbf{ETX}(0x03), \mathbf{HT}(0x09), \mathbf{VT}(0x0B), \mathbf{EOT}(0x04), \ldots\}$, and numbers in brackets are their hexadecimal values of ASCII coding.

Where **GS** and **RS** are the separators of ID-Value pairs; **HT** and **VT** are the table-controlling characters, and these two characters are treated equivalently to beginning identifier of table header and table records respectively, and **VT** is the terminator of table header simultaneously as well; **STX** and **ETX** are hierarchical structure-controlling characters, and they are treated equivalently to the characters "{" and "}"; **EOT** is the closing identifier of the whole data block.

(a) Syntax diagram of Sequential data model

(b) Syntax diagram of relational data model

(c) Syntax diagram of hierarchical data model

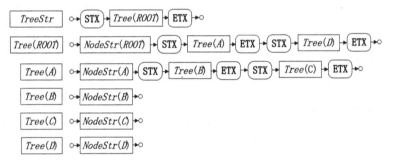

Fig. 5. The syntax diagram of three data models

4.2   Representation of Sequential Data

Representation method of sequential data is similar to that of Application Identifier or Data Identifier, which are the Key-Value pair-based storage method with self-described data in the RFID tags. This method adapts the 2-tuple Key-Value pair to describe the data content of items. The attribute metadata $a_i(i = 1, \ldots, n)$ and its corresponding value V_i constitute a Key-Value pair (a_i, V_i). If there are p feature values described in RFID tags, the data block is the collection of p Key-Value pairs about p features of Smart Object, and the keys of metadata are represented by their unique string *MID*.

$$P = \left\{ (a_{1'}, V_{1'}), (a_{2'}, V_{2'}), \ldots, (a_p, V_p) \right\}$$
$$= \left\{ (MID_{1'}, V_{1'}), (MID_{2'}, V_{2'}), \ldots, (MID_p, V_p) \right\}$$

Due to $|MID_{i'}| > |ID_i|$, in order to compress data coding and improve the storage efficiency, the unique string $\underline{ID}_i$ is used to represent its associated with metadata $a_{i'}$. This is, $P = P' = \{(\underline{ID}_{1'}, V_{1'}), (\underline{ID}_{2'}, V_{2'}), \ldots, (\underline{ID}_p, V_p)\}$. These ID-Value pairs are stored practically in Smart Objects.

In order to differentiate different ID-Value pairs, the nonprinting separator **GS** is inserted between two ID-Value pairs to separate them. The separators **RS** and **EOT** are used at the beginning and closing of the data block to identify the beginning and closing. The data sequence of storage in Smart Objects is shown as follows:

$$\mathbf{RS}, (ID_{1'}, V_{1'}), \mathbf{GS}, (ID_{2'}, V_{2'}), \mathbf{GS}, (ID_{3'}, V_{3'}), \mathbf{GS}, \ldots, (ID_p, V_p), \mathbf{EOT}.$$

The Identifier ID and its value V of ID-Value pair are connected directly and become an ID-Value string. Many ID-Value strings are connected with separator **GS** inserting between two ID-Value strings. The character **EOT** is used to identify the closing of the whole data block. The final string *SeqStr* in the memory of Smart Object is

$$SeqStr ::= \mathbf{RS}\underline{ID}_{1'}V_{1'}\mathbf{GS}\underline{ID}_{2'}V_{2'}\mathbf{GS}\underline{ID}_{3'}V_{3'}\mathbf{GS}\ldots\underline{ID}_pV_p\mathbf{EOT}.$$

The syntax diagram of *SeqStr* expression is shown in Fig. 5(a).

4.3   IDTable: Representation of Relational Data

In order to represent relational data in Smart Objects, the IDTable method [31] is adopted. This method defines table header in Smart Object, and then represent the corresponding table record data on the base of the table header definition.

Definition of Table Fields with Identifiers. Each field in table header is represented with an $\underline{ID}$ of the metadata from set B. The beginning of table header is identified with nonprinting character **HT** and its closing is identified with **VT**. Some separators **GS** are used between two $\underline{ID}$s to separate table fields. The table header is defined as follows:

$$\mathbf{HT}\underline{ID}_{1'}\mathbf{GS}\underline{ID}_{2'}\mathbf{GS}\underline{ID}_{3'}\mathbf{GS}\ldots\underline{ID}_{p'}\mathbf{GSVT}.$$

Representation of Table Record. According to above representation of sequential data, each record is represented with $\underline{ID}$-Value pair sequence $(\underline{ID}_{1'}, V_{1'}), (\underline{ID}_{2'}, V_{2'}), \ldots, (\underline{ID}_{p'}, V_{p'})$, and separators **GS** are used to separate two neighboring $\underline{ID}$-Value pairs and separators **RS** are used to separate two neighboring records. Since table fields are defined above, and each field is the same as the ID of the corresponding $\underline{ID}$-Value pair for each record, and these repeated $\underline{ID}$s can be removed to save memory. When these ID-Value pairs are parsed, the $\underline{ID}$s can be mapped to corresponding fields and the $\underline{ID}$-Value pairs are restored. Therefore, the format of the xth record can be built as follows.

$$Vx_{1'}\mathbf{GS}Vx_{2'}\mathbf{GS}\ldots Vx_{p'}\mathbf{RS}$$

The separator **EOT** is used to identify the close of all the records. Assume that *TabStr* is the final string of relational data in the memory of Smart Object. The syntax diagram of *TabStr* expression is shown in Fig. 5(b).

4.4   IDTree: Representation of Hierarchical Data

In order to represent the hierarchical data with the identifier set B, the IDTree method is presented to solve this problem. IDTree uses the two nonprinting characters **STX** and **ETX** in set *C* to control the structure among data, which are equivalent to "{" and "}". They appear in pairs to pack all the data of the node itself and its subtree node. All the data of each node can be packed the data of node-owned level and the data of its all subtree nodes with **STX** and **ETX**. **STX** represents the beginning of the package and **ETX** represents the closing of the package. By recursion, the data of the subtree node in the package is packed all the data of current node-level and its child-nodes with **STX** and **ETX**. When the node is a leaf-node, and then **STX** and **ETX** only pack the data of the leaf node-level.

For the node *x*, assume that this node-owned level data is *NodeStr(x)*, and *NodeStr(x)* does not include its subtree node data. *NodeStr(x)* can be represented with the method of sequential data in Sect. 4.2 or relational data in Sect. 4.3.

Take an example to illustrate the representation method of hierarchical data, which is shown in Fig. 6. The data of ROOT-level *NodeStr(ROOT)* and the data of its child-nodes *A* and *D* is packed with characters **STX** and **ETX**, named package P_{ROOT}. The data of ROOT node-level *NodeStr(ROOT)* is following the character **STX**. All the data of node *A*, which includes the data of current level *NodeStr(A)* and the data of their child-nodes P_B and P_C, is packed with **STX** and **ETX**, named P_A Similarly, the node *D* is packed with **STX** and **ETX**, named P_D. And then the data packages of each child-nodes P_A and P_D of the node *ROOT* is represented respectively following the *NodeStr (ROOT)* in order. In a similar way, all the data of subtree nodes *B* and *C* of node A is packed with **STX** and **ETX**, named P_B and P_C respectively. And data of their current level is *NodeStr(B)* and *NodeStr(C)*. With this nested way, all the nodes and their relationship are represented with **STX** and **ETX**.

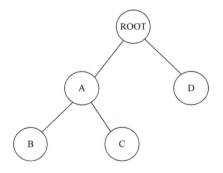

Fig. 6. An example for hierarchical data

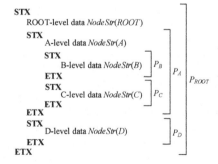

Fig. 7. Representation of hierarchical data

Assume that *TreeStr* is the final string of hierarchical data in the memory of Smart Object. Then the whole hierarchical data are represented as follows.

*TreeStr::=**STX**NodeStr(ROOT)**STX**NodeStr(A)**STX**NodeStr(B)**ETXSTX**NodeStr (C)**ETX ETXSTX**NodeStr(D)**ETXETX**.*

The syntax diagram of *TreeStr* expression is shown in Fig. 5(c). The unfolded structure of *TreeStr* string is shown in Fig. 7.

5 Evaluation

5.1 Performance Comparison of Representation

Table 1. The performances comparison among XML, EDI, JSON, YAML, ANSI and IDML

		XML	JSON	ANSI MH 10.8.2	IDML
Scalability		High	High	Medium	High
Interoperability		High	High	High	High
Compatibility		High	High	High	High
Data representation capability	Sequential data	Support	Support	Only for logistics	Support
	Relational data	Support	Support	Only for logistics	Support
	Hierarchical data	Support	Support	Only for logistics	Support

Since RDF and OWL have the capability of logic reason and proof and their representation is implemented with XML, XML is selected only instead of RDF and OWL for the performance comparison of data representation. Similarly, JSON-LD and JSON-TD is derived from JSON, then performance of JSON is the same as that of JSON-LD or that of JSON-TD. Therefore, according to the analysis in Sect. 2 and the features of IDML, this section compares IDML with XML, JSON and ANSI MH 10.8.2 standard in scalability, interoperability, compatibility and representation capability. The comparison results are shown in Table 1.

5.2 Calculation Analysis of Storage Efficiency

In order to quantitatively analyze the storage efficiency, a common scenario of container shipment is built to calculate the efficiency with different languages. Assume that there are P pallets in a shipping container, and there is $r_p(1 \leq p \leq P)$ items on the $p^{th}(1 \leq p \leq P)$ pallet. An active RFID tag is attached to the container to store all the data of items in the container. Assume that K features data is used to describe the container itself, and m features data is used to describe the pallet itself, and n features data is used to describe each kind of items on the pallet. And assume that the length of identifier ID is 4 bytes, and the length of its corresponding value is 8 bytes. Now memory requirement of RFID tag can be counted.

If all the node data are sequential data, the representation method is called sequential-node IDML; and if the node data are relational data, the method is called relational-node IDML. To store all the data of container items in active RFID tag, S_G, S_T, S_A and S_J are the byte number of storage space with sequential-node IDML method, relational-node IDML method, ANSI MH 10.8.2 and JSON respectively. They can be calculated with above variables. And expressions of S_G, S_T, S_A and S_J are simplified as follows.

$$S_G = 13K + P(2 + 13m) + (2 + 13n)\sum\nolimits_{p=1}^{P} r_p$$

$$S_T = 13K + P(2 + 13m + 5n) + 8n\sum\nolimits_{p=1}^{P} r_p$$

$$S_A = 6 + 13K + P(6 + 13m) + (6 + 13n)\sum\nolimits_{p=1}^{P} r_p$$

$$S_J = 2 + 18K + P(4 + 18m) + (1 + 18n)\sum\nolimits_{p=1}^{P} r_p$$

Where the expression $\sum_{p=1}^{P} r_p$ is the sum of all the items in the container, denoted as $R = \sum_{p=1}^{P} r_p$. Then the above S_G, S_T, S_A, and S_J are the functions that depend on the variables: number of pallets P and number of total number of items R. Since there is one item at least on a pallet, then the inequation $R > P$ is satisfied.

Comparison of Storage Efficiency. Under the conditions of $r_p > 1(1 \leq p \leq P)$, $K > 1$, $m > 1$, $n > 1$ and $R > P$, the constant of S_J is $2 + 18K$, and the coefficient of P is $4 + 18m$, and the coefficient of R is $1 + 18n$, the values of these three expressions are greater than that of S_G, S_T and S_A. Therefore, S_J is the greatest among the four solutions, that means the solution with JSON is the most memory. In the same way, the relations among S_G, S_T and S_A can be compared, and from the smallest to the largest, their byte number of storage memory is S_T, S_G, S_A and S_J in ascending order.

Calculation of Storage Efficiency in Typical Scenarios. To compare the storage efficiency of sequential-node IDML method and relational-node IDML method, on the basis of ANSI MH 10.8.2 and JSON respectively, the paper calculated the efficiency increase of above two IDML methods. The calculating expression is defined as follows.

$$\eta_{GA}(P, R) = (S_A - S_G)/S_A$$

$$\eta_{TA}(P, R) = (S_A - S_F)/S_A$$

$$\eta_{GJ}(P, R) = (S_J - S_G)/S_J$$

$$\eta_{TJ}(P, R) = (S_J - S_F)/S_J$$

In two possible typical scenarios, the efficiency increase is listed in Table 2.

Table 2. IDML efficiency increasing for two scenarios

$K = m = n = 4, P = 8, R = 50$			
η_{GA}	6.95%	η_{GJ}	26.5%
η_{TA}	34.4%	η_{TJ}	48.2%
$K = m = n = 4, P = 6, R = 60$			
η_{GA}	5.79%	η_{GJ}	26.4%
η_{TA}	37.4%	η_{TJ}	50.4%

6 Conclusion

Focusing on the balance between flexibility and efficiency for data representation of Smart Objects in WoT, this paper presents an identifier-based markup language for resource-constrained Smart Objects. After the paper proposes the method framework of IDML and main ideas. The data representation methods of sequential data, relational data, and hierarchical data are put forward. Compared with JSON and ANSI MH 10.8.2, IDML not only has the scalability and representation capability, not also has higher efficiency, and can meet the requirement of data representation for Smart Objects.

The contributions can be summarized as follows. (1) To make data representation efficient, the system framework is designed for IDentifier-based Markup Language. In this framework, based on the domain data dictionary, three ideas are presented, i.e., structuralization for associations between Keys and their Values, shortening the length of metadata identifiers and utilization nonprinting characters to control data structure. (2) To make data representation flexible, data representations for three data models are presented, namely, sequential data, relational data and hierarchical data.

References

1. Kortuem, G., Kawsar, F., Fitton, D., Sundramoorthy, V.: Smart objects as building blocks for the internet of things. IEEE Internet Comput. **4**(1), 44–51 (2010)
2. Web of Things. http://www.w3.org/IoT/
3. Gutierrez, C., Garbajosa, J., Diaz, J., Yague, A.: Providing a consensus definition for the term 'Smart Product'. In: Proceedings of the International Symposium and Workshop on Engineering of Computer Based Systems, pp. 203–211 (2013)
4. Meyer, G.G., Främling, K., Holmström, J.: Intelligent products: a survey. Comput. Ind. **60**(3), 137–148 (2009)
5. Marròn, P.J., Karnouskos, S., Minder, D.: The Emerging Domain of Cooperating Objects. Springer, Heidelberg (2011). https://doi.org/10.1007/978-3-642-28469-4
6. Ma, J.: Smart u-Things: challenging real world complexity. In: IPSJ Symposium Series, vol. 19, pp. 146–150 (2005)
7. Extensible Markup Language (XML). http://www.w3.org/XML/
8. Resource Description Framework (RDF). http://www.w3.org/RDF/
9. Web Ontology Language (OWL). http://www.w3.org/TR/owl-features/
10. Electronic Data Interchange. https://en.wikipedia.org/wiki/Electronic_data_interchange

11. JavaScript Object Notation. http://www.json.org/
12. YAML Ain't Markup Language. http://yaml.org/
13. SensorML. http://www.opengeospatial.org/sensorml
14. Ota, N., Kramer, W.T.C.: TinyML: Meta-data for Wireless Networks. https://people.eecs. berkeley.edu/~culler/cs294-f03/finalpapers/tinyml.pdf
15. Malewski, C., Simonis, I., Terborst, A., et al.: StarFL – a modularised metadata language for sensor descriptions. Int. J. Digi. Earth **7**(6), 450–469 (2014)
16. Physical Markup Language. http://web.mit.edu/mecheng/pml/
17. Upnp Forum: UPnP iotmc IoTManagementAndControl DataModel Service(v1). http://www. upnp.org/iotmc/UPnP-iotmc-IoTManagementAndControl-DataModel-v1-Service.pdf
18. Sensory Dataset Description Language (SDDL). https://www.cise.ufl.edu/~helal/ opensource/sddl.pdf
19. W3C Consortium: A JSON-based Serialization for Linked Data. https://www.w3.org/TR/ json-ld/
20. W3C Consortium: JSON-Thing Description. https://www.w3.org/ TR/2018/WD-IoT-thing-description-20180405/
21. SenML: simple building block for IoT semantic interoperability. https://www.iab.org/wp-content/IAB-uploads/2016/03/IAB_IOTSI_Keranen_Jennings_SenML.pdf
22. GS1.Tag Data Standards (V1.9). http://www.gs1.org/gsmp/kc/epcglobal/tds
23. Luo, W., Bolic, M., Wang, J., Qian, X.: Management of sensor-related data based on virtual TEDS in sensing RFID system. Int. J. Distrib. Sens. Netw. 1–11 (2015). https://doi.org/10. 1155/2015/969841
24. An Overview of IEEE 1451.4 Transducer Electronic Data Sheets. https://standards.ieee.org/ develop/regauth/tut/teds.pdf
25. Efficient XML Interchange (EXI) Format 1.0 (Second Edition). https://www.w3.org/TR/exi/
26. Concise Binary Object Representation. https://en.wikipedia.org/wiki/CBOR
27. W3C Consortium: WAP Binary XML Content Format. https://www.w3.org/TR/wbxml/
28. Information technology–ASN.1 encoding rules: Specification of Basic Encoding Rules (BER), Canonical Encoding Rules(CER) and Distinguished Encoding Rules(DER). ISO/IEC 8825-1-2008
29. Electronic Device Description Language (EDDL). http://www.eddl.org/
30. Part Traceability Data Standards-spec2000. http://www.spec2000.com/representations/ jona.pdf
31. Luo, W.: IDTable: self-describing relational data for resource-constraint smart objects. In: 2018 IEEE 24rd International Conference on Parallel and Distributed Systems (ICPADS), Singapore (2018)
32. Information technology–Automatic identification and data capture techniques–Syntax for high-capacity ADC media. ISO/IEC 15434-2006
33. Transfer Data syntax for High Capacity ADC Media. ANSI MH 10.8.3-2004

Understanding Decision Model and Notation: DMN Research Directions and Trends

Krzysztof Kluza(✉), Weronika T. Adrian, Piotr Wiśniewski, and Antoni Ligęza

AGH University of Science and Technology, al. Mickiewicza 30,
30-059 Krakow, Poland
{kluza,wta,wpiotr,ligeza}@agh.edu.pl

Abstract. Decision Model and Notation provides a modeling notation for decisions, supports decision management, and business rules specification. In this paper, we identify research directions concerning DMN standard, outline classification of DMN research areas and perspectives of this relatively new formalism.

Keywords: Decision Model and Notation (DMN) ·
Decision modeling · Research directions

1 Introduction

Decision Model and Notation (DMN) [1] constitutes a relatively new standard of Object Management Group (OMG). It is a part of a range of the OMG Business Modeling specifications that include such notations as Business Process Model and Notation (BPMN), Case Management Model and Notation (CMMN) or Semantics of Business Vocabulary and Business Rules (SBVR).

The Request For Proposal of DMN was presented in March 2011. Some leaks have been presented in Juner [2]. Version Beta 1 of DMN 1.0 was released in January 2014. Although it exposed several lackings in its metamodel (e.g. non-matching class namespaces, with regard to the name of the whole) which made its usage difficult [3], it has been accepted by several vendors who developed the modeling tools[1], as well as authors of handbooks [4,5]. Finally, OMG adopted DMN 1.0 in September 2015 and DMN 1.1 in June 2016. DMN filled the gap in the market of decision modeling and started to be often used with BPMN. After a couple years, it became a standardized solution for modeling decision.

In this paper, we provide a short overview of research directions concerning the DMN notation, as well as attempt to evaluate the state-of-the-art in the identified directions. Our objective is to provide a synthesized multi-aspect introduction to DMN, enriched with trends and perspectives.

The rest of this paper is organized as follows: Sect. 2 provides a brief overview of DMN, including the Model Driven Architecture (MDA) perspective. In Sect. 3,

---

[1] See: https://methodandstyle.com/dmn-tools-current-state-market/.

© Springer Nature Switzerland AG 2019
C. Douligeris et al. (Eds.): KSEM 2019, LNAI 11775, pp. 787–795, 2019.
https://doi.org/10.1007/978-3-030-29551-6_69

we briefly present our method of research papers selection, and the paper is summarized in Sect. 4.

2   Decision Model and Notation (DMN)

The aim of the DMN standard is to provide the notation for decision modeling so that the decision could be easily presented in diagrams and understandable by business users [6]. The main purposes of the notation are: modeling human decision-making, modeling the requirements for automated decision-making, and implementing automated decision-making [1]. DMN decision models are based on four types of elements: *Decision, Business Knowledge Model, Input Data*, and *Knowledge Source* (see Fig. 1).

Fig. 1. The types of DMN elements

Decisions are used to determine an output from a number of inputs using some decision logic. *Business Knowledge Models* encapsulates business knowledge, such as decision tables, business rules or analytic models. *Input Data* elements specify the input of a Decision or Business Knowledge Model. *Knowledge Sources* model authoritative knowledge sources in a decision model. These elements can be connected using different requirement connectors, such as *Information, Knowledge*, and *Authority*.

A higher level decision model can be represented as Decision Requirements Graph (DRG), which may be split into one or more Decision Requirements Diagrams (DRD), presenting a particular view of the model [1]. On the other hand, for the lower level of decision modeling, i.e. rules, DMN provides a dedicated language – Friendly Enough Expression Language (FEEL). Such rules can be evaluated using some dedicated FEEL environment or transformed into a more specific executable representation.

3   Overview of DMN Research Directions

In this section, we analyze the literature on Decision Model and Notation. First, we describe a strategy for our analysis, and then we sketch a landscape of research directions, with prominent papers representing each of them.

3.1 Paper Selection Strategy

Based on three databases of peer-reviewed literature: *Web of Science, Science Direct* and *Scopus*, using the query containing 5 different phrases (entire phrase):

```
(ALL("Decision Model and Notation") OR ALL("DMN model")
OR ALL("model DMN") OR ALL("DMN decision") OR ALL("decision DMN"))
```

we obtained 125 different records (limited to papers published after 2010). From these, we manually selected the documents regarding research related to the DMN notation. We excluded 18 results not related to the Decision Model and Notation[2]. As in many papers DMN is only mentioned, we excluded 27 results where DMN was briefly mentioned (but not as a close related or future work).

3.2 Analysis and Classification Attempt

Based on the conducted literature analysis, we categorized the research papers into seven research areas, divided into more specific research directions. Figure 2 presents the selected directions which are elaborated in the following subsections.

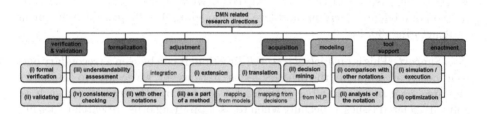

Fig. 2. Overview of the DMN related research directions

Verification and Validation of Models. It is a research direction that includes: (i) formal verification of models (in case of DMN these are mostly decision logic models i.e. decision tables), formal checking of selected model properties [7, 8], (ii) validating of the requirements or manual compliance checking [9], (iii) understandability assessment – checking if a model is easy to comprehend [10] (iv) consistency checking and correcting inconsistencies between models [11].

Formalization. DMN model may be formalized on different abstraction levels and for different purposes. Formalization can be used for defining clear semantics of the model [12–14], to provide a base for formal model checking [7], to accurately describe extension or integration scenarios [15] or to specify execution process [16].

---

[2] We rejected the papers where DMN has a different meaning, e.g. a model compound 2,6 -dimethynaphthalate, dichotomous markov noise, default mode networks, etc.

Adjustment. By adjustment of the model, we consider a group of research directions which provide some way of adaptation of the DMN for a specific purpose: (i) extension of models to support other perspectives, domain elements, environments, etc. [17–19], (ii) integration with other models in various notations (mostly BPMN) [15,20], (iii) integration within some modeling methods or methodologies; in which DMN constitutes a part responsible for modeling decisions [21–26].

Acquisition. Model acquisition is an essential step in the decision management life cycle. It can be done by manual decision modeling (see *Modeling*) or by: (i) model translation from other representations [27–29], (ii) mining decision from event logs [22,30,31], in particular from event-based logs containing extensive instance data, the so-called decision logs [32–34].

Modeling. In most of the analyzed papers, DMN was primarily used just for modeling decisions. Apart from using DMN as a part of the whole system modeling, there are attempts concerning applicability assessment for various domain areas. Moreover, there is a broad spectrum of modeling aspects which were considered by researchers, such as: (i) comparing DMN with other notations [35], (ii) analyzing various aspects of DMN [36], e.g. cognitive load [37], complexity [38], etc. method of modeling decisions and levels of modeling [15,39], possible refinement or refactoring [30,40].

Tool Support. This is an *applied research* direction. It can be seen as secondary one, as it mostly accompanies the primary research. However, we decided to emphasize this area, as it raises a number of topics not covered by other directions, such as: software-related issues, especially when tools supporting other research issues like verification or modeling are concerned [41–44], storing and serializing models [45], or issues of maintainability, scalability and portability [46].

Enactment. This covers various aspects of running DMN models in some environments, especially for the purpose of: (i) simulation [47] or execution [48–50] of decision logic, (ii) optimization of the executed logic [51].

3.3   Discussion of the Classification and Trends Analysis

The presented categories of research does not constitute a closed set of research directions, but can serve as a prototype of a broader and more formal taxonomy. As it can be noticed, some of the presented categories overlap. Moreover, most of the research directions could be also considered from another dimension (perspective). For example, when talking about model consistency, we can consider the consistency of the models on the following levels: a single DMN diagram (decision model) or decision table (decision logic), various abstraction levels of a single DMN model, two or more DMN models, a DMN model and other models, in particular integrated ones, or a DMN model and other knowledge resources (such as event logs, spreadsheets, natural language description, etc.). Figure 3 grasps the "popularity" of various directions over the last five years.

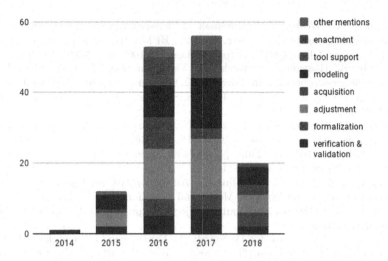

Fig. 3. The research directions observed among selected papers in each year

4 Concluding Remarks

Decision Model and Notation has recently attracted a considerable amount of research attention. In this paper, we identified the existing research directions concerning DMN standard, provided a preliminary classification of the research areas and quantitatively presented the collected data regarding the identified research directions. In our future work, we would like to extend the classification with new categories, covering all existing DMN related papers.

References

1. OMG: Decision Model and Notation (DMN). Version 1.1. Technical report formal/16-06-01, Object Management Group (2016)
2. Linehan, M., de Sainte Marie, C.: The relationship of decision model and notation (DMN) to SBVR and BPMN. Bus. Rules J. **12**(6) (2011)
3. Biard, T., Le Mauff, A., Bigand, M., Bourey, J.-P.: Separation of decision modeling from business process modeling using new "Decision Model and Notation" (DMN) for automating operational decision-making. In: Camarinha-Matos, L.M., Bénaben, F., Picard, W. (eds.) PRO-VE 2015. IAICT, vol. 463, pp. 489–496. Springer, Cham (2015). https://doi.org/10.1007/978-3-319-24141-8_45
4. Debevoise, T., Taylor, J., Sinur, J., Geneva, R.: The MicroGuide to Process and Decision Modeling in BPMN/DMN: Building More Effective Processes by Integrating Process Modeling with Decision Modeling. CreateSpace Independent Publishing Platform (2014)
5. Silver, B.: DMN Method & Style. Cody-Cassidy Press, Altadena (2016)
6. Taylor, J., Fish, A., Vanthienen, J., Vincent, P.: Emerging standards in decision modeling - an introduction to decision model & notation. In: iBPMS: Intelligent BPM Systems: Intelligent BPM Systems: Impact and Opportunity. BPM and Workflow Handbook Series, pp. 133–146. Future Strategies, Inc. (2013)

7. Batoulis, K., Weske, M.: Soundness of decision-aware business processes. In: Carmona, J., Engels, G., Kumar, A. (eds.) BPM 2017. LNBIP, vol. 297, pp. 106–124. Springer, Cham (2017). https://doi.org/10.1007/978-3-319-65015-9_7

8. Batoulis, K., Haarmann, S., Weske, M.: Various notions of soundness for decision-aware business processes. In: Mayr, H.C., Guizzardi, G., Ma, H., Pastor, O. (eds.) ER 2017. LNCS, vol. 10650, pp. 403–418. Springer, Cham (2017). https://doi.org/10.1007/978-3-319-69904-2_31

9. Batoulis, K., Baumgraß, A., Herzberg, N., Weske, M.: Enabling dynamic decision making in business processes with DMN. In: Reichert, M., Reijers, H.A. (eds.) BPM 2015. LNBIP, vol. 256, pp. 418–431. Springer, Cham (2016). https://doi.org/10.1007/978-3-319-42887-1_34

10. Dangarska, Z., Figl, K., Mendling, J.: An explorative analysis of the notational characteristics of the Decision Model and Notation (DMN). In: 2016 IEEE 20th International Enterprise Distributed Object Computing Workshop (EDOCW), pp. 1–9. IEEE (2016)

11. Janssens, L., Bazhenova, E., De Smedt, J., Vanthienen, J., Denecker, M.: Consistent integration of decision (DMN) and process (BPMN) models. In: Proceedings of the CAiSE'16 Forum, at the 28th International Conference on Advanced Information Systems Engineering (CAiSE 2016), Ljubljana, Slovenia, June 13–17, 2016, vol. 1612, pp. 121–128. CEUR-WS. org (2016)

12. Calvanese, D., Dumas, M., Laurson, Ü., Maggi, F.M., Montali, M., Teinemaa, I.: Semantics and analysis of DMN decision tables. In: La Rosa, M., Loos, P., Pastor, O. (eds.) BPM 2016. LNCS, vol. 9850, pp. 217–233. Springer, Cham (2016). https://doi.org/10.1007/978-3-319-45348-4_13

13. Calvanese, D., Dumas, M., Maggi, F.M., Montali, M.: Semantic DMN: formalizing decision models with domain knowledge. In: Costantini, S., Franconi, E., Van Woensel, W., Kontchakov, R., Sadri, F., Roman, D. (eds.) RuleML+RR 2017. LNCS, vol. 10364, pp. 70–86. Springer, Cham (2017). https://doi.org/10.1007/978-3-319-61252-2_6

14. Calvanese, D., Dumas, M., Laurson, Ü., Maggi, F.M., Montali, M., Teinemaa, I.: Semantics, analysis and simplification of DMN decision tables. Information Systems (2018)

15. Hasic, F., Vanwijck, L., Vanthienen, J.: Integrating processes, cases, and decisions for knowledge-intensive process modelling. In: Proceedings of the 1st International Workshop on Practicing Open Enterprise Modeling within OMiLAB (PrOse 2017), Leuven, Belgium, 22 November 2017 (2017)

16. Janssens, L., De Smedt, J., Vanthienen, J.: Modeling and enacting enterprise decisions. In: Krogstie, J., Mouratidis, H., Su, J. (eds.) CAiSE 2016. LNBIP, vol. 249, pp. 169–180. Springer, Cham (2016). https://doi.org/10.1007/978-3-319-39564-7_17

17. Horita, F.E., de Albuquerque, J.P., Marchezini, V., Mendiondo, E.M.: Bridging the gap between decision-making and emerging big data sources: an application of a model-based framework to disaster management in brazil. Decis. Support Syst. 97, 12–22 (2017)

18. Horita, F.E.A., Link, D., de Albuquerque, J.P., Hellingrath, B.: oDMN: an integrated model to connect decision-making needs to emerging data sources in disaster management. In: 2016 49th Hawaii International Conference on System Sciences (HICSS), pp. 2882–2891. IEEE (2016)

19. Perez-Alvarez, J.M., Gomez-Lopez, M.T., Parody, L., Gasca, R.M.: Process instance query language to include process performance indicators in DMN. In: 2016 IEEE 20th International Enterprise Distributed Object Computing Workshop (EDOCW), pp. 1–8. IEEE (2016)

20. Mertens, S., Gailly, F., Poels, G.: Enhancing declarative process models with DMN decision logic. In: Gaaloul, K., Schmidt, R., Nurcan, S., Guerreiro, S., Ma, Q. (eds.) CAISE 2015. LNBIP, vol. 214, pp. 151–165. Springer, Cham (2015). https://doi.org/10.1007/978-3-319-19237-6_10

21. Hasić, F., De Smedt, J., Vanthienen, J.: A service-oriented architecture design of decision-aware information systems: decision as a service. In: Panetto, H., et al. (eds.) OTM 2017. LNCS, vol. 10573, pp. 353–361. Springer, Cham (2017)

22. Hasić, F., De Smedt, J., Vanthienen, J.: Developing a modelling and mining framework for integrated processes and decisions. In: Debruyne, C., Panetto, H., Weichhart, G., Bollen, P., Ciuciu, I., Vidal, M.-E., Meersman, R. (eds.) OTM 2017. LNCS, vol. 10697, pp. 259–269. Springer, Cham (2018). https://doi.org/10.1007/978-3-319-73805-5_28

23. Ortner, E., Mevius, M., Wiedmann, P., Kurz, F.: Design of interactional decision support applications for e-participation in smart cities. Int. J. Electron. Gov. Res. (IJEGR) 12(2), 18–38 (2016)

24. Griesinger, F., Seybold, D., Domaschka, J., Kritikos, K., Woitsch, R.: A DMN-based approach for dynamic deployment modelling of cloud applications. In: Lazovik, A., Schulte, S. (eds.) ESOCC 2016. CCIS, vol. 707, pp. 104–111. Springer, Cham (2018). https://doi.org/10.1007/978-3-319-72125-5_8

25. Ghlala, R., Kodia Aouina, Z., Ben Said, L.: MC-DMN: Meeting MCDM with DMN involving multi-criteria decision-making in business process. In: Gervasi, O., et al. (eds.) ICCSA 2017. LNCS, vol. 10409, pp. 3–16. Springer, Cham (2017). https://doi.org/10.1007/978-3-319-62407-5_1

26. Abdelsalam, H.M., Shoaeb, A.R., Elassal, M.M.: Enhancing Decision Model Notation (DMN) for better use in Business Analytics (BA). In: Proceedings of the 10th International Conference on Informatics and Systems, pp. 321–322. ACM (2016)

27. Batoulis, K., Meyer, A., Bazhenova, E., Decker, G., Weske, M.: Extracting decision logic from process models. In: Zdravkovic, J., Kirikova, M., Johannesson, P. (eds.) CAiSE 2015. LNCS, vol. 9097, pp. 349–366. Springer, Cham (2015). https://doi.org/10.1007/978-3-319-19069-3_22

28. Bazhenova, E., Zerbato, F., Weske, M.: Data-centric extraction of DMN Decision Models from BPMN process models. In: Teniente, E., Weidlich, M. (eds.) BPM 2017. LNBIP, vol. 308, pp. 542–555. Springer, Cham (2018). https://doi.org/10.1007/978-3-319-74030-0_43

29. Paschke, A., Könnecke, S.: A RuleML - DMN translator. In: RuleML (Supplement) (2016)

30. Bazhenova, E., Weske, M.: Deriving decision models from process models by enhanced decision mining. In: Reichert, M., Reijers, H.A. (eds.) BPM 2015. LNBIP, vol. 256, pp. 444–457. Springer, Cham (2016). https://doi.org/10.1007/978-3-319-42887-1_36

31. Bazhenova, E., Buelow, S., Weske, M.: Discovering decision models from event logs. In: Abramowicz, W., Alt, R., Franczyk, B. (eds.) BIS 2016. LNBIP, vol. 255, pp. 237–251. Springer, Cham (2016). https://doi.org/10.1007/978-3-319-39426-8_19

32. De Smedt, J., van den Broucke, S.K.L.M., Obregon, J., Kim, A., Jung, J.-Y., Vanthienen, J.: Decision mining in a broader context: an overview of the current landscape and future directions. In: Dumas, M., Fantinato, M. (eds.) BPM 2016. LNBIP, vol. 281, pp. 197–207. Springer, Cham (2017). https://doi.org/10.1007/978-3-319-58457-7_15

33. Bazhenova, E., Haarmann, S., Ihde, S., Solti, A., Weske, M.: Discovery of fuzzy DMN decision models from event logs. In: Dubois, E., Pohl, K. (eds.) CAiSE 2017. LNCS, vol. 10253, pp. 629–647. Springer, Cham (2017). https://doi.org/10.1007/978-3-319-59536-8_39

34. Mannhardt, F., de Leoni, M., Reijers, H.A., van der Aalst, W.M.P.: Decision mining revisited - discovering overlapping rules. In: Nurcan, S., Soffer, P., Bajec, M., Eder, J. (eds.) CAiSE 2016. LNCS, vol. 9694, pp. 377–392. Springer, Cham (2016). https://doi.org/10.1007/978-3-319-39696-5_23

35. Kluza, K., Wiśniewski, P., Jobczyk, K., Ligęza, A., Mroczek, A.S.: Comparison of selected modeling notations for process, decision and system modeling. In: 2017 Federated Conference on Computer Science and Information Systems (FedCSIS), pp. 1095–1098. IEEE (2017)

36. Ochoa, L., González-Rojas, O.: Analysis and re-configuration of decision logic in adaptive and data-intensive processes (short paper). In: Panetto, H., et al. (eds.) OTM 2017. LNCS, vol. 10573, pp. 306–313. Springer, Cham (2017)

37. Figl, K., Mendling, J., Tokdemir, G., Vanthienen, J.: What we know and what we do not know about DMN. Enterp. Modell. Inf. Syst. Architect. 13, 1–2 (2018)

38. Hasic, F., De Smedt, J., Vanthienen, J.: Towards assessing the theoretical complexity of the Decision Model and Notation (DMN). In: Joint Proceedings of the Radar tracks at the 18th BPMDS, the 22nd EMMSAD, and the 8th EMISA workshop, Essen, Germany, June 12–13, 2017. (2017) 64–71

39. Bock, A.: How modeling language shapes decisions: problem-theoretical arguments and illustration of an example case. In: Schmidt, R., Guédria, W., Bider, I., Guerreiro, S. (eds.) BPMDS/EMMSAD -2016. LNBIP, vol. 248, pp. 383–398. Springer, Cham (2016). https://doi.org/10.1007/978-3-319-39429-9_24

40. Hasić, F., Devadder, L., Dochez, M., Hanot, J., De Smedt, J., Vanthienen, J.: Challenges in refactoring processes to include decision modelling. In: Teniente, E., Weidlich, M. (eds.) BPM 2017. LNBIP, vol. 308, pp. 529–541. Springer, Cham (2018). https://doi.org/10.1007/978-3-319-74030-0_42

41. Batoulis, K., Nesterenko, A., Repitsch, G., Weske, M.: Decision management in the insurance industry: standards and tools. In: Proceedings of the BPM 2017 Industry Track co-located with the 15th International Conference on Business Process Management (BPM 2017), Barcelona, Spain, 10–15 September 2017, pp. 52–63 (2017)

42. Laurson, Ü., Maggi, F.M.: A tool for the analysis of DMN decision tables. In: BPM (Demos), pp. 56–60 (2016)

43. Batoulis, K., Weske, M.: A tool for checking soundness of decision-aware business processes. In: BPM (Demos). CEUR-WS.org (2017)

44. Cánovas-Segura, B., et al.: A decision support visualization tool for infection management based on BMPN and DMN. In: Valencia-García, R., et al. (eds.) CITI 2017. CCIS, pp. 158–168. Springer, Cham (2017). https://doi.org/10.1007/978-3-319-67283-0_12

45. Ghlala, R., Aouina, Z.K., Said, L.B.: Decision-making harmonization in business process: using NoSQL databases for decision rules modelling and serialization. In: 2016 4th International Conference on Control Engineering & Information Technology (CEIT), pp. 1–6. IEEE (2016)

46. Proctor, M., Tirelli, E., Sottara, D., Silver, B., Feldman, J., Gauthier, M.: The effectiveness of DMN portability. In: Proceedings of the Doctoral Consortium, Challenge, Industry Track, Tutorials and Posters @ RuleML+RR 2017, London, UK, 11–15 July 2017 (2017)

47. Pufahl, L., Wong, T.Y., Weske, M.: Design of an extensible BPMN process simulator. In: Teniente, E., Weidlich, M. (eds.) BPM 2017. LNBIP, vol. 308, pp. 782–795. Springer, Cham (2018). https://doi.org/10.1007/978-3-319-74030-0_62
48. Nikaj, A., Batoulis, K., Weske, M.: REST-enabled decision making in business process choreographies. In: Sheng, Q.Z., Stroulia, E., Tata, S., Bhiri, S. (eds.) ICSOC 2016. LNCS, vol. 9936, pp. 547–554. Springer, Cham (2016). https://doi.org/10.1007/978-3-319-46295-0_34
49. Pufahl, L., Mandal, S., Batoulis, K., Weske, M.: Re-evaluation of decisions based on events. In: Reinhartz-Berger, I., Gulden, J., Nurcan, S., Guédria, W., Bera, P. (eds.) BPMDS/EMMSAD -2017. LNBIP, vol. 287, pp. 68–84. Springer, Cham (2017). https://doi.org/10.1007/978-3-319-59466-8_5
50. Dasseville, I., Janssens, L., Janssens, G., Vanthienen, J., Denecker, M.: Combining DMN and the knowledge base paradigm for flexible decision enactment. In: RuleML 2016 Supplementary Proceedings. New York, USA, 6–9 July 2016 (2016)
51. Bazhenova, E., Weske, M.: Optimal acquisition of input data for decision taking in business processes. In: Proceedings of the Symposium on Applied Computing, pp. 703–710. ACM (2017)

Data and Knowledge:
An Interdisciplinary Approach for Air
Quality Forecast

Cheng Feng$^{(\boxtimes)}$, Wendong Wang, Ye Tian, Xiangyang Gong, and Xirong Que

State Key Lab of Networking and Switching Technology,
Beijing University of Posts and Telecommunications, Beijing, China
{fengcheng124,wdwang,yetian,xygong,rongqx}@bupt.edu.cn

Abstract. Air pollution has become a critical problem in rapidly developing countries. Prior domain knowledge combined with data mining offers new ideas for air quality prediction. In this paper, we propose an interdisciplinary approach for air quality forecast based on data mining and air mass trajectory analysis. The prediction model is composed of a temporal predictor based on local factors, a spatial predictor based on geographical factors, an air mass predictor tracking air pollutants transport corridors and an aggregator for final prediction. Experimental results based on real world data show that the cross-domain data mining method can significantly improve the prediction accuracy compared with other baselines, especially in the period of severe pollution.

Keywords: Air quality prediction · Machine learning ·
Data and knowledge · Interdisciplinary approach

1 Introduction

Air pollution may increase risks of lung and cardiovascular disease [13]. Air pollution has drawn wide attention from industry and academia [2,12,14]. Air Quality Index (AQI) quantitatively describes air quality. Factors such as industrial processes, energy production and transportation make AQI prediction a difficult task [15].

Existing AQI prediction methods can be broadly divided into two categories: physical and chemical models [5,10] and data mining [6,15,16]. Physical and chemical models can be performed without historical data, but they demand sufficient knowledge of pollution sources that is hard to achieve. With the development of sensor networks [1,4], data mining is more suitable for finding complex relationships between pollutant concentration and potential predictors, but hard to extend to other scenarios and predict extreme points.

To predict AQI of Beijing precisely, we collect air quality readings, meteorology data and weather forecast of Beijing and surrounding cities. A temporal predictor is designed based on the target station's own historical conditions.

© Springer Nature Switzerland AG 2019
C. Douligeris et al. (Eds.): KSEM 2019, LNAI 11775, pp. 796–804, 2019.
https://doi.org/10.1007/978-3-030-29551-6_70

A spatial predictor is used by considering fine particles and gas can easily spread from one place to another. The two predictors are both based on data mining using data collected from Beijing. In a wider region, an air mass predictor is designed to evaluate the transport of air pollutants in surrounding cities. To the best of our knowledge, we are the first to combine data mining with air mass trajectory model at different dimensions. Experimental results show that air mass predictor coupled with temporal predictor and spatial predictor bring significant improvements to air quality prediction. As a final result, the mean absolute error can be reduced by 44.14% on average compared with other baselines and the relative absolute error can be reduced by 44.37%.

2 Related Work

Most existing air quality prediction methods in environmental science are based on physical and chemical models. These studies usually demand some sufficient knowledge, such as the real-time emissions, the accurate description of chemical reactions [5,10] or the physical processes under the planetary boundary layer [5].

Over the past decades, some statistic models [3,9] have been employed. For example, Perez et al. use an integrated neural network model to forecast PM_{10}. However, these methods put all features into a single model, ignoring multi-dimensional nature of data.

In recent years, with the development of data mining technology, researchers achieve the air quality predictions at multiple dimensions. For example, Zheng et al. [15] use data collected from meteorological authorities to forecast air quality at space-time dimensions. Chen et al. [6] combine social web data with physical sensor data to predict smog disaster in airports. Qi et al. [16] use a unified model for interpolation, prediction, feature selection and analysis of fine-grained air quality. However, these methods ignore the meteorology principles which can make great contributions to prediction of air pollution.

3 Features Engineering

3.1 Data Correlation Analysis

Divide Beijing into grids and we assume AQI of each grid is unified. Given a collection of grids $G = G_1 \bigcup G_2$, where $u.AQI$ ($u \in G_1$) is unknown and $v.AQI$ ($v \in G_1$) can be observed, we aim to infer AQI of each grid g ($g \in G$) in next 72 h based on data sets (air quality readings ($\mathcal{U}$), meteorological data ($\mathcal{M}$) and forecasting data ($\mathcal{F}$)).

Figure 1 shows the results between target AQI and the subclasses from data sets. Figure 1(a) shows the results of correlation analysis at GY station. GY station is five kilometers away from the target area, the subclass of AQI has the strongest correlation with the target AQI, while the correlation between RHU and target AQI is very weak. Figure 1(b) shows the results of stations with different distance. When the distance is within 10 km, the correlation is relatively strong, while when the distance is more than 30 km, the correlation is relatively weak. There is a obvious positive correlation between correlation and distance. Figure 1(c) shows the results of one station at different times. There also exists a obvious positive correlation between correlation and time. After 6 h, the correlation becomes very weak, which means it would be a very hard problem to offer accurate air quality prediction in a long period of time.

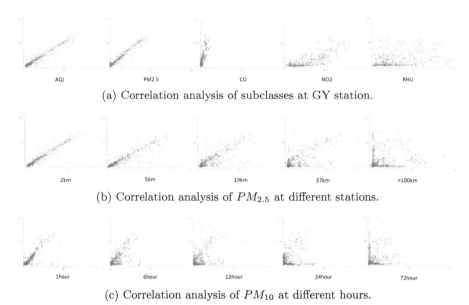

(a) Correlation analysis of subclasses at GY station.

(b) Correlation analysis of $PM_{2.5}$ at different stations.

(c) Correlation analysis of PM_{10} at different hours.

Fig. 1. Correlation analysis of the data.

3.2   Feature Construction

Temporal Feature. Every location has a lot of historical data. In this sub classifier, we only use the historical data of the target location.

Spatial Feature. We use data sets with the distance below 30 km (without the target's data) as target's surroundings. To reduce computational complexity, surroundings can be divided into four independent regions (NE,SE,SW,NW). We project other stations onto the four regions according to their geo-coordinates.

Air Mass Feature. Backward trajectories from Hybrid Single-Particle Lagrangian Integrated Trajectory (HYSPLIT) model were used to track air mass trajectories. The HYSPLIT model computes trajectories based on Global Data Assimilation System (GDAS) [8].

4   Hybrid Predictive Model

Fig. 2 shows the framework of the predictive model, consisting of four parts: temporal predictor, spatial predictor, air mass predictor and prediction aggregator.

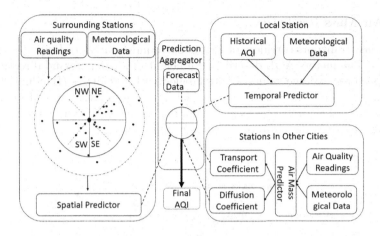

Fig. 2. Framework of the predictive model.

4.1 Temporal Predictor

We employ a linear regression to the model $y = w_0 + \sum_{i=1}^{n} w_i x_i$, where y is the target's AQI, n is the number of examples, x_i are the explanatory variables, such as $PM_{2.5}$ value of the past hour. Based on the least square method, the loss function

$$L\left(w\right) = \frac{1}{2n} \sum_{i=0}^{n} \left(y_w(x_i) - y^i\right)^2 = \frac{1}{2n} \left(XW - y\right)^T \left(XW - Y\right) \tag{1}$$

where $y_w(x_i)$ is the evaluation value, y^i is the true value of example i, X, W, Y are the matrix form of the variables.

4.2 Spatial Predictor

Given data set $\Re = \{(f_i, y_i)\} \, (|\Re| = n, f_i \in \mathbb{R}^m, y_i \in \mathbb{R})$ with n examples and m features, where $\mathbb{R}^m$ is the set of the final features and $\mathbb{R}$ is the set of AQI. We employ XGBoost [11] tree with K additive functions to predict the output $\hat{y}_i = \phi\left(f_i\right) = \sum_{k=1}^{K} \theta_k\left(f_i\right), \theta_k \in \mathbb{P}$, where $\mathbb{P} = \{\theta\left(x\right) = \omega_q\left(x\right)\} \left(q : \mathbb{R}^m \to T, \omega \in \mathbb{R}^T\right)$, q represents the structure of each tree and maps an example to the corresponding leaf index. T is the number of leaves. θ_k describes an independent tree with structure q and leaf weights ω. Score on ith leaf can be defined as ω_i. The regularized objective can be defined as the minimum value of the $\mathbb{L}\left(\phi\right)$

$$\mathbb{L}\left(\phi\right) = \sum_i l\left(\hat{y}_i, y_i\right) + \sum_k \gamma T + \frac{1}{2}\lambda \left\|\omega\right\|^2 \tag{2}$$

4.3 Air Mass Predictor

We tracked transport corridors of 24 h in surrounding areas of Beijing, as shown in Fig. 3. The meters AGL describes the height of air mass, wind direction and wind speed are average values. Cities labeled with red circles (Baoding, Tianjin and Tangshan) are industrial zones, which may cause large air pollution while the city labeled with green circle (Zhangjiakou) is considered as the major air pollutant diffusion direction of Jing-Jin-Ji region [12].

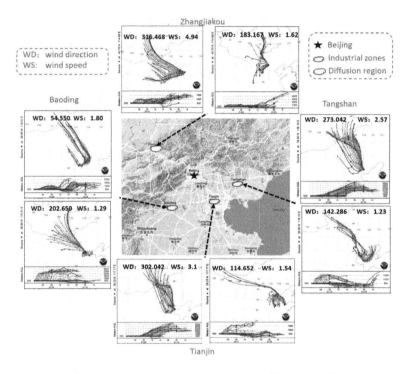

Fig. 3. Air mass trajectory analysis based on HYSPLIT.

We use two kinds of attributes to evaluate the air pollutant transportation and diffusion over the Jing-Jin-Ji region.

Transport Coefficient $T_A = C * WS_A * f_A \left(\cos \left(WD_A - D_A \right) \right) * AQI_A$, where C is a constant, WS_A and WD_A represent wind speed and wind direction of city A, D_A is the direction from A to Beijing, AQI_A is air pollutants concentration, f_A is used to describe the relationship between transmission characteristics and wind direction of city A. A linear fitting method is used to calculate f_A, the line is defined as $f_A \left(x \right) = ax + b$ and passes through two points $(1, MAXT)$, $(-1, MINT)$. $MAXT$ is the percentage of trajectories between A and Beijing to trajectories of all when the wind is on D_A, while when the wind is on the opposite direction, we can get $MINT$ in the same way.

The *Diffusion Coefficient* based on air pollutant diffusion direction can be defined as $D = C*WS*(1 + cos(WD - D_{diffusion}))$, where C is a constant, WS and WD represent the wind speed and wind direction, $D_{diffusion}$ is the diffusion direction, in this study, $D_{diffusion}$ is the direction from Beijing to Zhangjiakou.

4.4 Prediction Aggregator

Prediction aggregator is an artificial neural network (ANN) model based on multilayer perceptron (MLP) [7] and back propagation. Purelin function is used as the transfer function in the hidden layer. There are 13 variables in the input layer, including values provided by temporal and spatial predictors, transport and diffusion coefficients calculated by air mass predictor, forecast features published by meteorological authorities, timestamp (day of year and hour of day).

5 Evaluations

5.1 Experiment Settings

Data Sets. We collect data in Jng-Jin-Ji region, 2016/2/1-2017/3/10 (Table 1). Air quality readings record $PM_{2.5}$, PM_{10}, SO_2, NO_2, CO and O_3 concentrations. Meteorological data has 17 attributes related to wind, atmospheric pressure, temperature and humidity. Forecast data includes weather conditions, temperature, humidity, wind speed, wind direction and atmospheric pressure.

Table 1. Data sets details (Beijing, Tianjin, Tangshan, Baoding, Zhangjiakou).

Data Sets	Air Quality Readings					Meteorological Data					Forecast
Cities	BJ	TJ	TS	BD	ZJK	BJ	TJ	TS	BD	ZJK	BJ
Stations	35	14	12	7	10	18	12	5	7	11	15
Instances	336520	135408	115390	67498	96443	163664	115776	45490	63679	100094	46360
Interval	1h	1h	1h	1h	1h	1h	1h	1h	1h	1h	3h

Evaluation Indexes and Ground Truth. The ground truth of a station can be obtained from its later readings. As shown in Table 1, there are 35 stations in Beijing and the cross validation method is used. For the next 1–72 h, we measure the prediction of each hour $\widetilde{\sigma}_i$ against its ground truth σ_i with mean absolute error $e = \frac{\sum_i |\widetilde{\sigma}_i - \sigma_i|}{n}$ and relative absolute error $p = \frac{\sum_i |\widetilde{\sigma}_i - \sigma_i|}{\sum_i \sigma_i}$.

Baselines. (1) *Single Model:* linear regression (LR), gaussian process for regression (GP), and regression tree (RT). These baselines are used to justify the preference for using multiple models of different dimensions. (2)*Subsets:* This set of baselines justifies the necessity of each component of our method, e.g., temporal predictor (TP), spatial predictor (SP), and use all of them (TSA).

Table 2. Results with combined multiple models.

TIME	1-hour		3-hour		6-hour		12-hour		18-hour		24-hour		48-hour		72-hour	
MODEL	e	p	e	p	e	p	e	p	e	p	e	p	e	p	e	p
TP	8.8	0.11	25.4	0.32	39.5	0.49	54.9	0.67	65.1	0.79	66.0	0.81	67.9	0.85	71.0	0.88
SP	16.7	0.21	23.0	0.29	36.1	0.45	52.8	0.64	68.2	0.83	67.6	0.83	73.5	0.92	75.2	0.93
TP+SP	7.9	0.10	22.3	0.28	32.8	0.41	42.5	0.52	46.6	0.57	59.5	0.73	66.4	0.83	68.3	0.85
TSA	**3.9**	**0.05**	**18.7**	**0.24**	**29.7**	**0.37**	**30.8**	**0.38**	**31.2**	**0.38**	**44.3**	**0.54**	**43.0**	**0.53**	**48.9**	**0.61**

5.2   Results

Fig. 4 shows 12 h (e: 30.8, p: 0.38) and 72 h (e: 48.9, p: 0.61) predictions against the ground truth. As shown in Table 2, TP and SP have similar accuracy except 1 h. As time goes on, TSA outperforms TP and SP obviously. The air mass predictor and forecast data coupled with TP and SP bring improvements to air quality prediction.

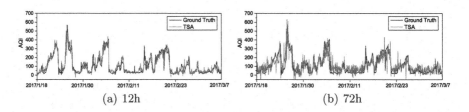

(a) 12h   (b) 72h

Fig. 4. Predictions vs groundtruth (GY Station, Beijing, 2017/1/18-2017/3/10).

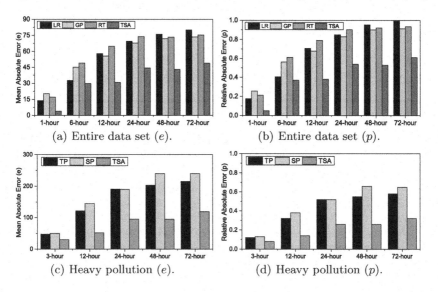

(a) Entire data set (e).   (b) Entire data set (p).

(c) Heavy pollution (e).   (d) Heavy pollution (p).

Fig. 5. Results of different data sets.

TSA outperforms all the baselines as shown in Fig. 5(a) and (b). The results justify the validity of multi-dimensional model compared with single model. The accurate prediction of heavy pollution can make great sense of protecting people from air pollutants. We use data of heavy pollution ($AQI > 300$) to justify the contribution of air mass predictor. As shown in Fig. 5(c) and (d), TP and SP make no senses for heavy pollution after 24 h, but TSA still keeps an acceptable accuracy even after 72 h.

6   Conclusion and Future Work

In this paper, we utilize multiple data sources including air quality readings, meteorological data and forecast data to forecast air quality in Beijing. We model the forecasting problem with methods from two unrelated academic areas: data mining methods based on data-driven models and the methods from atmospheric dynamics. In the future, we plan to further improve the prediction accuracy by considering the different chemical composition of air pollutants and the physical and chemical processes happened among the air pollutants.

Acknowledgement. This work was supported by National Natural Science Foundation of China (Grant No.61602051).

References

1. Zhang, B., et al.: Learning-based energy-efficient data collection by unmannedvehicles in smart cities. IEEE Trans. Industr. Inf. **14**(4), 1666–1676 (2018)
2. Feng, C., et al.: Estimate air quality based on mobile crowd sensing and big data. IEEE WoWMoM (2017)
3. Stadlober, E., et al.: Quality and performance of a PM10 daily forecasting model. Atmos. Environ. **42**(6), 1098–1109 (2008)
4. Gao, H., et al.: A survey of incentive mechanisms for participatory sensing. IEEE Commun. Surv. Tutorials (2017)
5. Djalalova, I., et al.: PM2.5 analog forecast and Kalman filter post-processing for the community multiscale air quality (CMAQ) model. Atmos. Environ. **108**, 76–87 (2015)
6. Chen, J., et al.: Smog disaster forecasting using social web data and physical sensor data. In: IEEE Big Data (2015)
7. Tang, J., et al.: Extreme learning machine for multilayer perceptron. IEEE Trans. Neural Networks Learn. Syst. **27**(4), 809–821 (2016)
8. Buehner, M.J., et al.: Four-dimensional ensemble-variational data assimilation for global deterministic weather prediction. Nonlinear Process. Geophys. **20**(5), 669–682 (2013)
9. Perez, P., et al.: An integrated neural network model for PM10 forecasting. Atmos. Environ. **40**(16), 2845–2851 (2006)
10. Kota, S.H., et al.: Evaluation of on-road vehicle CO and NO_x National Emission Inventories using an urban-scale source-oriented air quality model. Atmos. Environ. **82**, 99–108 (2014)

11. Chen, T., et al.: Xgboost: a scalable tree boosting system. In: ACM SIGKDD International Conference (2016)
12. Feng, X., et al.: Formation and dominant factors of haze pollution over Beijing and its peripheral areas in winter. Atmos. Pollut. Res. **5**(3), 528–538 (2014)
13. Morelli, X., et al.: Air pollution, health and social deprivation: a fine-scalerisk assessment. Environ. Res. **147**, 59–70 (2016)
14. Zheng, Y., et al.: U-air: When urban air quality inference meets big data. In: ACM SIGKDD International Conference (2013)
15. Zheng, Y., et al.: Forecasting fine-grained air quality based on big data. In: ACM SIGKDD International Conference (2015)
16. Qi, Z., et al.: Deep air learning: Interpolation, prediction, and feature analysis of air quality. IEEE Trans. Knowl. Data Eng. **30**(12), 2285–2297 (2018)

A Multi-label Active Learning Approach for Mobile App User Review Classification

Montassar Ben Messaoud[1], Ilyes Jenhani[2(✉)], Nermine Ben Jemaa[1], and Mohamed Wiem Mkaouer[3]

[1] LARODEC, ISG Tunis, Bardo, Tunisia
{montassar.benmassaoud,n.benjemaa}@isgs.u-sousse.tn
[2] College of Computer Engineering and Science,
Prince Mohammad Bin Fahd University, Khobar, Kingdom of Saudi Arabia
ijenhani@pmu.edu.sa
[3] Rochester Institute of Technology, Rochester, NY, USA
mwmvse@rit.edu

Abstract. User reviews of mobile applications convey useful feedback from users, e.g. feature requests, bug descriptions, etc. The increasing number of reviews that users submit daily makes it difficult for developers to manually analyze and classify them into proper review categories. Moreover, several review messages may contain more than one information. In this paper, we propose to use multi-label active learning as a convenient solution to the problem of mobile app user reviews classification. An unlabeled and structured dataset was built from the initially unstructured large set of review messages. Moreover, in order to reduce the effort needed to assign labels to each instance in the large constructed dataset, we opted for an Active Learning approach. Experimental results have shown that, by actively querying an oracle for labels during training a binary relevance-based classifier (with logistic regression as a base classifier), we obtained a classifier that outperformed well-known classifiers in terms of performance without the need to label the whole dataset.

1 Introduction

In this era of explosions in technological advances, with ever evolving technology at our fingertips, mobile applications (apps)[1] have become an indispensable part of our lives. A mobile application is not just a need but has become a necessity as well. These applications are available from mobile application distribution platforms (e.g., *Google Play Store, Apple App Store, etc.*) which provides app users with a variety of apps and services that are easy to search, download, and install. Users may also express their experience with the app through providing comments and reviews to the downloaded applications by giving a star rating and a textual feedback, and both are visible for public.

---

[1] For sake of simplicity, we will use the short name "app" to refer to a mobile application throughout this paper.

© Springer Nature Switzerland AG 2019
C. Douligeris et al. (Eds.): KSEM 2019, LNAI 11775, pp. 805–816, 2019.
https://doi.org/10.1007/978-3-030-29551-6_71

Mobile application reviews (or App reviews for short) are not only indicators that users rely on to finalize their purchasing decisions but also provide a rich source of information for the app programmers to better understand users' perceptions of their app and make the necessary changes and fixed to meet their requirements and desires. Therefore, app reviews is considered as a main source for enriching the backlog for the future updates of the app along with shaping it towards the accomplishment of various app improvement and maintenance tasks, for instance, adding new features or improving existing ones, fixing reported bugs and crashes, enhancing the app interface design and usability based on reported user experiences. Every day users leave a huge amount of reviews which makes it difficult for developers to filter relevant information. Moreover, those reviews may contain a lot of useless feedback like offensive material, spam, insulting comment and advertisement for other apps. Consequently, developers spend a long time searching for useful reviews among the huge number of available messages instead of focusing on other matters. Based on these observations, we propose an automated approach to the classification of user reviews to improve the efficiency of developers in maintaining their apps and making them suitable for the users' needs.

The classification and extraction of useful information contained in user reviews have been proposed in the literature but the majority of the existing studies handled the problem using multi-class classification where each review cannot belong to more than one category/class. Few studies [1,2] have used multi-label classification as a solution to allow reviews to be classified into multiple classes at the same time. Although existing studies focused on accurately classifying reviews, it is important to note that no research has considered the issue of annotating the abundant unlabeled data that developers are exposed to. In fact, unlabeled data is relatively easy to acquire through the daily received reviews, but labels are difficult, time-consuming, and expensive to obtain. In this context, Active Learning (AL) algorithms have emerged to solve this problem. With AL, it is possible to achieve similar (or greater) performance to using a fully labeled data-set with a fraction of the cost or time that it takes to label all the data and with fewer training labels.

In this paper, we address the classification diversity by enabling reviews to be multi-labeled. The expensive task related to the manual labeling of training instances is addressed by a multi-label active learning approach. The evaluation of our approach has demonstrated its ability to achieve an accuracy of 76%, outperforming other off-the-shelf classifiers with a reduced number of labeled training instances. We also provide the community with a labeled dataset as part of our replication package[2]. This paper is organized as follows: Sect. 2 introduces basic background knowledge relative to the different concepts used in our approach. Section 3 briefly overviews the different works related to the classification of user reviews. A detailed description of the proposed approach is provided in Sect. 4. The experimental design and results are outlined in Sect. 5. Finally, Sect. 6 draws conclusions and exposes future studies.

---

[2] https://smilevo.github.io/mareva/.

2 Background

2.1 App Review

User reviews serve as a communication channel between programmers and the actual app users. A user review (a.k.a App review in context of mobile application) refers to a review written by a user to express a particular attitude, opinion, position, impression based on his/her experience as user of the reviewed application. This review consists of a textual part and a quantitative part. Generally, the textual part includes the title and the body of the review. The quantitative part represents the metadata which is displayed on the app page or appearing on the search results. The star rating (on a scale of 1 to 5 stars) or the submission time is the most common.

Reviews are also valuable to developers and all software companies interested in analyzing user reviews and feedback. These reviews are crucial because the developer can easily know which bugs or problems the app is facing, which features need to be improved, and which ones need to be prioritized in the next update. In [3], authors demonstrated that developers who read and analyze user reviews are rewarded in terms of ratings.

App reviews have attracted much attention in the literature, different automated approaches has been proposed to classify app reviews into several types. In this paper, we aim at proposing an approach to classify user reviews into one or more classes from the following list of categories:

- **Bug reports**. Reviews that report app issues which should be fixed in the next update like crashes, erroneous behaviors, or performance issues.
- **Feature requests**. Reviews written by users to ask for missing/new features or missing content and request for improving existing features.
- **User experiences**. Reviews that describe what users felt while using the app.

2.2 Text Pre-processing via Natural Language Processing

In the last decade Natural Language Processing (NLP) and Machine learning have developed enormously and yet, we are able to comprehend natural language most of the time. In this paper, we used NLP techniques for text pre-processing. Pre-processing the reviews with common NLP techniques can help increase the classification accuracy of reviews. The NLP techniques used in this paper are briefly described in what follows.

Stopword Removal. Stopwords represent those words which appear frequently in text but which do not add any extra sense (e.g. the, in, that, of, are, is, those, for, etc) in a sentence. The removal of these stopwords from the review messages makes feature extraction techniques more focused on more informative terms like "issue" or "update".

Stemming and Lemmatization. When writing texts, grammatical rules force us to use different forms of a word (e.g. nouns, adjectives, adverbs, verbs, with added prefixes or suffixes, etc.). To enhance the performance of our app review classification approach, we used the stemming and lemmatization techniques to only keep one keyword that represents a set of keywords having the same meaning but written in different forms. **Stemming** usually refers to reducing the inflected words to their stem (basic) form by removing its postfix (e.g., *"goods" is replaced with "good"*). **Lemmatization** is the process that maps the various forms of a word to the canonical or citation form of the word, also known as the lexeme or lemma [4]. For instance, "changing", "changed", and "changes" become "change".

Bigrams. Sometimes word groups provide more benefits than only one word when explaining the meaning. A bigram is an n-gram (n = 2). Considering this sentence: "The app crashes frequently", we can split this sentence into three bigrams: "The, app", "app, crashes", "crashes, frequently". Besides, we can distinguish between these two bigrams "crashes frequently" and "never crashes" which are semantically different and can reveal two different review categories.

2.3   Multi-label Classification

Classification is a central topic in machine learning. It can be defined as the task of predicting the label(s) of unseen instances by using a model trained on a set of labeled instances (i.e. with known class labels) [5]. For many problems, e.g., bio-informatics, image labeling, sentiment analysis, music categorization and text mining, it has been shown that the standard multi-class approach is not appropriate since each training instance could be labeled with a subset of labels instead of a single label from a set of possible labels. This approach is known as multi-label classification. In the context of user review classification, in the multi-class setting, a review can be either classified as a bug report or a feature request but not both at the same time. Whereas, with multi-label classification, a review can be assigned more than one class at the same time (e.g. bug report and feature request) which is usually as it will be shown later.

2.4   Multi-label Active Learning

In supervised learning, classifiers are built from a fully labeled training sets. Some approaches aim at reducing the amount of time and effort needed to label a full training set. AL is one of these approaches [6]. AL helps reduce the cost induced by the labeling process. In fact, during an active learning process, the learner will ask the help of an oracle (e.g. a subject matter expert) to obtain the labels of selected unlabeled instances. Usually, the selected instances are those that the learner struggles with their classification. Doing so, AL can reduce the labeling effort by minimizing the total number of needed training instances, especially for large datasets and complicated problem domains. Initially, AL has

Table 1. Summary of studies about user review classification

Study	Sing/mult	Auto?	Classification method	Category
Panichella et al. 2015	Single	Yes	NLP text analysis sentiment analysis	Opinion asking/Information giving/Information seeking/Problem discovery/Feature request/Solution proposal
Guzman et al. [1]	Multi	Yes	Machine learning classifier	Bug report/User request/Usage scenario/Feature shortcoming/Feature strength/Complaints/Praise/Noise
Maalej et al. [8]	Single	Yes	Machine learning classifier	Feature requests/Bug reports/Ratings/User experiences
Deocadez et al. [7]	Single	Yes	Semi-supervised classification techniques	Functional non-functional
Zhang et al. [2]	Multi	Yes	Cost-sensitive learning method	Crashing/Update issue/Installation issue/Response time/Compatibility issue/Additional cost/Feature request/Network connection issue/Property safety/Content complaint/Privacy and ethical issue/Feature removal/Resource heavy/Functional complaint/User interface/Traffic wasting/Other
Our work 2019	**Multi-label**	**Yes**	**Multi-label active learning**	**Feature requests/Bug reports/User experiences**

been developed to support multi-class classification, where each training instance is labeled with one and only one class label. Several AL approaches have been proposed in the literature [6]. The most popular approach is the so-called *Pool-based sampling* where a large pool of unlabeled data is available. Instances to be queried for labeling will be selected from the pool based on some informativeness measure [6]. In this paper we use this most commonly used AL approach because we already have a large set of unlabeled reviews to learn from.

3 Related Work

Throughout its lifetime, the app is expected to continually improve and evolve to ensure its efficiency, utility and desirability to users. Thus, app developers need to continuously monitor and respond to the needs of their users in terms of newly requested features and/or bug-fix demands. A readily available resource for finding information about the users needs is the analysis if user app reviews. It is common to find users suggesting new features to meet their specific needs and users reporting some bugs or problems which need to be fixed in the next update. With this in mind, many efforts have been striving to manage the huge amount of information included in the app reviews and to classify them into appropriate classes. Different user review classification approaches have been proposed. We summarize the studies related to these approaches in Table 1. Some approaches have used a limited set of classes, for example, [7] introduced a novel approach that can help app developers to automatically classify apps reviews into two categories of functional and non-functional requirements using semi-supervised learning unlike [2] which proposed more extensive set of classes with 17 types of issues in a Chinese app store.

4   Methodology

Our App review classification approach is made up of 4 phases, as depicted in Fig. 1.

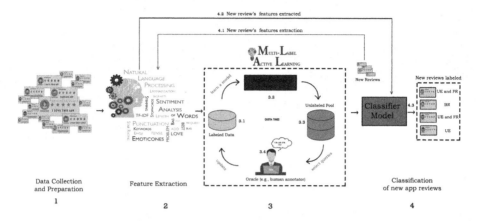

Fig. 1. The app user review classification process

4.1   Phase 1: Data Collection and Preparation

Due to the incredibly large total number of apps, only a small portion of apps need to be considered in our study. Firstly, we used a custom web crawler to automatically extract user reviews for different apps which fall into several categories (e.g., *multimedia, internet, security, games, etc.*) from the GitHub. In total, we collected 111143 reviews. All the available metadata (such as app purchase display name, submission date, app category, reviewer name and ratings) were also collected. Secondly, to create a representative dataset, we cleaned this dataset by removing the reviews which are not written in English. We also removed reviews that only contain numbers or non-character symbols. Next, we selected a random sample containing around 30000 reviews. From the initially selected 30000 reviews, we removed the user reviews which are shorter than 20 characters-long because these reviews are usually less informative and irrelevant for the developers. We ended up with a dataset of 10982 reviews.

4.2   Phase 2: Feature Extraction

In this section, we present the features that we have found in previous studies and we propose new ones that we believe are useful for the classification step.

Keywords-Related Features. The review is a textual message which is composed of multiple keywords. Some of these keywords are relevant and can help determine the category of the review. For this purpose, we use two different techniques, namely, String matching [8] and the Bag of words [8]. The String matching is a simple static technique used to check whether the review contains certain keywords. We compiled from the literature [8] a list of keywords associated with the appropriate review type and we extended this list with additional keywords. A sample of selected keywords includes: bug, problem, error, issue, fix, etc. (for bug reports); add, suggest, wish, change, request, etc. (for feature requests) and great, nice, help, cool, etc. (for user experience).

Bag of words is a technique used to automatically identifying and weighing the keywords using a supervised machine-learning approach. Before running the bag of words step, we must conduct some text preprocessing steps in order to reduce the noise from text data, identify the root word for the different words in text corpus and reduce the size of the text data. We used NLTK[3] (Natural Language ToolKit) which is a well-known NLP library written in Python.

We began our text preprocessing by applying the **Stemming** by using the PorterStemmer[4]. Then, we applied the **Lemmatization** using the Word-NetLemmatizer[5]. After finishing the text preprocessing step, we used TF-IDF (Term Frequency-Inverse Document Frequency) which assesses the importance of a word in a review message. We have used TF-IDF with word pairs called bigrams to better apprehend the context of the word in the review message.

Star Rating. The score provided by the app user (ranges from 1 to 5).

Tense. The past is narrative tense used for reporting and description, so the past might reveal a bug report or a user experience. **The future** tense is used for promise or a hypothetical scenario. Future might reveal an enhancement on existing feature or a feature request. Additionally, modal verbs (i.e., can, could, may, might, shall, should, will, would, must) might also reveal a feature request or an improvement of some features of the application.

Punctuation. Punctuation is vital to disambiguate the meaning of sentences. In our study, we focus on exclamation and interrogation marks that can prove to be strong indicators of opinions.

Length. In [9] Vasa et al. analyzed a large dataset of user reviews and found that user review length is characterized by an average of 117 characters and median at 69 characters. Therefore, the review length can also be considered as a reliable feature for the review classification where lengthy reviews are more likely to indicate user experience description and/or a bug report [8].

---

[3] https://www.nltk.org.
[4] https://www.nltk.org/api/nltk.stem.html.
[5] https://www.nltk.org/modules/nltk/stem/wordnet.html.

Sentiment Analysis-Based Feature. Analyzing user sentiments towards apps can be very profitable to app developers. App reviews usually reflect the positive and negative emotions of app users. The negative sentiment may reveal a bug report while positive sentiment may reveal a user experience. To extract the reviewer's sentiment for a given message, we used TextBlob[6] which is a Python library for processing textual data.

Emoticons. Emoticons (a.k.a, Emoji or smiley faces) represent a valuable feature which can substantially prove to be strong indicators of opinion. Currently, emoticons became an established common part of people's digital communication like e-mails, text messages, blogs and forums. This emoticons are also used in review message and can indicate the review type. For this reason, we created a dictionary of 248 different emojis and labeled them manually (positive, negative and neutral).

4.3 Phase 3: Multi-label Active Learning

Labeling all the review messages we have in our dataset is very time-consuming. A solution to avoid labeling all the reviews in our dataset is to use AL [6]. Compared with standard supervised learning algorithms, AL algorithms requires much lower number of labeled instances and actively query an oracle for labels during the learning process. For this reason, we used Libact [10] which is a Python package that implements several AL algorithms (also called query strategies) for Multi-label Classification. These include Binary Minimization (BinMin), Maximal Loss Reduction with Maximal Confidence (MMC), Multi-label Active Learning With Auxiliary Learner (MLALAL), etc. [10].

MLALAL is the most generalized framework that aims to address some limitations of MMC. In particular, this framework is composed of two learners. The first is called "major learner" which is used for making predictions. The second learner, namely, "auxiliary learner" is used in helping the query decisions. In addition, MLALAL uses a query criterion that measures the disagreement between the two learners [11]. We chose to use the MLALAL query strategy for our approach that we label Multi-label Active REView clAssification (MAREVA). The simple reason for adopting MLALAL query strategy for our MAREVA is that it is a general framework and both MMC and BinMin are special cases of MLALAL. Regarding the major learner, we chose the binary relevance with logistic regression as a base classifier. For the auxiliary learner, we chose binary relevance with support vector machines as a base classifier.

In this work, we used the Hamming loss reduction, a commonly-used loss function for multi-label classification [12]. More details about the setting of the multi-label active learning phase parameters will be provided in the experimentation section.

---

[6] https://textblob.readthedocs.io/en/dev/quickstart.html.

4.4   Phase 4: Classification of New Reviews

In this phase, the trained and built logistic regression model is be used to classify new review messages. For each message, the values of all the above-described features are calculated. Hence, the review message is transformed into a vector of feature values. The vector is then be handled by the classifier model, and its corresponding review type(s) are determined.

5   Experimentations

5.1   Experimental Setup and Dataset Description

As previously mentioned in Sect. 4.1, we conducted our experimentation on a dataset containing 10982 real reviews. These reviews correspond to different apps that have been developed between 2009 and 2017. The selected apps belong to different categories. In addition to the review messages, associated metadata (e.g., app name, app category, app developer, etc.) has been also extracted.

We have conducted an initial peer labeling of around 500 reviews. During this task, each review message was presented to two annotators working together at one workstation. Both annotators have in-depth knowledge of application review analysis and software engineering. Both read the review message and propose the associated class label(s). When they disagree, the proposed class label sets are merged. After that, we used Libact [10] Python package for the active learning (AL) step. Parameters of the selected AL approach are provided in what follows: **Query Strategy:** Multi-label AL With Auxiliary Learner; **Query Criterion:** Hamming Loss Reduction; **Major Learner:** Logistic Regression; **Auxiliary Learner:** Support Vector Machine (SVM); **Quota:** Based on several tests and on the size of our dataset, we chose to select 20 instances per iteration; **Stopping Criterion:** One possible stopping criterion could be the total number of queried instances. Another one could be the aimed performance value. For our study, we opted to perform 100 iterations and label 20% of the original dataset.

5.2   Results and Analyses

AL algorithms are usually evaluated by showing their underlying classification performance curves, which plot the performance value as a function of the running total of completed iterations [6]. For our experiments, we generated two curves: one for the hamming loss HL (Loss) and the other one for the F-measure. We performed 100 iterations. During each iteration, the two annotators were queried to label 20 instances. We ended up with 2000 additional labeled reviews.

As shown in Fig. 2, the curve is represented with a fluctuating red line showing the progress of the loss throughout 100 iterations. Generally, the loss decreases as the number of iterations increases. It falls quickly at first from 0.27 to 0.24 then goes down at a slower rate. This confirms that AL carefully selects the instances to label in each iteration which was not the case for our random selection of the initial 500 instances. The best score was obtained at the 82nd iteration.

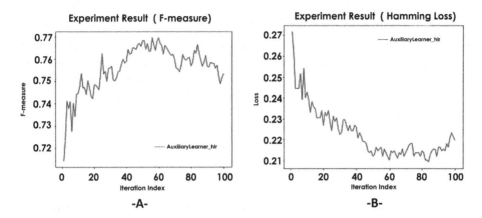

Fig. 2. F-measure (-A-) and Hamming Loss (-B-) scores across 100 iterations.

The slight increase in the loss after the 82nd iteration explains that the newly labeled reviews were not consistent with the previously labeled ones which means that these reviews were not easy to label by the two annotators. Moreover, Fig. 2 shows that the score of F-measure increases when the number of iterations increases. We started our experimentation with a 0.71 F1 score and we ended up with 0.75. However, the best overall score of 0.77 was reached at the 56th and at the 60th iterations.

As can be noticed, both curves show fluctuations throughout the scale due to the complexity of the problem. In fact, the human annotators (resp. the classifier itself) faced difficulties in labeling (resp. classifying) many of the reviews due to their low quality (i.e. informativeness, syntax, etc.). Moreover, it could be explained by the fact that there are many keywords that can pertain to different categories. For instance, when a word like "...issue" is detected..." in a review message, the classifier will most likely classify it as a bug report. However, in a message like: "it would be helpful to issue alerts...", clearly this is a feature request. Thus, the variety of the semantic of some keywords may increase the ambiguity and thus makes the classification task harder.

In another experiment, we reported the performance of MAREVA with that of the binary relevance multi-label approach using the following base classifiers: Decision Trees (TREE), K-Nearest Neighbors (KNN), Multilayer Perceptron Neural Networks (MLP) and Random Forests (RF). The choice of the base classifiers was based on their good fit with the binary relevance wrapper method [1,13]. For the multi-label approach, we used One-Vs-The-Rest strategy which corresponds to the implementation of binary relevance in the Scikit-learn library. This strategy consists in fitting one classifier per class. For each classifier, the class is fitted against all the other classes.

Figure 3 shows the HL and F1 values for the five approaches including MAREVA. The reported values are the result of a 10-folds cross validation testing strategy.

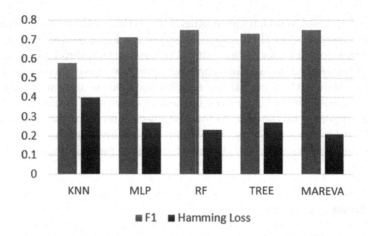

Fig. 3. Comparison of F1 (F-measure) and Hamming Loss (HL) values of MAREVA with those of other well-known classifiers.

Overall, we can notice that both MAREVA and RF outperform other classifiers by reaching an F-measure score of 0.75. In terms of loss, our approach shows a low HL value compared to the other classifiers. It is noticeable that KNN is showing the worst performance with a loss value reaching 0.4. This could be explained by the non appropriateness of the distance measure used with KNN. We believe that with a semantic distance, the performance of KNN could improve. On the other hand, MLP, TREE and RF show acceptable performances with respectively 0.27, 0.27 and 0.23 loss values. This is an interesting finding. In fact, it is not surprising that MAREVA slightly outperforms the other approaches since during the active learning process, the annotators helped the major and auxiliary learners (logistic regression and SVM) in classifying the "difficult" instances by labeling them. The good performance of the other approaches (TREE, RF and MLP) shows that the MLALAL strategy helps obtain a training set which is not only good for the major and auxiliary classifiers it uses.

6 Research Discussion and Conclusions

In this paper, we tackled the problem of classifying user reviews using a multi-label active learning solution. The use of multi-label classification has allowed a partial mitigation of the human bias in classifying user reviews. Initially, after performing the literature review, we adopted the four classes as defined in [8] i.e., Bug reports, Feature requests, User experiences and Rating. Generally, reviewers tend to express their emotions, their impression and their attitude when describing their experience. So, the classifier tends to return several cases of these messages during the iterations. To mitigate the ambiguity of these classes, we merged these two classes in one class which we called *User experience*. In the future, we plan on further improving our classification by taking into account the developer responses to reviews as another feature that enforces the learning process of our classifier since their responses can be used as a relevance indicator for reviews which contain information critical to the app that developers care about enough to respond. Also, another challenge which we have encountered during our classification, is the fact that few reviews may become outdated as they may describe features that no longer exist in the app or criticize technologies that are no longer supported by the app. As for now, there is no systematic way to detect these outlying reviews and thus, we plan on further investigating the possibility of correlating reviews with the current change logs publicly available for some of the apps.

References

1. Guzman, E., El-Haliby, M., Bruegge, B.: Ensemble methods for app review classification: an approach for software evolution (N). In: 30th IEEE/ACM International Conference on Automated Software Engineering, pp. 771–776 (2015)
2. Zhang, L., Huang, X., Jiang, J., Hu, Y.: CSLabel: an approach for labelling mobile app reviews. J. Comput. Sci. Technol. **32**(6), 1076–1089 (2017)
3. Palomba, F., et al.: Crowdsourcing user reviews to support the evolution of mobile apps. J. Syst. Softw. **137**, 143–162 (2018)
4. Bird, S., Klein, E., Loper, E.: Natural Language Processing with Python: Analyzing Text with the Natural Language Toolkit. O'Reilly Media Inc., Sebastopol (2009)
5. Herrera, F., Charte, F., Rivera, A.J., del Jesus, M.J.: Multilabel Classification - Problem Analysis, Metrics and Techniques. Springer, Cham (2016). https://doi.org/10.1007/978-3-319-41111-8
6. Settles, B.: Active learning literature survey. University of Wisconsin-Madison, Computer Sciences Technical report 1648 (2009)
7. Deocadez, R., Harrison, R., Rodríguez, D.: Automatically classifying requirements from app stores: a preliminary study. In: IEEE 25th International Requirements Engineering Conference Workshops, pp. 367–371 (2017)
8. Maalej, W., Kurtanovic, Z., Nabil, H., Stanik, C.: On the automatic classification of app reviews. Requirements Eng. **21**(3), 311–331 (2016)
9. Vasa, R., Hoon, L., Mouzakis, K., Noguchi, A.: A preliminary analysis of mobile app user reviews. In: Proceedings of the 24th Australian Computer-Human Interaction Conference, pp. 241–244 (2012)
10. Yang, Y., Lee, S., Chung, Y., Wu, T., Chen, S., Lin, H.: libact: pool-based active learning in python, vol. 6. CoRR (2017)
11. Hung, C.-W., Lin, H.-T.: Multi-label active learning with auxiliary learner. In: Asian Conference on Machine Learning, pp. 315–332 (2011)
12. Tai, F., Lin, H.-T.: Multilabel classification with principal label space transformation. Neural Comput. **24**(9), 2508–2542 (2012)
13. Zhang, M.-L., Zhou, Z.: A review on multi-label learning algorithms. IEEE Trans. Knowl. Data Eng. **26**(8), 1819–1837 (2014)

A Causality-Based Approach to Assessing Inconsistency for Multi-context Systems

Kedian Mu[(✉)]

School of Mathematical Sciences, Peking University,
Beijing 100871, People's Republic of China
mukedian@math.pku.edu.cn

Abstract. Nonmonotonic multi-context systems provide a promising starting point to interlink heterogeneous and decentralized knowledge contexts effectively by modeling the information exchange among contexts instead of logics of contexts uniformly by virtue of bridge rules. Inconsistency handling has been considered as one of the important issues in multi-context systems, since inconsistency makes a multi-context system useless. In this paper, we propose an approach to assessing the responsibility of each bridge rule of a multi-context system for the inconsistency of that system, which helps us better understand roles of bridge rules involved in inconsistency from the point of view of causality.

Keywords: Inconsistency · Multi-context systems · Causality

1 Introduction

The need of interlinking heterogeneous and decentralized knowledge contexts increasingly arises when a variety of knowledge is elicited or mined from data effectively. Nonmonotonic multi-context systems introduced by Brewka and Eiter [1,2] provide a good starting point to interlink heterogeneous and decentralized knowledge contexts. Instead of unifying logics of different contexts, multi-context systems model inter-contextual information exchange in a uniform way by bridge rules for cases where different contexts may use different logics and reasoning mechanisms. Roughly speaking, the bridge rule is similar to the logic programming rule in the form, which consists of two parts, i.e., the head and the body of the rule. Given a bridge rule, its head gives the context it belongs to and the information content that would be added to the context once the access of the context to others allowed by the body of rule is activated.

The notion of equilibrium has been proposed as semantics for multi-context systems [1]. Informally speaking, an equilibrium for a given multi-context system is a sequence of belief sets (each corresponding to a context in that system) such that each belief set is acceptable to the corresponding context when the knowledge base of the context is updated by all applicable bridge rules of the context in the sequence of belief sets.

© Springer Nature Switzerland AG 2019
C. Douligeris et al. (Eds.): KSEM 2019, LNAI 11775, pp. 817–828, 2019.
https://doi.org/10.1007/978-3-030-29551-6_72

Given a multi-context system, if there is no equilibrium for that system, we say that the multi-context system is inconsistent [4,5]. Inconsistency handling has been considered as one of the most important issues in multi-context systems because inconsistency makes a multi-context system useless. The dual notions of inconsistency explanation and diagnosis [4,5] have been introduced to characterize the inconsistency for multi-context systems. Roughly speaking, a diagnosis is a pair of sets of bridge rules such that the inconsistency of the system will disappear if we deactivate all the bridge rules in the first set, and activate all the bridge rules in the second one unconditionally. Each diagnosis can be considered as a potential proposal for resolving the inconsistency. In particular, the notion of diagnosis can be reduced to that of deletion-diagnosis for scenarios where deactivation of bridge rules is preferred to unconditional activation of rules [4,5]. Here a deletion-diagnosis is a set of bridge rules such that the deactivation of these bridge rules makes the inconsistency disappear. In this paper, we focus on the deletion-diagnoses for a given multi-context system.

How to select the desired diagnoses is still a challenge to the inconsistency handling for multi-context systems. Most approaches focus on ranking diagnoses based on either the preference order relation over diagnoses [6,7,16] or the preference order relation over bridge rules [14]. However, preference over diagnoses is often considered as meta-knowledge or prior knowledge about multi-context systems, and then is not easily obtained. Ranking diagnoses based on quantitative assessment of inconsistency provides a promising way to select desired ones in the absence of such prior knowledge [15]. Informally speaking, such approaches allow us to assess each diagnosis based on measures for bridge rules involved in inconsistency.

Intuitively, an inconsistency measure used to rank diagnoses should characterize the role of each bridge rule in the inconsistency of a multi-context system from the point of view of causality, that is, by the measure assigned to a bridge rule, we can know whether and to which extent the inconsistency depends on that bridge rule in causality. Such a characterization can help us connect the inconsistency measuring and ranking diagnoses for inconsistency resolving in a natural way. But the current inconsistency measure used for ranking diagnoses is slightly adapted from the inconsistency value MIV_C presented in [9,10], which does not take into account causality explicitly.

In this paper, we propose an approach to characterizing the role of each bridge rule in causing the inconsistency of that multi-context system from the point of view of Halpern-Pearl's causal model [8] and Chockler and Halpern's notion of responsibility [3], which provides a promising starting point to prioritize diagnoses from the perspective of causality in the absence of prior knowledge.

The rest of this paper is organized as follows. We give brief introductions to multi-context systems and Halpern-Pearl's causal model in Sect. 2, respectively. In Sect. 3, we formulate the inconsistency analysis for multi-context systems in the framework of Halpern-Pearl's causal model, and then define the responsibility of each bridge rule for the inconsistency. In Sect. 4, we extend our approach to cases where some bridge rules are protected from being modified. Finally, we conclude this paper in Sect. 5.

2   Preliminaries

The multi-context system presented by Brewka and Eiter aims to combine arbitrary monotonic and nonmonotonic logics [1]. Here an abstract logic (or just logic) L is defined as a triple (KB_L, BS_L, ACC_L), where KB_L is the set of well-formed knowledge bases of L, which characterizes the syntax of L; BS_L is the set of belief sets; and $ACC_L \colon KB_L \to 2^{BS_L}$ is a function describing the semantics of the logic by assigning to each knowledge base (a set of formulas) a set of acceptable sets of beliefs [1].

Given a sequence $\mathcal{L} = (L_1, L_2, \ldots, L_n)$ of logics. An L_k-bridge rule over $\mathcal{L}$, $1 \le k \le n$, is of the form

$$(k : s) \leftarrow (r_1 : p_1), \cdots, (r_j : p_j), \mathbf{not}\ (r_{j+1} : p_{j+1}), \cdots, \mathbf{not}\ (r_m : p_m), \quad (1)$$

where $kb \cup \{s\} \in KB_{L_k}$ for each $kb \in KB_{L_k}$, and for each $i \in \{1, 2, \ldots, m\}$, r_i is a logic identifier ($1 \le r_i \le n$), and p_i is an element of some belief set of L_{r_i} [1]. Roughly speaking, An L_k-bridge rule describes a potential information flow between the logic L_k and some other logics in the sequence.

A multi-context system $M = (C_1, C_2, \ldots, C_n)$ is a collection of contexts $C_i = (L_i, kb_i, br_i)$, $1 \le i \le n$, where $L_i = (KB_i, BS_i, ACC_i)$ is a logic, $kb_i \in KB_i$ is a knowledge base, and br_i is a set of L_i-bridge rules over $\mathcal{L} = (L_1, L_2, \ldots, L_n)$ [1].

We use br_M to denote the set of all bridge rules in M, i.e, $br_M = \cup_{i=1}^{n} br_i$. For the sake of simplicity, we use $\overline{D}$ to denote $br_M \setminus D$ for $D \subseteq br_M$ in an MCS M. Let R be a set of bridge rules, we use $M[R]$ to denote the MCS obtained from M by replacing br_M with R.

A belief state for $M = (C_1, C_2, \ldots, C_n)$ is a sequence $S = (S_1, S_2, \ldots, S_n)$ such that each $S_i \in BS_i$. A bridge rule r of the form (1) is *applicable* in a belief state $S = (S_1, S_2, \ldots, S_n)$ if for $1 \le i \le j$, $p_i \in S_{r_i}$ and for $j + 1 \le l \le m$, $p_l \notin S_{r_l}$. We use $app(br_i, S)$ to denote the set of all L_i-bridge rules that are applicable in belief state S.

In semantics, a belief state $S = (S_1, S_2, \ldots, S_n)$ of M is an equilibrium if, for $1 \le i \le n$, $S_i \in ACC_i(kb_i \cup \{\varphi(r)|r \in app(br_i, S)\})$ [1]. Essentially, an equilibrium is a belief state S such that each belief set S_i is acceptable to C_i when kb_i is enlarged by taking into account the heads of all the applicable bridge rules of C_i in S.

Not all the multi-context systems have at least one equilibrium. If an MCS has no equilibrium, we say that MCS is *inconsistent* [4]. We use $M \models \bot$ to denote that M is inconsistent. In this paper, we assume that every individual context is a consistent knowledge base if no bridge rules apply, i.e., $M[\emptyset] \not\models \bot$.

Now we use the following example taken from [14] to illustrate the notion of inconsistent MCS.

Example 1. Let $M_1 = (C_1, C_2, C_3)$ be an MCS, where L_1 is a propositional logic, whilst both L_2 and L_3 are ASP logics. Suppose that

- $kb_1 = \{a, b\}$, $br_1 = \{r_1 = (1 : c) \leftarrow (2 : e)\}$;
- $kb_2 = \{d \leftarrow e, e \leftarrow\}$, $br_2 = \{r_2 = (2 : p) \leftarrow (1 : c)\}$;
- $kb_3 = \{g \leftarrow, \bot \leftarrow q, \mathbf{not}\ h\}$, $br_3 = \{r_3 = (3 : q) \leftarrow (2 : p), (1 : a); r_4 = (3 : h) \leftarrow \mathbf{not}\ (1 : a)\}$.

Then all bridge rules, except r_4, are applicable. The three applicable bridge rules in turn add q to C_3, and then activate $\bot \leftarrow q, \mathbf{not}\ h$. So, M_1 has no equilibrium, i.e., $M_1 \models \bot$.

The notion of diagnosis has been proposed for characterizing inconsistency in a multi-context system from a perspective of restoring consistency [4]. Essentially, a diagnosis is exactly a pair of sets of bridge rules such that inconsistency will disappear if we deactivate the rules in the first set, and add the rules in the second set in unconditional form. In particular, the diagnosis with the empty set of bridge rules unconditionally activated is more preferred for cases where deactivation of bridge rules is preferred to unconditional activation of bridge rules. Such special diagnoses are also called deletion-diagnoses or s-diagnoses in [4,5]. We focus on deletion-diagnoses in this paper.

Definition 1 (Deletion-diagnosis [4,5]). *Given an MCS M, a deletion-diagnosis of M is a set D of bridge rules of M such that $M[\overline{D}] \not\models \bot$. We use $D_m^-(M)$ to denote the set of all $\subseteq$-minimal deletion-diagnoses of M.*

The notion of deletion-explanation (also termed s-inconsistency explanation) characterizes the inconsistency of a given MCS from a perspective of causing inconsistency.

Definition 2 (Deletion-explanation [4,5]). *Given an MCS M, a deletion-explanation of M is set E of bridge rules of M such that each R where $E \subseteq R \subseteq br_M$ satisfies $M[R] \models \bot$. We use $E_m^+(M)$ to denote the set of all $\subseteq$-minimal deletion-explanations of M.*

Example 2. Consider the MCS M_1 in Example 1 again. Then

$$D_m^-(M_1) = \{D_1, D_2, D_3\} \text{ and } E_m^+(M_1) = \{E_1 = \{r_1, r_2, r_3\}\},$$

where $D_1 = \{r_1\}, D_2 = \{r_2\}, D_3 = \{r_3\}$. This means we only need to deactivate one of the three bridge rules r_1, r_2, and r_3, in order to restore consistency for M_1.

It has been shown that there is a duality relation between deletion-diagnoses and deletion-explanations [4,5]:

Proposition 1. *Given an inconsistent MCS M, then* $\displaystyle\bigcup_{D \in D_m^-(M)} D = \bigcup_{E \in E_m^+(M)} E.$

Next we give very brief introductions to Halpern and Pearl's causal model [8] and Chockler and Halpern's notion of responsibility [3], respectively. For more material, please see Sects. 2 and 3 in [3].

We start with the signature of a causal model. A signature is a tuple $\mathcal{S} = \langle \mathcal{U}, \mathcal{V}, \mathcal{R} \rangle$, where $\mathcal{U}$ is a finite set of exogenous variables, whose values are determined by factors outside a causal model, $\mathcal{V}$ is a finite set of endogenous variables, whose values are ultimately determined by the exogenous variables, and $\mathcal{R}$ associates with every variable $Y \in \mathcal{U} \cup \mathcal{V}$ a finite nonempty set $\mathcal{R}(Y)$ of possible values for Y [3,8].

A causal model over signature $\mathcal{S}$ is a tuple $\mathcal{M} = \langle \mathcal{S}, \mathcal{F} \rangle$, where $\mathcal{F}$ associates with every endogenous variable $X \in \mathcal{V}$ a function F_X such that $F_X : ((\times_{U \in \mathcal{U}} \mathcal{R}(U)) \times (\times_{Y \in \mathcal{V} \setminus \{X\}} \mathcal{R}(Y))) \to \mathcal{R}(X)$ [3,8].

We use $\boldsymbol{X}$ and $\boldsymbol{x}$ to denote a (possibly empty) vector of variables in $\mathcal{V}$ and values for the variables in $\boldsymbol{X}$, respectively. We use $\boldsymbol{X} \leftarrow \boldsymbol{x}$ to denote the case of setting the values of the variables in $\boldsymbol{X}$ to $\boldsymbol{x}$. We use $\boldsymbol{u}$ to denote a setting for the variables in $\mathcal{U}$. Here we call $\boldsymbol{u}$ a context [3,8].

Given $\boldsymbol{X} \leftarrow \boldsymbol{x}$, a new causal model denoted $\mathcal{M}_{\boldsymbol{X} \leftarrow \boldsymbol{x}}$ over the signature $\mathcal{S}_{\boldsymbol{X}} = \langle \mathcal{U}, \mathcal{V} - \boldsymbol{X}, \mathcal{R}|_{\mathcal{V} - \boldsymbol{X}} \rangle$, is defined as $\mathcal{M}_{\boldsymbol{X} \leftarrow \boldsymbol{x}} = \langle \mathcal{S}_{\boldsymbol{X}}, \mathcal{F}^{\boldsymbol{X} \leftarrow \boldsymbol{x}} \rangle$, where $F_Y^{\boldsymbol{X} \leftarrow \boldsymbol{x}}$ is obtained from F_Y by setting the values of the variables in $\boldsymbol{X}$ to $\boldsymbol{x}$ [3,8].

Given a signature $\mathcal{S} = \langle \mathcal{U}, \mathcal{V}, \mathcal{R} \rangle$, a primitive event is a formula of the form $X = x$, where $X \in \mathcal{V}$ and $x \in \mathcal{R}(X)$ [3,8]. In general, for $\boldsymbol{X} = (X_1, X_2, \cdots, X_n)$ and $\boldsymbol{x} = (x_1, x_2, \cdots, x_n)$, we abbreviate $(X_1 = x_1) \wedge (X_2 = x_2) \wedge \cdots \wedge (X_n = x_n)$ as $\boldsymbol{X} = \boldsymbol{x}$.

A basic causal formula defined in [3,8] is in the form of $[\boldsymbol{Y} \leftarrow \boldsymbol{y}]\varphi$, where φ is a Boolean combination of primitive events. As explained in [3,8], $[\boldsymbol{Y} \leftarrow \boldsymbol{y}]\varphi$ means that φ holds in the counterfactual world that would arise if $\boldsymbol{Y}$ is set to $\boldsymbol{y}$.

A causal formula is a Boolean combination of basic causal formulas [3,8]. We use $(\mathcal{M}, \boldsymbol{u}) \models \varphi$ to denote that a causal formula φ is true in causal model $\mathcal{M}$ given a context $\boldsymbol{u}$. Given a recursive model M, $(\mathcal{M}, \boldsymbol{u}) \models [\boldsymbol{Y} \leftarrow \boldsymbol{y}](X = x)$ if the value of X is x in the unique vector of values for the endogenous variables that simultaneously satisfies all equations $F_Z^{\boldsymbol{Y} \leftarrow \boldsymbol{y}}, Z \in \mathcal{V} - \boldsymbol{Y}$ under the setting $\boldsymbol{u}$ of $\mathcal{U}$ [3,8]. Note that this definition can be extended to arbitrary causal formulas in the usual way.

Definition 3 (Cause [8]). *We say that $\boldsymbol{X} = \boldsymbol{x}$ is a cause of φ in $(\mathcal{M}, \boldsymbol{u})$ if the following three conditions hold:*

AC1. $(\mathcal{M}, \boldsymbol{u}) \models (\boldsymbol{X} = \boldsymbol{x}) \wedge \varphi$.

AC2. *There exists a partition $(\boldsymbol{Z}, \boldsymbol{W})$ of $\mathcal{V}$ with $\boldsymbol{X} \subseteq \boldsymbol{Z}$ and some setting $(\boldsymbol{x}', \boldsymbol{w}')$ of the variables in $(\boldsymbol{X}, \boldsymbol{W})$ such that if $(\mathcal{M}, \boldsymbol{u}) \models Z = z^*$ for $Z \in \boldsymbol{Z}$, then*

    (a) *$(\mathcal{M}, \boldsymbol{u}) \models [\boldsymbol{X} \leftarrow \boldsymbol{x}', \boldsymbol{W} \leftarrow \boldsymbol{w}']\neg\varphi$. That is, changing $(\boldsymbol{X}, \boldsymbol{W})$ from $(\boldsymbol{x}, \boldsymbol{w})$ to $(\boldsymbol{x}', \boldsymbol{w}')$ changes φ from true to false.*

    (b) *$(\mathcal{M}, \boldsymbol{u}) \models [\boldsymbol{X} \leftarrow \boldsymbol{x}, \boldsymbol{W} \leftarrow \boldsymbol{w}', \boldsymbol{Z}' \leftarrow \boldsymbol{z}^*]\varphi$ for all subsets $\boldsymbol{Z}'$ of $\boldsymbol{Z} - \boldsymbol{X}$. That is, setting $\boldsymbol{W}$ to $\boldsymbol{w}'$ should have no effect on φ as long as $\boldsymbol{X}$ has the value $\boldsymbol{x}$, even if all the variables in an arbitrary subset of $\boldsymbol{Z}$ are set to their original values in the context $\boldsymbol{u}$.*

AC3. $(\boldsymbol{X} = \boldsymbol{x})$ *is minimal, that is, no subset of $\boldsymbol{X}$ satisfies AC2.*

Based on Halpern-Pearl's causal model above, the notion of responsibility presented by Chockler and Halpern is given as follows:

Definition 4 (Degree of Responsibility [3]). *The degree of responsibility of $X = x$ for φ in $(\mathcal{M}, \boldsymbol{u})$, denoted $dr((\mathcal{M}, \boldsymbol{u}), (X = x), \varphi)$, is 0 if $X = x$ is not a cause of φ in $(\mathcal{M}, \boldsymbol{u})$; it is $\frac{1}{k+1}$ if $X = x$ is a cause of φ in $(\mathcal{M}, \boldsymbol{u})$ and there exists a partition $(\boldsymbol{Z}, \boldsymbol{W})$ and setting $x', \boldsymbol{w}'$ for which AC2 holds such that (a) k variables in $\boldsymbol{W}$ have different values in $\boldsymbol{w}'$ than they do in the context $\boldsymbol{u}$ and (b) there is no partition $(\boldsymbol{Z}', \boldsymbol{W}')$ and setting $x'', \boldsymbol{w}''$ satisfying AC2 such that only $k' < k$ variables have different values in $\boldsymbol{w}''$ than they do in the context $\boldsymbol{u}$.*

As explained in [3], the degree of responsibility of $X = x$ for φ in $(\mathcal{M}, \boldsymbol{u})$ captures the minimal number of changes that have to be made in $\boldsymbol{u}$ in order to make φ counterfactually depend on X.

3   The Responsibility of Bridge Rules

In this section, we formulate the problem of inconsistency in an MCS by Halpern and Pearl's causal model, and then identify the responsibility of each bridge rule of that MCS for the inconsistency.

Given an inconsistent MCS M and the set of all $\subseteq$-minimal deletion-explanations $E_m^+(M)$, to construct a causal model for the inconsistency of M,

- we associate every bridge rule $r \in br_M$ with a binary variable X_r, whose value is 0 if r is deactivated and 1 if r keeps unchanged. We use $\boldsymbol{X}$ to denote the vector of all the variables corresponding to bridge rules.
- we associate every bridge rule variable X_r a binary exogenous variable U_r. Moreover, we assume that the value of X_r depends on only the value of U_r. We use $\mathcal{U}_M$ and $\boldsymbol{U}$ to denote the set and the vector of all the exogenous variables.
- we associate every $\subseteq$-minimal deletion-explanation $E \in E_m^+(M)$ with a binary variable Y_E, whose value is 0 if at least one bridge rule in E is deactivated and 1 otherwise. We use $\boldsymbol{Y}$ to denote the vector of all the variables corresponding to $\subseteq$-minimal deletion-explanations.
- we use a binary variable I_M to describe the problem of inconsistency in M, whose value is 1 if M keeps inconsistent and 0 otherwise.

Let $\mathcal{V}_M = \{X_r | r \in br_M\} \cup \{Y_E | E \in E_m^+(M)\} \cup \{I_M\}$ be the set of all endogenous variables. Obviously, for each endogenous variable V, $\mathcal{R}_M(V) = \{0, 1\}$. Furthermore, we define the following functions to characterize the dependence relation between these variables:

- $F_{X_r}(\boldsymbol{U}, \boldsymbol{X} - X_r, \boldsymbol{Y}, I_M) = U_r$ ($X_r = U_r$ for short) for every bridge rule $r \in br_M$.

- $F_{Y_E}(U, X, Y - Y_E, I_M) = \prod_{r \in E} X_r$ ($Y_E = \prod_{r \in E} X_r$ for short) for every $E \in E_m^+(M)$.
- $F_{I_M}(U, X, Y) = \bigoplus_{E \in E_m^+(M)} Y_E$ ($I_M = \bigoplus_{E \in E_m^+(M)} Y_E$ for short) for inconsistency variable I_M, where $\bigoplus$ is the Boolean addition.

Roughly speaking, the function F_{X_r} represents the assumption that the value of bridge rule variable X_r is determined by only the value of the corresponding exogenous variable U_r. The function F_{Y_E} describes the nature of E being a $\subseteq$-minimal deletion-explanation, that is, E is a $\subseteq$-minimal set of bridge rules together causing inconsistency in M. The function F_{I_M} describes the characterization of inconsistency of M based on $\subseteq$-minimal deletion-explanations of M. We use $\mathcal{F}_M$ to denote the set of all the functions above for M, i.e.,

$$\mathcal{F}_M = \{F_{X_r} | r \in br_M\} \cup \{F_{Y_E} | E \in E_m^+(M)\} \cup \{F_{I_M}\}.$$

Then the causal model for the inconsistency of M, denoted $\mathcal{M}_M$, is defined as $\mathcal{M}_M = \langle \mathcal{S}_M, \mathcal{F}_M \rangle$, where $\mathcal{S}_M = \langle \mathcal{U}_M, \mathcal{V}_M, \mathcal{R}_M \rangle$. Recall that each bridge rule variable is determined by its exogenous variable, then we can use the context $u = 1 = (1, 1, \ldots, 1)$ to represent the case where no bridge rule is deactivated.

We use the following example to illustrate the causal model for inconsistent MCSes.

Example 3. Consider the MCS M_1 in Example 1 again. Recall that $E_m^+(M_1) = \{E_1 = \{r_1, r_2, r_3\}\}$.

Now we construct the causal model $\mathcal{M}_{M_1}$ for the problem of inconsistency in M_1 as follows:

- Let U_{r_i} and X_{r_i} be the exogenous and endogenous variables corresponding to bridge rule r_i, respectively. Then $X_{r_i} = U_{r_i}$ for all $i = 1, 2, 3, 4$.
- Let Y_{E_1} be the binary variable corresponding to E_1. Then

$$Y_{E_1} = X_{r_1} \times X_{r_2} \times X_{r_3}.$$

- Let I_{M_1} be the binary variable representing the inconsistency in M_1, then $I_{M_1} = Y_{E_1}$.

Given a context $u = 1$, then $(\mathcal{M}_{M_1}, u) \models (I_{M_1} = 1)$.

Furthermore, consider counterfactual worlds arising from $X_{r_1} \leftarrow 0$, $X_{r_2} \leftarrow 0$, $X_{r_3} \leftarrow 0$, and $X_{r_4} \leftarrow 0$, respectively, then

$$(\mathcal{M}_{M_1}, u) \models [X_{r_1} \leftarrow 0](I_{M_1} = 0), \ (\mathcal{M}_{M_1}, u) \models [X_{r_2} \leftarrow 0](I_{M_1} = 0).$$

$$(\mathcal{M}_{M_1}, u) \models [X_{r_3} \leftarrow 0](I_{M_1} = 0), (\mathcal{M}_{M_1}, u) \models [X_{r_4} \leftarrow 0](I_{M_1} = 1).$$

The first three items state that deactivating either the bridge rule r_1 or r_2 or r_3 makes inconsistency disappear, whilst the last one states that deactivating the bridge rule r_4 cannot make the MCS consistent.

Now we are ready to characterize the role of each bridge rule in the inconsistency of a given MCS, and then define the responsibility of a bridge rule for the inconsistency in an inconsistent MCS based on the causal model.

Proposition 2. *Given an inconsistent MCS M and $r \in br_M$ a bridge rule of M. Then $X_r = 1$ is a cause of $I_M = 1$ in $(\mathcal{M}_M, u)$ if and only if $\exists E \in E_m^+(M)$ s.t. $r \in E$.*

Proof. Let r be a bridge rule of M such that $\exists E \in E_m^+(M)$ s.t. $r \in E$. Then following Proposition 1, there exists at least one diagnosis $D \in D_m^-(M)$ s.t. $r \in D$. Let $\boldsymbol{X}_D$ be the vector of variables corresponding to bridge rules in D and $\boldsymbol{W} = \boldsymbol{X}_D - X_r$. Further, consider a partition $(\boldsymbol{Z}, \boldsymbol{W})$ of $\mathcal{V}_M$, where $\boldsymbol{Z} = \boldsymbol{X} - \boldsymbol{W}$. Then we can check that $(\mathcal{M}_M, u) \models (X_r = 1) \wedge (I_M = 1)$. Moreover, $(\mathcal{M}_M, u) \models [X_r \leftarrow 0, \boldsymbol{W} \leftarrow \boldsymbol{0}](I_M = 0)$, but $(\mathcal{M}_M, u) \models [X_r \leftarrow 1, \boldsymbol{W} \leftarrow \boldsymbol{0}, \boldsymbol{Z}' \leftarrow \boldsymbol{1}](I_M = 1)$ for all subsets $\boldsymbol{Z}'$ of $\boldsymbol{Z} - X_r$. So, $X_r = 1$ is a cause of $I_M = 1$ in $(\mathcal{M}_M, u)$.

On the other hand, suppose that $X_r = 1$ is a cause of $I_M = 1$ in $(\mathcal{M}_M, u)$. Then consider a partition $(\boldsymbol{Z}, \boldsymbol{W})$ of $\mathcal{V}_M$ satisfying condition AC2 such that $\boldsymbol{W}$ is $\subseteq$-minimal. Let $D_{\boldsymbol{W}}$ be the set of bridge rules corresponding to variables of $\boldsymbol{W}$. Then $D_{\boldsymbol{W}} \cup \{r\}$ is a $\subseteq$-minimal deletion-diagnosis. So, $r \in \bigcup_{D \in D_m^-(M)} D$. By Proposition 1, $\exists E \in E_m^+(M)$ s.t. $r \in E$.   □

Definition 5. *Let M be an inconsistent MCS and $r \in br_M$ a bridge rule of M. Then the degree of responsibility of r for the inconsistency of M, denoted $RI(r, M)$, is defined as $RI(r, M) = dr((\mathcal{M}_M, u), (X_r = 1), (I_M = 1))$, where $\mathcal{M}_M$ is the causal model of the inconsistency of M.*

Note that $0 \leq RI(r, M) \leq 1$ for all $r \in br_M$. In particular, the following proposition gives a characterization for bridge rules with null responsibility for the inconsistency.

Proposition 3. *Given an inconsistent MCS M and $r \in br_M$ a bridge rule of M. Then $RI(r, M) = 0$ if and only if $r \in \overline{\bigcup_{E \in E_m^+(M)} E}$.*

Proof. $RI(r, M) = 0 \Leftrightarrow X_r = 1$ is not a cause of $I_M = 1$. $\Leftrightarrow$ for all $E \in E_m^+(M)$, $r \notin E \Leftrightarrow r \in br_M - \bigcup_{E \in E_m^+(M)} E$.   □

This proposition shows that bridge rules not involved in deletion-explanations need not bear any responsibility for the inconsistency in an inconsistent MCS. Now we focus on bridge rules with nonzero responsibility for the inconsistency. The following proposition provides an alternative characterization for the degree of responsibility for the inconsistency.

Proposition 4. *Given an inconsistent MCS M and $r \in \bigcup_{E \in E_m^+(M)} E$ a bridge rule involved in deletion-explanations. Then*

$$RI(r, M) = \max\{\frac{1}{|D|} | D \in D_m^-(M) \ s.t. \ r \in D\}.$$

Proof. Let $r \in \bigcup_{E \in E_m^+(M)} E$, then X_r is a cause of $I_M = 1$. Then there exists a partition $(\mathbf{Z}, \mathbf{W})$ satisfying condition AC2 such that $\mathbf{W}$ is $\subseteq$-minimal in Halpern-Pearl's model. Let $D_{\mathbf{W}}$ be the set of bridge rules corresponding to variables of $\mathbf{W}$. Then $D_{\mathbf{W}} \cup \{r\} \in D_m^-(M)$. So, $\frac{1}{|\mathbf{W}|+1} = \frac{1}{|D_{\mathbf{W}} \cup \{r\}|}$ for all such $\mathbf{W}$s. Therefore, $RI(r, M) = \max\{\frac{1}{|D|} | D \in D_m^-(M) \ s.t. \ r \in D\}$.   □

According to Halpern-Pearl's causal model, given a bridge rule r involved in the inconsistency of M, deactivating the other bridge rules of a minimal deletion-diagnosis containing r exactly obtains a contingency where the inconsistency counterfactually depends on the bridge rule r. In this sense, the degree of responsibility of r for the inconsistency is determined by the minimal number of bridge rules deactivated to obtain a contingency where the inconsistency counterfactually depends on r. In particular, if there is no bridge rule deactivated to obtain such a contingency (i.e., there is no variable in $\mathbf{W}$), then $RI(r, M) = 1$. This implies that the inconsistency of M counterfactually depends on r. In such cases, we call $X_r = 1$ a counterfactual cause of $I_M = 1$.

The following proposition provides a characterization for the counterfactual cause of inconsistency.

Proposition 5. *Given an inconsistent MCS M and $r \in br_M$ a bridge rule of M. Then $RI(r, M) = 1$ if and only if $r \in \bigcap_{E \in E_m^+(M)} E$.*

Proof. Let r be a bridge rule of M. Suppose that $RI(r, M) = 1$, then $X_r = 1$ is a cause of $I_M = 1$ in the causal model $(\mathcal{M}_M, \mathbf{u})$. Moreover, $(\mathcal{M}_M, \mathbf{u}) \models [X_r \leftarrow 0](Y_E = 0)$ for all $E \in E_m^+(M)$. Then $r \in E$ for all $E \in E_m^+(M)$. So, $r \in \bigcap_{E \in E_m^+(M)} E$.

On the other hand, if $r \in \bigcap_{E \in E_m^+(M)} E$, then $(\mathcal{M}_M, \mathbf{u}) \models [X_r \leftarrow 1](I_M = 1)$ for all $E \in E_m^+(M)$, and $(\mathcal{M}_M, \mathbf{u}) \models [X_r \leftarrow 0](Y_E = 0)$ for all $E \in E_m^+(M)$. So, $(\mathcal{M}_M, \mathbf{u}) \models [X_r \leftarrow 0, \mathbf{Z}' \leftarrow 1](I_M = 1)$ for all subsets $\mathbf{Z}'$ of $\mathcal{V}_M - \{X_r\}$. Then we conclude that $X_r = 1$ is a cause of $I_M = 1$ and there exists $\mathbf{W} = \emptyset$ satisfying condition AC2. Therefore, $RI(r, M) = 1$.   □

We use the following example to illustrate the notion of responsibility of a bridge rule for the inconsistency.

Example 4. Consider the MCS M_1 in Example 1 again. Then

$$RI(r_1, M_1) = RI(r_2, M_1) = RI(r_3, M_1) = 1, \ RI(r_4, M_1) = 0.$$

This implies that the inconsistency of M_1 counterfactually depends on each of r_1, r_2, and r_3. In contrast, r_4 need not bear any responsibility for the inconsistency in M_1.

Note that all the variables involved in the causal model $\mathcal{M}_M$ are binary ones. Such a causal model is called the binary causal model, moreover, it has been shown that computing the degree of responsibility is $FP^{NP[\log n]}$-complete in binary causal models [3]. Then we can get the following result on computational complexity.

Proposition 6. *Computing the degree of responsibility of each bridge rule of an MCS for the inconsistency is $FP^{NP[\log n]}$-complete in cases where the set of all the $\subseteq$-minimal deletion-explanations is given.*

On the other hand, given an inconsistent MCS M, there exists at least one bridge rule bearing non-zero responsibility for the inconsistency in that MCS. Then we may use the responsibilities of bridge rules of M to assess the degree of inconsistency of MCS M. We use $\boldsymbol{RI}$ to denote the vector of responsibilities of bridge rules for the inconsistency corresponding to the vector $\boldsymbol{X}$.

Definition 6. *Let M be an MCS. Then the inconsistency measurement for M based on $\boldsymbol{RI}$, denoted $Ind(M)$, is defined as $Ind(M) = f(\boldsymbol{RI})$, where f is a function.*

Now we give the following instances, which describe the inconsistency from different perspectives.

$$- \; Ind_{\min}(M) = \begin{cases} \frac{1}{\max\limits_{r \in br_M} RI(r,M)}, & \text{if } M \models \perp, \\ 0, & \text{otherwise.} \end{cases}$$

$$- \; Ind_{\max}(M) = \begin{cases} \frac{1}{\min\{RI(r,M)|r \in \bigcup\limits_{E \in E_m^+(M)} E\}}, & \text{if } M \models \perp, \\ 0, & \text{otherwise.} \end{cases}$$

Note that $Ind_{\min}(M)$ gives the minimal number of bridge rules that have to be deactivated to restore the consistency of M, whilst $Ind_{\max}(M)$ gives the maximal number of bridge rules that have to be deactivated to restore the consistency of M. In addition, $Ind_{\min}(M)$ and $Ind_{\max}(M)$ may be combined by using f-measure statistic as follows:

$$- \; Ind_{F_\beta}(M) = \begin{cases} \frac{(1+\beta^2) \times Ind_{\min}(M) \times Ind_{\max}(M)}{Ind_{\min}(M) + \beta^2 \times Ind_{\max}(M)}, & \text{if } M \models \perp, \\ 0, & \text{otherwise.} \end{cases} \text{, where } \beta > 0 \text{ is a}$$
balance factor.

All the three measurements accord with the point of view that the cost of restoring consistency can be considered as an evaluation of the inconsistency presented in [11].

4   Discussion and Comparison

In this section, we consider scenarios where some bridge rules are protected from being either deactivated or activated unconditionally [6].

Given an inconsistent MCS M, let br_P be the set of protected bridge rules. Then we adapt the causal model $\mathcal{M}_M$ to the case where br_P are protected from being modified. We use $\mathcal{M}_{M|P}$ to denote the causal model for the case of protected bridge rules. We use a binary variable P to describe protected bridge rules, whose value is 0 if all the bridge rules in br_P are protected from modification and 1 otherwise. Then we add the following function F_P:

- $F_P(\boldsymbol{U}, \boldsymbol{X}, \boldsymbol{Y}, I_M) = \bigoplus\limits_{r \in br_P} (1 - X_r) \; (P = \bigoplus\limits_{r \in br_P} (1 - X_r) \text{ for short}).$

Further, we adapt the function F_{I_M} as follows:

- $F_{I_M}(\boldsymbol{U}, \boldsymbol{X}, \boldsymbol{Y}, P) = (\bigoplus\limits_{E \in E_m^+(M)} Y_E) \oplus P$

Then we can define the degree of responsibility of a bridge rule for the inconsistency given a set of protected bridge rules as follows:

Definition 7. *Let M be an inconsistent MCS and br_P a set of protected bridge rules. Let r be a bridge rule of M. Then the degree of responsibility of r for the inconsistency of M given br_P, denoted $RI(r, M|P)$, is defined as*

$$RI(r, M|P) = dr((\mathcal{M}_{M|P}, \boldsymbol{u}), (X_r = 1), (I_M = 1)),$$

where $\mathcal{M}_{M|P}$ is the causal model of the inconsistency of M given br_P.

Taking causality into account makes our approach different from inconsistency assessments used in [15], which uses the Shapley value, one of the well-known cooperation game models, to identify the responsibility of each bridge rule for the inconsistency. However, our approach can be considered as a generalization of approaches to assessing inconsistency for classical knowledge bases presented in [12,13] to the case of multi-context systems.

5   Conclusion

We have proposed an approach to identifying the degree of responsibility of each bridge rule in an inconsistent multi-context system for the inconsistency in that system based on Halpern-Pearl's causal model and Chockler and Halpern's notion of responsibility. Then we introduced some inconsistency measurements for the whole system based on the characterization of responsibilities of bridge rules. How to use these measurements to facilitate the inconsistency handling in multi-context systems is an interesting issue for future work.

Acknowledgements. This work was partly supported by the National Natural Science Foundation of China under Grant No. 61572002, No. 61170300, No. 61690201, and No. 61732001.

References

1. Brewka, G., Eiter, T.: Equilibria in heterogeneous nonmonotonic multi-context systems. In: Holte, R.C., Howe, A.E. (eds.) Proceedings of the Twenty-Second AAAI Conference on Artificial Intelligence, 22–26 July 2007, Vancouver, British Columbia, Canada, pp. 385–390. AAAI Press (2007)

2. Brewka, G., Eiter, T., Fink, M., Weinzierl, A.: Managed multi-context systems. In: Walsh, T. (ed.) Proceedings of the 22nd International Joint Conference on Artificial Intelligence, IJCAI 2011, Barcelona, Catalonia, Spain, 16–22 July 2011, pp. 786–791. IJCAI/AAAI Press (2011)
3. Chockler, H., Halpern, J.Y.: Responsibility and blame: a structural-model approach. J. Artif. Intell. Res. **22**, 93–115 (2004)
4. Eiter, T., Fink, M., Schüller, P., Weinzierl, A.: Finding explanations of inconsistency in multi-context systems. In: Lin, F., Sattler, U., Truszczynski, M. (eds.) Principles of Knowledge Representation and Reasoning: Proceedings of the Twelfth International Conference, KR 2010, Toronto, Ontario, Canada, 9–13 May 2010, pp. 329–339. AAAI Press (2010)
5. Eiter, T., Fink, M., Schüller, P., Weinzierl, A.: Finding explanations of inconsistency in multi-context systems. Artif. Intell. **216**, 233–274 (2014)
6. Eiter, T., Fink, M., Weinzierl, A.: Preference-based inconsistency assessment in multi-context systems. In: Janhunen, T., Niemelä, I. (eds.) JELIA 2010. LNCS (LNAI), vol. 6341, pp. 143–155. Springer, Heidelberg (2010). https://doi.org/10.1007/978-3-642-15675-5_14
7. Eiter, T., Fink, M., Weinzierl, A.: Preference-based diagnosis selection in multi-context systems. In: Eiter, T., Strass, H., Truszczyński, M., Woltran, S. (eds.) Advances in Knowledge Representation, Logic Programming, and Abstract Argumentation. LNCS (LNAI), vol. 9060, pp. 233–248. Springer, Cham (2015). https://doi.org/10.1007/978-3-319-14726-0_16
8. Halpern, J.Y., Pearl, J.: Causes and explanations: a structural-model approach. Part i: causes. Br. J. Philos. Sci. **56**(4), 843–887 (2005)
9. Hunter, A., Konieczny, S.: Measuring inconsistency through minimal inconsistent sets. In: Brewka, G., Lang, J. (eds.) Principles of Knowledge Representation and Reasoning: Proceedings of the Eleventh International Conference (KR 2008), pp. 358–366. AAAI Press (2008)
10. Hunter, A., Konieczny, S.: On the measure of conflicts: shapley inconsistency values. Artif. Intell. **174**(14), 1007–1026 (2010)
11. Konieczny, S., Lang, J., Marquis, P.: Quantifying information and contradiction in propositional logic through test actions. In: Gottlob, G., Walsh, T. (eds.) Proceedings of the Eighteenth International Joint Conference on Artificial Intelligence, IJCAI-03, Acapulco, Mexico, 9–15 August 2003, pp. 106–111. Morgan Kaufmann (2003)
12. Mu, K.: Responsibility for inconsistency. Int. J. Approx. Reason. **61**, 43–60 (2015)
13. Mu, K.: Measuring inconsistency with constraints for propositional knowledge bases. Artif. Intell. **259**, 52–90 (2018)
14. Mu, K., Wang, K., Wen, L.: Preferential multi-context systems. Int. J. Approx. Reason. **75**, 39–56 (2016)
15. Weinzierl, A.: Comparing inconsistency resolutions in multi-context systems. In: Lassiter, D., Slavkovik, M. (eds.) ESSLLI 2010-2011. LNCS, vol. 7415, pp. 158–174. Springer, Heidelberg (2012). https://doi.org/10.1007/978-3-642-31467-4_11
16. Weinzierl, A.: Inconsistency management under preferences for multi-context systems and extensions. Dissertation, Faculty of Informatics, Vienna University of Technology, Austria, pp. 1–228 (2014)

Extracting Hidden Preferences over Partitions in Hedonic Cooperative Games

Athina Georgara[(✉)], Dimitrios Troullinos, and Georgios Chalkiadakis

School of Electrical and Computer Engineering,
Technical University of Crete, Chania, Greece
{ageorgara, gehalk}@intelligence.tuc.gr, dtroullinos@isc.tuc.gr

Abstract. The prevalent assumption in *hedonic games* is that agents are interested solely on the composition of their own coalition. Moreover, agent preferences are usually assumed to be known with certainty. In our work, agents have *hidden* preferences over *partitions*. We first put forward the formal definition of hedonic games in partition function form (PFF-HGs), and extend well-studied classes of hedonic games to this setting. Then we exploit three well-known supervised learning models, *linear regression*, *linear regression with basis function*, and *feed forward neural networks*, in order to (approximately) extract the unknown hedonic preference relations over partitions. We conduct a systematic evaluation to compare the performance of these models on PFF-HGs; and, in the process, we develop an evaluation metric specifically designed for our problem. Our experimental results confirm the effectiveness of our work.

Keywords: Learning preferences or rankings · Cooperative games ·
Uncertainty in AI · Applications of supervised learning

1 Introduction

Hedonic games [2] is a class of cooperative games typically used to model settings where agents form coalitions based on their interpersonal relations with others. That is, agents are attracted to coalitions due to their membership, and their "payoff" corresponds to their satisfaction from the collaboration itself. Hedonic games can in fact be modeled as *non-transferable utility games* [7]. In most studies so far, complete information over essential components of such games is assumed. However, under a more realistic point of view, one has to deal with *uncertainty*. In this light, [15] and [9] explore learning methods applied in several classes of hedonic games to discover the underlying hidden aspects of the game.

To the best to our knowledge, all hedonic game papers so far assume that the utility an agent i assigns to a coalition C depends solely on the identities of agents in C [2,8]; however, the value of a coalition can intuitively be affected not only by its own composition, but also by that of other groups.[1] In other

---

[1] In [1], in fact, this is mentioned as a potential extension, but it is not studied there.

© Springer Nature Switzerland AG 2019
C. Douligeris et al. (Eds.): KSEM 2019, LNAI 11775, pp. 829–841, 2019.
https://doi.org/10.1007/978-3-030-29551-6_73

words, it is natural that the satisfaction yielded by a certain coalition differs depending on *coalition structure*. In cooperative game theory, such partition-wide preferences have been studied both in transferable and non-transferable utility games (games with externalities or in partition function form), but not specifically within the scope of hedonic games [7,16]. Here we provide the formal definition of hedonic games in partition function form (PFF-HGs), and extend well-studied sub-classes of hedonic games to ones with externalities.

We then proceed to employ supervised learning models such as linear regression, regression with basis functions, and feed-forward neural networks to discover *latent collaboration patterns* in PFF-HGs. In particular, we focus on specific classes of games in PFF-HG, and we exploit their properties to extract their unknown aspects: we consider the preference relation of each agent as the latent aspect of the game. In other words, in our framework agents themselves are unaware of their own preferences; and they *learn* the hidden preferences relation via observing past interactions with others. This is a realistic assumption when considering a vast partition-space: in fact, any competition involving teams or individuals, which can regroup over time and be 'revealed' to the participants, can be captured by the settings we describe in this work. Note that even with a few agents the partition-space is extremely large, e.g., even for 10 agents, we have $B_{10} = \sum_{k=0}^{9} \binom{9}{k} \cdot B_k = 115975$ partitions (B is the *Bell number* [7]).

For instance, consider n companies that establish synergies in order to acquire government contracts. In each competition the companies form different coalitions, and the bundling of the contracts leads to different satisfaction for each company. A series of such competitions provides a learning model with sufficient data that can help an involved company to plan forthcoming collaborations. Another example could be crowdsourcing online platforms, where given a complicated task and a specific time frame, individuals are to form work-groups that compete with each other to solve problems or puzzles; at the end of a task's period, the groups may reform into different coalitions. In such settings, the groupings naturally affect the final outcome, while the formation space is vast and thus own preferences are unknown.

In what follows, in Sect. 2 we formally define the PFF-HG games. In Sect. 3 we present the explicit application of the aforementioned learning models to our problem at hand. In Sect. 4 we describe the game environments within which we employed the learning process. Finally, in Sect. 4.3 we discuss our results, while Sect. 5 concludes this paper.

2   Hedonic Games in Partition Function Form

Let $N = \{1, \cdots, n\}$ be a finite, non-empty set of players of size $|N| = n$. A coalition $S \subseteq N \setminus \{\emptyset\}$ is a non-empty subset of players. The relative to player i coalitional space, consists of all coalitions which contain i, and is defined as $N_i = \{S \subseteq N : i \in S\}$. A *partition* or *coalition structure* is a set of coalitions $\pi = \{S_1, \cdots, S_m\}$ such that for each pair $i, j = 1, \cdots, m$ and $i \neq j$, $S_i \cap S_j = \emptyset$; and $\cup_{i=1,\cdots,m} S_i = N$. We denote with $\pi(i)$ the coalition within π that contains agent i. The set of all partitions of N is denoted as Π. The pair (S, π) is an *embedded coalition*, where $\pi \in \Pi$ is a partition, and $S \in \pi$ is a coalition within partition π. The set of all embedded coalitions over N is denoted with $\mathcal{E}_N$. The set of the embedded coalitions that contain agent i is denoted with $\mathcal{E}_N(i)$. The class of hedonic games is defined as:

Definition 1 (Hedonic Games [2]). *A hedonic game is given by a pair $G = (N, \succsim)$, where $\succsim$ is a preference profile that specifies for every agent $i \in N$ a reflexive, complete and transitive binary relation $\succsim_i$ on N_i.*

Both transferable (TU) and non-transferable (NTU) utility games have been expressed in partition function form (PFF). Hedonic games constitute a special class of NTU games:

Definition 2 (NTU games in Partition Function Form [14]). *A coalitional game in partition function form (PFF) with non-transferable utility (NTU) is defined by a pair $\langle N, V \rangle$, where N is the set of players, and V is a mapping such that for every $\pi \in \Pi$ and every coalition $S \subseteq N$, $S \in \pi$, $V(S, \pi)$ is a closed convex subset of $\mathbb{R}^{|S|}$ that contains the payoff vector that players in S can achieve. Alternatively, if we consider a payoff vector in $\mathbb{R}^n$ for every coalition $S \subseteq N$ (let for any $i \notin S$ the corresponding payoff be 0 or $-\infty$), then V can be viewed as a mapping $V \colon \mathcal{E}_N \to \mathbb{R}^n$ that assigns to n-vector of real numbers to each embedded coalition (S, π).*

We now provide the corresponding definition for *hedonic games in partition function form*, and extend common hedonic game classes to this setting.

Definition 3 (PFF-HGs). *A hedonic game (HG) in partition function form (PFF) is defined by a pair $\langle N, \succsim \rangle$, where N is the set of players, and $\succsim = \{\succsim^{\pi_1}, \cdots, \succsim^{\pi_m}\}$ with $|\Pi| = m$; and for all $\pi_j \in \Pi$ $\succsim^{\pi_j} = \{\succsim_1^{\pi_j}, \cdots, \succsim_n^{\pi_j}\}$, and each $\succsim_i^{\pi_j} \subseteq N_i \times N_i$ is a complete, reflexive and transitive preference relation describing agent i's preferences over coalitions it can participate in when π_j is in place.*

2.1 Additively Separable Hedonic Games (ASHGs)

In ASHGs [8], an agent's utility for a given coalition is the sum of the utilities it assigns to other members of that coalition. Formally, each agent $i \in N$ assigns to each agent $j \in N$ a value $b_i^j \in \mathbb{R}$,[2] and the utility of coalition S is defined as $v_i(S) = \sum_{j \in S} b_i^j$.

Generalizing ASHGs to partition function form, each agent assigns a value to any agent within each partition $\pi \in \Pi$, i.e, agent i assigns the value $b_i^j(\pi)$ to agent j when partition π is formed. Thus, the utility of embedded coalition (S, π) is now defined as $v_i(S, \pi) = \sum_{j \in S} b_i^j(\pi)$. As such, it is more natural to model ASHGs like NTU games due to their properties. Therefore, there is a mapping $V \colon \mathcal{E}_N \to \mathbb{R}$ such that for every embedded coalition there is an n-vector of reals:

---

[2] The agents assign a zero value to themselves, i.e., $b_i^i = 0$.

$$V(S, \pi) = \begin{bmatrix} v_1(S, \pi) \\ v_2(S, \pi) \\ \vdots \\ v_n(S, \pi) \end{bmatrix} = \begin{bmatrix} \sum_{j \in S} b_1^j(\pi) \\ \sum_{j \in S} b_2^j(\pi) \\ \vdots \\ \sum_{j \in S} b_n^j(\pi) \end{bmatrix}$$

Given this, each agent forms a preference relation that refers to embedded coalitions (rather than coalitions), and therefore to partitions. This preference relation is as follows: agent i prefers embedded coalition (S, π) to (T, π'), $(S, \pi) \succsim_i (T, \pi')$, if and only if $v_i(S, \pi) \geq v_i(T, \pi')$, even if S and T consist of exactly the same set of agents.[3]

2.2   Boolean Hedonic Games (BHGs)

Boolean hedonic games provide a concise representation of hedonic games with dichotomous preference relations [1]. According to the dichotomous preferences model, each agent i can partition $N_i = \{S \subseteq N \setminus \{\emptyset\} : i \in S\}$ into two disjoint sets N_i^+ and N_i^-; and i strictly prefers all coalitions in N_i^+ to those in N_i^-, and is indifferent about coalitions in the same set. In boolean hedonic games, each agent i, instead of explicitly enumerating the preference relation that leads to dichotomous preferences, defines a logic formula γ_i that intuitively represents its goal of being with preferred partners; and i is satisfied if its goal is achieved, or dissatisfied otherwise. This formula can be of any form of a propositional logic language, but γ_i in [1] involves only propositional variables *relative* to agent i, that is, denoting agents i wants or does not want to be grouped with.

Expanding BHGs to partition function form, the key idea is to partition the Π space into two disjoint sets P_i^+ and P_i^-, i.e. into a set with the partitions agent i prefers, and a set with the partitions i does not. In its generality, the use of propositional logic formulae allows us to have a compact representation, but γ_i in [1] was meant to capture i's preferences regarding the composition of its coalition only. We extend into PFF by introducing a specific form for γ_i, which is as follows: each γ_i is *not* restricted to variables relative to agent i, but consists of multiple pairs $\langle Incl_i, \overline{Incl_i} \rangle$ connected via the logical connective *or* ($\vee$). $\langle Incl_i, \overline{Incl_i} \rangle$ is a pair of two *disjoint* sets of subcoalitions. Now, each pair is interpreted as follows: $Incl_i$ is a set of "must-include" subsets of coalitions, while $\overline{Incl_i}$ is a set of "must-not-include" subsets of coalitions. In words, the set $Incl_i$ represents desirable patterns of collaborations that a preferable to i partition must contain; while the set $\overline{Incl_i}$ indicates cooperation among agents that must be excluded from a preferable partition. Thus, a partition π satisfies the pair $\langle Incl_i, \overline{Incl_i} \rangle$ if:

- $\forall c \in Incl_i \; \exists S \in \pi : c \subseteq S$; **and**
- $\forall c \in \overline{Incl_i} \; \nexists S \in \pi : c \subseteq S$

---

[3] Notice, that by simply changing the sum operator with max, min, or average, we can similarly express the $\mathcal{B} - Games$, $\mathcal{W} - Games$, and FHGs [2] in PFF, respectively.

that is, for every desirable pattern $c \in Incl_i$ there is a coalition $S \in \pi$ that contains c (i.e., $c \subseteq S$); while for each unwanted pattern $c \in \overline{Incl_i}$ there is no coalition $S \in \pi$ such that c is contained in S. In general, a formula γ_i is of the form: $\gamma_i = \langle Incl_{i,1}, \overline{Incl_{i,1}} \rangle \vee \langle Incl_{i,2}, \overline{Incl_{i,2}} \rangle \vee \cdots \vee \langle Incl_{i,p}, \overline{Incl_{i,p}} \rangle$, and a partition π satisfies γ_i (we write $\pi \models \gamma_i$) if there is a pair $\langle Incl_{i,j}, \overline{Incl_{i,j}} \rangle$ such that π satisfies $\langle Incl_{i,j}, \overline{Incl_{i,j}} \rangle$. Therefore, the partition space Π is the disjoint union of the sets: $P_i^+ = \{\pi \in \Pi : \pi \models \gamma_i\}$ and $P_i^- = \{\pi \in \Pi : \pi \not\models \gamma_i\}$.

3   Learning Models

Here we discuss learning models that we applied on PFF-HGs.

3.1   Linear Regression Model

The linear regression model (LRM) [6] is a simple but powerful data analysis tool. An LRM attempts to find the best *line* fitting the input observations ($\mathbf{x}$) and their target values ($\mathbf{t}$). Each observation can be an L-dimensional vector, that abbreviates multiple parameters. During the training phase, the LRM computes a weight vector $\mathbf{w} = (\mathbf{x}^T \mathbf{x})^{-1} \mathbf{x}^T \mathbf{t}$; while during the testing phase, the model compares each approximated value $\hat{y}_r = w_0 + \sum_{l=1}^{L} w_l \cdot x_{r,l}$ with its corresponding target value t_r.

We let each agent $i \in N (|N| = n)$ train and maintain its own learning model. Given a hedonic game G in PFF, an observation is a pair (partition, target value), encoded as follows: we use $\binom{n}{2}$ boolean variables, with each one indicating whether an unordered pair of agents co-exist in the same coalition within the given partition. That is, for each unordered pair (i,j) we use the indicator function $\mathbb{1}_{i \in \pi(j)} = 1$ if agents i, j are in the same coalition, and $\mathbb{1}_{i \in \pi(j)} = 0$ otherwise.[4] Thus, a partition π_k is encoded as $\mathbf{x}_k$ having $\binom{n}{2}$ elements as:

$$\mathbf{x_k} = [\underbrace{\mathbb{1}_{ag_2 \in \pi(ag_1)}, \mathbb{1}_{ag_3 \in \pi(ag_1)}, \cdots, \mathbb{1}_{ag_n \in \pi(ag_1)}}_{n-1 \text{ elements}}, \underbrace{\mathbb{1}_{ag_3 \in \pi(ag_2)}, \mathbb{1}_{ag_4 \in \pi(ag_2)}, \cdots, \mathbb{1}_{ag_n \in \pi(ag_2)}}_{n-2 \text{ elements}},$$

$$\underbrace{\mathbb{1}_{ag_4 \in \pi(ag_3)}, \mathbb{1}_{ag_5 \in \pi(ag_3)}, \cdots, \mathbb{1}_{ag_n \in \pi(ag_3)}}_{n-3 \text{ elements}}, \quad \cdots \cdots \cdots \cdots ,$$

$$\underbrace{\mathbb{1}_{ag_{i+1} \in \pi(ag_i)}, \mathbb{1}_{ag_{i+2} \in \pi(ag_i)}, \cdots, \mathbb{1}_{ag_n \in \pi(ag_i)}}_{n-i \text{ elements}}, \quad \cdots \cdots \cdots \cdots ,$$

$$\underbrace{\mathbb{1}_{ag_{n-1} \in \pi(ag_{n-2})}, \mathbb{1}_{ag_n \in \pi(ag_{n-2})}}_{2 \text{ elements}}, \mathbb{1}_{ag_n \in \pi(ag_{n-1})}]$$

As mentioned above, each agent trains its own model to learn its preferences, considering that each agent's target value for a given partition can be different. Training and testing samples contain partitions (π_k) encoded as $\mathbf{x}_k$, along with

---

[4] We remind the reader that $\pi(j) = S \in \pi : j \in S$.

the corresponding target value (t_k). For ASHGs, this value is equal to $t_k = v_i(S, \pi_k)$, whereas for BHGs, t_k will have a positive value $+c$, $(c > 0)$ if $\pi_k \in P_i^+$ or a negative value $-c$ if $\pi_k \in P_i^-$. In essence, learning an agent's preferences in BHGs can be described as a classification problem, and is examined as such; while ASHGs is a straightforward function approximation problem.

3.2 Linear Regression Model with Basis Functions

The linear regression model provides us with a linear function of the form $t_i \sim \alpha + \beta x_i$. However, the data may not be linear, and thus a line is not an appropriate function to use as predictor. Instead, we can empower the LRM by using M basis functions; i.e. a number of non-linear functions that help us to acquire a more appropriate predictor. The weight vector is now defined according to this set of basis functions, and $\mathbf{w}$ is computes as: $\mathbf{w} = (\boldsymbol{\Phi}^T \cdot \boldsymbol{\Phi})^{-1} \cdot \boldsymbol{\Phi}^T \cdot \mathbf{t}$, where

$$\boldsymbol{\Phi} = \begin{bmatrix} \phi_0(\mathbf{x}_1) & \phi_1(\mathbf{x}_1) & \cdots & \phi_{M-1}(\mathbf{x}_1) \\ \phi_0(\mathbf{x}_2) & \phi_1(\mathbf{x}_2) & \cdots & \phi_{M-1}(\mathbf{x}_2) \\ \vdots & & \ddots & \vdots \\ \phi_0(\mathbf{x}_K) & \phi_1(\mathbf{x}_K) & \cdots & \phi_{M-1}(\mathbf{x}_K) \end{bmatrix} \in \mathbb{R}^{K \times M}.$$ The number M of basis functions,

along with their form, depend essentially on the problem at hand; here we determine M with the TPE method described in Sect. 3.3. In our approach, we chose to work with *Gaussian Basis Functions*. These are of the form [6]:

$$\phi_i(\mathbf{x}) = exp\left\{ -\frac{\|\mathbf{x} - \mu_i\|^2}{2\sigma^2} \right\} \tag{2}$$

where μ_i reflects the location of each ϕ_i in the L-dimensional space, and σ the scale of each value, which is common for every ϕ_i. Now, each basis function ϕ_i is an exponential, related to a center vector $\mu_i \in \mathbb{R}^{\|X\|}$, and a standard deviation $\sigma \in \mathbb{R}^+$. For computing the center vector μ_i of each ϕ_i, we use the well-known *k-means* algorithm [12], while σ is the same for all ϕ_i.

3.3 Feed-Forward Neural Network (NN)

The aforementioned learning models are not in general appropriate for modelling complex preferences with great accuracy. Feed-Forward Neural Networks [6,10] are better at that task, and thus we also employ one here.

In each hidden layer, a non-linear activator is used, otherwise it would act similarly to an LR model. Depending on the PFF-HG class, we let the output layer have a different activator. That is, in ASHGs, a regression model is needed to approximate the function $t_k = v_i(S, \pi_k) \in \mathbb{R}$, so the output layer activator must be linear. In the case of BHGs, essentially we have a classification problem, thus we use a sigmoid activator at the output layer. By using a sigmoid function, the resulting target values lie in $\{0, 1\}$; thus we use the convention that when the target value of a given sample π_k is $t_k = 1$, it means that $\pi_k \in N_i^+$, and when $t_k = 0$ we have that $\pi_k \in N_i^-$.

The performance of an NN depends on the choice of some hyperparameters such as the optimization method, the number of nodes per layer, the activator function in each layer, etc.; while the chosen set of hyperparameters is highly dependent on the complexity of the to-be-learned preferences, i.e., the problem at hand. In this work, we use as an optimization method the *ADAM optimization* algorithm [3]. ADAM attempts to combine the benefits of two different variations of the stochastic gradient descent method, namely Adaptive Gradient Descent (AdaGrad) and the Root Mean Square Propagation (RMSprop) [13]. AdaGrad uses a different learning rate for each parameter to improve performance for sparse gradients, while in RMSprop and AdaDelta the learning rate of each parameter relies on a decaying average of recent gradients. The choice of the ADAM optimizer was made empirically, following a series of experiments with instances of our problem. This showed that ADAM outperformed AdaGrad, RMSprop and AdaDelta [13]. We focused on the above methods, since adaptive learning systems are generally suggested for sparse data, as discussed in [13]. The sparsity of the data is clearly indicated by the form of our observations' representation (see Sect. 3.1).

Having selected the optimization method, we let our architecture self-tune other hyperparameters of the network by using the Tree-structured Parzen Estimator (TPE) [5], an algorithm based on Bayesian optimization with the use of *hyperopt library* for python [4]. In general, hyperparameter optimizers attempt to find a value h_i that minimizes a function $f(h)$, i.e. $\mathrm{argmin}_h(f(h))$. In our apporach, f represents the loss function of the neural network, since this is the quantity we want to minimize. For a predefined number of steps, the algorithm produces sets of hyperparameters h_i, that are used to construct a neural network, which is then trained and tested given the input data. At the end of this process, our architecture yields the best set of hyperparameters h^*, along with the trained neural network that uses these h^*. The TPE allows us to optimize hyperparameters that are structurally dependent: for instance, if we set as a hyperparameter the number of hidden layers, we first optimize the number of layers, and then the hyperparameters for each layer. Figure 1 shows the architecture of the model for selecting the best hyperparameters for the neural network. In Sect. 4.2 we introduce an evaluation metric, which is used as the function f.

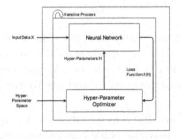

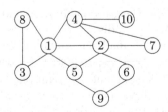

Fig. 1. Architecture for selecting network hyperparameters.

Fig. 2. Social graph g example

4   Experimental Results

Here we first describe the games' environment, i.e., how we generated the synthetic data used for our experiments. Then, we present the evaluation metrics of our work. The coding was in Python3; the experiments ran on a PC with an i7@2.7 GHz processor and 8 GB of RAM.

4.1   Games Environment Setup

The preference relations in hedonic games may be arbitrary. In the classes mentioned above, the preferences depend either on the values b_i^j with a known operator (summation, maximization, etc.), or on formulas. The values b_i^j may be arbitrary, follow some a priori known distribution, or follow some specific function. Here, we suggest that the values b_i^j are derived from a graph, reminiscent of a social network,[5] that describes the "communication links" between the agents.

Specifically, the value i assigns to j within partition π, comes from the graph structure. That is, $b_i^j(\pi)$ is related to the following three properties:

1. the distance between agent i and j; and
2. the distances between agent i and all coalitions in π.
3. the distances between agent j and all coalitions in π.

Intuitively, the distance between i and j, denoted as $\mathrm{dist}_g(i,j)$, represents a measurable metric for the expression "how close friends are i and j". Property 1 would have been enough in hedonic games with no externalities. However, when we study the games in partition function form, each agent values differently coalitions and agents depending on the formed coalition structure. Thus, we need to capture the partition's form. The distance between an agent i and a coalition S in π, intuitively represents i's 'motivation' to deviate in another existing coalition. Therefore, property 2 compensates i for collaborating with j instead of another set of people; while property 3 'honours' j for working with i.

The distance between two agents, $\mathrm{dist}_g(i,j)$, is defined as the shortest path that connects these agents; and the distance between an agent i and a coalition S is $\mathrm{dist}_g(i,S) = \sum_{j \in S} \frac{\mathrm{dist}_g(i,j)}{|S|}$. The value i assigns to j is defined as:

$$b_i^j(\pi|g) = \kappa_i \cdot \frac{1}{\mathrm{dist}(i,j)} + \lambda_i \cdot \sum_{S \in \pi} \mathrm{dist}_g(i,S) + \xi_i \cdot \sum_{S \in \pi} \frac{1}{\mathrm{dist}_g(j,S)},$$

where g is the graph, and κ_i, λ_i and ξ_i are constants related to agent i. In words, term $\lambda_i \cdot \sum_{S \in \pi} \mathrm{dist}_g(i,S)$ captures i's 'cost' to move to a different coalition and attributes a small/large amount for coalitions close/faraway to her. While term $\xi_i \cdot \sum_{S \in \pi} \frac{1}{\mathrm{dist}_g(j,S)}$ expresses i's degree of honour towards j, and attributes a small/large amount for coalitions faraway/close to j.

Note that each agent may consider a completely different social network than its peers. In other words, each i perceives differently the collaboration patterns

---

[5] We abusively use the term 'social network' to refer to a graph that give rise to personal values b_i^j; without considering any related literature on the term.

among players. Having defined values b_i^j in this way, we may therefore use any of the above suggested utility functions, e.g. summation, boolean, etc., to determine the coalitions' and partitions' utility.

Game Parameters. In all games we have $n = [5, 10, 20, 50]$ agents. For the ASHGs in PFF: in each game we constructed a social graph (see Fig. 2) with n nodes and $e \sim \mathcal{U}(n - 1, \frac{n \cdot (n-1)}{2})$ number of edges (uniformly chosen between the minimum number of edges that allow us to have a connected graph, and the maximum number of edges that results in a fully connected graph); each edge has a weight $w_{edge} \sim \mathcal{U}(1, 5)$. For the BGs in PFF: in each game, we use uniform distributions to construct a formula γ_i consisting of multiple pairs $\langle Incl_i, \overline{Incl_i} \rangle$ for each agent $i \in N$, depending on the number of agents in the game; and to let each pair involve a certain number of agents, as shown in Table 1.

Table 1. Game environment parameters

n	Graph			Formulae	
	κ, λ, ξ	$|edges|$	$edge_{weight}$	#$\langle Incl_i, \overline{Incl_i} \rangle$/agent	#agents/$\langle Incl_i, \overline{Incl_i} \rangle$
5	$\sim \mathcal{U}(0, 10)$	$\sim \mathcal{U}(4, 10)$	$\mathcal{U}(1, 5)$	$\mathcal{U}(2, 3)$	$\mathcal{U}(1, 4)$
10	$\sim \mathcal{U}(0, 10)$	$\sim \mathcal{U}(9, 45)$	$\mathcal{U}(1, 5)$	$\mathcal{U}(4, 7)$	$\mathcal{U}(4, 6)$
20	$\sim \mathcal{U}(0, 10)$	$\sim \mathcal{U}(19, 190)$	$\mathcal{U}(1, 5)$	$\mathcal{U}(9, 11)$	$\mathcal{U}(5, 7)$
50	$\sim \mathcal{U}(0, 10)$	$\sim \mathcal{U}(49, 1225)$	$\mathcal{U}(1, 5)$	$\mathcal{U}(12, 15)$	$\mathcal{U}(8, 12)$

4.2 Evaluation Metrics

In order to evaluate our experimental results, it is essential to determine the nature of the desirable outcomes. We work with hedonic games, a class of cooperative games which, unlike others, possesses some particular properties. Specifically, in such games, we care little about the actual coalitions' utilities, since our interest lies mainly on the preference relation formed. The modelling of the games studied within the scope of this paper (i.e., the interpretation of a game instance into input data for a learning model), allows us to extract the desired preferences. Thus, a question arises: do we care to learn the best function $\hat{u}_i(S, \pi)$ that resembles the actual $u_i(S, \pi)$; or do we desire a $\hat{u}_i(S, \pi)$ that encodes a preference relation best matching the actual one?

To be more accurate, we distinguish the following two evaluation metrics:

- the *Root Mean Square Error* (RMSE) between the predicted utility functions $\hat{u}_i(S, \pi)$, and the true function $u_i(S, \pi)$
- the *Qualitative Proximity* (QP) between the ordering described by $\hat{u}_i(S, \pi)$ and the true preference relation.

The first metric is straightforward, $\mathrm{RMSE}(u_i, \hat{u}_i) = \sqrt{\frac{1}{|D|} \sum_{(S,\pi) \in D} (u_i(S, \pi) - \hat{u}_i(S, \pi))^2}$, where D is the collection of testing data encoded as described in Sect. 3.1, and $|D|$

is the size of the collection D. The second metric, however, is more interesting. This metric indicates that even if the predicted $\hat{u}_i$ differs significantly from the true u_i in actual values, they are still equivalent. That is, functions $\hat{u}_i$ and u_i encode in the same way the preference relation between any two embedded coalitions (S,π) and (T,π'), e.g. both $(S,\pi) \succsim_i^{u_i} (T,\pi')$ and $(S,\pi) \succsim_i^{\hat{u}_i} (T,\pi')$ hold. QP in fact could be thought of as a variant of *Kendall Tau* metric [11].

Therefore, when a utility function of an agent i is "learned" based on the training data, we extract a preference relation, $\succsim_i^{\hat{u}_i}$, over partitions. Then we can measure the *percentage of equivalence* between u_i and $\hat{u}_i$ by counting the average of pairwise relations that are identically encoded by u_i and $\hat{u}_i$. Thus, we define Qualitative Proximity as follows:

$$QP(u_i, \hat{u}_i) = \frac{\sum_{(S,\pi),(T,\pi')\in D} CHK(u_i, \hat{u}_i, (S,\pi), (T,\pi'))}{|D|(|D|-1)/2}, \text{ where}$$

$$CHK(u_i, \hat{u}_i, (S,\pi), (T,\pi')) = \begin{cases} 1 & \text{if } ((S,\pi) \succsim_i^{u_i} (T,\pi') \\ & \wedge (S,\pi) \succsim_i^{\hat{u}_i} (T,\pi')) \\ 0 & \text{otherwise} \end{cases}.$$

One step further, we introduce a single metric that combines both RMSE and QP. According to this metric:

- the lower the error $RMSE(u_i, \hat{u}_i)$, the better $\hat{u}_i$ fits u_i
- the higher the $QP(u_i, \hat{u}_i)$, the better $\succsim_i^{\hat{u}_i}$ matches $\succsim_i^{u_i}$.

Thus, our *Overall Preference Accuracy (OPA)* metric can be defined as follows:

$$OPA(u_i, \hat{u}_i) = \frac{QP(u_i, \hat{u}_i)}{\epsilon + RMSE_{nrm}(u_i, \hat{u}_i)},$$

where $RMSE_{nrm}$ is the normalized RMSE regarding the test samples values' range. This normalized RMSE allows us to compare the performance in games with different value ranges. The intuitive interpretation of the OPA metric is that, we highly value the contribution of QP metric–since this actually measures the similarity of the original preference relation to the approximated one–but also take into some consideration the RMSE between the original and the approximated function. In order to avoid division with zero, we add a small positive $\epsilon = 10^{-5}$ to the denominator.

As mentioned above, we use OPA in the TPE for the hyperparameter selection. Specifically, we set the loss function TPE attempts to minimize to $f(h) = \frac{1}{OPA(u_i, \hat{u}_i)}$, where u_i is derived from the input (test) data, and the estimated $\hat{u}_i$ is related to the hyperparameters h for the neural network model.

4.3   Results

Table 2. Approximate time needed per game for training and testing.

	5			10			20			50		
	LRM	LRMRBF	NN	LRM	LRMRBF	NN	LRM	LRMRBF	NN	LRM	LRMRBF	NN
ASHGs	0.05 s	1.2 s	14 s	2.4 s	17 s	1.7 min	10 s	1.7 min	8.3 min	3.2 min	25.3 min	5.5 h
BHGs	0.04 s	1 s	45 s	1.3 s	12 s	2.9 min	5.5 s	1.2 min	8.4 min	1.7 min	30.6 min	2.5 h

Table 3. Samples per setting

n	Partition samples		
	Training	Testing	Validation
5	200	500	200
10	2000	5000	2000
20	5000	10000	5000
50	20000	40000	10000

We conducted a series of experiments for our evaluation, simulating both ASHGs and BHGs games. Table 3 shows the number of observation samples used in each setting (depending on the number of agents). Note that *Validation* refers to the process of optimizing the model's hyperparameters. For each (*type of game, number of agents*) setting, we trained each learning model for 5 game examples. In Fig. 3 we show the average scores of both OPA and QP metrics each learning model yielded per setting (*type of game, number of agents*). As we can see, NN models outperform LRM and LRMRBF, both in ASHGs and BHGs, especially as the number of agents increases. This is, in fact, an anticipated result since the hyper-parameters optimization makes our NN models more adaptive to the problem. However, the larger the number of agents is, the more computationally expensive the NN model is. This results from the hidden layers having many fully connected nodes. The number of layers is 1 or 2, while the nodes per layer are in $[\frac{n}{2}, \frac{n \cdot (n-1)}{2}]$, selected by TPE optimizer.

In BHGs, the complexity of our hidden preferences mainly depends on the number of different pairs $\langle Incl, \overline{Incl} \rangle$ each agent has, and on conflicts regarding the preference for a specific agent j (j may be "wanted" as part of a specific subcoalition, but not of some other). In our experiments we increased the "intricacy" of the preferences, as the number of agents increases (see Table 2). Thus, we observe that the LRM, in BHGs, lacks scalability; i.e., LRM is incapable to approximate highly "complex" preferences. However, for a small number of agents (i.e. 5), the fact that the formulae are considerably simple results to an average ~85% on QP; this, along with the fact that the NN is computationally expensive gives rise to a trade off between the two models–see the approximate time each model needs in Table 2. For ASHGs, due to their nature, both LRM and LRMRBF are very effective in terms of QP, and well-behaved regarding

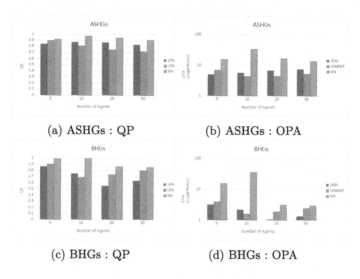

(a) ASHGs : QP (b) ASHGs : OPA

(c) BHGs : QP (d) BHGs : OPA

Fig. 3. QP and OPA scores (average over 5 games).

scalability. Once again NN outperforms the other models, however, the high computational load of this model makes the simple and more inexpensive models very appealing. Between the LRM and LRMRBF, the former is found to be more consistent for settings with many players. Note that all three learning methods exhibit performance ranging from adequate to extremely successful, operating with a small number of samples in huge partition space. For example, for 20 agents, we have $10^{13.71372}$ partitions in total, and we feed the models only with 5000 training samples, i.e., with the $9.66 \cdot 10^{-9}\%$ of the total space.

5   Conclusion and Future Work

In this paper, we put forward the formal definition of PFF-HGs, and extended well studied classes of HGs to partition function form. Then, we employed three learning models to approximate the hidden preference relations. Finally, we conducted a systematic evaluation that verified the effectiveness of our approach. As future work, we intend to test the learning process in other classes of hedonic games, such as $\mathcal{B}/\mathcal{W} - Games$, and Fractional HGs [2] in PFF.

References

1. Aziz, H., Harrenstein, P., Lang, J., Wooldridge, M.: Boolean hedonic games. In: Proceedings of the Fifteenth International Conference on Principles of Knowledge Representation and Reasoning, KR 2016, pp. 166–175. AAAI Press (2016)
2. Aziz, H., Savani, R., Moulin, H.: Hedonic games. In: Brandt, F., Conitzer, V., Endriss, U., Lang, J., Procaccia, A.D. (eds.) Handbook of Computational Social Choice, pp. 356–376. Cambridge University Press, Cambridge (2016)

3. Ba, J., Kingma, D.: Adam: a method for stochastic optimization. In: Proceedings of the 3rd International Conference on Learning Representations (ICLR-15) (2015)
4. Bergstra, J., Yamins, D., Cox, D.D.: Making a science of model search: hyperparameter optimization in hundreds of dimensions for vision architectures (2013)
5. Bergstra, J.S., Bardenet, R., Bengio, Y., Kégl, B.: Algorithms for hyper-parameter optimization. In: Proceedings of NIPS-2011, pp. 2546–2554 (2011)
6. Bishop, C.M.: Pattern Recognition and Machine Learning (Information Science and Statistics). Springer, Berlin (2006)
7. Chalkiadakis, G., Elkind, E., Wooldridge, M.: Computational Aspects of Cooperative Game Theory (Synthesis Lectures on Artificial Inetlligence and Machine Learning), 1st edn. Morgan & Claypool Publishers, San Rafael (2011)
8. Elkind, E., Wooldridge, M.: Hedonic coalition nets. In: Proceedings of The 8th International Conference on Autonomous Agents and Multiagent Systems, AAMAS 2009, Vol. 1, pp. 417–424 (2009)
9. Georgara, A., Ntiniakou, T., Chalkiadakis, G.: Learning hedonic games via probabilistic topic modeling. In: Slavkovik, M. (ed.) EUMAS 2018. LNCS (LNAI), vol. 11450, pp. 62–76. Springer, Cham (2019). https://doi.org/10.1007/978-3-030-14174-5_5
10. Goodfellow, I., Bengio, Y., Courville, A.: Deep Learning. MIT Press, Cambridge (2016)
11. Kendall, M.: Rank Correlation Methods. Griffin, London (1948)
12. MacQueen, J., et al.: Some methods for classification and analysis of multivariate observations. In: Proceedings of the Fifth Berkeley Symposium on Mathematical Statistics and Probability, Oakland, CA, USA, vol. 1, pp. 281–297 (1967)
13. Ruder, S.: An overview of gradient descent optimization algorithms (2016)
14. Saad, W., Han, Z., Zheng, R., Hjorungnes, A., Basar, T., Poor, H.V.: Coalitional games in partition form for joint spectrum sensing and access in cognitive radio networks. IEEE J. Sel. Top. Signal Process. **6**, 195–209 (2012)
15. Sliwinski, J., Zick, Y.: Learning hedonic games. In: Proceedings of the 26th IJCAI-17, pp. 2730–2736 (2017)
16. Thrall, R.M., Lucas, W.F.: N-person games in partition function form. Naval Res. Logist. Quart. **10**(1), 281–298 (1963)

Agent-Based Approach for Inventory Pre- and Post-disruption Decision Support

Maroua Kessentini[1,2]($\boxtimes$), Narjes Bellamine Ben Saoud[1], and Sami Sboui[2]

[1] Univ. Manouba, ENSI, RIADI LR99ES26,
Campus Universitaire Manouba, 2010 Manouba, Tunisia
`maroua.kessentini@gmail.com`
[2] SQLI Services, Technopole Manouba, 2010 Manouba, Tunisia

Abstract. Due to its global nature and highly dynamic and competitive environment, supply chain arguably is more exposed to disruptions. As supply chains continue to grow in scale and complexity, inventory management in a dynamic business environment is a challenging task. The aim of this paper is to propose a multi-agent approach to quantify the impact of inventory disruptions. Our objective is to analyze the capacities of supply chains to cope with disruptions before and after stockouts by including (proactive) mitigation strategies and reactive strategies. The proposed system allows providing advice to human users in the form of decision support. A prototype system is built and validated, which demonstrates the feasibility of the proposed approach. The experiments show that the implementation of multi-agent technology makes the system much more flexible to make the final decision.

Keywords: Inventory disruption management ·
Pre- and post-disruption · Multi-agent modeling and simulation ·
Decision support system

1 Introduction

In the recent past, the supply chain is driven by a low demand variability environments [2]. In this almost stable environment, much of the supply chain management efforts have focused on increasing the efficiency. Efficiency is expressed in terms of reduced costs while fulfilling the system requirements in terms of customer satisfaction and on-time delivery. Nowadays, the firm's perceptions are changed given the global nature and the turbulent and uncertain supply chain environment. In this complex dynamic and competitive environment, supply chains are more susceptible to disruptions [1]. The potential losses of disruptions imply for an effective disruption management.

Effective disruption management affects the success or the failure of the supply chain management. One of the most important perceptions in this field is

© Springer Nature Switzerland AG 2019
C. Douligeris et al. (Eds.): KSEM 2019, LNAI 11775, pp. 842–853, 2019.
https://doi.org/10.1007/978-3-030-29551-6_74

the inventory management. Inventory management in the disturbed environment is become more challenging. The challenging environment is characterized by a more and more shorten product life cycle, an increasing customization levels, and more partners geographically dispersed. Handling disruption under this global and dispersed environment calls for a higher levels of supply chain resilience. To model and design a resilient supply chain, mathematical programming are widely used [4]. Despite their potential, the uncertainty violates the required assumptions for many stochastic models [5]. As alternative to analytical modelling, simulation techniques provide an artificial environment to assess the dynamic behaviour of the system. For aforementioned challenge, the agent-based technology presents a good target.

The main goal of the presented work is to propose an approach that allows applying the resilience findings of supply chain management to the inventory disruption management processes. Our contribution is to define the inventory disruption problem and to provide solution(s) which minimized the disruption impact. These solutions will be analyzed and proposed to the human decision-maker to make the final decision.

2 Related Works

To manage disruption, companies need to follow a path from risk identification to disruption recovery. Risk identification refers to defining a list of risk events and to classifying them in different categories. One of the most common risk categorisation schemes is location-based classification. This classification distinguishes between three categories of risk sources - "internal to the company", "external to the company but internal to the network of the chain" and "external to the network" [6]. The actors in internal risks have more control on the cause of the disruption. However, external risks are more difficult to control [7].

Disruption recovery allows to amplify or absorb risk effects and to improve the performance. To limit the impact of disruptions, decision rules regarding order quantities, batch sizes, global sourcing [3] are important. In addition, the literature presents many key policies such as information sharing, partners collaboration [10], safety stocks [8] and flexibility [9]. Flexibility may includes supply flexibility, process flexibility (flexible manufacturing process) and demand flexibility (postponement, inter-changeably). These policies were among the most frequently mentioned supply chain handling strategies [6].

Handling disruption might include mitigation (proactive) and reactive strategies [7]. What firms do before and after the occurrence of the disruption are both important and should be implemented and coordinated. References [12] think that one of the future research directions is to integrate proactive and reactive strategies for managing disruptions. The combination of these perspectives has only been looked by two groups. Reference [13] give a method that integrates game theory and Bayesian belief networks to determine the optimal preventive and reactive strategies under resource constraints. Reference [14] present a process for managing supply chain operation "before, during, and after" product recall that include three main stages: "Readiness, Responsiveness, and Recovery". However, these works are either developed for a specific type of disruption or about analytical modelling for supply chains.

3   Problem Overview

In this paper, we consider a very common type of supply chain with a distributor firm of N finish products ($p_i \; for \; i = 1 \ldots N$). These products are supplied from M suppliers ($S_j \; for \; j = 1 \ldots M$) in order to meet K customers' orders ($CO_k \; for \; k = 1 \ldots K$). Each customer order is described by the requested product CO^p, the quantity needed CO^{amt}, the requested due date CO^{dd}, the customer location CO^{loc}, the customer priority CO^{prio} and the time when the order is placed CO^{time}. The suppliers are assumed to be located in disjoint geographic regions. They are characterized by the delivery time (LT_p product lead time) and the product purchase price $CostR_p$. The distributor firm receives customers' orders, meets their needs and communicates with suppliers in order to ask for the required products according to the used inventory procurement policies. The amount of the required product as well as the date of order placement for each customer order is a complicated task and is done based on the procedure that is described in [15]. In the case of disruption, the distributor firm aims to reduce the impact of disruption at a low cost (financial objective) and a high customer satisfaction level (logistical objective).

4   Inventory Disruption Management Model

Inventory system is compose of autonomous actors interconnected by physical, information and financial flow. Each actor is responsible for one or more activities and coordinate with others to execute their responsibilities in the system [11]. The inventory system has the same basic characteristics as an agent namely autonomy, social-ability, pro-activeness and dynamicity. In addition, the flexible behaviour of agent can be easily used to conceive many experiments. These experiments aims to study the effects of actors structure on the desired performance of the system. To conclude, agent-based modelling looks like an appropriate approach to model the inventory system as a decentralized and complex system.

As mentioned before, the inventory system in this work is composed of three types of actors: customer, supplier and the distributor firm itself. The distributor firm is the main actor that is modelled by an agent built upon three modules (see Fig. 1). The monitoring module responsible for providing the required monitoring information. By gathering and analyzing corresponding data from all parties of the supply chain, it can detect anomalies. Based on the available information, the decision module encompasses the general behavior of the agent such as computing, communicating and inferring and/or evaluating new solutions. The action module defines a variety of possible actions undertaken by the agent in the normal/abnormal supply chain operation. The normal supply chain operation is related to the order generation process, the order acceptance process (scheduling policy), and the inventory management process (procurement policy). In addition to this routine decisions, additional decisions should be made in case of disruptions.

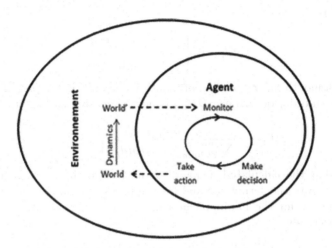

Fig. 1. The generic structure for distributor firm agent (adapted from [16]).

4.1 Order Generation

The input to this procedure is an estimated demand curve $DD_{p,d}$ (1) for each product p during one year ($\forall\ d\ \in D = 360\ days$). The first term of (1) represents the seasonal variation effect of a demand where CA_p is the cycle amplitude and CN_p is the number of cycles in one year (number of days in simulation horizon). The second term represents the annual gradual growth effect of a demand where BD_p is the base demand level and DG_p is the demand growth factor. The third term represents the daily uncertainty in demand curve where α_d is a uniform $[-1, 1]$ random variable and DDU_p is a daily demand uncertainty limit.

$$DD_{p,d} = CA_p\ sin(d\ CN_p\ \frac{\pi}{180}) + BD_p\ exp(d\ DG_p) + \alpha_d\ DDU_p \qquad (1)$$

The next step is to translate the demand curve into discrete orders by firstly determine the cumulative monthly demand $MD_{p,m}$ (2) where m represents the index for each month ($m = 1, 2, \ldots, \lceil(D/30)\rceil$).

$$MD_{p,m} = \sum_{d=30(m-1)+1}^{30m} (DD_{p,d}) \qquad (2)$$

After that, each monthly demand is re-distributed throughout the days in the month according to the order frequency index f_p. This last represents the probability of a customer order for the product p on a given day d, where $0 \leq f_p \leq 1$. We assume that, on each day, each customer can send at most one order for each product type. Then, a uniform $[0,1]$ random variable $\mu_{p,d}$ is generated every day in the month and compared to f_p to capture the uncertainty of order occurrence $ratd_{p,d}$ (3).

$$ratd_{p,d} = \begin{cases} \mu_{p,d} \ if \ \mu_{p,d} \leq f_p \\ 0 \ if \ \mu_{p,d} > f_p \end{cases} \tag{3}$$

For each month m, the portion of monthly demand that is placed on the day d following an order occurrence $DR_{p,d}$ is next generated as shown in (4).

$$DR_{p,d} = \frac{ratd_{p,d}}{\sum_{d=30(m-1)+1}^{30m}(ratd_{p,d})}(MD_{p,m}) \tag{4}$$

Given that the calculated demand amount might be unreasonably low or high, we generate the actual demand for the product p on the day d $AD_{p,d}$ (5) after accounting for the minimum and maximum order size limits, D_{min} and D_{max}, respectively.

$$AD_{p,d} = \begin{cases} 0 \ if \ DR_{p,d} < D_{min} \\ DR_{p,d} \ if \ D_{min} \leq DR_{p,d} \leq D_{max} \\ D_{max} \ if \ DR_{p,d} > D_{max} \end{cases} \tag{5}$$

$AD_{p,d}$ represents one customer order that will be created if $AD_{p,d} > 0$ for which $CO^{amt} = AD_{p,d}$, $CO^p = p$ and $CO^{time} = d$. The other order details $(CO^{dd}, CO^{prio}$ and $CO^{loc})$ are randomly generated from their pre-defined ranges shown in Table 1.

4.2   Order Acceptance

In this process, the daily customers' order-list is evaluated. Accordingly, acceptance/rejection/negotiation decisions are taken for each order in the list. The process is presented in Algorithm 1. The top order in the list is considered for evaluation, the decision is taken and again the new top order is considered until the list is empty. First, the profitability level of the order is checked. The order is considered profitable when it revenue is equal or larger than 20% of it incurred costs. If an order is profitable and there is enough inventories, the order will be accepted. In the case of profitable order for which there is not enough inventories or not-profitable order from an important customer for which there is enough inventory, the order attribute can be negotiated. Else (i.e. the order is not profitable and the customer is regular or customer is important but there is no enough inventories), the order will be rejected.

4.3   Inventory Management

Under the reorder point policy, the product will be purchased when its inventory level falls below the reorder point RR_p. The amount of the product p purchased at the day d $RP_p(d)$ is then calculated based on (6).

$$RP_p(d) = \begin{cases} RT_p - RF_p(d) & \text{if } RF_p(d) < RR_p \\ 0 & \text{otherwise} \end{cases} \tag{6}$$

Where RT_p represents the maximum capacity of storage tanks (i.e. the inventory top-up-to level "S") for the product p, $RF_p(d) = IR_p(d) + \sum RW_p(d)$ is the amount of the product p that will be found at the day d and RW_p is the amount of the product p that has been ordered but not yet arrived. The inventory level is calculated as follow: $(IR_p(d) = IR_p(d-1) + RA_p(d-1) - RU_p(d-1))$. Where $RA_p(d) = RP_p(d - ALT_p)$ represents the amount of the product p arriving at the day d and $RU_p(d)$ is the amount of the product p transferred to customer. The time lag between product purchase and its arrival incorporating uncertainty is $ALT_p = (1 + \lambda \ LTU_p) \ LT_p$. Where λ is a uniform $[0, 1]$ random variable for lead time uncertainty, LTU_p is the maximum delivery delay and LT_p is the nominal product lead time.

Algorithm 1 Order acceptance

Require: L_d // set of l customers' orders in a given day d
Ensure: action = accept, reject, negotiate //the decision undertaken for each customer order in the order-list
1: $i \leftarrow 1$ // Initialization
2: **while** $i \leq l$ //the order-list is NOT EMPTY **do**
3:     $p \leftarrow CO_i^p$, $dd \leftarrow CO_i^{dd}$, $loc \leftarrow CO_i^{loc}$
4:     Calculate IR_p // in terms of accepted orders
5:     Calculate the order's profit margin CO_i^{prof}
6:     **if** $CO_i^{prof} = true$ // revenue $\geq 20\%$ costs **then**
7:         **if** $CO_i^{amt} \leq IR_p(dd - loc)$ **then**
8:             $action \leftarrow accept$
9:         **else**
10:             $action \leftarrow negotiate$
11:         **end if**
12:     **else**
13:         **if** $CO_i^{prio} = 1$ // important customer **then**
14:             **if** $CO_i^{amt} \leq IR_p(dd - loc)$ **then**
15:                 $action \leftarrow negotiate$
16:             **else**
17:                 $action \leftarrow reject$
18:             **end if**
19:         **else**
20:             $action \leftarrow reject$
21:         **end if**
22:     **end if**
23:     $i \leftarrow i + 1$
24: **end while**

4.4 Disruption Management

A disruption analysis approach is used to model the different possible remedial actions and quantifies their impact on the supply chain performance. The first step is generating a disruption scenario. For each day in the simulation horizon, the occurrence of a disruption is checked by generating a uniform $[0, 1]$ random number and comparing it with the probability of a disruption to occur D_p. If the random number is less than D_p, so there is a disruption in that day ($DST = d$ presents the disruption start time). Next, the disruption duration DD is defined according to triangular distribution. So, the disruption end time $DET = DST + DD$ can be calculated.

Many different strategies can be defined and implemented to handle the potential disruption. Therefore, some of these strategies have been defined for experimentation with the model. Two prevention strategies are modelled: the inventory mitigation (the distribution firm carries some excess inventory) and the sourcing mitigation (the distribution firm sources from two suppliers kinds i.e. one global supplier and one backup high-cost supplier). In addition, three possible reactive strategies are presented. The emergency procurement: flowing the detection of disruption, the distributor firm starts looking for alternative suppliers and placing an emergency order. Each supplier, receives the emergency order, presents his proposal. When the distributor firm receives all proposals, it assigns the request to the supplier(s) with the nearest delivery time. The requested quantity can be delivered from a single supplier or distributed between different suppliers. Customer negotiation: the orders affected by the disruption are either orders accepted before or after the announcement of the disruption. For the first type of orders, the distribution firm begins to re-negotiate with some customers to extend their orders' due date. For the second type of orders, the distribution firm adjusts its order acceptance strategy. Orders re-allocation: the basic idea here is to exchange the orders affected by the disruption between the different resources currently available.

4.5 Performance Measuring

The performance can be measured through various key performance indicators: logistics performances (customer satisfaction, number of missed orders, number of late orders, total tardiness) and financial performances (profit). Customer satisfaction is measured as the percentage of on time deliveries NLO (7) out of the total number of orders accepted NCO during the simulation horizon. The total tardiness NLD is measured as follow: $NLD = NLD + \sum_{i=1}^{NCO} \max(0, CO_i^{dt} - CO_i^{dd})$ where CO^{dt} represents the time when the product is delivered to the customer.

$$NLO = \begin{cases} NLO + 1 & if\ CO_i^{dt} > CO_i^{dd},\ \forall\ i = 1 \ldots NCO \\ NLO & \text{otherwise} \end{cases} \qquad (7)$$

The Profit is measured as the revenue minus the various Costs. $Revenue = \sum_{i=1}^{NCO} Price_p \times CO_i^{amt}$ where $Price_p$ is the selling price of product p.

$Costs = CostTc + CostPen + CostPur + CostInv + CostFix.$ $CostTc = \sum_{i=1}^{NCO} CostD \times CO_i^{amt} \times CO_i^{loc}$ is the transportation cost where $CostD$ is the delivery cost per unit product per unit distance. $CostPen = \sum_{i=1}^{NCO} pen \times \max(0, CO_i^{dt} - CO_i^{dd})$ is the late delivery penalty where pen is the penalty cost per late day. $CostPur = \sum_p CostR_p \times RA_p(t)$ is the purchasing cost where $CostR_p$ is the price of the purchased product. $CostInv = \sum_p CostI \times IR_p(d)$ is the inventory cost where $CostI$ is the inventory cost per unit product per day. $CostFix(d) = CostOF \times d$ is the fixed operating cost where the fixed operating cost per day.

5   Experimental Results

Our simulator is developed using the multi-Agent platform JADE installed on ECLIPSE. The input values for the model are given in Table 1.

Table 1. Nominal values for model parameters

	Parameter description		Notation	Value(s)
General	simulation horizon (days)		D	360
	number of customer		NC	50
	number of supplier		NS	6
Customer data	cycle amplitude		CA_p	4
	number of cycles in one year		CN_p	2
	base demand level		BD_p	200
	demand growth factor		DG_p	8/37000
	daily demand uncertainty limit		DDU_p	5
	order frequency index		f_p	0.3
	maximum order size limit		D_{max}	5000
	minimum order size limit		D_{min}	500
	due date range (days)		dd	15-25
	customer location range (days)		loc	0-10
Supplier data	lead time (days)	global supplier	LT_p	7
		local supplier		4
	purchase price ($/unit)	global supplier	$CostR_p$	60
		local supplier		75
Distributor firm data	maximum capacity/top-up point (unit)		RT_p	2500
	fixed operating cost ($/day)		CostOF	2000
	inventory cost [$/(unit day)]		CostI	1
	late penalty ($/day)		Pen	500
	delivery cost $/[unit(unit distance)]		CostD	5
	initial inventory level (unit)		$IR_p(0)$	1500
	product price ($/unit)		$Price_p$	120

The simulator takes as input a set of customers' orders that are generated using Matlab. Fifty customers' orders are modelled each day (an order can be zero means that the customer don't place an order in that specific day). Each order seeks to one common product. We assume that there is only one product type in this paper. In addition, we consider that only one disruption is considered at the same time. The disruption considered for experimentation in this work is the supplier disruption. The probability of this disruption is Dp = 0,005 (or the expected frequency of once per 200 days). And the duration is sampled from a triangular distribution with a minimum value of 5 days, a most likely value of 10 days and a maximum value of 20 days. Using this input, different scenarios are generated in each simulation run. Thus, even for the same configuration, the outputs indicators performance were different. Accordingly, we run the model for 20 disruption scenarios and report the mean and standard deviation for each indicator performance measure. The capabilities of our simulator for decision support are illustrated using four case studies.

5.1   Case Study 1: Order Acceptance Process

This case study experiments three specific cases on order acceptance. The first case (case 1) concerns the no-negotiation case in which customer orders will be accepted as long as the product is available before the due date. The second case (case 2) is about the order selectivity case in which the level of profitability of the order is checked first. If the order is profitable, the availability of products before the delivery date will be verified. Subsequently, profitable orders for which the requested delivery time is achievable are accepted and all others are rejected. In the third case (case 3), an order that cannot be accepted will not be immediately rejected but will be negotiated to reach an agreement on the due date. The results of simulation are presented in Table 2.

Table 2. Simulation results of the order acceptance process cases

	Case 1	Case 2	Case 3
Accepted orders	473 (9)	174 (5)	386 (5)
Late orders	161 (9)	26 (4)	27 (4)
Profit (m$)	13.69 (0.86)	15.68 (0.87)	18.44 (1.45)

In the case of no-negotiation, the only criterion of acceptance of the orders is the availability of the products. Consequently, the total number of accepted orders is considerably higher than in the other two cases. However, the number of late orders in this case is much higher than in the other two cases. Delayed delivery not only hurts the company's reputation and the future behaviour of its customers, but also decreases the overall profile due to late penalty fees.

5.2   Case Study 2: Inventory Management Process

The inventory management process is impacted by the selection of the inventory management policy and the supplier characteristics. In this experiment, two category of supplier are available: a global supplier with delivery time of 7 days and a local supplier with delivery time of 4 days but with 25% higher unit product price. As the reorder point policy is used, we assume that the reorder point can be on 25% or 40% of the capacity of storage and that the inventory top-up-to level "S" is set as the maximum capacity of storage. The simulation results are presented in Table 3.

Table 3. Simulation results of the inventory management process

Policy (s, S)	Delivery time = 7 days		Delivery time = 4 days	
	s = 25%	s = 40%	s = 25%	s = 40%
Profit (m$)	13.68 (1.22)	19.69 (1.45)	15.94 (1.46)	19.51 (1.31)
Cr satisfaction (%)	68 (4)	91 (3)	73 (5)	92 (2)
Late orders	112 (9)	59 (5)	93 (9)	59 (5)

Simulation horizon 360 days
Number of orders ±250

The results shows that the delivery time can not generally be considered as an important factor in comparing it to the inventory management policy. The second obvious conclusion is that the policy (s, S) with s = 40% gives better results and can be considered as a point of reference. The implementation of an appropriate inventory management policy should therefore be considered as the main factor for improving the inventory management process. However, selecting a higher control point can increase the cost of storage and subsequently decrease the profit. In order to obtain an overview of the appropriate level for this parameter, a study of the control point variation and its impact on the chain performance must be conducted. This will be one of our short-term prospects.

5.3   Case Study 3: Pre-disruption Process

In this case study, the inventory mitigation (strategy 1) and the sourcing mitigation (strategy 2) are compared with each other and also with the case of no action (Table 4). The sourcing mitigation strategy was the dominant choice in terms of profit in most scenarios. As can be seen, by defining a prevention strategy, profit can be improved up to 13–42%. The average profit for sourcing mitigation strategy however is higher in comparison with the other two options. It can be concluded that this strategy is the appropriate strategy to manage supplier disruptions.

5.4   Case Study 4: Post-disruption Process

In this experiment, we considers that supplier disruption is occurs on day 148 of the simulation horizon. The abnormal event will result in 25 late orders with 46 late days. As mentioned before, three possible actions to react to this disruption:

Table 4. Effect of preventive strategies on the chain performance

	No action	Strategy 1	Strategy 2
Late orders	26 (17)	1 (1)	3 (2)
Delay (days)	57 (6)	30 (20)	1 (1)
Cr satisfaction (%)	80 (4)	98.4 (1)	97.6 (1)
Profit (m$)	7.58 (0.67)	8.60 (0.66)	10.77 (0.68)

Simulation horizon 360 days
Number of orders ±125

emergency demand (Policy 1), re-assignment of orders (Policy 2) and customer negotiation. For customer negotiation action, we run the simulation with two possible parameters. The probability of the customer agreeing to extend the delivery date is estimated at 35% for the optimistic case (Policy 3) and 15% for the pessimistic case (Policy 4). The result is presented in Table 5. As we can be shown, the re-assignment policy results in a considerable improvement in logistic performance. However, the other two policies can also improve the logistic performance of 25 late orders to an average of 15 late orders. In terms of financial performance, negotiation with the client is the most attractive policy.

Table 5. Effect of reactive policies on the chain performance

	Policy 1	Policy 2	Policy 3	Policy 4
Late orders	7 (5)	16 (7)	19 (5)	11 (4)
Delay (days)	22 (5)	37 (29)	40 (10)	25 (4)
Profit (m$)	10.11 (0.96)	10.03 (1.04)	10.42 (0.88)	10.47 (0.90)

Simulation horizon 360 days
Number of orders ±125

6 Conclusion and Perspectives

The main objective of this paper is to capitalize the know-how mitigation strategies of the supply chain in order to model inventory disruption management problem. According to this, we present how agent-based modeling can be used as a versatile tool for decision support in pre and post-disruption situations. The results of the experiments highlight the applicability of agent-based models to quantify the impacts of the key mitigation strategies on system performance. The perspectives of this research work can be formulated in several areas. Within a short time, the simulator can be extended and we can add new risks and strategies and implement other interaction protocols. In the future, integrating the optimization and the knowledge management in the decisional layer are important aspects to study.

References

1. Ambulkar, S., Blackhurst, J., Grawe, S.: Firm's resilience to supply chain disruptions: scale development and empirical examination. J. Oper. Manag. **33**, 111–122 (2015)
2. Kärkkäinen, M.: Increasing efficiency in the supply chain for short shelf life goods using RFID tagging. Int. J. Retail Distrib. Manag. **31**(10), 529–536 (2003)
3. Tsai, W.C.: A dynamic sourcing strategy considering supply disruption risks. Inter. J. Prod. Res. **54**(7), 2170–2184 (2016)
4. Gong, X., Chao, X., Zheng, S.: Dynamic pricing and inventory management with dual suppliers of different lead times and disruption risks. Prod. Oper. Manag. **23**(12), 2058–2074 (2014)
5. Wu, D.D., Chen, S.H., Olson, D.L.: Business intelligence in risk management: some recent progresses. Inform. Sci. **256**, 1–7 (2014)
6. Jüttner, U.: Supply chain risk management: understanding the business requirements from a practitioner perspective. Int. J. Logistics Manag. **16**(1), 120–141 (2005)
7. Behdani, B. , Adhitya, A., Lukszo, Z., Srinivasan, R.: How to handle disruptions in supply chains-an integrated framework and a review of literature (2012)
8. Ivanov, D., Sokolov, B., Dolgui, A.: The Ripple effect in supply chains: trade-off 'efficiency-flexibility-resilience' in disruption management. Int. J. Prod. Res. **52**(7), 2154–2172 (2014)
9. Esmaeilikia, M., Fahimnia, B., Sarkis, J., Govindan, K., Kumar, A., Mo, J.: Tactical supply chain planning models with inherent flexibility: definition and review. Ann. Oper. Res. **244**(2), 407–427 (2016)
10. Wakolbinger, T., Cruz, J.M.: Supply chain disruption risk management through strategic information acquisition and sharing and risk-sharing contracts. Int. J. Prod. Res. **49**(13), 4063–4084 (2011)
11. Kumar, V., Srinivasan, S.: A review of supply chain management using multi-agent system. Int. J. Comput. Sci. Issues (IJCSI) **7**(5), 198 (2010)
12. Behzadi, G., O'Sullivan, M.J., Olsen, T.L., Scrimgeour, F., Zhang, A.: Robust and resilient strategies for managing supply disruptions in an agribusiness supply chain. Int. J. Prod. Econ. **191**, 207–220 (2017)
13. Qazi, A., Dickson, A., Quigley, J., Gaudenzi, B.: Supply chain risk network management: a bayesian belief network and expected utility based approach for managing supply chain risks. Int. J. Prod. Econ. **196**, 24–42 (2018)
14. Pyke, D., Tang, C.S.: How to mitigate product safety risks proactively? Process, challenges and opportunities. Int. J. Logistics Res. Appl. **13**(4), 243–256 (2010)
15. Adhitya, A., Srinivasan, R.: Dynamic simulation and decision support for multisite specialty chemicals supply chain. Ind. Eng. Chem. Res. **49**(20), 9917–9931 (2010)
16. Joslyn, C., Rocha, L.: Towards semiotic agent-based models of socio-technical organizations. In: Proceedings AI, Simulation and Planning in High Autonomy Systems (AIS 2000) Conference, Tucson, Arizona, pp. 70–79 (2000)

Correction to: Spatio-Temporal Correlation Graph for Association Enhancement in Multi-object Tracking

Zhijie Zhong⬤, Hao Sheng⬤, Yang Zhang⬤, Yubin Wu⬤,
Jiahui Chen⬤, and Wei Ke⬤

Correction to:
Chapter "Spatio-Temporal Correlation Graph for Association Enhancement in Multi-object Tracking" in:
C. Douligeris et al. (Eds.): *Knowledge Science, Engineering and Management*, LNAI 11775,
https://doi.org/10.1007/978-3-030-29551-6_35

Unfortunately the authors failed to add an acknowledgment to their contribution. Correction has been updated in the book. The acknowledgment should have read as follows:

Acknowledgement:
This study is partially supported by the National Key R&D Program of China (No.2017YFC0806500), the National Natural Science Foundation of China (No.61861166002), the Science and Technology Development Fund of Macau SAR (File no. 0001/2018/AFJ) Joint Scientific Research Project, the Macao Science and Technology Development Fund (No.138/2016/A3), the Fundamental Research Funds for the Central Universities, the Open Fund of the State Key Laboratory of Software Development Environment (No. SKLSDE-2019ZX-04) and the China Scholarship Council State-Sponsored Scholarship Program (Grant No. 201806025026). Thank you for the support from HAWKEYE Group.

The updated version of this chapter can be found at
https://doi.org/10.1007/978-3-030-29551-6_35

Author Index

Printed in the United States
By Bookmasters